AMERICAN DECADES
PRIMARY SOURCES

1980–1989

AMERICAN DECADES
PRIMARY SOURCES
1980-1989

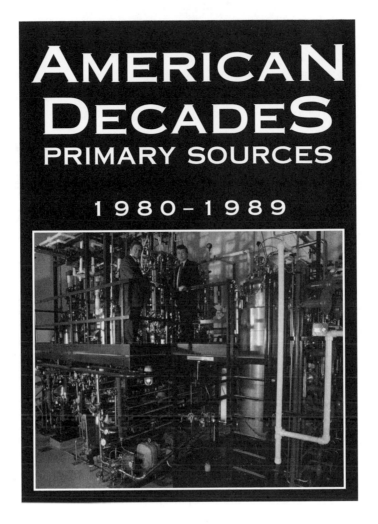

CYNTHIA ROSE, PROJECT EDITOR

GALE®

THOMSON

GALE

Detroit • New York • San Diego • San Francisco • Cleveland • New Haven, Conn. • Waterville, Maine • London • Munich

THOMSON
GALE

American Decades Primary Sources, 1980–1989

Project Editor
Cynthia Rose

Editorial
Jason M. Everett, Rachel J. Kain, Pamela A. Dear, Andrew C. Claps, Thomas Carson, Kathleen Droste, Christy Justice, Lynn U. Koch, Michael D. Lesniak, Nancy Matuszak, John F. McCoy, Michael Reade, Rebecca Parks, Mark Mikula, Polly A. Rapp, Mark Springer

Data Capture
Civie A. Green, Beverly Jendrowski, Gwendolyn S. Tucker

Permissions
Margaret Abendroth, Margaret A. Chamberlain, Lori Hines, Jacqueline Key, Mari Masalin-Cooper, William Sampson, Shalice Shah-Caldwell, Kim Smilay, Sheila Spencer, Ann Taylor

Indexing Services
Lynne Maday, John Magee

Imaging and Multimedia
Randy Bassett, Dean Dauphinais, Leitha Etheridge-Sims, Mary K. Grimes, Lezlie Light, Daniel W. Newell, David G. Oblender, Christine O'Bryan, Kelly A. Quin, Luke A. Rademacher, Denay Wilding, Robyn V. Young

Product Design
Michelle DiMercurio

Composition and Electronic Prepress
Evi Seoud

Manufacturing
Rita Wimberley

For permission to use material from this product, submit your request via Web at http://gale-edit.com/permissions, or you may download our Permissions Request form and submit your request by fax or mail to:

Permissions Department
The Gale Group, Inc.
27500 Drake Rd.
Farmington Hills, MI 48331-3535
Permissions Hotline:
248-699-8006 or 800-877-4253, ext. 8006
Fax: 248-699-8074 or 800-762-4058

Cover photographs reproduced by permission of AP/Wide World Photos (Bill Gates, right), Bettmann/Corbis (Michael Jordan, spine), The Library of Congress (Supreme Court justice Sandra Day O'Connor, left), Roger Ressmeyer/Corbis (Interferon production facility, Emeryville, California, background) and Wally McNamee/Corbis (President Ronald Reagan at the Brandenburg Gate, center).

LIBRARY OF CONGRESS CATALOGING-IN-PUBLICATION DATA

American decades primary sources / edited by Cynthia Rose.
    v. cm.
Includes bibliographical references and index.
Contents: [1] 1900-1909 — [2] 1910-1919 — [3] 1920-1929 — [4] 1930-1939 — [5] 1940-1949 — [6] 1950-1959 — [7] 1960-1969 — [8] 1970-1979 — [9] 1980-1989 — [10] 1990-1999.
    ISBN 0-7876-6587-8 (set : hardcover : alk. paper) — ISBN 0-7876-6588-6 (v. 1 : hardcover : alk. paper) — ISBN 0-7876-6589-4 (v. 2 : hardcover : alk. paper) — ISBN 0-7876-6590-8 (v. 3 : hardcover : alk. paper) — ISBN 0-7876-6591-6 (v. 4 : hardcover : alk. paper) — ISBN 0-7876-6592-4 (v. 5 : hardcover : alk. paper) — ISBN 0-7876-6593-2 (v. 6 : hardcover : alk. paper) — ISBN 0-7876-6594-0 (v. 7 : hardcover : alk. paper) — ISBN 0-7876-6595-9 (v. 8 : hardcover : alk. paper) — ISBN 0-7876-6596-7 (v. 9 : hardcover : alk. paper) — ISBN 0-7876-6597-5 (v. 10 : hardcover : alk. paper)
    1. United States—Civilization—20th century—Sources. I. Rose, Cynthia.
E169.1.A471977 2004
973.91—dc21
                                                    2002008155

CONTENTS

Entries are arranged in chronological order by date of primary source. For entries with one primary source, the entry title is the primary source title. Entries with more than one primary source have an overall entry title, followed by the titles of the primary sources.

Law and Justice

Lifestyles and Social Trends

The Media

Medicine and Health

Religion

Science and Technology

Sports

ADVISORS AND CONTRIBUTORS

Advisors

CARL A. ANTONUCCI JR. has spent the past ten years as a reference librarian at various colleges and universities. Currently director of library services at Capital Community College, he holds two master's degrees and is a doctoral candidate at Providence College. He particularly enjoys researching Rhode Island political history during the 1960s and 1970s.

KATHY ARSENAULT is the dean of library at the University of South Florida, St. Petersburg's Poynter Library. She holds a master's degree in Library Science. She has written numerous book reviews for *Library Journal,* and has published articles in such publications as the *Journal of the Florida Medical Association* and *Collection Management.*

JAMES RETTIG holds two master's degrees. He has written numerous articles and has edited *Distinguished Classics of Reference Publishing* (1992). University librarian at the University of Richmond, he is the recipient of three American Library Association awards: the Isadore Gibert Mudge Citation (1988), the G.K. Hall Award for Library Literature (1993), and the Louis Shores-Oryx Press Award (1995).

HILDA K. WEISBURG is the head library media specialist at Morristown High School Library and specializes in building school library media programs. She has several publications to her credit, including *The School Librarians Workshop, Puzzles, Patterns, and Problem Solving: Creative Connections to Critical Thinking,* and *Learning, Linking & Critical Thinking: Information Strategies for the K-12 Library Media Curriculum.*

Contributors

EUGENIA F. BELL is a freelance editor and publication manager who holds a bachelor's in philosophy from Pennsylvania State University. She spent four years as an editor of architecture and design books for the Princeton Architectural Press before working for a year as a publications manager for the Walker Art Center in Minneapolis, Minnesota. She is the author of *The Chapel at Ronchamp* (1999).
Chapter: Fashion and Design.

TIMOTHY G. BORDEN has contributed to such publications as *History Behind the Headlines, Michigan Historical Review, Polish American Studies,* and *Northwest Ohio Quarterly.* He also serves as reader/referee of Notre Dame University at Lebanon's *Palma Journal.*
Chapter: Lifestyles and Social Trends.

DENNIS A. CASTILLO received his doctorate in the history of Christianity from the University of Chicago. Currently an associate professor of Church History at Christ the King Seminary in East Aurora, New York, he is at work on his first book, *The Maltese Cross: A Military History of Malta.* A Detroit native, he now lives in Buffalo, New York.
Chapter: Religion.

PAUL G. CONNORS earned a doctorate in American History from Loyola University in Chicago. He has a strong interest in Great Lakes maritime history, and has contributed the article "Beaver Island Ice Walkers" to *Michigan History*. He has worked for the Michigan Legislative Service Bureau as a research analyst since 1996.

Essay: Using Primary Sources. *Chronologies:* Selected World Events Outside the United States; Government and Politics, Sports chapters. *General Resources:* General, Government and Politics, Sports.

CHRISTOPHER CUMO is a staff writer for *The Adjunct Advocate Magazine*. Formerly an adjunct professor of history at Walsh University, he has written two books, *A History of the Ohio Agricultural Experiment Station, 1882–1997,* and *Seeds of Change,* and has contributed to numerous scholarly journals. He holds a doctorate in History from the University of Akron.

Chapter: Science and Technology. *Chapter Chronologies and General Resources:* Business and the Economy, Education, Medicine and Health, Science and Technology.

JENNIFER HELLER holds bachelor's degrees in Religious Studies and English Education, as well as a master's in Curriculum and Instruction, all from the University of Kansas. She has been an adjunct associate professor at Johnson County Community College in Kansas since 1998. She is currently at work on a dissertation on contemporary women's religious literature.

Chapter Chronology and General Resources: Religion.

DAVID M. HOLFORD has worked as an adjunct instructor at Ohio University, Park College, and Columbus State Community College; education curator for the Ohio Historical Society; and held editorial positions at Glencoe/McGraw Hill and Holt, Rinehard, and Winston. He also holds a doctorate in History from Ohio State University. A freelance writer/editor since 1996, he as published *Herbert Hoover* (1999) and *Abraham Lincoln and the Emancipation Proclamation* (2002).

Chapter Chronologies and General Resources: Lifestyles and Social Trends, The Media.

MILLIE JACKSON is an associate librarian at Grand Valley State University in Allendale, Michigan. She has previously worked as an English teacher and as the special collections librarian at Oklahoma State University. Dr. Jackson's dissertation on ladies's library associations in Michigan won the American Library Association's Phyllis Dain Library History Dissertation Award in 2001.

Chapters: The Arts, Education, The Media.

JACQUELINE LESHKEVICH joined the Michigan Legislative Service Bureau as a science research analyst in 2000. She earned her Bachelor of Science in Biochemistry from Northern Michigan University and a master's degree, also in Biochemistry, from Michigan Technological University. A contributor to such publications as *Nature Biotechnology* and *Plant Cell,* she is also an amateur astronomer.

Chapters: Medicine and Health, Sports.

SCOTT A. MERRIMAN currently works as a part-time instructor at the University of Kentucky and is finishing his doctoral dissertation on Espionage and Sedition Acts in the Sixth Court of Appeals. He has contributed to *The History Highway* and *History.edu,* among others. Scott is a resident of Lexington, Kentucky.

Chapter: Law and Justice.

PATRICK D. REAGAN has taught history at Tennessee Technological University since 1982. He has written over forty book reviews and has contributed to such publications as *Designing a New America: The Origins of New Deal Planning, 1890–1943,* and *American Journey: World War I and the Jazz Age.* He is also the author of *History and the Internet: A Guide.*

Chapter: Business and the Economy.

LORNA BIDDLE RINEAR is the editor and coauthor of *The Complete Idiot's Guide to Women's History.* A Ph.D. candidate at Rutger's University, she holds a bachelor's from Wellesley College and a master's degree from Boston College. She resides in Bellingham, Massachusetts.

Chapter Chronologies and General Resources: The Arts, Fashion and Design.

AMY ROSE taught at the college level for ten years before becoming a freelance writer, editor, and instructional designer. She has published articles on such topics as ergonomics and labor relations. She holds a bachelor's and doctorate, both in Classical Studies, from the University of Colorado at Boulder.

Chapter: Fashion and Design.

MARY HERTZ SCARBROUGH earned both her bachelor's in English and German and her J.D. from the University of South Dakota. Prior to becoming a freelance writer in 1996, she worked as a law clerk in the Federal District Court for the District of South Dakota and as legal counsel for the Immigration and Naturalization Service. She lives in Storm Lake, Iowa.

Chapter Chronology and General Resources: Law and Justice.

ACKNOWLEDGMENTS

Following is a list of the copyright holders who have granted us permission to reproduce material in this volume of American Decades Primary Sources. *Every effort has been made to trace copyright, but if omissions have been made, please let us know.*

Copyrighted material in *American Decades Primary Sources, 1980–1989*, was reproduced from the following periodicals: *Alaska Science Forum*, March 4, 1985. Reproduced by permission of the University of Alaska Fairbanks Geophysical Institute and the authors. —*America*, v. 158, April 30, 1988. © 1988. All rights reserved. Reproduced with permission of America Press, Inc., 106 West 56th Street, New York, NY 10019. —*American Film*, July/August, 1988 for "Dialogue on Film: Steven Bochco." Reproduced by permission. —*Art in America*, December 1986 for "Wordsmith: An Interview with Jenny Holzer" by Bruce Ferguson. Copyright © 1986 by the author. Reprinted by permission of the author. —*ARTnews*, v. 84, November, 1985 for "When Is a Painting Finished?" by Paul Gardner. © 1985 ARTnews Associates. Reproduced by permission of the author. —*Arts Magazine*, v. 61, June, 1987 for "Barbara Kruger: Pictures and Words" by Jeanne Siegel; v. 62, October 1987 for "Mrs. Holladay and the Guerrilla Girls" by John Loughery. Copyright © 1987 by The Arts Digest Inc. Reprinted by permission of the publisher and the respective authors. —*The Atlantic*, December, 1981 for "The Education of David Stockman" by William Greider; v. 264, September, 1989 for "The Cholesterol Myth" by Thomas J. Moore. Reproduced by permission of the respective authors. —*Boston Globe*, October 26, 1986. Republished with permission of Boston Globe, conveyed through Copyright Clearance Center, Inc. —*Change*, v. 20, September/October, 1988. Copyright © 1988 Helen Dwight Reid Educational Foundation. Reproduced with permission of the Helen Dwight Reid Educational Foundation, published by Heldref Publications, 1319 18th Street, NW, Washington, D.C., 20036-1802. —*The Christian Century*, v. 104, June 17–24, 1987; v. 105, July 6–13, 1988. Reproduced by permission. —*Christian Social Action*, 1990. Reproduced by permission. —*Christianity and Crisis*, v. 47, March 2, 1987 for "Womanist Theology: Black Women's Voices" by Delores S. Williams. Reproduced by permission of the author. —*Commonweal*, April 25, 1986. Copyright © 1986 Commonweal Publishing Co., Inc. reproduced by permission of Commonweal Foundation. —*Editor & Publisher*, v. 119, August 30, 1986. Reproduced by permission. —*Educational Leadership*, v. 47, December, 1989/January, 1990; v. 46, February, 1989. Copyright © 1989 by the Association for Supervision and Curriculum Development. All rights reserved. Reprinted by permission of the publisher. —*Genentech*, September 6, 1978; October 19, 1982. Reproduced by permission. —From "Religion in America: 1981." The Gallup Organization, Inc. and The Princeton Religion Research Center, Inc., 1981. Copyright © 1981 by The Gallup Organization, Inc. All rights reserved. Reproduced by permission. —*The Independent Review*, v. 7, Winter, 2003 for "My Time with Supply-Side Economics" by Paul Craig Roberts. Reproduced by permission of the author. —*The Journal of the American Medical Association*, v. 253, June 21, 1985; v. 254, December 20, 1985. Reproduced by permission. —*Journal of Ecumenical Studies*, v. 20, Winter, 1983. Reproduced by permission. —*The Journal of Negro Education*, v. 52,

Summer, 1983 for "The Impact of Rule 48 Upon the Black Student Athlete: A Comment" by Alexander Williams, Jr. Reproduced by permission of the publisher and the author. —*Journal of Reading*, v. 29, March, 1986. Reproduced with permission of the International Reading Association. —*Life*, v. 6, March, 1983. Reproduced by permission. —*Maclean's*, v. 101, April 11, 1988. © 1988 by Maclean's Magazine. Reproduced by permission. —*Multinational Monitor*, January, 1990. Reproduced by permission. —*NASSP Bulletin*, v. 72, November, 1988. Copyright 1988 National Association of Secondary School Principals. www.principals.org. Reproduced by permission. —*National Geographic*, November, 1985. Reproduced by permission. —*Nature*, v. 325, January 1, 1987. Copyright 1987 Macmillan Publishers Ltd. Reproduced by permission. —*The NCAA News*, v. 20, January 19, 1983. Reproduced by permission. —*The New England Journal of Medicine*, v. 312, January 17, 1985. Copyright © 1985 Massachusetts Medical Society. All rights reserved. Reproduced by permission. —*The New York Review of Books*, May 14, 1981; March 12, 1987; December 20, 1990. Copyright © 1981, 1987, 1990 Nyrev, Inc. Reproduced with permission from The New York Review of Books. —*The New York Times*, August 13, 1980; November 29, 1983; July 18, 1984; January 29, 1986; October 14, 1988. Copyright © 1980, 1983, 1984, 1986, 1988 by The New York Times Company. Reproduced by permission. —*The New York Times Magazine*, July 19, 1987; June 11, 1989. Copyright © 1987 Stephen Jay Gould and 1989 Barbara Grizzuti Harrison respectively. Reproduced by permission. —*The New Yorker*, v. 62, April 21, 1986. Reproduced by permission. —Policy Statement adopted by the National Council of the Churches of Christ in the U.S.A., Racial Justice Working Group of the Division of Church and Society, 1984. Reproduced by permission. —*Respect Life*, 1984; 1985. Reproduced by permission. —*Rolling Stone*, July 22, 1982; August 10, 1989. © 1982, 1989 by Straight Arrow Publishers, Inc. All rights reserved. Reproduced by permission. —*Saturday Evening Post*, v. 257, April, 1985. Reproduced by permission. —*Science*, v. 208, June 6, 1980; v. 245, September 1, 1989. Copyright 1980, 1989 by AAAS. Reproduced by permission. —*Scientific American*, v. 246, February, 1982; v. 247, August, 1982; v. 249, August, 1983; v. 251, August, 1984; v. 257, October, 1987; v. 259, November, 1988. Copyright © 1982, 1983, 1984, 1987, 1988 by Scientific American, Inc. All rights reserved. Reproduced by permission. —*Sports Illustrated*, April 20, 1987; March 21, 1989. Reproduced by permission./ 1989 for "A Red-Letter Day" by Crosbie Cotton. Reproduced by permission of the author. —*St. Paul Pioneer Press*, June 21, 1987. Reproduced by permission. —*Time*, September 26, 1983; September 1, 1986; v. 134, October 9, 1989; v. 137, May 20, 1991. © 1983, 1986, 1989, 1991 Time Inc. Reproduced by permission. —*The Wall Street Journal*, April 14, 1983. © 1983 Dow Jones & Company, Inc. All rights reserved. Reproduced from The Wall Street Journal. —*Washington Post*, October, 1981; February, 1984; June 20, 1986. © 1981, 1984, 1986, Washington Post Book World Service/Washington Post Writers Group. Reproduced by permission.

Copyrighted material in *American Decades Primary Sources, 1980–1989*, was reproduced from the following books: Bakker, Jay. From *Son of a Preacher Man: My Search for Grace in the Shadows*. HarperSanFrancisco, a Division of HarperCollins Publishers, 2001. Copyright © 2001 by Jay Bakker. All rights reserved. Reproduced by permission of HarperCollins Publishers, Inc. —Bakker, Jim with Ken Abraham. From *I Was Wrong*. Thomas Nelson Publishers, 1996. Copyright © 1996 by Jim Bakker. All rights reserved. Reproduced by permission. —Bauman, Robert E. From *The Gentleman From Maryland: The Conscience of a Gay Conservative*. A Belvedere Book/Arbor House, 1986. Copyright © 1986 by Robert E. Bauman. All rights reserved. Reproduced by permission of HarperCollins Publishers. —Bayer, Ronald and Gerald M. Oppenheimer. From *AIDS Doctors: Voices From the Epidemic*. Oxford University Press, 2000. Copyright © 2000 by Ronald Bayer and Gerald M. Oppenheimer. All rights reserved. Used by permission of Oxford University Press, Inc. —Bloom, Allan. From *The Closing of the American Mind*. Simon and Schuster, 1987. Copyright © 1987 by Allan Bloom. All rights reserved. Reproduced by permission of Simon & Schuster Macmillan. —Carver, Raymond. From *Cathedral*. Alfred A. Knopf, 1983. Copyright © 1981, 1982, 1983 by Raymond Carver. All rights reserved. Reproduced by permission of Alfred A. Knopf, Inc. and International Creative Management, Inc. —Chandrasekhar, Subrahmanyan. From *Nobel Lectures, Physics 1981–1990*. World Scientific Publishing Co., 1993. Copyright © 1993 by Nobel Foundation. All rights reserved. Reproduced by permission. —Cisneros, Sandra. From *The House on Mango Street*. Vintage Contemporaries, 1991. Copyright © 1984 by Sandra Cisneros. All rights reserved. Reproduced by permission. —Cole, Lewis. From Prologue to *Never Too Young to Die: The Death of Len Bias*. Pantheon Books, 1989. Copyright © 1989 by Lewis Cole. All rights reserved. Reproduced in the U.S. by permission of Random House, Inc. Reproduced in the U.K. by permission of Sterling Lord Literistic, Inc. —Conner, Dennis with Bruce Stannard. From *Comeback: My Race for the America's Cup*. Edited by Paul C. Larsen. St. Martin's Press, 1987. Copyright © 1987 by Dennis Conner Sports, Inc. All rights reserved. Reprinted with permission of Palgrave Macmillan. —Drew, Elizabeth. From *Politics and Money: The New Road to Corruption*. Macmillan Publishing

From *You Cannot Be Serious*. G.P. Putnam's Sons, 2002. Copyright © 2002 John McEnroe. All rights reserved. Reproduced by permission of G.P. Putnam's Sons, a division of Penguin Putnam Inc. —Messner, Tammy Faye. From *Tammy: Telling It My Way*. Villard, 1996. Copyright © 1996 by T.F. Messner. All rights reserved. Reproduced by permission of Random House, Inc. —Naisbitt, John. From *Megatrends: Ten New Directions Transforming Our Lives*. Warner Books, 1982. Copyright © 1982 by John Naisbitt. All rights reserved. Reproduced by permission. —Navratilova, Martina with George Vecsey. From *Martina*. Alfred A. Knopf, 1985. Copyright © 1985 by Martina Enterprises, Inc. All rights reserved. Reproduced in the U.S. by permission of Alfred A. Knopf, Inc. Reproduced in the U.K. by permission of HarperCollins Publishers Ltd. (London). —North, Oliver L. with William Novak. From *Under Fire: An American Story*. HarperCollins Publishers, 1991. Copyright © 1991 by Oliver L. North. All rights reserved. Reproduced by permission of HarperCollins Publishers, Inc. —Oliver, Mary. From *Dream Work*. The Atlantic Monthly Press, 1986. Copyright © 1986 by Mary Oliver. All rights reserved. Reproduced by permission of Grove/Atlantic, Inc., and the author. —Payton, Walter with Don Yaeger. From *Never Die Easy: The Autobiography of Walter Payton*. Villard, 2000. Copyright © 2000 by Celebrity Appearances, Inc. and Don Yaeger. All rights reserved. Reproduced in the U.S. by permission of Villard Books, a division of Random House, Inc. Reproduced in the U.K. by permission of Vigliano Associates Ltd. —Prichard, Peter. From *The Making of McPaper: The Inside Story of USA Today*. Andrews, McMeel & Parker, 1987. Copyright © 1987 by Gannett New Media Services. All rights reserved. Reproduced by permission. —Sharpton, Al and Anthony Walton. *From Go and Tell Pharaoh: The Autobiography of the Reverend Al Sharpton*. Doubleday, 1996. Copyright © 1996 by Reverend Al Sharpton and Anthony Walton. All rights reserved. Reproduced in the U.S. by permission of Doubleday, a division of Random House, Inc. Reproduced in the U.K. by permission of Frances Goldin, Literary Agency. —Shilts, Randy. From *And the Band Played On: Politics, People, and the AIDS Epidemic*. St. Martin's Press, 1987. Copyright © 1987 by Randy Shilts. All rights reserved. Reprinted with permission of Palgrave Macmillan. —Simon, Paul. From *Advice & Consent*. National Press Book, 1992. Copyright © 1992 by Paul Simon. All rights reserved. Reproduced by permission of the author. —Simon, Paul. From "Graceland." Warner Bros. Records, 1986. Copyright © 1996 by P.S. Broadway Holdings, Inc. All rights reserved. Reproduced by permission of Paul Simon Music. —Slater, Lauren. From *Prozac Diary*. Random House, 1998. Copyright © 1998 by Lauren Slater. All rights reserved. Reproduced by permission of Random House,

Inc. —Stern, Robert A.M. From *Building and Projects 1987–1992*. Rizzoli, 1992. © Rizzoli 1992. Reproduced by permission. —Stewart, Martha. From *Entertaining*. Clarkson N. Potter, Inc./Publishers, 1982. Copyright © 1982 by Martha Stewart. All rights reserved. Reproduced in the U.S. by permission of Random House, Inc. Reproduced in the U.K. by permission of Susan Magrino Agency on behalf of Martha Stewart. —Stockman, David A. From *The Triumph of Politics: How the Reagan Revolution Failed*. Harper & Row, Publishers, 1986. Copyright © 1986 by David A. Stockman. All rights reserved. Reproduced by permission of HarperCollins Publishers. —The Schroeder Family with Martha Barnette. From *The Bill Schroeder Story*. William Morrow and Company, Inc., 1987. Copyright © 1987 by Martha Barnette, Margaret Schroeder, Melvin Schroeder, Stan Schroeder, Cheryl Schroeder, Terry Schroeder, Rod Schroeder and Monica Bohnert. All rights reserved. Reproduced by permission of HarperCollins Publishers. —Tower, John, Edmund Muskie and Brent Scowcroft. From *The Tower Commission Report: The Full Text of the President's Special Review Board*. Bantam Books/Times Books, 1987. Copyright © 1987 by Random House, Inc. All rights reserved. Reproduced by permission of Bantam Books, a division of Random House, Inc. —Viguerie, Richard A. From *The New Right: We're Ready to Lead*. The Viguerie Company, 1980. Copyright © 1980 by The Viguerie Company. All rights reserved. Reproduced by permission. —Walker, Alice. From *The Color Purple*. Harcourt Brace & Company, 1982. Copyright © 1982 by Alice Walker. All rights reserved. Reproduced by permission of Harcourt. —Wasserstein, Wendy. From *The Heidi Chronicles and Other Plays*. Harcourt Brace Jovanovich, 1990. Copyright © 1978, 1984, 1985, 1990 by Wendy Wasserstein. All rights reserved. Reproduced by permission of Harcourt, Inc. —Will, George F. From *The Morning After: American Successes and Excesses 1981–1986*. The Free Press, A Division of Macmillan, Inc., 1986. Copyright © 1986 by The Washington Post Company. All rights reserved. Reproduced by permission of The Free Press, an imprint of Simon & Schuster Macmillan. —Wilson, August. From *Fences: A Play by August Wilson*. A Plume Book, 1986. Copyright © 1986 by August Wilson. All rights reserved. Reproduced by permission of Plume Book, a division of Penguin Putnam Inc. —Wolfe, Tom. From *From Bauhaus to Our House*. McGraw-Hill Ryerson Ltd., 1981. Copyright © 1981 by Tom Wolfe. All rights reserved. Reproduced by permission of Farrar, Straus and Giroux, LLC.

Copyrighted material in *American Decades Primary Sources, 1980–1989*, was reproduced from the following web sites: Alamo, Tony, "The Pope's Secrets." Online at: http://www.alamoministries.com/Anti-Christ/popes_secrets.htm. 1984. Reprinted with permission. —"Interview Vyacheslav Fetisov." Online at: http://www.pbs.org/wgbh/pages/frontline/shows/hockey/interviews/fetisov.html. Published by pbs.org. Reprinted with permission. —"Statement of Commissioner A. Bartlett Giamatti." Online at: http://www.baseball1.com/bb-data/rose/abg _statement.html. Published by The Baseball Archive /www.baseball1.com, August 24, 1989. Reprinted with permission. —Warner, Margaret and Renzo Piano. From http://www.pbs.org/newshour/bb/entertainment/jan-june98 /piano_6-19.html. Reproduced by permission.

ABOUT THE SET

American Decades Primary Sources is a ten-volume collection of more than two thousand primary sources on twentieth-century American history and culture. Each volume comprises about two hundred primary sources in 160–170 entries. Primary sources are enhanced by informative context, with illustrative images and sidebars—many of which are primary sources in their own right—adding perspective and a deeper understanding of both the primary sources and the milieu from which they originated.

Designed for students and teachers at the high school and undergraduate levels, as well as researchers and history buffs, *American Decades Primary Sources* meets the growing demand for primary source material.

Conceived as both a stand-alone reference and a companion to the popular *American Decades* set, *American Decades Primary Sources* is organized in the same subject-specific chapters for compatibility and ease of use.

Primary Sources

To provide fresh insights into the key events and figures of the century, thirty historians and four advisors selected unique primary sources far beyond the typical speeches, government documents, and literary works. Screenplays, scrapbooks, sports box scores, patent applications, college course outlines, military codes of conduct, environmental sculptures, and CD liner notes are but a sampling of the more than seventy-five types of primary sources included.

Diversity is shown not only in the wide range of primary source types, but in the range of subjects and opinions, and the frequent combination of primary sources in entries. Multiple perspectives in religious, political, artistic, and scientific thought demonstrate the commitment of *American Decades Primary Sources* to diversity, in addition to the inclusion of considerable content displaying ethnic, racial, and gender diversity. *American Decades Primary Sources* presents a variety of perspectives on issues and events, encouraging the reader to consider subjects more fully and critically.

American Decades Primary Sources' innovative approach often presents related primary sources in an entry. The primary sources act as contextual material for each other—creating a unique opportunity to understand each and its place in history, as well as their relation to one another. These may be point-counterpoint arguments, a variety of diverse opinions, or direct responses to another primary source. One example is President Franklin Delano Roosevelt's letter to clergy at the height of the Great Depression, with responses by a diverse group of religious leaders from across the country.

Multiple primary sources created by particularly significant individuals—Dr. Martin Luther King, Jr. for example—reside in *American Decades Primary Sources*. Multiple primary sources on particularly significant subjects are often presented in more than one chapter of a volume, or in more than one decade, providing opportunities to see the significance and impact of an event or figure from many angles and historical perspectives. For example, seven primary sources on the controversial Scopes "monkey" trial are found in five chapters of the

1920s volume. Primary sources on evolutionary theory may be found in earlier and later volumes, allowing the reader to see and analyze the development of thought across time.

Entry Organization

Contextual material uses standardized rubrics that will soon become familiar to the reader, making the entries more accessible and allowing for easy comparison. Introduction and Significance essays—brief and focused—cover the historical background, contributing factors, importance, and impact of the primary source, encouraging the reader to think critically—not only about the primary source, but also about the way history is constructed. Key Facts and a Synopsis provide quick access and recognition of the primary sources, and the Further Resources are a stepping-stone to additional study.

Additional Features

Subject chronologies and thorough tables of contents (listing titles, authors, and dates) begin each chapter. The main table of contents assembles this information conveniently at the front of the book. An essay on using primary sources, a chronology of selected events outside the United States during the twentieth century, substantial general and subject resources, and primary source type and general indexes enrich *American Decades Primary Sources*.

The ten volumes of *American Decades Primary Sources* provide a vast array of primary sources integrated with supporting content and user-friendly features.

This value-laden set gives the reader an unparalleled opportunity to travel into the past, to relive important events, to encounter key figures, and to gain a deep and full understanding of America in the twentieth century.

Acknowledgments

A number of people contributed to the successful completion of this project. The editor wishes to acknowledge them with thanks: Luann Brennan, Katrina Coach, Pamela S. Dear, Nikita L. Greene, Madeline Harris, Alesia James, Cynthia Jones, Pamela M. Kalte, Arlene Ann Kevonian, Frances L. Monroe, Charles B. Montney, Katherine H. Nemeh, James E. Person, Tyra Y. Phillips, Elizabeth Pilette, Noah Schusterbauer, Susan Strickland, Karissa Walker, Tracey Watson, and Jennifer M. York.

Contact Us

The editors of *American Decades Primary Sources* welcome your comments, suggestions, and questions. Please direct all correspondence to:

Editor, *American Decades Primary Sources*
The Gale Group, Inc.
27500 Drake Road
Farmington Hills, MI 48331–3535
(800) 877–4253

For email inquiries, please visit the Gale website at www.gale.com, and click on the Contact Us tab.

ABOUT THE VOLUME

The United States in the 1980s saw several firsts: for women, the media, medicine, and science. Sandra Day O'Connor became the first woman appointed to the U.S. Supreme Court, and Sally Ride became the first woman in space. CNN was established as the first 24-hour news station. AIDS was identified for the first time, and DNA was first used to convict criminals. The science community faced a stunning setback, however, with the explosion of the space shuttle *Challenger*, which had among its crew the first teacher to go into space. President Ronald Reagan's administration became mired for a time in the Iran-Contra affair, which involved a plan to provide arms to rebels in Nicaragua and free Americans held hostage by terrorists. Terrorists bombed the U.S. Embassy in Beirut, and the U.S. Army introduced its slogan "Be All You Can Be." The following documents are just a sampling of the offerings available in this volume.

Highlights of Primary Sources, 1980–1989

- Excerpt from *The House on Mango Street,* by Sandra Cisneros

- Memorandum on air traffic controllers strike

- List of terms from *Cultural Literacy: What Every American Needs to Know*

- Illustrations from *The Official Preppy Handbook*

- Transcript from *Challenger*'s operational recorder

- "Be All That You Can Be," recruiting advertisement for the U.S. Army

- Oral history of AIDS doctors

- An interview with *Hill Street Blues* creator Stephen Bochco

- *In Memory of Her: A Feminist Theological Reconstruction of Christian Origins*

- Photograph of the eruption of Mount St. Helens

- "Mitochondrial DNA and Human Evolution," journal article and graphics

- Statement of Major League Baseball Commissioner Bart Giamatti banning Pete Rose from baseball

Volume Structure and Content

Front matter

- Table of Contents—lists primary sources, authors, and dates of origin, by chapter and chronologically within chapters.

- About the Set, About the Volume, About the Entry essays—guide the reader through the set and promote ease of use.

- Highlights of Primary Sources—a quick look at a dozen or so primary sources gives the reader a feel for the decade and the volume's contents.

- Using Primary Sources—provides a crash course in reading and interpreting primary sources.

- Chronology of Selected World Events Outside the United States—lends additional context in which to place the decade's primary sources.

Chapters:

- The Arts
- Business and the Economy
- Education
- Fashion and Design
- Government and Politics
- Law and Justice
- Lifestyles and Social Trends
- The Media
- Medicine and Health
- Religion
- Science and Technology
- Sports

Chapter structure

- Chapter table of contents—lists primary sources, authors, and dates of origin chronologically, showing each source's place in the decade.

- Chapter chronology—highlights the decade's important events in the chapter's subject.

- Primary sources—displays sources surrounded by contextual material.

Back matter

- General Resources—promotes further inquiry with books, periodicals, websites, and audio and visual media, all organized into general and subject-specific sections.

- General Index—provides comprehensive access to primary sources, people, events, and subjects, and cross-referencing to enhance comparison and analysis.

- Primary Source Type Index—locates primary sources by category, giving readers an opportunity to easily analyze sources across genres.

ABOUT THE ENTRY

The primary source is the centerpiece and main focus of each entry in *American Decades Primary Sources.* In keeping with the philosophy that much of the benefit from using primary sources derives from the reader's own process of inquiry, the contextual material surrounding each entry provides access and ease of use, as well as giving the reader a springboard for delving into the primary source. Rubrics identify each section and enable the reader to navigate entries with ease.

Entry structure

- Key Facts—essential information pertaining to the primary source, including full title, author, source type, source citation, and notes about the author.

- Introduction—historical background and contributing factors for the primary source.

- Significance—importance and impact of the primary source, at the time and since.

- Primary Source—in text, text facsimile, or image format; full or excerpted.

- Synopsis—encapsulated introduction to the primary source.

- Further Resources—books, periodicals, websites, and audio and visual material.

Navigating an Entry

Entry elements are numbered and reproduced here, with an explanation of the data contained in these elements explained immediately thereafter according to the corresponding numeral.

Primary Source/Entry Title, Primary Source Type

•1• | **"Ego"**
•2• | Magazine article

•1• **PRIMARY SOURCE/ENTRY TITLE** The entry title is the primary source title for entries with one primary source. Entry titles appear as catchwords at the top outer margin of each page.

•2• **PRIMARY SOURCE TYPE** The type of primary source is listed just below the title. When assigning source types, great weight was given to how the author of the primary source categorized it. If a primary source comprised more than one type—for example, an article about art in the United States that included paintings, or a scientific essay that included graphs and photographs—each primary source type included in the entry appears below the title.

Composite Entry Title

•3• **Debate Over *The Birth of a Nation***

•1• **"Capitalizing Race Hatred"**
•2• Editorial

•1• "Reply to the *New York Globe*"

•2• Letter

•3• COMPOSITE ENTRY TITLE An overarching entry title is used for entries with more than one primary source, with the primary source titles and types below.

Key Facts

•4• **By:** Norman Mailer

•5• **Date:** March 19, 1971

•6• **Source:** Mailer, Norman. "Ego." *Life* 70, March 19, 1971, 30, 32–36.

•7• **About the Author:** Norman Mailer (1923–) was born in Long Branch, New Jersey. After graduating from Harvard and military service in World War II (1939–1945), Mailer began writing, publishing his first book, the best-selling novel *The Naked and the Dead,* in 1948. Mailer has written over thirty books, including novels, plays, political commentary, and essay collections, as well as numerous magazine articles. He won the Pulitzer Prize in 1969 and 1979. ■

•4• AUTHOR OR ORIGINATOR The name of the author or originator of the primary source begins the Key Facts section.

•5• DATE OF ORIGIN The date of origin of the primary source appears in this field, and may differ from the date of publication in the source citation below it; for example, speeches are often given before they are published.

•6• SOURCE CITATION The source citation is a full bibliographic citation, giving original publication data as well as reprint and/or online availability (usually both the deep-link and home-page URLs).

•7• ABOUT THE AUTHOR A brief bio of the author or originator of the primary source gives birth and death dates and a quick overview of the person's life. This rubric has been customized in some cases. If the primary source is the autobiography of an artist, the term "author" appears; however, if the primary source is a work of art, the term "artist" is used, showing the person's direct relationship to the primary source. Terms like "inventor" and "designer" are used similarly. For primary sources created by a group, "organization" may have been used instead of "author." If an author is anonymous or unknown, a brief "About the Publication" sketch may appear.

Introduction and Significance Essays

•8• **Introduction**

. . . As images from the Vietnam War (1964–1975) flashed onto television screens across the United States in the late 1960s, however, some reporters took a more active role in questioning the pronouncements of public officials. The broad cul-

tural changes of the 1960s, including a sweeping suspicion of authority figures by younger people, also encouraged a more restive spirit in the reporting corps. By the end of the decade, the phrase "Gonzo Journalism" was coined to describe the new breed of reporter: young, rebellious, and unafraid to get personally involved in the story at hand. . . .

•8• INTRODUCTION The introduction is a brief essay on the contributing factors and historical context of the primary source. Intended to promote understanding and jump-start the reader's curiosity, this section may also describe an artist's approach, the nature of a scientific problem, or the struggles of a sports figure. If more than one primary source is included in the entry, the introduction and significance address each one, and often the relationship between them.

•9• **Significance**

Critics of the new style of journalism maintained that the emphasis on personalities and celebrity did not necessarily lead to better reporting. As political reporting seemed to focus more on personalities and images and less on substantive issues, some observers feared that the American public was ill-served by the new style of journalism. Others argued that the media had also encouraged political apathy among the public by superficial reporting. . . .

•9• SIGNIFICANCE The significance discusses the importance and impact of the primary source. This section may touch on how it was regarded at the time and since, its place in history, any awards given, related developments, and so on.

Primary Source Header, Synopsis, Primary Source

•10• **Primary Source**

The Boys on the Bus [excerpt]

•11• SYNOPSIS: A boisterous account of Senator George McGovern's ultimately unsuccessful 1972 presidential bid, Crouse's work popularized the term "pack journalism," describing the herd mentality that gripped reporters focusing endlessly on the same topic. In later years, political advisors would become more adept at "spinning" news stories to their candidates' advantage, but the essential dynamics of pack journalism remain in place.

•12• The feverish atmosphere was halfway between a high school bus trip to Washington and a gambler's jet junket to Las Vegas, where small-time Mafiosi were lured into betting away their restaurants. There was giddy camaraderie mixed with fear and low-grade hysteria. To file a story late, or to make one glaring factual error, was to chance losing everything—one's job, one's expense account, one's drinking buddies, one's mad-dash existence, and the methedrine buzz that comes from knowing stories that the public would not know for hours and secrets that the public would never know. Therefore reporters channeled their gambling instincts into late-night poker games and private bets on the outcome of the elections. When it came to writing a story, they were as cautious as diamond-cutters. . . .

•10• **PRIMARY SOURCE HEADER** The primary source header signals the beginning of the primary source, and "[excerpt]" is attached if the source does not appear in full.

•11• **SYNOPSIS** The synopsis gives a brief overview of the primary source.

•12• **PRIMARY SOURCE** The primary source may appear excerpted or in full, and may appear as text, text facsimile (photographic reproduction of the original text), image, or graphic display (such as a table, chart, or graph).

Text Primary Sources

The majority of primary sources are reproduced as plain text. The font and leading of the primary sources are distinct from that of the context—to provide a visual clue to the change, as well as to facilitate ease of reading. Often, the original formatting of the text was preserved in order to more accurately represent the original (screenplays, for example). In order to respect the integrity of the primary sources, content some readers may consider sensitive was retained where it was deemed to be integral to the source. Text facsimile formatting was used sparingly and where the original provided additional value (for example, Aaron Copland's typing and handwritten notes on "Notes for a Cowboy Ballet").

Narrative Break

•13•   I told him I'd rest and then fix him something to eat when he got home. I could hear someone enter his office then, and Medgar laughed at something that was said. "I've got to go, honey. See you tonight. I love you." "All right," I said. "Take care." Those were our last words to each other.

■ ■ ■

Medgar had told me that President Kennedy was speaking on civil rights that night, and I made a mental note of the time. We ate alone, the children and I. It had become a habit now to set only four places for supper. Medgar's chair stared at us, and the children, who had heard

about the President's address to the nation, planned to watch it with me. There was something on later that they all wanted to see, and they begged to be allowed to wait up for Medgar to return home. School was out, and I knew that Van would fall asleep anyway, so I agreed.

•13• **NARRATIVE BREAK** A narrative break appears where there is a significant amount of elided material, beyond what ellipses would indicate (for example, excerpts from a nonfiction work's introduction and second chapter, or sections of dialogue from two acts of a play).

Image Primary Sources

Primary source images (whether photographs, text facsimiles, or graphic displays) are bordered with a distinctive double rule. The Primary Source header and Synopsis appear under the image, with the image reduced in size to accommodate the synopsis. For multipart images, the synopsis appears only under the first part of the image; subsequent parts have brief captions.

•14• "Art: U.S. Scene": *The Tornado* by John Steuart Curry (2 OF 4)

•14• **PRIMARY SOURCE IMAGE HEADER** The primary source image header assists the reader in tracking the images in a series. Also, the primary source header listed here indicates a primary source with both text and image components. The text of the *Time* magazine article "Art: U.S. Scene," appears with four of the paintings from the article. Under each painting, the title of the article appears first, followed by a colon, then the title of the painting. The header for the text component has a similar structure, with the term "magazine article" after the colon. Inclusion of images or graphic elements from primary sources, and their designation in the entry as main primary sources, is discretionary.

Further Resources

•15• **Further Resources**

BOOKS
Dixon, Phil. *The Negro Baseball Leagues, 1867–1955: A Photographic History.* Mattituck, N.Y.: Amereon House, 1992.

PERIODICALS
"Steven Spielberg: The Director Says It's Good-Bye to Spaceships and Hello to Relationships." *American Film* 13, no. 8, June 1988, 12–16.

WEBSITES
Architecture and Interior Design for 20th Century America, 1935–1955. American Memory digital primary source collection, Library of Congress. Available online at http://memory.loc.gov/ammem/gschtml/gotthome

.html; website home page: http://memory.loc.gov /ammem/ammemhome.html (accessed March 27, 2003).

AUDIO AND VISUAL MEDIA

E.T.: The Extra-Terrestrial. Original release, 1982, Universal. Directed by Steven Spielberg. Widescreen Collector's Edition DVD, 2002, Universal Studios.

•15• **FURTHER RESOURCES** A brief list of resources provides a stepping stone to further study. If it's known that a resource contains additional primary source material specifically related to the entry, a brief note in italics appears at the end of the citation. For websites, both the deep link and home page usually appear.

USING PRIMARY SOURCES

The philosopher R.G. Collingwood once said, "Every new generation must rewrite history in its own way." What Collingwood meant is that new events alter our perceptions of the past and necessitate that each generation interpret the past in a different light. For example, since September 11, 2001, and the "War on Terrorism," the collapse of the Soviet Union seemingly is no longer as historically important as the rise of Islamic fundamentalism, which was once only a minor concern. Seen from this viewpoint, history is not a rigid set of boring facts, but a fascinating, ever-changing field of study. Much of this fascination rests on the fact that historical interpretation is based on the reading of primary sources. To historians and students alike, primary sources are ambiguous objects because their underlying meanings are often not crystal clear. To learn a primary document's meaning(s), students must identify its main subject and recreate the historical context in which the document was created. In addition, students must compare the document with other primary sources from the same historical time and place. Further, students must cross-examine the primary source by asking of it a series of probing investigative questions.

To properly analyze a primary source, it is important that students become "active" rather than "casual" readers. As in reading a chemistry or algebra textbook, historical documents require students to analyze them carefully and extract specific information. In other words, history requires students to read "beyond the text" and focus on what the primary source tells us about the person or group and the era in which they lived. Unlike chemistry and algebra, however, historical primary sources have the additional benefit of being part of a larger, interesting story full of drama, suspense, and hidden agendas. In order to detect and identify key historical themes, students need to keep in mind a set of questions. For example, Who created the primary source? Why did the person create it? What is the subject? What problem is being addressed? Who was the intended audience? How was the primary source received and how was it used? What are the most important characteristics of this person or group for understanding the primary source? For example, what were the authors' biases? What was their social class? Their race? Their gender? Their occupation? Once these questions have been answered reasonably, the primary source can be used as a piece of historical evidence to interpret history.

In each *American Decades Primary Sources* volume, students will study examples of the following categories of primary sources:

- Firsthand accounts of historic events by witnesses and participants. This category includes diary entries, letters, newspaper articles, oral-history interviews, memoirs, and legal testimony.

- Documents representing the official views of the nation's leaders or of their political opponents. These include court decisions, policy statements, political speeches, party platforms, petitions, legislative debates, press releases, and federal and state laws.

- Government statistics and reports on such topics as birth, employment, marriage, death, and taxation.

- Advertisers' images and jingles. Although designed to persuade consumers to purchase commodities or to adopt specific attitudes, advertisements can also be valuable sources of information about popular beliefs and concerns.

- Works of art, including paintings, symphonies, play scripts, photographs, murals, novels, and poems.

- The products of mass culture: cartoons, comic books, movies, radio scripts, and popular songs.

- Material artifacts. These are everyday objects that survived from the period in question. Examples include household appliances and furnishings, recipes, and clothing.

- Secondary sources. In some cases, secondary sources may be treated as primary sources. For example, from 1836 to 1920, public schools across America purchased 122 million copies of a series of textbooks called the McGuffey Reader. Although current textbooks have more instructional value, the Reader is an invaluable primary source. It provides important insights into the unifying morals and cultural values that shaped the worldview of several generations of Americans, who differed in ethnicity, race, class, and religion.

Each of the above-mentioned categories of primary sources reveals different types of historical information. A politician's diary, memoirs, or collection of letters, for example, often provide students with the politicians' unguarded, private thoughts and emotions concerning daily life and public events. Though these documents may be a truer reflection of the person's character and aspirations, students must keep in mind that when people write about themselves, they tend to put themselves at the center of the historical event or cast themselves in the best possible light. On the other hand, the politician's public speeches may be more cautious, less controversial, and limited to advancing his or her political party's goals or platform.

Like personal diaries, advertisements reveal other types of historical information. What information does the WAVES poster on this page reveal?

John Phillip Faller, a prolific commercial artist known for his *Saturday Evening Post* covers, designed this recruitment poster in 1944. It was one of over three hundred posters he produced for the U.S. Navy while enrolled in that service during World War II. The purpose of the poster was to encourage women to enlist in the WAVES (Women Accepted for Volunteer Emergency Service), a women's auxiliary to the Navy established in

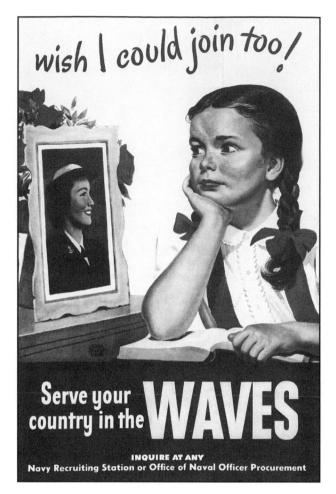

1942. It depicts a schoolgirl gazing admiringly at a photograph of a proud, happy WAVE (perhaps an older sister), thus portraying the military service as an appropriate and admirable aspiration for women during wartime. However, what type of military service? Does the poster encourage women to enlist in military combat like World War II male recruitment posters? Does it reflect gender bias? What does this poster reveal about how the military and society in general feel about women in the military? Does the poster reflect current military and societal attitudes toward women in the military? How many women joined the WAVES? What type of duties did they perform?

Like personal diaries, photographs reveal other types of historical information. What information does the next photograph reveal?

Today, we take electricity for granted. However, in 1935, although 90 percent of city dwellers in America had electricity, only 10 percent of rural Americans did. Private utility companies refused to string electric lines

THE LIBRARY OF CONGRESS.

to isolated farms, arguing that the endeavor was too expensive and that most farmers were too poor to afford it anyway. As part of the Second New Deal, President Franklin Delano Roosevelt issued an executive order creating the Rural Electrification Administration (REA). The REA lent money at low interest rates to utility companies to bring electricity to rural America. By 1950, 90 percent of rural America had electricity. This photograph depicts a 1930s tenant farmer's house in Greene County, Georgia. Specifically, it shows a brand-new electric meter on the wall. The picture presents a host of questions: What was rural life like without electricity? How did electricity impact the lives of rural Americans, particularly rural Georgians? How many rural Georgians did not have electricity in the 1930s? Did Georgia have more electricity-connected farms than other Southern states? What was the poverty rate in rural Georgia, particularly among rural African Americans? Did rural electricity help lift farmers out of poverty?

Like personal diaries, official documents reveal other types of historical information. What information does the next document, a memo, reveal?

From the perspective of the early twenty-first century, in a democratic society, integration of the armed services seems to have been inevitable. For much of American history, however, African Americans were prevented from joining the military, and when they did enlist they were segregated into black units. In 1940, of the nearly 170,000-man Navy, only 4,007, or 2.3 percent, were African American personnel. The vast majority of these men worked in the mess halls as stewards—or, as labeled by the black press, "seagoing bellhops." In this official document, the chairman of the General Board refers to compliance with a directive that would enlist African Americans into positions of "unlimited general service." Who issued the directive? What was the motivation behind the new directive? Who were the members of the General Board? How much authority did they wield? Why did the Navy restrict African Americans to the "messman branch"? Notice the use of the term "colored race." Why was this term used and what did it imply? What did the board conclude? When did the Navy become integrated? Who was primarily responsible for integrating the Navy?

CONFIDENTIAL

DOD Dir. 5200.10, June 29, 1960
NND by ⟨illegible⟩ date Oct 5, 1961

DOWNGRADED AT 3 YEAR INTERVALS;
DECLASSIFIED AFTER 12 YEARS
DOD DIR 5200.10 NARS-NT

G.B. No. 421
(Serial No. 201)
SECRET

Feb 3, 1942

From: Chairman General Board.
To: Secretary of the Navy.

Subject: Enlistment of men of colored race to other than
            Messman branch.

Ref: (a) SecNav let. (SC)P14-4/MM (03200A)/Gen of
            Jan 16, 1942.

1.   The General Board, complying with the directive
contained in reference (a), has given careful attention to the
problem of enlisting in the Navy, men of the colored race
in other than the messman branch.

2.   The General Board has endeavored to examine the
problem placed before it in a realistic manner.

A.   Should negroes be enlisted for **unlimited** general service?

(a) Enlistment for general service implies that the
individual may be sent anywhere, - to any ship or station where
he is needed. Men on board ship live in particularly close
association; in their messes, one man sits beside another; their
hammocks or bunks are close together; in their common tasks they
work side by side; and in particular tasks such as those of a
gun's crew, they form a closely knit, highly coordinated team.
How many white men would choose, of their own accord, that their
closest associates in sleeping quarters, at mess, and in a gun's
crew should be of another race? How many would accept such
conditions, if required to do so, without resentment and just
as a matter of course? The General Board believes that the
answer is "Few, if any," and further believes that if the issue were
forced, there would be a lowering of contentment, teamwork
and discipline in the service.

(b) One of the tennets of the recruiting service
is that each recruit for general service is potentially a leading
petty officer. It is true that some men never do become petty
officers, and that when recruiting white men, it is not possible
to establish which will be found worthy of and secure promotion
and which will not. If negroes are recruited for general service,
it can be said at once that few will obtain advancement to petty
officers. With every desire to be fair, officers and leading
petty officers in general will not recommend negroes for promotion
to positions of authority over white men.

DOWNGRADED AND
DECLASSIFIED

- 1 -

CONFIDENTIAL

The General Board is convinced that the enlistment of negroes for unlimited general service is unadvisable.

B.   Should negroes be enlisted in general service but detailed in special ratings or for special ships or units?

(a) The ratings now in use in the naval service cover every phase of naval activity, and no new ratings are deemed necessary merely to promote the enlistment of negroes.

(b) At first thought, it might appear that assignment of negroes to certain vessels, and in particular to small vessels of the patrol type, would be feasible. In this connection, the following table is of interest:

Type of Ship	Total Crew	Men in Pay Grades 1 to 4	Men in Pay Grades 5 to 7 (Non-rated)
Battleship	1892	666	1226
Light Cruiser (10,000 ton)	988	365	623
Destroyer (1630 ton)	206	109	97
Submarine	54	47	7
Patrol Boat (180 foot)	55	36	19
Patrol Boat (110 foot)	20	15	5

NOTE: Pay grades 1 to 4 include Chief Petty Officers and Petty Officers, 1st, 2nd and 3rd Class; also Firemen, 1st Class and a few other ratings requiring length of service and experience equal to that required for qualification of Petty Officers, 3rd class. Pay grades 5 to 7 include all other non-rated men and recruits.

There are no negro officers and so few negro petty officers in the Navy at present that any vessels to which negroes might be assigned must have white officers and white petty officers. Examination of the table shows the small number of men in other than petty officer ratings that might be assigned to patrol vessels and indicates to the General Board that such assignments would not be happy ones. The assignment of negroes to the larger ships, where well over one-half of the crews are non-rated men, with mixture of whites and negroes, would inevitably lead to discontent on the part of one or the other, resulting in clashes and lowering of the efficiency of the vessels and of the Navy.

- 2 -

The material collected in these volumes of *American Decades Primary Sources* are significant because they will introduce students to a wide variety of historical sources that were created by those who participated in or witnessed the historical event. These primary sources not only vividly describe historical events, but also reveal the subjective perceptions and biases of their authors. Students should read these documents "actively," and with the contextual assistance of the introductory material, history will become relevant and entertaining.

—*Paul G. Connors*

CHRONOLOGY OF SELECTED WORLD EVENTS OUTSIDE THE UNITED STATES, 1980-1989

1980

- Italian semiotics professor Umberto Eco publishes his medieval detective novel, *The Name of the Rose.*

- The Church of England replaces the Book of Common Prayer, used in services since 1569, with the Alternative Service Book.

- On January 6, voters reelect Indira Gandhi prime minister of India.

- On February 27, France announces the sale of weapons-grade uranium and a nuclear reactor to Iraq.

- On March 24, human rights activist Archbishop Oscar A. Romero is murdered in El Salvador.

- In April, the Organization of Petroleum Exporting Countries (OPEC) raises the price of a barrel of crude oil to thirty-two dollars.

- On April 12, Samuel K. Doe leads a military coup in deposing President William R. Tolbert in Liberia.

- On April 17, Donald A. Henderson, Johns Hopkins University physician and head of the World Health Organization campaign against smallpox, announces its eradication.

- On April 18, Zimbabwe, formerly known as Rhodesia, gains independence after years of civil war.

- From April 21 to September 26, a total of 125,262 Cubans flee to the U.S. to escape poverty and repression.

- On April 24, U.S. forces fail to rescue the fifty-two hostages held by Islamic revolutionaries in Iran.

- In May, Ian Curtis, lead singer of the British rock group Joy Division commits suicide.

- On May 20, Quebec citizens vote against independence, remaining part of Canada.

- On June 6, physicists Luis Alvarez and Walter Alvarez (father and son) propose that the collision of an asteroid with Earth caused the extinction of the dinosaurs 65 million years ago.

- On June 26, France announces the test of a neutron bomb.

- On June 27, Canada's House of Commons adopts "O, Canada" as the national anthem.

- On July 5, Swede Bjorn Borg beats American John McEnroe to win the Wimbledon tennis championship. The two battled through five sets for three hours and fifty-three minutes.

- On July 14, the American Defense Intelligence Agency (ADIA) announces that its members believe that South Africa exploded an atomic bomb in September 1979.

- On July 18, India launches its first staged rocket.

- On August 14, Polish shipyard workers in Gdansk strike to protest a rise in meat prices.

- On August 19, Willy Russell performs his play *Educating Rita* at London's Piccadilly Theatre following its opening at the Warehouse Theatre.

- On August 20, the Soviet Union, in response to continuing unrest in the East Bloc, jams western radio broadcasts in violation of the 1975 Helsinki accords.

- From September 4 to September 22, Iraqi planes and ten thousand troops attack Iranian airfields in the Shatt al Arab estuary, escalating border conflicts and beginning an eight-year war between Iran and Iraq.

- On September 17, gunmen assassinate former Nicaraguan dictator Anastasio Somoza Debayle in Asunción, Paraguay.

- On October 1, the European Economic Community (EEC) bans the use of growth hormones (steroids) in cattle feed.

- On October 4, a bomb explosion outside a Paris synagogue kills four, injures ten, and raises fear of neo-Nazi activities in France.

- In December, British unemployment reaches 2.5 million, the highest since 1935.

- On December 8, Polish-born poet Czeslaw Milosz receives the Nobel Prize in literature.

1981

- Physicians diagnose eight cases of Kaposi's Sarcoma, a rare cancer, in young gay men in New York City. These cases are the first that physicians document in what will become the Auto Immunodeficiency Syndrome (AIDS) pandemic.

- On January 17, Philippine president Ferdinand Marcos ends eight years of martial law and calls for free elections.

- On January 20, the day of U.S. president Ronald Reagan's inauguration, the United States releases almost $8 billion in Iranian assets, and Iran releases the fifty-two American diplomats held hostage for 444 days.

- On January 23, the Reagan administration suspends U.S. financial aid to the revolutionary Sandinista government of Nicaragua, charging that Nicaragua, with the aid of Cuba and the Soviet Union, is supplying arms to rebels in El Salvador.

- In February, the U.S. presidential administration of Ronald Reagan resumes grain exports to the Soviet Union and agrees that the United States will not suspend grain shipments in the future.

- In March, Spain legalizes divorce.

- On May 5, Irish nationalist Bobby Sands dies following a sixty-five-day hunger strike which Sands had hoped would gain worldwide sympathy for Irish independence.

- On May 6, the Reagan administration, accusing Libya of supporting terrorism, closes the Libyan embassy in Washington, D.C.

- On May 10, voters elect Socialist Party leader François Mitterrand president of France.

- On May 13, Pope John Paul II survives an assassination attempt in Rome, Italy by a Bulgarian-trained Turk.

- On June 7, Israeli jets destroy Iraq's Osirak nuclear reactor to prevent Iraqi production of plutonium.

- On June 22, Iranian president Abolhassan Bani-Sadr is removed from office and flees to France.

- On June 28, Islamic Republican Party chief Ayatollah Mohammed Beheshti, along with four aides, is killed in Teheran.

- On July 1, dramatist Nell Dunn premieres the play *Steaming* at London's Theatre Royal, Stratford East.

- On July 17, Britain completes the 4,626-foot Humber Bridge at Hull, the world's longest suspension bridge.

- On July 24, U.S. envoy Philip C. Habib negotiates a ceasefire following clashes between Israeli and Palestinian forces in Lebanon.

- On July 28, dramatist Simon Gray premieres the play *Quartermaine's Terms,* starring Edward Fox, at the Queen's Theatre in London.

- On July 29, Prince Charles of Great Britain, thirty-two, marries Lady Diana Spencer, twenty, at St. Paul's Cathedral in London.

- On August 19, two U.S. Navy planes shoot down two Soviet-made Libyan Air Force planes after the Libyans attacked them in air space above the Gulf of Sidra.

- On August 30, a bomb kills several top Iranian officials, including President Muhammad Ali Rajai and Prime Minister Mohammad Javar Bahonar.

- On September 11, a grenade kills Ayatollah Assadolah Madani, an aide to Iranian cleric and Islamic revolutionary leader Ayatollah Ruholla Khomeini.

- On September 21, British Honduras, renamed Belize, becomes an independent member of the British Commonwealth of Nations.

- On September 22, the TGV, a train that travels 236 mph, begins service from Paris to Lyon, France.

- On October 6, in Cairo, Islamic thugs murder Egyptian president, Nobel laureate, and fellow Muslim Anwar Sadat for his 1979 peace accord with Israel and recent crackdowns on political dissidents. Hosni Mubarak, fifty-three, will succeed Sadat as president.

- On November 1, the Caribbean islands of Antigua and Barbuda gain independence and unify as one state in the British Commonwealth of Nations.

- On December 10, Bulgarian-born writer Elias Canetti receives the Nobel Prize in literature.

- On December 13, Polish general Wojciech Jaruzelski, having become prime minister in February, declares martial law, outlaws the independent labor union Solidarity, and imprisons opposition leaders.

1982

- British actor Ben Kingsley plays the lead in British director Richard Attenborough's *Gandhi.*

- Italian tenor Placido Domingo stars in Italian director Franco Zeffirelli's movie version of Italian composer Giuseppe Verdi's opera *La Traviata.*

- A census reveals that China's population exceeds one billion.

- On March 1, two unmanned Soviet probes land on Venus, surviving long enough to transmit data on its soil and atmosphere.

- On March 23, the military overthrows the dictatorship of General Romeo Lucas Garcia in Guatemala.

- On April 1, Panama takes over the Panama Canal Area under the terms of a 1977 treaty with the United States.

- On April 2, Argentina invades the Falkland Islands in the southern Atlantic Ocean, over which it and Britain each claim possession.

- On April 12, Great Britain blockades the Falkland Islands in response to Argentina's invasion of the islands.

- On April 17, Queen Elizabeth II of Britain signs the Constitution Act in Ottawa, Canada, replacing the North American Act of 1867 with a constitution that acknowledges Canadian autonomy.
- On April 21, Israeli forces destroy Palestinian strongholds in southern Lebanon from which members of the Palestinian Liberation Organization (PLO) have launched guerrilla attacks.
- On April 25, Israel withdraws its last troops from the Sinai Peninsula under terms of the 1978 Camp David Accords and the 1979 Egyptian-Israeli peace treaty.
- On May 4, South African playwright Athol Fugard debuts *Master Harold . . . and the Boys* at New York City's Lyceum Theater.
- On May 14, British forces storm the Falkland Islands to reclaim them from Argentina.
- On May 24, Iranian forces retake the port city of Khurramshahr, seizing thirty thousand Iraqi prisoners.
- On June 3, terrorists wound the Israeli ambassador to Great Britain in London.
- On June 6, Israel invades Lebanon to destroy PLO sanctuaries.
- On June 14, Argentinean troops in the Falkland Islands surrender to the British.
- In July, Italy defeats West Germany, 3-1, to win the World Cup in international soccer competition.
- On July 17, doctors admit their inability to identify the cause of a new disease known as acquired severe immunodeficiency disease (ASID).
- On July 27, Israeli jets bomb West Beirut, killing 120 and injuring 232.
- On August 20, Mexico defaults on a $60 billion foreign debt, the first of several Third World nations to do so.
- On August 29, two British explorers complete a three-year circumnavigation of the globe by way of both the North and South poles.
- On August 30, British anthropologist Richard Leakey, son of Louis S. B. and Mary Leakey, and a team of anthropologists report the discovery in Kenya of a "humanlike" jawbone 8 million years old.
- On September 14, a bomb kills Christian Phalangist leader Bashir Gemayel, the president-elect of Lebanon.
- On September 16, Christian Phalangist militiamen massacre Palestinian civilians in refugee camps in West Beirut.
- On October 1, the Christian Democrats defeat the Socialists in West German elections.
- On October 29, Spanish voters elect Socialist leader Felipe González as prime minister.
- On November 5, Brazil and Paraguay complete construction of the sluice gates on the Itaipu Dam, the world's largest hydroelectric project.
- On November 10, Soviet Communist Party Secretary Leonid I. Brezhnev dies after seventeen years in power in the Soviet Union. Former KGB head Yuri V. Andropov succeeds him.
- On November 16, dramatist Tom Stoppard debuts *The Real Thing* at London's Strand Theatre.

- On December 8, Colombian novelist Gabriel García Márquez receives the Nobel Prize in literature.
- On December 9, the Centers for Disease Control and Prevention in Atlanta announces that the disease now known as acquired immunodeficiency syndrome (AIDS) is spreading to infants and children.
- On December 10, two Soviet cosmonauts set a record of 211 days in space.

1983

- The "New Romantic" style of British pop music, exemplified by artists such as A Flock of Seagulls, Duran Duran, and Culture Club, is popular in the United States and Europe.
- On March 9, dramatist Caryl Churchill premieres the play *Fen* at London's Almeida Theatre.
- On March 22, the German magazine *Stern* reveals the existence of what it claims to be Adolf Hitler's diaries. Scholars expose the diaries as a hoax.
- On March 30, dramatist Ray Cooney premieres the play *Run for Your Wives,* at London's Shaftesbury Theatre.
- On April 18, terrorists bomb the U.S. Embassy in Beirut, killing sixty-three people to punish the United States for supporting Israel.
- On May 11, the newly discovered IRAS-Araki-Alcock comet comes within 2.9 million miles of Earth, the closest a comet has come since 1770.
- In July, Australia strips the United States of the America's Cup for the first time since 1851 when the *Australia II* defeats *Liberty,* four races to three, in international sailboat racing.
- On August 6, the oil tanker *Castillo de Bellver* catches fire, spilling 250,000 tons of oil off the coast of Cape Town, South Africa.
- On August 21, Philippine senator Benigno S. Aquino returns to Manila after two years in exile to organize opposition to President Ferdinand Marcos.
- On August 29, mortar shells kill two and wound thirteen U.S. marines at their compound at the Beirut, Lebanon, airport.
- In September, Soviet haulers quit fishing the Aral Sea, once the source of 10 to 15 percent of their freshwater catch.
- On September 1, a Korean Air Lines Boeing 747 strays into Soviet airspace above Sakhalin Island in the north Pacific. A Soviet jet shoots it down, killing all 269 passengers.
- On September 15, Israeli prime minister Menachem Begin resigns. Foreign Minister Yitzhak Shamir succeeds him.
- On September 21, David Mamet's study of greed, *Glengarry Glen Ross,* opens at London's Cottlesloe Theatre.
- On October 8, the Metropolitan Teien Art Museum opens in Tokyo, Japan.
- On October 9, North Korean terrorists destroy a ceremonial mausoleum in Rangoon, Burma, killing nineteen and wounding forty-nine in an attempt to assassinate South Korean president Chun Doo Hwan.

- On October 12, a Tokyo court convicts former Japanese prime minister Kakuei Tanaka of accepting a $2.2 million bribe from Lockheed Corporation, fines him the amount of the bribe, and sentences him to four years in prison.

- On October 23, terrorists on suicide missions detonate trucks filled with explosives in the U.S. and French barracks in Lebanon, killing 241 U.S. marines and fifty-eight French paratroopers.

- On October 25, three thousand U.S. marines invade Grenada, an island in the Caribbean.

- On October 26, dramatist Hugh Williams debuts the play *Pack of Lies* at London's Lyric Theatre.

- On November 4, a suicide bomber attacks an Israeli military installation in Lebanon, killing sixty people.

- On November 26, masked gunmen steal $39 million in gold from Heathrow Airport in London.

- On December 8, Indian-born Subramanyan Chandrasekhar receives the Nobel Prize in physics for his work on stellar evolution.

- On December 11, Polish Solidarity leader Lech Walesa receives the Nobel Peace Prize.

- On December 31, Major General Mohammed Buhari overthrows Nigeria's five-year-old democracy.

1984

- Famine and drought in sub-Saharan Africa kill three hundred thousand.

- On January 1, France receives its first delivery of Soviet natural gas from the new European-Soviet pipeline.

- On January 4, the Centers for Disease Control and Prevention reports that AIDS can spread through heterosexual intercourse.

- On January 18, terrorists kill American University president Malcolm H. Kerr in Beirut, Lebanon.

- In February, Japan endures a scare as extortionists claim to have poisoned candy.

- On February 9, Soviet general secretary Yuri V. Andropov dies. Politburo member Konstantin U. Chernenko succeeds him.

- On February 10, the Soviet Union and China sign a $1.2 billion trade agreement.

- On March 16, South Africa and Mozambique sign a peace accord, the first between South Africa's white government and a black nation.

- On March 27, *Starlight Express,* a musical featuring roller skating, debuts at London's Apollo Theatre.

- On April 4, Michael Frayn debuts *Benefactors* at London's Vaudeville Theatre.

- On April 21, the Centers for Disease Control and Prevention confirms reports that French researchers have identified a virus thought to cause AIDS.

- In May, French sculptor Jean Dubuffet unveils his *Monument with Standing Beast* before the new State of Illinois building in Chicago.

- In May, voters elect Junta leader and political moderate José Napoleón Duarte president of El Salvador.

- In June, British pop star Bob Geldof organizes Band Aid, a high-profile pop music charity for African famine victims.

- From June 5 to June 6, Indian efforts to expel Sikh separatists from the Golden Temple at Amritsar cause a riot that kills six hundred to twelve hundred people.

- On June 30, Canadian prime minister Pierre Elliott Trudeau resigns and calls for national elections.

- On August 3, the African nation of Upper Volta changes its name to Burkina Faso.

- On August 22, British anthropologist Richard Leakey and American anthropologist Alan Walker announce the discovery in Kenya of eighteen-million-year-old bones of what they believe to be the common ancestor of humans and the African apes.

- On August 29, the World Court denounces the U.S. mining of Nicaraguan harbors as a violation of international law.

- On September 4, the Progressive Conservative Party wins 211 of 282 seats in the House of Commons in Canadian national elections.

- On September 14, no party earns a majority of votes in Israeli elections. The Knesset agrees to a coalition government headed first by Labor leader Shimon Peres, then by Likud head Yitzhak Shamir.

- In October, a national coal strike cripples mining in Britain.

- On October 1, Sikh extremists among her own bodyguards assassinate Indian prime minister Indira Gandhi. Her son Rajiv, succeeds her and wins the ministry in his own right by year's end.

- On October 19, the Polish security police murder pro-Solidarity priest Jerzy Popieluszko.

- On October 20, Beijing, China, allows businesses to seek profit for the first time since the communist revolution in 1949.

- On November 15, Chilean police arrest thirty-two thousand suspects in the Santiago slum of La Victoria and hold them in a soccer stadium for questioning after demonstrations against dictator Augusto Pinochet.

- On November 19, a natural gas explosion in Mexico City kills five hundred people.

- In December, Great Britain's Thatcher government privatizes its telephone service.

- On December 3, the Union Carbide insecticide plant in Bhopal, India, leaks poison gas, killing two thousand and injuring two hundred thousand.

- On December 11, Archbishop Desmond Tutu receives the Nobel Peace Prize.

- On December 19, Prime Minister Margaret Thatcher of Britain and Premier Zhao Ziyang of China sign an agreement in Beijing to transfer Hong Kong from Britain to China in 1997.

- On December 21, gunmen seize two Merrill Lynch couriers in Montreal, Canada, and escape with $51.3 million in securities.

1985

- British author D. H. Lawrence is enshrined in Poet's Corner at London's Westminster Abbey.

- On February 4, New Zealand refuses to allow a U.S. warship into its waters on the grounds that the ship carries nuclear arms.

- On February 17, British scientists report the existence of a "hole" in the ozone layer over Antarctica.

- In March, orchestras throughout the world sponsor Bach festivals to commemorate the three hundredth anniversary of German composer Johann Sebastian Bach's birthday.

- On March 11, Soviet Communist Party general secretary Konstantin Chernenko, seventy-three, dies. Agriculture Minister Mikhail Sergeyevich Gorbachev, fifty-four, succeeds him.

- On March 13, Prime Minister Margaret Thatcher of Britain commissions a group to study the problem of violence at soccer games following two widely publicized soccer riots.

- On March 16, Lebanese terrorists kidnap Terry Anderson, U.S. foreign correspondent for the Associated Press, in Beirut, Lebanon, and hold him until December 4, 1991.

- On May 1, President Ronald Reagan of the United States ends trade with Nicaragua, denouncing the Sandinista regime as a threat to U.S. security.

- On May 29, a soccer riot at the European Cup Finals in Brussels, Belgium, collapses a platform, killing thirty-eight.

- On July 10, the French secret service bombs the antinuclear protest ship *Rainbow Warrior* in Auckland harbor, New Zealand.

- On July 13, British pop star Bob Geldof stages Live Aid, simultaneous concerts in London and Philadelphia, for African famine relief.

- On July 20, South Africa declares an indefinite state of emergency, the first in twenty-five years in response to racial violence.

- On August 17, in the Iran-Iraq War, Iraq attacks the Iranian oil terminal of Kharg Island with French Exocet missiles.

- On September 1, explorer Robert D. Ballard, leading a joint French-U.S. team, discovers the wreck of the *Titanic* in the Atlantic Ocean five hundred miles south of Newfoundland.

- On September 13, Saudi Arabian oil minister Ahmad Zaki Yamani announces an oil discount, reducing oil prices for the next six months.

- On October 7, terrorists hijack the Italian cruise ship *Achille Lauro* in the Mediterranean Sea and kill an American passenger the next day.

- On October 8, *Les Misérables* debuts at London's Palace Theatre.

- On October 15, voters elect Gen. Samuel K. Doe president of Liberia despite accusations of election fraud.

- In November, British anthropologist Richard Leakey and American anthropologist Alan Walker make what biochemist and historian of paleoanthropology Roger Lewin called "the paleontological discovery of the century": a 1.6 million-year-old skeleton in Kenya missing only an arm bone and some bones in the hands and feet. The press dubbed the discovery the Turkana Boy because Leakey and Walker had found it near Lake Turkana, Kenya, and because the remains were of a nine-year-old boy, Leakey and Walker estimated.

- On November 3, Tanzanian president Julius K. Nyerere, who led his nation to independence, resigns after twenty-one years in power. Vice President Ali Hassan Mwinyi succeeds him.

- On November 9, Soviet chess master Gary Kasparov defeats world chess master Anatoly Karpov in Moscow.

- On November 11, Nicaraguan Sandinista president Daniel Ortega Saavedra rejects a peace plan of the Contradora (neutral Latin American) nations, citing the absence of a provision to forbid U.S. military maneuvers in the region.

- On November 21, Soviet leader Mikhail Gorbachev and President Ronald Reagan of the United States meet for a summit on foreign affairs.

- On November 25, the musical *Black and Blue,* featuring vaudeville songs from the 1920s and 1930s, debuts at Paris's Chatelet theater.

- On December 9, French novelist Claude Simon receives the Nobel Prize in literature.

- On December 10, Italian-born Franco Modigliani receives the Nobel Prize in economics.

- On December 27, terrorists kill eighteen and injure 111 at airports in Rome, Italy and Vienna, Austria.

- On December 30, Pakistani president General Mohammad Zia ul-Haq declares an end to eight and one-half years of martial law.

1986

- On January 1, President Ronald Reagan of the United States and Soviet general secretary Mikhail Gorbachev exchange New Year's greetings televised in the United States and Soviet Union.

- On January 6, General Samuel K. Doe is inaugurated as president of Liberia.

- On February 6, Haitian President-for-Life Jean-Claude "Baby Doc" Duvalier, thirty-four, flees to France following a week of protests.

- On February 11, the U.S.S.R. frees Russian dissident Anatoly Shcharansky in an East-West prisoner exchange.

- On February 26, engineers complete the Annacis Bridge in Vancouver, British Columbia, the world's longest cable-stayed bridge.

- On February 26, Philippine ruler Ferdinand Marcos flees to Hawaii after ten days of protest against election fraud.

- On February 28, Swedish prime minister and peace activist Olof Palme, fifty-nine, is assassinated in Stockholm.

- In March, Argentinean director Luis Puenzo's *La historia oficial* (The Official Story), wins an Oscar for best foreign film.

- On March 4, former United Nations secretary-general Kurt Waldheim wins election as president of Austria despite evidence he had been a Nazi during World War II.

- On March 7, President Pieter W. Botha of South African lifts martial law in effect in black districts since 1985.
- On March 14, the European Space Agency's *Giotto* spacecraft passes within 335 miles of the core of Halley's Comet.
- On March 15, voters elect Paris mayor Jacques Chirac to head a Conservative Parliament and share power with Socialist president François Mitterrand, who has been in power since 1981.
- On April 5, a terrorist bombing at a West Berlin discotheque kills two people, including a U.S. serviceman, and injures 230.
- On April 10, the U.S. government warns consumers not to drink Italian wine after some twenty people die in Italy from drinking wine contaminated with methanol.
- On April 13, Pope John Paul II visits Rome's main synagogue in what may be the first papal visit to a Jewish temple.
- On April 14, the Anglican Church appoints civil rights leader Desmond Tutu Archbishop of South Africa.
- On April 15, the United States bombs the Tripoli and Benghazi headquarters of Libyan leader Mu'ammar Gadhafi to punish Libya's bombing a West Berlin discotheque.
- On April 18, South Africa repeals laws that had restricted the movement of blacks.
- On April 26, an accident at the Chernobyl nuclear power plant near Kiev, Ukraine, releases a radioactive cloud into the atmosphere.
- In May, an international commission names the AIDS virus the human immunodeficiency virus (HIV).
- On May 1, nearly 1.5 million South Africans protest apartheid in the nation's largest strike.
- On May 24, Margaret Thatcher begins a three-day visit to Israel, the first by a British prime minister.
- On May 27, the United States agrees to comply with the 1979 Strategic Arms Limitation Treaty, suspended since the Soviet invasion of Afghanistan.
- On June 12, South Africa again declares a state of emergency in anticipation of protests to mark the tenth anniversary of the Soweto uprising.
- On June 26, voters reject a measure to end Ireland's ban on divorce.
- On June 27, the International Court of Justice at The Hague rules that the United States has broken international law by mining the harbors of Nicaragua and by aiding antigovernment rebels.
- On June 29, Argentina wins the World Cup in soccer by defeating West Germany, 3-2.
- On July 6, the Liberal Democratic Party and Prime Minister Yasuhiro Nakasone win reelection in parliamentary elections in Japan.
- On July 15, U.S. officials announce the dispatch of U.S. Army troops to Bolivia to help Bolivia stop the cultivation and sale of illegal drugs.
- On July 26, Shiite Muslim terrorists release American priest Lawrence Jenco from captivity in Lebanon following a Reagan administration secret arms trade to Iran.

- On August 18, the Soviet Union announces it will continue its moratorium on nuclear testing, which had expired on August 6.
- From August 21 to August 26, volcanic explosions release toxic gas, killing fifteen hundred to seventeen hundred people in Cameroon.
- On September 11, President Hosni Mubarak of Egypt and Prime Minister Shimon Peres of Israel meet in the first summit between the nations in five years.
- On September 16, the European Economic Community (ECC) issues economic sanctions against South Africa for oppressing blacks.
- In October, French physicians begin trials of the abortion drug, RU 486.
- On October 5, Nicaragua shoots down a U.S. cargo plane carrying arms and captures the pilot, Eugene Hasenfus of Wisconsin.
- On October 7, a politically neutral daily, *The Independent,* begins publication in London.
- On October 9, Andrew Lloyd Weber debuts the musical *The Phantom of the Opera,* starring Michael Crawford, at London's Majesty Theatre.
- On October 12, President Ronald Reagan of the United States offers Soviet general secretary Mikhail Gorbachev complete nuclear disarmament at a summit in Reykjavík, Iceland.
- On October 14, holocaust survivor and human rights activist Elie Wiesel wins the Nobel Peace Prize.
- On October 21, British playwright Hugh Whitemore debuts *Breaking the Code,* at London's Haymarket Theater.
- On November 1, a fire at the Sandoz pharmaceutical warehouse in Switzerland discharges one thousand tons of toxic chemicals into the Rhine River, killing millions of fish and contaminating the water.
- On November 2, Shiite extremists in Lebanon exchange American University administrator David Jacobsen for U.S. weapons.
- On November 25, Soviet general secretary Mikhail Gorbachev visits India, the first by a Soviet leader since 1980.
- On November 28, the United States violates the 1979 Strategic Arms Limitation Treaty with the Soviet Union by deploying a B-52 bomber capable of carrying cruise missiles.
- On November 30, Punjabi extremists hijack a public bus in India and kill twenty-two Hindus.
- On December 8, Prime Minister Jacques Chirac of France withdraws a bill to reform French universities following more than two weeks of student protests.
- On December 17, Nicaragua releases American pilot Eugene Hasenfus whom it had held since October 5.
- On December 20, some fifty thousand students march for democracy in Shanghai, China.

1987

- A Sicilian Mafia trial ends in prison sentences for 338 of 452 defendants charged with heroin trafficking.

- On January 1, a team of molecular biologists announces that evidence from mitochondrial DNA traces the ancestry of all modern humans to a single woman who lived in Africa between one hundred thousand and two hundred thousand years ago. The press dubbed her Mitochondrial Eve.

- On January 4, the Communist Party of China expels dissidents.

- On February 22, Syrian troops seize West Beirut in an attempt to end anarchy in the city for fear that violence in Lebanon might inflame tensions throughout the region.

- On March 6, the ferry *Herald of Free Enterprise* sinks in the English Channel, killing 192 people.

- On April 11, South Africa bans protests against its detention of blacks.

- On May 17, Iraqi missiles hit the U.S. frigate *Stark* in the Persian Gulf, killing thirty-seven men.

- On June 11, Prime Minister Margaret Thatcher of Britain wins a third term.

- On June 25, Soviet Party general secretary Mikhail Gorbachev announces Perestroika: economic reforms to raise Soviet factory and farm production.

- In July, the United States regains the America's Cup when *Stars and Stripes* sweeps Australia's *Kookaburra III* in international sailboat racing.

- On July 4, a French court sentences former Gestapo chief Klaus Barbie, seventy-three, to life in prison for war crimes during World War II.

- On August 1, Shiites and Sunni on hajj (pilgrimage) clash in Mecca, Saudi Arabia, killing nearly four hundred people.

- On August 7, five Central American nations agree to Costa Rican president Oscar Arias Sanchez's peace process.

- On October 1, Nicaragua's anti-Sandinista newspaper, *La Prensa,* resumes publication.

- On October 2, Great Britain begins tests of the French abortion pill, RU 486.

- On October 3, Canada and the United States sign a free-trade agreement.

- On October 27, dramatist Peter Shaffer premieres the play *Lettice and Lovage,* starring Maggie Smith, at London's Globe Theater.

- On November 9, a bomb explosion in Colombo, Sri Lanka, kills thirty-two and injures more than seventy.

- On December 7, Soviet leader Mikhail Gorbachev arrives in Washington for a three-day summit with President Ronald Reagan of the United States.

- On December 11, President Oscar Arias Sanchez of Costa Rica wins the Nobel Peace Prize.

- On December 16, voters elect Roh Tae Woo, whom South Korean military leader and president Chun Doo-Hwan had chosen to succeed him.

- On December 17, Milos Jakes, a Gorbachev-style reformer, replaces Czech Communist Party leader Gustav Husak, who has ruled for eighteen years.

- On December 31, the United States protests the release of Medellín drug lord Jorge Luis Ochoa from a Colombian prison.

1988

- Iranian novelist Salman Rushdie's satire, *The Satanic Verses,* incenses Muslim readers with alleged "blasphemies".

- Italian novelist Umberto Eco publishes the mystery *Foucault's Pendulum.*

- Floods in Bangladesh—the worst in seventy years—kill thousands and leave millions homeless.

- In January, Palestinians in the Gaza Strip launch an *intifada* (uprising) against Israeli occupation of Palestine.

- On January 28, the Canadian Supreme Court overturns a law restricting abortion.

- On February 5, a U.S. grand jury indicts Panamanian dictator and one-time CIA informant General Manuel Noriega on charges of accepting bribes from drug traffickers.

- On March 16, Iraqi troops kill four thousand to twelve thousand Kurdish civilians with poison gas in the town of Halabja.

- On April 14, the Soviet Union announces it will begin to withdraw from Afghanistan on May 17.

- In July, the U.S. *Stars and Stripes* successfully defends the America's Cup against New Zealand.

- On July 1, delegates to a Communist conference in Moscow endorse Mikhail Gorbachev's reforms, including transfer of power to a democratically elected legislature.

- On July 3, the U.S. warship *Vincennes* mistakes an Iran Air A300 Airbus for an attacking plane and shoots it down, killing all aboard.

- On July 8, French voters reelect President François Mitterrand.

- On July 13, Peace talks among Angola, South Africa, and Cuba end fighting in Angola and Namibia.

- On July 20, Iran and Iraq cease fire after nearly eight years of war.

- In August, Polish workers strike to pressure the government to rescind its ban on the union Solidarity.

- On August 18, President General Mohammad Zia ul-Haq of Pakistan and U.S. ambassador Arnold I. Raphel die in a midair explosion of a Pakistani Air Force plane.

- On September 24, France and China allow the public to use the abortion pill, RU 486.

- On December 1, voters elect Benazir Bhutto, daughter of former prime minister Zulfikar Ali Bhutto, prime minister of Pakistan.

- On December 5, the West German environmental ministry confirms a U.S. report of an accident at a nuclear power plant near Frankfurt in December 1987.

- On December 8, Egyptian novelist Naguib Mahfouz receives the Nobel Prize in literature.

- On December 21, a Pan Am 747 explodes in midair over Lockerbie, Scotland, killing all 259 passengers and eleven people on the ground.

1989

- On January 27, the World Health Organization estimates that the number of AIDS cases worldwide will increase from 450,000 to 5 million in 2000.

- From February 2 to February 3, the military overthrows Alfredo Stroessner, Paraguay's dictator for thirty-five years.

- On March 26, voters elect Moscow politician Boris N. Yeltsin, who had broken with the Communist Party, leader of the non-communist party.

- On March 30, the Louvre Museum in Paris reopens following renovations that feature a glass pyramid entrance designed by architect I. M. Pei.

- On April 15, Chinese students meet in Beijing's Tiananmen Square to mourn the death of Politburo member Hu Yaobang, seventy-three.

- On May 7, Panamanians vote to oust Gen. Manuel Noriega, but he ignores their decision.

- On May 11, Kenya calls for a worldwide ban on the trade of ivory to protect the African elephant from extinction.

- On May 14, Argentinean voters elect Peronist leader Carlos Saúl Menem president in the first peaceful transfer of power since 1927.

- On May 24, the Exxon *Valdez* hits a reef in Prince William Sound off the coast of Alaska, spilling ten million gallons of oil.

- On June 4, President Ayatollah Khomeini of Iran dies. Ali Akbar Hashemi Rafsanjani succeeds him.

- On June 8, Chinese troops fire on protesters in Tiananmen Square and execute leaders of the democratic movement.

- On July 23, Japan's ruling Liberal Democratic Party, mired in scandal, loses elections for the first time since 1955.

- On August 15, President Pieter W. Botha of South Africa resigns. His successor, F. W. de Klerk, permits anti-apartheid marches and releases some political prisoners in the fall.

- On August 18, the Polish government, following non-Communist victories in June parliamentary elections, forms a cabinet with non-Communist leaders, the first Polish multiparty government in forty years.

- On August 23, hundreds of thousands of Lithuanians, Latvians, and Estonians form a human chain across their three states to demand independence from the Soviet Union.

- On September 26, the last Vietnamese troops leave Cambodia after eleven years of occupation.

- From October 5 to October 7, Soviet leader Mikhail Gorbachev visits East Germany to celebrate its fortieth anniversary.

- On October 7, the Hungarian Communist Party renames itself the Hungarian Socialist Party and renounces communism in favor of democratic socialism.

- On October 9, the Supreme Soviet allows workers to strike under limited conditions for the first time since 1917.

- On October 19, the British Court of Appeals voids the conviction of the "Guildford Four," Irish prisoners convicted of 1974 bombings of pubs in Guildford and Woolwich.

- On October 23, Hungary declares itself a free republic on the thirty-third anniversary of the 1956 uprising.

- On October 28, Czech police disperse ten thousand people in Prague for staging a pro-democracy rally and arrest dissidents, including playwright Vaclav Havel.

- On November 3, nine thousand people demonstrate for democracy in Sofia, Bulgaria.

- On November 9, East Germany allows citizens to visit the West without visas.

- On November 10, President Todor Zhivkov of Bulgaria resigns after eighteen years in power.

- On November 11, the rebel Farabundo Marti National Liberation Front (FMLN) launches a "final offensive" in its ten-year civil war against the government in El Salvador.

- On November 23, Former Czechoslovakian leader Alexander Dubcek, who ushered in the reform "Prague Spring" of 1968, addresses seventy thousand pro-democracy demonstrators in Braislava.

- On November 24, the Czechoslovakian Communist Party Presidium, including General Secretary Milos Jakes, resigns en masse.

- On November 29, the southern republic of Serbia severs economic ties with the northern republic of Slovenia in Yugoslavia.

- On December 1, President Mikhail Gorbachev meets Pope John Paul II at the Vatican, the first meeting between a head of the Soviet Union and the Pope.

- On December 3, the entire leadership of East Germany's ruling Socialist Unity party resigns, including all 163 members of the Central Committee.

- On December 10, nearly fifty thousand people demonstrate in Sofia for an end to communist rule in Bulgaria.

- On December 10, Norwegian Trygve Haavelmo receives the Nobel Prize in economics.

- On December 11, two hundred thousand people demonstrate in Leipzig for the reunification of Germany.

- On December 15, demonstrators in Timisoara, Romania, surround a church to prevent the secret police from arresting a popular cleric, Reverend Laszlo Tokes.

- On December 16, the United States invades Panama City, "Operation Just Cause," after Panamanian soldiers kill a U.S. marine.

- On December 20, the Lithuanian Communist Party declares independence from the Soviet Communist Party.

- On December 22, Germans celebrate the opening of the Brandenburg Gate between East and West Berlin, symbolically reuniting East and West Germany and ending the Cold War.

- On December 29, voters elect dramatist Vaclav Havel president of Czechoslovakia.

1

THE ARTS

MILLIE JACKSON

Entries are arranged in chronological order by date of primary source. For entries with one primary source, the entry title is the same as the primary source title. Entries with more than one primary source have an overall entry title, followed by the titles of the primary sources.

Important Events in the Arts, 1980–1989

1980

- More than 1.5 million people tour a retrospective exhibit of one thousand works by Pablo Picasso at the Museum of Modern Art in New York City.

- President Jimmy Carter cancels a Washington exhibit of works from the Hermitage Museum in Leningrad to protest the Soviet invasion of Afghanistan.

- Mikhail Baryshnikov becomes director of the American Ballet Theater.

- The Metropolitan Opera receives a $5 million grant from Texaco.

- On March 29, the New York Metropolitan Opera production of *Manon Lescaut,* with Placido Domingo and Renata Scotto, is broadcast via satellite to twenty countries.

- On April 13, *Grease,* the longest running show on Broadway to date, closes after 3,388 performances.

- On September 6, the Whitney Museum buys Jasper Johns's *Three Flags* for $1 million, the highest price yet paid for a work by a living artist.

- On December 8, Former Beatle John Lennon is killed outside his apartment building in New York City by Mark David Chapman.

MOVIES: *Airplane!,* directed by Jim Abrahams and David Zucker and starring Robert Hays and Julie Hagerty; *Altered States,* directed by Ken Russell and starring William Hurt and Blair Brown; *American Gigolo,* directed by Paul Schrader and starring Richard Gere and Lauren Hutton; *The Blues Brothers,* directed by John Landis and starring John Belushi and Dan Aykroyd; *Caddyshack,* directed by Harold Ramis and starring Chevy Chase, Bill Murray, and Rodney Dangerfield; *Coal Miner's Daughter,* directed by Michael Apted and starring Sissy Spacek and Tommy Lee Jones; *Dressed to Kill,* directed by Brian De Palma and starring Michael Caine, Nancy Allen, and Angie Dickinson; *The Elephant Man,* directed by David Lynch and starring John Hurt, Anthony Hopkins, and Anne Bancroft; *The Empire Strikes Back,* directed by Irvin Kershner and starring Harrison Ford, Mark Hamill, and Carrie Fisher; *Fame,* starring Irene Cara; *The Great Santini,* starring Robert Duvall; *Melvin and Howard,* directed by Jonathan Demme and starring Paul LeMat, Mary Steenburgen, and Jason Robards; *Nine to Five,* directed by Colin Higgins and starring Jane Fonda, Lily Tomlin, and Dolly Parton; *Ordinary People,* directed by Robert Redford and starring Donald Sutherland, Mary Tyler Moore, and Timothy Hutton; *Private Benjamin,* directed by Howard Zieff and starring Goldie Hawn; *Raging Bull,* directed by Martin Scorsese and starring Robert De Niro; *The Shining,* directed by Stanley Kubrick and starring Jack Nicholson and Shelley Duvall; *The Stunt Man,* directed by Richard Rush and starring Peter O'Toole; *Tess,* directed by Roman Polanski and starring Nastassia Kinski; *Urban Cowboy,* directed by James Bridges and starring John Travolta and Debra Winger; *Xanadu,* directed by Robert Greenwald and starring Michael Beck, Olivia Newton-John, and Gene Kelly.

FICTION: Jean M. Auel, *The Clan of the Cave Bear;* Ann Beattie, *Falling in Place;* Thomas Berger, *Neighbors;* E.L. Doctorow, *Loon Lake;* Ken Follett, *The Key to Rebecca;* Cynthia Freeman, *Come Pour the Wine;* Shirley Hazzard, *The Transit of Venus;* Erica Jong, *Fanny;* Stephen King, *Firestarter;* Maxine Hong Kingston, *China Men;* Judith Krantz, *Princess Daisy;* Robert Ludlum, *The Bourne Identity;* James Michener, *The Covenant;* Wright Morris, *Plains Song for Female Voices;* Joyce Carol Oates, *Bellefleur;* Walker Percy, *The Second Coming;* Belva Plain, *Random Winds;* Tom Robbins, *Still Life With Woodpecker;* Sidney Sheldon, *Rage of Angels;* John Kennedy Toole, *A Confederacy of Dunces;* Anne Tyler, *Morgan's Passing;* Eudora Welty, *The Collected Stories;* Gene Wolfe, *The Shadow of the Torturer.*

POPULAR SONGS: Air Supply, "Lost in Love"; Pat Benatar, "Heartbreaker"; Blondie, "Call Me"; David Bowie, "Ashes to Ashes"; Captain and Tennille, "Do That to Me One More Time"; Irene Cara, "Fame"; The Clash, "Train in Vain"; The Commodores, "Still"; Christopher Cross, "Sailing" and "Ride Like the Wind"; Grandmaster Flash and the Furious Five, "Freedom"; Funkadelic, "Knee Deep"; Crystal Gayle, "Heart Mender"; Rupert Holmes, "Escape"; Jermaine Jackson, "Let's Get Serious"; Michael Jackson, "Don't Stop Til You Get Enough," "Off the Wall," and "Rock with You"; Billy Joel, "It's Still Rock & Roll to Me"; Kool & The Gang, "Ladies Night" and "Too Hot"; Lipps Inc., "Funkytown"; M, "Pop Muzik"; Paul McCartney, "Coming Up"; Bette Midler, "The Rose"; Ronnie Milsap, "In No Time at All"; Anne Murray, "Broken Hearted Me" and "Daydream Believer"; Willie Nelson, "On the Road Again"; Olivia Newton-John, "Magic" and "Xanadu"; Gary Numan, "Cars"; Tom Petty and the Heartbreakers, "Don't Do Me Like That" and "Refugee"; Pink Floyd, "Another Brick in the Wall"; The Pretenders, "Brass in Pocket"; Prince, "I Wanna Be Your Lover"; Queen, "Crazy Little Thing Called Love"; Smokey Robinson, "Cruisin'"; Kenny Rogers, "Coward of the County"; Rolling Stones, "Emotional Rescue"; Diana Ross, "Upside Down"; The S.O.S. Band, "Take Your Time"; Shalamar, "The Second Time Around"; Spinners, "Cupid/I've Loved You for a Long Time" and "Working My Way Back to You/Forgive Me Girl"; Sugar Hill Gang, "Rapper's Delight"; The Whispers, "And the Beat Goes On."

1981

- Broadway box offices take in almost $200 million.

- The Metropolitan Museum of Art in New York City opens The American Wing.

- Michael Cimino's movie *Heaven's Gate* loses $40 million, making Hollywood producers unwilling to finance other big-budget motion pictures by "auteur" directors.
- The portable Sony Walkman becomes a huge seller, popularizing "mobile" music.
- The Whitney Museum opens its first branch, in Stamford, Connecticut.
- The $7.2 million San Antonio Museum opens.
- The University of Pennsylvania Press publishes the complete, unexpurgated version of Theodore Dreiser's novel *Sister Carrie,* including thirty-six thousand words that the original publisher, Frank Doubleday, considered too sexually explicit.
- The Rolling Stones earn a record $25 million during their forty-city U.S. tour.
- On May 21, American collector Wendell Cherry buys Picasso's self-portrait *Yo Picasso* at Sotheby's auction house in New York City for $5.83 million, the highest price yet paid for a twentieth-century work of art.
- On August 1, MTV (Music Television) begins broadcasting. Its first video is the Buggles' "Video Killed the Radio Star."
- On October 4, *The Life and Adventures of Nicholas Nickleby* sets a record for Broadway ticket prices—one hundred dollars per seat.

MOVIES: *Arthur,* directed by Steve Gordon and starring Dudley Moore, Liza Minnelli, and John Gielgud; *Atlantic City,* directed by Louis Malle and starring Burt Lancaster and Susan Sarandon; *Blow Out,* directed by Brian De Palma and starring John Travolta and Nancy Allen; *Body Heat,* directed by Lawrence Kasdan and starring William Hurt and Kathleen Turner; *Endless Love,* starring Brooke Shields; *Escape from New York,* directed by John Carpenter and starring Kurt Russell; *The French Lieutenant's Woman,* directed by Karel Reisz and starring Meryl Streep and Jeremy Irons; *Heaven's Gate,* directed by Michael Cimino and starring Christopher Walken and Kris Kristofferson; *Mommie Dearest,* starring Faye Dunaway; *My Dinner with Andre,* directed by Louis Malle and starring Wallace Shawn and Andre Gregory; *On Golden Pond,* directed by Mark Rydell and starring Henry Fonda, Katharine Hepburn, and Jane Fonda; *Ragtime,* directed by Milos Forman and starring James Olson, Mary Steenburgen, Howard E. Rollins, Jr., and James Cagney; *Raiders of the Lost Ark,* directed by Steven Spielberg and starring Harrison Ford; *Reds,* directed by Warren Beatty and starring Beatty, Diane Keaton, Jack Nicholson, and Maureen Stapleton; *S.O.B.,* directed by Blake Edwards and starring William Holden and Julie Andrews; *Stripes,* directed by Ivan Reitman and starring Bill Murray; *Superman II,* directed by Richard Donner and Richard Lester and starring Christopher Reeve, Gene Hackman, and Margot Kidder.

FICTION: Thomas Berger, *Reinhart's Women;* Raymond Carver, *What We Talk About When We Talk About Love;* Howard Fast, *The Legacy;* Cynthia Freeman, *No Time for Tears;* Andrew M. Greeley, *The Cardinal Sins;* Frank Herbert, *God Emperor of Dune;* John Irving, *The Hotel New Hampshire;* Stephen King, *Cujo;* John D. MacDonald, *Free Fall in Crimson;* Leonard Michaels, *The Men's Club;* Toni Morrison, *Tar Baby;* Joyce Carol Oates, *Angel of Light;*

Harold Robbins, *Goodbye, Janet;* Philip Roth, *Zuckerman Unbound;* Lawrence Sanders, *The Third Deadly Sin;* Martin Cruz Smith, *Gorky Park;* John Updike, *Rabbit Is Rich;* Joseph Wambaugh, *The Glitter Dome.*

POPULAR SONGS: Air Supply, "The One That You Love"; Pat Benatar, "Hit Me with Your Best Shot"; Blondie, "Rapture" and "The Tide Is High"; Kim Carnes, "Bette Davis Eyes"; Rosanne Cash, "Seven Year Ache"; Eric Clapton and His Band, "I Can't Stand It"; The Commodores, "Lady (You Bring Me Up)"; Earl Thomas Conley, "Fire and Smoke"; Christopher Cross, "Arthur's Theme"; Devo, "Whip It"; Neil Diamond, "America," "Hello Again," and "Love on the Rocks"; Duran Duran, "Girls on Film" and "Planet Earth"; E.L.O., "Hold On Tight"; Sheena Easton, "For Your Eyes Only" and "Morning Train"; English Beat, "Mirror in the Bathroom"; Daryl Hall and John Oates, "Kiss on My List"; George Harrison, "All Those Years Ago"; Rick James, "Give It to Me Baby" and "Superfreak"; Kool & The Gang, "Celebration"; John Lennon, "Starting Over" and "Woman"; Manhattan Transfer, "Boy from New York City"; Ronnie Milsap, "No Gettin' Over Me"; Juice Newton, "Angel of the Morning" and "Queen of Hearts"; Oak Ridge Boys, "Elvira"; Dolly Parton, "9 to 5"; Pointer Sisters, "Slow Hand"; The Police, "De Do Do Do, De Da Da Da" and "Don't Stand So Close to Me"; Queen, "Another One Bites the Dust"; Eddie Rabbitt, "I Love a Rainy Night"; REO Speedwagon, "Keep on Loving You"; Kenny Rogers, "Lady" and "I Don't Need You"; Rolling Stones, "Start Me Up"; Diana Ross and Lionel Richie, "Endless Love"; Joey Scarbury, "The Theme from The Greatest American Hero"; Frankie Smith, "Double Dutch Bus"; Rick Springfield, "Jessie's Girl"; Bruce Springsteen, "Hungry Heart"; Billy Squier, "The Stroke"; Rod Stewart, "Passion"; Barbra Streisand, "Woman in Love"; Barbra Streisand and Barry Gibb, "Guilty" and "What Kind of Fool"; Styx, "The Best of Times" and "Too Much Time On My Hands"; Grover Washington, Jr., "Just the Two of Us"; Stevie Wonder, "Master Blaster."

1982

- Michael Jackson releases *Thriller,* which becomes the top-selling album in history.
- The Library of America begins publishing collected editions of works by major American authors.
- Compact discs are introduced by the Sony Corporation of Japan and Philips of the Netherlands.
- The Salvador Dali Museum opens in Saint Petersburg, Florida.
- Carnegie Hall in New York City undergoes a $20 million renovation.
- The J. Paul Getty Museum in Malibu, California, receives a $1.1 billion bequest from oil magnate J. Paul Getty, making it the best-endowed museum in America.
- Steven Spielberg's movie *E.T.: The Extra-Terrestrial* earns a record $235 million at the box office in only three months.
- On June 7, Graceland, the Memphis, Tennessee, home of the late Elvis Presley, is opened to the public as a tourist attraction.

• On October 7, *Cats,* a musical based on the poems of T.S. Eliot, opens on Broadway and becomes the most popular musical of the 1980s.

MOVIES: *Blade Runner,* directed by Ridley Scott and starring Harrison Ford; *Cat People,* directed by Paul Schrader and starring Nastassia Kinski and Malcolm McDowell; *Deathtrap,* directed by Sidney Lumet and starring Michael Caine and Christopher Reeve; *Diner,* directed by Barry Levinson and starring Steve Guttenberg, Kevin Bacon, Mickey Rourke, Daniel Stern, Timothy Daly, Paul Reiser, and Ellen Barkin; *Eating Raoul,* directed by Paul Bartel and starring Paul Bartel and Mary Woronov; *E.T., The Extra-Terrestrial,* directed by Steven Spielberg and starring Henry Thomas and Drew Barrymore; *Fast Times at Ridgemont High,* directed by Amy Heckerling and starring Sean Penn, Phoebe Cates, and Jennifer Jason Leigh; *First Blood,* starring Sylvester Stallone; *48 Hrs.,* directed by Walter Hill and starring Nick Nolte and Eddie Murphy; *Frances,* directed by Graeme Clifford and starring Jessica Lange; *Making Love,* directed by Arthur Hiller and starring Michael Ontkean, Kate Jackson, Harry Hamlin, and Wendy Hiller; *Missing,* directed by Constantin Cosa-Gavras and starring Sissy Spacek and Jack Lemmon; *My Favorite Year,* directed by Richard Benjamin and starring Peter O'Toole; *An Officer and a Gentleman,* directed by Taylor Hackford and starring Richard Gere and Debra Winger; *Personal Best,* starring Mariel Hemingway and Patrice Donnelly; *Poltergeist,* directed by Tobe Hooper and starring JoBeth Williams; *The Road Warrior,* directed by George Miller and starring Mel Gibson; *Sophie's Choice,* directed by Alan J. Pakula and starring Meryl Streep and Kevin Kline; *Star Trek II: The Wrath of Khan,* starring William Shatner, Leonard Nimoy, and Ricardo Montalban; *Tootsie,* starring Dustin Hoffman, Jessica Lange, and Teri Garr; *The Verdict,* directed by Sidney Lumet and starring Paul Newman; *Victor/Victoria,* directed by Blake Edwards and starring Julie Andrews, James Garner, and Robert Preston; *Wild Style,* directed by Charlie Ahearn and starring "Lee" Quinones, Sandra "Pink" Fabara, Fred Braithwaite, and Patti Astor; *The World According to Garp,* directed George Roy Hill and starring Robin Williams, Glenn Close, and John Lithgow.

FICTION: Isaac Asimov, *Foundation's Edge;* Jean M. Auel, *The Valley of Horses;* Ann Beattie, *The Burning House;* Saul Bellow, *The Dean's December;* Arthur C. Clarke, *2010: Odyssey Two;* Richard Condon, *Prizzi's Honor;* John M. Del Vecchio, *The 13th Valley;* Stephen R. Donaldson, *The One Tree;* Ken Follett, *The Man from St. Petersburg;* John Gardner, *Mickelsson's Ghosts;* John Jakes, *North and South;* Stephen King, *Different Seasons;* Judith Krantz, *Mistral's Daughter;* Robert Ludlum, *The Parsifal Mosaic;* Bobbie Ann Mason, *Shiloh and Other Stories;* James Michener, *Space;* Joyce Carol Oates, *A Bloodsmoor Romance;* Cynthia Ozick, *Levitation, Five Fictions;* Harold Robbins, *Spellbinder;* Mary Lee Settle, *The Killing Ground;* Sidney Sheldon, *Master of the Game;* Isaac Bashevis Singer, *The Collected Stories;* Danielle Steel, *Crossings;* Paul Theroux, *The Mosquito Coast;* Anne Tyler, *Dinner at the Homesick Restaurant;* Alice Walker, *The Color Purple;* William Wharton, *A Midnight Clear.*

POPULAR SONGS: Alabama, "Love in the First Degree" and "Mountain Music"; Afrika Bambaataa, "Planet Rock"; Toni Basil, "Mickey"; Big Country, "In a Big Country"; Laura Branigan, "Gloria"; Buckner and Garcia, "Pac-Man Fever"; The Cars, "Shake It Up"; Chicago, "Hard to Say I'm Sorry"; Joe Cocker and Jennifer Warnes, "Up Where We Belong"; John Cougar, "Hurts So Good" and "Jack and Diane"; Crosby, Stills & Nash, "Southern Cross" and "Wasted On the Way"; Paul Davis, " '65 Love Affair"; Dazz Band, "Let It Whip"; Earth, Wind & Fire, "Let's Groove"; Fleetwood Mac, "Hold Me" and "Gypsy"; A Flock of Seagulls, "I Ran"; Foreigner, "Waiting For a Girl Like You"; Aretha Franklin, "Jump To It"; J. Geils Band, "Centerfold" and "Freeze-Frame"; The Go-Go's, "Our Lips Are Sealed," "Vacation," and "We Got the Beat"; Daryl Hall and John Oates, "I Can't Go for That (No Can Do)" and "Private Eyes"; Human League, "Don't You Want Me"; Billy Idol, "Hot in the City"; Joan Jett and the Blackhearts, "I Love Rock 'n' Roll"; Journey, "Open Arms"; Loverboy, "Working for the Weekend"; Paul McCartney and Stevie Wonder, "Ebony and Ivory"; Men at Work, "Who Can It Be Now"; Steve Miller Band, "Abracadabra"; Ronnie Milsap, "Any Day Now"; The Motels, "Suddenly Last Summer" and "Only the Lonely"; Willie Nelson, "Always On My Mind"; Juice Newton, "Love's Been a Little Bit Hard on Me"; Olivia Newton-John, "Physical"; The Alan Parsons Project, "Eye in the Sky"; The Police, "Every Little Thing She Does Is Magic"; Prince, "Controversy"; Quarterflash, "Harden My Heart"; Ricky Skaggs, "Crying My Heart Out Over You"; Soft Cell, "Tainted Love/Where Did Our Love Go"; Rick Springfield, "Don't Talk to Strangers"; Rod Stewart, "Young Turks"; Survivor, "Eye of the Tiger"; Toto, "Rosanna"; Tommy Tutone, "867-5309 (Jenny)"; Twisted Sister, "We're Not Gonna Take It"; Vangelis, "Chariots of Fire"; Hank Williams, Jr., "A Country Boy Can Survive"; Stevie Wonder, "That Girl."

1983

• Conceptual artist Javacheff Christo surrounds eleven islands in Biscayne Bay, Florida, with pink polypropylene at a cost of $3 million.

• On Motown's twenty-fifth anniversay TV special, pop singer Michael Jackson does his moonwalk and brings street dancing into the spotlight.

• On April 22, the Dance Black America Festival in Brooklyn, New York, celebrates three hundred years of African American dance.

• On May 25, the movie *Return of the Jedi* sets an opening-day box-office record, $6.2 million.

• On September 29, after 3,389 performances, *A Chorus Line* becomes the longest-running show in the history of Broadway.

• On October 22, the Metropolitan Opera in New York City celebrates its one hundredth anniversary with a gala featuring one hundred performers.

MOVIES: *The Big Chill,* directed by Lawrence Kasdan and starring William Hurt, Glenn Close, Kevin Kline, Jeff Goldblum, Tom Berenger, JoBeth Williams, Mary Kay Place, and Meg Tilly; *Breathless,* directed by Jim McBride and starring Richard Gere; *Flashdance,* directed by Adrian Lyne and starring Jennifer Beals; *The King of Comedy,* directed by Martin Scorsese and starring Robert De Niro, Jerry Lewis, and Sandra Bernhard; *Lianna,* directed by John Sayles; *Local Hero,* directed by Bill Forsyth and starring Burt Lancaster; *Mr. Mom,* directed by Stan Dragoti and starring Michael Keaton and Teri Garr; *The Outsiders,* starring Matt Dillon, Patrick Swayze, Rob Lowe, Tom Cruise, Emilio Estevez, and Ralph Macchio; *Return of the Jedi,* directed by Richard Marquand and starring Harrison Ford, Mark Hamill, and Carrie Fisher; *The Right Stuff,* directed by Philip Kaufman and starring Sam Shepard, Scott Glenn, Ed Harris, Dennis Quaid, and Fred Ward; *Risky Business,* directed by Paul Brickman and starring Tom Cruise and Rebecca DeMornay; *Rumble Fish,* directed by Francis Ford Coppola and starring Matt Dillon and Mickey Rourke; *Scarface,* directed by Brian De Palma and starring Al Pacino and Michelle Pfeiffer; *Silkwood,* directed by Mike Nichols and starring Meryl Streep, Kurt Russell, and Cher; *Streamers,* directed by Robert Altman and starring Matthew Modine; *Sudden Impact,* starring Clint Eastwood; *Superman III,* starring Christopher Reeve and Richard Pryor; *Tender Mercies,* directed by Bruce Beresford and starring Robert Duvall; *Terms of Endearment,* directed by James L. Brooks and starring Shirley MacLaine, Debra Winger, and Jack Nicholson; *Trading Places,* directed by John Landis and starring Eddie Murphy and Dan Aykroyd; *Twilight Zone—The Movie,* starring Vic Morrow and John Lithgow; *Valley Girl,* directed by Martha Coolidge and starring Nicolas Cage and Deborah Foreman; *WarGames,* directed by John Badham and starring Matthew Broderick, Ally Sheedy, and Dabney Coleman; *The Year of Living Dangerously,* directed by Peter Weir and starring Mel Gibson, Sigourney Weaver, and Linda Hunt; *Yentl,* directed and produced by Barbra Streisand, starring Streisand and Mandy Patinkin; *Zelig,* directed by Woody Allen and starring Woody Allen and Mia Farrow.

FICTION: Isaac Asimov, *The Robots of Dawn;* Raymond Carver, *Cathedral;* Jackie Collins, *Hollywood Wives;* Stephen R. Donaldson, *White Gold Wielder;* George Garrett, *The Succession;* Mark Helprin, *Winter's Tale;* William Kennedy, *Ironweed;* Stephen King, *Pet Sematary* and *Christine;* Louis L'Amour, *The Lonesome Gods;* Norman Mailer, *Ancient Evenings;* Bernard Malamud, *The Stories;* Anne McCaffrey, *Moreta;* James Michener, *Poland;* Judith Rossner, *August;* Philip Roth, *The Anatomy Lesson;* Lee Smith, *Oral History;* Danielle Steel, *Changes;* Walter Tevis, *The Queen's Gambit;* John Edgar Wideman, *Sent for You Yesterday;* Roger Zelazny, *Unicorn Variations.*

POPULAR SONGS: ABC, "The Look of Love"; Bryan Adams, "Straight from the Heart"; After the Fire, "Der Kommisar"; Air Supply, "Making Love Out of Nothing at All"; John Anderson, "Swingin'"; Adam Ant, "Goody Two Shoes"; Patti Austin with James Ingram, "Baby Come to Me"; David Bowie, "China Girl," "Let's Dance," and "Modern Love"; Irene Cara, "Flashdance . . . What a Feeling"; The Clash, "Rock the Casbah"; George Clinton, "Atomic Dog"; Culture Club, "Do You Really Want to Hurt Me," "I'll Tumble 4 Ya," and "Time"; Def Leppard, "Photograph"; Dexy's Midnight Runners, "Come on Eileen"; Thomas Dolby, "She Blinded Me with Science"; Duran Duran, "Hungry Like the Wolf," "Is There Something I Should Know?," and "Rio"; Eurythmics, "Sweet Dreams (Are Made of This)"; Marvin Gaye, "Sexual Healing"; Golden Earring, "Twilight Zone"; Eddy Grant, "Electric Avenue"; Daryl Hall and John Oates, "Maneater"; Herbie Hancock, "Rockit"; Don Henley, "Dirty Laundry"; Michael Jackson, "Beat It," "Billie Jean," "Human Nature," and "Wanna Be Startin' Something"; Michael Jackson and Paul McCartney, "The Girl Is Mine"; Rick James, "Cold Blooded"; Billy Joel, "Allentown" and "Tell Her About It"; Journey, "Separate Ways"; Kajagoogoo, "Too Shy"; The Greg Kihn Band, "Jeopardy"; The Kinks, "Come Dancing"; Huey Lewis and the News, "Heart and Soul"; Men at Work, "Down Under"; Men Without Hats, "The Safety Dance"; Midnight Star, "Freak-a-zoid"; Mtume, "Juicy Fruit"; Musical Youth, "Pass the Dutchie"; The Police, "Every Breath You Take"; The Pretenders, "Back on the Chain Gang"; Charley Pride, "Night Games"; Prince, "1999," "Little Red Corvette," and "Delirious"; Eddie Rabbitt with Crystal Gayle, "You and I"; Lionel Richie, "My Love," "Truly," and "You Are"; Kenny Rogers and Sheena Easton, "We've Got Tonight"; Run-D.M.C., "It's Like That/Sucker M.C."; Bob Seger and the Silver Bullet Band, "Shame on the Moon"; Michael Sembello, "Maniac"; Stray Cats, "Sexy + 17" and "Stray Cat Strut"; Styx, "Mr. Roboto"; Donna Summer, "She Works Hard for the Money"; Talking Heads, "Speaking in Tongues"; Thompson Twins, "Lies"; Toto, "Africa"; Bonnie Tyler, "Total Eclipse of the Heart"; Shelly West, "Jose Cuervo."

1984

• The New York Philharmonic Orchestra presents *Horizons 84: The New Romanticism,* a program mixing computer, synthesizer, and performance art.

• After four years of renovation costing $55 million, the Museum of Modern Art in New York City reopens with a new wing that doubles its gallery space.

• The Equitable Life Assurance Society buys ten Thomas Hart Benton murals.

• Forty-five Renaissance masterworks at the Metropolitan Museum are discovered to be forgeries.

• The Getty Museum acquires the Ludwig collection of medieval manuscripts and several major photograph collections, becoming one of the world's finest photograph museums.

• Run-D.M.C.'s self-titled debut album becomes the first rap album to be certified gold.

• On February 28, Michael Jackson wins eight Grammy awards for his album *Thriller,* which tops 37 million in sales and also earns him seven American Music Awards.

• On June 19, the Motion Picture Association of America institutes the PG-13 rating.

MOVIES: *All of Me,* directed by Carl Reiner and starring Steve Martin and Lily Tomlin; *Amadeus,* directed by Milos Forman and starring F. Murray Abraham and Tom Hulce; *Beat Street,* directed by Stan Latham and starring Robert Taylor, Rae Dawn Chong, and Guy Davis; *Beverly Hills Cop,* directed by Martin Brest and starring Eddie Murphy; *Body Double,* directed by Brian De Palma and starring Melanie Griffith; *Body Rock,* directed by Marcelo Epstein and starring Lorenzo Lamas; *Breakin',* starring Lucinda

Dickey, Adolfo (Shabba-Doo) Quinones, and Michael (Boogaloo Shrimp) Chambers; *Broadway Danny Rose,* directed by Woody Allen and starring Woody Allen and Mia Farrow; *Choose Me,* directed by Alan Rudolph and starring Genevieve Bujold; *Country,* directed by Richard Pearce and starring Jessica Lange and Sam Shepard; *Footloose,* directed by Herbert Ross and starring Kevin Bacon and Lori Singer; *Ghostbusters,* directed by Ivan Reitman and starring Bill Murray, Dan Aykroyd, Rick Moranis, and Sigourney Weaver; *Gremlins,* directed by Joe Dante and starring Zach Galligan and Phoebe Cates; *Indiana Jones and the Temple of Doom,* directed by Steven Spielberg and starring Harrison Ford; *The Karate Kid,* directed by John G. Avildsen and starring Ralph Macchio and Pat Morita; *The Killing Fields,* directed by Roland Joffe and starring Sam Waterston and Haing S. Ngor; *Missing in Action,* directed by Joseph Zito and starring Chuck Norris; *Mrs. Soffel,* starring Diane Keaton; *The Natural,* directed by Barry Levenson and starring Robert Redford, Robert Duvall, and Glenn Close; *Once Upon a Time in America,* directed by Sergio Leone and starring Robert De Niro and James Woods; *Paris, Texas,* directed by Wim Wenders and starring Harry Dean Stanton and Nastassia Kinski; *Places in the Heart,* directed by David Lean and starring Sally Field; *Police Academy,* directed by Hugh Wilson and starring Steve Guttenberg; *Purple Rain,* directed by Albert Magnoli and starring Prince; *Reckless,* directed by James Foley and starring Aidan Quinn and Daryl Hannah; *Red Dawn,* directed by John Milius and starring Patrick Swayze; *Repo Man,* directed by Alex Cox and starring Emilio Estevez and Harry Dean Stanton; *The River,* starring Sissy Spacek and Mel Gibson; *Romancing the Stone,* directed by Robert Zemeckis and starring Kathleen Turner and Michael Douglas; *Sixteen Candles,* directed by John Hughes and starring Molly Ringwald and Anthony Michael Hall; *Splash,* directed by Ron Howard and starring Tom Hanks and Daryl Hannah; *Star Trek III: The Search for Spock,* directed by Leonard Nimoy and starring William Shatner and Leonard Nimoy; *Stop Making Sense,* directed by Jonathan Demme and starring Talking Heads; *Stranger Than Paradise,* directed by Jim Jarmusch; *Streets of Fire,* directed by Walter Hill and starring Michael Paré, Diane Lane, Rick Moranis, and Amy Madigan; *The Terminator,* directed by James Cameron and starring Arnold Schwarzenegger; *This Is Spinal Tap,* directed by Rob Reiner and starring Christopher Guest and Michael McKean; *The Woman in Red,* directed by Gene Wilder and starring Gene Wilder, Kelly LeBrock, and Gilda Radner.

FICTION: Rosellen Brown, *Civil Wars;* Mary Higgins Clark, *Stillwatch;* E.L. Doctorow, *Lives of the Poets: Six Stories and a Novella;* Louise Erdrich, *Love Medicine;* Ellen Gilchrist, *Victory Over Japan;* Robert A. Heinlein, *Job: A Comedy of Justice;* Joseph Heller, *God Knows;* Frank Herbert, *Heretics of Dune;* John Jakes, *Love and War;* Susan Kenney, *In Another Country;* Stephen King and Peter Straub, *The Talisman;* David Leavitt, *Family Dancing;* Robert Ludlum, *The Acquitaine Progression;* Alison Lurie, *Foreign Affairs;* Norman Mailer, *Tough Guys Don't Dance;* Jay McInerney, *Bright Lights, Big City;* Jayne Anne Phillips, *Machine Dreams;* Belva Plain, *Crescent City;* Mario Puzo, *The Sicilian;* Tom Robbins, *Jitterbug Perfume;* Helen Hooven Santmyer, " . . . *And Ladies of the Club*";

Danielle Steel, *Full Circle;* John Updike, *The Witches of Eastwick;* Leon Uris, *The Haj;* Gore Vidal, *Lincoln;* John Edgar Wideman, *Brothers and Keepers;* Richard Yates, *Young Hearts Crying.*

POPULAR SONGS: Art of Noise, "Beat Box"; Bananarama, "Cruel Summer"; Pat Benatar, "Love Is a Battlefield"; Berlin, "No More Words"; Laura Branigan, "Self Control"; Cameo, "She's Strange"; The Cars, "You Might Think" and "Drive"; Chicago, "Hard Habit to Break"; Phil Collins, "Against All Odds (Take a Look at Me Now)"; Culture Club, "Church of the Poison Mind," "Karma Chameleon," "Miss Me Blind," and "It's a Miracle"; Duran Duran, "Union of the Snake," "New Moon on Monday," and "The Reflex"; Sheila E., "The Glamorous Life"; Eurythmics, "Here Comes the Rain Again"; Frankie Goes to Hollywood, "Two Tribes" and "War"; The Go-Go's, "Head Over Heels"; Daryl Hall and John Oates, "Out of Touch" and "Say It Isn't So"; Corey Hart, "Sunglasses at Night"; Dan Hartman, "I Can Dream About You"; Julio Iglesias and Willie Nelson, "To All the Girls I've Loved Before"; Michael Jackson, "Thriller"; Michael Jackson and Paul McCartney, "Say Say Say"; The Jacksons, "State of Shock"; Rick James, "17"; Billy Joel, "Uptown Girl"; Elton John, "I Guess That's Why They Call It the Blues" and "Sad Songs (Say So Much)"; Howard Jones, "New Song"; The Judds, "Mama He's Crazy"; Chaka Khan, "I Feel for You"; Laid Back, "White Horse"; Cyndi Lauper, "Girls Just Want to Have Fun," "She Bop," and "Time After Time"; John Lennon, "Nobody Told Me"; Huey Lewis and the News, "I Want a New Drug," "If This Is It," and "The Heart of Rock 'n' Roll"; Kenny Loggins, "Footloose"; Madonna, "Holiday," "Borderline," "Material Girl" and "Lucky Star"; Barbara Mandrell, "Only a Lonely Heart Knows"; John Cougar Mellencamp, "Pink Houses"; Nena, "99 Luftballons"; Billy Ocean, "Caribbean Queen"; Ollie and Jerry, "Breakin' . . . There's No Stopping Us"; Ray Parker, Jr., "Ghostbusters"; The Alan Parsons Project, "Don't Answer Me"; The Pointer Sisters, "Automatic," "Jump (for My Love)," and "I'm So Excited"; Prince, "When Doves Cry" and "Purple Rain"; Prince & The Revolution, "Let's Go Crazy"; Psychedelic Furs, "Heartbeat"; Queen, "Radio Ga-Ga"; Quiet Riot, "Cum On Feel the Noize"; Ratt, "Round and Round"; Lionel Richie, "All Night Long," "Hello," "Running With the Night," and "Stuck on You"; Rockwell, "Somebody's Watching Me"; Kenny Rogers with Dolly Parton, "Islands in the Stream"; The Romantics, "Talking in Your Sleep"; Scandal featuring Patty Smyth, "The Warrior"; Peter Schilling, "Major Tom (Coming Home)"; Scorpions, "Rock You Like a Hurricane"; Shannon, "Let the Music Play"; Bruce Springsteen, "Born in the U.S.A.," "Cover Me" and "Dancing in the Dark"; George Strait, "Let's Fall to Pieces Together"; Talk Talk, "It's My Life"; Thompson Twins, "Hold Me Now"; Tina Turner, "What's Love Got to Do With It"; Twisted Sister, "We're Not Gonna Take It"; Conway Twitty, "I Don't Know a Thing About Love"; Van Halen, "Jump," "I'll Wait," and "Panama"; John Waite, "Missing You"; Wang Chung, "Dance Hall Days"; Wham!, "Wake Me Up Before You Go-Go"; Deniece Williams, "Let's Hear It for the Boy"; Stevie Wonder, "I Just Called to Say I Love You"; Yes, "Owner of a Lonely Heart"; Paul Young, "Come Back and Stay"; ZZ Top, "Legs."

1985

- Income from rental of movies on videocassette equals movie theater box office income.

- The Getty Museum buys Andrea Mantegna's *Adoration of the Magi* for a record $10.4 million.

- Sales of Bruce Springsteen's *Born in the U.S.A.* reach fifteen million.

- Madonna's *Like a Virgin* becomes the first album by a female artist to sell more than five million copies.

- The all-star recording "We Are the World," released under the name USA for Africa, becomes the hottest-selling single of the decade and raises $50 million for African famine relief.

- Michael Jackson buys ATV Music for $40 million, acquiring the rights to some 250 songs written by John Lennon and Paul McCartney.

- The art magazine *ARTnews* pressures the Austrian government to return thirty-nine hundred artworks seized by the Nazis to their owners, with unclaimed works to be auctioned for Jewish charities.

- Frank Zappa, Dee Snider of Twisted Sister, and John Denver are among the musicians who testify at Senate hearings on explicit lyrics in rock music.

- On July 13, the "Live Aid" concert held in London and Philadelphia is broadcast to more than 1.6 billion people and raises $70 million for African famine relief.

- On September 22, "Farm Aid," a concert organized by Willie Nelson, Neil Young, and John Cougar Mellencamp to raise funds for American farmers, is held in Champaign, Illinois.

- On October 2, movie actor Rock Hudson dies from an AIDS-related illness, raising public awareness of the disease.

- In November, the Whitney Museum opens a branch in the new $200 million Equitable Building in New York; Roy Lichtenstein contributes a sixty-eight-foot mural to its entrance.

- From November 10 to November 14, the first American Music Week at Alice Tully Hall in New York City features three hundred performances of music by new and established American composers, including John Cage, Aaron Copland, and Robert Erickson.

MOVIES: *After Hours*, directed by Martin Scorsese and starring Griffin Dunne; *Back to the Future*, directed by Robert Zemeckis and starring Michael J. Fox; *Blood Simple*, directed by Joel and Ethan Coen; *Brazil*, directed by Terry Gilliam and starring Jonathan Pryce, Kim Greist, and Robert De Niro; *The Breakfast Club*, starring Molly Ringwald, Emilio Estevez, Judd Nelson, Anthony Michael Hall, and Ally Sheedy; *Cocoon*, directed by Ron Howard and starring Jessica Tandy, Steve Guttenberg, Don Ameche, Wilford Brimley, and Hume Cronyn; *The Color Purple*, directed by Steven Spielberg and starring Whoopi Goldberg, Danny Glover, Oprah Winfrey, and Margaret Avery; *Desert Hearts*, starring Helen Shaver and Patricia Charbonneau; *Desperately Seeking Susan*, directed by Susan Seidelman and starring Rosanna Arquette, Aidan Quinn, and Madonna; *The Goonies*, starring Sean Astin, Josh Brolin, and Corey

Feldman; *Kiss of the Spider Woman*, directed by Hector Babenco and starring William Hurt and Raul Julia; *Lost in America*, starring Albert Brooks and Julie Hagerty; *Mad Max Beyond Thunderdome*, starring Mel Gibson and Tina Turner; *Mask*, starring Cher, Sam Elliott, and Eric Stolz; *National Lampoon's European Vacation*, starring Chevy Chase; *Out of Africa*, directed by Sydney Pollack and starring Meryl Streep and Robert Redford; *Pee-Wee's Big Adventure*, directed by Tim Burton and starring Pee-Wee Herman; *Prizzi's Honor*, directed by John Huston and starring Jack Nicholson, Kathleen Turner, and Anjelica Huston; *The Purple Rose of Cairo*, directed by Woody Allen and starring Mia Farrow; *Rambo: First Blood, Part 2*, starring Sylvester Stallone; *Rocky IV*, starring Sylvester Stallone; *St. Elmo's Fire*, starring Rob Lowe, Demi Moore, Andrew McCarthy, Ally Sheedy, Emilio Estevez, and Martin Balsam; *The Sure Thing*, starring John Cusack and Daphne Zuniga; *Sweet Dreams*, starring Jessica Lange and Ed Harris; *The Trip to Bountiful*, directed by Peter Masterson and starring Geraldine Page; *White Nights*, starring Mikhail Baryshnikov, Gregory Hines, and Isabella Rossellini; *Witness*, directed by Peter Weir and starring Harrison Ford and Kelly McGillis; *Young Sherlock Holmes*, starring Nicholas Rowe.

FICTION: Jean M. Auel, *The Mammoth Hunters*; Russell Banks, *Continental Drift*; Ann Beattie, *Love Always*; Barbara Taylor Bradford, *Hold the Dream*; Carolyn Chute, *The Beans of Egypt, Maine*; Tom Clancy, *The Hunt for Red October*; Jackie Collins, *Lucky*; Robin Cook, *Mindbend*; Don DeLillo, *White Noise*; E. L. Doctorow, *World's Fair*; Dominick Dunne, *The Two Mrs. Grenvilles*; Bret Easton Ellis, *Less Than Zero*; Cynthia Freeman, *Illusions of Love*; William Gaddis, *Carpenter's Gothic*; Mary Gordon, *Men and Angels*; Andrew M. Greeley, *Virgin and Martyr*; Robert A. Heinlein, *The Cat Who Walks Through Walls*; Frank Herbert, *Chapterhouse: Dune*; Rolando Hinojosa Smith, *Partners in Crime*; John Irving, *The Cider House Rules*; Garrison Keillor, *Lake Wobegon Days*; Stephen King, *Skeleton Crew*; Louis L'Amour, *Jubal Sackett*; Elmore Leonard, *Glitz*; John D. MacDonald, *The Lonely Silver Rain*; Bobbie Ann Mason, *In Country*; Larry McMurtry, *Lonesome Dove*; James Michener, *Texas*; Anne Rice, *The Vampire Lestat*; Philip Roth, *Zuckerman Bound*; Carl Sagan, *Contact*; Lawrence Sanders, *The Fourth Deadly Sin*; Erich Segal, *The Class*; Sidney Sheldon, *If Tomorrow Comes*; Danielle Steel, *Secrets* and *Family Album*; Irving Stone, *Depths of Glory*; Peter Taylor, *The Old Forest and Other Stories*; Anne Tyler, *The Accidental Tourist*; Kurt Vonnegut, *Galápagos*; Joseph Wambaugh, *Secrets of Harry Bright*; Herman Wouk, *Inside, Outside*.

POPULAR SONGS: ABC, "Be Near Me"; Bryan Adams, "Heaven," "Run to You," "Somebody," and "Summer of '69"; Animotion, "Obsession"; Artists United Against Apartheid, "Sun City"; Philip Bailey with Phil Collins, "Easy Lover"; Pat Benatar, "We Belong"; Jellybean Benitez, "Sidewalk Talk"; Bronski Beat, "Smalltown Boy"; Phil Collins, "Sussudio" and "One More Night"; The Commodores, "Nightshift"; Dead or Alive, "You Spin Me Round (Like a Record)"; DeBarge, "Rhythm of the Night"; Dire Straits, "Money for Nothing"; Duran Duran, "A View to a Kill" and "The Wild Boys"; Sheena Easton, "Strut" and "Sugar Walls"; Harold Faltermeyer, "Axel F";

Foreigner, "I Want to Know What Love Is"; Aretha Franklin, "Freeway of Love" and "Who's Zoomin' Who"; Glenn Frey, "The Heat Is On" and "You Belong to the City"; General Public, "Never You Done That"; Lee Greenwood, "Dixie Road"; Jan Hammer, "Miami Vice Theme"; Murray Head, "One Night in Bankok"; Don Henley, "The Boys of Summer"; The Hooters, "And We Danced"; Whitney Houston, "You Give Good Love" and "Saving All My Love for You"; Waylon Jennings, Willie Nelson, Johnny Cash, and Kris Kristofferson, "Highwayman"; Howard Jones, "Things Can Only Get Better"; Katrina and the Waves, "Walking on Sunshine"; Kool & The Gang, "Cherish," "Fresh," and "Misled"; Patti LaBelle, "New Attitude"; Julian Lennon, "Valotte"; Huey Lewis and the News, "The Power of Love"; Lisa Lisa and Cult Jam with Full Force, "I Wonder If I Take You Home"; Madonna, "Angel," "Crazy for You," "Dress You Up," "Into the Groove," "Like a Virgin," and "Material Girl"; John Cougar Mellencamp, "Lonely Ol' Night"; Miami Sound Machine, "Conga"; Ronnie Milsap, "Lost in the Fifties Tonight"; New Edition, "Cool It Now"; New Order, "The Perfect Kiss"; John Parr, "St. Elmo's Fire"; Prince & The Revolution, "Raspberry Beret" and "Pop Life"; Ready for the World, "Oh Sheila"; REO Speedwagon, "Can't Fight This Feeling"; David Lee Roth, "California Girls" and "Just a Gigolo"; Run-D.M.C., "King of Rock"; Sade, "Smooth Operator"; Simple Minds, "Don't You (Forget About Me)"; Simply Red, "Money's Too Tight to Mention"; Bruce Springsteen, "I'm on Fire," "Glory Days," and "My Hometown"; Starship, "We Built This City"; Sting, "If You Love Somebody Set Them Free" and "Fortress Around Your Heart"; Tears for Fears, "Everybody Wants to Rule the World," "Shout," and "Head Over Heels"; 'Til Tuesday, "Voices Carry"; The Time, "Jungle Love"; Tina Turner, "Better Be Good to Me," "Private Dancer," and "We Don't Need Another Hero (Thunderdome)"; USA for Africa, "We Are the World"; Wham!, "Careless Whisper" and "Everything She Wants"; Stevie Wonder, "Part-time Lover"; Paul Young, "Everytime You Go Away."

1986

- Dollywood, Dolly Parton's theme park in Pigeon Forge, Tennessee, opens to the public.

- Choreographer Martha Graham's dance company celebrates its sixtieth anniversary.

- The Joffrey Ballet celebrates its thirtieth anniversary.

- On February 26, Robert Penn Warren is named the first poet laureate of the United States.

- On May 5, Cleveland is chosen as the site for the Rock and Roll Hall of Fame.

MOVIES: *Aliens,* directed by James Cameron and starring Sigourney Weaver; *Blue Velvet,* directed by David Lynch and starring Kyle MacLachlan, Laura Dern, Dennis Hopper, Isabella Rossellini, and Dean Stockwell; *Children of a Lesser God,* directed by Randa Haines and starring William Hurt and Marlee Matlin; *The Color of Money,* directed by Martin Scorsese and starring Paul Newman and Tom Cruise; *Crimes of the Heart,* starring Diane Keaton, Sissy Spacek, and Jessica Lange; *Down and Out in Beverly Hills,* starring Nick Nolte, Bette Midler, and Richard Dreyfuss;

The Fly, directed by David Cronenberg and starring Jeff Goldblum and Geena Davis; *Hannah and Her Sisters,* directed by Woody Allen and starring Woody Allen, Mia Farrow, Dianne Wiest, and Michael Caine; *The Hitcher,* directed by Robert Harmon and starring Rutger Hauer, C. Thomas Howell, and Jennifer Jason Leigh; *The Mission,* directed by Roland Joffe and starring Robert De Niro and Jeremy Irons; *Mona Lisa,* directed by Neil Jordan and starring Bob Hoskins; *Peggy Sue Got Married,* starring Kathleen Turner and Nicolas Cage; *Platoon,* directed by Oliver Stone and starring Charlie Sheen, Tom Berenger, and Willem Dafoe; *Round Midnight,* starring Dexter Gordon; *Ruthless People,* directed by Jim Abrahams, David Zucker and Jerry Zucker, and starring Danny DeVito and Bette Midler; *Salvador,* directed by Oliver Stone and starring James Woods and James Belushi; *Shanghai Surprise,* starring Madonna and Sean Penn; *She's Gotta Have It,* directed by Spike Lee; *Sid and Nancy,* directed by Alex Cox and starring Gary Oldman and Chloe Webb; *Something Wild,* directed by Jonathan Demme and starring Melanie Griffith and Jeff Daniels; *Stand by Me,* directed by Rob Reiner and starring River Phoenix; *Star Trek IV: The Voyage Home,* starring William Shatner and Leonard Nimoy; *Top Gun,* directed by Tony Scott and starring Tom Cruise and Kelly McGillis; *Under the Cherry Moon,* starring Prince.

FICTION: Isaac Asimov, *Foundation and Earth;* Barbara Taylor Bradford, *Act of Will;* Tom Clancy, *Red Storm Rising;* Arthur C. Clarke, *The Songs of Distant Earth;* Jackie Collins, *Hollywood Husbands;* Pat Conroy, *The Prince of Tides;* Stephen Coonts, *Flight of the Intruder;* Patti Davis, *Homefront;* Stephen R. Donaldson, *Mordant's Need;* Louise Erdrich, *The Beet Queen;* Ken Follett, *Lie Down With Lions;* Richard Ford, *The Sportswriter;* Cynthia Freeman, *Seasons of the Heart;* Larry Heinemann, *Paco's Story;* Ernest Hemingway, *Garden of Eden;* Tama Janowitz, *Slaves of New York;* Stephen King, *It;* David Leavitt, *The Lost Language of Cranes;* Robert Ludlum, *The Bourne Supremacy;* Sue Miller, *The Good Mother;* Andre Norton, *Flight in Yiktor;* Belva Plain, *The Golden Cup;* Reynolds Price, *Kate Vaiden;* Sally Quinn, *Regrets Only;* Lawrence Sanders, *The Eighth Commandment;* Mary Lee Settle, *Celebration;* Clifford D. Simak, *Highway of Eternity;* Danielle Steel, *Wanderlust;* Robert Stone, *Children of Light;* Peter Taylor, *A Summons to Memphis;* John Updike, *Roger's Version.*

POPULAR SONGS: Carl Anderson and Gloria Loring, "Friends and Lovers"; Art of Noise featuring Duane Eddy, "Peter Gunn"; Atlantic Starr, "Secret Lovers"; B-52's, "Summer of Love"; Bananarama, "Venus"; Bangles, "Manic Monday" and "If She Knew What She Wants"; Berlin, "Take My Breath Away"; Bon Jovi, "You Give Love a Bad Name"; Boston, "Amanda"; James Brown, "Living in America"; Cameo, "Word Up"; Belinda Carlisle, "Mad About You"; Rosanne Cash, "Never Be You"; Phil Collins, "Take Me Home"; Culture Club, "Move Away"; The Dream Academy, "Life in a Northern Town"; Sheila E., "A Love Bizarre"; Erasure, "Oh L'Amour"; Falco, "Rock Me Amadeus"; Peter Gabriel, "Sledgehammer"; Genesis, "Invisible Touch"; Gwen Guthrie, "Ain't Nothin' Goin' On But the Rent"; Heart, "Never" and "These Dreams"; Whitney Houston, "How Will I Know" and

"Greatest Love of All"; Human League, "Human"; INXS, "What You Need"; Janet Jackson, "What Have You Done for Me Lately," "Nasty," and "When I Think of You"; The Jets, "Crush On You"; Grace Jones, "Slave to the Rhythm"; The Judds, "Have Mercy"; Patti LaBelle and Michael McDonald, "On My Own"; Cyndi Lauper, "True Colors"; Level 42, "Something About You"; Huey Lewis and the News, "Stuck with You"; Madonna, "Live to Tell," "Papa Don't Preach," and "True Blue"; Reba McEntire, "Whoever's in New England"; John Cougar Mellencamp, "R.O.C.K. in the U.S.A." and "Small Town"; Mr. Mister, "Broken Wings" and "Kyrie"; Eddie Murphy, "Party All the Time"; Nu Shooz, "I Can't Wait"; Orchestral Manoeuvres in the Dark, "If You Leave"; Robert Palmer, "Addicted to Love"; Pet Shop Boys, "West End Girls"; Prince & The Revolution, "Kiss" and "Mountains"; Regina, "Baby Love"; Lionel Richie, "Dancing on the Ceiling" and "Say You, Say Me"; Run-D.M.C., "Walk This Way"; Simply Red, "Holding Back the Years"; Stacey Q, "Two of Hearts"; Starship, "Sara"; The Statler Brothers, "Too Much On My Heart"; Jermaine Stewart, "We Don't Have to Take Our Clothes Off"; Timbuk 3, "The Future's So Bright, I Gotta Wear Shades"; Randy Travis, "On the Other Hand" and "1982"; Tina Turner, "Typical Male"; Dionne Warwick and Friends, "That's What Friends Are For"; Steve Winwood, "Higher Love"; Dwight Yoakam, "Honky Tonk Man" and "Guitars, Cadillacs"; ZZ Top, "Sleeping Bag."

1987

- Jasper Johns's *Out the Window* sells for $3.6 million; Rembrandt Peale's *Rubens Peale with a Geranium* fetches $4 million at auction.

- The Terra Museum of American Art opens in Chicago.

- Aretha Franklin is the first woman inducted into the Rock and Roll Hall of Fame.

- The Metropolitan Museum opens a $26 million wing dedicated to twentieth-century art.

- Tenor Luciano Pavarotti and cellist Yo-Yo Ma are among the performers at the AIDS benefit concert *Music for Life* held at Carnegie Hall in New York City.

- The Smithsonian Institution opens the Arthur M. Sackler Gallery of Asian and Near Eastern Art and the Museum of African Art in Washington, D.C.

- The Vienna Philharmonic performs the complete Beethoven symphonies and concerti at Carnegie Hall in New York.

- Christie's of New York sells Vincent van Gogh's *Sunflowers* for $39.9 million at auction; Sotheby's of New York sells his *Irises* for $53.9 million.

- George Michael's song "I Want Your Sex" is banned from many radio-station playlists because its lyrics are considered too suggestive to be heard by young listeners.

- On July 13, pop star Madonna, opera singer Leontyne Price, and rapper Queen Latifah are among the performers at an AIDS benefit concert held at Madison Square Garden in New York City.

- In August, more than fifty thousand fans gather in Memphis to commemorate the tenth anniversary of Elvis Presley's death.

- On October 5, thirteen New York dance companies perform a *Dancing for Life* benefit for AIDS research.

MOVIES: *Baby Boom,* starring Diane Keaton; *Beverly Hills Cop II,* starring Eddie Murphy; *The Big Easy,* directed by Jim McBride and starring Dennis Quaid and Ellen Barkin; *Broadcast News,* directed by James L. Brooks and starring Holly Hunter, William Hurt, and Albert Brooks; *Cry Freedom,* starring Kevin Kline and Denzel Washington; *Dirty Dancing,* directed by Emile Ardolino and starring Patrick Swayze and Jennifer Grey; *Empire of the Sun,* directed by Steven Spielberg and starring Christopher Bale, John Malkovich, and Miranda Richardson; *Fatal Attraction,* directed by Adrian Lyne and starring Michael Douglas and Glenn Close; *Full Metal Jacket,* directed by Stanley Kubrick and starring Matthew Modine; *Gardens of Stone,* directed by Francis Ford Coppola and starring James Caan, Anjelica Huston, and James Earl Jones; *Good Morning, Vietnam,* starring Robin Williams; *Hamburger Hill,* starring Anthony Barrile and Michael Patrick Boatman; *House of Games,* directed by David Mamet and starring Lindsay Crouse and Joe Mantegna; *Ishtar,* starring Warren Beatty and Dustin Hoffman; *Lethal Weapon,* directed by Richard Donner and starring Mel Gibson and Danny Glover; *The Lost Boys,* starring Jason Patric, Kiefer Sutherland, and Corey Haim; *Matewan,* directed by John Sayles; *Moonstruck,* directed by Norman Jewison and starring Cher, Nicolas Cage, Olympia Dukakis, and Danny Aiello; *Near Dark,* directed by Kathryn Bigelow and starring Adrian Pasdar and Jenny Wright; *Prick Up Your Ears,* starring Gary Oldman; *Radio Days,* directed by Woody Allen; *Raising Arizona,* directed by Joel and Ethan Coen and starring Nicolas Cage and Holly Hunter; *River's Edge,* starring Dennis Hopper and Keanu Reeves; *Robocop,* diected by Paul Verhoeven and starring Peter Weller and Nancy Allen; *Roxanne,* directed by Fred Schepisi and starring Steve Martin and Daryl Hannah; *Sign o' the Times,* starring Prince, Sheila E., and Sheena Easton; *The Stepfather,* directed by Joseph Ruben and starring Terry O'Quinn and Shelley Hack; *Superman IV: The Quest for Peace,* starring Christopher Reeve; *Suspect,* starring Cher; *Three Men and a Baby,* directed by Leonard Nimoy and starring Tom Selleck, Steve Guttenberg, and Ted Danson; *Tin Men,* directed by Barry Levinson and starring Richard Dreyfuss and Danny DeVito; *The Untouchables,* directed by Brian De Palma and starring Kevin Costner, Sean Connery, and Robert De Niro; *Wall Street,* directed by Oliver Stone and starring Charlie Sheen, Michael Douglas, Martin Sheen, and Daryl Hannah; *Who's That Girl?,* starring Madonna and Griffin Dunne; *The Witches of Eastwick,* directed by George Miller and starring Jack Nicholson, Cher, Susan Sarandon, and Michelle Pfeiffer.

FICTION: Isaac Asimov, *Fantastic Voyage II;* Saul Bellow, *More Die of Heartbreak;* Truman Capote, *Answered Prayers;* Tom Clancy, *Patriot Games;* Mary Higgins Clark, *Weep No More My Lady;* Arthur C. Clarke, *2061: Odyssey Three;* Robin Cook, *Outbreak;* Janet Dailey, *Heiress;* Carrie Fisher, *Postcards from the Edge;* Thomas Flanagan, *The Tenants of Time;* John Jakes, *Heaven and Hell;* Garrison Keillor, *Leaving Home;* Stephen King, *Misery, The Tommyknockers,* and *The Eyes of the Dragon;* Louis L'Amour, *The Haunted Mesa;* Larry McMurtry, *Texasville;* James

Michener, *The Legacy;* Toni Morrison, *Beloved;* Cynthia Ozick, *The Messiah of Stockholm;* Robert B. Parker, *Pale Kings and Princes;* Jayne Anne Phillips, *Fast Lanes;* Frederik Pohl, *The Annals of the Heechee;* Philip Roth, *The Counterlife;* Lawrence Sanders, *The Timothy Files;* Sidney Sheldon, *Windmills of the Gods;* Danielle Steel, *Kaleidoscope* and *Fine Things;* Scott Turow, *Presumed Innocent;* Kurt Vonnegut, *Bluebeard;* Tom Wolfe, *The Bonfire of the Vanities.*

POPULAR SONGS: Herb Alpert, "Diamonds"; Bangles, "Walk Like an Egyptian"; Beastie Boys, "(You Gotta) Fight for Your Right (to Party)"; Bon Jovi, "Livin' on a Prayer" and "Wanted Dead or Alive"; Bobby Brown, "Girlfriend"; Peter Cetera with Amy Grant, "The Next Time I Fall"; Club Nouveau, "Lean on Me"; The Robert Cray Band, "Smoking Gun"; Crowded House, "Don't Dream It's Over"; Cutting Crew, "(I Just) Died in Your Arms"; Chris de Burgh, "The Lady in Red"; Duran Duran, "Notorious"; Gloria Estefan and Miami Sound Machine, "Rhythm Is Gonna Get You"; Exposé, "Come Go With Me"; Samantha Fox, "Touch Me (I Want Your Body)"; Aretha Franklin and George Michael, "I Knew You Were Waiting for Me"; Kenny G, "Songbird"; Peter Gabriel, "Big Time"; Georgia Satellites, "Keep Your Hands to Yourself"; Genesis, "Land of Confusion"; Debbie Gibson, "Only in My Dreams"; Lou Gramm, "Midnight Blue"; Grateful Dead, "Touch of Grey"; Heart, "Alone"; Bruce Hornsby and the Range, "Mandolin Rain" and "The Way It Is"; Whitney Houston, "Didn't We Almost Have It All" and "I Wanna Dance With Somebody (Who Loves Me)"; Billy Idol, "Mony Mony"; Janet Jackson, "Control" and "Let's Wait Awhile"; Michael Jackson "Bad"; Michael Jackson with Siedah Garrett, "I Just Can't Stop Loving You"; Michael Johnson, "Give Me Wings"; The Judds, "Cry Myself to Sleep"; L.L. Cool J, "I Need Love"; Cyndi Lauper, "Change of Heart"; LeVert, "Casanova"; Huey Lewis and the News, "Hip to Be Square" and "Jacob's Ladder"; Lisa Lisa and Cult Jam, "Head to Toe" and "Lost in Emotion"; Los Lobos, "La Bamba"; Madonna, "Open Your Heart," "La Isla Bonita," "Who's That Girl," and "Causing a Commotion"; Reba McEntire, "What Am I Gonna Do About You"; Bill Medley and Jennifer Warnes, "(I've Had) The Time of My Life"; John Cougar Mellencamp, "Paper in Fire"; George Michael, "I Want Your Sex"; Robbie Nevil, "C'est la Vie"; K.T. Oslin, "80s Ladies"; Tom Petty and the Heartbreakers, "Jammin' Me"; Pink Floyd, "Learning to Fly"; Prince, "Sign O' the Times" and "U Got the Look"; R.E.M., "The One I Love"; Smokey Robinson, "Just to See Her"; Linda Ronstadt and James Ingram, "Somewhere Out There"; Bob Seger, "Shakedown"; Bruce Springsteen, "Brilliant Disguise"; Starship, "Nothing's Gonna Stop Us Now"; Tiffany, "I Think We're Alone Now"; Randy Travis, "Forever and Ever, Amen"; U2, "With or Without You," "I Still Haven't Found What I'm Looking For," and "Where the Streets Have No Name"; Luther Vandross, "Stop to Love"; Suzanne Vega, "Luka"; Billy Vera and the Beaters, "At This Moment"; Wang Chung, "Everybody Have Fun Tonight"; Jody Watley, "Looking for a New Love"; Whitesnake, "Here I Go Again"; Kim Wilde, "You Keep Me Hangin' On"; Bruce Willis, "Respect Yourself"; World Party, "Ship of Fools."

1988

• Whitney Houston becomes the first recording artist in *Billboard* history to have four number one songs from a single album; only one month later Michael Jackson breaks this record with five number one singles from his *Bad* album.

• Religious fundamentalists picket Martin Scorsese's controversial movie *The Last Temptation of Christ.*

• Novelist Toni Morrison wins the Pulitzer Prize for *Beloved.*

• Motown Records is sold to MCA and a Boston investment firm for $61 million.

• Total spending for cultural events ($3.4 billion) exceeds spending on spectator sports for the first time in American history.

• Picasso's *Acrobat and Young Harlequin* sells for $38.4 million, a record sum for a twentieth century artist; Jasper Johns's *False Starts* sets an auction record for a living artist, $17 million.

• On September 2, Bruce Springsteen, Sting, Peter Gabriel, and Tracy Chapman launch a benefit concert tour for Amnesty International.

MOVIES: *The Accidental Tourist,* directed by Lawrence Kasdan and starring William Hurt, Geena Davis, and Kathleen Turner; *The Accused,* directed by Jonathan Kaplan and starring Jodie Foster and Kelly McGillis; *Beetlejuice,* directed by Tim Burton and starring Michael Keaton, Alec Baldwin, Geena Davis, and Winona Ryder; *Big,* directed by Penny Marshall and starring Tom Hanks; *Big Business,* starring Bette Midler and Lily Tomlin; *Bright Lights, Big City,* starring Michael J. Fox; *Bull Durham,* directed by Ron Shelton and starring Kevin Costner, Susan Sarandon, and Tim Robbins; *Cocktail,* starring Tom Cruise; *Colors,* directed by Dennis Hopper and starring Sean Penn and Robert Duvall; *Coming to America,* starring Eddie Murphy; *A Cry in the Dark,* directed by Fred Schepisi and starring Meryl Streep and Sam Neill; *Dangerous Liaisons,* directed by Stephen Frears and starring Glenn Close, John Malkovich, and Michelle Pfeiffer; *Die Hard,* starring Bruce Willis; *A Fish Called Wanda,* directed by Charles Crichton and starring John Cleese, Jamie Lee Curtis, Kevin Kline, and Michael Palin; *The Good Mother,* starring Diane Keaton and Liam Neeson; *The Last Temptation of Christ,* directed by Martin Scorsese and starring Willem Dafoe; *Married to the Mob,* directed by Jonathan Demme and starring Michelle Pfeiffer; *Mississippi Burning,* directed by Alan Parker and starring Gene Hackman and Willem Dafoe; *The Naked Gun,* starring Leslie Nielsen, Priscilla Presley, and O.J. Simpson; *Rain Man,* directed by Barry Levinson and starring Dustin Hoffman and Tom Cruise; *Running on Empty,* starring Christine Lahti, River Phoenix, Judd Hirsch, and Martha Plimpton; *Tucker,* starring Jeff Bridges; *Twins,* starring Arnold Schwarzenegger and Danny DeVito; *The Unbearable Lightness of Being,* directed by Philip Kaufman and starring Daniel Day-Lewis, Lena Olin, and Juliette Binoche; *Who Framed Roger Rabbit?,* directed by Robert Zemeckis and starring Bob Hoskins; *Willow,* starring Val Kilmer; *Working Girl,* directed by Mike Nichols and starring Melanie Griffith, Harrison Ford, and Sigourney Weaver.

FICTION: Poul Anderson, *The Year of the Ransom;* Richard Bach, *One;* Barbara Taylor Bradford, *To Be the Best;* Nash

Candelaria, *The Day the Cisco Kid Shot John Wayne;* Raymond Carver, *Where I'm Coming From;* John Casey, *Spartina;* Tom Clancy, *The Cardinal of the Kremlin;* Jackie Collins, *Rock Star;* Joan Collins, *Prime Time;* Stephen Coonts, *Final Flight;* Don DeLillo, *Libra;* Pete Dexter, *Paris Trout;* Dominick Dunne, *People Like Us;* Louise Erdrich, *Tracks;* Alex Haley, *A Different Kind of Christmas;* Susan Isaacs, *Shining Through;* Dean R. Koontz, *Lightning;* Judith Krantz, *Till We Meet Again;* Robert Ludlum, *The Icarus Agenda;* Anne McCaffrey, *Dragonsdawn;* Larry McMurtry, *Anything for Billy;* James Michener, *Alaska;* Gloria Naylor, *Mama Day;* Belva Plain, *Tapestry;* Anne Rice, *The Queen of the Damned;* Lawrence Sanders, *Timothy's Game;* Erich Segal, *Doctors;* Sidney Sheldon, *The Sands of Time;* Lee Smith, *Fair and Tender Ladies;* Danielle Steel, *Zoya;* Peter Straub, *Koko;* Anne Tyler, *Breathing Lessons;* Leon Uris, *Mitla Pass.*

POPULAR SONGS: Aerosmith, "Angel" and "Rag Doll"; Rick Astley, "Never Gonna Give You Up" and "Together Forever"; Anita Baker, "Giving You the Best That I Got"; The Beach Boys, "Kokomo"; Bon Jovi, "Bad Medicine"; Breathe, "Hands to Heaven"; Edie Brickell and the New Bohemians, "What I Am"; Bobby Brown, "Don't Be Cruel" and "My Prerogative"; James Brown, "I'm Real"; Belinda Carlisle, "Circle in the Sand," "Heaven Is a Place on Earth," and "I Get Weak"; Eric Carmen, "Hungry Eyes"; Rosanne Cash, "If You Could Change Your Mind"; Tracy Chapman, "Fast Car"; Cheap Trick, "The Flame"; Cher, "I Found Someone"; The Church, "Under the Milky Way"; Phil Collins, "Groovy Kind of Love"; D.J. Jazzy Jeff and the Fresh Prince, "Parents Just Don't Understand"; Terence Trent D'Arby, "Sign Your Name" and "Wishing Well"; Taylor Dayne, "Tell It to My Heart," "Prove Your Love," and "I'll Always Love You"; Def Leppard, "Love Bites" and "Pour Some Sugar on Me"; Depeche Mode, "Route 66"; E.U., "Da'Butt"; Erasure, "Chains of Love"; The Escape Club, "Wild Wild West"; Gloria Estefan and Miami Sound Machine, "1-2-3" and "Anything for You"; Exposé, "Seasons Change"; Samantha Fox, "Naughty Girls (Need Love Too)"; Debbie Gibson, "Foolish Beat," "Out of the Blue," and "Shake Your Love"; Guns N' Roses, "Sweet Child O' Mine"; George Harrison, "Got My Mind Set on You"; Whitney Houston, "Where Do Broken Hearts Go," "One Moment in Time," and "So Emotional"; Ice-T, "Colors"; INXS, "Need You Tonight," "Devil Inside," "Never Tear Us Apart," and "New Sensation"; Michael Jackson, "Dirty Diana," "Man in the Mirror," and "The Way You Make Me Feel"; Jellybean, "Jingo (Remix)"; The Jets, "Make It Real" and "Rocket 2 U"; Elton John, "Candle in the Wind" and "I Don't Want to Go On with You Like That"; Johnny Kemp, "Just Got Paid"; Gladys Knight and the Pips, "Love Overboard"; L.L. Cool J, "I'm Goin Back to Cali"; M/A/R/R/S, "Pump Up the Volume"; Richard Marx, "Hold Onto the Nights"; Bobby McFerrin, "Don't Worry, Be Happy"; John Cougar Mellencamp, "Check It Out" and "Cherry Bomb"; George Michael, "Faith," "Father Figure," "Monkey," and "One More Try"; Midnight Oil, "Beds Are Burning"; New Edition, "If It Isn't Love"; New Kids On the Block, "Please Don't Go Girl"; Billy Ocean, "Get Outta My Dreams, Get Into My Car"; Robert Palmer, "Simply Irresistible"; Pebbles, "Girlfriend" and "Mercedes

Boy"; Pet Shop Boys and Dusty Springfield, "What Have I Done to Deserve This?"; Robert Plant, "Tall Cool One"; Prince, "Alphabet St." and "I Could Never Take the Place of Your Man"; Psychedelic Furs, "All That Money Wants"; Brenda Russell featuring Joe Esposito, "Piano in the Dark"; Salt-N-Pepa, "Push It"; Salt-N-Pepa featuring E.U., "Shake Your Thang"; Siouxsie and the Banshees, "The Killing Jar" and "Peek-A-Boo"; The Smithereens, "Only a Memory"; Al B. Sure!, "Nite and Day"; Patrick Swayze featuring Wendy Frazer, "She's Like the Wind"; Keith Sweat, "I Want Her"; Tiffany, "Could've Been"; U2, "Desire"; Van Halen, "Finish What Ya Started"; Whitesnake, "Is This Love"; Keith Whitley, "Don't Close Your Eyes"; Vanessa Williams, "The Right Stuff"; Steve Winwood, "Roll With It"; Stevie Wonder, "Skeletons"; Dwight Yoakam and Buck Owens, "Streets of Bakersfield."

1989

- A Picasso self-portrait sells for $47.85 million, a record sum for a twentieth century work; later this year the record is broken by Picasso's *Pierrette's Wedding,* which fetches $51.3 million.

- Willem de Kooning's *Interchange* sells for $20.7 million, a record for a living artist.

- Movies gross a record $5 billion.

- Bob Dylan is inducted into the Rock and Roll Hall of Fame.

- Sony Corporation buys Columbia Pictures for $3.4 billion.

- On March 5, amid controversy, artist Richard Serra's mammoth sculpture *Tilted Arc* is removed from Federal Plaza in New York.

- On March 30, the Louvre in Paris adds a new entrance, a glass and metal pyramid designed by American architect I.M. Pei.

- On June 21, the original script for the movie classic *Citizen Kane* (1941) is sold at auction for $210,000.

MOVIES: *Batman,* directed by Tim Burton and starring Jack Nicholson, Michael Keaton, and Kim Basinger; *Bill and Ted's Excellent Adventure,* starring Keanu Reeves and Alex Winter; *Born on the Fourth of July,* directed by Oliver Stone and starring Tom Cruise; *Casualties of War,* directed by Brian de Palma and starring Sean Penn and Michael J. Fox; *Crimes and Misdemeanors,* directed by Woody Allen; *Dead Poets Society,* directed by Peter Weir and starring Robin Williams; *Do the Right Thing,* directed by Spike Lee and starring Danny Aiello, Ossie Davis, Ruby Dee, John Turturro, and Lee; *Driving Miss Daisy,* directed by Bruce Beresford and starring Jessica Tandy and Morgan Freeman; *Drugstore Cowboy,* directed by Gus Van Sant and starring Matt Dillon and Kelly Lynch; *Enemies: A Love Story,* starring Ron Silver, Lena Olin, and Anjelica Huston; *The Fabulous Baker Boys,* directed by Steve Kloves and starring Jeff Bridges, Beau Bridges, and Michelle Pfeiffer; *Field of Dreams,* directed by Phil Alden Robinson and starring Kevin Costner; *Ghostbusters II,* starring Bill Murray and Dan Aykroyd; *Glory,* directed by Edward Zwick and starring Matthew Broderick, Denzel Washington, and Morgan Freeman; *Heathers,* starring Winona Ryder and Christian Slater; *Honey, I Shrunk the Kids,* starring Rick Moranis; *In Country,* starring Bruce Willis; *Indiana Jones and the Last*

Crusade, directed by Steven Spielberg and starring Harrison Ford, Sean Connery, and River Phoenix; *Look Who's Talking,* starring John Travolta and Kirstie Alley; *National Lampoon's Christmas Vacation,* starring Chevy Chase; *Parenthood,* directed by Ron Howard and starring Steve Martin and Dianne Wiest; *Say Anything,* starring John Cusack; *Scandal,* starring Joanna Whalley-Kilmer and John Hurt; *sex, lies and videotape,* directed by Steven Soderbergh and starring James Spader and Andie MacDowell; *Star Trek V: The Final Frontier,* starring William Shatner and Leoard Nimoy; *The War of the Roses,* directed by Danny DeVito and starring Michael Douglas and Kathleen Turner; *When Harry Met Sally,* directed by Rob Reiner and starring Billy Crystal and Meg Ryan.

FICTION: Jimmy Buffett, *Tales from Margaritaville;* Tom Clancy, *Clear and Present Danger;* Mary Higgins Clark, *While My Pretty One Sleeps;* Stephen Coonts, *Minotaur;* Len Deighton, *Spy Line;* E. L. Doctorow, *Billy Bathgate;* Ken Follett *The Pillars of the Earth;* John Grisham, *A Time to Kill;* Allan Gurganus, *The Oldest Living Confederate Widow Tells All;* John Irving, *A Prayer for Owen Meany;* John Jakes, *California Gold;* Stephen King, *The Dark Half;* Dean R. Koontz, *Midnight;* Larry McMurtry, *Some Can Whistle;* James Michener, *Caribbean;* Belva Plain, *Blessings;* Lawrence Sanders, *Capital Crimes;* Martin Cruz Smith, *Polar Star;* Danielle Steel, *Star;* Amy Tan, *The Joy Luck Club;* Alice Walker, *The Temple of My Familiar.*

POPULAR SONGS: Paula Abdul, "Straight Up," "Forever Your Girl," and "Cold Hearted"; Aerosmith, "Love in an Elevator"; Art of Noise featuring Tom Jones, "Kiss"; Rick Astley, "She Wants to Dance With Me"; B-52's, "Love Shack"; Bee Gees, "One"; Clint Black, "Better Man" and "Killin' Time"; Bon Jovi, "I'll Be There For You"; Boy Meets Girl, "Waiting for a Star to Fall"; Bobby Brown, "Every Little Step," "On Our Own," and "Roni"; Belinda Carlisle, "Leave a Light On"; Cher, "If I Could Turn Back Time"; Cher and Peter Cetera, "After All"; Neneh Cherry, "Buffalo Stance" and "Kisses on the Wind"; Chicago, "Look Away"; Phil Collins, "Another Day in Paradise" and "Two Hearts"; Alice Cooper, "Poison"; Elvis Costello, "Veronica"; Cowboy Junkies, "Sweet Jane"; The Cult, "Fire Woman"; The Cure, "Love Song" and "Fascination Street"; Taylor Dayne, "Don't Rush Me"; De La Soul, "Me, Myself and I"; Fine Young Cannibals, "She Drives Me Crazy" and

"Good Thing"; Lita Ford (duet with Ozzy Osbourne), "Close My Eyes Forever"; Debbie Gibson, "Lost in Your Eyes" and "Electric Youth"; Great White, "Once Bitten, Twice Shy"; Guns N' Roses, "Paradise City," "Patience," and "Welcome to the Jungle"; Heavy D & The Boyz, "We Got Our Own Thang"; Highway 101, "Setting Me Up"; Hoodoo Gurus, "Come Anytime"; Janet Jackson, "Miss You Much" and "Rhythm Nation"; Michael Jackson, "Smooth Criminal"; Billy Joel, "We Didn't Start the Fire"; Kon Kan, "I Beg Your Pardon"; Kool Moe Dee, "They Want Money"; L.L. Cool J, "I'm That Type of Guy"; K.D. Lang, "Pulling Back the Reins"; Living Colour, "Cult of Personality"; Love & Rockets, "So Alive"; Madonna, "Cherish," "Express Yourself," "Like a Prayer," and "Oh Father"; Ziggy Marley and the Melody Makers, "Tumblin' Down"; Maurice, "This Is Acid"; Bette Midler, "Wind Beneath My Wings"; Mike + The Mechanics, "The Living Years"; Milli Vanilli "Baby Don't Forget My Number," "Blame It on the Rain," "Girl I'm Gonna Miss You," and "Girl You Know It's True"; Bob Mould, "See a Little Light"; New Kids on the Block, "You Got It (The Right Stuff)," "I'll Be Loving You (Forever)," and "Hangin' Tough"; New Order, "Fine Time"; Roy Orbison, "You Got It"; Donny Osmond, "Soldier of Love"; Tom Petty, "Free Fallin'," "I Won't Back Down," and "Runnin' Down a Dream"; Pixies, "Here Comes Your Man"; Poison, "Every Rose Has Its Thorn"; Prince, "Batdance"; Public Enemy, "Fight the Power"; Public Image Ltd., "Disappointed"; R.E.M., "Orange Crush" and "Stand"; The Replacements, "I'll Be You"; Linda Ronstadt and Aaron Neville, "Don't Know Much"; Roxette, "The Look"; Skid Row, "18 and Life"; Soul II Soul featuring Caron Wheeler, "Back to Life" and "Keep on Movin'"; Rod Stewart, "My Heart Can't Tell You No"; The Stop the Violence Movement, "Self-Destruction"; Donna Summer, "This Time I Know It's for Real"; Tears for Fears, "Sowing the Seeds of Love"; Technotronic, "Pump Up the Jam"; Tone Loc, "Funky Cold Medina" and "Wild Thing"; Traveling Wilburys, "End of the Line"; Conway Twitty, "She's Got a Single Thing in Mind"; Stevie Ray Vaughan and Double Trouble, "Crossfire"; Warrant, "Heaven"; Karyn White, "Superwoman"; White Lion, "When the Children Cry"; Will to Power, "Baby I Love Your Way/Freebird Medley"; XTC, "The Mayor of Simpleton"; Young M.C., "Bust a Move."

"A Conversation with Steven Spielberg"

Interview

By: Michael Sragow

Date: 1982

Source: Sragow, Michael. "A Conversation with Steven Spielberg." Reprinted from *Rolling Stone*, July 22, 1982. In *Steven Spielberg Interviews.* Edited by Lester D. Friedman and Bret Notbohm. Jackson: University Press of Mississippi, 2000, 107–113.

About the Author: Michael Sragow is a film reviewer whose critiques have appeared in *New Yorker, The Baltimore Sun, Rolling Stone,* and other publications. He attended film school at New York University and later completed his degree in literature and history at Harvard. ∎

Introduction

Steven Spielberg was already a well-known film director by the time of his 1982 *Rolling Stone* interview with Michael Sragow. *Jaws* (1975) and *Close Encounters of the Third Kind* (1977) were blockbuster hits in the theaters. This interview took place prior to the release of *E.T.: The Extra Terrestrial* and *Poltergeist* in the summer of 1982.

Steven Spielberg knew he wanted to make movies when he was a child. His passion led him to film school, but he dropped out to actually make movies. Spielberg explains the importance of movies in his interview. He said movies, as opposed to films, are for audiences to enjoy. This is not to say that a film cannot be enjoyed; however, the difference in artistic purpose is what Spielberg tries to convey. He admires his contemporary colleagues, and speculates that there are two schools of moviemakers. While Spielberg is in the George Lucas *Star Wars* and *Raiders of the Lost Ark* camp, filmmakers such as Francis Ford Coppola and Martin Scorsese have their own style of depicting urban life and more artistically inclined subjects.

Spielberg's projects for the summer of 1982 were meant to make audiences laugh, cry, wonder, and fear. *E.T.: The Extra-Terrestrial* was a relatively low-budget film, made for ten million dollars. It would gross more than $700 million at the box office. Its story of a ten-year-old boy's friendship with an alien creature continued to sell well into the twenty-first century. The storyline of *Poltergeist,* a horror film, revolves around the strange paranormal phenomena that occurs in a family's home. Although it is a horror film, the story has moments that can make the audience laugh. Steven Spielberg captured the summer of 1982 with these now classic films. He continued to make enormously successful films into the twenty-first century.

Significance

Steven Spielberg's vision comes across in his interview with Michael Sragow. This includes his vision of the future of his industry, his own projects, his hopes and dreams and of life in twentieth-century America. Spielberg is an astute observer of American life. The hopes, dreams, and fears of children and from his own childhood are clearly communicated in his 1982 offerings.

E.T.: The Extra-Terrestrial is Spielberg's personal resurrection while *Poltergeist* is his personal nightmare. The two films represent versions of suburbia that most kids of Spielberg's age, and even younger, experienced as they grew up. The ever-present television featured comedy and drama, and commercials designed to turn viewers into a consumer society. Mothers of the 1950s gathered in kitchens to talk while children played outside in the neighborhood. Spielberg's use of this societal shift, from the rural or city life to the suburbs is important in his movies because it captures a generation's experience as they relate to the story. Further, his storylines revolving around children's lives, especially in *E.T.,* provide a different point of view from most movies. Spielberg addresses critical themes in the movies: dreams, discovery, loneliness, disconnection from the world, overcoming of prejudices, and creating friendships between cultures.

Perhaps one of the most vital aspects of Steven Spielberg's movies, not only in the summer of 1982 but also beyond, is the aspect of story. He realizes the need for stories in people's lives—not just for children, but also for adults. Stories provided emotional connections with the characters in the movies and with each other. Philip Taylor points out that "Together, claimed Time magazine, [*E.T.* and *Poltergeist*] establish the movie screen as magic lantern, where science plays tricks on the eye as an artist enters the heart and nervous system with images that bemuse and beguile.'"

Primary Source

"A Conversation with Steven Spielberg" [excerpt]

> **SYNOPSIS:** *E.T.* received four Academy Awards for Best Sound Effects Editing, Best Visual Effects, Best Score (John Williams), and Best Sound. The technical details caused both *E.T.* and *Poltergeist*

to rise above the ordinary childhood story. Spielberg recounts the movie's genesis in his own childhood in this interview.

At thirty-four, Steven Spielberg is, in any conventional sense, the most successful movie director in Hollywood, America, the Occident, the planet Earth, the solar system, and the galaxy. Three of his movies—*Jaws, Close Encounters of the Third Kind,* and *Raiders of the Lost Ark* are action-fantasy classics that rank among the biggest moneymakers of all time. Before the summer is out, they may well be joined by *E.T.: The Extra-Terrestrial,* a lyrical piece of sci-fi about the human, and alien, condition (conceived, coproduced, and directed by Spielberg), and a crowd-pleasing shocker, *Poltergeist* (coproduced and cowritten by Spielberg but directed by Tobe Hooper).

Spielberg is the scion of a suburban upbringing and a public-school education. His mother was a concert pianist and his father a computer scientist who moved his family of four children "from Ohio to New Jersey, Arizona, Saratoga, and Los Angeles." From age twelve on, Spielberg knew he did one thing best: make movies. When college time came, he enrolled in film school at Cal State Long Beach. In 1969, on the basis of a twenty-four-minute short called *Amblin',* Spielberg was able to sign with Universal, where he directed episodes of *Night Gallery, Marcus Welby,* and *Columbo,* the terrifying TV-movie *Duel*; his first feature, *The Sugarland Express*; and his breakthrough, "primal scream" thriller, *Jaws.*

E.T. The Extra-Terrestrial is another breakthrough for Spielberg. His previous movies have all been spectacles of some species, even the out-of-control slapstick epic *1941.* Their escapism grew out of Spielberg's childhood fantasy life: "When I didn't want to face the real world," he says, "I just stuck a camera up to my face. And it worked." Making *E.T.,* however, compelled Spielberg to face the reality of this childhood pain and left him feeling "cleansed." Now, he says, "I'm trying to make movies by shooting more from the hip and using my eyes to see the real world."

The day after a triumphant out-of-competition screening of *E.T.* at Cannes in May, I spoke to Spielberg in his New York City hotel suite. He exuded casualness, from his NASA cap to his stockinged feet, as well as confidence that his most intimate movie might also prove to be his best loved. Talking about *E.T., Poltergeist,* his favorite contemporary directors, and the troubled state of the motion-picture business, Spielberg seemed itching to take on the world.

Everything seems to have come together for you with E.T. Certainly few filmmakers have had such a good shot at being both profoundly personal and phenomenally popular.

You know the saying, the book wrote itself. This movie didn't make itself, but things began to happen from its inception in 1980 that told me this was a movie I was ready to make. I'm not into psychoanalysis, but *E.T.* is a film that was inside me for many years and could only come out after a lot of suburban psychodrama.

What do you mean by suburban psychodrama?

Growing up in a house with three screaming younger sisters and a mother who played concert piano with seven other women—I was raised in a world of women.

In a lot of your movies, the women or the girls are the more elastic characters, emotionally.

That's right, they are. I like women, I like working with women. *E.T.* had a plethora of them. A women coproducer, a woman writer, a woman film editor, a woman assistant director, woman costumer, women script person, women in construction, women in set design, a woman set dresser. I am less guarded about my feelings around women. I call it shoulder-pad syndrome; you can't cry on a shoulder that's wearing a shoulder pad. This is something from my school days of being a wimp in a world of jocks.

How much of a wimp were you?

The height of my wimpery came when we had to run a mile for a grade in elementary school. The whole class of fifty finished, except for two people left on the track—me and a mentally retarded boy. Of course *he* ran awkwardly, but I was just never able to run. I was maybe forty yards ahead of him, and I was only 100 yards away from the finish line. The whole class turned and started rooting for the young retarded boy—cheering him on, saying "C'mon, c'mon, beat Spielberg! Run, run!" It was like he came to life for the first time, and he began to pour it on but still not fast enough to beat me. And I remember thinking, "Okay, now how am I gonna fall and make it look like I really fell?" And I remember actually stepping on my toe and going face hard into the red clay of the track and actually scraping my nose. Everybody cheered when I fell, and then they began to really scream for this guy: "C'mon, John, C'mon, run, run!" I got up just as John came up behind me, and I began running as if to beat him but not really to win, running to let *him* win. We were nose to nose, and suddenly I laid back a step, then a half-step. Suddenly he was ahead, then he was a chest ahead,

Director Steven Spielberg with his arm around E.T. from the 1982 movie, *E.T.: The Extra-Terrestrial.* GETTY IMAGES. REPRODUCED BY PERMISSION.

then a length, and then he crossed the finish line ahead of me. Everybody grabbed this guy, and they threw him up on their shoulders and carried him into the locker room, into the showers, and I stood there on the track field and cried my eyes out for five minutes. I'd never felt better and I'd never felt worse in my entire life.

You once said you managed to win over some of the jocks by starring them in a film called Battle Squad. *By making films like* Jaws, *were you still trying to ingratiate yourself with hard guys?*

Yeah, hard liners. Hard, cynical liners. But not just three or four jocks in my elementary or junior high school. I'm talking about millions of people.

Do you mean that making movies is a way of showing off?

With the exception of *Close Encounters,* in all my movies before *E.T.,* I was giving *out,* giving *off* things before I would bring something *in.* There were feelings I developed in my personal life . . . that I had no place to put. Then, while working on *Raiders,* I had the germ of an idea. I was very lonely, and I remember thinking I had nobody to talk to. My girlfriend was in California, so was George Lucas. Harrison Ford had a bad case of the *turistas.* I remember

wishing one night that I had a friend. It was like, when you were a kid and had grown out of dolls or teddy bears or Winnie the Pooh, you just wanted a little voice in your mind to talk to. I began concocting this imaginary creature, partially from the guys who stepped out of the mother ship for ninety seconds in *Close Encounters* and then went back in, never to be seen again.

Then I thought, what if I were ten years old again—where I've sort of been for thirty-four years, anyway—and what if he needed me as much as I needed him? Wouldn't that be a great love story? So I put together this story of this boy meets creature, boy loses creature, creature saves boy, boy saves creature—with the hope that they will somehow always be together, that their friendship isn't limited by nautical miles. And I asked Melissa Mathison, who is Harrison Ford's girlfriend and a wonderful writer, to turn it into a screenplay.

Did you hire her because you admired her work on The Black Stallion?

I did admire *The Black Stallion,* but it was more because Melissa was one of the few people on the *Raiders* location I could talk to. I was pouring out my heart to Melissa all the time.

In E.T., *the view of growing up is both uplifting and painful. If Elliot hadn't befriended E.T., he'd still be one lonely kid.*

To me, Elliot was always the Nowhere Man from the Beatles song. I was drawing from my own feelings when I was a little kid and I didn't have that many friends and had to resort to making movies to become quasi-popular and to find a reason for living after school hours. Most of my friends were playing football or basketball or baseball and going out with girls. I didn't do those things until very late.

Is E.T. *your imaginary revenge—turning the Nowhere Man into a hero?*

Oh yeah, absolutely. When I began making *E.T.*, I thought that maybe the thing to do was to go back and make life the way it should have been. How many kids, in their Walter Mitty imaginations, would love to save the frogs or kiss the prettiest girl in class? That's every boy's childhood fantasy.

Have you been able to fulfill your own childhood fantasies?

Let me tell you an interesting story. The German director Wim Wenders called me yesterday and said, "Do an interview for me; I'm asking one question: what is the future of the movie business?" I agreed and showed up at three in the afternoon at the Carlton Hotel in Cannes. I walk into this room, and there's a 16-mm movie camera, a microphone, a Nagra [tape recorder] and lights and a crew of six people. They turn on the equipment and they leave me all alone in the room! Finally, I answer the question—straightforward, analytic, sort of like the *Wall Street Journal*. I'm proud of myself until I talk to Harrison Ford. He says *he* would have taken off all his clothes and sat there in the nude, not said a word for ten minutes, then, when the film had run out, walked out fully dressed and thanked them all for a pleasant experience. After all, they weren't going to see the film for forty-eight hours—it takes that long to process it! Now, that just shows me that I'm not as far along in my development as Harrison is. I guess I still haven't been able to shake off the anesthetic of suburbia.

The anesthetic of suburbia—that implies that it protects you from pain and from any kind of raw feeling.

And real life. Because the anesthetic of suburbia also involves having three parents—a mother, a father, and a TV set. Two of them are equilibriums, but one of them is more powerful, because it's always new and fresh and entertaining. It doesn't reach out and tell you what to do.

To me, the key suburban feeling is claustrophobia. Sitting in the den, waiting for the Good Humor truck to come.

I love that. Remember Pinky Lee? I used to sit in the den, listen for the Good Humor truck and watch Pinky Lee on TV. There was no privacy in suburbia because my mom's friends would come in the morning, drink coffee and gossip. And it *was* claustrophobic. It's a reality to kids: in suburbia you have to create a kid's world apart from an adult world—and the two will never eclipse. In an urban world, the adult world and the child world are inseparable. Everybody gets the same dose of reality every day. On the way to school, on the way to the drugstore, on the way home, on the way shopping, it's all the same. In suburbia, kids have secrets. And that's why I wanted *E.T.* to take place in suburbia. What better place to keep a creature from outer space a secret from the grown-ups?

How heavily did you base the movie on contemporary suburban experience, as opposed to your own memories?

In today's world, a twelve-year-old kid is what we were at sixteen and a half. So a transformation happened once I cast the film with real kids. Not stage Hollywood actors, you know—kids who've never been in a casting director's office or an art director's room. Real people, just real people—that's who we cast.

Diagolue changed considerably. I never would have called my brother, if I'd had one, "penis breath" in front of my mother. It's not the most popular word in the Pac Man generation's vernacular, but it's a word that's used every once in a while, and it conjures up quite gross and hilarious images. I wanted the kids to say something that would shake up the mother, 'cause I wanted her to laugh first, then reprimand, instead of just saying "How dare you say that in my house!" *That's* the Fifties mother, the one who got attacked by the Martians who ate the dog. *Today's* parent, being my age, would burst out laughing and then suddenly realize, "Omigosh, I'm the father, I can't laugh at that. Sit down, son, and never say that word again, or I'll pretend I'm *my* mom and dad back in the Fifties, and you'll have to learn from them.

I think kids tend to look at adults as just melodramatic excuses for people. A lot of kids look up to look down. And I found, even when I was giving Henry Thomas [Elliot] direction, that if I was out of touch with his reality, he would give me a look that seemed to say, "Oh brother, he's old." I could always tell when I was reaching Henry. He would smile and laugh, or he'd say "Yeah, yeah, right." I was constantly being rewarded or corrected by people three times less my age. I was moving *faster* than the kids. So I slowed myself down and began to metabolize according to them instead of Steven Spielberg.

Did that scare you?

The thing that I'm just scared to death of is that someday I'm gonna wake up and bore somebody with a film. That's kept me making movies that have tried to outspectacle each other. I got into the situation where my movies were real big, and I had a special-effects department and I was the boss of that and that was a lot of fun. Then I'd get a kick out of the production meetings—not with three or four people, but with fifty, sometimes nearer to 100 when we got close to production—because I was able to lead troops into Movie Wars. The power became a narcotic, but it wasn't power for power's sake. I really am attracted to stories that you can't see on television and stories that you can't get every day. So that attraction leads me to the Impossible Dream, and that Impossible Dream usually costs me $20 million.

François Truffaut helped inspire me to make *E.T.* simply by saying to me, on the *Close Encounters* set, "I like you with *keeds,* you are wonderful with *keeds,* you must do a movie just with *keeds.*" And I said, "Well, I've always wanted to do a film about kids, but I've got to finish this, then I'm doing *1941,* about the Japanese attacking Los Angeles." And Truffant told me I was making a big mistake. He kept saying, "You are the child."

To me, your biggest visual accomplishment is the contrast between suburbia in the harsh, daytime light, when everything looks the same, to the mysterious way it looks at night. By the end, you get a mothering feeling from the night.

Yeah, it *is* Mother Night. Remember in *Fantasia,* Mother Night's flying over with her cape, covering a daylight sky? When I was a kid, that's what night really looked like. The Disney Mother Night was a beautiful woman with flowing, blue-black hair, and arms extended outward, twenty miles in either direction. And behind her was a very inviting cloak. She came from the horizon in an arc and swept over you until everything was a blue-black dome. And then there was an explosion, and the stars were suddenly made in this kind of animated sky. I wanted the opening of *E.T.* to be that kind of Mother Night. You know,

you come down over the trees, you see the stars, and suddenly you think you're in space—wow, you're not, you're in a forest somewhere. You're not quite sure where; you might be in a forest on some distant planet. It was Melissa's idea to use the forest; at first, I thought of having the ship land in a vacant lot. But she said, "A forest is magical . . . there are elves in forests."

Further Resources

BOOKS

Ebert, Roger, Gene Siskel, and Martin Scorsese. *The Future of Movies: Interviews with Martin Scorsese, Steven Spielberg, and George Lucas.* Kansas City, Mo.: Andrews McMeel, 1991.

McBride, Joseph. *Steven Spielberg: A Biography.* New York: Simon & Schuster, 1997.

Taylor, Philip M. *Steven Spielberg: The Man, His Movies, and Their Meaning.* New York: Continuum, 1992.

PERIODICALS

Salamon, Julie. "Movie Mogul; Maker of Hit after Hit, Steven Spielberg is also a Conglomerate; But Hollywood's Superpower Disdains Tycoon Status; Snubbed at Oscar Time; A BMW With a Bodyguard." *Wall Street Journal,* February 9, 1987, 1.

"Steven Spielberg: The Director Says It's Good-Bye to Spaceships and Hello to Relationships." *American Film* 13, no. 8, June 1988, 12–16.

WEBSITES

DreamWorks SKG. Available online at http://www.dreamworks .com/ (accessed April 25, 2003).

E.T.: The Extra Terrestrial. Available online at http://www.et dvd.com/ (accessed April 25, 2003).

AUDIO AND VISUAL MEDIA

E.T.: The Extra-Terrestrial. Original release, 1975. Universal. Directed by Steven Spielberg. Widescreen Collector's Edition DVD, 2002. Universal Studios.

Poltergeist. Original release, 1982, Warner Bros. Directed by Steven Spielberg and Tobe Hooper. 1982. VHS, 1997. Warner Studios. Widescreen Collector's Edition DVD, 2002. Warner Home Video.

Crimes of the Heart

Play script

By: Beth Henley

Date: 1982

Source: Henley, Beth. *Crimes of the Heart.* New York: Penguin, 1982, 55–68.

About the Author: Beth Becker Henley (1952–) was born in Jackson, Mississippi. She received a B.F.A. from Southern

Playwright Beth Henley won a Pulitzer Prize for *Crimes of the Heart* when she was only 29. AP/WORLD WIDE PHOTOS. REPRODUCED BY PERMISSION.

Methodist University in 1974. She attended graduate school at the University of Illinois for a year to study acting. Henley sets her plays in the South and draws upon her background for characters and inspiration. She won the Pulitzer Prize for *Crimes of the Heart* in 1981; the New York Drama Critics Circle Award, 1981; and the Oppenheimer Award, 1981. She has written plays, screenplays, and television plays. ■

Introduction

Beth Henley wanted to be an actress but realized that there were not many parts for Southern women. She turned to playwriting and created several memorable female characters of Southern heritage. Influenced by her childhood in Mississippi, Henley relies on the oral traditions of the South to create the rich dialogue in her plays. She has been compared to both Tennessee Williams and Flannery O'Connor, fellow Southerners. She admits that she had not read O'Connor until the comparison was made. Her favorite authors are Anton Chekhov and Shakespeare.

Henley wrote her first play as a sophomore in a college playwriting class. The one-act *Am I Blue?* was produced in 1973 while she was still a student at Southern Methodist University. *Crimes of the Heart* was not written until 1978 when she was living in Los Angeles. She completed the play in three months.

Crimes of the Heart is about the three McGrath sisters, each eccentric in her own way. The setting is Hazelhurst, Mississippi, a small town where Henley spent childhood weekends with grandparents and relatives. Lenny, the oldest sister who turns thirty in the play, has remained at the family home. She worries that her life will be loveless. Meg, the middle sister, has returned from a failed attempt to become a singer in Hollywood. Babe, the youngest, shot her husband in the stomach because, as she says, "I just didn't like his stinking looks." The play revolves around the three sisters and their memories, dreams, and family bonds. In the family kitchen the kin gather to solve the problem of one of their own. In the process they rediscover the depth of family relationships that never go away.

Significance

Crimes of the Heart established Henley's career as a playwright. The play, notes Billy J. Harbin, "became the first drama to receive the Pulitzer Prize prior to its Broadway opening, and she, the first woman playwright to receive the award in twenty-three years." The play began in regional theater and Henley made changes after each performance. In December 1980, it began a five-week run off Broadway. On November 4, 1981, it opened at the John Golden Theater. The play ran for 535 performances. In addition to the Pulitzer, the play won the New York Drama Critics Circle Award for Best New Play, a George Oppenheimer/Newsday Playwriting Award, a Guggenheim, and a Tony nomination.

Henley was praised for her dialogue. The women in her plays reveal wit, charm, and their isolation. Comedy covers tragedy in Henley's plays. Themes examining death, disasters, and family bonds rest just beneath the surface of the whimsical dialogue. The sisters share memories of their mother's suicide and of growing up with grandparents who thought the cure for sadness was banana splits. The sisters continue to take solace in food as adults. The action in *Crimes of the Heart* reveals the sisters' endurance of their tragic lives as much as their ability to cope with the present situation of Babe's crime.

Critics greeted *Crimes of the Heart* with both praise and doubt. John Simon, reviewer for *New York Magazine,* writes that it is a play which "restores one's faith in theater." He praised Henley's creation of character and stated that she had an "authentically individual vision." Scot Haller discusses the other bizarre characters the viewer will see in the play that cause the action to become almost absurd. Walter Kerr, well known theater critic for *The New York Times,* wrote that despite "grinning" during the play, he did not find it believable enough be a lasting influence. Henley's play has lasted, however, and the delightful, offbeat McGrath sisters live on through stage performances throughout the country as well as in a 1986 film version starring Sissy Spacek, Diane Keaton, and Jessica Lange.

Primary Source

Crimes of the Heart [excerpt]

SYNOPSIS: As Act Two opens, Babe is meeting with her lawyer, Barnette Lloyd. She tries to explain what happened after she shot her husband, Zachary. Lenny re-enters the kitchen, upset with Meg for lying to their grandfather at the hospital. The differences in the sisters' lives and beliefs are highlighted as they recall the past and try to make sense of the present.

The lights go up on the kitchen. It is evening of the same day. Meg's suitcase has been moved upstairs. Babe's saxophone has been taken out of the case and put together. Babe and Barnette are sitting at the kitchen table. Barnette is writing and rechecking notes with explosive intensity. Babe, who has changed into a casual shift, sits eating a bowl of oatmeal, slowly.

Barnette, *to himself*: Mmm huh! Yes! I see, I see! Well, we can work on that! And of course, this is mere conjecture! Difficult, if not impossible, to prove. Ha! Yes. Yes, indeed. Indeed—

Babe: Sure you don't want any oatmeal?

Barnette: What? Oh, no. No, thank you. Let's see; ah, where were we?

Babe: I just shot Zackery.

Barnett, *looking at his notes*: Right. Correct. You've just pulled the trigger.

Babe: Tell me, do you think Willie Jay can stay out of all this?

Barnette: Believe me, it is in our interest to keep him as far out of this as possible.

Babe: Good.

Barnette, *throughout the following, Barnette stays glued to Babe's every word*: All right, you've just shot one Zackery Botrelle, as a result of his continual physical and mental abuse—what happens now?

Babe: Well, after I shot him, I put the gun down on the piano bench, and then I went out into the kitchen and made up a pitcher of lemonade.

Barnette: Lemonade?

Babe: Yes, I was dying of thirst. My mouth was just as dry as a bone.

Barnette: So in order to quench this raging thirst that was choking you dry and preventing any possibility of you uttering intelligible sounds or phrases, you went out to the kitchen and made up a pitcher of lemonade?

Babe: Right. I made it just the way I like it, with lots of sugar and lots of lemon—about ten lemons in all. Then I added two trays of ice and stirred it up with my wooden stirring spoon.

Barnette: Then what?

Babe: Then I drank three glasses, one right after the other. They were large glasses—about this tall. Then suddenly my stomach kind of swole all up. I guess what caused it was all that sour lemon.

Barnette: Could be.

Babe: Then what I did was . . . I wiped my mouth off with the back of my hand, like this . . . *She demonstrates.*

Barnette: Hmmm.

Babe: I did it to clear off all those little beads of water that had settled there.

Barnette: I see.

Babe: Then I called out to Zackery. I said, "Zackery, I've made some lemonade. Can you use a glass?"

Barnette: Did he answer? Did you hear an answer?

Babe: No. He didn't answer.

Barnette: So what'd you do?

Babe: I poured him a glass anyway and took it out to him.

Barnette: You took it out to the living room?

Babe: I did. And there he was, lying on the rug. He was looking up at my trying to speak words. I said, "What? . . . Lemonade? . . . You don't want it? Would you like a Coke instead? Then I got the idea—he was telling me to call on the phone for medical help. So I got on the phone and called up the hospital. I gave my name and address, and I told them my husband was shot and he was lying on the rug and there was plenty of blood. *She pauses a minute, as Barnette works frantically on his notes.* I guess that's gonna look kinda bad.

Barnette: What?

Babe: Me fixing that lemonade before I called the hospital.

Barnette: Well not . . . necessarily.

Babe: I tell you, I think the reason I made up the lemonade, I mean besides the fact that my mouth was bone dry, was that I was afraid to call the authorities. I was afraid. I—I really think I was afraid they would see that I had tried to shoot Zackary, in fact, that I *had* shot him, and they would accuse me of possible murder and send me away to jail.

Barnette: Well, that's understandable.

Babe: I think so. I mean, in fact, that's what did happen. That's what is happening—'cause here I am just about ready to go right off to the Parchment Prison Farm. Yes, here I am just practically on the brink of utter doom. Why, I feel so all alone.

Barnette: Now, now look—Why, there's no reason for you to get yourself so all upset and worried. Please don't. Please.

They look at each other for a moment.

Barnette: You just keep filling in as much detailed information as you can about those incidents on the medical reports. That's all you need to think about. Don't you worry, Mrs. Botrelle, we're going to have a solid defense.

Babe: Please don't call me Mrs. Botrelle.

Barnette: All right.

Babe: My name's Becky. People in the family call me Babe, but my real name's Becky.

Barnette: All right, Becky.

Barnette and Babe stare at each other for a long moment.

Babe: Are you sure you didn't go to Hazlehurst High?

Barnette: No, I went away to a boarding school.

Babe: Gosh, you sure do look familiar. You sure do.

Barnette: Well, I—I doubt you'll remember, but I did meet you once.

Babe: You did? When?

Barnette: At the Christmas bazaar, year before last. You were selling cakes and cookies and . . . candy.

Babe: Oh, yes! You bought the orange pound cake!

Barnette: Right.

Babe: Of course, and then we talked for a while. We talked about the Christmas angel.

Barnette: You do remember.

Babe: I remember it very well. You were even thinner then than you are now.

Barnette: Well, I'm surprised. I'm certainly . . . surprised.

The phone rings.

Babe, *as she goes to answer the phone*: This is quite a coincidence! Don't you think it is? Why, it's almost a fluke. *She answers the phone.* Hello . . . Oh, hello, Lucille . . . Oh, he is? . . . Oh, he does? . . . Okay. Oh, Lucille, wait! Has Dog come back to the house? . . . Oh, I see . . . Okay. Okay. *After a brief pause* Hello, Zackery? How are you doing? . . . Uh huh . . . uh huh . . . Oh, I'm sorry. . . . Please don't scream . . . Uh huh . . . uh huh . . . You want what? . . . No, I can't come up there now . . . Well, for one thing, I don't even have the car. Lenny and Meg are up at the hospital right now, visiting with Old Grandaddy . . . What? . . . Oh, really? . . . Oh really? Well I've got me a lawyer that's over here right right now, and he's building me up a solid defense! . . . Wait just a minute, I'll see. *To Barnette:* He wants to talk to you. He says he's got some blackening evidence that's gonna convict me of attempting to murder him in the first degree!

Barnette, *disgustedly*: Oh, bluff! He's bluffing! Here, hand me the phone. *He takes the phone and becomes suddenly cool and suave.* Hello, this is Mr. Barnette Lloyd speaking. I'm Mrs. . . . ah, Becky's attorney . . . Why, certainly, Mr. Botrelle, I'll be more than glad to check out any pertinent information that you may have . . . Fine, then I'll be right on over. Goodbye. *He hangs up the phone.*

Babe: What did he say?

Barnette: He wants me to come see him at the hospital this evening. Says he's got some sort of evidence. Sounds highly suspect to me.

Babe: Oooh! Didn't you just hate his voice? Doesn't he have the most awful voice? I just hate—I can't bear to hear it!

Barnette: Well, now—now, wait. Wait just a minute.

Babe: What?

Barnette: I have a solution. From now on, I'll handle all communications between you two. You can simply refuse to speak with him.

Jessica Lange, Sissy Spacek, and Diane Keaton in a scene from the movie *Crimes of the Heart*. THE KOBAL COLLECTION. REPRODUCED BY PERMISSION.

Babe: All right—I will. I'll do that.

Barnette, *starting to pack his briefcase*: Well, I'd better get over there and see just what he's got up his sleeve.

Babe, *after a pause*: Barnette.

Barnette: Yes?

Babe: What's the personal vendetta about? You know, the one you have to settle with Zackery.

Barnette: Oh, it's—it's complicated. It's a very complicated matter.

Babe: I see.

Barnette: The major thing he did was to ruin my father's life. He took away his job, his home, his health, his respectability. I don't like to talk about it.

Babe: I'm sorry. I just wanted to say—I hope you win it. I hope you win your vendetta.

Barnette: Thank you.

Babe: I think it's an important thing that a person could win a lifelong vendetta.

Barnette: Yes. Well, I'd better be going.

Babe: All right. Let me know what happens.

Barnette: I will. I'll get back to you right away.

Babe: Thanks.

Barnette: Goodbye, Becky.

Babe: Goodbye, Barnette.

Barnette exits. Babe looks around the room for a moment, then goes over to her white suitcase and opens it up. She takes out her pink hair curlers and a brush. She begins brushing her hair.

Babe: Goodbye, Becky. Goodbye, Barnette. Goodbye, Becky. Oooh.

Lenny enters. She is fuming. Babe is rolling her hair throughout most of the following scene.

Babe: Lenny, hi!

Lenny: Hi.

Babe: Where's Meg?

Lenny: Oh, she had to go by the store and pick some things up. I don't know what.

Babe: Well, how's Old Granddaddy?

Lenny, *as she picks up Babe's bowl of oatmeal*: He's fine. Wonderful! Never been better!

Babe: Lenny, what's wrong? What's the matter?

Lenny: It's Meg! I could just wring her neck! I could just wring it!

Babe: Why? Wha'd she do?

Lenny: She lied! She sat in that hospital room and shamelessly lied to Old Granddaddy. She went on and on telling such untrue stories and lies.

Babe: Well, what? What did she say?

Lenny: Well, for one thing, she said she was gonna have an RCA record coming out with her picture on the cover, eating pineapples under a palm tree.

Babe: Well, gosh, Lenny, maybe she is! Don't you think she really is?

Lenny: Babe, she sat here this very afternoon and told me how all that she's done this whole

year is work as a clerk for a dog-food company.

Babe: Oh, shoot. I'm disappointed.

Lenny: And then she goes on to say that she'll be appearing on the Johnny Carson show in two week's time. Two week's time! Why Old Grandaddy's got a TV set right in his room. Imagine what a letdown it's gonna be.

Babe: Why, mercy me.

Lenny, *slamming the coffeepot on*: Oh, and she told him the reason she didn't use the money he sent her to come home Christmas was that she was right in the middle of making a huge multimillion-dollar motion picture and was just under too much pressure.

Babe: My word!

Lenny: The movie's coming out this spring. It's called, *Singing in a Shoe Factory*. But she only has a small leading role—not a large leading role.

Babe, *laughing*: For heaven's sake—

Lenny: I'm sizzling. Oh, I just can't help it! I'm sizzling!

Babe: Sometimes Meg does such strange things.

Lenny, *slowly, as she picks up the opened box of birthday candy*: Who ate all this candy?

Babe, *hesitantly*: Meg.

Lenny: My one birthday present, and look what she does! Why she's taken one little bite out of each piece and then just put it back in! Ooh! That's just like her! That is just like her!

Babe: Lenny, please—

Lenny: I can't help it! It gets me mad! It gets me upset! Why, Meg's always run wild—she

started smoking and drinking when she was fourteen years old; she never made good grades—never made her own bed! But somehow she always seemed to get what she wanted. She's the one who got singing and dancing lessons, and a store-bought dress to wear to her senior prom. Why, do you remember how Meg always got to wear twelve jingle bells on her petticoats, while we were only allowed to wear three pieces? Why?! Why should Old Grandmama let her sew twelve golden jingle bells on her petticoats and us only three!

Babe, *who has heard all this before*: I don't know! Maybe she didn't jingle them as much!

Lenny: I can't help it! It gets me mad! I resent it. I do.

Babe: Oh, don't resent Meg. Things have been hard for Meg. After all, she's the one who found Mama.

Lenny: Oh, I know; she's the one who found Mama. But that's always been the excuse.

Babe: But I tell you, Lenny, after it happened, Meg started doing all sorts of these strange things.

Lenny: She did? Like what?

Babe: Like things I never even wanted to tell you about.

Lenny: What sort of things?

Babe: Well, for instance, back when we used to go over to the library, Meg would spend all her time reading and looking through this old black book called *Diseases of the Skin*. It was full of the most sickening pictures you've ever seen. Things like rotting-away noses and eyeballs drooping down the sides of people's faces, and scabs and sores and eaten-away places over all parts of people's bodies.

Lenny, *trying to pour her coffee*: Babe, please! That's enough!

Babe: Anyway, she'd spend hours and hours just forcing herself to look through this book. Why, it was the same way she'd force herself to look at the poster of crippled children stuck up in the window at Dixieland Drugs. You know, that one where they want you to give a dime. Meg would stand there and stare at their eyes and look at the braces on their crippled-up legs—then she'd purposely go and spend her dime on a double-scoop ice cream cone and eat it all down. She'd say to me,

"See, I can stand it. I can stand it. Just look how I'm gonna be able to stand it."

Lenny: That's awful.

Babe: She said she was afraid of being a weak person. I guess 'cause she cried in bed every night for such a long time.

Lenny: Goodness mercy. *After a pause:* Well, I suppose you'd have to be a pretty hard person to be able to do what she did to Doc Porter.

Babe: Oh shoot! It wasn't Meg's fault that hurricane wiped Biloxi away. I never understood why people were blaming all that on Meg—just because that roof fell in and crunched Doc's leg. It wasn't her fault.

Lenny: Well, it was Meg who refused to evacuate. Jim Craig and some of Doc's other friends were all down there, and they kept trying to get everyone to evacuate. But Meg refused. She wanted to stay on because she thought a hurricane would be—oh, I don't know—a lot of fun. Then everyone says she baited Doc into staying there with her. She said she'd marry him if he'd stay.

Babe, *taken aback by this new information:* Well, he has a mind of his own. He could have gone.

Lenny: But he didn't. 'Cause . . . 'cause he loved her. And then, after the roof caved in and they got Doc to the high school gym, Meg just left. She just left him there to leave for California—'cause of her career, she says. I think it was a shameful thing to do. It took almost a year for his leg to heal, and after that he gave up his medical career altogether. He said he was tired of hospitals. It's such a sad thing. We've called him Doc for years.

Babe: I don't know. I guess I don't have any room to talk, 'cause I just don't know. *Pause.* Gosh, you look so tired.

Lenny: I feel tired.

Babe: They say women need a lot of iron—so they won't feel tired.

Lenny: What's got iron in it? Liver?

Babe: Yeah, liver's got it. And vitamin pills.

Further Resources

BOOKS

"Beth Henley." In *Drama Criticism,* vol 14. Farmington Hills, Mich.: Gale, 2001, 307–328.

Gupton, Janet L. "Un-Ruling the Woman: Comedy and the Plays of Beth Henley and Rebecca Gilman." In *Southern Women Playwrights: New Essays in Literary History and Criticism.* Robert L. McDonald and Linda Rohrer Paige, ed. Tuscaloosa: University of Alabama Press, 2002. 124–138.

Kullman, Colby H., and Miriam Neuringer. "Beth Henley." In *American Playwrights Since 1945: A Guide to Scholarship, Criticism and Performance.* Philip C. Kolin, ed. New York: Greenwood Press, 1989, 169–178.

PERIODICALS

Haller, Scot. "Her First Play, Her First Pulitzer Prize." *Saturday Review* 8, no. 11, November 1981, 40–42.

Harbin, Billy J. "Familial Bonds in the Plays of Beth Henley." *The Southern Quarterly* 25, no. 3, Spring 1987, 81–94.

Kerr, Walter. "Offbeat–But a Beat Too Far." *The New York Times,* November 15, 1981, Section D, 3, 31.

Simon, John. "Sisterhood is Beautiful." *New York Magazine* 14, no. 2, January 12, 1981, 42, 44–46.

WEBSITES

"Beth Henley." The Mississippi Writers Page, University of Mississippi Department of English. Available online at http://www.olemiss.edu/depts/english/ms-writers/dir/henley_beth/; website home page: http://www.olemiss.edu/depts/english/ms-writers/dir/henley_beth/ (accessed April 25, 2003).

AUDIO AND VISUAL MEDIA

Crimes of the Heart. Original release, 1986. Directed by Bruce Beresford. VHS, 1996. Anchor Bay Entertainment.

"Cathedral"

Short story

By: Raymond Carver

Date: 1983

Source: Carver, Raymond. "Cathedral." In *Cathedral: Stories* New York: Knopf, 1983, 209–212.

About the Author: Raymond Carver (1938–1988), was born in Clatskanie, Oregon. He attended Humboldt State College (now California State University, Humboldt), receiving an A.B. degree in 1963, and the University of Iowa, receiving a M.F.A. degree in 1966. He was a short story writer. In addition, he wrote poetry and prose. Carver taught at Syracuse University before moving to the West Coast. His award-winning stories have been published in collections, magazines, and anthologies. Carver was married to writer Tess Gallagher. He was awarded the National Endowment for the Arts Discovery Award for poetry, 1970; the Levinson Prize for poetry, 1985; and the Creative Arts Award citation from Brandeis University, 1988. ■

Introduction

Raymond Carver published two volumes of short stories before *Cathedral* appeared in 1983. With this

Master short-story writer Raymond Carver often explored forbidden topics and places in his works. GETTY IMAGES. REPRODUCED BY PERMISSION.

volume, a new writing style emerged. The stories were more hopeful. The characters experience redemption and concentrate less on the dreariness of life than in earlier Carver works such as *Will You Please Be Quiet, Please?* (1976) and *What We Talk About When We Talk About Love* (1981). Nelson Hathcock writes that Carver changed "the potential power in his characters, the power to reconstruct their lives through language and, in the process, arrive at some understanding or intuitive accord."

The sparseness of Carver's sentences and images has been compared to the styles of other great American writers of the twentieth century, namely, Ernest Hemingway, Sherwood Anderson, and Flannery O'Connor. The angst and the heartache that characters experience when they realize just how fragile their lives are can terrorize the reader. Ordinary life can change with one coincidental event or meeting in Carver's world.

In the title story, Bub, the narrator and an alcoholic, displays the unsavoriness of a jealous, mean man. He reveals his ignorance when Robert, a blind man who his wife once worked for, visits the house. Bub plays mean little tricks on Robert until his wife leaves them alone for a time, watching television. Bub suddenly understands that Robert can not visualize what he takes for granted as they "watch" a show on cathedrals. Through his encounter with the man, primarily through language and later "reading" a drawing of a cathedral, Bub understands blindness for the first time as he closes his eyes and tries to read the drawing with only his fingers. Whether he internalizes this lesson is left for the reader to decide.

The stories in *Cathedral* are connected in subtle ways but the reader does not have to read from beginning to end in order to understand the characters or plot. However, reading the entire collection enhances the understanding of Carver's place as a fine writer.

Significance

The lonely and isolated characters that inhabit Carver's fictional world come from his life experiences. In essays, he revealed the difficulty of his early life and marriage and the struggles that caused him and his wife to lose hope. *The New York Times* reviewer Irving Howe notes that the characters are "lacking an imagination, for strangeness, they succumb to the strangeness of their trouble." Married couples often do not communicate well in Carver's stories, or if they begin to, life breaks down and they do not know how to go on with it. Howe comments, "the commonplace is unnerving" for the both characters and reader. Carver's brilliance as a writer is as evident in "Cathedral" as it is in the other eleven in the collection. The characters in the stories reveal more, are more human, and sometimes more humane—these are not the very spare, "cut to the marrow" stories of his previous collections. These are still not characters one necessarily wants to meet, but they are human.

Carver still portrays the suffering better than the good in life, but this collection signals the turning point in a fine writer's work.

Primary Source

"Cathedral" [excerpt]

SYNOPSIS: "Cathedral," the final story in the collection by the same name, was first published in the *Atlantic Monthly*. It also appeared in the 1982 volume of *Best American Short Stories*. The characters in the story and the collection possess the potential for change and understanding that had not been apparent in Carver's earlier work.

This blind man, an old friend of my wife's, he was on his way to spend the night. His wife had died. So he was visiting the dead wife's relatives in Connecticut. He called my wife from his in-laws'. Arrangements were made. He would come by train, a five-hour trip, and my wife would meet him at the station. She hadn't seen him since she worked for him one summer in Seattle ten years ago. But she and the blind man had kept in touch. They made tapes and mailed them back and forth. I wasn't enthusiastic about his visit. He was no one I knew. And his being blind bothered me. My idea of blindness came from the movies. In the movies, the blind moved slowly and never laughed. Sometimes they were led by seeing-eye dogs. A blind man in my house was not something I looked forward to.

That summer in Seattle she had needed a job. She didn't have any money. The man she was going to marry at the end of the summer was in officer's training school. He didn't have any money, either. But she was in love with the guy, and he was in love with her, etc. She'd seen something in the paper: HELP WANTED—*Reading to Blind Man,* and a telephone number. She phoned and went over, was hired on the spot. She'd worked with this blind man all summer. She read stuff to him, case studies, reports, that sort of thing. She helped him organize his little office in the county social-service department. They'd become good friends, my wife and the blind man. How do I know these things? She told me. And she told me something else. On her last day at the office, the blind man asked if he could touch her face. She agreed to this. She told me he touched his fingers to every part of her face, her nose—even her neck! She never forgot it. She even tried to write a poem about it. She was always trying to write a poem. She wrote a poem or two every year, usually after something really important had happened to her.

When we first started going together, she showed me the poem. In the poem, she recalled his fingers and the way they had moved over her face. In the poem, she talked about what she had felt at the time, about what went through her mind when the blind man touched her nose and lips. I can remember I didn't think much of the poem. Of course, I didn't tell her that. Maybe I just don't understand poetry. I admit it's not the first thing I reach for when I pick up something to read.

Anyway, this man who'd first enjoyed her favors, the officer-to-be, he'd been her childhood sweetheart. So okay. I'm saying that at the end of the summer she let the blind man run his hands over her face, said goodbye to him, married her childhood etc., who was now a commissioned officer, and she moved away from Seattle. But they'd kept in touch, she and the blind man. She made the first contact after a year or so. She called him up one night from an Air Force base in Alabama. She wanted to talk. They talked. He asked her to send him a tape and tell him about her life. She did this. She sent the tape. On the tape, she told the blind man about her husband and about their life together in the military. She told the blind man she loved her husband but she didn't like it where they lived and she didn't like it that he was a part of the military-industrial thing. She told the blind man she'd written a poem and he was in it. She told him she was writing a poem about what it was like to be an Air Force officer's wife. The poem wasn't finished yet. She was still writing it. The blind man made a tape. He sent her the tape. She made a tape. This went on for years. My wife's officer was posted to one base and then another. She sent tapes from Moody AFB, McGuire, McConnell, and finally Travis, near Sacramento, where one night she got to feeling lonely and cut off from people she kept losing in that moving-around life. She got to feeling she couldn't go it another step. She went in and swallowed all the pills and capsules in the medicine chest and washed them down with a bottle of gin. Then she got into a hot bath and passed out.

But instead of dying, she got sick. She threw up. Her officer—why should he have a name? he was the childhood sweetheart, and what more does he want?—came home from somewhere, found her, and called the ambulance. In time, she put it all on a tape and sent the tape to the blind man. Over the years, she put all kinds of stuff on tapes and sent the tapes off lickety-split. Next to writing a poem every year, I think it was her chief means of recreation. On one tape, she told the blind man she'd decided to live away from her officer for a time. On another tape, she told him about her divorce. She and I began going out, and of course she told her blind man about it. She told him everything, or so it seemed to me. Once she asked me if I'd like to hear the latest tape from the blind man. This was a year ago. I was on the tape, she said. So I said okay, I'd listen to it. I got us drinks and we settled down in the living room. We made ready to listen. First she inserted the tape into the player and adjusted a couple of dials. Then she pushed a lever. The tape squeaked and someone began to talk in this loud voice. She lowered the volume. After a few minutes of harmless chitchat, I heard my own name in the mouth of this stranger, this blind man I didn't even know! And then this: "From all you've said about him, I can only conclude—" But we were interrupted, a knock on the door, something, and we didn't ever get back to the tape. Maybe it was just as well. I'd heard all I wanted to.

Now this same blind man was coming to sleep in my house.

Further Resources

BOOKS

Nesset, Kirk. *The Stories of Raymond Carver: A Critical Study.* Athens: Ohio University Press, 1995.

Saltzman, Arthur M. *Understanding Raymond Carver.* Columbia: University of South Carolina Press, 1988.

PERIODICALS

Facknitz, Mark A. R. "'The Calm,' 'A Small Good Thing,' and 'Cathedral': Raymond Carver and the Rediscovery of Human Worth." *Studies in Short Fiction* 23, no. 3, Summer 1986, 287–296.

Hathcock, Nelson. "The Possibility of Resurrection: Re–Vision in Carver's 'Feathers' and 'Cathedral.'" *Studies in Short Fiction* 28, no. 1, Winter 1991, 31–39.

Howe, Irving. "Stories of Our Loneliness." *The New York Times Book Review,* September 11, 1983, 1, 42–43.

Wickenden, Dorothy. "Old Darkness, New Light." *The New Republic,* November 14, 1983, 38–39.

AUDIO AND VISUAL MEDIA

Carver, Raymond, and Kay Bonetti. "Interview." Columbia, Mo.: American Audio Prose Library, 1983. Cassette.

The House on Mango Street
Novel

By: Sandra Cisneros

Date: 1984

Source: Cisneros, Sandra. *The House on Mango Street.* 1984. Reprint, New York: Vintage, 1991, 3–5.

About the Author: Sandra Cisneros (1954–) was born in Chicago and grew up in Humboldt Park, Illinois. She earned an undergraduate B.A. degree from Loyola University in 1976 and an M.F.A. degree from the University of Iowa Writers Program in 1978. Cisneros is a Chicano activist and feminist, traits that are reflected in her fiction and poetry. She was awarded the National Endowment for the Arts fellow, 1982, 1988; the Lannan Foundation Literary Award, 1991; and the MacArthur fellow, 1995. ∎

Introduction

The House on Mango Street was first published by a small press, Arte Publico, in 1984. When it was republished in 1989 by Vintage Books, a division of Random House, the book gained a broader readership beyond the Chicano and Latino community. Sandra Cisneros has been called a "representative" of her culture and has been one of the authors credited with revitalizing interest in Chicano writing.

Cisneros has discussed her background and what she faced in college. In an interview for *Southwest Review,* she noted that "Coming from a working class background, an ethnic community, an urban community, a family that did not have books in the house, I did not have the same frames of reference as my classmates." She talks about the disconnection she felt from both subject and training while acknowledging her good fortune of having the privilege to attend prestigious programs. As she rebelled against the middle class life surrounding her in college, she found her voice. Out of her background, she discovered the "street child's voice" and the stories that comprise *The House on Mango Street.*

The House on Mango Street is the eloquently told story of life in the Hispanic quarter of Chicago. Rather than journeying to a far-off place, like Huck Finn, Esperanza Cordero watches the world around her. Her dream for a better house is a basic American motif. The local junk store, the bum who lives in the attic, the drunks on the street, and the children's past times are all subjects for the vignettes that become the collective picture of life for the determined narrator.

Significance

The narrator of Sandra Cisneros's *The House on Mango Street* is Esperanza Cordero, a young girl growing up in Chicago. She has been compared to Huck Finn and to Holden Caulfield as a spokesperson for her age and culture. She is also credited with continuing the tradition of Virginia Woolf's *A Room of One's Own.* Esperanza's narrative is a coming-of-age story in which she gains understanding of her family, her world, and herself.

The novel is not written in a traditional format, yet it contains the themes of the classic *bildungsroman*—a novel about the moral and psychological growth of its characters. Told in vignettes, the story conveys moments in the lives of the neighborhood and the culture of the Chicano people who inhabit it. Esperanza observes especially the women, as she shapes her own identity and dreams. She realizes that her place as a woman in a racial minority allows her fewer opportunities but that education can provide a way to a different life. Cisneros' training as a writer and her Chicano identity allowed her to break the rules of novel writing while telling a story that contains the traditional dreams and fears people experience.

Felicia Cruz notes that Cisneros challenges "accepted literary form, gender inequities, and the cultural and economic subordination of minorities." She addresses class and ethnic identification up front. Her book appeals to a broad readership and has been translated in languages throughout the world. The basic theme of her work, wanting something better for one's life, is one of the appealing factors to both adult and younger readers. She "shows us the world through someone else's eyes" comments Thomas O'Malley. "Things like racism, sex, friendship, dreams, fears, and family are not just issues. They are experiences." For these reasons *The House on Mango Street* has become a standard on reading lists in American literature, women's studies, and cultural studies courses across the country. Accessible language and poignancy makes the novel popular with a wide range of readers.

Primary Source

The House on Mango Street [excerpt]

SYNOPSIS: The book begins and ends with the same litany of the moves that Esperanza's family made throughout her life. The hope for a home comes to her when she realizes that a flat is not truly a house. In the end, she continues to hope to leave Mango Street and she records her thoughts so the "ghost does not ache so much."

We didn't always live on Mango Street. Before that we lived on Loomis on the third floor, and before that we lived on Keeler. Before Keeler it was Paulina, and before that I can't remember. But what I remember most is moving a lot. Each time it seemed there'd be one more of us. By the time we got to Mango Street we were six—Mama, Papa, Carlos, Kiki, my sister Nenny and me.

The House on Mango Street is ours, and we don't have to pay rent to anybody, or share the yard with the people downstairs, or be careful not to make too much noise, and there isn't a landlord banging on the ceiling with a broom. But even so, it's not the house we thought we'd get.

We had to leave the flat on Loomis quick. The water pipes broke and the landlord wouldn't fix them because the house was too old. We had to leave fast. We were using the washroom next door and carrying water over in empty milk gallons. That's why Mama and Papa looked for a house, and that's why we moved into the house on Mango Street, far away, on the other side of town.

They always told us that one day we would move into a house, a real house that would be ours for always so we wouldn't have to move each year. And our house would have running water and pipes that worked. And inside it would have real stairs, not hallway stairs, but stairs inside like the houses on T.V. And we'd have a basement and at least three washrooms so when we took a bath we wouldn't have to tell everybody. Our house would be white with trees around it, a great big yard and grass growing without a fence. This was the house Papa talked about when he held a lottery ticket and this was the house Mama dreamed up in the stories she told us before we went to bed.

Writer Sandra Cisneros is best known for *The House on Mango Street*, a volume of loosely structured vignettes that has been classified as both a short-story collection and a series of prose poems. AP/WORLD WIDE PHOTOS. REPRODUCED BY PERMISSION.

But the house on Mango Street is not the way they told it at all. It's small and red with tight steps in front and windows so small you'd think they were holding their breath. Bricks are crumbling in places, and the front door is so swollen you have to push hard to get in. There is no front yard, only four little elms the city planted by the curb. Out back is a small garage for the car we don't own yet and a small yard that looks smaller between the two buildings on either side. There are stairs in our house, but they're ordinary hallway stairs, and the house has only one washroom. Everybody has to share a bedroom—Mama and Papa, Carlos and Kiki, me and Nenny.

Once when we were living on Loomis, a nun from my school passed by and saw me playing out front. The laundromat downstairs had been boarded up because it had been robbed two days before and the owner had painted on the wood YES WE'RE OPEN so as not to lose business.

Where do you live? she asked.

There, I said, pointing up to the third floor.

You live *there*?

There, I had to look where she pointed—the third floor, the paint peeling, wooden bars Papa had nailed on the windows so we wouldn't fall out. You live *there?* The way she said it made me feel like nothing. *There.* I lived *there.* I nodded.

I knew then I had to have a house. A real house. One I could point to. But this isn't it. The house on Mango Street isn't it. For the time being, Mama says. Temporary, says Papa. But I know how these things go.

Further Resources

BOOKS

TuSmith, Bonnie. *All My Relatives: Community in Contemporary Ethnic American Literatures.* Ann Arbor: University of Michigan Press, 1993.

Yarbro-Bejarao, Yvonne. "Chicana Literature from a Chicana Feminist Perspective." In *Feminisms: An Anthology of Literary Theory and Criticism.* Robyn R. Warhol and Diane Price Herndl, ed. New Brunswick, N.J.: Rutgers University Press, 1991, 732–737.

PERIODICALS

Cisneros, Sandra. "Return to One's House: An Interview with Sandra Cisneros." Interview with Martha Satz. *Southwest Review* 82, no. 2, 1997, 166–185.

Cruz, Felicia J. "On the 'Simplicity' of Sandra Cisneros's *House on Mango Street.*"*MFS: Modern Fiction Studies* 47, no. 4, Winter 2001, 910–946.

O'Malley, Thomas F. "A Ride Down Mango Street." *English Journal* 86, no. 8, December 1997, 35–37.

WEBSITES

"Sandra Cisneros." Las Mujeres. Available online at http://www.lasmujeres.com/sandracisneros/; website home page: http://www.lasmujeres.com/ (accessed April 26, 2003).

"Sandra Cisneros." Voices from the Gaps: Women Writers of Color. University of Minnesota. Available online at http://voices.cla.umn.edu/authors/CISNEROSsandra.html; website home page: http://voices.cla.umn.edu/ (accessed April 26, 2003).

AUDIO AND VISUAL MEDIA

Cisneros, Sandra. *The House on Mango Street.* Random House Audiobooks, 1998. Cassette.

"God Bless the U.S.A."
Song

By: Lee Greenwood

Date: 1984

Source: Greenwood, Lee. "God Bless the U.S.A." MCA Music, 1984.

About the Artist: Lee Greenwood (1942–), born in Los Angeles, grew up on a farm near Sacramento, California. He re-ceived a saxophone for his tenth birthday to encourage a musical career. He formed his first band, The Moonbeams, while in high school, then played in casinos and lounges in Nevada. He later moved to Nashville. In 1983 and 1984 he was selected Male Vocalist of the Year by the Country Music Association (CMA). ∎

Introduction

Lee Greenwood understands both the business and entertainment sides of country music. "*Show business* is two words," he told Judy Corwin of the *Baylor Business Review.* "You've got to know as much about the business as you know about the show, or you may never survive." Knowing this has helped Greenwood move from the casino lounges of Nevada to the stage of country music. In 1980 he signed with MCA in Nashville and began recording albums and touring. In 1981 his first hit, "It Turns Me Inside Out" remained on the charts for 22 weeks and made Greenwood a star.

Greenwood toured extensively in the first years after moving to Nashville. In addition to the large venues and the fair circuit, Greenwood played private conventions and participated in military USO tours with Bob Hope. A composer as well as a performer, he began concentrating more on writing music while slowing down on his tours. In addition to country music, Greenwood writes rhythm and blues.

"God Bless the U.S.A" was written in 1984. The patriotic lyrics were an instant hit, and the song became identified with Greenwood. The song was included on Greenwood's 1992 album, *American Patriot.*

Significance

The year Lee Greenwood composed "God Bless the U.S.A." he was named Country Music Association's Male Vocalist of the Year for the second year in a row. In addition, he won a Grammy for the Best Country Music Album of the Year. In 1985, "God Bless the U.S.A." received the CMA Song of the Year Award. The honors brought further attention to Greenwood and his music, but it was the patriotic message of the song that drew listeners. "The patriotic pull of this song has thrilled Americans from coast to coast and around the world. It has become so firmly entrenched in Americana music that President George Bush asked [Greenwood] to perform the song during presidential inauguration festivities this past January [1989]," Corwin reported.

Greenwood's understanding of the importance of the military in American life is reflected in his lyrics, "And I won't forget the men who died, who gave that right to me/ And I'd gladly stand up next to you and defend her still today." His sensitivity to the image of the military originated from observing his father's naval career. Following World War II (1939–1945), the military was still honored in the country, and his father would wear his uniform if he needed to hitch a ride. The image of the military became negative after the Korean conflict (1950–1953) and Vietnam War (1964–1975), however. The visits to military bases provided, as Corwin notes, "the need for giving inspiration to our servicemen and women not only stateside but also at our bases throughout the world."

Greenwood's song became the anthem of the Persian Gulf War. Played on radio stations throughout the country, the lyrics reflected the pride of patriotism and love of freedom. It returned again following the September 11, 2001, bombing of the World Trade Center and the Pentagon and attained the number two position on the charts in October 2001. Then again in 2003, as American troops liberated Iraq, Greenwood's words and music were heard across the airwaves. It is a song that will remain a patriotic anthem.

Primary Source

"God Bless the U.S.A."

SYNOPSIS: Patriotic melodies have always been popular with Americans and Lee Greenwood's "God Bless the U.S.A." is no exception. The song emphasizes traditional American values of family, pride, and freedom.

If tomorrow all the things were gone
I'd worked for all my life,
And I had to start again
with just my children and my wife,
I'd thank my lucky stars
to be livin' here today,
'cause the flag still stands for freedom
and they can't take that away.

I'm proud to be an American
where at least I know I'm free,
And I won't forget the men who died
who gave that right to me,
And I gladly stand up next to you
and defend her still today,
'Cause there ain't no doubt I love this land
God Bless the U.S.A.

From the lakes of Minnesota
to the hills of Tennessee,
across the plains of Texas,
from sea to shining sea.
From Detroit down to Houston
and New York to LA.,
Well, there's pride in every American heart
and it's time to stand and say:

I'm proud to be an American
where at least I know I'm free,
And I won't forget the men who died
who gave that right to me,
And I gladly stand up next to you
and defend her still today,

Lee Greenwood sings at the Music City News Country Awards in 1984. **AP/WORLD WIDE PHOTOS. REPRODUCED BY PERMISSION.**

'Cause there ain't no doubt I love this land
God Bless the U.S.A.

Further Resources

BOOKS

Daley, Dan. *Nashville's Unwritten Rules: Inside the Business of Country Music.* Woodstock, N.Y.: Overlook Press, 1998.

Kingsbury, Paul, ed. *The Encyclopedia of Country Music: The Ultimate Guide to the Music.* New York: Oxford University Press, 1998.

Richards, Tad, and Melvin B. Shestack. *The New Country Music Encyclopedia.* New York: Simon & Schuster, 1993.

PERIODICALS

Corwin, Judy. "The Business of Making Music: The Case of Country Music Artist Lee Greenwood." *Baylor Business Review* 7, no. 2, Summer 1989, 9–15.

Theokas, Christopher. "Patriotism Leads Hit Parade." *USA Today,* October 25, 2001, D1.

WEBSITES

"God Bless the U.S.A." American Dreams Collection. Available online at http://www.usdreams.com/Greenwood79.html; website home page: http://www.usdreams.com/ (accessed April 26, 2003).

Lee Greenwood Online. Available online at http://www.leegreenwood.com/ (accessed April 26, 2003).

AUDIO AND VISUAL MEDIA

Greenwood, Lee. *Best of Lee Greenwood.* Capitol/EMI Records 89650, CD, 2000.

"We Are the World"

Song

By: Michael Jackson; Lionel Richie

Date: 1985

Source: Jackson, Michael, and Lionel Richie. "We Are the World." Secaucus, N.J.: Mijac Music & Brockman Music, 1985.

About the Artists: Michael Jackson (1958–) and Lionel Richie (1949–) are both singers and songwriters. Jackson began his career singing with his brothers in the Jackson Five during the 1960s. In 1976 the group split and Jackson began pursuing a solo career. Richie sang with the group the Commodores from the 1960s until 1981, when he began a solo career. ■

Introduction

Recording stars raising funds for needy causes became a larger enterprise in the 1980s compared to previous decades. In 1984, a group of artists in the United Kingdom known as BandAid recorded "Do They Know It's Christmas?" USA for Africa (United Support of Artists for Africa) recorded "We Are the World" in January 1985. Other "aid" organizations—such as Farm Aid to raise money for farmers—formed throughout the 1980s to solicit funds for a variety of causes.

"We are the World" was organized by Ken Kragen, Richie's manager, in response to an idea by Harry Belafonte, who originally planned a benefit concert by black musicians to raise funds for Africa. In two hours' time, Jackson and Richie composed the lyrics and music that would be recorded by 45 artists. The lyrics were meant to present a message of hope and unity for a country that lacked food and basic needs.

Goron Crovitz, writing in the *Wall Street Journal,* sheds light on the situation in Ethiopia:

> In most of Africa, government meddling has ruined farming. The situation is worse in Ethiopia, where the greatest horror is the special famine forced by the government on opponents of the Marxist-Leninist regime. Western relief groups are stymied when they try to get aid to the rebels in the north, especially those in the province of Tigre. The people there are being "resettled" by the government. The Ethiopian military, which distributes the Western aid, is in the business of killing the Tigreans, not feeding them. Conceding that Ethiopia hasn't allowed aid to the rebels, who've pleaded for a "food truce," USA for Africa organizers say politics could become a problem.

Significance

Harry Belafonte's idea motivated 45 artists to join as one to record a song that would reach the top of the charts in March 1985, raising $50 million for famine relief in Ethiopia. Quincy Jones produced the single. The singers included stars such as Stevie Wonder, Paul Simon, Kim Carnes, Gordon Lightfoot, Bob Dylan, Anne Murray, Kenny Rogers, Tina Turner, Billy Joel, and Dionne Warwick. The recording was scheduled to follow the American Music Awards, so that the largest number of artists would be available.

The power of celebrity to sell is, of course, nothing new. The recording of "We Are the World" is significant not only for the cross section of vocalists it drew, but also for the attention it attracted by record purchasers and radio stations. On one day in March, 1985, five thousand radio stations played the song simultaneously. It won the Grammy for Best Song in 1985.

Not everyone was wowed by the charity of the artists. Crovitz noted that "Although they've announced that 35% of the funds will go to Africa for medical care, 35% for grain and seeds, 20% for 'long-term development' and 10% for the homeless in the U.S., the USA (United Support of Artists) for Africa organizers haven't, in fact, given much thought to what aid they are going to deliver how, to whom and when. A spokesman just says, 'USA for Africa personages' plan to fly to Ethiopia with aid sometime in June." For Crovitz, the lyrics did not match the severity of the situation. Ken Kragen responded to Crovitz's criticism in the editorial section of the *Wall Street Journal.* He wrote that "the lyrics were meant to be an anthem of the times," not a realistic politically accurate statement. He also noted that support, rather than negative comments, were needed to solve the problems. "We Are the World" did raise money for famine relief. Stars donated their time, record companies donated potential royalties and production expertise, and people purchased the record.

Primary Source

"We Are the World"

> **SYNOPSIS:** The single, record, and video for "We Are the World" brought attention to the famine in Africa. Selling millions of copies, the song raised funds for famine relief.

There comes a time when we need a certain call
When the world must come together as one
There are people dying
Oh, and it's time to lend a hand to life
The greatest gift of all

We can't go on pretending day by day
That someone, somehow will soon make a change
We're all a part of God's great big family
And the truth—you know love is all we need
(CHORUS)
We are the world, we are the children
We are the ones who make a brighter day
so let's start giving

Music and movie stars, including Michael Jackson, Diana Ross, and Lionel Richie, sing "We Are the World" in January 1986. © BETTMANN/CORBIS. REPRODUCED BY PERMISSION.

There's a choice we're making
We're saving our own lives
It's true we'll make a better day
Just you and me

Well, send 'em your heart
So they know that someone cares
And their lives will be stronger and free
As God has shown us
By turning stone to bread
And so we all must lend a helping hand

(CHORUS)

When you're down and out
There seems no hope at all
But if you just believe
There's no way we can fall
Well, well, well, let's realize
That one change can only come
When we stand together as one

(REPEAT CHORUS AND FADE)

Further Resources

BOOKS

Berger, Gilda. *USA for Africa: Rock Aid in the Eighties.* New York: F. Watts, 1987.

Breskin, David, Chery McCall, and Roger Hilburn. *We Are the World.* New York: Perigee Books, 1985.

PERIODICALS

Crovitz, Gordon. "Critique: Can Rock Stars Stem Ethiopian Hunger?" *The Wall Street Journal,* April 24, 1985, 28 (Eastern ed.), 30 (Western ed.).

Howes, David. "We Are the World" and its Counterparts: Popular Songs as Constitutional Discourses." *International Journal of Politics, Culture and Society* 3, no. 3, Spring 1990, 315–339.

Kragen, Ken. "'Naive' Anthem May Make a World of Difference." *The Wall Street Journal,* May 16, 1985, 33 (Eastern ed.), 31 (Western ed.).

WEBSITES

"We Are the World." Available online at http://www.inthe80s .com/weworld.shtml; website home page: http://www .inthe80s.com/ (accessed April 27, 2003).

AUDIO AND VISUAL MEDIA

We Are the World. Polygram 824 822, LP, 1985. PGD/Polygram 4228 24822, CD, 1991.

We Are the World USA for Africa. Original release, 1985. VHS, 1988. Columbia Tristar Home Video.

Speed-the-Plow

Play script

By: David Mamet

Date: 1985

Source: Mamet, David. *Speed-the-Plow*. New York: Gove Weidenfeld, 1985, 3–10.

About the Author: Playwright, screenwriter, director, and producer, David Mamet (1947–) was born in Chicago. Attending Goddard College and receiving a B.A. degree in 1969, Mamet studied at the Neighborhood Playhouse School of the Theater in New York from 1968–69. In addition to writing plays, Mamet has taught at Yale and New York University. ■

Introduction

Critics have proclaimed David Mamet one of the primary playwrights of the late twentieth century. His play *American Buffalo,* first produced in 1975, established his reputation as a national figure. *Glengarry Glen Ross* (1983), which opened in England, extended his reputation and won the Pulitzer Prize. Many of Mamet's plays premiere in Chicago, his hometown, prior to opening on Broadway.

Author Joycelyn Trigg notes that Mamet has "consistently acknowledged his indebtedness to Thorstein Veblen's *Theory of the Leisure Class* in numerous interviews." He also cites Karl Marx, Sigmund Freud, Bruno Bettelheim, and Joseph Campbell for helping form his moral vision. These writers explore the economics of culture and the influences on the culture. Commercial gain is one of the primary motives of the two movie moguls in *Speed-the-Plow*. Class considerations and the effects of wealth are also part of the theories. His language and style have been compared to Harold Pinter, a renowned British playwright. Minimalism is a key aspect in both playwrights' work.

Speed-the-Plow tells the story of Bobby Gould and Charlie Fox, two old-time movie collaborators. They quibble over percentages of the gross and film deals. Gould and Fox agree to make a safe film that they feel will make lots of money, even if the script is bad. Karen, a young aspiring woman and Gould's secretary, will do anything to succeed. Using her sex appeal, she convinces him to change plans and produce a movie based on a novel about radiation and the end of the world instead. Fox is angry at his friend's decision but personal loyalty wins in the end. Madonna made her Broadway debut in the play. Joe Mantegna played Bobby, and Ron Silver portrayed Charlie.

Significance

Speed-the-Plow enjoyed great success from the beginning. Advanced press caused the Broadway opening to be moved to Royale Theater at Lincoln Center instead of the original venue, the Mitzi E. Newhouse theater. Reviewer Robert Brustein of *The New Republic* wrote that Mamet's twelfth play "is the deftest and funniest of Mamet's works." The play is a spare one: The set has no walls and furniture is draped over with dust covers. The characters act only in the present.

Part of the draw for the Broadway opening in 1988 was Madonna, whose appearance helped to fill the theater with sellout crowds. However, critics called her performance less than satisfying. Richard Hornby, theater reviewer for *The Hudson Review,* reported that "her performance was unexceptional, deprived of an echo chamber, she has little voice, and her features are small and relatively inexpressive, but she is relaxed and sincere on stage, and hence easy to watch."

Critics disagreed about the meaning of the play. Some saw it as a satire of Hollywood while others saw it as a play about the tests of friendship. Those who saw personal loyalty as a primary theme cited the decaying society and corrupt values as the test of loyalty. The motifs are clear, however. The competition between Gould and Fox; their loathing of having to work while accepting that it is part of life—these appear throughout the play. In his review for *Modern Drama,* Tony Stafford pointed out that there are "well over one hundred different references to such words as 'job,' 'work,' 'position,' 'desk,' 'office,' 'business,' 'deal' (as in work agreement), 'hire,' and 'do' (as a synonym for 'work')." The definition of a work ethic, an American ideal, is a central theme of the play.

Speed-the-Plow is performed in a mere ninety minutes, a short time for a Broadway play. Mamet's skill with language and subtle comedy continue his ongoing dissection of American life and values.

Primary Source

Speed-the-Plow [excerpt]

SYNOPSIS: The source of the title is a play by Thomas Morton performed in 1800. The motifs of work are similar to those found in Mamet's play. The title is also a medieval blessing. It can be interpreted that the two hucksters bless their moneymaking ventures.

ONE

Gould's office. Morning. Boxes and painting materials all around. Gould is sitting, reading, Fox enters.

Gould: When the gods would make us mad, they answer our prayers.

Fox: Bob . . .

Gould: I'm in the midst of a wilderness.

Fox: Bob . . .

Gould: If it's not quite "Art" and it's not quite "Entertainment," it's here on my desk. I have inherited a monster.

Fox: . . . Bob . . .

Gould: Listen to this . . . *(Reads)*: "How are things made round? Was there one thing which, originally, was round . . . ?"

Fox: . . . Bob . . .

Gould: *(leafing through the book he is reading, reads)*: "A certain frankness came to it . . ." *(He leafs.)* "The man, downcast, then met the priest, under the bridge, beneath that bridge which stood for so much, where so much had transpired *since* the radiation."

Fox: . . . yeah, Bob, that's great . . .

Gould: Listen to this: "and with it brought grace. But still the questions persisted . . . that of the Radiation. That of the growth of animalism, the decay of the soil. And it said 'Beyond terror. Beyond grace' . . . and caused a throbbing . . . machines in the void . . ." *(He offers the book to Fox.)* Here: take a page.

Fox: I have to talk to you.

Gould: Chuck, Chuck, Chuck, *Charles*: you get too old, too busy to have 'fun' this business, to have 'fun,' then what are you . . . ?

Fox: . . . Bob . . .

Gould: What are you?

Fox: What am I . . . ?

Gould: Yes.

Fox: What am I when?

Gould: What are you, I was saying, if you're just a slave to commerce?

Fox: If I'm just a slave to commerce?

Gould: Yes.

Fox: I'm nothing.

Gould: No.

Fox: You're absolutely right.

Gould: You got to have fun. You know why?

Fox: Okay: why?

Gould: Because, or else you'll die, and people will say "he never had any fun."

Fox: How close are you to Ross?

Gould: How close am I to Ross . . . ? I don't know. How close should I be?

Fox: I have to ask you something.

David Mamet's comedy *Speed-the-Plow* was first presented on Broadway in 1988. AP/WORLD WIDE PHOTOS. REPRODUCED BY PERMISSION.

Gould *(pause)*: Go ahead, Charl.

Fox: You wanna' greenlight a picture? What's your deal, what's your new deal?

Gould: What's my new deal, that's all you can talk about?

Fox: What's your new deal?

Gould: Alright. Over ten mil I need Ross's approval. Under ten mil, I can greenlight it. So what. *(Pause.)*

Fox: This morning, Bob.

Gould: . . . Yes . . . ?

Fox: This morning a man came to me.

Gould: . . . a man came to you. Whaddayou, already, you're here to "Promote" me . . . ?

Fox: Bob . . .

Gould: You here to promote me? Charl? Because, Charl, one thing I don't need . . .

Fox: Bob.

Gould: When everybody in this jolly *town* is tryin' to promote me, do you wanna see my messages . . . ?

Ron Silver, left, Madonna, and Joe Mantegna take a curtain call after the premier of David Mamet's *Speed-the-Plow* in New York on May 4, 1988. **AP/WORLD WIDE PHOTOS. REPRODUCED BY PERMISSION.**

Fox: Bob.

Gould: "Get Him While He's Hot" . . .

Fox: Yes, yes, but . . .

Gould: My good, my "good" friend, Charles Fox . . .

Fox: Bob . . .

Gould: That's why we have "channels."

Fox: Uh huh.

Gould: All these "little" people out there, that we see. Y'unnerstand? Fellow asks, "what are they *there* for?" Well, Charl. We Don't Know. But we *think,* you give the thing to *your* boy, gives it to *my* boy, these people get to *eat,* they don't have to go *beg,* and get in everybody's face the *airport* the whole time. This morning the phone won't stop ringing. Do you know who's calling? Everybody says they met me in *Topeka,* 1962, and do I want to make their movie. Guys want me to do remakes of films haven't been made yet.

Fox: . . . Huh, huh . . .

Gould: I'm drowning in "coverage." *(He picks up a script and reads:)* "The Story of a Horse and the Horse Who Loved Him." *(He drops script.)* . . . Give me a breather from all those fine folk suddenly see what a great "man" I am. N'when I *do* return my calls, Charl, do you know what I'll tell those people?

Fox: No.

Gould: I'm going to tell them, "Go through Channels." This protects me from them. And from folk, fine as they are, like you, Charl, when you come to me for favors. Or did you come up here to congratulate me on my new promotion?

Fox: Congratulations.

Gould: Do I deserve it?

Fox: Yes. You do, Bob.

Gould: Why?

Fox: Because you're a prince among men and you're Yertle the Turtle.

Gould: Alright, then, that's enough. What did you bring me?

Fox: This morning, Bob.

Gould: Yes?

Fox: This morning Doug Brown came to me.

Gould: . . . Doug Brown.

Fox *(pause)*: He came to my *house*, Bob. How would you *like* . . . How would you like Doug Brown to "cross the street" to do a picture for us? *(Pause.)* Bob? How would you *like,* a script that I got him. He's *nuts* for it, he's free, we could start to shoot next *month,* I have his word and he'll come to the studio, and do the film for us. Doug Brown will cross the street and do a film for us next month.

Gould *(picks up the phone)*: Get me Ross. *(Pause.)*

Fox: . . . do you see what I'm telling you?

Gould: . . . he came to your house . . .

Fox: . . . can you believe what I'm saying to you . . . ?

Gould: Douggie Brown.*(Into phone:)* Ross *(pause)* Richard Ross . . . no, no, no, *don't* look in the book . . . there's a button on the console . . . Richard R. . . . just push the button on the . . . *(Pause.)* There's a button on the console . . . Richard Ross . . . just . . . *Thank you. (Hangs up the phone. Pause.)* Are you alright?

Fox: I'm fine. I'm fine, I just need coffee.

Gould: We'll get it for you. Tell mmm . . .

Fox: Alright, I, this is some time ago.

Gould: . . . uh huh . . .

Fox: That I get the script to Brown . . .

Gould: What script . . . ?

Fox: You don't know it, a prison script . . .

Gould *(simultaneously with "script")*: One of ours . . . ?

Fox: I found it in the file. I *loved* it . . . all the time I'm thinking . . .

Gould: Uh huh . . .

Fox: How to do this script, I, one day . . .

Gould: Uh huh . . .

Fox: . . . so . . .

Gould: So, you give the script to Brown . . .

Fox: Not "him," his . . .

Gould: Uh huh . . .

Fox: . . . his . . .

Gould: . . . I know . . .

Fox: His "guy."

Gould: Yes.

Fox: *Gives* Douggie the script . . . *(Phone rings. Gould picks up the phone.)*

Gould *(into phone)*: Yes. Thank you. *(Hangs up.)* Ross'll get back to us . . .

Fox: . . . His guy *gives* Douggie the scri . . .

Gould: He gives Douggie the script.

Fox: Yes.

Gould: Mmm . . .

Fox: *Months* ago, alright? *I* don't know. *Today,* alright . . . ? Today. *(Pause.)* I'm having coffee.

Gould: Umm hmmm . . .

Fox: Who drives up?

Gould: . . . coffee at your house . . .

Fox: Who drives up?

Gould: Douggie Brown.

Fox: Douglas Brown drives up to my house. *(Pause.)* He says, "I Want To Do Your Script I've got this other thing to deal with, and we'll settle it tomorrow. Call me ten o'clock tomorrow morning. I'll come in and sign *up.*" *(Phone rings.)*

Gould *(into phone)*: *Hello* . . . who? No calls. *No* calls. Just Richard Ross. And we need coffee . . . okay? *Got* it . . . ? *(Hangs up.)*

Fox: . . . cross the street to shoot it . . . ? And he says "why not." *(Pause.)*

Gould: . . . *huh* . . .

Fox: *Huh* . . . ?

Gould: . . . He'd come over here to shoot it . . .

Fox: Sonofabitch like out of some damn fairytale.

Gould: . . . he drove to your house . . .

Fox: . . . I'm looking out the window . . .

Gould: . . . son of a bitch . . .

Fox: . . . Douglas Brown drives up . . .

Further Resources
BOOKS

Hudgins, Christopher G., and Leslie Kane, eds. *Gender and Genre: Essays on David Mamet.* New York: Palgrave, 2001.

Kane, Leslie, ed. *David Mamet: A Casebook.* New York: Garland, 1992.

Trigg, Joycelyn. "David Mamet." In *American Playwrights Since 1945: A Guide to Scholarship, Criticism and Perfor-*

mance. Philip C. Kolin, ed. New York: Greenwood Press, 1989, 259–288.

PERIODICALS

Brustein, Robert. "Speed-the-Plow." *The New Republic* 198, no. 23, June 6, 1988, 29–33.

Hornby, Richard. "Review of Speed the Plow." *The Hudson Review* 41, no. 3, Autumn 1988, 516–518.

Kolin, Phillip C. "Performing Scripts in David Mamet's Speed-the-Plow." *Notes on Contemporary Literature* 28, no. 5, November 1998, 5–6.

Stafford, Tony J. "*Speed-the-Plow* and *Speed the Plough*: The Work of the Earth." *Modern Drama* 36, no. 1, March 1993, 38–47.

WEBSITES

Charnick, Jason. "David Mamet Info Page." Available online at http://www.mindspring.com/~jason-charnick/mamet.html; website home page: http://www.mindspring.com/~jason-charnick/ (accessed April 27, 2003).

The Salon Interview: David Mamet. Salon.com. Available online at http://www.salon.com/feature/1997/10/cov_si_24 mamet.html; website home page: http://www.salon.com/ (accessed April 27, 2003).

"When is a Painting Finished?"

Magazine article

By: Paul Gardner

Date: 1985

Source: Gardner, Paul. "When is a Painting Finished?" *ARTnews* 84, November 1985, 89–97.

About the Author: Paul Gardner worked for *The New York Times* as a staff writer and assistant editor of the Sunday Arts & Leisure section. He was a contributor to *A Faulkner Perspective,* Franklin Library. He wrote the screenplay *La Decade Prodigieuse,* with Claude Chabrol. Notable assignments include an exclusive interview with Leni Riefenstahl, the German film director. He was also a contributor to periodicals, including *Transatlantic Review, Plays & Players, ARTnews,* and *London Sunday Observer.* ∎

Introduction

As with all arts, painters approach their work in a variety of ways. Paul Gardner chose fourteen painters to whom he posed the question "When is a painting finished?" The answers vary as much as the art they create. Just as writers revise their works, many artists attempt to improve what they view as flaws in their paintings.

Several of the artists refer to a "gut feeling"; in other words, they just know when something is finished. Jim Dine says that "a painting is finished when the romance is over." Robert Longo knows a painting is not done if

he wakes in the "middle of the night, really, really bothered." The process varies for artists as their art varies. The contributors to this article work with various mediums: oil, mixed media, and acrylics. There is no one school or movement that characterizes the group.

Significance

The artists' statements represent in words what they attempt to complete on canvas. Through the descriptions of their art, their explanations about how they work, and their feelings about when a painting is done, the reader senses the great variety in the world of contemporary art. Their reflections are a key to understanding not only the question of a "finished" painting, but the work of an artist in general.

The artist may describe an exhibit or an entire body of work. Reflections on earlier movements shows the way artists develop in their work and thinking. Al Held, for example, discusses the Abstract Expressionism of the 1950s and 60s. He recalls constant discussions about when a piece was truly finished. His theory in 1985 developed into one of knowing when he has reached a certain point and can let go. This theme runs through many of the statements. If there is an aspect, a color, an image that is just not quite right they do not want to let their vision and creation out into the world. When it is ready, art, like children, can go forth and be admired by the waiting public.

Primary Source

"When is a Painting Finished?" [excerpt]

> **SYNOPSIS:** Most of the artists in this group of artists' statements had been refining their craft for decades. In the 1980s they were the names that the art world knew and was drawn to.

A painting is never finished—it simply stops in interesting places. This aphorism has often been used, yet artists tend to find it more fanciful than true. At least this is what we discovered than we asked 14 artists of various styles, ages, and backgrounds, "How do you know when a painting is finished?"

Although their answers are as diverse as their paintings, their working routines turn out to be surprisingly similar. Most find it essential to be working on two pieces at the same time, and most find it equally important to put aside a supposedly "finished" canvas for several days, weeks or even months in order to look at the piece with a cold, critical eye.

Many artists retouch finished work. In one unusual case, an artist discovered during a museum retrospective that a major painting had a "flaw" and he later corrected it—some 12 years after he had "completed" the work. By contrast, another artist contends that once his work is sent to the gallery, his participation is over; his "duty" is to quickly send "information out to the world."

A feeling of surprise or of romance rewarded or a mystery solved are also cited as cues to when work is finished. Other artists remark on distinct physical sensations. Some, who plan carefully in advance, see the finish as a logical conclusion of sketches realized, while others remark that the end is a spontaneous act. All the artists seem to agree that today's "mistakes" are mentally stored away and rectified in the future.

Keith Haring

I consider my work the record of a moment, so it starts and ends during one session. I almost never rework an image. When it's done, it's done. This happens quickly, and I don't look back and try to do it another way.

Graffiti art is an instant gesture, like calligraphy. And because I'm capturing that instant, I do not believe in mistakes. The image won't change, though I may touch up a spot that seems fuzzy. Each day I draw differently anyway, so there'd be no point in going over yesterday's output.

I've been working on a series of black-and-white paintings and just finished one in an hour. I feel a heightened sense of reality when I'm working—that's why it is important that each painting be finished quickly, or the power of the moment is lost.

I don't sit around and doodle; I don't sketch. However, often my drawing board for ideas is an empty advertising panel in the subway stations. (The cops like me, though I got a $15 ticket last week.) Usually I don't have the time to go out every day and hunt up unsold advertising panels.

Basically, I work as fast as I can, maybe doing five paintings a day. Some artists need time for reflection because they're dealing with subtle colors, but my work is more about drawing. If my first rendering isn't strong enough, then I know that it needs more lines—more embellishment. I wasn't satisfied with a self-portrait, so I filled in black vein lines and it was complete. There was never any question of doing it over again. This may be a fault, but it's me, it's how I work. I find it more interesting to start something new than to keep agonizing over the same piece. I will add what I call sytlistic touches, such as X symbols, that tend to pull together lines, dots, stripes.

The lines themselves just naturally find their own given space. Once they're there, they're there. The most exciting aspect is when I'm painting and I'm not sure what will emerge. I'm aware of what I'm doing, whether it's starving hands reaching for money or a medical examiner stealing the eyes of a police victim, but I also like to feel a sense of abandonment.

I admire the Japanese and feel a kinship with them. Their painting is a ritual, an act. The power of the line is important in Japanese art. Chance plays a big role too. This appeals to me. Essentially, the information is in the line. My position is: get the information out fast, don't keep it for your eyes only in the studio.

Janet Fish

When necessary, I make changes or rethink a piece as I go along, which is why the "finished" moment is not something I dread.

For the last five years I've been doing still lifes—breakfast kitchen scenes, or just objects on a table. Since I work from life, the still life is an actual sketch. In one piece, *Eggs and Cereal,* I arranged breakfast things on a table—flowers, orange juice, a morning newspaper and shirred eggs in ceramic containers. I had to cook the eggs three times, which took longer than it did to paint them. I started with some wallpaper. The paper was "springy," so I wanted the scene to evoke a sunny morning. Anyway, as the painting neared completion, I realized that it wasn't complete at all. There were too many shadows. They were dead in quality. I repainted the shadows, making them a brighter blue and giving them light. A decision about such details, a decision that's correct, is important in finishing a painting. And I make these decisions as I work

With *Pencils and Crayons,* I moved pencils and crayons around even as I painted them because I wanted a specific type of diagonal line in the painting. I also had selected a violet-colored dish as an element, but after it was painted I felt the edges weren't sharp enough. Immediately I repainted, so there was a transition from pale green to violet.

The paintings grow as I work on them, and I don't hesitate to alter the original set-up. There are exceptions: sometimes a picture won't grow, it just seems stuck. I once attempted a painting of a woman rolling cookies. A model posed for about 30 hours. When I considered the result, I saw too much tension in her figure, in the way she held her head. Then I realized that during our studio sessions she had been tense, and so had I. It was clearly visible in the work, and the tension could not be painted out. I put the painting away—it's unfinished, although there are things I like in it. I allow myself a lot of creative freedom, but I am, I think, an objective critic.

You can be blind to a painting, or you may find you're sick of it. When a work is finished and I'm satisfied, I'll hang it on the wall and study it while talking on the telephone or doing routine studio chores. I may alter a color here or there.

But I've never had a problem knowing when a painting is finished because I begin with an idea of images and color and build up gradually to the resolution of that idea, always stepping back at certain stages to see how the colors relate. I know how I *want* them to relate. It's my own system of checks and balances. It also means that *I* have to relate to what I'm looking at.

Joan Snyder

Frequently while I'm in the middle of a painting, some friends come by and say, "Leave it alone. Don't do another thing." When that happens I know I must keep going, even if there's a possibility of destroying a painting. There's also the possibility that I might make it even better. When I feel that what has been put on canvas cannot be disturbed, I leave it alone, even if it's not perfect. Nothing is perfect. It's risk.

I never rigidly plan in advance. I'm not patient with pencil and paper, so whatever ideas I have are usually sketched on scraps of paper, very informally, and I may do studies. I admire Jackson Pollock, who liberated us all. However, I still love the German Expressionists. My ancestors are from Russia and Germany, and that angst is part of me.

In the studio these days I constantly listen to classical vocalists and to opera—Mozart, Strauss. Music, which can be so complex structurally, has taught me more about structure than other art forms. It's also inspirational. I want to have the angels in my studio. Sometimes they're suffering, but that's okay.

Painting for me is like music. There can be so many emotional possibilities in a piece of music, and that's what I try to do in a painting. There was a time, for example, when a painting would start in the upper left corner and work toward the upper right corner, as if moving toward a crescendo. The bottom right corner would be the resolution. This was certainly the process in my "Symphony" paintings.

I just completed a large piece, *Can We Turn Our Rage Into Poetry?,* and while working on it I collaged pieces of velvet, chips of mirror and sequins on a canvas in which grays, browns and black represent the rage, while the very bright colors represent the poetry. But I was hung up on one purple square. I did it over and over again until I felt totally satisfied. Finishing can be agonizing. But when I decide to stop, I don't later retouch or change ideas. Once I've made my statement, I've done all I can and finally I feel peaceful with the work.

When you paint your guts out, it's like having an orgasm. You just *know* when you're done.

Tom Wesselmann

Determining when a painting is finished depends on the nature of the work and the work process. Over the past 25 years, I've had a wide variety of form changes, and I realize that you can't separate the nature of the process from that of the final judgement.

During the '60s, when I was doing collage still lifes and "Great American Nudes," my work process was mainly to move proposed elements around until the composition seemed right. To a large extent, "right" meant exciting. When I experienced, as I often did, a distinct physical thrill in my stomach, I knew it was my eyes telling me the painting was "right." I had first experienced this visceral thrill as an art student while looking at a Motherwell "Elegy." It was my first esthetic reaction to art.

In the '60s I had rather definite esthetic conditions, intellectually applied, that I tried to meet. But into the late '60s and beyond, I relied increasingly on intuitive judgement. Also my work process included more and more preliminary studies—at times, ridiculously many. With these preliminary studies, the image works up in stages and "finishing" takes place all along the way. Into the '70s, when I was mostly doing intense, compressed oil-on-canvas paintings, the image was quite fully restored in small studies. By the time the big work was tackled, it was mainly a matter of properly transferring from small to large.

In all my work I paint the image twice. After the first run-through the image is there, but not alive. The second painting-through is intensely done, perfecting colors and details. It's here that the art goes in and the painting springs to life. Here it is mainly my having, over the course of the process, become sensitive to the image—and as the final image declares itself forcefully, I know when it's right.

In my giant standing still lifes, finishing meant finding the exact relationship between the huge free-standing sections. In maquette form, the elements were chosen and assembled in a proper position. But at giant scale, such as a 35-foot pair of sunglasses, the precise positioning was crucial in making the overall image come together with convincing forcefulness. It finally came down to trial-and-error movements involving fractions of an inch: even one-quarter of an inch could make a difference.

In my newest work, all in cutout metal, I must work out the preliminary study with unusual thoroughness because it's technically unpleasant to effect changes once the image is cut and painted through. Finishing the work is recognizing when the potential spelled out in the study has been realized.

My old visceral thrill is largely atrophied, although I still get flashes of it at times. It's been replaced by a kind of certainty, an intellectual thrill that an image has lived up to my expectations and seems fully formed and resolved.

It's kind of love at first sight.

Robert Motherwell

An advantage of a retrospective is that you can make comparisons within a large body of work. When I recently had my retrospective at the Guggenheim Museum, I felt for the first time that there was some flaw in a large painting, *Elegy to the Spanish Republic #132,* done about 12 years ago. When the show was over, I had it brought back to my studio instead of putting it in storage. It was an important picture in my oeuvre, but, at my age, I would rather wreck a picture than feel it to be off-key. . . .

The problem was not the image, but a big area of salmon color in the background acting itself as an image, though secondarily so. I modulated this area in an earth color without shape. The work then took on a coherent spatial character. Amazing that something so seemingly simple markedly changed the feeling of the work. What I was doing involved repainting over about one-eighth of the work, which might have wrecked it, but as soon as I finished, I felt on target. You just go on a gut feeling of recognition, of hearing and accepting your own voice. It is a tentative process, involving shifting and revising, trying to sense what the picture itself is trying to express.

Elegy to the Spanish Republic #132 was one of about 150 pieces in the retrospective and, oddly enough, most people would not notice the difference between the painting as it was and as it is now. The expressive image was unaltered. But its space, essentially a "wall," had gained clarity and coherence.

I sometimes think of pictures as analogues to human relations. There is an interactive between the canvas and oneself, with many levels of feeling. Art is an experience, not an "object." If you look at a work as an object and find yourself noticing the machinery of it all, something is wrong. A picture is finished when you experience it vividly, when it makes you aware of the resonance and mystery of a realized expression.

The "finishing" of a painting varies as much as the various works themselves and, in fact, depends on the individual work. There is no rule for me, though I cannot paint in an empty studio. I need to be surrounded by my own work—paintings, collages, drawings, etchings and the rest. I do not work on one painting at a time, but on several at once. This permits comparison: when one painting seems more realized or stronger than the others I try to raise the remaining works to the same level. In a sense the paintings are all in competition with each other, but at the same time they help each other through mutual criticism.

When the original impulse that started it all has realized itself, the finish line has been reached—though to some observers that impulse has not been pushed far enough, while to others it's been pushed too far.

Neil Jenney

When I hear artists talk too much about finishing a painting, it often suggests to me that they're working "for" a show—on deadline. That really makes me nervous because I can't be ruled by the deadlines; they're not a valid priority. In fact, I refuse to work with deadlines. They are foreign to me. And I don't make paintings "for" a show.

I love the inspiration that goes into starting a new work, and then I usually stay at it—months, years—until I screw up. Then I put it aside, hang it on a wall and move on to another piece and later go back to it. I reject deadlines and I reject being pushed along. Deadlines and being rushed smack of art-world commercialism that is bad for you creatively and technically. I may complete about four and a half paintings a year. This year I'll compete less.

The best art is fine-tuned, and it's never *really* done. I admire Flaubert's dictum that you do it over and over again. The problem is that if you're a perfectionist, you can never reach perfection. But you can develop an understanding of your work and grow with it as it gains a life and personality of its own. On some level, I'm disappointed with everything I do. Actually, I hate to finish a work. It's just nit-grit craft. I'd much rather sit in my chair and think of new things.

My work goes through such long periods of gestation that it's not within my game plan to be uncertain about it when the end is in sight. Occasionally I get a "Eureka, I've got it!" attitude, but it's mostly just getting through the slow tedium of the work. The major format—the statement—is decided before I start mixing paint: I know what's going on, there's never been any confusion. Some artists seem to be at a Ping-Pong table, hitting in multiple directions.

I construct very precise sculptural frames for my paintings, and if the frame isn't enhancing the illusion I want, I make adjustments. The frame is part of the overall work. When I make changes on the painting itself, I'm governed by my internal judgement. I want to eliminate weak spots or soft spots. In *North America Abstracted,* an abstract landscape with formal clouds—not puffy clouds—floating in a late afternoon sky, I reworked and fine-tuned areas, making some darker, some cooler, some lighter. I wanted to achieve a three-dimensional quality.

Although I feel a painting is never done, I show it when, finally, I feel *comfortable.*

David Hare

As long as a painting is alive, it's never finished—and it's not alive as long as you are working on it. If this sounds like a confusing paradox, it's meant to be, for the question of when a painting is finished is crucial to the act of creation.

Giving a painting a life of its own is extremely precarious, like dancing on the edge of a cliff. It's usually best just before it becomes a cliché, so you have to know when to pull back, to keep yourself from slipping. I started as a sculptor and switched to painting 12 years ago. A painting is an illusion. Sculpture stinks of reality. The most exciting time in painting is just after I've started, when I'm full of expectation and hope. I don't approve of setting out with concepts that are absolute, because then you never let in the new. Since I'm willing to risk new ideas after I've begun work, I think exaggerated changes often give a canvas high-voltage energy.

For example, I was working on a piece now called *Dog Elephant.* I wanted to paint an elephant in a landscape, with a flat background. The image was evolving into an abstract elephant, and it didn't seem to go anywhere. I added an ear, which made the trunk look like a drooped ear of a hound dog, and then I added an upper lip and an eye. The figure became half dog, half-elephant. The result now teases the mind, which I'm all in favor of as I certainly was not trying to copy nature. *Feather Man,* collage and canvas, started as an abstract landscape with sky. As I improved the detail, it changed from a landscape to a figure with a strong head that blends into the sky, and the painting acquired a definite personality.

When I achieve an image that overwhelms both the canvas and me, then I know—paradox aside—that the painting is done. What happens next is editorial work—strengthening color and line. Some might find editing boring, but I consider it a pleasant aspect or the last dance with a desperate obsession, for that is what each work is—an obsession.

Elizabeth Murray

I nag myself to get a painting done because usually I've been working so hard for such a long time that I feel, okay, by now it should be finished. On the other hand, it's a kind of fight, an entanglement—an affair you'd like to get out of but sometimes can't.

I start haphazardly. I don't do color sketches or maquettes. I first cut out various shapes, and when I get the color I know I'm beginning to realize the painting. It's extremely difficult to explain how I decide on color and shape—it depends on how I feel at the moment and, initially, what's in my paintbox, though later, as the painting develops, my decision about color becomes more specific. There *is* significant interplay between color and shape.

As I work on a piece over a period of time, my vision becomes clearer. I know more about myself in relation to a painting and how I might trick myself into prematurely thinking that it's done. I suppose it sounds dramatic, but there's an agony about beginning and an agony about ending although I don't have a feeling of panic anymore.

In a new work, *Sunday Morning*—a sort of cantilevered S in which you can see a woman seated on a chair, though most of her body isn't visible—I wanted to leave more canvas than usual showing, so I had to restrict myself. I worked on it for about two weeks and then spent six weeks deciding if it was finished. I was particularly bothered by the feet, painting and repainting them. One day an artist friend said he thought the feet were too explicit. A remark like that will either hook me or irritate me. But he was right. I painted the feet again, making them less explicit. Now, I was satisfied. It was like an exorcism.

Sometimes I pretend a painting is done—walk away from it for a few weeks, then come back and make radical changes. With a piece called *Mouse Cup,* I made a major color alteration after I thought I was finished. The predominant color was red. I had a preconceived notion about using red, and what happened demonstrates how preconceptions usually go out the window. I was haunted by that work for an entire summer. The red really began to bug me. I eventually repainted it from red to mousy gray colors. That's why it's necessary to have paintings around, to live with them.

In a way, a painting is like a mystery. Once the shapes and colors are established to my satisfaction, the mystery is solved.

Further Resources

BOOKS

Albers, Josef, Emile De Antonio, and Mitch Tuchman. *Painters Painting: A Candid History of the Modern Art Scene, 1940–1970.* New York: Abbeville Press, 1984.

Robertson, Jack. *Twentieth-Century Artists on Art: An index to Artists' Writings, Statements, and Interviews.* Boston: G.K. Hall, 1985.

Siegel, Jeanne, ed. *Artwords 2: Discourse on the Early 80s.* Ann Arbor, Mich.: UMI Research Press, 1988.

PERIODICALS

"Artists' Statements and Interviews on Conceptual Art." *Flash Art* 143, November/December 1988, 112–117.

Fences

Play script

By: August Wilson

Date: 1986

Source: Wilson, August. *Fences.* New York: New American Library, 1986, 1–20.

About the Author: August Wilson (1945–), born in Pittsburgh, Pennsylvania, dropped out of high school after being accused of plagiarism. He educated himself in a local library. He wrote and submitted poems to literary publications at the University of Pittsburgh. In 1968 he co-founded a theatre company, Black Horizons on the Hill, located in Pittsburgh. He pursued his dream to write first as a poet, and later as a playwright. Wilson draws characters for plays from his life, his environment, and his background. He has won the Pulitzer Prize twice and has been awarded numerous fellowships, including a Guggenheim in 1986. ■

Introduction

August Wilson provides a voice to those who have been disenfranchised by society. The setting of his plays is often Pittsburgh, where he grew up. Over a five-year period, *Fences* was subjected to drafts, revisions, and workshops around the country. The first reading of *Fences* was in 1982 at the New Dramatists in New York. In July 1983 it was accepted as a Eugene O'Neill Theater workshop play. At this time the play was still three and a half hours long. In 1985 Wilson worked on the play at the Yale Repertory Theater and at the Goodman Theater in Chicago. By the time it reached the 46th Street Theater on Broadway it lasted two hours and fifteen minutes, a far more manageable length for audiences. The history of the production is important because of the influences on Wilson's writing and the changes he made in the characters. The development is "a study in refining the level of responsibility in each of the characters, responsibility both to themselves and to those around them," according to researcher Joan Fishman. One of the goals was to create a positive, African American male.

Fences tells the story of Troy, a father of three children. His son from his first marriage receives whatever he asks for, partially out of guilt because Troy was in prison and could not be a father to him. With Cory, the son of his second marriage, he is stricter. He does not want Cory's dreams dashed as his were when he wanted to be an athlete. Troy lives in the past, with a deconstructionist attitude and slave ancestry, reflecting when African Americans were still not treated equally and the color barrier had not been broken. After an affair, Troy delivers a daughter to his wife and asks her to help raise the child. She agrees, as the mistress had died and the child would have no home if they did not take her in. Troy pushes limits that his wife meets. At the end of the play, however, the finished fence restricts Troy from the outside world. His life is finished, along with his chances to amend the wrongs he has wrought.

Significance

The symbolic fence that Troy builds throughout the play is key to the understanding of Wilson's message and the character's lives. The scars of three generations are revealed through story and action. Over an eight-year period the father-son and brother-to-brother relationships grow and develop. The fence is a measure of healing and division, of mortality and death. It inhibits or protects the characters, as the father is trying to protect the son; the son sees his actions as holding him back. Troy feels fenced off from society because he has not had the opportunities for advancement in his job and because of the time he lost in prison. His sons, especially Cory, feel as if Troy is limiting their possibilities in the world.

Wilson utilizes a poetic language to convey his character's personalities and their trials in life. Classic themes are evident in August Wilson's *Fences.* Mary Bogumil points out that the "powerful but destructive central character; the house as a central location" and the "concern about professional success" are all present. Sports and metaphors of sports are central to the play and the lives of the family. The historic events of the civil rights era are not overtly employed, but are nonetheless present. Attitudes and confrontations between the characters are influenced by what is going on in the world outside the home.

Although the plot centers on the male characters, Rose is also critical. Troy's wife, Rose, has given up her own dreams and hopes to provide a home for her family. When trust is betrayed, she is devastated, yet she rises above Troy's affair to care for a child that is not her own. Rose's only desire was for a family and the kind of home she never had as a child.

Wilson's play is more complex than it may seem on the surface. The issues he presents depict a specific time in America and the pressures that characters endure in life.

Primary Source

Fences [excerpt]

SYNOPSIS: Lloyd Richards introduces the play in this edition. Wilson met Richards, an actor and director, in 1982 when he was working on his earlier acclaimed work, *Ma Rainey's Black Bottom*. Richards became his mentor and has guided him ever since.

Act One

Scene One

It is 1957. Troy and Bono enter the yard, engaged in conversation. Troy is fifty-three years old, a large man with thick, heavy hands; it is this largeness that he strives to fill out and make an accommodation with. Together with his blackness, his largeness informs his sensibilities and the choices he has made in his life.

Of the two men, Bono is obviously the follower. His commitment to their friendship of thirty-odd years is rooted in his admiration of Troy's honesty, capacity for hard work, and his strength, which Bono seeks to emulate.

It is Friday night, payday, and the one night of the week the two men engage in a ritual of talk and drink. Troy is usually the most talkative and at times he can be crude and almost vulgar, though he is capable of rising to profound heights of expression. The men carry lunch buckets and wear or carry burlap aprons and are dressed in clothes suitable to their jobs as garbage collectors.

Bono: Troy, you ought to stop that lying!

Troy: I ain't lying! The nigger had a watermelon this big. *(He indicates with his hands.)* Talking about . . ."What watermelon, Mr. Rand?" I liked to fell out! "What watermelon, Mr. Rand?" . . . And it was sitting there big as life.

Bono: What did Mr. Rand say?

Troy: Ain't said nothing. Figure if the nigger too dumb to know he carrying a watermelon, he wasn't gonna get much sense out of him. Trying to hide that great big old watermelon under his coat. Afraid to let the white man see him carry it home.

Bono: I'm like you . . . I ain't got no time for them kind of people.

Troy: Now what he look like getting mad cause he see the man from the union talking to Mr. Rand?

Bono: He come to me talking about . . ."Maxson gonna get us fired." I told him to get away from me with that. He walked away from me calling you a troublemaker. What Mr. Rand say?

Troy: Ain't said nothing. He told me to go down the Commissioner's office next Friday. They called me down there to see them.

Bono: Well, as long as you got your complaint filed, they can't fire you. That's what one of the white fellows tell me.

Troy: I ain't worried about them firing me. They gonna fire me cause I asked a question? That's all I did. I went to Mr. Rand and asked him, "Why? Why you got the white mens driving and the colored lifting?" Told him, "what's the matter, don't I count? You think only white fellows got sense enough to drive a truck. That ain't no paper job! Hell, anybody can drive a truck. How come you got all whites driving and the colored lifting?" He told me "take it to the union." Well, hell, that's what I done! Now they wanna come up with this pack of lies.

Bono: I told Brownie if the man come and ask him any questions . . . just tell the truth! It ain't nothing but something they done trumped up on you cause you filed a complaint on them.

Troy: Brownie don't understand nothing. All I want them to do is change the job description. Give everybody a chance to drive the truck. Brownie can't see that. He ain't got that much sense.

Bono: How you figure he be making out with that gal be up at Taylor's all the time . . . that Alberta gal?

Troy: Same as you and me. Getting just as much as we is. Which is to say nothing.

Bono: It is, huh? I figure you doing a little better than me . . . and I ain't saying what I'm doing.

Troy: Aw, nigger, look here . . . I know you. If you had got anywhere near that gal, twenty minutes later you be looking to tell somebody. And the first one you gonna tell . . . that you gonna want to brag to . . . is gonna be me.

Bono: I ain't saying that. I see where you be eyeing her.

Troy: I eye all the women. I don't miss nothing. Don't never let nobody tell you Troy Maxson don't eye the women.

Bono: You been doing more than eyeing her. You done bought her a drink or two.

Troy: Hell yeah, I bought her a drink! What that mean? I bought you one, too. What that mean cause I buy her a drink? I'm just being polite.

Bono: It's alright to buy her one drink. That's what you call being polite. But when you wanna be buying two or three . . . that's what you call eyeing her.

Troy: Look here, as long as you known me . . . you ever known me to chase after women?

Bono: Hell yeah! Long as I done known you. You forgetting I knew you when.

Troy: Naw, I'm talking about since I been married to Rose?

Bono: Oh, not since you been married to Rose. Now, that's the truth, there. I can say that.

Troy: Alright then! Case closed.

Bono: I see you be walking up around Alberta's house. You supposed to be at Taylors' and you be walking up around there.

Troy: What you watching where I'm walking for? I ain't watching after you.

Bono: I seen you walking around there more than once.

Troy: Hell, you liable to see me walking anywhere! That don't mean nothing cause you see me walking around there.

Bono: Where she come from anyway? She just kinda showed up one day.

James Earl Jones, right, and Mary Alice act out a scene from the play *Fences.* RON SCHERL/AP WIDE WORLD PHOTOS. REPRODUCED BY PERMISSION.

Troy: Tallahassee. You can look at her and tell she one of them Florida gals. They got some big healthy women down there. Grow them right up out the ground. Got a little bit of Indian in her. Most of them niggers down in Florida got some Indian in them.

Bono: I don't know about the Indian part. But she damn sure big and healthy. Woman wear some big stockings. Got them great big old legs and hips as wide as the Mississippi River.

Troy: Legs don't mean nothing. You don't do nothing but push them out of the way. But them hips cushion the ride!

Bono: Troy, you ain't got no sense.

Troy: It's the truth! Like you riding on Goodyears!

(*Rose enters from the house. She is ten years younger than Troy, her devotion to him stems from her recognition of the possibilities of her life without him: a succession of abusive men and their babies, a life of partying and running the streets, the Church, or aloneness with its attendant pain and frustration. She recognizes Troy's spirit as a fine and illuminating one and she either ignores or forgives his faults, only some of which she recognizes. Though she doesn't drink, her presence is an integral part of the Friday night rituals. She alternates between the porch and the kitchen, where supper preparations are under way.)*

Rose: What you all out here getting into?

Troy: What you worried about what we getting into for? This is men talk, woman.

Rose: What I care what you all talking about? Bono, you gonna stay for supper?

Bono: No, I thank you, Rose. But Lucille say she cooking up a pot of pigfeet.

Troy: Pigfeet! Hell, I'm going home with you! Might even stay the night if you got some pigfeet. You got something in there to top them pigfeet, Rose?

Rose: I'm cooking up some chicken. I got some chicken and collard greens.

Troy: Well, go on back in the house and let me and Bono finish what we was talking about. This is men talk. I got some talk for you later. You know what kind of talk I mean. You go on and powder it up.

Rose: Troy Maxson, don't you start that now!

Troy: *(Puts his arm around her.)* Aw, woman . . . come here. Look here, Bono . . . when I met this woman . . . I got out that place, say "Hitch up my pony, saddle my mare . . . there's a woman out there for me somewhere. I looked here. Looked there. Saw Rose and latched on to her." I latched on to her and told her—I'm gonna tell you the truth—I told her, "Baby, I don't wanna marry, I just wanna be your man." Rose told me . . . tell him what you told me, Rose.

Rose: I told him if he wasn't the marrying kind, then move out the way so the marrying kind could find me.

Troy: That's what she told me. "Nigger, you in my way. You blocking the view! Move out the way so I can find me a husband." I thought it over two or three days. Come back—

Rose: Ain't no two or three days nothing. You was back the same night.

Troy: Come back, told her . . .": Okay, baby . . . but I'm gonna buy me a banty rooster and put

him out there in the backyard . . . and when he sees a stranger come, he'll flap his wings and crow . . ." Look here, Bono, I could watch the front door by myself . . . it was that back door I was worried about.

Rose: Troy, you ought not talk like that. Troy ain't doing nothing but telling a lie.

Troy: Only thing is . . . when we first got married . . . forget the rooster . . . we ain't had no yard!

Bono: I hear you tell it. Me and Lucille was staying down there on Logan Street. Had two rooms with the outhouse in the back. I ain't mind the outhouse none. But when that goddam wind blow throught there in the winter . . . that's what I'm talking about! To this day I wonder why in the hell I ever stayed there for six long years. But see, I didn't know I could do no better. I thought only white folk had inside toilets and things.

Rose: There's a lot of people don't know they can do no better than they doing now. That's just something you got to learn. A lot of folks still shop at Bella's.

Troy: Ain't nothing wrong with shopping at Bella's. She got fresh food.

Rose: I ain't said nothing about if she got fresh food. I'm talking about what she charge. She charge ten cents more than the A & P.

Troy: The A & P ain't never done nothing for me. I spends my money where I'm treated right. I go down to Bella, say, "I need a loaf of bread, I'll pay you Friday." She give it to me. What sense that make when I got money to go and spend it somewhere else and ignore the person who done right by me? That ain't in the Bible.

Rose: We ain't talking about what's in the Bible. What sense it make to shop there when she overcharge?

Troy: You shop where you want to. I'll do my shopping where the people been good to me.

Rose: Well, I don't think it's right for her to overcharge. That's all I was saying.

Bono: Look here . . . I got to get on. Lucille going be raising all kind of hell.

Troy: Where you going, nigger? We ain't finished this pint. Come here, finish this pint.

Bono: Well, hell, I am . . . if you ever turn the bottle loose.

Troy: *(Hands him the bottle.)* The only thing I say about the A & P is I'm glad Cory got that job down there. Help him take care of his school clothes and things. Gabe done moved out and things started getting tight around here. He got that job . . . He can start to look out for himself.

Rose: Cory done went and got recruited by a college football team.

Troy: I told that boy about that football stuff. The white man ain't gonna let him get nowhere with that football. I told him when he first come to me with it. Now you come telling me he done went and got more tied up in it. He ought to go and get recruited in how to fix cars or something where he can make a living. . . .

Further Resources

BOOKS

Bogumil, Mary L. *Understanding August Wilson.* Columbia: University of South Carolina Press, 1999.

Fishman, Joan. "Developing His Song: August Wilson's Fences." In *August Wilson: A Casebook.* Marilyn Elkins, ed. New York: Garland, 1994, 161–181.

Shannon, Sandra G. *The Dramatic Vision of August Wilson.* Washington, D.C.: Howard University Press, 1995.

PERIODICALS

Hornby, Richard. "Fences." *The Hudson Review* 40, no. 3, Autumn 1987, 465–472.

Wessling, Joseph H. "Wilson's 'Fences.'" *The Explicator* 57, no. 2, Winter 1999, 123–127.

WEBSITES

"August Wilson." Wyoming Council for the Humanities. Available online at http://www.uwyo.edu/wch/bdpmmf.htm; website home page: (accessed April 28, 2003).

"August Wilson at Dartmouth." Dartmouth College. Available online at http://www.dartmouth.edu/~awilson/; website home page: http://www.dartmouth.edu/ (accessed April 28, 2003).

Two Poems from *Dream Work*

"Wild Geese"; "The Journey"

Poems

By: Mary Oliver

Date: 1986

Source: Oliver, Mary. "Wild Geese" and "The Journey." In *Dream Work.* New York: Atlantic Monthly Press, 1986, 14, 38.

About the Author: Mary Oliver (1935–) was born in Cleveland, Ohio, and attended both Ohio State University (1955–56) and Vassar (1956–57). She won the Pulitzer Prize for Poetry in 1984 for the collection *American Primitive,* and was also awarded a National Book Award for Poetry in 1992 for *New and Selected Poems.* Oliver frequently teaches poetry workshops at colleges and universities. In 2003, she was the Catharine Osgood Foster Professor at Bennington College. ■

Introduction

Mary Oliver says that she never took interesting jobs so that she could concentrate on her writing. An interesting job, Oliver claims, distracts her thoughts and takes energy away from what she feels is the most important part of her life. Oliver has not yet been the subject of sustained writings about her life or poetry, but her poetry has drawn the attention of other poets and has earned critical acclaim.

Dream Work is Oliver's seventh book of poetry. In the collection she crafts forty-five poems that explore the themes of nature, the spirit, and solitude. Oliver examines the mythic relationships between nature and women.

Douglas Burton-Christie writes that "Oliver places herself in a long and ancient company of seekers, for whom the discipline of *memento mori* represented the surest way of retaining a firm grasp on his life." Meditation on death, part of all nature, is often part of Oliver's poetry. Through her observations and spiritual musings, Burton-Christie notes that Oliver focuses "carefully on the details of the ordinary, the everyday—especially in the natural world." Her poetry questions nature and the reader, often presenting contradictions. The reader may not notice these complexities of Oliver's work on a first reading; however, as one delves into her poetry the multiple meanings become evident.

Oliver also contemplates human nature in her poetry. In *Dream Work* she explores the subjects of the Holocaust, incest, and starvation. Her poems echo the sins of earlier poets and artists, including William Butler Yeats, Walt Whitman, and Vincent Van Gogh. Her vision encompasses physical nature and spirituality. "Wild Geese" and "The Journey" question how one chooses to live life. Is it a life that one loves or merely a life one lives?

Significance

Mary Oliver is an observer of nature: of the moths, the trees, the sky, and the geese. Oliver's poetry explores the "solitary and difficult labors of the spirit" and the "truth of the individual's world." She joins nature with the writer and with the reader.

In her review of *Dream Work,* Sandra M. Gilbert comments that "Oliver's poems are deliberately impersonal, almost anti-confessional." This is not meant to be

Mary Oliver's poems reflect more a pastoral life lived with plants and animals than with human beings. **AP/WORLD WIDE PHOTOS. REPRODUCED BY PERMISSION.**

a negative opinion. Gilbert adds that Oliver is "never less than expert in her crafting of verse and her precision of language." She cites the poem "Orion," in which Oliver "meditates on the alternative consciousness, the being in a perpetual present that might liberate the lives of plants and animals from what human beings experience as the burden of the past." Alicia Ostriker writes that Oliver's "verse feels increasingly confident, smoother, and thus bolder" and that "she is among our finest poets, and still growing."

The rhythm in Oliver's poetry joins the reader with the subject. Rhyme, however, is often hidden within the poem. She allows for epiphanies and discoveries of the truths of life in her poetry. Like many of her poems, "Wild Geese" and "The Journey" explore solitary paths in life. Connections with a larger world and with a world beyond the earthly one are also present in Oliver's work. She is linked to a romantic tradition as well as a spiritual/mystical tradition of poetry.

Primary Source

Two Poems from *Dream Work*

SYNOPSIS: Mary Oliver explores the solitary life while the world continues on around her. Her poems ask as many questions as they answer and leave the reader to decide on what should be and what is right. In the selections here the subject is clearly part of the larger "family of things" and is concerned with finding a place in the world.

"Wild Geese"
You do not have to be good.
You do not have to walk on your knees
for a hundred miles through the desert, repenting.
You only have to let the soft animal of your body
love what it loves.
Tell me about despair, yours, and I will tell you mine.
Meanwhile the world goes on.
Meanwhile the sun and the clear pebbles of the rain
are moving across the landscapes,
over the prairies and the deep trees,
the mountains and the rivers.
Meanwhile the wild geese, high in the clean blue air,
are heading home again.
Whoever you are, no matter how lonely,
the world offers itself to your imagination,
calls to you like the wild geese, harsh and exciting—
over and over announcing your place
in the family of things.

"The Journey"
One day you finally knew
what you had to do, and began,
though the voices around you
kept shouting
their bad advice—
though the whole house
began to tremble
and you felt the old tug
at your ankles.
"Mend my life!"
each voice cried.
But you didn't stop.
You knew what you had to do,
though the wind pried
with its stiff fingers
at the very foundations,
though their melancholy
was terrible.
It was already late
enough, and a wild night,
and the road full of fallen
branches and stones.
But little by little,
as you left their voices behind,
the stars began to burn
through the sheets of clouds,
and there was a new voice
which you slowly
recognized as your own,
that kept you company
as you strode deeper and deeper
into the world,
determined to do
the only thing you could do—
determined to save
the only life you could save.

Further Resources

BOOKS

Bryson, J. Scott, ed. *Ecopoetry: A Critical Introduction.* Salt Lake City: University of Utah Press, 2002.

Oliver, Mary. *A Poetry Handbook: A Prose Guide to Understanding and Writing Poetry.* San Diego, Calif.: Harcourt Brace, 1994.

Ratiner, Steven, comp. *Giving Their Word: Conversations with Contemporary Poets.* Amherst: University of Massachusetts Press, 2002.

PERIODICALS

Burton-Christie, Douglas. "Nature, Spirit, and Imagination in the Poetry of Mary Oliver." *Cross Current* 46, no.1, Spring 1996, 77–87.

Gilbert, Sandra M. "*Dream Work* by Mary Oliver, Atlantic Monthly Press." *Poetry* 150, no. 2, May 1987, 113–116.

McNew, Janet. "Mary Oliver and the Tradition of Romantic Nature Poetry." *Contemporary Literature* 30, no.1, Spring 1989, 59–77.

Ostriker, Alicia. "Review of *Dream Work*." *The Nation* 243, no. 5, August 30, 1986, 149–151.

WEBSITES

Brunner, Edward. "Mary Oliver." *Modern American Poetry* [Online Journal]. Available online at http://www.english.uiuc.edu/maps/poets/m_r/oliver/oliver.htm; website home page: http://www.english.uiuc.edu/maps/ (accessed April 28, 2003).

"Mary Oliver." The Academy of American Poets. Available online at http://www.poets.org/poets/poets.cfm?prmID=269; website home page: http://www.poets.org/ (accessed April 28, 2003).

"Graceland"
Song

By: Paul Simon

Date: 1986

Source: Simon, Paul. "Graceland." Available online at http://www.paulsimon.com/index_collection.html (accessed April 29, 2003).

About the Artist: Paul Simon (1941–) began his successful solo career in 1972 after the breakup of Simon and Art Garfunkel, the 1960s folk duo. His first solo album had actually been released in 1965, but only in the United Kingdom. Both a singer and a songwriter, Simon was inducted into the Rock and Roll Hall of Fame in 2001. ■

Introduction

Paul Simon is "disinclined to honor artificial borders when it comes to music and culture," according to the online Rock and Roll Hall of Fame. He has experimented with different styles and types of music since beginning his solo career in the 1970s.

Simon collaborated with South African musicians on the *Graceland* album. Because of the political climate in South Africa and the issues surrounding apartheid, this became controversial for many. Simon attempted to separate himself from the politics to present international music but it was a difficult claim to make when he included exiled South African musicians in the Graceland tour.

Paul Simon discovered the "township jive," or mbaqanga sound originating from Soweto, in the summer of 1984. A friend gave him a tape that would influence the Graceland album's sound and style as well as that of his future albums.

Regarding the title song, Jay Cocks of *Time* reports Simon as asserting that "Graceland" is "not about Elvis Presley, or his Memphis home but about a 'state of peace.'" Certainly Presley is who most American listeners, hearing the word, might think of first, but upon reflecting on the lyrics one can understand that they express a hope for peace, a place where all will be received. The other tracks capture the rhythms and humor that Simon has become known for on his albums.

Significance

The musical success of the *Graceland* album was accompanied by sharp criticism for Paul Simon. When he visited South Africa to work with musicians, he violated the United Nations' cultural ban. James Victor Gbeho, Ghanaian ambassador and the chair of the United Nations Special Committee Against Apartheid, said "Mr. Simon is taking a position against us, against the United Nations, against the international community," reported Rob Tannenbaum in *Rolling Stone*. Simon was censored for visiting South Africa and people were discouraged from buying the album. Other antiapartheid groups supported Simon. According to Tannenbaum, the Pan-Africanist Congress asserted that "the album 'is helping the oppressed people' in South Africa by exposing their culture to an international audience." Despite the criticism, the album was a tremendous success, earning four Grammy nominations and selling four million copies by February 1987.

Significant in the release and making of the album was inclusion of the South African musicians—they are featured on nine of its eleven songs. Simon began recording in South Africa and then brought three of the musicians to New York to continue the work. The South African a cappella group Ladysmith Black Mambazo became well known in the United States after *Graceland* was released, following it with records of their own.

The Graceland Tour brought additional exposure to the album, its musicians, and exiled musicians who joined the tour. Rather than opening in South Africa, the tour

Paul Simon, left, performs on stage during a tour to promote his *Graceland* album, a blend of South African styles, zydeco, and Mexican rock. © **PENNY TWEEDIE/CORBIS. REPRODUCED BY PERMISSION.**

began in Rotterdam, the Netherlands. Despite protests outside, the music inside was a hit. "People went wild, just wild," reported David Fricke in *Rolling Stone.* In the end the infectious rhythms and funky sounds that Simon and the South African musicians produced on the Graceland album and in the concerts won a popularity that outlasted the criticism and controversy. Simon's revolutionary album changed his music and exposed the world to musicians and songs they may have otherwise never have heard.

Primary Source

"Graceland"

> **SYNOPSIS:** Paul Simon told Jay Cocks that after the lines "Losing love/Is like a window in your heart/ Everybody sees you're blown apart" came to him that everything else on the album flowed. He called the line a "catharsis" and remembered that after that line, the funny songs were written.

The Mississippi Delta was shining
Like a National guitar
I am following the river
Down the highway
Through the cradle of the civil war

I'm going to Graceland
Graceland
In Memphis Tennessee
I'm going to Graceland
Poorboys and Pilgrims with families
And we are going to Graceland
My traveling companion is nine years old
He is the child of my first marriage
But I've reason to believe
We both will be received
In Graceland

She comes back to tell me she's gone
As if I didn't know that
As if I didn't know my own bed
As if I'd never notice
The way she brushed her hair from
Her forehead
And she said losing love
Is like a window in your heart
Everybody sees you're blown apart
Everybody sees the wind blow

I'm going to Graceland
Memphis Tennessee
I'm going to Graceland
Poorboys and Pilgrims with families
And we are going to Graceland
And my traveling companions
Are ghosts and empty sockets
I'm looking at ghosts and empties

But I've reason to believe
We all will be received
In Graceland

There is a girl in New York City
Who calls herself the human trampoline
And sometimes when I'm falling, flying
Or tumbling in turmoil I say
Oh, so this is what she means
She means we're bouncing into
Graceland
And I see losing love
Is like a window in your heart
Everybody sees you're blown apart
Everybody sees the wind blow

In Graceland, In Graceland
I'm going to Graceland
For reasons I cannot explain
There's some part of me wants to see
Graceland
And I may be obliged to defend
Every love, every ending
Or maybe there's no obligations now
Maybe I've a reason to believe
We all will be received
In Graceland.

Further Resources

PERIODICALS

Cocks, Jay. "Tall Gumboots at Graceland: Dancing in the Penumbra with Rhymin' Simon." *Time,* September 15, 1986, 84.

Fricke, David. "Paul Simon's Amazing Graceland Tour: The World is Suddenly Dancing to a South African Beat, Much to the Dismay of Some Antiapartheid Activists." *Rolling Stone,* July 2, 1987, 42–44, 46, 48, 59.

Meinjtes, Louise. "Paul Simon's *Graceland,* South Africa, and the Mediation of Musical Meaning." *Ethnomusicology* 34, Winter 1990, 37–73.

Tannenbaum, Rob. "UN Group Attacks Paul Simon; Says 'Graceland' Broke Cultural Boycott of South Africa." *Rolling Stone,* February 12, 1987, 11, 104.

WEBSITES

Paul Simon: Rock and Roll Hall of Fame. Available online at http://www.rockhall.com/hof/inductee.asp?id=1143; website home page: http://www.rockhall.com/ (accessed April 29, 2003).

Ellen Foster

Novel

By: Kaye Gibbons

Date: 1987

Source: Gibbons, Kay. *Ellen Foster.* 1987. First Vintage Contemporaries Edition. New York: Vintage, 1988.

About the Author: Kaye Gibbons (1960–) was born in Nash County, in rural North Carolina. She attended North Carolina State University and the University of North Carolina, Chapel Hill. The author of several books set in the South, Gibbons won the Sue Kaufman Prize for First Fiction for the novel *Ellen Foster.* ∎

Introduction

Kaye Gibbons is one of a long line of Southern women writers who have created memorable female characters such as Ellen Foster, Ruby Pitts Woodrow Stokes, Charlie Kate, and Hattie Barnes—all of whom leave an impression upon the reader. Her women are survivors who are often fiercely independent. Ellen Foster is the thirteen-year-old girl who the reader encounters in Gibbons's first novel, published in 1987. She began the book as part of a graduate seminar at the University of North Carolina, Chapel Hill. Kaye Gibbons won the Sue Kaufman Prize from the American Academy and Institute of Arts and Letters, a Special Citation from the Ernest Hemingway Foundation, and the Louis D. Rubin Writing Award for *Ellen Foster.*

Gibbons's work often contains autobiographical threads. In *Ellen Foster* the mother's suicide and the drunken and abusive father are similar to the author's own family. Like Ellen, she "was handed off among, what she calls 'various bizarre, kleptomaniac, hypochondriac, pathological-liar, sociopath relatives' until she found a safe haven foster mother," says Liz Seymour in her online article.

Ellen Foster narrates the story of her life with courage and humor. At a young age, Ellen has become a survivor. She attempts to create order in her chaotic life, but even with her determination she can not overcome some of the odds she faces. Ellen finds a happy home with Julia, a teacher at her school, but is then placed with her mama's mama (who she never calls her grandmother) and an aunt, who are hateful toward her because they hated her parents. In the end, Ellen finally finds a place to belong with a new mama and a foster family.

Significance

Home, friendship, and humor are all crucial parts of Ellen Foster's story. Ellen's quest is for a home where she belongs and where she feels comfortable. She overcomes the inherited prejudice of her Southern upbringing and realizes the value in her friendship with Starletta, a young, silent black girl. The often unintentional humor of Ellen's narratives knits these journeys together.

Ellen sets out to look for a family of her own. Raised in poverty and in a brutal backwoods environment, she seeks the peace and compassion she has never known. After her mamma's mamma dies, Ellen makes a list of what she wants in a family because, she says, "I thought I would soon bust open if I did not get one of them for

Kaye Gibbons authored a group of novels predominantly set in rural Southern communities, including *Ellen Foster*. © JERRY BAUER. REPRODUCED BY PERMISSION.

my own self soon." What she finds is a foster family that appears to her as a loving, clean, happy group of children with a mother. She does not fully understand that this is not a traditional family, yet it does not matter to her because she finds what she values there. She adopts the last name of "Foster" when the court awards her to the new family. The reader never hears her given surname, an important point because Ellen never feels that she is wanted by them.

Starletta is Ellen's only friend throughout most of the novel. Although Starletta's family takes her in when she runs from her drunken daddy, Ellen remains cautious. She does not feel comfortable eating the food or sleeping on the sheets in her black friend's house. The cultural conditioning that Ellen has received is not surprising here. By the end of the novel Ellen realizes the value of Starletta's friendship and that Starletta is not different from herself in most ways. She overcomes her upbringing to see beyond race to Starletta's qualities as a human.

Barbara Bennet notes that throughout *Ellen Foster* the reader finds the "humor that is an intricate part of many southern women writers' works." Humor defines Ellen's voice, making the reader see her, and not just her painful life, while softening the harsh realities that

Ellen faces. Ellen usually does not mean to be funny even though her expressions and her way of describing the events of her life come across to the reader as humorous.

Alice Hoffman, also a novelist, writes in her *New York Times Book Review* article that "there is a dual narrative. In one, Ellen's ordeals are followed consecutively; in the other, she looks back to tell her story." Hoffman praises Gibbons characterization that is not "grim [or] melodramatic" and that "focuses on Ellen's strengths rather than her victimization, presenting a memorable heroine who rescues herself." As Veronica Makowsky points out, in Gibbons' subsequent novels the reader continues to find a "search for order in an unstable world." *Ellen Foster* was the beginning of a marvelous writer's career.

Primary Source

Ellen Foster [excerpt]

SYNOPSIS: Ellen's daddy has been a problem throughout her life. When he shows up at school, Ellen takes over the class in the teacher's absence and tries to control the situation that she knows is impossible. In her matter of fact way, Ellen reflects on what happens and how the other children in her class are likely to remember it. She uses the same deadpan style in her descriptions of her attendance at church and the food-related activities that follow.

My daddy came my way. I did not go his.

He stayed in that house I know stewing thinking how to wring my neck.

He came to the school one day during naptime. We always put our heads on the desks to rest for a while. I cannot sleep in that position so I fake it. There is nothing to do but fill up your pencil tray with spit.

The day my daddy came to school nobody got a good nap.

My room then was on the front of the school that looks like a red shoebox. I heard a car sound outside and I knew without thinking long that it had to be him. My whole self knew at the same time and my eyes had spots.

I dreaded to look at him. If I had seen this on television he might have looked funny but since it was me and real life I could not see the humor.

The teacher had to be on coffee break so I took over.

Everybody sit back down and stay quiet, I said loud. They all wanted to see what was outside.

He did not know exactly what room I was in so he made a general announcement for the whole building.

Get the hell out here is what he told me to do.

He had parked his truck in the flower bed the special handicapped children had planted. Later that day when they saw the mashed ground and the obvious dead marigolds they each threw little separate fits. The kind you would throw if somebody said the end of the world was coming up shortly.

He stepped out of the truck waving some cash money and telling Ellen dammit to come back he would pay for it.

Then my teacher came back in the room and looked at me like I invited him. She told the children to finish their naps but who would sleep when that man Ellen's daddy is outside?

You have to wonder what they will remember when they are big. A man coming to school? A man waving dollars and screaming? One man my daddy waving dollars, yelling and undoing his britches during naptime?

I told the teacher I could make him stop. Just give me a pistol and then go out there and scoop him up.

It does not even make me squint to see that in my head anymore.

I yelled for him to put his dollars on the ground and go back home. There was no sense in him leaving with the money.

When he heard me he stopped like a bird dog when you blow the silent whistle. He wondered where my sound was coming from.

The police came in awhile and slapped the bracelets on. We all watched him go away.

Somebody sent for Julia and she came to me finally. Her art room is in the back apart from the rest of the school so she had not seen the time but she pulled my head to her stomach and said to let's go home.

When we got home I stopped feeling dazey and wondered if he had left the money. She took the dollars out of her purse and then I had them.

Hot damn I thought.

It was back normal for a while until Julia and Roy came in my room for a chat. He did most of the talking. She mainly patted the bed beside her and held her fingertips up to her nose holes.

He told me the court believes you should be with your family now.

I do not believe it. It sounds crazy to me because the three of us could pass for a family on the street.

But it was true and the next week I went in front of the judge.

Julia bought me a dress for court we both hated. She said it is not exactly our style but there are some times when you have to play the game she learned the hard way.

It had a sailor neck collar and she said here is the worst part. Lace stockings and black patting leather shoes. Conformity she said.

When we went in the court I thought staying in the middle of Roy and Julia was best. My daddy was over there in the middle of two police but you still have to be careful.

And lo and behold my mama's mama.

I had not seen her since the graveyard and there she is again to watch this time.

They talked mainly above my head. Usually I can jump in and hang on to what you are saying but I felt so dazey in my head again that not a word made sense.

Then the judge in the box who was extra old to have a job talked right to me. He said he had grandchildren of his own and could certainly understand her point.

Whose point? I needed to know.

Then I caught on it was she my mama's mama. She was it. I knew when she looked down the row at me with the kind of eyes that say ha ha I got you now.

All the arrangements are made they said so why bring me in here and do this in front of everybody like Julia who wants to scream she says. What do you do when the judge talks about the family society's cornerstone but you know yours was never a Roman pillar but is and always has been crumbly old brick? I was in my seat frustrated like when my teacher makes a mistake on the chalkboard and it will not do any good to tell her because so quick she can erase it all and on to the next problem.

He had us all mixed up with a different group of folks.

■ ■ ■

On Sunday the food at my new mama's is as good as it can be.

The only thing is you have to go to church before you can have one bite.

Usually a child will make a fuss about going to church but we do not. You might expect us to tug at our hats and kick the pews but we know better. We behave like we are somebody because my new mama gets part of the collection money every week. That goes for our support, our food and clothes.

You go in that church and act genuine. Even if you think what he has to say that week is horse manure or even if you believe it is a lie you sit there and be still. Worse could happen than for you to sit for an hour. You could be where you came from.

I mostly read the stain glass windows and wonder all about who they are in memory of.

We have windows like the Pope has but his are art. I know all about that.

The preacher says that today yes even on this very day his word will free us from the torments and distractions of the mind.

It is hard to be a hypocrite. I look at the preacher and at my new mama and fix my face to look like hers. We all sit lined up with faces like hers. She says to be appropriate.

It is hard too when you want to smile at the collection plates set up on the altar spilling over with folding money. Every Sunday she gets her fair share. Reach down and give! I want to announce to the sinners.

All of us but the baby boy Roger is expected to be here on Sunday. Some teenage women tend to him in the nursery. He is much like Starletta except he is white and a baby boy.

We always get in here and to our places before the organ prelude. That way folks can see us and rest sure that their money is well spent.

Dora and her mama attend this church on special holidays like the Lord's Supper and Thanksgiving. They both glide down the row and wish they had mink stoles to flag in our faces. They stay too dressed.

When I had to live with them a while we would come to this church even before I learned the name of my new mama. Of all the ladies in the church that could make into a new mama she of all people was the one for me. Even when I got back to Dora's house I thought about her and all that she looked like to me.

I watched her in the churchyard when she would walk straight and square down the steps like she might be a Queen or a lady going to be executed with dignity. Down the steps she would go by the

gossipy ladies quiet and I always tried to catch her eyes. Lord eyes that would flush all the ugly out of your system and leave in you too much air to breathe.

She certainly was a oddity and I had to step back when I saw her and was not looking for anything in particular but knew her time was what all that I needed to grab. I would think when I went to the house and write down ways and tricks of how to have her.

Now it is done. It worked and I pat myself on the back each Sunday I walk down the steps close as I can be up next to her.

When or if you come to my house now after church you will smell all the things that have been simmering on low. It has been waiting for me and me for it.

If I am very hungry my dress comes off me in a heartbeat. Sometimes I hurry too fast and I forget to unzip my back. It is helpless to smell lunch through a dress that is hung on your face. I have busted a zipper and ripped two neck collars trying to strip and my new mama told me some things about patience.

I stay starved though.

Everything we do almost on Sundays has to do with food. When we finish the meal on hand it is time to prepare chicken salad, ham salad, bread, three bean soup, or what have you for that week's lunch boxes. That way my new mama says she has a head start and will not need to go crazy in the morning times when there is already breakfast to get in you and coats to get on you.

I know that ten years from now I will be a member of the food industry. Or I might read or do art. I have seen many pictures drawed or painted of food. They always appeal to me.

Everybody like me, Stella, Francis, my new mama, Jo Jo, but not the baby are involved in this Sunday cooking. Only Stella and me came with useful experience so we get to work the stove. My new mama says I fry a mean egg.

Today it is bread and soup. It does not sound like much but it is hardy and I like to show it off in the lunchroom when all the other people have a measly tray of this or that.

When we are in the kitchen we are a regular factory. It is just on Sundays we all get to cook supervised. The rest of the week we learn one at a time.

Jo Jo gets time off from the kitchen to practice dancing to her records. Not rock and roll but slow and no singing music. Some of the records I cannot tell apart but some of them I get in my head and use them for background music for my old stories.

I myself am dying to put on the froufrou skirt and slick top Jo Jo dances around in. Not for somebody to see me but to stand in the hall mirror and observe myself private and practice my style of posing.

She has been taking lessons at the lady's school all year and does she evermore love it. You can see her dancing even when she is only in one place or eating supper.

I myself can dance like I already said but not like Jo Jo. I had rather shake a leg.

My new mama says for me to wash the flour off my arms and do my homework. If you are like me you will put it off until the last minute and then Wild Kingdom comes on but that is just too bad.

I have a donated desk and chair in my room.

If the door is not shut good baby Roger will crawl in here by mistake. That low it is hard to tell where you are at.

If I do not feel like company I turn him back toward the door and motion for him to leave. If he stays he is always hot to find something of mine to break or gnaw on. I keep my old microscope and art supply out of reach.

I usually hand him my gloves because they will not fit down his throat.

When it dawns on him to leave on his own will he heads off for another room. He has a mama here but he did not get a daddy.

Further Resources

BOOKS

Bennett, Barbara. *Comic Visions, Female Voices: Contemporary Women Novelists and Southern Humor.* Baton Rouge: Louisiana State University Press, 1998.

Jones, J. Sydney. "Kaye Gibbons." In *Something About the Author,* vol. 117. Farmington Hills, Mich.: Gale, 2000, 63–68.

Makowsky, Veronica. "Kaye Gibbons." In *The History of Southern Women's Literature.* Carolyn Perry and Mary Louise Weaks, eds. Baton Rouge: Louisiana State University Press, 2002, 604–609.

PERIODICALS

Bell, Pearl K. "Southern Discomfort." *The New Republic* 198, no. 9, February 29, 1988, 38–41.

Hoffman, Alice. "Shopping for a New Family." *New York Times Book Review,* May 31, 1987, 13.

Monteith, Sharon. "Between Girls: Kaye Gibbons' *Ellen Foster* and Friendship as a Monologic Formulation." *Journal of American Studies* 33, no. 1, 1999, 45–46.

WEBSITES

"Kaye Gibbons, Afternoon Seminar Transcript, April 23, 1998." (transcript). New York State Writers Institute. Writers Online Magazine. Available online at http://www.albany.edu/writers-inst/olv5n1.html#gibbons; website home page: http://www.albany.edu/writers-inst/ (accessed April 29, 2003).

Seymour, Liz. "Kaye Gibbons—Making it up as she goes along." Bookmagazine.com. Available online at http://www.bookmagazine.com/archive/issue4/gibbons.shtml; website home page: http://www.bookmagazine.com/ (accessed April 29, 2003).

AUDIO AND VISUAL MEDIA

Ellen Foster. Original release, 1997. Hallmark Hall of Fame. Directed by John Erman. VHS, 2003. Hallmark Home Entertainment.

Gibbons, Kaye. "Interviews." In *New Southerners.* Research Triangle Park, N.C.: National Humanities Center, 1995. 7 Audiocassettes.

Barbara Kruger's Statement of Multi-Media Art

"Barbara Kruger: Pictures and Words"

Magazine article

By: Jeanne Siegel

Date: 1987

Source: Siegel, Jeanne. "Barbara Kruger: Pictures and Words." *Arts Magazine* 61, no. 10, Summer 1987, 17–21.

About the Author: Jeanne Siegel (1932–) is a former associate editor of *Arts Magazine.* She has written extensively on art and artists, including the books *Artwords: Discourse and the 60s and 70s* (1985), *Art Talk: The Early 80s* (1990), and *Painting After Pollock: Structures of Influence* (1999). Siegel is also a curator and is currently chair of the Fine Arts Department and the Advanced Art History Seminars at the School of Visual Arts in New York.

Untitled

Works of Art

By: Barbara Kruger

Date: 1987

Source: *Untitled* 1987. Mary Boone Gallery, New York. ∎

Introduction

Barbara Kruger uses text and images to create her art. She attended art school at Parsons School of Design in New York, then worked as a graphic designer and in advertising before making the transition to visual art.

Similar to Jenny Holzer, Kruger uses words to make people think. She draws from aphorisms, truisms, fragments of sentences, and opinions when creating her art. Her work appears in public spaces, such as on billboards, as well as in galleries and museums. Kruger sees art museums as becoming "dense theaters of receivership." Unlike Holzer, Kruger adds images to her text, often in the form of photographs.

Kruger dislikes binary terms. She does not believe in pro-con or either-or relationships. In an interview with W.J.T. Mitchell, she says, "I feel that there are many of us who are working to make certain changes, who are invested in questions, rather than the surety of knowledge." This theme is present throughout the interviews that have been published with Kruger, and also in her work. By choosing fragments, rather than entire texts or images, Kruger is subversive. She questions the codes that society has in place and what the public expects when it views media. By upsetting those codes, Kruger challenges the viewer to think and reappraise what it so readily accepts as truth.

Significance

Kruger rejects labeling; she refuses to be put in a box where she may be stuck. As the art critic Jeanne Siegel questions her in a 1987 *Arts Magazine* interview, this fact becomes quite evident.

Kruger's words are carefully chosen, in her art and in her interviews. She uses pronouns to invite viewers into the art with her. She attacks myths of modern society regarding images of women, or what society is dictating women to be. Kruger is intent on raising issues of power, sexuality, and representation. She started her public shows in 1974, but they did not draw much attention until the 1980s, when her worked shifted to include a more political message. Consumerism and the effect of pressures on people are themes of Kruger's work. During the 1980s she participated in solo shows and group shows, and created a number of public projects for groups or causes. She designed a number of posters and billboards addressing women's reproductive rights that appeared in subway stations and on busses, and were posters for marches. This kind of work draws attention to both the issue and the creator. Her billboards that are anti-consumerism (e.g., "I shop therefore I am") have appeared on T-shirts, billboards, and in knock-off ads imitating her style.

Kruger's strong opinions can be seen in all of the work she creates. Even if she rejects labels, she makes statements and uses imagery to make people think and reconsider a phrase or a photo they may have viewed in another less political context.

Primary Source

"Barbara Kruger: Pictures and Words" [excerpt]

SYNOPSIS: Kruger is a master at using her graphic design and advertising background to create art. The

multi-media message, which became the venue for many 1980s artists, is in skilled hands. Kruger expanded into film and television criticism and audio media in the 1990s. The combined text and imagery continues to be important.

. . . Jeanne Siegel: You had your first solo show in 1974 at Artists Space. But it seems that you didn't get any serious critical attention until 1982—the kind of critical attention that raised issues that we're still discussing today. Why do you think there was that time gap and why do you think it happened in 1982?

Barbara Kruger: Why things "happen" as you say, in the art world as they do, does not differ greatly from the mechanisms of other "professional" groupings. Why certain productions emerge and are celebrated is usually due to a confluence of effective work and fortuitous social relations, all enveloped by a powerful market structure. Of course, just what the effectiveness of work is becomes pivotal and it is this area which is of interest to me. I see my production as being procedural, that is, a constant series of attempts to make certain visual and grammatical displacements. I didn't pop into the world with a beret on clutching a pair of scissors and a stack of old magazines. I don't think that an artist instantly materializes chock full of dizzying inspirations and masterpieces waiting to be hatched. I think the work that people do can be determined to some degree by where and when they've been born, how they've been touched, the color of their skin, their gender, and what's been lavished upon or withheld from them. I think it took me a while to determine what it could mean to call myself an artist and how I could do work that was questioning, yet pleasurable, for both myself and others.

JS: How did that transition actually take place?

BK: I attended art school and college for only about two years, but even in that short time, the educational system had begun to do its unfortunate work. I remember being at Parsons and asking a teacher whether an artist could work with photographs and magic marker. I was told in no uncertain terms that if I was planning to be an artist I would have to hide out in a garret for ten years and learn how to grind pigment. I have no doubt that if I had been at Cal Arts in 1973, my educational experience would have been a bit different. Well, anyway, I left school and worked as a graphic designer for quite a while, doing mostly magazine work and book covers. When I finally began doing so-called *artwork*, it was the processes of painting and stitching to which I gravitated. That lasted about four

We don't need another hero

Primary Source

"Untitled" (We don't need another hero)

SYNOPSIS: Barbara Kruger's work challenges contemporary assumptions and perceptions of society and women's place in it. The work above, *Untitled (We don't need another hero),* features a Norman Rockwell image from a *Saturday Evening Post* of a girl admiring the bicep of a boy. COURTESY MARY BOONE GALLERY, NEW YORK. PHOTO BY ZINDMAN/FREMONT.

years, and although it offered me some really pleasurable, cozy-wozy studio activity, I simply couldn't continue doing it. The sirenlike call of photography and magic markers was continuing to beckon me and I guess I was determined to follow it.

JS: But it took until the early '80s for you to shift to a more political work that caught the critical attention to which I referred a moment ago.

BK: It always amuses me that when an artist chooses to foreground the tray of stylistic hors d'oeuvres from which they are obliged to make their choice of visual signature, people react with a kind of impatience. I find the labeling of my more recent work as *political* to the exclusion of my earlier activity, to be problematic. First, I am wary of the categorization of so-called political and feminist work, as this mania for categorization tends to ghettoize certain practices, keeping them out of the discourse of contemporary picture-making. My early work was relegated to the category of the decorative, long before the short-lived celebration of "Decorative Art." Turning to craftlike procedures was a conventional, historically grounded way for women to define themselves through visual work. However, I don't subscribe to the uncritical celebration of this work, which might suggest that women have a genetic proclivity

toward the decorative arts. Women were allowed to develop certain virtuoso visual effects within the interiorized, domestic space of the home. I had the pleasures and problems of indulging in this type of artistic activity for a while, and I think that the relations which produced the sanctioning of this work certainly do constitute a politic.

JS: What followed?

BK: I started writing and performing narrative and verse while I was still painting and found that the entry of words into my work soon brought my painting to a grinding halt. By 1978 I was working with photographs and words.

JS: However, the general climate in the country was shifting too at that particular time. Reagan was elected in 1980.

BK: My work went through big changes around 1976, if we have to get numerical about it. And although changes in electoral leadership can symbolically affect how people live their lives, I think that a number of artists working today developed an awareness of the mechanics of power and dispersal that predated the election of Ronald Reagan. To get really concrete about things, my disenchantment with my own work and the subculture which con-

Primary Source

Untitled (I shop therefore I am)
In *Untitled (I shop therefore I am)* Barbara Kruger juxtaposes a bold image of a hand with a striking phrase. COURTESY MARY BOONE GALLERY, NEW YORK. PHOTO BY ZINDMAN/FREMONT.

tained it coincided with a period of forced economic exile from New York. Having no money, I was fortunate to get a number of visiting artist jobs which removed me from the city for scattered semesters over a period of about four years. During this time, I read a lot, drove around a lot, went to lots of movies, and generally tried to rethink my connections to my work, to the art world, and most importantly, to the games

and relations that congeal, disperse, and make the world go round.

JS: Were you more conscious of Reagan in California? Perhaps already aware of Reagan as the quintessential figure of "appearance" or "illusion," a point which is fundamentally made in your work?

BK: Ronald Reagan is an actor. He is directed and produced. He stands where he's supposed to stand and says what he's told to say. He was president of the Screen Actors Guild and a government informer. He and his directors know that television elects Presidents.

JS: His growing media image coincided with a second possible framework for the new development in your work. That is the change in attitude in the art world toward photography, which came about at about the same time—in the late '70s or early '80s. In the '70s photography had extremely limited exposure in the art world. Perhaps we could pinpoint this change in receptivity in terms of artists, for example, in 1977 Laurie Anderson used media images in her performances.

BK: If you want me to name names one would have to talk about Warhol, and then later Ed. Ruscha, John Baldessari, and later on David Salle, Richard Prince, Sherry Levine, Sarah Charlesworth, Troy Brauntuch, Laurie Simmons, Jack Goldstein, Cindy Sherman, and Robert Longo. The "Pictures" exhibition at Artists Space was organized in 1977.

JS: Do you feel that made a difference for you?

BK: I think there are precedents for working with pictures excised from the media which go back a long way. But of course, I had friendships with many of the artists who were developing a vernacular sort of signage. However, the use of words lent my work a kind of uncool explicitness. I have to say that the biggest influence on my work, on a visual and formal level, was my experience as a graphic designer—the years spent performing serialized exercises with pictures as words. So, in a sort of circular fashion, my "labor" as a designer became, with a few adjustments, my "work" as an artist.

JS: Specifically, what do you think you held onto from that experience?

BK: Almost everything. I learned how to deal with an economy of image and text which beckoned and fixed the spectator. I learned how to think about a kind of quickened effectivity, an accelerated seeing and reading which reaches a near apotheosis in television. . . .

Further Resources

BOOKS

Goldstein, Ann. *Barbara Kruger: Thinking of You.* Cambridge, Mass.: M.I.T. Press, 1999.

Mitchell, W.J.T. "An Interview with Barbara Kruger." In *Art and The Public Sphere.* W.J.T. Mitchell, ed. Chicago: University of Chicago Press, 1992, 234–248.

PERIODICALS

Linker, Kate. "Eluding Definition." *Artforum International* 23, December 1984, 61–67.

Morgan, Robert C. "Mary Boone Gallery, New York: Exhibit."*Arts Magazine* 63, April 1989, 96–97.

WEBSITES

"Barbara Kruger Online." Artcyclopedia. Available online at http://www.artcyclopedia.com/artists/kruger_barbara.html; website home page: http://www.artcyclopedia.com/ (accessed April 29, 2003).

AUDIO AND VISUAL MEDIA

Barbara Kruger: Pictures and Words. VHS, 1996.

Women in the World of Art

"Mrs. Holladay and the Guerrilla Girls"

Magazine article

By: John Loughery

Date: 1987

Source: Loughery, John. "Mrs. Holladay and the Guerrilla Girls." *Arts Magazine* 62, no. 2, October 1987, 63 65.

About the Author: John Loughery (1953–) has worked as an English teacher in New York City and as a freelance journalist. His art criticism, film reviews, and reviews of galleries and openings have appeared in many art journals, particularly *Arts Magazine.* In 1990 he became the full-time art critic for *The Hudson Review.* Loughery has edited and authored several books and anthologies, including *John Sloan: Painter and Rebel* (1995), *The Other Side of Silence: Men's Lives and Gay Identities* (1998), and *Eloquent Essay: An Anthology of Classic & Creative Nonfiction* (1999).

Do Women Have to Be Naked to Get Into the Met. Museum?

Billboard

By: Guerrilla Girls

Date: 1989

Source: Guerrilla Girls. *Do Women Have to Be Naked to Get Into the Met. Museum?* 1989. Available online at http://www.guerrillagirls.com (accessed June 10, 2003). ∎

Introduction

Mrs. Holladay (Wilhelmina Cole Holladay) and the Guerrilla Girls employed very different methods to attain the same goal: to increase the opportunities for women artists to exhibit their work. Holladay was born in 1922 in Elmira, New York. She earned a bachelor's degree in art history at Cornell University, and also attended some postgraduate classes at the University of Paris and the University of Virginia. A private collector and socialite in Washington, D.C., Holladay used her connections to corporate America to fund a museum for women's art that opened in 1987. This museum was not greeted with overwhelming enthusiasm because the collection was not viewed as an outstanding representation of women's art. Up the coast, the Guerrilla Girls were beginning their activist protests against underrepresentation of women in major art museums and in the art world in general. This more radical approach drew attention by the media and the public to the plight of women artists. The Guerrilla Girls were a group of female artists and other interested persons connected to the art world who organized around 1985 in New York, California, and England to expose the alleged sexism and racism in the art world and culture on the whole. They remained anonymous, wearing fake brown fur and gorilla masks.

The difference between Mrs. Holladay and the Guerrilla Girls can be compared to the difference between feminine and feminist exhibits. Feminine women exhibited art that was acceptable, even if it was not always the best example of art. Controversial artworks by contemporary women were usually not exhibited. The feminist and politically motivated Guerrilla Girls challenged the feminine and the conservative art world that favored male artists. Taking on the personas of dead female artists, the Guerrilla Girls spoke for women dead and living who were generally unknown even if they had produced large bodies of work.

The style may be different, but the intent is similar. Both Holladay and the Guerrilla Girls want female artists to be noticed and honored. The National Women's Museum of Art (NWMA) broadened its policies for exhibits and collecting. In 2002 exhibits of "Feminism and Art: Selections from the Permanent Collection" and a retrospective of "Judy Chicago" appeared. The Guerrilla Girls have expanded their causes to include literature, the media, the press, and any other entity they view as sexist or discriminatory.

Significance

John Loughery examines the clash of culture between the Guerrilla Girls and Holladay's museum. Loughery points out the problems of the NMWA, calling its lobby "Early Nieman Marcus . . . a pastiche that is completely out of place in this day and age." While his comments may be seen as overly critical considering the museum's laudable intentions to provide a permanent home for women's art in America, the question to be asked is how should art be selected and who should decide? Is it enough to provide access to what was a private collection and call it representative of women's art? Or is the Guerrilla Girls' "in your face" approach the way to obtain more representation?

Loughery makes a good point in his question "Is this really it?" when viewing the NMWA opening exhibit.

Other writers, such as Barbara Quick, have questioned whether women's art should be housed in a separate museum at all, as this practice may further isolate women artists. The history of the museum has been controversial in art and feminist circles; however, its collection has expanded in subsequent years and the museum has gained a reputation for providing access to art that may not be available elsewhere.

The Guerrilla Girls' actions and activities rest on the opposite end of the spectrum from Holladay's. As Lucy Lippard notes, they "provide a link, if only a link, between the art world and the grass roots political activism of other feminist artists across the country." This connection is vital in their work. The Guerrilla Girls' antics, advertising, demonstrations, and speeches all attract attention to the hidden agendas of the art world and of the arts in general.

A single strategy for attracting attention to women's art is not enough. The Guerrilla Girls' anonymity and brazen messages will appeal to some, while the conventional activism of those such as Holladay will draw support from others.

Primary Source

"Mrs. Holladay and the Guerrilla Girls" [excerpt]

SYNOPSIS: John Loughery compares the conservative with the outrageous in his article highlighting different approaches to valuing female artists. The National Women's Art Museum was the first museum devoted solely to art by women. The museum did not take risks with collecting in its first years. The Guerrilla Girls, however, are known for risk taking and speaking out.

Enter the Guerrilla Girls. In the two and a half years since their founding, this anonymous activist group has done a fair amount of education and unsettling in New York, in print even more than in their public appearances. Their trademark is well established by now—the ever-present gorilla mask—but their tactics are varied and still evolving. They've appeared, in costume, to make their point at panel discussions. They've plastered SoHo with posters, publicly naming and shaming "the bad guys"—the galleries who don't represent women artists, the critics who ignore their shows. (An updated version of this infamous list is promised in the near future.) They publish ads to show the percentages of reviewer coverage of women's shows by the different art magazines and the number of solo shows held in New York museums in recent years. This year the Guerrilla Girls put together their own documentary exhibition, "The Guerrilla Girls Strike Back," an assault

Primary Source

Do Women Have to Be Naked to Get Into the Met. Museum?

SYNOPSIS: The Guerrilla Girls designed this billboard for the Public Art Fund in New York. The image, based on Ingre's *Odalisque,* was rejected because the PAF said the design wasn't clear enough. The group then rented advertising space on New York City buses and ran the image themselves. The bus company later cancelled the lease saying that the image was too suggestive. COURTESY WWW.GUERRILLAGIRLS.COM. REPRODUCED BY PERMISSION.

on sexism at the Whitney. Their campaign consists of old-fashioned consciousness-raising; their methods, though, are vehemently 80s—with heavy emphasis on theatrical effect and pointed advertising.

The membership in names and numbers, is a well-guarded secret, but it would seem to include not only artists but some museum and gallery people as well. (Be assured, "in every institution there is a Guerrilla Girl lurking," is all a spokeswoman will say.) This mysteriousness—the member's disguises, the silence about numbers—serves more than one purpose. The attention paid to most political groups in our society usually has to do with celebrity and even more with size. Numbers equals clout. But if no one other than the members themselves know how many Guerrilla Girls there are, that standard of judgment is rendered meaningless. Similarly, problems of ego and "reprisal" are eliminated. No one woman can use her involvement to advance her reputation or simply to become better known in the art world, and no one woman need fear having to pay a price for insulting a dealer, curator, or critic the group may have miffed along the way. "The art world today is centered on gossip, not politics or issues," a Guerrilla Girl commented recently. The masks and the whole strategy of anonymity and vagueness, so obnoxious or silly to some critics, are, the Guerrilla Girls feel, the key to their success. Without any personalities or careers to gossip about, their audience

is left with only the facts and the issues to ponder and debate.

The Guerrilla Girls are also reluctant to be pinned down about their goals. They don't want a quota system for Biennials or theme shows. They're not talking about a feminist version of affirmative action. They are interested, one gathers, in something larger—more like a deeper perception of the ways in which this delimiting of women's talent and achievements takes place, an awareness which in itself might yield a different future. For if the group came into existence on the heels of the MoMA show, it clearly saw that single exhibition (and even that one museum) as only a small part of the problem, a symbolic affront. A little research showed that the track record of the other New York museums was just as bad—ironically, the regional museums do far better by women than the major metropolitan institutions, the Guerrilla Girls point out—as were the attitudes in the press and the galleries.

Nor did all the obstacles the Guerilla Girls defined in their first months originate with the opposite sex. A symbol as potent as McShine's survey was Mary Boone's gallery. Boone's was one of the most high-powered of the SoHo galleries to emerge in the late '70s, but its roster until recently was exclusively male—Salle, Schanbel, Fischl, et al.—and in some cases was seen as almost misogynistic. Mary Boone's response to the criticism has been to dismiss the Guerrilla Girls as artists disgruntled for professional reasons, as people who haven't "made it." (Here the value of anonymity comes into play again. How do we know the group doesn't include successful artists represented by profitable galleries?) The fact that this year Boone finally elected to take on two women, Barbara Kruger and Sherrie Levine, has been happily interpreted by the Guerrilla Girls as evidence of their effectiveness as agitators. This is a claim Boone rejects, of course, but the timing is coincidental. Hastening the end of the male-dominated gallery and the decline of the hyper-masculine aura that has pervaded American art from Pollock through the Neo-Expressionists is undoubtedly an aim the Guerrilla Girls do see as one of their own.

A culmination for the moment of the group's activities was the exhibition organized last May, timed to coincide with the Biennial, whose intent was a nitty-gritty exposé of the policies of the Whitney Museum. It was an unusual show, intentionally belligerent and comic. Unlike a Sunday visit to the Museum of Women in the Arts a few doors up from Pennsylvania Avenue, a weekend visit to "The Guerrilla Girls Strike Back" on the ramshackle top floor of the Clocktower Building in lower Manhattan required a bit of fortitude, a sense of purpose. The curiosity of the idle gallery browser didn't apply here, and there was something fitting in that. One had to *want* to see this exhibition. The Clocktower Building on Leonard Street, south of SoHo and three blocks north of City Hall, is a massive, ancient, uninviting office building, largely deserted on Saturdays. A sign in the empty lobby directed visitors to take an elevator to the twelfth floor and walk up one flight. After reaching the thirteenth floor (coping with two defective elevators en route), we wandered past file cabinets, blackboards, and boxes in a dusty, high-ceilinged rotunda toward a long passageway lined with empty artist's studios. At the end of the corridor a woman in black (maskless) sat smoking a cigarette behind a table stacked with brochures and xeroxes, which led into the gallery. Visitors at the Clocktower show were a long way from West Broadway chic, let alone the pink marble of 13th Street and New York Avenue.

The exhibition managed to be several things at once: droll, dour, grimly didactic, ruthless, entertaining, and genuinely informative. (Similar dissections of other museums are planned for the years ahead.) The provocateurs had turned statisticians and researchers for this enterprise, and what we were treated to essentially was an assortment of wall displays advertising and interpreting the Whit-

ney's abysmal record on women in the arts. Some of the posters, charts, graphs, and illustrations were quite funny—I liked the banana motif, which seemed appropriate—while others were meant to be stark and chilling. No small part of this information extravaganza was directed toward the money-politics of museum life, inextricably linked as that is to sexual politics, and we learned more than a few intriguing professional biographical facts about the Whitney's trustees, director, and curators and about the museum's long-questioned relationship with a few preferred galleries and their male favorites. The museum's love affair with corporate sponsors, institutions which are not exactly in the vanguard of equal opportunity struggles, and the more subtle ties of male corporate influence on the trustees and curators was another prominent theme of "The Guerrilla Girls Strike Back."

One of the most startling of the exhibition's statements wasn't about the low numbers of women included in past Biennials, a regular source of complaint over the years, but addressed the fact that, of all the full-scale, main-gallery exhibitions the Whitney has organized in the last five years, not one has been devoted to women. While even young male artists, men far from their prime, enjoyed retrospectives between 1982 and 1987, not one of the many talented, prolific, critically recognized women in their forties, fifties, or sixties had the same privilege. (According to the Guerrilla Girls, even the two shows on the latest Whitney Schedule that are of work by women—the Cindy Sherman and Elizabeth Murray shows—came to the museum by default, by way of the Broida, and not as a result of the Whitney's own initiation.) For an art institution founded by a woman, Gertrude Vanderbilt Whitney, and guided through its first years by a woman, the remarkable Julian Force, the Whitney would seem to have done pretty badly by America's women artists, if the picture the Clocktower exhibition has provided is a true one.

Is there any reason to doubt the show's contention that the Whitney is biased, or at least hopelessly enmeshed in the usual seamy art world politics? The Whitney has declined to comment in any way, which suggests at least that a raw nerve has been touched here. But then, as the Guerilla Girls spokeswoman told me this summer, their exhibitions on the other New York museums that will follow are going to reveal a record that is every bit as sorry.

The Guerilla Girls have brought a note of energetic humor into the art world of the '80s that's refreshing and long overdue. But beyond the entertainment element, they're as earnest as any of their less flamboyant activist predecessors and they're making some of the targets uncomfortable in useful ways. Mrs. Holladay may have described her museum as an institutional equivalent of Sandra Day O'Connor, a genteel and indirect force for women's rights, but the Guerrilla Girls see themselves as less roundabout, less polite, more eager to make waves.

How large those waves will have to be, though, remains to be seen. And that's the problem: the most aggressive feminist group around today is still, and is likely to remain, a small-scale enterprise, too easily dismissed by the skeptical, the indifferent, or the offended. Given what anyone imagines the size and resources of the Guerrilla Girls to be, their effect is necessarily going to be local rather than regional or national, and of a hit-and-run nature. Long gone are the direct, vigorous confrontations and meditations of the early '70s—something the Guerrilla Girls were never intending to revive anyway—and with them the possibility of accountability and immediate reactions to protest. (How easy it is now for the Whitney, the "bad guy" galleries, and the "bad guy" magazines and writers to ignore the whole thing.) There are other risks, too. The dangers of courting a style of action that will keep many sympathetic and less adventurous women at bay, of adhering to tactics that are likely to wear thin as time passes, and finally of preaching more to the committed than to the uninformed, surround this whole endeavor.

As we inch our way toward equality of the sexes in the next century, the art world mirrors our social history with agonizing vividness. In the years following the defeat of ERA, radicalism is lost from sight only to emerge in the guise of show-biz politics, while Establishment conservatives garner the funds and cloud the issues.

Further Resources

BOOKS
Guerrilla Girls. *Confessions of the Guerrilla Girls.* New York: HarperPerennial, 1995.

Lippard, Lucy R. *The Pink Glass Swan: Selected Essays on Feminist Art.* New York: New Press, 1995.

PERIODICALS
Gablik, Suzi. "We Spell It Like the Freedom Fighters": A Conversation with the Guerrilla Girls." *Art in America* 82, no. 1, January 1994, 43–45.

Quick, Barbara E. "Is a Woman's Place in a Woman's Museum?" *U.S. News & World Report,* April 20, 1987, 70.

WEBSITES
"Guerrilla Girls—Feminists are Funny!" Available online at http://www.guerrillagirls.info/ (accessed April 30, 2003).

"Guerrilla Girls: Fighting Discrimination with Facts, Humor and Fake Fur." Available online at http://www.guerrillagirls .com/ (accessed April 30, 2003).

"National Museum of Women in the Arts." Available online at http://www.nmwa.org/ (accessed April 30, 2003).

AUDIO AND VISUAL MEDIA
Guerrillas in our Midst. Directed by Amy Harrison. VHS, 1992. Women Make Movies, Inc.

The Heidi Chronicles
Play script

By: Wendy Wasserstein

Date: 1988

Source: Wasserstein, Wendy. *The Heidi Chronicles and Other Plays.* 1988. Reprint, New York: Vintage Books, 1991, 162–167.

About the Author: Wendy Wasserstein (1950–) was born in Brooklyn, New York, and grew up in Manhattan. She earned a bachelor's degree in 1971 from Mt. Holyoke College before pursuing a graduate degree in 1973 in creative writing at City College of New York. Wasserstein also attended Yale University School of Drama in 1976 where she studied with Robert Brustein, a prestigious drama critic. ∎

Introduction

Wendy Wasserstein's first professional play was *Any Woman Can't*, a farce about a woman who tried to become independent in the male–dominated world. Produced in 1973, the play began Wasserstein's career and her quest to create women in drama who weren't just stereotypes. Wasserstein's other plays include *Uncommon Women and Others* (1975), *Isn't It Romantic* (1981), and *The Sisters Rosensweig* (1992).

The Heidi Chronicles began in workshop productions at the Seattle Repertory Theatre in April 1988. It opened in New York on December 12, 1988, moving to Broadway's Plymouth Theatre on March 9, 1989. The play won numerous awards, including a Tony Award and Pulitzer Prize.

Wendy Wasserstein is concerned with many of the issues affecting women in her generation in her eleventh play. *The Heidi Chronicles* covers Heidi Holland's life from high school in 1965 through her decision to become a single parent in the 1980s. Heidi, an art historian, is intelligent and has participated in many of the activities of her baby boomer generation. She attended a 1968 Eugene McCarthy rally and consciousness-raising session, and participated in a 1974 protest trying to gain attention for

Pulitzer Prize winning playwright Wendy Wasserstein celebrates her comedy, *The Heidi Chronicles,* about a woman who experiences the student activism of the late 1960s, the feminist consciousness-raising of the early 1970s, and the tough-minded careerism of the 1980s. © BETTMANN/CORBIS. REPRODUCED BY PERMISSION.

women in the arts. Heidi also attends her friends' showers and observes them as their families grow. She feels isolated and abandoned by her friends and by the women's movement in general. In her attempt to find a fulfilling life, she adopts a baby girl. Susan Johnston is Heidi's friend who changes as trends do. The play includes two male characters: Peter Patrone is Heidi's gay friend and soul mate while Scoop Rosenbaum, an editor, is insensitive to Heidi but is a charismatic presence. Rather than marrying the intelligent Heidi, Scoop opts for the stereotypical Southern belle Lisa.

Significance

The Heidi Chronicles mirrors Wendy Wasserstein's own experiences. Gail Ciociola reports that in interviews Wasserstein has said, "I wasn't married, and I was beginning to feel like the odd man out at baby showers. I didn't know whether the sacrifices I had made were worth the road I was taking." She reflects upon the unhappy comments she has heard from feminists as well as on the key events of the Baby Boomer generation. Wasserstein depicts a character who make choices for her life and then winds up "living with the consequences of choices made early in the play, choices inextricably bound with her eventual allegiance to feminism," according to Ciociola. *The Heidi Chronicles* explores sisterhood, feminism, and idealistic attitudes about "having it all," where one finds fulfillment in life.

Despite the awards the play received, reviews were mixed. Mel Gussow, theater reviewer for *The New York Times,* writes that the play is an "enlightening portrait of [Wasserstein's] generation." He also notes that "theater-

goers are left with tantalizing questions about women today and tomorrow." Mimi Kramer calls Wasserstein's play a "bangup production" and declares it "Wasserstein's best work to date." Writing for *The Nation,* however, Moira Hodgson, labels it a "successful bad play" and states that the "evening drags." Helene Keyssar finds the play "disturbing" and says that it "is aggressively monologic, self-contained, a seemingly perfect picture without loopholes of a particular historic moment that is so pleasing to some and distressing to others." The conclusion of the play is often debated; is Wasserstein showing the hope for the future through Heidi's adoption of Judy or is the ending a "cop-out," as some critics claim?

Through Heidi's character, Ciociola asserts, Wasserstein "dares to probe the relationship of the women's movement to societal models of success and consumerism." The changes in life that result from making one choice rather than another and the changes in society that often are out of personal control may ultimately be the key to understanding Heidi and what she hopes for in life.

Primary Source

The Heidi Chronicles [excerpt]

SYNOPSIS: This scene, depicting Heidi and Susan at age sixteen, reveals the differences between the two: Susan, anxious to comport herself according to male expectations yet not without underlying shrewd manipulation; and Heidi, agreeable to Susan but less eager to impress boys, letting one "get away" and encountering Peter for the first time.

Scene 1

1965. A high-school dance, with folding chairs, streamers, and a table with a punch bowl. Two sixteen-year-old girls enter, SUSAN, *wearing a skirt and a cardigan sweater, and* HEIDI *in a traditional A-line dress. The girls find a corner and look out at the dance floor as they sing and sway to the music. "The Shoop Shoop Song" is playing. "Does he love me? I wanna know. How can I tell if he loves me so."*

Susan: Is it in his eyes?

Heidi: Oh, nooooooo, you'll be deceived.

Susan: Is it in his eyes?

Heidi: Oh no, he'll make believe.

Susan: Heidi! Heidi! Look at the guy over at the radiator.

Heidi: Which one?

Susan: In the blue jeans, tweed jacket, and the Weejuns.

Heidi: They're all wearing that.

Susan: The one in the vest, blue jeans, tweed jacket, and Weejuns.

Heidi: Cute.

Susan: Looks kinda like Bobby Kennedy.

Heidi: Kinda. Yup, he's definitely cute.

Susan: Look! He can twist and smoke at the same time. I love that! *Susan unbuttons her sweater and pulls a necklace out of her purse.*

Heidi: Susan, what are you doing?

Susan: Heidi, men rely on first impressions. Oh, God, he's incredible! Heidi, move!

Heidi: What, Susie?

Susan: Just move! The worst thing you can do is cluster. 'Cause then it looks like you just wanna hang around with your girlfriend. But don't look desperate. Men don't dance with desperate women. Oh my God! There's one coming. Will you start moving! Trust me.

Heidi begins to move. She doesn't notice a boy, Chris Boxer, coming over to her.

Chris: Hi.

Heidi: Hi.

Chris: Hi. I'm Chris Boxer, Student Council president here.

Heidi: I'm Heidi Holland, editor of the newspaper somewhere else.

Chris: Great. I knew I could talk to you. Do you want to dance? *(Begins to twist.)*

Heidi: I'm sorry, I can't leave my girlfriend. *(Moves back to Susan.)*

Susan: I don't believe this.

Heidi: This is my girlfriend, Susan Johnston. We came to the dance together.

Chris: Oh, I thought you were alone.

Susan: She is. We just met.

Chris: Well, very nice to meet you both. *(Begins to walk away.)*

Susan: Chris, don't go.

Heidi: Please don't go. We can all dance together. We can form a line and hully-gully, baby.

Chris *(uncomfortable, looks around)*: Well, that's the headmaster. I guess I have to go, and, uh, ask him how it's going. Keep the faith. *(He snaps his fingers.)*

Heidi: We will.

Chris begins to walk away again.

Susan *(calls after him)*: Nice meeting you. *(Begins whispering to Heidi.)* I can't believe you did that. Heidi, we're at a dance! You know, girl meets boy. They hold hands walking in the sand. Then they go to the Chapel of Love. Get it?

Heidi: Got it.

"Satisfaction" begins to play.

Voice: The next dance is gonna be a Ladies' Choice.

Susan *(thrilled)*: All right. Let's get organized here. Heidi, stand in front of me. I can't ask Twist and Smoke to dance with my skirt this long. What should I say to him? *(Susan rolls up her skirt.)*

Heidi: Ask him how he coordinates the twisting with the smoking.

Susan: You know, as your best friend, I must tell you frankly that you're going to get really messed up unless you learn to take men seriously.

Heidi: Susan, there is absolutely no difference between you and me and him. Except that he can twist and smoke at the same time and we can get out of gym with an excuse called "I have my monthly."

Susan: S . . . ! It's still too long. *(Continues to roll the waist of her skirt until it is midthigh.)* Can you get home all right by yourself?

Heidi: He'll never even suspect I even know you.

Susan: Wish me luck!

Heidi *(kisses her on the cheek)*: Luck!

Susan *(jumps back in horror)*: Heidi! Don't!

Heidi: Keep the faith! *(Snaps her fingers as Chris Boxer did.)*

Susan: Shhhhh! Don't make me laugh or my skirt will roll down.

Heidi: I'll call you tomorrow.

Susan exits as she waves good-bye to Heidi. Heidi sits on a chair, takes out a book, reads it for a moment, then puts it on her lap as she stares out. "Play with Fire" is played. Peter, a young man in a St. Mark's school blazer, approaches. He looks at her. She smiles and looks down.

Peter: You must be very bright.

Heidi: Excuse me?

Peter: You look so bored you must be very bright.

Heidi: I'm sorry?

Peter: Don't be sorry. I appreciate bored people. Bored, depressed, anxious. These are the qualities I look for in a woman. Your lady friend is dancing with the gentleman who looks like Bobby Kennedy. I find men who smoke and twist at the same time so dreary.

Heidi: Not worth the coordination, really.

Peter: Do you have any?

Heidi: I can sit and read at the same time.

Peter: What book is that?

Heidi: *Death Be Not Proud.*

Peter: Of course.

Heidi: A favorite of mine at dances.

Peter: I was drawn to you from the moment I saw you shielding that unfortunate wench rolling up her garments in the tempest.

Heidi: I'm sorry.

Peter: Please. Don't apologize for being the most attractive woman on this cruise.

Heidi: Cruise?

Peter: She docks tonight in Portsmouth. And then farewell to the *Queen Mary.* Forever to harbor in Long Beach, California. *C'est triste, n'est pas?*

Heidi: Ce n'est pas bon.

Peter (*excitedly*): Our tragic paths were meant to cross. I leave tomorrow for the sanatorium in Zurich. (*Coughs.*)

Heidi: How odd! I'm going to the sanatorium in Milan. (*Coughs. He offers her his handkerchief. She refuses.*)

Peter: My parents are heartbroken. They thought I was entering Williams College in the fall.

Heidi: My parents put down a deposit at Vassar.

Peter: We've only this night together. I'm Peter, a small noise from Winnetka. I tried to pick out your name . . . Amanda, Lady Clara, Estelle . . .

Heidi: It's . . .

Peter: No, don't tell me. I want to remember you as you are. Beside me in the moonlight, the stars above us . . .

Heidi: The sea below us.

Peter: Glenn Miller and the orchestra. It's all so peaceful.

Heidi: Mmmmmm. Quite peaceful.

"The Shoop Shoop Song" is heard again.

Peter: The twist-and-smokers are heaving themselves on their lady friends. This must be the final song. Would you do me the honor of one dance?

Heidi: Certainly.

Peter: Ahhh! "The Shoop Shoop Song." Baroque but fragile.

Heidi: Melodic but atonal.

Peter: Will you marry me?

Heidi: I covet my independence.

Peter: Perhaps when you leave the sanatorium, you'll think otherwise. I want to know you all my life. If we can't marry, let's be great friends.

Heidi: I will keep your punch cup, as a memento, beside my pillow.

Peter: Well, shall we hully-gully, baby?

Heidi: Really, I . . .

Peter: Don't worry, I'll teach you.

He begins to do a form of shimmy line dance. Holding Heidi's hand, he instructs her. The dance is somewhat interpretive and becomes a minuet. They sing as they dance together.

Peter: How 'bout the way he acts?

Heidi: Oh noooo, that's not the way.

Peter: And you're not listenin' to all I say. If you wanna know if he loves you so . . .

Takes Heidi's waist and dips her.

Peter: It's in his kiss.

Heidi & Peter: Oh yeah! It's in his kiss!

They continue to dance as the lights fade.

Further Resources

BOOKS

Ciociola, Gail. *Wendy Wasserstein: Dramatizing Women, Their Choices and Their Boundaries.* Jefferson, N.C.: McFarland, 1998.

Gillespie, Patti P. "Wendy Wasserstein." In *American Playwrights Since 1945: A Guide to Scholarship, Criticism, and Performance.* Philip C. Koln, ed. New York: Greenwood, 1989, 469–477.

Watermeier, Daniel J. "The Search for Self: Attachment, Loss, and Recovery in *The Heidi Chronicles.* In *Staging Difference: Cultural Pluralism in American Theatre and Drama.* Marc Maufort, ed. New York: Lang, 1995, 351–362.

PERIODICALS

Gussow, Mel. "A Modern-Day Heffalump in Search of Herself." *The New York Times,* December 12, 1988, C13.

Hodgson, Moira. "The Heidi Chronicles." *The Nation,* May 1, 1989, 605–606.

Keyssar, Helene. "Drama and the Dialogic Imagination: *The Heidi Chronicles* and *Fefu and Her Friends.*" *Modern Drama* 34, no. 1, March 1991, 88–106.

Kramer, Mimi. "Portrait of a Lady." *The New Yorker* 64, no. 45, December 26, 1988, 81–82.

WEBSITES

"Wendy Wasserstein." Indiana University Home Pages. Available online at http://www.homepages.indiana.edu/033001 /text/conversations.html; website home page: http://www .homepages.indiana.edu/ (accessed April 30, 2003).

"Just Say Know: Interview with Keith Haring"

Interview

By: David Sheff

Date: 1989

Source: Sheff, David. "Just Say Know: Interview with Keith Haring." *Rolling Stone* 558, August 10, 1989, 58, 66, 102.

About the Author: David Sheff has conducted interviews and contributed articles to such publications as *The New York Times Magazine, Los Angeles Times Magazine, Esquire, Rolling Stone, Playboy,* and *Wired,* as well as *The Observer* in England and publications in Russia and Japan. Among the people he has interviewed are Ansel Adams, John Lennon, Gore Vidal, Steve Jobs, Tom Hanks, Betty Friedan, and nuclear physicist Ted Taylor. Sheff has also produced documentaries for National Public Radio. ∎

Introduction

Keith Haring (1958–1990) was born in New York and began drawing comics when he was a child. He enjoyed the work and, after trying graphic design school, decided to pursue a degree and a career in making his own art. Like many of the other public artists of his generation, Keith Haring wanted to bring art to the people. His bright drawings done with chalk began appearing in the subways of New York. One of the most familiar drawings of Haring's is called "Radiant Baby"—a baby, surrounded by energy rays, that has appeared on T-shirts, posters, buttons, and other items. Other regular characters were his barking dogs and colorful people, who showed up in numerous places.

As Haring's reputation grew, so did demand for his art. Haring created stories to accompany his artwork and worked with children on special projects. He also created art that brought attention to AIDS.

Haring did not only create small drawings and figures—often his work filled walls or floors with color and design. His sculptures stand in parks and gardens throughout the world in the early 2000s. Contemplating Andy Warhol's death, Haring wrote in one of his journals, "Art is, after all, about the image we have before us, the lasting impact and effect that image has on us, not only the ego of the artist whose obsession with himself prevents him from seeing the larger picture." Haring's art has had a lasting impact that will continue long after his death from AIDS in 1990.

Significance

Haring once wrote that he expected to die young, though not of a long-lasting disease. He believed his death would result from an accident of some kind. He used the fact that he had AIDS as an incentive to live each day as a special day, relishing life and the simple pleasures it held.

His discussion with David Sheff highlights his background and the inspiration for his artwork. Haring reflects upon his adolescence and abstract art that came out of using drugs. He did not realize that the cartoon characters he enjoyed drawing could also be considered art until much later. Haring discovered that art could be something a person enjoyed doing, not through the cliché that declared artists must be miserable, but through finding models to emulate. His creations grew as he realized that doing what he enjoyed was more important than fitting into an established category.

Haring's influences included his contemporaries working in multimedia and language, such as Jenny Holzer, and artists and writers from the beat and pop age, in particular William Burroughs and Andy Warhol. Haring worked with words early in his career, experimenting with how a word, phrase, or typeface would stop people and make them think or at least react.

Haring felt the tension between commercialism and art. Once his art became a commodity, did it change? Haring's recognition increased after his Absolut vodka ad campaign, which continued to appear in magazines in the beginning of the twenty-first century, and his AIDS-related and safe-sex campaigns. These campaigns were commercially successful and gained social attention. The AIDS campaign caused people to talk about issues that society was not comfortable discussing. Keith Haring was not afraid to confront the political, the controversial, or topics beyond the ordinary. For him, nothing is trivial at a time when he felt he was "summing up" his life and work.

Primary Source

"Just Say Know: Interview with Keith Haring" [excerpt]

SYNOPSIS: Keith Haring and David Sheff cover a broad spectrum of topics in this 1989 interview. Haring talks openly about AIDS and his personal battle with the disease, he discusses being openly gay and the reactions of his family, and recalls how he began creating his art. The familiar red, yellow, blue, and green figures are more than cartoons, they are symbols for what Haring values—living life.

Mayor Richard M. Daley has declared it Keith Haring Week in Chicago. The artist is here to work with some 300 public-high-school kids on a mural, and Daley has issued an official proclamation with lots of official-sounding whereases. For example, "Whereas Keith Haring is internationally recognized as one of the most important artists of his generation and is acknowledged to have popularized and expanded the audience for the art forms of painting and sculpture." Or this one, Haring's favorite: "Whereas he is respected for committing his life and work to the democratic ideals of social justice, equality, and compassion for his fellow man."

A 520-foot ribbon of whitewashed plywood has been constructed in Grant Park across from the city's Cultural Center. Haring and the kids will spend several days painting the wall, which will then be moved to a building construction site near downtown Chicago and eventually broken up into panels that will be placed permanently in the participating schools. Haring encourages and coaches the kids as they add to his dancing figures and abstract creatures and shapes. De la Soul plays from the boombox. One kid paints dancing fairies. Another writes, I WOULD FLY IF I HAD WINGS AND SOMEWHERE TO FLY. Others: NO SEX UNTIL MARIGE and DON'T USE DRUGS.

One day it begins to rain, so the kids are asked to come back to paint the next day. Before they go, they swarm around the artist, asking him to draw on and sign their hats. They walk away in Keith Haring hats and T-shirts. One girl in a cluster of seniors says to him, "I really got to thank you." Another pipes in, "Yeah, not many people pay attention to us." The first girl says, "Most people consider us an eyesore." A tall boy who has been silently watching adds, "Like we don't exist."

In Haring's hotel room, one of the students, a seventeen-year-old junior named Joe Asencios, orders a well-done steak from room service. Haring has invited Asencios to see the Cirque du Soleil, a theatrical circus, tonight. "I haven't ever taken art," Asencios says. "I'll take it next year." This experience has transformed him. Asencios, who lives with this father, an exterminator, and hasn't seen his mother except twice in nine years, says Haring is the nicest person he has ever met in his life.

His last day in Chicago, Haring paints two walls in Rush–Presbyterian–St. Luke's Medical Center. The next morning he will jet off to Iowa to visit an elementary school where he painted a mural five years ago, then he will return to New York to work on a series of etchings and to paint a mural in the Lesbian and Gay Community Services Center. In June he travels to Antwerp for the opening of an exhibition of his newest paintings. After this, he's off to Paris, where he and Soviet painter Eric Bulatov are painting huge canvases that will fly over Paris on opposite sides of a blimp. From there he travels to Pisa to paint a mural on a historic site within the walled city.

It's an exhausting schedule, but Haring, 31, has rarely set down his paintbrush since he first gained attention in the late 1970s for his drawings in the New York City subways. With white chalk, he made simple, powerful and distinctive figures—crawling babies, dogs, flying saucers and the like—that were cartoonlike, reflecting his earliest influences which included Walt Disney and his father, an engineer whose hobby was cartooning.

The Harings lived in Kutztown, Pennsylvania, where Keith had an unextraordinary childhood of paper routes and odd jobs. He experienced the Sixties via television; he was ten when Robert Kennedy and Martin Luther King Jr. were shot. In his early teens, he was, for a time, a Jesus freak. He later became an ersatz hippie, hitchhiking across the country, selling Grateful Dead and anti-Nixon T-shirts he made and experimenting with drugs. The one constant throughout was his art. He had his first exhibition when he was only nineteen, at what is now the Pittsburgh Center for the Arts.

He arrived in New York in 1978, enrolled in the School of Visual Arts and became immersed in the art and social scene of the East Village. It was a vibrantly exciting period from which emerged such artists as Jean-Michel Basquiat, Kenny Scharf and a singer named Madonna. Four years after arriving, Haring had his first major exhibition. Andy Warhol, who became his close friend, Roy Lichtenstein, Robert Rauschenberg and Sol Le Witt attended.

His work in and out of studios became more and more well known. He made huge sculptures for playgrounds and public spaces and murals for inner-city walls, clubs and children's wards of hospitals. Much of his art contained political messages about AIDS, crack and apartheid. He also began to work with inner-city children all over the country. For the hundredth anniversary of the Statue of Liberty, he and

Artist Keith Haring sits in front of his "Crack is Wack" mural in Manhattan, New York, New York, 1987. © OWEN FRANKEN/CORBIS. © THE KEITH HARING ESTATE. REPRODUCED BY PERMISSION.

1000 kids made a building-size painting. In 1986 he painted on the Berlin Wall. He had fast become one of the most popular artists in the world, although his ascent was controversial. Some viewed him as a pop, commercial media manipulator, while others took him very seriously, describing his work as an assimilation of some or all of Warhol, Lichtenstein, the minimalists, aboriginal art, American Indian art and primitivism. Prices for his paintings soared—one canvas recently sold for $100,000—and Haring's images became some of the most familiar of our time, partly because they were circulated on T-shirts, buttons, posters, billboards, watches, walls and even clothes, many of which are now sold at the Pop Shop, his store in New York City.

Haring is openly gay, and he has used his art to benefit gay causes. Since the AIDS epidemic began, he has been an advocate of safe sex, and the disease that has taken the lives of some of his close friends has been an inspiration in his work. Two years ago, Haring himself was tested HIV positive, and he has since developed Kaposi's sarcoma, a form of cancer that often accompanies AIDS. While KS can be fatal, his illness hasn't slowed Haring down at all. To the observer, the only noticeable effect is lesions, faint plum-colored splotches behind his ear and on his forehead.

A sticker on the heavy industrial door of Haring's lower-Broadway studio reads, JUST SAY KNOW—TIM LEARY. Through the door, the studio is like the inside of a kaleidoscope. There are Warhol soup cans, Mobil flying horses, a Mona Lisa with colored nails smashed into her face, toys—a talking Pee-wee and Chairry and a Roger Rabbit Super Flexie—and stacks of art books. There are wrapped wall-size canvases, a huge hot-pink phallus, a larger-than-life black-and-white sculpture of a headless man and shelves of paints. There are photographs of Brooke Shields and Michael Jackson, a poster of Grace Jones painted like a warrior and a pair of fluorescent bikes.

Haring is wearing paint-splattered jeans, untied Nike Delta Force high tops and one of his SAFE SEX T-shirts. . . . He is thin and pale, eyes wide behind think-rimmed gray glasses, sort of like Sherman of Peabody and Sherman.

We begin our interview—the first of a half-dozen extensive, late-night sessions in Manhattan and Chicago—while Haring paints a new series of canvases. There are several abstractions obviously influenced by his recent trip to Morocco and a two-part black-and-white series painting. The first canvas has a skeleton peeing on a small sunflower. In the sec-

ond, the flower has blossomed. Keith talks like he paints. It comes out in a line, a spontaneous, smooth line.

What made you want to be an artist?

My father made cartoons. Since I was little, I had been doing cartoons, creating characters and stories. In my mind, though, there was a separation between cartooning and being a quote-unquote artist. When I made the decision to be an artist, I began doing these completely abstract things that were as far away from cartooning as you could go. It was around the time that I was taking hallucinogens—when I was sixteen or so. Psychedelic shapes would come like automatic writing, come out of my unconscious. The drawings were abstract, but you'd see things in them.

Were you taking drugs because is was fashionable?

Drugs were a way to rebel against what was there and at the same time to sort of not be there. And I remember that all the antidrug things on television at the time only made me want to do them more. They showed all these things to scare you: a gas burner turning into a beautiful flower. I thought, that's great! You mean I can see like *that?*

Drugs showed me a whole new world. It completely changed me. I was a terror when I was a teenager, an embarrassment to the family, really a mess on drugs. I ran away. I came home stoned out of my mind on downs. I got arrested—for stuff like stealing liquor from a firehouse, on my newspaper route, no less. Me and my friends were making and selling angel dust.

If you had conformed to your parents' expectations, what would you have been like?

We were in a little, conservative town. You grew up there, went to high school there, stayed there, married someone from there, had kids there, and your kids stayed, too. I had been a good little kid. My parents had taken us to church and things like that, but I became this little Jesus freak, and my parents were appalled. I had fallen into the movement out of a lack of any other thing to believe in and out of wanting to be part of something. Part of deciding I wanted to try drugs was realizing that it was time to start thinking for myself instead of blindly following just to be part of a group.

When did you decide to go to art school?

I'd been convinced to go by my parents and guidance counselor. They said that if I was going to seriously pursue being an artist, I should have some commercial-art background. I went to a commercial-art school, where I quickly realized that I didn't want to be an illustrator or a graphic designer. The people I met who were doing it seemed really unhappy; they said that they were only doing a job while they did their own art on the side, but in reality that was never the case—their own art was lost. I quit the school. I went to a huge retrospective by Pierre Alechinsky at the Carnegie Museum of Art. It was the first time that I had seen someone who was older and established doing something that was vaguely similar to my little abstract drawings. It gave me this whole new boost of confidence. It was the time I was trying to figure out if I was an artist, why and what that meant. I was inspired by the writings of Jean Dubuffet, and I remember seeing a lecture by Christo and seeing the film on his work *Running Fence.*

How did these artists inspire you?

The thing I responded to most was their belief that art could reach all kinds of people, as opposed to the traditional view, which has art as this elitist thing. The fact that these influences quote-unquote *happened* to come along changed the whole course I was on. Then another so-called coincidence happened. I applied at a public-employment place for work and happened to get placed in a job at what's now the Pittsburgh Center for the Arts. I was painting walls and repairing the roof and things. I started using their facilities to do bigger and bigger paintings. When someone cancelled an exhibition and they had an empty space, the director offered me an exhibit in one of the galleries. For Pittsburgh, this was a big thing, especially for me, being nineteen and showing in the best place I could show in Pittsburgh besides the museum. From that time, I knew I wasn't going to be satisfied with Pittsburgh anymore or with the life I was living there. I had started sleeping with men. I wanted to get away from the girl I was living with. She said she was pregnant. I was in the position of having to get married and be a father or making a break. One thing I knew for sure: I didn't want to stay there and be a Pittsburgh artist and married with a family. I decided to make a major break. New York was the only place to go.

What did you do once you got there?

At first I was just working in the same style as I was at home. But then all kinds of things started to happen. Maybe the most important was that I learned about William Burroughs. I learned about him almost by accident—like almost everything else that has happened to me, sort of by accident-chance-coincidence.

Apparently, you believe in fate.

From the time that I was little, things would happen that seemed like chance, but they always meant more, so I came to believe there was no such thing as chance. If you accept it that there are no coincidences, you use whatever comes along.

How did Burroughs influence you?

Burrough's work with Brion Gysin with the cut-up method became the basis for the whole way that I approached art then. The idea of their book, *The Third Mind,* is that when two separate things are cut up and fused together, completely randomly, the thing that is born of that combination is this completely separate thing, a third mind with its own life. Sometimes the result was not that interesting, but sometimes it was prophetic. The main point was that by relying on so-called chance, they would uncover the essence of things, things below the surface that were more significant than what was visible.

How did you use the concepts?

I used the idea when I cut up headlines from the *New York Post* and put them back together and then put them up on the streets and handbills. That's how I started work on the street. There was a group of people using the streets for art then, like Jenny Holzer, who was putting out these handbills with things she was calling truisms, these absurd comments. I was altering advertisements and making these fake *Post* headlines that were completely absurd: REAGAN SLAIN BY HERO COP or POPE KILLED FOR FREED HOSTAGE. I'd post them all over the place.

With what intent?

The idea was that people would be stopped in their tracks, not knowing whether it was real or not. They'd stop because it had familiar words like *Reagan* or *pope* and it was in a familiar typeface—so they had to confront it and somehow deal with it.

What was it like living in the East Village at that time?

It was just exploding. All kinds of new things were starting. In music, it was the punk and New Wave scenes. There was a migration of artists from all over America to New York. It was completely wild. And we controlled it ourselves. There was the group of artists called COLAB—Collaborative Projects—doing exhibitions in abandoned buildings. And there was the club scene—the Mudd Club and Club 57, at St. Mark's Place, in the basement of a Polish church, which became our hangout, a clubhouse, where we could do whatever we wanted. We started doing theme parties—beatnik parties that were satires of the Sixties and parties with porno movies and stripteases. We showed early Warhol films. And there was this art out on the streets. Before I knew who he was, I became obsessed with Jean-Michel Basquiat's work.

Was this the period in which Basquiat was doing his early graffiti?

Yeah, but the stuff I saw on the walls was more poetry than graffiti. They were sort of philosophical poems that would use the language the way Burroughs did—in that it seemed like it could mean something other than what it was. On the surface they seemed really simple, but the minute I saw them I knew that they were more than that. From the beginning he was my favorite artist.

And how was your art developing?

I'd gone from the abstract drawings to the word pieces but I decided that I was going to draw again. But if I was going to draw again, I couldn't go back to the abstract drawings; it had to have some connection to the real world. I organized a show at Club 57 for Frank Holliday and me. I bought a roll of oaktag paper and cut it up and put it all over the floor and worked on this whole group of drawings. The first few were abstracts, but then these images started coming. There were humans and animals in different combinations. Then flying saucers were zapping the humans. I remember trying to figure out where this stuff came from, but I have no idea. It just grew into this group of drawings. I was thinking about these images as symbols, as a vocabulary of things. In one a dog's being worshipped by these people. In another one the dog is being zapped by a flying saucer. Suddenly it made sense to draw on the street, because I had something to say. I made this person crawling on all fours, which evolved into the quote-unquote baby. And there was an animal being, which now has evolved into the dog. They really were representational of human and animal. In different combinations they were about the difference between human power and the power of animal instinct. It all came back to the ideas I learned from semiotics and the stuff from Burroughs—different juxtapositions would make different meanings. I was becoming more and more involved in the underground art scene, doing graffiti, and then I would use people's studios and do paintings. It was one of the first times graffiti was being considered art, and there were shows. In the summer of 1980, COLAB organized an exhibition of a lot of these artists in the Times Square Show. It was the first time the art world really paid attention to graffiti and to these other outsider artists. It was written about in the *Village Voice* and in the art magazines. Jean-Michel and I got singled out of the group then.

How did you begin drawing in the subways?

One day, riding the subway, I saw this empty black panel where an advertisement was supposed to go. I immediately realized that this was the perfect place to draw. I went back above ground to a card shop and bought a box of white chalk, went back down and did a drawing on it. It was perfect— soft, black paper, chalk drew on it really easy.

I kept seeing more and more of these black spaces, and I drew on them whenever I saw one. Because they were so fragile, people left them alone and respected them; they didn't rub them out or try to mess them up. It gave them this other power. It was this chalk-white fragile thing in the middle of all this power and tension and violence that the subway was. People were completely enthralled.

Except the police.

Well, I was arrested, but since it was chalk and could easily be erased, it was like a borderline case. The cops never knew how to deal with it. The other part that was great about it was the whole thing was a performance. When I did it, there were inevitably people watching—all kinds of people. After the first month or two I started making buttons because I was so interested in what was happening with the people I would meet. I wanted to have something to make some other bonding between them and the work. People were walking around with little badges with the crawling baby with glowing rays around it. The buttons started to become a thing, now, too; people with them would talk to each other, there was a connection between people in the subway.

The subway pictures became a media thing, and the images started going out into the rest of the world via headlines and television. I became associated with New York and the hip-hop scene, which was all about graffiti and rap music and break dancing. It had existed for five years or more, but it really hadn't started to cross over into the general population. It was incredibly interesting to me that it was reaching all kinds of people in different levels from different backgrounds. Then, in 1982, I had my first one-man show in New York at a big gallery, Tony Shafrazi, in SoHo.

What happened to your resolve to stay away from the traditional, snobbish art scene?

As an art student and being sort of the underground and having very precise and cynical ideas about the art world, the traditional art-dealer gallery represented a lot that I hated about the art world. But people started to see an opportunity to make a lot of money buying my work. I got disillusioned with letting dealers and collectors come to my studio. They would come in and, for prices that were nothing, a couple hundred dollars, go through all the paintings and then not get anything or try to bargain. I didn't want to see those people anymore. I wanted to sell paintings because it would enable me to quit my job, whether as a cook or delivering house plants or whatever else I was doing—and paint full time. But I had to have a gallery just to give me distance.

Was it hard to accept the fact that the paintings were commodities?

Yes, but it's not that way for everyone. People get something from living with a painting. I love living with paintings.

What do you have on the wall in your apartment?

One of my favorite Warhol paintings that I ever got from Andy—a small hand-painted portrait of Christ at the Last Supper. Two George Condo paintings. One Basquiat. A small Lichtenstein drawing. A Picasso etching. A Clemente monoprint and a Kenny Scharf. I also have a television painted by Kenny that is incredible. And one piece of mine, a metal mask that I made for an exhibition a few years ago in New York. In the collection, I have a lot of things, from Jean Tinguely to Robert Mapplethorpe photographs to a lot more Warhols and Basquiats.

Had you met Warhol by the time of your first show?

Before I knew him, he had been an image to me. He was totally unapproachable. I met him finally through [photographer] Christopher Makos, who brought me to the Factory. At first Andy was very distant. It was difficult for him to be comfortable with people if he didn't know them. Then he came to another exhibition at the Fun Gallery, which was soon after the show at Shafrazi. He was more friendly. We started talking, going out. We traded a lot of works at that time.

How do you feel about the publication of the Warhol diaries?

He wanted them to be published. That's why he kept them. The weirdest thing to me is to see his insecurity. It was all ridiculous, because he had nothing to be insecure about; this was after he'd already safely carved himself a permanent notch in our history, probably the most important notch since Picasso. It's nice going through the diaries, though, because he tells enough of the story that it takes me back to the exact moment, and I can fill in all the rest.

Further Resources

BOOKS

Haring, Keith. *Keith Haring: I Wish I Didn't Have to Sleep.* New York: Prestel, 1997.

Thompson, Robert Farris. *Keith Haring Journals.* New York: Viking, 1996.

PERIODICALS

Adams, Brooks. "Keith Haring: Radiant Picaresque."*Art in America* 86, no. 4, April 1998, 94–99.

Galloway, David. "Keith Haring: Made in Germany." *Art in America* 79, no. 3, March 1991, 118–124.

WEBSITES

Keith Haring. Available online at http://www.haring.com/ (accessed April 30, 2003).

"Haring Kids." Keith Haring Foundation. Available online at http://www.haringkids.com/ (accessed April 30, 2003).

2

BUSINESS AND THE ECONOMY

PATRICK D. REAGAN

Entries are arranged in chronological order by date of primary source. For entries with one primary source, the entry title is the same as the primary source title. Entries with more than one primary source have an overall entry title, followed by the titles of the primary sources.

Important Events in Business and the Economy, 1980–1989

1980

- Clothing manufacturer Calvin Klein features Brooke Shields in ads, launching a designer jeans fad.

- Low-fare People Express Airline, founded by Donald Barr, begins no-frills service in the Northeast.

- United Steelworkers and big steel manufacturers attempt to revitalize the steel industry by creating labor-management participation teams in imitation of Japanese practices.

- AT&T begins a telephone 900 service.

- AT&T is convicted of antitrust violations and fined $1.8 billion.

- The prime interest rate averages 15.26 percent.

- Inflation averages 12.5 percent, the highest in thirty-three years despite high interest rates to contract the money supply.

- Unemployment averages 7.1 percent.

- Japanese investors operate some 225 U.S. manufacturing firms.

- On January 1, the average car costs $7,574.

- On February 8, President Jimmy Carter announces a $13 million cut in federal spending in hopes of curbing inflation.

- In March, brothers Nelson Bunker Hunt and William Herbert Hunt fail to corner the silver market as the value of silver drops.

- In March, the Dow-Jones Industrial Average reaches 1,000.

- In June, the Motor Carrier Act deregulates the trucking industry.

- In June, Henry Ford II retires a chairman of Ford Motor Company.

- On July 14, the United States announces that it imported 14 percent less crude oil during the first six months of 1980 than during the same period in 1979.

- On July 22, Ted Turner creates Cable News Network (CNN) to televise round-the-clock news.

- On August 18, the price of gold reaches a high of $802 on the New York market, rising $159 in one week.

- On August 23, Congress deregulates the banking industry.

- On October 3, Congress removes ceilings on the interest rates that savings and loans can pay depositors.

- On October 23, a ninety-four-day strike by the Screen Actors Guild and the American Federation of Television and Radio Artists (the longest in the unions' history) ends with a new contract.

- On November 4, voters elect Ronald Reagan president. His agenda includes a reduction in federal spending and a tax cut for wealthy Americans.

- On December 19, the United States prime interest rate reaches a record high, 21.5 percent, as the Federal Reserve Board tries to contract the money supply by discouraging people and businesses from borrowing money.

1981

- U.S. agricultural exports reach a record high, $43.8 billion.

- U.S. Steel buys Marathon Oil for $6.3 billion.

- On February 5, President Ronald Reagan makes his first television address as president, asking for cuts in income taxes and federal spending.

- On February 18, President Ronald Reagan proposes a federal budget $41.4 billion less than former President Jimmy Carter's budget.

- In March, President Ronald Reagan urges Congress to require welfare recipients to work for their benefits.

- In March, President Reagan urges Congress to cut taxes and the budget by $130.5 billion.

- On March 6, Reagan cautions that federal agencies may need to lay off workers to save money.

- On March 27, the United Mine Workers of America (UMWA) contract expires. Coal miners in the eastern states go on strike.

- On March 28, after reaching a high of $40 per ounce in January, and a low of $4, the price of silver stabilizes at $12 per ounce.

- On April 24, President Ronald Reagan ends a fifteen-month grain embargo on the USSR, reopening the country to U.S. grain exports.

- On May 7, the United Automobile Workers (UAW) reaffiliates with the American Federation of Labor and Congress of Industrial Organizations (AFL-CIO) after thirteen years apart.

- On May 1, Japan announces plans to limit car exports to the United States after American officials threaten to impose quotas on Japanese imports.

- On May 13, President Ronald Reagan proposes to cut Social Security 10 percent, but senior-citizen outrage kills the idea.

- On May 26, OPEC (the Organization of Petroleum Exporting Countries) freezes oil prices at $32 per barrel and announces a 10 percent cut in production, raising fears that OPEC's real intent is to raise prices.

- In June, inflation falls to 10.4 percent, demonstrating that the Fed's policy of raising interest rates is working, though inflation remains higher than the roughly 3 percent Americans enjoy in 2003.

- In June, the Children's Defense Fund estimated that black children are four times more likely than white children to live in poverty in the U.S.

- On June 12, baseball players go on strike.

- On August 3, thirteen thousand members of the Professional Air Traffic Controllers Organization (PATCO) go on strike after rejecting a federal proposal of a new contract.

- On August 15, President Ronald Reagan fires more than ten thousand PATCO strikers, replacing them with nonunion workers.

- From October to December, the U.S. Gross National Product (GNP) drops 5 percent as car and home sales fall.

1982

- Female business leaders create the Committee of two hundred to promote the achievements of women in business.

- The Japanese auto manufacturer Honda begins making cars at Marysville, Ohio.

- Gannett Publishing Company launches *USA Today,* a national daily newspaper.

- U.S. industries cut more than 1.25 million jobs.

- On January 1, 34 million Americans live below the poverty line.

- In January, McDonald's passes Sears as the world's largest owner of real estate.

- In January, the U.S. Justice Department orders telecommunications giant American Telephone and Telegraph (AT&T) to dissolve into several companies to permit competition and innovation in telecommunications.

- In January, the EPCOT Center (Experimental Prototype Community of Tomorrow), which had been visualized by Walt Disney in 1966 as a self-sustaining utopian community, opens at Disney World.

- In March, Secretary of the Interior James Watt opens one billion acres of American coast-line to oil and gas drilling.

- On May 18, Congress deregulates the savings-and-loan industry, allowing speculative investments.

- In June, U.S. unemployment hits 9.4 percent, the highest since 1941, with 10.3 million unemployed.

- On June 7, Congress approves a three-year, 25 percent reduction in personal and business income taxes.

- In July, the U.S. Department of Labor reports 14 percent of Americans below the poverty line, the highest percentage since 1967.

- In August, a bull market begins on Wall Street.

- In October, Congress raises federal insurance for each savings and loan depositor from forty thousand dollars to one hundred thousand dollars.

- In December, inflation falls to 6.1 percent.

1983

- The Public Power Supply System of Washington State defaults on more than $2 billion in municipal bonds, the worst government default in U.S. history.

- Frank Lorenzo, head of Texas Air, bought Continental Airlines, declared bankruptcy, fired its workers and offered to rehire them at half their old pay.

- In January, more than 11.5 million Americans are unemployed.

- In April, inflation falls to 3.2 percent.

- On April 20, President Ronald Reagan signs Social Security legislation that aims to keep the system out of debt for the next seventy-five years.

- In November, Drexel Burnham Lambert executive Michael Milken develops the idea of using high-yield "junk" bonds that are repaid by pledging assets of the target company to facilitate company takeovers and corporate buying of public stock.

- On December 23, two U.S. railroads merge to create Santa Fe Southern Pacific.

1984

- General Motors buys Texknowledge and Electronic Data Systems from H. Ross Perot for $2.5 billion.

- The Hewlett-Packard Company introduces the laptop computer.

- The computer language MS-DOS, developed by Microsoft for IBM, is used in two million computers and in more than 90 percent of IBM personal computers and compatible equipment.

- On January 25, President Ronald Reagan announces, in his State of the Union address, plans to simplify the tax code, which Congress would enact in the 1986 Tax Reform Act.

- On February 1, the Senate confirms Elizabeth Hanford Dole as Secretary of Transportation.

- In August, inflation rises to 4.3 percent.

- In August, the U.S. House Select Committee on Children, Youth and Families reports that the number of poor children grew by two million from 1980 to 1982.

- In October, two hundred Yale University clerical workers go on strike to protest low pay and demeaning treatment from professors and administrators.

1985

- A record forty-three thousand farms go bankrupt as land prices fall and interest rates soar.

- Banks and savings-and-loan institutions go bankrupt in Texas, Oklahoma, and other oil states when oil prices fall.

- As high-yield "junk" bonds finance company takeovers, the number of U.S. corporate mergers and buyouts increases—with twenty-four involving more than $1 billion each.

- On February 6, President Reagan calls for tax cuts to stimulate economic growth in his State of the Union address.

- In May, inflation falls to 3.6 percent.

- On September 16, the U.S. Department of Commerce announces that the United States has become a debtor nation for the first time since 1914.
- On December 12, President Ronald Reagan signs the Gramm-Rudman-Hollings Act, limiting Congressional spending in an effort to eliminate the federal deficit by 1991.

1986

- Entrepreneur Rupert Murdoch launches the non-cable network Fox.
- The average weekly wage for U.S. workers is $171.07.
- The value of U.S. farmland drops to $392 billion—approximately half its value in 1980.
- On March 4, Congress passes the Tax Reform Act, reducing taxes on the wealthiest Americans, just as Congress had reduced taxes on the wealthy throughout the 1920s.
- On April 7, Microsoft Corporation, led by William Henry Gates III, offers stock for sale to the public.
- On November 14, Wall Street businessman Ivan Boesky plea bargains with government officials, admitting he had bought stock after receiving tips about forthcoming merger bids.
- In December, U.S. international debt reaches $269 billion.

1987

- In January, the U.S. Commerce Department predicts that technology companies will grow faster than manufacturing companies.
- On January 6, the Reagan administration, the Federal Reserve Board, and some private economists predict the economy will continue to expand for the fifth straight year.
- On January 10, the U.S. Labor Department announces that consumer prices rose only 2.5 percent in 1986, the least in thirty-seven years thanks to low oil prices.
- On January 11, representatives from business, academia, and labor form the Competitiveness Council to promote U.S. exports.
- On January 17, the Federal Reserve Board reports that industrial production rose 0.5 percent in November, an increase over past reports.
- On January 23, the U.S. Commerce Department reports that the economy grew at a slower rate than the Reagan administration had expected.
- On January 25, Treasury Secretary James A. Baker tells President Reagan that the dollar's two-year fall in value relative to other currencies has been good for the economy.
- On January 27, President Ronald Reagan stresses in his State of the Union address the need for U.S. businesses to compete in a global market.

- On February 18, low interest rates and low oil prices combine with a weak dollar to boost corporate profits.
- On February 20, the U.S. Commerce Department announces that the economy grew 1.3 percent after inflation, a lower rate than had been predicted.
- On February 27, the Commerce Department reports that orders to factories for durable goods fell 7.5 percent in January, the biggest drop in seven years despite a 51 percent increase in military orders.
- On March 15, evidence suggests that American consumers are ending their four-year buying spree because of high debt.
- On March 23, an independent study suggests that outmoded accounting methods may explain the failure of American companies to modernize production.
- On April 7, the Commerce Department reports to Congress that Japanese companies are increasing their investments in the United States despite the fear that the steady decline of the dollar against the yen might prompt Japanese investors to pull out of the United States.

1988

- In February, the IRS estimates that 15 percent of Americans underreport their income.
- On May 3, the American Association for the Advancement of Science reports that scientists in business and industry earn, on average, twice the salaries of scientists in academe and government.
- In July, the U.S. Department of Agriculture reports that the average American family spends roughly 25 percent of income on food.
- On October 9, the American Bar Association lists corporate law as the most lucrative specialty with a median income of $78,000.
- On November 17, the Bureau of Labor Statistics reports that the median income for African American families is less than half the median income of white families.

1989

- On January 1, one-third of homeless Americans are families with children.
- On January 1, 40 percent of poor Americans are children.
- In June, the U.S. Department of Housing and Urban Development reports that only 15 percent of twenty-five year-olds could afford a home.
- On July 4, four thousand striking miners and their supporters hold a rally in St. Paul, Virginia, to bring their plight to national attention.

President Ronald Reagan's Inaugural Address, January 20, 1981

Speech

By: Ronald W. Reagan

Date: January 20, 1981

Source: Reagan, Ronald W. President Ronald Reagan's Inaugural Address, January 20, 1981. *The Public Papers of President Ronald W. Reagan, 1981–1988*. Ronald Reagan Presidential Library Official Web Site. Available online at http://www.reagan.utexas.edu/resource/speeches/1981/12081a. htm; website home page: http://www.reagan.utexas.edu/ (accessed May 6, 2003).

About the Author: Ronald Reagan (1911–), born in Tampico, Illinois, built his political appeal on criticizing government spending, arguing that federal programs led to high taxes and slow growth. He served as California governor from 1966 to 1974, losing bids for the Republican presidential nomination in 1968 and 1976. In 1980, Republican nominee Reagan defeated Democrat Jimmy Carter (served 1977–1981) for the presidency. He was elected to a second term in 1984. In 1994 he retired from public life, revealing that he had been diagnosed as having Alzheimer's Disease. ∎

Introduction

In 1980, Americans suffered from an annual price inflation rate of around twelve percent. Many were tired of the Great Society programs of the 1960s that had sparked economic growth. When prices and unemployment began rising after 1968, Americans encountered an economic situation that economists had previously stated was not possible, dubbed "stagflation"—high inflation and high unemployment existing at the same time. This problem caused millions of ordinary people to fear losing their jobs in the 1970s.

In the 1980 presidential election Republican candidate Ronald Reagan claimed that the "misery index" (the combination of the unemployment and inflation rates) had skyrocketed under Democrat Jimmy Carter. He urged people to ask themselves whether they were better off than they had been four years ago. Voters responded with a major shift in political values symbolized by the move from a moderate Democratic president to a conservative Republican.

Reagan's inaugural address captured this discontent when he said that "government is not the solution to our problem; government is the problem." By appealing to the hopes and fears of ordinary Americans in the working and middle classes, Reagan set the stage for a move away from the spending policies of the turbulent 1960s to a new focus on private businesses, individual efforts, and lower taxes. He promised to replace the older economic policies of federal spending with a new set of Republican policies. Reagan called for massive tax cuts that would take money out of the hands of government officials and place it into the hands of private investors and business firms. Through this means, the nation could increase the rate of economic growth, create more jobs, and lower taxes. By lowering the cost of interest payments on private and public loans, the Federal Reserve Board could play a central part in attacking high prices. Consumers would purchase more goods and services. Reagan called on the historic traditions of hard work, individual initiative, and private business activity to rebuild the nation's economy while improving the nation's reputation overseas.

Significance

Historians often cite from famous inaugural addresses to point to the central focus of a new president's vision for the future. This selection from Ronald Reagan's speech emphasizes the political strategy and economic values that would mark his administration. By blaming Democratic policies for the rapid and high price increases of the late 1970s, Reagan set the groundwork for his own very different vision of the country's economic path. Rejecting the idea of government spending to invest in building the economic future, he argued that Americans must return to traditional values of hard work, risky investment, and leadership by private economic institutions to rebuild the national economy.

Since leaving his career as a Hollywood actor in the 1930s and 1940s to enter politics, Reagan had practiced giving speeches on these ideas. His nationwide television address in favor of Republican presidential candidate Barry Goldwater's conservative policies in 1964 was too early. By the late 1970s, the economic circumstances had changed dramatically away from the prosperity and low unemployment of the mid-1960s. Reagan's call for a new kind of economic policy set a positive tone for the economic activities of the early 1980s that benefited private firms at the cost of ignoring the need to repair the economy for all Americans. His popular appeals to the ordinary American sounded much like the words of liberal Democrat Franklin D. Roosevelt (served 1933–1945) in

Ronald Reagan delivers his inaugural address in front of the Capitol on January 20, 1981. **AP/WIDE WORLD PHOTOS. REPRODUCED BY PERMISSION.**

the 1930s. However, his policies, in part constrained by a Congress reluctant to reduce government spending, ended up improving the fortunes of only a small percentage of Americans in the 1980s. Critics would soon claim that the Reagan policies had a much different social impact than what he predicted in this 1981 inaugural address.

Primary Source

President Ronald Reagan's Inaugural Address, January 20, 1981 [excerpt]

> **SYNOPSIS:** President Ronald W. Reagan (served 1981–1989) called for new federal economic policies in the 1980s that would lower prices, cut government spending, decrease taxes, and increase investment.

The business of our nation goes forward. These United States are confronted with an economic affliction of great proportions. We suffer from the longest and one of the worst sustained inflations in our national history. It distorts our economic decisions, penalizes thrift, and crushes the struggling young and the fixed-income elderly alike. It threatens to shatter the lives of millions of our people.

Idle industries have cast workers into unemployment, human misery, and personal indignity. Those who do work are denied a fair return for their labor by a tax system which penalizes successful achievement and keeps us from maintaining full productivity.

But great as our tax burden is, it has not kept pace with public spending. For decades we have piled deficit upon deficit, mortgaging our future and our children's future for the temporary convenience of the present. To continue this long trend is to guarantee tremendous social, cultural, political, and economic upheavals.

You and I, as individuals, can, by borrowing, live beyond our means, but for only a limited period of time. Why, then, should we think that collectively, as a nation, we're not bound by that same limitation? We must act today in order to preserve tomorrow. And let there be no misunderstanding: We are going to begin to act, beginning today.

The economic ills we suffer have come upon us over several decades. They will not go away in days, weeks, or months, but they will go away. They will go away because we as Americans have the capacity now, as we've had in the past, to do whatever needs to be done to preserve this last and greatest bastion of freedom.

In this present crisis, government is not the solution to our problem; government is the problem. From time to time we've been tempted to believe that society has become too complex to be managed by self-rule, that government by an elite group is superior to government for, by, and of the people. Well, if no one among us is capable of governing himself, then who among us has the capacity to govern someone else? All of us together, in and out of government, must bear the burden. The solutions we seek must be equitable, with no one group singled out to pay a higher price.

We hear much of special interest groups. Well, our concern must be for a special interest group that has been too long neglected. It knows no sectional boundaries or ethnic and racial divisions, and it crosses political party lines. It is made up of men and women who raise our food, patrol our streets, man our mines and factories, teach our children, keep our homes, and heal us when we're sick pro- fessionals, industrialists, shopkeepers, clerks, cab- bies, and truck drivers. They are, in short, "We the people," this breed called Americans.

Well, this administration's objective will be a healthy, vigorous, growing economy that provides equal opportunities for all Americans with no barri- ers born of bigotry or discrimination. Putting Amer- ica back to work means putting all Americans back to work. Ending inflation means freeing all Ameri- cans from the terror of runaway living costs. All must share in the productive work of this "new beginning," and all must share in the bounty of a revived econ- omy. With the idealism and fair play which are the core of our system and our strength, we can have a strong and prosperous America, at peace with itself and the world.

Further Resources

BOOKS

Boaz, David. *Assessing the Reagan Years*. Washington, D.C.: Cato Institute, 1988.

Cannon, Lou. *President Reagan: The Role of a Lifetime*. New York: Simon & Schuster, 1991.

Dallek, Robert. *Ronald Reagan: The Politics of Symbolism*. Cambridge, Mass.: Harvard University Press, 1999.

Johnson, Haynes B. *Sleepwalking Through History: America in the Reagan Years*. New York: Norton, 1991.

Kiewe, Amos, and Davis W. Houck. *A Shining City on a Hill: Ronald Reagan's Economic Rhetoric, 1951–1989*. New York: Praeger, 1991.

Niskanen, William A. *Reaganomics: An Insider's Account of the Policies and the People*. New York: Oxford University Press, 1988.

Noonan, Peggy. *What I Saw at the Revolution: A Political Life in the Reagan Era*. New York: Random House, 1990.

Reagan, Ronald. *An American Life*. New York: Simon and Schuster, 1990.

Rogin, Michael Paul. *Ronald Reagan, the Movie and Other Episodes in Political Demonology*. Berkeley: University of California Press, 1987.

Schaller, Michael. *Reckoning with Reagan: America and Its President in the 1980s*. New York: Oxford University Press, 1992.

Sloan, John W. *The Reagan Effect: Economics and Presiden- tial Leadership*. Lawrence: University Press of Kansas, 1999.

Wills, Garry. *Reagan's America: Innocents at Home*. Garden City, N.Y.: Doubleday, 1987.

Yergin, Daniel, and Joseph Stanislaw. *The Commanding Heights: The Battle for the World Economy*. New York: Si- mon & Schuster, 2002.

WEBSITES

"Commanding Heights: The Battle for the World Economy." PBS. Available online at http://www.pbs.org/wgbh/com- mandingheights/; website home page: http://www.pbs.org/ (accessed May 6, 2003). *This website is intended to ac- company the television series of the same title, based on the book by Daniel Yergin and Joseph Stanislaw.*

"Inaugural Addresses of the Presidents of the United States." Bartleby.com. Available online at http://www.bartleby.com /124/; website home page: http://www.bartleby.com/ (ac- cessed May 6, 2003). *This website contains inaugural ad- dresses in full text for every president since George Washington.*

"Reagan: Actor, Governor, President—The Biography of a Pop- ular but Contradictory Man." The Presidents Series, The American Experience, Public Broadcasting System. Avail- able online at http://www.pbs.org/wgbh/amex/reagan/; web- site home page: http://www.pbs.org/ (accessed May 6, 2003). *This website contains still photos and entire transcript from the PBS series on American Presidents along with brief bib- liographies and a selection of related websites.*

"Ronald Wilson Reagan." Presidents of the United States (PO- TUS), Internet Public Library. Available online at http:// www.ipl.org/div/potus/rwreagan.html; website home page: http://www.ipl.org/ (accessed May 6, 2003). *This website contains a brief biography, links to key documents, and a selection of sound clips from President Reagan's speeches.*

Woolley, John, and Gerhard Peters. "The American Presidency Project." University of California, Santa Barbara. Available online at http://www.presidency.ucsb.edu/index.php (accessed May 6, 2003). *This website contains additional primary sources including presidential election data; presidential portraits; the public papers and speeches of presidents from Herbert Hoover through Gerald Ford, Jimmy Carter, and George H.W. Bush; inaugural addresses and state of the union addresses for presidents from George Washington through George W. Bush; the Fireside Chats of Franklin D. Roosevelt; Saturday radio addresses for presidents from William J. Clinton through George W. Bush; and national political party platforms since 1840.*

AUDIO AND VISUAL MEDIA

The American Experience: Ronald Reagan. Directed by Andrea Kalin and Jacqueline Shearer. VHS, 1998. PBS Home Video.

Restoring Economic Growth and Stability in the Eighties

Report

By: President's Commission for a National Agenda for the Eighties

Date: January 1981

Source: President's Commission for a National Agenda for the Eighties. "Restoring Economic Growth and Stability in the Eighties." Chapter 3 in *A National Agenda for the Eighties.* New York: New American Library, 1981, 24–27, 31–33.

About the Organization: In October 1979, President Jimmy Carter (served 1977–1981) appointed forty-five citizens to the President's Commission for a National Agenda for the Eighties. Chaired by Columbia University president William J. McGill, the group included thirteen women, four African Americans, two Hispanic Americans, four labor union leaders, and representatives from religious, environmental, consumer, and public interest institutions. Many came from backgrounds in banking, large corporations, and small businesses. ■

Introduction

By the end of the 1970s, Americans were increasingly divided as a result of the Vietnam War (1964–1975), the Watergate scandal, and ambitious social policies. The national economy was stagnant in the face of rising prices and growing uncertainty about the future. Creation of the President's Commission for a National Agenda for the Eighties reflected President Carter's concern about how to address Americans' declining faith in a range of institutions. Businesses, government, labor unions, churches, schools, and voluntary associations had cemented the social fabric since World War II (1939–1945). Unlike President Dwight Eisen-

hower's (served 1953–1961) blue-ribbon President's Commission on National Goals (1959–1960), the Carter commission reflected the increasing diversity of individuals and groups within the economy, society, and culture in the wake of the many changes of the 1960s and 1970s.

The earlier commission had consisted of ten white males from the Northeast who agreed on the postwar consensus in American life about economic growth, a moderate liberal ideology, and a two-party democratic system dominated by New Deal Democrats and Modern Republicans. Carter's group came from more varied backgrounds and was a more accurate representation of the American population.

Some members of the Carter commission were better known to the broad American public than others. These included historian Daniel Boorstin, poet Gwendolyn Brooks, director Marian Wright Edelman of the Children's Defense Fund, president Benjamin Hooks of the National Association for the Advancement of Colored People, American Federation of Labor-Congress of Industrial Organizations (AFL-CIO) leader Lane Kirkland, former Secretary of Commerce Juanita Kreps, religion historian Martin Marty, and former Pennsylvania governor William Scranton. Not surprisingly, in the course of their research and deliberations, they would have a much more difficult time, compared to the members of Eisenhower's commission, in reaching consensus among themselves as to the future direction of the country.

Significance

The final report of the President's Commission for a National Agenda for the Eighties appeared in January 1981 after Republican Ronald W. Reagan (served 1981–1989) defeated Democrat Jimmy Carter in the 1980 presidential election. Commission members focused on the nation's economic woes. The issues raised in the report dominated political debate, economic policymaking, and private sector business management decision making throughout the 1980s.

Since 1945, the American economy had experienced dramatic economic growth, low levels of unemployment, and ups and downs in prices that were regular developments of the business cycle. As this report indicated, while many Americans had come to expect such long-term growth as the national norm, in historical terms it was the exception rather than the rule. More women and the postwar baby boom generation entered the workforce to become consumers. Economic slowdown began in the early 1970s, a situation which worsened throughout the decade. By the late 1970s, price inflation had reached annual double-digit figures, while the unemployment rate remained inexplicably high. This problem of "stagflation" baffled economists, stymied policymakers, and challenged political leaders at the White House and in Congress. Recognition of the impact of global trade and the role of the Organization of Petroleum Exporting Countries (OPEC) in sparking rapid increases in oil prices left Americans wondering what the future might bring.

Commission members concluded that there were only two choices: The U.S. could accept slower economic growth, or the nation could promote growth by redirecting capital from consumption and government expenditures. Commissioners argued that only the path of increased growth would make for a better future for all Americans. Lower federal taxes, a possible increase in the number of Americans living in poverty, and growth of the total "American pie" would result in higher productivity, lower rates of inflation and unemployment, and renewal of the postwar mass consumption society that most people took for granted as a permanent feature of American life.

Primary Source

Restoring Economic Growth and Stability in the Eighties [excerpt]

> **SYNOPSIS:** In recommending increased productivity, lower prices, and more jobs as the solution to the economic challenges of the late 1970s, this blue ribbon report hinted that economic policies in the 1980s would place less emphasis on government spending and more on private investors and business firms.

An Agenda for Government, Business, and Labor

From the end of World War II through the 1960s, the United States experienced an unprecedented period of rapid and sustained growth. Rapid growth served in part as a political solvent. As long as everyone could have more, issues involving the reallocation of resources were less divisive. And there were psychological as well as material dividends. Whereas previous generations of Americans had aspirations for success in the future while they made sacrifices in the present, the phenomenon of postwar affluence gave rise to a new set of attitudes. Prosperity was accompanied by a sense that it was no longer necessary to defer certain pleasures, that one could enjoy current consumption and still look forward to an even more affluent future.

American economic performance in the Seventies—in terms of inflation, unemployment, and growth—was substantially worse than in the previous two decades. The 7.1 percent average annual rate of inflation of the Seventies was more than three times the average in the previous two decades, while the average unemployment rate of 6.2 percent was about 1.5 percentage points higher. Similarly, our economic growth was significantly slower than that to which we had become accustomed. GNP increased an average of 3.1 percent annually, down from 4 percent in the previous two decades and from the average of 3.3 percent since 1890. However, because the Fifties and Sixties were periods of unusually high growth, our perceptions of the growth achieved in the Seventies may be unduly pessimistic.

Nevertheless, the Seventies were a decade of shock and disappointment for many Americans. If the Eighties are to be different, our highest economic priorities must be to reduce inflation and unemployment and to restore substantial economic growth—especially in the sense of sustained increases of real output and income per person. In the short run, the policies required to do this will entail social and economic costs. In the long run, however, our ability to achieve a wide range of objectives will be enhanced, making the "hard choices" among these objectives less painful.

We are very sensitive to the problems that intensified economic stringencies pose for those at the lowest levels of the economy. We also understand all too clearly that vague assurances about long-range benefits are insufficient if the long range is so distant as to trap people in poverty and dependence. Nevertheless, we believe that economic growth is necessary if we are successfully to avoid a divisive struggle over the allocation of resources in the long run. That outcome will benefit no one, least of all the poor, the elderly, and the dependent.

Perhaps more important than the actual slowing of growth is that the sources of our growth in the Seventies were different from those in the past. Unusually rapid growth of the labor force was largely responsible for the expansion in total output that took place in the last decade. Productivity increases were much smaller than before, so that output per hour worked and real compensation per hour worked grew more slowly than in the previous two decades.

Nonetheless, three factors enabled us to maintain, on average, nearly the Sixties' rate of growth in real after-tax income and consumption per person: the increased number of women entering the labor force, the arrival of the baby boom generation at working age, and a reduction in our savings rates. But we cannot count on these factors to cushion our economic difficulties in the coming decade. Hence,

The final meeting of the President's Commission for a National Agenda for the Eighties, formed by Jimmy Carter and focusing on the nation's economic woes, dominated political debate, economic policymaking, and private sector business management decision making throughout the 1980s. © **FRANK MCMAHON/CORBIS. REPRODUCED BY PERMISSION.**

if the trend toward slower growth is not reversed, the entire public will feel the consequences in real disposable income. Therefore, the Commission advocates a national commitment to restoring substantial economic growth in the United States. Reattaining such growth may prove difficult—it is by no means inevitable, but it is not beyond our reach.

In our view, the slowdown of the past decade is not the result of a systematic illness. The Seventies saw the U.S. economy buffeted by severe and unforeseen dislocations, notably the stunning rise in the price of petroleum. Immediate adjustment to that change would have entailed sharp disruptions in the lives of many citizens. Policies that kept U.S. energy prices temporarily below world levels had the effect of spreading the process of adjustment over time. One cost of these policies was a temporary reduction in our overall growth rate, a cost that we may not have understood adequately at the time. Ad-

justments to a world of scarce, expensive energy are now under way, reducing this impediment to future growth; of course, a major disruption in the flow of oil from the Middle East would still seriously affect our growth. Moreover, the labor force will increase more slowly in the Eighties, and its average experience level will increase, developments that should facilitate higher productivity growth.

It is important to understand that part of the reason for the slower growth in our Gross National Product (GNP) during the Seventies was an increased desire by many Americans for additional leisure, a cleaner environment, a less pressured job, or other improvements in the quality of their lives. Attitudes and values changed. Conventional economic growth enjoyed a lower relative priority than in the past. Choices and preferences with respect to alternative types of economic and technological growth will continue to evolve in the Eighties.

Just as the rate of growth attainable in the Eighties may not equal that of the Fifties and Sixties, so will the pattern of growth differ. For example, private decisions will respond to the social and economic criteria implicit in higher energy prices and more stringent environmental standards. The result will be less intensive use of natural resources and more conservation. The service sector will absorb a growing share of the labor force, continuing a long-term trend. As a result of technological advances and changing patterns of international competition, growth will probably be most rapid in areas such as information and communications.

To achieve economic stability and growth will require policy initiatives in a number of areas. Inflation must be brought under control without delay, while at the same time we must adopt policies to achieve our long-term objectives of growth in employment and output. A number of these policies would benefit the country as a whole but might impose costs on a part of the population, at least during the transition from old policies to new ones. It is important, for reasons of both equity and political realism, to be aware of the adverse side effects of desirable politics. Protection of "safety nets" for those who may be harmed should be integral parts of policy changes designed to combat inflation and to produce long-term growth in productivity and employment. . . .

The economic outlook for the Eighties is brighter than recent experience would suggest. Some of the factors that retarded growth in the Seventies will probably be less important in the Eighties. Yet there is no room for complacency. Over the long run, the growth of income and consumption per person cannot exceed the growth of productivity. To avoid a sharp slowdown in the growth in income per person in the Eighties, we must restore substantial growth in productivity.

Essentially, there are two alternatives. The first is to accept the slower growth rates that have characterized the past few years. The advantage of this alternative is that it would not require short-run deferrals of consumption in order to expand our productive capacity. The disadvantage is that it would require a substantial readjustment of expectations. Americans could no longer reasonably expect the substantial improvements in the standard of living that were such a prominent feature of the post-World War II decades.

A second alternative—the one we endorse—is to place a higher priority on achieving economic growth. It is important to realize that economic growth, like any other national goal, has a price tag. More rapid economic growth would require more investment of capital in plant and equipment, and that would require deferring other expenditures. But we believe this is the more desirable course.

Economic growth is important because it is the best means of attaining many other objectives. Growth is desirable to the extent that it improves the quality of life for Americans when the noneconomic side effects of growth are properly taken into account. Appropriate environmental, health, safety, and land-use policies can succeed in directing growth in a manner that minimizes the negative side effects that have accompanied some economic activities in the past.

Only a sustained increase in real output will enable the United States to achieve a broad range of national and international goals—from a general rise in the standard of living to improved social benefits for the needy; from retraining and providing jobs for the unemployed to improving the nation's competitiveness in exports and enhancing its leadership role in the world community. . . .

Even goals not customarily associated with economic growth, such as increased longevity, an improved environment, and increased safety, are more easily afforded in an expanding rather than a stagnating economy. Economic growth would ease the difficulties that individuals and communities will face in making adjustments to economic and technological change. It would, finally, enhance the prospects for recreating the national consensus that is so sorely needed.

No matter how successful we are in restoring economic growth, there will be a gap between expectations and reality, perhaps especially for the baby boom generation whose expectations were formed in the Fifties and Sixties, a gap which could well result in significant social and political problems. We will therefore need to develop strategies to respond to this gap and to prepare the public for the new resource and entitlement realities of the Eighties. How painful a process this will be depends largely on the degree to which we are able to achieve substantial economic growth.

Restoring growth will, as noted, entail costs and some difficult short-term trade-offs. Both technological innovation and capital investment require real resources, and if they are to claim an increased share of GNP, other things—personal consumption and government expenditures—must receive a declining share. Moreover, the private sector will make most of the decisions to adopt new technologies and to expand investment. It will do so only if government restores a stable, growth-producing economic environment. Public policies to restore growth must, therefore, affect government tax revenues and/or expenditures. For example, tax reductions to induce savings and investment would, in the short run at least, diminish the amount of revenue available for the expansion of government programs. Higher direct subsidies or tax incentives for research and development would have a similar effect. Thus, without new revenue sources that do not themselves discourage growth, government expenditures will have to grow less rapidly than we have become accustomed to since the mid-Sixties. Calls for substantial real increases in specific components of federal expenditures—defense, energy, entitlement programs, or anything else—cannot all be accommodated simultaneously if growth is to be restored.

One source of objections to the policy changes that are necessary to restore economic growth is a fear that they will be undertaken at the expense of the needy. We are well aware of the potential asymmetries of economic growth, but it need not follow that the poor will be selectively harmed. The lot of the disadvantaged can be improved both by policies directed at stimulating the growth of the economy and by programs that directly transfer income or services to them. Both kinds of policies have an important role. . . .

An expanding economy will ameliorate and reverse this effect in two ways. Increased job opportunities will raise the income of the poor and reduce the number who need government assistance, thereby permitting more generous assistance to those remaining in poverty. Moreover, growth creates a larger "pie" from which transfers can be made, allowing for further expansion of transfer programs in the future. And, of course, even in the short run, transfer programs need not be the only—or even a primary—source of funds for promoting growth. Choosing an appropriate mix of policies—to assist the needy, to invigorate the economy, and to pursue many other objectives while fairly distributing necessary sacrifices—will be a principal item on our agenda during the Eighties.

Further Resources

BOOKS

Biven, W. Carl. *Jimmy Carter's Economy: Policy in an Age of Limits.* Chapel Hill: University of North Carolina Press, 2002.

Campagna, Anthony S. *Economic Policy in the Carter Administration.* Westport, Conn.: Greenwood, 1995.

Denison, Edward Fulton. *Trends in American Economic Growth, 1929–1982.* Washington D.C.: Brookings Institution, 1982.

Feldstein, Martin, ed. *The American Economy in Transition.* Chicago: University of Chicago Press, 1980.

Hargrove, Erwin C. *Jimmy Carter as President: Leadership and the Politics of Public Good.* Baton Rouge: Louisiana State University Press, 1988.

Kaufman, Burton I. *The Presidency of James Earl Carter, Jr.* Lawrence: University Press of Kansas, 1993.

Piore, Michael J., and Charles F. Sabel. *The Second Industrial Divide: Possibilities for Posterity.* New York: Basic Books, 1984.

Sloan, John W. *The Reagan Effect: Economics and Presidential Leadership.* Lawrence: University Press of Kansas, 1999.

Yergin, Daniel, and Joseph Stanislaw. *The Commanding Heights: The Battle for the World Economy.* New York: Simon & Schuster, 2002.

Zieger, Robert H. "The Quest for National Goals." In *The Carter Presidency: Policy Choices in the Post-New Deal Era.* Gary M. Fink and Hugh Davis Graham, eds. Lawrence: University Press of Kansas, 1998.

WEBSITES

"Carter: The Crises of Confidence." Program in Presidential Rhetoric, Department of Communication, Texas A & M University. Available online at http://www.tamu.edu/scom/pres/speeches/jccrisis; website home page: http://www.tamu.edu/comm/ (accessed May 7, 2003). *This website presents the text of the speech given by President Jimmy Carter on July 15, 1979.*

"Commanding Heights: The Battle for the World Economy." PBS. Available online at http://www.pbs.org/wgbh/commandingheights/; website home page: http://www.pbs.org/ (accessed May 6, 2003). *This website is intended to accompany the television series of the same title, based on the book by Daniel Yergin and Joseph Stanislaw.*

Council of Economic Advisors. Available online at http://www.whitehouse.gov/cea/; website home page: http://www.whitehouse.gov/cea/ (accessed May 7, 2003). *Established by the Employment Act of 1946, the CEA works with the President and the Cabinet to draft the annual Economic Report of the President. The Report is submitted to the Congress, which uses it to draft legislation for the annual federal budget and appropriation legislation.*

"Jimmy Carter." The President's Series, The American Experience, Public Broadcasting System. Available online at http://www.pbs.org/wgbh/amex/carter/; website home page: http://www.pbs.org/ (accessed May 7, 2003).

Jimmy Carter Library and Museum. Available online at http://carterlibrary.galileo.peachnet.edu/ (accessed May 7, 2003). *This website of the Carter Presidential Library includes many primary sources from the Carter administration along with photographs and links to related websites.*

Joint Economic Committee Homepage. Available online at http://jec.senate.gov/ (accessed May 7, 2003). *Established by the Employment Act of 1946, the congressional JEC works with the President and the Cabinet to draft legislation for the annual federal budget and appropriation legislation.*

Woolley, John, and Gerhard Peters. "The American Presidency Project." University of California, Santa Barbara. Available online at http://www.presidency.ucsb.edu/index.php (accessed May 6, 2003). *This website contains additional primary sources including presidential election data; presidential portraits; the public papers and speeches of presidents from Herbert Hoover through Gerald Ford, Jimmy Carter, and George H.W. Bush; inaugural addresses and state of the union addresses for presidents from George Washington through George W. Bush; the Fireside Chats of Franklin D. Roosevelt; Saturday radio addresses for presidents from William J. Clinton through George W. Bush; and national political party platforms since 1840.*

"How to Wreck the Economy"

Journal article

By: Lester C. Thurow

Date: May 14, 1981

Source: Thurow, Lester C. "How to Wreck the Economy." *New York Review of Books,* May 14, 1981, 3–4.

About the Author: Lester C. Thurow (1938–) was born in Livingston, Montana. Former Dean of the Sloan School of Management at the Massachusetts Institute of Technology, Thurow became an important public commentator in the wake of the publication of two books, *The Zero Sum Society: Distribution and the Possibilities for Economic Change* (1980) and *The Zero Sum Solution: Building a World-Class American Economy* (1985). During the 1980s, he became increasingly critical of the Reagan economic policies as being too politically driven. He argued that economic policies needed to focus on increasing productivity, replacing consumption with productive investments, and rebuilding the necessary public infrastructure to support private sector growth. ∎

Introduction

In this May 1981 essay, Lester Thurow, a professor of economics and management at the Massachusetts Institute of Technology, analyzes the proposed federal budget of the new administration of Ronald Reagan (served 1981–1989). While many Americans rarely paid close attention to such complex policy documents, Thurow carefully read and thought about the Reagan economic strategy for its first two years. He concluded that increasing national defense spending to three times its Vietnam era size would divert resources away from civilian production and fail to address the issue of how to increase civilian productivity. Tax cuts for individuals would lead to more consumption rather than the savings needed to invest in building a strong economy for the future. Speed-

ing up the rate at which businesses could take tax breaks for aging equipment (accelerated depreciation) would encourage unproductive investments such as shopping malls rather than state-of-the-art industrial plants.

Trained as a professional academic economist, Thurow also noted that the human impact of the proposed Reagan tax cuts would be most heavily borne by Americans living just above the official poverty line. In sum, this mainstream economist rejected the assumptions and effects of the new economic policy based on "supply-side" economics held by many of the key advisers in the early Reagan administration. He argued that investment in private sector plants, productive resources, and more jobs were needed. The Reagan policies of increased defense spending, speculative investment, and enriching the wealthy (thereby creating a "trickle-down" effect that would benefit the rest of society) were based on a flawed economic theory of "supply-side" economics.

Significance

In the wake of slowed economic growth, rising unemployment, and increased prices since the early 1970's, many Americans were ready to try new economic policies in the 1980s. Combining the traditional support of Main Street businesses for tax cuts, the ideas of advocates of "supply-side" economics, and the interest-group power of corporations, the proposed Reagan budgets for 1981 and 1982 received much positive press when first offered. Yet when trained economists such as Lester Thurow looked at the details of these budgets, they found much to criticize. While agreeing that increased productivity was the key to renewed growth in the 1980's, supporters and critics of the Reagan proposals differed in their economic, political, and social assumptions of how to achieve growth. Thurow and other critics saw weaknesses in the ideas behind "supply-side" economics, argued for the central importance of investment in the right kinds of economic activities, and remained concerned about the possible negative social costs of these policies on Americans from the middle class on down the social structure.

Later events proved the critics largely correct. Economic productivity did increase faster in the 1980s compared to the late 1970s, but not as fast as in the postwar period of 1945 to 1973. Investment went up, but into more speculative ventures rather than into the creation of new plants, products, and jobs. Consumption soared past the national savings rate, which led to Americans buying more goods from trading partners such as Canada and Japan than to selling U.S. goods overseas. This in turn meant that the balance of trade between America and her trading partners dramatically rose at a period when America needed to save more at home and sell more goods and services abroad.

Primary Source

"How to Wreck the Economy" [excerpt]

SYNOPSIS: In the essay below, MIT economist Lester Thurow analyzes the budget proposals for 1981 and 1982. Early in the Reagan years, he criticizes the assumptions and effects of "supply-side" economics held by advocates of the new economic policy.

The recent discussion of President Reagan's budget has largely overlooked its most alarming feature, so far as the U.S. economy is concerned. Reagan is proposing to increase defense expenditures by $142 billion, from $162 billion for the fiscal year 1981 in the current budget to $304 billion in fiscal year 1985, the last budget of his first term. If reelected he is planning a further $39 billion increase, to $343 billion in fiscal 1986.

This $181 billion increase over five years can be understood only if it is compared with the build-up of military spending during the Vietnam War. In the five years between 1965 and 1970 military spending rose by $24.2 billion, and soon after rose to a peak of $26.9 billion. After correcting for inflation, a $26.9 billion increase then would be equivalent to a $59 billion increase now.

As a result the military build-up that is currently being contemplated is three times as large as the one that took place during the Vietnam War. Whether an increase of this magnitude is really necessary depends on an analysis of foreign affairs and military readiness that is beyond this review. Some defense experts and legislators are questioning whether many items in the new military budget are actually needed and whether some of them endanger national security more than they protect it. Such questions are certainly important and must be raised. But if such a build-up is necessary, then it is important that it be done in such a way that it does the least possible damage to the economy.

The Reagan budget has not been clearly understood because, perhaps deliberately, it has been presented as a set of subtractions from or additions to the Carter budget. The policies of President Carter are now irrelevant. It makes no difference what he proposed. Everything that is in the budget is now a Reagan proposal. The only questions to be resolved turn on what President Reagan wants.

In addition to the increase in the military budget, civilian expenditures are scheduled to rise by $76 billion—from $493 billion to $569 billion. After correcting for inflation, we can see that civilian expenditures are down substantially by 16 percent, although they rise in money terms. As a result the total budget increases from $655 billion in fiscal 1981 to $912 billion in fiscal 1986. In addition, President Reagan is proposing a 16 percent reduction in federal tax collections—$196 billion in fiscal 1986—in order to stimulate savings and investment. . . .

President Reagan wants both dramatic tax cuts to encourage investment and an even more extensive military build-up. But he cannot have both without wrecking the economy further unless he is willing to raise taxes dramatically on private consumption. He has chosen not to do so. If his current program is carried out, he too will wreck the economy.

Military spending is a form of consumption. It does not increase our ability to produce more goods and services in the future. While it may be necessary, it is consumption nonetheless. And as in any private budget, if you allocate more to one form of consumption, you must allocate less to some other form of consumption.

This means equivalent cuts must be made in other forms of consumption. The proposed military increase is so large that it cannot be fully paid for with cuts in civilian expenditures unless the president is willing to abolish major social programs such as Social Security. If he is not willing to do this, taxes must be raised to cut private consumption.

While President Reagan is only preparing for war and not actively engaging in one, the economic problems of military spending spring from the rapid production of weapons, not from their use. The capacity to produce capital goods and equipment, skilled manpower, and raw materials must all be quickly redirected to military production. In shifting both human and capital resources from civilian to military activities tremendous strains are placed on the domestic economy, unless measures are taken to restrain private consumption. Without tax increases the military can get only the necessary capital capacity, skilled manpower, and raw materials by paying more than the civilian economy is willing to pay. This drives up prices and creates civilian shortages.

The problem is compounded if tax breaks are to be given for investment, as is contemplated by Reagan's economic plan. The capital goods industries cannot produce enough equipment to build both military factories and civilian factories. The investment tax reductions therefore encourage private investors to get into a bidding war with the military for the industrial equipment that is available. The result would be a rapid rate of inflation in capital goods that would eventually lead to inflation in consumer goods. Inflation would break out, as it did during the Vietnam War, but this time the U.S. would be adding inflation to an economic system that already has an 11 percent rate of inflation rather than to a system that had an inflation rate of less than 2 percent. . . .

Our slowdown in productivity is caused by many factors, including an increasing movement toward services, and sharp declines in construction and mining productivity. These are not going to end suddenly. And the same slow transition will occur in the part of the economy on which the Reagan administration is focusing most of its attention—investment. New investment takes time. Major new industrial facilities typically take from five to ten years to complete, so we will have no output from them for five to ten years. Consequently they will not be raising productivity for five to ten years.

If a little extra investment would cure our productivity problem we would not have such a problem at all. When productivity was growing at more than 3 percent per year, from 1948 to 1965, Americans invested 9.5 percent of their GNP in industrial plant and equipment. While productivity was falling 0.5 percent a year from 1977 to 1980, Americans invested 11.3 percent of their GNP in industrial plant and equipment. We need more investment, but investment cannot cure the productivity problem in the short run. . . .

These economic difficulties will also be magnified by the plans for the civilian budget. A 16 percent cut in taxes is supposed to stimulate savings and investment but it is directed at the wrong targets. Any across-the-board tax cut such as Kemp-Roth must confront the fact that the average American family saved only 5.6 percent of its income in 1980. Past experience strongly suggests that given a $100 tax cut, the average American will save and invest $5.60, but will also consume $94.40. In view of our needs for investment and of the military program the administration demands, we simply cannot afford to add private consumption of this magnitude to our economic system. We should be cutting consumption.

Similarly, many of the investment tax cuts proposed by Reagan are poorly conceived. A cut in the capital gains tax that includes both investment in plant and equipment and speculative investment— in land, homes, gold, antiques, paintings, etc—may suck investment funds out of productive investments and into speculative investments, since speculative investments pay off faster than productive investments. But we need productive investments not

MIT economist Lester Thurow evaluates Ronald Reagan's 1982 budget proposals. © BETTMANN/CORBIS. REPRODUCED BY PERMISSION.

speculative investments. If supply-side economics were to make sense, it would include tax increases for speculative investments.

The current proposal for accelerated depreciation on a "10–5–3" basis gives the largest breaks to commercial buildings and may well encourage the construction of more shopping centers rather than industrial factories. Here again the largest tax breaks should favor new industrial facilities.

The administration's cuts in the civilian budget have relatively little to do with economics. They are good or bad depending upon your view of what constitutes adequate provision for the needy in a good society. My ethics tell me that there is something wrong with cutting nutrition programs for poor pregnant women. Mr. Stockman's ethics tell him that they are precisely the group whose benefits should be cut. Perhaps that is the difference between learning ones' ethics and economics in a department of economics rather than at a divinity school.

There is, however, one major economic problem with the proposed cuts in expenditures. Most of the cuts focus on the working poor—essentially the group that is above the poverty line but within

$3,000 of it. This group is going to be faced with a choice. The Reagan administration assumes that a cut in the social welfare benefits for the working poor will force them to work more. It is more likely that it will encourage them to work less to regain eligibility for the programs that they have just lost.

Further Resources

BOOKS

Bowles, Samuel, David M. Gordon, and Thomas E. Weiskopf. *After the Waste Land: A Democratic Economics for the Year 2000.* Armonk, N.Y.: M.E. Sharpe, 1990.

Campagna, Anthony S. *The Economy in the Reagan Years: The Economic Consequences of the Reagan Administrations.* Westport, Conn.: Greenwood, 1994.

Executive Office of the President and Office of Management and Budget. *America's New Beginning: A Program for Economic Recovery Budget.* Washington, D.C.: White House, Office of the Press Secretary, 1981.

Friedman, Benjamin M. *Day of Reckoning: The Consequences of American Economic Policy Under Reagan and After.* New York: Random House, 1988.

Krugman, Paul K. *Peddling Prosperity: Economic Sense and Nonsense in the Age of Diminished Expectations.* New York: Norton, 1994.

Lekachman, Robert F. *Greed Is Not Enough: Reaganomics.* New York: Pantheon Books, 1982.

————. *Visions and Nightmares: America After Reagan.* New York: Macmillan, 1987.

McQuaid, Kim. *Big Business and Presidential Power: From FDR to Reagan.* New York: Morrow, 1982.

Thurow, Lester C. *Dangerous Currents: The State of Economics.* New York: Random House, 1983.

————. *The Zero Sum Society: Distribution and the Possibilities for Economic Change.* New York: Basic Books, 1980.

————. *The Zero Sum Solution: Building a World-Class Economy.* New York: Simon & Schuster, 1985.

PERIODICALS

Thurow, Lester C. "Death by a Thousands Cuts." *New York Review of Books,* December 17, 1981, 3–4.

————. "How to Rescue a Drowning Economy." *New York Review of Books,* April 1, 1982, 3–4.

————. "Sentimental Education." *New York Review of Books,* October 7, 1982, 6–8.

WEBSITES

Brookings Institution. http://www.brookings.org/ (accessed May 6, 2003). *This website has policy research on a variety of topics from a centrist perspective from one of the earliest American think tanks founded in the early twentieth century.*

Center on Budget and Policy Priorities. http://www.cbpp.org/ (accessed May 6, 2003). *This website includes data, analysis, and policy recommendations by policy analysts from a centrist to liberal perspective.*

Economic Policy Institute. http://www.epinet.org/ (accessed May 6, 2003). *This website includes alternative perspectives on economic policy from a social democratic perspective.*

Professor Lester Thurow Web Site. http://www.lthurow.com/ (accessed May 6, 2003). *This website includes biographical information, articles, speaking engagements, and other information by the professor of economics and management at the Massachusetts Institute of Technology in Cambridge, Massachusetts.*

Memorandum About Federal Employment of Discharged Air Traffic Controllers

Memo

By: Ronald W. Reagan

Date: December 9, 1981

Source: Reagan, Ronald W. Memorandum About Federal Employment of Discharged Air Traffic Controllers. Ronald Reagan Presidential Library. Available online at http://www.reagan.utexas.edu/resource/speeches/1981/120981b.htm; website home page: http://www.reagan.utexas.edu/ (accessed May 6, 2003).

About the Author: Ronald Reagan (1911–), born in Tampico, Illinois, built his political appeal on criticizing government spending, arguing that federal programs led to high taxes and slow growth. He served as California governor from 1966 to 1974, losing bids for the Republican presidential nomination in 1968 and 1976. In 1980, Republican nominee Reagan defeated Democrat Jimmy Carter (served 1977–1981) for the presidency. He was elected to a second term in 1984. In 1994 he retired from public life, revealing that he had been diagnosed as having Alzheimer's Disease. ■

Introduction

On August 3, 1981, nearly all 13,000 air traffic controllers working for the Federal Aviation Administration (FAA) at the nation's airports went on strike, despite the fact that as federal employees they were not legally permitted to do so. Most print and broadcast media focused on demands of the Professional Air Traffic Controllers Organization (PATCO) for wage increases of $10,000 (to salaries already well above the national average), a thirty-two hour work week, and a better retirement plan. Yet the strike arose from longtime conflicts between the FAA and controllers over such issues as long hours, constant high levels of stress on the job, and poor labor-management relations. The real issue was who controlled the workplace in the high-volume, fast-paced, overworked control towers which directed traffic in American airways.

Within twenty-four hours of the start of the strike, President Ronald Reagan (served 1981–1989) issued an ultimatum demanding that the controllers return to their jobs within forty-eight hours. When the deadline expired, he fired the 11,350 controllers, about seventy percent of the controller labor force, who had not returned to work. He also banned rehiring any of the striking controllers for lifetime from working for the FAA. This December 1981 memorandum announced at a public press conference represented the formal notice of Reagan's decision and marked the start of a very bleak decade for American workers and organized labor unions. In point of fact, labor relations between the FAA and PATCO had been deteriorating for more than a decade as a result of harsh FAA leadership, lack of sufficient controllers to handle increasing airplane traffic in the nation's skies, and old equipment that made an already stressful job more difficult. Controllers had to bring a high level of education, dedication, and focus to the job that, due to a high rate of "burnout," usually lasted only into the controllers' early thirties. Many FAA managers and controllers came from a military background that led to a tightly regulated workplace that left controllers working long hours, using obsolete technology, and facing little time with their families. Little of the social environment of this very specialized job was discussed in extensive press coverage of the 1981 strike.

Significance

At the start of the 1981 PATCO strike, many Americans took little notice of the harsh conditions, long hours, and short career spans of air traffic controllers. FAA managers at airports emphasized the need for passenger safety, efficient business operations, and high rates of productivity judged by numbers of planes landing and taking off from airports. While PATCO officials originally issued ninety-seven demands, president Robert Poli soon fixed on higher pay, better retirement benefits, and a shorter work week. Once President Reagan demanded that controllers return to work or risk losing their jobs, the 1,650 returning strikers, managers, and military people took over operation of the air control system through the United States by working forty-eight hours per week during six-day weeks for months. Ironically, most of the issues that were at the heart of the strike continued to plague the new workforce. Addition of newer technology led to replacement of many human controllers by machines. Over the rest of the decade, government officials and private employers led a major campaign that weakened labor-management relations in many industries. Union membership in affiliates of the American Federation of Labor-Congress of Industrial Organizations (AFL-CIO) continued to decline from the postwar high of the mid-1950s. Many employers took the vigorous anti-union stance of the Reagan administration as a message that they could take strong stands in union negotiations, hire

In 1981, during the Professional Air Traffic Controller Strike, 11,350 controllers, or seventy percent of the workforce, who did not return to their jobs within forty-eight hours, were fired and banned from being rehired during their lifetimes. AP/WIDE WORLD PHOTOS. REPRODUCED BY PERMISSION.

labor spies, and break unions. Labor historians noted that the PATCO strike set the precedent for a worsening of relations between American workers and their employers which haunted the national economy throughout the Reagan years.

Primary Source

Memorandum About Federal Employment of Discharged Air Traffic Controllers

> **SYNOPSIS:** In December 1981, President Ronald Reagan issued a public memo calling for a ban on the hiring of striking air traffic controllers by the Federal Aviation Administration at the nation's airports.

December 9, 1981

Memorandum for the Director of the Office of Personnel Management
Subject: Federal Employment of Discharged Air Traffic Controllers

The Office of Personnel Management has established the position that the former air traffic controllers who were discharged for participating in a strike against the Government initiated on August 3, 1981 shall be debarred from federal employment for a period of three years. Upon deliberation I have concluded that such individuals, despite their strike participation, should be permitted to apply for federal employment outside the scope of their former employing agency.

Therefore, pursuant to my authority to regulate federal employment, I have determined that the Office of Personnel Management should permit federal agencies to receive applications for employment from these individuals and process them according to established civil service procedures. Your office should perform suitability determinations with respect to all such applicants according to established standards and procedures under 5 CFR, Part 731.

After reviewing reports from the Secretary of Transportation and the Administrator of the Federal Aviation Administration, I have further determined that it would be detrimental to the efficiency of operations at the Federal Aviation Administration and to the safe and effective performance of our national air traffic control system to permit the discharged air traffic controllers to return to employment with that agency. Therefore, these former federal employees should not be deemed suitable for employment with the Federal Aviation Administration.

I direct you to process their applications for reemployment with the federal government accordingly.

Ronald Reagan

Further Resources

BOOKS

Aronowitz, Stanley. *Working Class Hero: A New Strategy for Labor.* New York: Adama Books, 1983.

Brody, David. *Workers in Industrial America: Essays on the Twentieth-Century Struggle.* New York: Oxford University Press, 1993.

Bluestone, Barry, and Bennett Harrison. *The Deindustrialization of America: Plant Closings, Community Abandonment, and the Dismantling of Basic Industry.* New York: Basic Books, 1982.

Lichtenstein, Nelson. *State of the Union: A Century of American Labor.* Princeton, N.J.: Princeton University Press, 2002.

Moody, Kim. *An Injury to All: The Decline of American Unionism.* London and New York: Verso, 1988.

Piore, Michael J., and Charles F. Sabel. *The Second Industrial Divide: Possibilities for Prosperity.* New York: Basic Books, 1984.

Shostak, Arthur B., and David Skocik. *The Air Controllers' Controversy: Lessons from the PATCO Strike.* New York: Human Sciences Press, 1986.

Zieger, Robert H., and Gilbert J. Gall. *American Workers, American Unions,* 3rd ed. Baltimore, Md.: Johns Hopkins University Press, 2002.

PERIODICALS

Moberg, David. "The Consequences of the Air Traffic Controllers' Strike, 20 Years Later." *The Progressive Media Project,* July 21, 2001. Available online at http://www.progressive.org/pmp0701/pmpmj2601.html; website home page: http://www.progressive.org (accessed May 6, 2003).

——. "Terminal Flight: The Air Traffic Controllers' Strike of 1981." *Journal of American Studies* 18, August 1984, 165–183.

Pells, Virginia. "The Pressures of PATCO: Strikes and Stress in the 1980s." *Essays in History* 37, 1995. Available online at http://etext.lib.Virginia.edu/journals/EH/EH37/Pels.html; website home page: http://etext.virginia.edu/journals/EH/ (accessed May 6, 2003).

WEBSITES

AFL–CIO: America's Union Movement. Available online at http://www.aflcio.org/ (accessed May 6, 2003). *This website of the American Federation of Labor–Congress of Industrial Organizations includes information about the labor force, union organizing, and institutional work of the largest umbrella group for craft and industrial unions in the United States.*

"The Air Traffic Controllers' Strike." The Eighties Club. Available online at http://eightiesclub.tripod.com/id241.htm; website home page: http://eightiesclub.tripod.com/ (accessed March 2, 2003).

Labor and Working-Class History Association. http://www.lawcha.org/ (accessed May 6, 2003).

"Labor History on the Internet." Department of History, Tennessee Technological University. Available online at http://www.tntech.edu/history/labor.html; website home page: http://www.tntech.edu/history (accessed May 6, 2003). *This site contains links to many information sources about American labor history including professional groups, libraries and archives, specialized sites, and current labor issues.*

McCartin, Joseph A. "Marking a Tragic Anniversary" History News Service. Available online at http://www2.h-net.msu.edu/~hns/articles/2001/080301a.html; website home page: http://www2.h-net.msu.edu/ (accessed May 6, 2003).

The Professional Air Traffic Controllers Organization. Available online at http://www.patco81.com/ (accessed May 6, 2003). *This website is the official site of the PATCO labor union, and an affiliate of the American Federation of State, County, and Municipal Employes union. It includes information about current strikes, organizing activities, and links to a range of sites dealing with labor issues.*

"The Education of David Stockman"

Journal article

By: William Greider

Date: December 1981

Source: Greider, William. "The Education of David Stockman." *The Atlantic Monthly* 248, December 1981, 27–50.

About the Author: William Greider (1939–), a newspaper, magazine, and television reporter, gained access to the inside discussions of Reagan administration economic policymakers through a series of interviews in 1981 with David Stockman, director of the Office of Management and Budget. Among his numerous books on politics and economics are *Who Will Tell the People: The Betrayal of American Democracy* (1992); *One World, Ready or Not: The Manic Logic of Global Capitalism* (1997), and *Fortress America: The American Military and the Consequences of Peace* (1999). ∎

Introduction

When Ronald Reagan (served 1981–1989) assumed the presidency in January 1981, he promised the American people a new direction in federal economic policy. Combining the concerns of a minority of academic economists advocating "supply-side" economic policies, the traditional interests in tax cuts of Main Street business leaders, and the interest-group power of corporate managers represented in the Business Roundtable, the Reagan economic policies emerged from the complicated politics of the budget-making process. When he first took over as the director of the Office of Management and Budget (created in 1921), David Stockman hoped to implement a conservative vision of economic growth and prosperity. During the turbulent 1960s, Stockman had worked as a New Left political activist in the Students for a Democratic Society (SDS) organization, the main New Left institution of the early and mid-1960s. Over time, Stockman's political and economic views became more conservative.

Once he joined the Reagan revolution, Stockman hoped to build on his conservative Midwestern roots to restrain federal spending that went toward the building of what he considered wasteful, interest-group bureaucracies in Washington, D.C. He saw the Reagan administration as an opportunity to fight to control an overblown federal government machinery. Yet during his first year as budget director, Stockman learned that politics and power trumped ideology and vision. While Reagan officials presented the American public with a vision of economic growth, balanced federal budgets, and deep tax cuts, the reality of the policy process was the desire of conservative politicians in Congress to help their interest group constituencies and supporters by adding more dollars and programs to the annual federal budget.

Significance

Ronald Reagan and his supporters came to Washington, D.C., with plans to cut back on the size of the federal government, free up investment capital in the private sector, and increase economic growth. Some of the Reagan team were true believers in the secular religion of "supply-side" economics. They wanted to promote rising supplies of goods and services from the private sector rather than increasing demand from consumers through government spending or installment debt. Others were practical business leaders hoping to gain tax cuts to invest as they saw fit. Still others represented powerful corporations who had learned the value of establishing connections with political leaders in the federal government. Budget director David Stockman was one of the true believers who had shifted from New Left activism in the 1960s to conservative economic policies by the 1980s.

In the course of his first year as head of the Office of Management and Budget, Stockman reluctantly learned the hard realities of political life in Washington, D.C. While engaged in the budget process, he found that members of both houses of Congress as well as lobbyists representing various business interests were not interested in participating in any kind of conservative revolution in economic policy. They wanted results in the form of hard cash to invest. This selection from an article by journalist William Greider based on interviews with Stockman traces the growing disillusionment of Stockman during the negotiations over the 1981 federal budget.

Primary Source

"The Education of David Stockman" [excerpt]

> **SYNOPSIS:** Reagan budget director David Stockman describes political wrangling over the 1981 budget, especially the multi-year tax cuts that led to dramatic increases in annual deficits and total federal debt.

While ideology would guide Stockman in his new job, he would be confronted with a large and tangible political problem: how to resolve the three-sided dilemma created by Ronald Reagan's contradictory campaign promises. In private, Stockman agreed that his former congressional mentor, John Anderson, running as an independent candidate for President in 1980, had asked the right question: How is it possible to raise defense spending, cut income taxes, and balance the budget, all at the same time? Anderson had taunted Reagan with that question, again and again, and most conventional political

During a Cabinet meeting, Ronald Reagan passes his jelly bean jar to Budget Director David Stockman. © BETTMANN/CORBIS. REPRODUCED BY PERMISSION.

thinkers, from orthodox Republican to Keynesian liberal, agreed with Anderson that it could not be done.

But Stockman was confident, even cocky, that he and some of his fellow conservatives had the answer. It was a theory of economics—the supply-side theory—that promised an end to the twin aggravations of the 1970's: high inflation and stagnant growth in America's productivity. "We've got to figure out a way to make John Anderson's question fit into a plausible policy path over the next three years," Stockman said. "Actually, it isn't all that hard to do."

The supply-side approach, which Stockman had only lately embraced, assumed first of all, that dramatic action by the new President, especially the commitment to a three-year reduction of the income tax, coupled with tight monetary control, would signal investors that a new era was dawning, that the growth of government would be displaced by the robust growth of the private sector. If economic behavior in a climate of high inflation is primarily based on expectations about the future value of money, then swift and dramatic action by the President could reverse the gloomy assumptions in the disordered financial markets. As inflation abated, interest rates

dropped, and productive employment grew, those marketplace developments would, in turn, help Stockman balance the federal budget.

"The whole thing is premised on faith," Stockman explained. "On a belief about how the world works." As he prepared the script in his mind, his natural optimism led to bullish forecasts, which were even more robust than the Reagan Administration's public promises. "The inflation premium melts away like the morning mist," Stockman predicted. "It could be cut in half in a very short period of time if the policy is credible. That sets off adjustments and changes in perception that cascade through the economy. You have a bull market in '81, after April, of historic proportions." . . .

In early January, Stockman and his staff were assembling dozens of position papers on program reductions and studying the internal forecasts for the federal budget and the national economy. The initial figures were frightening—"absolutely shocking," he confided—yet he seemed oddly exhilarated by the bad news, and was bubbling with new plans for coping with these horrendous numbers. An OMB computer, programmed as a model of the nation's economic behavior, was instructed to estimate the impact of Reagan's program on the federal budget. It predicted that if the new President went ahead with his promised three-year tax reduction and his increase in defense spending, the Reagan Administration would be faced with a series of federal deficits without precedent in peacetime—ranging from $82 billion in 1982 to $116 billion in 1984. Even Stockman blinked. If those were the numbers included in President Reagan's first budget message, the following month, the financial markets that Stockman sought to reassure would instead be panicked. Interest rates, already high, would go higher; the expectation of long-term inflation would be confirmed.

Stockman saw opportunity in these shocking projections. "All the conventional estimates just wind up as mud," he said. "As absurdities. What they basically say, to boil it down, is that the world doesn't work."

. . . The budget politics of 1981, which produced such clear and dramatic rhetoric from both sides, was, in fact, based upon a bewildering set of numbers that confused even those, like Stockman, who produced them.

"None of us really understands what's going on with all these numbers," Stockman confessed at one point. "You've got so many different budgets out and so many different baselines and such complexity now in the interactive parts of the budget between policy action and the economic environment and all the internal mysteries of the budget, and there are a lot of them. People are getting from A to B and it's not clear how they are getting there. It's not clear how we got there and it's not clear how Jones is going to get there." . . .

Reagan's policy-makers knew that their plan was wrong, or at least inadequate to its promised effects, but the President went ahead and conveyed the opposite impression to the American public. With the cool sincerity of an experienced television actor, Reagan appeared on network TV to rally the nation in support of the Gramm-Latta resolution, promising a new era of fiscal control and balanced budgets, when Stockman knew they still had not found the solution. This practice of offering the public eloquent reassurances despite privately held doubts was not new, of course. Every contemporary President—starting with Lyndon Johnson, in his attempt to cover up the true cost of the war in Vietnam—had been caught, sooner or later, in contradictions between promises and economic realities. The legacy was a deep popular skepticism about anything a President promised

about the economy. Barely four months in office, Ronald Reagan was already adding to the legacy.

Stockman himself had been a late convert to supply-side theology, and now he was beginning to leave the church. The theory of "expectations" wasn't working. He could see that. And Stockman's institutional role as budget director forced him to look constantly at aspects of the political economy that the other supply-siders tended to dismiss. Whatever the reason, Stockman was creating some distance between himself and the supply-side purists; eventually, he would become the target of their nasty barbs. For his part, Stockman began to disparage the grand theory as a kind of convenient illusion— new rhetoric to cover old Republican doctrine. . . .

"The hard part of the supply-side tax cut is dropping the top rate from 70 to 50 percent—the rest of it is a secondary matter," Stockman explained. "The original argument was that the top bracket was too high, and that's having the most devastating effect on the economy. Then, the general argument was that, in order to make this palatable as a political matter, you had to bring down all the brackets. But, I mean, Kemp-Roth was always a Trojan horse to bring down the top rate."

A Trojan horse? This seemed a cynical concession for Stockman to make in private conversation while the Reagan Administration was still selling the supply-side doctrine to Congress. Yet he was conceding what the liberal Keynesian critics had argued from the outset–the supply-side theory was not a new economic theory at all but only new language and argument to conceal a hoary old Republican doctrine: give the tax cuts to the top brackets, the wealthiest individuals and largest enterprises, and let the good effects "trickle down" through the economy to reach everyone else. Yes, Stockman conceded, when one stripped away the new rhetoric emphasizing across-the-board cuts, the supply-side theory was really new clothes for the unpopular doctrine of the old Republican orthodoxy. "It's kind of hard to sell 'trickle down,'" he explained, "so the supply-side formula was the only way to get a tax policy that was really 'trickle down.' Supply-side is 'trickle-down' theory."

Further Resources

BOOKS

Anderson, Martin. *Revolution.* San Diego, Calif.: Harcourt Brace Jovanovich, 1988.

Burch, Philip H. *Reagan, Bush, and Right-Wing Politics: Elites, Think Tanks, Power and Policy.* Westport, Conn.: JAI Press, 1997.

Campagna, Anthony S. *The Economy in the Reagan Years: The Economic Consequences of the Reagan Administrations*. Westport, Conn.: Greenwood, 1994.

Executive Office of the President and Office of Management and Budget. *America's New Beginning: A Program for Economic Recovery Budget*. Washington, D.C.: White House, Office of the Press Secretary, 1981.

Gilder, George F. *Wealth and Poverty*. New York: Basic Books, 1981.

Greider, William. *The Education of David Stockman and Other Americans*. New York: Dutton, 1982.

Greenya, John, and Anne Urban. *The Real David Stockman*. New York: St. Martin's Press, 1986.

Kiewe, Amos, and Davis W. Houck. *A Shining City on a Hill: Ronald Reagan's Economic Rhetoric, 1951–1989*. New York: Praeger, 1991.

Niskanen, William A. *Reaganomics: An Insider's Account of the Politics and the People*. New York: Oxford University Press, 1988.

Roberts, Paul Craig. *The Supply-Side Revolution: An insider's Account of Policymaking in Washington*. Cambridge, Mass.: Harvard University Press, 1984.

Sloan, John W. *The Reagan Effect: Economics and Presidential Leadership*. Lawrence: University Press of Kansas, 1999.

Spulber, Nicolas. *Managing the American Economy, from Roosevelt to Reagan*. Bloomington: Indiana University Press, 1989.

Stein, Herbert. *Presidential Economics: The Making of Economic Policy from Roosevelt to Reagan and Beyond*. New York: Simon & Schuster, 1985.

Stockman, David. *The Triumph of Politics: Why the Reagan Revolution Failed*. New York: Harper and Row, 1986.

Thompson, Kenneth W., ed. *Reagan and the Economy: Nine Intimate Perspectives*. Lanham, Md.: University Press of America; Charlottesville, Va.: Miller Center, 1994.

Ullman, Owen. *Stockman: The Man, the Myth, the Future*. New York: Fine, 1986.

Wanniski, Jude. *The Way the World Works*. New York: Simon and Schuster, 1979.

PERIODICALS

Easterbrook, Greg. "Ideas Move Nations: How Conservative Think Tanks Have Helped to Transform the Terms of Political Debate." *The Atlantic* 257, no.1, January 1986, 66–80. Available online at http://www.theatlantic.com/politics/poli big/eastidea.htm; website home page: http://www.theatlantic .com/ (accessed May 6,. 2003).

WEBSITES

Cato Institute: Individual Liberty, Limited Government, Free Markets, and Peace. Available online at http://www.cato.org/ (accessed May 6, 2003). *This website contains speeches, press releases, memoranda, and publications of libertarian policy activists and scholars who often influenced Reagan administration policies.*

Heritage Foundation: Policy Research & Analysis. Available online at http://www.heritage.org/ (accessed May 6, 2003). *This website contains policy documents, press releases, and publications of conservative policy activists and scholars whose work proved among the most influential from any think tanks on various Reagan administration economic policies.*

"Inaugural Addresses of the Presidents of the United States." Bartleby.com. Available online at http://www.bartleby.com /124/; website home page: http://www.bartleby.com/ (accessed May 6, 2003). *This website contains inaugural addresses in full text for every president since George Washington.*

Office of Management and Budget. Executive Office of the President. http://www.whitehouse.gov/omb/; website home page: http://www.whitehouse.gov/ (accessed May 6, 2003).

"Reagan: Actor, Governor, President—The Biography of a Popular but Contradictory Man." The Presidents Series, The American Experience, Public Broadcasting System. Available online at http://www.pbs.org/wgbh/amex/reagan/; website home page: http://www.pbs.org/ (accessed May 6, 2003). *This website contains still photos and entire transcript from the PBS series on American Presidents along with brief bibliographies and a selection of related websites.*

Ronald Reagan Presidential Library Official Web Site. Available online at http://www.reagan.utexas.edu/ (accessed May 6, 2003). *This website contains primary sources in the form of speeches and writings by President Reagan.*

"Ronald Wilson Reagan." Presidents of the United States (POTUS), Internet Public Library. Available online at http:// www.ipl.org/div/potus/rwreagan.html; website home page: http://www.ipl.org/ (accessed May 6, 2003). *This website contains a brief biography, links to key documents, and a selection of sound clips from President Reagan's speeches.*

Woolley, John, and Gerhard Peters. "The American Presidency Project." University of California, Santa Barbara. Available online at http://www.presidency.ucsb.edu/index.php (accessed May 6, 2003). *This website contains additional primary sources including presidential election data; presidential portraits; the public papers and speeches of presidents from Herbert Hoover through Gerald Ford, Jimmy Carter, and George H.W. Bush; inaugural addresses and state of the union addresses for presidents from George Washington through George W. Bush; the Fireside Chats of Franklin D. Roosevelt; Saturday radio addresses for presidents from William J. Clinton through George W. Bush; and national political party platforms since 1840.*

The IBM Personal Computer

Photograph

By: IBM (International Business Machines Corporation)

Date: 1981

Source: AP/Wide World Photos.

About the Organization: IBM traces its history back to 1896, with the formation of the Tabulating Machine Com-

Primary Source

The IBM Personal Computer

SYNOPSIS: This picture of an IBM personal computer represents an important symbol of the growing centrality of information, data processing, and data exchange in the knowledge economy of 1980's America. AP/WIDE WORLD PHOTOS. REPRODUCED BY PERMISSION.

pany by Herman Hollerith, who had invented the punch card, tabulating machine, and sorter adopted by the U.S. Census Bureau in 1890. This company merged with International Time Recording Company and Computing Scale Company of America in 1911, to form the Computing-Tabulating-Recording Company, or C-R-T. In 1924, C-R-T changed its name to International Business Machines Corporation—IBM ■

Introduction

While the history of the computing machine goes back much farther in time than most people are aware, its impact on broader society and culture came during the 1980s and 1990s with the widespread use of the personal computer and the Internet. The federal government, especially the U.S. military, had purchased one hundred percent of all microchips for use in government computers during the 1950s, helping to make the computer industry possible. During the 1960s, large corporations began employing mainframe computers manufactured by the International Business Machines Corporation (IBM) to organize production lines, track inventories, keep company records, and perform routine tasks.

In August 1981, IBM joined the growing number of American companies producing a smaller "personal" computer for use on desktops in homes, offices, businesses, government agencies, and student dorm rooms. While initially reluctant to shift its corporate focus from the mainframe to the personal computer, IBM entered the PC revolution by introducing its IBM PC, which employed a software operating system designed by Bill Gates, head of a then small firm called Microsoft. With the MicroSoft Disk Operating System (MS-DOS) software and the personal computer hardware design, IBM set the industry standard for a new generation of computers that would dramatically change the day-to-day lives of millions of Americans. Throughout the 1980s, the "IBM clone"—a personal computer manufactured by any of many companies but modeled on the design of the IBM PC—served as the standard for desktop machines that replaced typewriters, calculating machines, and paper records in private and public offices, schools, libraries, and factories. Americans living through the decade did not necessarily understand the implications of this "knowledge revolution" immediately, but over time

Businesses and employees, accustomed to working with typewriters, carbon paper, file cards, preprinted forms, and specially printed accounting paper, found themselves learning to use PCs, a symbol of the new era of economic development. © **ROGER RESSMEYER/CORBIS. REPRODUCED BY PERMISSION.**

they changed habits of an earlier industrial age. Businesses and employees accustomed to working with typewriters, carbon paper, file cards, preprinted forms, and specially printed accounting paper to balance books found themselves learning to use this new technology. The image of the IBM PC became a symbol of this new era of economic development.

Significance

In the immediate postwar years after 1945, few Americans knew or cared about the existence of specialized business machines beyond the ever-present telephone and the newly popular television set. The nation's first automated computers were designed for and purchased by the U.S. military to track huge amounts of data that no human being could possibly collect, collate, and analyze in reasonable periods of time. By the 1950s, a small but growing semiconductor industry sold its products to government agencies, particularly the nation's armed forces, to wage the Cold War against the Soviet Union. As had happened in a number of other cases, new technology developed for the military eventually saw transfer to the civilian economy where it was

used in ways never foreseen by the original inventors. In the 1960s, computers were used by an increasing number of government agencies and private firms to keep track of inventories of goods and services, archive engineering designs and quality control records, and calculate assets and debits on balance sheets. While this first generation of large mainframe computers would later appear quite primitive, at the time they were cutting edge technology. During the 1970s, inventors and corporate research departments began designing increasingly smaller and faster chips that one day could be paired with miniaturization of other hardware components to make possible small computers that could fit on the top of a desk. By the end of the 1980s, advocates, futurists, and even sober economists had begun predicting that the advent of the personal computer and whatever might follow in its wake would raise productivity, lower labor costs, and improve efficiency rates to such an extent that the United States and the world might be on the verge of creating an entirely "new economy." In the decade to follow, more and more Americans came to hear, believe, and trust in the emergence of "the new economy."

Further Resources

BOOKS

Akera, Atsushi, and Frederik Nebeker, eds. *From 0 to 1: An Authoritative History of Modern Computing.* New York: Oxford University Press, 2002.

Barnouw, Erik, ed. *International Encyclopedia of Communications.* 4 vols. New York: Oxford University Press, 1989.

Campbell-Kelly, Martin. *From Airline Reservations to Sonic the Hedgehog: A History of the Software Industry.* Cambridge, Mass.: MIT Press, 2003.

———, and Williams Aspray. *Computer: A History of the Information Machine.* New York: Basic Books, 1996.

Chandler, Alfred D., and James W. Cortada, eds. *A Nation Transformed by Information: How Information Has Shaped the United States from Colonial Times to the Present.* New York: Oxford University Press, 2000.

Reagan, Patrick D. *History and the Internet: A Guide.* New York: McGraw–Hill, 2002.

Shaiken, Harley. *Work Transformed: Automation and Labor in the Computer Age.* New York: Holt, Rinehart and Winston, 1984.

Temin, Peter, ed. *Inside the Business Enterprise: Historical Perspectives on the Use of Information.* Chicago: University of Chicago Press, 1991.

Zuboff, Shoshana. *In the Age of the Smart Machine: The Future of Work and Power.* New York: Basic Books, 1988.

PERIODICALS

John, Richard H., ed. "Special Issue: Computers and Communications Networks." *Business History Review* 75, Spring 2001, 1–176.

WEBSITES

"Charles Babbage Institute: Center for the History of Information Technology." University Libraries, University of Minnesota. Available online at http://www.cbi.umn.edu/ (accessed May 12, 2003). *This website acts as a clearinghouse for detailed information on the history of computers, software, and computing.*

Computer History Museum Home Page. Available online at http://www.computerhistory.org/ (accessed May 12, 2003). *This website has a cornucopia of textual, image, and digital information about the history of computing including pictures of now obsolete computers.*

Muuss, Mike, comp. "History of Computing Information." U.S. Army Research Laboratory. Available online at http://ftp.arl.mil:80/~mike/comphist/; website home page: http://ftp.arl.army.mil/ (accessed May 12, 2003). *This website, maintained by a U.S. Army officer, contains valuable primary sources and many pictures regarding the early history of computers in the post–World War II years.*

"Research History Highlights." IBM. Available online at http://www.research.ibm.com/about/past_history.shtml; website home page: http://www.research.ibm.com/ (accessed May 11, 2003). *This website of the IBM Corporation describes some of the technical advances in computer design in the post–1945 period by the firm which later set the industry standard when it introduced the IBM PC in 1981.*

"The Blight on Wall Street"
Journal article

By: Felix Rohatyn
Date: March 12, 1987
Source: Rohatyn, Felix. "The Blight on Wall Street." *New York Review of Books,* March 12, 1987, 21–23.
About the Author: Financier Felix Rohatyn (1928–), as chairman of the Municipal Assistance Corporation of the City of New York, led the effort to bring New York City out of its financial crisis in the 1970s as chairman of the New York Municipal Authority. During the 1980s, he publicly commented on the need to rebuild roads, bridges, factories, and other physical facilities. Rohatyn served as the U.S. ambassador to France from 1997 to 2000. ∎

Introduction

The "supply-side" economic policies of the 1980s were intended to lead the way to a rebirth of American productivity and growth. The key to its economic plan lay in bringing forth new investment capital to allow individuals and companies to expand demand which would then result in more consumption. Once the process began, it would continue in a cyclic pattern with supply, demand, consumption, jobs, rising income, and increased rates of growth and employment. Yet the decade saw much of this investment taking place by speculative and unethical investors seeking quick earnings with little regard for its impact on the national economy.

From August 1982 until the crash in October 1987, the stock market entered a bullish period that brought euphoria among brokers, traders, investors, bankers, corporate managers, and dealers in "junk bonds." By investing in low-quality bonds that delivered a high rate of return but with high risk, dealers such as Ivan Boesky became cultural celebrities. In his 1985 graduation speech at the University of California at Berkeley, Boesky bluntly stated that "Greed is all right, by the way. I want you to know that. I think greed is healthy. You can be greedy and still feel good about yourself." Two years later actor Michael Douglas, playing the character of Gordon Gecko, pronounced that "greed is good" in filmmaker Oliver Stone's film *Wall Street.* Americans discussed the latest phenomenon—the prosperity of the young, urban professionals—without a hint of irony or sarcasm. Corporations hired growing numbers of newly graduated students from prestigious M.B.A. (Master's degree in Business Administration) programs.

Significance

Financier Felix Rohatyn, as head of the New York City Municipal Authority, had plenty of experience with financial crisis management. In a series of hard-hitting

This illustration of Ivan Boesky appeared in Felix Rohatyn's article, "The Blight on Wall Street." Investing in low-quality bonds that delivered a high rate of return but with high risk, dealer Ivan Boesky bluntly stated that, "You can be greedy and still feel good about yourself."
ILLUSTRATION BY DAVID LEVINE. REPRODUCED BY PERMISSION.

essays, Rohatyn took speculators, financial institutions, and public policymakers to task for failing to rebuild the country's aging public infrastructure of roads, bridges, schools, airports, and other public facilities that desperately needed attention. Few Americans listened. Many were so busy working and taking care of their families that they had little time to make sense of the complicated twists and turns of public and private finance which had turned a small number of Americans into wealthy, famous people very quickly.

At the start of the 1980s, most politicians, economic leaders, economists, and policy advisers agreed on the need for the United States to increase the rate of productivity that had hit zero and started going into negative territory. The economic policies followed by the Ronald Reagan (served 1981–1989) and George Bush (served 1989–1993) administrations for most of the decade created advantages for investors through personal

and business tax cuts, accelerated depreciation of business costs, and the shifting of large sums of money from public spending to private markets. While the 1970s had earned the nickname of the "Me Decade," by 1985, the 1980s were being referred to as the "Decade of Greed." Speculative investment in a booming bull market brought fame and fortune to individuals and institutions, but failed to spark the kinds of capital spending necessary to drive up productivity. Despite considerable loosening of the nation's regulatory laws under the free market philosophy of the Republican administrations, eventually these dangerous practices came under fire and investigation. The catalyst came in the form of the October 1987 stock market crash, after which scandal after scandal appeared in the headlines of newspapers across the country.

Primary Source

"The Blight on Wall Street" [excerpt]

SYNOPSIS: In this essay, financier Felix Rohatyn points to the impact of stock speculation on the financial markets. Short-term investment hurts such key financial institutions as banks, savings and loans associations, insurance companies, and stock brokerage houses on Wall Street according to Rohatyn.

As the revelations of illegality and excesses in the financial community begin to be exposed, those of us who are part of this community have to face a hard truth: a cancer has been spreading in our industry, and how far it will go will only become clear as the Securities and Exchange Commission and Federal prosecutors pursue the various investigations currently under way. The cancer is called greed.

It has grown in a more feverish climate of speculation than any we have seen since the 1920s; and it is not wholly unrelated to our continued huge fiscal deficits. It is encouraged by deregulation and the prevailing market ideology; it is specifically concentrated in the recent wave of huge takeovers financed by junk bonds—high-yielding bonds with relatively small backing—and on the various financial activities related to them. Its most deeply disturbing aspect, so far, has been the Ivan Boesky affair, involving the illegal use of insider information in the trading of securities.

The stock market is at an all-time high, while business is relatively slow and major sectors of our economy are in serious difficulty. Furthermore, looking to the future, aside from the devaluation of the dollar, which cuts two ways, we see little or no evidence of a realistic willingness on the part of government to

In the film *Wall Street,* Michael Douglas, playing the character of Gordon Gecko, pronounced that "greed is good." **THE KOBAL COLLECTION/20TH CENTURY FOX. REPRODUCED BY PERMISSION.**

solve our most fundamental economic problems: our budget deficit, our trade deficit, and the vulnerability of our banking system. The financial markets now have a life of their own, seemingly unrelated to any underlying economic realities. The need for productive investment in this country, together with the risks created by the level of existing speculation, makes it more important than ever that the integrity of the financial markets be assured and that capital be used to build and not to speculate. . . .

As a result of these developments, financial structures are being seriously eroded. In recent years, some of the largest takeovers came about as a result of raids, financed by junk bonds, on the target companies. Many of these companies were then acquired by third parties. A large part of the oil industry has been reorganized as a result. The mergers of Chevron and Gulf, Occidental and Cities Service, and Mobil and Superior all occurred as a result of raids or the threat of raids. The deterioration in their combined balance sheets has been dramatic. Far from benefiting from a healthy restructuring, the oil companies involved are cutting

exploration sharply, a practice our country will pay for dearly when the next energy crisis occurs. With their high levels of debt, the oil companies could be in serious difficulty if the price of oil declines again. If one were to conceive a scheme to get the US into trouble as far as energy is concerned, it would be difficult to improve on what has happened.

The use of junk bonds is particularly hazardous in large takeovers. High-yield, low-rated debt, in reasonable amounts, is a perfectly acceptable means of financing for many companies ineligible for investment-grade credit ratings. It is a different story, however, when this sort of debt, in the tens of billions of dollars, is used to substitute for equity in the takeovers of very large companies. . . .

Between $75 and $100 billion of junk bonds have been placed over the last five or six years. Possibly more than half this amount has been directly related to takeovers, leveraged buy-outs, and restructurings. Only financial institutions can provide purchasing power in such size. The cornerstone of junk-bond takeovers is the willingness of financial institutions—with legal responsibilities as "fiduciaries" toward depositors, retirees, and policyholders—to acquire this paper in vast amounts. Insurance companies, savings and loans, pension funds, commercial banks—all want to show short-term profits from high-yielding assets; so far, the experiment has largely been a success. Interest rates have declined steadily over the last five years and the stock market has boomed. But what will happen in a downturn, especially if that downturn is accompanied by rising interest rates as a result of the flight of foreign capital from the US? Of the several financial time bombs ticking in our closet, this is potentially one of the largest and most dangerous. And if large-scale defaults occur in the junk bond market as a result of a recession, it will, as always, be the taxpayer who ultimately pays. The government will not allow large financial institutions to go down in a time of crisis.

The dangers of the proliferation of large-scale takeovers actively financed by excessive use of high-cost debt should be made clear:

- At a time when we should be trying to encourage long-term investment, this activity encourages speculation and short-term trading.

- At a time when we should be trying to strengthen our important industries to make them more competitive, this activity weakens many of our companies by stripping away their equity and replacing it with high-cost debt. Borrowing can promote growth when the borrowed funds are used by a company to make new investments in order to meet future market needs and to be more competitive. It is quite another story when leverage is created to pay out shareholders today at the expense of growth tomorrow.

- At a time when many of our financial institutions (banks, savings banks, insurance companies) are under considerable pressure, this activity preempts more and more general credit and causes the weakest sectors of the economy to acquire large amounts of risky and possibly illiquid paper in order to show a strong performance. Much of this paper has never been tested in a period of economic downturn.

- At a time when we need to continue attracting capital from throughout the world, our securities markets appear to be more and more under the control of professionals and insiders.

. . . The picture of greed and corruption currently in the headlines could unleash a vicious backlash against financial institutions as well as individuals.

Those who break the law must be punished; institutions should be reformed. The securities industry has been heavily and successfully regulated since the 1930s. The notion that additional legislation would interfere with the workings of a free market is a myth in this particular case.

Further Resources
BOOKS
Bruck, Connie. *The Predators' Ball: The Junk Bond Raiders and the Man Who Staked Them.* New York: American Lawyer/Simon and Schuster, 1988.

Friedman, Benjamin M. *Day of Reckoning: The Consequences of American Economic Policy Under Reagan and After.* New York: Random House, 1988.

Geisst, Charles R. *Wall Street: A History.* New York: Oxford University Press, 1997.

Gordon, John Steele. *The Great Game: The Emergence of Wall Street as a World Power, 1653–2000.* New York: Scribner, 1999.

Greider, William. *Secrets of the Temple: How the Federal Reserve Runs the Country.* New York: Simon & Schuster, 1987.

Krugman, Paul R. *Peddling Prosperity: Economic Sense and Nonsense in the Age of Diminished Expectations.* New York: Norton, 1994.

Lekachman, Robert F. *Greed Is Not Enough: Reaganomics.* New York: Pantheon Books, 1982.

———. *Visions and Nightmares: America After Reagan.* New York: Macmillan, 1987.

McCraw, Thomas K. *Prophets of Regulation: Charles Francis Adams, Louis D. Brandeis, James M. Landis, Alfred E. Kahn.* Cambridge, Mass.: Harvard University Press, 1984.

Rohatyn, Felix G. *The Twenty-Year Century: Essays on Economics and Public Finance.* New York: Random House, 1983.

Schaller, Michael. *Reckoning with Reagan: America and Its President in the 1980s.* New York: Oxford University Press, 1992.

Seligman, Joel. *The Transformation of Wall Street: A History of the Security and Exchange Commission and Modern Corporate Finance.* Boston: Houghton Mifflin, 1982.

Sobel, Robert. *The Big Board: A History of the New York Stock Market.* Washington, D.C.: Beard, 2000.

———. *Dangerous Dreamers: The Financial Innovators from Charles Merrill to Michael Milken.* New York: Wiley, 1993.

———. *The New Game on Wall Street.* New York: Wiley, 1987.

Stevens, Mark. *The Insiders: The Truth Behind the Scandal Rocking Wall Street.* New York: Putnam, 1987.

Werner, Walter, and Steven T. Smith. *Wall Street.* New York: Columbia University Press, 1991.

White, Lawrence J. *The S & L Debacle: Public Policy Lessons for Bank and Thrift Legislation.* New York: Oxford University Press, 1991.

Zey, Mary. *Banking on Fraud: Drexel, Junk Bonds, and Buyouts.* New York: Aldine de Gruyter, 1993.

PERIODICALS

Rohatyn, Felix G. "The Coming Emergency and What Can Be Done About It." *New York Review of Books* 27, no. 19, December 4, 1980.

———. "New York and the Nation." *New York Review of Books* 28, no. 21/22, January 21, 1982, 26–29.

———. "Reconstructing America." *New York Review of Books* 28, no. 3, March 5, 1981, 16–19.

WEBSITES

American Stock Exchange. Available online at http://www.amex.com/ (accessed May 8, 2003). *This website of the AMEX includes information about stocks and bonds available for purchase and sale by investors and brokers interested in securities of smaller firms not listed on the New York Stock Exchange.*

Filings and Forms (EDGAR). U.S. Securities and Exchange Commission. Available online at http://www.sec.gov/edgar.shtml; website home page: http://www.sec.gov. (accessed May 8, 2003). *This section of the SEC's website provides investor and broker access to legal filings required by federal law for firms using the stock exchanges to raise investment capital.*

New York Stock Exchange. Available online at http://www.nyse.com/ (accessed May 8, 2003). *This website contains an enormous amount of information for brokers and investors of stocks and bonds listed on the NYSE.*

U.S. Securities and Exchange Commission. http://www.sec.gov/ (accessed May 8, 2003). *This website of the governmentally operated SEC established in 1933 to regulate activities in the nation's securities exchanges provides detailed information about various regulatory policies applicable to the buying and selling of stocks and bonds.*

AUDIO AND VISUAL MEDIA

Wall Street. Original release, 1987. Directed by Oliver Stone. VHS, 1996. Twentieth Century Fox. Widescreen DVD, 2003. Twentieth Century Fox Home Video.

"Things Were Better Before 1973: Selected Indicators of Prosperity and Progress"

Table

By: Robert Heilbroner

Date: October 23, 1988

Source: Heilbroner, Robert. "Things Were Better Before 1973: Selected Indicators of Prosperity and Progress." *New York Times Book Review,* October 23, 1988, 43.

About the Author: Economist Robert Heilbroner (1919–) regularly reviews newly published works in major newspapers and journals. Best known as the author of *The Worldly*

Philosophers: The Lives, Times, and Ideas of the Great Economic Thinkers (seven editions from 1953 to 1999), Heilbroner has written a number of works in economic history, current economic policy, and the future direction of economic growth. ∎

Introduction

In a 1988 article for the prestigious *New York Times Book Review,* economist Robert Heilbroner includes a revealing table showing the mixed economic record of the 1980s. One of the difficulties in making sense of economic policies in any period arises from the short-term statistics which may, and often do, hide more historically significant long-term changes. Economists, policy analysts, politicians, advocates, and critics in the 1980s often made claims based either on their own political and economic values or on figures that told only part of the broader story. In this case, Heilbroner presents a summary table that provides perspective on the economy of the 1980s.

The table reveals several important trends. Figures in the first column show the long-term postwar prosperity of the 1948–1973 years. The changes in the 1973–1987 period can be compared with those of the longer postwar period to place them in historical perspective. Additionally, the changes of the post–1973 period are subdivided into the years 1973–1980 and 1980–1987, facilitating an evaluation of the strengths and weaknesses of the economic policies of the 1970s and the 1980s. Heilbroner uses such categories as the average civilian unemployment rate in percentages and the average growth in civilian employment to assess changes in job growth and decline. Differences in the inflation rates show how that key economic indicator changed in each period. Changes in the average growth of Real GNP (the total value of all goods and services produced adjusted for inflation) and output per hour suggest long-term changes in productivity. Finally, the changes in average growth of real compensation (wages and salaries adjusted for inflation) and the percent of Americans in poverty indicate the human impact of economic change over time.

Significance

Sometimes statistical figures arranged in tabular form can tell much more about change over time than many words. This 1988 table shows a large gap between the economic projections of the Reagan administration and the actual performance of the American economy in the 1980s.

Seen from the perspective of post–1945 economic prosperity, the record of the 1970s and 1980s seems quite anemic. While the average postwar unemployment rate for the period of 1948–1973 was only 4.8 percent, the

Things Were Better Before 1973: Selected Indicators of Prosperity and Progress

Period	1948–73	1973–87	1973–80	1980–87
Average civilian unemployment rate (percent)	4.8	7.3	6.8	7.8
Average growth in civilian unemployment (percent per year)	1.5	2.0	2.2	1.8
Average inflation per year (G.N.P. Price Index)	3.0	6.2	7.8	4.5
Average growth of real G.N.P. (percent per year)	3.6	2.4	2.1	2.6
Average growth of output per hour, business sector (percent per year)	2.8	1.0	0.5	1.5
Average growth of real compensation per hour (percent per year)	2.96	0.36	0.19	0.52
Persons in poverty (percent)				
Beginning of period	30.0*	11.1	11.1	13.0
End of period	11.1	13.7	13.0	13.7

*Unofficial estimate for 1950

SOURCE: Tobin, James. "The Rise and Fall of the American Economy." *New York Times Book Review*, October 23, 1988, 43.

Primary Source

"Things Were Better Before 1973: Selected Indicators of Prosperity and Progress"

SYNOPSIS: Economist Robert Heilbroner provides figures for key economic indicators of the 1980s in a summary table in a 1988 *New York Times Book Review* article.

rate for the 1970s was higher at 6.8 percent, while that for the 1980s was even higher at 7.8 percent. Price inflation in the 1970s at 7.8 percent was much higher than the postwar rate of 3.0 percent. The inflation rate in the 1980s dropped to 4.5 percent, lower than the 1970s rate, but still higher than the average postwar rate. GNP and output rose in the 1980s compared with the 1970s, but still remained below that of the postwar averages. Wages and salaries (compensation) that had lagged in the 1970s improved in the 1980s, but remained considerably behind the average rate of almost 3 percent in the postwar period. The poverty rate, which had declined dramatically from 30 percent in 1948 to 11 percent in 1973, rose to 13.0 percent in 1980, then to 13.7 percent by 1987.

In sum, the economic record of the 1980s was at best a mixed one. The economic policies of the Federal Reserve Board under Paul Volcker (appointed in 1979) did bring price inflation under control during the course of the 1980s. Yet the average rate of civilian unemployment growth increased in the 1980s compared with the 1970s, even though real GNP increased faster in the 1980s than in the 1970s. While wages and salaries grew faster in the 1980s, other research shows that these increased much more quickly for individuals and families in the upper ranges of the income structure (especially the top five percent and top twenty percent) than for most Americans. The percentage of Americans living in poverty increased over the entire period of the 1970s and 1980s. While the official poverty rate grew less slowly in the 1980s than in the 1970s, this may have been a result of changes in the Bureau of Labor Statistics' definition of the poverty rate in the 1980s which meant that

Americans who would have been counted as poor in the 1970s disappeared from the official poverty figures in the 1980s—they were no longer counted as poor. The advocates of "supply-side" economics had promised that economic growth would increase markedly. Decreased social spending, tax cuts, increased defense spending, and better monetary policies by the Federal Reserve Board would lead to more jobs, higher production, and more total tax revenues. The Reagan economic vision proved more utopian theory than practice. By the end of the Reagan years (1981–1989), the federal debt had tripled. By the end of the Bush years (1989–1993), it had quadrupled.

Further Resources

BOOKS

Barrett, Laurence I. *Gambling with History: Ronald Reagan in the White House.* Garden City, N.Y.: Doubleday, 1983.

Berman, Larry, ed. *Looking Back on the Reagan Presidency.* Baltimore, Md.: Johns Hopkins University Press, 1990.

Blumenthal, Sidney. *Our Long National Daydream: A Political Pageant of the Reagan Era.* New York: Harper & Row, 1988.

———, and Thomas Byrne Edsall, eds. *The Reagan Legacy.* New York: Pantheon Books, 1988.

Campagna, Anthony S. *The Economy in the Reagan Years: The Economic Consequences of the Reagan Administrations.* Westport, Conn.: Greenwood, 1994.

Conley, Richard S., ed. *Reassessing the Reagan Presidency.* Lanham, Md.: University Press of America, 2003.

Friedman, Benjamin M. *Day of Reckoning: The Consequences of American Economic Policy Under Reagan and After.* New York: Random House, 1988.

People line up to claim unemployment benefits in September, 1980, at an office of the Michigan Employment Security Commission.
© BETTMANN/CORBIS. REPRODUCED BY PERMISSION.

————, and National Bureau of Economic Research. *What Have We Learned from the Reagan Deficits and Their Disappearance?* Cambridge, Mass.: National Bureau of Economic Research, 2000.

Judis, John B. *The Paradox of American Democracy: Elites, Special Interests, and the Betrayal of Public Trust.* New York: Routledge, 2001.

Krugman, Paul R. *Peddling Prosperity: Economic Sense and Nonsense in the Age of Diminished Expectations.* New York: Norton, 1994.

Lampman, Robert. *The Share of Top Wealth-Holders in National Wealth, 1922–56.* Princeton, N.J.: Princeton University Press, 1962.

Levy, Frank. *Dollars and Dreams: The Changing American Income Distribution.* New York: Norton, 1988.

Levy, Peter B. *Encyclopedia of the Reagan–Bush Years.* Westport, Conn.: Greenwood, 1996.

Sloan, John W. *The Reagan Effect: Economics and Presidential Leadership.* Lawrence: University Press of Kansas, 1999.

Wolff, Edward N., ed. *International Comparisons of the Distribution of Household Wealth.* New York: Oxford University Press, 1987.

————. *Top Heavy: The Increasing Inequality of Wealth in America and What Can Be Done About It.* New York: The New Press, 2002.

WEBSITES

"Commanding Heights: The Battle for the World Economy." PBS. Available online at http://www.pbs.org/wgbh/commandingheights/; website home page: http://www.pbs.org/ (accessed May 6, 2003). *This website is intended to accompany the television series of the same title, based on the book by Daniel Yergin and Joseph Stanislaw.*

Council of Economic Advisors. Available online at http://www.whitehouse.gov/cea/; website home page: http://www.whitehouse.gov/ (accessed May 9, 2003). *Established by the Employment Act of 1946, the CEA works with the President and the Cabinet to draft the annual "Economic Report of the President." The Report is submitted to the Congress, which uses it to draft legislation for the annual federal budget and appropriation legislation.*

Joint Economic Committee. U.S. Congress. http://jec.senate.gov/ *Established by the Employment Act of 1946, the congressional JEC works with the President and the Cabinet to draft legislation for the annual federal budget and appropriation legislation.*

EH.Net: Economic History Services. Available online at http://www.eh.net/ (accessed May 9, 2003). *This website provides a range of resources on economic history from the major professional groups including an encyclopedia, book reviews, datasets, and cost calculators at different points in history.*

National Bureau of Economic Research. Available online at http://www.nber.org/ (accessed May 9, 2003). *Founded in*

1920, the NBER is the most widely known and respected scholarly source of statistical economic collection and analysis in the United States conducted by the nation's leading economists. NBER director Martin Feldstein served as President Reagan's key economic adviser.

"National Income Accounts Data." Bureau of Economic Analysis. Available online at http://www.bea.doc.gov/bea/dn1 .htm; website home page: http://www.bea.gov/ (accessed May 9, 2003). *Since the development of national income and accounts time series by scholars in the 1930's, the BEA has conducted ongoing research, analysis, and distribution of updated statistical tables that place current economic productivity and growth figures into a longer term historical context as well as providing policymakers with detailed information for the economic policy–making process.*

Steckel, Richard H. "A History of the Standard of Living in the United States." EH.Net Encyclopedia. Robert Whaples, ed. Available online at http://www.eh.net/encyclopedia/steckel .standard.living.us.php; website home page: http://www.eh .net/encyclopedia/ (accessed May 9, 2003).

U.S. Census Bureau. Available online at http://www.census .gov/ (accessed May 9, 2003). *This website contains a wealth of detailed statistical information on a wide range of areas of American demographic, economic, social, ethnic, gender, and racial life. Many of the Census Bureau's specialized publications are included here in digital formats for easy download such as the annual "Statistical Abstract of the United States" and summary reports from decennial censuses as they become available.*

"Transplanted to the U.S.A."

Journal article

By: Mike Parker

Date: January 1990

Source: Parker, Mike. "Transplanted to the U.S.A." *Multinational Monitor,* January 1990. Available online at http:// multinationalmonitor.org/hyper/issues/1990/01/mm0190_11 .html; website home page: http://multinationalmonitor.org/ (accessed May 10, 2003).

About the Author: Mike Parker (1940–), a labor activist and industrial electrician specializing in automation, contributes to *Labor Notes.* He has written *Inside the Circle: A Union Guide to QWL* (1985) and co-authored, with Jane Slaughter, *Choosing Sides: Unions and the Team Concept* (1988). ∎

Introduction

American economic activity in the 1980s faced increasing economic competition from abroad. In the automobile manufacturing industry, General Motors, Ford, and Chrysler, along with American Motors, continued to focus on high volume, mass production of cars that changed with each new model year. From the early 1970s

on, Japanese car manufacturers such as Honda, Nissan, Toyota, Mazda, Mitsubishi, and Subaru made inroads into the domestic car market with less expensive, smaller, and more fuel efficient models that appealed to American consumers in the wake of the two oil embargoes of the Jimmy Carter years (1977–1981).

Since the 1930s, the American automobile industry had employed the single largest segment of the industrial work force, with millions more workers indirectly involved in the steel, rubber, glass, oil, and service industries. The Japanese challenge to U.S. economic dominance in the postwar period peaked in the 1980s with particular strength in the car market. Using new styles of business management and labor relations, Japanese companies started to build automobile "transplant" factories in America that created jobs and hope for millions of American workers. Some of these new plants received wide press coverage in local, state, and national media, such as the Honda plant in Lordstown, Ohio, the Nissan truck plant in Smyrna, Tennessee, and the Toyota factory in Georgetown, Kentucky. Later, Japanese and American managers built several joint plants such as the Toyota-General Motors plant in Fremont, California.

While consumers celebrated the availability of inexpensive, high-quality automobiles the Japanese entry brought, workers had a very different perspective. In this article, Mike Parker details the origins, managerial style, impact on labor relations, and social costs of the Japanese transplant factories.

Significance

The U.S. economy confronted a growing challenge from global competition that became increasingly stronger during the 1980s. Dominated by American workers since the early twentieth century, the automobile industry represented the smoothly running national economy at its best. Facing challenges from Japanese transplants, American car manufacturers and autoworkers had to deal with new ideas and practices for management and labor. Introduction of lean "just-in-time" supply systems, new machine technology, and automated workplaces led to issues of managerial authority, unionization, work rules, and job practices that seemed to overwhelm the U.S. car industry. Most of the Japanese firms insisted on a non-union work environment in order to control labor costs, the degree of automation, and work rules. American autoworkers and union officials saw this as a threat to their control of the workplace as well as the size of paychecks and range of benefits.

Parker's analysis of changes in the auto industry captures many of the consequences of changes in the workplace during the decade, while focusing on the social impact of new technology and economic change that would

At a time when challenges were facing American managers, workers, and communities in the auto industry from transplanted Japanese car plants, a sign saying "NO JAPANESE VEHICLES" at an auto parts store, informs people that no Japanese vehicles are allowed in their front parking lot. © JAMES MARSHALL/CORBIS. REPRODUCED BY PERMISSION.

continue to affect the lives of millions of working Americans for the remainder of the century. He notes the importance of the structure of the car industry that began separating the geographical location of high–skill, high–paying jobs from more routine, lower–paying work. Increased use of high-speed machinery placed growing pressure on workers to produce more cars at a faster rate while shrinking the size of the total automobile work force. Unions had to contend with the issues of how to react to new technology, who would control its use, and how workers would be compensated for the time, education, and stamina required to keep up with new technology. Managers had to decide whether to accept the demand of Japanese corporations for nonunion work or change the postwar tradition of labor relations negotiations and compromises on the work floor. Business leaders, citizens, and potential employees in local communities had to choose whether to face the possibility of permanent long-term economic decline or accept new outside management, lower wages, and global suppliers. Many of these issues expanded into a wide range of U.S. industries, which had to adjust to global competition that had not existed for most of the post-World War II period—when the American economy dominated world trade.

Primary Source

"Transplanted to the U.S.A." [excerpt]

SYNOPSIS: Labor journalist and industrial electrician Mike Parker describes the challenges facing American managers, workers, and communities in the auto industry from transplanted Japanese car plants in the 1980s.

Seven Japanese auto companies and one Korean firm built automobile assembly plants in North America. By 1992, the new Japanese-owned or managed auto assembly "transplants" could have a capacity of roughly three million vehicles, roughly 20 percent of domestic production. . . .

The Shape of the Industry

From William F. Buckley to the Bush administration to liberal economists like Lester Thurow, there is a broad consensus that foreign investment is good for the U.S. economy. But economist Candice Howes of the Rutgers Program on Regional and Industrial Economics argues that each investment must be analyzed to determine its effect. In the case of the auto transplants, she says, the Japanese are "transferring only a part of their system—the limbs are coming but the body is left behind." The transplants focus on the assembly and stamping operations and parts which are relatively easy to manufacture. The complex and engineering-intensive sections of manufacturing tend to stay abroad. This division of labor dramatically affects job possibilities. If the more highly skilled jobs are maintained overseas, there are limited possibilities for U.S. employees to advance within the company. Engineering-intensive manufacturing offers low-level workers the possibility of obtaining better and higher paying jobs. Many transplant managers are also concerned about where the important business decisions are made. . . .

The Introduction of Technology

In the early 1980s, General Motors developed a strategy of rapid automation in order to boost productivity and reduce the workforce. Many believed that the Japanese system of management offered an alternative, relying on the efficient use of labor instead of automation. The NUMMI plant, which is jointly owned by GM and Toyota, was cited as an example. As it turns out, the new Japanese plants are deriving the benefits of the intensification of automation as well as of labor. Honda claims that its new East Liberty, Ohio plant will have nine totally automated final assembly functions. At Honda, the entire die change is so automated that on the world's biggest stamping press a die change can be accomplished by just one person in 5 minutes. Only a few years ago, die changing a line took a half dozen people several hours or even shifts. Transplants have overcome many of the difficulties associated with introducing new technology which displaces workers . . .

Worker participation in solving problems greatly shortens the automation "debugging" period. According to studies at the Massachusetts Institute of Technology, transplants tend to have twice as many robots per unit output as U.S.-owned plants. But the use of robots and other technology does not necessarily create large numbers of highly skilled jobs in the United States. Most of the technology in the transplants is designed and developed in Japan. The units are designed for modular replacement to min-

imize the need for skilled repair work on the site. Typically, entire transplant operations are set up and tested in Japan and then moved to the United States for installation.

Remaking Management-Labor Relations

From a management point of view, the transplants seem enormously successful. The Honda plants set the industry standards for quality and productivity. The NUMMI plant is not far behind. GM has a special office to study NUMMI and a program which rotates management officials through NUMMI for training.

The other U.S. partners use their joint ventures in the same way. To some extent, the low costs of the transplants come simply because the plants are physically new and require less maintenance. Their new workers are also younger, healthier and stronger. These mitigating factors notwithstanding, the transplants have all but wiped out U.S. management interest in exploring alternative production systems, such as those in Sweden, which might increase productivity without restricting workers' rights. Instead, management holds up the transplant productivity figures and demands union concessions and adoption of transplant-type work organization in order to become "competitive." Such "competitive" labor agreements include the team concept and "just-in-time production" (in which subcontractors must deliver relatively small batches of parts as they are needed by the assembly plant), and allow management to freely contract out or speed up work— in short, to adopt all the features which have made the transplants so successful from management's point of view. Under the rubric of new forms of teamwork, management gains increased flexibility at the expense of working conditions and work rules that workers have long regarded as their factory bill of rights. Management has been significantly aided in its crusade to roll back workers' shop floor rights by top UAW leaders' endorsement of the systems at NUMMI and Mazda.

Unionization

The transplants have been antagonistic to unions, particularly traditional "American-style" unions. They have located in areas not traditionally sympathetic to unions in order to prevent the unionization of their workforces. One bank researcher who prepares location studies for smaller Japanese companies says that "non-union area" tops the list of new-site requirements. . . . When the UAW has tried

A public relations photo for Honda, taken in 1983 during the height of anti-Japanese sentiment among those in the auto industry, shows an American man and Japanese man shaking hands. **AMERICAN AUTOMOBILE ASSOCIATION. REPRODUCED BY PERMISSION.**

to organize the transplants, the Japanese companies have resisted the union's efforts. Nissan aggressively waged a successful campaign to keep the UAW out of its Smyrna, Tennessee plant. In the 1989 representation election, 70 percent of the workers at the Smyrna plant voted against the UAW. Honda has generally taken a softer line on unionization, avoiding public attacks on the UAW and allowing that workers are free to choose to be represented by a union. But Honda has also made it clear to its workforce that it does not look favorably on pro-union attitudes. This approach has been successful in rebuffing the UAW; in 1985 the union withdrew a request for an election at Honda's Marysville, Ohio plant, fearing it could not win. In contrast, those plants which are joint ventures with the U.S. Big Three—NUMMI, Diamond Star and CAMI—are all unionized. . . . The UAW has become a booster and has assisted in spreading the management system to other U.S. plants. President Owen Bieber declares that NUMMI's "worker-centered atmosphere" should

"point to a bright future for the domestic auto industry." UAW regional director Bruce Lee attacks critics of NUMMI as "old-guard unionists" or "1960s-era leftists." In fact, in organizing the transplants, the UAW's focus seems not to be entirely on the workers; the union appears more concerned with convincing management that it can be a good partner in production. . . .

More importantly, however, U.S. management has its own agenda for the joint venture experiments: to see if so-called Japanese management techniques can be applied not just to a U.S. workforce but to a unionized workforce. So called Japanese management techniques can work only with no union or with a compliant union; the question for the U.S. companies is whether the UAW is sufficiently docile. Though the results have generally been favorable to the companies, the final verdict is not in. At NUMMI, a large and significant bloc within the union is critical of management. At Mazda, the victory of the system's critics in 1989 union elections and subsequent union-won changes regulating the use of temporary workers and limiting absentee penalties resulted in a management shake-up. . . . The industry's increased reliance on subcontracting of parts production ("outsourcing") and just-in-time production has forced the parts production plants to move wherever the new assembly plants locate. Even where a new assembly plant is unionized, virtually none of its supplier plants are.

Social Costs

The transplants have very low cost figures. What is often ignored is the high social cost paid to achieve the low plant costs. In a variety of ways, the transplants pass on costs to society which were once internalized by corporations. First, the transplants shift the burden of taking care of "used up" workers to their families and the taxpayers. The new sites can hire younger, stronger workers and set work standards accordingly. But when workers grow older or get injured, they are not able to maintain the same pace. These workers are then forced out because the management system employed in the transplants does not make lighter jobs available for those with seniority. This process improves plant productivity and profit figures—but at the expense of the discarded workers. Second, the transplants exacerbate the problems of over-capacity in the auto industry. . . . Because of the excess capacity in the auto industry, building a new plant at one site means shutting down a plant elsewhere. These plant closings devastate communities such as Detroit or Flint which have depended on car factories for their economic well-being. Third, the transplants, as well as the new-site U.S.-owned factories, demand massive subsidies from communities before they commit to a particular location. In every case, plants choose to locate in new areas only after gathering the proceeds of bidding wars between communities and states which provide training money, roads, sewers, tax breaks and, in some cases, Japanese instruction in schools. Given the limit in available public funds, such uses of taxpayer dollars mean cuts in other public services.

Effect on Blacks

Most of the transplants have been located away from metropolitan areas, furthering a larger trend of companies leaving the urban areas where blacks live in large numbers, such as Detroit, Cleveland, Flint and Pontiac, for predominantly white, semi-rural areas. Moreover, the Japanese-owned plants hire a smaller percentage of blacks out of the available workforce than U.S.-owned plants, according to a recent study by University of Michigan sociologists Robert Cole and Donald Deskins. . . . Japanese auto parts suppliers have located in areas which, on average, are 12 percent black, but only 8 percent of their workers are black. New U.S.-owned auto assembly plants have also tended to avoid heavily black metropolitan areas, but their hiring records are much better. On the average they located in areas which were 16.6 percent black but 25.4 percent of their workers were black, reflecting the disproportionably high minority participation in blue-collar work in the United States.

The hiring gaps appear too great to be accidental. In 1988, the Equal Employment Opportunity Commission reached a $6 million settlement with Honda over a charge that the company discriminated against black and women workers. The reason that the new-site U.S. plants do so much better than transplants in hiring blacks, Cole and Deskins suggest, may not be because of responsible U.S. corporate policy but rather because union contracts often allow workers to follow their work to new plants. Indeed, the one transplant which has a significantly higher minority percentage than its surrounding area, NUMMI, was forced to recruit its workers from the former GM plant workforce.

Who is Responsible?

It is as wrong as it is easy to blame the Japanese for the problems facing U.S. industrial workers. The Japanese are not responsible for centuries of race and gender inequities in the United States. Nor are the Japanese responsible for our economic system or legislation which allows corporations to relocate to escape unions, shift costs to society or choose to build in over-capacity industries. Indeed, the policies of the Japanese-managed corporations are not significantly different from those of U.S.-owned companies. U.S.-owned corporations are as involved in globalizing production as the Japanese. U.S. companies have initiated the joint ventures and experimented with so-called Japanese management techniques because they want to adopt them as quickly as possible. U.S. corporations as much as the Japanese are seeking to replace skilled unionized workers with automation or non-union workers. U.S. corporations are spending millions to bypass unions or render them ineffective through team-concept schemes. Like the Japanese companies, U.S. firms are attempting to move to non-union areas, demanding local community taxbreaks and outsourcing extensively to non-union firms. General Motors, for example, located its acclaimed Saturn project in a right-to-work state and almost all of its announced non-GM suppliers are non-union. The transplants have quickly become the standard-bearers for U.S. management. The fundamental public policy issue is not the racial or national ownership of the transplants, but the corporate policies of disregard for workers and communities which they are spearheading.

Further Resources

BOOKS

Aronowitz, Stanley. *Working Class Hero: A New Strategy for Labor.* New York: Adena Books, 1983.

Bernstein, Michael A., and David E. Adler, eds. *Understanding American Economic Decline.* New York: Cambridge University Press, 1994.

Blackford, Mansel G. *A History of Small Business in America.* New York: Twayne Publishers, 1991.

Brody, David. *Workers in Industrial America: Essays on the Twentieth-Century Struggle.* New York: Oxford University Press, 1993.

Bluestone, Barry, and Bennett Harrison. *The Deindustrialization of America: Plant Closings, Community Abandonment, and the Dismantling of Basic Industry.* New York: Basic Books, 1982.

Dertozous, Michael L., Richard Lester, and Robert Solow. *Made in America: Regaining the Productive Edge.* Cambridge, Mass.: MIT Press, 1989.

Dubofsky, Melvyn, and Foster Rhea Dulles. *Labor in America: A History,* 6th ed. Wheeling, Ill.: Harlan Davidson, 1999.

Gelsanliter, David. *Jump Start: Japan Comes to the Heartland.* New York: Farrar Straus Giroux, 1990.

Halberstam, David. *The Reckoning.* New York: Morrow, 1986.

Harrison, Bennett, and Barry Bluestone. *The Great U-Turn: Corporate Restructuring and the Polarizing of America.* New York: Basic Books, 1988.

Lichtenstein, Nelson. *State of the Union: A Century of American Labor.* Princeton, N.J.: Princeton University Press, 2002.

———, and Howell John Harris, eds. *Industrial Democracy in America: The Ambiguous Promise.* Washington, D.C.: Woodrow Wilson Center, 1993.

Lichtenstein, Nelson, and Stephen Meyers, eds. *On the Line: Essays in the History of Auto Work.* Urbana: University of Illinois Press, 1989.

Milkman, Ruth. *Farewell to the Factory: Auto Workers in the Late Twentieth Century.* Berkeley: University of California Press, 1997.

Moody, Kim. *An Injury to All: The Decline of American Unionism.* London, Eng.: Verso, 1988.

Obey, David, and Paul Sarbanes, eds. *The Changing American Economy: Papers from the Fortieth Anniversary Symposium of the Joint Economic Committee of the United States Congress.* New York: Blackwell, 1986.

Parker, Mike. *Inside the Circle: A Union Guide to QWL.* Boston: South End Press, 1985.

———, and Jane Slaughter. *Choosing Sides: Unions and the Team Concept.* Boston: South End Press, 1988.

Piore, Michael J., and Charles F. Sabel. *The Second Industrial Divide: Possibilities for Prosperity.* New York: Basic Books, 1984.

Shaiken, Harley. *Work Transformed: Automation and Labor in the Computer Age.* New York: Holt, Rinehart and Winston, 1984.

Sherman, Joe. *In the Rings of Saturn.* New York: Oxford University Press, 1993.

Thurow, Lester. *Head to Head: The Coming Economic Battle Among Japan, Europe, and America.* New York: Morrow, 1992.

Tolliday, Steven, and Jonathan Zeitlin, eds. *The Automobile Industry and Its Workers: Between Fordism and Flexibility.* New York: St. Martin's Press, 1987.

Wolff, Michael, Peter Rutten, Albert F. Bayers, III, and the World Rank Research Team. *Where We Stand: Can America Make It in the Global Race for Wealth, Health, and Happiness?* New York: Bantam, 1992.

Zieger, Robert H., and Gilbert J. Gall. *American Workers, American Unions,* 3rd ed. Baltimore, Md.: Johns Hopkins University Press, 2002.

WEBSITES

AFL–CIO: America's Union Movement. http://www.aflcio.org/ *This website of the American Federation of Labor–Congress of Industrial Organizations includes information about the labor force, union organizing, and institutional work of the largest umbrella group for craft and industrial unions in the United States.*

Labor and Working-Class History Association. http://www.lawcha.org/ (accessed May 10, 2003). *The website for the major professional organization of labor historians.*

"Labor History on the Internet." Department of History, Tennessee Technological University. Available online at http://www.tntech.edu/history/labor.html; website home page: http://www.tntech.edu/history/ (accessed May 10, 2003). *This site contains links to many information sources about American labor history including professional groups, libraries and archives, specialized sites, and current labor issues.*

"Welcome to the UAW." United Automobile, Aerospace, and Agricultural Implement Workers of America. Available online at http://www.uaw.org/ (accessed May 11, 2003). *This website includes information about organizing efforts in the automobile industry among the Big Three automakers (GM, Ford, Daimler–Chrysler) and some of the Japanese transplant factories.*

AUDIO AND VISUAL MEDIA

The Automobile Story. Produced by WGBH Science Unit. Films for the Humanities & Sciences, 1992.

"Reagan Lives!"

Magazine article

By: Benjamin M. Friedman

Date: December 20, 1990

Source: Friedman, Benjamin M. "Reagan Lives!" *New York Review of Books* 37, no. 20, December 20, 1990, 29–33.

About the Author: Economist Benjamin Friedman (1944–) has worked for the Federal Reserve Banks of New York and Boston, the Board of Governors of the Federal Reserve System, Morgan Stanley, and as program director in Financial Markets and Monetary Economics of the National Bureau of Economic Research. He has served as chair of the Economics Department at Harvard University, where he has held the William Joseph Maier Professorship in Political Economy since 1989. ■

Introduction

Harvard University economist Benjamin Friedman evaluates the legacy of Ronald Reagan administration's economic policies and their impact on proposed economic policies by his Republican successor George H. W. Bush (served 1989–1993), in this essay. Having increased both the annual federal budget deficit and the total federal debt by huge amounts of government spending, especially through the defense buildup of the 1980s, the United States now had to figure out how to pay the nation's bills. As Friedman makes clear in this analysis of the impact of President Bush and the Congress drafting and passing a budget that raised taxes and began the long process of paying back the expenditures of the previous decade, the American public was not happy. Accustomed to Reagan's promises of social entitlements to middle-class Americans and defense spending without raising federal taxes, many were not ready to accept a new era of fiscal responsibility in the 1990s.

The Reagan legacy had sizeable costs. High-skill, well-paying jobs were replaced with low–skill jobs at lower wages and salaries. The U.S. balance of trade with its trading partners such as Canada, Mexico, Japan, and Western Europe had gone into negative territory in the mid-1980s. For the first time since 1920, the United States owed its trading partners more money for imports than American businesses sold abroad in the form of exports. America had shifted from a creditor to a debtor nation which in turn lowered the value of the U.S. dollar relative to other nations' currencies such as the Japanese yen and the West German mark. When Iraqi dictator Saddam Hussein invaded the Persian Gulf state of Kuwait in August 1990, President Bush's quick action to turn back the attack led to an increase in the economic reverses that had begun before the invasion. Above all, Friedman argues that the American people refused to admit that rising income inequality and lowered average family income raise central questions of social responsibility, fairness, and long-term economic and social stability.

Significance

The 1970s had ended in national disillusionment just a few short years after the nation's bicentennial celebration in 1976. Economic stagnation, double-digit price inflation, President Jimmy Carter's (served 1977–1981) call for national sacrifice, and the chaos of the Iranian hostage crisis left Americans numb. Many felt that their future looked bleak unless something new were done. When Ronald Reagan (served 1981–1989) promised a new era of economic growth and prosperity in the 1980 campaign, in contrast to the economic malaise experienced under Carter, it was little wonder that he won the election. In his 1981 inaugural address Reagan claimed that "government is the problem," while calling for a new economic policy based on "supply-side" economics. Cuts in government spending for social programs, three years of dramatic federal income tax cuts, and accelerated depreciation for new investments by businesses heralded a new age. Reagan, a former Hollywood actor and governor of California, told U.S. citizens that it was "morning in America" again. With active business leadership and support, Reagan implemented his new economic policies with much fanfare.

While the 1980s saw heated debate over Reaganomics among scholars and some politicians, most Americans chose to believe in Reagan's vision. They hoped it would spark productivity increases, millions of new jobs, higher wages and salaries, and the return of prosperity that in the 1960s had seemed as if it would last forever. Yet careful examination of the economic record of the 1980s suggests, at best, a very mixed performance. While price inflation was brought under control by the Federal Reserve Board led by Paul Volcker (appointed in 1979), the tax cuts of the early Reagan years failed to result in useful investments in new products and technology to create more high-skilled, high-paying jobs. Growth measured in terms of higher Gross National Product and output per hour improved in the 1980s compared with the 1970s, yet nowhere near as fast as during the 1945–1975 period. The social costs of economic change took a high toll on most Americans, except for the very wealthy in the top five percent of individuals and families. The 1980s was only one of two decades in twentieth-century U.S. history in which the relative distribution of income shifted significantly. In the 1940s, relative income shares had moved away from the top into the hands of the lower middle, middle, and upper middle classes. In the 1980s, income shifts that had begun in the 1970s continued taking shares away from the lowest 80 percent of families and putting it into the hands of the top twenty percent (and even more so to the top five percent). The

Internal Revenue Service employees process income tax forms at a center in Ogden, Utah. The Reagan administration cut federal income taxes and reduced federal spending in the early 1980s. © ROGER RESSMEYER/CORBIS. REPRODUCED BY PERMISSION.

Reagan policies during a time of structural change away from the older industrial economy toward the newer service and information economy resulted in millions of jobs lost. These jobs were replaced by newer ones that paid lower wages and salaries, often included minimal or no benefits, and provided little chance for upward social mobility. It would take another decade and different economic policies to rebuild the national economy in time for the twenty-first century.

Primary Source

"Reagan Lives!" [excerpt]

> **SYNOPSIS:** Benjamin Friedman discusses the economic and social legacy of the Reagan economic policies of the 1980s.

The legislation enacting Reaganomics may now be mostly gone, but the economic legacy of Ronald Reagan remains. Perhaps more important, the political attitudes that made many Americans so receptive to the Reagan program in the first place remain as well. One of the most significant lessons to be drawn from the exhausting 1990 battle over federal tax and spending policies is simply that so many Americans are no more willing today to make the sacrifices needed to rectify the nation's fiscal imbalance—either to cut back middle-class entitlements or to eliminate jobs in defense industries, and certainly not to pay higher taxes—than they were when Ronald Reagan first assured them there was no need to do so. . . .

Even so, the Reagan legacy—the consequence of having sustained that imbalance for so long—is still very much with us. By now the objective realities created by an entire decade of over-borrowing and under-investing, including especially the shrinking supply of "good" jobs and the parallel failure of the average worker's wage to keep up with inflation, are familiar enough. So too are the signs, increasingly frequent and ever harder to ignore, of the loss of American influence in international economic relations following a decade of borrowing from abroad and selling off national assets. This summer's Persian Gulf invasion marked the first international crisis in decades in which the dollar fell instead of rallying. Since then Americans have watched the spectacle of our public officials, from Secretary of State Baker on down, going about the world, begging bowl in hand, soliciting contributions to finance what we can no longer afford on our own. Because no change in fiscal policy can suddenly wish into being the factories and machines that the nation failed to build during the last ten years, or magically erase the debts that it incurred, these aspects of the Reagan legacy will continue to shape our economic prospects for years to come, no matter how much we now raise taxes or cut government spending.

More fundamentally, when we consider the moral obligations that the members of any society either do or do not accept in their relationships with one another, both individually and in the aggregate, it seems still to be true that many Americans reject any notion of their own responsibility for the government's chronic fiscal imbalance and its consequences, as well as any need that they should join in correcting it. Who, after all, thinks he pays too little in taxes? Who thinks his Social Security check is too big? Who thinks his parents pay too little for medical care? Whatever people may believe about the abstractions that so often dominate the public debate over our nation's fiscal policies, the 1990 budget battle showed that many Americans even now remain unwilling to accept the basic truth of the matter. Despite all the self-reassuring accusations to the effect that "they" (Are they the poor? the ill? the elderly? defense contractors? farmers?) are bleeding "our" pocketbooks, our basic problem is that members of the average American family insist on government services—for themselves, for their parents, and for their children—that cost more than what they are willing to pay in taxes.

Economic Fundamentals: Opportunity or Danger?

. . . First, the dramatic increase in economic inequality among Americans in recent years inevitably brought into sharp focus the question of how to distribute whatever sacrifices the new fiscal measures would entail. Before the 1980s, a standard way to duck potentially fractious debates about whether the American system of mixed capitalism tended toward a more or less equal distribution of wealth and incomes was to complain that, because of the paucity of hard data about who owns what, no one could really say. That answer no longer suffices. Within the last ten years the difference between rich and poor has widened in ways that are easily visible despite the continuing absence of precise data.

Even within the limited sphere of wages earned by those who are working, the change has been startling. In 1979, college-educated workers earned 47 percent more on average than those with just high-

school educations. Today the gap is 67 percent. Ten years ago the chief executive officers of the nation's 300 largest companies made on average 29 times what the typical manufacturing worker made. Now the multiple is 93 to 1. The enormous changes in asset values in recent years—and hence the widening gap between families who already owned houses before the price explosion of the 1970s and those who now can't afford to buy one, or between investors who participated in the 1982–1987 stock market boom and everyone who didn't—only exaggerate the overall distortion.

Especially against the background of this widening inequality, any call for sacrifice by large numbers of families would naturally have raised the issue of "fairness." But concerns over inequality carry a different burden when, on average, incomes are rising from when incomes are stagnant or even falling. If most families were earning more today than they were a few years ago, the air would be full of talk about how a rising tide lifts most boats, albeit by uneven amounts, and unfortunately leaves a few behind. The reality, and hence the prevailing attitude, is far different. In 1990 not that many Americans are, in Ronald Reagan's famous phrase, better off than they were, four (or even eight) years ago.

The second economic development of the 1980s that powerfully influenced the political environment within which the 1990 budget battle took place is simply that the average American family is losing ground, and knows it. The steep decline in earning power that began with the first OPEC oil shock and, after a respite in the late 1970s, extended through the Reagan-Volcker recession was bad enough. But at least the families who suffered through it could see some identifiable problems on which to lay the blame, including oil prices that went in two stages from $3 per barrel to $30, and then the need for a period of economic slack—in fact, the most severe business downturn since the depression of the 1930s—to halt spiraling inflation. By the mid-1980s, however, with oil prices falling and inflation under control, and the Reagan administration proclaiming a new era of economic expansion, people thought they had earned the right to incomes that would once again be rising.

They were wrong. In 1983, the first year of the new expansion of the economy, the average American worker in business earned $281 per week. That expansion will probably end soon, if it has not ended already, but even so it has fulfilled one part of the promise held out for it by becoming the longest running economic expansion in American peacetime experience. It has failed, however, to deliver the rising real wages that have accompanied previous expansions. Wage increases outdistanced inflation (barely) in only two years out of the next seven, and by mid-1990 the average worker was earning just $267 per week in 1983 dollars.

These two fundamental economic developments of the 1980s, widening inequality and a declining average income, are not independent of each other; nor is either unrelated to the fiscal policies that the nation has pursued. On average since 1980 the federal government's borrowing has absorbed nearly three fourths of all net saving done by American families and businesses combined. As a result, the share of the nation's income devoted to net investment in new plants and equipment has been lower than at any time since World War II. The absence of new factories and new machines has, in turn, not only restricted productivity growth and therefore wage growth in the nation's basic industries but also sharply curtailed the supply of jobs that these industries have to offer.

Jobs in manufacturing still pay about one third more, on average, than jobs in other industries, just as they did in the late 1970s. The difference is that today there are fewer of them. In 1979 American manufacturing firms employed just over 21 million workers. By the time the 1981–1982 recession ended, 18.2 million were left. Today, after nearly eight years of recovery and expansion, there are just 19.1 million. This makes the 1980s the first decade since the Industrial Revolution in which the number of Americans working in manufacturing has fallen.

From one perspective, of course, the fact that two thirds of the manufacturing jobs lost in the 1981–1982 recession disappeared permanently meant "leaner and meaner" companies that could afford to pay higher executive salaries and still generate ample profit to stimulate sharply rising stock prices. But an entire decade of shrinking employment in the sector of the economy that has traditionally provided the nation's largest source of high-wage jobs has also depressed living standards on average throughout the work force. And it has importantly contributed to widening inequality by taking away what used to be the greatest opportunity for most workers who could not afford college. After we allow for inflation, young high-school-educated males—the group most likely to compete for manufacturing jobs—now earn 18 percent less on average than in 1979.

The combination of widening inequality and a declining average wage may be understandable as the result of the economic policies America has followed during the last ten years, but that does not make the combination any the less potent as a political force. Indeed, most observers who have recognized these fundamental developments, and have inferred that they work to the advantage of one political party or the other (typically the Democrats), have probably underestimated the variety and the volatility of the likely public responses. Awareness that one's own economic situation has deteriorated, envy toward those who have somehow gotten ahead, frustration over the nation's increasing impotence in world affairs, and a general sense of discouragement that any of these trends will be reversed in the future—these all breed the kind of popular reaction that can be difficult for conventional politicians of either party to address. The result is a political climate in which departures from the norm in all directions, ranging from the promisingly innovative to the frighteningly ugly, may flourish.

Further Resources

BOOKS

Berman, Larry, ed. *Looking Back on the Reagan Presidency.* Baltimore, Md.: Johns Hopkins University Press, 1989.

Bernstein, Michael A., and David E. Adler, eds. *Understanding American Economic Decline.* New York: Cambridge University Press, 1994.

Blumenthal, Sidney, and Thomas Byrne Edsall, eds. *The Reagan Legacy.* New York: Pantheon Books, 1988.

Burch, Philip H. *Reagan, Bush, and Right-Wing Politics: Elites, Think Tanks, Power and Policy.* Greenwich, Conn.: JAI Press, 1997.

Conley, Richard S., ed. *Reassessing the Reagan Presidency.* Lanham, Md.: University Press of America, 2003.

Ehrenreich, Barbara. *Fear of Falling: The Inner Life of the Middle Class.* New York: Pantheon Books, 1989.

———. *The Worst Years of Our Lives: Irreverent Notes From a Decade of Greed.* New York: Pantheon Books, 1990.

Feldstein, Martin. *Revolution: The Reagan Legacy.* Stanford, Calif.: Hoover Institution, 1990.

Friedman, Benjamin M. *Day of Reckoning: The Consequences of American Economic Policy Under Reagan and After.* New York: Random House, 1988.

———, and National Bureau of Economic Research. *What Have We Learned from the Reagan Deficits and Their Disappearance?* Cambridge, Mass.: National Bureau of Economic Research, 2000.

Harrison, Bennett, and Barry Bluestone. *The Great U-Turn: Corporate Restructuring and the Polarizing of America.* New York: Basic Books, 1988.

Johnson, Haynes B. *Sleepwalking Through History: America in the Reagan Years.* New York: 1991.

Judis, John B. *The Paradox of American Democracy: Elites, Special Interests, and the Betrayal of Public Trust.* New York: Routledge, 2001.

Krugman, Paul R. *Peddling Prosperity: Economic Sense and Nonsense in the Age of Diminished Expectations.* New York: 1994.

Levy, Peter B. *Encyclopedia of the Reagan-Bush Years.* Westport, Conn.: Greenwood Press, 1996.

Obey, David, and Paul Sarbanes, eds. *The Changing American Economy: Papers from the Fortieth Anniversary Symposium of the Joint Economic Committee of the United States Congress.* New York: Blackwell, 1986.

Palmer, John, and Isabel Sawyer. *The Reagan Record: An Assessment of America's Changing Domestic Priorities.* Washington, D.C.: The Urban Institute, 1984.

Pemberton, William E. *Exit with Honor: The Life and Presidency of Ronald Reagan.* Armonk, N.Y.: M.E. Sharpe, 1997.

Peterson, Wallace C. *Silent Depression: The Fate of the American Dream.* New York: Norton, 1994.

Phillips, Kevin. *Boiling Point: Democrats, Republicans, and the Decline of Middle-Class Prosperity.* New York: HarperPerennial, 1994.

———. *The Politics of Rich and Poor: Wealth and the American Electorate in the Reagan Aftermath.* New York: Random House, 1990.

Schaller, Michael. *Reckoning with Reagan: America and Its President in the 1980s.* New York: Oxford University Press, 1992.

Schor, Juliet B. *The Overworked American: The Unexpected Decline of Leisure.* New York: Basic Books, 1992.

Yergin, Daniel, and Joseph Stanislaw. *The Commanding Heights: The Battle for the World Economy.* New York: Simon & Schuster, 2002.

PERIODICALS

Zinsmeister, Karl. "Summing Up the Reagan Era." *The Wilson Quarterly* 14, no. 1, Winter 1990, 110–117.

WEBSITES

""Commanding Heights: The Battle for the World Economy." PBS. Available online at http://www.pbs.org/wgbh/commandingheights/; website home page: http://www.pbs.org/ (accessed May 6, 2003). *This website is intended to accompany the television series of the same title, based on the book by Daniel Yergin and Joseph Stanislaw.*

Council of Economic Advisors. Available online at http://www.whitehouse.gov/cea/; website home page: http://www.whitehouse.gov/ (accessed May 9, 2003). *This website includes the annual "Economic Report of the President," which contains detailed economic information used in tracking economic productivity, growth, and income.*

EH.Net: Economic History Services. Available online at http://www.eh.net/ (accessed May 9, 2003). *This website provides a range of resources on economic history from the major professional groups including an encyclopedia, book reviews, datasets, and cost calculators at different points in history.*

National Bureau of Economic Research. Available online at http://www.nber.org/ (accessed May 9, 2003). *Founded in 1920, the NBER is the most widely known and respected scholarly source of statistical economic collection and analysis in the United States conducted by the nation's leading economists. NBER director Martin Feldstein served as President Reagan's key economic adviser.*

"National Income Accounts Data." Bureau of Economic Analysis. Available online at http://www.bea.doc.gov/bea/dn1.htm; website home page: http://www.bea.gov/ (accessed May 9, 2003). *Since the development of national income and accounts time series by scholars in the 1930's the BEA has conducted ongoing research, analysis, and distribution of updated statistical tables that place current economic productivity and growth figures into a longer term historical context as well as providing policymakers with detailed information for the economic policy–making process.*

Steckel, Richard H. "A History of the Standard of Living in the United States." EH.Net Encyclopedia. Robert Whaples, ed. Available online at http://www.eh.net/encyclopedia/steckel.standard.living.us.php; website home page: http://www.eh.net/encyclopedia/ (accessed May 9, 2003).

U.S. Census Bureau. Available online at http://www.census.gov/ (accessed May 9, 2003). *This website contains a wealth of detailed statistical information on a wide range of areas of American demographic, economic, social, ethnic, gender, and racial life. Many of the Census Bureau's specialized publications are included here in digital formats for easy download such as the annual "Statistical Abstract of the United States" and summary reports from decennial censuses as they become available.*

"Distribution of Family Income, 1973–1989"

Table

By: Sheldon Danziger and Peter Gottschalk

Date: 1992

Source: Danziger, Sheldon, and Peter Gottschalk, eds. "Distribution of Family Income, 1973–1989." In *Uneven Tides: Rising Inequality in America.* New York: Russell Sage Foundation, 1992.

About the Authors: Economist and professor of social work Sheldon Danziger (1948–), co-director of the National Poverty Research Center at the University of Michigan in the early 2000s, served as director of the University of Wisonsin's Institute for Research on Poverty from 1983 to 1988. Danziger was a Woodrow Wilson fellow, 1970, and National Science Foundation fellow, 1970–1972. He received his Ph.D. in 1975 from the Massachusetts Institute of Technology.

Economist Peter Gottschalk of Boston College is co-author of many works with Danziger. ∎

Introduction

In flowing rhetoric, President Ronald Reagan promised the American people that it was "morning in America again." Yet careful examination of the impact of economic changes on the income of families over the course of the period from the early 1970s to the late 1980s told a very different story. Economic researchers Danziger and Gottschalk conducted detailed study and analysis of family incomes, using the years 1973 and 1989 as baselines, to determine how they had changed over time. Statistical analysis of family income in America is often categorized in terms of "quintiles," consisting of twenty-percent blocks of the entire family population, in order to evaluate the ebb and flow of equality and inequality of income over relatively longer periods of time than just a year or two.

Danziger and Gottschalk's figures reveal a glaring change between 1973 and 1989—while the bottom eighty percent of American families saw their share of national income decline, the top twenty percent benefited from a dramatic increase of 3.5 percent. The second highest twenty percent saw declines of only 0.3 percent, but the middle and second lowest twenty-percent segments experienced drops of 1.0 and 1.3 percent. The lowest 20 percent had a decline in income of 0.9 percent. The overall pattern sug-

Distribution of Family Income, 1973–1989

Share of Income	1973	1989	% change, 1973–89
Top 20%	41.1%	44.6%	+3.5%
2nd highest 20%	24.0%	23.7%	−0.3%
Middle 20%	17.5%	16.5%	−1.0%
2nd lowest 20%	11.9%	10.6%	−1.3%
Lowest 20%	5.5%	4.6%	−0.9%

SOURCE: Danziger, Sheldon and Peter Gottschalk, eds. *Uneven Tides: Rising Inequality in America*. New York: Russel Sage Foundation, 1993.

Primary Source

"Distribution of Family Income, 1973–1989"

SYNOPSIS: Economists Sheldon Danziger and Peter Gottschalk's 1993 study traces the impact of economic policies on family income from 1973 to 1989, presenting a summary table of changes in family income over the 1970s and 1980s.

gests that between 1973 and 1989, the vast majority of American families saw their relative share of national income go down, while the top 20 percent of families received not only the only relative gain, but a large gain equal to that of the loss of the remaining 80 percent of families.

Ivana and Donald Trump relax on their yacht in 1988. The 1980s saw greater inequality in the nation's distribution of wealth. © **BETTMANN/CORBIS.**
REPRODUCED BY PERMISSION.

Significance

Political and economic language as used in election campaigns and by the mass media often obscures as much as it clarifies significant matters of public policy. While it is easy for politicians and economic leaders to employ words such as "opportunity," "equality," "democracy," "free enterprise," "the marketplace," and "government bureaucracy" to gain Americans' attention for their partisan recommendations, scholarly analysts must follow conventional rules of statistical sampling, measurable amounts, change over time, adjustments for changes in the cost of living, prices, and wages.

Although careful analyses of the impact of economic policies on Americans and their families at all income levels were conducted during the 1980s, they were largely lost in the noise of simpler rhetorical claims by advocates, critics, and opponents of new economic policies. By the end of the decade, a number of careful studies based on reliable statistics began showing a common threat of rising inequality of income for most Americans over the course of the 1970s and 1980s. Accustomed to seeing images of upper middle and upper class lifestyles on television and movie screens, many Americans came to believe the overheated rhetoric of the time, unaware that sober examination clearly revealed that the most dramatic change in the distribution of family incomes since the 1940s was a shift away from equality in a more ominous direction of rising inequality in relative terms. Additional studies of changes in the distribution of wealth among individuals and the distribution of wealth broken down by quintiles showed similar trends, although small differences emerged in terms of exact numbers. When future social and labor historians write the history of the 1980s, their accounts will reflect both the language of the decade and the economic realities in the declining fortunes of most American families.

Further Resources

BOOKS

Bartlett, Donald L., and James B. Steele. *America: What Went Wrong?* Kansas City, Mo.: Andrews and McMeel, 1992.

Campagna, Anthony S. *The Economy in the Reagan Years: The Economic Consequences of the Reagan Administrations.* Westport, Conn.: Greenwood Press, 1994.

Conley, Richard S., ed. *Reassessing the Reagan Presidency.* Lanham, Md.: University Press of America, 2003.

Ehrenreich, Barbara. *Fear of Falling: The Inner Life of the Middle Class.* New York: Pantheon Books, 1989.

———. *The Worst Years of Our Lives: Irreverent Notes From a Decade of Greed.* New York: Pantheon Books, 1990.

Friedman, Benjamin M. *Day of Reckoning: The Consequences of American Economic Policy Under Reagan and After.* New York: Random House, 1988.

Fuchs, Victor. *How We Live: An Economic Perspective on Americans from Birth to Death.* Cambridge, Mass.: Harvard University Press, 1983.

Krugman, Paul R. *Peddling Prosperity: Economic Sense and Nonsense in the Age of Diminished Expectations.* New York: Norton, 1994.

Lampman, Robert. *The Share of Top Wealth–Holders in National Wealth, 1922–56.* Princeton, N.J.: Princeton University Press, 1962.

Lekachman, Robert F. *Greed is Not Enough: Reaganomics.* New York: Pantheon Books, 1982.

———. *Visions and Nightmares: America After Reagan.* New York: Macmillan, 1987.

Levy, Frank. *Dollars and Dreams: The Changing American Income Distribution.* New York: Norton, 1988.

Peterson, Wallace C. *Silent Depression: The Fate of the American Dream.* New York: Norton, 1994.

Phillips, Kevin P. *Boiling Point: Democrats, Republicans, and the Decline of Middle-Class Prosperity.* New York: Harper-Perennial, 1994.

———. *The Politics of Rich and Poor: Wealth and the American Electorate in the Reagan Aftermath.* New York: Random House, 1990.

Wolff, Edward N. *Top Heavy: The Increasing Inequality of Wealth in America and What Can Be Done About It.* New York: The New Press, 1996.

———, ed. *International Comparisons of the Distribution of Household Wealth.* New York: Oxford University Press, 1987.

WEBSITES

Council of Economic Advisors. Available online at http://www.whitehouse.gov/cea/ (accessed May 10, 2003). *This website includes the annual* Economic Report of the President, *which contains detailed economic information used in tracking economic productivity, growth, and income.*

National Bureau of Economic Research. Available online at http://www.nber.org/ (accessed May 10, 2003). *Founded in 1920, the NBER is the most widely known and respected scholarly source of statistical economic collection and analysis in the United States conducted by the nation's leading economists. NBER director Martin Feldstein served as President Reagan's key economic advisor.*

"National Income Accounts Data." Bureau of Economic Analysis, U.S. Department of Commerce. Available online at http://www.bea.doc.gov/bea/dn1.htm; website home page: http://www.bea.doc.gov/ (accessed May 10, 2003). *Since the development of national income and accounts time series by scholars in the 1930's, the BEA has conducted ongoing research, analysis, and distribution of updated statistical tables that place current economic productivity and growth figures into a longer term historical context as well as providing policymakers with detailed information for the economic policy-making process.*

Steckel, Richard H. "A History of the Standard of Living in the United States." EH.Net Encyclopedia. Robert Whaples, ed. Available online at http://www.eh.net/encyclopedia/steckel.standard.living.us.php; website home page: http://www.eh.net/ (accessed May 10, 2003).

U.S. Census Bureau. Department of Commerce. Available online at http://www.census.gov/ (accessed May 10, 2003). *This website contains a wealth of detailed statistical information on a wide range of areas of American demographic, economic, social, ethnic, gender, and racial life. Many of the Census Bureau's specialized publications are included here in digital formats for easy download such as the annual "Statistical Abstract of the United States" and summary reports from decennial censuses as they become available.*

"My Time with Supply-Side Economics"

Journal article

By: Paul Craig Roberts

Date: 2003

Source: Roberts, Paul Craig. "My Time with Supply-Side Economics." *The Independent Review* 7, no 3, Winter 2003, 393–396.

About the Author: Economist Paul C. Roberts (1939–) played a key role in discussions within the Ronald Reagan administration about sparking economic growth. An advocate of "supply-side economics," Roberts was able to mediate between economic theories, professional economic policymakers, and politicians who put together the 1981 Reagan tax cuts. He is author of *The Supply-Side Revolution* (1984). Roberts later joined the conservative Hoover Institution at Stanford University. ∎

Introduction

In the late 1970s, economists moved away from the older tradition of government spending as a way to invest in national economic growth for the future. A small group of academic economists and policy activists began taking a second look at the idea of using federal tax cuts to promote economic growth. If taxes that would otherwise go into government coffers were redistributed to individuals and businesses, they believed, growth would emerge from the supply side of producers of goods and services. Rather than waiting for government spending to create economic demand, investors, entrepreneurs, and business corporations could call forth expansion. By creating new products, expanding marketing and advertising, and investing in new technologies and plants, businesses would increase the nation's total volume of goods and services (known as the Gross National Product—GNP).

In adopting this new policy, the Reagan administration (1981–1989) would be able to address the economic difficulties of the Jimmy Carter years (1977–1981). By making it harder for people and firms to take out loans

by changes in the nation's money supply through the Federal Reserve Board and raising production with lower taxes and higher investment, "supply-side" economic policy could in theory lead to economic growth.

Economists such as Arthur Laffer and Milton Friedman called for a change in economic thinking about investment, the money supply, and taxes. Once federal taxes were lowered, growth would take off making possible productivity increases, more jobs, lower prices, and a greater amount of revenue to pay government bills. Members of Congress such as New York Republican Representative Jack Kemp began supporting the idea of a large tax cut to spark renewed prosperity in the 1980s. In its first economic report to the Congress, the Reagan administration advocated sizeable tax cuts over three years, which the national legislature quickly adopted. Here economist Roberts presents the administration's view of this major change in national economic policy that came about in the early years of the first Reagan administration.

Significance

By the late 1970s, economic policies first adopted in the 1960s came under increasing criticism from academic economists, business leaders, politicians, and policymakers. Advocates of "supply-side economics" began claiming that by changing the monetary policies of the Federal Reserve Board and lowering federal taxes, productivity could be dramatically improved. While the federal tax rate charged to businesses and individuals would go down, the volume of economic activity would increase so much that the total revenue collected from federal taxes would rise. This would make payment of the federal debt and decreases in the annual budget of the U.S. government possible, while creating millions of new jobs that would allow Americans to buy more consumer goods and services. In theory, "supply-side" economics sounded convincing, but in practice the effects of the Reagan tax cuts, combined with a Congress that would not rein in government spending on domestic programs, was disastrous. Annual deficits as a result of large increases in national defense expenditures rose for most of the decade. Tax cuts did not result in more revenues for the federal government. Instead, annual government budget deficits kept going up during the administrations of President Ronald Reagan (served 1981–1989) and George H. W. Bush (1989–1993).

Primary Source

"My Time with Supply-Side Economics" [excerpt]

> **SYNOPSIS:** Conservative economist Paul Craig Roberts explains the origins and his role in the "supply-side" economic policies of the early 1980s.

Former chairmen of the Council of Economic Advisors testify before the Senate Banking Committee on anti-inflation prices in 1980. Rising inflation during the Carter administration was one of the issues that led the Reagan government to bring about economic reform.
© BETTMANN/CORBIS. REPRODUCED BY PERMISSION.

Supply-side economics presented a fundamental challenge to Keynesian demand management. Keynesian multiplier rankings, which showed government spending to be a more effective stimulus to the economy than tax-rate reduction, had turned demand management into a ramp for government spending programs. Powerful vested interests organized in support of this policy. All Republicans could do was to bemoan the deficits necessary to maintain full employment. . . .

Supply-side economics came out of the policy process. It was the answer to the "malaise" of the Carter years," stagflation," and the worsening "Phillips curve" trade-offs between inflation and unemployment. Supply-side economists convinced policymakers, both Democrat and Republican, that "stagflation" resulted from a policy mix that pumped up demand with easy money while restricting output with high tax rates. This argument carried the day with policymakers before it did with academic economists, who resented the diminution of their policy influence and human capital.

I played a lead role in the economic policy change (Roberts 1984), but Norman Ture and Robert Mundell were the first supply-side theorists. Art Laffer recalls that Mundell discussed the relative-price effects of fiscal policy at the University of Chicago in the early 1970s, when Laffer joined the economics faculty. Laffer also recalls many conversations with Ture in Washington, D.C., in 1967 and 1968 in which Ture, a Chicago Ph.D., described the relative-

price effects of fiscal policy. My conversations with Ture in 1975 solidified my own thinking.

The interest-rate approach to the cost of capital predates the income tax. Supply-side economics brought the insight that marginal tax rates enter directly into the cost of capital. A reduction in marginal tax rates makes profitable investment opportunities that previously could not return a normal profit after meeting tax and depreciation charges.

This perspective provided a more promising policy for stimulating investment than the Keynesian idea of using monetary policy to drive market interest rates below the marginal return on plant and equipment. In a world of global capital markets, central banks cannot alter the real interest rate in financial markets independently of the technological, tax, and risk factors that determine the cost of capital. During the 1970s, such attempts in the United States resulted in higher nominal interest rates and a rise in inflation.

The conventional view, which stressed the interest rate as the important factor in the cost of capital, suffered from the misconception that higher government revenues from increased taxation can spur capital investment by lowering deficits and interest rates or by creating budget surpluses and retiring debt. Because taxation reduces investment and economic activity, the only certain way to reduce "crowding out" is to cut government expenditure.

Supply-side economics also added the insight that the total resources claimed by government (tax revenues plus borrowing) is an inadequate measure of the tax burden because it ignores the production that is lost owing to disincentives. In this perspective, a tax cut can be real even if it is not matched dollar for dollar with a spending cut. The relative-price effects will expand economic activity, thus making the tax cut partially self-financing even if people expect that taxes will be raised in the future to pay off government debt incurred by cutting tax rates.

As a policy, supply-side economics first won over Republicans in the House. Jack Kemp was the leader. Next, it won over important Democratic committee chairmen in the Senate, such as Joint Economic Committee chairman Lloyd Bentson and Finance Committee chairman Russell Long. For example, in 1979 and 1980 the annual report of the Joint Economic Committee abandoned demand management and called for the implementation of a supply-side policy. By the time of Ronald Reagan's election as president, there was bipartisan support in Congress for a supply-side change in the policy mix. Inflation would be restrained with monetary policy, and output would be expanded by lowering the after-tax cost of labor and capital.

President Reagan's economic program was contained in a document called *A Program for Economic Recovery,* published on February 18, 1981. Contrary to many uninformed academic economists' assertions, the administration did not base its program on a "Laffer curve" forecast that the tax cut would pay for itself. The administration decided not to fight the battle for a dynamic revenue forecast and used the standard static revenue forecasting still in use today. Tables in the document show that the administration assumed that every dollar of tax cut would result in a dollar of lost revenue.

The tax cut was expected to slow the growth of revenues. Receipts as a percentage of gross national product (GNP) were expected to fall from 21.1 percent in 1981 to 19.6 percent in 1986. To avoid rising deficits, the budget plan showed the necessity of slowing the growth of spending below the contemporary policy projections.

The "Reagan deficits" occurred because inflation fell substantially below the budget assumptions, and therefore real spending rose above projections. As the budget deficits resulted from the unexpected rate at which inflation declined, the deficits themselves could not be a source of inflation and high interest rates. The economic establishment and Wall Street mistook a result of unanticipated disinflation as a potential cause of inflation. Consequently, the inflation and high interest rates predicted by many economists never materialized.

Reagan's economic policy caused an increase in the willingness to hold dollars. The decline in velocity, together with tight monetary policy and a smaller tax component in the cost of labor and capital, broke the back of inflation more rapidly than forecasts, constrained by concepts such as "core inflation," had predicted. The decline in the income velocity of money during the 1980s is proof that the long recovery was not a Keynesian demand phenomenon. A demand-led recovery would have increased the income velocity of money.

Supply-side economics provides a different explanation of the U.S. current and capital accounts during the 1980s than the critique that blames the "twin deficits" on an excessive Keynesian expansion. The 1981 business tax cut and the reductions

in personal income tax rates in mid-1982 and mid-1983 raised the after-tax rate of return on real investment in the United States relative to that in the rest of the world. Consequently, instead of exporting capital, the United States retained it. U.S. balance of payments statistics show that a collapse in U.S. capital outflows accounts for the shift of the net capital inflow from negative to positive between 1982 and 1983. U.S. capital outflows declined $71 billion. Foreign capital inflow fell by $9 billion.

During the 1982–84 period, when the story of foreign money pouring into the United States to finance overconsumption was fixed firmly in the world's consciousness, there was no significant change in the inflow of foreign capital into the United States. U.S. capital outflow, however, collapsed from $121 billion to $24 billion, a decline of 80 percent. The money stayed at home, and we financed our own deficit.

The collapse in U.S. capital outflow is clearly the origin of the large trade deficit, which by definition is a mirror image of the capital surplus. Not until 1986, with the dollar falling and U.S. interest rates low, did the foreign capital inflow increase significantly. The "twin deficits" theory was just another Keynesian hoax.

Among politicians, Democrats moved early to identify with supply-side economics. Republicans, however, were divided. The Republican establishment had no stake in a policy identified with outsiders such as Jack Kemp and Ronald Reagan. With a view to the succession, establishment Republicans portrayed Reagan's policy as extreme and in need of their moderate hand. Political self-serving by the Republican establishment aided and abetted the Keynesian misinterpretation of Reagan's supply-side policy.

Further Resources
BOOKS
Anderson, Martin. *Revolution.* New York: Harcourt Brace Jovanovich, 1988.

Boskin, Michael J. *Reagan and the Economy: The Successes, Failures, and Unfinished Agenda.* San Francisco, Calif.: Institute for Contemporary Studies, 1987.

Campagna, Anthony S. *The Economy in the Reagan Years: The Economic Consequences of the Reagan Administrations.* Westport, Conn.: Greenwood, 1994.

Executive Office of the President, and Office of Management and Budget. *America's New Beginning: A Program for Economic Recovery Budget.* Washington, D.C.: U.S. Government Printing Office, 1981.

_____. *Fiscal Year 1982 Budget Revisions Budget.* Washington, D.C.: U.S. Government Printing Office, 1981.

Gilder, George F. *Wealth and Poverty.* New York: Basic Books, 1981.

Niskanen, William A. *Reaganomics: An Insider's Account of the Policies and the People.* New York: Oxford University Press, 1988.

———, Stephen Moore, and Cato Institute. *Supply-Side Tax Cuts and the Truth about the Reagan Economic Record.* Washington, D.C.: Cato Institute, 1996.

Regan, Donald T. *For the Record: From Wall Street to Washington.* San Diego: Harcourt Brace Jovanovich, 1988.

Roberts, Paul Craig. *The Supply-Side Revolution: An Insider's Account of Policymaking in Washington.* Cambridge, Mass.: Harvard University Press, 1984.

Sloan, John W. *The Reagan Effect: Economics and Presidential Leadership.* Lawrence: University Press of Kansas, 1999.

Spulber, Nicolas. *Managing the American Economy, from Roosevelt to Reagan.* Bloomington: Indiana University Press, 1989.

Stein, Herbert. *Presidential Economics: The Making of Economic Policy from Roosevelt to Reagan and Beyond.* New York: Simon and Schuster, 1984.

Tobin, James, and Murray L. Weidenbaum. *Two Revolutions in Economic Policy: The First Economic Reports of Presidents Kennedy and Reagan.* Cambridge, Mass: MIT Press, 1988.

Wanniski, Jude. *The Way the World Works.* New York: Simon and Schuster, 1979.

Weidenbaum, Murray L., and Kenneth W. Thompson. *Reagan and the Economy: Nine Intimate Perspectives.* Lanham, Md.: University Press of America; Charlottesville, Va.: Miller Center, 1994.

PERIODICALS

Carroll, James D., A. Lee Fritschler, and Bruce L. R. Smith. "Supply-Side Management in the Reagan Administration." *Public Administration Review* 45, no. 6, November/December 1985, 805–814.

Easterbrook, Greg. "Ideas Move Nations: How Conservative Think Tanks Have Helped to Transform the Terms of Political Debate." *The Atlantic* 257, January 1986, 66–80. Available online at http://www.theatlantic.com/politics/poli big/eastidea.htm

Reynolds, Alan, and Paul Craig Roberts. "What Really Happened in 1981." *The Independent Review* 5, no. 2, 2000, 279–281.

WEBSITES

Cato Institute: Individual Liberty, Limited Government, Free Markets, and Peace. Available online at http://www.cato .org/ (accessed May 12, 2003). *This website contains speeches, press releases, memoranda, and publications of libertarian policy activists and scholars who often influenced Reagan administration policies.*

Heritage Foundation: Policy Research & Analysis. Available online at http://www.heritage.org/ (accessed May 12, 2003). This website contains policy documents, press releases, and publications of conservative policy activists and scholars whose work proved among the most influential from any think tanks on various Reagan administration economic policies.

"Reagan: Actor, Governor, President—The Biography of a Popular but Contradictory Man." The Presidents Series, The American Experience, Public Broadcasting System. Available online at http://www.pbs.org/wgbh/amex/reagan/; website home page: http://www.pbs.org/ (accessed May 6, 2003). *This website contains still photos and entire transcript from the PBS series on American Presidents along with brief bibliographies and a selection of related websites.*

Ronald Reagan Presidential Library. Available online at http://www.reagan.utexas.edu/ (accessed May 12, 2003). *This website contains additional primary sources in the form of speeches and writings by President Reagan.*

"Ronald Wilson Reagan." Presidents of the United States (POTUS), Internet Public Library. Available online at http://www.ipl.org/div/potus/rwreagan.html; website home page: http://www.ipl.org/ (accessed May 6, 2003). *This website contains a brief biography, links to key documents, and a selection of sound clips from President Reagan's speeches.*

Tax History Project. http://www.taxhistory.org/ (accessed May 12, 2003). *This website contains articles on various topics related to changes in taxation over time.*

Woolley, John, and Gerhard Peters. "The American Presidency Project." University of California, Santa Barbara. Available online at http://www.presidency.ucsb.edu/index.php (accessed May 6, 2003). *This website contains additional primary sources including presidential election data; presidential portraits; the public papers and speeches of presidents from Herbert Hoover through Gerald Ford, Jimmy Carter, and George H.W. Bush; inaugural addresses and state of the union addresses for presidents from George Washington through George W. Bush; the Fireside Chats of Franklin D. Roosevelt; Saturday radio addresses for presidents from William J. Clinton through George W. Bush; and national political party platforms since 1840.*

3

EDUCATION

MILLIE JACKSON

Entries are arranged in chronological order by date of primary source. For entries with one primary source, the entry title is the same as the primary source title. Entries with more than one primary source have an overall entry title, followed by the titles of the primary sources.

Important Events in Education, 1980–1989

1980

- A Gallup poll shows that parents believe the top four problems in schools are discipline, drug use, poor curriculum, and low standards.

- Poll results show that African Americans from the Northeast gave public schools a "D."

- Seventy-nine percent of respondents favor instruction in morals.

- Dade County Florida School District decides not to provide special programs for twenty thousand refugees inundating south Florida.

- A court orders Rand-McNally Corporation, a publisher of junior-high chemistry textbooks, to pay $155,000 to two eighth graders injured while conducting an experiment outlined in their text.

- In July, a federal judge strikes down a Texas law excluding most illegal alien children from public schools, saying "the rights of man are not a function of immigration status."

- On July 4, the National Education Association (NEA) endorses Democrat Jimmy Carter for a second term as president. The NEA and other teacher unions have traditionally endorsed Democratic candidates because the party spends more than Republicans on education.

- On July 17, a U.S. Circuit Court of Appeals upholds a decision ordering New York school districts to provide signing interpreters for deaf children.

- In August, the Republican presidential platform in New York supports an end to busing and abolition of the U.S. Department of Education.

- On August 18, the U.S. Supreme Court strikes down a Kentucky law allowing public schools to post the Ten Commandments as a violation of the Establishment Clause of the First Amendment.

- In September, one million fewer children begin kindergarten than in 1979.

- On September 2, Franklin Military School, authorized by the Richmond, Virginia, Board of Education, opens as one of few public military academies. Known as a "miniature West Point," the school is hailed as a balance to the "open" schools elsewhere in Richmond.

- On October 1, science teachers publish the Mount St. Helens Curriculum Materials Project, materials that convert the volcano's eruption into lessons.

- In November, the Rand Corporation reports that schools that desegregate voluntarily offer a better education than those that desegregate under court order.

1981

- In January, a U.S. Circuit Court of Appeals rules that the First Amendment "does not permit public school officials to allow student prayer meetings in classrooms before school."

- On January 19, the last day of the Jimmy Carter administration, the U.S. Department of Education publishes a new, stricter interpretation of Title I regulations.

- On January 20, the Heritage Foundation, a conservative think tank, publishes "Agenda for Progress," recommending "the eventual goal of complete elimination of federal funding" for schools.

- In March, the Ronald Reagan administration downgrades the nutritional requirements of school lunches and defines ketchup and pickle relish as vegetables.

- In March, New York City schools, having identified an extra twenty thousand handicapped students to comply with a court order, find themselves with seven thousand handicapped students but no teachers.

- On March 5, parents of six public-school students sue the Philadelphia Board of Education for more than $20 million, claiming the students had been exposed to harmful levels of asbestos, a carcinogen.

- On April 5, the District of Columbia announces it will retain more than six thousand children in grades one through three under the schools' new competency-based curriculum.

- In October, a U.S. Circuit Court upholds the right of police to use police dogs to sniff the school locker of a student suspected of harboring drugs or alcohol.

1982

- In June, the South Dakota Supreme Court upholds the right of a public school to fire a biology teacher for "devoting too much instructional time to the Biblical account of creation."

- On August 10, a federal judge affirms the testimony of scientists and philosophers, many of them with international reputations, in rejecting a Louisiana creationism suit. The 1981 Louisiana law had required balanced treatment of creationism and evolution.

- In September, the National Assessment of Educational Progress announces that in five years Hispanic nine-year-olds have improved their reading skills twice as much as the average for children that age.

- In November, teacher unions in fourteen states declare Democratic gubernatorial victories to be "victories for education."

- On November 1, the College Board reports that the SAT for college-bound seniors in 1982 rose for the first time in nineteen years. The average verbal score was 425 and the average math score 467.

1983

- Chicago school officials announce they are investigating charges that school-bus drivers smoke marijuana and drink alcohol on the job.

- A U.S. Education Department survey of fifteen thousand kids reveals that children of working mothers scored lower on reading and math tests than those students with mothers who stay home.

- In January, a federal appeals court strikes down sex bias rules of the Department of Education, ruling that the department can regulate only those school programs that receive federal funds.

- On January 24, a U.S. Circuit Court of Appeals rules that handicapped students in Peoria, Illinois must pass minimum competency tests for a diploma if Illinois mandates the test for all students.

- On February 7, a U.S. district judge in Philadelphia rules that once a school district has integrated faculty, it need not maintain racial balance by reshuffling teachers' assignments.

- On February 21, school finance experts predict states will do little to equalize funding among districts the next decade because revenue shortfalls will leave states little discretionary money.

- On March 5, the director of curriculum in New York announces that teachers will assign all students a minimum amount of homework each night.

- On March 21, the U.S. Supreme Court hears the case of an unmarried teacher fired after she gave birth.

- On April 4, the American Association of School Administrators finds that schools spend Chapter II block grants on equipment not staff.

- On April 18, school security directors say most districts' computer files are vulnerable to hackers. Students' favorite ploy is to change grades in data banks.

- On May 16, a federal judge in Florida upholds denial of diplomas to seniors failing that state's minimum competency exam. The judge does not rule the exam biased, although African Americans are 57 percent of the failures but only 20 percent of students.

- On May 30, only half the students in Coalinga, California, return to their elementary schools, a week and a half after an earthquake measuring 6.5 on the Richter scale hit the town.

- On June 24, the U.S. Supreme Court upholds a lower court approval of New York's state aid to public schools despite the disparity it leaves between wealthy and poor districts.

- On July 11, the U.S. Supreme Court upholds a ban on sweep searches of students by dogs.

- On September 26, school officials from five areas sue the U.S. Department of Agriculture in hopes of suspending its verification procedure for free or reduced-price lunches. The suit charges that each verification costs the district eighteen dollars.

- On October 10, a long-range study finds that the low pay of Catholic school teachers (top pay of eighteen thousand dollars) compared to pay in the public schools (top of about thirty thousand dollars) contributes to the 20 percent turnover in Catholic school faculty.

- On November 21, in the first Wisconsin case of a teacher taking a student to court for battery, a Wisconsin teacher wins twenty-three thousand dollars in punitive damages from a student who hit him three times in the face.

- On December 19, a Vatican research group urges parochial schools to strengthen sex education.

1984

- On January 16, the Pasadena, Maryland, school board rejects a request from a fundamentalist Christian parent who wants teachers to tell the "truth" about Santa Claus to first graders.

- On February 27, a state superintendent-appointed committee in Alabama finds that teachers have too little time to sell class rings, caps, gowns, yearbooks, and the other paraphernalia desired by high-school seniors.

- On February 28, the Cincinnati, Ohio school district becomes the latest to end years of struggle against desegregation by designing a voluntary system that uses magnet schools.

- On March 26, Dr. Robert Graham, a member of Ronald Reagan's Task Force on Food Assistance, suggests a universal school-lunch program that taxes parents for the value of kids' meals as income.

- On May 6, Congress authorizes $425 million in fiscal 1984 for new programs in math, science, and foreign languages over the next five years.

- On May 7, Texas repeals a 1974 textbook restriction requiring the Big Bang theory to be presented as "only one of several explanations" of how the universe began.

- On June 4, a Hicksville, New York, school district approves a referendum reinstating a period of silent meditation at the beginning of the school day. A parent vows to sue with the help of the New York Civil Liberties Union if the period exists when her daughter begins school in September.

- On July 9, the installation of a computer system capable of phoning the parents of everyone absent without permission and doing so in English, Spanish, and Vietnamese reduces class cutting 45 percent in Arlington, Virginia high schools.

- On September 11, Los Angeles, California officials require students to maintain a C average with no failures to participate in extracurricular activities.

- In October, 200 Yale University clerical workers strike to protest low pay and demeaning treatment from professors and administrators. Strikers staged a peaceful blockade of the Yale president's house to bring their plight to national attention.

- In October, a judge in Schuylkill County, Pennsylvania, upholds the decision of Catholic school officials who kicked a sixteen-year-old football player off the team for getting another student pregnant.

- On October 8, the U.S. Supreme Court agrees to hear an Oklahoma City case in which a school district claims authority to fire homosexual teachers who espouse homosexuality.

- On December 17, ten Arkansas teachers sue to block the state from requiring them to take a literacy test and a competency exam in their subject areas.

- On December 18, the National Council for Better Education, a conservative group, announces plans to recruit teachers who want an alternative to the National Education Association.

1985

- A study reports that one-third of U.S. teachers are uncomfortable using computers; nearly all want more training.

- A jury requires U.S. Gypsum to pay $675,000 to School District Five of Lexington and Richland Counties in South Carolina for asbestos removal from Irmo High School after learning that the company's safety director knew of dangers as early as 1955.

- The nation's 2.1 million teachers receive an average 7.3 percent pay raise, for an average 1984–1985 salary of $23,546.

- An annual Gallup poll on education shows a split among teachers, principals, and the public on the worst problem facing education. Principals claim lack of money; teachers claim too much paperwork; the public claims discipline.

- On January 3, Secretary of Education Terrel H. Bell reports that none of the states with top SAT students—Wisconsin, New Hampshire, Iowa, and Minnesota—spent the most money on public education.

- On January 7, the Chicago school board reaches an agreement with twenty thousand striking teachers, out for two weeks, by offering a 4.5 percent salary increase.

- In February, a random sample of student achievement before and after five Colorado school districts went to a four-day week shows performance unaffected.

- On February 4, the U.S. Supreme Court affirms "reasonable" searches of students—upholding a New Jersey vice principal who searched the purse of a fourteen-year-old drug dealer.

- On February 5, Montgomery County, Maryland, announces plans to send school information such as report cards and newsletters to both divorced parents, not just the custodial parent.

- In May, Johns Hopkins University researchers give students at Pimlico Middle School in Baltimore tokens worth thirty-five cents for attending classes. Students may spend the tokens at the school store or cafeteria.

- On May 7, *Science,* the journal of the American Association for the Advancement of Science, publishes a study of more than one thousand scientific and technical journals during a three-year period to determine if evidence of creationism was being suppressed. Of more than 135,000 articles submitted, only eighteen concerned creationism, and none was written by an author skilled in the scientific method.

- In June, the ACT announces that trade and technology jobs have replaced social-services occupations as the most popular career choices among eighth and eleventh graders.

- On June 10, the U.S. Agriculture Department scraps its ban on the sale of junk food at public schools. Nevertheless, schools may not sell junk-food in the cafeteria or at lunchtime.

- On June 15, the U.S. Supreme Court strikes down a 1981 Alabama law granting public schools the right to allow silent prayer as a violation of the Establishment Clause of the First Amendment.

- In July, a study by the Southern Regional Education Board finds that education majors take less-demanding courses than most students.

- On July 8, the Youth Suicide Center says the last person a suicidal teen would confide in is a school counselor—and that 11 percent of U.S. high-school seniors have attempted suicide sometime in their lives.

- On August 5, sixty years after John Scopes went on trial in Tennessee for teaching the theory of evolution in a high-school biology class, a federal appeals court strikes down a four-year-old Louisiana law mandating the teaching of creationism.

- On August 27, the U.S. Supreme Court, in *New Jersey v. T.L.O.,* affirms the right of public schools to search the possessions of a student suspected of an infraction without first obtaining a search warrant.

- In September, the journal *Phi Delta Kappan* reprints Ohio University professor Myron Lieberman's 1959 article calling for an independent national board to certify superior teachers modeled on similar bodies that exist for lawyers and doctors.

- On September 23, a Metropolitan Life Insurance poll claims that by 1990 one of every four teachers will have left the job because of low pay and poor work conditions. Only 36 percent of teachers believe merit pay and teacher bonuses benefit education.

- On October 8, the National Center for Education Statistics announces that high-school students in 1982 did less homework than peers in 1972, but more than students in 1980.

- On October 15, fitness expert Bonnie Prudden tells a U.S. Senate subcommittee that today's sixteen-year-olds did worse on fitness tests than students did thirty years ago. Fifty-eight percent of American students, but only 8 percent of Europeans, failed a standard fitness test.

- On December 13, the *Journal of the American Medical Association* reports that students and teachers run a high risk of contracting hepatitis B virus from mentally retarded children mainstreamed into classrooms.

1986

- The U.S. Department of Education announces in the first federal study of U.S. teachers in fifteen years that most put in long workweeks, are likely to have an advanced degree, and earn $22,701. One-third of male and one-fifth of female teachers have a second job.

- Parents, in the annual Gallup poll of education, say for the first time that drugs are the worst problem in schools, replacing the perennial favorite: discipline.

- In January, the American Association of School Administrators reports, for the first time in its twelve years of keeping records, that a principal surpasses seventy thousand dollars in salary.

- In February, for the fifth time in five years, President Ronald Reagan requests a reduction in federal spending for education. For fiscal year 1987 the total is $15.2 billion, down $3.2 billion from fiscal year 1986.

- On February 24, the Council for Basic Education reports that minimum competency tests for students are at best a "waste of time, at worst, a form of consumer fraud."

- On March 10, the American Association of School Administrators releases a study of the 154 best high schools. Their commonalities are "the hardest to pin down": a positive climate, strong administrative leadership, and excellent teachers.

- On March 24, a study shows that women are increasing their representation on U.S. school boards: from 12 percent in 1972 to 38 percent in 1985.

- In April, Broughton High School in Raleigh, North Carolina, is the first public school in the nation to establish a private endowment. The endowment of one hundred thousand dollars gives the school's two best teachers a five thousand dollar bonus in 1986.

- On May 5, the National Council on Year-Round Education estimates that more than two hundred students in some three hundred schools are in year-round schools. Most common is the 45/15 plan, in which students spend forty-five days in class, then fifteen days on vacation.

- On June 16, a teachers union charges bias in a test given in March to two hundred thousand Texas teachers. One percent of white teachers failed the test, but 18 percent of African American teachers and 6 percent of Hispanic teachers failed.

- On August 28, Nobel laureates denounce creationism at a news conference, saying that to "teach that the statements of Genesis are scientific truths is to deny all the evidence."

- On September 9, the National Education Association says that social ills are schools' biggest problems. Teachers cannot solve suicide, teen pregnancy, and teen drug use.

- On September 14, the U.S. Department of Education announces that the per-pupil expenditure for this school year has reached a high of $4,263.

- On September 22, a University of Minnesota study finds that 80 percent of latchkey children like being home alone, and that nearly 30 percent of children in K-3 go home to a situation with no adult custodian.

- On October 6, a National Assessment of Educational Progress survey shows that of thirty-six hundred adults ages twenty-one to twenty-five, only 40 percent could understand a newspaper editorial; only 20 percent could use a bus schedule to plan a trip; and only 10 percent could interpret a four-line poem by Emily Dickinson.

- On October 20, a House-Senate committee sets the Education Department's budget for fiscal year 1987 at $19.2 billion, more than 25 percent above President Ronald Reagan's request for $15.2 billion.

- On October 30, Education Secretary William Bennett and Defense Secretary Caspar Weinberger hold a press conference to promote military retirees as candidates for teaching positions. They present a new brochure, "A Second Career for You," published by the Department of Education to military retirees.

- On November 3, U.S. Surgeon General C. Everett Koop urges schools to launch programs at the "lowest grade possible" to warn children of the dangers of AIDS (acquired immunodeficiency syndrome).

- On November 17, in the first case of its kind, a student athlete at the University of Colorado challenges a school-run drug testing program as a violation of the Fourth Amendment's ban on unreasonable search and seizure.

- On December 1, in a nationwide study of teacher evaluations, the Rand Corporation concludes that most schools do not put enough resources into the program, and that "even fewer put the results into action."

1987

- In February, Education Secretary William Bennett reports no improvement on SAT scores and a drop in graduation rates in thirty-three states.

- On February 9, the U.S. Supreme Court announces it will consider in *Karcher v. May* the legality of a New Jersey law allowing one minute of "silent contemplation" at the start of the school day.

- On February 23, a Kent State University researcher creates an interactive video simulation of violence in schools to train prospective teachers.

- On May 4, the New Jersey Supreme Court, in a 7-0 decision, requires schools to admit students with AIDS.

- On June 15, a survey shows that graduates of vocational education programs in Ohio earn 21 percent more than students with no vocational training.

- On July 25, the U.S. Supreme Court strikes down a Louisiana law that had required public schools to teach creationism alongside evolution.

- On August 17, the California Board of Education, setting what could be a mandate for textbook publishing nationwide, unanimously passes a measure requiring more information on religion in history textbooks.

- On September 1, the U.S. Department of Education notifies nearly a million student-loan defaulters that they must pay by October 1 or pay collection costs plus repayment loans, adding up to 45 percent to their bills.

- On September 28, Columbia University Teachers College finds that U.S. secondary-school students know less about science than their predecessors did in 1970 and that they lag behind students in England and Japan.

- On November 9, a group of twelve conservative historians and education writers attacks American history text publishers, accusing them of filling student texts with "cowardice, commercialism, condescension, and crassness" and serving as "cheerleaders for minorities at the expense of central stories that mark the nation's development."

- On December 7, a coalition of urban school superintendents releases a plan to decrease the nation's dropout rate; it includes early intervention, a positive school climate, high expectations for students, and strong teachers.

1988

- On January 18, the Education Commission of the States reports that the majority of illiterates in America are white.

- On February 1, the U.S. Supreme Court gives school administrators wide latitude over student newspapers in *Hazelwood v. Kuhlmeier*. In a 5-3 decision, the majority writes, "A school need not tolerate student speech that is inconsistent with its mission, even though government could not censor similar speech outside school."

- On February 12, the National Center for Educational Information reports that public-school administrators, mostly male, white, and well paid, have higher opinions of schools than does the public.

- On March 14, the fifth annual Department of Education "wall chart" shows SAT scores unchanged.

- On May 23, the National Endowment for the Arts reports that American education produces "artistic and cultural illiterates."

- On June 28, the National Council of State Legislatures warns that most states will need to increase taxes to reform public education.

- In September, Lauro Cavazos replaces William Bennett as Secretary of Education.

- On September 12, the Rand Corporation recommends recruiting homemakers and career switchers to fill a shortage of qualified math and science teachers.

- On September 26, the U.S. Education Department reports that special education costs less in the mainstream. The cost to educate a student in special-ed classes is $8,649 per year, but in regular classes the cost drops to $3,847.

- In November, seven thousand schools receive a series of ten videos to dissuade children from drug use. The Drug-Free Schools and Communities Act funded these videos.

- On December 19, principals from several districts report that student uniforms have improved their school climate and have support from 97 percent of parents.

1989

- In January, a NAACP Defense Fund survey says poor African Americans rely on education to catapult their children from poverty.

- In February, a New Jersey court affirmed the right of schools to grant or refuse tenure to a teacher. Tenure guarantees employment for the duration of a person's career barring illegal conduct or dereliction of duty.

- On February 27, the National Research Council reports that three of four American students do not master enough math to cope in college or on the job.

- On March 13, the American Association of School Administrators (AASA) reports that principals' salaries outpace inflation, with the average principal earning $52,987.

- On April 24, the Education Writers Association labels a quarter of the nation's eighty-eight thousand school buildings a threat to children's safety.

- In May, the Texas Supreme Court rules, 9-0, that the state's school-finance system is unconstitutional because it offers poor children a poor education. Texas must devise a new funding formula by May 1990.

- On May 8, the EPA finds high radon levels in schools in sixteen states. Twenty-two percent of the three thousand classrooms tested exceeded standards for radon gas.

- On July 17, the U.S. Supreme Court rules that states are immune from parent suits for tuition reimbursement for private-school special education. Local school districts must continue bearing the burden alone.

- On September 11, a study shows that children from small families outstrip their classmates from large families in educational attainment.

- On September 25, the Women's Sports Foundation analyzed data on thirteen thousand students and found that female high-school athletes are more likely to enter college than nonathletes.

- On October 23, a survey reveals that fewer students are drinking alcohol and using drugs than two years ago, but more are smoking cigarettes.

- In December, the American Institute for Research announces that forty-four states require teachers to pass competency tests, up from just ten in 1980.

- On December 4, the Virginia State Board of Education declares that parents need not tell school officials if their child has AIDS.

- On December 18, the U.S. Supreme Court refuses to review a ruling that no child is too handicapped to receive services from school districts.

Why Johnny Still Can't Read: A New Look at the Scandal of Our Schools

Nonfiction work

By: Rudolf Flesch

Date: 1981

Source: Flesch, Rudolf. *Why Johnny Still Can't Read: A New Look at the Scandal of Our Schools.* New York: Harper & Row, 1981, 1–5.

About the Author: Rudolf Flesch (1911–1986) was an expert on literacy and writing. He was born in Vienna and became a citizen of the United States in 1938. He earned a B.S. (1940), M.A. (1942), and a Ph.D. (1943) from Columbia. Flesch, who believed that the phonetic approach was the best way to teach reading, wrote *Why Johnny Can't Read* in 1955. ∎

Introduction

Rudolf Flesch's 1955 *Why Johnny Can't Read* examined the crisis in teaching reading as he saw it. His companion volume, *Why Johnny Still Can't Read: A New Look at the Scandal of Our Schools,* published in 1981, reiterates his concern with the contemporary methods of teaching reading in the elementary schools. He contrasts the use of phonics to teach reading with what he calls the "look and say" method of learning.

The controversy about how to teach reading was nothing new in 1981. However, the popularity of whole language and reading and writing across the entire curriculum was gaining ground in the schools. These methods concentrated on using books to teach children to read, instead of the drills associated with phonics. In the meantime, parents and public reports were requesting phonics training for young children. Programs such as *Hooked on Phonics,* published by the Gateway Co., were being advertised as home instruction methods for parents to use. Adult illiteracy studies and lower standardized test scores were used as proof that children were not being taught to read effectively. Jeanne Chall, a well-respected reading researcher, noted that the lower scores on SAT tests corresponded with the years that the students attended first and second grade. This seemed proof that the "look and say" method had failed children.

Rudolf Flesch questions educators who say that phonics is being taught, and that it is only a partial method of teaching reading. He cites studies going back to the 1940s to support his view that "phonics first" is the only way to teach children to be successful readers. Flesch's "ten alibis," presented in Chapter 5, outline his favorite excuses from educators. In subsequent chapters, he expands upon these alibis—noting what is wrong with each one in his opinion. Rudolf Flesch was not the last author to take on the "phonics vs. whole language methods" of teaching reading. The controversy still existed at the beginning of the twenty-first century.

Significance

Rudolf Flesch's anger was apparent from his tone and the examples cited in the opening chapters of *Why Johnny Still Can't Read.* Flesch lists the "Phonics Five" and the "Dismal Dozen" series of readers. The latter teach what he calls the "look and say" method of reading which he rejected. His book is intended for parents, as much as the educational community. Flesch calls for parental involvement in the selection of textbooks, and in monitoring how their children are taught.

Reviewers of the book noted that politics play an important part in the decisions about how to teach reading. Joseph Featherstone, a headmaster and widely published author on educational issues, states that "Rudolf Flesch is clearly a man of terrific conviction, and his writing has the vigor that flows from a single powerful idea." Featherstone goes on to say that reading is far more complicated than Flesch describes. "Questions about what stirs hearts and minds" must be considered when analyzing why students cannot or do not read. John Merrow, an educational commentator, hopes that "this book reaches a wide audience, because Flesch is right about phonics." Merrow does not agree with Flesch on every point, however, noting that Flesch "offers no proof" of the conspiracies he outlines in the book.

Although the movement in reading research was leaning toward literacy research at the beginning of the 1980s, phonics research and promotion were not dead. This is especially clear in the 1990 publication of Marilyn Adams' *Beginning to Read.* That book caused a furor at the beginning of the next decade because Adams, like Flesch, proposed the use of phonics to teach young children to read.

Why Johnny Still Can't Read is important because it was published at a time when teaching reading was shifting toward a more integrated approach of learning. Researchers were looking at the whole child and the whole curriculum for ways to encourage and teach. Flesch, though controversial, never abandoned the basic skills that he viewed as vital to the process of reading and the foundation of learning.

Children work on an English problem at the chalkboard during a language lesson. AP/WIDE WORLD PHOTOS. REPRODUCED BY PERMISSION.

Primary Source

Why Johnny Still Can't Read: A New Look at the Scandal of Our Schools [excerpt]

SYNOPSIS: Flesch points out specific problems with the major reading series used in the schools. He delves into the teacher's manuals to provide examples of the methods of teaching which these series, such as Scott Foresman and Ginn, advocate.

Are you worrying about your child's education? You should be. There's an 85 percent chance that your Johnny or Mary will never learn to read properly.

There are two schools of thought about how to teach a child to read. One is called "intensive phonics" or "systematic phonics" or, more recently, "decoding" or "code emphasis." In this book, to avoid confusion, I'll call it "phonics-first." The other is called the "look-and-say" or "whole-word" or "sight-reading" method or—so help me—"psycholinguistics." I'll use "look-and-say."

When I wrote my book *Why Johnny Can't Read* twenty-five years ago, look-and-say ruled supreme.

Almost all American schools used it. Phonics-first was a poor orphan, used only in a handful of schools.

I said in my book that phonics-first worked splendidly and should be used in all schools, while look-and-say was wretchedly poor and should be abandoned at once.

Unfortunately my advice fell on deaf ears. With heart-breaking slowness, phonics-first crept into some 15 percent of our schools, but an estimated 85 percent of them still stick to old, discredited look-and-say.

The results of this mass miseducation have been disastrous. America is rapidly sinking into a morass of ignorance. The official statistics are appalling.

In 1975 the U.S. Office of Education sponsored the so-called APL (Adult Performance Level) study, conducted by Dr. Norvel Northcutt of the University of Texas in Austin. It was designed to find out how many Americans had the skills to cope with modern life. It showed that 21.7 percent of adults between eighteen and sixty-five—or 23 million people—couldn't read a want ad, a job application form, a label on a medicine bottle, or a safety sign at a workplace.

Of those 23 million, 16 percent had never gone beyond third grade. This left 19 million who'd had four or more years of schooling but never learned how to read. Why? Because almost all of them were taught by look-and-say, and the method doesn't work.

And what happened at the other end of the educational scale? How did our brightest young people do at college age after they'd been taught reading by look-and-say in first grade? For them, look-and-say worked like a time bomb. In 1963 the nationwide college entrance test (Scholastic Aptitude Test or SAT) scores began to drop. They've been dropping steeply ever since, with no end in sight. Verbal SAT averages, which stood at 478 in 1963, were down to 424 in 1980—a staggering drop of 9 percent of the whole 200–800-point range in seventeen years.

In 1977 a blue-ribbon twenty-one-member advisory panel, headed by former Secretary of Labor Willard Wirtz, issued a report on the decline in the SAT scores. "The panel members," it said, "share strongly the national concern about the increasing signs of functional illiteracy . . . [but they could find] no *one* cause of the SAT score decline."

However, in an appendix to the report, Professor Jeanne Chall of Harvard University offered a clue to that one basic cause. The students' low SAT scores, she wrote, had a "clearcut" statistical relationship to the reading instruction program used ten years earlier in first grade. The program had been based on a series of "look-and-say" readers.

There's little doubt that we'll soon have doctors who can't easily read medical journals, lawyers who have difficulty researching a case, scientists who stumble through their professional literature. In the 1990s we'll have to import top professionals from abroad. We'll join the ranks of such under-educated Third World countries as the Ivory Coast, Saudi Arabia, and Zambia. And there'll be few, if any, Nobel Prize winners who learned to read in an American school.

I've earned the right to say that these grim prospects are the direct results of look-and-say teaching in our schools. Twenty-five years ago I studied American methods of teaching reading and warned against educational catastrophe. Now it has happened.

Surely you don't want your Johnny or Mary to grow up as a functional illiterate or educational crip-

ple. In this book I'll show you what you can do to help your child get a good education.

I'll start with the difference between phonics-first and look-and-say.

Learning to read is like learning to drive a car. You take lessons and learn the mechanics and the rules of the road. After a few weeks you've learned how to drive, how to stop, how to shift gears, how to park, and how to signal. You've also learned to stop at a red light and understand road signs. When you're ready, you take a road test, and if you pass, you can drive.

Phonics-first works the same way. The child learns the mechanics of reading, and when he's through, he can read.

Look-and-say works differently. The child is taught to read *before* he's learned the mechanics—the sounds of the letters. It's like learning to drive by starting your car and driving ahead. You'd learn to recognize and remember certain landmarks. First, on your street, you pass by the big yellow garage, the house with a plastic stork on the lawn, and the dentist's house. You turn right and pass the plumber, the florist, and the Italian restaurant. You turn again and drive by the stationery store, the carpenter, the podiatrist, the funeral home, and the bank. Then you come to the big intersection with the Exxon and the Texaco gas stations. You turn again and pass the diner, the gift shop, the drugstore, the optometrist, the little knit shop, and the pediatrician. One more turn and you're back home.

Continuing that "look-and-say" method of learning how to drive, you would repeat that lesson for three or four months until you'd be fully familiar with all the landmarks—the yellow garage, the plastic stork, the dentist, the plumber, the florist, the Italian restaurant, the stationery store, the carpenter, the podiatrist, the funeral home, the bank, the Exxon station, the Texaco station, the diner, the gift shop, the drugstore, the optometrist, the knit shop, and the pediatrician. You'd have learned to drive around the block.

Then you'd be allowed to go farther. Three months and you would have learned how to drive to the Catholic church and the supermarket. By the time you've fully learned those other landmarks, it would be the end of the school year and you would have a "landmark vocabulary" of 350 items. Next year you'd learn to drive to the railroad station and the Protestant church on the hill.

And the mechanics of driving? You'd pick those up as you go along. After three months you'd learn how to step on the brake, after another two months you'd learn how to signal. Next year you'd learn about traffic lights.

Now let's see how these two methods work with reading. With phonics-first the child is first taught the letters of the alphabet and what sounds they stand for. Since English has only twenty-six letters to express about forty-four sounds, this is done in a strict sequence so that the child sees only words whose letter sounds he has already learned. For instance, a sentence in the first Lippincott reader says, "Ann and Dan pin up the map." Before they get to that sentence, the children have learned the sounds of *n, d, p, m,* short *a,* short *i,* and short *u.* They've also learned the word *the,* one of a handful of special words taught out of sequence to make it possible to tell a story.

At the end of a semester or a year or two years, depending on which phonic system you use, children can read an estimated 24,000 words in their speaking or listening vocabulary. They can then go on to grammar, composition, literature, social studies, and science—in other words, they can start on their education.

And how does look-and-say work? It works on the principle that children learn to read by reading. It starts with little "stories" containing the most-often-used words in English and gradually builds up a "sight vocabulary." The children learn to read by seeing those words over and over again. By the end of first grade they can recognize 349 words, by the end of second grade 1,094, by the end of third grade 1,216, and by the end of fourth grade 1,554. (I got those numbers from the Scott, Foresman series, but all look-and-say series teach about the same number of words.)

The Scott, Foresman cumulative fourth-grade list contains the words *anteater, chariot, freckle, Hawaiian, laryngitis, peccary, Siberian, skunk,* and *toothpick.* But it does *not* contain the words *boil, cell, cheap, church, coal, cost, crime, due, fact, pain, pray, pride, puff, root, steam, stock, sum, tax, twelve,* and *vote.* These are words a look-and-say-trained child may *not* be able to read by the end of fourth grade. Of course, if he'd been taught phonics-first, he'd be able to read his full speaking or listening vocabulary, which has been estimated at 40,000 words.

Further Resources
BOOKS
Adams, Marilyn Jager. *Beginning to Read: Thinking and Learning about Print.* Cambridge, Mass.: The MIT Press, 1990.

Pearson, P. David. "Reading." In *Encyclopedia of Educational Research.* Vol. 3, 6th ed., New York: Macmillan Publishing, 1992, 1075–1085.

PERIODICALS
Featherstone, Joseph. "Teaching & Learning." *The New York Times Book Review,* August 9, 1981, 10–11, 21.

Frager, Alan M. "Three Faces of Reading." *Clearing House,* 59, no. 4, December 1985, 158–161.

Merrow, John. "Home from School." *New Republic,* 185, December 23, 1981, 38–40.

WEBSITES
Leman, Nicholas. "The Reading Wars." The Atlantic Monthly Online. Available online at http://www.theatlantic.com/issues/97nov/read.htm; website home page http://www.theatlantic.com (accessed May 11, 2003).

AUDIO AND VISUAL MEDIA
Hooked on Phonics. Gateway Productions, Ltd., Audiocassettes, 1988.

Ways With Words: Language, Life and Work in Communities and Classrooms
Nonfiction work

By: Shirley Brice Heath
Date: 1983
Source: Heath, Shirley Brice. *Ways With Words: Language, Life, and Work in Communities and Classrooms.* Cambridge: Cambridge University Press, 1983, 44–47.
About the Author: Shirley Brice Heath is the Margery Bailey Professor of English and Dramatic Literature at Stanford University. She is an anthropologist, linguist, and social historian. Her research focuses on oral and written language, youth development, race relations, and organizational learning. She has published several books and over 100 articles and book chapters. Heath was a MacArthur Foundation Fellow in 1984. ∎

Introduction
Ethnographers study other cultures to discover what is unique about their ways of life and behaviors. The research combines elements of social history with anthropology and education. Shirley Brice Heath studied two communities and classrooms in the rural Southeast of the United States to discover how children learned language at home and at school. The communities she visited are known as "Roadville," a white working class community, and "Trackton," a black working class community. Roadville residents had worked in the textile mills for generations, while the older generations of Trackton residents

farmed, and the current generation worked in mills. The additional group of townspeople are black and white middle class.

Heath's study began during the 1960s when desegregation was changing the way of life in the South. She was teaching at a university in the Piedmont region of the Carolinas when her students raised the question central to her study: "What were the effects of preschool home and community environments on the learning of those language structures and uses that were needed in classrooms and job settings?" Answering this question lead Heath to do field work between 1969 and 1978 in the two communities. She lived and worked in both cities, gaining entry and trust through residents she knew. Roadville and Trackton each had fewer than 150 residents. Shirley Brice Heath presents the oral traditions and the written traditions that shape the children's language. Understanding the culture which children bring to school is an important part of understanding how to teach children new skills. The study is not a model for other studies. While children in other communities can be studied, this was a unique time and place, as well as a unique pair of communities. What we learn from Heath is how people communicate, and how they come to understand one another.

Significance

Shirley Brice Heath's book *Ways With Words* has been described as an "international classic." Originally published in 1983, it was reissued in 1996 with a postepilogue. The book is "arguably the most widely cited study of children's language use in and out of school." This long term study documents how the way children learn language affects their integration into the academic and work community.

National Council Teachers of English awarded *Ways with Words* the 1985 David H. Russell Award. This study "reminds us of the complexities of language learning and the importance of understanding the social context of language development and use." Further, Heath's work recognized interdisciplinary studies and the importance of understanding social backgrounds as a way to improve teaching. The teachers in Heath's study learned how to use the children's backgrounds and language practices for "creating innovative learning opportunities and adjusting their classrooms and teaching strategies." Researchers, including Brian Street, have built on Heath's work to explain sociolinguistic differences in communities.

Heath's findings now seem to be common knowledge in the educational community. She observed the importance of nonverbal cues, as well as verbal ones. She noted that teams were important for working and learning, and that families and schools play a part in the child's development and language skills. Teachers must recognize that all children do not learn in the same manner, and they do not have the same linguistic background. For these observations, Heath's work is valuable for educational research. However, her work is also vital for its insight into community life and its recommendations for conducting fieldwork over time. Heath has devoted her career to studying the language of children and youth. A thirty-year follow up study was planned for "Roadville" and "Trackton."

Primary Source

Ways With Words: Language, Life, and Work in Communities and Classrooms [excerpt]

SYNOPSIS: In this section, Brice Heath explains the "paradox" of school. While the Roadville parents understand that education is valuable, they do not become involved in their children's education—as middle class parents often do. The adults, especially women, seek education to find what they missed in their younger years. They also look for the secrets of middle class life.

The Role of Schooling

Families with teenagers advise those with preschoolers: "Enjoy it while you can, teach 'em all you can now. When they get on up in school, you can't teach 'em anything." Roadville parents of junior and senior high level students therefore both depend on and resent the school; the bringing together of differences in student backgrounds, extracurricular activities, and expectations of behavior have undermined their closed community's control and left them less able to relate to the school of today than to any other institution which touches their lives.

They puzzle over the paradox that school, longfamiliar in their own lives and the dreams of their parents, is now so changed. They remember their preparations with and their hopes for their preschoolers. When these hopes are clearly not being fulfilled, they blame teachers, school administrators, the blacks, and the federal government. Their children fail to get out of school what education always promised, and they wonder at their children's assertions that they do not need school to get ahead.

Once children begin school, Roadville parents see their responsibilities as restricted to seeing that their children attend regularly, bring their books home, and stay out of trouble. They do not ask about homework, and they offer little help on homework projects. Children rarely ask their parents for assistance, and when projects call for materials or knowledge not available from the classroom, most Roadville students do not complete assignments.

They do not bring books home to read for pleasure, and their afternoon activities—beyond the barest attention to mathematics assignments or straightforward fill-in-the blanks homework—include ballgames, helping around the house, visiting friends, or attending Scout meetings. Roadville parents expect their children to be good students, and they accept C students as good. They do not express dismay when their children get occasional Ds. They praise, admire, and are surprised by their A and B students. Peggy and Lee Brown's older child, Martin, was as a sixth grader an excellent student. Peggy, at any opportunity, expressed their pride in Martin: "He's twelve years old, 'n we're very proud of him, that he's turnin' out to be a *good boy,* an excellent student." Mothers take more interest in their children being good students than do fathers, and mothers are those who brag about their children's grades, while fathers brag about their children's participation in athletic events, cheerleading, and clubs at school.

Adult education classes in Gateway attract Roadville women who quit school to get married and quit the mill to have children. Betty and Peggy both returned to adult education to get their high school diplomas after they were married, and they often spoke of Martha's older sister who did the same. Among the young folks, all the wives have more education than their husbands. The difference between Mrs. Macken's schooling and her husband's is the most marked—and the most talked about by both that family and others. She finished college; he had only a high school education. Martha completed the eleventh grade, her husband quit at the ninth. Betty and Peggy were getting their high school diplomas; their husbands had none. Mrs. Turner had two years of college; her husband finished only high school. Many of the women believe they "know" more than their husbands, but they must keep their knowledge away from their husbands and exert their school knowledge in ways which their husbands will not notice. Mothers serve as Scout "den-mothers" and room mothers for their children's classrooms, and work in the parent-teacher organization in the elementary school. They usually belong to no other organizations, however; those who work in the mill do not have the time, and those who stay home with their children keep busy with gardening and other "hobbies" such as sewing and canning.

In their adult education classes, Roadville women seek out secrets of the educated middle-class townspeople. They observe and listen to town women talk whenever they can; they want to know how middle-class children succeed in school when their own children do not. However, Roadville women see and hear talk of only some few habits of the townspeople: their purchases, their dress, their travel. In their attempt to "do for their children," Roadville mothers therefore try to sew their clothes in new styles, plan more travel in the camper, and pay more attention to what the public media say one "should" do for children. They take their families to Alberta to the coliseum for flower shows and country music concerts. No matter that the educated and the school recommend visits to the museum and art shows; the Roadville family as a whole will tolerate only the flower show. There, they can find ideas and tasks to link to home practices and situations.

Their own expectation that hard work brings results, causes them to urge their children to "work hard" in school, and they ask for evidence of such hard work in practices familiar to them spelling words, "learnin' lessons," and doing homework. Yet on those rare occasions when their children confront them with what they must do at school, they cannot grasp the ultimate purpose of the activities called for; as Lisa put it: "we have to look up definitions all the time, 'n when we have a test, we look up answers to questions in science, 'n such as that." These tasks always seem to point to something else, to suggest that they will have some purpose, some place to be put to use. But neither Roadville parents nor children see and participate in these ultimate occasions for use. The average, and even the good, students seem to do only minimally what is asked of them to conform. They do not engage themselves creatively in making use of school tasks, in plugging them into some activity where they might make a difference. They see no reason to use the word whose definition was learned in English class last week in either a conversation at home, or in an essay for this week's American History class. Roadville students' social vitality and creativity seem to turn back into their own sense of dress and talk of cars and music. By the time they reach high school, they have written off school as not making any difference for what they want. At their age, they feel sure success in school tasks will threaten their social relations with those whose company they value. The jobs they want seem unrelated to the tasks school sets up for them. They recognize no situational relevance; they do not see that the skills and attitudes their teachers promote make any difference in the jobs they seek: flying, nursing, selling, etc. They want to get out now, or as soon as possible, to get on with the business for which they feel prepared: setting up homes and families, working to make money, and planning to get ahead. Meanwhile, in their own homes with their parents, the good meals and talk of the future go on, the winter gardens grow, mothers attentively sew new dresses for the school dance, and the sun shines on the chimneys of the mill.

Further Resources

BOOKS

Cazden, C.B. "Heath, Shirley Brice." In *Concise Encyclopedia of Sociolinguistics.* New York: Elsevier, 2001.

Edwards, A.D. "Oral Language, Culture and Class." In *Encyclopedia of Language and Education.* Vol. 3. Dordrecht: Kluwer Academic Publishers, 1997.

PERIODICALS

Daniell, Beth. "Narratives and Literacy: A Story about the Perils of Not Paying Attention." *College, Composition and Communication* 50, no. 3, February 1999, 393–410.

Ong S.J., Walter J. "Literacy and Orality in Our Times." *ADE Bulletin,* no. 58, September 1978, 1–7.

Prendergast, Catherine. "The Water in the Fishbowl: Historicizing *Ways with Words.*" *Written Communication,* 17, no. 4, October 2000, 452–490.

WEBSITES

Shirley Brice Heath. Available online at http://shirleybriceheath .com/ (accessed May 10, 2003).

Secretary of Education Terrel Bell. AP/WIDE WORLD PHOTOS. REPRODUCED BY PERMISSION.

A Nation at Risk

Report

By: The National Commission on Excellence in Education.
Date: 1983
Source: The National Commission on Excellence in Education. *A Nation at Risk: The Imperative for Educational Reform.* Washington, D.C.: The Commission, April 1983, 5–12.
About the Organization: T.H. Bell, Secretary of Education, formed the National Commission on Excellence in Education on August 26, 1981. Its eighteen members came from higher education, school boards, secondary classrooms and business. They were charged with studying education in the United States and returning a report of their findings within eighteen months. ∎

Introduction

Secretary of Education T.H. Bell gave the National Commission on Excellence in Education six tasks in its charter: assess the quality of teaching and learning in all of the nation's schools, including private and public; compare our schools to those in other nations; study the relationships between college admissions and student achievement in high school; identify programs that foster success in college; assess how social and educational

changes in the twenty-five preceding years affected student achievement; and define the problems to be faced and overcome by the nation's schools. The findings were to be reported to the nation as a whole, and suggestions for implementation of the Commission's recommendations were to be included in the report. The Commission sought input from a broad range of experts and the public. Hearings, commissioned papers and analysis, letters and descriptions of outstanding programs that already existed were all considered.

The conclusions of the Commission reflected the concern of the public that something truly was wrong in education. The findings included data indicating that standardized test scores had fallen, more adults were illiterate, and students were not prepared for college or for the workforce. The increasing number of remedial courses at the college level was noted, as were the lack of rigorous standards and grading. The course load and number of hours students spent in school in the United States compared poorly with other advanced countries. The Commission recommended implementation of a more rigorous curriculum that included English, math, science and foreign languages, as well as setting higher expectations for teachers. The Commission noted that their recommendations "are based on the beliefs that everyone can learn, that everyone is born with an *urge* to learn that can be nurtured, that a solid high school education is within the reach of virtually all, and that lifelong learning will equip people with the skills required for new careers and for citizenship (emphasis in the original)."

Significance

Media reactions and responses to the report *A Nation at Risk: The Imperative for Educational Reform* were predictable. The country's schools were failing our children, and we were not keeping up with other industrialized countries or ready for the dawning of the technological age. Reactions to the report, and others that followed it, noted the oversimplification of its findings. Schools are not all equal, and all children cannot be taught in the same way. Funding for schools and programs to improve education is not readily available to all districts or all colleges. Educators saw the report as "posing simple answers to complex questions" and "thinking that all questions have answers."

The overall conclusion of the Commission was that education was being "eroded by a rising tide of mediocrity." This alone raised concerns with the public, and it put education at the top of the nation's agenda. While the core curriculum of four years of English, three years of math, science and social studies and a semester of computer science was viewed as laudable, it was not seen as the only solution. The report focused on productivity and on its own version of excellence—rigid standards and high standardized test scores. The issues ignored included many of the global problems facing the nation at the beginning of the twenty-first century; social injustices, hunger, terrorism and religious persecution. Even in 1983, these problems were noted by critics of the findings.

Since its release, experts in the field of education have reflected on *A Nation at Risk*. In 1984, William Gardner pointed out that the report's "quick fix" approach was not the answer to what had occurred in education. It noted the same problems that educators had been discussing for decades. However, the "clear, readable" report, endorsed by politicians, drew attention that educators never enjoyed. A decade after releasing the report, Terrel H. Bell, former Secretary of Education, reflected on its findings and success. He admitted that the report was far more negative than he anticipated, and that its findings and statistics were not read with the cautions intended. Bell also noted the societal factors and influences of the home that the report ignored. Twenty years after the report was released, Pam Grossman, professor of education at Stanford, notes that the same wars are still being fought. She concludes that "teachers are still fighting for professional recognition and respect," and that education is once again at a crossroad. To fix education requires recognition that solutions are not simple, and that it takes more than a list of recommendations to solve the problems.

Primary Source

A Nation at Risk [excerpt]

SYNOPSIS: The Secretay of Education is free to form a commission to study educational goals and needs under 20 United States Code 1233a. These commissions are meant to be advisory in nature and to return information that will aid the country in improving education.

Our Nation is at risk. Our once unchallenged preeminence in commerce, industry, science, and technological innovation is being overtaken by competitors throughout the world. This report is concerned with only one of the many causes and dimensions of the problem, but it is the one that undergirds American prosperity, security, and civility. We report to the American people that while we can take justifiable pride in what our schools and colleges have historically accomplished and contributed to the United States and the well-being of its people, the educational foundations of our society are presently being eroded by a rising tide of mediocrity that threatens our very future as a Nation and a people. What was unimaginable a generation ago has begun to occur—others are matching and surpassing our educational attainments.

If an unfriendly foreign power had attempted to impose on America the mediocre educational performance that exists today, we might well have viewed it as an act of war. As it stands, we have allowed this to happen to ourselves. We have even squandered the gains in student achievement made in the wake of the Sputnik challenge. Moreover, we have dismantled essential support systems which helped make those gains possible. We have, in effect, been committing an act of unthinking, unilateral educational disarmament.

Our society and its educational institutions seem to have lost sight of the basic purposes of schooling, and of the high expectations and disciplined effort needed to attain them. This report, the result of 18 months of study, seeks to generate reform of our educational system in fundamental ways and to renew the Nation's commitment to schools and colleges of high quality throughout the length and breadth of our land.

That we have compromised this commitment is, upon reflection, hardly surprising, given the multitude of often conflicting demands we have placed on our Nation's schools and colleges. They are routinely called on to provide solutions to personal, social, and political problems that the home and other institutions either will not or cannot resolve. We must understand that these demands on our schools and colleges often exact an educational cost as well as a financial one.

On the occasion of the Commission's first meeting, President Reagan noted the central importance of education in American life when he said: "Certainly there are few areas of American life as important to our society, to our people, and to our families as our schools and colleges." This report, therefore, is as much an open letter to the American people as it is a report to the Secretary of Education. We are confident that the American people, properly informed, will do what is right for their children and for the generations to come.

The Risk

History is not kind to idlers. The time is long past when America's destiny was assured simply by an abundance of natural resources and inexhaustible human enthusiasm, and by our relative isolation from the malignant problems of older civilizations. The world is indeed one global village. We live among determined, well-educated, and strongly motivated competitors. We compete with them for international standing and markets, not only with products but also with the ideas of our laboratories and neighborhood workshops. America's position in the world may once have been reasonably secure with only a few exceptionally well-trained men and women. It is no longer.

The risk is not only that the Japanese make automobiles more efficiently than Americans and have government subsidies for development and export. It is not just that the South Koreans recently built the world's most efficient steel mill, or that American machine tools, once the pride of the world, are being displaced by German products. It is also that these developments signify a redistribution of trained capability throughout the globe. Knowledge, learning, information, and skilled intelligence are the new raw materials of international commerce and are today spreading throughout the world as vigorously as miracle drugs, synthetic fertilizers, and blue jeans did earlier. If only to keep and improve on the slim competitive edge we still retain in world markets, we must dedicate ourselves to the reform of our educational system for the benefit of all—old and young alike,

affluent and poor, majority and minority. Learning is the indispensable investment required for success in the "information age" we are entering.

Our concern, however, goes well beyond matters such as industry and commerce. It also includes the intellectual, moral, and spiritual strengths of our people which knit together the very fabric of our society. The people of the United States need to know that individuals in our society who do not possess the levels of skill, literacy, and training essential to this new era will be effectively disenfranchised, not simply from the material rewards that accompany competent performance, but also from the chance to participate fully in our national life. A high level of shared education is essential to a free, democratic society and to the fostering of a common culture, especially in a country that prides itself on pluralism and individual freedom.

For our country to function, citizens must be able to reach some common understandings on complex issues, often on short notice and on the basis of conflicting or incomplete evidence. Education helps form these common understandings, a point Thomas Jefferson made long ago in his justly famous dictum:

> I know no safe depository of the ultimate powers of the society but the people themselves; and if we think them not enlightened enough to exercise their control with a wholesome discretion, the remedy is not to take it from them but to inform their discretion.

Part of what is at risk is the promise first made on this continent: All, regardless of race or class or economic status, are entitled to a fair chance and to the tools for developing their individual powers of mind and spirit to the utmost. This promise means that all children by virtue of their own efforts, competently guided, can hope to attain the mature and informed judgment needed to secure gainful employment and to manage their own lives, thereby serving not only their own interests but also the progress of society itself.

Indicators of the Risk

The educational dimensions of the risk before us have been amply documented in testimony received by the Commission. For example:

> International comparisons of student achievement, completed a decade ago, reveal that on 19 academic tests American students were never first or second and, in comparison with other industrialized nations, were last seven times.

Some 23 million American adults are functionally illiterate by the simplest tests of everyday reading, writing, and comprehension.

About 13 percent of all 17-year-olds in the United States can be considered functionally illiterate. Functional illiteracy among minority youth may run as high as 40 percent.

Average achievement of high school students on most standardized tests is now lower than 26 years ago when Sputnik was launched.

Over half the population of gifted students do not match their tested ability with comparable achievement in school.

The College Board's Scholastic Aptitude Tests (SAT) demonstrate a virtually unbroken decline from 1963 to 1980. Average verbal scores fell over 50 points and average mathematics scores dropped nearly 40 points.

College Board achievement tests also reveal consistent declines in recent years in such subjects as physics and English.

Both the number and proportion of students demonstrating superior achievement on the SATs (i.e., those with scores of 650 or higher) have also dramatically declined.

Many 17-year-olds do not possess the "higher order" intellectual skills we should expect of them. Nearly 40 percent cannot draw inferences from written material; only one-fifth can write a persuasive essay; and only one-third can solve a mathematics problem requiring several steps.

There was a steady decline in science achievement scores of U.S. 17-year-olds as measured by national assessments of science in 1969, 1973, and 1977.

Between 1975 and 1980, remedial mathematics courses in public 4-year colleges increased by 72 percent and now constitute one-quarter of all mathematics courses taught in those institutions.

Average tested achievement of students graduating from college is also lower.

Business and military leaders complain that they are required to spend millions of dollars on costly remedial education and training programs in such basic skills as reading, writing, spelling, and computation. The Department of the Navy, for example, reported to the Com-

mission that one-quarter of its recent recruits cannot read at the ninth grade level, the minimum needed simply to understand written safety instructions. Without remedial work they cannot even begin, much less complete, the sophisticated training essential in much of the modern military.

These deficiencies come at a time when the demand for highly skilled workers in new fields is accelerating rapidly. For example:

Computers and computer-controlled equipment are penetrating every aspect of our lives—homes, factories, and offices.

One estimate indicates that by the turn of the century millions of jobs will involve laser technology and robotics.

Technology is radically transforming a host of other occupations. They include health care, medical science, energy production, food processing, construction, and the building, repair, and maintenance of sophisticated scientific, educational, military, and industrial equipment.

Analysts examining these indicators of student performance and the demands for new skills have made some chilling observations. Educational researcher Paul Hurd concluded at the end of a thorough national survey of student achievement that within the context of the modern scientific revolution, "We are raising a new generation of Americans that is scientifically and technologically illiterate." In a similar vein, John Slaughter, a former Director of the National Science Foundation, warned of "a growing chasm between a small scientific and technological elite and a citizenry ill-informed, indeed uninformed, on issues with a science component."

But the problem does not stop there, nor do all observers see it the same way. Some worry that schools may emphasize such rudiments as reading and computation at the expense of other essential skills such as comprehension, analysis, solving problems, and drawing conclusions. Still others are concerned that an over-emphasis on technical and occupational skills will leave little time for studying the arts and humanities that so enrich daily life, help maintain civility, and develop a sense of community. Knowledge of the humanities, they maintain, must be harnessed to science and technology if the latter are to remain creative and humane, just as the humanities need to be informed by science and technology if they are to remain relevant to the human condition. Another analyst, Paul Copperman, has drawn a sobering conclusion. Until now, he has noted:

> Each generation of Americans has outstripped its parents in education, in literacy, and in economic attainment. For the first time in the history of our country, the educational skills of one generation will not surpass, will not equal, will not even approach, those of their parents.

It is important, of course, to recognize that *the average citizen* today is better educated and more knowledgeable than the average citizen of a generation ago—more literate, and exposed to more mathematics, literature, and science. The positive impact of this fact on the well-being of our country and the lives of our people cannot be overstated. Nevertheless, *the average graduate* of our schools and colleges today is not as well-educated as the average graduate of 25 or 35 years ago, when a much smaller proportion of our population completed high school and college. The negative impact of this fact likewise cannot be overstated.

Hope and Frustration

Statistics and their interpretation by experts show only the surface dimension of the difficulties we face. Beneath them lies a tension between hope and frustration that characterizes current attitudes about education at every level.

We have heard the voices of high school and college students, school board members, and teachers; of leaders of industry, minority groups, and higher education; of parents and State officials. We could hear the hope evident in their commitment to quality education and in their descriptions of outstanding programs and schools. We could also hear the intensity of their frustration, a growing impatience with shoddiness in many walks of American life, and the complaint that this shoddiness is too often reflected in our schools and colleges. Their frustration threatens to overwhelm their hope.

What lies behind this emerging national sense of frustration can be described as both a dimming of personal expectations and the fear of losing a shared vision for America.

On the personal level the student, the parent, and the caring teacher all perceive that a basic promise is not being kept. More and more young people emerge from high school ready neither for college nor for work. This predicament becomes more acute as the knowledge base continues its rapid expansion, the number of traditional jobs shrinks, and new jobs demand greater sophistication and preparation.

On a broader scale, we sense that this undertone of frustration has significant political implications, for it cuts across ages, generations, races, and political and economic groups. We have come to understand that the public will demand that educational and political leaders act forcefully and effectively on these issues. Indeed, such demands have already appeared and could well become a unifying national preoccupation. This unity, however, can be achieved only if we avoid the unproductive tendency of some to search for scapegoats among the victims, such as the beleaguered teachers.

On the positive side is the significant movement by political and educational leaders to search for solutions—so far centering largely on the nearly desperate need for increased support for the teaching of mathematics and science. This movement is but a start on what we believe is a larger and more educationally encompassing need to improve teaching and learning in fields such as English, history, geography, economics, and foreign languages. We believe this movement must be broadened and directed toward reform and excellence throughout education.

Further Resources

BOOKS

Gordon, David T., ed. *A Nation Reformed? American Education Twenty Years after A Nation at Risk.* Cambridge, Mass.: Harvard Education Press, 2003.

Ravitch, Diane. *What Do Our 17 Year Olds Know? A Report on the First National Assessment of History and Literature.* New York: Harper & Row, 1987.

PERIODICALS

Bell, Terrel H. "Reflections One Decade after A Nation at Risk." *Phi Delta Kappan* 74, no. 8, April 1993, 592–597.

Gardner, William E. "A Nation at Risk: Some Critical Comments." *Journal of Teacher Education,* 35, no. 1, January-February 1984, 13–15.

Nash, Robert J., and Edward R. Ducharme. "Where There is no Vision, the People Perish: A Nation at Risk" *Journal of Teacher Education* 34, no. 4, July-August 1983, 38–46.

WEBSITES

Grossman, Pam. "Teaching: From A Nation at Risk to a Profession at Risk?" Harvard Education Letter Research Online. Available online at http://www.edletter.org/past/issues /2003-jf/nation.shtml; website home page http://www.edletter .org (accessed May 10, 2003).

Bob Jones University v. U.S.

Supreme Court decision

By: Warren Burger

Date: 1983

Source: Burger, Warren. *Bob Jones University v. United States,* 461 U.S. 574, 578, 580–581, 585–588, 592–593, 595–596 (1983). Available online at http://laws.findlaw.com /us/461/574.html; website home page http://laws.findlaw.com (accessed May 10, 2003).

About the Author: Warren Burger (1908–1995) served as chief justice of the United States Supreme Court from 1969 to 1986. Appointed by President Richard Nixon (served 1969–1974), Burger was viewed as a conservative and advocate of judicial restraint, in contrast to his immediate predecessor as chief justice, Earl Warren. ∎

Introduction

The battle over the tax-exempt status of Bob Jones University (BJU) began in 1970. BJU, located in Greenville, South Carolina, was founded in 1927 by Dr. Bob Jones Sr. The college is a non-denominational, liberal arts school that advocates "old time religion and the absolute authority of the Bible" The regulations issued by IRS 501(c)(3) did not allow an institution which discriminated based on race to have tax exempt status. Prior to 1970, "any otherwise qualified private school that engaged in racially discriminatory practices could obtain tax-exempt status, according to the IRS policy, if it did not receive aid from a State or one of its political subdivisions whereby its operation was in violation of the Constitution or existing Federal law." This changed when a group of African American parents in Mississippi filed suit against private schools which refused to admit their children. The courts upheld the 1964 Civil Rights legislation and added language to the tax code prohibiting private schools from becoming tax exempt if they discriminated based on race.

Private schools are not necessarily religious. This is where the problems of Bob Jones University began. Asserting a constitutional right to freedom of religion, BJU stated that it should be tax-exempt and allowed to act on its beliefs, based on its interpretation of the Bible—which, among other things, did not allow African American students admission. When African Americans were admitted, only married couples were allowed to attend. In 1975, when single African American students were admitted, BJU's strict rule forbidding interracial marriage and dating drew much attention.

Chief Justice Warren Burger delivered the Supreme Court's ruling on May 24, 1983. In an 8-1 decision, the Court held that Bob Jones University was not a charitable institution entitled to tax-exempt status under IRS 501(c)(3). Bob Jones University denied that it was discriminatory in its admissions practices. The ruling also included the Goldsboro Christian Schools, who freely admitted that they discriminated based on race.

Significance

The U.S. Court of Appeals for the Fourth Circuit had already revoked Bob Jones University's tax exempt status. The Supreme Court's affirmation of the denial of tax-exempt status for BJU was a significant step in declaring that racial discrimination would not be tolerated. The ruling came near the end of the session, and many thought that the court might delay its decision until the following year. The debate escalated in January 1982, when President Ronald Reagan (served 1981–1989) "called off the IRS and restored tax-exempt status to the 111 private schools, including Bob Jones University, that were ruled ineligible for tax-exempt certificates." Reagan declared that the decision to determine who could be tax exempt should be made by Congress, not the IRS. This decision further muddied the waters, and caused the suit to go forward to the Supreme Court.

The case centered on public policy and the university's ban on interracial relationships and marriage. If a school was to receive tax exemption, then it must uphold certain public policy or public beliefs. The main issue was whether the university could deny individual rights in the name of religious freedom, based on its interpretation of the Bible, yet still receive tax-exempt status. Tax-exemption is a vital part of funding nonprofit institutions. It allows not only for exemptions from paying taxes, it also allows donations to be tax deductible. The decision made the university liable for over a half-million dollars in back taxes.

The case created strange alliances. Citizens of Greenville, South Carolina—not enamored with BJU— supported the university on the principle of freedom to think and believe as one chooses. Some religious leaders supported BJU for similar reasons. Dean M. Kelley, executive for religious and civil liberty of the National Council of Churches, found the confinement of the ruling to education disturbing and feared for the future of churches' tax-exempt status.

Bob Jones University is still not tax exempt, nor does it accept federal funds for financial aid. The university, self-proclaimed as "the world's most unusual university," continues to practice its religious beliefs over capitulating to receive tax-exempt status.

Primary Source

Bob Jones University v. U.S. [excerpt]

SYNOPSIS: Sections A and B of the Supreme Court decision outlined the revisions to the IRS rulings on charitable groups and prior cases that influenced the decision. The admissions policies of Bob Jones University were also detailed. Students and faculty at the university are required to sign documents stating that they agree with the policies of the university in order to attend.

Chief Justice Burger delivered the opinion of the Court.

We granted certiorari to decide whether petitioners, nonprofit private schools that prescribe and enforce racially discriminatory admissions standards on the basis of religious doctrine, qualify as tax-exempt organizations under 501(c) (3) of the Internal Revenue Code of 1954.

I

A

Until 1970, the Internal Revenue Service granted tax-exempt status to private schools, without regard to their racial admissions policies, under 501(c)(3) of the Internal Revenue Code, 26 U.S.C. 501(c)(3), 1 and granted charitable deductions for contributions to such schools under 170 of the Code, 26 U.S.C. 170.

On January 12, 1970, a three-judge District Court for the District of Columbia issued a preliminary injunction prohibiting the IRS from according tax-exempt status to private schools in Mississippi that discriminated as to admissions on the basis of race. *Green v. Kennedy,* 309 F. Supp. 1127, appeal dism'd sub nom. *Cannon v. Green,* 398 U.S. 956 (1970). Thereafter, in July 1970, the IRS concluded that it could "no longer legally justify allowing tax-exempt status [under 501(c)(3)] to private schools which practice racial discrimination." IRS News Release, July 7, 1970, reprinted in App. in No. 81-3, p. A235. At the same time, the IRS announced that it could not "treat gifts to such schools as charitable deductions for income tax purposes." Ibid. By letter dated November 30, 1970, the IRS formally notified private schools, including those involved in this litigation, of this change in policy, "applicable to all private schools in the United States at all levels of education." See id., at A232. . . .

B

Bob Jones University is a nonprofit corporation located in Greenville, S.C. . . .

The sponsors of the University genuinely believe that the Bible forbids interracial dating and marriage.

To effectuate these views, Negroes were completely excluded until 1971. From 1971 to May 1975, the University accepted no applications from unmarried Negroes, but did accept applications from Negroes married within their race.

Following the decision of the United States Court of Appeals for the Fourth Circuit in *McCrary v. Runyon,* 515 F.2d 1082 (1975), aff'd, 427 U.S. 160 (1976), prohibiting racial exclusion from private schools, the University revised its policy. Since May 29, 1975, the University has permitted unmarried Negroes to enroll; but a disciplinary rule prohibits interracial dating and marriage. That rule reads:

There is to be no interracial dating.

1. Students who are partners in an interracial marriage will be expelled.

2. Students who are members of or affiliated with any group or organization which holds as one of its goals or advocates interracial marriage will be expelled.

3. Students who date outside of their own race will be expelled.

4. Students who espouse, promote, or encourage others to violate the University's dating rules and regulations will be expelled.

The University continues to deny admission to applicants engaged in an interracial marriage or known to advocate interracial marriage or dating. Id., at A277. . . .

II

A

In Revenue Ruling 71-447, the IRS formalized the policy, first announced in 1970, that 170 and 501(c)(3) embrace the common-law "charity" concept. Under that view, to qualify for a tax exemption pursuant to 501(c)(3), an institution must show, first, that it falls within one of the eight categories expressly set forth in that section, and second, that its activity is not contrary to settled public policy.

Section 501(c)(3) provides that "[c]orporations . . . organized and operated exclusively for religious, charitable . . . or educational purposes" are entitled to tax exemption. Petitioners argue that the plain language of the statute guarantees them tax-exempt status. They emphasize the absence of any language in the statute expressly requiring all exempt organizations to be "charitable" in the common-law sense, and they contend that the disjunctive "or" separating the categories in 501(c)(3) precludes such a

Bob Jones III (center left, in grey), the president of Bob Jones University, stands next to his father Bob Jones Jr. (r), in front of the U.S. Supreme Court on October 12, 1982. © BETTMANN/CORBIS. REPRODUCED BY PERMISSION.

reading. Instead, they argue that if an institution falls within one or more of the specified categories it is automatically entitled to exemption, without regard to whether it also qualifies as "charitable." The Court of Appeals rejected that contention and concluded that petitioners' interpretation of the statute "tears section 501(c)(3) from its roots." 639 F.2d, at 151.

It is a well-established canon of statutory construction that a court should go beyond the literal language of a statute if reliance on that language would defeat the plain purpose of the statute . . .

Section 501(c)(3) therefore must be analyzed and construed within the framework of the Internal Revenue Code and against the background of the congressional purposes. Such an examination reveals unmistakable evidence that, underlying all relevant parts of the Code, is the intent that entitlement to tax exemption depends on meeting certain common-law standards of charity—namely, that an institution seeking tax-exempt status must serve a public purpose and not be contrary to established public policy.

This "charitable" concept appears explicitly in 170 of the Code. That section contains a list of organizations virtually identical to that contained in 501(c)(3). It is apparent that Congress intended that list to have the same meaning in both sections. In 170, Congress used the list of organizations in defining the term "charitable contributions." On its face, therefore, 170 reveals that Congress' intention was to provide tax benefits to organizations serving charitable purposes. The form of 170 simply makes plain what common sense and history tell us: in enacting both 170 and 501(c)(3), Congress sought to provide

tax benefits to charitable organizations, to encourage the development of private institutions that serve a useful public purpose or supplement or take the place of public institutions of the same kind.

Tax exemptions for certain institutions thought beneficial to the social order of the country as a whole, or to a particular community, are deeply rooted in our history, as in that of England. The origins of such exemptions lie in the special privileges that have long been extended to charitable trusts. . . .

When the Government grants exemptions or allows deductions all taxpayers are affected; the very fact of the exemption or deduction for the donor means that other taxpayers can be said to be indirect and vicarious "donors." Charitable exemptions are justified on the basis that the exempt entity confers a public benefit—a benefit which the society or the community may not itself choose or be able to provide, or which supplements and advances the work of public institutions already supported by tax revenues. History buttresses logic to make clear that, to warrant exemption under 501(c)(3), an institution must fall within a category specified in that section and must demonstrably serve and be in harmony with the public interest. The institution's purpose must not be so at odds with the common community conscience as to undermine any public benefit that might otherwise be conferred.

B

We are bound to approach these questions with full awareness that determinations of public benefit and public policy are sensitive matters with serious implications for the institutions affected; a declaration that a given institution is not "charitable" should be made only where there can be no doubt that the activity involved is contrary to a fundamental public policy. But there can no longer be any doubt that racial discrimination in education violates deeply and widely accepted views of elementary justice. Prior to 1954, public education in many places still was conducted under the pall of *Plessy v. Ferguson,* 163 U.S. 537 (1896); racial segregation in primary and secondary education prevailed in many parts of the country. See, e. g., Segregation and the Fourteenth Amendment in the States (B. Reams & P. Wilson eds. 1975). This Court's decision in *Brown v. Board of Education,* 347 U.S. 483 (1954), signalled an end to that era. Over the past quarter of a century, every pronouncement of this Court and myriad Acts of Congress and Executive Orders attest a firm national policy to prohibit racial segregation and discrimination in public education. . . .

Given the stress and anguish of the history of efforts to escape from the shackles of the "separate but equal" doctrine of *Plessy v. Ferguson,* 163 U.S. 537 (1896), it cannot be said that educational institutions that, for whatever reasons, practice racial discrimination, are institutions exercising "beneficial and stabilizing influences in community life," *Walz v. Tax Comm'n,* 397 U.S. 664, 673 (1970), or should be encouraged by having all taxpayers share in their support by way of special tax status.

There can thus be no question that the interpretation of 170 and 501(c)(3) announced by the IRS in 1970 was correct. That it may be seen as belated does not undermine its soundness. It would be wholly incompatible with the concepts underlying tax exemption to grant the benefit of tax-exempt status to racially discriminatory educational entities, which "exer[t] a pervasive influence on the entire educational process." *Norwood v. Harrison,* supra, at 469. Whatever may be the rationale for such private schools' policies, and however sincere the rationale may be, racial discrimination in education is contrary to public policy. Racially discriminatory educational institutions cannot be viewed as conferring a public benefit within the "charitable" concept discussed earlier, or within the congressional intent underlying 170 and 501(c)(3).

Further Resources

BOOKS

Dalhouse, Mark Taylor. *An Island in the Lake of Fire: Bob Jones University, Fundamentalism, and the Separatists Movement.* Athens: University of Georgia Press, 1996.

United States Commission on Civil Rights. *Discriminatory Religious Schools and Tax Exempt Status.* Washington, D.C.: United States Commission on Civil Rights, 1982.

PERIODICALS

Connell, Christopher. "Bob Jones University: Doing Battle in the Name of Religion and Freedom." *Change,* 15, no. 4, May/June 1983, 38–47.

Kelley, Dean M. "The Supreme Court Redefines Tax Exemption." *Society,* 21, no. 4, May/June 1984, 23–28.

Rabkin, Jeremy. "Behind the tax-exempt schools debate." *The Public Interest,* 68, Summer 1982, 21–36.

WEBSITES

Bob Jones University. Available online at http://www.bju.edu/index.xml (accessed May 10, 2003).

"The Impact of Rule 48 Upon the Black Student Athlete: A Comment"

Journal article

By: Alexander Williams Jr.

Date: 1983

Source: Williams Jr., Alexander. "The Impact of Rule 48 Upon the Black Student Athlete: A Comment." *Journal of Negro Education* 52, no. 3, Summer 1983, 362–363, 370–372.

About the Author: Alexander Williams Jr. (1948–) was educated at Howard University and Temple University. As President Clinton's first African American nominee to the federal bench, he was appointed to the United States District Court in Maryland on August 18, 1994. Judge Williams served as a prosecutor for Prince George's County, practiced law in Washington D.C. and Maryland, and taught law at Howard Law School. ■

Introduction

At its convention in 1983, the National Collegiate Athletic Association (NCAA) adopted Rule 48, a proposition regarding eligibility for participating in football and basketball at Division I schools. The Rule took effect August 1, 1986, but not without much criticism and debate. Rule 48 has three parts. First, a high school senior must have a 2.0 grade point average on a 4.0 scale to be eligible for athletic participation. Second, the student must have taken eleven core classes in high school, including three in English, two in math, two in social studies, and two in natural or physical science. Finally, the student must have a combined score of 700 on the Scholastic Assessment Test (SAT), or a composite of fifteen on the American College Test (ACT). Many in and out of the educational community viewed them as racist.

Alexander Williams Jr., then an associate professor at Howard University Law School, outlined the inequities of Rule 48. As a lawyer, he questioned the legalities of the rule given the practice of leaving admissions standards to the state and local educational authorities. Williams also pointed out the biases of standardized testing that favor upper and middle class white students. This bias was also pointed out by many other critics and has been well documented since the early 1980s. His main concerns revolved around the legal authority of the NCAA to set policy for one group of students which created a dual admissions standard; and how students who are admitted as freshman would become eligible to play sports. As Williams pointed out, a student cannot teach himself to read and write in one year.

Significance

Rule 48 was enacted in August 1986 despite the fury that surrounded it. Supporters stated that it would end the recruiting violations of the past. Joe Paterno, football coach of the Penn State Nittany Lions, said that it would end "the exploitation of a generation and a half of black athletes," but realized that declaring athletes ineligible for Division I play was not a solution. Coaches from historically black colleges declared that it was a move to eliminate African American athletes from their programs and from the programs of larger institutions.

Williams and most other opponents questioned how the test scores had been devised. No data was presented to the NCAA regarding athletes' test scores; however, data was available from Educational Testing Service (ETS) outlining the mean scores of black and white students from 1976 to 1982. The lowest average score was 707 for black students in 1982. This was over 200 points lower than the average score for white students in the same year. It is assumed that the committee writing the guidelines used this data to arrive at its standards. Even officials from the ETS were quoted as saying that the SAT and ACT should not be used in this way.

High schools faced a larger burden to prepare athletes for the standards of Rule 48. An additional question that Rule 48 raised was the responsibility of colleges and universities for athletes. Williams questioned the availability of remedial courses for students who did not meet the freshman requirement. Further, he and others pointed out that a year to acclimate to college would not cure the deficiencies of the student. Adding a rigorous Division I schedule to classes does not address the question of academic preparation.

Data from studies on athletes affected by Rule 48 shows gains in graduation rates. These gains are most often seen in the non-revenue generating sports, however. The questions about student athletes persist, and have yet to be completely solved.

Primary Source

"The Impact of Rule 48 Upon the Black Student Athlete: A Comment" [excerpt]

SYNOPSIS: Williams spells out his fears and frustrations with Rule 48. The NCAA role in this decision is also in question. A 1996 study released by the NCAA showed an increase in graduation rates and in minority athletes. Still, the Rule 48 continued to be debated by the NCAA and by colleges and universities in the early twenty-first century.

Introduction

On August 1, 1986, Rule 48 of the National Collegiate Athletic Association (NCAA) will become ef-fective. Just what will be the actual effect of its implementation is as yet unknown. However, it is more than mere conjecture that Rule 48 will have a major impact upon the black athlete with college aspirations. Moreover, few will dispute the notion that this impact will foster profound litigious ramifications.

Will the impact of Rule 48 be positive or negative? The response to such an inquiry lies in one's point of view concerning both the role of athletics in the educational system and the validity of the proposed standards under Rule 48 in measuring worthiness to attend college. With the invocation of Rule 48, educators, academicians, lawyers, civil rights leaders, coaches, and athletes have postulated their varied views on these two issues. Some would argue that Rule 48 is long overdue, that black student athletes have been exploited in the past and will be beneficiaries of more stringent academic requirements. Others argue, however, that the rule will adversely affect black colleges which desire to retain their Division I status; that the standarized test requirement of Rule 48 reflects a cultural bias that is unfair to black athletes; and that Rule 48 triggers an awareness of broader issues that affect those in this nation who are not of the predominant culture.

This paper discusses these divergent views while exploring the nexus between the standards of Rule 48 and the considerations posited by the NCAA for establishing them. In doing so, some conclusions are drawn as to the probable effect(s) of Rule 48 upon the black athlete, the black institution and, consequently, the black community.

Background: Rule 48 Content and Proposed Objective

At its 1983 convention, the NCAA adopted No. 48 Eligibility Rule, referred to as Rule 48 [Division I only]. In substance it provides that:

> A 2.000 qualifier as used herein is defined as one who is a high school graduate and at the time of graduation from high school presented an accumulative six, seven or eight semesters minimum grade-point average of 2.000 (based on a maximum of 4.000) in a core curriculum of at least 11 academic courses including at least three in English, two in Mathematics, two in Social Science and two in Natural or Physical Science (including at least one laboratory class, if offered by the high school) as certified on the high school transcript or by official correspondence, as well as a 700 combined score on the verbal and math sections of the SAT or a 15 composite score on the ACT.

The Rule had been drafted by the ad hoc athletic committee of the American Council on Education (ACE), for the NCAA, with the proposed "intent to establish a specific core curriculum for which a student must present a minimum grade average and test score for initial eligibility at a Division I institution." . . .

(D) Rule 48 and Its Desired Goal

One of the chief criticisms that remains for consideration is that the Rule 48 standards are not reasonably calculated to, nor are they the best and most effective method for, achieving the desired result—elimination of educational deficiencies in the college athlete. Rule 48 requires that a high school senior seeking freshman eligibility in a Division I school have a 2.000 minimum grade point average in a core curriculum of 11 courses. The questionable lack of authority in the NCAA to set curriculum standards for schools, especially public schools, has already been explored. The concern here is that the curriculum requirement serves to blame the victim of a deficient educational system and to hamper his further participation, rather than to correct his educational deficiencies.

Prior to Rule 48, NCAA regulations required only that an entering student athlete have an overall 2.0 average in high school. Rule 48 purports to determine from what courses that average must be derived. In effect, it directs high schools to set up a "core curriculum" and requires those who would aspire to participate in football or basketball (and no other sports), to take that core curriculum and maintain a 2.0 grade point average.

Again, public school policy is to be decided only by the state and local officials imbued with the authority and responsibility for setting academic priorities and standards. As Justice Rehnquist emphatically put it in *Board of Curators of the University of Missouri v. Horowitz*, "by and large, public education in our Nation is committed to the control of state and local authorities." No other should intrude on that historical control in academic priorities.

Further, if the fundamental goal of Rule 48 is the elimination of educational deficiencies in college athletes, what justifiable reason could there be for not applying Rule 48 to all schools, in all divisions, in all sports covered by the National Collegiate Athletic Association? Notwithstanding, it is highly questionable what elimination from sports participation for one year would accomplish if the deficiencies are

as serious as claimed. An athlete who can neither read nor write cannot teach himself to do so, with college proficiency, in one year—especially without remedial assistance. In addition, if getting the athlete acclimated to "college life" is the goal, what will be the effect of the sudden adjustment he must make when he begins to play in his second year and his disengagement as a regular non-athlete student has been eliminated?

It seems highly unlikely that holding an athlete from participation his first year addresses the root of the problem. What is really needed to cure any existing or supposed educational deficiencies in college athletes is significant remedial and tutorial assistance. The NCAA argues that athletes must cease leaving college without minimal academic and educational skills. Rule 48 has the practical effect of placing the onus upon the individual high school to insure that the athlete who aspires to a Division I college has those skills. Since the NCAA cannot legitimately mandate educational policy for high schools, especially public high schools, the focus should be upon providing a source and means from which the athlete can acquire the skills as the NCAA claims he needs before he is in college.

Further Resources

BOOKS

Benson, Martin T., ed. *A Comparison of College Graduation Rates of Freshman Student-Athletes before and after Proposition 48. NCAA Research Report 92–01.* Overland Park, Kans.: National Collegiate Athletic Association, 1993.

PERIODICALS

Atwell, Robert H. "Keeping the Amateur in Athletics." *Educational Record* 64, no. 3, Summer 1983, 16–17.

Blum, Debra E. "Graduation Rate of Scholarship Athletes Rose After Proposition 48 Was Adopted, NCAA Reports." *The Chronicle of Higher Education*, July 7, 1993, A42–A44.

Clark, Vernon L. et al. "NCAA Rule 48: Racism or Reform?" *Journal of Negro Education* 55, no. 2, Spring 1986, 162–170.

Zingg, Paul J. "No Simple Solution: Proposition 48 and the Possibilities of Reform." *Educational Record* 64, no. 3, Summer 1983, 6–12.

WEBSITES

NCAA Rules and Eligibility. Available online at http://www.ncaa.org/index1.html; website home page http://www.ncaa.org (accessed May 10, 2003).

"Commentary: Conversations with a New Literate"

Journal article

By: Henry C. Amoroso Jr.

Date: 1986

Source: Amoroso Jr., Henry C. "Commentary: Conversations with a New Literate." *Journal of Reading* 29, no. 6, March 1986, 484–488.

About the Author: Henry C. Amoroso, Jr. is a Professor of Education at the University of Southern Maine, Gorham. He also taught at George Peabody College for Teachers at Vanderbilt University, and has served as a Volunteers in Service to America (VISTA) Volunteer/Supervisor. Amoroso's research centers on critical theory, literacy, and reading. ∎

Introduction

A 1989 national study of adult literacy rates showed that twenty to thirty million adults in the United States had "inadequate basic skills" and were "already out of school." Illiteracy was seen as not only an educational problem, but also as a social and economic problem which would not be solved easily. The report suggested that the Adult Basic Skills Act and federal money could help solve the educational needs of adults. While some of those with lower skills were immigrants, others were school dropouts or learning disabled.

Studies of illiterate prisoners differ somewhat from the general population. Most of the prisoners in a 1994 study had not graduated from high school. Also, the average proficiency of prisoners is lower than the general population. There were also good statistics in this report. "Over sixty percent of the inmate population reported being involved in education and/or vocational programs in prison." These inmates had a higher level of literacy than those not involved in educational programs.

The interview by Henry C. Amoroso Jr. of Tony, a prisoner who learned to read, shows that there is more to literacy than learning the meanings of words and sentences. Tony, tutored in a prison program, discussed the level of concern his tutor showed him as a key part in learning to read. Self-esteem, the feeling that he had dignity and that he could learn to read, seemed as important as the reading skills themselves. He was also able to pass the skills on to another inmate, showing that he had gained confidence and internalized what he had learned.

Significance

Adult illiteracy affects the ability to gain employment and many other needs that adults have. Statistics show that illiterate adults are more often at or below the poverty level. Correlation with prisoners and the general public is not always accurate in these studies, because of the differences in representation of the general population within the prison population.

Tony's story was not only about learning to read in a prison program, however. It also reflected the condition of schools and the care and concern shown for children in school. While studies like *A Nation at Risk* pushed for higher standards in the curriculum, what more often was needed was a caring adult in a child's life. Overworked teachers and overcrowded classrooms did not allow teachers to pay attention to students who needed more assistance with work, or those who had special needs.

The opportunity for research and growth of adult literacy studies showed how the schools have failed large numbers of children. Creating better schools with smaller classes requires increased funding. This is always the problem when trying to improve conditions, particularly in the inner city school districts. Anecdotal reports, which accompany the hard statistics usually presented in research studies, bring a human face to the illiteracy problem and demonstrate the cost children and adults pay for missing an education far better than a bar graph.

Primary Source

"Commentary: Conversations with a New Literate" [excerpt]

SYNOPSIS: The interviewer was able to elicit answers and stories from Tony which showed the lack of care he experienced in school. While this is one side of a story, it reflects the price paid not only by this man, but by millions of adults across the country. Tutoring programs, such as the one used in this case, help some to read later in life, but demonstrate how opportunities are often missed because of a lack of this skill.

What follows is an interview with an 18-year-old prisoner soon after he learned how to read and write. This is a man who, in today's euphemisms, would be called a dysfunctional learner. The conversation affords the reader a simple, direct, and moving account of how he learned about reading and how he learned how to learn. The power of this interview lies in the fact that it underscores the central importance to the illiterate adult of a caring, connected relationship established by the teacher. The interview format generates insights into the learner's world and into the part teachers can play in promoting authentic learning.

Did your tutor help you with your reading?

Yeah.

What did he do? Tell me a little bit about it.

He started with little words and stuff and finally I got through real good and I just started to learn how to read in the last year since I first come and he'd keep giving me books until he got to one that I liked. He's still doing this, too.

Kind of experimenting?

Yeah.

Sometimes he may bring in something that you like and sometimes not, right?

Yeah.

I mean it's not that you have to read everything. What you like, you read.

He tells me to read 15 pages out of each one and if I don't like it by then, put it down and get another one.

Has progress been very slow or very fast?

It's been coming fast because words I didn't know in a book (the definition and stuff), I'd have a whole bunch of 'em. Now I just have about eight or nine.

Every time you come down here for these sessions do you feel that you're getting a little better?

Yeah.

Do you ever feel that you're not making progress fast enough? Do you get impatient with yourself?

No. 'Cause everybody's been telling that I've been doing real good 'cause they see the stuff I've been writing. They can look at it and say I coming along real good.

Well, what is it exactly that is helping you concentrate on your reading?

I guess knowing that I ain't the only one that cares about me knowing how to read and knowing all that stuff.

Are you doing anything with the reading?

Yeah.

I know you've been writing stories.

Yeah. Telling people about it. See, I know stuff that I didn't know before. When somebody starts a conversation about something I had done read, shoot, I can jump right off into it. Use to I'd just sit down and listen to 'em talk. Now I can tell some stories.

Did your tutor ever ask you what you were interested in and write stories about that and then bring them down and read with you?

Yeah, the first time he come he asked us what all we like and I told him women, cars, and a whole bunch of stuff and he wrote some stories about it

and I caught him on a mistake about it, too. Yeah, he wrote a story and he put two pages of the same thing in there.

Do you ever remember in grade school a teacher who tried that with you? Asked you what you were interested in or kind of met you half-way?

No. Yeah, I do. A teacher, when I was in the sixth grade at Richland School . . . a teacher named Miss Scrushal . . . yeah she was a crazy teacher. She asked me all kind of stuff and she knowed I didn't know how to read and she'd tell me. Gave me a book that had pictures of the words and I could read that. It had an eye for I and a car for car and all that stuff.

When you were in the sixth grade were there other students like you?

I'm not really sure 'cause everybody could read except this little girl and me.

One of the other students in the class?

It ended up me and her was going together for a while.

Think back now as far as you can go—first grade, second grade, third grade—how exactly do you think the things Lee has been doing with you have been different than what you've done in grade school in learning to read?

Well, I don't know if it was me that didn't care. Here I care and Lee, he cares. At least that's my impression anyway and I don't know if it was me that didn't care or the teachers that didn't care.

Did they treat you any differently than Lee has been treating you?

Yeah. You know they'd be giving spelling tests and stuff and I'd done skipped 3 or 4 days and I didn't know what was going on. She'd tell me to put my head down on the desk and if I didn't know a word she'd give me a dictionary and tell me to look it up. And here I am I don't even know how to spell the word. She'd have me go to the dictionary and look the word up. In here, if I don't know a word, Lee'll try to tell me a definition of it. If he can't come up with a good one he'll look in the dictionary for it.

If somehow we could go back to the sixth grade and meet your teachers, what would you tell them about how they should have been teaching you to read?

Instead of them picking out what you should read, you should be allowed to pick out what you want to read. They like certain things and we like certain things.

They never did that?

No.

If you had a chance right now, to teach someone in the unit to read, what would you do and how would you do it?

There was Dan here who didn't know how to read.

Tell me a little bit about that.

Well, he couldn't hardly write his own name. I remember when I was like that. So, I started doing like Lee did. I'd stay in there with him about 2 or 3 hours. I had him write 'cat.' He had a spelling test on it. I had him write it about 20 times until he knowed it. He had about 15 words and then I'd give him a little old test on 'em and he'd spell 'em and I'd just sit there until he got 'em right.

If there is a word that your friend comes to and he doesn't know how to pronounce it, how would you teach him that word?

Look in there and find a word that I do know. First I'd break it down and sound out the other word. I had a word 'undistinguishable' and I didn't know what the hell that word was. He broke it down and said 'Un' is always the opposite and then he said, "What is this word right here?" Then I said "Distinguished." He said "All right." He put 'able' on it and I said, "Undistinguishable."

Have you tried it?

Yeah, I'm working hard and I done good last night.

What would happen if you went up there and you just gave this friend a book, a pencil and a piece of paper and said, "Do the work."

Well, it won't work. If a person don't know nothing he ain't going to learn nothing like that. You know, you got to spend a little time with him . . . let him know that you care just as much as you can.

Further Resources

BOOKS

Haigler, Karl O. *Literacy Behind Prison Walls: Profiles of the Prison Population from the National Adult Literacy Survey.* Washington, D.C.: National Center for Educational Statistics, 1994.

National Advisory Council on Adult Education (U.S.) Literacy Committee. *Illiteracy in America: Extent, Causes, and Suggested Solutions.* Washington, D.C.: The Council, 1986.

PERIODICALS

Chisman, Forrest P. "The Federal Role in Adult Literacy." *The Education Digest* 55, no. 2, October 1989, 11–14.

Greenberg, Daphne, et al. "Implementaion Issues In a Reading Program for Low Reading Adults." *Journal of Adolescent & Adult Literacy* 45, no. 7, April 2002, 626–632.

WEBSITES

Henry C. Amoroso Jr. Courses. Available online at http://www.usm.maine.edu/~amoroso/courses/; website home page http://usm.maine.edu (accessed May 10, 2003).

National Assessments of Adult Literacy. Available online at http://nces.ed.gov/naal/; website home page http://nces.ed.gov (accessed May 10, 2003).

Cultural Literacy: What Every American Needs to Know

Nonfiction work

By: E.D. Hirsch Jr.

Date: 1987

Source: Hirsch Jr., E.D, et. al. *Cultural Literacy: What Every American Needs to Know.* Boston: Houghton Mifflin, 1987, 146, 148, 152–153, 160, 161

About the Author: E.D. Hirsch Jr. (1928–) was educated at Cornell University (B.A.1950) and Yale University (M.A., 1953, Ph.D., 1957). He spent ten years teaching at Yale, before moving to the University of Virginia, where he is the William R. Kenan Professor of English. Hirsch has received both a Fulbright (1955) and a Guggenheim (1964–1965) award. ■

Introduction

The 1980s witnessed several dire reports of a nation of mediocre students. Falling test scores, dismal reports on school curriculum, and illiteracy rates all caused concern for the public and educators. E.D. Hirsch's book, *Cultural Literacy: What Every American Needs to Know*, created further concern by illustrating that students do not share the common terms and concepts of society. His book was a bestseller, but it was also highly controversial.

Hirsch does not assert that students are illiterate, but rather that they do not understand what they are reading in most of their courses. Because they cannot identify allusions or references to historical, literary, scientific or geographical events or concepts, they fail to fully comprehend the meanings and connections of what teachers and texts attempt to convey. Hirsch spelled out what could be done about the lack of knowledge and provided a lengthy list of "What Literate Americans Know" in the appendix of the book.

Hirsch began pursuing ideas of cultural literacy in the late 1970s. He presented talks at a conference honoring Mina Shaughnessy in 1980, and at the Modern Language Association in 1981. His preliminary ideas were published in both the *Journal of Basic Writing* and in *The*

American Scholar. Following the presentations and publications, Hirsch was encouraged by fellow scholars to expand his ideas into book form. Joseph Kett, a historian, and James Trefil, a scientist, assisted Hirsch with compiling a preliminary list of terms. The men later coauthored the *Dictionary of Cultural Literacy.*

Significance

Hundreds of articles have been written in response to E.D. Hirsch's book on cultural literacy. Many of the educators who have written, in part or whole, about Hirsch's theories are negative about the methods in his text. Conservative thinkers tend to be positive about its suggestions.

Wayne J. Urban reviewed Hirsch's book along with Alan Bloom's *Closing of the American Mind* and Diane Ravitch and Chester E. Finn Jr's. *What Do Our 17-Year-Olds Know?* These books were commonly grouped together in reviews. Urban criticizes Hirsch's reliance on the SAT (a multiple choice format) as establishing conclusively that students are not culturally literate. He also expresses concern that "nowhere in Hirsch's book is the issue addressed of how those things should come to be known." Wayne Booth, professor of English at University of Chicago, wrote Hirsch an open letter in *Change.* Booth agrees with Hirsch that the state of education is a mess, but like many others, he does not see the value of lists.

Not everyone disagreed with Hirsch. George Steiner, a literary scholar writing for *New Yorker* states that "Hirsch is emphatically right" in what he writes. Steiner calls the list "intrinsically fascinating." He worked to form groups to write core curriculums based on the ideas in this book and ideas developed throughout his teaching career. Schools have adopted these curricula across the country, resulting in higher test scores. Hirsch actually warns about lists for lists' sake in the book, even though many ignored that information. In a 1997 interview published in *Phi Delta Kappan,* Hirsch explains the background for the book. He witnessed the differences between students at the University of Virginia and at a community college in Richmond, Virginia when he conducted a study. The community college students could usually read the words of a text but had no understanding of the meaning. They did not know who men like Robert E. Lee or Ulysses S. Grant were. Hirsch notes that he realizes students attend school in a classroom and are schooled at home. He also discusses social injustices that he sees in schools because there is not a core curriculum that all students must master. These troubling realizations led him to write his book and to found the Core Knowledge Foundation, which publishes books meant to alleviate what Hirsch views as a problem for America. The troubles on the other side, of course, involve how the book was interpreted, and how the lists were taught as fact, instead of in context.

Primary Source

"What Literate Americans Know," *Cultural Literacy: What Every American Needs to Know* [excerpt]

SYNOPSIS: The selections below come from the list of terms and concepts that Hirsch included in the appendix of his book. The list may have been one of the most controversial sections of the book because critics asserted that it took education back to a time when rote memorization of facts, names and dates was valued. Hirsch argues that the context of the items included in the list is what is important to understand.

The geographical names, historical events, famous people, and patriotic lore need no special comment. They are words and phrases that appear in newspapers, magazines, and books without explanation. Famous persons are identified as they are normally alluded to, sometimes without first names, e.g. Cervantes. We are not encyclopedists; we want to reflect the culture. We have provided a rather full listing of grammatical and rhetorical terms because students and teachers will find them useful for discussing English grammar and style. . . .

Because there is little broad knowledge of science even among educated people, the kind of criteria used to compile our lists for the humanities and social sciences—for example, Would a literate person be familiar with this term?—simply can't be used for the natural sciences. The gap between the essential basic knowledge of science and what the general reader can be expected to know has become too large. Our criterion for choosing a science entry has been that the candidate must be truly essential to a broad grasp of a major science. This criterion may not assure true scientific literacy, but it should at least help overcome serious illiteracy. . . .

The List

1066
1492
1776
1861-1865
1914-1918
1939-1945
abbreviation (written English)
abolitionism

abominable snowman

abortion

Abraham and Isaac

Absence makes the heart grow fonder.

absenteeism

absolute monarchy

absolute zero

abstract expressionism

academic freedom

a cappella

accelerator, particle

accounting

AC/DC (alternating current/direct current)

Achilles

Achilles' heel

acid

acid rain

acquittal

acronym

acrophobia

Acropolis

Actions speak louder than words.

active voice

act of God

actuary

acupuncture

A.D. (anno domini)

Adam and Eve

Adams, John

Adams, John Quincy

adaptation

Addams, Jane

ad hoc

ad hominem

adieu

Adirondack Mountains

adjective

Adonis

adrenal gland

adrenaline (fight or flight)

Adriatic Sea

adultery

adverb

AEC (Atomic Energy Commission)

Aegean Sea

Aeneas

Aeneid, The (title)

aerobic

Aeschylus

Aesop's Fables (title)

aesthetics

affirmative action

affluent society

Afghanistan

aficionado

AFL–CIO

Africa

Agamemnon

. . .

Baa, Baa, Black Sheep (text)

Babbitt

Babel, Tower of

Babylon

bacchanalian

Bacchus

Bach, Johann Sebastian

bacillus

Bacon, Sir Francis

Baconian method (scientific method, induction)

bacteria

Bad news travels fast.

bad penny always turns up, A

bad workman blames his tools, A

Baghdad

Bahamas

bail

baker's dozen

balance of nature

balance of payments

balance of power

balance of terror

balance sheet

Balkans

ballad

ballerina

ballet

ballistic missile

Baltic Sea

Baltimore, Maryland

Balzac

banana republic

Bangkok

bank run

bankruptcy

baptism

Baptist

Barber of Seville, The (title)

Barcelona

Bard of Avon

baritone

bark is worse than his bite, His

bar mitzvah

Barnum, P.T.

barometer (barometric pressure)

baroque

Barrymores, the

Barton, Clara

basal metabolism

basalt

base (chemistry)

basilica

bas relief

bass

bass drum

bass fiddle

basso

bassoon

basta

Bastille

bat mitzvah

Battle Hymn of the Republic (song)

Battle of Britain

Battle of Bunker Hill

Battle of Concord

Battle of Gettysburg

Battle of Hastings

Battle of Lexington

Battle of Marathon

Battle of Midway

Battle of Stalingrad

Battle of the Bulge

Battle of Waterloo

Battle of Yorktown

Baudelaire

. . .

Bunker Hill, Battle of

Bunyan, Paul

buoyancy

bureaucracy

bureaucrat

burgher

Burke, Edmund

Burma

Burns, Robert

burnt child fears the fire, The

burn the candle at both ends

burn the midnight oil

burn with a hard, gemlike flame

Burr, Aaron

Burr-Hamilton duel

bury the hatchet

business before pleasure

business cycle

bust (economic)

buy a pig in a poke

buyer's market

Byron, Lord

Byronic

byte

Byzantine (complexity)

Byzantine empire

cabinet (government)

cadre

Caesar, Julius

Caesar Augustus

Caesarean section

Cain and Abel

Cairo

calculus

Calcutta

Calder

. . .

Central America

Central Intelligence Agency (CIA)

centrifugal force

centripetal force

Cerberus

cerebellum

cerebral cortex

Ceres (Demeter)

Cervantes

Ceylon

Cézanne

cf. (confer)

chain reaction

chain store

Chamberlain, Neville

. . .

Further Resources

BOOKS

Ravitch, Diane, and Chester E. Finn Jr. *What Do Our 17-Year-Olds Know?* New York: Harper & Row, 1987.

PERIODICALS

Booth, Wayne C. "Cultural Literacy and Liberal Learning: An Open Letter to E.D. Hirsch, Jr." *Change,* July/August 1988, 10–21.

Goldberg, Mark F. "An Interview with E.D. Hirsch Jr: Doing What Works." *Phi Delta Kappan* 79, no. 2, September 1997, 83–85.

Steiner, George. "Review of *Cultural Literacy.*" *New Yorker* 63, June 1, 1987, 106.

Urban, Wayne J. "Book Reviews: The Closing of the American Mind; Cultural Literacy; What Do Our 17-Year-Olds Know?" *The Journal of American History* 75, no.3, December 1988, 869–874.

WEBSITES

Core Knowledge. Available online at http://www.coreknowledge.org/ (accessed May 10, 2003).

E.D. Hirsch Jr's Homepage. Available online at http://www-hoover.stanford.edu/bios/hirsch.html; website home page http://www-hoover.stanford.edu (accessed May 10, 2003).

The Closing of the American Mind
Nonfiction work

By: Allan Bloom

Date: 1987

Source: Bloom, Allan. *The Closing of the American Mind: How Higher Education has Failed Democracy and Impoverished the Souls of Today's Students.* New York: Simon & Schuster, 1987, 62–67.

About the Author: Allan Bloom (1930–1993) was a professor of political philosophy at the University of Chicago. He was also a member of the Committee on Social Thought. Bloom earned his Ph.D. at the University of Chicago, and then taught at University of Chicago, Yale, Cornell and the University of Toronto, before returning to Chicago. Bloom also wrote about Shakespeare, and translated editions of Plato's *Republic* and Rousseau's *Emile*. ∎

Introduction

Allan Bloom joined E.D. Hirsch Jr., Diane Ravitch and Chester E. Finn Jr. in chastising the American educational system for what students did not know. Bloom's target was the elite university, but his arguments share common themes with the authors with whom he was compared in 1987. Bloom concentrated on values and morals in his work. He cited the great philosophers as either helping or hindering education as it stood in the late 1980s. His book was more personal than the others published the same year. He drew on thirty years of teaching at Ivy League universities and the thousands of students he encountered for his sadness over the state of knowledge at the end of the twentieth century.

In the preface, Bloom wrote that the book was a "meditation on the state of our souls," and that it was a "report from the front." Bloom advocated a return to the Great Book curriculum, rather than what he views as a watered down mixture of courses "relevant" to students lives. He claims, similarly to Hirsch, that understanding classic allusions provide context and richness for a person's life. Bloom gives examples of Dickens's characters who students do not know at all—or who they may have "grazed" in high school. Bloom was critical of the lack of preparation in lower grades; however, that was not his concentration. He bemoaned the 1960s when students protested, and he felt that the universities, particularly the humanities, gave in and gave up.

Significance

The Closing of the American Mind hit the bestseller list just as *Cultural Literacy* did. In an article reflecting on the book a decade later, S.J.D. Green, a fellow at All Soul's College, Oxford, recalls an anecdote about the concern Simon & Schuster had over printing an unknown author's work. They "insisted upon a foreword from Bloom's old friend, the then rather better-known Saul Bellow" hoping to help book sales. It turns out this was unnecessary.

In the 1980s—when reports were constantly being issued about the lack of learning and knowledge of American students—the public welcomed this kind of treatise. Academics have never fully accepted it, however. Like its companions, the book caused a storm of controversy over curricula and the state of universities. William Kristol, then chief of staff to the secretary of the U.S. Department of Education (now co-publisher of *The Weekly Standard*), reviewed the book for *The Wall Street Journal*. He wrote that it "brilliantly knits together such astute perceptions of the contemporary scene with such depth of scholarship and philosophical learning" like no other recent book. Kristol described the book with words such as "witty," "lively and deep," and "outrageous and so sensible." His assessment was positive. However, as Green points out a decade later, these positive assessments typically led to no concrete reforms.

Neil Postman, in a 1989 review, called Bloom's book an answer to Hirsch's questions. He noted that Bloom did not address the fact that American education has never been devoted to the Great Books that Professor Bloom loves—but he does see a necessity in Bloom's thinking. "Bloom is arguing that students need stories, narratives, tales, theories (call them what you will) that will serve as moral and intellectual frameworks." Stories are vital, as most would agree. The problem with Bloom's book and with others in the category was whose stories should we value in American education? That is the key element that continues to be debated when curriculums are being written and proposed.

In his book *The Closing of the American Mind* Allan Bloom decries the lack of reading and the lack of heroes in his students. **COPYRIGHT © 1987 BY ALLAN BLOOM. ALL RIGHTS RESERVED. REPRODUCED BY PERMISSION OF SIMON & SCHUSTER MACMILLAN.**

Primary Source

The Closing of the American Mind [excerpt]

SYNOPSIS: Bloom decries the lack of reading and the lack of heroes in his students. The blank faces that met him support his thesis that students in college lack morals and values, in part, because they do not know classic literature. Bloom blamed everything from feminism to the popularity of films and entertainment for his students lack of knowledge.

Books

I have begun to wonder whether the experience of the greatest texts from early childhood is not a prerequisite for a concern throughout life for them and for lesser but important literature. The soul's longing, its intolerable irritation under the constraints of the conditional and limited, may very well require encouragement at the outset. At all events, whatever the cause, our students have lost the practice of and the taste for reading. They have not learned how to read, nor do they have the expectation of delight or improvement from reading. They are "authentic," as against the immediately preceding university generations, in having few cultural pretensions and in refusing hypocritical ritual bows to high culture.

When I first noticed the decline in reading during the late sixties, I began asking my large introductory classes, and any other group of younger students to which I spoke, what books really count for them. Most are silent, puzzled by the question. The notion of books as companions is foreign to them. Justice Black with his tattered copy of the Constitution in his pocket at all times is not an example that would mean much to them. There is no printed word to which they look for counsel, inspiration or joy. Sometimes one student will say "the Bible." (He learned it at home, and his Biblical studies are not usually continued at the university.) There is always a girl who mentions Ayn Rand's *The Fountainhead,* a book, although hardly literature, which, with its sub-Nietzschean assertiveness, excites somewhat eccentric youngsters to a new way of life. A few students mention recent books that struck them and supported their own self-interpretation, like *The Catcher in the Rye.* (Theirs is usually the most genuine response and also shows a felt need for help in self-interpretation. But it is an uneducated response. Teachers should take advantage of the need expressed in it to show such students that better writers can help them more.) After such sessions I am pursued by a student or two who wants to make it clear that he or she is really influenced by books, not just by one or two but by many. Then he recites a list of classics he may have grazed in high school.

Imagine such a young person walking through the Louvre or the Uffizi, and you can immediately grasp the condition of his soul. In his innocence of the stories of Biblical and Greek or Roman antiquity, Raphael, Leonardo, Michelangelo, Rembrandt and all the others can say nothing to him. All he sees are colors and forms—modern art. In short, like almost everything else in his spiritual life, the paintings and statues are abstract. No matter what much of modern wisdom asserts, these artists counted on immediate recognition of their subjects and, what is more, on their having a powerful meaning for their viewers. The works were the fulfillment of those meanings, giving them a sensuous reality and hence completing them. Without those meanings, and without their being something essential to the viewer as a moral, political and religious being, the works lose their essence. It is not merely the tradition that is lost when the voice of civilization elaborated over millennia has been stilled in this way. It is being itself that vanishes beyond the dissolving horizon. One of the most flattering things that ever happened to me as a teacher occurred when I received a postcard from a very good student on his first visit to Italy, who wrote, "You are not a professor of political philosophy but a travel agent." Nothing could have better expressed my intention as an educator. He thought I had prepared him to see. Then he could begin thinking for himself with something to think about. The real sensation of the Florence in which Machiavelli is believable is worth all the formulas of

metaphysics ten times over. Education in our times must try to find whatever there is in students that might yearn for completion, and to reconstruct the learning that would enable them autonomously to seek that completion.

In a less grandiose vein, students today have nothing like the Dickens who gave so many of us the unforgettable Pecksniffs, Micawbers, Pips, with which we sharpened our vision, allowing us some subtlety in our distinction of human types. It is a complex set of experiences that enables one to say so simply, "He is a Scrooge." Without literature, no such observations are possible and the fine art of comparison is lost. The psychological obtuseness of our students is appalling, because they have only pop psychology to tell them what people are like, and the range of their motives. As the awareness that we owed almost exclusively to literary genius falters, people become more alike, for want of knowing they can be otherwise. What poor substitutes for real diversity are the wild rainbows of dyed hair and other external differences that tell the observer nothing about what is inside.

Lack of education simply results in students' seeking for enlightenment wherever it is readily available, without being able to distinguish between the sublime and trash, insight and propaganda. For the most part students turn to the movies, ready prey to interested moralisms such as the depictions of Gandhi or Thomas More—largely designed to further passing political movements and to appeal to simplistic needs for greatness—or to insinuating flattery of their secret aspirations and vices, giving them a sense of significance. *Kramer vs. Kramer* may be up-to-date about divorces and sex roles, but anyone who does not have *Anna Karenina* or *The Red and the Black* as part of his viewing equipment cannot sense what might be lacking, or the difference between an honest presentation and an exercise in consciousness-raising, trashy sentimentality and elevated sentiment. As films have emancipated themselves from the literary tyranny under which they suffered and which gave them a bad conscience, the ones with serious pretensions have become intolerably ignorant and manipulative. The distance from the contemporary and its high seriousness that students most need in order not to indulge their petty desires and to discover what is most serious about themselves cannot be found in the cinema, which now only knows the present. Thus, the failure to read good books both enfeebles the vision and strengthens our most fatal tendency—the belief that the here and now is all there is.

The only way to counteract this tendency is to intervene most vigorously in the education of those few who come to the university with a strong urge for *un je ne sais quoi,* who fear that they may fail to discover it, and that the cultivation of their minds is required for the success of their quest. We are long past the age when a whole tradition could be stored up in all students, to be fruitfully used later by some. Only those who are willing to take risks and are ready to believe the implausible are now fit for a bookish adventure. The desire must come from within. People do what they want, and now the most needful things appear so implausible to them that it is hopeless to attempt universal reform. Teachers of writing in state universities, among the noblest and most despised laborers in the academy, have told me that they cannot teach writing to students who do not read, and that it is practically impossible to get them to read, let alone like it. This is where high schools have failed most, filled with teachers who are products of the sixties and reflecting the pallor of university-level humanities. The old teachers who loved Shakespeare or Austen or Donne, and whose only reward for teaching was the perpetuation of their taste, have all but disappeared.

The latest enemy of the vitality of classic texts is feminism. The struggles against elitism and racism in the sixties and seventies had little direct effect on students' relations to books. The democratization of the university helped dismantle its structure and caused it to lose its focus. But the activists had no special quarrel with the classic texts, and they were even a bit infected by their Frankfurt School masters' habit of parading their intimacy with high culture. Radicals had at an earlier stage of egalitarianism already dealt with the monarchic, aristocratic and antidemocratic character of most literary classics by no longer paying attention to their manifest political content. Literary criticism concentrated on the private, the intimate, the feelings, thoughts and relations of individuals, while reducing to the status of a literary convention of the past the fact that the heroes of many classic works were soldiers and statesmen engaged in ruling and faced with political problems. Shakespeare, as he has been read for most of this century, does not constitute a threat to egalitarian right thinking. And as for racism, it just did not play a role in the classic literature, at least in the forms in which we are concerned about it today, and no great work of literature is ordinarily considered racist.

But *all* literature up to today is sexist. The Muses never sang to the poets about liberated women. It's the same old *chanson* from the Bible and Homer through Joyce and Proust. And this is particularly grave for literature, since the love interest was most of what remained in the classics after politics was purged in the academy, and was also what drew students to reading them. These books appealed to eros while educating it. So activism has been directed against the content of books. The latest translation of Biblical text—sponsored by the National Council of the Churches of Christ—suppresses gender references to God, so that future generations will not have to grapple with the fact that God was once a sexist. But this technique has only limited applicability. Another tactic is to expunge the most offensive authors—for example, Rousseau—from the education of the young or to include feminist responses in college courses, pointing out the distorting prejudices, and using the books only as evidence of the misunderstanding of woman's nature and the history of injustice to it. Moreover, the great female characters can be used as examples of the various ways women have coped with their enslavement to the sexual role. But never, never, must a student be attracted to those old ways and take them as models for him or herself. However, all this effort is wasted. Students cannot imagine that the old literature could teach them anything about the relations they want to have or will be permitted to have. So they are indifferent.

Having heard over a period of years the same kinds of responses to my question about favorite books, I began to ask students who their heroes are. Again, there is usually silence, and most frequently nothing follows. Why should anyone have heroes? One should be oneself and not form oneself in an alien mold. Here positive ideology supports them: their lack of hero-worship is a sign of maturity. They posit their own values. They have turned into a channel first established in the *Republic* by Socrates, who liberated himself from Achilles, and picked up in earnest by Rousseau in *Emile.* Following on Rousseau, Tolstoy depicts Prince Andrei in *War and Peace,* who was educated in Plutarch and is alienated from himself by his admiration for Napoleon. But we tend to forget that Andrei is a very noble man indeed and that his heroic longings give him a splendor of soul that dwarfs the petty, vain, self-regarding concerns of the bourgeoisie that surrounds him. Only a combination of natural sentiment and unity with the spirit of Russia and its history can, for Tolstoy, produce human beings superior to Andrei, and even they are only ambiguously superior. But in America we have only the bourgeoisie, and the love of the heroic is one of the few counterpoises available to us. In us the contempt for the heroic is only an extension of the perversion of the democratic principle that denies greatness and wants everyone to feel comfortable in his skin without having to suffer unpleasant comparisons. Students have not the slightest notion of what an achievement it is to free oneself from public guidance and find resources for guidance within oneself. From what source within themselves would they draw the goals they think they set for themselves? Liberation from the heroic only means that they have no resource whatsoever against conformity to the current "role models." They are constantly thinking of themselves in terms of fixed standards that they did not make. Instead of being overwhelmed by Cyrus, Theseus, Moses or Romulus, they unconsciously act out the roles of the doctors, lawyers, businessmen or TV personalities around them. One can only pity young people without admirations they can respect or avow, who are artificially restrained from the enthusiasm for great virtue.

In encouraging this deformity, democratic relativism joins a branch of conservatism that is impressed by the dangerous political consequences of idealism. These conservatives want young people to know that this tawdry old world cannot respond to their demands for perfection. In the choice between the somewhat arbitrarily distinguished realism and idealism, a sensible person would want to be both, or neither. But, momentarily accepting a distinction I reject, idealism as it is commonly conceived should have primacy in an education, for man is a being who must take his orientation by his possible perfection. To attempt to suppress this most natural of all inclinations because of possible abuses is, almost literally, to throw out the baby with the bath. Utopianism is, as Plato taught us at the outset, the fire with which we must play because it is the only way we can find out what we are. We need to criticize false understandings of Utopia, but the easy way out provided by realism is deadly. As it now stands, students have powerful images of what a perfect body is and pursue it incessantly. But deprived of literary guidance, they no longer have any image of a perfect soul, and hence do not long to have one. They do not even imagine that there is such a thing.

Following on what I learned from this second question, I began asking a third: Who do you think is evil? To this one there is an immediate response: Hitler. (Stalin is hardly mentioned.) After him, who else? Up until a couple of years ago, a few students said Nixon, but he has been forgotten and at the

same time is being rehabilitated. And there it stops. They have no idea of evil; they doubt its existence. Hitler is just another abstraction, an item to fill up an empty category. Although they live in a world in which the most terrible deeds are being performed and they see brutal crime in the streets, they turn aside. Perhaps they believe that evil deeds are performed by persons who, if they got the proper therapy, would not do them again—that there are evil deeds, not evil people. There is no *Inferno* in this comedy. Thus, the most common student view lacks an awareness of the depths as well as the heights, and hence lacks gravity.

Further Resources

BOOKS

Hirsch, Jr., E.D. *Cultural Literacy: What Every American Needs to Know.* Boston: Houghton Mifflin, 1987.

PERIODICALS

Green, S.J.D. "The Closing of the American Mind, Revisited." *The Antioch Review* 56, no. 1, Winter 1998, 371–382.

Kristol, William. "Bookshelf: Troubled Souls: Where We Went Wrong." *The Wall Street Journal,* April 22, 1987, Eastern ed., 1.

Postman, Neil. "Learning by Story." *The Atlantic,* December 1989, 119–124.

Mozert v. Hawkins County Board of Education

Court case

By: Pierce Lively

Date: 1987

Source: Lively, Pierce. *Mozert v. Hawkins County Board of Education,* 827 F.2d 1058 (1987). Available online at http://www.soc.umn.edu/~samaha/cases/mozert%20v%20hawkins%20co%20schools.htm; website home page http://www.soc.umn.edu (accessed May 12, 2003).

About the Author: Pierce Lively (1920–) was born in Louisville, Kentucky. After graduating from Centre College, Lively enlisted in the Navy during World War II (1939–1945). He then attended the University of Virginia Law School, before practicing law in Kentucky. President Nixon (served 1969–1974) appointed Lively to the United States Court of Appeals, Sixth Circuit in 1972, and Lively served as chief judge of that court from 1983 until his retirement in 1997. As of 2003, Judge Lively was teaching at Centre College. ∎

Introduction

The plaintiffs in the case against the Hawkins County Board of Education included Bob and Alice Mozert,

Vicki Frost, and other concerned parents. The Tennessee school district required students to use the Holt, Rinehart, Winston reading series which contained materials the plaintiffs found offensive. Their lawsuit proceeded to the U.S. Court of Appeals, Sixth Circuit.

Vicki Frost, a parent of three children, read a few of the stories in her child's reading textbook. What she read deeply offended her beliefs as a born-again Christian. When she approached school officials about the content of the text, she was told that alternate readings could be provided. This accommodation lasted only a short time. In November 1983, the school board voted not to provide alternatives to the Holt reading series that had been adopted for grades 1–8 in the Hawkins County Schools. Students who did not participate in reading were suspended from school. The district said that the curriculum was integrated, and that students could be discussing ideas from the reading at any point of the day. There was not an isolated reading lesson or time, even though reading was taught as a separate subject in the upper grades. This decision caused students and parents to file a lawsuit against the district.

Vicki Frost was not alone in her concerns about the content of stories. Families joined together to form "Citizens Organized for Better Schools" (COBS) to fight what they viewed as morally offensive works. The group fought the case as a First Amendment violation. They argued that the schools should respect their fundamentalist Christian beliefs. They did not want their children exposed to anything that differed from their interpretation of the Bible. It is important to note that the families came from different denominations; therefore, this was not a single church against the schools. The case began in the U.S. District Court of Eastern Tennessee, where it was initially dismissed. The Sixth Circuit court returned it to the District Court, however, and District Court Judge Hull ruled in favor of the parents. This led to the decision excerpted below.

Significance

A number of critical issues were considered in *Mozert v. Hawkins County Board of Education*. These included the First Amendment rights of the students and parents, the rights of parents to control what their children learn, and the freedom of the schools to act in good faith for the majority of the students.

Vicki Frost "testified that she spent more than 200 hours reviewing the Holt series and found numerous passages that offended her religious beliefs." She stated that there were seventeen categories—including evolution, supernaturalism, pacifism, and magic—that caused her concern. The press frequently cited *The Wizard of Oz* as an example, but her concerns went deeper. She also ob-

jected to the teacher's manuals and lesson suggestions that accompanied the Holt series. Mrs. Frost and the other parents did not want their children role playing or doing anything that would foster false imagination. They objected to what the children were being taught—what they were required to recognize as "truths" from the texts.

Educators were concerned about this suit on several levels. It was not the first lawsuit to charge that a school or district was violating a student's First Amendment rights. The series was selected because it incorporated "critical reading" or critical thinking skills into the curriculum. Texts, concepts, and ideas could be incorporated throughout the day, and were not isolated to a single period for reading. The development of thought and openness to new ideas is an important educational value. Restricting students to a few alternative texts, limited their exposure. Educators worried about further censorship of texts. Would they include controversial topics in a text if challenges were constantly being filed? The main argument by the School District was that public education was to serve all students in the best manner possible. There were alternatives available to the parents, including private schools, church schools, and home schooling. In the end, the school district won, and the Supreme Court refused to hear the case. However, questions about reading, use of imagination, and how children should be taught have not ended.

Primary Source

Mozert v. Hawkins County Board of Education [excerpt]

> **SYNOPSIS:** Who decides how a child should be educated? In this case, the courts ruled that the school district was acting in accordance with its mission to provide a fair education for all students. Other cases ruling for challenging parents and students were distinguished. The *Yoder* case, in which the family refused to send their children to school, did not apply, though it addressed freedom of religion. Other options were available to the students and parents if they disagreed with the school's reading curriculum.

School children and their parents brought action seeking injunctive relief and money damages for alleged violation of their First Amendment right to free exercise of religion. The United States District Court for the Eastern District of Tennessee, 579 F.Supp. 1051, limited plaintiffs' allegations and subsequently granted defendants' motion to dismiss, 582 F.Supp. 201, and plaintiffs appealed. The Court of Appeals, 765 F.2d 75, reversed and remanded. On remand, the District Court, 647 F.Supp. 1194, Thomas Gray Hull J., held that requiring children to

Vicki Frost points to text in her child's school textbook. She and other parents of the Hawkins County School District found the text to be offensive to their beliefs. **KNOXVILLE JOURNAL.**

read from textbooks they found offensive to their religious beliefs burdened students' rights of free exercise of religion, granted injunction against required reading and awarded damages. Appeal was brought. The Court of Appeals, Lively, Chief Judge, held that requirement that public school students study basic reader series chosen by school authorities did not create unconstitutional burden under free exercise clause.

Reversed and remanded with directions to dismiss complaint.

Cornelia G. Kennedy and Boggs, Circuit Judges, concurred and filed opinions. . . .

I

A

Early in 1983 the Hawkins County, Tennessee Board of Education adopted the 1060 Holt, Rinehart and Winston basic reading series (the Holt series) for use in grades 1–8 of the public schools of the county. In grades 1–4, reading is not taught as a separate subject at a designated time in the school day. Instead, the teachers in these grades use the reading texts throughout the day in conjunction with other subjects. In grades 5–8, reading is taught as a separate subject at a designated time in each class. However, the schools maintain an integrated curriculum which requires that ideas appearing in the reading programs reoccur in other courses. By statute public schools in Tennessee are required to include "character education" in their curricula. The pupose of this requirement is "to help each student develop positive values and to improve student conduct as students learn to act in harmony with their positive values and learn to become good citizens in their school, community, and society." Tennessee Code Annotated (TCA) 49–6–1007 (1986 Supp.).

Like many school systems, Hawkins County schools teach "critical reading" as opposed to reading exercises that teach only word and sound recognition. "Critical reading" requires the development of higher order cognitive skills that enable students to evaluate the material they read, to contrast the ideas presented, and to understand complex characters that appear in reading material. Plaintiffs do not dispute that critical reading is an essential skill which their children must develop in order to succeed in other subjects and to function as effective participants in modern society. Nor do the defendants dispute the fact that any reading book will do more than teach a child how to read, since reading is instrumental in a child's total development as an educated person.

The plaintiff Vicki Frost is the mother of four children, three of whom were students in Hawkins County public schools in 1983. At the beginning of the 1983–84 school year Mrs. Frost read a story in a daughter's sixth grade reader that involved mental telepathy. Mrs. Frost, who describes herself as a "born again Christian," has a religious objection to any teaching about mental telepathy. Reading further, she found additional themes in the reader to which she had religious objections. After discussing her objections with other parents, Mrs. Frost talked with the principal of Church Hill Middle School and obtained an agreement for an alternative reading program for students whose parents objected to the assigned Holt reader. The students who elected the alternative program left their classrooms during the reading sessions and worked on assignments from an older textbook series in available office or library areas. Other students in two elementary schools were excused from reading the Holt books.

B.

In November 1983 the Hawkins County School Board voted unanimously to eliminate all alternative reading programs and require every student in the public schools to attend classes using the Holt series. Thereafter the plaintiff students refused to read the Holt series or attend reading classes where the series was being used. The children of several plaintiff students were suspended for brief periods for this refusal. Most of the plaintiff students were ultimately taught at home, or attended religious schools, or transferred to public schools outside Hawkins County. One student returned to school because his family was unable to afford alternate schooling. Even after the board's order, two students were allowed some accommodation, in that the teacher either excused them from reading the Holt stories, or specifically noted on worksheets that the students were not required to believe the stories.

On December 2, 1983, the plaintiffs, consisting of seven families—14 parents and 17 children—filed this action pursuant to 42 U.S.C. 1983. In their complaint the plaintiffs asserted that they have sincere religious beliefs which are contrary to the values taught or inculcated by the reading textbooks and that it is a violation of the religious belief and convictions of the plaintiff students to be required to read the books and a violation of the religious beliefs of the plaintiff parents to permit their children to read the books. The plaintiffs 1061 sought to hold the defendants liable because "forcing the student-plaintiffs to read school books which teach or inculcate choices in areas where the Bible provides the answer. . . .

Quite recently the Supreme Court quoted Justice Douglas, concurring in *Sherbert v. Verner,* 374 U.S. at 412, 83 S.Ct. at 1798, as follows:

[T]he Free Exercise Clause is written in terms of what the government cannot do to the individual, not in terms of what the individual can extract from the government. *Bowen v. Roy,* 476 U.S. 693, 106 S.Ct. 2147, 2152, 90 L.Ed.2d 735 (1986).

Paraphrasing this thought, the Court wrote:

The Free Exercise Clause affords an individual protection from certain forms of governmental compulsion; it does not afford an individual a right to dictate the conduct of the Government's internal procedures.

Since we have found none of the prohibited forms of governmental compulsion in this case, we conclude that the plaintiffs failed to establish the existence of an unconstitutional burden. Having determined that no burden was shown, we do not reach the issue of the defendants' compelling interest in requiring a uniform reading series or the question, raised by the defendant, of whether awarding damages violated the Establishment Clause.

Judge Boggs concludes that the majority reverses the district court because it found the plaintiffs' claims of First Amendment protection so extreme as obviously to violate the Establishment Clause. This is not the holding of the majority. We do point out that under certain circumstances the plaintiffs, by their own testimony, would only accept accommodations that would violate the Establishment Clause. However, this is not the holding. What we do hold is that the requirement that public school students study a basal reader series chosen by the school authorities does not create an unconstitutional burden under the Free Exercise Clause when the students are not required to affirm or deny a belief or engage or refrain from engaging in a practice prohibited or required by their religion. There was no evidence that the conduct required of the students was forbidden by their religion. Rather, the witnesses testified that reading the Holt series "could" or "might" lead the students to come to conclusions that were contrary to teachings of their and their parents' religious beliefs. This is not sufficient to establish an unconstitutional burden. . . .

The judgment of the district court granting injunctive relief and damages is reversed, and the case is remanded with directions to dismiss the complaint. No costs are allowed. The parties will bear their own costs on appeal.

Further Resources

BOOKS

Brinkley, Ellen Henson. *Caught Off Guard: Teachers Rethinking Censorship and Controversy.* Boston: Allyn and Bacon, 1999.

DelFattore, Joan. *What Johnny Shouldn't Read: Textbook Censorship in America.* New Haven, Conn.: Yale University Press, 1992.

Edwards, June. *Opposing Censorship in the Public Schools: Religion, Morality, and Literature.* Mahwah, N.J.: L. Erlbaum Associates, 1998.

PERIODICALS

Flygare, Thomas J. "Some Thoughts on the Tennessee Textbook Case. Mozert v. Hawkins County Schools." *Phi Delta Kappan* 68, February 1987, 474–475.

Hulsizer, Donna. "Public Education on Trial." *Educational Leadership* 44, no. 8, May 1987, 12–16.

Jorstad, Eric. "What Johnny Can't Read: Parents, Textbooks, & the Courts." *Commonweal* 115, no. 12, June 17, 367–370.

WEBSITES

The Council of Parent and Attorneys and Advocates. Available online at http://www.copaa.net/resources/tracking.html; website home page: http://www.copaa.net (accessed May 12, 2003).

Holt, Rinehart and Winston. http://www.hrw.com/ (accessed May 12, 2003).

AUDIO AND VISUAL MEDIA

Censorship In Our Schools, Hawkins County, Tennessee. Directed by Grady Watts. People for the American Way: Videocassette, 1988.

"Student Press Freedom: One View of the *Hazelwood* Decision"

Journal article

By: Mark Goodman

Date: 1988

Source: Goodman, Mark. "Student Press Freedom: One View of the *Hazelwood* Decision," *NASSP Bulletin* 72, no. 511, November 1988, 39–44.

About the Author: Mark Goodman is the Executive Director of the Student Press Law Center (SPLC) in Arlington, Virginia. Goodman attended journalism school at the University of Missouri and Duke University Law School. The Student Press Law Center is an advocate for students' rights and provides legal assistance to students and educators who require it. ■

Introduction

Hazelwood School District v. Kuhlmeier focused on the rights of student journalists in public high schools. The main question decided was: "Do students or school officials have the right to determine the content of school-sponsored student publications?" In 1983, the case began with censorship at Hazelwood East High School in suburban St. Louis, Missouri. A principal removed personal stories about student pregnancies and students of divorced parents. He found these to be offensive and inappropriate for the school newspaper. The students took the school district to court for violating the First Amendment rights of student journalists.

The United States Court of Appeals was the only court to uphold student rights. Both the United States District Court and the Supreme Court ruled in favor of the rights of school officials to censor student publications. This suit dealt with publications related to classes held in school or completed on campus. Rights of students to distribute publications completed off campus was determined in *Burch v. Barker,* a 1983 lawsuit, filed by the American Civil Liberties Union (ACLU)-Washington on behalf of students, against Lindbergh High School in Renton, Washington. In that case, the court ruled for the students because they had produced the newspaper off campus and at their own expense. The distinction between on and off campus publications was important in *Hazelwood,* as was the interpretation of the courts regarding First Amendment rights.

The Hazelwood decision curtailed the freedom of students and their advisors to decide what could be printed in a school-sponsored publication. The school officials could censor publications that they felt would be harmful. They must, however, show that they have a valid reason for censorship, and could not stop publication merely because they held a different point of view.

Significance

A free press for students has many advantages. Teachers and advisors can help students tackle the controversial subjects that they face on a daily basis. Student editors and writers can learn to interpret facts and use critical thinking to write a story that will be fair and just to the parties involved. Students, who have freedom to publish the viewpoints they see as important to their peers, may consider careers in journalism. Squelching students' freedom of speech can reverse all of these positive factors. This has been the fear since the Supreme Court issued its decision in *Hazelwood v. Kuhlmeier.*

The court's 5-3 decision stated that a school-sponsored student publication was not a public forum for student expression. Three factors applied to the decision of viewing a publication as a public forum. Is a there a faculty sponsor? Does the publication teach students or audience particular skills or knowledge? And, are the school name or resources used? In some cases, under these criteria, an extracurricular activity can be subject to the *Hazelwood* decision. It is also significant that the decision only applies to public high schools.

Schools continue to treat student publications in different ways. Some take advantage of the *Hazelwood* ruling, reading the articles prior to publication and determining whether they are appropriate for the school's population. Other principals grant editorial freedom for student journalists, allowing them to decide what should be printed in the student newspaper. In a 1998 article, Clara G. Hoover writes "the alarm that swept through the academic, journalism and civil rights communities following *Hazelwood* seems to have subsided a bit in the last 10 years." As noted on the Student Press Law Center website, however, Mark Goodman and his colleagues still see the threat of censorship as a major factor in student publications. Despite the court's decision, censorship and freedom of the press for high school students continues to be debated. The best approach, according to SPLC and journalism groups, is adopting a clear policy regarding the responsibilities of student journalists. This may be the best way to eliminate problems.

Primary Source

"Student Press Freedom: One View of the *Hazelwood* Decision" [excerpt]

> **SYNOPSIS:** Goodman is concerned about the freedom of students to express opinions that may not be popular with school officials. *Hazelwood* effectively prohibits this expression with the threat of censorship. Goodman points out that libel is difficult for the courts to decide, and that school officials who use this as a rationale are bound to encounter problems.

On January 13, 1988, the United States Supreme Court decided its first case ever involving the First Amendment rights of high school journalists working on a school-sponsored newspaper. That case, *Hazelwood School District v. Kuhlmeier,* focused on a debate that has been raging for years: Do students or school officials have the right to determine the content of school-sponsored student publications?

For many years, national organizations of high school publications advisers like the Journalism Education Association and the Columbia Scholastic Press Advisers Association have supported the free press rights of students. The Student Press Law Center, the Quill and Scroll journalism honorary society, and the National Scholastic Press Association are only three of the dozens of national, regional, and state organizations on both the high school and college level that have taken similar positions in support of high school student press freedom.

A Review of *Hazelwood*

The Supreme Court decided the *Hazelwood* case as a matter of law. However, the Court left it up to school districts across the country to look at censorship as a matter of educational policy. *Hazelwood* provides every principal an opportunity to examine the practical reasons why thousands of journalism educators reject censorship of student publications as being both morally offensive and educationally unsound.

The *Hazelwood* case focused on the student newspaper *Spectrum* at Hazelwood East High School in suburban St. Louis. In the spring of 1983, students on the *Spectrum* staff prepared two pages of stories on the problems teenagers face. The Hazelwood East principal saw the newspaper before it went to press and felt that two of the stories were inappropriate.

One, about teenage pregnancy, included the personal accounts of three unnamed Hazelwood East students who described their own pregnancies. Another, about the impact of divorce on children, contained quotes from students whose parents had been divorced. The principal removed the two pages of stories from *Spectrum.* Some students on the newspaper staff strongly objected to his action and eventually took the school district to court, claiming First Amendment infringement.

In 1985, a United States district court in Missouri upheld the school's action. The court said that because *Spectrum* was produced by a journalism class, it was a part of the school's curriculum that school officials had the right to control.

The students appealed that decision, and the United States Court of Appeals in St. Louis reversed. The court of appeals said, in its July 1986 decision, that although *Spectrum* was produced in relationship to a journalism class, it was more than a curricular exercise. The court said that *Spectrum* was a forum for student expression; as such, it could only be censored when school officials could show that the content they objected to would result in financial liability for the school or would create a material and substantial disruption of school activities.

The court said the school had not met that standard. On January 20, 1987, the Supreme Court accepted the school's request to review the case and heard oral argument on October 13.

Supreme Court review of the First Amendment rights of student journalists had been a long time coming. Back in 1969, the Court stated that neither students nor teachers "shed their constitutional rights to freedom of speech or expression at the schoolhouse gate." In deciding that a school could not punish students who wore black armbands to school in protest of the Vietnam war, the Court said that student expression was protected unless it "materially disrupts classwork or involves substantial disorder or invasion of the rights of others."

Subsequently, courts across the nation applied this holding to student publications. But the Supreme Court had never taken the opportunity to rule specifically on a case involving a student newspaper, yearbook, or magazine at the secondary school level. Thus, the *Hazelwood* case provided the Supreme Court with the opportunity to focus on the student press for the first time.

Disappointment for Journalism Teachers

The decision the Court reached was a disappointing one for many journalism educators. Rather than follow the tried and true *Tinker* standard, the five-member majority of the Court said *Tinker* did not apply.

In the eyes of the majority, the practice at Hazelwood had been for the adviser to exercise complete editorial control over student publications; no policy of the school indicated an intention to create a forum where students could exercise their own editorial discretion. When it coupled these determinations with the fact that the *Spectrum* was a school-sponsored curricular program, the majority said the student newspaper was not a forum for student expression. In this non-forum, school officials would

be allowed to censor when they could demonstrate "legitimate pedagogical concerns."

This new standard, while still leaving the burden of justifying censorship on school officials, gave Hazelwood much more authority to censor than had been available under the *Tinker* standard. . . .

Accepting Full Responsibility

School officials who take on the task of censoring their student publications should be prepared to bear the consequences of their actions. From the moment they begin to censor it will be clear that they are the ones who accept full responsibility for whatever might appear in a student publication. Before, they could have relied on the fact that both the law and sound educational practice prohibited them from censoring and protected them from blame. Now, when the inevitable mistakes are made, the community will point a finger at a school principal and will probably be far less understanding than it would if the mistakes were those of students.

Principal W. Ben Nesbit of Spring Valley High School in Columbia, S.C., notes some pragmatic reasons why he has been a long-time defender of student press freedom.

"If you don't allow students to speak out on issues that affect them, (issues such as) pregnancy, AIDS, abuse of alcohol and drugs, in their student publications, they will speak out in ways that may not be socially acceptable and that may be embarrassing to the school," Nesbit says.

A likely avenue for their expression? What we once called underground newspapers. The courts have clearly established that students have the right to distribute such publications on school grounds during the school day. With alternative publications there is no adviser to offer input or to help students learn the responsibility that goes with their position. Students do not get the same lessons in journalism from an independent publication, but a school will likely have the same if not greater concerns.

"Letting students speak out in student publications encourages creativity and prompts them to stretch and grow," says Nesbit. "That creativity is something you don't see in a stagnant and repressed environment where censorship is practiced."

Conclusion

The Supreme Court decision in *Hazelwood School District v. Kuhlmeier* may result in some significant changes in student publications. Calls received by the Student Press Law Center indicated some schools are using *Hazelwood* as a justification to censor when they never censored before.

But the Supreme Court's decision has not changed the reasons that those who are most actively involved with journalism education believe that we have nothing to fear from student press freedom. Rather, we believe a free student press can provide innumerable benefits to our students as well as to our schools.

Further Resources

BOOKS

Fuller, Sarah Betsy. *Hazelwood v. Kuhlmeir: Censorship in School Newspapers.* Springfield, N.J.: Enslow, 1998.

Ingelhart, Louis E. *Press Law and Press Freedom for High School Publications: Count Cases and Related Decisions Discussing Free Expression Guarantee and Limitations for High School Students and Journalists.* New York: Greenwood Press, 1986.

PERIODICALS

Dickson, Thomas V. "Attitudes of High School Principals about Press Freedom after Hazelwood." *Journalism Quarterly* 66, no. 1, Spring 1989, 169–173.

"Hazelwood Decision: The Complete Text of the January 13, U.S. Supreme Court 5 3 Decision." *Quill and Scroll* 62, no. 3, February/March 1988, 11–18.

Hoover, Clara G. "The Hazelwood Decision: A Decade Later." *NASSP Bulletin* 82, no. 599, September 1998, 48–56.

WEBSITES

Student Press Law Center. Available online http://www.splc.org/ (accessed May 12, 2003).

Hazelwood School District v. Kuhlmeier, 484 U.S. 260 (1988) Available online http://www.splc.org/law_library.asp?id=1; website home page: http://www.splc.org (accessed May 12, 2003).

"AIDS, Youth, and the University: An Interview with Admiral Watkins"

Interview

By: Admiral James D. Watkins

Date: 1988

Source: Watkins, James D. "AIDS, Youth, and the University: An Interview with Admiral Watkins." *Change* 20, no. 5, September/October 1988, 39–44.

About the Author: Admiral James D. Watkins (1927–) graduated from the U.S. Naval Academy in 1949. During his career in the navy he held such positions as commander-in-chief of the U.S. Pacific Fleet and Chief of Naval Operations. After Watkins retired, President Ronald Reagan (served 1981–1989) appointed him chairman of the Presidential Commission on the Human Immunodeficiency Virus Epidemic (AIDS) from 1987–1988. ∎

Introduction

AIDS and HIV became prominent problems of society in the 1980s. Identified in 1981, the HIV/AIDS epidemic became an issue with the United States government in 1983. In 1988, every household in the country received an educational brochure about AIDS from the U.S. Health Service. In addition, President Reagan formed the Presidential Commission on the Human Immunodeficiency Virus Epidemic (AIDS) in 1987—naming Admiral James D. Watkins, U.S. Navy, (retired) as chairman. Watkins became a vocal advocate for AIDS education in the broadest sense of the word. He had no prior health policy experience, but he led a group who issued a landmark report in June 1988. The Commission studied the issues surrounding the epidemic and ways to educate both the public and the medical community. Youth and college students were of particular interest because of the overwhelming attitude that they were immune from contracting the disease.

Education is the focus of the interview with Frank Newman in the September/October 1988 issue of *Change*. Watkins believed that if health workers did not know the facts about the disease, how could the public expect children and young adults to know? Myths about AIDS and HIV were exposed throughout the meetings, seminars and hearings the Commission held. Well-educated people still thought that AIDS could be transmitted by mosquito bites or through physical exposure to a person with the disease. Watkins also pushed for education at the college level, with the belief that an educated college population would carry the message to the younger generations. Another important factor for the Commission was to address the prejudicial feelings and discrimination displayed to those with HIV or AIDS. Through education, these fears and feelings can be lessened or eliminated.

Significance

The interview with Admiral Watkins pointed to a number of important factors about AIDS education in the United States during the 1980s. While the epidemic was growing, education was not necessarily keeping pace. False views spread through media, word of mouth, and fear of the unknown. Prejudice against the homosexual population was widespread regarding AIDS. The general population, and especially the youth, did not necessarily connect AIDS or HIV as a risk to themselves. They saw it as a disease other people contracted. Also a problem not widely acknowledged was a lack of awareness on the part of those with AIDS that they themselves had this

Admiral James Watkins, U.S. Navy (ret.), the Chairman of the Presidential Commission on the Human Immunodeficiency Virus Epidemic (AIDS) from 1987 to 1988. © **WALLY MCNAMEE/CORBIS. REPRODUCED BY PERMISSION.**

disease. The barriers could be broken only with well-planned education, and if those who had been exposed came forward and informed others.

Administrators on college campuses were particularly interested in educating their students about AIDS. *The Chronicle of Higher Education* frequently printed articles about this concern and students attitudes. The accompanying problems of drinking and drug use were also usually mentioned in these articles. Programs spread across campuses, some voluntary and others mandatory. At Assumption College in Worchester, Massachusetts, a mandatory program was held in residence halls with trained staff. Though some students resented the program at first, "97% of those who attended indicated that they learned new information which they considered of value to them in making decisions in their lives." Students also appreciated the concern shown for their health. A study conducted in 1987, 1991, and 1995 revealed "weak spots" in the knowledge of college students about how AIDS was spread, and its early warning signs.

The Commission's findings indicated that through support and commitment to educational training, people would learn the facts about AIDS. The future generation's lives and well-being were at stake, making this a vital issue for society to take seriously. At the time of the report, drugs for AIDS and HIV were just beginning to be developed. At the beginning of the twenty-first century, several were available. Education remains the key factor in preventing this disease and in seeking a cure.

Primary Source

"AIDS, Youth, and the University: An Interview with Admiral Watkins" [excerpt]

> **SYNOPSIS:** Without a broad educational program, knowledge about HIV/AIDS will remain a mystery to most people. This not only affects health care workers, but also the general population. Attitudes about AIDS are shaped in the home, church, school, and community.

Newman: Jim, you've just devoted nine months of your life to an intensive look at the AIDS situation. What's the most important thing you learned?

Watkins: I think the lesson that has come home to me throughout these months is the fact that education is the principal weapon we have for dealing with the virus. After all, we have no cure and no vaccine at this point.

When I speak of "education," though, I speak of a term misunderstood by many people who, too quickly, focus solely on the schoolroom environment—say, in the high schools. But our look at education should be much broader. For example, what we are seeing is a poorly educated health-care community—doctors, nurses, dentists, who simply don't know much about the virus. Or, we see religious leaders engaged in bigotry about this epidemic because they lack education about the virus. So we need a more comprehensive, far-reaching approach to education. We mean education for the workplace, for those not in the workplace, for those in the schools, for that quarter of our kids who should be in the high schools, but are not. We are talking about health-care provider education, and about educating volunteers, community-based organizations, and public health officials that have to be involved with this epidemic. So we are talking about every single aspect of education in order to reach all segments of society, particularly those segments out of the mainstream who are at highest risk.

Newman: Where do you find the locus for that? Who's got to take the leadership?

Watkins: I think the federal government, state governments, and all the people who work in health fields have to come together and develop new concepts of educating for broad, fundamental understanding of our own human biology, so that youngsters themselves can begin to participate and be part of the solution to the many health-related ills that society faces.

For example, we know about low birth weight and teen pregnancy and what it does to slow down cognitive processes in the early school grades. We know we are dealing with things like nutritional problems; inadequate participation in Head Start; the teen pregnancy issue; and substance abuse, whether it's alcohol, smoking, or drugs. So we are looking at an opportunity here to completely restructure the way we focus our efforts to understand what a healthy lifestyle is all about. Too often we *assume* that a child in this nation will be healthy. That may have been true years ago, but society is markedly changing. For example, one-third of youngsters today are born into poverty: now we are hardening an underclass with inadequate health-care availability, and our studies show a strong linkage or overlay between that underclass and AIDS. The overlays are direct and frightening to me. With the rapidly changing demographics, this underclass will consist mainly of Hispanic and black Americans.

What emerges is a much larger specter hanging over the nation than just this virus alone. AIDS brings into focus a variety of flaws in our system—flaws well known to professionals in education, business, and health—major flaws in the ways we approach youth at risk and adolescent development generally. All those flaws are brought into sharp focus for the American people by our look at society through the HIV lens. The job of educators of all kinds, then, is to help people learn in a fundamental way about human biology and their own bodies so they can possess lifelong strategies for healthy, wholesome lifestyles, not only for their personal good and human dignity, but with respect to others.

Newman: So when you say "education," you mean more than simply knowing about what causes AIDS. You are talking about trying to get at health-care problems by getting students to understand the nature of human biology.

Watkins: Absolutely. That larger understanding is far more important than HIV-specific issues. I know we have to do things in the near term because there is so much misunderstanding out there, but we have to start talking now about how young people can become real players in solving the health threats that face them across the board.

You know, if youngsters learned from kindergarten through the sixth grade, for example, how to

approach the complex transitional period to puberty, about the physiological changes in themselves as they move into new, more worldly environments, then AIDS instruction would have a chance. It would build on an educational base, so that when we talk to our young people about AIDS they'd understand from what they learned earlier about human biology. We would engage them at a point when they could begin to make their own decisions—sound decisions based on solid knowledge of their own bodies. And somehow, if we don't take advantage of the concern created by the HIV threat, we'll miss a great opportunity to expand our approach to education at a time when the nation desperately needs young people aware of their own uniqueness and human dignity, key underpinnings of solidifying self-esteem.

Further Resources

BOOKS

Keeling, Richard P. *Effective AIDS Education on Campus.* San Francisco: Jossey Bass, 1992.

Steinbach, Sheldon Elliott. *AIDS on Campus: Emerging Issues for College and University Administrators.* Washington, D.C.: American Council on Education, 1985.

United States. National Commission on Acquired Immune Deficiency Syndrome. *AIDS: An Expanding Tragedy: The Final Report of the National Commission on AIDS.* Washington, D.C.: The Commission, 1993.

PERIODICALS

Castronovo, Neil Ryan. "Acquired Immune Deficiency Syndrome Education on the College Campus: The Mandate and the Challenge." *Journal of Counseling & Development* 68, May/June 1990, 578–580.

McCormack, Arlene Smith. "Revisiting College Students Knowledge and Attitudes about HIV/AIDS: 1987, 1991 and 1995." *College Student Journal* 31, September 1997, 356–363.

WEBSITES

HIV/AIDS and College Students: A CDC Pathfinder. Available online at http://www.aegis.com/PUBS/CDC_FACT_SHEETS/1995/CPATH003.html; website home page: http://www.aegis.com (accessed May 12, 2003).

AIDS on Today's Campuses. Available online at http://www.eriche.org/crib/aids.html; website home page: http://www.eriche.org (accessed May 12, 2003).

AUDIO AND VISUAL MEDIA

The Education of Admiral Watkins: AIDS Update; A Death in the Family. Directed by Admiral James Watkins. WGBH Educational Foundation, Videocassette, 1989.

"A Letter to the Alumni and Faculty of Georgetown"
Letter

By: Timothy S. Healy

Date: 1988

Source: Healy, Timothy S. "A Letter to the Alumni and Faculty of Georgetown." *America* 158, no. 17, April 30, 1988, 455–458.

About the Author: Timothy S. Healy (1923–1992) was an ordained Roman Catholic priest in the Society of Jesus (Jesuit). He served as a faculty member and president of Georgetown University from 1976 to 1989. While there he was credited with helping Georgetown become a top-ranked university. Healy also taught at other institutions and served as the president of the New York Public Library. ∎

Introduction

In March 1988, Georgetown University settled an ongoing legal battle with two groups of homosexual students—one from the university's main campus and one from the law school. The Gay Rights Coalition of Georgetown University requested full recognition by the university, in order to obtain funding for their campus activities. The university refused, stating that homosexuality violated the beliefs of the Catholic Church, and that supporting them would be morally wrong. The eight-year battle ended when the university deciding not to appeal to the United States Supreme Court, and to negotiate a settlement with the groups after an adverse Court of Appeals decision.

The Georgetown case was complicated by religious freedoms, as well as issues regarding discrimination. The gay students accused the university of violating Washington, D.C.'s Human Rights Act, which guarantees rights for all people. The Superior Court ruled that the university had violated the D.C. act, but later decided that the university had the right to do so under the First Amendment. The Court of Appeals heard the case twice. In the end, the Court decided that the students' rights and the interest of eliminating discrimination prevented the university from "deny[ing] tangible benefits to homosexual student groups on basis of their sexual orientation." However, the Court said they could not force the university to recognize the groups.

President Timothy S. Healy's letter to alumni addressed the history of the legal battle and the struggle of the board to comply with court orders. Georgetown officials decided not to appeal to the Supreme Court because they did not think they had built a strong enough case over the years. Also, the Supreme Court's refusal to issue a stay from the lower court's decision suggested that Georgetown would lose in the Supreme Court—possibly

creating a national precedent, rather than one limited to the District of Columbia.

Significance

In this complicated case, the school argued that the tenets of the Catholic Church did not "teach a sexual ethic based merely on personal preferences." The students argued that they deserved recognition. The issue of the use of campus facilities and funding were at stake in the case, as well as moral issues. The fine lines between recognition, endorsing a lifestyle, and the availability of "tangible benefits" were critical points in the case.

Georgetown was founded in 1789, and it is the oldest Catholic university in America. When the Court upheld the right of the students, the university worked hard to negotiate a plan that would preserve the beliefs it had held for nearly two centuries. The settlement included the following provisions: gay student groups were not allowed the use of religious services or facilities, non-campus activities were prohibited, and homosexual acts were not condoned by the University. The university was also concerned about the use of its name in relation to gay student activities. Ramifications of the decision spread beyond the campus walls. Following the court's decision, President Reagan (served 1981–1989) and Congress called for the District of Columbia to change the Human Rights Act so religious schools would not be affected. This was seen as a political move, and as a way to force each member of Congress to vote on homosexual rights.

In the more than twenty years since this case was decided, Georgetown has changed. The website for the university spells out the "Access to Benefits" that resulted from the lawsuit, and explains what is and is not supported. There is now a "SafeZone" for those with questions about different lifestyles. In the spring of 2003, the university advertised for a coordinator of LGBTQ (Lesbian, Gay, Bisexual, Transgender, Questioning) Resources in the Office of Student Affairs. This signals the distance that Georgetown has traveled since the 1980s on this issue.

Primary Source

"A Letter to the Alumni and Faculty of Georgetown" [excerpt]

SYNOPSIS: Healy explains why a Catholic university permits meeting space and other college benefits to homosexual students. In the letter, Healy distinguishes between allowing them student's rights that other campus groups are allowed, and recognition or endorsement of a practice that the Catholic Church does not recognize.

For the past eight years Georgetown University has been engaged as the defendant in a lawsuit brought by two groups of homosexual students, one on the University's Main Campus and one at the Law School. At the end of March, the University arrived at an acceptable agreement with its opponents for the order that the trial court must issue in this matter. For that reason the University did not appeal the case to the Supreme Court. I am writing to give you the history of this long affair, and also the University's reasons for settling at this point rather than carrying it further.

In 1977, a group of students at the University formed an organization called "Gay People of Georgetown University" (G.P.G.U.). In 1979 and again in 1980, G.P.G.U. requested and received "student body endorsement," a status requiring approval only by the student government and not by the University. This endorsement entitled the group to advertise in student publications and to apply for lecture funds; it also granted them a limited use of University facilities. The group, however, wanted more than student body endorsement. It demanded full University recognition. That recognition would have meant that the University endorsed the activities of the organization, and would also have afforded it more extensive benefits, including University funding.

The University rejected G.P.G.U.'s request for University recognition on the grounds that the group presented a homosexual life style as morally acceptable. Among the group's stated purposes was "fostering theories of sexual ethics consonant with one's personal beliefs." The University stated that norms governing sexual conduct were objective, and that Catholicism does not teach a sexual ethic based merely on personal preference. Georgetown emphasized that "while it supports and cherishes the individual lives and rights of its students, it cannot subsidize this cause because it would be an inappropriate endorsement for a Catholic University."

At this point, local government became involved. The District of Columbia has an ordinance called the Human Rights Act. Under that act it would be an unlawful discrimination for an educational institution "to deny, restrict, or to abridge or condition the use of, or access to, any of its facilities and services to any person otherwise qualified, wholly or partially, for a discriminatory reason based upon the race, color, religion, national origins, sex, age, marital status, personal appearance, sexual orientation, family responsibilities, political affiliation, source of income or physical handicap of any individual. . . ." Under the same act, sexual orientation is defined as "male

Georgetown, founded in 1789, is the oldest Catholic University in the United States. © RICHARD T. NOWITZ/CORBIS. REPRODUCED BY PERMISSION.

or female homosexuality, heterosexuality and bisexuality, by preference or practice."

Under the provisions of this statute, G.P.G.U. field suit in the Superior Court for the District of Columbia alleging that the University had violated the Human Rights Act. The District of Columbia itself promptly intervened as a plaintiff to obtain enforcement of the act.

In October 1983, the Superior Court, in the person of Judge Sylvia Bacon, declared the act unenforceable against Georgetown under the "free exercise" clause of the Constitution. The court found that under Catholic doctrine, to which Georgetown adheres, no one "affiliated with the Roman Catholic Church may condone, endorse, approve or be neutral about homosexual orientation, homosexual life style or homosexual acts." The trial court thus found that "the District of Columbia Human Rights Act must yield to the Constitutional guarantees of religious freedom."

The plaintiffs then went to the Court of Appeals of the District of Columbia. In July 1985, a three-judge panel reversed the trial court by vote of 2 to 1. That same day, however, the Court of Appeals issued a spontaneous order vacating the smaller panel's opinion and setting the case for consideration by the whole court. Twenty-five months after the case was heard *en banc,* the court issued its decision in November 1987. Each judge wrote separately, and there was no opinion for the court. The court was shy one judge, and another judge, a former Georgetown dean, recused himself.

Despite its scattering of opinions, however, the holding of the court is clear: The District of Columbia has a compelling interest in eradicating discrimination against homosexuals, and that overrides the First Amendment protection of Georgetown's religious objections to subsidizing homosexual rights' organizations. The Court of Appeals held as a matter of statutory interpretation that the act does not require Georgetown to give the groups formal University recognition, which the court labeled an intangible. Instead, the court said, "The act only requires Georgetown to grant the groups the tangible benefits associated with University recognition." The court, therefore, accepted the distinction in principle between officially recognizing an organization and underwriting its activities.

Further Resources

BOOKS

Evans, Nancy J., and Vernon A. Wall. *Beyond Tolerance: Gays, Lesbians, and Bisexuals on Campus.* Alexandria, Va.: American College Personnel Association, 1991.

Gay Rights Coalition of Georgetown University v. Georgetown University, 496 A.2d 567, 27 Ed. Law Rep. 167 (D.C. Jul 30, 1985) (NO. 84-50, 84-51)

Gay Rights Coalition of Georgetown University Law Center v. Georgetown University, 536 A.2d 1, 56 USLW 2295, 44 Ed. Law Rep. 309 (D.C. Nov 20, 1987) (NO. 84-50, 84-51)

Wall, Vernon A., and Nancy J. Evans. *Toward Acceptance: Sexual Orientation Issues on Campus.* Lanhan, Md.: University Press of America, 2000.

PERIODICALS

Blumenstyk, Goldie. "In Wake of Georgetown U. Case, District of Columbia Told to Change Anti–Bias Law." *The Chronicle of Higher Education* 35, no. 7, October 12, 1988, A25.

Parlow, Matthew J. "Revisiting *Gay Rights Coalition of Georgetown Law Center v. Georgetown University* A Decade Later: Free Exercise Challenges and the Nondiscrimination Laws Protecting Homosexuals." *Texas Journal of Women and the Law* 9, no. 2, Spring 2000, 219–249.

WEBSITES

Georgetown University Access to Benefits. Available online at http://osp.georgetown.edu/benefits/access_to_benefits.htm; website home page: http://osp.georgetown.edu (accessed May 12, 2003).

Georgetown University SafeZone. Available online http://safezone.georgetown.edu/ (accessed May 12, 2003).

"On Creating *Ganas*: A Conversation with Jaime Escalante"

Interview

By: Jaime Escalante

Date: 1989

Source: Escalante, Jaime. "On Creating *Ganas*: A Conversation with Jaime Escalante."*Educational Leadership* 46, no. 5, February 1989, 46–47.

About the Author: Jaime Escalante (1930–) was born in La Paz, Bolivia. Not knowing how to speak English, and lacking any teaching credentials, he attended night school when he came to the United States. In 1976 he began teaching at Garfield High School, in East Los Angeles, California. Escalante was able to motivate a small group of students to take, and pass the AP calculus exam in 1982. Escalante became a national hero almost overnight. ∎

Introduction

Jaime Escalante was born in La Paz, Bolivia, where he had taught physics and math for fourteen years. After immigrating to the United States in 1964, he discovered that his teaching credentials would not transfer to a United States school. To remedy this situation and to learn English, he attended night school and accepted a teaching position at Garfield High School in East Los Angeles in the 1973–74 school year. Because he valued education, he was not prepared for the disrespect and disregard for education exhibited by the students and their parents at the new school. Yet, he understood these children, since he had been suspended from school several times as a child.

Drugs, gangs, and violence were common problems in the innercity schools. These problems were difficult to fight and deterred the ability to teach, or even to control a classroom. Escalante was not discouraged, however, viewing the problems as challenges. He has been quoted as saying, "The day someone quits school, he is condemning himself to a future of poverty," This theory, together with the belief that students must have desire and be motivated, pushed Escalante to be an award-winning teacher. Escalante claims he is only a math teacher. But he has shown the world that students will learn if a teacher believes in them, even those who feel incapable of learning.

Significance

"Ganas" means desire in Spanish. Jaime Escalante creates this in students. He has proven that motivation is

Actor Edward James Olmos (left) stands next to high-school teacher Jaime Escalante (right). Olmos portrayed Escalante in *Stand and Deliver,* the 1988 film based on Escalante's achievements. **AP/WIDE WORLD PHOTOS. REPRODUCED BY PERMISSION.**

as important—or more important—than previous training for his high school students to succeed in math. Escalante's program is focused on teamwork and turning students into leaders. The change in students did not happen overnight, or even in one year, however. The movie version of his classroom, *Stand and Deliver,* gave a false impression that students can neglect their studies for several years, and then be redeemed by a few months of hard work.

Escalante believed in students' ability enough to put them in front of the class and make them explain an answer to a math problem. Great change happened at Garfield High School because of Escalante's hard work—and the hard work of other teachers and administrators who believed in academics. His students gained confidence and began to perform better, reaching levels they never imagined. Escalante expected much from his students, from studying to being prepared to answer questions orally. He also encouraged students to think about further education. He made that "one of the requirements" of his class.

Escalante rejected the divisions of students into gifted and ordinary. Everyone has a talent or a gift. Everyone can learn. He believes most in the power of teachers. "We all remember the first teacher who really touched our lives, or gave us some encouragement, or at least appreciated our best." With this philosophy, Es-

calante challenged his students to prepare for the Advanced Placement Calculus exam. Knowledge, motivation, and understanding that they were valued as people helped these students excel on the test. When the first group of students were forced to retest because they were suspected of cheating, they did even better. This demonstrated the success of Escalante and his methods.

Escalante left Garfield High School in 1991 due to differences with the new administration. Unfortunately the program declined after his departure. He moved on to other teaching positions, and hosted a math-related television show, *Futures,* on Public Broadcasting System (PBS).

Jaime Escalante was honored with a Presidential Medal of Excellence (1998) and induction into the National Teachers Hall of Fame (1999). However, what honors him the most is the success of his students.

Primary Source

"On Creating *Ganas*: A Conversation with Jaime Escalante"

SYNOPSIS: The interviewer talks to Jaime Escalante, a teacher who worked with at-risk students in East Los Angeles. Escalante was the subject of the movie *Stand and Deliver.*

How did you, a teacher at Garfield High School, become the subject of a movie?

I don't know really. I just helped my students reach the highest possible degree of personal development. I have knowledge, and I have a deep love for my students. When I came to this school in 1973–74, the students were not interested in education. The parents were not interested in education.

It wasn't what you expected?

No, and my first day was not really enjoyable. I noticed the language these kids used, and I noticed the kids without any supplies. I was disappointed. I decided to go back to my job—I had a good job, I was working with computers.

Going back home, I changed my mind. I said, "First, I'm going to teach them responsibility, and I'm going to teach them respect, and *then* I'm going to quit." I started trying to attract some of the students. My intention was to capture the minds of these kids to build an image, a college image, a school image, a university image—that you can educate yourselves to be Somebody.

So it was discouraging at first, but you were determined.

I took it as a challenge. I said, "We're going to see, kids."

Where did you get your determination?

I started teaching when I was only 22 years old. I taught mathematics back home in Bolivia for 11 years. However, when I came to the U.S., none of my credentials would count. That's why I had to go back and start from scratch. I always had in mind to go back to my first love, which was teaching. And I did that; finally, when I got my teaching credentials, I picked Garfield. But I didn't know Garfield was in bad shape. There were too many gang kids, too many fights inside the school. It was never unusual to see the police car every five minutes at school. That was the beginning. But now the school is different.

You have a thorough knowledge of mathematics.

Yes, and also I have a strong background in skills—in other words, how to communicate and how to teach these kids. Really, it's not just the knowledge of math. Because to have the knowledge is one thing, and to use that knowledge is another, and to know how to teach or how to motivate these kids is the combination of both. My skills are really to motivate these kids, to make them learn, to give them *ganas*—the desire to do something—to make them believe they can learn.

How do you convey this belief, this self-confidence, to them?

I use the team approach. I make them believe that we have a team which is going to prepare for the Olympics. And our Olympics is the advanced placement calculus exam. I always talk to them and tell them, "Look, we prepared two years for this competition, and you have to play strong defense. Don't let the test put you down. You're the best." And every time the kids go to take the advanced placement calculus exam, they wear the jacket with a bulldog, which is the school mascot, and the kids go to the testing room yelling "Defense! Defense! Defense!"

Why does this work with your students?

Because in 1982 we had the controversial year in which ETS believed these kids could not pass the advanced placement calculus exam, and they showed they could do it. ETS thought two of my students had cheated, and all of them had to retake the exam, and then their scores were even higher.

On top of that, every year we double the number of students interested in advanced calculus. We double the number of students interested in mathematics. This school has so many students in chemistry, biology, and physics—it's because they believe they can do it. One of the things the kids always repeat in front of me is "You said, 'I believe in what you're doing.'" And the kids sense that they are going to be Somebody someday.

And then the teamwork reinforces their confidence.

Right. Suppose I have a student who does not feel confident with math or doesn't like it too much. In order to motivate her or him, I say, "Look, you're going to be the class leader. So they're going to be asking questions, and you should be able to answer questions, and I'm going to help. Come over here, and I'm going to be explaining to you. The only thing you have to do is pay attention and repeat everything I'm going to say."

And the kids start producing. Then I give my assignment. I say, "I want you to teach this tomorrow. We're going to surprise the whole class, nobody knows, so we need to understand what I'm going to teach. So I'm going to call you early, and you're going to explain on the board. But play it cool."

They keep ready, and then I call on that kid, and he or she does the work on the board. The next day the kid comes to me and asks "How did I do?"

I say, "You did extremely well, but you can do better. So next time I'll let you know what you're going to be doing." That way they start building up confidence.

Once they build that confidence, it's easy going. It's not difficult, I just start pushing and keep working more and more. Once there's a team, we have no problem. So I take the kid for the summer; and the next year, especially when he or she is a senior, that kid will be my teaching assistant. They make money. That's when I prove this is easy—you know a little, enough to make a little money; if you go to college, you're going to make more money.

And how does this work out? Are these children now going on to college?

Yes, that's one of the requirements. The first day when these kids walk into my room, I have a bunch of names of schools and colleges on the chalkboard. I ask each student to memorize one. The next day I pick one kid and ask, "What school did you pick?" He says USC or UCLA or Stanford, MIT, Colgate, and so on. So I say, "Okay, keep that in mind. I'm going to bring in somebody who'll be talking about the schools." So in fact I talk to the college adviser, and he comes and talks, and I ask him to choose the school they want. The only thing I have to supply, which I call *ganas,* is the desire to do it. The money is going to come if the kids are working.

They have been able to finance their college careers?

Yes, they do, we do. We have a foundation, the Foundation for Advancement in Science and Education, which collects money to help these kids. We use the money to pay the teaching assistants and to help kids go to college. We find scholarship for them, too.

What is Garfield High School like now?

We've become one of the best schools At Garfield we're so proud of our students. I feel great when I see our kids going to the best colleges now. It looks like a private school; everybody wants to come to this school. But we don't have enough desks, we don't have enough teachers to be able to continue with our program in the way we'd like.

What made you so sure that these kids could learn like this?

I don't think kids cannot learn. That's my own philosophy. Anybody, any kid can learn if he or she

has the desire to do it. That's what *ganas* is about. The teacher plays an important role in education—we all remember the first teacher who really touched our lives, or gave us some encouragement, or at least appreciated our best. The teacher gives us the desire to learn, the desire to be Somebody.

What would you say to teachers who find themselves teaching students like yours?

The teacher has to have the energy of the hottest volcano, the memory of an elephant, and the diplomacy of an ambassador. . . . Really, a teacher has to possess love and knowledge and then has to use this combined passion to be able to accomplish something. Don't teach from the desk, no. Don't teach for the money.

When we talk about education, we're talking about the future of our country—the teacher plays an important role in that. The owner of the future will be the person who is the owner of his or her own human resources, and human resources are the product of high quality in education.

Further Resources

BOOKS

Donmoyer, Robert, and Raylene Kos. *At-Risk Students: Portraits, Policies, Programs and Practices.* Albany, N.Y.: SUNY Press, 1993.

Means, Barbara, et al., eds. *Teaching Advanced Skills to At-Risk Students: Views from Research and Practice.* San Francisco: Jossey Bass, 1991.

PERIODICALS

Jehlen, Alain. "How to Advance Minority Students." *NEA Today* 21, no. 4, January 2003, 26–27.

"Stand and Deliver Revisited." *Resource* 34, no. 3, July 2002, 34–39.

WEBSITES

Excellence: Do it Right the First Time. Available online at http://www.govtech.net/magazine/visions/feb98vision/escalante.phtml; website home page: http://www.govtech.net (accessed May 12, 2003).

Hall of Fame–Jaime Escalante. Available online at http://www.boliviaweb.com/hallfame/escalante.htm; website home page: http://www.boliviaweb.com (accessed May 12, 2003).

AUDIO AND VISUAL MEDIA

Stand and Deliver. Directed by Ramon Menendez. Warner Home Video, Videocassette, 1988.

4

FASHION AND DESIGN

EUGENIA F. BELL

Entries are arranged in chronological order by date of primary source. For entries with one primary source, the entry title is the same as the primary source title. Entries with more than one primary source have an overall entry title, followed by the titles of the primary sources.

Important Events in Fashion and Design, 1980–1989

1980

- American designers abandon synthetics for natural fabrics and more-expensive weaves.
- Skirts become shorter and shorter.
- Knits in a wide variety of textures, and colors take a significant place in fashion—even as dress-up clothes.
- Norma Kamali shows her successful collection of cotton fleece-sweats separates modeled after exercise-dance clothes.
- *The Official Preppy Handbook,* edited by Lisa Birnbach, is published.
- The preppie look reappears—navy blazers, button-down shirts, and challis skirts.
- The latest fad is the Rubik's cube.
- Yellow ribbons are everywhere in memory of the American hostages held in Iran.
- On November 21, an estimated eighty-three million Americans watch an episode of the television series *Dallas* to find out "Who shot J. R.?" T-shirts printed with the question had been appearing in stores all over the country.

1981

- Postmodernist slogan "Less is a Bore" replaces modernism's "Less is More."
- Tom Wolfe's *From Bauhaus to Our House* is published; the book criticizes the architectural profession for creating abstract buildings that do not properly celebrate American capitalism.
- Ralph Lauren introduces "retro cowgirl" look that becomes a fad: petticoats and denim skirts worn with boots.
- Sailor-theme clothes are shown by Chloe, Geoffrey Beene, Yves Saint Laurent, and others.
- IBM comes out with a 288K memory chip.
- On January 20, Ronald Reagan is inaugurated as president; his wife, Nancy, wears a white, one-shouldered inaugural-ball gown designed by James Galanos; her complete inaugural wardrobe reportedly costs twenty-five thousand dollars.

1982

- Perry Ellis shows a new silhouette for women's clothing: boxy jacket with long, pleated skirt; this theme—long and full or short and lean—would continue to be popular for the rest of the decade.
- White, cream, and pastels are popular colors for the summer.
- Computers reach 1.5 million homes.
- Hot items are Smurfs and E.T. stuff.
- "Valley girl" stereotypes spawn two phrases: "grody to the max," and "gag me with a spoon."
- The first part of the Vietnam Veterans Memorial, the Wall, designed by Yale-educated architect Maya Ying Lin, is dedicated in Washington, D.C.

1983

- According to *The World Almanac,* young Americans' "top hero" is Michael Jackson; his look is widely copied.
- A study by the Society of Podiatrists reports that one in every ten women now wears a size ten or larger shoe as a result of increased participation in dancing, aerobics, or jogging.
- Ray-Ban sunglasses, worn by Tom Cruise in the movie *Risky Business,* are popular.
- Break dancing hits the mainstream consciousness.
- Cabbage Patch dolls, complete with birth certificates, are popular with girls and their mothers.
- The oversized coat becomes a trend.
- The pop singer Madonna shows her navel and wears underwear as outer-wear.
- The designers Kamali and Ellis show narrow, midi-length skirts that flare slightly at the hem.
- The High Museum of Art, designed by Richard Meier and Partners, is built in Atlanta.
- Diplaying the glass and steel severity of the International Style in an Art Deco inspired design, the Transco Tower is built in Houston; the architects are Philip Johnson and John Burgee.

1984

- The "men's skirt"—pants with wide legs, one of which folds over the other—is introduced; despite heavy press coverage, it fails to become popular.
- The movie *Flashdance* inspires an off-the-shoulder sweat-shirts fad.
- Michael Jackson travels the country on his Victory tour, and his album *Thriller* sells thirty-eight million copies, inspiring youths to wear one glove, mock military jackets, and black patent leather shoes.
- Bustiers, inspired by the 1950s, are worn with contemporary minis, boxer shorts, or gathered skirts.
- The television shows *Dallas* and *Dynasty* inspire shoulder pads and short skirts—the bold and alluring look.
- The television series *Miami Vice* influences men's styles: unconstructed sport coats worn over T-shirts, both in pastel colors.
- Trivial Pursuit is the hot new board game.

1985

- The female silhouette is softer and ultrafeminine, with full skirts and scooped necklines.
- Curvier, more athletic-looking models replace the malnourished "Twiggy look" in fashion magazines.
- Lingerie—from garter belts to one-piece body suits with lace inserts—becomes popular.
- *Dynasty* costumer Nolan Miller launches a commercial collection of extravagant clothes.
- Anne Klein shows a pale pink cashmere blazer with classic but strong lines that becomes a quintessential garment of the mid 1980s and will still be copied late in the decade.
- Linen, popularized by Giorgio Armani, is chic for men.
- Street style, the deliberately underdressed look of youth, is the height of fashion.
- Dietary concerns, such as potentially hazardous additives and the importance of calcium, influence eating habits.
- "New Coke" is withdrawn from the market after three months.

1986

- *American Vogue* shows sweater twin sets with Grace Kelly-inspired scarves and bags.
- The T-shirt dress, in plain matte colors, is popular.
- The movie *Out of Africa*, starring Robert Redford and Meryl Streep, inspires safari jackets.
- For men, the conservative preppy look still dominates.
- Aerobics is the new health fad.

1987

- The fashion industry attempts to revive the short skirt and fails.
- The average woman spends $569 on clothes this year.
- Men's suits return to favor.
- The punk-rock influence in fashion is waning.
- Video presentations, using computer graphics, are a standard requirement for architectural competitions.
- Forty states and hundreds of cities restrict smoking in public buildings.
- Sixty percent of American kitchens have microwaves.
- On October 19, the stock market crashes; the fashion industry attempts to recover by raising prices.

1988

- The fashion industry experiences a lull as career women refuse to pay top prices for impractical, trendy clothes.
- *Modern Classicism,* by Robert Stern and Ramon Gastil, is published.
- The Ford Motor Company introduces the Probe.
- On November 8, George Bush is elected president; his wife, Barbara, will influence women's fashions with such accoutrements as her three-strand fake-pearl necklace.

1989

- Increasingly, models of diverse ethnic backgrounds are seen in fashion magazines as the Caucasian "all-American" face wanes in popularity.
- Brocade is popular with women's casual clothes.
- The sarong shape is seen in women's pants, skirts, and bathing suits.
- Big, beaded necklaces are piled one on top of the other, often in vivid colors and geometric shapes.
- Rockefeller Plaza West, designed by Kohn Pederson Fox Associates, is completed in New York City; it evokes the 1920s-style skyscraper.
- The World Financial Center and Winter Garden, designed by Cesar Pelli, are completed in New York City. The glass-enclosed 45,000 square foot Winter Garden, completed October 1988, is the centerpiece of the World Financial Center.
- Peter Eisenman's deconstructivist modern glass, steel and concrete Wexler Center for the Arts is completed on the Ohio State University campus in Columbus, Ohio.
- Frank Gehry and Associates win the commission to design the Walt Disney Concert Hall, home of the Los Angeles Philharmonic, in Los Angeles.
- *Progressive Architecture* magazine reports that diversity is the only common thread in contemporary American architecture.
- A computer-operated camera that calculates the buyer's measurements and prints out a custom-made bathing suit is used in eighteen stores.
- Frozen yogurt and Teenage Mutant Ninja Turtles are the hot new items.

"Prep Persona No. 3"

Illustration

By: Lisa Birnbach

Date: 1980

Source: Birnbach, Lisa, "Prep Persona Number 3." *The Official Preppy Handbook.* New York: Workman Publishing, 1980, 98–99.

About the Author: Lisa Birnbach (1959–) graduated from Brown University and achieved notoriety in the United States upon the publication in 1980 of *The Official Preppy Handbook,* a guide to the etiquette, dress codes, and mannerisms of the "preppy" culture. The book was number one on *The New York Times* bestseller list for thirty-eight weeks. ∎

Introduction

The origins of a preppy style can be traced to the 1890s when the growing number of private schools in England—also referred to as preparatory or prep schools—became increasingly exclusive and competitive. Schools and students perpetuated an image of exclusivity and status by wearing a school uniform which incorporated regal elements such as emblems or coats of arms, ties and ribbons in unique combinations of school colors, and monogrammed shirts and sweaters. This privileged look changed following World War I, when students began wearing their khaki-colored military uniforms to school. This blend of casual and classy became the defining mark of the "preppy look." The preppy style reached a new popularity in the 1970s and 1980s when mass culture adopted the classic preppy elements for everyday dressing—rep ties, Izod tennis shirts, and Bermuda shorts.

The preppy style, which exploded in the 1980s with Lisa Birnbach's *The Official Preppy Handbook,* was not a fad when the author wrote her tongue-in-cheek lampoon of Izod shirts (worn collar up), nicknames (Buffy for girls, Trip for boys), penny loafers, and classic clothiers (J. Press and Brooks Brothers). The advice and guidelines satirically set forth mocked a classic way of American dress and behavior that was linked to New England, prep schools, and Ivy League universities. Deeply rooted in "WASP" (White Anglo-Saxon Protestant) stereotypes, the preppy lifestyle was most often associated with those who belonged to the country club, wore corduroy pants embroidered with whales, or sent their children to posh boarding schools.

Significance

Although Lisa Birnbach's *The Official Preppy Handbook,* was intended as a satire of the pretentious manners and mores of Ivy Leaguers, many readers took the book seriously, and it ended by glamorizing the culture it lampooned. The book covers topics ranging from traditions, mannerisms, and etiquette that make a prep school kid to the pets one should keep. It describes proper party and social behavior, provides a preppy lexicon, and describes what clothes to wear at every stage of life. The book's advice and lingo were taken up by prep schoolers and college-bound students for whom oxford cloth and pearls were mandatory.

A preppy's wardrobe was characteristically masculine. Most clothing was either from the boys' department or similar in style to men's clothing. The same colors, including pink, were de rigeur for both men and women. More recently, clothing chains such as Abercrombie and Fitch and The Gap have offered preppy-style clothing that highlights feminine shapes and details.

The subtitle of the book, "Look, Muffy, a Book for Us!" telegraphs its intended wit and sarcasm. The handbook has become a timeless cult classic. In 2001, clothier Lands End devoted a full spread in a catalogue to an essay by Lisa Birnbach. In the piece titled "Muffy Rides Again!," Birnbach shares her insights on what preppy is and isn't, echoing the humorous profiles of fictional Muffys and Trips from her book. The signifiers of preppy include the classic, the sporty, and the casual—all at the same time. Wardrobe staples include the Izod Lacoste polo shirt, anything plaid, blazers, pleated khaki pants, tennis-white skirts or dresses, and anything sporting monogrammed initials—socks, totes or shirts. The preppy style has enjoyed countless revivals over the years. The look is unlikely ever to go out of fashion.

Further Resources

BOOKS

De La Haye, Amy, Cathie Dingwall, and Danny McGrath. *Surfers, Soulies, Skinheads and Skaters: Subcultural Style from the Forties to the Nineties.* New York: Overlook, 1996.

PERIODICALS

Larocca, Amy. "Prep Back: Preppy Look is Back." *New York,* April 2, 2001, 15.

THE COLLEGE YEARS. The boy is on the left; the girl, right. For the first time they are in a community of many different types of people, and this very functional uniform helps them to identify one another in the crowd. By now they have learned that they are different from everyone else, and they band together in a group even more tightly knit than their sweaters.

dark green Lacoste shirt collar up, defying gravity

extra crocodile added in lewd position

pink oxford cloth shirt

green down vest (the temperature is 55°)

Norwegian sweater from L.L. Bean, shoulders dirty from gatoring

in pockets: keys to Jeep; ID with forged year; phone number of JoAnne, a typist; slip of paper with call number of book but not the title; $4.59

rust colored wide wale corduroy pants

cuffs (of course)

no socks

Bean rubber moccasins, even though it's sunny

dazed look from too much beer last night or 8:30 Econ lecture

bench has been stolen 5 times already this year, and is now bolted into the sidewalk

ambush for pouring beer on the unsuspecting

Same Econ

needlepoint made by ex-girlfriend

pale blue

down vest

school ring, immediately recognizable from 25 yards

PREP PERSONA No. 3

short hair (stays out of her eyes during squash games)

gold hoop earrings, concession to femininity

navy blue cotton Skyr turtleneck collar pulled up to chin

Fair Isle sweater, blue with yellow yoke — her mother's, bought in Edinburgh in 1962

yellow oxford cloth shirt, monogrammed on pocket —cuffs turned back over sweater

with three sleeves, it's hard to bend your arms

old Timex men's watch with blue and green ribbon band

in pockets of khakis: Trident gum, cinnamon flavor; keys to room; ticket stubs from an ice hockey game; $3.62

khakis, men's, without a cuff because she let them down

Bean boots (also worn with kilts)

Primary Source

"Prep Persona No. 3"

SYNOPSIS: *The Official Preppy Handbook* is a satirical guide to the behavior and dress demanded by those who wish to be truly preppy. The five "Prep Persona" sections are spaced throughout the book chronologically by age. Prep Persona No. 3 depicts two preppy college students. ILLUSTRATION BY OLIVER WILLIAMS. WORKMAN PUBLISHING. REPRODUCED BY PERMISSION.

Calvin Klein Jeans Advertisement

Advertisement

By: Calvin Klein

Date: 1980

Source: Calvin Klein Jeans Advertisement. 1980. AP/Wide World Photos. Available online at http://www.apwideworld .com/WWP_HOME/index.html (accessed May 9, 2003).

About the Designer: Designer Calvin Klein (1942–) was born in the Bronx, New York. Interested in fashion at an early age, he taught himself to sew and sketch. Klein attended the High School of Art and Design in Manhattan. He graduated from New York's Fashion Institute of Technology

in 1964, and went on to a successful career as a fashion designer. In the early 1980s Klein led the industry in offering more affordable designer jeans to the market. ■

Introduction

Before the 1950s made denim jeans fashionable, they were mainly worn and regarded as work clothing. That image changed as stars like James Dean began to sport denim jeans in the movies. In 1968, designer Calvin Klein and longtime friend Barry Schwartz opened an apparel company that offered a line of men's and women's coats. Klein was responsible for the design work while Schwartz used his business skills to launch their new company, Calvin Klein Limited. Klein had a chance meeting with a buyer from Bonwit Teller, one of the more

Primary Source

Calvin Klein Jeans Advertisement

SYNOPSIS: Fashion designer Calvin Klein pioneered the drive to draw young consumers to his designer jeans. Using the young model and actress Brooke Shields in the first of a career-long series of controversial advertisements, Klein proved himself to be a marketing visionary who has followed up his early achievements with continued success in the fashion industry. AP/WIDE WORLD PHOTOS. REPRODUCED BY PERMISSION.

fashionable New York department stores, who was impressed with the coats and made a substantial order for the store. Klein's design achievements soon earned recognition in the world of fashion, and his rise to a remarkable career in fashion design began.

Both the fashion media and clothing retailers were impressed with the clean lines and spare shapes of Klein's coats, and he was encouraged to expand his offering by introducing a collection of sportswear. Klein's simple designs were greatly admired in New York fashion circles and became very popular with consumers. Klein's success also helped to smooth the way for the brilliant careers of other American minimalist fashion designers, such as Giorgio Armani.

Through the 1970s, Calvin Klein gained growing attention for the sophistication and sexiness of his expanding range of women's apparel, which eventually encompassed sportswear and a full ready-to-wear line. In

the late 1970s, the company revolutionized fashion—and advertising—when they introduced Calvin Klein Jeans, the original designer jeans.

Significance

Klein is generally credited for inaugurating the designer jeans trend. His television ads in the 1980s featured the young, slender, and alluring Brooke Shields in skin-tight Kleins purring, "You know what comes between me and my Calvins? Nothing." Seductive print ads photographed by Richard Avedon not only changed advertising, but they prompted anti-pornography groups to hound Klein for the unsuitability of his ads. The controversial ads generated consumer attention and interest and helped to define a new role for blue jeans in fashion history.

Klein is quoted as saying:

I don't hard sell anything. There is no way to

advertise jeans today by trying to push the jeans and make them interesting; it's been done. The only way to advertise is by not focusing on the product. Some people feel that what we're doing makes no sense, that it's just a waste of money. But it's working. My attitude is 'If you want to sell jeans, don't talk about it.'

Calvin Klein jeans remained a popular choice even as other players swiftly entered the market, and designers like Gloria Vanderbilt and Jordache went head-to-head with Klein. Since there was sufficient demand and enough designer jeans on the market to keep prices reasonable, all the designers fared quite well as long as the look was popular. Calvin Klein is no longer the major player in the denim market, but he moved on to combine his marketing and fashion genius to offer successful and popular lines of men's wear, children's clothing, unisex fragrances, cosmetics, and home furnishings.

Further Resources

BOOKS

Churcher, Sharon. *Obsession: The Lives and Times of Calvin Klein.* New York: Avon, 1995.

PERIODICALS

Bennetts, Leslie. "Our Miss Brooke." *Vanity Fair,* December 1994, 212–215.

Foltz, Kim. "A Kinky New Calvinism." *Newsweek,* March 11, 1985, 65.

WEBSITES

"Calvin Klein: A Case Study." Media Awareness Network. Available online at http://www.media-awareness.ca/english /resources/educational/handouts/ethics/calvin_klein_case_ study.cfm; website home page: http://www.media-aware ness.ca/english/index.cfm (accessed May 20, 2003).

Vietnam Veterans Memorial

Design Submission for Vietnam Veterans Memorial Competition

Statement

By: Maya Lin

Date: March 1981

Source: Lin, Maya. Design Submission for Vietnam Veterans Memorial Competition. March 1981. "Vietnam Veterans Memorial: Evolution of the Memorial." Available online at http://www.nps.gov/vive/memorial/evolution.htm#; website home page: http://www.nps.gov (accessed July 17, 2003).

Vietnam Veterans Memorial

Work of art

By: Maya Lin

Date: 1984

Source: Schwartz, Ira. Vietnam Veterans Memorial, September 21, 1984. Associated Press/Wide World Photos. Available online at http://www.apwideworld.com/WWP_HOME /in dex.html (accessed May 23, 2003).

About the Artist: Maya Lin (1959–) was born in Athens, Ohio. At the age of twenty-one, while still an architecture student at Yale University, Lin won the design competition for the Vietnam Memorial in the Washington Mall. Lin works as both an architect and a sculptor. Although she has designed numerous buildings, her public monuments have brought her the most recognition. ∎

Introduction

Trained as an artist and architect, Lin's sculptures, parks, monuments, and architectural projects are linked by her ideal of making a place for individuals within the landscape. Lin first captured public attention when, as a senior at Yale University, she submitted the winning design in the national competition for the Vietnam Veterans Memorial. The competition judges chose Lin's design unanimously. They favored the design for promoting no particular political point of view and for effectively complementing the nearby Washington Monument and Lincoln Memorial.

The idea for a Vietnam Veterans Memorial came from Jan Scruggs, an infantry corporal in Vietnam from 1969 to 1970. He envisioned a memorial that would commemorate the service and sacrifice of all Americans who had served in the Vietnam conflict. The Vietnam Veterans Memorial Fund was formed in 1979 to raise money and support for the project. Early legislative help came from U.S. Senators Charles Mathias and John Warner. In July 1980, then-President Jimmy Carter signed legislation to provide a site for the memorial in Constitution Gardens near the Lincoln Memorial and the reflecting pool. The design and plans were finalized in March 1982, and, with federal approval, the work commenced almost immediately. Groundbreaking took place on March 26, 1982, and the memorial was dedicated on November 13, 1982. It took two more years for all the components of the Vietnam Veteran Memorial Park—including the Wall, a bronze statue, and a flag—to be completed.

Significance

The Wall, as it has come to be known by veterans and their families, was widely criticized when the plan was unveiled. Critics, mainly veterans of the Vietnam War, claimed that the memorial demeaned the sacrifices made by the veterans it honored. They found the Wall's

Primary Source

Vietnam Veterans Memorial

SYNOPSIS: The Vietnam Veterans Memorial in Washington, D.C. is Maya Lin's most admired work. Although it aroused controversy when Lin won the design competition, the Memorial has become a sacred place and has set a new standard for graceful memorial design around the world. AP/WIDE WORLD PHOTOS. REPRODUCED BY PERMISSION.

design austere and meaningless. A bronze sculpture depicting three battle-weary soldiers, designed by Frederic Hart, was later added at the site to appease the memorial's detractors.

Lin, a Chinese-American, also encountered racial prejudice and opposition from planning officials when she insisted on supervising the construction of the project. Disheartened by her experience and the controversy, Lin left her graduate studies in architecture soon after the monument was dedicated in 1982. She later returned to complete her graduate work.

The Vietnam Veterans Memorial is especially significant and poignant because it commemorates those who died fighting a war that the United States lost. The memorial combines two long, joined, symmetrical walls upon which the names of all the men and women killed or missing during the Vietnam conflict are inscribed.

The two halves of the Wall have a combined length of 493.5 feet. Each segment is made of seventy, ten-foot-high panels inscribed with a total of 58,229 names. The

names appear in chronological order, alphabetized according to the date of casualty, starting with two names from July 8, 1959. An inscription reads:

In honor of the men and women of the Armed Forces of the United States who served in the Vietnam War. The names of those who gave their lives and of those who remain missing are inscribed in the order they were taken from us.

Primary Source

Design Submission for Vietnam Veterans Memorial Competition [excerpt]

SYNOPSIS: This statement was written by Maya Lin while she was an architecture student at Yale University as a part of her submission for the proposed memorial.

Walking through this park-like area, the memorial appears as a rift in the earth—a long, polished

Maya Lin shows a model of her design for the Vietnam Veterans Memorial in 1981. © BETTMANN/CORBIS. REPRODUCED BY PERMISSION

black stone wall, emerging from and receding into the earth. Approaching the memorial, the ground slopes gently downward, and the low walls emerging on either side, growing out of the earth, extend and converge at a point below and ahead. Walking into the grassy site contained by the walls of the memorial we can barely make out the carved names upon the memorial's walls. These names, seemingly infinite in number, convey the sense of overwhelming numbers, while unifying those individuals into a whole. For this memorial is meant not as a monument to the individual but rather, as a memorial to the men and women who died during this war, as a whole.

The memorial is composed not as an unchanging monument, but as a moving composition, to be understood as we move into and out of it; the passage itself is gradual, the descent to the origin slow, but it is at the origin that the meaning of the memorial is to be fully understood. At the intersection of these walls, on the right side, at the wall's top, is carved the date of the first death. It is followed by the names of those who have died in the war, in chronological order. These names continue on this wall, appearing to recede into the earth at the wall's end. The names resume on the left wall, as the wall emerges from the earth, continuing back to the origin, where the date of the last death is carved, at the bottom of this wall. Thus the war's beginning and end meet; the war is "complete," coming full circle, yet broken by the earth that bounds the angle's open side, and contained within the earth itself. As we turn to leave, we see these walls stretching into the distance, directing us to the Washington Monument, to the left, and the Lincoln Memorial, to the right, thus bringing the Vietnam Memorial into an historical context. We the living are brought to a concrete realization of these deaths.

Brought to a sharp awareness of such a loss, it is up to each individual to resolve or come to terms with this loss. For death, is in the end a personal and private matter, and the area contained with this memorial is a quiet place, meant for personal reflection and private reckoning. The black granite walls, each two hundred feet long, and ten feet below ground at their lowest point (gradually ascending toward ground level) effectively act as a sound barrier, yet are of such a height and length so as not to appear threatening or enclosing. The actual area is wide and shallow, allowing for a sense of privacy, and the sunlight from the memorial's southern exposure along with the grassy park surrounding and within its walls, contribute to the serenity of the area. Thus this memorial is for those who have died, and for us to remember them.

Further Resources

BOOKS

Lin, Maya. *Boundaries.* New York: Simon and Schuster, 1999.

———. *Public/Private.* New York: Distributed Art Publishers, 1994.

PERIODICALS

Danto, Arthur. "The Vietnam Veterans Memorial." *The Nation,* August 31, 1985, 152–155.

Niebuhr, Gustav. "More Than a Monument: The Spiritual Dimension of These Hallowed Walls." *The New York Times,* November 11, 1994, A12.

Sorkin, Michael. "What Happens When a Woman Designs a War Monument?" *Vogue,* May 1983, 120.

Stein, Judith E. "Space and Place." *Art in America,* December 1994, 66–71.

AUDIO AND VISUAL MEDIA

Maya Lin: A Strong Clear Vision. Directed by Freida Lee Mock. American Film Foundation, VHS, 1994.

From Bauhaus to Our House

Nonfiction work

By: Tom Wolfe

Date: 1981

Source: Wolfe, Tom. *From Bauhaus to Our House.* New York: Farrar, Straus, Giroux, 1981.

About the Author: Tom Wolfe (1931–) was born in Richmond, Virginia. He was educated at Washington and Lee University and earned his Ph.D. at Yale. During a ten-year journalism career, Wolfe wrote for the *Springfield* (Massachusetts) *Union,* served as Latin American correspondent for the *Washington Post,* and wrote for both the *New York Herald Tribune* and *New York Magazine.* In 1963, Wolfe wrote a forty-two page "memo" on a custom car show in Los Angeles for *Esquire* that the magazine printed in full. Eventually, that memo became his very successful first book, *The Kandy-Kolored Tangerine Flake Streamline Baby.* Considered the father of the New Journalism movement, Wolfe has published a number of bestsellers in both fiction and nonfiction. ∎

Introduction

In the late 1920s, American architects and designers began to abandon traditional American design principles and to adopt a European style based on the teachings of the avant-garde Bauhaus school in Weimar, Germany. The Bauhaus (German for "house for building") was a design philosophy developed in response to the economic devastation of World War I and the need to rebuild Germany. Originally applied to worker housing, the Bauhaus favored a "rational" and pragmatic approach to building design, featuring clean, unornamented, and highly functional designs, free from "bourgeois" details, and characterized by open floor plans, simple shapes, and functional furnishings. Although quite influential on twentieth century architecture (especially the now-standard American kitchen), the Bauhaus style had its critics, who found the machine-made and "sanitized" designs lacking in human touch and deplored their impersonal, even demeaning, effects.

In 1975, Tom Wolfe wrote *The Painted Word,* a scathing attack on modern art. The book traces the social history of modern art from its origins in revolution to its present state, which Wolfe considers a parody of itself in the way that it has become the very thing it set out to criticize. Something of a sequel to that treatise, *From Bauhaus to Our House* explores the contradiction between the spare, impersonal, and highly abstract architecture and the society it serves.

Significance

Wolfe's attack on Modernist trends in architecture is a landmark critique of a movement he believed had outlasted its effectiveness. Wolfe argues that social and intellectual trends have become the chief basis for aesthetic form. He claims that architects have willingly abandoned their personal visions, their originality, and their artistic motivations to create work that is primarily a reaction to immediate fashions and simultaneously dehumanizing of the spaces for their users and inhabitants. The book has aroused controversy in part because Wolfe is not an architect and is unconnected with the profession. His iconoclastic book denounces a movement held sacred, and it speaks to non-architects in trenchant terms about the tendency of modern architecture to be ruled by theory and out of touch with the society it accommodates.

The opening lines sum up what Wolfe is attacking:

O beautiful, for spacious skies, for amber waves of grain, has there ever been another place on earth where so many people of wealth and power have paid for and put up with so much architecture they detested as within these blessed borders today?

He censures modern architecture that is "built for the sake of building it" and he takes architects to task for disregarding the effects of their designs on the people who inhabit such architecture. In sum, Wolfe lays bare the pretentiousness of the Modern Art community.

A model of an Illinois Institute of Technology building designed by Ludwig Mies Van Der Rohe. © BETTMANN/CORBIS. REPRODUCED BY PERMISSION.

From Bauhaus to Our House initiated a challenge to an orthodoxy that has long kept architecture within the province of the elite. Wolfe urged readers to trust their own responses to architecture and art. He invites them to resist the social pressures that compel them to praise what leaves them cold or to pretend to be unmoved by work which give them pleasure. Directing readers to seek more authentic aesthetic experiences, Wolfe calls for a return of art to the province of the people.

Primary Source

From Bauhaus to Our House [excerpt]

SYNOPSIS: Wolfe's anti-Modernist creed was hailed as a groundbreaking book de-mysticizing the theory-laden practice and teaching of modern architecture. A leader in the "New Journalism" movement, Wolfe made it acceptable to be a non-expert writing on matters normally associated with the academy.

In short, the reigning architectural style in this, the very Babylon of capitalism, became worker housing. Worker housing, as developed by a handful of architects, inside the compounds, amid the rubble of Europe in the early 1920s, was now pitched up high and wide, in the form of Ivy League art-gallery annexes, museums for art patrons, apartments for the rich, corporate headquarters, city halls, country estates. It was made to serve every purpose, in fact, except housing for workers.

It was not that worker housing was never built for workers. In the 1950s and early 1960s the federal government helped finance the American version of the Dutch and German Siedlungen of the 1920s. Here they were called public housing projects. But somehow the workers, intellectually undeveloped as they were, managed to avoid public housing. They called it, simply, "the projects," and they avoided it as if it had a smell. The workers—if by workers we mean people who have jobs—headed out instead to the suburbs. They ended up in places like Islip, Long Island, and the San Fernando Valley of Los Angeles, and they bought houses with pitched roofs and shingles and clapboard siding, with no structure expressed if there was any way around it, with gaslight-style front-porch lamps and mailboxes set up on lengths of stiffened chain that seemed to defy gravity—the more cute and antiquey touches, the better—and they loaded these houses with "drapes" such as baffled all description and wall-to-wall

Designed by Ludwig Mies Van Der Rohe, the Barcelona chair is named for its debut at the Barcelona International Fair in 1929. Its classic modern design made it a popular, yet expensive piece in the 1980s. © FRANCESCO VENTURI/CORBIS. REPRODUCED BY PERMISSION.

carpet you could lose a shoe in, and they put barbecue pits and fishponds with concrete cherubs urinating into them on the lawn out back, and they parked the Buick Electras out front and had Evinrude cruisers up on tow trailers in the carport just beyond the breezeway.

As for the honest sculptural objects designed for worker-housing interiors, such as Mies' and Breuer's chairs, the proles either ignored them or held them in contempt because they were patently uncomfortable. This furniture is today a symbol of wealth and privilege, attuned chiefly to the tastes of the businessmen's wives who graze daily at the D & D Building, the major interior-decoration bazaar in New York. Mies' most famous piece of furniture design, the Barcelona chair, retails today for $3,465 and is available only through decorators. The high price is due in no small part to the chair's worker-housing honest nonbourgeois materials: stainless steel and leather. Today the leather can be ordered only in black or shades of brown. In the early 1970s, it seems, certain bourgeois elements were having them made in the most appalling variations . . . zebra skin, Holstein skin, ocelot skin, and *pretty fabrics.*

The only people left trapped in worker housing in America today are those who don't work at all and are on welfare—these are the sole inhabitants of "the projects"—and, of course, the urban rich who live in places such as the Olympic Tower on Fifth Avenue in New York. Since the 1950s the term "luxury highrise" has come to denote a certain type of apartment house that is in fact nothing else but the Siedlungen of Frankfurt and Berlin, with units stacked up thirty, forty, fifty stories high, to be rented or sold to the bourgeoisie. Which is to say, pure nonbourgeois housing for the bourgeoisie only. Sometimes the towers are of steel, concrete, and glass; sometimes of glass, steel, and small glazed white or beige bricks. Always the ceilings are low, often under eight feet, the hallways are narrow, the rooms are narrow, even when they're long, the bedrooms are small (Le Corbusier was always in favor of that), the walls are thin, the doorways and windows have no casings, the joints have no moldings, the walls have no baseboards, and the windows don't open, although small vents or jalousies may be provided. The construction is invariably cheap in the pejorative as well as the literal sense. That builders could present these boxes in the 1950s, without a twitch of the nostril, as luxury, and that well-educated men and women could accept them, without a blink, as luxury—here is objective testimony, from those too dim for irony, to the aesthetic sway of the compound aesthetic, of the Silver Prince and his colonial legions, in America following the Second World War.

Every respected instrument of architectural opinion and cultivated taste, from *Domus* to *House & Garden,* told the urban dwellers of America that this was *living.* This was the good taste of today; this was modern, and soon the International Style became known simply as modern architecture. . . .

So what if you were living in a building that looked like a factory and felt like a factory, and paying top dollar for it? Every modern building of quality looked like a factory. That was *the look of today.* . . .

The truth was, this was inescapable. The compound style, with its *nonbourgeois* taboos, had so reduced the options of the true believer that every building, the beach house no less than the skyscraper, was bound to have the same general look.

And so what? The terms *glass box* and *repetitious,* first uttered as terms of opprobrium, became badges of honor. Mies had many American imitators, Philip Johnson, I. M. Pei, and Gordon Bunshaft being the most famous and the most blatant. And the

Bauhaus in the 1950s

By the 1950s, Bauhaus architecture held sway across the United States. With its acres of visible steel, its rows of wide-open windows, and offices separated by "curtained space" (dividers) rather than walls, Bauhaus was extremely popular in both industrial and private settings. Born in Germany in the severe poverty following World War I (1914–1918), the Staatliches Bauhaus school produced works characterized by an anti-bourgeoisie attitude that led to stripped-down designs and an absence of ornamentation. Bauhaus architects wanted to bring out the natural aesthetic qualities of their materials, not, as previous generations of architects had done, by contrasting one material with another, but instead by arranging the base materials in the available space.

Born in 1886, Bauhaus architect Ludwig Mies Van Der Rohe studied art under Peter Behrens from 1908 to 1912. His aesthetic style was influenced by artists like Karl Frederich Schinkel and schools of thought like Russian constructivism. His design ethic "less is more" became as famous as his architecture. Van Der Rohe was the director of the Bauhaus school in Germany until the 1930s. When the Nazis closed down the Bauhaus school in Germany, some of its chief architects, Mies Van Der Rohe among them, came to the United States. Van Der Rohe then spearheaded the American Bauhaus movement.

The United States was wide open to the new design movement. Civilians in the United States had taken part in the war effort during World War II (1939–1945) in a variety of ways. Ordinary citizens conserved resources and energy for the troops overseas and cultivated victory gardens to feed their families. People took pride in their thriftiness and in their ability to sacrifice more than their neighbors. This tendency resulted in a country that was wide open to a stripped-down architecture like Bauhaus. As the war ended, the economy continued to grow, and wartime rationing ceased. People looked for wise ways to spend their hard-saved money. Soldiers coming home from the war were ready to get married, buy houses, have children, and live the American dream.

At the end of the war, Bauhaus had re-appeared as the postwar style that would prevail in the United States for the next decade or more. The Illinois Institute of Technology, designed by Mies Van Der Rohe himself, and Harvard University's Graduate School of Design were both seats of the movement.

Bauhaus appealed to both the corporate world and private individuals because it seemed both practical and economical. Its large, well-lit rooms with banks of windows provided significant cost-savings to companies. This was the era of the man in the gray flannel suit, and few workers publicly objected to the uniformity of Bauhaus design. Mass production of identical materials lowered production costs, making new homes accessible to average people, who were fleeing to the suburbs in droves. Though Bauhaus had little influence on the actual buildings most suburbanites lived in, when furnishing their new homes many families chose practical, economical, mass-produced Bauhaus-style furniture.

The uniformity of style of the Bauhaus movement did not go entirely without comment. Architect Frank Lloyd Wright hated it, though he got along personally with Mies Van Der Rohe. But in the 1950s, Americans were suffering from (and perpetuating) McCarthyism and Cold War anticommunism. It was important to look and act like your neighbors in order to avoid arousing suspicion. Thus, Americans embraced Bauhaus with zeal and incorporated it into their homes and businesses alike. Indeed, though the style has changed and has far more critics now than it did in the 1950s, Bauhaus architecture remains highly popular today, especially in corporate settings.

most unashamed. Snipers would say that every one of Philip Johnson's buildings was an imitation of Mies van der Rohe. And Johnson would open his eyes wide and put on his marvelous smile of mock innocence and reply, "I have always been delighted to be called Mies van der Johnson." Bunshaft had designed Lever House, corporate headquarters for the Lever Brothers soap and detergent company, on Park Avenue. The building was such a success that it became the prototype for the American glass box, and Bunshaft and his firm, Skidmore, Owings & Merrill, did many variations on this same design. To the charge that glass boxes were all he designed, Bunshaft liked to crack: "Yes, and I'm going to keep on doing them until I do one I like."

For a hierophant of the compound, confidence came easy! What did it matter if they said you were imitating Mies or Gropius or Corbu or any of the rest? It was like accusing a Christian of imitating Jesus Christ.

Further Resources

BOOKS

Blaser, Werner. *Mies Van Der Rohe.* Boston: Birkhauser, 1997.

Johnson, Philip. *Mies Van Der Rohe.* New York: Museum of Modern Art, 1978.

Kentgens-Craig, Margret. *The Bauhaus and America: First Contacts, 1919–1936.* Cambridge: MIT Press, 1999.

Whitford, Frank. *Bauhaus.* London: Thames and Hudson, 1984.

PERIODICALS

Hines, Thomas. "Conversing with the Compound." *Design Book Review 1987,* no.13, Fall, 13–19.

WEBSITES

"Bauhaus Architecture." ArtandCulture. Available online at http://www.artandculture.com/arts/movement?movementId=21; website home page: http://www.artandculture.com (accessed March 25, 2003).

"Architect Ludwig Mies Van Der Rohe." Great Buildings Online. Available online at http://www.greatbuildings.com/architects/Ludwig_Mies_van_der_Rohe.html (accessed March 25, 2003).

AUDIO AND VISUAL MEDIA

Dessau's Bauhaus. Directed by Frederic Compain. Films for the Humanities. Videocassette, 2002.

Apple IIc Computer

Photograph

By: FrogDesign and Steve Jobs

Date: 1984

Source: "Apple Computer President and Co-Founders." April 24, 1984. Corbis. Image no. BE023357. Available online at pro.corbis.com (accessed June 16, 2003).

About the Designers: FrogDesign was founded in 1969 in Germany by designer Hartmut Esslinger. Esslinger and his team had produced the brand images for Sony, Louis Vuitton, and several German industrial firms before expanding to the United States in 1983 to develop a design language for Apple Computers.

Steve Jobs (1955–) was born in Los Altos, California. At age twenty-one, Jobs co-founded the Apple Computer Corporation with Steve Wozniak and was a millionnaire by age 30. Jobs left Apple in 1985 to pursue other ventures. ∎

Introduction

Apple Computer co-founder Steve Jobs was from the outset deeply committed to effective and compelling industrial design for Apple products. He believed that intelligent graphics and products with proven usability did not merely determine how the consumer judged or identified with a company's product—successful design could also enhance the user's understanding of how a product worked and increase user comfort with the product. At a time when personal computers were still novel, Jobs considered it especially vital for his products to be accessible rather than intimidating.

Jobs played a directive role at Apple in the development of products that were both elegant and tasteful. He was centrally involved in the conception of the original packaging, manual design, and advertising. It was Jobs's idea to package every component of a machine—keyboard, mouse, disks, cords, manual, and the combined CPU and screen unit—in a separate compartment, compelling the user to become familiar with each item as he or she unpacked and set it up.

Initially it was the Apple Design Guild, an informal in-house industrial design team, that shaped Jobs's ideas into functional—and increasingly popular—computer systems. However, Jobs then began to look for what he considered a "world-class" designer to develop and apply a uniform design language to all Apple products. The company conducted a competition among a random selection of international designers by the Apple Design Guild. It took a year to select the finalists, who were then asked to design prototypes named after the seven dwarves from *Snow White.* Although the finalists included a popular Apple in-house designer and an established and successful British firm, it was a virtually unknown German designer named Hartmut Esslinger who was the unanimous choice among Apple executives. Esslinger and his team moved to California in 1983 to form Frogdesign, Inc., and he became Apple's exclusive identity and product designer.

Significance

The importance that Steve Jobs placed on appearance is most vividly revealed in Apple's commitment to innovative industrial design. The products that were developed during and after Jobs's tenure at the company reflect this concern. Frogdesign's initial proposal, which won them the exclusive contract with Apple, was to transform the appearance of Apple computers and garner many awards. Hartmut Esslinger and Steve Jobs, whose rapport is legendary, shared a vision of uncompromising innovation. Jobs relied on Esslinger to develop a universal visual vocabulary for Apple. The computers were to be recognizable as Apple's. The graphic components of packaging and documentation would use a typeface unique to Apple. Instructions would be user-friendly and easy to follow. Advertisements would reflect Apple's grand design agenda. It was up to Esslinger and his FrogDesign team to synthesize these requirements into a singular Apple identity. Esslinger's work for Apple ended in 1987 when he joined Jobs (who had left the company in 1985) at an unsuccessful new enterprise called NeXT Computer. Esslinger's work at Apple not only changed how the personal computer would look for many years, but also helped to create and popularize a unified branding strategy that has been adopted throughout the corporate world.

Primary Source

Apple IIc Computer

SYNOPSIS: FrogDesign's visual concept for Apple computers reflected a growing commitment to user-friendly industrial design. (Left to right) Steve Jobs, John Sculley and Steve Wozniak present the Apple IIc at a conference in San Francisco in April 1984. The IIc received the Industrial Design Excellence award that year. © BETTMANN/CORBIS. REPRODUCED BY PERMISSION.

Further Resources

BOOKS

Bürdek, Bernhard E. *The Apple Macintosh.* Frankfurt am Main: Verlag Form, 1997.

Sweet, Fay. *Frog: Form Follows Emotion.* New York: Watson-Guptill, 1999.

PERIODICALS

Burrows, Peter. "Bye-bye, Beige Box." *Business Week,* June 3, 1996, 77.

Dyett, Linda. "Lily pad." *House Beautiful,* November 2000, 138–142.

Hafner, Katie. "Hartmut Esslinger: High Tech's One-Man Bauhaus." *Business Week,* August 17, 1987, 59.

WEBSITES

"The Design Revolution: 1983-85." Available online at http://www.landsnail.com/apple/local/design/design.html; website home page: http://www.landsnail.com (accessed May 9, 2003).

AUDIO AND VISUAL MEDIA

Triumph of the Nerds: Impressing Their Friends. John Gau Productions and Oregon Public Broadcasting. Videocassette, 1996.

Air Jordans

Advertisement

By: Nike

Date: 1985

Source: Nike Air Advertisment, 1985. The Advertising Archive. Image no. 30502939.

About the Designer: Peter Moore was Nike's lead designer during the 1980s. His original sketches for the Air Jordan line—to be named after basketball star Michael Jordan and first manufactured in 1985—featured the shoes among an array of other sports clothing including warm-up suits and basketball jerseys. ∎

Introduction

In 1984, the Chicago Bulls drafted North Carolina's star player, Michael Jordan. Jordan was the third overall pick in that year's draft. Nike saw Jordan's potential as a player in the National Basketball Association (NBA), and his potential as a spokesperson for their shoes.

The winning formula ultimately combined Jordan, who was voted NBA Rookie of the Year with the vision of Peter Moore. Moore had the inspiration to use Jordan, a rising star in the sports world who had considerable charisma, as the defining icon for a new product. In 1985, Nike launched the Air Jordans, a boldly red and black and surprisingly awkward-looking sports shoe. In the past, sneakers had always been white, with rare and no-table exceptions: a pair of green and white Converse Weapons for Celtics' Larry Bird and a purple and yellow pair for Magic Johnson of the Los Angeles Lakers. When the new shoe appeared on the market, many consumers wondered how something so ugly could succeed in the marketplace.

In April 1986, Nike introduced the Air Jordans in six test cities. They were an immediate success. The demand was so great that some retailers sold the $64.95 high-tops for as much as a hundred dollars a pair. The shoes created a controversy in the NBA, which banned the shoe for a time because of the air pockets in the soles. Yet teenagers treasured Air Jordans as a mark of prestige worth fighting over. With total sales of $55 million on the first orders, Nike was quickly hailed as a fearless innovator.

Moore quit Nike soon after the Air Jordan was launched, claiming that the company had become too big and unwieldy. Moore became the lead designer at Nike's competitor, Adidas. He later joined forces with another sports shoe manufacturer, Reebok.

Significance

Almost no other fashion item of the past twenty-five years has made such a mark on the world's sense of style as Moore's Air Jordans. Moore's design was novel and unappealing at first, especially to older sports fans. In a November 1967 issue of *Sports Illustrated,* journalist Curry Kirkpatrick called the new shoes "extraordinarily ugly red and black clodhoppers." But the younger generation had a different reaction and lined up to buy the shoes, confident that the shoes would improve their image with peers if not their athletic prowess. Nike followed up on its initial success by offering a new model of Air Jordans every year, each with its unique color combination and cut.

Moore's inspiration has since become the standard for sports shoe design. The Air Jordan, in its proliferation of styles and colors, is still one of the most popular sports shoes on the market. But prestige had its price—the intense demand for the shoe fueled violent incidents among urban teens in the 1980s and early 1990s. Some who couldn't afford to buy the shoes resorted to stealing them, and reportedly some urban gangs offered pairs of Air Jordans as an incentive to attract new members.

The designer once told an interviewer, "True innovation ultimately must strike an emotional chord." Without doubt, Air Jordans did just that. Although the style has since become a form of conventional wisdom for sports shoe makers, Peter Moore was responsible for bringing a concept to life and launching a style that has become exceedingly popular.

MICHAEL JORDAN 1
ISAAC NEWTON 0

Primary Source

Air Jordans

SYNOPSIS: The popular Nike Air Jordan was introduced in 1985 amid excitement and controversy. After numerous design revisions and color combinations, Nike continued to produce the shoe in 2003. THE ADVERTISING ARCHIVE, LTD. REPRODUCED BY PERMISSION.

Further Resources

BOOKS

Andrews, David L., editor. *Michael Jordan, Inc.: Corporate Sport, Media Culture, and Late Modern America.* Albany: State University of New York Press, 2001.

Goldman, Robert. *Nike Culture: The Sign of the Swoosh.* London: Sage Publications, 1998.

Katz, Donald. *Just Do It: The Nike Spirit in the Corporate World.* New York: Random House, 1994.

PERIODICALS

"Air Jordan Takes Off. Nike's Shoe Named After Basketball Star." *Newsweek,* June 17, 1985, p. 79.

WEBSITES

Cave, Damien. "Masterpiece: Air Jordan." Salon.com. Available online at http://archive.salon.com/ent/masterpiece/2002/08/05/air_jordan/; website home page: http://www.salon.com (accessed May 9, 2003).

"Selling a Dream of Elegance and the Good Life"

Magazine article

By: Stephen Koepp

Date: September 1, 1986

Source: Koepp, Stephen. "Selling a Dream of Elegance and the Good Life." *Time,* September 1, 1986, 55–58.

About the Designer: Ralph Lauren (1939–) is a native of the Bronx, New York, and studied at the City College there. He began his fashion career in 1967, designing ties for the Beau Brummell Tie Company. One year later, with a fifty-thousand dollar loan and a headful of tie designs, he founded Polo Fashions. Ralph Lauren has received numerous awards from the fashion industry, including the coveted Council of Fashion Designers of America's Lifetime Achievement Award. ■

Introduction

Ralph Lifshitz was born into a family of poor Russian Jews. He was too short to become a baseball player, and he did not do well enough to become a rabbi, as his mother had wished. Lauren changed his surname at the age of sixteen. After a brief stint in the army, he got his

Fashion designer Ralph Lauren. AP/WIDE WORLD PHOTOS.
REPRODUCED BY PERMISSION.

start in the fashion business by working as a salesperson for Brooks Brothers. From there, he set about designing ties for men. Although a full inch wider than the prevailing fashion, Lauren's ties were extraordinarily successful in the New York department stores, especially at Bloomingdale's, which was the first store to take on his expanded lines of first men's and, later, women's clothing.

Lauren designed his first men's wear collection in 1968, the same year he founded Polo Fashions. Four years later, he ventured into women's clothing. The opportunity that secured his fame came when he costumed the cast of 1974 movie version of F. Scott Fitzgerald's *The Great Gatsby,* starring Robert Redford. When Diane Keaton was choosing her wardrobe for the title character in *Annie Hall,* she chose the the Ralph Lauren "look."

Lauren's love for the styles of the rugged American West—denim jeans, turquoise belts, coats made from Native American textiles—was translated into a high-end line of clothing. Lauren's designs reflect his admiration—and talent—for the classic look in men's and women's clothes. Not all his ventures were successful. Although his late-1970s Western Wear collection made a name for him in ready-to-wear, it was a failure financially. This proved to be one of a handful of Lauren's failed business

ventures. By the 1980s, Lauren had expanded his designs into a home collection that included furniture and linens.

Significance

Ralph Lauren came a long way from his Bronx childhood to become a dominant figure in American sportswear design. Lauren has made a name for himself by combining comfortable elegance, durability, and traditionalism in his designs. His designs appeal especially to professionals and other upwardly mobile men and women. Few clothing designers have achieved a product range so various, a retailing network so extensive, or a marketing image so well defined. Some of Lauren's success can be attributed to his providing a wide market with the finely tailored clothes of high-quality materials that were traditionally available only to the high-end market. He has achieved this by bringing his clothing lines to the seventeen hundred department stores that currently carry his brand, as well as to his own factory outlets.

Lauren, who once sold his wares store-to-store dressed in a bomber jacket and jeans, has amassed a lifestyle empire with annual revenues of $1.47 billion and profits of $120 million. An important factor in Lauren's success is the development of a brand image which incorporates the man himself as a key element. This approach has allowed him to expand his vision to market everything from suits to suitcases and sofas to soccer balls. The Lauren empire includes twenty-six licensees who sell $4 billion in everything from tableware to towels, along with 224 retail stores and outlet centers.

Lauren creates not just clothes, but entire environments and identities, suggesting that even tradition can be purchased. His continued success—despite occasional setbacks—in an ever-changing world is a testimony to his abilities both as a businessman and as a designer of clothing and fragrances.

Primary Source

"Selling a Dream of Elegance and the Good Life" [excerpt]

SYNOPSIS: Ralph Lauren has not so much invented a new kind of American fashion, as he has put his signature on garments that are timeless classics of American fashion. In this way, Lauren has become one of the most important fashion designers of the twentieth century.

Lauren sells an image of ready-to-wear prosperity, but there was nothing instant about his success in New York City's gritty garment district. He worked hard, sold hard and survived countless trials and errors. His early lack of strategic planning brought him close to bankruptcy in 1972. In the late 1970s, his Western Wear collection thrust Lauren into the fashion spotlight but failed financially.

More often, Lauren manages to find a lucrative combination of what he likes and what will sell, a spectrum that has ranged from Polo shirts to his Santa Fe collection. In terms of his standing in the industry, he has become fashion's equivalent of an old-time movie mogul who creates, directs and lives out his own view of high style. Lauren possesses the financial and personal clout to put his name on just about any product, or roomful of products, he pleases.

No matter how diverse they become, Lauren's wares reflect a rigid design philosophy, a kind of "Polo Manifesto" that his advertising brochures proclaim as "originality, but always with integrity and a respect for tradition." His newest venture, coming this fall, is a line of upholstered furniture ranging from $535 ottomans to $5,500 sofas. "I want to make all the things I love," he says. "A lot of people have nice taste. I have dreams."

To sell his vision of the lush life, Lauren is building an ever larger retail network. The designer now sells his products in 48 franchised Polo shops, 132 department store boutiques and 16 discount outlets. In April he opened what his company calls the world's largest one-designer store, Polo/Ralph Lauren, in a 20,000-sq.-ft. renovated mansion on Manhattan's tony Madison Avenue shopping strip. The Polo palace, which is the first retail store Lauren has owned outright, represents a gamble that one designer can produce enough strong-selling goods to support a department store-size emporium. . . .

Young Ralph was preoccupied with basketball, stickball and the exploits of Joe DiMaggio and Mickey Mantle, but he started showing a flair for clothes in his early teens. "The kids I grew up with were wearing leather motorcycle jackets like Marlon Brando," he recalls. "But at the same time I saw there was a collegiate side of the world. I was inspired by it. I was always very preppie." Klein remembers that Lauren cut a distinctive figure in the neighborhood by mixing olive-drab Army clothes with tweeds. At 15, Ralph got his first fashion commission: to design red satin warm-up jackets for his baseball team.

It was Lauren's older brother Jerry, now the head of Polo's menswear design department, who suggested when Ralph was 16 that the siblings change their surname. "Lifshitz was a burden," Jerry recalls. "I was in the Air Force reserve, and I got tired of be-

ing on the defensive at mail call with somebody fooling around with the sound of my name. It was silly to live with it. It wasn't some family dynasty." Ralph and Jerry rattled off potential names to each other and settled almost randomly on Lauren, which sounded euphonious to them.

At DeWitt Clinton High School in the Bronx, Lauren attended business classes but paid little attention to studies. His adolescent idols were British and American style setters: the Duke of Windsor, for example, and Katharine Hepburn, who stole the show in *The Philadelphia Story* with her pants-and-pearls look. Lauren's early fashion education was basically a home-study course that he recalls being a "combination of movies and reading *Esquire.* "Says he: "Whether that world exists or not, I don't know. I saw things as they should have been, not as they were."

Lauren worked part time, accepting returned garments in a budget-price department store, to earn money to buy classically cut clothes at Manhattan's Brooks Bros. In his high school yearbook, Lauren confidently listed his ambition as "millionaire." The entry was a gag, he claims today, but his brother Jerry remembers that Ralph had a "constant urge to make something happen. He was always reaching for more."

Ralph tried a stint at New York's City College but decided to drop out, at least partly, he says, because it was an aesthetic letdown. "There was no wonderful campus with boys and girls wearing V-neck sweaters," he explains, as though he still feels he missed something in life.

Lauren subsequently served a hitch in the Army reserve, then got a seasonal job at Brooks Bros. as a clerk during the Christmas rush. At 22 he went to work as a New York regional salesman for Abe Rivetz, a Boston necktie manufacturer. Lauren made the rounds of his Long Island wholesale customers dressed in tweeds and driving a British Morgan convertible. Pondering fashion trends as he traveled, he decided around 1964 that the men who wore the narrow ties of the early '60s were ready for a change to wider, more colorful designs. While Lauren was not a particularly gifted sketch artist, he knew how to put together a fashionable ensemble. "I would walk [into a room] and my clients would say, 'I want what you are wearing.' My instincts were there. I didn't think I was a designer, but I had ideas."

In those days, garment company bosses generally called the shots in the fashion business, and American clothing designers were only beginning to achieve acceptance as entrepreneurs. Lauren managed to persuade his employers to let him design a few innovative cravats, but when new management took over the firm the budding designer was told the world was not ready for Ralph Lauren. He migrated to a larger men's-furnishings company, Beau Brummel, which agreed to manufacture his original neckwear. Lauren needed a brand name and wanted something that sounded tweedy and British. Cricket? Rugby? Polo! That was it, even though Lauren had never been to a match. "We thought of everything," says Lauren with a grin. "I couldn't call it Basketball."

Further Resources

BOOKS

Diamonstein, Barbaralee. *Fashion: The Inside Story.* New York: Rizzoli, 1985.

Gross, Michael. *Genuine Authentic: The Real Life of Ralph Lauren.* New York: Harper Collins, 2003.

McDowell, Colin. *Ralph Lauren: The Man, the Vision, the Style.* New York: Rizzoli, 2003.

PERIODICALS

"The Dream Maker." *U.S. News & World Report,* February 8, 1988, 78.

Ferretti, Fred." The Business of Being Ralph Lauren." *The New York Times Magazine,* September 18, 1983, 112–114.

"Casting Center, Walt Disney World"

Essay

By: Robert A.M. Stern

Date: 1986

Source: Kraft, Elizabeth, ed. "Casting Center, Walt Disney World." *Robert A.M. Stern: Buildings and Projects, 1987–1992.* New York: Rizzoli, 1992.

About the Architect: Robert A.M. Stern (1939–) was born in Brooklyn and practices in New York City. He also serves as Dean of the prestigious School of Architecture at Yale University. Stern's architecture unites tradition with innovation, and he strives to create a meaningful sense of place in his buildings. His firm has won numerous awards for design excellence, and Stern has written and edited more than twenty books. ∎

Introduction

Walt Disney's vision of amusement parks and town squares was fully realized in Disneyland and Walt Disney World. When he began developing the theme parks, Disney hired artists and scene painters, many of them from Hollywood studios, to bring the imaginative visions of his animated films to life in Anaheim, California, and Orlando, Florida. It was an amusement park in Holland, featuring reproductions of architectural landmarks, that first gave Disney the idea of making his American amusement parks architecturally as well as artistically significant. He hired a young Californian architect, Welton Becket—known for his stately homes for movie stars and famous for his design of the Capitol Records Tower in Los Angeles—and other architects who would give the Disney parks architectural distinction.

In the early 1980s, Walt Disney Company's chief executive, Michael Eisner, renewed the tradition of innovative architecture at the parks and began commissioning some of the most renowned contemporary architects—Robert Venturi, Robert A.M. Stern, Arata Isozaki, Frank Gehry, Aldo Rossi, and Michael Graves among them—to design important buildings for the company. In the process Disney set new standards for postmodern architecture and became one of its leading patrons in the world. The resulting projects, which include idiosyncratic, fantastic theme parks, hotels, resorts, movie studios, and offices, blend Disney's popular, often surreal, imagery and iconography into the architects' individual styles.

Significance

Robert A. M. Stern and his team have developed several Disney commissions, all exemplifying the power of architecture to create an inhabitable fantasy world. Robert Stern's Casting Center is an employee hiring and training area located near Orlando, Florida. Stern wanted the building to express the spirit of Disney and also to reflect its Floridian locale. Stern drew upon early twentieth-century Florida building styles, especially the "Mediterranean Revival" style, which incorporates Venetian imagery with elements of Florida's environment and climate. The result is a building which resembles a Venetian palazzo adorned with fanciful details, such as the classically styled columns topped with gold-leaf Disney characters.

The facade has an Italianate harlequin pattern, while the entry is protected by a sweeping canopy that recalls Disney's futuristic Tomorrowland. Other details, such as doorknobs inspired by *Alice in Wonderland* call to mind a Disney theme park castle. Stein wanted the visitor to experience something of Disney prior to their arrival at the reception desk, "Let them wander. Let them get a taste for Disney before they get there," he explained. He achieved this by designing a long ramp flanked by frescoed walls that leads visitors through a Disney landscape to the second-floor reception desk.

Stern's work provides Disney with a compelling blend of the seriousness and the fanciful—it is an architectural approach to a fantastical world.

Primary Source

"Casting Center, Walt Disney World"

SYNOPSIS: Robert A.M. Stern was one of a number of prominent architects hired by Disney in the 1980s to design buildings for the company's various studios and theme parks. Stern's casting building for Disney is both playful and exaggerated, yet it reflects the classical notion of architecture for which Stern is so well known.

Lake Buena Vista, Florida, 1987–89

The Casting Center faces Interstate 4 but is entered from Buena Vista Drive within Walt Disney World proper. The sole representation of the Disney company along the interstate, the building is intended not only to house personnel functions but also to convey the company spirit to prospective employees. It accommodates the central hiring facility as well as offices for the Employee Relations Division and the Labor Relations Department. The design of the 360-by-80-foot, 61,000-square-foot building—organized as two blocklike abutments and a bridge spanning a marsh—represents a journey from unemployment to employment. The southern end of the bridge houses the entrance rotunda, while the northern end contains the building's principal room, the General Employment Lobby, located on the second floor.

Inside and out, the casting building abounds in imagery culled from Disney's movies and theme parks: campanile-like skylights, turrets, finials, futuristic airfoil shapes, and elaborately tiled surfaces, as well as Mickey Mouse water scuppers. Visitors enter under the airfoil canopy, open bronze doors with handles modeled on a character from *Alice in Wonderland,* and move through a processional sequence of spaces that starts in an oval rotunda adorned with twelve gilt statues of Disney's most illustrious characters illuminated from above by a glazed campanile. Continuing along a 150-foot-long skylit ramp lined with trompe-l'oeil panels that offer highly interpretive views of Disney World as well as the immediate roadside context, the job seeker is introduced to the heart of the building without violating the privacy of workers who occupy the two floors of offices. The ramp is not only a way to effectively handle the large crowds of job applicants but also a surrogate for the visitor's experience in the Disney parks, where ramps are used to channel crowds and heighten the sense of expectation for individual attractions. The trip up the ramp culminates in the General Employment Lobby, located under the second campanile.

Further Resources

BOOKS

Dunlop, Beth, and Vincent Scully. *Building a Dream: The Art of Disney Architecture.* New York: Abrams, 1996.

Marling, Karal Ann. *Designing Disney's Theme Parks: The Architecture of Reassurance.* Paris: Flammarion, 1997.

PERIODICALS

Cramer, Ned. "Defending Disney." *Architecture,* August 1997, 3.

Young, Dwight. "Frisky Buildings." *Preservation,* September/October 1996, 144.

WEBSITES

"1994 Life Dream House Architect: Robert A.M. Stern." Life.com. Available online at http://www.life.com/Life/dreamhouse/stern/sternbio.html; website home page: http://www.life.com (accessed May 21, 2003).

Wexner Center for the Arts

Photograph; Illustration

By: Peter Eisenman and Richard Trott

Date: 1989

Source: "Wexner Center for the Visual Arts." Axonometric illustration. In Rifkind, Carole. *A Field Guide to Contemporary American Architecture.* New York: Penguin, 1998, 173; Smith, G.E. Kidder. "Wexner Center for the Arts at Ohio State University." 1989. Corbis. Image no. GE001356. Available online at http://pro.corbis.com (accessed May 9, 2003).

About the Architects: Peter Eisenman (1932–) was born in Newark, New Jersey. He studied architecture at Cornell, Columbia, and Cambridge Universities. He was a protégé of Philip Johnson. Eisenman is the founder and director of the Institute for Architecture and Urban Studies in New York City. He also started the architecture journal, *Oppositions.* Eisenman has designed large housing and urban projects, educational facilities, and private houses. He is the author of numerous publications and has won many awards for his work.

Richard Trott, a Columbus-native, graduated from Ohio State University College of Engineering in 1961. In 1965 he founded Trott and Bean Architects, a reknowned Columbus firm. He co-designed the Wexner Center, as well as the Greater Columbus Convention Center, with Peter Eisenman. In 1998 Ohio State University established a professorship in his honor. ■

Introduction

Peter Eisenman is among the most influential and controversial architects active today. His eccentric designs have generated both praise and outrage. Eisenman creates an architecture which is deliberately disconnected

Primary Source

Wexner Center for the Arts: Photograph

SYNOPSIS: Peter Eisenman's design for the Wexner Center at Ohio State University was the physical manifestation of his anti-Postmodern architectural philosophy. Both hailed and assailed by critics, the building has earned more defenders over time. However, at just over ten years old, the building required major restoration for which the university provided a budget of ten million dollars. © CORBIS. REPRODUCED BY PERMISSION.

from the traditional. His buildings feature such unexpected elements as tilted walls, split ceilings, and odd angles. Some are designed to look unfinished. Others appear to be in process of demolishment. Eisenman believes that his buildings should examine ideas. His early work used shapes and forms deriving from what he calls the "tenuous relationship" between language and underlying structure. This relationship is the central interest of the philosophical deconstructionists, and Eisenman acknowledges the influence of such theorists as Friedrich Nietzsche, Noam Chomsky, and Jacques Derrida on his work.

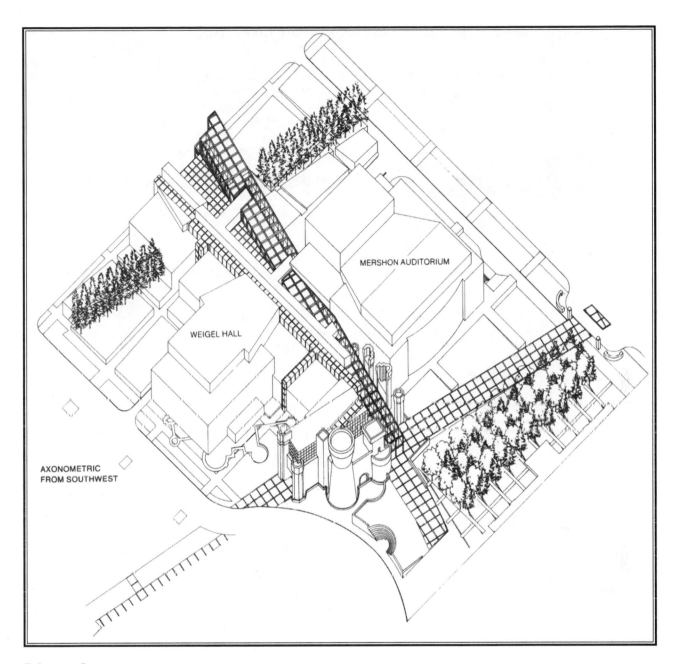

WEIGEL HALL

MERSHON AUDITORIUM

AXONOMETRIC
FROM SOUTHWEST

Primary Source

Wexner Center for the Arts: Illustration

The Wexner Center for the Arts is composed of several buildings, constructed to display and promote all different forms of art. The grid shown is a white metal structure made to resemble scaffolding. ILLUSTRATION FROM *A FIELD GUIDE TO CONTEMPORARY AMERICAN ARCHITECTURE*. REPRODUCED BY PERMISSION OF DUTTON, A DIVISION OF PENGUIN PUTNAM, INC.

Few of Eisenman's designs have been built, but even his ideas attract attention. Eisenman's vision is often regarded as repellant. He himself claims to be "exploring the possibility of a truly horrific environment." He wants his architecture to disturb, to disrupt the viewer's expectations. Few in the field believed that Eisenman would ever succeed selling his unique visions. Yet he found a benefactor in businessman Leslie H. Wexner, who hired Eisenman to design the Wexner Center at Ohio State University.

Significance

The Wexner Center for the Visual Arts at Ohio State University was Peter Eisenman's first major public project to be built and a key commission. Peter Eisenman's design was an architectural attempt to

Architect Peter Eisenman. Eisenman's designs are inspired from his philosophical theories. © CORBIS. REPRODUCED BY PERMISSION

Further Resources

BOOKS

Eisenman, Peter, and Victoria Mulgrave. *Eisenman Architects: Selected and Current Works.* Melbourne: Images Publishing Group, 1995.

Steele, James, ed. *Museum Builders.* London: Academy Editions, 1994.

PERIODICALS

Andersen, Kurt. "A Crazy Building in Columbus." *Time,* November 20, 1989, 84.

McGuigan, Cathleen. "Eisenman's Gridlocked Mind Game." *Newsweek,* November 20, 1989, 74.

"Peter Eisenman." Interview. *Current Biography,* October 1997, 17–20.

WEBSITES

Lamster, Mark. "The Wexner Center." Metropolismag.com. Available online at http://www.metropolismag.com/html /content_0701/ob/ob09.html; website home page: http://www .metropolismag.com (accessed May 21, 2003).

AUDIO AND VISUAL MEDIA

Peter Eisenman: Making Architecture Move. Michael Blackwood Productions. Videocassette, 1995.

expose the "bankruptcy of conventional reality." Opening in 1989, the center is designed around superimposed grids—the city grid and the grid of the university campus—which underpin the building's complex geometry.

The Wexner Center reflects Eisenman's interest in questioning basic precepts of order and function. There is no façade. Its windows are set directly along the floor. Columns stop in midair. Illogical angles and unexpected juxtapositions surprise the visitor at every turn. The galleries are oddly shaped and not suitable for every type of art. Theaters specially designed for film and performance are also incorporated.

Not everyone is impressed by the center. Fellow architects accuse Eisenman of excessive concern about form at the cost of function. After a little more than ten years of use, the building needed major repairs to correct leaks, improve environmental controls, and resolve operational inefficiencies involving space planning and patterns of use. Architects are not the only critics. In an interview with Metropolismag.com, art historian Andrew McClellan said, "There's no balance between architecture and display. I can't imagine a single curator in the country would endorse the Wexner as an ideal space to exhibit art."

Empire Bay Tracksuit Advertisement

Advertisement

By: Empire Bay

Date: 1980s

Source: Empire Bay Tracksuit Advertisement. The Advertising Archive. Image no. 30506691. ∎

Introduction

By the late 1970s, sportswear and fashion were merging. A growing interest in fitness and exercise and an increase in body consciousness among Americans combined to create a new demand for fashionable exercise clothing. In the 1970s, the fashion industry began to respond by providing more appealing exercise clothing to replace the traditional gym shorts and old sweatshirt.

In the 70s and 80s, various influences were brought to bear on the new exercise fashions. The tracksuit was born when matching bottoms were added to the jacket tops athletes wore. Zip-fronted suits were inspired by the astronaut suits of the late 1960s. Fabrics normally used for casual, at-home, or workout attire, such as stretch velour and terrycloth, became stylish for party wear. Even cashmere, once reserved for expensive sweaters, began to be used for sweatshirts. Close-fitting Spandex tights, torn sweatshirts studded with rhinestones, and expensive sneakers made by L.A. Gear or Reebok became indispensable for the fashion-conscious, both in and out of the gym.

Primary Source

Empire Bay Tracksuit Advertisement

SYNOPSIS: The growing popularity of fitness and exercise, combined with the fashion influence of films such as *Fame* and *Flashdance,* fueled the popularity of fashionable and stylish workout clothes that are designed for use on the street or in the gym. THE ADVERTISING ARCHIVE, LTD. REPRODUCED BY PERMISSION.

Many people appreciated the comfort and easy care of sports clothes, and soon clothes designed for the gym or the dance studio were being worn in the streets. Baggy sweatshirts, leg warmers, "scrunch" socks, and super-wide headbands became elements of the 1980s aerobics look. Scrunch socks were often worn with the popular high-top Reebok shoes, and leg warmers were worn with everything from leotards to jeans to mini skirts and high-heeled shoes. Stylish athletic clothing was becoming big business as designers from all stylistic backgrounds began to put their signatures on athletic clothing or sports shoes.

The 1980s also saw the arrival of the lightweight, front-zippering warm-up suit, a nylon jacket matched with loose bottom trousers with elasticated cuffs and waist. The newer styles often featured neon colors and contrasting piping along the sleeves or pants seams.

Significance

The trend in fashionable exercise clothing was reinforced by the increasing popularity of sports and exercise. Yoga was very popular throughout the 1960s and 1970s. Other enthusiasts played squash, handball, or tennis, while many took up jogging or joined health clubs for aerobics classes or weight work. By 1980, exercise had become a routine part of life for many Americans. Dance studios offering jazz, tap, exercise, and step classes also became popular. Pop music bands like Bananarama and the Go-Gos helped popularize the new trendy look, while movies like *Fame* and *Flashdance* decisively moved women's fashion in the same direction.

As the fad for exercise has persisted, casual sporty clothing has become the preferred wear for almost any occasion. Fitness fashion, now referred to as "leisure wear," has been a lucrative business since the 1970s. Sneakers have taken over the footwear industry, and many fashion designers have developed lines of clothing to answer the demand.

Further Resources

BOOKS

McDowell, Colin. *McDowell's Dictionary of Twentieth Century Fashion.* London: Muller, 1984.

Mulvagh, Jane. *Vogue History of Twentieth-Century Fashion.* New York: Viking, 1988.

PERIODICALS

Mosher, Cheryl. "Functional Fashion." *Women's Sports & Fitness* 7, May 1985, 12.

Reed, J. D. "Body and Soles." *Money* 15, May 1986, 174–176.

"Oldfangled New Towns"

Magazine article

By: Kurt Andersen
Date: May 20, 1991
Source: Andersen, Kurt. "Oldfangled New Towns." *Time,* November 4, 1985, 52–55. ∎

Introduction

In 1946, Florida businessman J.S. Smolian bought eighty acres of beachfront property on Florida's northwest coast near the town of Seagrove. After failing to realize his vision for a company summer resort, Smolian used the property as a family getaway. There was almost no building on the site until Smolian's grandson, Robert Davis, an award-winning developer in Miami, decided to develop the property. His vision for Seaside was inspired by the desire to revive the architectural traditions of Northwest Florida—wood-frame cottages adapted to the climate.

The cottages Davis remembered from his childhood summers in the area featured deep roof overhangs for shade and ample windows for cross-ventilation in all the rooms. The cottages were built of wood and other low-maintenance materials that could survive several generations of homeowners. Davis asked Miami architects and urban planners Andres Duany and Elizabeth Plater-Zyberk (DPZ) to help him plan a community that could combine these traditions with a modern approach in order to create a year-round community. DPZ seized the chance to execute a visionary urban design. The husband-and-wife design team is perhaps the most significant contributor to the debate on New Urbanism and New Towns. They have completed designs for over 250 new and existing communities, and they have won numerous awards for their innovative town planning designs.

Duany and Plater-Zyberk undertook extensive research to study local building traditions and to plan an ideal community that would answer Davis's requirements. They traveled throughout the South, especially in Florida, seeking examples of the building type Davis wanted represented in his new community. Armed with cameras, sketch pads, and tape measures, the architects developed a thorough set of standards and rules for making recreating buildings that would be historically accurate, faithfully evoke Davis's memories, and fulfill his ideal for a recreated community.

Most of the buildings DPZ studied were located in small coastal towns, and gradually the idea evolved that the small town was an appropriate model for the layout of streets and squares and the location of the town's various elements. After assessing the particular needs, circumstances, and expectations for Davis's Seaside, the designers created a town plan for a brand new community.

Significance

The most famous of DPZ's "New Towns" is Seaside, Florida, Robert Davis's childhood vacation retreat that has been recreated from the ground up as a year-round village. Seaside has been hailed as the first and greatest example of how a New Town should work. The project gave DPZ a chance to realize their innovative concept for addressing through community design the ill effects of urban sprawl on people who live in and around modern cities. DPZ planned not only how the structures in the town were to be built and where they should be located, but they also planned the town from scratch, designing an architecture that is various rather than monotonous. The town plan is compact and de-emphasizes the automobile, helping to make Seaside more self-contained and ecologically conscientious. The town is especially safe and navigable for pedestrians.

DPZ developed and followed a strict set of codes for details of design and construction in the Seaside project. For example, the *Regulating Plan,* fixing the street grid of the town; the *Architectural Regulations,* specifying the styles, materials, heights, and even colors for buildings; and the *Street Types Regulation* setting standards for the design and landscaping of streets, boulevards, and highways.

Seaside has inspired a number of other projects in "smart growth" community designs around the country as other architects and real estate developers are attracted to the DPZ's vision. However, both the town and the planners have their detractors. Some criticize the creation of what they called "glorified suburbs," hardly differing from the communities that sprawl around cities throughout the U.S. and lacking the cultural diversity the New Towns purportedly invite.

Primary Source

"Oldfangled New Towns" [excerpt]

For Americans with even a little money, to live anywhere but a suburb is to make a statement. If you are comfortable, you are naturally a suburbanite; living out in the country or in the heart of the city has become a lifestyle declaration only slightly less exotic than a commitment to vegetarianism or the Latin Mass. In 1950 moving out to some spick-and-span new subdivision was the very heart of the American dream. In 1990 suburban living is simply a middle-class entitlement—it is how people live.

New census figures show, in fact, that suburbanites will soon be the American majority, up from being about a third of the population back in 1950. Yet as America's cities and villages have dissolved into vast suburban nebulas, no one seems entirely happy with the result. From Riverside County in southern California to Fairfax County in northern Virginia, new American suburbs tend to be disappointments, if not outright failures. Traffic jams are regularly as bad as anything in the fearsome, loathsome city. Waste problems can be worse. Boundaries are ill defined; town centers are nonexistent. Too often, there's no there there. [sic]

The critique is not new. Until recently, however, nearly all the dissidents have sneered and carped from on high, dismissing not just the thoughtless, ugly way suburbs have developed, but also the very hopes and dreams of those who would live there. Today, for the first time, the most articulate, convincing critics of American suburbia are sympathetic to suburbanites and are proposing a practical cure.

For more than a decade, Andres Duany and Elizabeth Plater-Zyberk, a Miami-based husband-and-wife team of architects and planners, have been reinventing the suburb, and their solution to sprawl is both radical and conservative: they say we must return to first principles, laying out brand-new towns according to old-fashioned fundamentals, with the locations of stores, parks and schools precisely specified from the outset, with streets that invite walking, with stylistic harmony that avoids the extremes of either architectural anarchy or monotony.

Duany and Plater-Zyberk are no pie-in-the-sky theorists, but deeply pragmatic crusaders who barnstorm the country, lecturing, evangelizing, designing, bit by bit repairing and redeeming the American landscape. So far the couple and their colleagues have proposed, at the behest of developers, more than 30 new towns ranging from Tannin, a 70-acre hamlet in Alabama, to Nance Canyon, a 3,050-acre, 5,250-unit New Age town near Chico, Calif. Half a dozen such towns are already under construction. Seaside, their widely publicized prototype town in northern Florida, is more than half built. At Kentlands, a new town on the edge of Maryland suburbia outside Washington, the first families have just moved in, and vacant lots are selling despite the

Strict building codes for homes in the planned resort community of Seaside, Florida, help create a Victorian-era appearance for the entire town. © DAVE G. HOUSER/CORBIS. REPRODUCED BY PERMISSION

housing slump. In addition, the two, among the Prince of Wales' favorite architects, have helped design a town Charles plans to build in Dorset.

Duany and Plater-Zyberk are not alone. Sharing roughly the same principles, scores of other architects—most notably Peter Calthorpe in San Francisco, the partners Alexander Cooper and Jacquelin Robertson in New York City, and William Rawn in Boston—are designing deeply old-fashioned new towns and city neighborhoods. Most important, developers are buying into the latest view of how suburbs ought to be built. "I still have a memory of the kind of place Duany is talking about," says Joseph Alfandre, 39, the veteran Maryland developer who has already invested millions in Kentlands. "It is the kind of place I grew up in, that I have always dreamed of re-creating. When I was five years old [in 1956 in Bethesda]. I was independent—I could walk into town, to the bowling alley, the movie theater, the drugstore. Duany just reminded me of it."

Andres Duany is Mr. Outside to Elizabeth Plater-Zyberk's Ms. Inside. He inspires, he charms, he gives the stirring, witty lectures. She organizes, she

teaches, she makes the heartfelt case for a particular scheme. Both are relentless and smart and talented, and both are American baby boomers (he left communist Cuba as a child in 1960; her parents left communist Poland in the late '40s), who met as Princeton undergraduates in the early '70s.

It was in 1980, when Duany and Plater-Zyberk were hired by quixotic developer Robert Davis to turn 80 acres of Gulf Coast scrubland into a resort, that they ceased being merely interesting architects and started becoming visionary urban planners. As with all revolutions, the essential idea was simple: instead of building another dull cluster of instant beach-front high-rises, the developer and designers wondered, why not create a genuine town, with shops and lanes and all the unpretentious grace and serendipitous quirks that have always made American small towns so appealing? Thus was born the town of Seaside—and with it, the movement to make new housing developments real places again.

Their intent is not to reproduce any particular old-fashioned place. Rather, Duany and Plater-Zyberk have meticulously studied the more-than-skin-deep particulars of traditional towns and cities from Charleston to New Orleans to Georgetown, and of the great prewar suburbs, such as Mariemont, Ohio. They've looked at how streets were laid out, how landmarks were placed, the intermingling of stores and houses, the rough consistency of buildings' cornice lines and materials. They've measured the optimal distances between houses across the street and next door, figured out just what encourages walking (narrow streets, parked cars, meaningful destinations) and reckoned the outer limit of a walkable errand (a quarter mile). They have tried to discern, beyond surface style, exactly what makes deeply charming places deeply charming.

In the standard new suburb, built as quickly as possible by developers working exclusively to maximize short-term profit, little thought is given to making a rich, vital whole. New suburban streets meander arbitrarily, making navigation almost impossible for outsiders. The houses are often needlessly ugly mongrels. Even worse, they are plopped down on lots with almost no regard for how the houses might exist together, as pieces of a larger fabric. They are too far apart to provide the coziness of small-town or city streets, too close to create the splendor of country privacy. Corner stores or neighborhood post offices are almost unheard of.

The single biggest difference between modern suburbs and authentic towns is the dominance of the automobile. Suburban street-design standards have been drafted by traffic engineers, and so the bias is in favor of—you guessed it—traffic. It is now a planning axiom that streets exist almost exclusively for cars, and for cars going as fast as possible.

Duany and Plater-Zyberk challenge the urban-planning orthodoxies that, they say, encourage traffic congestion. With dead-end suburban cul-de-sacs leading to "collector roads" that in turn funnel all traffic to the highway, every driver is jammed onto the same crowded road. Why not have shops reached by small neighborhood streets, thus keeping errand runners off the highway? Why not have stores' parking lots connected so shoppers could drive from place to place without heading back out to the main road? Because local codes, drafted by experts, won't permit it.

Thomas Brahms is the executive director of the Institute of Transportation Engineers, the field's main professional association. He is patronizing, even contemptuous, toward the new movement. "It would be nice to turn the clock back to the walking cities of the early 1800s," Brahms says, "but I don't think we can do that. It would be utopian to think that you could draw a circle and think that people would stay within that circle and not leave it."

Duany, Plater-Zyberk, Calthorpe and the rest agree that five minutes is as far as most people will generally go for an errand on foot, which means that the natural size for a neighborhood, equipped with the basic shops and services, is 200 acres—an area a bit larger than one-half mile square. No one is suggesting that people will remain locked within these neighborhoods, only that they should not be *required* to leave any time they want to shop or work. "These pedestrian neighborhoods create a stronger sense of community," says Calthorpe, who has produced designs for a score of such places, mainly on the West Coast. "They re-create the glue that used to hold together our communities before they were slashed apart by the big expressways."

Plater-Zyberk have gone further by developing an appealing and practical process for designing new towns efficiently. After a developer hires the firm, the planners start collecting information about the area—quirks of geography, regional traditions. A sympathetic local architect may be incorporated into the team of designers, planners, renderers and engineers, always led by Duany or Plater-Zyberk. The group descends on the site. About one week and $80,000 to $300,000 later, they will have produced detailed plans and preliminary construction drawings for a new town, complete with a marketing scheme and an artist's slick conceptions of particular streets and possible houses. At each step of the way, citizens and officials are invited to inspect and react to the work-in-progress. "People really see what they're getting," Duany says of this quasi-democracy, instead of being presented with a mystifying fait accompli.

The couple seldom design particular houses or buildings for the towns they plan—an almost heroic act of restraint for architects. Instead, they conjure a tangible vision of the place they mean to germinate, then draft the rules that architects and builders will follow after they go. The result is towns that are authentic patchworks, not the plainly fake diversity that is inevitable when a single hand creates all the architecture. . . . but most Duany–Plater-Zyberk towns in the eastern U.S. carry similar prescriptions: houses must be clad in wood clapboard, cedar shingles, brick or stone, and roofs (of cedar shake, metal or slate) must be gabled or hipped, and pitched at traditional angles. . . .

What worries Duany and Plater-Zyberk most are their pseudo followers, developers and architects who apply a gloss of ye-olde-towne charm without supplying any of the deeper, more fundamental elements of old-fashioned urban coherence. Calthorpe agrees emphatically. "You can have nice streets, and you can put trees back on them, and you can make beautiful buildings with front porches again, but if the only place it leads is out to the expressway, then we are going to have the same environment all over again."

Further Resources

BOOKS

Bressi, Todd. *The Seaside Debates.* New York: Rizzoli, 2002.

Mohney, David. *Seaside: Making a Town in America.* New York: Princeton Architectural Press, 1991.

PERIODICALS

Dunlop, Beth. "Coming of Age." *Architectural Record,* July 1989, 96–103.

Goldberger, Paul. "The Truman Show." *The New Yorker,* June 22–29, 1998, 41.

WEBSITES

Seaside. Available online at http://www.seasidefl.com (accessed May 23, 2003).

Power Suiting

Managing Lives: Corporate Women and Social Change

Nonfiction work

By: Sue Joan Mendelson Freeman

Date: 1990

Source: Freeman, Sue Joan Mendelson. *Managing Lives: Corporate Women and Social Change.* Amherst: University of Massachusetts Press, 1990, 184.

About the Author: Sue Freeman (1944–) is a psychologist and professor of education at Smith College. Her research concentrates on women's moral development and on women and careers. She also works on the Project on Women and Social Change at Smith College, which uses a multidisciplinary approach to study women in the American workforce.

Calvin Klein Woman's Suit Advertisement

Advertisement

By: Calvin Klein

Date: 1980s

Source: The Advertising Archive Ltd. Image no. 30523208. ∎

Introduction

Although women were making significant progress in the American workplace in the late 1960s and through the 1970s, the number of women entering corporate leadership positions dramatically increased in the 1980s. With the exception of the rare female executive, however, many women continued to hold corporate positions for which they were paid less than their male counterparts. These positions were sometimes referred to as "Mommy Track" jobs, meaning that the woman was expected to move on if she had a baby during the course of her employment. Very few of these jobs were high-powered, high-paying positions.

Many people believed that women were finally becoming equals to men in the workplace. In reality, the treatment of women employees and their compensation compared to men did not support this perception. Although attitudes about women's abilities in the corporate world were slowly changing, professional women continued to struggle against the sexist outlook.

The nature of professional women's dress reinforced this discriminatory attitude. Business suits for women were available at the time, but, except for the pantsuit, the prevailing fashion featured decidedly feminine elements: Skirts were knee-length. Jackets were shorter than men's and were often fitted at the waist. Lapels were softly shaped, and the suits were often worn with blouses adorned with bows, ruffles, and other fripperies. Professional clothing for women seemed hopelessly out of date. What's more, the appearance of a woman in a dowdy skirt suit and soft ruffles may have actually strengthened the perception that she was less capable and less presentable than a male counterpart in an important meeting or as a representative for a company. Nevertheless, a more favorable image of the corporate woman prevailed, and women's suit dressing underwent a drastic change in the early to mid 1980s.

Significance

Gradually women discovered that dressing in a more masculine style meant that they were taken more seriously in the office. The 1980s look for a woman's professional wardrobe was tailored and styled after the man's suit and was influenced by a variety of models and media moments. These included the effects on fashion of television dramas such as "Dynasty" and "Dallas," programs that featured powerful—and powerfully dressed—women. Corporate business suit dressing was also shaped by international influences such as Margaret Thatcher, Britain's first female prime minister, who always appeared in a tailored day or evening suit. Fashionable blouses often had collars with a cravat or tie effect, but the use of silk, polyester satin, or crepe de chine fabrics softened the severe masculine tailoring of the garments.

Primary Source

Calvin Klein Woman's Suit Advertisement

SYNOPSIS: Neutral and dark-colored suits with shoulder pads were worn by women seeking to get ahead in business. The model's masculine posture in this Calvin Klein advertisement reflects the notion that if a woman looks more like a man she may be treated as well as one. THE ADVERTISING ARCHIVE, LTD. REPRODUCED BY PERMISSION.

As the fashion for a female identity in the workplace took hold, shoulder widths grew. Increasingly large shoulder pads were used to support the wider cut of sleeves in suit jackets. Designers tried to promote wide shoulders of football-player dimensions in the clothing of the early 1980s, and although women at first rejected the style, shoulder widths eventually reached dimensions not seen before in the twentieth century.

In *Managing Lives,* author Sue Freeman explored the conflicting perceptions of women executives taking on traditionally men's roles. She interviewed dozens of women at different phases of their careers about their struggle to be accepted as professionals and about their own assumptions about their roles as women professionals. Part of Freeman's research on self-image revolved around dressing and how it affected others' perceptions of the women. Some interviewees believed it was necessary to their success to wear a "power suit" and high heels, while others claimed to be intimidated by women who did dress that way when they themselves did not. Through the exploration of these attitudes and impressions, Freeman's book proved that clothing really does matter in the workplace.

Primary Source

Managing Lives: Corporate Women and Social Change [excerpt]

SYNOPSIS: Masculine suits with broad shoulders characterized the professional wardrobe of women who were rising in the corporate workplace during the 1980s. Dubbed "power dressing," the fashion trend served to improve the professional image of women executives on equal footing with their male counterparts, if not in terms of salary, at least in terms of authority.

A professional image is composed of many elements, from those that are obviously job-related to personal behavior and appearance. Being professional means looking the part and being businesslike, making the right decisions, and putting the company's success first. The implication is that the company's success spells success for the individual.

To behave in what one believes to be a professional manner is not enough, however. The meanings that are attached to behavior by its observers and recipients come to define it and thereby influence its effectiveness. Women have frequently been characterized in ways that are contrary to their self-perceptions and to their intended purposes. Camilla is surprised to discover the connotation attached to a slight variation in her wardrobe.

Once I started to wear a suit to work every single day religiously, there was a change in attitude. And I was told when I was reviewed,

"Well, I see you're looking a little more professional." Not that I ever didn't; I always wore skirts and blouses and jackets. [*What does "professional-looking" mean?*] I think sterner. I think they mean sterner and a little more powerful, or maybe more in control of the situation.

Further Resources

BOOKS

Dunseath, Kirsty, ed. *A Second Skin: Women Write about Clothes.* London: Women's Press, 1998.

Fischer-Mirkin, Toby. *Dress Code: Understanding the Hidden Meanings of Women's Clothes.* New York: Clarkson Potter, 1995.

Pante, Robert. *Dressing to Win.* New York: Doubleday 1984.

PERIODICALS

Nonkin, Lesley Jane. "Fear-of-Power Dressing." *Vogue,* September 1986, 316.

Urquhart, Rachel. "Whom Do Women Dress For?" *Vogue,* November 1994, 320–326.

High Museum of Art
Architectural design

By: Richard Meier

Date: 1993

Source: Krist, Bob. "Entrance to Atlanta's High Museum of Art." Corbis. Image no. RI002142. Available online at http://pro.corbis.com (accessed May 20, 2003).

About the Architect: Richard Meier (1930–) was born in Newark, New Jersey. He graduated from Cornell University and worked with several architectural firms before establishing his own practice in 1963. Just two years later, in 1965, Meier won national acclaim for his design of the Smith House in Darien, Connecticut. He next achieved fame in 1979, with the opening of his Visitors' Center at the utopian community of New Harmony, Indiana. In 1984, Meier became the youngest architect ever to be awarded the prestigious Pritzker Prize. He won the AIA Gold Medal in 1997. ■

Introduction

The High Museum of Art was founded in 1905 as the Atlanta Art Association. In 1926, Atlanta benefactor Mrs. Joseph High donated her home to the Association for a museum and art school, and the High Museum opened to the public in 1928. In 1955, a new building was opened to accommodate a significant collection of Renaissance paintings donated to the museum. The museum collection doubled in the 1960s, again threatening to outgrow its exhibition spaces. The museum hired Richard Meier in 1980 to design a new signature building.

Meier was well suited to accept the museum's commission. After studying architecture at Cornell University, Meier moved to New York City in the late 1950s and briefly worked for Marcel Breuer, one of the key figures in architecture's Modernist movement. He also painted for a while, sharing a studio with Frank Stella. However, it was architecture where Meier excelled. He made his mark in the 1970s with lean designs for several houses and some modest but impressive institutional buildings. It was in these projects that he perfected the use of the white, porcelain-glazed steel panels that have become his trademark.

Meier says of his influences:

> Le Corbusier was a great influence, but there are many influences and they are constantly changing. . . . We are all affected by Le Corbusier, Frank Lloyd Wright, Alvar Aalto, and Mies van der Rohe. But no less than Bramante, Borromini and Bernini. Architecture is a tradition, a long continuum. Whether we break with tradition or enhance it, we are still connected to that past. We evolve.

Significance

In 1980, when the High Museum approached Meier to design a new building to house their growing collection, the architect and many of his colleagues were working within the confines of the Modern movement. Like Le Corbusier and Van der Rohe, the pioneers of the movement, Meier used technology rather than traditional decorative details to determine a building's look. Meier refined the Modernist tradition to adapt and apply tech-

Architect Richard Meier. GETTY IMAGES. REPRODUCED BY PERMISSION.

Richard Meier on the Study of Architecture

"My area of study is architecture and its cultural manifestations, and such a quest for historical knowledge, especially of the arts, arises from my own need for a deeper understanding of the essence of architecture. Too frequently, the merely historical understanding of architecture is considered the complete and authentic understanding: whereas the sense of spiritual activity expressed in architectonic forms should be related to speculative interest in the nature of architectural forms more directly than to a historical interest in forms already realized, already claimed by the past. The one affords us the promise of architecture; the other, too often, ends in historicist ideology.

SOURCE: Meier, Richard. *Richard Meier, Architect: 1964–1984*. New York: Rizzoli, 1984, 6.

---

nology in an innovative way. Unlike his predecessors, who sought a universal architectural solution that defined a way of life, Meier regarded architecture as a tool for solving a variety of smaller architectural problems. "Each situation, each project," he says, "is different." The new Modernist's technological approach was reaching its apex of popularity in the United States at this time. Many practitioners were teaching in the universities and building the lean, streamlined structures typified by Meier's High Museum.

Meier's museum building is constructed of concrete slabs and steel columns. The facade features Meier's characteristic white, porcelain-enameled steel panels. The base of the building is enclosed by granite panels of equal size. A series of windows completes the exterior. The entrance features a gracefully curved pavilion that proceeds into an airy four-story-high, glass-roofed atrium. The interior ramp system providing access to the galleries allows the art to be viewed from various angles and at different levels and distances. The design brings natural light into the galleries, while various devices are used to provide visual variety. These include framed vistas of the surrounding park-like landscape and glimpses into other galleries, the atrium, and the building's exterior.

Primary Source

High Museum of Art

SYNOPSIS: Richard Meier's design for Atlanta's High Museum of Art is a defining work for the architect, who has remained true to his own design philosophy and largely disregarded the trends of modern architecture. The building successfully combines Meier's interests in livability and harmony in his designs. The High Museum is considered one of the best of its kind in terms of how art is exhibited and viewed. © BOB KRIST/CORBIS. REPRODUCED BY PERMISSION

Further Resources

BOOKS

High Museum of Art: The New Building, a Chronicle of Planning, Design, and Construction. Atlanta: High Museum of Art, 1983.

Meier, Richard. *Richard Meier, Architect: 1964–1984.* New York: Rizzoli International Publications, 1984.

PERIODICALS

Fox, Catherine. "A New High for Atlanta." *Art News,* November 1983, 102–106.

Kuhn, Irene Corbally. "Atlanta's High Museum." *Gourmet,* December 1984, 48–53.

"Master Builder"

Interview

By: Renzo Piano and Margaret Warner

Date: June 19, 1998

Source: Piano, Renzo. "Master Builder." Interview by Margaret Warner. *MacNeil/Lehrer Newshour.* PBS program transcript. June 19, 1998. Available online at http://www.pbs.org/newshour/bb/entertainment/jan-june98/piano_6-19.html; website home page: http://www.pbs.org (accessed May 23, 2003).

About the Author: Architect Renzo Piano (1937–) was born in Genoa, Italy, into a family of builders. At seventeen, Renzo announced his decision to study architecture. After graduating from Milan Polytechnic Architecture School in 1964, Piano worked for several years in his father's construction company. In 1970, he formed a partnership with the now-renowned British architect, Richard Rogers. Piano and Rogers became leaders in the "High-Tech" movement popular throughout the 1970s and 1980s. ■

Located in Houston, Texas, the Menil Collection houses approximately 15,000 works of art. **PHOTO BY HICKEY-ROBERTSON, HOUSTON; COURTESY OF THE MENIL COLLECTION, HOUSTON.**

Introduction

Renzo Piano first attracted notice in 1971 when, at age 33, he and his partner Richard Rogers won the competition to design the Pompidou Center in Paris. When the Pompidou was completed in 1977, it caused considerable controversy, owing mainly to its unusual and non-traditional look. With color-coded structural and service elements (blue for air conditioning, green for water, red for security, stairs, and elevators, and yellow for electricity—visible on the building's exterior) the Center presented a sharp contrast with its setting in an old Parisian neighborhood. In the interview excerpt below, Piano justified his design by saying:

> The Marie . . . is an old neighborhood, but this spaceship landing from somewhere in the middle of Marie is exactly what medieval cathedral has been long time ago. They are a spaceship. And in every city you have always some element, monuments normally, that are out of scale. If they have

an important job to do, that makes sense, and the Centre Pompidou has an important job to do. It has been visited by 150 million persons in 20 years. So it's a very important job.

The community eventually accepted the center, which has become a popular tourist spot.

Like other practitioners of the "High-Tech" movement, Piano and Rogers used technology as the starting point for the design of the Pompidou. They took pains, however, not to allow the building's unusual form to distract from its purpose to provide a useful and comfortable space for visitors. In his more recent works, Piano has applied similar innovative structural experiments to a range of projects, creating some of the most graceful and culturally significant buildings of the late twentieth century.

Significance

The Menil Collection in Houston opened in 1987 to exhibit the art collection of John and Dominique de Menil.

Renzo Piano, designer of the Menil Collection, has also been lauded for his innovative structures in Europe, such as Potsdamer Platz in Berlin and the Pompidou Centre in Paris. GETTY IMAGES. REPRODUCED BY PERMISSION.

Regarded as one of the most important private collections of primarily twentieth-century art, the Menil Collection includes about fifteen thousand paintings, sculptures, prints, drawings, and photographs.

The Menil Collection was designed by Renzo Piano and his firm, Building Workshop. Piano's design provides quiet, contemplative spaces that are ideal for exhibiting and viewing art. An inventive roof and skylight system uses high-tech louvers, or sun-shades, to provide shade in the glass-roofed galleries. These sun-shades, along with garden atriums and plate-glass windows, fill the galleries with natural light and bring the changes of weather, season, and time of day into the building. The Menil Collection's exterior is a long facade of white steel and gray cypress wood siding. Unlike the Pompidou, the building harmonizes with its neighborhood of 1920s-era bungalows on quiet tree-lined streets. In addition to the Menil Collection, several other architecturally significant galleries have been built by the Menil Foundation elsewhere in the immediate neighborhood, creating a cultural oasis in the sprawling city of Houston while preserving the integrity of its tranquil neighborhood.

Piano's international reputation secured him other significant commissions, including the San Nicola Soc-cer Stadium in Bari, Italy, and the Kansai Air Terminal in Osaka, Japan. The Kansai is considered by many to be Piano's greatest contribution to architecture. One of the largest buildings ever built, the Kansai survived an earthquake in 1995 without so much as a broken pane of glass, a testimony to the precision and sturdiness of the design.

Primary Source

"Master Builder" [excerpt]

> **SYNOPSIS:** Renzo Piano's minimalist, airy building houses the art collection of John and Dominique de Menil. The building is lit by diffused natural light and is tailor-made to suit the artwork on exhibit. In 1998, Piano was awarded the Pritzker Prize, architecture's most prestigious honor.

Margaret Warner: Well, we thought we'd look at a couple of specific works of yours and talk a little bit more about your work. And I think we have a slide that we're going to put up, the first one, which is the Pompidou Center in Paris, which, as you know, but to our viewers, was completed in 1977. Now, you entered a competition for this, and you were a very young man at the time. What were you trying to achieve?

Renzo Piano: I did that competition in 1971, together with Richard Rogers, who is one of my best friends, and we are still great friends, and we were very young. I was 33 years. Richard was 36, I guess. We were bad boys. We were really bad boys. And what we wanted to do was mainly to be disobedient to-institution-and [sic] build in the middle of Paris. At that time Paris was full of institutions building very, very severe, austere, made of stone-we-we [sic] wanted to break that sensation of intimidating building. And we wanted to create actually totally different emotion, that is, the one of creating curiosity. Curiosity is much better emotion than intimidation.

Margaret Warner: So is that why you took all these machinery elements like ventilation and so on and made them design elements?

Renzo Piano: As usual, in architecture there is never one reason why you do this or that way. One reason for taking the machine out was, in fact, create that effect of a factory, but also there was another very important practical reason. By doing this we-we [sic] were making free the platform from fixed elements. And, you know, when you are 33 and you are asked to make a building for culture, that may last three or four hundred years, that is what people told us, I mean, you are in great trouble.

You don't even understand what culture is about. How can you understand what culture will be in 200 years? So the idea was to create a few piazzas, one above the other, and to take all the fixed elements like lifts, elevators, air conditioning, all out from the platform, so that the building is actually made by five platforms, one above the other, totally flexible, and this actually did work very well.

Margaret Warner: Well, it's been very, very popular with tourists and visitors, but as I know you know it's also been criticized for kind of standing apart from the neighborhood.

Renzo Piano: From one point of view I agree. The Marie—is that neighborhood there—is an old neighborhood, but this spaceship landing from somewhere in the middle of Marie is exactly what medieval cathedral has been long time ago. They are a spaceship. And in every city you have always some element, monuments normally, that are out of scale. If they have an important job to do, that makes sense, and the Centre Pompidou has an important job to do. It has been visited by 150 million persons in 20 years. So it's a very Important job.

Margaret Warner: All right. Let's turn now to the Menil Collection Museum in Houston, which was completed really 10 years later in 1987, another museum but so different, at least to the untutored eye looks different, very serene, very subtle. Was that your intention? What were you trying to do there?

Renzo Piano: You may feel a bit funny what they're saying, but the Menil Collection Museum in Houston is in a sense also provocation like Beauborg was in Paris, except that in Paris it was a city full of memory, too much memory. In Houston, Texas, that is a city with very little memory you can say. I mean, we got built up, the opposite, the secularity of a museum, and, of course, the Menil was the right client for that. She was extremely bright, extremely subtle, and intelligent.

Margaret Warner: This was the woman with the great art collection.

Renzo Piano: Yes. Dominique De Menil was the collector, and she died at the beginning of this year. And then in some way the Menil Collection, quite a building, it was quite a provocation, but it was a sacred place, almost a temple, for contemplation of art, where you almost feel like taking off your shoes and getting gently inside. And so, you know, every kind of building has a different story and is in different place, and you cannot consider coherence to make the building equal. I mean, coherence is to be able to understand the situation and to make a good interpretation.

On the Menil Collection Building

Art collector Dominique de Menil was thinking not simply of a new home for her growing collection, but also of a center for music, literature, theatre, and cultural educational activities when she planned this new building in a small park surrounded by low residential housing. It was to be free of all stylistic borrowings, flexible and open, and above all was to be illuminated with natural light, a specification to which Piano subordinated all other design stages. The solution was a roof of 'leaves' of thin ferro-cement which would span both the free areas as well as the display rooms of the flat building, and to which additional lights could be easily attached. Above this, a sealed superstructure contains the 'treasury'—an air-conditioned storage space for works of art not on display. The traditional timbering of the outside walls is a reference to the surrounding houses: 'Demonumentalization' was the motto.

Margaret Warner: And you created an interesting way of letting in the light with those what they call leaves on the roof.

Renzo Piano: Yes, yes.

Margaret Warner: Can you explain that in a way we could understand.

Renzo Piano: Well, it's very easy. I mean, we call those elements of concrete, very tiny piece of concrete, and we call leaves because like the leaves of a tree they make impossible to the sun to get in directly, and you cannot, of course, have the sun directly on the painting. So by doing those forms that are like that and so the sun bunch all time twice before coming in, we were able to avoid direct sun, and, of course, to cut down the infrared rays and light. And this was just a system for aiding natural light inside. It's not the only one, but, of course, we did use the shape of those leaves from inside to create a sense of the space, because it's not true that a good museum is totally neutral. If you make a museum like a white box and you put a piece of art inside, you kill the piece of art. A museum should be not neutral, totally neutral, must have a character.

Further Resources

BOOKS

Goldberger, Paul. *Renzo Piano and Building Workshop: Buildings and Projects, 1971-1989.* New York: Rizzoli, 1989.

Pizzi, Emilio. *Renzo Piano.* Basel: Birkhauser, 2003.

PERIODICALS

Betsky, Aaron. "Minimalism Meets the Public." *Metropolitan Home,* March 1997, 78, 81.

Covington, Richard. "The Incredible Lightness of Being Renzo Piano." *Smithsonian Magazine,* June 1999.

WEBSITES

Renzo Piano Building Workshop. Available online at http://www.rpwf.org/ (accessed May 23, 2003).

"Renzo Piano: Pritzker Architecture Prize Laureate 1998." Priztkerprize.com. Available online at http://www.pritzkerprize.com/98piano.htm; website home page: http://www.pritzkerprize.com (accessed May 23, 2003).

5

GOVERNMENT AND POLITICS

PAUL G. CONNORS

Entries are arranged in chronological order by date of primary source. For entries with one primary source, the entry title is the same as the primary source title. Entries with more than one primary source have an overall entry title, followed by the titles of the primary sources.

Important Events in Government and Politics, 1980–1989

1980

- On January 4, President Jimmy Carter reacts to the Soviet invasion of Afghanistan on December 29, 1979 by withdrawing the SALT II arms-control treaty from consideration by the United States Senate. He also places an embargo on the sale of grain and some types of electronic equipment to the Soviet Union.

- On January 7, President Carter signs a bill guaranteeing $1.5 billion in loans to bail out the Chrysler Corporation.

- On February 2, the news media report the results of a two-year sting operation (code name: Abscam) in which an FBI agent posing as a wealthy Arab offered bribes to elected officials. Among those arrested and eventually convicted on bribery or related charges are Sen. Harrison Williams, Jr. (D-N.J.), and Representatives John W. Jenrette, Jr. (D-S.C.), Richard Kelly (R-Fla.), Raymond Lederer (D-Pa.), John M. Murphy (D-N.Y.), Michael Myers (D-Pa.), and Frank Thompson, Jr. (D-N.J.).

- On April 2, President Carter signs the Crude Oil Windfall Profits Tax Act of 1980. In conjunction with decontrolling oil prices, this act is expected to collect $227 billion in revenues in the next ten years.

- On April 12, at the urging of President Carter, the United States Olympic Committee votes to boycott the 1980 summer games in Moscow to protest the Soviet invasion of Afghanistan.

- On June 3, the National Bureau of Economic Research reports that the United States has been in a recession since January.

- On July 1, President Carter signs a bill deregulating the trucking industry.

- On July 14, President Carter's brother Billy Carter registers with the government as an agent of the Libyan government, a terrorist regime, and reports that he has received more than $220,000 in the last seven months.

- On July 16, the Republican National Convention nominates Ronald Reagan for president. The next day the convention nominees George H. Bush for vice president.

- On August 14, the Democratic National Convention renominates President Carter and Vice President Mondale.

- On August 20, the Defense Department announces the development of the Stealth aircraft, which can elude detection by radar.

- On August 25, the independent presidential candidate John Anderson of Illinois chooses Patrick J. Lucey of Wisconsin as his running mate.

- On October 2, Representative Michael Myers, who was convicted on charges stemming from the Abscam probe, is expelled from the House of Representatives. This is the first time since 1861 that the House has removed from office one of its own members.

- On October 14, President Carter signs the Staggers Rail Act, which deregulates the nation's railroads.

- On November 4, Republican Ronald Reagan is elected president of the United States with 51.6 percent of the popular vote to 41.7 percent for incumbent president Jimmy Carter and 6.7 percent for third-party candidate John Anderson.

1981

- On January 20, the Iran hostages are freed.

- Ronald Reagan is inaugurated president of the United States. In his first official act, he freezes all government hiring.

- On January 28, President Reagan lifts most oil price controls.

- On January 29, President Reagan orders a sixty-day freeze on all pending federal regulations.

- On February 18, in his State of the Union Address, President Reagan calls for tax reduction and budget cuts of $41.4 billion. He also proposes to increase the military budget from 24 percent to 32 percent.

- In March, President Reagan directs the CIA to assist "Contra" guerrilla forces opposed to the Marxist Sandinista government of Nicaragua.

- On March 6, President Reagan announces the cutting of thirty-seven thousand federal government jobs.

- On March 30, John W. Hinckley, Jr., shoots President Reagan in the chest as he walks to his limousine after delivering a speech at the Washington Hilton Hotel. Press Secretary James S. Brady receives a serious but nonfatal head wound, and two law-enforcement officers are also shot.

- On April 11, President Reagan returns to the White House after eleven days in the hospital following the March 30 assassination attempt.

- On April 24, President Reagan lifts the Soviet grain embargo.

- On July 7, President Reagan nominates Sandra Day O'Connor to be the first woman justice on the United States Supreme Court.

- On August 4, Congress passes President Reagan's tax-cut measures, which features a 5 percent across-the-board cut in individual tax rates on October 1, 1981 and another 10 percent cut July 1, 1982, and another 10 percent cut on July 1, 1983.

- On October 22, President Reagan decertifies the air traffic controllers union, PATCO, thereby firing the workers who have been striking since August 3.

• On November 23, President Reagan vetoes a bill to pay for the current operation of the federal government. Congress votes to continue funding at present levels and the president signs the bill.

1982

• The United States adopts a Defense Guidance Plan, which outlines a $1.6 trillion increase in defense expenditures over a five-year period.

• On January 26, in his State of the Union Address, President Reagan proposes a "New Federalism," a transfer of social programs to the states.

• On February 15, the National Savings and Loan League asks Congress to provide the financially distressed industry with a $15.5 billion bailout.

• On June 30, the proposed Equal Rights Amendment is defeated after failing to be ratified from the required thirty-eight states. The amendment fell three states short of ratification.

• On August 5, the United States House of Representatives votes down a nuclear-freeze resolution.

• On August 19, Congress approves a tax increase of $98.3 billion.

• On December 3, unemployment reaches 10.8 percent, the highest rate since 1940.

• On December 8, Congressman Edward Boland (D-Mass.) successfully sponsors an amendment making it illegal to use U.S. funds to overthrow the Sandinista government of Nicaragua. Congress renews the amendment in 1983, 1984, and 1985, extending it through the 1986 fiscal year.

• On December 23, Congress approves a five-cent-per-gallon gasoline tax increase.

1983

• On January 21, President Reagan tells Congress that El Salvador has made progress in reducing human rights abuses and is therefore entitled to military aid.

• On March 21, William D. Ruckelshaus is named to head to Environmental Protection Agency, replacing Anne Gorsuch Burford, who resigned on March 9.

• On March 23, President Reagan proposes the development of a space defense shield to intercept incoming missiles. Formally called the Strategic Defense Initiative (SDI), this proposal becomes popularly known as "Star War."

• On March 25, Congress passes legislation to prevent the Social Security system from going bankrupt.

• In April, the American public learns that the CIA assisted a Contra attack on Nicaraguan oil terminals.

• On May 14, President Reagan refuses to pardon Watergate felons Jeb Stuart Magruder and E. Howard Hunt, Jr.

• On July 28, Congress repeals the 10 percent withholding tax on dividend and interest income.

• On September 1, Senator Henry M. "Scoop" Jackson of Washington State dies at the age of seventy-one. One the last New Deal Democrats, Jackson served almost forty-three years in Congress.

• On October 9, the embattled United States Secretary of the Interior James G. Watt resigns from the Reagan administration.

• On November 2, President Reagan signs into law a bill designating the third Monday in January as a federal holiday in honor of Reverend Martin Luther King.

1984

• On January 11, a blue-ribbon presidential commission headed by former secretary of state Henry Kissinger recommends an $8 billion increase in economic assistance and further military aid for El Salvador.

• On January 22, Attorney General William French Smith resigns pending congressional approval of his successor, Edwin Meese III, whose confirmation hearings are suspended in March pending an inquiry into his financial dealings.

• On April 10, by a vote of 84-12, the Senate passes a nonbinding resolution opposing the use of federal funds to mine Nicaraguan harbors. Two days later the House approves it by 281–111.

• On July 6, the unemployment rate falls to 7 percent the lowest since the spring of 1980.

• On July 17, Congress passes a bill that cuts federal highway funding for states that fail to raise their minimum drinking age to twenty-one.

• On July 18, the Democratic National Convention nominates former Vice President Walter Mondale for president. The next day, the convention nominates Representative Geraldine A. Ferraro of New York for vice president.

• On July 25, President Reagan says that Mondale and Ferraro are "so far to the left they've left America."

• On August 22, the Republican National Convention renominates President Ronald Reagan and Vice President George H. Bush.

• On October 1, Secretary of Labor Raymond J. Donovan is indicted on charges of grand larceny and keeping false records.

• On November 6, President Reagan is elected to a second term in a landslide victory over Democrat Walter Mondale, who wins only the District of Columbia and his home state of Minnesota. The margin of the Reagan victory is the second largest in American history.

• On December 4, the United States House Ethics Committee finds that as a member of Congress Geraldine Ferraro violated House rules by not reporting the personal income of her husband.

• On December 5, the United States House Intelligence Committee charges that the CIA violated federal law in some of its aid to Contra rebels.

1985

• On January 8, President Reagan announces that White House Chief of Staff James A. Baker III and Treasury Secretary Donald T. Regan will trade jobs.

• On January 20, President Reagan takes the oath of office marking the beginning of his second term. Because of the bitter cold, public ceremonies are postponed until January 21.

- On February 6, in his State of the Union Address, President Reagan calls for cuts in domestic spending and more military spending.

- On February 23, the United States Senate confirms Meese's appointment as attorney general more than a year after his nomination.

- On April 23, former North Carolina Senator Sam Ervin, who headed the Senate Select Committee on Watergate, dies in Winston-Salem at the age of eighty-eight.

- On May 1, the United States bans trade with Nicaragua.

- On May 28, President Reagan announces his plan to overhaul the federal tax code.

- In July, at the urging of the Reagan administration, Congress repeals the Clark Amendment of 1975, which has prevented the United States from aiding either side in the Angolan civil war. The Reagan administration begins sending aid to the UNITA faction, which is also backed by France, Saudi Arabia, and South Africa.

- On July 13, President Reagan undergoes abdominal surgery to remove cancer from his large intestine. He is out of the hospital in two weeks.

- On August 29, President Reagan orders a fifteen-month freeze on the pay of federal civil servants.

- On October 28, AFL-CIO President Lane Kirkland, at the federation's thirtieth anniversary celebration, calls President Reagan an "enemy of labor," along with the "bastards" at the National Labor Relations Board.

- On November 27, the Dow Jones Industrial Averages closes at a record high of 1475.69.

- On December 11, Congress passes the Gramm-Rudman Act requiring a balanced federal budget.

1986

- On January 28, President Reagan's public opinion approval rating is 65 percent.

- On January 31, the Dow Jones Industrial Average reaches a record high of 1570.99.

- On February 11, the Equal Employment Opportunity Commission (EEOC), under the direction of Chairman Clarence Thomas, abandons the use of hiring quotas to compensate for job discrimination.

- On March 1, pursuant to the Gramm-Rudman balanced-budget act of 1985, appropriations to hundreds of federal programs are cut by 4.3 percent.

- On June 25, the United States House of Representatives approves $100 million in humanitarian and economic aid to the Contras.

- On July 7, the United States Supreme Court rules that a key provision of the Gramm-Rudman Act that provides for automatic spending cuts violates the separation of powers because its vests executive authority in the legislative comptroller general office.

- On July 23, EEOC Chairman Thomas, in reaction to a recent United States Supreme Court decision, states that his agency will resume hiring quotas to counter job discrimination.

- On August 4, President Reagan declares a "national mobilization" against illegal drug use.

- On September 15, President Reagan orders drug testing for federal employees in sensitive jobs.

- On September 17, the United States Senate confirms Antonin Scalia to the United States Supreme Court and William H. Rehnquist as Chief Justice.

- On September 27, Congress passes the most sweeping tax-reform bill since the 1940s. The act reduces the number of income tax brackets for individuals and businesses and lowers the maximum tax rates.

- On October 2, Congress overrides President Reagan's veto of the Comprehensive Anti-Apartheid Act, which condemns racial separation in South Africa, institutes an embargo on most South African imports, and bans most American investment in that nation.

- On October 3, Congress passes legislation requiring schools to inspect for asbestos hazards and to protect against related health risks.

- On October 17, President Reagan signs into law a $9 billion Superfund toxic waste cleanup bill.

- On October 27, as part of his "War on Drugs," President Reagan signs into law a $1.7 billion bill to combat illegal drugs.

- On November 3, a Lebanese newspaper with ties to Iran reveals that contrary to its stated policy of not negotiating with terrorists, the United States has been trading arms for hostages.

- On November 6, President Reagan signs a sweeping immigration law reform bill that prohibits the hiring of illegal aliens and offers amnesty to those already in the United States.

- On November 13, President Reagan says the United States has sent Iran a few defensive weapons and spare parts, but he denies any attempt to exchange weapons for hostages.

- On November 19, President Reagan acknowledges missile sales to Iran and asks Attorney General Edwin Meese to investigate.

- On November 23, Attorney General Meese announces that he has discovered that proceeds from the sale of arms to Iran have been diverted to the Contras.

- On November 26, President Reagan appoints former senator John Tower, former secretary of state Edmund Muskie, and former national security adviser Brent Scowcroft as a commission to investigate what has become know as the Iran-Contra affair.

1987

- On January 8, President Reagan recovers from prostate surgery and undergoes a battery tests to diagnosis the possible reoccurrence of intestinal cancer.

- On January 8, the Dow Jones Industrial Average for the first time in history surpasses the 2000 mark to reach 2002.25.

- On February 4, Congress overrides President Reagan's veto of a $20 billion Clean Water Act. It is identical to an act he vetoed successfully in 1986.

- On February 26, the Tower Commission report places chief blame for the Iran-Contra affair on National Security Council director Robert McFarlane, Lt. Col. Oliver North, Adm. John Poindexter, and former CIA director William Casey. It also criticizes the president for remaining too remote from the planning process.

- On February 27, White House Chief-of-Staff Donald Regan resigns over his role in the Iran-Contra scandal and is replaced by former Senate majority leader Howard Baker of Tennessee.

- On March 4, in a televised speech President Reagan accepts "full responsibility" for the Iran-Contra affair. At a March 19 news conference he denies knowing that profits from Iranian arms sales went to the Contras.

- On April 2, Congress overrides President Reagan's veto of an $87.5 billion highway and transit bill that also allows states to raise speed limits to 65 mph on interstate highways in sparsely populated areas.

- On April 17, President Reagan imposes a 100 percent import tariff worth $300 million on personal computers, television sets, and power tools from Japan in response to allegations that Japan violated an export agreement on computer chips.

- From May 5 to August 3, Congress holds public hearings on the Iran-Contra affair.

- On May 8, Democratic presidential frontrunner Senator Gary Hart of Colorado pulls out of the race after reports of infidelity aboard the sailboat "Monkey Business."

- On October 19, the Dow Jones Industrial Average plummets 508.32 points, ending the bull market that had risen steadily since August 1982.

- On October 23, the United States Senate rejects the nomination of the conservative jurist Robert Bork to the United States Supreme Court.

- On November 11, President Reagan nominates Anthony M. Kennedy to the Supreme Court. He is confirmed on February 2 1988.

- On November 18, in its final report on the Iran-Contra hearings, Congress criticizes those involved in the operation for "secrecy, deception and disdain for the law."

- From December 8 to December 10, during a summit meeting in Washington, D.C., President Reagan and Premier Gorbachev sign the Intermediate Nuclear Forces (INF) Treaty, agreeing to eliminate intermediate-range weapons from their nuclear arsenals.

1988

- On January 15, President Reagan is given a clean bill of health after his annual physical reveals no reoccurrence of colon or intestinal cancer.

- On February 3, the United States Senate unanimously confirms the politically liberal Judge Kennedy to the United States Supreme Court.

- On February 4, two federal grand juries in Florida indict Panamanian dictator Manuel Noriega on drug-trafficking charges.

- On March 11, Robert McFarlane pleads guilty on four counts of illegally withholding information from Congress in connection with the Iran-Contra affair. On March 3, 1989, he is sentenced to two years' probation and fined twenty thousand dollars.

- On March 16, a federal grand jury in Washington, D.C., indicts Poindexter, North, and two others on charges relating to their involvement in the Iran-Contra affair.

- On March 22, Congress overrides President Reagan's veto of the Civil Rights Restoration Act, which extends federal antibias laws to an entire school or other organization if any of its programs receive federal funding.

- On March 29, two top Justice Department officials resign over concerns with the investigation into alleged legal violations committed by Attorney General Meese.

- On April 8, President Reagan freezes all Panamanian assets in the United States.

- On July 1, President Reagan signs legislation expanding Medicare to protect the handicapped and elderly from "catastrophic" medical costs.

- On July 5, Attorney General Meese resigns, claiming that although he has been "completely exonerated" by James C. McKay, the independent prosecutor investigating his finances, the lengthy investigation has undermined his support on Capitol Hill.

- On July 13, Congress passes a bill requiring a sixty-day notice to employees of plant closings or large layoffs.

- On July 18, independent prosecutor McKay issues a report stating that Meese "probably" violated the law four times while in office by allowing a false income-tax return to be filed for him, late payment of capital gains taxes, and twice violating conflict-of-interest laws.

- On July 20, the Democratic National Convention nominates Massachusetts Governor Michael S. Dukakis for President.

- On July 28, a national poll shows that Democratic presidential nominee Dukakis holds a 51 percent to 37 percent lead over Vice President George H. Bush for president.

- On August 10, President Reagan signs a bill that extends a national apology and reparations to Japanese-Americans interned during World War II.

- On August 18, the Republican National Convention nominates Vice-President George H. Bush for president and Senator Daniel Quayle of Indiana for vice president.

- On September 13, President Reagan signs a bill extending the Fair Housing Act of 1968 to protect the disabled and families with children.

- On October 22, Congress passes a Taxpayer's Bill of Rights for taxpayers in dealing with the Internal Revenue Serivice.

- On October 26, President Reagan pocket vetos the Whistleblowers bill which would have protected the federal workforce from retribution for exposing waste, fraud, and abuse. The measure had passed both houses of Congress without a dissenting vote.

- On November 8, Republican George Bush is elected president, defeating Democrat Michael Dukakis by a margin of 53.4 to 45.6 percent.
- On December 12, President Reagan blames the increase of the federal budget and budget deficit on the "iron triangle" consisting of Congress, the press, and special interest groups.

1989

- On January 14, President Reagan, in his final national radio address, boasts that the "economy is booming," domestic problems are under control, and the "Soviet menace show some signs of relenting."
- On January 18, a national poll shows that President Reagan leaves office with a 68 percent approval rating. This is the highest approval rating of any outgoing president since 1945.
- On January 20, George H. Bush is inaugurated president of the United States.
- On March 9, the United States Senate confirms William J. Bennett as the first director of the cabinet-level Office of National Drug Control Policy.
- On March 9, the United States Senate rejects John Tower's nomination as secretary of defense by a margin of 53-47.
- On April 10, President Bush signs into law the Whistle-blower Protection Act, which had previously been vetoed by President Reagan.
- On April 17, House Speaker James C. Wright, Jr., is charged by the House Ethics Committee with accepting improper gifts and violating rules that limit outside income.

- On May 4, in the Iran-Contra affair, Oliver North is found guilty on three felony charges: obstructing a congressional inquiry, destroying documents, and accepting an illegal gift. On July 5 he is fined twenty thousand dollars, given a three-year suspended prison sentence, placed on probation for two years, and ordered to perform twelve hundred hours of community service. Poindexter's trial is set to begin in January 1990.
- On May 19, for the first time since the stock market crash of 1987, the Dow Jones Industrial Average surpasses the 2,500 mark.
- On June 13, President Bush vetoes a bill that would raise the minimum wage to $4.55 a hour. He states that the bill would have cost young Americans thousands of jobs.
- On August 9, President Bush signs into law a $166 billion bill to bailout the savings and loan industry. It is the largest federal rescue bill in United States history.
- On November 8, Congress passes a compromise minimum wage bill, raising it to $4.25 by 1991. However, it sets a lower minimum wage for teenagers. President Bush signs it into law on November 17.
- On December 22, the United States Senate Ethics Committee begins formal inquiries into the collapse of the Lincoln Savings and Loan Association. The investigation centers on allegations that Senators Allan Cranston of California, John Glenn of Ohio, John McCain of Arizona, Donald W. Riegle of Michigan, and Dennis DeConcini of Arizona acted improperly.

Edward M. Kennedy's Speech on Economic Issues, 1980 Democratic Convention

Speech

By: Ted Kennedy

Date: August 12, 1980

Source: Kennedy, Ted. "Transcript of Kennedy's Speech on Economic Issues at Democratic Convention." *The New York Times,* August 13, 1980.

About the Author: Ted Kennedy (1932–) was born in Boston, Massachusetts, the youngest of Joseph and Rose Kennedy's nine children. After high school graduation, Kennedy entered the U.S. Army, serving from 1951 to 1953. After leaving the army, Kennedy graduated from Harvard and the University of Virginia Law School. In 1962, he was elected to the U.S. Senate to finish the term of his older brother, President John F. Kennedy (served 1961–1963). He since has been re-elected to seven terms, and he is the third most senior member of the Senate. ∎

Introduction

In 1978, Democratic voters favored Senator Edward "Ted" Kennedy (D-Mass) by an astounding 2-to-1 margin over his rival, incumbent President Jimmy Carter (served 1977–1981) for the 1980 Democratic presidential nomination. Carter was unpopular because the nation was besieged by high interest rates, unemployment, a faltering economy, and high gasoline prices. At one point, the president's approval ratings plummeted to twenty-six percent, lower than President Richard Nixon's during the Watergate scandal.

On July 15, 1979, Carter stated in a national address to the American people that the nation was suffering from a "crisis of confidence." Many Americans believed that the president was causing the suffering, at least in part. Among those who held this opinion was Senator Kennedy. In 1972 and 1976, Kennedy, in light of past ethical lapses, had refused to run for president despite polls showing that he was the overwhelming Democratic favorite. Despite his past, however, Kennedy announced that he would challenge Carter for the party nomination in November 1979. In response, Carter said, "I'll whip his ass."

The Carter-Kennedy campaign was fascinating. Rarely do candidates with such an important power base in Washington as Kennedy's challenge an incumbent president of their own party. Moreover, Kennedy and Carter were very different kinds of men. Carter was a rural southerner from Georgia who did not readily identify with ethnic groups or labor unions—the core constituencies of the Democratic Party. In turn, Kennedy was a political product of the urban, multi-ethnic, labor-dominated Northeast. Unfortunately for Kennedy, four days after he declared his candidacy, Iranian militants seized the U.S. embassy in Tehran, taking fifty-two hostages. The crisis temporarily improved Carter's public standing, as Americans rallied around their president. Although Carter's approval ratings began to tumble again in March 1980, Kennedy was unable to capture enough primary delegates to win the nomination. At the Democratic convention in August, Carter was nominated on the first ballot—but the convention's high point was Kennedy's rousing concession speech.

Significance

Following Kennedy's concession speech, Convention Chairman Tip O'Neil could not bring the rowdy convention to order. For thirty-five minutes, unyielding cheers of "We Want Ted! We Want Ted!" reverberated within Madison Square Garden. To Kennedy supporters, Carter may have defeated their hero in the primaries, but they would return the favor on the convention floor when adopting the party's platform.

Unlike the Democratic National Convention in 1976, Carter had no ideological control over the delegates. He was at the mercy of Democratic Party regulars—elected officials and labor unions prepared to draft a party platform somewhat more liberal than Carter, and considerably more liberal than the American public. For the next seventeen hours, delegates fiercely debated twenty unresolved issues on the convention floor. In the end, Kennedy supporters won several major concessions, including provisions that seemingly repudiated the Carter record. For example, the platform called for a twelve billion dollar anti-recession program to create 800,000 new jobs. In a jab at Carter, it stated that the party would not pursue a policy of high interest rates and unemployment to fight inflation. The platform also opposed a balanced budget constitutional amendment. On social issues, the platform called for federal funding of abortions—a position Carter opposed, while supporting legal abortion. For the first time in American political convention history, the platform specifically opposed discrimination based on "sexual orientation." The platform also called for

Senator Ted Kennedy waves to the crowd at the Democratic Convention, August 12, 1980. © BETTMANN/CORBIS. REPRODUCED BY PERMISSION.

universal health insurance and, against Carter's objections, denied support to all candidates not supporting the Equal Rights Amendment.

In the end, the platform was so skewed to the party's liberal base that it alienated America's middle class. Carter had no choice but to endorse the platform, however halfheartedly. The platform—together with the wide appeal of Ronald Reagan's (served 1981–1989) conservative message, the continuing Iran hostage crisis, and the third party candidacy of John Anderson—contributed to Carter becoming the first incumbent to lose the presidency since Herbert Hoover (served 1929–1933) in 1932.

Primary Source

Edward M. Kennedy's Speech on Economic Issues, 1980 Democratic Convention [excerpt]

SYNOPSIS: On August 12, 1980, Ted Kennedy gave one of the most notable political speeches of his career. Drawing on traditional Democratic themes enunciated by Woodrow Wilson (served 1913–1921), Franklin D. Roosevelt (served 1933–1945), and his brother, John F. Kennedy (served 1961–63), Senator Kennedy, in a subtle jab at President Carter, said, "let us offer new hope, new hope to an Amer-

ica uncertain about the present, but unsurpassed in its potential for the future."

Fairness and Compassion

The commitment I seek is not to out-worn views, but to old values that will never wear out. Programs may sometimes become obsolete, but the ideal of fairness always endures. Circumstances may change but the work of compassion must continue. It is surely correct that we cannot solve problems by throwing money at them, but it is also correct that we dare not throw out our national problems onto a scrap heap of inattention and indifference. The poor may be out of political fashion, but they are not without human needs. The middle class may be angry, but they have not lost the dream that all Americans can advance together.

The demand of our people in 1980 is not for smaller government or bigger government but for better government. Some say that government is always bad and that spending for basic social programs is the root of our economic evils. But we reply, the present inflation and recession costs our economy $200 billion a year. We reply, inflation and unemployment are the biggest spenders of all.

The task of leadership in 1980 is not to parade scapegoats or to seek refuge in reaction but to match our power to the possibilities of progress.

While others talked of free enterprise, it was the Democratic Party that acted—and we ended excessive regulation in the airline and trucking industry. We restored competition to the marketplace. And I take some satisfaction that this deregulation legislation that I sponsored and passed in the Congress of the United States.

As Democrats, we recognize that each generation of Americans has a rendevous with a different reality. The answers of one generation become the questions of the next generation, but there is a guiding star in the American firmament. It is as old as the revolutionary belief that all people are created equal, and as clear as the contemporary condition of Liberty City and the South Bronx. Again and again, Democratic leaders have followed that star, and they have given new meaning to the old values of liberty and justice for all.

We are the party of the New Freedom, the New Deal and the New Frontier. We have always been the party of hope. So this year, let us offer new hope—new hope to an America uncertain about the present but unsurpassed in its potential for the future.

To all those who are idle in the cities and industries of America, let us provide new hope for the dignity of useful work. Democrats have always believed that a basic civil right of all Americans is that their right to earn their own way. The party of the people must always be the party of full employment.

To all those who doubt the future of our economy, let us provide new hope for the reindustrialization of America. And let our vision reach beyond the next election or the next year to a new generation of prosperity. If we could rebuild Germany and Japan after World War II, then surely we can reindustrialize our own nation and revive our inner cities in the 1980's.

To all those who work hard for a living wage, let us provide new hope that their price of their employment shall not be an unsafe work place and a death at an earlier age.

To all those who inhabit our land, from California to the New York island, from the Redwood forest to the Gulf Stream waters, let us provide new hope that prosperity shall not be purchased by poisoning the air, the rivers and the natural resources that are the greatest gift of this continent.

Further Resources

BOOKS

Clymer, Adam. *Edward M. Kennedy: A Biography*. New York: Perennial, 2000.

Drew, Elizabeth. *Portrait of an Election: The 1980 Presidential Campaign*. New York: Simon and Schuster, 1981.

Leamer, Laurence. *The Kennedy Men: 1901-1963*. New York: Harper, 2002.

PERIODICALS

Cadden, Vivian. "What Happened at Chappaquiddick." *McCall's*, August 1974.

Honan, William H. "The Kennedy Network." *The New York Times Magazine*, June 17, 1979.

WEBSITES

The Carter Center. Available online at http://www.cartercenter.org (accessed June 9, 2003).

"Senator Edward M. Kennedy: Online Office." *United States Senate*. Available online at http://kennedy.senate.gov (accessed June 9, 2003).

The Holloway Report

Report

By: James Holloway

Date: August 23, 1980

Source: Holloway, James. *The Holloway Report*. Joint Chiefs of Staff, August 23, 1980. Available online at http://www.gwu.edu/~nsarchiv/NSAEBB/NSAEBB63/doc8.pdf; website home page: http://www.gwu.edu (accessed June 9, 2003).

About the Author: Admiral James L. Holloway (1922–) was born in Charleston, South Carolina, the son of a naval admiral. Holloway graduated from the U.S. Naval Academy in 1942, and during World War II (1939–1945), he earned a Bronze Star as a gunnery officer in the Pacific theater. After the war, Holloway became a jet fighter, earning the Distinguished Flying Cross in two tours of combat in the Korean War (1950–1953). In 1974, he became the Chief of Naval Operations until his retirement four years later. Holloway led an investigation into the failed rescue attempt to free hostages held in Iran, issuing "The Holloway Report" to the Joint Chiefs of Staff on August 23, 1980. ∎

Introduction

In 1953, the Central Intelligence Agency (CIA) launched Operation Ajax to prevent the nationalization of Iranian petroleum reserves and the elimination of that country's existing monarchy. In doing so, the covert operation assisted in the overthrow of Iranian premier Mohammed Mossadeq, a strong proponent of Iranian nationalism, and the installation of Muhammad Reza Pahlavi to the royal seat. Pahlavi, commonly known as "the shah of Iran," had previously opposed Mossadeq before fleeing the country. He acquired U.S. support and returned to Iran as a key player in the CIA's overthrow plans. As a bulwark against communism, the shah served as an important ally to the United States in the Cold War. He also served as a major purchaser of U.S. military goods and provider of oil. Both the United States and the shah benefitted significantly from their relationship.

Within Iran, however, the shah and the United States were unpopular. To consolidate his power, the shah repressed opposition political parties and restricted the press. The CIA-trained secret police, the SAVAK, was particularly unpopular as it brutally suppressed the shah's opponents. Additionally, widespread government corruption and rapid inflation sparked economic discontent. Reform efforts proved ineffective until the land reform, electoral law changes, and other initiatives implemented in the shah's White Revolution. These measures pleased a large sector of the public, but failed to improve conditions for the poorer classes. Muslim clerics in particular objected to women being granted the right to vote. The shah's pro-Western orientation angered many Muslim religious leaders in Iran, who believed that Islamic and Iranian cultural values and identity were being undermined by Western influences. In 1963, Ayatollah Sayyid Ruhollah Musavi Khomeini, a religious leader, gave a speech in which he fervently and directly attacked the shah's leadership. He was arrested and three days of rioting ensued before being fiercely suppressed.

Iranian army officers and Ayatollah Sadegh Khalkali view the wreckage of a U.S. C-130 cargo plane used in the aborted commando raid to rescue U.S. embassy hostages. **AP/WIDE WORLD PHOTOS. REPRODUCED BY PERMISSION.**

After being released from jail, Khomeini continued to speak out against the shah. He was exiled from Iran, but persisted in voicing his opposition to the government. While Khomeini was in exile, underground groups formed in Iran. Young people, discontent with what they perceived to be the ineffectiveness of the legal opposition to the U.S.-backed shah and inspired by guerrilla efforts elsewhere in the world, formed two main groups—the Marxist Fedayan and the religious-based Mojahedin. Public unrest and violence increased along with the shah's unpopularity, and large-scale demonstrations resulted from the mistrust and alienation felt across the stratas of Iranian society. When Khomeini returned to Iran in 1979, he was welcomed by millions of enthusiastic Iranians who felt that he could effect change. Members of the military approached him with their loyalty and urged him to affect a coup against the shah.

Revolutionaries in the underground, emboldened by Khomeini's return, took to the streets. The army withdrew from fighting the insurrection, effectively signalling its lack of support for the government. This resulted in a general uprising from which the shah fled and Khomeini became the ultimate ruler. President Jimmy Carter (served 1977–1981) admitted the deposed shah, who was suffering from cancer, into the United States for medical treatment. Fearing that previous U.S. support for the shah—and the coup that led him to power—might replay itself, Khomeini, on November 4, 1979, denounced the United States as the "Great Satan" and ordered 400-armed radicals to seize the U.S. Embassy in Tehran. Fifty-two Americans were taken hostage. For the next fourteen months, the Iranian hostage crisis paralyzed the Carter administration. Each night, pictures of blindfolded hostages were beamed to television sets throughout the world.

Significance

In April 1980, eight Sea Stallion helicopters took off from the USS *Nimitz* in the Gulf of Oman to carry out Operation Eagle Claw. Ninety members of Delta Force were flown six hundred miles at night and at low altitude to a refueling site in the Iranian desert. From there, the men were to be airlifted by helicopter to Tehran and rescue the hostages. During the operation mechanical problems grounded three helicopters. With only five operational helicopters, the mission was cancelled. As the forces withdrew, a C-130 transport aircraft collided with a helicopter, killing eight servicemen. After that, ammunition aboard the aircraft exploded, damaging several helicopters. The Sea Stallions were abandoned, and their crews transported back to the *Nimitz* aboard the remaining C-130s. The next day, Americans watched triumphant Iranian broadcasts showing captured American military equipment and charred aircraft shells.

The disastrous hostage rescue attempt was symbolic of the United States' perceived military impotence, particularly in Special Forces operations, in decline throughout the 1970s. In domestic politics, the catastrophe further eroded the public's confidence in the U.S. government, especially in the Carter administration. Although the failing national economy was the primary issue in the 1980 presidential election, President Carter's handling of the Iranian crisis played a vital role in his loss to Ronald Reagan (served 1981–1989). While Eagle Claw contributed to Carter's image as a weak, ineffectual leader, it was probably fortunate that the mission was aborted. The military projected that if the operation had proceeded, numerous hostages and rescuers would have been killed and that the more than 200 Americans remaining in Tehran would have been taken hostage. Eagle Claw was not a complete disaster, as it forced the Department of Defense to reform Special Operations forces. The lessons learned from Eagle Claw were instrumental to the future successes of Operation Just Cause in Panama, Desert Shield/Desert Storm in Iraq and Kuwait, Joint Endeavor in Bosnia, Enduring Freedom in Afghanistan, and Iraqi Freedom.

Primary Source

The Holloway Report

SYNOPSIS: After the Eagle Claw catastrophe, the Joint Chiefs of Staff commissioned a Special Operations Review group, headed by Admiral James L. Holloway III, to examine the hostage rescue mission as a basis for recommending future improvement. The report, which was released on August 23, 1980, revealed significant failings in planning, training, and equipment.

IV. Conclusions

The conclusions drawn in this chapter derive from the determination of fact presented in Chapter II and the analysis of issues discussed in Chapter III.

Specific Conclusions

The concept of a small clandestine operation was valid and consistent with national policy objectives.

The review group concludes that the concept of a small, clandestine operation was sound. A larger, overt attempt would probably have resulted in the death of the hostages before they could be reached. It offered the best chance of getting the hostages out alive and the least danger of starting a war with Iran. Further, the large-scale military thrust required by an overt operation would have triggered early hostile reaction, possibly resulting in widespread Iranian casualties and giving strong credence to probably Iranian allegations that the rescue attempt was an act of war. Conversely, a small operation with Iranian casualties essentially limited to the act of freeing the hostages would have better supported the contention that it was a rescue, not a punitive raid.

The operation was feasible and probably represented the plan with the best chance of success at the time the mission was launched.

Despite all the complexities, the inherent difficulties, and the human and equipment performance required, the review group unanimously concludes that the risks were manageable, the overall probability of success good, and the operation feasible. Under these conditions, decision to execute was justified.

The plan for the unexecuted portion of the mission was soundly conceived and capable of successful execution. It appeared to be better than other alternatives—a realistic option with the best chance for success at the time of mission execution. Based upon the review group's visit with the ground rescue force and a comparison with the capabilities of CT forces of other nations, it appears that selection, training, and equipment of the ground forces were excellent.

The group believes it virtually impossible to precisely appraise the remaining part of the operation and to measure probability of success. During that portion of the mission, the inevitability of hostile reaction would have become a major factor. The dynamics inherent in a recovery of the type envisioned would have produced a level of complexity that makes the study of probabilities essentially a matter of conjecture.

The rescue mission was a high-risk operation.

The mission had to be considered high risk because people and equipment were called upon to perform at the upper limits of human capacity and equipment capability. There was little margin to compensate for mistakes or plain bad luck.

Furthermore, possible measures to reduce the high risk factor could conceivably introduce new elements of risk. For example, the JTF considered that adding more helicopters and crews to improve the chances of having more helicopters en route would result in an unnecessary increase in the OPSEC risk. A delay in execution for additional training could increase the risk.

The first realistic capability to successfully accomplish the rescue of the hostages was reached at the end of March.

Confidence in the probability of mission success grew after the final training exercise in the western United States. With the possible exception of several items of communications equipment, essentially all mechanical means used in the rescue operation—helicopters, aircraft, and special equipment—were available on 4 November 1979.

OPSEC was an overriding requirement for a successful operation.

Rescue depended upon surprising the captors in the Embassy compound before the hostages could be harmed. If this surprise could not be achieved, the mission would fail—either canceled or aborted, with high probability of the hostages being removed or executed. Further, recognizing the importance of the element of surprise, the group is reluctant to criticize, even constructively, the OPSEC standards for being too strict, as secrecy was successfully preserved until after withdrawal of the aircraft from Iran.

Nevertheless, throughout the planning and execution phases, decisions were made and actions taken or not taken because of OPSEC that the group believed could have been done differently. Furthermore, most, if not all, of the suggested alternatives could have been implemented without an adverse OPSEC impact had there been a more precise OPSEC plan developed early after the formation of the JTF organization and with specific responsibilities assigned.

Command and control was excellent at the upper echelons, but became more tenuous and fragile at the intermediate level.

The command and control arrangements at the higher echelons from the NCA through the Joint Chiefs of Staff to COMJTF were ideal. Further down the operational chain, command relationships were less well defined and not as well understood.

External resources adequately supported the JTF and were not a limiting factor.

The effectiveness of the special supply system for the helicopters was commendable, especially considering the problems imposed by OPSEC.

Planning was adequate except for the number of backup helicopters and the provisions for weather contingencies.

More helicopters aboard NIMITZ would have increased the chances of the required number of "Up" helicopters being available at each stage of the operation. Additional RH-53Ds with crews could have been deployed to NIMITZ without crowding or impacting other mission requirements if the carrier and without a reduction in OPSEC. The use of C-130 aircraft to lead the Rh-53 flight to Desert One would have decreased the probability of a mission abort due to weather. C-130 pathfinders and spare RH-53Ds could have been added to the mission without requiring additional fuel at Desert One.

Preparation for the mission was adequate except for the lack of comprehensive, full-scale training.

OPSEC considerations mitigated against such a rehearsal and, while the review group recognized the inherent risk in bringing all of the forces together in the western US training site, the possible security disadvantages of such a rehearsal seem to be outweighed by the advantages to be gained.

Increasing familiarity of element leaders with one another, both during the operation and in the ensuing debriefing critique.

Exposing the command and control relationships to the pressures of a full-scale combination of airplanes, helicopters, troops, and vehicles, maneuvering in the crowded parking area under the confusing conditions of noise, dust, and darkness.

Two factors combined to directly cause the mission abort: Unexpected helicopter failure rate, and low visibility flight conditions en route to Desert One.

If the dust phenomenon had not occurred, Helicopter #5 would have arrived at Desert One, or if one more helicopter had remained up, six would have arrived at Desert One despite the dust.

There were alternatives available that would have reduced the probability of an abort due to these factors, and they have been discussed in detail in terms of planning and preparation.

The siting of Desert One near a road probably represented a higher risk than indicated by the JTF assessment.

The intrusion of the Iranian vehicles at Desert One significantly increased the chances of Iranians' identifying the intent and timing of the operation. Although there was a workable plan to handle the bus passengers, the burned-out truck, empty bus, and abandoned heavy-lift helicopter near a well-traveled road could have resulted in early discovery by Iranian authorities. The group, however, realizes that the location may have been the best available.

General Conclusions

Although the specific conclusions cover a broad range of issues relating to the Terms of Reference, two fundamental concerns emerge in the review group's consensus which are related to most of the major issues:

The ad hoc nature of the organization and planning is related to most of the major issues and underlies the group's conclusions.

By not utilizing an existing JTF organization, even with a small staff and only cadre units assigned, would have provided an organizational framework of professional expertise around which a larger tailored force organization could quickly coalesce.

The important point is that the infrastructure would have existed—the trusted agents, the built-in OPSEC, the secure communications. At a minimum, COMJTF would have had a running start and could have devoted more hours to plans, operations, and tactics rather than to administration and logistics

Operations Security

Many things, which in the opinion of the review group could have been done to enhance mission success, were not done because of strict OPSEC considerations. The review group considers that most of these alternatives could have been incorporated without an adverse OPSEC impact had there been a more precise OPSEC plan. A carefully structured JTF organization would have inherently provided an OPSEC environment within which a selective process could have allowed a wider initial disclosure policy—still a very stringent need-to-know policy—but based upon selective disclosure rather than minimum disclosure.

Further Resources

BOOKS

Beckwith, Charlie A., and Donald Know. *Delta Force.* San Diego: Harcourt, Brace, and Jovanovich, 1983.

Bolger, Daniel P. *Americans At War 1975-1986: An Era of Violent Peace.* Navato, Calif.: Presidio Press, 1988.

Sick, Gary. *All Fall Down: America's Tragic Encounter with Iran.* New York: Random House, 1985.

PERIODICALS

"Another Rescue Mission: Special Report." *Newsweek,* vol. 95, no. 19, May 12, 1980, 26–53.

Brzezinski, Zbignew. "The Failed Mission." *The New York Times Magazine,* April 18, 1982, 28–31.

WEBSITES

"Iran Hostage Crisis." University of St. Francis. Available online at http://www.stfrancis.edu/hi/victa/stuweb/~tl8241/id26.htm; website home page: http://www.stfrancis.edu (accessed June 9, 2003).

"Operation Eagle Claw." *Federation of American Scientists.* Available online at http://www.fas.org/man/dod-101/ops/eagle_claw.htm; website home page: http://www.fas.org (accessed June 9, 2003).

Executive Order 12291

Executive order

By: Ronald Reagan

Date: February 17, 1981

Source: Reagan, Ronald. "Proclamation and Executive Orders dated February 17, 1981." Available online at http://www.reagan.utexas.edu/resource/speeches/1981/21781c.htm; website home page: http://www.reagan.utexas.edu (accessed June 9, 2003). *Contains full text of Executive Order 12291.*

About the Author: Ronald Reagan (1911–) was born in Tampico, Illinois. After graduating from Eureka College, Reagan worked as a sports broadcaster for a Davenport, Iowa radio station. In 1937, while covering spring training in California, Reagan signed a contract with Warner Brothers, a movie studio. Reagan eventually starred in over fifty films. In 1964, he retired from acting and was elected governor of California. In 1980, Reagan was elected president (served 1981–1989). After serving two terms, he retired to his ranch in California. ∎

Introduction

In 1787, the Constitutional Convention at Philadelphia implemented a revolutionary political concept, federalism. Under this concept, more than one level of government exists within the same territory, and each maintains real autonomy over some decision-making. Prior to this time, most political theorists believed that federalism was impossible to achieve because competing sovereigns would eventually battle against each other until one reigned supreme. The Constitutional Convention was convened to reform the Articles of Confederation, the first American charter of government that vested sovereignty within the individual thirteen states. Among the Articles' many problems were that states were too weak to solve their boundary disputes, prevent their neighbors from imposing tariffs on interstate commerce, or financially support the Confederation. In the end, the constitutional delegates scrapped the Articles, creating the first modern federal state with the drafting of the Constitution. The Constitution, while providing for a strong national government, granted states the power to tax,

Ronald Reagan's term in office saw an increase in power handed over to the states. THE LIBRARY OF CONGRESS.

borrow money, pass their own laws, establish their own courts, charter banks, and administer elections.

In the twentieth century, state autonomy came under increasing attack by the federal government. In 1913, the Sixteenth Amendment gave Congress the power to levy income taxes. During the Great Depression, President Franklin Roosevelt (served 1933–1945) broadly expanded federal jurisdiction. With millions of Americans living hand-to-mouth, state governments were unable to cope with the situation. Under the New Deal initiatives, Roosevelt centralized authority in Washington, D.C., by forcing states to cede authority in return for job programs, welfare to mothers with dependent children, and social security to the aged. In the 1960s, President Lyndon Johnson's (served 1963–1969) War on Poverty promoted federally subsidized vocational education, job training, food stamps, Medicare, and Medicaid. The election of President Reagan (served 1981–1989) in 1980 marked the resurgence of conservatism, concluding that after forty years "big government" had failed to effectively deal with poverty and other social ills.

Significance

In 1981, President Ronald Reagan was elected on his promise to "curb the size and influence of the federal es-

tablishment" because "the federal government is not part of the solution, but part of the problem." Instead of empowering Americans, big government had become unsympathetic and unresponsive, its regulations overly burdensome. The president attempted to redefine federalism through *Reaganomics.*

In 1981, Congress passed the largest tax cut in history, partially offset by $39 billion in cuts to food stamps, job training, health services, and other entitlement programs. Instead of using the saved revenue to reduce the national debt, the money was plowed into defense. By 1986, the budget deficit soared to a record $220 billion. The Reagan administration also eliminated many federal regulations affecting the workplace, health care, consumer protection, the environment, and banking—which played a part in the Savings and Loan crisis.

In October 1987, President Reagan issued Executive Order No. 12612, limiting the power of the federal government by stressing adherence to the original intentions of the founding fathers. Nevertheless, after two terms in office, Reagan failed to reduce the size or scope of government. In 1994, for the first time in forty years, the Republicans controlled Congress. Following in Reagan's footsteps, conservatives had successfully campaigned on the issue of reducing the federal government. Two years later, President Bill Clinton (served 1993–2001) declared that "the era of big government is over." Clinton supported welfare reform, giving states greater control in administering the program, and signed legislation preventing the federal government from imposing unfunded mandates on the states. However, in 1998, Clinton issued Executive Order No. 13088, revoking Reagan's earlier order and granting the federal bureaucracy broad powers to intervene in state affairs. Under tremendous political pressure, Clinton withdrew the order a few months later.

Primary Source

Executive Order 12291 [excerpt]

SYNOPSIS: Two days after his inauguration, President Reagan authorized a committee to propose ways of reducing economic and social regulations. On February 17, 1981, Reagan launched his conservative agenda by issuing Executive Order No. 12291, requiring all proposed regulations to be subject to review and cost-benefit analysis prior to approval. By 1983, the number of new proposed regulations declined by one-third.

By the authority vested in me as President by the Constitution and laws of the United States of America, and in order to reduce the burdens of existing and future regulations, increase agency accountability for regulatory actions, provide for presidential oversight of the regulatory process, minimize duplication and conflict of regulations, and insure well-reasoned regulations, it is hereby ordered as follows:

■ ■ ■

Sec. 2. General Requirements. In promulgating new regulations, reviewing existing regulations, and developing legislative proposals concerning regulation, all agencies, to the extent permitted by law, shall adhere to the following requirements:

(a) Administrative decisions shall be based on adequate information concerning the need for and consequences of proposed government action;

(b) Regulatory action shall not be undertaken unless the potential benefits to society from the regulation outweigh the potential costs to society;

(c) Regulatory objectives shall be chosen to maximize the net benefits to society;

(d) Among alternative approaches to any given regulatory objective, the alternative involving the least net cost to society shall be chosen; and

(e) Agencies shall set regulatory priorities with the aim of maximizing the aggregate net benefits to society, taking into account the condition of the particular industries affected by regulations, the condition of the national economy, and other regulatory actions contemplated for the future.

Sec. 3. Regulatory Impact Analysis and Review.

(a) In order to implement Section 2 of this Order, each agency shall, in connection with every major rule, prepare, and to the extent permitted by law consider, a Regulatory Impact Analysis. Such Analyses may be combined with any Regulatory Flexibility Analyses performed under 5 U.S.C. 603 and 604.

(b) Each agency shall initially determine whether a rule it intends to propose or to issue is a major rule, provided that, the Director, subject to the direction of the Task Force, shall have authority, in accordance with Sections 1(b) and 2 of this Order, to prescribe criteria for making such determinations, to order a rule to be treated as a major rule, and to require any set of related rules to be considered together as a major rule.

(c) Except as provided in Section 8 of this Order, agencies shall prepare Regulatory Impact Analyses of major rules and transmit them, along with all notices of proposed rulemaking and all final rules, to the Director as follows:

(1) If no notice of proposed rulemaking is to be published for a proposed major rule that is not an emergency rule, the agency shall prepare only a final Regulatory Impact Analysis, which shall be transmitted, along with the proposed rule, to the Director at least 60 days prior to the publication of the major rule as a final rule;

(2) With respect to all other major rules, the agency shall prepare a preliminary Regulatory Impact Analysis, which shall be transmitted, along with a notice of proposed rulemaking, to the Director at least 60 days prior to the publication of a notice of proposed rulemaking, and a final Regulatory Impact Analysis, which shall be transmitted along with the final rule at least 30 days prior to the publication of the major rule as a final rule;

(3) For all rules other than major rules, agencies shall submit to the Director, at least 10 days prior to publication, every notice of proposed rulemaking and final rule.

(d) To permit each proposed major rule to be analyzed in light of the requirements stated in Section 2 of this Order, each preliminary and final Regulatory Impact Analysis shall contain the following information:

(1) A description of the potential benefits of the rule, including any beneficial effects that cannot be quantified in monetary terms, and the identification of those likely to receive the benefits;

(2) A description of the potential costs of the rule, including any adverse effects that cannot be quantified in monetary terms, and the identification of those likely to bear the costs;

(3) A determination of the potential net benefits of the rule, including an evaluation of effects that cannot be quantified in monetary terms;

(4) A description of alternative approaches that could substantially achieve the same regulatory goal at lower cost, together with an analysis of this potential benefit and costs and a brief explanation of the legal reasons why such alternatives, if proposed, could not be adopted; and

(5) Unless covered by the decription required under paragraph (4) of this subsection, an explanation of any legal reasons why the rule cannot be based on the requirements set forth in Section 2 of this Order.

(e) (1) The Director, subject to the direction of the Task Force, which shall resolve any issues raised under this Order or ensure that they are presented to the President, is authorized to review any preliminary or final Regulatory Impact Analysis, notice of proposed rulemaking, or final rule based on the requirements of this Order.

(2) The Director shall be deemed to have concluded review unless the Director advises an agency to the contrary under subsection (f) of this Section:

(A) Within 60 days of a submission under subsection (c)(1) or a submission of a preliminary Regulatory Impact Analysis or notice of proposed rulemaking under subsection (c)(2);

(B) Within 30 days of the submission of a final Regulatory Impact Analysis and a final rule under subsection (c)(2); and

(C) Within 10 days of the submission of a notice of proposed rulemaking or final rule under subsection (c)(3).

(f) (1) Upon the request of the Director, an agency shall consult with the Director concerning the review of a preliminary Regulatory Impact Analysis or notice of proposed rulemaking under this Order, and shall, subject to Section 8(a)(2) of this Order, refrain from publishing its preliminary Regulatory Impact Analysis or notice of proposed rulemaking until such review is concluded.

(2) Upon receiving notice that the Director intends to submit views with respect to any final Regulatory Impact Analysis or final rule, the agency shall, subject to Section 8(a)(2) of this Order, refrain from publishing its final Regulatory Impact Analysis or final rule until the agency has responded to the Director's views, and incorporated those views and the agency's response in the rulemaking file.

(3) Nothing in this subsection shall be construed to as displacing the agencies' responsibilities delegated by law.

(g) For every rule for which an agency publishes a notice of proposed rulemaking, the agency shall include in its notice:

(1) A brief statement setting forth the agency's initial determination whether the proposed rule is a major rule, together with the reasons underlying that determination; and

(2) For each proposed major rule, a brief summary of the agency's preliminary Regulatory Impact Analysis.

(h) Agencies shall make their preliminary and final Regulatory Impact Analyses available to the public.

(i) Agencies shall initiate reviews of currently effective rules in accordance with the purposes of this Order, and perform Regulatory Impact Analyses of currently effective major rules. The Director, subject to the direction of the Task Force, may designate currently effective rules for review in accordance with this Order, and establish schedules for reviews and Analyses under this Order.

Sec. 4. Regulatory Review. Before approving any final major rule, each agency shall:

(a) Make a determination that the regulation is clearly within the authority delegated by law and consistent with congressional intent, and include in the Federal Register at the time of promulgation a memorandum of law supporting that determination.

(b) Make a determination that the factual conclusions upon which the rule is based have substantial support in the agency record, viewed as a whole, with full attention to public comments in general and the comments of persons directly affected by the rule in particular.

■ ■ ■

Sec. 7. Pending Regulations.

(a) To the extent necessary to permit reconsideration in accordance with this Order, agencies shall, except as provided in Section 8 of this Order, suspend or postpone the effective dates of all major rules that they have promulgated in final form as of the date of this Order, but that have not yet become effective, excluding:

   (1) Major rules that cannot legally be postponed or suspended;

   (2) Major rules that, for good cause, ought to become effective as final rules without reconsideration. Agencies shall prepare, in accordance with Section 3 of this Order, a final Regulatory Impact Analysis for each major rule that they suspend or postpone.

(b) Agencies shall report to the Director no later than 15 days prior to the effective date of any rule that the agency has promulgated in final form as of the date of this Order, and that has not yet become effective, and that will not be reconsidered under subsection (a) of this Section:

   (1) That the rule is excepted from reconsideration under subsection (a), including a brief statement of the legal or other reasons for that determination; or

   (2) That the rule is not a major rule.

(c) The Director, subject to the direction of the Task Force, is authorized, to the extent permitted by law, to:

   (1) Require reconsideration, in accordance with this Order, of any major rule that an agency has issued in final form as of the date of this Order and that has not become effective; and

   (2) Designate a rule that an agency has issued in final form as of the date of this Order and that has not yet become effective as a major rule in accordance with Section 1(b) of this Order.

(d) Agencies may, in accordance with the Administrative Procedure Act and other applicable statutes, permit major rules that they have issued in final form as of the date of

this Order, and that have not yet become effective, to take effect as interim rules while they are being reconsidered in accordance with this Order, provided that, agencies shall report to the Director, no later than 15 days before any such rule is proposed to take effect as an interim rule, that the rule should appropriately take effect as an interim rule while the rule is under reconsideration.

(e) Except as provided in Section 8 of this Order, agencies shall, to the extent permitted by law, refrain from promulgating as a final rule any proposed major rule that has been published or issued as of the date of this Order until a final Regulatory Impact Analysis, in accordance with Section 3 of this Order, has been prepared for the proposed major rule.

(f) Agencies shall report to the Director, no later than 30 days prior to promulgating as a final rule any proposed rule that the agency has published or issued as of the date of this Order and that has not been considered under the terms of this Order:

   (1) That the rule cannot legally be considered in accordance with this Order, together with a brief explanation of the legal reasons barring such consideration; or

   (2) That the rule is not a major rule, in which case the agency shall submit to the Director a copy of the proposed rule.

(g) The Director, subject to the direction of the Task Force, is authorized, to the extent permitted by law, to:

   (1) Require consideration, in accordance with this Order, of any proposed major rule that the agency has published or issued as of the date of this Order; and

   (2) Designate a proposed rule that an agency has published or issued as of the date of this Order, as a major rule in accordance with Section 1(b) of this Order.

(h) The Director shall be deemed to have determined that an agency's report to the Director under subsections (b), (d), or (f) of this Section is consistent with the purposes of this Order, unless the Director advises the agency to the contrary:

(1) Within 15 days of its report, in the case of any report under subsections (b) or (d); or

(2) Within 30 days of its report, in the case of any report under subsection (f).

(i) This Section does not supersede the President's Memorandum of January 29, 1981, entitled "Postponement of Pending Regulations", which shall remain in effect until March 30, 1981.

(j) In complying with this Section, agencies shall comply with all applicable provisions of the Administrative Procedure Act, and with any other procedural requirements made applicable to the agencies by other statutes.

Sec. 8. Exemptions.

(a) The procedures prescribed by this Order shall not apply to:

(1) Any regulation that responds to an emergency situation, provided that, any such regulation shall be reported to the Director as soon as is practicable, the agency shall publish in the Federal Register a statement of the reasons why it is impracticable for the agency to follow the procedures of this Order with respect to such a rule, and the agency shall prepare and transmit as soon as is practicable a Regulatory Impact Analysis of any such major rule; and

(2) Any regulation for which consideration or reconsideration under the terms of this Order would conflict with deadlines imposed by statute or by judicial order, provided that, any such regulation shall be reported to the Director together with a brief explanation of the conflict, the agency shall publish in the Federal Register a statement of the reasons why it is impracticable for the agency to follow the procedures of this Order with respect to such a rule, and the agency, in consultation with the Director, shall adhere to the requirements of this Order to the extent permitted by statutory or judicial deadlines.

(b) The Director, subject to the direction of the Task Force, may, in accordance with the purposes of this Order, exempt any class or category of regulations from any or all requirements of this Order.

Sec. 9. Judicial Review. This Order is intended only to improve the internal management of the Federal government, and is not intended to create any right or benefit, substantive or procedural, enforceable at law by a party against the United States, its agencies, its officers or any person. The determinations made by agencies under Section 4 of this Order, and any Regulatory Impact Analyses for any rule, shall be made part of the whole record of agency action in connection with the rule.

Sec. 10. Revocations. Executive Orders No. 12044, as amended, and No. 12174 are revoked.

Ronald Reagan
The White House,
February 17, 1981.

Further Resources

BOOKS

Eastland, Terry. *Energy in the Executive: The Case for the Strong Presidency.* New York: Free Press, 1992.

Noonan, Peggy. *What I Saw at the Revolution: A Political Life in the Reagan Era.* New York: Random House. 1990.

Riker, William H. *Federalism: Origin, Operation, Significance.* Boston: Little, Brown, 1964.

PERIODICALS

Beer, Samuel H. "Federalism, Nationalism and Democracy in America," *The American Political Science Review,* vol. 72, Issue 1, March 1978, 9–21.

Brinkley, Alan. "Liberty, Community and the National Idea." *The American Prospect,* no. 29, November-December 1996, 53–59.

WEBSITES

"History of U.S. Federalism." Website of Kala Ladenheim. Available online at http://www.min.net/~kala/fed/history .htm; website home page: http://www.min.net/~kala (accessed June 9, 2003). *The site provides comprehensive analysis of federal-state relations throughout American history.*

"Reagan 2000: Federalism and the New Republicans." *The Federalist,* Available online at http://www.reagan2000.com/in-dex.asp (Accessed June 9, 2003).

"Question-and-Answer Session with Reporters Helen Thomas and Jim Gerstenzang on the President's Recovery Period"

Press conference

By: Ronald Reagan

Date: April 22, 1981

Source: Reagan, Ronald. "Question-and-Answer Session With Reporters Helen Thomas and Jim Gerstenzang on the President's Recovery Period." Available online at http://www.reagan.utexas.edu/resource/speeches/1981/42281a .htm; website home page: http://www.reagan.utexas.edu (accessed June 9, 2003).

About the Author: Ronald Reagan (1911–) was born in Tampico, Illinois. After graduating from Eureka College, Reagan worked as a sports broadcaster for a Davenport, Iowa radio station. In 1937, while covering spring training in California, Reagan signed a contract with Warner Brothers, a movie studio. Reagan eventually starred in over fifty films. In 1964, he retired from acting and was elected governor of California. In 1980, Reagan was elected president (served 1981–1989). After serving two terms, he retired to his ranch in California. ∎

Introduction

A little more than two months into his presidency, Ronald Reagan nearly died in an assassination attempt. At 2:30 P.M. on March 30, after the president had delivered a speech to the Building Trades Conference of the AFL-CIO at the Washington Hilton, he exited the hotel. Four secret service agents and two aides accompanied the president. Outside, a light rain was falling as Reagan headed toward the presidential limousine. Awaiting the president was John W. Hinckley, Jr., a mentally unbalanced youth. Positioned in a combat crouch with a two-handed hold on his .22 caliber Rohm R6-14 revolver, Hinckley carefully tracked the president's movements. As Reagan passed a crowd of reporters, a journalist yelled out a question. Reagan turned to respond. In less than two seconds, six gun shots rang out.

Secret Service Agent Jerry Parr grabbed Reagan by the waist and pushed him headlong into the limousine. A bullet careened off the side of the vehicle, striking the diving president. The bullet entered his body near the left armpit, deflected off his seventh rib, rupturing the lung. The bullet lodged near Reagan's heart. A semi-conscious Reagan was wheeled into George Washington University's trauma unit. Having lost 2,100 cc of blood, much of it filling his left pleural cavity, Reagan's condition was

very serious. Once stabilized, he regained enough composure to ask his nurse who was holding his hand, "Does Nancy know about us?" When the First Lady arrived moments later, he told her, "Honey, I forgot to duck." As he was hoisted up on the operating table, he looked up at the doctors and said, "I hope you are all Republicans." It took the surgeon more than thirty minutes to cut through the 71-year-old president's barrel chest to remove the bullet.

Significance

In June 1982, John W. Hinckley was found not guilty by reason of insanity in the attempted assassination of President Reagan. The would-be murderer was sent to St. Elizabeth's Mental Hospital in Washington, D.C. On the day of the shooting, Hinckley had written the actress Jodie Foster, describing his plan to kill the president. Hinkley became obsessed with Foster after seeing her play a teenage prostitute in the 1976 film *Taxi Driver*.

Hinckley's plot to kill the president had a significant impact on Reagan's presidency. Since the 1950s, this was the fourth assassination attempt on Reagan's life. This near death experience, however, was different because he came to believe that God had spared his life for a divine purpose. A firm anti-communist for forty years, he interpreted his survival as a reminder from God to dedicate the rest of his life to defeating this godless evil.

Reagan's recovery also boosted his political fortunes. This was the fourth time in less than two decades that American presidents had become assassins' targets. Moments after Hinckley emptied his chamber, the nation was on high alert, waiting anxiously to learn Reagan's fate. Unlike in Dallas in 1963, the president survived and the country let out a collective sigh of relief. Reagan's ease and humor in the face of adversity raised him to almost folk-hero status with the American people. The year before, Reagan defeated Carter, receiving only fifty-one percent of the vote, and only fifty-two percent of eligible voters cast ballots. Reagan's election was no clear mandate for change. His newly found popularity, however, translated into political capital. Within three months of the attempted assassination, the Democratically-controlled Congress voted for Reagan's tax cuts, reduced government expenditures on domestic programs, and increased appropriations to military and national defense establishments to combat the Soviets.

Primary Source

Question-and-Answer Session with Reporters Helen Thomas and Jim Gerstenzang on the President's Recovery Period

SYNOPSIS: On April 22, 1981, twenty-three days after the attempted assassination, Reagan was back

Ronald Reagan was shot by John Hinckley just moments after leaving the Washington, D.C., Hilton in 1981. The attempted assassination wounded Reagan and critically injured James Brady, who was behind Reagan at the time. © CORBIS. REPRODUCED BY PERMISSION.

to work at the White House. At noon, he spoke of that fateful day with two veteran reporters. His casual attitude toward the ordeal, his refusal to change his daily routine, and his sympathy for his assailant's family was much admired by the American people.

Ms. Thomas: All the reports seem to be true, rosy-cheeked and—

The President [laughing]: No, I'm feeling fine.

Ms. Thomas: Can you tell us a little bit about how you felt at the time of the shooting? Did you ever feel you were in mortal danger? I know you didn't even know you were hit, but—

The President: No, that's right, and as a matter of fact, it still seems unreal. I knew there had to be shots, and my first instinct was to take a look and see what was going on from where they were. But the Secret Service man behind me had a different idea, and the next thing I knew I found myself pushed into the car. But it still seems kind of unreal.

Ms. Thomas: It's unreal to us, too, because we've come out of that hotel so many times and—

The President: Yeah. . . .

Mr. Gerstenzang: What were your first thoughts when you realized that you had been hit?

The President: Actually, I can't recall too clearly. I knew I'd been hurt, but I thought that I'd been hurt by the Secret Service man landing on me in the car. And it was, I must say, it was the most paralyzing pain. I've described it as if someone had hit you with a hammer.

But that sensation, it seemed to me, came after I was in the car, and so I thought that maybe his gun or something, underneath, when he had come down on me, had broken a rib. But when I sat up on the seat and the pain wouldn't go away, and suddenly I found that I was coughing up blood, we both decided that maybe I'd broken a rib and punctured a lung. So, that's when we headed for the hospital. And I walked in and gave them my own diagnosis, and the next thing I knew I was on a cart and it was then, I guess, that they found the wound and that I actually had been shot.

Ms. Thomas: Then, you were awake and everything? I mean—

The President: Oh, yes.

Ms. Thomas:—but had lost a lot of blood and—

The President: Yes. And my main concern, even as I was getting to the hospital, was that—and I voiced this several times to them—that the more I tried to breathe and the deeper I tried to breathe, it kept seeming as if I was getting less air—and you know that panic that you can get if you're strangling on something. I almost had the feeling that it was going to diminish to the place where I wouldn't be getting any. And then they shut me up by sticking a pipe down my throat and oxygen on, and that's when I had to start writing notes—[laughter]—because I couldn't talk with that pipe in there.

Ms. Thomas: But you always felt that you were alert enough to know what was going on and—

The President: Oh, yes. Yeah, I knew that in the manner in which I was unclothed that I probably wouldn't wear that suit again.

Ms. Thomas: Do you have any feelings about going out again? I mean, are there any—is there trauma or instants that you say, "Oh, God, do I have to face this again?" Or do you feel that, you know—

The President: I have a hunch I'll be more alert in going again.

Ms. Thomas: We will, too.

The President: That's the other thing.

I look back now in some of these reviews that they've shown of the first few months and so forth. I see some of the milling in crowds and so forth that we've done, and I find myself wondering, "Well, why didn't this happen 27 times before?" But, no, there's not going to be any change in the way we do things. . . .

Ms. Thomas: How do you actually feel? I mean, do you hurt at times and you feel good at times?

The President: Well, as the doctors will tell you, I have never had a chest injury before. They will tell you that it is one of the longest enduring discomforts, and it doesn't go away. There is just that kind of pain or discomfort there constantly that you hope day by day is getting less, and I think is getting less and less. But other than that—I've resumed at a little slower pace my regimen of exercises that I've always done for keeping fit. And I don't think

I'm going to hurdle any tables in the room here for a while, but, really, the recovery is astonishing to me as I think it is, in the reaction, to the doctors, because the only comparison I have to go by is I once had pneumonia, and that was 36 years ago when I was making a picture. And I lost 17 pounds at the time and was months in regaining strength or anything. And I'm so far ahead in this than I was then, that I have to—

Ms. Thomas: You are. I know we keep pushing because we keep forgetting what a short time it's actually been. . . .

Ms. Thomas: When do you think you'll be feeling well enough to go back to the Oval Office, or do you like working in the family quarters or—

The President: Well, actually, I don't think I'd be doing anything different. And I'm just going to, you know, I'm going to do it my way. It's convenient this way, because there still are calls by the doctors who want to come and check. There is the convenience of being able to get up and, for example, the telephone calling that I've been doing, which I'd be doing from the office, but I can get up in the morning without bothering to get dressed yet, put on a robe, and sit and do the calls.

So this, you know, with the Congress on recess, I don't think there'd be anything different or I'd be doing anything different than I've done other than possibly some appearances that have been scheduled and which had to be canceled or which George Bush substituted for me. But other than that I've been doing what I'd be doing. Remember, the schedule actually called for me to be in California for a few days. . . .

Mr. Gerstenzang: Could you, maybe in describing how you are working up there each day, sort of show how your day goes?

The President: Well, they vary from day to day. Usually we start with a staff meeting, and we do that—which was normal before. Yesterday I had a series of meetings, finishing up with almost an hour's meeting with those Governors who came to see me. We have security briefings.

So, that some days—now, today, for example, has been—well, there's been some sizeable amount of paper signing and so forth that went on, and then mainly after the staff meeting, the telephone calling, which I've been doing. And that will continue, because you don't get them the first call.

Ms. Thomas: You might find them at a radio station. [Laughter]

The President: And believe me, that was a total accident. They didn't make it sound exactly that way. Usually I say to them, "Where did we find you?" And I'll tell you why I say that, because early in the calls, I called a Congressman and we'd found him in New Zealand at 4 a.m. [Laughter]

Ms. Thomas: You mean recently?

The President: Yes.

Ms. Thomas: Oh, my God.

The President: I wanted to tell him that I was somebody else. [Laughter] It was too late. He knew who it was. [Laughter]

Ms. Thomas: Was he awake?

The President: Yes, I must say he was most pleasant about the whole thing. So, I usually ask that. And yesterday I asked that question, "Where'd I find you?" and he told me, "In Beaver Falls, at this radio station." He said, "I'm on a talk show here." And I said, "You mean, we're on the talk show now?" And he said, "Well, no, they've put me on another phone for this call." But he said, "I think they'd appreciate it very much if you'd say hello to their"—well, his forum. "They know you're on the phone." And I said, "Well, okay."

So, they put him on the other phone, the one that is audible to the radio audience, and we carried on our conversation there on the talk show.

Ms. Thomas: Do you go to bed earlier now? Do you take naps? Do you sort of try to ease into it?

The President: The only routine that I'm continuing is an afternoon nap. And that was never—in spite of some stories to the contrary—that was never a habit of mine. As a matter of fact, I've never been one who naps very well in the daytime. Everybody else sacks out on the plane and everything else, and I don't.

But I have found that I do go to sleep and sleep for a brief period. So, I guess that is part of the recovery.

Ms. Thomas: Do you think your life has changed?

The President: Only temporarily, such as not getting on a horse for a while yet.

Ms. Thomas: It's not like in the movies.

The President: Oh, I thought you meant just changed in—

Ms. Thomas: I mean the impact itself, of everything that's happened in terms of the Presidency, yourself—

The President: Well, of course, you know, I had 8 years of a job that was similar enough that there hasn't been any great surprises to me in this. But I'm enjoying it, to be able to deal directly with the things I've heretofore talked about. I enjoy doing that.

Ms. Thomas: You don't want to hang up your cleats or anything because of this incident?

The President: No, no.

Ms. Thomas: Does it give you any kind of new sense of—I mean, I think the country's kind of worried about your security and—

The President: Well, again, you get—maybe this is part of it—that you get a little used to it. In all those 8 years and those hectic times when I was Governor, I was aware that there were constant threats. And I could usually tell when there was a slight difference in the security precautions and the normal—something new must have been suggested. And in the two campaigns, having had national-type security, Secret Service, no, I've been—you're aware of that. And you sometimes wonder in your mind when and how it's going to happen or any attempt or what it would be like.

You remember '76; there was that fellow with the toy gun. Well, I never saw that; I was busy saying hello to someone. And I didn't see this.

Ms. Thomas: Do you have any feelings about your assailant? Of course there's nothing you can really feel, I guess. It's something that's senseless.

The President: Well, yes, the feeling is I hope, indeed I pray, that he can find an answer to his problem. He seems to be a very disturbed young man. He comes from a fine family. They must be devastated by this. And I hope he'll get well too.

Ms. Thomas: That's very kind of you. You don't have any feelings of real anger, then, or—

The President: Well, I don't know how I could ask

for help for myself and feel that way about someone else.

Mr. Gerstenzang: If you were to speak to his parents, what would you tell them?

The President: Well, I think I'd tell them that I understand and—[pause]—hope for a good outcome there, to end their problem. . . .

Mr. Gerstenzang: Has this in any way changed your thinking on gun control at all?

The President: No, and let me explain why. I'm not just being closed-minded or stubborn.

We have the laws now. Granted that all States aren't uniform. But I don't know of any place—there may be some—but I don't know of any place in the country where it is now not against the law to carry a concealed weapon. Now, we've found that that can't prevent someone. Your District of Columbia here has such a law. But a man was carrying a concealed weapon. So, I don't see where we believe that adding another law that probably will be just as unenforceable as this one is going to make a difference.

In fact, if anything, I'm a little disturbed that focusing on gun control as an answer to the crime problem today could very well be diverting us from really paying attention to what needs to be done if we're to solve the crime problem.

Ms. Thomas: Which is?

The President: Well, I do think we're showing the results of several decades of growing permissiveness, unwillingness to hold individuals responsible for their misdeeds, blaming society instead. In other words, quicker, more effective justice.

Mr. Deaver: One more.

Ms. Thomas: One more. We've got to make this one good. [Laughter] In terms of [Press Secretary] Brady, will he continue on? Are you going to keep the slot open for him?

The President: Oh, you bet. And I think all of us—as I say, when I finally did learn that three others had been hit, including the agent who deliberately placed himself between me and the gunman—but Jim, of course, was the most serious, and I am so gratified by the optimism about his recovery that that's a daily prayer.

Ms. Thomas: A miracle.

The President: Yes. For him.

Ms. Thomas and Mr. Gerstenzang: Thank you very much.

Further Resources

BOOKS

Blumenthal, Sidney. *Our Long National Daydream: A Political Pageant of the Reagan Era.* New York: Harper & Row, 1988.

Brookheiser, Richard. *The Outside Story: How Democrats and Republicans Reelected Reagan.* New York: Doubleday, 1986.

Willis, Garry. *Reagan's America: Innocents at Home.* New York: Doubleday, 1987.

PERIODICALS

"Covering Up for a Sick President." *Newsweek,* vol. 110, October 5, 1987, 56.

Morris, Edmund. "The Gipper's 'Long Goodbye': In the Twilight, the Former President, a Victim of Alzheimer's, Slips Away." *Newsweek.* vol. 134, October 4, 1999, 40.

WEBSITES

"Doctors Recommend Hinckley Be Given Unsupervised Trips Off Hospital Grounds." *CNN,* April 11, 2000. Available online at http://www.cnn.com/2000/US/04/11/hinckley.visits.02/index.html; website home page http://www.cnn.com (accessed June 9, 2003).

"The John Hinckley Trial." *The University of Missouri-Kansas City Law School.* Available online at http://www.law.umkc.edu/faculty/projects/ftrials/hinckley/hinckleytrial.html; website home page: http://www.law.umkc.edu (accessed June 9, 2003).

"Remarks and a Question-and-Answer Session with Reporters on the Air Traffic Controllers' Strike"

Press conference

By: Ronald Reagan

Date: August 3, 1981

Source: Reagan, Ronald. "Remarks and a Question-and-Answer Session With Reporters on the Air Traffic Controllers Strike." Available online at http://www.reagan.utexas.edu/resource/speeches/1981/80381a.htm; website home page: http://www.reagan.utexas.edu (accessed June 9, 2003).

About the Author: Ronald Reagan (1911–) was born in Tampico, Illinois. After graduating from Eureka College, Reagan worked as a sports broadcaster for a Davenport, Iowa, radio station. In 1937, while covering spring training in

Air traffic controllers walk the picket line in New York. AP/WIDE WORLD PHOTOS. REPRODUCED BY PERMISSION.

California, Reagan signed a contract with Warner Brothers, a movie studio. Reagan eventually starred in over fifty films. In 1964, he retired from acting and was elected governor of California. In 1980, Reagan was elected president (served 1981–1989). After serving two terms, he retired to his ranch in California. ∎

Introduction

On August 3, 1981, some 13,000 members of the Professional Air Traffic Controllers Organization (PATCO) went on strike against the Federal Aviation Administration (FAA), resulting in the cancellation of sixty percent of the nation's commercial air traffic. The strikers' aim was to cripple the nation's commercial traffic to the extent that the FAA would yield to PATCO demands. PATCO wanted an across-the-board pay increase of $10,000 a year for all controllers, whose annual salaries ranged between $20,000 and $49,000. PATCO also sought a reduction of the five-day, 40-hour workweek to a four-day, 32-hour workweek. The demands totaled $770 million and were to be paid for by taxpayers. The FAA rejected PATCO's demands, in part because if the controllers prevailed, other public sector unions would follow suit. Instead, it made a $40 million counteroffer,

including a shorter workweek. Ninety-five percent of PATCO's membership rejected the offer.

Since they were federal employees, the air traffic controllers' strike was illegal, violating the no-strike clause of their employment contracts. Though Congress prohibited federal employees from striking in 1955, twenty-two unauthorized federal strikes had occurred. PATCO organized nationwide slowdowns and sickouts in 1968, 1969, 1970, 1974, 1975, and 1978 and had suffered little retribution. To better its bargaining position, PATCO went on strike during the peak summer travel season. The nation's air traffic controllers supervised 14,000 commercial flights a day, carrying 800,000 passengers and 10,000 tons of air cargo. The strike threatened to devastate the $30 billion-a-year industry, inflict major carriers with $30 million a day in losses, and force airlines to layoff 340,000 other employees. Hours after PATCO went on strike, President Ronald Reagan, the first president to be a lifetime member of the AFL-CIO, held a press conference in the White House Rose Garden.

Significance

Within 48 hours of the strike, over 11,000 air traffic controllers were fired—while 1,200 strikers returned to work. In October, the Federal Labor Relations Authority decertified PATCO, and the union was disbanded. In anticipation of a strike, the FAA had developed a contingency plan for 3,000 supervisors, 2,000 non-striking controllers, and 900 military controllers to take command of the nation's airport towers. The FAA ordered airlines operating at the major hubs to scale back scheduled flights by fifty percent during peak hours. Almost sixty small airport towers were closed until further notice. To ensure passenger safety, the 33,000-member Air Line Pilots Association performed extra traffic monitoring duties. The FAA's training school in Oklahoma—typically training 1,500 new controllers every five-month session—graduated 5,500 new controllers. The contingency plan was successful, as nearly eighty percent of all fights were soon operating as scheduled.

Not only did the Reagan administration effectively replace the air traffic controllers, he won the public relations battle. Reagan undermined PATCO support by focusing on union demands for a $10,000 raise and a four-day workweek. The public had little sympathy for PATCO members, already earning well above the national income average. In the end, sixty-five percent of the American people supported Reagan's handling of the controversy. Reagan was seen as a strong, decisive leader, in sharp contrast to their view of his predecessor, Jimmy Carter (served 1977–1981). The strike also had an important impact on foreign affairs. It convinced Soviet leaders that they were dealing with a man of conviction who would not be easily intimidated. The strike also marked an important transition point in American collective bargaining, for public and private sector unions were increasingly unable to protect their interests and force management into concessions.

Primary Source

Remarks and a Question-and-Answer Session With Reporters on the Air Traffic Controllers Strike

SYNOPSIS: On August 3, 1981, Reagan held a question-and-answer session with reporters concerning the air traffic controllers strike. In his opening announcement, he quoted the solemn oath taken by federal employees promising not to strike when they accepted their jobs. He gave the employees two days to return to work or be terminated. His tough stance was very popular with the American people.

The President: This morning at 7 a.m. the union representing those who man America's air traffic control facilities called a strike. This was the culmination of 7 months of negotiations between the Federal Aviation Administration and the union. At one point in these negotiations agreement was reached and signed by both sides, granting a $40 million increase in salaries and benefits. This is twice what other government employees can expect. It was granted in recognition of the difficulties inherent in the work these people perform. Now, however, the union demands are 17 times what had been agreed to—$681 million. This would impose a tax burden on their fellow citizens which is unacceptable.

I would like to thank the supervisors and controllers who are on the job today, helping to get the nation's air system operating safely. In the New York area, for example, four supervisors were scheduled to report for work, and 17 additionally volunteered. At National Airport a traffic controller told a newsperson he had resigned from the union and reported to work because, "How can I ask my kids to obey the law if I don't?" This is a great tribute to America.

Let me make one thing plain. I respect the right of workers in the private sector to strike. Indeed, as president of my own union, I led the first strike ever called by that union. I guess I'm maybe the first one to ever hold this office who is a lifetime member of an AFL-CIO union. But we cannot compare labor-management relations in the private sector with government. Government cannot close down the assembly line. It has to provide without interruption the protective services which are government's reason for being.

It was in recognition of this that the Congress passed a law forbidding strikes by government employees against the public safety. Let me read the solemn oath taken by each of these employees, a sworn affidavit, when they accepted their jobs: "I am not participating in any strike against the Government of the United States or any agency thereof, and I will not so participate while an employee of the Government of the United States or any agency thereof."

It is for this reason that I must tell those who fail to report for duty this morning they are in violation of the law, and if they do not report for work within 48 hours, they have forfeited their jobs and will be terminated.

[Reporter:] Mr. President, are you going to order any union members who violate the law to go to jail?

The President: Well, I have some people around here, and maybe I should refer that question to the Attorney General.

[Reporter:] Do you think that they should go to jail, Mr. President, anybody who violates this law?

The President: I told you what I think should be done. They're terminated.

The Attorney General: Well, as the President has said, striking under these circumstances constitutes a violation of the law, and we intend to initiate in appropriate cases criminal proceedings against those who have violated the law.

[Reporter:] How quickly will you initiate criminal proceedings, Mr. Attorney General?

The Attorney General: We will initiate those proceedings as soon as we can.

[Reporter:] Today?

The Attorney General: The process will be underway probably by noon today.

[Reporter:] Are you going to try and fine the union $1 million per day?

The Attorney General: Well, that's the prerogative of the court. In the event that any individuals are found guilty of contempt of a court order, the penalty for that, of course, is imposed by the court.

[Reporter:] How much more is the government prepared to offer the union?

The Secretary of Transportation: We think we had a very satisfactory offer on the table. It's twice what other Government employees are going to get—11.4 percent. Their demands were so unreasonable there was no spot to negotiate, when you're talking to somebody 17 times away from where you presently are. We do not plan to increase our offer to the union.

[Reporter:] Under no circumstances?

The Secretary of Transportation: As far as I'm concerned, under no circumstance.

[Reporter:] Will you continue to meet with them?

The Secretary of Transportation: We will not meet with the union as long as they're on strike. When they're off of strike, and assuming that they are not decertified, we will meet with the union and try to negotiate a satisfactory contract.

[Reporter:] Do you have any idea how it's going at the airports around the country?

The Secretary of Transportation: Relatively, it's going quite well. We're operating somewhat in excess of 50 percent capacity. We could increase that. We have determined, until we feel we're in total control of the system, that we will not increase that. Also, as you probably know, we have some rather severe weather in the Midwest, and our first priority is safety.

[Reporter:] What can you tell us about possible decertification of the union and impoundment of its strike funds?

The Secretary of Transportation: There has been a court action to impound the strike fund of $3.5 million. We are going before the National Labor Relations Authority this morning and ask for decertification of the union.

[Reporter:] When you say that you're not going to increase your offer, are you referring to the original offer or the last offer which you've made? Is that still valid?

The Secretary of Transportation: The last offer we made in present value was exactly the same as the first offer. Mr. Poli (Robert Poli, Professional Air Traffic Controllers Organization) asked me about 11 o'clock last evening if he could phase the increase in over a period of time. For that reason, we phased it in over a longer period of time. It would have given him a larger increase in terms of where he would be when the next negotiations started, but in present value it was the $40 million originally on the table.

[Reporter:] Mr. Attorney General, in seeking criminal action against the union leaders, will you seek to put them in jail if they do not order these people back to work?

The Attorney General: Well, we will seek whatever penalty is appropriate under the circumstances in each individual case.

[Reporter:] Do you think that is an appropriate circumstance?

The Attorney General: It is certainly one of the penalties that is provided for in the law, and in appropriate cases, we could very well seek that penalty.

[Reporter:] What's appropriate?

The Attorney General: Well, that depends upon the fact of each case.

[Reporter:] What makes the difference?

[Reporter:] Can I go back to my "fine" question? How much would you like to see the union fined every day?

The Attorney General: Well, there's no way to answer that question. We would just have to wait until we get into court, see what the circumstances are, and determine what position we would take in the various cases under the facts as they develop.

[Reporter:] But you won't go to court and ask the court for a specific amount?

The Attorney General: Well, I'm sure we will when we reach that point, but there's no way to pick a figure now.

[Reporter:] Mr. President, will you delay your trip to California or cancel it if the strike is still on later this week?

The President: If any situation should arise that would require my presence here, naturally I will do that. So, that will be a decision that awaits what's going to happen. May I just—because I have to be back in there for another appointment—may I just say one thing on top of this? With all this talk of penalties and everything else, I hope that you'll emphasize, again, the possibility of termination, because I believe that there are a great many of those people—and they're fine people—who have been swept up in this and probably have not really considered the result—the fact that they had taken an oath, the fact that this is now in violation of the law, as that one supervisor referred to with regard to his children. And I am hoping that they will in a sense remove themselves from the lawbreaker situation by returning to their posts.

I have no way to know whether this had been conveyed to them by their union leaders, who had been informed that this would be the result of a strike.

[Reporter:] Your deadline is 7 o'clock Wednesday morning for them to return to work?

The President: Forty-eight hours.

The Secretary of Transportation: It's 11 o'clock Wednesday morning.

[Reporter:] Mr. President, why have you taken such strong action as your first action? Why not some lesser action at this point?

The President: What lesser action can there be? The law is very explicit. They are violating the law. And as I say, we called this to the attention of their leadership. Whether this was conveyed to the membership before they voted to strike, I don't know. But this is one of the reasons why there can be no further negotiation

President Ronald Reagan, flanked by Attorney General William French Smith, speaks publicly to striking federal air traffic controllers.
© BETTMANN/CORBIS. REPRODUCED BY PERMISSION.

while this situation continues. You can't sit and negotiate with a union that's in violation of the law.

The Secretary of Transportation: And their oath.

The President: And their oath.

[Reporter:] Are you more likely to proceed in the criminal direction toward the leadership than the rank and file, Mr. President?

The President: Well, that again is not for me to answer.

[Reporter:] Mr. Secretary, what can you tell us about the possible use of military air controllers—how many, how quickly can they get on the job?

The Secretary of Transportation: In answer to the previous question, we will move both civil and criminal, probably more civil than criminal, and we now have papers in the U.S. attorneys offices, under the Attorney General, in about 20 locations around the country where would be involved two or three principal people.

As far as the military personnel are concerned, they are going to fundamentally be backup to the supervisory personnel. We had 150 on the job, supposedly, about a half-hour ago. We're going to increase that to somewhere between 700 and 850.

[Reporter:] Mr. Secretary, are you ready to hire other people should these other people not return?

The Secretary of Transportation: Yes, we will, and we hope we do not reach that point. Again as the President said, we're hoping these people come back to work. They do a fine job. If that does not take place, we have a training school, as you know. We will be advertising. We have a number of applicants right now. There's a waiting list in terms of people that want to be controllers, and we'll start retraining and reorganize the entire FAA traffic controller group.

[Reporter:] Just to clarify, is your deadline 7 a.m. Wednedsay or 11 o'clock?

The Secretary of Transportation: It's 11 a.m. Wednesday. The President said 48 hours, and that would be 48 hours.

[Reporter:] If you actually fire these people, won't it put your air traffic control system in a hole for years to come, since you can't just cook up a controller in—[inaudible]?

The Secretary of Transportation: That obviously depends on how many return to work. Right now we're able to operate the system. In some areas, we've been very gratified by the support we've received. In other areas, we've been disappointed. And until I see the numbers, there's no way I can answer that question.

[Reporter:] Mr. Lewis, did you tell the union leadership when you were talking to them that their members would be fired if they went out on strike?

The Secretary of Transportation: I told Mr. Poli yesterday that the President gave me three instructions in terms of the firmness of the negotiations: one is there would be no amnesty; the second there would be no negotitaions during the strike; and third is that if they went on strike, these people would no longer be government employees.

[Reporter:] Mr. Secretary, you said no negotiations. What about informal meetings of any kind with Mr. Poli?

The Secretary of Transportation: We will have no meetings until the strike is terminated with the union.

[Reporter:] Have you served Poli at this point? Has he been served by the Attorney General?

The Attorney General: In the civil action that was filed this morning, the service was made on the attorney for the union, and the court has determined that that was appropriate service on all of the officers of the union.

[Reporter:] My previous question about whether you're going to take a harder line on the leadership than rank and file in terms of any criminal prosecution, can you give us an answer on that?

The Attorney General: No, I can't answer that except to say that each case will be investigated on its own merits, and action will be taken as appropriate in each of those cases.

[Reporter:] Mr. Lewis, do you know how many applications for controller jobs you have on file now?

The Secretary of Transportation: I do not know. I'm going to check when I get back. I am aware there's a waiting list, and I do not have the figure. If you care to have that, you can call our office, and we'll tell you. Also, we'll be advertising and recruiting people for this job if necessary.

[Reporter:] Mr. Secretary, how long are you prepared to hold out if there's a partial but not complete strike?

The Secretary of Transportation: I think the President made it very clear that as of 48 hours from now, if the people are not back on the job, they will not be government employees at any time in the future.

[Reporter:] How long are you prepared to run the air controller system—[inaudible]?

The Secretary of Transportation: For years, if we have to.

[Reporter:] How long does it take to train a new controller, from the waiting list?

The Secretary of Transportation: It varies; it depends on the type of center they're going to be in. For someone to start in the system and work through the more minor office types of control situations till they get to, let's say, a Chicago or a Washington National, it takes about 3 years. So in this case, what we'll have to do if some of the major metropolitan areas are shut down or a considerable portion is shut down, we'll be bringing people in from other areas that are qualified and then start bringing people through the training schools in the smaller cities and smaller airports.

[Reporter:] Mr. Secretary, have you definitely made your final offer to the union?

The Secretary of Transportation: Yes, we have.

[Reporter:] Thank you.

Further Resources

BOOKS

Johnson, Haynes. *Sleepwalking Through History: America in the Reagan Years.* New York: Doubleday 1991.

Reagan, Ronald. *An American Life.* New York: Simon and Schuster, 1990.

Shostak, Arthur, and David Skocik. *Air Controllers' Controversy.* New York: Human Sciences Press, 1986.

PERIODICALS

Alter, Jonathan. "Featherbedding in the Tower: How the Controllers Let the Cat Out of the Bag." *The Washington Monthly,* vol. 13, October 1981, 22–27.

Morganthau, Tom. "Who Controls the Air?" *Newsweek,* vol. 98, August 17, 1981, 18–24.

WEBSITES

"Ronald Reagan." *Reagan Foundation.* Available online at http://www.reaganfoundation.org/reagan/ (accessed June 9, 2003).

"Ronald Reagan Presidential Library." *University of Texas.* Available online at http://www.reagan.utexas.edu/ (Accessed June 9, 2003).

Sandra Day O'Connor became the first woman appointed to the U.S. Supreme Court. AP/WIDE WORLD PHOTOS. REPRODUCED BY PERMISSION.

Nomination of Sandra Day O'Connor

Testimony

By: Sandra Day O'Connor

Date: September 11, 1981

Source: *Nomination of Sandra Day O'Connor: Hearings Before the Committee on the Judiciary, United States Senate, Ninety-seventh Congress, first session, on the nomination of Judge Sandra Day O'Connor, of Arizona, to serve as an associate justice of the Supreme Court of the United States, September 9, 19, and 11, 1981.* Washington, D.C.: U.S. Government Printing Office, 1981, 237–242.

About the Author: Sandra Day O'Connor (1930–) was born in El Paso, Texas, and raised on a 155,000-acre ranch near the Arizona-New Mexico border. After graduating from high school, she enrolled at Stanford University and completed her undergraduate and law degrees in five years. In 1972, she became the Arizona Senate Majority Leader. Seven years later, she was appointed to Arizona's Court of Appeals. President Ronald Reagan (served 1981–1989) appoint her to the United States Supreme Court, where she became the first woman to serve on the United States' highest court. She serves as an associate justice. ∎

Introduction

President Jimmy Carter (served 1977–1981) was the first president since Andrew Johnson (served 1865–69) who did not have the opportunity to appoint at least one United States Supreme Court Justice. However, Carter appointed more members to the federal bench than all but four American presidents. Under the Omnibus Judgeship Act of 1978, Carter selected people to fill 152 newly established federal judgeships. Overall, Carter nominated 300 federal judges, or forty percent of the entire federal judiciary. Carter's judicial selections are controversial because of the weight he placed on his nominees' gender and race. In the name of "diversity," Carter nominated nearly one hundred federal judges who were women, African American, and/or Hispanic. This selection process was controversial, as Carter admitted that his nominees were generally less qualified than available white male candidates. Carter's selections were also controversial because they were often "activists" on social issues. Instead of interpreting the law, these liberal judges made social policy by legislating from the bench, especially on such controversial issues as abortion, school prayer, gay rights, and affirmative action.

In part, President Ronald Reagan (served 1981–1989) was elected because of the support of evangelical Christian groups, including the Moral Majority. These groups argued that liberal activist judges violated the constitutional separation of powers doctrine by implementing contentious social policies, bypassing the appropriate elected representative bodies—Congress, state legislatures, town councils, and public school boards. As a result, federal judges were imposing a radical agenda contrary to majority opinion. In the 1980 presidential election, President Ronald Reagan promised to some day nominate the most qualified woman to the Supreme Court. His opportunity arrived when Justice Potter Stewart announced his retirement in 1981. In choosing his replacement, Reagan required that the nominee be a strict constructionist, rather than a liberal judicial activist, and personally oppose abortion. He settled on 51-year old jurist Sandra Day O'Connor.

Significance

The main reason Reagan nominated O'Connor was because she was a woman. Reagan was the first president to acknowledge the political power of the gender gap. Not only did women made up fifty-one percent of the electorate, but, additionally, Reagan had captured only forty-seven percent of the female vote. Therefore, O'Connor's nomination was, in part, an attempt by Reagan to close the gender gap. As a strict constructionalist, O'Connor also received the recommendation of Arizona's influential senator Barry Goldwater of Arizona. Feminists and other liberals, including Senator Ted Kennedy (D-Mass.) supported her nomination, believing that O'Connor would uphold a woman's right to an abortion. In contrast, the Moral Majority sharply criticized the O'Connor nomination because of her pro-abortion votes as an Arizona legislator. They accused the Reagan administration of pandering to women voters by failing to nominate the most qualified candidate. The American Bar Association had given O'Connor only a "qualified" rating because of her limited experience as a judge and practicing attorney.

On September 15, 1981, the Senate Judiciary Committee approved O'Connor's nomination unanimously. The Senate confirmed the nomination by a vote of 99–0. Therefore, after some two hundred years and the nomination of one hundred men, the country finally had a female Supreme Court Justice. On the bench, O'Connor has been an independent, moderately conservative centrist. On abortion, she has supported state legislative restrictions, but has refused to reexamine the constitutional validity of *Roe v. Wade*. Though in O'Connor he failed to obtain a doctrinaire conservative to the Supreme Court, Reagan fared better in the lower courts. During his eight years in office, he nominated almost fifty percent of the federal judiciary, making 404 federal court appointees, virtually all more conservative than O'Connor.

Primary Source

Nomination of Sandra Day O'Connor [excerpt]

SYNOPSIS: During Judge O'Connor's otherwise smooth Senate confirmation hearing, she was re-

peatedly asked to explain her views on abortion, particularly *Roe v. Wade*. Conservatives argue that the 1973 Supreme Court decision is a classic example of liberal judicial activism. On September 11, 1981, Senator Jeremiah Denton questions O'Connor's abortion views.

Senator Denton: Thank you, Mr. Chairman.

Good morning, Judge O'Connor.

Judge O'Connor: Good morning.

Senator Denton: At the outset, let me clear up what amounted to a misunderstanding on my part yesterday. I had questioned you on your personal views on abortion, and you stated during that exchange, "It remains offensive at all levels," and stated that you think it is a problem at any level.

Then I thought I heard you say that you would not be in favor of abortion even to save the life of the mother. After several others had thought the same thing, and then having been questioned by some news people, I did look at the transcript and so forth and find out that that is not what you said.

You actually said, "Would I personally object to drawing the line to saving the life of the mother? No, I would not." You went on to say: "Are there other areas?" Then you said, "Possibly."

Therefore, I would have to withdraw my statement since it was based on error in understanding you. I misunderstood you. I would have to say that it appears that indeed you are not more conservative than I thought on that issue, and I would remind you that legislatively the Congress has done what it could to outlaw or forbid payments of government funding of abortion except to save the life of the mother.

That is where Congress drew the line but we could not go any further than just stop Government funding for it. We could not get into the legislation of abortion with respect to the public because we were preempted by a Supreme Court manifestation of judicial activism in the *Roe v. Wade* decision. Therefore, there is a real problem of that judicial activism, and I am sure that not all of my colleagues would agree that it is the wrong kind but, nevertheless, there was that example.

Therefore, I have learned that you are less conservative than I, and as I go into the Kenneth Starr memorandum I would refer you to a previous statement of yours which said that you felt that your personal feelings should not constitute the basis of decisions made on this matter or any other matter in the Supreme Court, but rather that if there is a constitutional principle which applies, it should be the determining factor.

I submit that in the Declaration we do have the statement, "all men created equal," et cetera, "endowed by their Creator with certain inalienable rights. Among these are life . . ." Then in the Constitution, in the Bill of Rights, article 5, "No person can be deprived of life without due process of law."

Senator East, as you know, has been conducting hearings to determine whether or not a fetus is a person. I agree that this is a very difficult question. I do not agree that it is difficult to determine that it is human life. I believe that that is irrefutable. . . .

I believe that abortion is the opposite of compassion for that being which needs it the most. I believe that history will prove that once a nation goes that way, from an ethic like ours, as Nazi Germany did, you immediately get involved with infanticide, euthanasia, genocide, and the whole idea of selective murder. This brings into play the question of the convenience of the existence of that person which is based on human judgement. That is why I feel so strongly about what might be called fotal rights, the right to survival on the part of that human life.

I do not believe, with you, that learning more about fetuses will ever change the fact that there is life there, God-given life which we do not understand, and we do not even know what makes grass grow. How can we get into the process of deciding, for convenience or for money—because that kid is going to cost money if it is born—or embarrassment that we want to spare that 13- or 14-year-old girl—and you have said that you are opposed to it for birth control purposes.

However, I want to know what you meant yesterday when you said, "Are there other areas?"—besides saving the life of the mother—and then you said, "Possibly." I would have to say that that is less conservative than that which Congress has indicated as its collective will, and it leaves me befud-

dled as to where you are. I feel I have gotten nowhere, in that you have said possibly there are other areas. We could go on for perhaps a month, and if that is all the specific you are going to be, I would not know at all where you are coming from philosophically on that issue.

Judge O'Connor: Senator Denton, I believe that I recounted previously for the committee my vote in the legislature on funding in connection with the bill for providing medical care to indigents, where I did support a measure that provided for certain exclusions in addition to what was necessary to save the life of the mother. In that instance it included instances of rape and incest, criminal actions, and I supported that.

Senator Denton: However, the criminal action—a little baby to be—is not involved in.

Judge O'Connor: I simply was trying to indicate, Senator Denton, where I had had occasion to vote as a legislator because, of course, people—many people—share your very eloquent views and your very perceptive views on this most pressing problem.

There are others who, perhaps out of different concerns, might draw the line in some slightly different fashion or indeed in some substantially different fashion, and these are the troubling issues that come before a legislator when asked to specifically draw the line. I appreciate that problem. I think I can simply indicate to you how I voted at that time on that issue.

Senator Denton: OK. Well, with respect to some of those votes, then, I would like to go into the document which has become known as the Starr memorandum. I would preface that by a question. You feel abortion is personally abhorrent and repugnant. Would it follow that you believe the unborn ought to be legally protected? If so, how and at what stage of their development?

Judge O'Connor: Senator Denton, excuse me. Is that your question?

Senator Denton: Yes. You have stated that you feel it is personally abhorrent and repugnant, and that it is a legislative matter to deal with it. Do you mean by that that we should legally protect the unborn? If so, how, considering the *Roe v. Wade* activism from the judicial branch?

Judge O'Connor: Well, Senator Denton, a legislative body at the State level today would be limited in that effort by the limitations placed in the *Roe v. Wade* decision. I recognize that. If a State legislature today were to try to draw the lines, it would have to reckon with that decision, which of course places substantial limitations on the freedom of State legislative bodies presently.

Senator Denton: Until that decision is changed or if something comes up to render it subject to change, it makes your appointment extremely important and your philosophy on that matter extremely important. Therefore, I hope you can appreciate the interest of those tens of millions—and there are tens of millions on the other side—who are interested in your position on that. I am not clear that we have drawn much out. Let me get on this.

Judge O'Connor: Senator Denton, I do appreciate the concerns and the strongly held views of so many people on this issue.

Senator Denton: I understand that.

On July 7, you had two telephone conversations with Kenneth W. Starr, counselor to the Attorney General of the United States.

Judge O'Connor: Excuse me. On what date, please?

Senator Denton: July 7, 1981, is my information.

Did you state in one or both of those conversations that you "know well the Arizona leader of the right-to-life movement, a prominent female physician in Phoenix, and have never had any disputes or controversies with her"?

Judge O'Connor: Senator Denton, I am sure that I indicated that I knew Dr. Gerster. Indeed, she lives in the same community in which I live, the Scottsdale-Paradise Valley Area.

Senator Denton: Yes, and you are acquaintances.

Judge O'Connor: We have children who have attended the same school, and I have seen her on any number of occasions.

I had occasion, of course, to see her in 1974 in my capacity as a legislator as well. She at that time was interested in the house memorial 2002, dealing with the question of whether the Arizona legislature should recommend to the Congress an amendment of the U.S. Constitution as a means of addressing the *Roe v. Wade* decision. Dr. Gerster—

Senator Denton: Excuse me. I do not mean to be impolite but in the interest of trying to stay within the time, the only part of the question that I am—the question deals with whether or not you said that you had never had any disputes or controversies with that leader, Dr. Gerster. Did you say that, because the Starr memorandum is quoted as having had you saying that?

Judge O'Connor: Senator Denton, I am sure that I did indicate that and I would like to explain precisely why I said that.

As a legislator, I had many instances in which people would come before the legislature and espouse a particular position with regard to a particular bill. I as a legislator was obligated to listen to those views along with the views of others, and then ultimately cast a vote. My receiving of information of that sort and ultimately casting a vote, even if it were cast in a manner other than that being espoused by the speaker, did not cast me in my view in the role of being an adversary.

I did not feel that in my position as a legislator, that every time I voted against a measure that someone in the public sector was supporting publicly in front of me, that I became an adversary. I was not a leader in connection with the passage or defeat of house memorial 2002. I was a legislator—

Senator Denton: I understand. I really do understand the thrust of your answer. It does appear, however, that the thrust that one would take from that answer which was quoted is that you and the right-to-life movement leader there really had no disputes on probably that issue. That I think might have been gleaned from that statement. I leave that to speculation. It certainly would have been my inference from it.

Judge O'Connor: Well, Senator Denton, I think that it is important to recognize that what I am trying to reflect is that because I may have voted differently than Dr. Gerster would have, had she been a legislator, does not mean that we are adversaries.

Senator Denton: Yes, I understand. However, there has been much opposition to your nomination and public statements by Dr. Gerstner, which probably we will hear some of later, concerning her opposition to many of your past legislative decisions. Therefore, there was an inconsistency, not in what your attitude was or what your statement was but I think with respect to the thrust of what that inclusion in Mr. Starr's report might have been interpreted as meaning.

Did you tell Mr. Starr that you did not remember how you voted on a bill to legalize abortion in Arizona, or that there is no record of how you voted on legislation to legalize abortion in Arizona? I believe we heard you say that you had some difficulty remembering one, and you had to get it out of a newspaper because it was not in the legislative records. Somebody in Arizona has said that that was the equivalent of not remembering how one would have voted on the Panama Canal issue.

Judge O'Connor: Senator Denton, as I explained I think in the first day of these hearings, with respect to house bill 20 I frankly had no recollection of the vote. We voted on literally thousands of measures and that bill never went to the floor for a vote. I tended to remember with more clarity those measures which required a vote on the merits on the floor. Committee votes are something else: Technically speaking, you are not voting on the merits in a committee vote. You are voting to put it out of committee with a certain recommendation.

In the year 1970, as reflected in the newspaper articles which I eventually unearthed, house bill 20 was not a major issue at that time in terms of having many people at a committee hearing, in any other way. It was simply not a measure that attracted that much attention.

In addition, house bill 20 was destined never to go to the floor in the State senate. I think it was widely known and believed even when it was in committee that it would never emerge from the Republican caucus. The votes were never there. It was a dead bill.

Senator Denton: Yes. Then it might be relevant to follow up: You stated that some change in Arizona statutes was appropriate, and "had a bill been presented to me that was less sweeping than H.B. 20, I would have supported that. It was not." You broke off, but you meant it was not introduced. Is that correct?"

Judge O'Connor: That is correct.

Senator Denton: Can you then remember why you did not support S.B. 216, which was a more conservative bill regarding abortion which was pending in the Senate Judiciary Committee after March 23, 1970, roughly a month before the committee's vote on H.B. 20?

Judge O'Connor: Senator Denton, was that Senator McNulty's bill, if you know?

Senator Denton: The bill provided for therapeutic abortions in cases involving rape, incest, or the life of the mother.

I have just been informed that my time is up.

It was Senator McNulty's bill, yes.

May she finish the answer to this question, Mr. Chairman?

The Chairman: She may finish the answer to your question.

Judge O'Connor: Senator Denton, as I recall that bill it provided for an elaborate mechanism of counseling services and other mechanisms for dealing with the question, and I was not satisfied that the complicated mechanism and structure of that bill was a workable one.

Senator Denton: OK. Thank you, Judge O'Connor.

Further Resources

BOOKS

Abraham, Henry J. *Justices, Presidents, and Senators: A History of the U.S. Supreme Court Appointments from Washington to Clinton*. Lanham, Md.: Rowman & Littlefield Publishers, 1999.

O'Connor, Sandra Day, and H. Alan Day. *Lazy B: Growing Up on a Cattle Ranch in the American Southwest*. New York: Random House, 2002.

PERIODICALS

"Justice—At Last." *Time*, July 20, 1981.

Sperling, Gene. "Justice in the Middle." *The Atlantic*, vol. 261, March 1988, 26–33.

Witt, Elder. "A Different Justice: Reagan and the Supreme Court." *Congressional Quarterly*, 1986.

WEBSITES

"Supreme Court Justice Sandra Day O'Connor Discusses Her New Autobiography *Lazy B* with Senior Correspondent Gwen Ifill." *PBS NewsHour with Jim Lehrer*, February 1, 2002. Available online at http://www.pbs.org/newshour/bb /entertainment/jan-june02/oconnor_2-1.html; website home page: http://www.pbs.org (accessed June 9, 2003).

Supreme Court of the United States. Available online at http:// www.supremecourtus.gov (accessed June 9, 2003).

The Bombing of the Marine Barracks in Lebanon

U.S. Marines Headquarters, Beirut, Lebanon, Before Bombing; U.S. Marines Headquarters, Beirut, Lebanon, After Bombing

Photographs

Date: October 23, 1983

Source: U.S. Marines' BLT Headquarters building prior to bombing. Photograph. Long Commission Report, *U.S. Marines in Lebanon 1982–1984*. History and Museums Division, Headquarters, U.S.M.C., Washington, D.C.; U.S. Marine barracks after bombing. Photograph, October 23, 1983. AP/Wide World Photos.

About the Organization: The 24th Marine Expeditionary Unit (MEU) is one of three Marine Air/Ground Logistics

Task Forces that routinely deploys from Marine Corps Base Camp Lejeune, North Carolina to the Mediterranean Sea aboard amphibious ready group shipping. In 1982, it was renamed as the 24th MAU (Marine Amphibious Unit) and was deployed twice to Lebanon as part of an international peacekeeping force. Six years later, it was renamed again as the 24th MEU. ■

Introduction

President Ronald Reagan's (served 1981–1989) foreign policy in the Middle East was similar to his predecessors'. He supported a strong Israel, the only Western-style democracy in the region, and "moderate" Arab monarchies. Together, they sought to limit Soviet influence in the region and ensure the continued exportation of Persian Gulf oil. The Reagan administration, however, was confronted with a very difficult problem: the Lebanese Civil War. Lebanon is a country approximately the size of Connecticut that borders the Mediterranean Sea between the Israel and Syria. In 1983, Lebanon's nearly three million people were divided among

Primary Source

U.S. Marines Headquarters, Beirut, Lebanon, Before Bombing

SYNOPSIS: On October 23, 1983, a Mercedes truck driven by terrorists, carrying 2,600 pounds of explosives, plowed though barbed wire fences and gates and crashed into the Marines' headquarters at the Beirut airport. In a matter of seconds, the four-story building was a mound of rubble. Two hundred forty-one members of the 24th MAU and sailors were killed in the suicide bombing. This is the U.S. Marine headquarters as it stood prior to the 1983 terrorist bombing. PHOTO FROM THE LONG COMMISSION REPORT.

Primary Source

U.S. Marines Headquarters, Beirut, Lebanon, After Bombing
Rescue crews get to work after the bombing of the U.S. Marine headquarters in Beirut, which resulted in 241 deaths.
AP/WIDE WORLD PHOTOS. REPRODUCED BY PERMISSION

seventeen religious sects and two-dozen extra-legal militias. Christians battling Muslims for control further complicated Lebanon's situation. The West-leaning Christians, allied with the Israelis and the Americans, dominated the political scene even though they were outnumbered by Muslims, aligned with the Syrians and the Palestinian Liberation Organization (PLO)—both receiving Soviet aid.

In June 1982, Israel invaded southern Lebanon to secure its border from attacks by PLO terrorists. In less than a week, Israel devastated the PLO and Syrian troops and laid siege to Beirut to root out the PLO. The United States brokered a deal whereby the PLO surrendered its heavy weapons and evacuated 15,000 personnel from Beirut. In return, Israel allowed them to leave unharmed. The United States agreed to send in the 24th Marine Amphibious Unit (MAU) to serve as a part of an international peacekeeping force. The 24th MAU left Lebanon in September, only to return two weeks later following the assassination of Lebanon's new Christian president. Next, the Israeli army moved back into Beirut and turned

a blind eye to revenging Christian forces killing 700 Palestinian civilians. The Lebanese government then disintegrated amid a civil war between Christians and Muslims. On September 29, 1983, 1,600 Marines took control of the Beirut airport.

Significance

The airport was a controversial place for the Americans to establish a base because it was vulnerable to attack from the surrounding Shouf Mountains. From the military's point of view, however, that vulnerability was a signal to potential enemies that their mission was purely peacekeeping and that they would not intervene in the civil war. The American position was naïve because Imad Mughniyah, leader of the Lebanese-based terrorist group Hezbollah, viewed the Americans as allies of the Lebanese Christians, as well as the Israelis, who were occupying southern Lebanon to creat a security zone from attacks into Israel. He therefore ordered and masterminded the Beirut bombing with the intent of driving the Americans out of Lebanon.

President Reagan composes his address to the nation after terrorists bombed the U.S. Marine headquarters in Beirut, Lebanon. © CORBIS. REPRODUCED BY PERMISSION.

In the early morning on October 23, 1983, a truck carrying a 12,000-pound explosive crashed through the security gates of the U.S. compound in a suicide attack. The explosion killed 241 American military personnel and wounded 80. In a simultaneous attack against the French presence in Lebanon, a 400-pound bomb hit a French military compound that same morning, killing 58 French troops.

On October 27, 1983, four days after the Beirut bombing, President Reagan, in a nationally televised address, with American integrity on the line, vowed to keep the Marines in Beirut. He stated, "Let me ask those who say we should get out of Lebanon: If we were to leave Lebanon now, what message would that send to those who foment instability and terrorism?" However, with the 1984 election on the horizon and Congress and public opinion firmly in favor of withdrawing the Marines from another Vietnam War (1964–1975) "quagmire," Reagan relented. In February 1984, Reagan ordered the withdrawal of the Marines, giving the impression that he

had acceded to the demands of Mughniyah, the Hezbollah terrorist. This is important because Mughniyah was a mentor to Osama bin Laden and his al-Qaeda terrorist network. Bin Laden realized that if the Americans could be forced to retreat from Lebanon, perhaps they could be forced to retreat from Saudi Arabia. With this intent, bin Laden organized numerous terrorist attacks on America, including the almost simultaneous attacks against the American embassies in Tanzania and Kenya in 1998, the USS *Cole* in Yemen in 2000, and the World Trade Center on September 11, 2001.

Further Resources

BOOKS

Frank, Benis M. *U.S. Marines in Lebanon, 1982-1984.* Washington, D.C.: G.P.O. 1987.

Hammel, Eric M. *The Roots: The Marines in Beirut, August 1982-February 1984.* Pacifica, Calif.: Pacifica Press, 1993.

Petit, Michael. *Peacekeepers at War: A Marine's Account of the Beirut Catastrophe.* New York: Faber and Faber, 1986.

PERIODICALS

Alexander, A.N. "A Personal Account of the Bombing of the American Embassy in Beirut." *Business America,* vol. 6, May 30, 1983, 16–18.

Friedman, Thomas. "Buildings Blasted. Truck Loaded With TNT Wrecks Headquarters of a Marine Unit. *The New York Times,* October 23, 1983. Available online at http://www.nytimes.com/learning/general/onthisday/991023onthisday_big.html#article; website home page: http://www.nytimes.com (accessed June 9, 2003).

WEBSITES

The Beirut Memorial. Available online at http://www.beirut memorial.org/history/brochure.html; website home page: http://www.beruit-memorial.org (accessed June 9, 2003).

"Report of the DOC Commission on the Beirut International Airport Terrorist Attack." The United States Department of Defense. December 20, 1983. Available online at http://www.ibiblio.org/hyperwar/AMH/XX/MidEast/Lebanon-1982-1984/DOD-Report/index.html#toc; website home page: http://www.ibiblio.org (accessed June 9, 2003).

"Excerpts from Jackson Appeal to Convention Delegates for Unity in Party"

Transcript

By: Jesse Jackson

Date: July 18, 1984

Source: Jackson, Jesse. "Excerpts from Jackson Appeal to Convention Delegates for Unity in Party." *The New York Times,* July 18, 1984.

About the Author: Jesse Jackson (1941–) was born in Greenville, South Carolina. In 1968, the Chicago Theological Seminary ordained Jackson a Baptist minister. In 1971, Jackson formed Operation PUSH (People United to Save Humanity) to expand educational and employment opportunities for minorities and the disadvantaged. Jackson made two unsuccessful campaigns for the Democratic Party presidential nomination in the 1980s. He remained one of the best known African American political and civil rights leaders into the twenty-first century. ∎

Introduction

During the Chicago mayoral primary in 1983, Jesse Jackson first considered running for the presidency. In that race, Jackson supported African American congressman Harold Washington's bid to unseat the incumbent, Mayor Jane Byrne. To his dismay, Senator Ted Kennedy supported Byrne, while former vice president Walter Mondale endorsed Richard J. Daley, the eldest son of Chicago's longtime mayor, Richard Daley. Jackson was particularly troubled by Mondale's endorsement because, in the 1980 presidential election, African American support helped the Carter-Mondale ticket carry Chicago. Moreover, Jackson had campaigned for President Carter (served 1977–1981) in twenty-nine states and seventy-two cities. Washington, who won the Chicago Democratic primary, defeated his Republican opponent in the general election, receiving only twenty percent of the white vote. Jackson concluded that white political leaders refused to endorse African American candidates, and that white voters, for the most part, would not elect African American candidates. Consequently, it was time for African Americans to help themselves. In October 1983, Jackson appeared on CBS's *60 Minutes.* Before an audience of over forty million, Jackson announced his intention to run for Democratic presidential nomination in 1984.

After Senator Kennedy announced that he would not contend for the 1984 Democratic presidential nomination, Mondale was widely considered the Democratic frontrunner. Another leading contender was Senator Gary Hart (D-Colo.), whose "John Kennedy-esque" style appealed to young urban professionals—nicknamed "yuppies." The other major contender was Jesse Jackson. All three candidates were from the liberal wing of the party. Each agreed that if elected president, top priorities would be to cut defense spending, impose higher taxes on the rich, increase spending on entitlement programs, and remain committed to affirmative action and race-based hiring quotas. Unlike his opponents, however, Jackson reached out to African Americans and other racial and ethnic minorities—gays, women, and the poor—a self-described "Rainbow Coalition." Although Jackson finished third in the primaries, his 400 committed delegates were enough to garner Jackson a prime time, nationally televised speech at the convention.

Significance

Jackson's candidacy was important, as he was the first African American to make a serious run for the presidential nomination of a major party. Politically energized, millions of African Americans gave Jackson a formidable power base, especially within the Democratic Party. Millions, especially in the South, responded to his charisma and powerful message to register and vote in the coming election. In eleven southern states, the number of African Americans registered to vote increased from 4.3 million in 1980 to 5.5 million in 1984—a thirty percent increase. In these eleven southern states, more new African American voters registered than whites, and in nine of the states, new African American voter registrations more than doubled new white registrations. In 1984 more African Americans voted than ever before, and during the 1984 general election, approximately 740,000 more African Americans voted than in 1980.

In addition to the significant rise in African American voter turnout Jackson's campaign inspired, his candidacy was also important because increased African American registration allowed the Democrats to take control of the United States Senate in 1986. In response, or so it has been argued by Democrats, Republicans began to "clean up" voter rolls by purging thousands of African American voters from the rolls. Prior to the 1988 primaries, millions of voters were purged from the rolls from Virginia through Texas. In contrast, Republicans argued that they were merely enforcing the rules and trying to clean up the rolls that for generations had been rife with corruption. As state and local governments had different criteria for purging voter rolls, Congress passed the 1993 National Voter Registration Act, also known as the Motor Voter Law, establishing uniform guidelines. South Carolina, Mississippi, and Virginia unsuccessfully sued to halt the enforcement of the law.

Reverend Jesse Jackson speaks at the Democratic National Convention, July 18, 1984. Reverend Jackson was the first African American to make a serious run at a major-party presidential nomination. AP/WIDE WORLD PHOTOS. REPRODUCED BY PERMISSION.

Primary Source

"Excerpts from Jackson Appeal to Convention Delegates for Unity in Party" [excerpt]

SYNOPSIS: At the Democratic National Convention in San Francisco on July 18, 1984, Jesse Jackson became the first African American to address a major political convention at length. For fifty minutes, he spoke directly, without interruption, to a national audience. More people watched this address than any other part of the convention. To the astonishment of television executives, the television audience grew during Jackson's speech.

Tonight we come together bound by our faith in a mighty God, with genuine respect and love for our country, and inheriting the legacy of a great party, the Democratic Party, which is the best hope for redirecting our nation on a more humane just and peaceful course.

This is not a perfect party. We are not a perfect people. Yet, we are called to a perfect mission: Our mission, to feed the hungry, to clothe the naked, to house the homeless, to teach the illiterate, to provide jobs for the jobless and to choose the human race over the nuclear race. . . .

My constituency is the desperate, the damned, the disinherited, the disrespected, and the despised.

They are restless and seek relief. They've voted in record numbers. They have invested faith, hope and trust that they have in us. The Democratic Party must send them a signal that we care. I pledge my best to not let them down. . . .

Courage and Initiative

With courage and initiative, leaders change things. No generation can choose the age or circumstance in which it is born, but through leadership it can choose to make the age in which it is born an age of enlightenment—an age of jobs and peace and justice.

Only leadership—that intangible combination of gifts, the discipline, information, circumstance, courage, timing, will and divine inspiration—can lead us out of the crisis in which we find ourselves. . . .

There is a proper season for everything. There is a time to sow and a time to reap. There is a time to compete, and a time to cooperate.

I ask for your vote on the first ballot as a vote for a new direction for this party and this nation; a vote of conviction, a vote of conscience.

But I will be proud to support the nominee of this convention for the Presidency of the United States of America.

Cites Respect for Opponents

I have . . . watched the leadership of our party develop and grow. My respect for both Mr. Mondale and Mr. Hart is great.

I've watched them struggle with the crosswinds and cross fires of being public servants, and I believe they will both continue to try to serve us faithfully. I am elated by the knowledge that for the first time in our history a woman, Geraldine Ferraro, will be recommended to share our ticket.

Throughout this campaign, I've tried to offer leadership to the Democratic Party and the nation.

If in my high moments, I have done some good, offered some service, shed some light, healed some wounds, rekindled some hope, or stirred someone from apathy and indifference, or in any way along the way helped somebody, then this campaign has not been in vain.

For friends who loved and cared for me, and for a God who spared me, and for a family who understood, I am eternally grateful.

If in my low moments, in word, deed or attitude, through some error of temper, taste or tone, I have caused anyone discomfort, created pain or revived someone's fears, that was not my truest self.

If there were occasions when my grape turned into a raisin and my joy bell lost its resonance, please forgive me. Charge it to my head and not to my heart. I am—my head, so limited in its finitude; my heart, which is boundless in its love for the human family. I am not a perfect servant. I am a public servant doing my best against the odds. As I

develop and serve, be patient. God is not finished with me yet.

A Brighter Side Somewhere

This campaign has taught me much: that leaders must be tough enough to fight, tender enough to cry, human enough to make mistakes, humble enough to admit them, strong enough to absorb the pain and resilient enough to bounce back and keep on moving. For leaders, the pain is often intense. But you must smile through your tears and keep moving with the faith that there is a brighter side somewhere.

Our flag is red, white and blue, but our nation is a rainbow—red, yellow, brown, black and white—and we're all precious in God's sight. America is not like a blanket—one piece of unbroken cloth, the same color, the same texture, the same size. America is more like a quilt—many patches, many pieces, many colors, many sizes, all woven and held together by a common thread.

The white, the Hispanic, the black, the Arab, the Jew, the woman, the native American, the small farmer, the businessperson, the environmentalist, the peace activist, the young, the old, the lesbian, the gay and the disabled make up the American quilt.

All of Us Fit Somewhere

Even in our fractured state, all of us count and all of us fit somewhere. We have proven that we can survive without each other. But we have not proven that we can win and progress without each other. We must come together.

From Fannie Lee Hamer in Atlantic City in 1964 to the Rainbow Coalition in San Francisco today, from the Atlantic to the Pacific, we have experienced pain but progress as we ended American apartheid laws, we got public, accommodation, we secured voting rights, we obtained open housing, as young people got the right to vote, we lost Malcolm, Martin, Medgar, Bobby, John and Viola.

The team that got us here must be expanded, not abandoned. . . .

We are co-partners in a long and rich religious history—the Judeo-Christian traditions. Many blacks and Jews have a shared passion for social justice at home and peace abroad. We must seek a revival of the spirit inspired by a new vision and new possibilities. We must return to higher ground. We are bound by Moses and Jesus, but also connected with Islam and Mohammed.

Search for Common Ground

These three great religions, Judaism, Christianity and Islam, were all born in the revered and holy city of Jerusalem. We are bound by Dr. Martin Luther King Jr. and Rabbi Abraham Heschel, crying out from their graves for us to reach common ground.

We are bound by shared blood and shared sacrifices. We are much too intelligent; much too bound by our Judeo-Christian heritage; much too victimized by racism, sexism, militarism and anti-Semitism; much too threatened as historical scapegoats to go on divided one from another: We must turn from finger pointing to clasped hands. We must share our burdens and our joys with each other once again. We must turn to each other and not on each other and choose higher ground.

Twenty years later, we cannot be satisfied by just restoring the old coalition. Old wine skins must make room for new wine.

We must be unusually committed and caring as we expand our family to include new members. All of us must be tolerant and understanding as the fears and anxieties of the rejected and of the party leadership express themselves in so many different ways. Too often what we call hate—as if it were some deeply rooted in philosophy or strategy—it is simply ignorance, anxiety, paranoia, fear and insecurity. To be strong leaders, we must be long-suffering as we seek to right the wrongs of our party and our nation. . . . That is our mission in 1984.

We are often reminded that we live in a great nation—and we do. But it can be greater still. The Rainbow is mandating a new definition of greatness. We must not measure greatness from the mansion down but from the manger. . . .

President Reagan says the nation is in recovery. Those 90,000 corporations that made a profit last year but paid no Federal taxes are recovering. The 37,000 military contractors who have benefited from Reagan's more than doubling of the military budget in peace-time surely they are recovering. The big corporations and rich individuals who received the bulk of a three-year, multibillion tax cut from Mr. Reagan are recovering. But no such recovery is under way for the least of these. Rising tides don't lift all boats, particularly those stuck at the bottom.

For the boats stuck at the bottom there's a misery index. This Administration has made life more miserable for the poor. Its attitude has been contemptuous. Its policies and programs have been cruel and unfair to working people.

The Nation's Poorest Region

Many say that the race in November will be decided in the South. President Reagan is depending on the conservative South to return him to office. But the South, I tell you, is unnaturally conservative. The South is the poorest region in our nation and, therefore, the least to conserve. In his appeal to the South, Mr. Reagan is trying to substitute flags and prayer cloths for food, and clothing, and education, health care and housing.

Mr. Reagan will ask us to pray—and I believe in prayer. I've come this way by the power of prayer. But we must watch false prophecy. He cuts energy assistance to the poor, cut breakfast programs from children, cut lunch programs from children, cut job training from children and then says to an empty table, "Let us pray." Apparently, he is not familiar with the structure of a prayer. You thank the Lord for the food that you're about to receive, not the food that just left.

I think that we should pray. But don't pray for the food, but let's pray for the man that took the food to leave. We need a change. We need a change in America. . . .

Fears of Nuclear War

Under this administration, we've lost the lives of our boys in Central America, in Honduras, in Grenada, in Lebanon, a nuclear standoff in Europe. Under this Administration, one-third of our children believe they will die in a nuclear war. The danger index is increasing in this world.

All the talk about a defense against Russia—the Russian submarines are closer, and their missiles are more accurate. We live in a world of might more miserable and a world more dangerous.

While Reaganomics and Reaganism is talked about often, so often we miss the real meaning. Reaganism is a spirit. Does Reaganomics represent the real economic facts of life?

Economic Policy Criticized

In 1980, Mr. George Bush, a man with reasonable access to Mr. Reagan did an analysis of Mr. Reagan's economic plan. Mr. George Bush concluded that Reagan's plan was "voodoo economics." He was right. Third-party candidate John Anderson said a combination of military spending, tax cuts and a balanced budget by 84 would be accomplished with blue smoke and mirrors. They were both right. . . .

President Reagan curbed inflation by cutting consumer demand. He cut consumer demand with conscious and callous fiscal and monetary policies. He used the Federal budget to deliberately induce unemployment and curb social spending. He then weighed and supported tight monetary policies of the Federal Reserve Board to deliberately drive up interest rates—again to curb consumer demand created through borrowing. . . .

Mr. Reagan brought inflation down by destabilizing our economy and disrupting family life.

He promised—he promised in 1980 a balanced budget. But instead we now have a record toward a billion dollar budget deficit. Under Mr. Reagan, the cumulative budget deficit for his four years is more than the sum total of deficits from George Washington through Jimmy Carter combined. I tell you, we need a change. How is he paying for these short-term jobs? Reagan's economic recovery is being financed by deficit spending—$200 billion a year. Military spending, a major cause of this deficit, is projected, over the next five years, to be nearly $2 trillion, and will cost about $40,000 for every tax-paying family.

Deficit and Interest Rates

When the Government borrows $200 billion annually to finance the deficit, this encourages the private sector to make its money off of interest rates as opposed to development and economic growth. Even money abroad, we don't have enough money domestically to finance the debt, so we are now borrowing money abroad, from foreign banks, governments and financial institutions: $40 billion is 1983; $70–80 billion in 1964 (40 percent of our total), and over $100 billion (50 percent of our total) in 1985. By 1989, it is projected that 50 percent of all individual income taxes will be going just to pay for interest on the debt. The United States used to be the largest exporter of capital, but under Mr. Reagan we will quite likely become the largest debtor nation.

Our vision is clear. . . . Our party can win. But we must provide hope, which will inspire people to struggle and achieve; provide a plan that shows a way out of our dilemma; and then lead the way. . . .

As I leave you now, we vote in this convention and get ready to go back across this nation in a couple of days. In this campaign I tried to be faithful to my promise. I have lived in el barios, ghettoes and in reservations and housing projects. I have a message for our youth. I challenge them to put hope in their brains and not to open their veins. I told them that like Jesus I, too, was born in the slum, but just because you're born in a slum does not mean the slum is born in you and you can rise above it if your mind is made up.

Two Sides to Every Slum

I told them in every slum there are two sides. When I see a broken window that's the slummy side. Train some youth to become a glazier, that's the sunny side. When I see a missing brick, that's the slummy side. Let that child in a union and become a brick mason and build, that's the sunny side. When I see a missing door, that's the slummy side. Train some youth to become a carpenter, that's the sunny side. When I see the vulgar words and hieroglyphics of destitution on the walls, that's the slummy side. Train some youth to be a painter and artist, that's the sunny side. We leave this place looking for the sunny side because there's a brighter side somewhere.

I'm more convinced than ever that we can win. We have fought up the rough side of the mountain. We can win. I just want young America to do me one favor, just one favor: exercise the right to dream. You must face reality, that which is. But then dream of a reality that ought to be, that must be. Live beyond the pain of reality with the dream of a bright tomorrow. Use hope and imagination as weapons of survival and progress.

'Choose the Human Race'

Use love to motivate you and obligate you to serve the human family. Young America, dream. Choose the human race over the nuclear race. Bury the weapons and don't burn the people.

Dream.

Dream of a new value system. Teachers who teach for life and not just for a living, teach because they can't help it.

Dream of lawyers more concerned about justice than a judgeship.

Dream of doctors more concerned about public health than personal wealth.

Dream of preachers and priests who will prophesy and not just profiteer. Preach and dream.

Our time has come. Our time has come.

Suffering breeds character. Character breeds faith, and in the faith will not disappoint.

Our time has come. Our faith, hope and dreams have prevailed. Our time has come. Weeping has endured for nights but that joy cometh in the morning. Our time has come. No grave can hold our body down. Our time has come. No time can live forever. Our time has come. We must leave the racial battle ground and come to the economic common ground and moral higher ground. America, our time has come. We come from this grace to amazing grace. Our time has come.

Give me your tired, give me your poor, your huddled masses who learn to breathe free and come November, there will be a change because our time has come. Thank you and God bless you.

Further Resources

BOOKS

Faw, Bob, and Nancy Skelton. *Thunder In America.* Austin: Texas Monthly Press, 1986.

Marshall, Frady. *Jesse: The Life and Pilgrimage of Jesse Jackson.* New York: Random House, 1996.

Timmerman, Kenneth R. *Shakedown: Exposing the Real Jesse Jackson.* Washinton, D.C.: Regnery, 2002.

PERIODICALS

"Aid to Dr. King Vows to Try to Restore Calm in Chicago." *Chicago Tribune,* April 6, 1968.

Joyce, Fay S. "Leaders of Blacks Debate Conditions on Aid to Mondale," *The New York Times,* August 29, 1984.

WEBSITES

"Frontline: The Pilgrimage of Jesse Jackson." *PBS.* Available online at http://www.pbs.org/wgbh/pages/frontline/jesse; website home page http://www.pbs.org (accessed June 9, 2003).

Rainbow/PUSH Coalition. Available online at http://www.rainbowpush.org (accessed May 18, 2003).

Ferraro: My Story

Autobiography

By: Geraldine Ferraro

Date: 1985

Source: Ferraro, Geraldine A., and Linda Bird Francke. *Ferraro: My Story.* New York: Bantam Books, 1985.

About the Author: Geraldine Ferraro (1935–) was born in Newburgh, New York. At sixteen, she graduated high school and earned a college scholarship. She worked her way through Fordham Law School as a public school teacher. In 1978, Ferraro was elected to Congress and served three terms. She served as Walter Mondale's vice presidential running mate in 1984, becoming the first woman nominated to a major party presidential ticket. In 1993, she was appointed as a delegate to the United Nations Human Rights Commission ∎

Introduction

In 1984, after a bitter primary fight with Colorado senator Gary Hart, Walter Mondale won the Democratic presidential nomination. Despite the hard-earned victory, Mondale's political future was uncertain. On July 1, 1983, a Gallup poll showed him trailing President Ronald Reagan (served 1981–1989) by nineteen percentage points. To shake up the campaign and energize his liberal base, Mondale needed to make a dramatic, historic move. After considering Tom Bradley and Wilson Goode as his vice presidential running mates, the mayors of Los Angeles and Philadelphia respectively and both African American, as well as San Antonio mayor Henry Cisneros, and San Francisco mayor Dianne Feinstein, Mondale selected the relatively inexperienced Geraldine Ferraro, a three-term congresswoman from New York. Ferraro was chosen for her popularity with blue-collar, Catholic voters, and because she embodied the all-American values of perseverance and hard work. She was also feisty, opinionated, and charming—everything Mondale was not.

More importantly, Ferraro was chosen because of the alleged "gender gap." In 1980, Reagan won fifty-six percent of the male vote, but only forty-seven percent of the female vote. This nine-point gender gap in a national election was nearly the largest in U.S. history to that time. Also in 1980, for the first time in U.S. history, more women voted than men. Not only were women emerging as an important voting bloc, but also they were winning political offices. From 1971 to 1983, the number of women in Congress rose from 15 to 24, and in state legislatures from 362 to 992. In addition, women's attitudes on social, environmental, and national security issues differed dramatically from men's. Following Ferraro's bracing convention acceptance speech, sixty-five percent of American voters considered her qualified to be vice president. The Mondale-Ferraro ticket earned a post-convention bump, as the Democrats held a precarious forty-eight to forty-six percent lead over the Republican Party's Ronald Reagan and George H. Bush shortly after Ferraro joined the ticket.

Significance

Between October and the November election, Ferraro traveled over 30,000 miles to drum up support. Despite this frantic pace, Mondale's campaign was in trouble. It was nearly impossible to defeat a popular president in a booming national economy with inflation and unemployment at decade lows. On election day, CBS news called the election for Reagan by 8 P.M. Reagan won by an eighteen-point margin, and 523 to 13 in the electoral college. The landslide victory ranked close to those of Franklin D. Roosevelt in 1936 and Richard Nixon in 1972. Mondale carried only the District of Co-

Democratic vice presidential candidate Geraldine Ferraro speaks at the National Italian American Foundation dinner on September 15, 1984. Ferraro was the first woman to grace a major party presidential ticket. © **BETTMANN/CORBIS. REPRODUCED BY PERMISSION.**

lumbia and Minnesota, his home state. The Democratic strategy of nominating a woman for vice president in an attempt to bolster Mondale's appeal failed. As in 1980, the nine-point gender gap persisted in 1984—as sixty-four percent of men voted Republican, together with fifty-five percent of women. Compared with 1980, Reagan attracted eight percent more women voters in 1984.

The most significant aspect of the Mondale candidacy was that it spelled the end of the Democratic liberal agenda on the national scene. In the 1972 and 1984 presidential elections, both featuring Mondale on the ticket, the Democrats lost in the electoral college a combined 1,104 to 62. Moreover, Republicans had won four of the last five presidential elections. In those four elections, they won 82.4 percent of the electoral votes, approaching Roosevelt's four-election achievement of 88.3 percent of the electoral votes cast. The collapse of the liberal agenda—defense spending cuts, tax hikes, increased spending on social programs, and unqualified support for affirmative action—continued with the victories of George H. Bush (served 1989–1993) in 1988 and George W. Bush (served 2001–present) in 2000. Between the Bush presidencies, Bill Clinton (served 1993–2001) won the White House twice as a "New Democrat." Clinton successfully moved to the political cen-

ter, borrowing Republican themes of law and order, individualism, and welfare reform.

Primary Source

Ferraro: My Story [excerpt]

SYNOPSIS: After the Democratic Convention, Ferraro hit the campaign trail for 103 consecutive days, having to adjust to Secret Service agents watching her every move. As the first female candidate in a national election, her wardrobe was a constant concern to the scrutinizing press, as well as the press's taboo that she and Mondale never touch hands.

On the Road

Never has a political candidacy drawn so much curiosity—and rarely so many enthusiasts. From sea to shining sea, it seemed, everyone wanted to get a look at the first woman vice-presidential candidate.

I was just as fascinated to see all these people as they were to see me, to look at the endless crowds while I stood on hastily constructed podiums, auditorium stages, the steps of town halls all over the country. As far as my eye could see were the faces of America; young, old, well-to-do, poor, of every possible ethnic descent, business executives, blue-collar workers, often people in wheelchairs—and women. "I never thought I'd live to see this day," one eighty-year-old said to me in Minneapolis. At a fundraiser in St. Paul a week later I repeated her comment. As I was leaving, an elderly woman beckoned me over and said: "You know the story you just told about the eighty-year-old woman? Well, I'm ninety-one and I never thought I'd live to see this day, either."

The pace was backbreaking. In the next three months I would travel over fifty-five thousand miles, campaign stumping in eighty-five cities in eighty-seven days. It wasn't always easy. At one rally in Portland, Oregon, the pouring rain dissolved my best lines, which I had just penned into my remarks, prompting the Oregon Historical Society to request the soggy papers as a souvenir. At a September picnic in Bayonne, New Jersey, the platform nearly collapsed, the sound system was terrible, and there was no podium. I asked the man standing next to me to take the pages of my speech as I finished delivering them. The only trouble was he became so engrossed in reading the speech over my shoulder that he started taking the pages out of my hands before I'd finished with them. I almost ended up delivering the speech while reading it over *his* shoulder. Total craziness.

There were other funny moments. After a long, grueling day in Montgomery, Alabama, I arrived exhausted at my hotel room only to watch the Secret Service agents try unsuccessfully to get my door open. "What's with you guys?" I twitted them. "Just shoot the lock off with your guns."

But they were above that. "Congresswoman Ferraro," one agent said to me gravely. "Would you happen to have a hairpin?"

The Secret Service agents were one of the best things about the campaign. They were fabulous, professional and courteous—both my details, headed by Paul Hackenberry and William Wasley, and John's, headed by Benny Crosby and Mike Johnston. It was not Gerry Ferraro they were guarding so much as the office I was running for. And they took the job very seriously. When I reached out to one crowd the Secret Service was a little worried . . . I looked up to see Mike Goehring moving through the crowd parallel to me, using his own body as a buffer between me and anyone who might try to do me harm. Every time I got out of the car, the agent would hold his hand over my head; I'm not sure if it was so I wouldn't bump it or because people getting in and out of cars are most vulnerable, and a head is an

easy and almost always fatal target. Cars and airports made the Secret Service particularly nervous. From the first airport, in Lake Tahoe, the agents would scan the rooftops as I moved from the plane to the car or vice-versa, keeping their fingers on the triggers of their automatic Israeli submachine guns, called Uzis, which they carried on their shoulders like pocketbooks.

It was hard at first to get used to. At Lake Tahoe, John and I had been awakened in the middle of the night by voices right outside our window. In Queens that meant one thing. You were about to be broken into. "Relax," John had said. "It's just the Secret Service." In the morning I explained my Queens paranoia to them, and we never heard another word. Whenever we got home during the campaign, I never felt more secure in my life. The Secret Service doused the light on our front porch so they wouldn't be direct targets, and stationed themselves around the yard and the street. That was just fine with me. Throughout the campaign I was the only person in New York City who went to bed without thinking of locking her front door.

I got impatient with them only once. In early September I had been campaigning on the West Coast, and John, immediately after a hernia operation, was with me on the trip, just to get away. But it had been a mistake for him to travel so soon, and he was really in bad shape. I had to make a stop in New Jersey and urged him to go directly home.

After the event I was naturally anxious to see him. But instead of following the direct route home, which takes only twenty minutes on city streets, the Secret Service wanted to take the longer highway route. It was safer, they explained to me. The stopping and starting at traffic lights made me an easier target. And there was no way they could get the entire motorcade filled with staff and press through all the lights together. I was angry because we always seemed to take the most time-consuming ways to get home. Outside of New York I didn't feel it, but this was my city, and I wanted to be in my own house. So I crabbed and fumed in the backseat en route. They did it my way, but of course, they were right. And I felt terrible about it afterward.

They were wrong, though, in the number of women agents the Secret Service employed, and my candidacy proved to be somewhat embarrassing to them. Since 1971, the Secret Service had assimilated only around eighty women into its force of close to eighteen hundred (the Secret Service never releases exact numbers), and often there wasn't a woman agent available for my detail. The lack of women agents was highlighted by my trips to public rest rooms. Every time we would look for one, it created a minor crisis. The agents would then have to "secure" the ladies' room, going in and peering under the stalls to make sure there was no one lurking inside. It was a ludicrous situation. After a while I started going into the ladies' room ahead of them, bending down to check out the stalls myself and then yelling, "All clear!" But the agents were behaving correctly. Their job was to protect me. And there always was the possibility that someone could have been in there who wanted to do me harm.

Only once did the Secret Service mess up. And it wasn't my security that was lost. It was my luggage. On September 15, Fritz and I were scheduled to attend the biannual National Italian American Foundation dinner in Washington, along with Ronald Reagan and George Bush. It was a formal dinner and the only time all four candidates would be seen together during the campaign. But when I flew into Washington from Elmira, New York, where I had spoken to a student group, the dress bag containing my evening dress and John's tuxedo was not there. Instead of being sent to Washington, the dress bag was locked in the trunk of a Secret Service car in our driveway in Queens.

My staff was getting hysterical. Protocol called for the presidential and vice-presidential candidates to enter the dinner first, to be in place when the incumbent President and Vice President arrived. But without our evening clothes, we couldn't go anywhere, and time was running out. Three substitute dresses owned by various staff members were rushed to the hotel, as was a tuxedo for John. Nothing fit. "I'll just wear my business suit," John said agreeably, but that was vetoed. So were the emergency dresses—by me. "I will not appear on a podium with the other three candidates on national television feeling uncomfortable," I said firmly to my staff, who were leaning hard on me.

This was nothing new. They had heard it before in San Francisco. I wanted my speech to be delivered well, and I wanted my people to be proud.

While our dress bag was in the air, the NIAF dinner began—without us. I used the time to meet with two of my lawyers and go over the Washington Legal Foundation's complaint lodged with the House Committee on Standards of Official Conduct about my congressional disclosure statements. And Fritz was wonderful about the dilemma, quite content to wait until our luggage came through, which it finally

did. Then we went down to the dinner together, well after Reagan and Bush had arrived. I began my speech by saying, "It is wonderful to be here with that other Italian on the ticket, Fritz Mondali." I was back in stride. . . .

Clothes were another area that became a subject of discussion because I was the first female candidate in a national campaign. Everybody seemed to have an opinion about what I should wear, including some of the press, who would often start off the day by saying: "Don't wear that color. It will blend into the background in pictures. You need a bright color." Wear suits, not dresses, came the constant advice from Barbara Roberts Mason, my senior policy adviser. According to the Business and Professional Women's Association, Barbara kept telling me, suits made any woman look more professional. I didn't think looking professional had anything to do with the suit versus dress controversy.

In at least one city, the laws of probability turned against me. In Pittsburgh, I was asked to autograph a picture from my previous trip to that marvelous city. When I looked down to sign it, there I was, wearing the same skirt and blouse I had on then. The people in Pittsburgh must have thought I had only one outfit.

Flowers, too, made their debut in national politics, though my staff had much more of a problem with them than I did. I love flowers. But there was some feeling in the campaign that my being given flowers, as happened constantly, was a kind of put-down. What nonsense, I told them. In no way was I going to deny my femininity during the campaign, and being given a dozen roses almost daily was one of the little pleasures on the campaign trail. I would take them back to the hotel and stick them in a vase so I could at least enjoy them overnight.

What to do with the flowers immediately after they were handed to me was a problem, however. On the one hand, there was Geraldine Ferraro, a person who loves flowers. On the other hand, there was Geraldine Ferraro, the vice-presidential candidate who was not going to walk around looking like a bridesmaid. So I'd thank the donor very much and instantly hand the flowers to Eleanor to hold. I drew the line, however, at wrist corsages. I didn't want to look like someone going to a prom.

Corsages notwithstanding, the whole issue of my being the first female candidate made other people feel far more awkward than it did me. There had been such a fuss in the campaign and the media about Fritz and me not touching at all, not even raising our joined hands, that it put everybody else off as well. Whenever we landed at an airport there would be fifteen or twenty official greeters, both men and women, lined up in the rain, in the cold, any time of the day or night. Often they were old friends, congressional colleagues, Democratic mayors, senators, or governors. And always, they would hesitate when they first saw me.

"I really wish I could give you a hug," they'd say.

"Go ahead," I'd tell them. "The only one who can't is Fritz Mondale."

I was also running a thin line being careful not to promote one group at the expense of another. Wherever I went, in addition to flowers, local people would give me a T-shirt to wear, a hat, or a sweatshirt. If it was presented as part of the official program, I would put it on. The audience would usually roar their approval, as in Boston, when I wore the Celtics T-shirt Senator Ted Kennedy gave me. But if it was handed to me by someone in the crowd, I reluctantly had to decline, not wanting to single out any specific group. It was hard. At one labor rally, a union member gave me his chapter hat to wear. "Thank you," I said, and put it on my lap.

"Wear it," he urged me.

"No," I said, not wanting to offend him, but not wanting to alienate anyone else at the same time.

His was a specific union within the whole group that makes up labor, many of whom were represented at that rally. How could I put on his hat and not one from the nurses or teachers or NOW? The only times I wore hats given to me were during the pouring rain in Wisconsin and Oregon, when I needed them to keep the rain off my glasses so that I could see my speech.

Further Resources

BOOKS
Gillon, Steven M. *The Democrats' Dilemma: Walter F. Mondale and the Liberal Legacy.* New York: Columbia Press, 1995.

Lewis, Finlay. *Walter Mondale: Portrait of an American Politician.* New York: Harper Collins, 1980.

PERIODICALS
Miller, John J. "The Dinosaur: The Bizarre Return of Walter Mondale." *The National Review,* October 28, 2002. Available online at http://www.nationalreview.com/miller/miller 102802.asp; website home page http://www.nationalreview.com (accessed June 9, 2003).

Will, George. "Mondale: Bullied and Buried." *The Washington Post,* November 8, 1994.

WEBSITES
"Debating Our Destiny: Geraldine Ferraro." *PBS.* Available online at http://www.pbs.org/newshour/debatingourdestiny /interviews/ferraro.html; website home page: http://www .pbs.org (accessed June 9, 2003).

"Debating Our Destiny: Vice President Walter Mondale." *PBS.* Available online at http://www.pbs.org/newshour/debatin gourdestiny/interviews/mondale.html; website home page: http://www.pbs.org (accessed June 9, 2003).

The Space Shuttle *Challenger* Accident

"Transcript of the *Challenger* Crew Comments from the Operational Recorder"
Transcript

By: NASA

Date: January 28, 1986

Source: "Transcript of the *Challenger* Crew Comments from the Operational Recorder." January 28, 1986. NASA Headquarters. Available online at http://www.hq.nasa.gov/office /pao/History/transcript.html; website home page: http://www .hq.nasa.gov (accessed June 9, 2003).

About the Organization: The National Aeronautics and Space Administration (NASA) began operation on October 1, 1958, in the aftermath of the Soviet Union launching Sputnik, the world's first artificial satellite. Fearing that the Soviets would next launch ballistic nuclear missiles at the United States, Congress passed the National Aeronautics and Space Act in July 1958. This act combined the National Advisory Committee for Aeronautics and other government agencies to form NASA. The creation of NASA marked the start of the U.S.-Soviet space race.

"A President's Eulogy"
Eulogy

By: Ronald Reagan

Date: January 31, 1986

Source: Reagan, Ronald. "A President's Eulogy." January 31, 1986. Available online at http://www.chron.com/content /interactive/special/challenger/docs/eulogy.html (accessed May 23, 2003).

About the Author: Ronald Reagan (1911–) in 1932 became a sportscaster at radio station WOC in Davenport, Iowa. In 1937, he turned to acting in television and movies. Initially a Democrat, Reagan switched to the Republican Party in 1962 and served as California's governor from 1966 to 1974. Between 1981 and 1989, he was president of the United States. Since leaving office, he has suffered from Alzheimer's disease. ∎

Introduction

In September 1969, two months after *Apollo XI* landed on the moon, NASA began to explore a more economical, reusable launch system. It was proposed that NASA commit itself to an Earth-orbiting space station and a space shuttle linking it to Earth. Due to budgetary constraints, however, President Richard M. Nixon (served 1969–1974) deferred the space station pending the development of a space shuttle. The first shuttle test was carried out in 1977 at the Dryden Flight Research Facility in California. The *Enterprise,* containing no engines or other systems needed for orbital flight, was piggybacked atop a modified Boeing 747. To test its aerodynamics and flight control characteristics, the *Enterprise* was carried to a high altitude and released for a gliding approach and landing in the Mojave Desert. From 1982—when the space shuttle launched its first operational mission—to January 1986, the program launched twenty-five successful missions.

The shape of the space shuttle is similar to a mid-size airline transport. Its cargo bay is fifteen feet wide and sixty feet long, and it is designed to deliver payloads of 65,000 pounds. Unlike airplanes, the space shuttle was designed to enter orbit on a repeated basis. The key to developing the shuttle was protecting it from the withering heat caused by friction with the atmosphere when the craft returns to Earth—along the edge of the wing, temperatures during entry may reach 2,750 degrees Fahrenheit and 600 degrees along the fuselage, the "coldest" area. The space shuttle is equipped with three rocket engines, generating 375,000 pounds of thrust. The external tank carries 143,000 gallons of oxygen propellant and 383,000 gallons of hydrogen propellant for a combined weight of 790 tons. The shuttle reenters orbit at speeds of 17,500 miles per hour and lands at 225 miles per hour.

Significance

At 11:38 A.M., January 28, 1986, the space shuttle *Challenger,* named after the 1870s British naval research vessel, *H.M.S. Challenger,* lifted off from Cape Canaveral, Florida. The shuttle's payloads included a satellite that would have been deployed into orbit to observe Halley's comet. From liftoff to when the signal from the shuttle was lost, there was no indication of a problem. All crew voice communications were normal, and no alarms sounded in the cockpit. The first evidence of a problem came from live video just .678 seconds into flight. A wisp of gray smoke was detected streaming from a joint on the right rocket booster. At 59.788 seconds, a small flame was detected. At 73 seconds, the *Challenger* reached an altitude of 46,000 feet and exploded in the reddish brown colors of an intense burn.

In twenty-five years of space exploration, seven Americans had died. With the *Challenger*'s short flight,

The *Challenger* crew leave their quarters at Kennedy Space Center to board the space shuttle. AP/WIDE WORLD PHOTOS. REPRODUCED BY PERMISSION.

however, this number doubled in just over one minute. That evening, President Ronald Reagan (served 1981–1989) went on national television to address a grieving nation. He said, "We will never forget them, nor the last time we saw them this morning as they prepared for their journey and waved goodbye and slipped the surly bonds of earth to touch the face of God." Reagan called for an immediate investigation into the disaster, but vowed that the space program would continue in honor of the dead astronauts. In June 1986, "The President's Commission on the Space Shuttle *Challenger* Accident" concluded that a fuel leak through faulty rubber O-rings that sealed joint sections of the rocket booster caused the accident. There were no further manned flights until September 1988. There were no further accidents until February 1, 2003, when the space shuttle *Columbia* disintegrated upon re-entry after a sixteen-day mission.

Primary Source

"Transcript of the *Challenger* Crew Comments from the Operational Recorder"

> **SYNOPSIS:** Forty-three days after the *Challenger* accident, the vessel's tape recorder was retrieved from the ocean floor. NASA released the tape transcript

The Space Shuttle *Challenger,* moments before exploding over the Kennedy Space Center in Florida, January 28, 1986. © BETTMANN/CORBIS. REPRODUCED BY PERMISSION.

that revealed the crew's comments from T-2.05 to T+73 seconds (meaning 2:05 minutes prior to take-off until 73 seconds into the flight). *The New York Times,* believing that the crew may have been aware of the impending danger, sued to force NASA to release the audio recording. The U.S. Supreme Court rejected the suit because it would have violated the *Challenger* families' privacy. In the transcript, "CDR" refers to the flight commander, Francis R. Scobee; "PLT" refers to the pilot, Michael J. Smith; "MS 1" refers to the aeronautical engineer Ellison S. Onizuka; and "MS 2" refers to the electrical engineer, Judith A. Resnik, all of whom perished, along with three other colleagues, when the *Challenger* ex-

ploded. NASA's explanatory comments to the Presidential Commission that investigated the tragedy are also noted.

T-2:05. MS 2: Would you give that back to me?

T-2:03. MS 2: Security blanket.

T-2:02. MS 2: Hmm.

T-1:58. CDR: Two minutes downstairs; you gotta watch running down there?

(NASA: Two minutes till launch.)

T-1:47. PLT: OK there goes the lox arm.

(NASA: Liquid oxygen supply arm to ET.)

T-1:46. CDR: Goes the beanie cap.

(NASA: Liquid oxygen vent cap.)

T-1:44. MS 1: Doesn't it go the other way?

T-1:42. (Laughter.)

T-1:39. MS 1: Now I see it; I see it.

T-1:39. PLT: God I hope not Ellison.

T-1:38. MS 1: I couldn't see it moving; it was behind the center screen.

(NASA: Obstructed view of liquid oxygen supply arm.)

T-1:33. MS 2: Got your harnesses locked?

(NASA: Seat restraints.)

T-1:29. PLT: What for?

T-1:28. CDR: I won't lock mine; I might have to reach something.

T-1:24. PLT: Ooh kaaaay.

T-1:04. MS 1: Dick's thinking of somebody there.

T-1:03. CDR: Unhuh.

T-59. CDR: One minute downstairs.

(NASA: One minute till launch.)

T-52. MS 2: Cabin Pressure is probably going to give us an alarm.

(NASA: Caution and warning alarm. Routine occurrence during prelaunch).

T-50. CDR: OK.

T-47. CDR: OK there.

T-43. PLT: Alarm looks good.

(NASA: Cabin pressure is acceptable.)

T-42. CDR: OK.

T-40. PLT: Ullage pressures are up.

(NASA: External tank ullage pressure.)

T-34. PLT: Right engine helium tank is just a little bit low.

(NASA: SSME supply helium pressure.)

T-32. CDR: It was yesterday, too.

T-31. PLT: OK.

T-30. CDR: Thirty seconds down there.

(NASA: 30 seconds till launch.)

T-25. PLT: Remember the red button when you make a roll call.

(NASA: Precautionary reminder for communications configuration.)

T-23. CDR: I won't do that; thanks a lot.

T-15. CDR: Fifteen.

(NASA: 15 seconds till launch.)

T-6. CDR: There they go guys.

(NASA: SSME Ignition.)

MS 2: All right.

CDR: Three at a hundred.

(NASA: SSME thrust level at 100% for all 3 engines.)

T+0. MS 2: Aaall riiight.

T+1. PLT: Here we go.

(NASA: Vehicle motion.)

T+7. CDR: Houston, Challenger roll program.

(NASA: Initiation of vehicle roll program.)

T+11. PLT: Go you Mother.

T+14. MS 1: LVLH.

(NASA: Reminder for cockpit switch configuration change. Local vertical/local horizontal).

T+15. MS 2: (Expletive) hot.

T+16. CDR: Ooohh-kaaay.

T+19. PLT: Looks like we've got a lotta wind here today.

T+20. CDR: Yeah.

T+22. CDR: It's a little hard to see out my window here.

T+28. PLT: There's ten thousand feet and Mach point five.

(NASA: Altitude and velocity report.)

T+30. (Garble.)

T+35. CDR: Point nine.

(NASA: Velocity report, 0.9 Mach).

T+40. PLT: There's Mach one.

(NASA: Velocity report, 1.0 Mach).

T+41. CDR: Going through nineteen thousand.

(NASA: Altitude report, 19,000 ft.)

T+43. CDR: OK we're throttling down.

(NASA: Normal SSME thrust reduction during maximum dynamic pressure region.)

T+57. CDR: Throttling up.

(NASA: Throttle up to 104% after maximum dynamic pressure.)

T+58. PLT: Throttle up.

T+59. CDR: Roger.

T+60. PLT: Feel that mother go.

T+60. Woooohoooo.

T+1:02. PLT: Thirty-five thousand going through one point five.

(NASA: Altitude and velocity report, 35,000 ft., 1.5 Mach).

T+1:05. CDR: Reading four eighty six on mine.

(NASA: Routine airspeed indicator check.)

T+1:07. PLT: Yep, that's what I've got, too.

T+1:10. CDR: Roger, go at throttle up.

(NASA: SSME at 104 percent.)

T+1:13. PLT: Uhoh.

T+1:13. LOSS OF ALL DATA.

Primary Source

"A President's Eulogy"

> **SYNOPSIS:** In the following eulogy, President Reagan praises the *Challenger*'s crew for their selfless pursuit of scientific knowledge. He reminds the nation that the quest to expand the boundaries of knowledge can end in tragedy, though he vows not to let the *Challenger*'s explosion derail the space shuttle program.

We come together today to mourn the loss of seven brave Americans, to share the grief we all feel and, perhaps in that sharing, to find the strength to bear our sorrow and the courage to look for the seeds of hope.

Our nation's loss is first a profound personal loss to the family and the friends and loved ones of our shuttle astronauts. To those they have left behind—the mothers, the fathers, the husbands and wives, brothers, sisters, and yes, especially the children—all of America stands beside you in your time of sorrow.

What we say today is only an inadequate expression of what we carry in our hearts. Words pale in the shadow of grief; they seem insufficient even to measure the brave sacrifice of those you loved and we so admired. Their truest testimony will not be in the words we speak, but in the way they led their lives and in the way they lost those lives—with dedication, honor and an unquenchable desire to explore this mysterious and beautiful universe.

The best we can do is remember our seven astronauts—our *Challenger* Seven—remember them as they lived, bringing life and love and joy to those who knew them and pride to a nation.

They came from all parts of this great country— from South Carolina to Washington State; Ohio to Mohawk, New York; Hawaii to North Carolina to Concord, New Hampshire. They were so different, yet in their mission, their quest, they held so much in common.

We remember Dick Scobee, the commander who spoke the last words we heard from the space shuttle *Challenger.* He served as a fighter pilot in Vietnam, earning many medals for bravery, and later as a test pilot of advanced aircraft before joining the space program. Danger was a familiar companion to Commander Scobee.

We remember Michael Smith, who earned enough medals as a combat pilot to cover his chest, including the Navy Distinguished Flying Cross, three Air Medals—and the Vietnamese Cross of Gallantry with Silver Star, in gratitude from a nation that he fought to keep free.

We remember Judith Resnik, known as J.R. to her friends, always smiling, always eager to make a contribution, finding beauty in the music she played on her piano in her off-hours.

We remember Ellison Onizuka, who, as a child running barefoot through the coffee fields and macadamia groves of Hawaii, dreamed of someday traveling to the Moon. Being an Eagle Scout, he said, had helped him soar to the impressive achievement of his career.

We remember Ronald McNair, who said that he learned perseverance in the cotton fields of South Carolina. His dream was to live aboard the space station, performing experiments and playing his saxophone in the weightlessness of space; Ron, we will miss your saxophone and we will build your space station.

We remember Gregory Jarvis. On that ill-fated flight he was carrying with him a flag of his university in Buffalo, New York—a small token he said, to the people who unlocked his future.

We remember Christa McAuliffe, who captured the imagination of the entire nation, inspiring us with her pluck, her restless spirit of discovery; a teacher, not just to her students, but to an entire people, instilling us all with the excitement of this journey we ride into the future.

We will always remember them, these skilled professionals, scientists and adventurers, these artists and teachers and family men and women, and we will cherish each of their stories—stories of triumph and bravery, stories of true American heroes.

Members of the President's Commission on the Space Shuttle *Challenger* Accident, Cape Canaveral, Florida, February 14, 1986. They inspect the joint of a solid rocket booster. It is believed that a failure in one such joint was responsible for the *Challenger*'s explosion. © **BETTMANN/CORBIS. REPRODUCED BY PERMISSION.**

On the day of the disaster, our nation held a vigil by our television sets. In one cruel moment, our exhilaration turned to horror; we waited and watched and tried to make sense of what we had seen. That night, I listened to a call-in program on the radio: people of every age spoke of their sadness and the pride they felt in "our astronauts." Across America, we are reaching out, holding hands, finding comfort in one another.

The sacrifice of your loved ones has stirred the soul of our nation and, through the pain, our hearts have been opened to a profound truth—the future is not free, the story of all human progress is one of a struggle against all odds. We learned again that this America, which Abraham Lincoln called the last best hope of man on Earth, was built on heroism and noble sacrifice. It was built by men and women like our seven star voyagers, who answered a call beyond duty, who gave more than was expected or required, and who gave it with little thought to worldly reward.

We think back to the pioneers of an earlier century, and the sturdy souls who took their families and their belongings and set out into the frontier of the American West. Often, they met with terrible hardship. Along the Oregon Trail you can still see the grave markers of those who fell on the way. But grief only steeled them to the journey ahead.

Today, the frontier is space and the boundaries of human knowledge. Sometimes, when we reach for the stars, we fall short. But we must pick ourselves up again and press on despite the pain. Our nation is indeed fortunate that we can still draw on immense reservoirs of courage, character and fortitude—that we are still blessed with heroes like those of the space shuttle *Challenger*.

Dick Scobee knew that every launching of a space shuttle is a technological miracle. And he said, if something ever does go wrong, I hope that doesn't mean the end to the space shuttle program. Every family member I talked to asked specifically that we continue the program, that that is what their departed loved one would want above all else. We will not disappoint them.

Today, we promise Dick Scobee and his crew that their dream lives on; that the future they worked so hard to build will become reality. The dedicated men and women of NASA have lost seven members of their family. Still, they too, must forge ahead, with a space program that is effective, safe and efficient, but bold and committed.

Man will continue his conquest of space. To reach out for new goals and ever greater achievements—that is the way we shall commemorate our seven *Challenger* heroes.

Dick, Mike, Judy, El, Ron, Greg and Christa—your families and your country mourn your passing. We bid you goodbye. We will never forget you. For those who knew you well and loved you, the pain will be deep and enduring. A nation, too, will long feel the loss of her seven sons and daughters, her seven good friends. We can find consolation only in faith, for we know in our hearts that you who flew so high and so proud now make your home beyond the stars, safe in God's promise of eternal life.

May God bless you all and give you comfort in this difficult time.

Further Resources

BOOKS

Burgess, Colin, and Grace George Corrigan. *Teacher in Space: Christa McAuliffe and the Challenger Legacy.* Lincoln, Neb.: Bison Books, 2000.

Lieurance, Suzanne. *The Space Shuttle Challenger Disaster in American History.* Berkley Heights, N.J.: Enslow Publishers, 2001.

Vaughan, Diane. *The Challenger Launch Decision: Risky Technology, Culture and Defiance at NASA.* Chicago: University of Chicago Press, 1997.

PERIODICALS

Brown, Stuart F. "Twenty Years After Apollo: Is the U.S. Lost in Space?" *Popular Science,* vol. 235, July 1989, 63–75.

Kluger, Jerry. "NASA's Orbiting Dream House." *Discover,* vol. 10, May 1989, 68–72.

WEBSITES

"*Challenger* Space Shuttle." Hawaii State Public Library System Guide to Resources and Services. Available online at http://www.hcc.hawaii.edu/hspls/challeng.html; website home page: http://www.hcc.hawaii.edu/hspls/ (accessed May 23, 2003).

"51-L: The *Challenger* Accident." Space Policy Project, Federation of American Scientists. Available online at http://www.fas.org/spp/51L.html; website home page: http://www.fas.org/spp/ (accessed May 23, 2003).

"Report of the Presidential Commission on the Space Shuttle *Challenger* Accident." NASA Space Shuttle Missions, Kennedy Space Center. Available online at http://science.ksc.nasa.gov/shuttle/missions/51-l/docs/rogers-commission/table-of-contents.html; website home page: http://science.ksc.nasa.gov/shuttle/missions/ (accessed May 23, 2003).

VIDEOCASSETTES

The "Challenger" Explosion. MPI Home Video, 1989, VHS.

Disaster: Point of No Return. Films for the Humanities and Sciences, 1997, VHS.

It Was No Accident: An Insider's View of the Unethical Decision-Making Process that Doomed the Space Shuttle "Challenger." State University of New York, Binghamton, 1988, VHS.

"Implementing Decisions of the Geneva Summit (C)"
Memo

By: Ronald Reagan

Date: February 4, 1986

Source: Reagan, Ronald. "Implementing Decisions of the Geneva Summit (C)," National Security Decision Directive Number 209, February 4, 1986. Available online at: http://www.fas.org/irp/offdocs/nsdd/nsdd-209.htm; website home page: http://www.fas.org (accessed June 9, 2003).

About the Author: Ronald Reagan (1911–) was born in Tampico, Illinois. After graduating from Eureka College, Reagan worked as a sports broadcaster for a Davenport, Iowa, radio station. In 1937, while covering spring training in California, Reagan signed a contract with Warner Brothers, a movie studio. Reagan eventually starred in over fifty films. In 1964, he retired from acting and was elected governor of California. In 1980, Reagan was elected president (served 1981–1989). After serving two terms, he retired to his ranch in California. ∎

Introduction

During the 1950s and 1960s, the U.S. nuclear arsenal was overwhelmingly superior to the Soviets'. During the presidency of John F. Kennedy (1961–1963), the United States devised a strategy to overcome a potential Soviet first-strike. The military outpaced the Soviets in the development of air, land, and sea-based nuclear weapons, thereby ensuring the survival of ample numbers of strategic weapons to annihilate the Soviet Union. Following the 1962 Cuban Missile Crisis debacle, the Soviet Union increased its production of land-based intercontinental ballistic missiles (ICBMs) to deter a possible American first-strike. By the end of the 1960s, the Soviets had reached nuclear parity with the United States. Now both sides had the capacity to sustain a first-strike and execute a withering nuclear counteroffensive. Thus, Mutual Assured Destruction (MAD) became the cornerstone of the U.S.-Soviet strategic relationship.

Throughout the 1970s, the Soviet Union and the United States entered into a series of nuclear arms control agreements to maintain parity, the key to mutual de-

UNCLASSIFIED

SYSTEM II
90055

THE WHITE HOUSE

WASHINGTON

February 4, 1986

UNCLASSIFIED

NATIONAL SECURITY DECISION
DIRECTIVE NUMBER 209

IMPLEMENTING DECISIONS OF THE GENEVA SUMMIT (C)

My meetings with General Secretary Gorbachev produced a fresh
start in U.S.-Soviet relations in the sense that it established a
framework for bilateral negotiations of some of our outstanding
differences. It is now our task to make use of this framework to
move us toward the goals I have set for U.S.-Soviet relations.
This will also be a key component in the substantive preparations
for my meeting with Mr. Gorbachev in the United States this year.
(U)

In order to ensure vigorous pursuit of a dialogue and, where
appropriate, negotiations in those areas where the Joint
U.S.-USSR Statement at Geneva indicated that progress is
possible, I hereby designate the following agencies to take the
lead in coordinating the United States position and pursuing it
actively with representatives of the Soviet Union: (U)

1. Negotiations on Nuclear and Space Arms: The Senior Arms
Control Group will continue to have responsibility for
coordinating views of U.S. positions to be taken, which will then
be reviewed by the National Security Council. (C)

2. Regional Conflicts: The Secretary of State will have
responsibility for developing concrete new ways to pursue my
initiative to end regional conflicts, as outlined in my speech to
the United Nations General Assembly last October, and for
conducting regular consultations with the Soviet Union. This
issue is a major one, and the Department of State should also
take the lead in ensuring that it receives an appropriate share
of public attention. (C)

3. People-to-People Contacts and Information Exchange: The
Director of the United States Information Agency will have the
responsibility for implementing the initiatives I have made in
this area. Policy matters will be considered by an
Interdepartmental Group chaired by the National Security Council

Declassified/Released on 3/13/96
under provisions of E.O. 12958
by J. Saunders, National Security Council

Declassify on: OADR

COPY 1 OF 10 COPIES

CONFIDENTIAL
UNCLASSIFIED

Primary Source

"Implementing Decisions of the Geneva Summit (C)" (1 OF 3)

SYNOPSIS: On February 4, 1986, President Reagan signed National Security Decision Directive Number 209. This document is important because following the Geneva Summit it established a new framework for bilateral negotiations on some significant differences between the United States and Soviet Union. Reagan orders various executive agencies to coordinate the American foreign policy position in several areas and to pursue it "actively" with the Soviet Union. FROM FAS.ORG (FEDERATION OF AMERICAN SCIENTISITS).

2

Staff. I would note in this connection that the areas for expansion of contacts noted in the U.S.-USSR Joint Statement are only a start toward the objective I have set for a radical expansion of contacts. Therefore, efforts should concentrate not merely on implementing those programs to which the Soviets agreed at Geneva, but to expanding their scope and size in accord with the proposals made by the United States before the Geneva Summit. (C)

4. Chemical Weapons: The Director of the Arms Control and Disarmament Agency shall, in coordination with the Interdepartmental Group on Chemical and Biological Weapons Arms Control, have primary responsibility for preparing the United States position for talks with the Soviets on verification measures to enforce a chemical weapons ban, and on measures to combat the proliferation of chemical weapons. In case of interagency disagreement, the issues should be referred to the Senior Arms Control Group. (C)

5. Risk Reduction Centers: The Staff of the National Security Council, working with the existing ad hoc interagency group on this subject, will retain primary responsibility for the development and implementation of the U.S. approach to be taken in the exploratory, expert-level discussions on the concept of risk reduction centers. (C)

6. Thermonuclear Fusion: The Secretary of Energy shall have the responsibility of coordinating the United States position for the study of the feasibility of an international effort to build a prototype fusion power plant. (C)

7. Cancer Research: The Secretary of Health and Human Services, in cooperation with the National Institutes of Health, shall be responsible for developing a cooperative program in this area, utilizing the U.S.-USSR Agreement on Cooperation in the Field of Medical Science and Public Health as a framework for implementation. (U)

8. Environmental Research: The Director of the Environmental Protection Agency will have the responsibility for implementing cooperation in this area, utilizing the U.S.-USSR Agreement on Cooperation in the Field of Environmental Protection. (U)

9. Humanitarian Issues: The Secretary of State will be responsible for conducting a vigorous effort, based primarily on private diplomacy, for achieving United States objectives in this area. (C)

COPY __1__ OF __10__ COPIES

Primary Source

"Implementing Decisions of the Geneva Summit (C)" (2 OF 3)
Page 2 of NSDD 209. FROM FAS.ORG (FEDERATION OF AMERICAN SCIENTISTS).

UNCLASSIFIED

CONFIDENTIAL

In all of these areas, the normal interagency process will be utilized to ensure that steps taken are in the interest of the United States. While I wish to ensure that these issues are pursued vigorously with the Soviet Union, all should be discussed and negotiated strictly on their merits. In negotiating with the Soviet Union no artificial deadlines should be set, nor any concessions made merely because another meeting with General Secretary Gorbachev will be scheduled for this year. (C)

UNCLASSIFIED

COPY 1 OF 10 COPIES

CONFIDENTIAL

Primary Source

"Implementing Decisions of the Geneva Summit (C)" (3 OF 3)
Page 3 of NSDD 209. FROM FAS.ORG (FEDERATION OF AMERICAN SCIENTISITS).

Mikhail Gorbachev and Ronald Reagan stand together in the White House library. GETTY IMAGES. REPRODUCED BY PERMISSION.

terrence. In 1972, President Richard M. Nixon (served 1969–1974) and General Secretary Leonid Brezhnev signed SALT I (Strategic Arms Limitation Talks), freezing the number of existing ballistic missiles at present levels, and the Anti-Ballistic Missile Treaty (ABM), preventing either side from creating a defense system to counter ICBMs. The rationale for the ABM Treaty was that any defensive technological advance would trigger an expensive arms race and destabilize U.S-Soviet relations by triggering a further buildup of offensive countermeasures. In 1980, President Ronald Reagan attacked the ABM Treaty, believing that technology had reached the point where an effective ABM system was achievable. In 1983, Reagan delivered his "Star Wars" speech, proposing that the Pentagon develop and deploy a space-based missile defense system costing in excess of $95 billion. In 1985, Soviet general secretary Mikhail Gorbachev came to power advocating a more conciliatory foreign policy towards the West.

Significance

Though the Geneva summit produced no important agreements, it was a political victory for President Reagan. By meeting with the Soviet general secretary, Reagan projected the image of a tough negotiator. At the summit, Gorbachev needed to reach an arms control agreement. He knew that military spending had to be reduced in order to stimulate his sinking domestic economy. To justify such cuts, Gorbachev needed Reagan to agree to similar military cuts. As a result, Gorbachev proposed reducing the strategic nuclear arsenals of both countries by fifty percent. To his surprise, Reagan refused because, in return, the United States would have to abandon its Strategic Defense Initiative (SDI). Reagan supported SDI because he believed that the doctrine of mutual assured destruction (MAD) was immoral. The United States had the moral obligation to defend its citizens from certain destruction by Soviet ICBMs. Reagan also believed that Moscow could not afford to be drawn into a technological race with Washington. If the Soviets attempted to develop and deploy their own system, it would further undermine their domestic economy by diverting badly needed financial resources to the military.

In October 1986, Reagan and Gorbachev met in Reykjavik, Iceland. The Soviet Union shocked the world by proposing that both nations eliminate their nuclear ballistic missiles. This proposal would have given America nuclear superiority because it did not apply to the nuclear arsenal aboard air force bombers. In a controversial decision, Reagan again rejected the offer because he would not abandon SDI or do anything to sustain the imploding Soviet economy. The president's decision was significant because it contributed to the collapse of the Soviet economy and the demise of the "Evil Empire" three years later. In addition, Reagan's faith in SDI paid dividends in Operation Iraqi Freedom in 2003, when Patriot missile batteries were successfully deployed against incoming Iraqi missiles.

Further Resources

BOOKS

Schultz, George P. *Turmoil and Triumph: My Years as Secretary of State.* New York: Charles Scribner's Sons, 1993.

Schweizer, Peter. *Reagan's War: The Epic Story of His Forty-Year Struggle and Final Triumph Over Communism.* New York: Doubleday 2002.

Winik, Jay. *On the Brink: The Dramatic Behind-the-Scenes Saga of the Reagan Era and the Men and Women Who Won the Cold War.* New York: Simon and Schuster, 1996.

PERIODICALS

Davis, Mark W. "Reagan's Real Reason for SDI." *Policy Review,* No. 103, October 2000. Available online at http://www.policyreview.org/oct00/davis_print.html; website home page: http://www.policyreview.org (accessed June 9, 2003).

Lewis, George. "Why National Missile Defense Won't Work." *Scientific American,* August 1999, 36–41.

WEBSITES

"Reagan-Gorbachev Transcripts, Reykjavik, Iceland, October 11–16, 1986." *CNN.* Available online at http://www.cnn.com/SPECIALS/cold.war/episodes/22/documents/reykjavik;

website home page http://www.cnn.com (accessed May 17, 2003).

"The Secret History of The ABM Treaty, 1969–1972." The National Security Archives. Available online at http://www.gwu.edu/~nsarchiv/NSAEBB/NSAEBB60; website home page: http://www.gwu.edu (accessed June 9, 2003).

The Tower Commission Report

Report

By: John Tower, Edmund Muskie, and Brent Scowcroft
Date: February 26, 1987
Source: Tower, John, et al. *The Tower Commission Report.* New York: Random House, February 1987.
About the Author: John Tower (1925–1991) was born in Houston, Texas. In 1943, he enlisted in the United States Navy, serving in the Pacific theater in World War II (1939–1945) until 1946. He was a 1953 graduate of Southern Methodist University, and in 1961, Tower became the youngest man ever to become a U.S. senator at age thirty-six. Tower was appointed chairman of the powerful Senate Armed Services Committee in 1981. He retired from public office in 1984, and worked as a defense consultant. ■

Introduction

In 1979, leftist rebels in Nicaragua ousted dictator Anastasio Somoza. The new, popularly elected Sandinista government held a Marxist ideology, and the Russians and Cubans supported it. After the 1980 presidential election—with the Cold War well underway—U.S. president Ronald Reagan (served 1981–1989) sought to undermine the communist government by supporting its adversaries, the contras—Spanish for "against"—who were waging a guerrilla war. In 1981, Reagan persuaded Congress to provide these "freedom fighters" with military arms.

In October 1984, Congress passed an amendment sponsored by Representative Edward P. Boland to bar further military assistance to the rebels. The Democratically-controlled Congress, fearing that continued military assistance would result in U.S. troops becoming involved in another Vietnam conflict (1964–1975), passed the measure. To avoid the ban, the Reagan administration instructed John Poindexter's National Security Council (NSC), not specifically covered by the Boland Amendment, to coordinate secret military aid to the contras.

At the time, Iran and Iraq had been engaged in a bloody war since 1980. Reagan was concerned that since the United States had no diplomatic relations with Iran, the Islamic nation was growing politically closer to the

Russians. Reagan was also troubled that Iranian sympathizers in Lebanon were holding four Americans hostage. In 1985, Reagan hoped to influence Iranian foreign policy in a pro-Western direction and gain the release of the hostages by authorizing the sale of missiles to Iran via Israel. In return, two American hostages were released. The profits from the arms sales were used to fund the contras. In November 1986, Lebanese newspapers broke the story. Reagan first denied the allegation, but later acknowledged that weapons were sold to Iran and that profits were diverted to the contras. He denied, however, that the arms were sold to win the release of American hostages. In December 1986, Reagan appointed a special review board to investigate the NSC.

Significance

Lieutenant Colonel Oliver North, an aid to Admiral Poindexter at the NSC, devised the covert diversion of funds. North used $12 million in arms sale profits to provide weapons for the contras, arguably a violation of the spirit of the congressional ban. In a memorandum, North detailed the transaction to Poindexter, who later testified under oath that he did not show it to Reagan in order to spare the president any possible embarrassment. When the American press began investigating the matter, North shredded hundreds of documents; but one document linking the White House to the plan survived. White House officials testified that President Reagan knew nothing of the diversion. Critics pointed out that, if this was true, Reagan had lost control of his administration. North was found guilty of destroying government documents to obstruct Congress, and Poindexter was convicted of conspiracy and lying to Congress. On appeal, both convictions were vacated because the defendants had entered into immunity agreements with the Senate when it had launched its investigation.

Though most Americans believed that President Reagan knew more of the details of what became known as the Iran-contra affair than he admitted, he remained popular with the public. Journalists dubbed him the "Teflon" president, commenting on Reagan's seemingly uncanny ability to deflect political embarrassments or bear responsibility for the actions of his administration. Yet, Reagan's influence with a furious Congress deteriorated. Critics contended that NSC officials had violated the Boland Amendment and interfered with the constitutional provision granting Congress oversight and control of the appropriations process. Reagan's supporters countered that neither federal statutes nor constitutional provisions were violated. They maintained that the executive branch was forced to turn to the NSC because of congressional interference with the president's authority to conduct foreign policy. The Reagan administration was

Members of the Tower Commission (from left to right) National Security Advisor Lieutenant General Brent Scowcroft, Senator John Tower, and Secretary of State Edmund Muskie field questions at the White House. © BETTMANN/CORBIS. REPRODUCED BY PERMISSION.

unable to pass any meaningful legislation for the remainder of the term.

Primary Source

The Tower Commission Report [excerpt]

> **SYNOPSIS:** In the report, Chairman John Tower states that although Reagan was "deeply committed" to the release of the hostages held by Iranian sympathizers, he concluded that the president had been lax in management over the situation. Reagan never publicly disagreed with Tower's findings.

Introduction

The pages you are about to read stand apart from past appraisals of Reagan and his era. We used to be told that the failures in Washington in his time were not his failures; his were the successes of rekindling in the American people confidence in themselves, in their country, in their political institutions, in their historical purpose and righteousness. Rambo America was America rampant—too materialistic, too self-obsessed, too superficial, critics said, but nevertheless a forceful presence once again on the grand stage of global power.

But as the report makes clear, the Iran-contra affair constituted a pair of grievous missteps: first, the covert sale of arms to Iran at a time when official American policy continued to call for the isolation of Ayatollah Khomeini and all his works; and second, the diversion of some of the profits to the Nicaraguan rebels at a time when Congress had

ruled out direct or indirect American governmental aid. . . .

In the months after the disclosure of the broad outlines of the scandal, bits and pieces of the story leaked out. The President and his associates tried several times to "cauterize the wound," as one of them put it, with a singular lack of success. Inevitably, the investigations began—one by the Senate intelligence committee; two by select committees of the Congress; one by a special prosecutor, Lawrence E. Walsh, and the one by the special review board, which was charged specifically with studying what went wrong in the National Security Council, the President's own foreign-policy staff apparatus, which under the leadership of Robert C. McFarlane and then Vice Adm. John M. Poindexter appears to have run wild, with an obscure, zealous Marine Lieutenant Colonel named Oliver L. North making key foreign-policy decisions for the mightiest nation in the free world.

The report of the review board is a first draft, as it were, prepared without the testimony of a number of key figures—Admiral Poindexter, Colonel North, and General Richard V. Secord, a key intermediary—whose accounts are expected to become available later if, as anticipated, they are granted limited immunity from prosecution. The board itself concedes that "the whole matter cannot be fully explained," that some aspects remain an enigma.

Nonetheless, the report represents not only the first detailed official look at the matter, but also a major political event in itself. It is given weight by the reputation of the men who signed it: former Senator John Tower, Republican of Texas, a conservative with special expertise in national security, who was the board's chairman; former Senator and former Secretary of State Edmund S. Muskie, Democrat of Maine, a onetime Presidential candidate known for his probity and level-headedness, and Brent Scowcroft, a retired Air Force general who served several Republican presidents as a key foreign-policy adviser. It is given weight by the fact that the President asked for it to be compiled. And it is given weight by its compellingly sober tone. . . .

More important, the board painted a picture of Ronald Reagan very different from that the world had become accustomed to in the last six years. No trace here of the lopsided smile, the easy wave, the confident mien that carried him through every past crisis; this portrait is of a man confused, distracted, so remote that he failed utterly to control the implementation of his vision of an initiative that would free American hostages and re-establish American influence in Iran, with all of its present and future strategic importance. At times, in fact, the report makes the President sound like the inhabitant of a never-never land of imaginary policies. . . .

Senator Tower was blunt when he answered the questions of reporters a few minutes after the report was released. He summed up his conclusions this way: "I believe the President was poorly advised and poorly served. I think that he should have followed up more and monitored this operation more closely. I think he was not aware of a lot of things that were going on and the way the operation was structured and who was involved in it. He very clearly didn't understand all of that." . . .

His buoyancy conspicuously absent, Reagan had little to say in a brief public statement just before the board held its press conference, except for a pledge to "do whatever is necessary to enact the proper reforms and to meet the challenges ahead." The problem with that was that all three members of the board made it plain that they considered this a policy blunder caused not by institutions but by individuals. . . .

■ ■ ■

B. Failure of Responsibility

The NSC system will not work unless the President makes it work. After all, this system was created to serve the President of the United States in ways of his choosing. By his actions, by his leadership, the President therefore determines the quality of its performance.

By his own account, as evidenced in his diary notes, and as conveyed to the Board by his principal advisors, President Reagan was deeply committed to securing the release of the hostages. It was this intense compassion for the hostages that appeared to motivate his steadfast support of the Iran initiative, even in the face of opposition from his Secretaries of State and Defense.

In his obvious commitment, the President appears to have proceeded with a concept of the initiative that was not accurately reflected in the reality of the operation. The President did not seem to be aware of the way in which the operation was implemented and the full consequences of U.S. participation. . . .

The President's management style is to put the principal responsibility for policy review and implementation on the shoulders of his advisors. Never-

theless, with such a complex, high-risk operation and so much at stake, the President should have ensured that the NSC system did not fail him. He did not force his policy to undergo the most critical review of which the NSC participants and the process were capable. At no time did he insist upon accountability and performance review. Had the President chosen to drive the NSC system, the outcome could well have been different. As it was, the most powerful features of the NSC system—providing comprehensive analysis, alternatives and follow-up—were not utilized. . . .

Beyond the President, the other NSC principals and the National Security Advisor must share in the responsibility for the NSC system.

President Reagan's personal management style places an especially heavy responsibility on his key advisors. Knowing his style, they should have been particularly mindful of the need for special attention to the manner in which this arms sale initiative developed and proceeded. On this score, neither the National Security Advisor nor the other NSC principals deserve high marks.

It is their obligation as members and advisors to the Council to ensure that the President is adequately served. The principal subordinates to the President must not be deterred from urging the President not to proceed on a highly questionable course of action even in the face of his strong conviction to the contrary.

In the case of the Iran initiative, the NSC process did not fail, it simply was largely ignored. The National Security Advisor and the NSC principals all had a duty to raise this issue and insist that orderly process be imposed. None of them did so. . . .

Mr. Regan also shares in this responsibility. More than almost any Chief of Staff of recent memory, he asserted personal control over the White House staff and sought to extend this control to the National Security Advisor. He was personally active in national security affairs and attended almost all of the relevant meetings regarding the Iran initiative. . . . He must bear primary responsibility for the chaos that descended upon the White House when such disclosure did occur.

Mr. McFarlane appeared caught between a President who supported the initiative and the cabinet officers who strongly opposed it. While he made efforts to keep these cabinet officers informed, the Board heard complaints from some that he was not always successful. VADM Poindexter on several

U.S.-supported Contras clean their weapons at a base camp in Honduras in 1985. © BILL GENTILE/CORBIS. REPRODUCED BY PERMISSION.

occasions apparently sought to exclude NSC principals other than the President from knowledge of the initiative. Indeed, on one or more occasions Secretary Shultz may have been actively misled by VADM Poindexter.

VADM Poindexter also failed grievously on the matter of Contra diversion. Evidence indicates that VADM Poindexter knew that a diversion occurred, yet he did not take the steps that were required given the gravity of that prospect. He apparently failed to appreciate or ignored the serious legal and political risks presented. His clear obligation was either to investigate the matter or take it to the President—or both. He did neither. Director Casey shared a similar responsibility. Evidence suggests that he received information about the possible diversion of funds to the Contras almost a month before the story broke. He, too, did not move promptly to raise the matter with the President. Yet his responsibility to do so was clear.

The NSC principals other than the President may be somewhat excused by the insufficient attention on the part of the National Security Advisor to the need to keep all the principals fully informed. Given the importance of the issue and the sharp policy di-

vergences involved, however, Secretary Shultz and Secretary Weinberger in particular distanced themselves from the march of events. Secretary Shultz specifically requested to be informed only as necessary to perform his job. Secretary Weinberger had access through intelligence to details about the operation. Their obligation was to give the President their full support and continued advice with respect to the program or, if they could not in conscience do that, to so inform the President. Instead, they simply distanced themselves from the program. . . . They were not energetic in attempting to protect the President from the consequences of his personal commitment to freeing the hostages.

Director Casey appears to have been informed in considerable detail about the specifics of the Iranian operation. He appears to have acquiesced in and to have encouraged North's exercise of direct operational control over the operation. Because of the NSC staff's proximity to and close identification with the President, this increased the risks to the President if the initiative became public or the operation failed.

There is no evidence, however, that Director Casey explained this risk to the President or made clear to the President that LtCol North, rather than the CIA, was running the operation. The President does not recall ever being informed of this fact. Indeed, Director Casey should have gone further and pressed for operational responsibility to be transferred to the CIA. . . .

Finally, Director Casey, and, to a lesser extent, Secretary Weinberger, should have taken it upon themselves to assess the effect of the transfer of arms and intelligence to Iran on the Iran/Iraq military balance, and to transmit that information to the President. . . .

■■■

D. Aftermath—The Efforts To Tell the Story

From the first hint in late-October, 1986 that the McFarlane trip would soon become public, information on the Iran initiative and Contra activity cascaded into the press. The veiled hints of secret activities, random and indiscriminate disclosures of information from a variety of sources, both knowledgeable and otherwise, and conflicting statements by high-level officials presented a confusing picture to the American public. The Board recognized that conflicts among contemporaneous documents and statements raised concern about the management of the public presentation of facts on the Iran initiative. Though the Board reviewed some evidence on events after the exposure, our ability to comment on these events remains limited.

The Board found evidence that immediately following the public disclosure, the President wanted to avoid providing too much specificity or detail out of concern for the hostages still held in Lebanon and those Iranians who had supported the initiative. In doing so, he did not, we believe, intend to mislead the American public or cover-up unlawful conduct. By at least November 20, the President took steps to ensure that all the facts would come out. From the President's request to Mr. Meese to look into the history of the initiative, to his appointment of this Board, to his request for an Independent Counsel, to his willingness to discuss this matter fully and to review his personal notes with us, the Board is convinced that the President does indeed want the full story to be told.

Those who prepared the President's supporting documentation did not appear, at least initially, to share in the President's ultimate wishes. Mr. McFarlane described for the Board the process used by the NSC staff to create a chronology that obscured essential facts. Mr. McFarlane contributed to the creation of this chronology which did not, he said, present "a full and completely accurate account" of the events and left ambiguous the President's role. This was, according to Mr. McFarlane, done to distance the President from the timing and nature of the President's authorization. He told the Board that he wrote a memorandum on November 18, which tried to, in his own words, "gild the President's motives." This version was incorporated into the chronology. Mr. McFarlane told the Board that he knew the account was "misleading, at least, and wrong, at worst." Mr. McFarlane told the Board that he did provide the Attorney General an accurate account of the President's role.

The Board found considerable reason to question the actions of LtCol North in the aftermath of the disclosure. The Board has no evidence to either confirm or refute that LtCol North destroyed documents on the initiative in an effort to conceal facts from threatened investigations. The Board found indications that LtCol North was involved in an effort, over time, to conceal or withhold important information. The files of LtCol North contained much of the historical documentation that the Board used to construct its narrative. Moreover, LtCol North was the primary U.S. government official involved in the details of the operation. The chronology he produced has many inaccuracies. These "histories" were to be the basis of the "full" story of the Iran initiative. These inaccuracies lend some evidence to the proposition that LtCol North, either on his own or at the behest of others, actively sought to conceal important information.

Out of concern for the protection of classified material, Director Casey and VADM Poindexter were to brief only the Congressional intelligence committees on the "full" story; the DCI before the Committees and VADM Poindexter in private sessions with the chairmen and vice-chairmen. The DCI and VADM Poindexter undertook to do this on November 21, 1986. It appears from the copy of the DCI's testimony and notes of VADM Poindexter's meetings, that they did not fully relate the nature of events as they had occurred. The result is an understandable perception that they were not forthcoming.

The Board is also concerned about various notes that appear to be missing. VADM Poindexter was the official note taker in some key meetings, yet no notes for the meetings can be found. The reason for the lack of such notes remains unknown to the Board. If they were written, they may contain very important information. We have no way of knowing if they exist.

Further Resources

BOOKS

Draper, Theodore. *A Very Thin Line: The Iran-Contra Affair.* New York: Hill and Wang, 1991.

Martin, Al. *The Conspirators: Secrets of an Iran-Contra Insider.* Pray, Mont.: National Liberty Press, 2002.

Walsh, Lawrence. *Firewall: The Iran-Contra Conspiracy and Cover Up.* New York: W.W. Norton, 1997.

PERIODICALS

Elkin, Steven. "Contempt of Congress: The Iran-Contra Affair and the American Constitution." *Congress and the Presidency,* vol. 18, Spring 1991, 1–16.

"Iran-Contra: As the Shadows Lengthen." *Newsweek,* vol. 134, no. 14, 1999, 36–38.

WEBSITES

"Final Report of the Independent Counsel for Iran/Contra Matters." *Federation of American Scientists.* Available online at http://www.fas.org/irp/offdocs/walsh/; website home page: http://www.fas.org (accessed June 9, 2003).

"The Iran-Contra Affair: The Making of a Scandal, 1983–1988." *National Security Archives.* Available online at http://nsarchive.chadwyck.com/icintro.htm; website home page: http://nsarchive.chadwyck.com (accessed June 9, 2003).

Ronald Reagan's Remarks at the Brandenburg Gate

Speech

By: Ronald Reagan

Date: June 12, 1987

Source: Reagan, Ronald. Transcript of "Remarks at the Brandenburg Gate." West Berlin, West Germany, June 12, 1987. Available online at http://www.ronaldreagan.com/sp_11.html; website home page: http://www.ronaldreagan.com (accessed June 9, 2003).

About the Author: Ronald Reagan (1911–) was born in Tampico, Illinois. After graduating from Eureka College, Reagan worked as a sports broadcaster for a Davenport, Iowa, radio station. In 1937, while covering spring training in California, Reagan signed a contract with Warner Brothers, a movie studio. Reagan eventually starred in over fifty films. In 1964, he retired from acting and was elected governor of California. In 1980, Reagan was elected president (served 1981–1989). After serving two terms, he retired to his ranch in California. ∎

Introduction

In May 1987, President Ronald Reagan prepared to travel to West Berlin to celebrate the German city's 750th anniversary. West Berlin officials suggested that Reagan speak in front of the Reichstag, the German parliament. The Reichstag was a short distance from the Berlin Wall, the Cold War barricade built by the Soviets in 1961 to prevent freedom-seeking East Berliners from fleeing to the West. Reagan, however, decided that he wanted to speak before the Brandenburg Gate, the two-hundred-year-old arch incorporated into the Berlin Wall. The West Berliners feared that a major speech before the symbol of Soviet totalitarianism would be too provocative and worsen relations between East and West. The *Stasi,* East Germany's secret police force, was also alarmed at Reagan's intentions. Knowing that the president had a history of delivering controversial speeches, the *Stasi* issued a general alert warning its agents to be extra vigilant, as Reagan may encourage East Berliners to defect.

Once the trip to West Berlin was confirmed, Peter Robinson, Reagan's speechwriter, and other members of White House advance team flew to Berlin to gauge the mood of the city. Robinson was invited to dine with Dieter Eltz, a retired World Bank official, and a dozen other West Berliners. When Robinson asked whether West Berliners had gotten used to the Wall, one man said, "My sister lives twenty miles in that direction but I haven't seen her in more than two decades. Do you think I can get used to that?" Next, Robinson's hostess clenched her fist and slammed it into her other palm and said, "If this man Gorbachev is serious with his talk of *glasnost* and *perestroika,* he can prove it. He can get rid of this wall." With that simple, passionate comment, Robinson had the central passage of the upcoming speech. When Reagan delivered his speech before an enthusiastic crowd, he exhorted the Soviet leader to "tear down this wall."

Significance

Two years later, on November 12, 1989, joyous Berliners hammered down the twenty-eight mile Berlin Wall, and with it Soviet communism was left on the "ash-heap of history." By October 1990, the two Germanys, split since the end of World War II (1939–1945) were reunited. The revolution spread immediately throughout Eastern Europe, toppling communist regimes in its wake. In Poland, Lech Walesa, leader of the ten-year-old Solidarity movement, found himself president of a free Poland. In Czechoslovakia, under Soviet domination for two decades, playwright Vaclav Havel was elected president in what was called the Velvet Revolution. In Bulgaria, Hungary, Romania, Yugoslavia, and Albania, this script was repeated.

Since the fall of the Berlin Wall, historians have debated the underlying reasons for the collapse of Soviet communism. The political left contends that Mikhail Gorbachev deserves the credit for liberalizing the Soviet economy and its political structure, while reducing the size of its military. They argue that if Reagan had not been a staunch Cold War warrior, Gorbachev would have retained power and prevented the country from breaking up into numerous unstable, nuclear-armed states. Others argue that the American Cold War victory was the result of President Harry Truman's (served 1945–1953) containment policy of the 1940s. By containing the Soviet menace for five decades, the United States had outlasted her enemies in a nerve-wracking battle of attrition. Conservatives, on the other hand, cite Great Britain's prime minister Margaret Thatcher who said, "Ronald Reagan won the Cold War without firing a shot." According to this view, Reagan was not satisfied with merely "containing" the Soviets, but wanted to challenge them ideologically, economically, technologically, militarily, and through indirect and direct attacks on the Soviet empire through support of Third World resistance movements. This direct challenge, articulated in National Security Decision Directive 75, forced Gorbachev to enact ever more far-reaching reforms until the regime collapsed in a muddle of economic and social strife.

Primary Source

Ronald Reagan's Remarks at the Brandenburg Gate

SYNOPSIS: On June 12, 1987, Reagan, against the advice of the U.S. State Department, delivered his Brandenburg Gate speech. It is widely considered to be the most patriotic speech ever delivered by a twentieth-century president. In its most memorable line, Reagan called on Mikhail Gorbachev, general secretary of the Soviet Union, to bring peace to Eastern Europe and the Soviet Union by tearing down the Berlin Wall.

Chancellor Kohl, Governing Mayor Diepgen, ladies and gentlemen:

Twenty-four years ago, President John F. Kennedy visited Berlin, speaking to the people of this city and the world at the City Hall. Well, since then two other presidents have come, each in his turn, to Berlin. And today, I, myself, make my second visit to your city.

We come to Berlin, we American presidents, because it's our duty to speak, in this place, of freedom. But I must confess, we're drawn here by other things as well: by the feeling of history in this city, more than five hundred years older than our own nation; by the beauty of the Grunewald and the Tiergarten; most of all, by your courage and determination.

Perhaps the composer Paul Lincke understood something about American presidents. You see, like so many presidents before me, I come here today because wherever I go, whatever I do: Ich hab noch einen Koffer in Berlin. [I still have a suitcase in Berlin.]

Our gathering today is being broadcast throughout Western Europe and North America. I understand that it is being seen and heard as well in the East. To those listening in East Berlin, a special word: Although I cannot be with you, I address my remarks to you just as surely as to those standing here before me. For I join you, as I join your fellow countrymen in the West, in this firm, this unalterable belief: Es gibt nur ein Berlin. [There is only one Berlin.]

Behind me stands a wall that encircles the free sectors of this city, part of a vast system of barriers that divides the entire continent of Europe. From the Baltic, south, those barriers cut across Germany in a gash of barbed wire, concrete, dog runs, and guard towers. Farther south, there may be no visible, no obvious wall. But there remain armed guards and checkpoints all the same—still a restriction on the right to travel, still an instrument to impose upon ordinary men and women the will of a totalitarian state. Yet is is here in Berlin where the wall emerges most clearly; here, cutting across your city, where the news photo and the television screen have imprinted this brutal division of a continent upon the mind of the world. Standing before the Brandenburg Gate, every man is a German, separated from his fellow men. Every man is a Berliner, forced to look upon a scar.

President von Weizsacker has said, "The German question is open as long as the Brandenburg Gate is closed." Today I say: As long as the gate is closed, as long as this scar of a wall is permitted to stand, it is not the German question alone that remains open, but the question of freedom for all mankind. Yet I do not come here to lament. For I find in Berlin a message of hope, even in the shadow of this wall, a message of triumph.

In this season of spring in 1945, the people of Berlin emerged from their aid-raid shelters to find devastation. Thousands of miles away, the people of the United States reached out to help. And in 1947 Secretary of State—as you've been told—George Marshall announced the creation of what would become known as the Marshall Plan. Speaking precisely forty years ago this month, he said: "Our policy is directed not against any country or

President Reagan addresses a crowd before the Brandenburg Gate in West Berlin, June 12, 1987. In his speech, he urged Gorbachev to "tear down this wall." © WALLY MCNAMEE/CORBIS. REPRODUCED BY PERMISSION.

doctrine, but against hunger, poverty, desperation, and chaos."

In the Reichstag a few moments ago, I saw a display commemorating this fortieth anniversary of the Marshall Plan. I was struck by the sign on a burnt-out, gutted structure that was being rebuilt. I understand that Berliners of my own generation can remember seeing signs like it dotted throughout the western sectors of the city. The sign read simply: "The Marshall Plan is helping here to strengthen the free world." A strong, free world in the West, that dream became real. Japan rose from ruin to become an economic giant. Italy, France, Belgium—virtually every nation in Western Europe saw political and economic rebirth; the European Community was founded.

In West Germany and here in Berlin, there took place an economic miracle, the Wirtschaftswunder. Adenauer, Erhard, Reuter, and other leaders understood the practical importance of liberty—that just as truth can flourish only when the journalist is given freedom of speech, so prosperity can come about only when the farmer and businessman enjoy economic freedom. The German leaders reduced tariffs, expanded free trade, lowered taxes. From 1950 to 1960 alone, the standard of living in West Germany and Berlin doubled.

Where four decades ago there was rubble, today in West Berlin there is the greatest industrial output of any city in Germany—busy office blocks, fine homes and apartments, proud avenues, and the spreading lawns of parkland. Where a city's culture seemed to have been destroyed, today there are two great universities, orchestras and an opera, countless theaters, and museums. Where there was want, today there's abundance—food, clothing, automobiles—the wonderful goods of the Ku'damm. From devastation, from utter ruin, you Berliners have, in freedom, rebuilt a city that once again ranks as one of the greatest on earth. The Soviets may have had other plans. But my friends, there were a few things the Soviets didn't count on—Berliner Herz, Berliner Humor, ja, and Berliner Schnauze. [Berliner heart, Berliner humor, yes, and a Berliner Schnauze.] [Laughter]

In the 1950s, Khrushchev predicted: "We will bury you." But in the West today, we see a free world that has achieved a level of prosperity and well-being unprecedented in all human history. In the Communist world, we see failure, technological backwardness, declining standards of health, even want of the most basic kind—too little food. Even today, the Soviet Union still cannot feed itself. After these four decades, then, there stands before the entire world one great and inescapable conclusion: Freedom leads to prosperity. Freedom replaces the ancient hatreds among the nations with comity and peace. Freedom is the victor.

And now the Soviets themselves may, in a limited way, be coming to understand the importance of freedom. We hear much from Moscow about a new policy of reform and openness. Some political prisoners have been released. Certain foreign news broadcasts are no longer being jammed. Some economic enterprises have been permitted to operate with greater freedom from state control.

Are these the beginnings of profound changes in the Soviet state? Or are they token gestures, intended to raise false hopes in the West, or to strengthen the Soviet system without changing it? We welcome change and openness; for we believe that freedom and security go together, that the advance of human liberty can only strengthen the cause of world peace. There is one sign the Soviets can make that would be unmistakable, that would advance dramatically the cause of freedom and peace.

General Secretary Gorbachev, if you seek peace, if you seek prosperity for the Soviet Union and Eastern Europe, if you seek liberalization: Come here to this gate! Mr. Gorbachev, open this gate! Mr. Gorbachev, tear down this wall!

I understand the fear of war and the pain of division that afflict this continent—and I pledge to you my country's efforts to help overcome these burdens. To be sure, we in the West must resist Soviet expansion. So we must maintain defenses of unassailable strength. Yet we seek peace; so we must strive to reduce arms on both sides.

Beginning ten years ago, the Soviets challenged the Western alliance with a grave new threat, hundreds of new and more deadly SS-20 nuclear missiles, capable of striking every capital in Europe. The Western alliance responded by committing itself to a counterdeployment unless the Soviets agreed to negotiate a better solution; namely, the elimination of such weapons on both sides. For

many months, the Soviets refused to bargain in earnestness. As the alliance, in turn, prepared to go forward with its counterdeployment, there were difficult days—days of protests like those during my 1982 visit to this city—and the Soviets later walked away from the table.

But through it all, the alliance held firm. And I invite those who protested then—I invite those who protest today—to mark this fact: Because we remained strong, the Soviets came back to the table. And because we remained strong, today we have within reach the possibility, not merely of limiting the growth of arms, but of eliminating, for the first time, an entire class of nuclear weapons from the face of the earth.

As I speak NATO ministers are meeting in Iceland to review the progress of our proposals for eliminating these weapons. At the talks in Geneva, we have also proposed deep cuts in strategic offensive weapons. And the Western allies have likewise made far-reaching proposals to reduce the danger of conventional war and to place a total ban on chemical weapons.

While we pursue these arms reductions, I pledge to you that we will maintain the capacity to deter Soviet aggression at any level at which it might occur. And in cooperation with many of our allies, the United States is pursuing the Strategic Defense Initiative—research to base deterrence not on the threat of offensive retaliation, but on defenses that truly defend; on systems, in short, that will not target populations, but shield them. By these means we seek to increase the safety of Europe and all the world. But we must remember a crucial fact: East and West do not mistrust each other because we are armed; we are armed because we mistrust each other. And our differences are not about weapons but about liberty. When President Kennedy spoke at the City Hall those twenty-four years ago, freedom was encircled, Berlin was under siege. And today, despite all the pressures upon this city, Berlin stands secure in its liberty. And freedom itself is transforming the globe.

In the Philippines, in South and Central America, democracy has been given a rebirth. Throughout the Pacific, free markets are working miracle after miracle of economic growth. In the industrialized nations, a technological revolution is taking place—a revolution marked by rapid, dramatic advances in computers and telecommunications.

In Europe, only one nation and those it controls refuse to join the community of freedom. Yet in this age of redoubled economic growth, of information and innovation, the Soviet Union faces a choice: It must make fundamental changes, or it will become obsolete.

Today thus represents a moment of hope. We in the West stand ready to cooperate with the East to promote true openness, to break down barriers that separate people, to create a safe, freer world. And surely there is no better place than Berlin, the meeting place of East and West, to make a start. Free people of Berlin: Today, as in the past, the United States stands for the strict observance and full implementation of all parts of the Four Power Agreement of 1971. Let us use this occasion, the 750th anniversary of this city, to usher in a new era, to seek a still fuller, richer life for the Berlin of the future. Together, let us maintain and develop the ties between the Federal Republic and the Western sectors of Berlin, which is permitted by the 1971 agreement.

And I invite Mr. Gorbachev: Let us work to bring the Eastern and Western parts of the city closer together, so that all the inhabitants of all Berlin can enjoy the benefits that come with life in one of the great cities of the world.

To open Berlin still further to all Europe, East and West, let us expand the vital air access to this city, finding ways of making commercial air service to Berlin more convenient, more comfortable, and more economical. We look to the day when West Berlin can become one of the chief aviation hubs in all central Europe.

With our French and British partners, the United States is prepared to help bring international meetings to Berlin. It would be only fitting for Berlin to serve as the site of United Nations meetings, or world conferences on human rights and arms control or other issues that call for international cooperation.

There is no better way to establish hope for the future than to enlighten young minds, and we would be honored to sponsor summer youth exchanges, cultural events, and other programs for young Berliners from the East. Our French and British friends, I'm certain, will do the same. And it's my hope that an authority can be found in East Berlin to sponsor visits from young people of the Western sectors.

One final proposal, one close to my heart: Sport represents a source of enjoyment and ennoblement, and you may have noted that the Republic of Korea—South Korea—has offered to permit cer-

tain events of the 1988 Olympics to take place in the North. International sports competitions of all kinds could take place in both parts of this city. And what better way to demonstrate to the world the openness of this city than to offer in some future year to hold the Olympic games here in Berlin, East and West?

In these four decades, as I have said, you Berliners have built a great city. You've done so in spite of threats—the Soviet attempts to impose the East-mark, the blockade. Today the city thrives in spite of the challenges implicit in the very presence of this wall. What keeps you here? Certainly there's a great deal to be said for your fortitude, for your defiant courage. But I believe there's something deeper, something that involves Berlin's whole look and feel and way of life—not mere sentiment. No one could live long in Berlin without being completely disabused of illusions. Something instead, that has seen the difficulties of life in Berlin but chose to accept them, that continues to build this good and proud city in contrast to a surrounding totalitarian presence that refuses to release human energies or aspirations. Something that speaks with a powerful voice of affirmation, that says yes to this city, yes to the future, yes to freedom. In a word, I would submit that what keeps you in Berlin is love—love both profound and abiding.

Perhaps this gets to the root of the matter, to the most fundamental distinction of all between East and West. The totalitarian world produces backwardness because it does such violence to the spirit, thwarting the human impulse to create, to enjoy, to worship. The totalitarian world finds even symbols of love and of worship an affront. Years ago, before the East Germans began rebuilding their churches, they erected a secular structure: the television tower at Alexander Platz. Virtually ever since, the authorities have been working to correct what they view as the tower's one major flaw, treating the glass sphere at the top with paints and chemicals of every kind. Yet even today when the sun strikes that sphere—that sphere that towers over all Berlin—the light makes the sign of the cross. There in Berlin, like the city itself, symbols of love, symbols of worship, cannot be suppressed.

As I looked out a moment ago from the Reichstag, that embodiment of German unity, I noticed words crudely spray-painted upon the wall, perhaps by a young Berliner: "This wall will fall. Beliefs become reality." Yes, across Europe, this wall will fall. For it cannot withstand faith; it cannot withstand truth. The wall cannot withstand freedom.

And I would like, before I close, to say one word. I have read, and I have been questioned since I've been here about certain demonstrations against my coming. And I would like to say just one thing, and to those who demonstrate so. I wonder if they have ever asked themselves that if they should have the kind of government they apparently seek, no one would ever be able to do what they're doing again.

Thank you and God bless you all.

Further Resources

BOOKS

Dallek, Robert. *Ronald Reagan: The Politics of Symbolism.* Cambridge, Mass.: Harvard Press, 1999.

Fitzgerald, Frances. *Way Out There in the Blue.* New York: Simon and Schuster, 2000.

Schweizer, Peter. *Reagan's War: The Epic Story of His Forty-Year Struggle and Final Triumph Over Communism.* New York: Doubleday, 2002.

PERIODICALS

Kaplan, Lawrence, F. "We're All Cold Warriors Now." *The Wall Street Journal,* January 18, 2000.

Krauthammer, Charles. "The Reagan Doctrine." *Time,* April 1, 1985.

WEBSITES

"A Concrete Curtain: The Life and Death of the Berlin Wall." *Deutches Historisches Museum.* Available online at http://www.wall-berlin.org/gb/berlin.htm; website home page: http://www.wall-berlin.org (accessed June 9, 2003).

"National Security Decision Directive 75." *Federation of American Scientists.* Available online at http://www.fas.org/irp/offdocs/nsdd/nsdd-075.htm; website home page: http://www.fas.org (accessed May 26, 2003).

U.S. Embassy Beijing to Department of State June 4, 1989

Telegram

By: James R. Lilley

Date: June 4, 1989

Source: Lilley, James R. U.S. Embassy Beijing to Department of State, June 4, 1989. National Security Archives, document 14. Available online at http://www.gwu.edu/~nsarchiv/NSAEBB/NSAEBB16/documents/14-01.htm; website home page: http://www.gwu.edu/~nsarchiv/ (accessed July 30, 2003).

About the Author: James R. Lilley is a renowned expert on East Asian affairs. Born in China, he moved to the United States in 1940. From 1975 to 1978, Lilley worked as a national intelligence officer in China, and then taught at Johns Hopkins School of Advanced International Studies until 1980. The following year, Lilley was appointed ambassador to China. After two years in Beijing, he was appointed ambassador to South Korea. He is a senior fellow with the American Enterprise Institute. ■

Introduction

In 1989, Tiananmen Square, meaning "Gate of Heavenly Peace," was the site of one of the bloodiest massacres in Chinese history. That April, student protesters from fifteen universities formed the Democracy Movement. Disillusioned with the false promises of communism, the students wanted the government to take dramatic steps toward democracy, including freedom of the press, speech, and assembly, free elections, the end of political corruption, and capitalistic reforms in order to better compete in the world market. At the time, the government was divided between reform-minded communist party members who believed that political liberalization would stimulate the economy, and hardliners who believed that if the government loosened its iron ideological grip, society would crumble and lead to capitalism.

On April 15, following the death of a noted government reformer and student sympathizer, the Democracy Movement organized massive demonstrations in his honor at Tiananmen Square. Within two weeks, the demonstrations became overtly political. On April 26, the leading communist newspaper printed an editorial accusing the protesters of being unpatriotic, deeply wounding the students who believed they were acting in China's best interest. In early May, the movement called for hunger strikes to draw attention to their plight and to force the government to negotiate with them, thereby winning the support of intellectuals, the working class, and agrarians. By May 17, one million Beijing protesters called on government leaders to resign. Three days later, the government declared martial law. Over the next two weeks, the number of students in the square had dropped to two thousand. On May 29, students smuggled into the square, on top of their bicycles, three enormous portions of plaster and Styrofoam. They fashioned the materials into a 35-foot replica of the Statute of Liberty, which they called the "Goddess of Democracy." On June 2, the government decided to implement a military crackdown and clear the square.

Significance

In response to the Tiananmen Square Massacre, President George H.W. Bush (served 1989–1993) suspended government-to-government and commercial arms sales to communist China, recommended that the World Bank postpone new development loans to China, together with implementing a host of other economic and commercial

---

sanctions. He refused, however, to withdraw from China most-favored nation (MFN) status—a reciprocal trading status that provides a country with the lowest available tariffs on its exports to the United States. The United States granted MFN status to all its trading partners in 1934. In 1951, during the early days of the Cold War, the policy was amended to require the president to suspend MFN status to all Chinese and Soviet bloc countries. In 1974, Congress passed a trade act that provided for the restoration of MFN status to countries with "non-market economies." The act also stipulated that MFN status would have to be renewed every year. In 1979, President Jimmy Carter (served 1977–1981) restored MFN status to China, and President Ronald Reagan (served 1981–1989) renewed it every year of his administration.

Unlike his immediate predecessors, President Bush was under tremendous pressure not to renew MFN because of the Tiananmen Square massacre. That year, Congresswoman Nancy Pelosi (D- Calif.) and Senator George Mitchell (D-Minn.) sponsored legislation that would have required Bush to deny MFN status to China if it had not made "overall significant progress" in human rights. Bush vetoed the legislation because he believed that conditional MFN status would have severely undermined Western-oriented reformers in China and further emboldened opposition to democracy and economic market reform. In addition, Bush feared that without MFN status, China—purchasers of $9 billion annually in U.S. goods, primarily aircraft, machinery, and agricultural products—would reduce its American imports, costing upwards of 150,000 high-tech U.S. jobs. Despite a worsening human rights record, China continues to maintain its MFN status.

Primary Source

U.S. Embassy Beijing to Department of State
June 4, 1989

SYNOPSIS: On June 4, 1989, the U.S. Embassy in Beijing sent a confidential cable to the Secretary of State in Washington, D.C. The embassy reported that approximately 10,000 troops had entered Tiananmen Square and confronted about 3,000 demonstrators when shooting broke out. In the end, hundreds of people were killed, though the exact number is unknown, and the Chinese government quashed the Democracy Movement in a brutal response reported around the world.

ADP492
CONFIDENTIAL

PAGE 01/BEIJIN/15424/01 OF 03/041023Z

ACTION EAP-00. . . .

O 0406368 JUN 99 ZFF4
FM AMEMBASSY BEIJING
TO SECSTATE WASHDC WIACT IMMEDIATE 0066
AMEMBASSY TOKYO IMMEDIATE
AMEMBASSY SEOUL IMMEDIATE
AMEMBASSY MOSCOW IMMEDIATE
AMEMBASSY LONDON IMMEDIATE
AMEMBASSY PARIS IMMEDIATE
AMEMEBASSY BANGKOK IMMEDIATE
AMCONSUL HONG KONG IMMEDIATE
AIT TAIPEI IMMEDIATE
USCENCPAC HONOLULU HI IMMEDIATE
AMCONSUL GUANGZHOU IMMEDIATE
AMCONSUL SHANGHAI IMMEDIATE
AMCONSUL SHENYANG IMMEDIATE
DIA WASHDC IMMEDIATE
AMCONSUL CHENGDU POUCH)

C O N F I D E N T I A L SECTION 01 OF 03
BEIJING 15424

CINCPAC FOR FPA FINNET

NSC FOR DOUG PAAL

E.O. 12366:DECL:OADR
TAGS: PGOV, PHUN, SOCI, CH, CASC
SUBJECT: SITREP NO. 32: THE MORNING OF JUNE 4

1. CONFIDENTIAL - ENTIRE TEXT

CONFIDENTIAL

CONFIDENTIAL

PAGE 02/BEIJIN/15424/01 OF 03/041023Z

2. SUMMARY. VIOLENCE CONTINUED THE MORNING OF JUNE FOURTH IN THE TIANANMEN SQUARE AREA. PROTESTORS CONTINUED TO SHOUT DEFIANCE AT THE TROOPS WHO THEN OPENED FIRE ON THEM. WE HAVE CONFIRMED THAT ONE AMERICAN WAS INJURED IN THE FIGHTING AND THAT AT LEAST ONE AMERICAN, A CBS EMPLOYEE, IS MISSING. CONSULATE CHENGDU REPORTS SOME 300 PROTESTORS MAY HAVE BEEN INJURED IN THAT CITY BUT THAT HAS OF THE EARLY AFTERNOON THERE WERE NO REPORTS OF DEATHS. END SUMMARY.

-

THE TIANANMEN AREA

——————.. . . .

3. AS OF ABOUT 0330 HOURS LOCAL TROOPS WERE IN CONTROL OF TIANANMEN SQUARE, BUT PEOPLE REMAINED IN THE SURROUNDING STREETS. SPORADIC GUNFIRE CONTINUED TO BE HEARD

The peaceful May 1989 protest in Tiananmen Square, and the Chinese government's subsequent violent crackdown, generated debate in the United States over granting China the "most-favored nation" trade designation. © PETER TURNLEY/CORBIS. REPRODUCED BY PERMISSION.

THROUGHOUT THE CITY. BY 0430 TROOPS HAD TAKEN UP POSITION ACROSS CHANGAN BOULEVARD FACING EAST WITH A LINE OF APCS BEHIND THEM. STUDENTS IN TURN LINED UP ON CHANGAN FACING WEST TOWARD THE TROOPS. MEANWHILE, A LARGE CONVOY OF TROOPS BEGAN ENTERING TIANANMEN SQUARE FROM THE WEST. SOME 10,000 TROOPS IN THE SQUARE FORMED CONCENTRIC RINGS, ONE FACING INWARD TOWARD SOME 3,000 REMAINING DEMONSTRATORS, AND THE OTHER FACING OUTWARD. AT 0530 A COLUMN OF ABOUT 50 APCS, TANKS, AND TRUCKS ENTERED TIANANMEN FROM THE EAST. DEMONSTRATORS SHOUTED ANGRILY AT THE CONVOY AND PLA TROOPS IN TIANANMEN OPENED A BARRAGE OF RIFLE AND MACHINE GUN FIRE. WHEN THIS GUNFIRE ENDED AT 0545, A NUMBER OF CASUALTIES REMAINED LYING ON THE GROUND. AT 0620, A SECOND COLUMN OF ABOUT 40 APCS, TANKS, AND TRUCKS

CONFIDENTIAL

CONFIDENTIAL

PAGE 03/BEIJIN/15424/01 OF 03/041023Z

ENTERED TIANANMEN BY THE SAME ROUTE AND THE STUDENTS AGAIN MOVED INTO THE ROAD. PLA TROOPS IN TIANANMEN OPENED FIRE WITH RIFLES AND MACHINE GUNS, ONCE MORE CAUSING A LARGE NUMBER OF CASUALTIES.

-

4. A SIMILAR STAND-OFF CONTINUED THROUGHOUT THE MORNING AND AFTERNOON OF JUNE 4. POLOFF REPORTED FROM THE BEIJING HOTEL THAT AT 1300 AND AGAIN AT 1500 DEMONSTRATORS APPROACHED TROOPS IN TIANANMEN SQUARE. THE DEMONSTRATORS SHOUTED IN DEFIANCE AT THE TROOPS WHO, IN EACH INSTANCE, EVENTUALLY OPENED FIRE ON THE CROWDS. THIS PATTERN APPEARS TO HAVE PERSISTED SINCE EARLIER IN THE DAY ACCORDING TO OTHER DIPLOMATIC REPORTS. AS THE CROWDS ON CHANGAN EAST OF TIANANMEN WOULD APPROACH THE TROOPS, THE TROOPS WOULD MOVE FORWARD, OFTEN OPENING FIRE, AND THE CROWDS WOULD RETREAT HURRIEDLY. AT 1020 MASSIVE MACHINE-GUN FIRE WAS REPORTED. TROOPS THEN ADVANCED IN FORMATION. THE CROWDS FLED IN PANIC AND SOON THE WHOLE OF

CHANGAN BOULEVARD WAS TEMPORARILY CLEAR. AT LEAST ONE BODY WAS OBSERVED LYING IN THE STREET. AT ABOUT 1215 SOME TEN STUDENTS REPORTEDLY WENT FROM THE BEIJING HOTEL AREA TO TALK TO THE SOLDIERS AND WERE GUNNED DOWN BY THE TROOPS. TWO EXPLOSIONS WERE ALSO HEARD BETWEEN THE BEIJING HOTEL AND TIANANMEN SQUARE.

-

THE JIANGUOMENWAI INTERSECTION

—————..···

5. AT THE INTERSECTION OF JIANGUOMENWAI (THE EASTERN EXTENSION OF CHANGANDAJIE) AND THE SECOND RING ROAD, LARGE NUMBERS OF RESIDENTS CONTINUED TO BLOCK TROOP TRUCKS AS OF ABOUT 0500 HOURS LOCAL.

CONFIDENTIAL

Further Resources

BOOKS

Fairbank, John, et al. *Children of the Dragon: The Story of the Tiananmen Massacre.* New York: Macmillan, 1990.

Salisbury, Harrison E. *Tiananmen Diary: 13 Days in June.* Boston: Little, Brown, 1989.

Schell, Orville. *Mandate of Heaven: The Legacy of Tiananmen Square and the Next Generation of Chinese Leaders.* New York: Simon and Schuster, 1995.

PERIODICALS

Beach, Sophie. "Tiananmen Plus Ten." *The Nation,* June 14, 1999.

Doder, Louise. "A Bloodbath in Beijing." *Maclean's,* June 12, 1989.

WEBSITES

"Tiananmen Revisited." *CNN.* Available online on http://edition.cnn.com/SPECIALS/2001/tiananmen; website home page: http://edition.cnn.com (accessed June 9, 2003).

Operation Just Cause Pamphlet

Pamphlet

By: PSYOP Operations

Date: December 20, 1989

Source: PSYOP Pamphlet announcing Money for Guns program in Panama in December 1989. Available online at http://www.psywarrior.com/panamaposter1.html; website home page: http://www.psywarrior.com (accessed June 9, 2003).

About the Group: The 4th Psychological Operations Group (Airborne) is headquartered at Fort Bragg, North Carolina. It is the only active duty U.S. Army Psychological Operations Group, and it consists of about 1,100 soldiers and 50 civilian analysts. The purpose of PSYOP is to demoralize the enemy by causing chaos among its ranks, while at the same time convince the local population to support American troops. ■

Introduction

In 1983, following the death of Panamanian dictator Omar Torrijos, General Manuel Noriega took control of the country. Panama is the tiny isthmus country that joins Central America to the South American country of Colombia. Only 400 miles long and 50 miles wide, it is about the size of South Carolina. Noriega had received military training in the United States, and he likely had ties to the Central Intelligence Agency (CIA). Noriega also worked with the notorious Colombian Medellín drug cartel. During President Ronald Reagan's (served 1981–1989) administration, the United States overlooked Noriega's criminal activities because he provided support to the U.S.-sponsored contras in their struggle against the Marxist Sandinista regime in Nicaragua. In February 1988, a Florida court indicted Noriega for assisting the Medellín cartel in transporting two tons of cocaine to the United States through Panama for $4.5 million. The indictment also accused him of constructing a cocaine-processing plant in Panama and providing drug runners with safe harbor.

In 1988, the United States engaged in a secret operation to remove Noriega from power. The plan, however, was halted after the American press leaked the story. In 1989, President George H.W. Bush (served 1989–1993) declared a "War on Drugs" and decided that the government could no longer support a dictator-drug lord. That October, however, the United States botched an attempted coup of the Noriega regime. Afterward, the dictator declared a state of national emergency and increased his persecution of Americans in Panama. In December, the Panamanian National Assembly declared that a state of war existed with the United States. Noriega publicly speculated that some day the "bodies of our enemies" would float down the Panama Canal. The next evening, three American soldiers were shot, one fatally. Intelligence reports indicated that Noriega was preparing to attack American citizens in a residential neighborhood, forcing Bush to invade Panama.

Significance

Operation Just Cause was the first American use of force since World War II (1939–1945) that was not related to the Cold War. The invasion was also the first major deployment of American troops since Vietnam (1964–1975). From December 20–24, 1989, 9,000

ES TU DEBER

MAXIMO QUE SE PAGARA:

$25 POR SUFICIENTE CANTIDAD DE MUNICIÓN

$25 POR GRANADA

$50 POR GRANADA RPG

$100 POR PISTOLA

$125 POR ESCOPETA

$150 POR RIFLE AUTOMATICO

$150 POR MINA

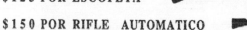

$5000 MAXIMO
POR ALMACENAMIENTOS DE ARMAS

COOPERA CON NOSOTROS HOY

Primary Source

Operation Just Cause Pamphlet (1 OF 2)

SYNOPSIS: In addition to using loudspeakers to demoralize Noriega, the PSYOP (Psychological Operations) successfully delivered over one million leaflets and handbills, 50,000 posters, 550,000 newspapers, and 125,000 pieces of miscellaneous printing material in Spanish urging the Panamanian military and civilians to turn in their weapons for money. Presented here is the front and back of a pamphlet encouraging the citizens of Panama to turn over their weapons to the U.S. military in exchange for money. U.S. MILITARY DOCUMENT. IMAGES COURTESY OF ED ROUSE, WWW.PSYWARRIOR.COM.

RECOMPENSA MAXIMA POR ALMACENAMIENTOS DE ARMAS
$5,000

PUNTOS DE ENTREGA

-Departamento de Policia cerca de la parte de atras del fuerte Albrook

-Gimnasio Nacional (Frente al Ancon Inn)

-Las armas seran aceptadas solamente en estos lugares diariamente de 7 de la manana a 5 de la tarde

PROCEDIMIENTOS DE ENTREGA

1. REMUEVE EL CARGADOR Y MUNICIONES DEL ARMA.

2. ATA UN PAÑO BLANCO AL ARMA.

3. ACERCATE CON EL ARMA SOSTENIDA BIEN EN ALTO POR EL CAÑON.

4. SIGUE LAS INSTRUCCIONES DE LAS AUTORIDADES.

COOPERA CON TU GOBIERNO Y AYUDA A
LAS FUERZAS ARMADAS ESTADOUNIDENSES
UNIDOS ALCANZAREMOS LA LEY, EL ORDEN Y
LA SEGURIDAD PUBLICA
SINTONIZA A A.M. 1160

Primary Source

Operation Just Cause Pamphlet (2 OF 2)
The back of the pamphlet encourages people to turn in their arms in exchange for as much as $5,000. U.S. MILITARY DOCUMENT. IMAGES COURTESY OF ED ROUSE, WWW.PSYWARRIOR.COM.

Marines, with the assistance of 13,000 U.S. troops already stationed in Panama, routed the 4,000-man Panamanian Defense Force. When Noriega eluded capture, President Bush offered a $1 million bounty. After searching two of Noriega's residences, special operation forces discovered pictures of Hitler, an extensive pornography collection, $283,000 in cash, Swiss bank account numbers, and a "witches diary" that recorded the activities of two Brazilian witches who were tutoring Noriega in black magic. On Christmas Eve, Noriega was granted refuge in the home of the Papal Nuncio, the Vatican's representative to Panama, until he could gain entry into Cuba. To prevent the press from eavesdropping on negotiations between the United States and Catholic officials—and to psychologically unnerve Noriega—the military ordered the blaring of rock music around-the-clock at the residence.

On December 29, the United States gave permission for the Archbishop of Panama to visit Noriega's "witch house" in order to "gain insight into the man's soul." Afterward, the archbishop recommended to Pope John Paul II that Noriega be turned over to the United States because he committed torture, murder, practiced devil worship and voodoo, and stockpiled weapons to conduct a long-term guerrilla campaign. On January 3, Catholic officials persuaded the dictator to surrender on the condition that he would not face the death penalty in the United States. He was immediately flown to Florida. In April 1992, Noriega was convicted of smuggling cocaine and sentenced to forty years imprisonment. In the end, the United States suffered twenty-three casualties and 330 wounded, and the Panamanian military suffered 297 dead and 129 wounded.

Primary Source

Operation Just Cause Pamphlet

SYNOPSIS: Below is the translation for the front and back of the PSYOP (Psychological Operations) pamphlet. The pamphlet was but one type of communication used by the new President of Panama, Guillermo Endara, to the Panamanian masses in the hours after the U.S. invasion of Panama began.

Translation—Front

"What We Will Pay"

- $25.00 for Information on Munitions
- $25.00 for Grenades
- $50.00 for RPG Grenades
- $100.00 for Pistols
- $125 for Automatic Rifles
- $150.00 for Mines

A maximum of $5000 will be paid for the above weapons.

Back

Maximum reimbursement (payment) for warehousing of weapons—$5000

Places for Delivery

- Police Department near the back of Albrook fountain
- National Gymnasium (front of Ancon Inn)
- Arms (weapons) will be accepted only at these places daily from 7am to 5pm

Delivery Procedures

1. Remove the loader and ammunition from the weapon
2. Attach a white cloth to the weapon
3. Approach with weapon held high by its barrel
4. Follow the instructions given by the authorities

Cooperate with your Government and help the American (United States) armed forces.

United we will have law, order, and public security (safety).

Further Resources

BOOKS

Buckley, Kevin. *Panama: The Whole Story.* New York: Simon and Schuster, 1991.

Donnelly, Thomas. *Operation Just Cause: The Storming of Panama.* New York: Lexington Books, 1991.

Scranton, Margaret. *The Noriega Years.* Boulder, Colo.: Westview, 1991.

PERIODICALS

"Army Psywarriors: A History of U.S. Army Psychological Operations." *Special Warfare,* vol. 5, October 1992, 18–25.

Hersch, Seymour. "Panama Strongman Said to Trade in Drugs, Arms and Illicit Money." *The New York Times,* June 12, 1986.

WEBSITES

"Operation Just Cause." *Federation of American Scientists.* Available online at http://www.fas.org/man/dod-101/ops /just_cause.htm; website home page: http://www.fas.org (accessed June 9, 2003).

Rouse, Ed. "Psywarrior: Psychological Operations: Links" Available online at http://www.psywarrior.com/links.html; website home page: http://http://www.psywarrior.com (accessed June 9, 2003). *This page contains links to detailed descriptions of psychological warfare by the United States military in specific wars and situations.*

6

LAW AND JUSTICE

SCOTT A. MERRIMAN

Entries are arranged in chronological order by date of primary source. For entries with one primary source, the entry title is the same as the primary source title. Entries with more than one primary source have an overall entry title, followed by the titles of the primary sources.

Important Events in Law and Justice, 1980–1989

1980

- On January 19, retired Supreme Court justice William O. Douglas dies.

- On January 21, the Supreme Court holds that prisoners who do not turn themselves in immediately following their escape are not entitled to introduce evidence at trial that harsh prison conditions justified their escape.

- On February 3, media reports tell of an FBI investigation into corruption in high offices, code-named Abscam.

- On February 8, another FBI undercover sting operation makes the news. This one, named Brilab (for bribery labor) involves southwestern labor leaders and politicians.

- On February 14, indictments against 55 persons in ten states are handed down in an undercover FBI investigation into child pornography distribution called Miporn.

- On March 10, Dr. Herman Tarnower, author of the "Scarsdale Diet," is shot to death in Purchase, New York.

- On March 12, John Wayne Gacy, Jr., is found guilty in Chicago in the deaths of thirty-three men and boys.

- On March 13, an Indiana jury acquits Ford Motor Company of reckless homicide charges in the deaths of three women in a fiery Ford Pinto crash.

- On March 15, terrorists of the Puerto Rican proindependence group FALN (Armed Forces of National Liberation) invade Carter and Bush political headquarters, tie up staff members, and spray paint the walls of the offices with anti-statehood slogans. No injuries are reported.

- On April 2, former associate justice of the Supreme Court, Stanley Reed, dies. Appointed to the high court in 1938, he retired in 1957.

- On June 30, the Supreme Court rules in *Harris v. McRae* that states participating in Medicaid program were not required to fund medically necessary abortions under Title XIX of the Social Security Act.

- On July 2, the Supreme Court hands down its decision in *Richmond Newspapers Inc. v. Virginia.* The court rules that a decision to close a murder trial to the media and the public violated the Constitution because the right to attend trials is "implicit in the guarantees of the First Amendment."

- On November 17, the Supreme Court, voting 5-4 in *Stone v. Graham,* overturns a Kentucky law requiring the display of the Ten Commandments in every public school classroom in the state.

- On December 8, former Beatle John Lennon is shot outside his New York apartment building. Killer Mark David Chapman is sentenced to twenty years to life on August 24, 1981.

1981

- On January 26, the Supreme Court rules, 8-0, that states may allow cameras into courtrooms if they so choose, in *Chandler* and *Florida.*

- On March 9, the Supreme Court decides, 8-1, that a defendant who remains silent in a criminal case is entitled to have the judge instruct a jury that no inference of guilt may be drawn from his decision not to testify in his own behalf.

- On March 23, the Supreme Court rules that states may require, with some exceptions, parental notification when a minor female seeks an abortion.

- On March 30, President Reagan is severely wounded in an assassination attempt. Press Secretary James Brady, a Secret Service agent, and a Washington, D.C., police officer are also wounded. All recover, but Brady suffers permanent brain damage.

- On June 16, Potter Stewart announces his retirement effective July 3 after twenty-three years on the Supreme Court.

- On September 25, Sandra Day O'Connor takes the oath of office and becomes the first woman to sit on the Supreme Court.

- On November 6, former FBI officials Mark Felt and Edward Miller are convicted of conspiring to violate the rights of Americans during searches they authorized for bombing suspects in 1972 and 1973. They are later pardoned by President Reagan.

- On November 25, Ford Motor Company agrees with the Equal Employment Opportunity Commission to pay $23 million in damages and other benefits to women and minorities as a result of complaints of discriminatory employment practices.

1982

- On January 6, William G. Bonin is convicted as Los Angeles' "freeway killer" in the murder of fourteen men and boys.

- On January 8, in a deal with the Justice Department to settle an antitrust lawsuit, AT&T agrees to divest itself of twenty-two Bell System companies.

- On January 23, Federal district court judge Prentice Marshall enjoins the U.S. Immigration and Naturalization Service from surrounding or invading homes or factories and questioning Hispanic Americans as to their citizenship status.

- On February 27, Wayne Williams is found guilty in the murder of two young black males. Twenty eight bodies of young black males were found in Atlanta over a twenty-two-month period.

- On March 24, the Supreme Court rules, 5-4, that states must have "clear and convincing" proof of child abuse or neglect before removing children from the custody of their natural parents.

- On April 5, former associate justice of the Supreme Court, Abe Fortas, dies.

- On June 15, the Supreme Court invalidates a Texas law which withheld funds for the education of chidren of illegal aliens. The ruling in *Plyler v. Doe* is based on the Equal Protection Clause of the Fourteenth Amendment.

- On June 18, the Supreme Court rules unanimously that mentally retarded people in state institutions are guaranteed all of the constitutional rights afforded to citizens by the Due Process Clause of the Fourteenth Amendment.

- On June 21, John Hinkley, Jr., is found innocent by reason of insanity in the 1981 shooting of President Reagan and three others.

- On June 23, the Supreme Court rules, 5-4, that a confession of a suspected criminal, even if obtained through legitimate interrogation, cannot be used as evidence if the subject had been arrested without probable cause to believe that a crime had been committed.

- On June 24, the Supreme Court rules that the president "is entitled to absolute immunity from damages liability predicated on his official acts." The case, *Nixon v. Fitzgerald.*, stems from President Richard M. Nixon's 1969 firing of a civilian analyst for the Air Force.

- On September 29, cyanide-laced Extra Strength Tylenol capsules kill seven in the Chicago area.

- On December 7, the first person to be executed by lethal injection in the United States is put to death in Huntsville, Texas.

1983

- On January 17, the Supreme Court rules in *Sony Corporation* and *Universal City Studios* that the sale of video tape recorders to the general public does not constitute contributory infringement of copyrighted public broadcasts.

- On March 2, the Supreme Court rules that state employees are covered by the federal law that prohibits discrimination on the basis of age.

- On March 6, a woman in New Bedford, Massachusetts reports being gang-raped at a tavern. Eventually four men are convicted of the crime.

- On May 24, the Supreme Court rules that the Internal Revenue Service acted permissibly when it revoked Bob Jones Universitys's tax exempt status on the ground that the University's prohibitions against interracial dating and marriage were racist.

- On June 3, tax protestor Gordon Kahl is killed in a shootout in Arkansas. Kahl had been wanted for the slaying of two U.S. marshals.

- On July 5, the Supreme Court rules in *Marsh v. Chambers* that the Nebraska Legislature's practice of opening each legislative session with prayer does not violate the Establishment Clause of the First Amendment.

- On July 6, the Supreme Court rules that an employer-sponsored retirement plan cannot pay women a lower monthly benefit based on the fact that women statistically live longer than men.

1984

- On January 17, the Supreme Court rules that there is no time limit on the collection of taxes owed on a fraudulent or false tax return, even if the taxpayer has subsequently filed a true tax return.

- On March 5, the Supreme Court rules in *Lynch v. Donelly* that the inclusion of a nativity scene in a city's holiday display did not violate the First Amendment's Establishment Clause.

- On April 1, singer Marvin Gaye is shot to death in Los Angeles by his father.

- On April 24, the Supreme Court rules in *Palmore v. Sidoti* that the Equal Protection Clause of the Fourteenth Amendment was violated when a Caucasian father was awarded custody of a child because the child's Caucasian mother began cohabitating with an African American. The lower court used the racially mixed household as a basis for awarding custody.

- On May 7, Viet Nam veterans obtain a $180 million out-of-court settlement in the Agent Orange class-action suit. Veterans claimed they had suffered injury from the defoliant.

- On May 10, a federal district court judge in Salt Lake City, Utah, holds that the federal government had been negligent in above-ground testing of nuclear weapons in Nevada between 1951 and 1962 and awards $6.2 million in damages to nine victims or their families.

- On June 11, the Supreme Court rules unanimously that evidence obtained illegally is admissible if the police could prove that the evidence would have been inevitably discovered by lawful means.

- On July 3, the Supreme Court rules in *Roberts v. U.S. Jaycees* that the Jaycees must admit women to its membership.

- On July 5, in *U.S. v. Leon,* the Supreme Court finds a "good faith exception" to the exclusionary rule of search and seizure. In other words, evidence will not be excluded from a trial where police act in good faith on a warrant issued by a judge, where that warrant later turns out be insufficient.

- On July 18, a gunman kills twenty-one at a McDonald's in San Ysidro, California. Police kill the gunman.

- On December 22, Bernhard Goetz shoots four African American youths on a New York subway. Goetz says the four were going to rob him.

1985

- On January 15, the Supreme Court rules, 6-3, in *New Jersey* and *T.L.O.* that public school officials can legally search public school students if they reasonably believe the search would result in evidence of a violation of school rules or the law.

- On March 18, the Supreme Court rules in *Federal Election Commission v. National Conservative Political Action*

Committee that the Federal Election Campaign Act violated the First Amendment rights of free speech and association when it prohibited independent political action committees from spending more than one thousand dollars to support the election of a presidential candidate.

- On March 19, the Supreme Court upholds the right of public employees to a hearing before being terminated from their jobs.

- On March 27, the Supreme Court rules that police do not have the right to shoot fleeing suspects who are not armed or dangerous.

- On May 13, in Philadelphia a confrontation between law enforcement and radical group MOVE ends when police drop an explosive onto the group's headquarters, killing eleven.

- On June 4, the Supreme Court rules in *Wallace v. Jaffree* that an Alabama statute authorizing one minute of silence during the school day "for meditation or voluntary prayer" violated the Establishment Clause of the First Amendment.

- On June 10, Klaus von Bulow is acquitted in Providence, Rhode Island, for attempting to murder his heiress wife, Sunny.

- On November 21, Jonathan Jay Pollard, a former U.S. Navy intelligence analyst, is arrested and accused of spying for Israel. He eventually pleads guilty and is sentenced to life in prison.

- On December 7, Potter Stewart, associate justice of the Supreme Court from 1958 to 1981, dies.

- On December 16, reputed mobster Paul Castellano is shot and killed outside a New York City restaurant.

1986

- On February 25, in *Renton v. Playtime Theatres Inc.,* the Supreme Court holds that a zoning ordinance that prohibited adult motion picture theaters from locating with in 1,000 feet of any residential zone, single- or multiple-family dwelling, church, park, or school does not violate the First or Fourteenth Amendments

- On March 25, the Supreme Court rules that Air Force regulations did not violate the Free Exercise Clause of the First Amendment, where they forbade a Jewish Air Force officer from wearing his yarmulke while on duty and in uniform. Congress passed legislation reversing the decision in 1987, permitting "neat and conservative" religious apparel.

- On April 30, in *Batson v. Kentucky,* the Supreme Court rules that a prosecutor's use of peremptory challenges to remove African Americans from a jury violated an African American defendant's rights guaranteed under the Sixth and Fourteenth Amendments when the resulting jury was composed only of whites.

- On May 19, the Supreme Court rules in *California v. Ciraolo* that the warrantless, aerial observation of an accused's back yard by police in a private plane from an altitude of 1,000 feet did not constitute an illegal search under the Fourth Amendment.

- On May 19, the Supreme Court rules in *Wygant v. Jackson Board of Education* that an affirmative action plan under

which African American schoolteachers retained their jobs while some white teachers who had more seniority were laid off violated the Equal Protection Clause of the Fourteenth Amendment.

- On June 19, in *Meritor Savings Bank v. Vinton,* the Supreme Court announces that a "hostile working environment" caused by discrimination or harassment is actionable under Title VII of the Civil Rights Act of 1964.

- On June 19, the Supreme Court rules in *Bowers v. Hardwick,* that there is no constitutional protection afforded for acts of consensual sodomy.

- On July 7, the Supreme Court ruled in *Bethel School District No. 403 v. Fraser* that the First Amendment does not prevent schools from prohibiting vulgar and lewd speech.

- On August 14, a U.S. Senate Judiciary Committee approves Justice William Rehnquist as the new chief justice and Antonin Scalia as a new associate justice of the Supreme Court.

- On August 21, Kerr-McGee Corporation settles a lawsuit brought a decade earlier by the estate of the late Karen Silkwood. Kerr-McGee agrees to pay $1.38 million for the nuclear contamination lawsuit.

- On November 15, Ivan Boesky is fined $100 million by the Securities and Exchange Commission for insider trading.

1987

- On March 31, a New Jersey court awards custody of "Baby M" to the baby's natural father and his wife. Mary Beth Whitehead, the baby's biological mother, was artificially inseminated with the father's sperm as the result of a contract entered into with the father. After giving birth, Whitehead decided to keep the baby. A New Jersey appellate court later granted Whitehead visitation rights to the child.

- On April 20, the United States, for the first time, deports an accused war criminal for trial in another country.

- On April 27, for the first time, the United States bars a head of state of a friendly nation from entering the United States. The U.S. bars Kurt Waldheim, former secretary general of the United Nations and president of Austria, because of his links to war crimes committed while a member of the Nazi Party.

- On May 4, in *Rotary International v. Rotary Club,* the Supreme Court rules that a California law requiring California Rotary Clubs to admit women members did not violate Rotary International's First Amendment rights of association.

- On June 15, in *Booth v. Maryland,* the Supreme Court holds that it was a violation of the Eighth Amendment for a jury to consider a "victim impact statement" during the sentencing phase of a death penalty case.

- On June 15, in *Airport Commissioners v. Jews for Jesus,* the Supreme Court holds that an ordinance forbidding any "First Amendment activities" at the Los Angeles International Airport violated the First Amendment.

- On June 19, in *Edwards v. Aguillard,* the Supreme Court holds that a Louisiana law violates the Establishment

Clause of the First Amendment when it required the teaching of "creation science" along with the theory of evolution.

- On June 26, Louis F. Powell, Jr., retires as an associate justice of the Supreme Court, having served since 1972.

- On August 21, Marine Clayton Lonetree is convicted of spying for the KGB.

- On November 7, Judge Douglas Ginsburg withdraws from consideration for a seat on the Supreme Court after admitting that he used marijuana several times in the 1970s while a professor at Harvard University Law School.

- On December 18, Ivan F. Boesky receives a three year prison sentence for his involvement in a Wall Street insider-trading scandal.

1988

- On January 13, U.S. Supreme Court rules in *Hazelwood School District v. Kuhlmeier* that the First Amendment permits schools to exercise editorial control over student speech so long as it is "reasonably related to legitimate pedagogical concerns."

- On February 5, Panamanian military leader, Manuel Noriega, is indicted in Florida on bribery and drug trafficking charges.

- On February 18, U.S. Appeals Court judge Anthony Kennedy is sworn into office as an associate justice of the Supreme Court.

- On February 24, the Supreme Court rules that the First Amendment protects a parody by *Hustler* magazine of Fundamentalist minister and public figure Jerry Falwell.

- On May 4, almost 1.4 million illegal aliens meet a deadline to file for legal status under an amnesty program.

- On March 24, Oliver L. North and John M. Poindexter, former national security aides, along with businessmen Richard V. Secord and Albert Hakim, enter not guilty pleas to charges stemming from the Iran-Contra scandal.

- On March 25, Robert E. Chambers, Jr., pleads guilty to first-degree manslaughter in the death of eighteen-year-old Jennifer Levin, in New York, in what is known as the "preppie murder case."

- On May 16, the Supreme Court rules in *California v. Greenwood* that a warrantless search and seizure of an accused's garbage that has been placed curbside does not violate the Fourth Amendment.

- On June 13, a New Jersey jury finds a tobacco company partly responsible for the death of a woman who had used their product in the past.

- On June 29, the Supreme Court rules in *Thompson v. Oklahoma* that the Eight Amendment prohibits executing anyone under the age of sixteen.

- On July 5, Attorney General Edwin Meese announces that he will resign from his position after a report by an independent counsel had found that he had probably violated criminal law four times while in office but recommended no further action, as there was no financial gain or corrupt intention.

- On August 12, Former Pennsylvania governor Richard Thornburgh is sworn in as attorney general.

- On October 21, a federal grand jury in New York indicts former Philippine President Ferdinand E. Marcos and his wife, Imelda, on fraud and racketeering charges. Marcos dies before his trial. Imelda is acquitted in 1990.

1989

- On January 13, Bernhard H. Goetz receives one year in prison for possessing an unlicensed gun that he used to shoot four youths in December 1984 on the New York subway that he said were going to rob him.

- On January 16, three days of rioting begin in Miami, after police officers shoot and kill a black motorcyclist.

- On January 23, the Supreme Court rules in *Richmond v. J.A. Crosnan Co.* that a city regulation that required companies awarded city construction contracts to subcontract 30 percent of their business to minority business enterprises violated the Equal Protection Clause of the Fourteenth Amendment.

- On January 24, serial killer Ted Bundy is executed in Florida.

- On March 21, the Supreme Court rules in *Skinner v. Railway Labor Executives' Association* that mandatory blood and urine tests of railroad employees involved in certain train accidents did not violate employees' Fourth Amendment rights involving search and seizure.

- On March 21, the Supreme Court rules in *Treasury Employees v. Von Raab* that a Customs Service drug testing program for employees who carry firearms, are involved in intercepting drugs entering the country, or are in high level positions involving classified information, does not violate employees' Fourth Amendment search and seizure rights.

- On April 3, the Supreme Court rules that drug agents may briefly detain airline passengers who fit the profile of a drug courier.

- On June 21, the Supreme Court rules *Texas v. Johnson* that a Texas statute barring flag desecration conflicts with the First Amendment.

- On June 26, the Supreme Court rules in *Stanford v. Kentucky* that the imposition of the death sentence on convicted capital offenders below the age of eighteen years old does not necessarily violate the Eighth Amendment.

- On July 18, actress Rebecca Schaeffer is shot and killed at her Los Angeles home by a stalker. Her death prompts California to enact a stalking law, the first of its kind.

- On August 22, Black Panther co-founder Huey P. Newton is shot to death in Oakland, California. His killer, Tyrone Robinson, is later sentenced to thirty-two years to life in prison.

- On August 30, Leona Helmsley of New York hotel fame is found guilty of income tax evasion and not guilty of extortion.

- On September 29, actress Zsa Zsa Gabor is convicted of battery. She had slapped a Beverly Hills police officer after he stopped her for expired license plates. Gabor spent three days in jail.

- On October 5, televangelist Jim Baker is convicted of using his *PTL* show to defraud watchers.

• On November 3, U.S. district court judge Walter Nixon, Jr., of Biloxi, Mississippi, is impeached and removed from the bench because of his conviction in 1986 of lying to a grand jury.

• On December 16, Judge Robert Vance of the U.S. Court of Appeals for the Eleventh Circuit is killed at his home in Birmingham, Alabama, by a pipe bomb that had been mailed to him.

Fullilove v. Klutznick

Supreme Court decision

By: Warren Burger

Date: July 2, 1980

Source: Burger, Warren. *Fullilove v. Klutznick,* 448 U.S. 448. Available online at http://laws.findlaw.com/us/448/448.html; website home page: http://laws.findlaw.com (accessed April 17, 2003).

About the Author: Warren Burger (1907–1995) was born in St. Paul, Minnesota. He practiced law until President Dwight Eisenhower (served 1953–1960) appointed him assistant attorney general, then to bench in the U.S. Court of Appeals. In 1969, President Richard Nixon (served 1969–1974) appointed him chief justice of the U.S. Supreme Court, where he served until 1986. His judicial record reflected his belief in "strict constructionism," meaning that justices are obligated to construe the Constitution narrowly. ∎

Introduction

After slavery was ended by the Thirteenth Amendment to the Constitution, the Fourteenth Amendment in 1868 required "equal protection of the laws" regardless of race. Individual states, however, passed laws that effectively denied people equal protection and equal opportunities based on race. This state of affairs continued for nearly a century, with the Supreme Court ruling that separate but equal facilities for different races were legal. Not until the 1954 *Brown v. Board of Education* case did the Court recognize that separate facilities are inherently unequal. Congress followed up in 1964 with the passage of the Civil Rights Act. At this point, equality of treatment was the law of the land.

Implementing civil rights, however, proved to be difficult. One problem was that whites had numerous built-in advantages, such as previously established business contacts, more experience because of past preferences, and positions of power in most labor unions. African Americans often did not even have the opportunity to compete equally. To remedy this, some federal programs began to require that a certain percentage of federal grants had to be given to minority owned businesses, regardless of whether or not they submitted the lowest bids. Then in 1977 the federal government passed the Public Works

Employment Act to create local works projects and relieve unemployment. One requirement under the act was that 10 percent of the funds had to be given to minority businesses. This act came under challenge in *Fullilove.*

Significance

Fullilove was an early test of the federal government's affirmative action programs. In its decision, written by Chief Justice Warren Burger, the Court upheld this program, holding that the federal government had demonstrated a compelling rationale for it, as it was needed to redress past discrimination. The Court also held, importantly, that the act allowed for a waiver of the 10 percent provision if it could be proved that there were no minority-owned businesses in the area, or if the minority-owned businesses were charging unreasonable fees. The flexibility of this program was a key reason it was upheld, and the Court stated that racial preferences were subject to "a most searching examination." After *Fullilove,* few federal programs adopted broad affirmative action guidelines.

State, college, and business affirmative action programs, though, were frequently the subject of challenges. When the federal courts imposed hiring quotas and goals on companies and city agencies that had discriminated in the past, these quotas were upheld. Similarly, voluntary affirmative action programs by cities to consider race as one factor in promotions were upheld at first. In 1989, however, a program in Richmond, Virginia, requiring that 30 percent of contracts be given to minority-owned businesses was struck down. The Court found that Richmond had not demonstrated past discrimination in city contracts and that there was no rational basis for the 30 percent figure. Since 1989, the Court has become more conservative, generally striking down or restricting many affirmative action programs. The public has turned against them as well, with several states passing referendums preventing affirmative action in higher education, among other places.

Primary Source

Fullilove v. Klutznick [excerpt]

SYNOPSIS: Writing for the Court majority, Burger first outlines the 10 percent set-aside program under the minority business enterprise (MBE) provision of the Public Works Employment Act of 1977 and argues that the program is within the bounds of Congress's power. He then states that Congress has the power under the Fourteenth Amendment to remedy past discrimination, that the program is within Congress's rights, and that the program is narrowly tailored to accomplish its goal, allowing for waivers and exemptions where necessary.

Mr. Chief Justice Burger announced the judgment of the Court. . . .

We granted certiorari to consider a facial constitutional challenge to a requirement in a congressional spending program that, absent an administrative waiver, 10% of the federal funds granted for local public works projects must be used by the state or local grantee to procure services or supplies from businesses owned and controlled by members of statutorily identified minority groups. . . .

When we are required to pass on the constitutionality of an Act of Congress, we assume "the gravest and most delicate duty that this Court is called on to perform." . . . A program that employs racial or ethnic criteria, even in a remedial context, calls for close examination; yet we are bound to approach our task with appropriate deference to the Congress, a co-equal branch charged by the Constitution with the power to "provide for the . . . general Welfare of the United States" and "to enforce, by appropriate legislation," the equal protection guarantees of the Fourteenth Amendment. . . .

Here we pass, not on a choice made by a single judge or a school board, but on a considered decision of the Congress and the President. However, in no sense does that render it immune from judicial scrutiny, and it "is not to say we 'defer' to the judgment of the Congress . . . on a constitutional question," or that we would hesitate to invoke the Constitution should we determine that Congress has overstepped the bounds of its constitutional power. . . .

The clear objective of the MBE provision is disclosed by our necessarily extended review of its legislative and administrative background. The program was designed to ensure that, to the extent federal funds were granted under the Public Works Employment Act of 1977, grantees who elect to participate would not employ procurement practices that Congress had decided might result in perpetuation of the effects of prior discrimination which had impaired or foreclosed access by minority businesses to public contracting opportunities. The MBE program does not mandate the allocation of federal funds according to inflexible percentages solely based on race or ethnicity. . . .

In enacting the MBE provision, it is clear that Congress employed an amalgam of its specifically delegated powers. The Public Works Employment Act of 1977, by its very nature, is primarily an exercise of the Spending Power. . . . This Court has recog-

nized that the power to "provide for the . . . general Welfare" is an independent grant of legislative authority, distinct from other broad congressional powers. *Buckley v. Valeo* . . . Congress has frequently employed the Spending Power to further broad policy objectives by conditioning receipt of federal moneys upon compliance by the recipient with federal statutory and administrative directives. This Court has repeatedly upheld against constitutional challenge the use of this technique to induce governments and private parties to cooperate voluntarily with federal policy. . . .

The legislative history of the MBE provision shows that there was a rational basis for Congress to conclude that the subcontracting practices of prime contractors could perpetuate the prevailing impaired access by minority businesses to public contracting opportunities, and that this inequity has an effect on interstate commerce. Thus Congress could take necessary and proper action to remedy the situation. . . .

It is not necessary that these prime contractors be shown responsible for any violation of antidiscrimination laws. Our cases dealing with application of Title VII of the Civil Rights Act of 1964, . . . express no doubt of the congressional authority to prohibit practices "challenged as perpetuating the effects of [not unlawful] discrimination occurring prior to the effective date of the Act." . . . Insofar as the MBE program pertains to the actions of private prime contractors, the Congress could have achieved its objectives under the Commerce Clause. We conclude that in this respect the objectives of the MBE provision are within the scope of the Spending Power.

In certain contexts, there are limitations on the reach of the Commerce Power to regulate the actions of state and local governments. . . . To avoid such complications, we look to 5 of the Fourteenth Amendment for the power to regulate the procurement practices of state and local grantees of federal funds. . . . A review of our cases persuades us that the objectives of the MBE program are within the power of Congress under 5 "to enforce, by appropriate legislation," the equal protection guarantees of the Fourteenth Amendment. . . .

With respect to the MBE provision, Congress had abundant evidence from which it could conclude that minority businesses have been denied effective participation in public contracting opportunities by procurement practices that perpetuated the effects of prior discrimination. . . .

We now turn to the question whether, as a means to accomplish these plainly constitutional objectives, Congress may use racial and ethnic criteria, in this limited way, as a condition attached to a federal grant. We are mindful that "[i]n no matter should we pay more deference to the opinion of Congress than in its choice of instrumentalities to perform a function that is within its power," . . . However, Congress may employ racial or ethnic classifications in exercising its Spending or other legislative powers only if those classifications do not violate the equal protection component of the Due Process Clause of the Fifth Amendment. We recognize the need for careful judicial evaluation to assure that any congressional program that employs racial or ethnic criteria to accomplish the objective of remedying the present effects of past discrimination is narrowly tailored to the achievement of that goal. . . .

Our review of the regulations and guidelines governing administration of the MBE provision reveals that Congress enacted the program as a strictly remedial measure; moreover, it is a remedy that functions prospectively, in the manner of an injunctive decree. . . .

As a threshold matter, we reject the contention that in the remedial context the Congress must act in a wholly "color-blind" fashion. In *Swann v. Charlotte-Mecklenburg Board of Education* . . . we rejected this argument in considering a court formulated school desegregation remedy on the basis that examination of the racial composition of student bodies was an unavoidable starting point and that racially based attendance assignments were permissible so long as no absolute racial balance of each school was required. . . . Here we deal, as we noted earlier, not with the limited remedial powers of a federal court, for example, but with the broad remedial powers of Congress. It is fundamental that in no organ of government, state or federal, does there repose a more comprehensive remedial power than in the Congress, expressly charged by the Constitution with competence and authority to enforce equal protection guarantees. Congress not only may induce voluntary action to assure compliance with existing federal statutory or constitutional antidiscrimination provisions, but also, where Congress has authority to declare certain conduct unlawful, it may, as here, authorize and induce state action to avoid such conduct. . . .

A more specific challenge to the MBE program is the charge that it impermissibly deprives nonminority businesses of access to at least some por-

tion of the government contracting opportunities generated by the Act. It must be conceded that by its objective of remedying the historical impairment of access, the MBE provision can have the effect of awarding some contracts to MBE's which otherwise might be awarded to other businesses, who may themselves be innocent of any prior discriminatory actions. Failure of nonminority firms to receive certain contracts is, of course, an incidental consequence of the program, not part of its objective; similarly, past impairment of minority-firm access to public contracting opportunities may have been an incidental consequence of "business as usual" by public contracting agencies and among prime contractors. It is not a constitutional defect in this program that it may disappoint the expectations of nonminority firms. When effectuating a limited and properly tailored remedy to cure the effects of prior discrimination, such "a sharing of the burden" by innocent parties is not impermissible. . . . The actual "burden" shouldered by nonminority firms is relatively light in this connection when we consider the scope of this public works program as compared with overall construction contracting opportunities. Moreover, although we may assume that the complaining parties are innocent of any discriminatory conduct, it was within congressional power to act on the assumption that in the past some nonminority businesses may have reaped competitive benefit over the years from the virtual exclusion of minority firms from these contracting opportunities. . . .

The history of governmental tolerance of practices using racial or ethnic criteria for the purpose or with the effect of imposing an invidious discrimination must alert us to the deleterious effects of even benign racial or ethnic classifications when they stray from narrow remedial justifications. Even in the context of a facial challenge such as is presented in this case, the MBE provision cannot pass muster unless, with due account for its administrative program, it provides a reasonable assurance that application of racial or ethnic criteria will be limited to accomplishing the remedial objectives of Congress and that misapplications of the program will be promptly and adequately remedied administratively.

It is significant that the administrative scheme provides for waiver and exemption. Two fundamental congressional assumptions underlie the MBE program: (1) that the present effects of past discrimination have impaired the competitive position of businesses owned and controlled by members of minority groups; and (2) that affirmative efforts to

Three Argentine men stand in the New York butcher shop they own. **AP/WORLD WIDE PHOTOS. REPRODUCED BY PERMISSION.**

eliminate barriers to minority-firm access, and to evaluate bids with adjustment for the present effects of past discrimination, would assure that at least 10% of the federal funds granted under the Public Works Employment Act of 1977 would be accounted for by contracts with available, qualified, bona fide minority business enterprises. Each of these assumptions may be rebutted in the administrative process.

The administrative program contains measures to effectuate the congressional objective of assuring legitimate participation by disadvantaged MBEs. Administrative definition has tightened some less definite aspects of the statutory identification of the minority groups encompassed by the program. There is administrative scrutiny to identify and eliminate from participation in the program MBEs who are not "bona fide" within the regulations and guidelines; for example, spurious minority-front entities can be exposed. A significant aspect of this surveillance is the complaint procedure available for reporting "unjust participation by an enterprise or individuals in the MBE program." . . . And even as to specific contract awards, waiver is available to avoid dealing with an MBE who is attempting to exploit the remedial as-

pects of the program by charging an unreasonable price, i. e., a price not attributable to the present effects of past discrimination. . . . We must assume that Congress intended close scrutiny of false claims and prompt action on them.

Grantees are given the opportunity to demonstrate that their best efforts will not succeed or have not succeeded in achieving the statutory 10% target for minority firm participation within the limitations of the program's remedial objectives. In these circumstances a waiver or partial waiver is available once compliance has been demonstrated. A waiver may be sought and granted at any time during the contracting process, or even prior to letting contracts if the facts warrant. . . .

That the use of racial and ethnic criteria is premised on assumptions rebuttable in the administrative process gives reasonable assurance that application of the MBE program will be limited to accomplishing the remedial objectives contemplated by Congress and that misapplications of the racial and ethnic criteria can be remedied. . . . Any preference based on racial or ethnic criteria must necessarily receive a most searching examination to make sure that it does not conflict with constitutional guarantees. This case is one which requires, and which has received, that kind of examination. This opinion does not adopt, either expressly or implicitly, the formulas of analysis articulated in such cases as *University of California Regents v. Bakke.* . . . However, our analysis demonstrates that the MBE provision would survive judicial review under either "test" articulated in the several Bakke opinions. The MBE provision of the Public Works Employment Act of 1977 does not violate the Constitution.

Further Resources

BOOKS

Curry, George E., and Cornel West, *The Affirmative Action Debate.* Reading, Mass.: Addison-Wesley, 1996.

Galub, Arthur L. *The Burger Court, 1968–1984.* Danbury, Conn.: Grolier, 1995.

Maltz, Earl M. *The Chief Justiceship of Warren Burger, 1969–1986.* Columbia, S.C.: University of South Carolina Press, 2000.

Raza, M. Ali, A. Janell Anderson, and Harry Glynn Custred. *The Ups and Downs of Affirmative Action Preferences.* Westport, Conn.: Praeger, 1999.

Spann, Girardeau A. *The Law of Affirmative Action: Twenty-Five Years of Supreme Court Decisions on Race and Remedies.* New York: New York University Press, 2000.

Urofsky, Melvin I. *A Conflict of Rights: The Supreme Court and Affirmative Action.* New York: Scribner's, 1991.

Yarbrough, Tinsley E. *The Burger Court: Justices, Rulings, and Legacy.* Santa Barbara, Calif.: ABC-CLIO, 2000.

WEBSITES

Race-Conscious Remedies Resource Site. Available online at http://www.law.ucla.edu/faculty/bios/crenshaw/racerem /contracting-p1.html; website home page: http://www.law .ucla.edu (accessed February 13, 2003).

Akron v. Akron Center for Reproductive Health

Supreme Court decision

By: Lewis F. Powell and Sandra Day O'Connor

Date: June 15, 1983

Source: Powell, Lewis F. and Sandra Day O'Connor. *Akron v. Akron Center for Reproductive Health,* 462 U.S. 416. Available online at http://laws.findlaw.com/us/462/416.html; website home page: http://laws.findlaw.com (accessed April 18, 2003).

About the Authors: Lewis Powell (1907–1998) graduated from Harvard Law School, became president of the American

Bar Association in 1964, and championed legal services for the poor. He was nominated to the U.S. Supreme Court in 1971 and served until 1987, acting as a moderate.

Sandra Day O'Connor (1930–) attended Stanford Law School, graduating third in her class. Because of gender bias, no firm would hire her, so she worked as a deputy county attorney. In 1981, she was the first woman appointed to the U.S. Supreme Court. ■

Introduction

In the United States, the states began to take more of an interest in the issue of abortion in the nineteenth century, in large part because abortion was risky and became more so when surgery was involved. Abortion, though, when performed in a medical setting, had become a much safer procedure during the twentieth century.

During this time as well, the legal system became much more interested in the rights of the individual. The Supreme Court shifted its focus from economic regulations to individual rights. Louis Brandeis argued for the "right to be let alone" as part of a right to privacy as early as 1928. Later, the Supreme Court built upon this right to overturn a Connecticut ban on the use of contraceptives. The right to privacy was used in 1972 to strike down a Texas law banning abortions in *Roe v. Wade.* There, Justice Blackmun argued that the right to privacy outweighed any state interest in regulating abortion up to the point of viability; after viability, abortions could be banned. Appropriate medical regulations to safeguard the health of the woman undertaking the abortion could, however, be instituted from the end of the first trimester of pregnancy.

This decision provoked a firestorm of controversy, and many candidates for public office argued for constitutional amendments that would overturn *Roe v. Wade.* Ronald Reagan (served 1981–1989), while running for the presidency, promised to appoint Supreme Court justices who would oppose *Roe.* The Supreme Court, though, continued to uphold its ruling. Then in 1983, regulations enacted by the city of Akron, Ohio, came before the Court.

Significance

The Supreme Court in this case struck down all of Akron's attempts to regulate abortion, including a parental consent requirement, an informed consent requirement, and the requirement that all abortions be performed in a hospital. Three justices dissented, though, including Sandra Day O'Connor, President Reagan's first appointee. Some argued that if Reagan could appoint two more justices, *Roe* could be overturned. In 1986 and 1987, Reagan appointed Justices Antonin Scalia and Anthony Kennedy—it seemed as if *Roe* might be overturned.

The question was directly addressed in 1992, in *Planned Parenthood of Southeastern Pennsylvania v. Casey.* Justice O'Connor led a plurality of three justices, including Kennedy, in an opinion that directly upheld *Roe* and argued that there was no compelling reason to reexamine the case. The Court did rework *Roe,* arguing that the key issue was not what trimester of pregnancy one was in but whether the fetus was viable, and that before viability, no legislation was allowed that placed an "undue burden" on a woman seeking an abortion. That decision has largely been upheld since, even though some regulations requiring waiting periods and prohibiting the use of public funds for abortions have been upheld. Those seeking abortions have also been hampered by protesters and by the fact that few doctors and clinics perform abortions in many towns. Even though it has been assailed, *Roe* still stands.

Primary Source

Akron v. Akron Center for Reproductive Health
[excerpt]

> **SYNOPSIS:** Justice Powell first reaffirms the holding of *Roe v. Wade.* He then argues that any regulation which puts a "significant obstacle" in the way of a woman's right to an abortion, except as allowed in *Roe,* is unconstitutional. He uses this standard to strike down most of Akron's regulations. Justice O'Connor dissents, arguing for discarding the trimester approach of *Roe* and suggesting that most of these regulations do not impose an undue burden.

Justice Powell delivered the opinion of the Court.

In this litigation we must decide the constitutionality of several provisions of an ordinance enacted by the city of Akron, Ohio, to regulate the performance of abortions. . . .

These cases come to us a decade after we held in *Roe v. Wade,* . . . that the right of privacy, grounded in the concept of personal liberty guaranteed by the Constitution, encompasses a woman's right to decide whether to terminate her pregnancy. Legislative responses to the Court's decision have required us on several occasions, and again today, to define the limits of a State's authority to regulate the performance of abortions. And arguments continue to be made, in these cases as well, that we erred in interpreting the Constitution. Nonetheless, the doctrine of stare decisis, while perhaps never entirely persuasive on a constitutional question, is a doctrine that demands respect in a society governed by the rule of law. We respect it today, and reaffirm *Roe v. Wade.* . . .

We reaffirm today, . . . that a State's interest in health regulation becomes compelling at approximately the end of the first trimester. The existence of a compelling state interest in health, however, is only the beginning of the inquiry. The State's regulation may be upheld only if it is reasonably designed to further that state interest. . . . And the Court in *Roe* did not hold that it always is reasonable for a State to adopt an abortion regulation that applies to the entire second trimester. A State necessarily must have latitude in adopting regulations of general applicability in this sensitive area. But if it appears that during a substantial portion of the second trimester the State's regulation "depart[s] from accepted medical practice," . . . the regulation may not be upheld simply because it may be reasonable for the remaining portion of the trimester. Rather, the State is obligated to make a reasonable effort to limit the effect of its regulations to the period in the trimester during which its health interest will be furthered.

There can be no doubt that 1870.03's second-trimester hospitalization requirement places a significant obstacle in the path of women seeking an abortion. A primary burden created by the requirement is additional cost to the woman. . . . Thus, a second-trimester hospitalization requirement may force women to travel to find available facilities, resulting in both financial expense and additional health risk. It therefore is apparent that a second-trimester hospitalization requirement may significantly limit a woman's ability to obtain an abortion.

Akron does not contend that 1870.03 imposes only an insignificant burden on women's access to abortion, but rather defends it as a reasonable health regulation. This position had strong support at the time of *Roe v. Wade,* . . . Since then, however, the safety of second-trimester abortions has increased dramatically. . . .

These developments, and the professional commentary supporting them, constitute impressive evidence that—at least during the early weeks of the second trimester—D & E abortions may be performed as safely in an outpatient clinic as in a full-service hospital. We conclude, therefore, that "present medical knowledge," . . . convincingly undercuts Akron's justification for requiring that all second-trimester abortions be performed in a hospital.

. . . By preventing the performance of D & E abortions in an appropriate nonhospital setting, Akron has imposed a heavy, and unnecessary, burden on women's access to a relatively inexpensive, otherwise accessible, and safe abortion procedure. Section 1870.03 has "the effect of inhibiting . . . the vast majority of abortions after the first 12 weeks," . . . and therefore unreasonably infringes upon a woman's constitutional right to obtain an abortion. . . .

In these circumstances, we do not think that the Akron ordinance, as applied in Ohio juvenile proceedings, is reasonably susceptible of being construed to create an "opportunity for case-by-case evaluations of the maturity of pregnant minors." . . . We therefore affirm the Court of Appeals' judgment that 1870.05(B) is unconstitutional. The Akron ordinance provides that no abortion shall be performed except "with the informed written consent of the pregnant woman, . . . given freely and without coercion." 1870.06(A). Furthermore, "in order to insure that the consent for an abortion is truly informed consent," the woman must be "orally informed by her attending physician" of the status of her pregnancy, the development of her fetus, the date of possible viability, the physical and emotional complications that may result from an abortion, and the availability of agencies to provide her with assistance and information with respect to birth control, adoption, and childbirth. 1870.06(B). In addition, the attending physician must inform her "of the particular risks associated with her own pregnancy and the abortion technique to be employed . . . [and] other information which in his own medical judgment is relevant to her decision as to whether to have an abortion or carry her pregnancy to term." 1870.06(C). . . .

Viewing the city's regulations in this light, we believe that 1870.06(B) attempts to extend the State's interest in ensuring "informed consent" beyond permissible limits. First, it is fair to say that much of the information required is designed not to inform the woman's consent but rather to persuade her to withhold it altogether. Subsection (3) requires the physician to inform his patient that "the unborn child is a human life from the moment of conception," a requirement inconsistent with the Court's holding in *Roe v. Wade* that a State may not adopt one theory of when life begins to justify its regulation of abortions. . . . Moreover, much of the detailed description of "the anatomical and physiological characteristics of the particular unborn child" required by subsection (3) would involve at best speculation by the physician. And subsection (5), that begins with the dubious statement that "abortion is a major surgical procedure" and proceeds to describe numerous possible physical and psychological compli-

Anti-abortion demonstrators gather in Washington D.C. in 1983. The Supreme Court decision in *Akron v. Akron Center for Reproductive Health* invalidated the regualtions of Akron, Ohio against the abortion clinic. © **BETTMANN/CORBIS. REPRODUCED BY PERMISSION.**

cations of abortion, is a "parade of horribles" intended to suggest that abortion is a particularly dangerous procedure. . . .

We are not convinced, however, that there is as vital a state need for insisting that the physician performing the abortion, or for that matter any physician, personally counsel the patient in the absence of a request. The State's interest is in ensuring that the woman's consent is informed and unpressured; the critical factor is whether she obtains the necessary information and counseling from a qualified person, not the identity of the person from whom she obtains it. Akron and intervenors strongly urge that the non-physician counselors at the plaintiff abortion clinics are not trained or qualified to perform this important function. The courts below made no such findings, however, and on the record before us we cannot say that the woman's consent to the abortion will not be informed if a physician delegates the counseling task to another qualified individual. . . .

We find that Akron has failed to demonstrate that any legitimate state interest is furthered by an arbitrary and inflexible waiting period. There is no evidence suggesting that the abortion procedure will be performed more safely. Nor are we convinced that the State's legitimate concern that the woman's decision be informed is reasonably served by requiring a 24-hour delay as a matter of course. The decision whether to proceed with an abortion is one as to which it is important to "affor[d] the physician adequate discretion in the exercise of his medical judgment." . . . In accordance with the ethical standards of the profession, a physician will advise the patient to defer the abortion when he thinks this will be beneficial to her. But if a woman, after appropriate counseling, is prepared to give her written informed consent and proceed with the abortion, a State may not demand that she delay the effectuation of that decision.

Section 1870.16 of the Akron ordinance requires physicians performing abortions to "insure that the remains of the unborn child are disposed of in a humane and sanitary manner." The Court of Appeals found that the word "humane" was impermissibly vague as a definition of conduct subject to criminal prosecution. The court invalidated the entire provision, declining to sever the word "humane" in order to uphold the requirement that disposal be "sanitary . . . We affirm this judgment. . . .

We affirm the judgment of the Court of Appeals invalidating those sections of Akron's "Regulations of Abortions" ordinance that deal with parental consent, informed consent, a 24-hour waiting period, and the disposal of fetal remains. The remaining portion of the judgment, sustaining Akron's requirement that all second-trimester abortions be performed in a hospital, is reversed. . . .

Justice O'Connor, with whom Justice White and Justice Rehnquist join, dissenting.

. . . Nonetheless, it is apparent from the Court's opinion that neither sound constitutional theory nor our need to decide cases based on the application of neutral principles can accommodate an analytical framework that varies according to the "stages" of pregnancy, where those stages, and their concomitant standards of review, differ according to the level of medical technology available when a particular challenge to state regulation occurs. The Court's analysis of the Akron regulations is inconsistent both with the methods of analysis employed in previous cases dealing with abortion, and with the Court's approach to fundamental rights in other areas. . . .

The trimester or "three-stage" approach adopted by the Court in *Roe,* and, in a modified form, employed by the Court to analyze the regulations in these cases, cannot be supported as a legitimate or useful framework for accommodating the woman's right and the State's interests. The decision of the Court today graphically illustrates why the trimester approach is a completely unworkable method of accommodating the conflicting personal rights and compelling state interests that are involved in the abortion context. . . .

The Court adheres to the *Roe* framework because the doctrine of stare decisis "demands respect in a society governed by the rule of law." Ante, at 420. Although respect for stare decisis cannot be challenged, "this Court's considered practice [is] not to apply stare decisis as rigidly in constitutional as in nonconstitutional cases." . . . Although we must be mindful of the "desirability of continuity of decision in constitutional questions . . . when convinced of former error, this Court has never felt constrained to follow precedent. In constitutional questions, where correction depends upon amendment and not upon legislative action this Court throughout its history has freely exercised its power to reexamine the basis of its constitutional decisions." . . .

Even assuming that there is a fundamental right to terminate pregnancy in some situations, there is no justification in law or logic for the trimester framework adopted in *Roe* and employed by the Court today on the basis of stare decisis. For the reasons stated above, that framework is clearly an unworkable means of balancing the fundamental right and the compelling state interests that are indisputably implicated. . . .

The fallacy inherent in the *Roe* framework is apparent: just because the State has a compelling interest in ensuring maternal safety once an abortion may be more dangerous than childbirth, it simply does not follow that the State has no interest before that point that justifies state regulation to ensure that first-trimester abortions are performed as safely as possible.

The state interest in potential human life is likewise extant throughout pregnancy. In *Roe,* the Court held that although the State had an important and legitimate interest in protecting potential life, that interest could not become compelling until the point at which the fetus was viable. The difficulty with this analysis is clear: potential life is no less potential in the first weeks of pregnancy than it is at viability or afterward. At any stage in pregnancy, there is the potential for human life. Although the Court refused to "resolve the difficult question of when life begins," . . . the Court chose the point of viability—when the fetus is capable of life independent of its mother— to permit the complete proscription of abortion. The choice of viability as the point at which the state interest in potential life becomes compelling is no less arbitrary than choosing any point before viability or any point afterward. Accordingly, I believe that the State's interest in protecting potential human life exists throughout the pregnancy. . . .

In determining whether the State imposes an "undue burden," we must keep in mind that when we are concerned with extremely sensitive issues, such as the one involved here, "the appropriate forum for their resolution in a democracy is the legislature. We should not forget that 'legislatures are ultimate guardians of the liberties and welfare of the people in quite as great a degree as the courts.' . . . This does not mean that in determining whether a regulation imposes an "undue burden" on the *Roe* right we defer to the judgments made by state legislatures. "The point is, rather, that when we face a complex problem with many hard questions and few easy answers we do well to pay careful attention to how the other branches of Government have addressed the same problem." . . .

We must always be mindful that "[t]he Constitution does not compel a state to fine-tune its statutes so as to encourage or facilitate abortions. To the contrary, state action 'encouraging childbirth except in the most urgent circumstances' is 'rationally related to the legitimate governmental objective of protecting potential life.' . . .

Section 1870.03 of the Akron ordinance requires that second-trimester abortions be performed in hospitals. . . .

For the reasons stated above, I find no justification for the trimester approach used by the Court to analyze this restriction. I would apply the "unduly burdensome" test and find that the hospitalization

requirement does not impose an undue burden on that decision. . . .

Section 1870.07 of the Akron ordinance requires a 24-hour waiting period between the signing of a consent form and the actual performance of the abortion, except in cases of emergency. . . .

Assuming, arguendo, that any additional costs are such as to impose an undue burden on the abortion decision, the State's compelling interests in maternal physical and mental health and protection of fetal life clearly justify the waiting period. As we acknowledged in Danforth . . . , the decision to abort is "a stressful one," and the waiting period reasonably relates to the State's interest in ensuring that a woman does not make this serious decision in undue haste. The decision also has grave consequences for the fetus, whose life the State has a compelling interest to protect and preserve. "[N]o other [medical] procedure involves the purposeful termination of a potential life." . . . The waiting period is surely a small cost to impose to ensure that the woman's decision is well considered in light of its certain and irreparable consequences on fetal life, and the possible effects on her own.

Further Resources

BOOKS

Drucker, Dan. *Abortion Decisions of the Supreme Court, 1973 through 1989: A Comprehensive Review with Historical Commentary.* Jefferson, N.C.: McFarland, 1990.

Goldstein, Leslie Friedman. *Contemporary Cases in Women's Rights.* Madison, Wis.: University of Wisconsin Press, 1994.

Guitton, Stephanie, and Peter H. Irons. *May It Please the Court: Arguments on Abortion.* New York: New Press, 1993.

Harrison, Maureen, and Steve Gilbert. *Abortion Decisions of the United States Supreme Court: The 1980's.* Beverly Hills, Calif.: Excellent Books, 1993.

Jeffries, John Calvin. *Justice Lewis F. Powell, Jr.* New York: Scribner's, 1994.

Van Sickel, Robert W. *Not a Particularly Different Voice: The Jurisprudence of Sandra Day O'Connor.* New York: P. Lang, 1998.

WEBSITES

National Public Radio. *30th Anniversary of Roe v. Wade. Timeline.* Available online at http://www.npr.org/news/specials /roevwade/timeline.html; website home page: http://www .npr.org/ (accessed February 13, 2003).

AUDIO AND VISUAL MEDIA

Weddington, Sarah Ragle. *The Constitution: How its Principles Apply to Today's Controversies.* Brookings, S.D.: South Dakota State University, 1989.

Mueller v. Allen

Supreme Court decision

By: William H. Rehnquist and Thurgood Marshall

Date: June 29, 1983

Source: Rehnquist, William H. and Thurgood Marshall. *Mueller v. Allen,* 463 U.S. 388. Available online at http://laws.findlaw.com/us/463/388.html; website home page: http://laws.findlaw.com (accessed April 17, 2003).

About the Authors: William Rehnquist (1924–) attended Stanford for his law degrees. In 1971, he was named to the U.S. Supreme Court, and in 1986, he was appointed chief justice. He is generally regarded as a conservative.

Thurgood Marshall (1908–1993) served as counsel for the National Association for the Advancement of Colored People (NAACP). In 1967, he became the first African American appointed to the U.S. Supreme Court, where he served until 1991. ∎

Introduction

Most American colonies had established churches. Religious freedom, though, was a motivating factor for many colonists, who came to believe that a separation of church and state was needed. For this reason, the First Amendment to the U.S. Constitution reads, in part, "Congress shall make no law respecting an establishment of religion, or prohibiting the free exercise thereof. . . ." The amendment's meaning was not generally tested in the nineteenth century because the Bill of Rights, which included the First Amendment, was held to apply only to the actions of the federal government.

In the twentieth century, though, things began to change. In the 1920s and 1930s, the Supreme Court began to hold that the First Amendment was part of our "liberty," which was applied against the states through the Fourteenth Amendment, prohibiting states from denying liberty and equal protection under the law. Religion also became a public part of American policy, as America was locked in a battle with the "godless communism" of the Soviet Union. The Supreme Court began to interpret the freedom of religion segment of the First Amendment in the 1960s. In *Engel* (1962), the Court struck down a requirement that schools begin their day with a prayer led by the teachers and repeated voluntarily by the students. The Court held that such a prayer was an endorsement of religion by the schools. In 1971, the Court developed a test (the *Lemon* test) for determining if aid to religious schools was constitutional. For the aid to be constitutional, it had to have a "secular purpose," had to neither help nor hurt religion, and had to not foster "an excessive entanglement of religion" with the state. In that case, the Court struck down a program of purchasing secular education from religious schools for students who normally attended those schools. The question of allow-

ing state income tax deductions for certain educational expenses, regardless of whether they were at a religious or secular school, was the issue in *Mueller v. Allen.*

Significance

The Supreme Court, in a 5 to 4 vote, upheld the Minnesota statute that allowed taxpayers to deduct expenses incurred at parochial schools. The majority held that the purpose of this statute was to encourage education, that the program did not directly help or hinder religion, and that even though state officials had to determine if certain expenses were for educational rather than religious purposes, this did not cause an "excessive entanglement." Those who dissented from the majority argued that most of the benefits go to religious schools, and so this tax deduction directly supports religion in a way prohibited by the First Amendment.

Later cases dealing with religion in education have consistently prohibited prayer in public schools and have struck down statutes requiring equal teaching of evolution and "creation science." Federal grants to charitable groups, both religious and secular, however, have been upheld. Aid to schools in educational areas have met mixed results—for instance, providing maps, periodicals, and photographs have been denied, but giving textbooks and reimbursing private schools for the costs of state tests have been allowed.

The issue of state involvement in religion, directly and indirectly, remains in the news. Ever since *Engel,* some conservatives have pushed for a constitutional amendment allowing prayer in public schools. States continue to try to force the posting of the Ten Commandments in courthouses and public schools, but these efforts have consistently been struck down at the federal government level. President George W. Bush (served 2001–) advocated providing federal aid to churches and religious groups to help with their charitable activities.

Primary Source

Mueller v. Allen [excerpt]

> **SYNOPSIS:** Justice Rehnquist, who wrote the majority opinion, details the Minnesota plan and outlines the *Lemon* test. He then argues that the tax deduction has the secular goal of advancing education, does not aid religion because it aids all schools, and does not excessively entangle the state in religion. Writing in dissent, Marshall argues that since the vast majority of the people helped by the statute attend religious schools, it violates the First Amendment.

Justice Rehnquist delivered the opinion of the Court. . . .

Minnesota, . . . permits state taxpayers to claim a deduction from gross income for certain expenses incurred in educating their children. The deduction is limited to actual expenses incurred for the "tuition, textbooks and transportation" of dependents attending elementary or secondary schools. . . .

Today's case is no exception to our oft-repeated statement that the Establishment Clause presents especially difficult questions of interpretation and application. It is easy enough to quote the few words constituting that Clause—"Congress shall make no law respecting an establishment of religion." It is not at all easy, however, to apply this Court's various decisions construing the Clause to governmental programs of financial assistance to sectarian schools and the parents of children attending those schools. . . .

One fixed principle in this field is our consistent rejection of the argument that "any program which in some manner aids an institution with a religious affiliation" violates the Establishment Clause. . . .

Notwithstanding the repeated approval given programs . . . , our decisions also have struck down arrangements resembling, in many respects, these forms of assistance. . . . In this case we are asked to decide whether Minnesota's tax deduction bears greater resemblance to those types of assistance to parochial schools we have approved, or to those we have struck down. Petitioners place particular reliance on our decision in *Committee for Public Education v. Nyquist,* supra, where we held invalid a New York statute providing public funds for the maintenance and repair of the physical facilities of private schools and granting thinly disguised "tax benefits," actually amounting to tuition grants, to the parents of children attending private schools. . . .

The general nature of our inquiry in this area has been guided, since the decision in *Lemon v. Kurtzman,* supra, by the "three-part" test laid down in that case:

> First, the statute must have a secular legislative purpose; second, its principal or primary effect must be one that neither advances nor inhibits religion . . . ; finally, the statute must not foster "an excessive government entanglement with religion."

. . . While this principle is well settled, our cases have also emphasized that it provides "no more than [a] helpful signpos[t]" in dealing with Establishment Clause challenges. . . .

Little time need be spent on the question of whether the Minnesota tax deduction has a secular purpose. . . .

A State's decision to defray the cost of educational expenses incurred by parents—regardless of the type of schools their children attend—evidences a purpose that is both secular and understandable. . . .

All these justifications are readily available to support 290.09, . . . and each is sufficient to satisfy the secular purpose inquiry of Lemon.

We turn therefore to the more difficult but related question whether the Minnesota statute has "the primary effect of advancing the sectarian aims of the nonpublic schools." . . . In concluding that it does not, we find several features of the Minnesota tax deduction particularly significant. . . .

Other characteristics of 290.09, . . . argue equally strongly for the provision's constitutionality. Most importantly, the deduction is available for educational expenses incurred by all parents, including those whose children attend public schools and those whose children attend nonsectarian private schools or sectarian private schools. . . .

Unlike the assistance at issue in *Nyquist,* 290.09, . . . permits all parents—whether their children attend public school or private—to deduct their children's educational expenses. . . . a program, like 290.09, . . . that neutrally provides state assistance to a broad spectrum of citizens is not readily subject to challenge under the Establishment Clause. . . .

The Establishment Clause of course extends beyond prohibition of a state church or payment of state funds to one or more churches. We do not think, however, that its prohibition extends to the type of tax deduction established by Minnesota. The historic purposes of the Clause simply do not encompass the sort of attenuated financial benefit, ultimately controlled by the private choices of individual parents, that eventually flows to parochial schools from the neutrally available tax benefit at issue in this case.

Petitioners argue that, notwithstanding the facial neutrality of 290.09, . . . in application the statute primarily benefits religious institutions. Petitioners rely, as they did below, on a statistical analysis of the type of persons claiming the tax deduction. . . .

We need not consider these contentions in detail. We would be loath to adopt a rule grounding the constitutionality of a facially neutral law on annual reports reciting the extent to which various classes of private citizens claimed benefits under the law.

Such an approach would scarcely provide the certainty that this field stands in need of, nor can we perceive principled standards by which such statistical evidence might be evaluated. Moreover, the fact that private persons fail in a particular year to claim the tax relief to which they are entitled—under a facially neutral statute—should be of little importance in determining the constitutionality of the statute permitting such relief.

Finally, private educational institutions, and parents paying for their children to attend these schools, make special contributions to the areas in which they operate. . . . If parents of children in private schools choose to take especial advantage of the relief provided by 290.09, . . . it is no doubt due to the fact that they bear a particularly great financial burden in educating their children. More fundamentally, whatever unequal effect may be attributed to the statutory classification can fairly be regarded as a rough return for the benefits, discussed above, provided to the State and all taxpayers by parents sending their children to parochial schools. In the light of all this, we believe it wiser to decline to engage in the type of empirical inquiry into those persons benefited by state law which petitioners urge.

Thus, we hold that the Minnesota tax deduction for educational expenses satisfies the primary effect inquiry of our Establishment Clause cases.

Turning to the third part of the Lemon inquiry, we have no difficulty in concluding that the Minnesota statute does not "excessively entangle" the State in religion. The only plausible source of the "comprehensive, discriminating, and continuing state surveillance," . . . necessary to run afoul of this standard would lie in the fact that state officials must determine whether particular textbooks qualify for a deduction. . . . Making decisions such as this does not differ substantially from making the types of decisions approved in earlier opinions of this Court. . . .

Justice Marshall, with whom Justice Brennan, Justice Blackmun, and Justice Stevens join, dissenting.

The Establishment Clause of the First Amendment prohibits a State from subsidizing religious education, whether it does so directly or indirectly. In my view, this principle of neutrality forbids not only the tax benefits struck down in *Committee for Public Education v. Nyquist,* . . . but any tax benefit, including the tax deduction at issue here, which subsidizes tuition payments to sectarian schools. I also believe that the Establishment Clause prohibits the tax deductions that Minnesota authorizes for the cost of books and other instructional materials used for sectarian purposes. . . .

Contrary to the majority's suggestion, . . . the bulk of the tax benefits afforded by the Minnesota scheme are enjoyed by parents of parochial school children not because parents of public school children fail to claim deductions to which they are entitled, but because the latter are simply unable to claim the largest tax deduction that Minnesota authorizes. Fewer than 100 of more than 900,000 school-age children in Minnesota attend public schools that charge a general tuition. Of the total number of taxpayers who are eligible for the tuition deduction, approximately 96% send their children to religious schools. . . .

That this deduction has a primary effect of promoting religion can easily be determined without any resort to the type of "statistical evidence" that the majority fears would lead to constitutional uncertainty. . . . The only factual inquiry necessary is the same as that employed in Nyquist. . . . whether the deduction permitted for tuition expenses primarily benefits those who send their children to religious schools. . . .

Because Minnesota, like every other State, is committed to providing free public education, tax assistance for tuition payments inevitably redounds to the benefit of nonpublic, sectarian schools and parents who send their children to those schools.

The majority also asserts that the Minnesota statute is distinguishable from the statute struck down in Nyquist in another respect: the tax benefit available under Minnesota law is a "genuine tax deduction," whereas the New York law provided a benefit which, while nominally a deduction, also had features of a "tax credit." . . . Under the Minnesota law, the amount of the tax benefit varies directly with the amount of the expenditure. Under the New York law, the amount of deduction was not dependent upon the amount actually paid for tuition but was a predetermined amount which depended on the tax bracket of each taxpayer. The deduction was designed to yield roughly the same amount of tax "forgiveness" for each taxpayer.

This is a distinction without a difference. Our prior decisions have rejected the relevance of the majority's formalistic distinction between tax deductions and the tax benefit at issue in Nyquist. . . . Like the tax benefit held impermissible in Nyquist, the tax deduction at issue here concededly was designed to "encourag[e] desirable expenditures for educational purposes." . . .

As previously noted, . . . the Minnesota tuition tax deduction is not available to all parents, but only to parents whose children attend schools that charge tuition, which are comprised almost entirely of sectarian schools. More importantly, the assistance that flows to parochial schools as a result of the tax benefit is not restricted, and cannot be restricted, to the secular functions of those schools.

In my view, Minnesota's tax deduction for the cost of textbooks and other instructional materials is also constitutionally infirm. The majority is simply mistaken in concluding that a tax deduction, unlike a tax credit or a direct grant to parents, promotes religious education in a manner that is only "attenuated." . . . A tax deduction has a primary effect that advances religion if it is provided to offset expenditures which are not restricted to the secular activities of parochial schools.

The instructional materials which are subsidized by the Minnesota tax deduction plainly may be used to inculcate religious values and belief. . . .

There is no reason to treat Minnesota's tax deduction for textbooks any differently. Secular textbooks, like other secular instructional materials, contribute to the religious mission of the parochial schools that use those books. . . .

In any event, the Court's assumption in Allen that the textbooks at issue there might be used only for secular education was based on the fact that those very books had been chosen by the State for use in the public schools. In contrast, the Minnesota statute does not limit the tax deduction to those books which the State has approved for use in public schools. Rather, it permits a deduction for books that are chosen by the parochial schools themselves. Indeed, under the Minnesota statutory scheme, textbooks chosen by parochial schools but not used by public schools are likely to be precisely the ones purchased by parents for their children's use. . . .

There can be little doubt that the State of Minnesota intended to provide, and has provided, "[s]ubstantial aid to the educational function of [church-related] schools," and that the tax deduction for tuition and other educational expenses "necessarily results in aid to the sectarian school enterprise as a whole." . . . For the first time, the Court has upheld financial support for religious schools without any reason at all to assume that the support will be restricted to the secular functions of those schools and will not be used to support religious instruction. This result is flatly at odds with the fundamental principle that a State may provide no financial support whatsoever to promote religion. I dissent.

Further Resources

BOOKS
Davis, Sue Justice. *Rehnquist and the Constitution.* Princeton, N.J.: Princeton University Press, 1989.

Eastland, Terry. *Religious Liberty in the Supreme Court: The Cases that Define the Debate over Church and State.* Washington, D.C.: Ethics and Public Policy Center, 1993.

Noonan, John Thomas, and Edward McGlynn Gaffney. *Religious Freedom: History, Cases, and Other Materials on the Interaction of Religion and Government.* New York: Foundation Press, 2001.

Smolla, Rodney A. *The First Amendment: Freedom of Expression, Regulation of Mass Media, Freedom of Religion.* Durham, N.C.: Carolina Academic Press, 1999.

Sullivan, Kathleen M., and Gerald Gunther, *First Amendment Law.* New York: Foundation Press, 1999.

PERIODICALS
Allsberry, Gregory K. "Tax Deductions for Parochial School Tuition: 'Mueller v. Allen,'" *Washington University Journal of Urban and Contemporary Law* 26, 107–121.

WEBSITES
Minnesota in the Supreme Court: Lessons on Supreme Court Cases Involving Minnesota. Available online at http://www.ccle.fourh.umn.edu/mueller.pdf; website home page: http://www.ccle.fourh.umn.edu (accessed February 13, 2003).

New York v. Quarles
Supreme Court decision

By: William H. Rehnquist, Sandra Day O'Connor, and Thurgood Marshall

Date: June 12, 1984

Source: Rehnquist, William H., Sandra Day O'Connor, and Thurgood Marshall. *New York v. Quarles,* 467 U.S. 649. Available online at http://laws.findlaw.com/us/467/649.html; website home page: http://laws.findlaw.com (accessed April 18, 2003).

About the Authors: William Rehnquist (1924–) attended Stanford for his law degrees. In 1971, he was named to the U.S. Supreme Court, and in 1986, he was appointed chief justice. He is generally regarded as a conservative.

Sandra Day O'Connor (1930–) attended Stanford Law School, graduating third in her class. Because of gender bias, no firm would hire her, so she worked as a deputy county attorney. In 1981, she was the first woman appointed to the U.S. Supreme Court.

Thurgood Marshall (1908–1993) served as counsel for the National Association for the Advancement of Colored People (NAACP) and in 1967 became the first African American appointed to the U.S. Supreme Court. He served on the Court until 1991. ∎

Introduction

The Bill of Rights, the first ten amendments to the Constitution, was added to the Constitution in 1791. The meaning of these amendments has not always been clear, especially with regard to the criminal justice system. Until the 1960s, different criminal procedures and constitutional protections applied at the state level and the federal level, creating fifty-one different sets of constitutional protections. Also, the police often had incentives for encouraging people not to pursue their rights, especially the right to remain silent or to contact an attorney. It was also unclear under the Constitution whether accused persons were supposed to be informed of their rights.

In the 1960s, the U.S. Supreme Court, under the leadership of Chief Justice Earl Warren, began increasing the constitutional protections for criminal defendants, and applying those protections in either state or federal courts. The Warren Court held that the right to counsel was fundamental. It applied the right against self-incrimination, which had existed for decades in federal court, to state court matters. It also held that a confession obtained when a defendant was not able to consult a lawyer and was not informed of the right to remain silent, was inadmissible in state courts. Finally, in 1966, in *Miranda v. Arizona,* the Supreme Court ruled that a defendant must be informed of the right to remain silent, to have a counsel present during questioning, and statements obtained without these warnings were not admissible in criminal court.

This decision caused a firestorm of controversy, even though many studies indicated that it had only a minimal effect on the actual practice of police work. Many politicians, including Richard Nixon, ran for office denouncing the *Miranda* decision. In the 1970s, the Burger Court narrowed the *Miranda* ruling, creating exceptions to it. In 1984, the Supreme Court considered the *Miranda* warning again in *New York v. Quarles,* a case involving a defendant, who before being given his Miranda warning, had admitted the location in a supermarket where he had tossed a gun after being chased by police.

Significance

The Supreme Court, by a vote of 6 to 3, upheld the use of the gun in court to obtain a conviction. The majority, led by Chief Justice Rehnquist, held that the issue of public safety allowed for the question to be asked and held that public safety was more important than the defendant's rights, and thus outweighed them. Justice

O'Connor would have allowed the use of the gun but not allowed a statement made by the defendant at the same time. Justice Marshall's dissent pointed out that the highest court of New York had found that there was no issue of public safety involved but only the desire of the police officer to obtain a conviction.

Since *Quarles,* the Supreme Court has generally narrowed the protections of *Miranda.* The Court has ruled that trickery and the deliberate withholding of information from a defendant were permitted. The Miranda warning is not required in brief traffic stops, and the Court allowed a confession that was obtained after a Miranda warning, but followed a previous confession obtained without that warning. Thus, the protections of Miranda have been somewhat limited. The Supreme Court did, though, disallow a confession that had been obtained after the defendant had asked for counsel but before that counsel had been provided.

Primary Source

New York v. Quarles [excerpt]

SYNOPSIS: Chief Justice Rehnquist opens by holding that the Miranda requirements do not apply to this case, because there was an issue of "public safety," creating an exception to Miranda. Justice O'Connor dissents in part, arguing that the statements gained without Miranda are inadmissible, but that the gun found before the Miranda warning was given was admissible. Justice Marshall dissents, arguing that the majority opinion destroys the clarity of the Miranda requirement, which was never about public safety but about coerced confessions.

Justice Rehnquist delivered the opinion of the Court. . . .

We conclude that under the circumstances involved in this case, overriding considerations of public safety justify the officer's failure to provide Miranda warnings before he asked questions devoted to locating the abandoned weapon.

. . . The Fifth Amendment guarantees that "[n]o person . . . shall be compelled in any criminal case to be a witness against himself." In *Miranda* this Court for the first time extended the Fifth Amendment privilege against compulsory self-incrimination to individuals subjected to custodial interrogation by the police. . . . The Fifth Amendment itself does not prohibit all incriminating admissions; "[a]bsent some officially coerced self-accusation, the Fifth Amendment privilege is not violated by even the most damning admissions. . . . The Miranda Court, however, presumed that interrogation in certain custodial circumstances is inherently coercive and held

A police officer reads Miranda rights to a handcuffed suspect. © **KIM KULISH/CORBIS SABA. REPRODUCED BY PERMISSION.**

that statements made under those circumstances are inadmissible unless the suspect is specifically informed of his Miranda rights and freely decides to forgo those rights. The prophylactic Miranda warnings therefore are "not themselves rights protected by the Constitution but [are] instead measures to insure that the right against compulsory self-incrimination [is] protected." . . . Requiring Miranda warnings before custodial interrogation provides "practical reinforcement" for the Fifth Amendment right. . . .

In this case we have before us no claim that respondent's statements were actually compelled by police conduct which overcame his will to resist. . . . Thus the only issue before us is whether Officer Kraft was justified in failing to make available to respondent the procedural safeguards associated with the privilege against compulsory self-incrimination since *Miranda*.

The New York Court of Appeals was undoubtedly correct in deciding that the facts of this case come within the ambit of the *Miranda* decision as we have subsequently interpreted it. We agree that respondent was in police custody. . . . As the New York

Court of Appeals observed, there was nothing to suggest that any of the officers were any longer concerned for their own physical safety. . . . The New York Court of Appeals' majority declined to express an opinion as to whether there might be an exception to the *Miranda* rule if the police had been acting to protect the public, because the lower courts in New York had made no factual determination that the police had acted with that motive. . . .

We hold that on these facts there is a "public safety" exception to the requirement that Miranda warnings be given before a suspect's answers may be admitted into evidence, and that the availability of that exception does not depend upon the motivation of the individual officers involved. In a kaleidoscopic situation such as the one confronting these officers, where spontaneity rather than adherence to a police manual is necessarily the order of the day, the application of the exception which we recognize today should not be made to depend on post hoc findings at a suppression hearing concerning the subjective motivation of the arresting officer. Undoubtedly most police officers, if placed in Officer Kraft's position, would act out of a host of different,

The Miranda rights are a basic set of simple statements that are read to accused persons prior to questioning. **CONNECTICUT STATE POLICE.**

instinctive, and largely unverifiable motives—their own safety, the safety of others, and perhaps as well the desire to obtain incriminating evidence from the suspect.

Whatever the motivation of individual officers in such a situation, we do not believe that the doctrinal underpinnings of *Miranda* require that it be applied in all its rigor to a situation in which police officers ask questions reasonably prompted by a concern for the public safety. The *Miranda* decision was based in large part on this Court's view that the warnings which it required police to give to suspects in custody would reduce the likelihood that the suspects would fall victim to constitutionally impermissible practices of police interrogation in the presumptively coercive environment of the station house. . . . The dissenters warned that the requirement of Miranda warnings would have the effect of decreasing the number of suspects who respond to police questioning. . . . The Miranda majority, however, apparently felt that whatever the cost to society in terms of fewer convictions of guilty suspects, that cost would simply have to be borne in the interest of enlarged protection for the Fifth Amendment privilege.

The police in this case, in the very act of apprehending a suspect, were confronted with the immediate necessity of ascertaining the whereabouts of a gun which they had every reason to believe the suspect had just removed from his empty holster and discarded in the supermarket. So long as the gun was concealed somewhere in the supermarket, with its actual whereabouts unknown, it obviously posed more than one danger to the public safety: an accomplice might make use of it, a customer or employee might later come upon it.

In such a situation, if the police are required to recite the familiar Miranda warnings before asking the whereabouts of the gun, suspects in Quarles' position might well be deterred from responding. Procedural safeguards which deter a suspect from responding were deemed acceptable in *Miranda* in order to protect the Fifth Amendment privilege; when the primary social cost of those added protections is the possibility of fewer convictions, the Miranda majority was willing to bear that cost. Here, had Miranda warnings deterred Quarles from responding to Officer Kraft's question about the whereabouts of the gun, the cost would have been something more than merely the failure to obtain evidence useful in convicting Quarles. Officer Kraft needed an answer to his question not simply to make his case against Quarles but to insure that further danger to the public did not result from the concealment of the gun in a public area.

We conclude that the need for answers to questions in a situation posing a threat to the public safety outweighs the need for the prophylactic rule protecting the Fifth Amendment's privilege against self-incrimination. We decline to place officers such as Officer Kraft in the untenable position of having to consider, often in a matter of seconds, whether it best serves society for them to ask the necessary questions without the Miranda warnings and render whatever probative evidence they uncover inadmissible, or for them to give the warnings in order to preserve the admissibility of evidence they might uncover but possibly damage or destroy their ability to obtain that evidence and neutralize the volatile situation confronting them.

In recognizing a narrow exception to the *Miranda* rule in this case, we acknowledge that to some degree we lessen the desirable clarity of that rule. At least in part in order to preserve its clarity, we have over the years refused to sanction attempts to expand our *Miranda* holding. . . . As we have in other contexts, we recognize here the importance of a workable rule "to guide police officers, who have only limited time and expertise to reflect on and balance the social and individual interests involved in the specific circumstances they confront." . . . But as we have pointed out, we believe that the exception which we recognize today lessens the necessity of that on-the-scene balancing process. The exception will not be difficult for police officers to apply because in each case it will be circumscribed by the exigency which justifies it. We think police officers can and will distinguish almost instinctively between questions necessary to secure their own safety or the safety of the public and questions designed solely to elicit testimonial evidence from a suspect.

The facts of this case clearly demonstrate that distinction and an officer's ability to recognize it. Officer Kraft asked only the question necessary to locate the missing gun before advising respondent of his rights. It was only after securing the loaded revolver and giving the warnings that he continued with investigatory questions about the ownership and place of purchase of the gun. The exception which we recognize today, far from complicating the thought processes and the on-the-scene judgments of police officers, will simply free them to follow their

legitimate instincts when confronting situations presenting a danger to the public safety. . . .

Justice O'Connor, concurring in the judgment in part and dissenting in part.

In *Miranda v. Arizona,* . . . the Court held unconstitutional, because inherently compelled, the admission of statements derived from in-custody questioning not preceded by an explanation of the privilege against self-incrimination and the consequences of forgoing it. Today, the Court concludes that overriding considerations of public safety justify the admission of evidence—oral statements and a gun—secured without the benefit of such warnings. . . . In so holding, the Court acknowledges that it is departing from prior precedent, . . . and that it is "lessen[ing] the desirable clarity of [the *Miranda*] rule," . . . Were the Court writing from a clean slate, I could agree with its holding. But *Miranda* is now the law and, in my view, the Court has not provided sufficient justification for departing from it or for blurring its now clear strictures. Accordingly, I would require suppression of the initial statement taken from respondent in this case. On the other hand, nothing in *Miranda* or the privilege itself requires exclusion of nontestimonial evidence derived from informal custodial interrogation, and I therefore agree with the Court that admission of the gun in evidence is proper. . . .

Justice Marshall, with whom Justice Brennan and Justice Stevens join, dissenting. . . .

The majority's treatment of the legal issues presented in this case is no less troubling than its abuse of the facts. Before today's opinion, the Court had twice concluded that, under *Miranda v. Arizona,* . . . police officers conducting custodial interrogations must advise suspects of their rights before any questions concerning the whereabouts of incriminating weapons can be asked. . . . Now the majority departs from these cases and rules that police may withhold Miranda warnings whenever custodial interrogations concern matters of public safety. . . .

Before today's opinion, the procedures established in *Miranda v. Arizona* had "the virtue of informing police and prosecutors with specificity as to what they may do in conducting custodial interrogation, and of informing courts under what circumstances statements obtained during such interrogation are not admissible." . . . In a chimerical quest for public safety, the majority has abandoned the rule that brought 18 years of doctrinal tranquility to the field of custodial interrogations.

As the majority candidly concedes, a public-safety exception destroys forever the clarity of *Miranda* for both law enforcement officers and members of the judiciary. The Court's candor cannot mask what a serious loss the administration of justice has incurred.

This case is illustrative of the chaos the "public-safety" exception will unleash. The circumstances of Quarles' arrest have never been in dispute. After the benefit of briefing and oral argument, the New York Court of Appeals, as previously noted, concluded that there was "no evidence in the record before us that there were exigent circumstances posing a risk to the public safety." . . . Upon reviewing the same facts and hearing the same arguments, a majority of this Court has come to precisely the opposite conclusion: "So long as the gun was concealed somewhere in the supermarket, with its actual whereabouts unknown, it obviously posed more than one danger to the public safety. . . ."

If after plenary review two appellate courts so fundamentally differ over the threat to public safety presented by the simple and uncontested facts of this case, one must seriously question how law enforcement officers will respond to the majority's new rule in the confusion and haste of the real world. As The Chief Justice wrote in a similar context: "Few, if any, police officers are competent to make the kind of evaluation seemingly contemplated. . . ." . . . Not only will police officers have to decide whether the objective facts of an arrest justify an unconsented custodial interrogation, they will also have to remember to interrupt the interrogation and read the suspect his Miranda warnings once the focus of the inquiry shifts from protecting the public's safety to ascertaining the suspect's guilt. Disagreements of the scope of the "public-safety" exception and mistakes in its application are inevitable.

The end result, as Justice O'Connor predicts, will be "a finespun new doctrine on public safety exigencies incident to custodial interrogation, complete with the hair-splitting distinctions that currently plague our Fourth Amendment jurisprudence." . . . In the meantime, the courts will have to dedicate themselves to spinning this new web of doctrines, and the country's law enforcement agencies will have to suffer patiently through the frustrations of another period of constitutional uncertainty. . . .

Whether society would be better off if the police warned suspects of their rights before beginning an interrogation or whether the advantages of giving such warnings would outweigh their costs did not in-

form the *Miranda* decision. On the contrary, the Miranda Court was concerned with the proscriptions of the Fifth Amendment, and, in particular, whether the Self-Incrimination Clause permits the government to prosecute individuals based on statements made in the course of custodial interrogations. . . .

In fashioning its "public-safety" exception to *Miranda,* the majority makes no attempt to deal with the constitutional presumption established by that case. The majority does not argue that police questioning about issues of public safety is any less coercive than custodial interrogations into other matters. The majority's only contention is that police officers could more easily protect the public if *Miranda* did not apply to custodial interrogations concerning the public's safety. But *Miranda* was not a decision about public safety; it was a decision about coerced confessions. Without establishing that interrogations concerning the public's safety are less likely to be coercive than other interrogations, the majority cannot endorse the "public-safety" exception and remain faithful to the logic of *Miranda v. Arizona.*

Further Resources

BOOKS

Davis, Sue Justice. *Rehnquist and the Constitution.* Princeton, N.J.: Princeton University Press, 1989.

Irons, Peter H. *Brennan vs. Rehnquist: The Battle for the Constitution.* New York: Knopf, 1994.

Leo, Richard A., and George C. Thomas. *The Miranda Debate: Law, Justice, and Policing.* Boston: Northeastern University Press, 1998.

Tushnet, Mark V. *Making Constitutional Law: Thurgood Marshall and the Supreme Court, 1961–1991.* New York: Oxford University Press, 1997.

Van Sickel, Robert W. *Not a Particularly Different Voice: The Jurisprudence of Sandra Day O'Connor.* New York: P. Lang, 1998.

White, Welsh S. *Miranda's Waning Protections: Police Interrogation Practices after Dickerson.* Ann Arbor, Mich.: University of Michigan Press, 2001.

WEBSITES

"Beyond Miranda." Available online at http://www.landmark-cases.org/miranda/beyond.html (accessed February 13, 2003).

AUDIO AND VISUAL MEDIA

Butler, Rex L. *Knowing and Protecting Your Rights: Miranda Was Never Enough.* Rex Attorneys. Videocassette. 2001.

Roberts v. U.S. Jaycees

Supreme Court decision

By: William J. Brennan and Sandra Day O'Connor

Date: July 3, 1984

Source: Brennan, William J. and Sandra Day O'Connor. *Roberts v. United States Jaycees,* 468 U.S. 609. Available on-line at http://laws.findlaw.com/us/468/609.html; website home page: http://laws.findlaw.com (accessed April 19, 2003).

About the Authors: William Brennan (1906–1997) attended law school at Harvard. In 1952, he was appointed to New Jersey's highest court. He joined the U.S. Supreme Court in 1957 and served until 1990.

Sandra Day O'Connor (1930–) attended Stanford Law School, graduating third in her class. Because of gender bias, though, no firm would hire her, so she worked as a deputy county attorney. In 1981, she was the first woman appointed to the U.S. Supreme Court. ∎

Introduction

Two issues that often pull in contradictory directions are gender discrimination and freedom of association. Only in the twentieth century was gender discrimination attacked. In 1868, Congress passed the Fourteenth Amendment, which reaffirmed the right to equal protection under the law, but the amendment did not extend to gender discrimination. Women lost their fight to extend the Fifteenth Amendment, which gave African Americans the right to vote, to women. Finally, in 1920, women obtained the right to vote. In 1964, Congress banned sexual discrimination in employment in the Civil Rights Act.

Freedom of association is not specifically mentioned in the First Amendment, but such a freedom is implied in freedom of speech or freedom to "assemble and petition the Government for a redress of grievances," both specifically mentioned in the First Amendment. In 1958, the U.S. Supreme Court held that freedom of association was guaranteed by the Fourteenth Amendment. In 1981, the Court held that the Democratic Party of Wisconsin could not be forced to seat a certain delegation, reaffirming the right of freedom of association.

Many groups, however, have excluded certain people from their membership. Country clubs, for example, excluded minorities and women, and some civic groups did not admit women as well. One such group was the Jaycees, formed in the 1920s to train young men for leadership, both in the community and in business. The group limited regular membership to men ages eighteen to thirty-five; women and men over thirty-five were admitted only as associate members who could not vote or hold office.

After Minnesota passed a law forbidding discrimination in public accommodation, several Minnesota Jaycee chapters began to admit women as full members,

Justice William J. Brennan delivered the majority opinion of the Court for *Roberts v. United States Jaycees.* **THE SUPREME COURT OF THE UNITED STATES. REPRODUCED**

and the national organization moved to revoke their charters. The Minnesota Department of Human Rights ordered the Jaycees to stop discriminating. That case, *Roberts v. U.S. Jaycees,* made its way to the Supreme Court in 1984.

Significance

A lower court had ruled that the Jaycees did not have to admit women because they were protected by freedom of association. The Supreme Court unanimously reversed the lower court's ruling. The Court held that freedom of association applied only to activities that dealt with the raising and creating of a family, such as marriage and childbirth. While the Court noted that people had the right to gather together for expressive purposes, it held that this right was not absolute. Further, the court held that the order to admit women as full members did not infringe on free speech to any great extent, and the Court balanced the right of free speech with the state's "legitimate interests." The Jaycees were ordered to admit women.

Since *Roberts,* the Supreme Court has generally upheld state requirements that force organizations to admit people regardless of sex or creed. Rotary Clubs in California and private organizations in New York have both been forced to admit people of any sex or race, and these orders have been upheld in the Supreme Court.

Primary Source

Roberts v. U.S. Jaycees [excerpt]

> **SYNOPSIS:** Justice Brennan, who wrote the majority opinion, agrees that freedom of association exists but holds that it is fundamental only in certain areas. He then details why the Jaycees are not fully protected by freedom of association, which means that Minnesota can order them to admit women. In a concurrence, Justice O'Connor holds that the Jaycees can be ordered to admit women, but the group's commercial nature rather than its message determines how much they are protected by the First Amendment.

Justice Brennan delivered the opinion of the Court. . . .

The Court has long recognized that, because the Bill of Rights is designed to secure individual liberty, it must afford the formation and preservation of certain kinds of highly personal relationships a substantial measure of sanctuary from unjustified interference by the State . . . Without precisely identifying every consideration that may underlie this type of constitutional protection, we have noted that certain kinds of personal bonds have played a critical role in the culture and traditions of the Nation by cultivating and transmitting shared ideals and beliefs; they thereby foster diversity and act as critical buffers between the individual and the power of the State. . . . Moreover, the constitutional shelter afforded such relationships reflects the realization that individuals draw much of their emotional enrichment from close ties with others. Protecting these relationships from unwarranted state interference therefore safeguards the ability independently to define one's identity that is central to any concept of liberty. . . .

The personal affiliations that exemplify these considerations, and that therefore suggest some relevant limitations on the relationships that might be entitled to this sort of constitutional protection, are those that attend the creation and sustenance of a family—marriage . . . ; childbirth . . . ; the raising and education of children, . . . and cohabitation with one's relatives. . . . Family relationships, by their nature, involve deep attachments and commitments to the necessarily few other individuals with whom one shares not only a special community of thoughts, experiences, and beliefs but also distinctively personal aspects of one's life. . . . Conversely, an association lacking these qualities—such as a large business enterprise—seems remote from the concerns giving rise to this constitutional protection. Accordingly, the Constitution undoubtedly imposes constraints on the State's power to control the selection of one's spouse that would not apply to regulations affecting the choice of one's fellow employees. . . .

Between these poles, of course, lies a broad range of human relationships that may make greater or lesser claims to constitutional protection from particular incursions by the State. Determining the limits of state authority over an individual's freedom to enter into a particular association therefore unavoidably entails a careful assessment of where that relationship's objective characteristics locate it on a spectrum from the most intimate to the most attenuated of personal attachments. . . . We need not mark the potentially significant points on this terrain with any precision. We note only that factors that may be relevant include size, purpose, policies, selectivity, congeniality, and other characteristics that in a particular case may be pertinent. In this case, however, several features of the Jaycees clearly place the organization outside of the category of relationships worthy of this kind of constitutional protection.

The undisputed facts reveal that the local chapters of the Jaycees are large and basically unselective groups. . . . Apart from age and sex, neither the national organization nor the local chapters employ any criteria for judging applicants for membership, and new members are routinely recruited and admitted with no inquiry into their backgrounds. . . .

In short, the local chapters of the Jaycees are neither small nor selective. . . .

An individual's freedom to speak, to worship, and to petition the government for the redress of grievances could not be vigorously protected from interference by the State unless a correlative freedom to engage in group effort toward those ends were not also guaranteed. . . . According protection to collective effort on behalf of shared goals is especially important in preserving political and cultural diversity and in shielding dissident expression from suppression by the majority. . . . Consequently, we have long understood as implicit in the right to engage in activities protected by the First Amendment a corresponding right to associate with others in pursuit of a wide variety of political, social, economic, educational, religious, and cultural ends. . . .

Kathy Ebert, former vice-president of the Minneapolis chapter of the Jaycees, was one of the three women who filed the original brief with the Minnesota Department of Human Rights. **AP/WIDE WORLD PHOTOS. REPRODUCED BY PERMISSION.**

The right to associate for expressive purposes is not, however, absolute. Infringements on that right may be justified by regulations adopted to serve compelling state interests, unrelated to the suppression of ideas, that cannot be achieved through means significantly less restrictive of associational freedoms. . . . We are persuaded that Minnesota's compelling interest in eradicating discrimination against its female citizens justifies the impact that application of the statute to the Jaycees may have on the male members' associational freedoms.

On its face, the Minnesota Act does not aim at the suppression of speech, does not distinguish between prohibited and permitted activity on the basis of viewpoint, and does not license enforcement authorities to administer the statute on the basis of such constitutionally impressible criteria. . . .

In applying the Act to the Jaycees, the State has advanced those interests through the least restrictive means of achieving its ends. Indeed, the Jaycees has failed to demonstrate that the Act imposes any serious burdens on the male members'

freedom of expressive association. . . . To be sure, as the Court of Appeals noted, a "not insubstantial part" of the Jaycees' activities constitutes protected expression on political, economic, cultural, and social affairs. . . . There is, however, no basis in the record for concluding that admission of women as full voting members will impede the organization's ability to engage in these protected activities or to disseminate its preferred views. The Act requires no change in the Jaycees' creed of promoting the interests of young men, and it imposes no restrictions on the organization's ability to exclude individuals with ideologies or philosophies different from those of its existing members. . . .

In any event, even if enforcement of the Act causes some incidental abridgment of the Jaycees' protected speech, that effect is no greater than is necessary to accomplish the State's legitimate purposes. As we have explained, acts of invidious discrimination in the distribution of publicly available goods, services, and other advantages cause unique evils that government has a compelling interest to prevent—wholly apart from the point of view such conduct may transmit. Accordingly, like violence or other types of potentially expressive activities that produce special harms distinct from their communicative impact, such practices are entitled to no constitutional protection. . . . In prohibiting such practices, the Minnesota Act therefore "responds precisely to the substantive problem which legitimately concerns" the State and abridges no more speech or associational freedom than is necessary to accomplish that purpose. . . .

We turn finally to appellee's contentions that the Minnesota Act, as interpreted by the State's highest court, is unconstitutionally vague and overbroad.. . . .

We have little trouble concluding that these concerns are not seriously implicated by the Minnesota Act, either on its face or as construed in this case. . . . The state court's articulated willingness to adopt limiting constructions that would exclude private groups from the statute's reach, together with the commonly used and sufficiently precise standards it employed to determine that the Jaycees is not such a group, establish that the Act, as currently construed, does not create an unacceptable risk of application to a substantial amount of protected conduct. . . .

Justice O'Connor, concurring in part and concurring in the judgment. . . .

I agree with the Court that application of the Minnesota law to the Jaycees does not contravene the First Amendment, but I reach that conclusion for reasons distinct from those offered by the Court. I believe the Court has adopted a test that unadvisedly casts doubt on the power of States to pursue the profoundly important goal of ensuring nondiscriminatory access to commercial opportunities in our society. At the same time, the Court has adopted an approach to the general problem presented by this case that accords insufficient protection to expressive associations and places inappropriate burdens on groups claiming the protection of the First Amendment. . . .

Whether an association is or is not constitutionally protected in the selection of its membership should not depend on what the association says or why its members say it. The Court's readiness to inquire into the connection between membership and message reveals a more fundamental flaw in its analysis. . . . The Court entirely neglects to establish at the threshold that the Jaycees is an associ-

ation whose activities or purposes should engage the strong protections that the First Amendment extends to expressive associations.

On the one hand, an association engaged exclusively in protected expression enjoys First Amendment protection of both the content of its message and the choice of its members. . . . A ban on specific group voices on public affairs violates the most basic guarantee of the First Amendment—that citizens, not the government, control the content of public discussion.

On the other hand, there is only minimal constitutional protection of the freedom of commercial association. . . .

Many associations cannot readily be described as purely expressive or purely commercial. . . . Clearly the standard must accept the reality that even the most expressive of associations is likely to touch, in some way or other, matters of commerce. The standard must nevertheless give substance to the ideal of complete protection for purely expressive association, even while it readily permits state regulation of commercial affairs.

In my view, an association should be characterized as commercial, and therefore subject to rationally related state regulation of its membership and other associational activities, when, and only when, the association's activities are not predominantly of the type protected by the First Amendment. . . . The purposes of an association, and the purposes of its members in adhering to it, are doubtless relevant in determining whether the association is primarily engaged in protected expression. . . . Even the training of outdoor survival skills or participation in community service might become expressive when the activity is intended to develop good morals, reverence, patriotism, and a desire for self-improvement.

The considerations that may enter into the determination of when a particular association of persons is predominantly engaged in expression are therefore fluid and somewhat uncertain. But the Court has recognized the need to draw similar lines in the past. . . .

In summary, this Court's case law recognizes radically different constitutional protections for expressive and nonexpressive associations. The First Amendment is offended by direct state control of the membership of a private organization engaged exclusively in protected expressive activity, but no First

Amendment interest stands in the way of a State's rational regulation of economic transactions by or within a commercial association. The proper approach to analysis of First Amendment claims of associational freedom is, therefore, to distinguish nonexpressive from expressive associations and to recognize that the former lack the full constitutional protections possessed by the latter.

Minnesota's attempt to regulate the membership of the Jaycees chapters operating in that State presents a relatively easy case for application of the expressive-commercial dichotomy. Both the Minnesota Supreme Court and the United States District Court, which expressly adopted the state court's findings, made findings of fact concerning the commercial nature of the Jaycees' activities. The Court of Appeals, which disagreed with the District Court. . . .

There is no reason to question the accuracy of this characterization.

Notwithstanding its protected expressive activities, the Jaycees—otherwise known as the Junior Chamber of Commerce—is, first and foremost, an organization that, at both the national and local levels, promotes and practices the art of solicitation and management. The organization claims that the training it offers its members gives them an advantage in business, and business firms do indeed sometimes pay the dues of individual memberships for their employees. Jaycees members hone their solicitation and management skills, under the direction and supervision of the organization, primarily through their active recruitment of new members." . . .

Recruitment and selling are commercial activities, even when conducted for training rather than for profit. The "not insubstantial" volume of protected Jaycees activity found by the Court of Appeals is simply not enough to preclude state regulation of the Jaycees' commercial activities. The State of Minnesota has a legitimate interest in ensuring nondiscriminatory access to the commercial opportunity presented by membership in the Jaycees. The members of the Jaycees may not claim constitutional immunity from Minnesota's antidiscrimination law by seeking to exercise their First Amendment rights through this commercial organization.

For these reasons, I agree with the Court that the Jaycees' First Amendment challenge to the application of Minnesota's public accommodations law is meritless.

Further Resources

BOOKS

Cushman, Clare, and Talbot D'Alemberte. *Supreme Court Decisions and Women's Rights: Milestones to Equality.* Washington, D.C.: CQ Press, 2001.

Eastland, Terry. *Freedom of Expression in the Supreme Court: The Defining Cases.* Lanham, Md.: Rowman and Littlefield, 2000.

Gold, Susan Dudley. *Roberts v. U.S. Jaycees (1984): Women's Rights.* New York: Twenty-First Century Books, 1995.

Hoff, Joan. *Law, Gender, and Injustice: A Legal History of U.S. Women.* New York: New York University Press, 1991.

Rosenkranz, E. Joshua, and Bernard Schwartz. *Reason and Passion: Justice Brennan's Enduring Influence.* New York: Norton, 1997.

Van Sickel, Robert W. *Not a Particularly Different Voice: The Jurisprudence of Sandra Day O'Connor.* New York: P. Lang, 1998.

WEBSITES

The Freedom Not to Associate. Available online at http://www.law.umkc.edu/faculty/projects/ftrials/conlaw/association.htm; website home page: http://www.law.umkc.edu (accessed February 13, 2003).

U.S. v. Leon

Supreme Court decision

By: Byron White and William J. Brennan

Date: July 5, 1984

Source: White, Byron and William J. Brennan. *United States v. Leon,* 468 U.S. 897. Available online at http://laws.findlaw.com/us/468/897.html; website home page: http://laws.findlaw.com (accessed April 19, 2003).

About the Authors: Byron White (1917–2002) was a Rhodes scholar and talented athlete in college. In 1938, he led the National Football League in rushing. He served as deputy attorney general in the Kennedy administration. From 1962 to 1993, he served on the U.S. Supreme Court.

William Brennan (1906–1997) attended law school at Harvard. In 1952, he was appointed to New Jersey's highest court. He joined the U.S. Supreme Court in 1957 and served until 1990. ■

Introduction

A sizable number of American colonists made their living by smuggling goods into the United States. To bring an end to this practice, the British issued general warrants allowing any area to be searched and any illegal items to be seized, a practice that outraged many colonists. Accordingly, the Bill of Rights includes the Fourth Amendment, which states that "the right of the people to be secure . . . against unreasonable searches and seizures, shall not be violated, and no Warrants shall issue, but upon probable cause . . . and particularly describing the place to be searched, and the persons or things to be seized." This amendment, though, provides no penalty for violations, and throughout the nineteenth century, courts generally allowed the use of evidence seized illegally.

In 1914, the Supreme Court created the "exclusionary rule": evidence seized without a warrant cannot be used in trial in a federal court. It was unclear, though, whether this rule applied to the states. In 1949 and 1954, the Supreme Court refused to apply the Fourth Amendment to the states. The question arose again in 1961, when the Supreme Court extended the exclusionary rule to the states in *Mapp v. Ohio*. This ruling was heavily criticized by those who felt that the exclusionary rule allowed criminals to go free because of a "technicality." Some justices on the Supreme Court began to argue for a "good faith" exception, allowing evidence seized with an invalid warrant as long as the officers with that warrant were acting in "good faith," believing the warrant to be valid. This issue arose in *U.S. v. Leon*.

Significance

At issue in *Leon* was the legality of a drug search. On the basis of a search warrant that appeared to be valid, police officers conducted a search and found incriminating evidence. Later, though, it was determined that the warrant was not valid, and the accused moved to suppress all evidence seized based on the warrant. When the lower court and court of appeals agreed, the government appealed to the Supreme Court. The Supreme Court overturned the lower courts and upheld the legality of the search, even though it had been undertaken with an invalid warrant. Thus, by a 6 to 3 vote, the Court created a "good faith" exception to the exclusionary rule. The majority opinion of Justice White "balanced" the costs to the defendant versus the "benefits" to society, and ruled that that benefits to society outweigh the costs to the defendant. The three dissenters, however, pointed out that privacy and liberty guaranteed by the Fourth Amendment were being sacrificed for the goal of crime prevention.

Since *Leon,* the Supreme Court has generally narrowed the Fourth Amendment. Without a warrant, in some circumstances, it has allowed mandatory drug testing of employees and students. This drug testing is not a "seizure" in the Fourth Amendment sense of the word. The Court has also given police increased latitude in their searches and has generally restricted the rights of those already convicted.

Primary Source

U.S. v. Leon [excerpt]

> **SYNOPSIS:** Justice White comments that the exclusionary rule is not required by the Fourth Amend-

ment and has "cost" society a great deal. White then argues for a "good faith" exception, stating that in this case, the exclusionary rule has no deterrent effect. Justice Brennan, in his dissent, argues that the "good faith" exception destroys the Fourth Amendment and that "weighing" the costs to the defendant of his loss of rights against the "benefits" to society destroys important freedoms.

Justice White delivered the opinion of the Court. . . .

The Fourth Amendment contains no provision expressly precluding the use of evidence obtained in violation of its commands, and an examination of its origin and purposes makes clear that the use of fruits of a past unlawful search or seizure "work[s] no new Fourth Amendment wrong." . . . The wrong condemned by the Amendment is "fully accomplished" by the unlawful search or seizure itself, ibid., and the exclusionary rule is neither intended nor able to "cure the invasion of the defendant's rights which he has already suffered." . . .

The substantial social costs exacted by the exclusionary rule for the vindication of Fourth Amendment rights have long been a source of concern. . . . An objectionable collateral consequence of this interference with the criminal justice system's truth-finding function is that some guilty defendants may go free or receive reduced sentences as a result of favorable plea bargains. Particularly when law enforcement officers have acted in objective good faith or their transgressions have been minor, the magnitude of the benefit conferred on such guilty defendants offends basic concepts of the criminal justice system. . . .

As yet, we have not recognized any form of good-faith exception to the Fourth Amendment exclusionary rule. But the balancing approach that has evolved during the years of experience with the rule provides strong support for the modification currently urged upon us. As we discuss below, our evaluation of the costs and benefits of suppressing reliable physical evidence seized by officers reasonably relying on a warrant issued by a detached and neutral magistrate leads to the conclusion that such evidence should be admissible in the prosecution's case in chief.

Because a search warrant "provides the detached scrutiny of a neutral magistrate, which is a more reliable safeguard against improper searches than the hurried judgment of a law enforcement officer 'engaged in the often competitive enterprise of ferreting out crime,'" . . . we have expressed a strong preference for warrants and declared that "in a doubtful or marginal case a search under a warrant may be sustainable where without one it would fall." . . . Reasonable minds frequently may differ on the question whether a particular affidavit establishes probable cause, and we have thus concluded that the preference for warrants is most appropriately effectuated by according "great deference" to a magistrate's determination. . . .

Deference to the magistrate, however, is not boundless. It is clear, first, that the deference accorded to a magistrate's finding of probable cause does not preclude inquiry into the knowing or reckless falsity of the affidavit on which that determination was based. . . . Second, the courts must also insist that the magistrate purport to "perform his 'neutral and detached' function and not serve merely as a rubber stamp for the police." . . . A magistrate failing to "manifest that neutrality and detachment demanded of a judicial officer when presented with a warrant application" and who acts instead as "an adjunct law enforcement officer" cannot provide valid authorization for an otherwise unconstitutional search. . . .

Third, reviewing courts will not defer to a warrant based on an affidavit that does not "provide the magistrate with a substantial basis for determining the existence of probable cause." . . .

Only in the first of these three situations, however, has the Court set forth a rationale for suppressing evidence obtained pursuant to a search warrant; in the other areas, it has simply excluded such evidence without considering whether Fourth Amendment interests will be advanced. To the extent that proponents of exclusion rely on its behavioral effects on judges and magistrates in these areas, their reliance is misplaced. First, the exclusionary rule is designed to deter police misconduct rather than to punish the errors of judges and magistrates. Second, there exists no evidence suggesting that judges and magistrates are inclined to ignore or subvert the Fourth Amendment or that lawlessness among these actors requires application of the extreme sanction of exclusion.

Third, and most important, we discern no basis, and are offered none, for believing that exclusion of evidence seized pursuant to a warrant will have a significant deterrent effect on the issuing judge or magistrate. Many of the factors that indicate that the exclusionary rule cannot provide an effective "special" or "general" deterrent for individual offending law enforcement officers apply as well to judges or magistrates. And, to the extent that the rule is thought to operate as a "systemic" deterrent

on a wider audience, it clearly can have no such effect on individuals empowered to issue search warrants. Judges and magistrates are not adjuncts to the law enforcement team; as neutral judicial officers, they have no stake in the outcome of particular criminal prosecutions. The threat of exclusion thus cannot be expected significantly to deter them. Imposition of the exclusionary sanction is not necessary meaningfully to inform judicial officers of their errors, and we cannot conclude that admitting evidence obtained pursuant to a warrant while at the same time declaring that the warrant was somehow defective will in any way reduce judicial officers' professional incentives to comply with the Fourth Amendment, encourage them to repeat their mistakes, or lead to the granting of all colorable warrant requests. . . .

We have frequently questioned whether the exclusionary rule can have any deterrent effect when the offending officers acted in the objectively reasonable belief that their conduct did not violate the Fourth Amendment. . . .

This is particularly true, we believe, when an officer acting with objective good faith has obtained a search warrant from a judge or magistrate and acted within its scope. In most such cases, there is no police illegality and thus nothing to deter. It is the magistrate's responsibility to determine whether the officer's allegations establish probable cause and, if so, to issue a warrant comporting in form with the requirements of the Fourth Amendment. . . . Penalizing the officer for the magistrate's error, rather than his own, cannot logically contribute to the deterrence of Fourth Amendment violations.

We conclude that the marginal or nonexistent benefits produced by suppressing evidence obtained in objectively reasonable reliance on a subsequently invalidated search warrant cannot justify the substantial costs of exclusion. . . .

Suppression therefore remains an appropriate remedy if the magistrate or judge in issuing a warrant was misled by information in an affidavit that the affiant knew was false or would have known was false except for his reckless disregard of the truth. . . .

In so limiting the suppression remedy, we leave untouched the probable-cause standard and the various requirements for a valid warrant. . . .

In the absence of an allegation that the magistrate abandoned his detached and neutral role, suppression is appropriate only if the officers were dishonest or reckless in preparing their affidavit or could not have harbored an objectively reasonable belief in the existence of probable cause. Only respondent Leon has contended that no reasonably well trained police officer could have believed that there existed probable cause to search his house; significantly, the other respondents advance no comparable argument. Officer Rombach's application for a warrant clearly was supported by much more than a "bare bones" affidavit. The affidavit related the results of an extensive investigation and, as the opinions of the divided panel of the Court of Appeals make clear, provided evidence sufficient to create disagreement among thoughtful and competent judges as to the existence of probable cause. Under these circumstances, the officers' reliance on the magistrate's determination of probable cause was objectively reasonable, and application of the extreme sanction of exclusion is inappropriate. . . .

Justice Brennan, with whom Justice Marshall joins, dissenting.

. . . in case after case, I have witnessed the Court's gradual but determined strangulation of the rule. It now appears that the Court's victory over the Fourth Amendment is complete. That today's decisions represent the piece de resistance of the Court's past efforts cannot be doubted, for today the Court sanctions the use in the prosecution's case in chief of illegally obtained evidence against the individual whose rights have been violated—a result that had previously been thought to be foreclosed.

The Court seeks to justify this result on the ground that the "costs" of adhering to the exclusionary rule in cases like those before us exceed the "benefits." But the language of deterrence and of cost/benefit analysis, if used indiscriminately, can have a narcotic effect. It creates an illusion of technical precision and ineluctability. It suggests that not only constitutional principle but also empirical data support the majority's result. When the Court's analysis is examined carefully, however, it is clear that we have not been treated to an honest assessment of the merits of the exclusionary rule, but have instead been drawn into a curious world where the "costs" of excluding illegally obtained evidence loom to exaggerated heights and where the "benefits" of such exclusion are made to disappear with a mere wave of the hand.

The majority ignores the fundamental constitutional importance of what is at stake here. . . . what the Framers understood . . . remains true today—that the task of combating crime and convicting the guilty will in every era seem of such critical and pressing concern that we may be lured by the temptations of expediency into forsaking our commitment to protecting individual liberty and privacy. . . .

At bottom, the Court's decision turns on the proposition that the exclusionary rule is merely a "'judicially created remedy designed to safeguard Fourth Amendment rights generally through its deterrent effect, rather than a personal constitutional right.'" . . . The germ of that idea is found in *Wolf v. Colorado* . . . and although I had thought that such a narrow conception of the rule had been forever put to rest by our decision in *Mapp v. Ohio* . . . it has been revived by the present Court and reaches full flower with today's decision. . . . This reading of the Amendment implies that its proscriptions are directed solely at those government agents who may actually invade an individual's constitutionally protected privacy. The courts are not subject to any direct constitutional duty to exclude illegally obtained evidence, because the question of the admissibility of such evidence is not addressed by the Amendment. This view of the scope of the Amendment relegates the judiciary to the periphery. Because the only constitutionally cognizable injury has already been "fully accomplished" by the police by the time a case comes before the courts, the Constitution is not itself violated if the judge decides to admit the tainted evidence. Indeed, the most the judge can do is wring his hands and hope that perhaps by excluding such evidence he can deter future transgressions by the police. Such a reading appears plausible, because, as critics of the exclusionary rule never tire of repeating, the Fourth Amendment makes no express provision for the exclusion of evidence secured in violation of its commands. A short answer to this claim, of course, is that many of the Constitution's most vital imperatives are stated in general terms and the task of giving meaning of these precepts is therefore left to subsequent judicial decisionmaking in the context of concrete cases. The nature of our Constitution, as Chief Justice Marshall long ago explained, "requires that only its great outlines should be marked, its important objects designated, and the minor ingredients which compose those objects be deduced from the nature of the objects themselves." . . .

A more direct answer may be supplied by recognizing that the Amendment, like other provisions of the Bill of Rights, restrains the power of the government as a whole; it does not specify only a particular agency and exempt all others. The judiciary is responsible, no less than the executive, for ensuring that constitutional rights are respected. . . .

The Amendment . . . must be read to condemn not only the initial unconstitutional invasion of privacy—which is done, after all, for the purpose of securing evidence—but also the subsequent use of any evidence so obtained.

The Court evades this principle by drawing an artificial line between the constitutional rights and responsibilities that are engaged by actions of the police and those that are engaged when a defendant appears before the courts. According to the Court, the substantive protections of the Fourth Amendment are wholly exhausted at the moment when police unlawfully invade an individual's privacy and thus no substantive force remains to those protections at the time of trial when the government seeks to use evidence obtained by the police.

I submit that such a crabbed reading of the Fourth Amendment casts aside the teaching of those Justices who first formulated the exclusionary rule, and rests ultimately on an impoverished understanding of judicial responsibility in our constitutional scheme. For my part, "[t]he right of the people to be secure in their persons, houses, papers, and effects, against unreasonable searches and seizures" comprises a personal right to exclude all evidence secured by means of unreasonable searches and seizures. The right to be free from the initial invasion of privacy and the right of exclusion are coordinate components of the central embracing right to be free from unreasonable searches and seizures. . . .

Moreover, the good-faith exception will encourage police to provide only the bare minimum of information in future warrant applications. The police will now know that if they can secure a warrant, so long as the circumstances of its issuance are not "entirely unreasonable," . . . all police conduct pursuant to that warrant will be protected from further judicial review. The clear incentive that operated in the past to establish probable cause adequately because reviewing courts would examine the magistrate's judgment carefully . . . has now been so completely vitiated that the police need only show that it was not "entirely unreasonable" under the circumstances of a particular case for them to believe that the warrant they were issued was valid. . . . The long-run effect unquestionably will be to undermine the integrity of the warrant process. . . .

When the public, as it quite properly has done in the past as well as in the present, demands that those in government increase their efforts to combat crime, it is all too easy for those government officials to seek expedient solutions. In contrast to such costly and difficult measures as building more prisons, improving law enforcement methods, or hiring more prosecutors and judges to relieve the overburdened court systems in the country's metropolitan areas, the relaxation of Fourth Amendment standards seems a tempting, costless means of meeting the public's demand for better law enforcement. In the long run, however, we as a society pay a heavy price for such expediency, because as Justice Jackson observed, the rights guaranteed in the Fourth Amendment "are not mere second-class rights but belong in the catalog of indispensable freedoms." . . . Once lost, such rights are difficult to recover. There is hope, however, that in time this or some later Court will restore these precious freedoms to their rightful place as a primary protection for our citizens against overreaching officialdom.

I dissent.

Further Resources

BOOKS

Alderman, Ellen, and Caroline Kennedy. *In Our Defense: The Bill of Rights in Action.* New York: Morrow, 1991.

Greenhalgh, William W. *The Fourth Amendment Handbook: A Chronological Survey of Supreme Court Decisions.* Chicago: Criminal Justice Section, American Bar Association, 1995.

Hutchinson, Dennis J. *The Man Who Once Was Whizzer White: A Portrait of Justice Byron R. White.* New York: Free Press, 1998.

Levy, Leonard Williams. *Origins of the Bill of Rights.* New Haven, Conn.: Yale University Press, 1999.

MacCoun, Robert J., and Peter Reuter. *Drug War Heresies: Learning from Other Vices, Times, and Places.* Cambridge, England: Cambridge University Press, 2001.

Rosenkranz, E. Joshua, and Bernard Schwartz. *Reason and Passion: Justice Brennan's Enduring Influence.* New York: Norton, 1997.

Wetterer, Charles M. *The Fourth Amendment: Search and Seizure.* Springfield, N.J.: Enslow, 1998.

WEBSITES

Criminal Due Process. Available online at http://www.maxwell.syr.edu/plegal/Lessons/Dpr/dpr8.html; website home page: http://www.maxwell.syr.edu (accessed February 13, 2003).

Fassoulas v. Ramey

Court case

By: Florida Supreme Court

Date: 1984

Source: Florida Supreme Court. *Fassoulas v. Ramey,* 450 So 2nd 822 (Fla. 1984). Reprinted in Hall, Kermit L., William M. Wiecek, and Paul Finkelman, ed. *American Legal History: Cases and Materials.* 2nd ed. New York: Oxford University Press, 1996, 508–509.

About the Organization: The Supreme Court of Florida was created soon after Florida's incorporation as a state in 1845. Initially, the justices were the circuit court justices, but the supreme court was given its own justices in 1851. As of 2003 the justices are appointed by the legislature to serve six-year terms, and the chief justice is chosen by the justices of the court. ■

Introduction

In the United States, the practice of medicine has greatly changed over the years. Originally, most doctors worked by themselves and were general practitioners. During the middle and late twentieth century, doctors began to specialize more. This meant that a patient no longer had only one doctor, decreasing the personal ties between the doctor and patient and increasing the probability of a lawsuit. Doctors also have steadily increased their rate of success, and the public is aware of this fact. Often, when a medical procedure fails, the patient wants someone to blame. Many in the public also know that all doctors have malpractice insurance. Thus, a faceless insurance company rather than the doctor is the one which compensates the patient in the event of a lawsuit.

Changes in the legal profession have also promoted more lawsuits. Lawyers now take cases on a contingency fee basis, which means that they take a percentage of any settlement or judgment without requiring the client to pay legal fees up front. In the eyes of many critics, this system encourages specious suits and quick settlements. Specialists in personal injury, or tort law, know personal injury law, which makes filing lawsuits easier. One subspecialty related to tort law is medical malpractice.

In Florida, the Fassoulases did not want any more children because their two previous children had been born with birth defects, so John had a vasectomy from Dr. Ramey. The vasectomy failed, and the Fassoulases had two more children. They sued for malpractice and won, and the case was appealed to the Florida Supreme Court.

Significance

The court upheld the lower court's verdict, but reduced the judgment for the Fassoulases, who were only allowed to recover the "extraordinary" expenses of raising a child with birth defects. Their experience is typical of many who win medical malpractice and tort judgments, then see their awards reduced on appeal. Rarely do these modifications make the front-page news.

Cases like this one bring into relief the ongoing struggle between law and medicine. On the one hand, doctors blame the large number of malpractice suits on the legal profession. On the other hand, a recent study found that 50 percent of malpractice lawsuits are filed against 6 percent of the doctors, suggesting that in many cases, doctors bring malpractice suits upon themselves. While the legal profession may have incentive to increase the number of medical malpractice suits filed, *Fassoulas v. Ramey* demonstrates that not all of these suits are without merit—many awards are reduced on appeal, and real issues need to be addressed by the medical community as well.

Primary Source

Fassoulas v. Ramey [excerpt]

SYNOPSIS: The court first discusses the vasectomy performed and how two children were born after this procedure. It then discusses the suit and the findings of the trial court. The court rules that a parent cannot be damaged by the birth of a normal and healthy child and also cannot be damaged by the normal "everyday" expenses of raising a child with birth defects. The court concludes by holding that the parents can recover only the extra costs of raising the child with birth defects.

Per curiam . . .

Plaintiffs, Edith and John Fassoulas, were married and had two children, both of whom had been born with severe congenital abnormalities. After much consideration, they decided not to have any more children due to the fear of having another physically deformed child and the attendant high cost of medical care. They then decided that John would undergo a vasectomy. This medical procedure was performed in January 1974 by defendant, Dr. Ramey. However, due to the negligence of the defendant in performing the operation, in giving medical advice concerning residual pockets of sperm, and in examining and judging the viability of sperm samples, Edith twice became pregnant and gave birth to two children. The first of these, Maria, was born in November 1974 and had many congenital deformities. Roussi, the second of the post-vasectomy children and the fourth Fassoulas child, was born in September 1976 with a slight physical deformity which was corrected at birth; he is now a normal, healthy child.

The plaintiffs sued Dr. Ramey and his clinic in tort based on medical malpractice for the two "wrongful births." They sought as damages Edith's past and future lost wages, her anguish and emotional distress at twice becoming pregnant, her loss of the society, companionship and consortium of her husband, John's mental anguish and emotional distress, his loss of the society, companionship and consortium of his wife, medical and hospital expenses and the expenses for the care and upbringing of the two new children until the age of twenty-one.

At trial, the jury found in favor of the plaintiffs, finding the defendant 100% negligent with reference to Maria and 50% negligent with reference to Roussi. The plaintiffs were found to be comparatively negligent as to the birth of Roussi. Damages were assessed in the amount of $250,000 for the birth of Maria and $100,000 for the birth of Roussi, the latter sum being reduced to $50,000 because of the plaintiff's comparative negligence. . . .

The rule in Florida is that "a parent cannot be said to have been damaged by the birth and rearing of a normal, healthy child." "[I]t has been imbedded in our law for centuries that the father and now both parents or legal guardians of a child have the sole obligation of providing the necessaries in raising the child, whether the child be wanted or unwanted." "The child is still the child of the parents, not the physician, and it is the parents' legal obligation, not the physician's, to support the child." For public policy reasons, we decline to allow rearing damages for the birth of a healthy child.

The same reasoning forcefully and correctly applies to the ordinary, everyday expenses associated with the care and upbringing of a physically or mentally deformed child. We likewise hold as a matter of law that ordinary rearing expenses for a defective child are not recoverable as damages in Florida.

We agree with the district court below that an exception exists in the case of special upbringing expenses associated with a deformed child. Special medical and educational expenses, beyond normal rearing costs, are often staggering and quite debilitating to a family's financial and social health; "indeed the financial and emotional drain associated with raising such a child is often overwhelming to the affected parents." There is no valid policy argument against parents being recompensed for these costs of extraordinary care in raising a deformed child to majority. We hold these special upbringing costs associated with a deformed child to be recoverable.

[The court allowed only the extraordinary rearing costs associated with Maria; it permitted nothing for the birth of Roussi.]

Further Resources

BOOKS

Aiken, Tonia D. *Legal and Ethical Issues in Health Occupations.* Philadelphia: W.B. Saunders, 2002.

Bhat, Vasanthakumar N. *Medical Malpractice: A Comprehensive Analysis.* Westport, Conn.: Auburn House, 2001.

Goldstein, Marc, and Michael Feldberg. *The Vasectomy Book: A Complete Guide to Decision Making.* Los Angeles: J.P. Tarcher, 1982.

Horn, Carl, Donald H. Caldwell, and D. Christopher Osborn. *Law for Physicians: An Overview of Medical Legal Issues.* Chicago: American Medical Association, 2000.

Jasper, Margaret C. *The Law of Medical Malpractice.* Dobbs Ferry, N.Y.: Oceana Publications, 2001.

Morreim, E. Haavi. *Holding Health Care Accountable: Law and the New Medical Marketplace.* New York: Oxford University Press, 2001.

Rostow, Victoria P., and Roger J. Bulger. *Medical Professional Liability and the Delivery of Obstetrical Care.* Washington, D.C.: National Academy Press, 1989.

WEBSITES

Hinshaw Report: Torts. Available online at http://www .hinshawlaw.com/library/torts/summer1996.cfm; website homepage: http://www.hinshawlaw.com (accessed February 13, 2003).

Garcia v. San Antonio Metropolitan Transit Authority

Supreme Court decision

By: Harry Blackmun, Lewis Powell, William Rehnquist, and Sandra Day O'Connor

Date: February 19, 1985

Source: Blackmun, Harry, Lewis Powell, William Rehnquist, and Sandra Day O'Connor. *Garcia v. San Antonio Metropolitan Transit Authority,* 469 U.S. 528. Available online at http://laws.findlaw.com/us/469/528.html; website home page: http://laws.findlaw.com (accessed April 19, 2003).

About the Authors: Harry Blackmun (1908–1999) served on the Supreme Court from 1970 to 1994. Lewis Powell (1907–1998) served on the Supreme Court from 1971 to 1987. William Rehnquist (1924–) was named to the Supreme Court in 1971. In 1986, he was appointed chief justice. In 1981, Sandra Day O'Connor (1930–) became the first woman appointed to the Supreme Court. ∎

Introduction

In the late nineteenth century, most American industrial workers worked ten-hour days six days a week. Conditions were worse in the steel industry, where

Justice Harry Blackmun delivered the majority opinion of the Court for *Garcia v. San Antonio Metropolitan Transit Authority.* GETTY IMAGES. REPRODUCED BY PERMISSION.

twelve-hour workdays were the norm. Although conditions were better for state workers, reformers called for minimum-wage and maximum-hours laws. One of the first reforms passed by many states was a requirement that employees would not work more than eight hours a day on state projects.

These laws were sometimes followed up by laws forcing a maximum work week on employers in general. Employers frequently challenged such laws in court, and throughout the late nineteenth and early twentieth centuries, the Supreme Court agreed with employers, holding that maximum-hour laws were an infringement of the workers' "freedom of contract." These decisions remained in force until the 1930s, when the federal government passed the 1938 Fair Labor Standards Act, which set up a maximum work week of forty-four hours (later reduced to forty) and a minimum wage of twenty-five cents an hour. This law was upheld by the Supreme Court, and the nation has had a maximum work week (without overtime) and a minimum wage for most workers ever since.

As the federal bureaucracy expanded in the twentieth century, many people looked to the federal government for solutions to problems, and many new federal programs were created. By the 1970s, though, critics thought that the federal government was the problem, not the solution, and called upon it to cede more power to the states. In 1974, in the midst of this spirit, Congress extended the Fair Labor Standards Act (FLSA), as it had several times before—each time the extension had been held constitutional. The 1974 amendments extended the FLSA to force cities to pay overtime for certain city employees. In response, the National League of Cities sued and won, as the Supreme Court held that the federal government had overstepped its commerce powers and that the Tenth Amendment required that the states be allowed to manage their own affairs. The same issue arose in *Garcia.*

Significance

In *Garcia,* the Court held that the Tenth Amendment did not protect cities and states from congressional legislation. The concept of "traditional government functions," which *National League of Cities* had said was not subject to congressional mandates, was unworkable, and that judgment was overturned. The Court majority held that a city or a state's main protection was within the political framework. The dissenting justices claimed that the Court's decision encroached on the authority of the states, eradicated federalism, and ignored the Tenth Amendment. Regardless of who had the better historical argument, the dissenters have had more success on the Court since *Garcia.* Appointments in the late twentieth century, including Justice Antonin Scalia, have used both the Tenth and Eleventh Amendments to strengthen the position of states and to limit the federal government.

Primary Source

Garcia v. San Antonio Metropolitan Transit Authority [excerpt]

SYNOPSIS: Justice Blackmun, who delivered the majority opinion, opens by noting that the Court was overruling *National League of Cities.* He then discusses the difficulties in determining what were "uniquely governmental functions" and so rules that this criteria should be abandoned. He then holds that states are protected by the political process. Justice Powell in dissent argues that this decision destroys federalism. Justice Rehnquist, also dissenting, says that federalism will rise again, and Justice O'Connor, dissenting, holds that the autonomy of states, ignored by the majority, is necessary to our republic.

Justice Blackmun delivered the opinion of the Court.

We revisit in these cases an issue raised in *National League of Cities v. Usery,* . . . In that litigation, this Court, by a sharply divided vote, ruled that the Commerce Clause does not empower Congress to enforce the minimum-wage and overtime provisions of the Fair Labor Standards Act (FLSA) against the States "in areas of traditional governmental functions." . . . Although National League of Cities supplied some examples of "traditional governmental functions," it did not offer a general explanation of how a "traditional" function is to be distinguished from a "nontraditional" one. Since then, federal and state courts have struggled with the task, thus imposed, of identifying a traditional function for purposes of state immunity under the Commerce Clause. . . .

Our examination of this "function" standard applied in these and other cases over the last eight years now persuades us that the attempt to draw the boundaries of state regulatory immunity in terms of "traditional governmental function" is not only unworkable but is also inconsistent with established principles of federalism and, indeed, with those very federalism principles on which National League of Cities purported to rest. That case, accordingly, is overruled. . . .

Were SAMTA a privately owned and operated enterprise, it could not credibly argue that Congress exceeded the bounds of its Commerce Clause powers in prescribing minimum wages and overtime rates for SAMTA's employees. Any constitutional exemption from the requirements of the FLSA therefore must rest on SAMTA's status as a governmental entity rather than on the "local" nature of its operations. . . .

Thus far, this Court   has made little headway in defining the scope of the governmental functions deemed protected under National League of Cities. In that case the Court set forth examples of protected and unprotected functions, . . . but provided no explanation of how those examples were identified. . . .

Many constitutional standards involve "undoubte[d] . . . gray areas," . . . and, despite the difficulties that this Court and other courts have encountered so far, it normally might be fair to venture the assumption that case-by-case development would lead to a workable standard for determining whether a particular governmental function should be immune from federal regulation under the Commerce Clause. A further cautionary note is sounded, however, by the Court's experience in the related field of state immunity from federal taxation. . . .

Even during the heyday of the governmental/proprietary distinction in intergovernmental tax-

immunity doctrine the Court never explained the constitutional basis for that distinction. . . .

The distinction the Court discarded as unworkable in the field of tax immunity has proved no more fruitful in the field of regulatory immunity under the Commerce Clause. Neither do any of the alternative standards that might be employed to distinguish between protected and unprotected governmental functions appear manageable. . . . Reliance on history as an organizing principle results in line-drawing of the most arbitrary sort; the genesis of state governmental functions stretches over a historical continuum from before the Revolution to the present, and courts would have to decide by fiat precisely how longstanding a pattern of state involvement had to be for federal regulatory authority to be defeated.

A nonhistorical standard for selecting immune governmental functions is likely to be just as unworkable as is a historical standard. The goal of identifying "uniquely" governmental functions, for example, has been rejected by the Court in the field of government tort liability in part because the notion of a "uniquely" governmental function is unmanageable. . . . Another possibility would be to confine immunity to "necessary" governmental services, that is, services that would be provided inadequately or not at all unless the government provided them. . . . The set of services that fits into this category, however, may well be negligible. . . .

We believe, however, that there is a more fundamental problem at work here, a problem that explains why the Court was never able to provide a basis for the governmental/proprietary distinction in the intergovernmental tax-immunity cases and why an attempt to draw similar distinctions with respect to federal regulatory authority under National League of Cities is unlikely to succeed regardless of how the distinctions are phrased. The problem is that neither the governmental/proprietary distinction nor any other that purports to separate out important governmental functions can be faithful to the role of federalism in a democratic society. . . .

We therefore now reject, as unsound in principle and unworkable in practice, a rule of state immunity from federal regulation that turns on a judicial appraisal of whether a particular governmental function is "integral" or "traditional." Any such rule leads to inconsistent results at the same time that it disserves principles of democratic self-governance, and it breeds inconsistency precisely because it is divorced from those principles. If there are to be limits on the Federal Government's power to interfere with state functions—as undoubtedly there are—we must look elsewhere to find them. We accordingly return to the underlying issue that confronted this Court in National League of Cities—the manner in which the Constitution insulates States from the reach of Congress' power under the Commerce Clause.

The central theme of National League of Cities was that the States occupy a special position in our constitutional system and that the scope of Congress' authority under the Commerce Clause must reflect that position. . . . National League of Cities reflected the general conviction that the Constitution precludes "the National Government [from] devour[ing] the essentials of state sovereignty." . . . In order to be faithful to the underlying federal premises of the Constitution, courts must look for the "postulates which limit and control."

What has proved problematic is not the perception that the Constitution's federal structure imposes limitations on the Commerce Clause, but rather the nature and content of those limitations. . . .

We doubt that courts ultimately can identify principled constitutional limitations on the scope of Congress' Commerce Clause powers over the States merely by relying on a priori definitions of state sovereignty. In part, this is because of the elusiveness of objective criteria for "fundamental" elements of state sovereignty, a problem we have witnessed in the search for "traditional governmental functions." There is, however, a more fundamental reason: the sovereignty of the States is limited by the Constitution itself. A variety of sovereign powers, for example, are withdrawn from the States by Article I, {section} 10. . . . Finally, the developed application, through the Fourteenth Amendment, of the greater part of the Bill of Rights to the States limits the sovereign authority that States otherwise would possess to legislate with respect to their citizens and to conduct their own affairs.

The States unquestionably do "retai[n] a significant measure of sovereign authority." . . . They do so, however, only to the extent that the Constitution has not divested them of their original powers and transferred those powers to the Federal Government. . . .

With rare exceptions, like the guarantee, in Article IV, 3, of state territorial integrity, the Constitution does not carve out express elements of state sovereignty that Congress may not employ its delegated powers to displace. . . . In short, we have no license to employ freestanding conceptions of state sovereignty when measuring congressional authority under the Commerce Clause. . . .

Apart from the limitation on federal authority inherent in the delegated nature of Congress' Article I powers, the principal means chosen by the Framers to ensure the role of the States in the federal system lies in the structure of the Federal Government itself. It is no novelty to observe that the composition of the Federal Government was designed in large part to protect the States from overreaching by Congress. . . .

In short, the Framers chose to rely on a federal system in which special restraints on federal power over the States inhered principally in the workings of the National Government itself, rather than in discrete limitations on the objects of federal authority. State sovereign interests, then, are more properly protected by procedural safeguards inherent in the structure of the federal system than by judicially created limitations on federal power. . . .

The fact that some federal statutes such as the FLSA extend general obligations to the States cannot obscure the extent to which the political position of the States in the federal system has served to minimize the burdens that the States bear under the Commerce Clause.

. . . against this background, we are convinced that the fundamental limitation that the constitutional scheme imposes on the Commerce Clause to protect the "States as States" is one of process rather than one of result. Any substantive restraint on the exercise of Commerce Clause powers must find its justification in the procedural nature of this basic limitation, and it must be tailored to compensate for possible failings in the national political process rather than to dictate a "sacred province of state autonomy." . . . This analysis makes clear that Congress' action in affording SAMTA employees the protections of the wage and hour provisions of the FLSA contravened no affirmative limit on Congress' power under the Commerce Clause. The judgment of the District Court therefore must be reversed.

Of course, we continue to recognize that the States occupy a special and specific position in our constitutional system and that the scope of Congress' authority under the Commerce Clause must reflect that position. But the principal and basic limit on the federal commerce power is that inherent in all congressional action—the built-in restraints that our system provides through state participation in federal governmental action. The political process ensures that laws that unduly burden the States will not be promulgated. In the factual setting of these cases the internal safeguards of the political process have performed as intended. . . .

We do not lightly overrule recent precedent. We have not hesitated, however, when it has become apparent that a prior decision has departed from a proper understanding of congressional power under the Commerce Clause. . . . Due respect for the reach of congressional power within the federal system mandates that we do so now.

National League of Cities v. Usery, . . . is overruled. . . .

Justice Powell, with whom The Chief Justice, Justice Rehnquist, and Justice O'Connor join, dissenting. . . .

Despite some genuflecting in the Court's opinion to the concept of federalism, today's decision effectively reduces the Tenth Amendment to meaningless rhetoric when Congress acts pursuant to the Commerce Clause. The Court holds that the Fair Labor Standards Act (FLSA) "contravened no affirmative limit on Congress' power under the Commerce Clause" to determine the wage rates and hours of employment of all state and local employees . . . I note that it does not seem to have occurred to the Court that it—an unelected majority of five Justices—today rejects almost 200 years of the understanding of the constitutional status of federalism. In doing so, there is only a single passing reference to the Tenth Amendment. Nor is so much as a dictum of any court cited in support of the view that the role of the States in the federal system may depend upon the grace of elected federal officials, rather than on the Constitution as interpreted by this Court. . . .

In our federal system, the States have a major role that cannot be pre-empted by the National Government. As contemporaneous writings and the debates at the ratifying conventions make clear, the States' ratification of the Constitution was predicated on this understanding of federalism. Indeed, the Tenth Amendment was adopted specifically to ensure that the important role promised the States by the proponents of the Constitution was realized. . . .

This history, which the Court simply ignores, documents the integral role of the Tenth Amendment in our constitutional theory. It exposes as well, I believe, the fundamental character of the Court's error today. Far from being "unsound in principle," . . . judicial enforcement of the Tenth Amendment is essential to maintaining the federal system so carefully designed by the Framers and adopted in the Constitution.

Although the Court's opinion purports to recognize that the States retain some sovereign power, it does not identify even a single aspect of state authority that would remain when the Commerce Clause is invoked to justify federal regulation. . . .

As I view the Court's decision today as rejecting the basic precepts of our federal system and limiting the constitutional role of judicial review, I dissent. . . .

Justice Rehnquist, dissenting. . . .

I do not think it incumbent on those of us in dissent to spell out further the fine points of a principle that will, I am confident, in time again command the support of a majority of this Court.

Justice O'Connor, with whom Justice Powell and Justice Rehnquist join, dissenting.

The Court today surveys the battle scene of federalism and sounds a retreat. . . .

In my view, federalism cannot be reduced to the weak "essence" distilled by the majority today. . . . If federalism so conceived and so carefully cultivated by the Framers of our Constitution is to remain meaningful, this Court cannot abdicate its constitutional responsibility to oversee the Federal Government's compliance with its duty to respect the legitimate interests of the States. . . .

Just as surely as the Framers envisioned a National Government capable of solving national problems, they also envisioned a republic whose vitality was assured by the diffusion of power not only among the branches of the Federal Government, but also between the Federal Government and the States. . . .

It is not enough that the "end be legitimate"; the means to that end chosen by Congress must not contravene the spirit of the Constitution. Thus many of this Court's decisions acknowledge that the means by which national power is exercised must take into account concerns for state autonomy. . . . The Court today rejects National League of Cities and washes its hands of all efforts to protect the States. In the process, the Court opines that unwarranted federal encroachments on state authority are and will remain "'horrible possibilities that never happen in the real world.'" . . . There is ample reason to believe to the contrary. . . .

Instead, the autonomy of a State is an essential component of federalism. If state autonomy is ignored in assessing the means by which Congress regulates matters affecting commerce, then federalism becomes irrelevant simply because the set of activities remaining beyond the reach of such a commerce power "may well be negligible." . . . That the Court shuns the task today by appealing to the "essence of federalism" can provide scant comfort to those who believe our federal system requires something more than a unitary, centralized government. I would not shirk the duty acknowledged by National League of Cities and its progeny, and I share Justice Rehnquist's belief that this Court will in time again assume its constitutional responsibility.

I respectfully dissent.

Further Resources

BOOKS

Davis, Sue Justice. *Rehnquist and the Constitution.* Princeton, N.J.: Princeton University Press, 1989.

Jeffries, John Calvin. *Justice Lewis F. Powell, Jr.* New York: Scribner's, 1994.

Linder, Marc. *"Moments are the Elements of Profit": Overtime and the Deregulation of Working Hours under the Fair Labor Standards Act.* Iowa City, Iowa: Fanpìhuà Press, 2000.

Van Sickel, Robert W. *Not a Particularly Different Voice: The Jurisprudence of Sandra Day O'Connor.* New York: P. Lang, 1998.

PERIODICALS

Breyer, Stephen G. "In Memoriam, Justice Harry A. Blackmun: Principle and Compassion." *Columbia Law Review* 99, no. 6, October 1999, 1393–1408.

"Symposium, the Jurisprudence of Justice Harry A. Blackmun." *Hastings Constitutional Law Quarterly* 26, no. 1, Fall 1998.

WEBSITES

The Tenth and Eleventh Amendments. Available online at http://www.law.umkc.edu/faculty/projects/ftrials/conlaw/tenth.htm; website home page: http://www.law.umkc.edu (accessed February 7, 2003).

Bowers v. Hardwick

Supreme Court decision

By: Byron White, Warren Burger, Lewis F. Powell, and Harry Blackmun

Date: June 30, 1986

Source: White, Byron, Warren Burger, Lewis F. Powell, and Harry Blackmun. *Bowers v. Hardwick,* 478 U.S. 186. Available online at http://laws.findlaw.com/us/478/186.html; website home page: http://laws.findlaw.com (accessed April 19, 2003).

About the Authosr: Byron White (1917–2002), a Rhodes scholar and talented athlete in college, graduated from Yale

University and served on the Supreme Court from 1962 to 1993. Warren Burger (1907–1995) was appointed chief justice of the Supreme Court in 1969 and served until 1986. Lewis F. Powell (1907–1998) served on the Court from 1971 to 1987. Harry Blackmun (1908–1999) was appointed to the Supreme Court in 1970 and remained there until 1994. ■

Introduction

For much of the history of the United States, homosexual behavior has been illegal. Sodomy was a crime in all thirteen states when the Constitution was enacted. These laws were not enforced very consistently, but their existence was a constant threat to homosexuals. Thus they were inhibited in their lifestyle, forced either to hide their true nature or else avoid the public eye entirely.

In the mid-twentieth century, attitudes toward homosexuals began to change in the United States. The Kinsey Reports of the 1940s and 1950s revealed that homosexuality was more common than was previously believed. They also showed that many Americans, both hetero- and homosexual, engaged in illegal sexual behavior like sodomy and oral sex. In part because of these revelations, a so-called sexual revolution swept the United States in the 1960s and 1970s, and sodomy laws began to be loosened.

Many states, though, did not repeal their laws against sodomy, including Georgia, which imposed a twenty-year jail term, even for conduct between consenting adults. While serving an outdated, unrelated warrant, a police officer arrested Michael Hardwick for sodomy, but later the charges were dropped. Hardwick used this arrest to challenge Georgia's sodomy law, and this challenge reached the Supreme Court.

Significance

In *Bowers v. Hardwick,* the Supreme Court narrowly sustained Georgia's sodomy law by a 5 to 4 decision, holding homosexual sodomy, even if engaged in consensually and privately, had no constitutional safeguards. Burger concurred, arguing strongly that there was no fundamental right to something banned in "Judeo-Christian moral and ethical standards." Justice Powell stuck a middle ground, holding that there was no fundamental right but that the punishment of twenty years in jail was excessive, and that if Georgia had imposed such a jail term on Hardwick, he might have voted to reverse. The dissent argued that part of our essential freedom to choose is the freedom to make different choices, even sexual ones. The Georgia sodomy law was eventually struck down, not by a federal court, but by the Georgia Supreme Court, which held that it violated Georgia's state constitution.

Homosexuality and personal freedom returned to the forefront of the news in the 1990s when President Clinton (served 1993–2001) attempted to first reverse the ban on gays in the military but then announced a "don't ask, don't tell" policy aimed at keeping the issue private. In the 2002–2003 term, the Court overturned a conviction under a Texas law that makes homosexual sodomy a misdemeanor, with a $200 fine, and does not criminalize heterosexual sodomy. The ruling essentially struck down all sodomy laws as violations of the Due Process Clause, and characterized such laws as thinly veiled attempts to criminalize homosexuality.

Primary Source

Bowers v. Hardwick [excerpt]

SYNOPSIS: Writing for the majority, Justice White first says the only issue is whether there is a constitutional right to conduct sodomy; he holds that there is not, and that this practice does not fall under the types of liberty deemed fundamental to the Constitution. Justice Burger argues that sodomy has always been criminalized and there is nothing in the Constitution to change that. Justice Powell suggests that the law is constitutional but that the twenty-year sentence far outweighs the seriousness of the crime. In his dissent, Justice Blackmun argues that the Georgia law is unconstitutional because people deserve to be "left alone."

Justice White delivered the opinion of the Court. . . .

The issue presented is whether the Federal Constitution confers a fundamental right upon homosexuals to engage in sodomy and hence invalidates the laws of the many States that still make such conduct illegal and have done so for a very long time. The case also calls for some judgment about the limits of the Court's role in carrying out its constitutional mandate. . . .

Accepting the decisions in these cases and the above description of them, we think it evident that none of the rights announced in those cases bears any resemblance to the claimed constitutional right of homosexuals to engage in acts of sodomy that is asserted in this case. No connection between family, marriage, or procreation on the one hand and homosexual activity on the other has been demonstrated, either by the Court of Appeals or by respondent. Moreover, any claim that these cases nevertheless stand for the proposition that any kind of private sexual conduct between consenting adults is constitutionally insulated from state proscription is unsupportable. . . .

Precedent aside, however, respondent would have us announce, as the Court of Appeals did, a fundamental right to engage in homosexual sodomy. This we are quite unwilling to do. . . .

Striving to assure itself and the public that announcing rights not readily identifiable in the Constitution's text involves much more than the imposition of the Justices' own choice of values on the States and the Federal Government, the Court has sought to identify the nature of the rights qualifying for heightened judicial protection . . . A different description of fundamental liberties appeared in *Moore v. East Cleveland* . . . where they are characterized as those liberties that are "deeply rooted in this Nation's history and tradition." . . .

It is obvious to us that neither of these formulations would extend a fundamental right to homosexuals to engage in acts of consensual sodomy. Proscriptions against that conduct have ancient roots. . . . Sodomy was a criminal offense at common law and was forbidden by the laws of the original 13 States when they ratified the Bill of Rights. . . . Against this background, to claim that a right to engage in such conduct is "deeply rooted in this Nation's history and tradition" or "implicit in the concept of ordered liberty" is, at best, facetious.

Nor are we inclined to take a more expansive view of our authority to discover new fundamental rights imbedded in the Due Process Clause. The Court is most vulnerable and comes nearest to illegitimacy when it deals with judge-made constitutional law having little or no cognizable roots in the language or design of the Constitution. . . . There should be, therefore, great resistance to expand the substantive reach of those Clauses, particularly if it requires redefining the category of rights deemed to be fundamental. Otherwise, the Judiciary necessarily takes to itself further authority to govern the country without express constitutional authority. The claimed right pressed on us today falls far short of overcoming this resistance.

Respondent, however, asserts that the result should be different where the homosexual conduct occurs in the privacy of the home. . . .

Plainly enough, otherwise illegal conduct is not always immunized whenever it occurs in the home. Victimless crimes, such as the possession and use of illegal drugs, do not escape the law where they are committed at home. . . . And if respondent's submission is limited to the voluntary sexual conduct between consenting adults, it would be difficult, except by fiat, to limit the claimed right to homosexual conduct while leaving exposed to prosecution adultery, incest, and other sexual crimes even though they are committed in the home. We are unwilling to start down that road.

Even if the conduct at issue here is not a fundamental right, respondent asserts that there must be a rational basis for the law and that there is none in this case other than the presumed belief of a majority of the electorate in Georgia that homosexual sodomy is immoral and unacceptable. This is said to be an inadequate rationale to support the law. The law, however, is constantly based on notions of morality, and if all laws representing essentially moral choices are to be invalidated under the Due Process Clause, the courts will be very busy indeed. Even respondent makes no such claim, but insists that majority sentiments about the morality of homosexuality should be declared inadequate. We do not agree, and are unpersuaded that the sodomy laws of some 25 States should be invalidated on this basis.

Accordingly, the judgment of the Court of Appeals is

Reversed. . . .

Chief Justice Burger, concurring.

I join the Court's opinion, but I write separately to underscore my view that in constitutional terms there is no such thing as a fundamental right to commit homosexual sodomy.

As the Court notes . . . the proscriptions against sodomy have very "ancient roots." . . . Homosexual sodomy was a capital crime under Roman law. . . . Blackstone described "the infamous crime against nature" as an offense of "deeper malignity" than rape, a heinous act "the very mention of which is a disgrace to human nature," and "a crime not fit to be named." . . . To hold that the act of homosexual sodomy is somehow protected as a fundamental right would be to cast aside millennia of moral teaching.

This is essentially not a question of personal "preferences" but rather of the legislative authority of the State. I find nothing in the Constitution depriving a State of the power to enact the statute challenged here.

Justice Powell, concurring.

I join the opinion of the Court. I agree with the Court that there is no fundamental right—i. e., no substantive right under the Due Process Clause—such as that claimed by respondent Hardwick, and found to exist by the Court of Appeals. This is not to suggest, however, that respondent may not be protected by the Eighth Amendment of the Constitution. The Georgia statute at issue in this case . . . authorizes a court to imprison a person for up to 20 years for a single private, consensual act of sodomy. In my view, a prison sentence for such conduct—certainly a sentence of long duration—would create a serious Eighth Amendment issue. Under the Georgia statute a single act of sodomy, even in the private setting of a home, is a felony comparable in terms of the possible sentence imposed to serious felonies such as aggravated battery . . . first-degree arson, . . . and robbery . . .

In this case, however, respondent has not been tried, much less convicted and sentenced. Moreover, respondent has not raised the Eighth Amendment issue below. For these reasons this constitutional argument is not before us. . . .

Justice Blackmun, with whom Justice Brennan, Justice Marshall, and Justice Stevens join, dissenting.

This case is no more about "a fundamental right to engage in homosexual sodomy," as the Court purports to declare . . . than *Stanley v. Georgia* . . . was about a fundamental right to watch obscene movies. . . . Rather, this case is about "the most comprehensive of rights and the right most valued by civilized men," namely, "the right to be let alone." . . .

But the fact that the moral judgments expressed . . . may be "natural and familiar . . . ought not to conclude our judgment upon the question whether statutes embodying them conflict with the Constitution of the United States." . . . Like Justice Holmes, I believe that "[i]t is revolting to have no better reason for a rule of law than that so it was laid down in the time of Henry IV. It is still more revolting if the grounds upon which it was laid down have vanished long since, and the rule simply persists from blind imitation of the past." . . . I believe we must analyze respondent Hardwick's claim in the light of the values that underlie the constitutional right to privacy. If that right means anything, it means that, before Georgia can prosecute its citizens for making choices about the most intimate aspects of their lives, it must do more than assert that the choice they have made is an "abominable crime not fit to be named among Christians." . . .

I need not reach either the Eighth Amendment or the Equal Protection Clause issues because I believe that Hardwick has stated a cognizable claim that 16-6-2 interferes with constitutionally protected interests in privacy and freedom of intimate association. But neither the Eighth Amendment nor the Equal Protection Clause is so clearly irrelevant that a claim resting on either provision should be peremptorily dismissed. The Court's cramped reading of the issue before it makes for a short opinion, but it does little to make for a persuasive one. . . .

Only the most willful blindness could obscure the fact that sexual intimacy is "a sensitive, key relationship of human existence, central to family life, community welfare, and the development of human personality." . . .

In a variety of circumstances we have recognized that a necessary corollary of giving individuals freedom to choose how to conduct their lives is acceptance of the fact that different individuals will make different choices. . . . The Court claims that its decision today merely refuses to recognize a fundamental right to engage in homosexual sodomy; what the Court really has refused to recognize is the fundamental interest all individuals have in controlling the nature of their intimate associations with others. . . .

"The right of the people to be secure in their . . . houses," expressly guaranteed by the Fourth Amendment, is perhaps the most "textual" of the various constitutional provisions that inform our understanding of the right to privacy, and thus I cannot agree with the Court's statement that "[t]he right pressed upon us here has no . . . support in the text of the Constitution." . . . Indeed, the right of an individual to conduct intimate relationships in the intimacy of his or her own home seems to me to be the heart of the Constitution's protection of privacy. . . .

I cannot agree that either the length of time a majority has held its convictions or the passions with which it defends them can withdraw legislation from this Court's security. . . . It is precisely because the issue raised by this case touches the heart of what makes individuals what they are that we should be especially sensitive to the rights of those whose choices upset the majority.

The assertion that "traditional Judeo-Christian values proscribe" the conduct involved, . . . cannot provide an adequate justification. . . . That certain, but by no means all, religious groups condemn the behavior at issue gives the State no license to impose their judgments on the entire citizenry. The legitimacy of secular legislation depends instead on whether the State can advance some justification for its law beyond its conformity to religious doctrine. . . . Thus, far from buttressing his case, petitioner's

invocation of Leviticus, Romans, St. Thomas Aquinas, and sodomy's heretical status during the Middle Ages undermines his suggestion that 16-6-2 represents a legitimate use of secular coercive power. A State can no more punish private behavior because of religious intolerance than it can punish such behavior because of racial animus. "The Constitution cannot control such prejudices, but neither can it tolerate them. Private biases may be outside the reach of the law, but the law cannot, directly or indirectly, give them effect." . . . No matter how uncomfortable a certain group may make the majority of this Court, we have held that "[m]ere public intolerance or animosity cannot constitutionally justify the deprivation of a person's physical liberty." . . .

Statutes banning public sexual activity are entirely consistent with protecting the individual's liberty interest in decisions concerning sexual relations: the same recognition that those decisions are intensely private which justifies protecting them from governmental interference can justify protecting individuals from unwilling exposure to the sexual activities of others. But the mere fact that intimate behavior may be punished when it takes place in public cannot dictate how States can regulate intimate behavior that occurs in intimate places. . . .

This case involves no real interference with the rights of others, for the mere knowledge that other individuals do not adhere to one's value system cannot be a legally cognizable interest . . . let alone an interest that can justify invading the houses, hearts, and minds of citizens who choose to live their lives differently. . . .

It took but three years for the Court to see the error in its analysis in *Minersville School District v. Gobitis*, . . . and to recognize that the threat to national cohesion posed by a refusal to salute the flag was vastly outweighed by the threat to those same values posed by compelling such a salute. . . . I can only hope that here, too, the Court soon will reconsider its analysis and conclude that depriving individuals of the right to choose for themselves how to conduct their intimate relationships poses a far greater threat to the values most deeply rooted in our Nation's history than tolerance of nonconformity could ever do. Because I think the Court today betrays those values, I dissent.

Further Resources
BOOKS
Baird, Robert M., and M. Katherine Baird. *Homosexuality: Debating the Issues.* Amherst, N.Y.: Prometheus Books, 1995.

D'Emilio, John, William B. Turner, and Urvashi Vaid. *Creating Change: Sexuality, Public Policy, and Civil Rights*. New York: St. Martin's Press, 2000.

Irons, Peter H., and Stephanie Guitton. *May It Please the Court: The Most Significant Oral Arguments Made Before the Supreme Court Since 1955*. New York: New Press, 1984.

Jeffries, John Calvin. *Justice Lewis F. Powell, Jr.* New York: Scribner's, 1994.

PERIODICALS

Breyer, Stephen G. "In Memoriam, Justice Harry A. Blackmun: Principle and Compassion." *Columbia Law Review* 99, no. 6, October 1999, 1393–1408.

WEBSITES

Sodomy Laws. Available online at http://www.sodomylaws .org/bowers/bowers.htm; website home page: http://www .sodomylaws.org (accessed February 13, 2003).

Johnson v. Transportation Agency

Supreme Court decision

By: William J. Brennan and Antonin Scalia

Date: March 25, 1987

Source: Brennan, William J. and Antonin Scalia. *Johnson v. Transportation Agency, Santa Clara County,* 480 U.S. 616. Available online at http://laws.findlaw.com/us/480/616.html; website home page: http://laws.findlaw.com (accessed April 20, 2003).

About the Authors: William Brennan (1906–1997) received his law degree from Harvard. After serving as a trial court judge, then an appellate court judge, he was appointed to the U.S. Supreme Court in 1957. He retired from the Court for health reasons in 1990.

Antonin Scalia (1936–) graduated from Harvard Law School in 1961. After teaching at the University of Virginia and Georgetown University, he was appointed to the U.S. Supreme Court in 1986. He is noted as a consistent advocate of "textualism," or holding the Constitution to its literal meaning only. ∎

Introduction

The Fourteenth Amendment, ratified in 1868, reaffirmed the principle that everyone was entitled to equal protection under the laws. This protection, though, was not always extended to women. It was not until 1920 that women were granted the right to vote. In the decades that followed, women continued to be barred from equal opportunity in education, employment, and the professions. For example, Sandra Day O'Connor was appointed to the U.S. Supreme Court in 1981, a testament to her legal skills. Yet, after graduating third in her class from Stan-

ford in the early 1950s, O'Connor could not find a job in a law firm because none would hire a woman.

In 1964, Congress attempted to remedy this situation by passing the Civil Rights Act, which banned, among other practices, sexual discrimination in employment. Inequalities, though, continued to plague the workplace. Men continued to be given preferential treatment, and often had advantages in promotion because of seniority, previously established business contacts, more experience, or leadership positions in labor. Federal programs to remedy this and other discrimination, sometimes required affirmative action. Affirmative action refers to a program or policy that gives preferential treatment to women and/or minority groups that were discriminated against in the past. The intention is to counteract the advantages held by white men because of past discrimination. Some state and county governments adopted voluntary affirmative action programs of their own. The legality of one such plan was challenged in *Johnson v. Transportation Agency*.

Significance

The transportation agency of Santa Clara County in California adopted an affirmative action plan intended to correct the gender imbalance in certain job classifications. After he was passed over for promotion in favor of a woman, Paul Johnson sued, claiming that his rights had been violated under the Civil Rights Act. The trial court agreed, but the court of appeals reversed this decision. The Supreme Court affirmed the decision of the court of appeals, upholding the county's voluntary affirmative action plan. Unlike strict quota plans, which require that a certain number of jobs or promotions be given to women, this plan required that when candidates were equally qualified, a woman could be hired or promoted based on gender. The Supreme Court has generally rejected quota programs, unless they were imposed by a court that found the specific company or organization involved had engaged in a long pattern of past discrimination. In his dissent, Justice Scalia argued that Title VII of the 1964 Civil Rights Act, which guaranteed "gender-blind" hiring, had instead guaranteed gender conscious employment. Since *Johnson*, the Supreme Court has generally looked with disfavor on affirmative action plans.

Primary Source

Johnson v. Transportation Agency [excerpt]

SYNOPSIS: Justice Brennan, writing for the majority, notes that women have been underrepresented in the job dispatcher category and that the affirmative action plan did not set quotas. He then notes that a qualified applicant had been promoted, and that using gender as one of many factors to be considered was reasonable to remedy past discrimination, making the hiring decision legal. Justice Scalia dissents, arguing that the wrong goals are being pursued and that the court is legitimizing discrimination.

Justice Brennan delivered the opinion of the Court.

Respondent, Transportation Agency of Santa Clara County, California, unilaterally promulgated an Affirmative Action Plan applicable . . . , to promotions of employees. In selecting applicants for the promotional position of road dispatcher, the Agency, pursuant to the Plan, passed over petitioner Paul Johnson, a male employee, and promoted a female employee applicant, Diane Joyce. . . .

Relevant to this case, the Agency Plan provides that, in making promotions to positions within a traditionally segregated job classification in which women have been significantly underrepresented, the Agency is authorized to consider as one factor the sex of a qualified applicant. . . .

As for the job classification relevant to this case, none of the 238 Skilled Craft Worker positions was held by a woman. . . .

The Agency's Plan thus set aside no specific number of positions for minorities or women, but authorized the consideration of ethnicity or sex as a factor when evaluating qualified candidates for jobs in which members of such groups were poorly represented. One such job was the road dispatcher position that is the subject of the dispute in this case. . . .

As a preliminary matter, we note that petitioner bears the burden of establishing the invalidity of the Agency's Plan. . . . Once a plaintiff establishes a prima facie case that race or sex has been taken into account in an employer's employment decision, the burden shifts to the employer to articulate a nondiscriminatory rationale for its decision. The existence of an affirmative action plan provides such a rationale. If such a plan is articulated as the basis for the employer's decision, the burden shifts to the plaintiff to prove that the employer's justification is pretextual and the plan is invalid. As a practical matter, of course, an employer will generally seek to avoid a charge of pretext by presenting evidence in support of its plan. That does not mean, however, as petitioner suggests, that reliance on an affirmative action plan is to be treated as an affirmative defense requiring the employer to carry the burden of proving the validity of the plan. The burden of proving its invalidity remains on the plaintiff.

The assessment of the legality of the Agency Plan must be guided by our decision in *Weber,* . . . In that case. . . .

We upheld the employer's decision to select less senior black applicants over the white respondent, for we found that taking race into account was consistent with Title VII's objective of "break[ing] down old patterns of racial segregation and hierarchy." . . . Our decision was grounded in the recognition that voluntary employer action can play a crucial role in furthering Title VII's purpose of eliminating the effects of discrimination in the workplace, and that Title VII should not be read to thwart such efforts. . . .

In reviewing the employment decision at issue in this case, we must first examine whether that decision was made pursuant to a plan prompted by concerns similar to those of the employer in *Weber.* Next, we must determine whether the effect of the Plan on males and nonminorities is comparable to the effect of the plan in that case.

The first issue is therefore whether consideration of the sex of applicants for Skilled Craft jobs was justified by the existence of a "manifest imbalance" that reflected underrepresentation of women in "traditionally segregated job categories." . . . The requirement that the "manifest imbalance" relate to a "traditionally segregated job category" provides assurance both that sex or race will be taken into account in a manner consistent with Title VII's purpose of eliminating the effects of employment discrimination, and that the interests of those employees not benefiting from the plan will not be unduly infringed. . . .

It is clear that the decision to hire Joyce was made pursuant to an Agency plan that directed that sex or race be taken into account for the purpose of remedying underrepresentation. . . .

As an initial matter, the Agency adopted as a benchmark for measuring progress in eliminating underrepresentation the long-term goal of a work force that mirrored in its major job classifications the percentage of women in the area labor market. Even as it did so, however, the Agency acknowledged that such a figure could not by itself necessarily justify taking into account the sex of applicants for positions in all job categories. For positions requiring specialized training and experience, the Plan observed that the number of minorities and women "who possess the qualifications required for entry into such job classifications is limited.." . . . The

Plan therefore directed that annual short-term goals be formulated that would provide a more realistic indication of the degree to which sex should be taken into account in filling particular positions. . . .

By contrast, had the Plan simply calculated imbalances in all categories according to the proportion of women in the area labor pool, and then directed that hiring be governed solely by those figures, its validity fairly could be called into question. This is because analysis of a more specialized labor pool normally is necessary in determining underrepresentation in some positions. . . .

The Agency's Plan emphatically did not authorize such blind hiring. It expressly directed that numerous factors be taken into account in making hiring decisions, including specifically the qualifications of female applicants for particular jobs. Thus, despite the fact that no precise short-term goal was yet in place for the Skilled Craft category in mid-1980, the Agency's management nevertheless had been clearly instructed that they were not to hire solely by reference to statistics. . . .

Furthermore, in considering the candidates for the road dispatcher position in 1980, the Agency hardly needed to rely on a refined short-term goal to realize that it had a significant problem of underrepresentation that required attention. Given the obvious imbalance in the Skilled Craft category, and given the Agency's commitment to eliminating such imbalances, it was plainly not unreasonable for the Agency to determine that it was appropriate to consider as one factor the sex of Ms. Joyce in making its decision. The promotion of Joyce thus satisfies the first requirement enunciated in *Weber,* since it was undertaken to further an affirmative action plan designed to eliminate Agency work force imbalances in traditionally segregated job categories.

We next consider whether the Agency Plan unnecessarily trammeled the rights of male employees or created an absolute bar to their advancement. . . . [T]he Plan sets aside no positions for women. The Plan expressly states that "[t]he 'goals' established for each Division should not be construed as 'quotas' that must be met." . . . Rather, the Plan merely authorizes that consideration be given to affirmative action concerns when evaluating qualified applicants. As the Agency Director testified, the sex of Joyce was but one of numerous factors he took into account in arriving at his decision. . . .

In addition, petitioner had no absolute entitlement to the road dispatcher position. Seven of the applicants were classified as qualified and eligible, and the Agency Director was authorized to promote any of the seven. Thus, denial of the promotion unsettled no legitimate, firmly rooted expectation on the part of petitioner. Furthermore, while petitioner in this case was denied a promotion, he retained his employment with the Agency, at the same salary and with the same seniority, and remained eligible for other promotions. . . .

The Agency has identified a conspicuous imbalance in job categories traditionally segregated by race and sex. It has made clear from the outset, however, that employment decisions may not be justified solely by reference to this imbalance, but must rest on a multitude of practical, realistic factors. It has therefore committed itself to annual adjustment of goals so as to provide a reasonable guide for actual hiring and promotion decisions. The Agency earmarks no positions for anyone; sex is but one of several factors that may be taken into account in evaluating qualified applicants for a position. As both the Plan's language and its manner of operation attest, the Agency has no intention of establishing a work force whose permanent composition is dictated by rigid numerical standards.

We therefore hold that the Agency appropriately took into account as one factor the sex of Diane Joyce in determining that she should be promoted to the road dispatcher position. The decision to do so was made pursuant to an affirmative action plan that represents a moderate, flexible, case-by-case approach to effecting a gradual improvement in the representation of minorities and women in the Agency's work force. Such a plan is fully consistent with Title VII, for it embodies the contribution that voluntary employer action can make in eliminating the vestiges of discrimination in the workplace. . . .

Justice Scalia, with whom The Chief Justice joins, and with whom Justice White joins in Parts I and II, dissenting. . . .

Ever so subtly, without even alluding to the last obstacles preserved by earlier opinions that we now push out of our path, we effectively replace the goal of a discrimination-free society with the quite incompatible goal of proportionate representation by race and by sex in the workplace. Part I of this dissent will describe the nature of the plan that the Court approves, and its effect upon this petitioner. Part II will discuss prior holdings that are tacitly overruled, and prior distinctions that are disregarded. Part III will describe the engine of discrimination we have finally completed. . . .

Road dispatcher Diane Joyce won a landmark 6-3 Supreme Court ruling for affirmative action. The decision upheld Santa Clara County, California's right to give her a promotion over an arguably more qualified man. © BETTMANN/CORBIS. REPRODUCED BY PERMISSION.

Not only was the plan not directed at the results of past sex discrimination by the Agency, but its objective was not to achieve the state of affairs that this Court has dubiously assumed would result from an absence of discrimination—an overall work force "more or less representative of the racial and ethnic composition of the population in the community." . . . Rather, the oft-stated goal was to mirror the racial and sexual composition of the entire county labor force, not merely in the Agency work force as a whole, but in each and every individual job category at the Agency. In a discrimination-free world, it would obviously be a statistical oddity for every job category to match the racial and sexual composition of even that portion of the county work force qualified for that job; it would be utterly miraculous for each of them to match, as the plan expected, the composition of the entire work force. Quite obviously, the plan did not seek to replicate what a lack of discrimination would produce, but rather imposed racial and sexual tailoring that would, in defiance of normal expectations and laws of probability, give each protected racial and sexual group a governmentally determined "proper" proportion of each job category. . . .

The most significant proposition of law established by today's decision is that racial or sexual discrimination is permitted under Title VII when it is intended to overcome the effect, not of the employer's own discrimination, but of societal attitudes that have limited the entry of certain races, or of a particular sex, into certain jobs. . . .

In fact, however, today's decision goes well beyond merely allowing racial or sexual discrimination in order to eliminate the effects of prior societal discrimination. The majority opinion often uses the phrase "traditionally segregated job category" to describe the evil against which the plan is legitimately (according to the majority) directed. . . . There are, of course, those who believe that the social attitudes which cause women themselves to avoid certain jobs and to favor others are as nefarious as conscious, exclusionary discrimination. Whether or not that is so (and there is assuredly no consensus on the point equivalent to our national consensus against intentional discrimination), the two phenomena are certainly distinct. And it is the alteration of social attitudes, rather than the elimination of discrimination, which today's decision approves as justification for state-enforced discrimination. This is an enormous expansion, undertaken without the slightest justification or analysis. . . .

It is impossible not to be aware that the practical effect of our holding is to accomplish de facto what the law . . . forbids anyone from accomplishing de jure: in many contexts it effectively requires employers, public as well as private, to engage in intentional discrimination on the basis of race or sex. . . . A statute designed to establish a color-blind and gender-blind workplace has thus been converted into a powerful engine of racism and sexism, not merely permitting intentional race- and sex-based discrimination, but often making it, through operation of the legal system, practically compelled.

It is unlikely that today's result will be displeasing to politically elected officials, to whom it provides the means of quickly accommodating the demands of organized groups to achieve concrete, numerical improvement in the economic status of particular constituencies. Nor will it displease the world of corporate and governmental employers (many of whom have filed briefs as amici in the present case, all on the side of Santa Clara) for whom the cost of hiring less qualified workers is often substantially less—and infinitely more predictable—than the cost of litigating Title VII cases and of seeking to convince federal agencies by nonnumerical means that no discrimination exists. In fact, the only losers in the process are the Johnsons of the country, for whom Title VII has been not merely repealed but actually inverted. The irony is that these individuals—predominantly unknown, unaffluent, unorganized—suffer this injustice at the hands of a Court fond of thinking itself the champion of the politically impotent. I dissent.

Further Resources

BOOKS

Brisbin, Richard A. *Justice Antonin Scalia and the Conservative Revival.* Baltimore, Md.: Johns Hopkins University Press, 1997.

Curry, George E., and Cornel West. *The Affirmative Action Debate.* Reading, Mass.: Addison-Wesley, 1996.

Raza, M. Ali, A. Janell Anderson, and Harry Glynn Custred. *The Ups and Downs of Affirmative Action Preferences.* Westport, Conn.: Praeger, 1999.

Rosenkranz, E. Joshua, and Bernard Schwartz. *Reason and Passion: Justice Brennan's Enduring Influence.* New York: Norton, 1997.

Schultz, David A., and Christopher E. Smith, *The Jurisprudential Vision of Justice Antonin Scalia.* Lanham, Md.: Rowman and Littlefield, 1996.

Spann, Girardeau A. *The Law of Affirmative Action: Twenty-Five Years of Supreme Court Decisions on Race and Remedies.* New York: New York University Press, 2000.

Urofsky, Melvin I. *A Conflict of Rights: The Supreme Court and Affirmative Action.* New York: Scribner's, 1991.

WEBSITES

"Milestones in the History of the Equal Employment Opportunity Commission." Available online at http://www.eeoc.gov /35th/milestones/1987.html; website home page: http:// www.eeoc.gov/ (accessed February 13, 2003).

Edwards v. Aguillard

Supreme Court decision

By: William J. Brennan and Antonin Scalia

Date: June 19, 1987

Source: Brennan, William J. and Antonin Scalia. *Edwards v. Aguillard,* 482 U.S. 578. Available online at http://laws .findlaw.com/us/482/578.html; website home page: http://laws .findlaw.com (accessed April 20, 2003).

About the Authors: William Brennan (1906–1997) received his law degree from Harvard. After serving as a trial court judge, then an appellate court judge, he was appointed to the U.S. Supreme Court in 1957. He retired from the Court for health reasons in 1990.

Antonin Scalia (1936–) graduated from Harvard Law School in 1961. After teaching at the University of Virginia and Georgetown University, he was appointed to the U.S. Supreme Court in 1986. He is noted as a consistent advocate of "textualism," or holding the Constitution to its literal meaning. ■

Introduction

When the nineteenth-century naturalist Charles Darwin published his theory of evolution—that plants and animals had evolved over a long period of time from earlier and simpler forms of life and that man was a "codescendant" with other mammals from a common ancestor—he challenged the fundamental religious beliefs of millions of people. In particular, Protestant fundamentalists, especially in the rural American South, condemned Darwin's theories and wanted them banned from public schools. In 1925, Tennessee passed the Butler Act, which made it illegal to teach evolution. Several people in Dayton, Tennessee, wanted to generate tourist income for the town, so they recruited John T. Scopes, a math teacher at the high school, to challenge the law. The case attracted national attention, and people flocked to Dayton. William Jennings Bryan joined the prosecution team, while Clarence Darrow, the period's most famous criminal defense lawyer, volunteered for the defense. Scopes was convicted and ordered to pay a $100 fine, but the conviction was overturned on appeal. Those favoring laws like the Butler Act were restrained by the negative press and experience of the Scopes trial.

The issue did not fade away, though. Even though the teaching of evolution was legal in all states, many biology teachers, either because they were fundamentalists themselves or they did not wish to run afoul of the school board, simply skipped the topic. Textbooks selected by committees often slighted the topic of evolution. Other states passed—or tried to pass—laws similar to the Butler Act. In the early 1980s, Louisiana passed a law requiring that "creation science"—the belief in the existence of a supernatural creator—and the theory of evolution be given equal treatment in the schools. This law was challenged, and the U.S. Supreme Court in *Edwards* affirmed the judgment of the district court and the court of appeals that the law was unconstitutional.

Significance

The Supreme Court, by a vote of 7 to 2, struck down the Louisiana law, holding that the law violated the establishment clause of the First Amendment to the Constitution and that it "impermissibly endorses religion." In their dissent, Justices Scalia and Rehnquist accept the state's contention that creation science is valid science and does not advance any particular religion.

Edwards has become a landmark case in this history of American jurisprudence concerning the meaning of the First Amendment, particularly the tension between the establishment clause (the state cannot "establish," or favor, a particular religion) and the free exercise clause (the state cannot interfere with the expression of religious beliefs). Dissension over the meaning of that amendment continues to this day. On the one hand are those who oppose *any* encroachment of religion into secular affairs, such as government and education, arguing that the First Amendment creates a "wall of separation" between church and state. Proponents of this view oppose not only the teaching of creationism in public schools but also, for example, religious displays on government grounds during traditional Christian holidays such as Christmas. On the other hand are those who argue that the purpose of the First Amendment was not to exclude religion from government but to prevent the state from favoring one religion over another (the establishment clause); the historical basis of their view in large part was the religious persecution found in England, with its state-sponsored Anglican Church. Proponents of this view argue that the nation's founders recognized the existence of God and never intended to exclude reference to the diety in public affairs; rather, they wanted American society to reflect a tolerance for all religious views (free exercise clause) without the state lending its support to one over the others.

Primary Source

Edwards v. Aguillard [excerpt]

SYNOPSIS: Justice Brennan, writing for the majority, first summarizes the Creationism Act and notes the three-part test (the *Lemon* test) for state involvement in religion. He concludes that the act violates the test's first part because it lacked a secular purpose and violates the second part because it advances religion. Scalia dissents, holding that the act's stated secular purpose was to advance academic freedom. He also argues that statutes should not be constitutionally required to have a secular purpose.

Justice Brennan delivered the opinion of the Court. . . .

The Creationism Act forbids the teaching of the theory of evolution in public schools unless accompanied by instruction in "creation science." . . . No school is required to teach evolution or creation science. If either is taught, however, the other must also be taught. Ibid. The theories of evolution and creation science are statutorily defined as "the scientific evidences for [creation or evolution] and inferences from those scientific evidences." . . .

The Establishment Clause forbids the enactment of any law "respecting an establishment of religion." The Court has applied a three-pronged test to determine whether legislation comports with the Establishment Clause. First, the legislature must have adopted the law with a secular purpose. Second, the statute's principal or primary effect must be one that neither advances nor inhibits religion. Third, the statute must not result in an excessive entanglement of government with religion. . . .

Lemon's first prong focuses on the purpose that animated adoption of the Act. . . . In this case, appellants have identified no clear secular purpose for the Louisiana Act. True, the Act's stated purpose is to protect academic freedom. . . . Even if "academic freedom" is read to mean "teaching all of the evidence" with respect to the origin of human beings, the Act does not further this purpose. The goal of providing a more comprehensive science curriculum is not furthered either by outlawing the teaching of evolution or by requiring the teaching of creation science.

While the Court is normally deferential to a State's articulation of a secular purpose, it is required that the statement of such purpose be sincere and not a sham. . . . It is clear from the legislative history that the purpose of the legislative sponsor, Senator Bill Keith, was to narrow the science curriculum. . . . Such a ban on teaching does not promote–indeed, it undermines—the provision of a comprehensive scientific education. It is equally clear that requiring schools to teach creation science with evolution does not advance academic freedom. . . .

Thus we agree with the Court of Appeals' conclusion that the Act does not serve to protect academic freedom, but has the distinctly different purpose of discrediting "evolution by counterbalancing its teaching at every turn with the teaching of creationism."

. . . . we need not be blind in this case to the legislature's preeminent religious purpose in enacting this statute. . . .

The preeminent purpose of the Louisiana Legislature was clearly to advance the religious viewpoint that a supernatural being created humankind. . . . The legislative history therefore reveals that the term "creation science," as contemplated by the legislature that adopted this Act, embodies the religious belief that a supernatural creator was responsible for the creation of humankind.

. . . Because the primary purpose of the Creationism Act is to advance a particular religious belief, the Act endorses religion in violation of the First Amendment. . . .

The Louisiana Creationism Act advances a religious doctrine by requiring either the banishment of the theory of evolution from public school classrooms or the presentation of a religious viewpoint that rejects evolution in its entirety. The Act violates the Establishment Clause of the First Amendment because it seeks to employ the symbolic and financial support of government to achieve a religious purpose. The judgment of the Court of Appeals therefore is

Affirmed.

Justice O'Connor joins all but Part II of this opinion. . . .

Justice Scalia, with whom The Chief Justice joins, dissenting.

Even if I agreed with the questionable premise that legislation can be invalidated under the Establishment Clause on the basis of its motivation alone, without regard to its effects, I would still find no justification for today's decision. The Louisiana legislators who passed the . . . Balanced Treatment Act . . . each of whom had sworn to support the Constitution, were well aware of the potential Es-

tablishment Clause problems and considered that aspect of the legislation with great care. After seven hearings and several months of study, . . . they approved the Act overwhelmingly and specifically articulated the secular purpose they meant it to serve. Although the record contains abundant evidence of the sincerity of that purpose (the only issue pertinent to this case), the Court today holds, essentially on the basis of "its visceral knowledge regarding what must have motivated the legislators," . . . that the members of the Louisiana Legislature knowingly violated their oaths and then lied about it. I dissent. Had requirements of the Balanced Treatment Act that are not apparent on its face been clarified by an interpretation of the Louisiana Supreme Court, or by the manner of its implementation, the Act might well be found unconstitutional; but the question of its constitutionality cannot rightly be disposed of on the gallop, by impugning the motives of its supporters. . . .

We have relatively little information upon which to judge the motives of those who supported the Act. About the only direct evidence is the statute itself and transcripts of the seven committee hearings at which it was considered. . . . Nevertheless, there is ample evidence that the majority is wrong in holding that the Balanced Treatment Act is without secular purpose. . . .

Before summarizing the testimony of Senator Keith and his supporters, I wish to make clear that I by no means intend to endorse its accuracy. But my views (and the views of this Court) about creation science and evolution are (or should be) beside the point. Our task is not to judge the debate about teaching the origins of life, but to ascertain what the members of the Louisiana Legislature believed. The vast majority of them voted to approve a bill which explicitly stated a secular purpose; what is crucial is not their wisdom in believing that purpose would be achieved by the bill, but their sincerity in believing it would be. . . .

The Act's reference to "creation" is not convincing evidence of religious purpose. The Act defines creation science as "scientific evidenc[e]," . . . and Senator Keith and his witnesses repeatedly stressed that the subject can and should be presented without religious content. . . . We have no basis on the record to conclude that creation science need be anything other than a collection of scientific data supporting the theory that life abruptly appeared on earth. . . . Creation science, its proponents insist, no more must explain whence life came than evolution must explain whence came the inanimate materials from which it says life evolved. . . .

The legislative history gives ample evidence of the sincerity of the Balanced Treatment Act's articulated purpose. . . .

In sum, even if one concedes, for the sake of argument, that a majority of the Louisiana Legislature voted for the Balanced Treatment Act partly in order to foster (rather than merely eliminate discrimination against) Christian fundamentalist beliefs, our cases establish that that alone would not suffice to invalidate the Act, so long as there was a genuine secular purpose as well. We have, moreover, no adequate basis for disbelieving the secular purpose set forth in the Act itself, or for concluding that it is a sham enacted to conceal the legislators' violation of their oaths of office. I am astonished by the Court's unprecedented readiness to reach such a conclusion, which I can only attribute to an intellectual predisposition created by the facts and the legend of Scopes . . . an instinctive reaction that any governmentally imposed requirements bearing upon the teaching of evolution must be a manifestation of Christian fundamentalist repression. In this case, however, it seems to me the Court's position is the repressive one. The people of Louisiana, including those who are Christian fundamentalists, are quite entitled, as a secular matter, to have whatever scientific evidence there may be against evolution presented in their schools, just as Mr. Scopes was entitled to present whatever scientific evidence there was for it. Perhaps what the Louisiana Legislature has done is unconstitutional because there is no such evidence, and the scheme they have established will amount to no more than a presentation of the Book of Genesis. But we cannot say that on the evidence before us in this summary judgment context, which includes ample uncontradicted testimony that "creation science" is a body of scientific knowledge rather than revealed belief. . . . Yet that illiberal judgment, that Scopes-in-reverse, is ultimately the basis on which the Court's facile rejection of the Louisiana Legislature's purpose must rest. . . .

Because I believe that the Balanced Treatment Act had a secular purpose, which is all the first component of the Lemon test requires, I would reverse the judgment of the Court of Appeals and remand for further consideration.

I have to this point assumed the validity of the Lemon "purpose" test. In fact, however, I think the pessimistic evaluation that The Chief Justice made of the totality of Lemon is particularly applicable to the "purpose" prong: it is "a constitutional theory [that] has no basis in the history of the amendment it seeks to interpret, is difficult to apply and yields unprincipled results. . . ."

Our cases interpreting and applying the purpose test have made such a maze of the Establishment Clause that even the most conscientious governmental officials can only guess what motives will be held unconstitutional. . . .

Given the many hazards involved in assessing the subjective intent of governmental decisionmakers, the first prong of Lemon is defensible, I think, only if the text of the Establishment Clause demands it. That is surely not the case. The Clause states that "Congress shall make no law respecting an establishment of religion." One could argue, I suppose, that any time Congress acts with the intent of advancing religion, it has enacted a "law respecting an establishment of religion"; but far from being an unavoidable reading, it is quite an unnatural one. . . . It is, in short, far from an inevitable reading of the Establishment Clause that it forbids all governmental action intended to advance religion; and if not inevitable, any reading with such untoward consequences must be wrong.

In the past we have attempted to justify our embarrassing Establishment Clause jurisprudence on the ground that it "sacrifices clarity and predictability for flexibility." One commentator has aptly characterized this as "a euphemism . . . for . . . the absence of any principled rationale." I think it time that we sacrifice some "flexibility" for "clarity and predictability." Abandoning Lemon's purpose test—a test which exacerbates the tension between the Free Exercise and Establishment Clauses, has no basis in the language or history of the Amendment, and, as today's decision shows, has wonderfully flexible consequences—would be a good place to start.

Further Resources

BOOKS

Brisbin, Richard A. *Justice Antonin Scalia and the Conservative Revival.* Baltimore, Md.: Johns Hopkins University Press, 1997.

Gould, Stephen Jay. *Ever Since Darwin: Reflections in Natural History.* New York: Norton, 1977.

Haught, John F. *God After Darwin: A Theology of Evolution.* Boulder, Col.: Westview, 2000.

Irons, Peter H., and Stephanie Guitton. *May It Please the Court: The Most Significant Oral Arguments Made Before the Supreme Court Since 1955.* New York: New Press, 1984.

Larson, Edward J. Summer. *For the Gods: the Scopes Trial and America's Continuing Debate over Science and Religion.* New York: BasicBooks, 1997.

Miller, Kenneth R. *Finding Darwin's God: A Scientist's Search For Common Ground Between God and Evolution.* New York: Cliff Street Books, 1999.

Numbers, Ronald L. *The Creationists.* New York: Knopf, 1992.

WEBSITES

The Talk.origins Archive. Available online at http://www.talkorigins.org/ (accessed February 13, 2003).

Morrison v. Olson

Supreme Court decision

By: William H. Rehnquist and Antonin Scalia

Date: June 29, 1988

Source: Rehnquist, William H. and Antonin Scalia. *Morrison v. Olson,* 487 U.S. 654. Available online at http://laws.findlaw.com/us/487/654.html; website home page: http://laws.findlaw.com (accessed April 20, 2003).

About the Authors: William Rehnquist (1924–) received his law degree from Stanford University. In 1971, he was named to the Supreme Court, and in 1986, he was appointed chief justice.

Antonin Scalia (1936–) graduated from Harvard Law School in 1961. He taught at the University of Virginia and Georgetown University. In 1986, he was appointed to the Supreme Court. ∎

Introduction

The Articles of Confederation, written during the American Revolution, provided for no executive branch (and no judiciary). Early Americans resisted having a strong executive because of abuses they had suffered under the British monarchy as colonists. This system of government, however, was too weak and ineffective, so the Constitution, to strengthen it, erected three branches of the federal government: the legislative to make laws, the executive to enforce the laws, and the judiciary to interpret the laws.

For the first century and a half, the federal government was limited in size (the post office was its largest agency), and played a small role in people's lives, especially the executive branch. With President Franklin Roosevelt's (served 1933–1945) New Deal and and Lyndon Johnson's (served 1963–1969) Great Society, however, the executive branch ballooned in size and, through the FBI and the CIA, developed intelligence capabilities that were too frequently used against American citizens.

Fears of an unchecked executive branch reached their peak during the Watergate scandal of the early

1970s, when funds from Republican Richard Nixon's (served 1969–1974) campaign were used to pay for a break-in at the Democratic National Headquarters in Washington, D.C.'s Watergate building. Nixon then authorized a cover-up, stymied the Department of Justice inquiry into the affair, and even fired the special prosecutor looking into it.

Even though the scandal eventually led to Nixon's resignation from office, Congress wanted to ensure that future presidents could not thwart justice by their misuse of federal law enforcement. As a result, Congress passed the 1978 Ethics in Government Act, which set up a three-judge panel that could appoint an independent counsel if the U.S. attorney general requested one; the counsel could be fired only for "good cause." In 1985, following a dispute over the Environmental Protection Agency's (EPA) enforcement of the Superfund legislation, an independent counsel was appointed. This brought the constitutionality of the Ethics in Government Act before the Supreme Court in *Morrison v. Olson.*

Significance

At issue in this case was the traditional separation of powers among the three branches of government. In a 7 to 1 vote, the Supreme Court upheld the constitutionality of the Ethics in Government Act. The Court held that the act does not violate the constitutional separation of powers, because the attorney general still must request the appointment of an independent counsel. In his closely reasoned dissent, Justice Scalia argued that the Ethics in Government Act, with its provision of an independent counsel, was an unconstitutional encroachment by Congress on the power of the executive branch of government and an unwarranted intrusion into the privacy of those who hold public office.

The Court's ruling would have important consequences in the 1990s. Kenneth Starr was appointed independent counsel in 1994 to investigate President Bill Clinton's (served 1993–2001) land dealings in the Whitewater case. Five years later, Starr produced a report advocating impeachment of Clinton for lying under oath about his relationship with presidential intern Monica Lewinsky. Clinton was eventually impeached by the House of Representatives but was not removed by the Senate.

Primary Source

Morrison v. Olson [excerpt]

SYNOPSIS: Justice Rehnquist upholds the Ethics in Government Act, noting that the independent counsel is an inferior officer and so can be appointed outside the executive branch. He then notes that controls on when and how the president can remove the independent counsel do not unbearably limit the executive branch. Scalia dissents, arguing that the independent counsel encroaches on the power of the executive branch and so violates the separation of powers.

Chief Justice Rehnquist delivered the opinion of the Court.

This case presents us with a challenge to the independent counsel provisions of the Ethics in Government Act of 1978, . . . We hold today that these provisions of the Act do not violate the Appointments Clause of the Constitution, . . . or the limitations of Article III, nor do they impermissibly interfere with the President's authority under Article II in violation of the constitutional principle of separation of powers.

Briefly stated, Title VI of the Ethics in Government Act . . . allows for the appointment of an "independent counsel" to investigate and, if appropriate, prosecute certain high ranking Government officials for violations of federal criminal laws. . . .

With respect to all matters within the independent counsel's jurisdiction, the Act grants the counsel "full power and independent authority to exercise all investigative and prosecutorial functions and powers of the Department of Justice, the Attorney General, and any other officer or employee of the Department of Justice." . . .

Finally, the Act provides for congressional oversight of the activities of independent counsel. An independent counsel may from time to time send Congress statements or reports on his or her activities. . . .

The line between "inferior" and "principal" officers is one that is far from clear, and the Framers provided little guidance into where it should be drawn. . . . We need not attempt here to decide exactly where the line falls between the two types of officers, because in our view appellant clearly falls on the "inferior officer" side of that line. Several factors lead to this conclusion.

First, appellant is subject to removal by a higher Executive Branch official. . . . Second, appellant is empowered by the Act to perform only certain, limited duties. An independent counsel's role is restricted primarily to investigation and, if appropriate, prosecution for certain federal crimes. . . .

Third, appellant's office is limited in jurisdiction. . . . Finally, appellant's office is limited in tenure. . . .

This does not, however, end our inquiry under the Appointments Clause. Appellees argue that even

if appellant is an "inferior" officer, the Clause does not empower Congress to place the power to appoint such an officer outside the Executive Branch.

. . . we see no reason now to depart from the holding of Siebold that such appointments are not proscribed by the excepting clause.

We also note that the history of the Clause provides no support for appellees' position. . . .

We do not mean to say that Congress' power to provide for interbranch appointments of "inferior officers" is unlimited. . . . we do not think that appointment of the independent counsel by the court runs afoul of the constitutional limitation on "incongruous" interbranch appointments. . . .

We now turn to consider whether the Act is invalid under the constitutional principle of separation of powers. Two related issues must be addressed: The first is whether the provision of the Act restricting the Attorney General's power to remove the independent counsel to only those instances in which he can show "good cause," taken by itself, impermissibly interferes with the President's exercise of his constitutionally appointed functions. The second is whether, taken as a whole, the Act violates the separation of powers by reducing the President's ability to control the prosecutorial powers wielded by the independent counsel. . . .

Considering for the moment the "good cause" removal provision in isolation from the other parts of the Act at issue in this case, we cannot say that the imposition of a "good cause" standard for removal by itself unduly trammels on executive authority. . . . Although the counsel exercises no small amount of discretion and judgment in deciding how to carry out his or her duties under the Act, we simply do not see how the President's need to control the exercise of that discretion is so central to the functioning of the Executive Branch as to require as a matter of constitutional law that the counsel be terminable at will by the President.

Nor do we think that the "good cause" removal provision at issue here impermissibly burdens the President's power to control or supervise the independent counsel, as an executive official, in the execution of his or her duties under the Act. This is not a case in which the power to remove an executive official has been completely stripped from the President, thus providing no means for the President to ensure the "faithful execution" of the laws. Rather, because the independent counsel may be terminated for "good cause," the Executive, through

Theodore Olson, U.S. assistant attorney general, was under investigation for obstructing justice in the investigation of the Environmental Protection Agency in the mid-1980s. **AP/WORLD WIDE PHOTOS. REPRODUCED BY PERMISSION.**

the Attorney General, retains ample authority to assure that the counsel is competently performing his or her statutory responsibilities in a manner that comports with the provisions of the Act. . . .

The final question to be addressed is whether the Act, taken as a whole, violates the principle of separation of powers by unduly interfering with the role of the Executive Branch. . . .

We observe first that this case does not involve an attempt by Congress to increase its own powers at the expense of the Executive Branch. . . .

Similarly, we do not think that the Act works any judicial usurpation of properly executive functions. . . .

Finally, we do not think that the Act "impermissibly undermine[s]" the powers of the Executive Branch . . . or "disrupts the proper balance between the coordinate branches [by] prevent[ing] the Executive Branch from accomplishing its constitutionally assigned functions," . . . It is undeniable that the Act reduces the amount of control or supervision that the Attorney General and, through him, the President exercises over the investigation and prosecution of a certain class of alleged criminal activity. . . .

Notwithstanding the fact that the counsel is to some degree "independent" and free from executive supervision to a greater extent than other federal prosecutors, in our view these features of the Act give the Executive Branch sufficient control over the independent counsel to ensure that the President is able to perform his constitutionally assigned duties.

In sum, we conclude today that it does not violate the Appointments Clause for Congress to vest the appointment of independent counsel in the Special Division; that the powers exercised by the Special Division under the Act do not violate Article III; and that the Act does not violate the separation-of-powers principle by impermissibly interfering with the functions of the Executive Branch. The decision of the Court of Appeals is therefore

Reversed . . .

Justice Scalia, dissenting.

It is the proud boast of our democracy that we have "a government of laws and not of men." . . . Without a secure structure of separated powers, our Bill of Rights would be worthless, as are the bills of rights of many nations of the world that have adopted, or even improved upon, the mere words of ours.

The principle of separation of powers is expressed in our Constitution in the first section of each of the first three Articles. Article I, {section} 1, provides that "[a]ll legislative Powers herein granted shall be vested in a Congress of the United States, which shall consist of a Senate and House of Representatives." Article III, {section}1, provides that "[t]he judicial Power of the United States, shall be vested in one supreme Court, and in such inferior Courts as the Congress may from time to time ordain and establish." And the provision at issue here, Art. II, {section}1, cl. 1, provides that "[t]he executive Power shall be vested in a President of the United States of America." . . .

That is what this suit is about. Power. The allocation of power among Congress, the President, and the courts in such fashion as to preserve the equilibrium the Constitution sought to establish—so that "a gradual concentration of the several powers in the same department," . . . can effectively be resisted. Frequently an issue of this sort will come before the Court clad, so to speak, in sheep's clothing: the potential of the asserted principle to effect important change in the equilibrium of power is not immediately evident, and must be discerned by a careful and perceptive analysis. But this wolf comes as a wolf. . . .

To repeat, Article II, {section}1, cl. 1, of the Constitution provides:

> The executive Power shall be vested in a President of the United States.

As I described at the outset of this opinion, this does not mean some of the executive power, but all of the executive power. It seems to me, therefore, that the decision of the Court of Appeals invalidating the present statute must be upheld on fundamental separation-of-powers principles if the following two questions are answered affirmatively: (1) Is the conduct of a criminal prosecution (and of an investigation to decide whether to prosecute) the exercise of purely executive power? (2) Does the statute deprive the President of the United States of exclusive control over the exercise of that power? Surprising to say, the Court appears to concede an affirmative answer to both questions, but seeks to avoid the inevitable conclusion that since the statute vests some purely executive power in a person who is not the President of the United States it is void. . . .

As I have said, however, it is ultimately irrelevant how much the statute reduces Presidential control. The case is over when the Court acknowledges, as it must, that "[i]t is undeniable that the Act reduces the amount of control or supervision that the Attorney General and, through him, the President exercises over the investigation and prosecution of a certain class of alleged criminal activity." . . . It is not for us to determine, and we have never presumed to determine, how much of the purely executive powers of government must be within the full control of the President. The Constitution prescribes that they all are. . . .

The purpose of the separation and equilibration of powers in general, and of the unitary Executive in particular, was not merely to assure effective government but to preserve individual freedom. Those who hold or have held offices covered by the Ethics in Government Act are entitled to that protection as much as the rest of us, and I conclude my discussion by considering the effect of the Act upon the fairness of the process they receive. . . .

It is, in other words, an additional advantage of the unitary Executive that it can achieve a more uniform application of the law. Perhaps that is not always achieved, but the mechanism to achieve it is there. The mini-Executive that is the independent counsel, however, operating in an area where so little is law and so much is discretion, is intentionally cut off from the unifying influence of the Justice De-

partment, and from the perspective that multiple responsibilities provide. . . . How admirable the constitutional system that provides the means to avoid such a distortion. And how unfortunate the judicial decision that has permitted it. . . .

Worse than what it has done, however, is the manner in which it has done it. A government of laws means a government of rules. Today's decision on the basic issue of fragmentation of executive power is ungoverned by rule, and hence ungoverned by law. It extends into the very heart of our most significant constitutional function the "totality of the circumstances" mode of analysis that this Court has in recent years become fond of. Taking all things into account, we conclude that the power taken away from the President here is not really too much. The next time executive power is assigned to someone other than the President we may conclude, taking all things into account, that it is too much. That opinion, like this one, will not be confined by any rule. We will describe, as we have today (though I hope more accurately) the effects of the provision in question, and will authoritatively announce: "The President's need to control the exercise of the [subject officer's] discretion is so central to the functioning of the Executive Branch as to require complete control." This is not analysis; it is ad hoc judgment. And it fails to explain why it is not true that—as the text of the Constitution seems to require, as the Founders seemed to expect, and as our past cases have uniformly assumed—all purely executive power must be under the control of the President.

The ad hoc approach to constitutional adjudication has real attraction, even apart from its work saving potential. It is guaranteed to produce a result, in every case, that will make a majority of the Court happy with the law. The law is, by definition, precisely what the majority thinks, taking all things into account, it ought to be. I prefer to rely upon the judgment of the wise men who constructed our system, and of the people who approved it, and of two centuries of history that have shown it to be sound. Like it or not, that judgment says, quite plainly, that "[t]he executive Power shall be vested in a President of the United States."

Further Resources

BOOKS

Brisbin, Richard A. *Justice Antonin Scalia and the Conservative Revival.* Baltimore, Md.: Johns Hopkins University Press, 1997.

Davis, Sue Justice. *Rehnquist and the Constitution.* Princeton, N.J.: Princeton University Press, 1989.

Dole, Robert J. *Project on the Independent Counsel Statute: Report and Recommendations.* Washington, D.C.: American Enterprise Institute, 1999.

Greenberg, Gerald S. *Historical Encyclopedia of U.S. Independent Counsel Investigations.* Westport, Conn.: Greenwood, 2000.

Johnson, Charles A., and Danette Brickman. *Independent Counsel: The Law and the Investigations.* Washington, D.C.: CQ Press, 2001.

Schmidt, Susan, and Michael Weisskopf. *Truth at Any Cost: Ken Starr and the Unmaking of Bill Clinton.* New York: HarperCollins, 2000.

Schultz, David A., and Christopher E. Smith. *The Jurisprudential Vision of Justice Antonin Scalia.* Lanham, Md.: Rowman and Littlefield, 1996.

AUDIO AND VISUAL MEDIA

Smaltz, Donald C., Peter J Boyer, and Michael Kirk. *Secrets of an Independent Counsel.* PBS Video. Videocassette. 1998.

Richmond v. J.A. Croson Co.

Supreme Court decision

By: Sandra Day O'Connor, John Paul Stevens, Antonin Scalia, Thurgood Marshall, and Harry Blackmun

Date: January 23, 1989

Source: O'Connor, Sandra Day, John Paul Stevens, Antonin Scalia, Thurgood Marshall, and Harry Blackmun. *Richmond v. J.A. Croson Co.,* 488 U.S. 469. Available online at http://laws.findlaw.com/us/488/469.html; website home page: http://laws.findlaw.com (accessed April 21, 2003).

About the Authors: Sandra Day O'Connor (1930–) in 1981 became the first woman appointed to the U.S. Supreme Court. John Paul Stevens (1920–) was appointed to the Supreme Court by President Gerald Ford in 1975. Antonin Scalia (1936–) graduated from Harvard in 1961 and was appointed to the Supreme Court in 1986. Thurgood Marshall (1908–1993) was the first African American appointed to the Supreme Court, serving from 1967 to 1991. Harry Blackmun (1908–1999), was appointed to the Court in 1970 and served until 1994. ∎

Introduction

In the 1960s, the federal government began to take action to end racial discrimination in the United States. In theory, such behavior had been outlawed by the Fourteenth Amendment to the Constitution in 1868. In practice, many states passed laws that denied African Americans and other minorities equal rights with white Americans, largely excluding them from white society. Not until the 1954 Supreme Court decision in *Brown v. Board of Education* did the federal government begin to intervene to secure the rights of minorities. Congress followed up in 1964 with the passage of the Civil Rights Act, the 1965 Voting Rights Act, and the 1968 Civil Rights Act. At this point, equality of treatment was the law of the land.

Implementing civil rights, however, proved to be difficult. One problem was that whites had numerous built-in advantages, such as previously established business contacts, more experience because of past preferences, and positions of power and leadership in most labor unions. African Americans often did not even have the opportunity to compete equally. To remedy this, some federal programs began to require that a certain percentage of federal grants had to be given to minority owned businesses, regardless of whether they submitted the lowest bid. A program of this sort was upheld in 1980 in the case of *Fullilove v. Klutznick.* The city of Richmond, Virginia, passed a similar affirmative action program, requiring that 30 percent of contracts had to be given to businesses owned primarily by members of various minority groups. A construction company brought suit, alleging that the plan was unconstitutional, and the case made its way to the U.S. Supreme Court.

Significance

This is one of the first U.S. Supreme Court decisions to strike down an affirmative action program. For such a program to be constitutional, the Court applied in this case a more demanding test than the one it had applied in *Fullilove.* The earlier case had required a "most searching examination" to determine if the government's remedy for past discrimination was constitutional; in *Richmond,* the Court required a "strict scrutiny" analysis, meaning that the program in question had to be the least restrictive means to accomplish a compelling state interest. On this basis, the Richmond plan was unconstitutional. The Court majority also objected to the program because Richmond had not established that it was guilty of past discrimination and hence needed remedial programs. In addition, the Court objected to a 30 percent quota as being overly rigid.

For those cities wishing to enact affirmative action programs, *Richmond v. Croson* set a high bar. Federal affirmative action programs had a lower bar, in part because proving discrimination on a nationwide scale was an easier undertaking. In 1995, however, federal programs were subjected to the same "strict scrutiny" standard that state and local programs had been since *Richmond.* Increasingly, in the eyes of the courts and much of the public, affirmative action programs were no longer an effective and fair way to solve the problem of past discrimination.

Primary Source

Richmond v. J.A. Croson Co. [excerpt]

SYNOPSIS: Justice O'Connor notes that affirmative action is allowable only where it has been shown that the city or state discriminated. She next holds that Richmond's plan is not narrowly tailored to counteract past discrimination and that past discrimination was not demonstrated, making the plan unconstitutional. Stevens concurs, arguing that affirmative action stigmatizes its beneficiaries. Scalia concurs in the judgment but argues that all affirmative action is unconstitutional because it establishes classifications based on race. Marshall dissents, arguing that Richmond has a right and a reason to adopt affirmative action and that affirmative action is allowable. Blackmun also dissents, suggesting that the majority is not true to the Constitution.

Justice O'Connor announced the judgment of the Court and delivered the opinion of the Court with respect to Parts I, III-B, and IV, an opinion with respect to Part II, in which The Chief Justice and Justice White join, and an opinion with respect to Parts III-A and V, in which The Chief Justice, Justice White, and Justice Kennedy join.

On April 11, 1983, the Richmond City Council adopted the Minority Business Utilization Plan (the Plan). The Plan required prime contractors to whom the city awarded construction contracts to subcontract at least 30% of the dollar amount of the contract to one or more Minority Business Enterprises (MBE's). . . .

. In *Fullilove,* we upheld the minority set aside . . . against a challenge based on the equal protection component of the Due Process Clause. . . .

That Congress may identify and redress the effects of society-wide discrimination does not mean that, a fortiori, the States and their political subdivisions are free to decide that such remedies are appropriate. . . .

It would seem equally clear, however, that a state or local subdivision (if delegated the authority from the State) has the authority to eradicate the effects of private discrimination within its own legislative jurisdiction. . . .

Thus, if the city could show that it had essentially become a "passive participant" in a system of racial exclusion practiced by elements of the local construction industry, we think it clear that the city could take affirmative steps to dismantle such a system. . . .

While there is no doubt that the sorry history of both private and public discrimination in this country has contributed to a lack of opportunities for black entrepreneurs, this observation, standing alone, cannot justify a rigid racial quota in the awarding of public contracts in Richmond, Virginia. Like the claim that discrimination in primary and secondary schooling justifies a rigid racial preference in medical school admissions, an amorphous claim that there has been past discrimination in a particular industry cannot justify the use of an unyielding racial quota. . . .

In sum, none of the evidence presented by the city points to any identified discrimination in the Richmond construction industry. We, therefore, hold that the city has failed to demonstrate a compelling interest in apportioning public contracting opportunities on the basis of race. . . .

As noted by the court below, it is almost impossible to assess whether the Richmond Plan is narrowly tailored to remedy prior discrimination since it is not linked to identified discrimination in any way. We limit ourselves to two observations In this regard.

First, there does not appear to have been any consideration of the use of race-neutral means to increase minority business participation In city contracting. . . .

Second, the 30% quota cannot be said to be narrowly tailored to any goal, except perhaps outright racial balancing. It rests upon the "completely unrealistic" assumption that minorities will choose a particular trade in lockstep proportion to their representation in the local population.

We think it obvious that such a program is not narrowly tailored to remedy the effects of prior discrimination. . . .

Because the city of Richmond has failed to identify the need for remedial action in the awarding of its public construction contracts, its treatment of its citizens on a racial basis violates the dictates of the Equal Protection Clause. Accordingly, the judgment of the Court of Appeals for the Fourth Circuit is.

Affirmed.

Justice Stevens, concurring in part and concurring in the judgment. . . .

There is a special irony in the stereotypical thinking that prompts legislation of this kind. Although it stigmatizes the disadvantaged class with the unproven charge of past racial discrimination, it actually imposes a greater stigma on its supposed beneficiaries. For, as I explained in my opinion in *Fullilove*:

Supreme Court Associate Justice Sandra Day O'Connor delivered the majority opinion of the Court for *Richmond v. J.A. Croson Co.* **THE LIBRARY OF CONGRESS.**

[E]ven though it is not the actual predicate for this legislation, a statute of this kind inevitably is perceived by many as resting on an assumption that those who are granted this special preference are less qualified in some respect that is identified purely by their race. . . .

Accordingly, I concur in Parts I, III-B, and IV of the Court's opinion, and in the judgment. . . .

Justice Scalia, concurring in the judgment. . . .

I do not agree, however, with Justice O'Connor's dictum suggesting that, despite the Fourteenth Amendment, state and local governments may in some circumstances discriminate on the basis of race in order (in a broad sense) "to ameliorate the effects of past discrimination." . . . The benign purpose of compensating for social disadvantages, whether they have been acquired by reason of prior discrimination or otherwise, can no more be pursued by the illegitimate means of racial discrimination than can other assertedly benign purposes we have repeatedly rejected. . . . The difficulty of overcoming the effects of past discrimination is as nothing compared with the difficulty of eradicating from our soci-

ety the source of those effects, which is the tendency—fatal to a Nation such as ours—to classify and judge men and women on the basis of their country of origin or the color of their skin. A solution to the first problem that aggravates the second is no solution at all. . . . At least where state or local action is at issue, only a social emergency rising to the level of imminent danger to life and limb—for example, a prison race riot, requiring temporary segregation of inmates . . . can justify an exception to the principle embodied in the Fourteenth Amendment that "[o]ur Constitution is colorblind, and neither knows nor tolerates classes among citizens" . . .

Where injustice is the game, however, turnabout is not fair play.

In my view there is only one circumstance in which the States may act by race to "undo the effects of past discrimination": where that is necessary to eliminate their own maintenance of a system of unlawful racial classification. . . .

Apart from their societal effects, however, which are "in the aggregate disastrous," . . . it is important not to lose sight of the fact that even "benign" racial quotas have individual victims, whose very real injustice we ignore whenever we deny them enforcement of their right not to be disadvantaged on the basis of race. . . . When we depart from this American principle we play with fire, and much more than an occasional DeFunis, Johnson, or Croson burns. . . .

Since I believe that the appellee here had a constitutional right to have its bid succeed or fail under a decisionmaking process uninfected with racial bias, I concur in the judgment of the Court.

Justice Marshall, with whom Justice Brennan and Justice Blackmun join, dissenting. . . .

More fundamentally, today's decision marks a deliberate and giant step backward in this Court's affirmative-action jurisprudence. Cynical of one municipality's attempt to redress the effects of past racial discrimination in a particular industry, the majority launches a grapeshot attack on race-conscious remedies in general. The majority's unnecessary pronouncements will inevitably discourage or prevent governmental entities, particularly States and localities, from acting to rectify the scourge of past discrimination. This is the harsh reality of the majority's decision, but it is not the Constitution's command. . . .

Richmond has two powerful interests in setting aside a portion of public contracting funds for minority-owned enterprises. The first is the city's interest in eradicating the effects of past racial discrimination. . . .

Richmond has a second compelling interest in setting aside, where possible, a portion of its contracting dollars. That interest is the prospective one of preventing the city's own spending decisions from reinforcing and perpetuating the exclusionary effects of past discrimination. . . .

The majority pays only lipservice to this additional governmental interest. . . . But our decisions have often emphasized the danger of the government tacitly adopting, encouraging, or furthering racial discrimination even by its own routine operations. . . .

The more government bestows its rewards on those persons or businesses that were positioned to thrive during a period of private racial discrimination, the tighter the deadhand grip of prior discrimination becomes on the present and future. Cities like Richmond may not be constitutionally required to adopt setaside plans. . . . But there can be no doubt that when Richmond acted affirmatively to stem the perpetuation of patterns of discrimination through its own decisionmaking, it served an interest of the highest order. . . .

In sum, to suggest that the facts on which Richmond has relied do not provide a sound basis for its finding of past racial discrimination simply blinks credibility. . . .

In any event, the majority's criticisms of individual items of Richmond's evidence rest on flimsy foundations. . . .

No one, of course, advocates "blind judicial deference" to the findings of the city council or the testimony of city leaders. . . . By disregarding the testimony of local leaders and the judgment of local government, the majority does violence to the very principles of comity within our federal system which this Court has long championed. . . .

When the legislatures and leaders of cities with histories of pervasive discrimination testify that past discrimination has infected one of their industries, armchair cynicism like that exercised by the majority has no place. . . .

Finally, I vehemently disagree with the majority's dismissal of the congressional and Executive Branch findings noted in *Fullilove* as having "extremely limited" probative value in this case. . . .

Of course, Richmond could have built an even more compendious record of past discrimination, one including additional stark statistics and additional individual accounts of past discrimination. But nothing in the Fourteenth Amendment imposes such onerous documentary obligations upon States and localities once the reality of past discrimination is apparent. . . .

Today, for the first time, a majority of this Court has adopted strict scrutiny as its standard of Equal Protection Clause review of race-conscious remedial measures. . . . This is an unwelcome development. A profound difference separates governmental actions that themselves are racist, and governmental actions that seek to remedy the effects of prior racism or to prevent neutral governmental activity from perpetuating the effects of such racism. . . .

Racial classifications "drawn on the presumption that one race is inferior to another or because they put the weight of government behind racial hatred and separatism" warrant the strictest judicial scrutiny because of the very irrelevance of those rationales. . . . By contrast, racial classifications drawn for the purpose of remedying the effects of discrimination that itself was race based have a highly pertinent basis: the tragic and indelible fact that discrimination against blacks and other racial minorities in this Nation has pervaded our Nation's history and continues to scar our society. . . .

In concluding that remedial classifications warrant no different standard of review under the Constitution than the most brutal and repugnant forms of state-sponsored racism, a majority of this Court signals that it regards racial discrimination as largely a phenomenon of the past, and that government bodies need no longer preoccupy themselves with rectifying racial injustice. I, however, do not believe this Nation is anywhere close to eradicating racial discrimination or its vestiges. In constitutionalizing its wishful thinking, the majority today does a grave disservice not only to those victims of past and present racial discrimination in this Nation whom government has sought to assist, but also to this Court's long tradition of approaching issues of race with the utmost sensitivity.

. . . it is too late in the day to assert seriously that the Equal Protection Clause prohibits States— or for that matter, the Federal Government, to whom the equal protection guarantee has largely been applied . . . from enacting race-conscious remedies. Our cases in the areas of school desegregation, voting rights, and affirmative action have demonstrated time and again that race is constitutionally germane, precisely because race remains dismayingly relevant in American life. . . .

The fact is that Congress' concern in passing the Reconstruction Amendments, and particularly their congressional authorization provisions, was that States would not adequately respond to racial violence or discrimination against newly freed slaves. To interpret any aspect of these Amendments as proscribing state remedial responses to these very problems turns the Amendments on their heads. . . .

In short, there is simply no credible evidence that the Framers of the Fourteenth Amendment sought "to transfer the security and protection of all the civil rights . . . from the States to the Federal government." . . . But nothing in the Amendments themselves, or in our long history of interpreting or applying those momentous charters, suggests that States, exercising their police power, are in any way constitutionally inhibited from working alongside the Federal Government in the fight against discrimination and its effects.

The majority today sounds a full-scale retreat from the Court's longstanding solicitude to race-conscious remedial efforts "directed toward deliverance of the century-old promise of equality of economic opportunity." . . . The new and restrictive tests it applies scuttle one city's effort to surmount its discriminatory past, and imperil those of dozens more localities. I, however, profoundly disagree with the cramped vision of the Equal Protection Clause which the majority offers today and with its application of that vision to Richmond, Virginia's, laudable set-aside plan. The battle against pernicious racial discrimination or its effects is nowhere near won. I must dissent. . . .

Justice Blackmun, with whom Justice Brennan joins, dissenting.

I join Justice Marshall's perceptive and incisive opinion revealing great sensitivity toward those who have suffered the pains of economic discrimination in the construction trades for so long.

I never thought that I would live to see the day when the city of Richmond, Virginia, the cradle of the Old Confederacy, sought on its own, within a narrow confine, to lessen the stark impact of persistent discrimination. But Richmond, to its great credit, acted. Yet this Court, the supposed bastion of equality, strikes down Richmond's efforts as though discrimination had never existed or was not demonstrated in this particular litigation. Justice Marshall

convincingly discloses the fallacy and the shallowness of that approach. History is irrefutable, even though one might sympathize with those who—though possibly innocent in themselves—benefit from the wrongs of past decades.

So the Court today regresses. I am confident, however, that, given time, it one day again will do its best to fulfill the great promises of the Constitution's Preamble and of the guarantees embodied in the Bill of Rights—a fulfillment that would make this Nation very special.

Further Resources

BOOKS

Brisbin, Richard A. *Justice Antonin Scalia and the Conservative Revival*. Baltimore, Md.: Johns Hopkins University Press, 1997.

Curry, George E., and Cornel West, *The Affirmative Action Debate*. Reading, Mass.: Addison-Wesley, 1996.

Van Sickel, Robert W. *Not a Particularly Different Voice: The Jurisprudence of Sandra Day O'Connor*. New York: P. Lang, 1998.

PERIODICALS

Joyce Holmes Benjamin. "The Supreme Court Decision [City of Richmond v. J.A. Croson Co.] and the Future of Race-conscious Remedies." *Government Finance Review* 5, no. 2, April 1989, 21–24.

"Constitutional Scholars' Statement on Affirmative Action after City of Richmond v. J.A. Croson Co." *Yale Law Journal* 98, no. 8, July 1989, 1711–1716.

WEBSITES

Affirmative Action Defended by W.B. Allen. Available online at http://www.msu.edu/~allenwi/essays_and_misc/Affirmative_Action_Defended.htm; website home page: http://www.msu.edu (accessed February 11, 2003).

Treasury Employees v. Von Raab

Supreme Court decision

By: Anthony Kennedy and Antonin Scalia

Date: March 21, 1989

Source: Kennedy, Anthony and Antonin Scalia. *Treasury Employees v. Von Raab*, 489 U.S. 656. Available online at http://laws.findlaw.com/us/489/656.html; website home page: http://laws.findlaw.com (accessed April 21, 2003).

About the Authors: Anthony Kennedy (1936–) graduated from Stanford University and Harvard Law School. He was appointed to the Supreme Court in 1988 after President Reagan's first two nominees failed. Kennedy has been more liberal than many conservatives had hoped.

Antonin Scalia (1936–) graduated from Harvard Law School in 1961. After teaching at the University of Virginia and George-town University, he was appointed to the U.S. Supreme Court in 1986. He is noted as a consistent advocate of "textualism," or holding the Constitution to its literal meaning. ■

Introduction

Many citizens in the late eighteenth century believed that the new U.S. Constitution gave too much power to the federal government and left the people vulnerable. To prevent governmental abuses, the First Congress added the Bill of Rights, the first ten amendments, to the Constitution. Included in the Bill of Rights is the Fourth Amendment, requiring that "the right of the people to be secure . . . against unreasonable searches and seizures, shall not be violated, and no Warrants shall issue, but upon probable cause . . . and particularly describing the place to be searched, and the persons or things to be seized."

For many years, this amendment was applied primarily to searches of homes or possessions. Twentieth-century concerns about substance abuse, combined with the medical technology to detect and measure substance abuse, however, tested the limits of the Fourth Amendment. Those charged with drunken driving, for example, were tested to see how much they had drunk. Urinalysis could detect the presence of illegal drugs in a person's system. Individual, targeted drug testing made sense for those suspected of a crime, particularly since a warrant could be obtained. A gray area that emerged, however, was wider scale drug testing of, for example, a class of employees. As part of the U.S. "War on Drugs," the government required drug testing of certain Customs Service employees. The constitutionality of that program was challenged in *Treasury Employees v. Von Raab*.

Significance

The Supreme Court upheld the constitutionality of the Customs Service program requiring a urinalysis test of those holding jobs involving drug interdiction, firearms, or classified materials. Writing for the majority, Justice Kennedy held that in some (but not all) of the job categories, the government had proven the necessary connection between the jobs and the risks posed by drug use. In his dissent, Justice Scalia pointed out that no rampant problem of drug use had been found that would justify this invasion of civil liberties by "searching and seizing" without warrants. In his view, this program was designed more for public relations than for any real threat. The majority opinion, though, has withstood legal challenges so that, for example, some school districts in the early twenty-first century required random drug testing of athletes.

Primary Source

Treasury Employees v. Von Raab [excerpt]

SYNOPSIS: Justice Kennedy notes the relevance of the Fourth Amendment prohibition against search and seizure. He concludes, however, that the search must only be reasonable and that required drug testing of certain employees in most cases is reasonable. Justice Scalia dissents, holding that these tests are an affront to human dignity and are not supported by evidence demonstrating drug problems in the Customs Service.

Justice Kennedy delivered the opinion of the Court.

We granted certiorari to decide whether it violates the Fourth Amendment for the United States Customs Service to require a urinalysis test from employees who seek transfer or promotion to certain positions. . . .

The United States Customs Service, a bureau of the Department of the Treasury, is the federal agency responsible for processing persons, carriers, cargo, and mail into the United States, collecting revenue from imports, and enforcing customs and related laws. . . . An important responsibility of the Service is the interdiction and seizure of contraband, including illegal drugs. . . . In the routine discharge of their duties, many Customs employees have direct contact with those who traffic in drugs for profit. Drug import operations, often directed by sophisticated criminal syndicates, . . . may be effected by violence or its threat. . . .

In May 1986, the Commissioner announced implementation of the drug testing program. Drug tests were made a condition of placement or employment for positions that meet one or more of three criteria. The first is direct involvement in drug interdiction or enforcement of related laws, an activity the Commissioner deemed fraught with obvious dangers to the mission of the agency and the lives of Customs agents. . . . The second criterion is a requirement that the incumbent carry firearms, as the Commissioner concluded that "[p]ublic safety demands that employees who carry deadly arms and are prepared to make instant life or death decisions be drug free." . . . The third criterion is a requirement for the incumbent to handle "classified" material, which the Commissioner determined might fall into the hands of smugglers if accessible to employees who, by reason of their own illegal drug use, are susceptible to bribery or blackmail. . . .

We granted certiorari. . . . We now affirm so much of the judgment of the Court of Appeals as upheld the testing of employees directly involved in drug interdiction or required to carry firearms. We vacate the judgment to the extent it upheld the testing of applicants for positions requiring the incumbent to handle classified materials, and remand for further proceedings. . . .

In *Skinner v. Railway Labor Executives' Assn.,* . . . decided today, we held that federal regulations requiring employees of private railroads to produce urine samples for chemical testing implicate the Fourth Amendment, as those tests invade reasonable expectations of privacy. Our earlier cases have settled that the Fourth Amendment protects individuals from unreasonable searches conducted by the Government, even when the Government acts as an employer, . . . and, in view of our holding in *Railway Labor Executives* that urine tests are searches, it follows that the Customs Service's drug-testing program must meet the reasonableness requirement of the Fourth Amendment. While we have often emphasized, and reiterate today, that a search must be supported, as a general matter, by a warrant issued upon probable cause, . . . our decision in *Railway Labor Executives* reaffirms the longstanding principle that neither a warrant nor probable cause, nor, indeed, any measure of individualized suspicion, is an indispensable component of reasonableness in every circumstance. . . . As we note in *Railway Labor Executives,* our cases establish that where a Fourth Amendment intrusion serves special governmental needs, beyond the normal need for law enforcement, it is necessary to balance the individual's privacy expectations against the Government's interests to determine whether it is impractical to require a warrant or some level of individualized suspicion in the particular context. . . .

The Customs Service has been entrusted with pressing responsibilities, and its mission would be compromised if it were required to seek search warrants in connection with routine, yet sensitive, employment decisions.

Furthermore, a warrant would provide little or nothing in the way of additional protection of personal privacy. . . .

Even where it is reasonable to dispense with the warrant requirement in the particular circumstances, a search ordinarily must be based on probable cause. . . . Our precedents have settled that, in certain limited circumstances, the Government's need to discover such latent or hidden conditions, or to prevent their development, is sufficiently compelling to justify the intrusion on privacy entailed by conducting such searches without any measure of individualized suspicion. . . . We think the Government's need to conduct the suspicionless searches required by the Customs program outweighs the privacy interests of employees engaged directly in drug interdiction, and of those who otherwise are required to carry firearms. . . .

It is readily apparent that the Government has a compelling interest in ensuring that front-line interdiction personnel are physically fit, and have unimpeachable integrity and judgment. Indeed, the Government's interest here is at least as important as its interest in searching travelers entering the country. . . .

While these operational realities will rarely affect an employee's expectations of privacy with respect to searches of his person, or of personal effects that the employee may bring to the workplace . . . , it is plain that certain forms of public employment may diminish privacy expectations even with respect to such personal searches. . . .

We think Customs employees who are directly involved in the interdiction of illegal drugs or who are required to carry firearms in the line of duty likewise have a diminished expectation of privacy in respect to the intrusions occasioned by a urine test. Unlike most private citizens or government employees in general, employees involved in drug interdiction reasonably should expect effective inquiry into their fitness and probity. Much the same is true of employees who are required to carry firearms. Because successful performance of their duties depends uniquely on their judgment and dexterity, these employees cannot reasonably expect to keep from the Service personal information that bears directly on their fitness. . . . While reasonable tests designed to elicit this information doubtless infringe some privacy expectations, we do not believe these expectations outweigh the Government's compelling interests in safety and in the integrity of our borders. . . .

In light of the extraordinary safety and national security hazards that would attend the promotion of drug users to positions that require the carrying of firearms or the interdiction of controlled substances, the Service's policy of deterring drug users from seeking such promotions cannot be deemed unreasonable. . . .

In sum, we believe the Government has demonstrated that its compelling interests in safeguarding our borders and the public safety outweigh the privacy expectations of employees who seek to be promoted to positions that directly involve the interdiction of illegal drugs or that require the incumbent to carry a firearm. We hold that the testing of

Customs agents unload a bag of smuggled cocaine they seized off Key West, Florida in 1989. The *Treasury Employees v. Von Raab* decision upheld a drug testing requirement by the United States Customs Service for employees who wanted to move into positions dealing directly with narcotics.
© BETTMANN/CORBIS. REPRODUCED BY PERMISSION.

these employees is reasonable under the Fourth Amendment. . . .

We are unable, on the present record, to assess the reasonableness of the Government's testing program insofar as it covers employees who are required "to handle classified material." We readily agree that the Government has a compelling interest in protecting truly sensitive information from those who, "under compulsion of circumstances or for other reasons, . . . might compromise [such] information." . . .

We also agree that employees who seek promotions to positions where they would handle sensitive information can be required to submit to a urine test under the Service's screening program, especially if the positions covered under this category require background investigations, medical examinations, or other intrusions that may be expected to diminish their expectations of privacy in respect of a urinalysis test. . . .

It is not clear, however, whether the category defined by the Service's testing directive encompasses only those Customs employees likely to gain access to sensitive information. Employees who are tested under the Service's scheme include those holding such diverse positions as "Accountant," "Accounting Technician," "Animal Caretaker," "Attorney (All)," "Baggage Clerk," "Co-op Student (All)," "Electric Equipment Repairer," "Mail Clerk/Assistant," and "Messenger." . . .

We cannot resolve this ambiguity on the basis of the record before us, and we think it is appropriate to remand the case to the Court of Appeals for such proceedings as may be necessary to clarify the scope of this category of employees subject to testing. Upon remand the Court of Appeals should examine the criteria used by the Service in determining what materials are classified and in deciding whom to test under this rubric. In assessing the reasonableness of requiring tests of these employees, the court should also consider pertinent information bearing upon the employees' privacy expectations, as well as the supervision to which these employees are already subject. . . .

We hold that the suspicionless testing of employees who apply for promotion to positions directly involving the interdiction of illegal drugs, or to positions that require the incumbent to carry a firearm, is reasonable. The Government's compelling interests in preventing the promotion of drug users to positions where they might endanger the integrity of our Nation's borders or the life of the citizenry outweigh the privacy interests of those who seek promotion to these positions, who enjoy a diminished expectation of privacy by virtue of the special, and obvious, physical and ethical demands of those positions. We do not decide whether testing those who apply for promotion to positions where they would handle "classified" information is reasonable because we find the record inadequate for this purpose.

The judgment of the Court of Appeals for the Fifth Circuit is affirmed in part and vacated in part, and the case is remanded for further proceedings consistent with this opinion.

It is so ordered. . . .

Justice Scalia, with whom Justice Stevens joins, dissenting. . . .

Until today this Court had upheld a bodily search separate from arrest and without individualized suspicion of wrong-doing only with respect to prison inmates, relying upon the uniquely dangerous nature of that environment. . . . Today, in *Skinner,* we allow a less intrusive bodily search of railroad employees involved in train accidents. I joined the Court's opinion there because the demonstrated frequency of drug and alcohol use by the targeted class of employees, and the demonstrated connection between such use and grave harm, rendered the search a reasonable means of protecting society. I decline to join the Court's opinion in the present case because neither frequency of use nor connection to harm is demonstrated or even likely. In my view the Customs Service rules are a kind of immolation of privacy and human dignity in symbolic opposition to drug use. . . .

The Court's opinion in the present case, however, will be searched in vain for real evidence of a real problem that will be solved by urine testing of Customs Service employees. . . .

It is not apparent to me that a Customs Service employee who uses drugs is significantly more likely to be bribed by a drug smuggler, any more than a Customs Service employee who wears diamonds is significantly more likely to be bribed by a diamond smuggler—unless, perhaps, the addiction to drugs is so severe, and requires so much money to maintain, that it would be detectable even without benefit of a urine test. Nor is it apparent to me that Customs officers who use drugs will be appreciably less "sympathetic" to their drug-interdiction mission, any more than police officers who exceed the speed limit in their private cars are appreciably less sympathetic to their mission of enforcing the traffic laws. . . . Nor, finally, is it apparent to me that urine tests will be even marginally more effective in preventing gun-carrying agents from risking "impaired perception and judgment" than is their current knowledge that, if impaired, they may be shot dead in unequal combat with unimpaired smugglers—unless, again, their addiction is so severe that no urine test is needed for detection. . . .

But if such a generalization suffices to justify demeaning bodily searches, without particularized suspicion, to guard against the bribing or blackmailing of a law enforcement agent, or the careless use of a firearm, then the Fourth Amendment has become frail protection indeed. . . .

The only plausible explanation, in my view, is what the Commissioner himself offered in the concluding sentence of his memorandum to Customs Service employees announcing the program: "Implementation of the drug screening program would set an important example in our country's struggle with this most serious threat to our national health and security." . . . Or as respondent's brief to this Court asserted: "[I]f a law enforcement agency and its employees do not take the law seriously, neither will the public on which the agency's effectiveness depends." . . . What better way to show that the Government is serious about its "war on drugs" than to subject its employees on the front line of that war to this invasion of their privacy and affront to their dignity? To be sure, there is only a slight chance that it will prevent some serious public harm resulting from Service employee drug use, but it will show to the world that the Service is "clean," and—most important of all—will demonstrate the determination of the Government to eliminate this scourge of our society! I think it obvious that this justification is unacceptable; that the impairment of individual liberties cannot be the means of making a point; that symbolism, even symbolism for so worthy a cause as the abolition of unlawful drugs, cannot validate an otherwise unreasonable search.

There is irony in the Government's citation, in support of its position, of Justice Brandeis' statement in *Olmstead v. United States* . . . that "[f]or good or for ill, [our Government] teaches the whole people by its example." . . . Brandeis was there dissenting from the Court's admission of evidence obtained through an unlawful Government wiretap. He was not praising the Government's example of vigor and enthusiasm in combatting crime, but condemning its example that "the end justifies the means" . . . An even more apt quotation from that famous Brandeis dissent would have been the following:

> [I]t is . . . immaterial that the intrusion was in aid of law enforcement. Experience should teach us to be most on our guard to protect liberty when the Government's purposes are beneficent. Men born to freedom are naturally alert to repel invasion of their liberty by evil-minded rulers. The greatest dangers to liberty lurk in insidious encroachment by men of zeal, well-meaning but without understanding. . . .

Those who lose because of the lack of understanding that be-got the present exercise in symbolism are not just the Customs Service employees, whose dignity is thus offended, but all of us—who suffer a coarsening of our national manners that ultimately give the Fourth Amendment its content, and who become subject to the administration of federal officials whose respect for our privacy can hardly be greater than the small respect they have been taught to have for their own.

Further Resources

BOOKS

Brisbin, Richard A. *Justice Antonin Scalia and the Conservative Revival.* Baltimore, Md.: Johns Hopkins University Press, 1997.

Gilliom, John. *Surveillance, Privacy, and the Law: Employee Drug Testing and the Politics of Social Control.* Ann Arbor, Mich.: University of Michigan Press, 1994.

Italia, Bob, and Paul J. Deegan. *Anthony Kennedy.* Edina, Minn.: Abdo and Daughters, 1992.

Jussim, Daniel. *Drug Tests and Polygraphs: Essential Tools or Violations of Privacy?* New York: Messner, 1987.

Schultz, David A., and Christopher E. Smith. *The Jurisprudential Vision of Justice Antonin Scalia.* Lanham, Md.: Rowman and Littlefield, 1996.

Yarbrough, Tinsley E. *The Rehnquist Court and the Constitution.* Oxford: Oxford University Press, 2000.

WEBSITES

ACLU's Testimony on Drug Testing in the Workplace. Available online at http://www.cleartest.com/testinfo/aclu_on_drug_testing.htm; website home page: http://www.cleartest.com (accessed February 11, 2003).

Advice and Consent
Memoir

By: Paul Simon

Date: 1992

Source: Simon, Paul. *Advice and Consent: Clarence Thomas, Robert Bork and the Intriguing History of the Supreme Court's Nomination Battles.* Washington, D.C.: National Press Books, 1992, 50–51, 54–56, 57, 58, 59, 61, 65–66, 67–68.

About the Author: Paul Simon (1928–) entered college at age sixteen to study journalism and dropped out of college at nineteen to become an editor-publisher. He created a chain of nineteen newspapers and gained a reputation for exposing vice and corruption. Simon served fourteen years in the Illinois legislature, one term as lieutenant governor of Illinois, eight years in the U.S. House of Representatives, and twelve years in the U.S. Senate. He wrote many books and ran an unsuccessful campaign for the U.S. presidency in 1988. ∎

Introduction

Under the Constitution, the U.S. Senate is given the power to approve or deny appointments to the Supreme Court. The Constitution reads, "and by and with the advice and consent of the Senate, [the President] shall appoint . . . Judges of the Supreme Court." Most Supreme Court nominations have been approved with little controversy, but not all, raising the issue of the balance of power between the presidency and the Senate and

Supreme Court Associate Justice nominee Robert Bork (middle) listens as former President Gerald Ford (left) introduces the nominee to the Senate Judiciary Committee. At right is Senator Robert Dole, who also made a statement on Bork's behalf. **AP/WIDE WORLD PHOTOS. REPRODUCED BY PERMISSION.**

whether "advice and consent" means that the Senate can block a president's nominee because of that nominee's "liberalism" or "conservatism." Louis D. Brandeis, selected by President Wilson (served 1913–1921), was a controversial nominee in 1916 because he was Jewish and progressive. In the 1930s, President Franklin Roosevelt (served 1933–1945), to garner judicial support for his New Deal policies, wanted to appoint up to six new justices in his "court-packing" plan, but the plan was soundly rejected by the Senate. Later, President Richard Nixon (served 1969–1974) encountered difficulties with nominees who were strong defenders of "law and order," and the Senate rejected both Clement Haynesworth and G. Harrold Carswell because of their extremely conservative, pro-segregation views.

President Ronald Reagan (served 1981–1989), also, encountered resistance to some of his Supreme Court nominees. The first to provoke significant debate was William Rehnquist. Questions arose regarding his opinion about the *Brown v. Board of Education* case in 1954.

While the Senate eventually confirmed Rehnquist, it rejected Judge Robert Bork in 1987.

Significance

As Senator Paul Simon notes in *Advice and Consent,* most people perceived Bork as intellectually qualified. Bork was rejected wholly because he was viewed as far too conservative. His conservatism, however, was based not on political affiliation but on his view of the role of a Supreme Court justice in relation to the Constitution.

Throughout American history, it has been the job of the Supreme Court to interpret the Constitution and to apply its somewhat general provisions to new circumstances—circumstances that the nation's founders could not even have imagined. Broadly speaking, justices bring one of two judicial philosophies to the bench. One philosophy is that the Constitution is a flexible document that must be adapted and interpreted to take into account changed circumstances. Thus, for example, the Constitution never specifies anything called a "right to privacy," but in the latter half of the twentieth century, the Supreme Court in effect created such a right in a number of areas such as reproductive rights. Some judicial scholars and judges, however, oppose this view of the jurist's role. They argue that such a view allows judges to, in effect, make law from the bench, thus usurping the constitutional role of Congress. Proponents of this view, often called strict constructionists, maintain that in their rulings the Supreme Court must adhere strictly to what the Constitution says. Thus, if the Constitution does not specify a right to privacy, such a right does not legally exist, and any judicial ruling that relies on such a right is suspect.

The struggle between strict constructionists and those who took a more flexible view of the Constitution was particularly acute from the 1960s into the 1980s. The liberal Warren Court had expanded the interpretation of the Constitution in a number of areas, including civil rights, the rights of accused criminals, and reproductive rights. The more conservative Reagan administration wanted a Supreme Court that would interpret the Constitution more literally. It was in this context that President Reagan nominated Robert Bork, whose nomination touched off a firestorm of controversy. He was perceived, rightly or wrongly, as opposed to civil rights legislation and legislation that strengthened the rights of persons accused of crimes. Feminists were particularly concerned that he would favor overturning *Roe v. Wade*, the landmark case that affirmed a woman's right to abortion. In these and other areas, Bork believed that the courts had overstepped their boundaries and created rights not enumerated in the Constitution or created law that the legislature had not passed.

Primary Source

Advice and Consent [excerpt]

SYNOPSIS: Simon opens by commenting on how important the Bork nomination was and why Bork's views created concerns. He then summarizes Bork's view of the Ninth Amendment, which reserves to the states rights not granted specifically to the federal government. Simon notes how many believed that Bork's appointment would have been a threat to the Constitution and how Bork had opposed civil rights advances. Simon closes by noting the witnesses who opposed and supported Bork, what doomed Bork's nomination, and how President Reagan mishandled the nomination process.

The "swing seat" on the Court often was Justice Powell, and in June 1987, he announced his retirement. Because Chief Justice Burger generally would be labeled a conservative, Burger's replacement by Scalia as a vote on the Court, when Rehn-

quist moved to Chief Justice, did not cause as much concern among many Court observers as the replacement for the Powell seat.

Reagan chose a man long talked about for the Court, a man of unquestioned intellectual skills and long a favorite of the right wing of the Republican Party, Appellate Court Justice Robert Bork. Once a poll-watcher for Socialists, he gradually drifted rightward, delivering literature for Adlai E. Stevenson in 1952 on the Bork trek to the right. In making the announcement the President described Bork as "well prepared, evenhanded and openminded." Although he had been confirmed unanimously for the Appellate Court, his move to the highest court immediately set off fireworks.

Whether in a speech such as one at the University of Michigan questioning whether free speech and freedom of the press have gone too far, or an address at Catholic University suggesting that the Supreme Court had created rights—specifically the right to use contraceptives and the right of a woman to have an abortion—that are not in the Constitution, Bork had stimulated the thinking of his audiences—and he obviously enjoyed that. However, most of us in the Senate knew more by reputation than from reading what he wrote. I had read a little—and like reading William Buckley—found Bork thought-provoking even when I disagreed, though his style is much more ponderous than the Buckley prose.

Robert Bork criticized the "one man, one vote" decision of the Court, as well as civil rights rulings. Sometimes he appeared to make extreme statements either to please the audience or to stimulate discussion. Those talks gave him a following—and led to difficulty. In the *National Catholic Reporter*, Father Robert Drinan, a former U.S. House member and a professor of law at Georgetown University, wrote:

> Bork's anti-civil rights positions are almost unbelievable. He wrote in 1971 that the Supreme Court was wrong in 1948 when it ruled that the 14th amendment forbade state-court enforcement of racially restrictive covenants. . . . Bork has even stated that the Supreme Court's decision in 1966 striking down Virginia's poll tax was "wrongly decided."

One Yale observer called Bork "intensely cynical about the law and the possibility for what it can do"—and that appealed to some and repelled others. One writer commented that Bork's problem was not his conservatism, but that he "looked like a warrior in that cause.". . .

We did not expect him to answer questions on how he might rule on *Roe v. Wade.* A potential Justice properly can decline to answer that direct question, though if the nominee has specific views, they could be disclosed with the cautionary word that a general attitude might not dictate how the nominee would vote on a specific case that would come before the Court. There are critics who say that what Bork said before the nomination and what he has written afterward suggest a clear course of evasion on his part in the hearings.

The question of privacy, however, is beyond dispute a legitimate area of inquiry. Bork's views on the privacy issue concerned some of us, what he called "the general and undefined 'right of privacy' invented in *Griswold v. Connecticut,*" the decision that said a state could not outlaw the use of contraceptives.

While the Constitution does not speak directly of a general right of privacy in Amendments III and IV of the Bill of Rights, it does speak about specific examples of privacy: "No Soldier, shall, in time of peace be quartered in any house, without the consent of the Owner, nor in time of war, but in a manner prescribed by law" (Amendment III). And in the next amendment: "The right of the people to be secure in their persons, houses, papers, and effects, against unreasonable searches and seizures, shall not be violated, and no Warrants shall issue, but upon probable cause, supported by Oath or affirmation, and particularly describing the place to be searched and the persons or things to be seized."

These two amendments speak about specific aspects of privacy. When these are combined with the little noticed but extremely important Ninth Amendment, the spirit of the Constitution is clear. Madison drafted the Ninth Amendment because Alexander Hamilton wrote to him that if he spelled out certain basic rights, there will be some who claim that these are the only rights people have. So the Ninth Amendment became part of the Constitution: "The enumeration of certain rights shall not be construed to deny or disparage others retained by the people." Combine all three amendments, and there is a strong spirit for protecting the privacy of citizens.

The Supreme Court recognized the liberty clause of the Fourteenth Amendment as an additional source of protection for the fundamental right of privacy. The Court relied on the Fourteenth Amendment in *Roe v. Wade,* holding that the right to privacy includes the right of a woman to decide whether or not to have an abortion.

Bork's testimony made clear that the Ninth Amendment is not high on a list of Constitutional amendments that are significant to him. In a 1986 speech about abuses of the Constitution, he mentioned as one abuse that

> a few judges, and even more academics, flirt with the Ninth Amendment as yet another . . . source of substantive rights to be created by the federal judiciary.

In other speeches he referred to the Ninth Amendment as an ink blot or a water blot on the Constitution, a meaningless smudge. When Senator Thurmond asked him, "What do you believe the Ninth Amendment means?" the Judge responded:

> That is an extremely difficult question. . . . I have seen . . . some historical research appearing in the *Virginia Law Review* which suggests . . . that the enumeration of Federal rights in the Bill of Rights shall not be construed to deny or disparage the right retained by the people in their constitutions. And that is the only explanation that has any plausibility to it that I have seen so far.

That is a rigidly narrow interpretation of rights "retained by the people." When witnesses testified that Bork had a limited view of civil liberties and civil rights, the evidence was not only his numerous writings and court decisions, but also testimony before the Committee, particularly as it related to the Ninth Amendment. In response to Senator Kennedy, he also said that "a generalized, undefined right of privacy is not in the Bill of Rights.". . .

All the witnesses praised his ability; that never came into question. But many respected witnesses said approving him would be too great a risk for the nation. Historian John Hope Franklin testified: "There is no indication in his writings, his teachings or his rulings that this nominee has any deeply held commitment to the eradication of the problem of race or even its mitigation. One searches his record in vain to find a civil rights advance that he supported from its inception. Legal scholar John Frank observed:

> Bork is a judicial activist beyond anything Earl Warren ever dreamed of. The differences between Judge Bork and his predecessor Justice Powell, is very dramatic; Justice Powell was a conservative judge who restricted his necessary lawmaking to new situations. Judge Bork . . . makes law as though precedent were meaningless and the Congress were in permanent recess. . . .

But if he had an array of star witnesses opposing him, the nominee also had an array of star supporters, including the former Chief Justice, Warren

Burger, describing him as "well qualified." Lloyd Cutler, Washington attorney and former counsel to President Jimmy Carter, called him "a highly qualified, conservative jurist, who is closer to the moderate center than to the extreme right." Governor James Thompson of Illinois, a former U.S. Attorney, testified for him. Former Attorney General Griffin Bell, who served under President Carter, told the Committee, "I would vote to confirm Judge Bork, and I do so on the view that he is sensitive and he has never taken any right away from anyone.". . .

Bork's pattern of coming out fairly consistently on the side of the financially powerful bothered some of us. Senator Leahy compounded that problem for Bork when he questioned whether he had done any *pro bono* work (free legal service) for those less fortunate, either while in private practice or while teaching at Yale. Bork said, "To tell you the truth, Senator, I was not asked, and I was busy working on other things and I didn't think about it." The American Bar Association's Model Rules of Professional Conduct include this admonition: "A lawyer should render public interest legal service." When my turn came for questioning, I said:

> I was a little surprised to hear your response to Senator Leahy on *pro bono* work. One of the things that is important for a Justice on the Court . . . to have is some understanding of those less fortunate in our society. Are there other things that you have done with the less fortunate in your sixty years . . . helping or volunteering to work with the retarded or whatever it may be?

Bork responded, "No, Senator, I can't claim a record of that sort." . . .

The Judiciary Committee voted 9–5 not to confirm Judge Bork, all Democrats voting no, joined by Senator Specter. Although the hearings started with a majority for him, the vote gradually changed. This shifting of votes is difficult to pinpoint, but after some experience with a legislative body, members and observers develop a sense of what is happening. Two things were clear: Bork portrayed himself as both rigid and professorial—Senators were the students receiving the lectures—and the small signals in comments from the members, both private and public, did not signal a favorable omen. The two factors that tipped the decision for me were his restrictive view of civil liberties and a lack of any empathy for the less fortunate. Before the hearings started, most observers agreed with *Newsweek*: "Bork is likely to be confirmed." What changed the Committee vote was not a mail or media campaign,

nor even the testimony of other witnesses, but the testimony of the nominee himself. . . .

On October 23rd the Senate voted: all one hundred Senators were present. Judge Bork lost, 58–42, the largest vote against a Supreme Court nominee in history. In the words of Senator Specter, the Senate rejected him "because his views were so extreme." Six Republicans voted with an almost solid group of Democrats. Two Democrats, Senator Ernest Hollings of South Carolina and Senator David Boren of Oklahoma, voted for Bork. The attempt to sell the nominee as a moderate, similar to the retiring Justice Powell, simply did not wash. . . .

Bork lost in the Senate, yet even those of us who voted against confirmation came away with respect for him. Most Senators at least partially agree with the writer who commented:

> Few compare in the seriousness of their lifelong engagement with the fundamental questions of constitutional law . . . It is a tragedy that the Republic should repay him for his decades of service by publicly humiliating him.

I would vote against him—as he would vote against me—because of our differing political philosophies. But he will contribute significantly to the continuing dialogue that is so essential for a free people. . . .

How had Bork become the nominee? Former Senator Howard Baker, highly esteemed on the Washington scene, served as President Reagan's chief-of-staff after Donald Regan had been fired, with a not co-gentle nudge from Nancy Reagan and others. Baker and the President had their regular 9:00 a.m. meeting to talk over the day's events and other matters, a meeting not to be interrupted except for an emergency. A message came that the Chief Justice was on the phone for the President. Reagan asked Baker to take the call, and they learned that Justice Powell had submitted his resignation. The President asked for a list of possible nominees. Baker, Attorney General Edwin Meese, and White House Counsel A. B. Culvahouse prepared a list of five names and gave it to the President. The four of them discussed the names, with Meese pushing Bork, and Baker having another choice. "Meese at no time strong-armed the President on this as some accounts have charged," Baker said. Baker went on to the Senate and talked to Senators Biden, Thurmond, Bob Dole of Kansas and Robert Byrd of West Virginia. He mentioned they were in the process of selecting a nominee but took great pains to be discreet so that names would not appear in the newspapers. He did drop the names of two or three possibilities. Baker's recollection is that Biden indicated storm signals for Bork.

Senator Biden, in Chicago in the midst of his campaign for the 1988 Democratic presidential nomination, received a phone call from the White House that the President wanted to see him. Biden had to be in Houston that evening for a televised debate. He flew to Washington to meet with Reagan, who showed him a list of five possible nominees, to get Biden's advice. Without committing himself, Biden gave an analysis of various possibilities. One name on the list, Robert Bork, caused Biden to tell the President, "If you nominate him, you'll have trouble on your hands." Biden flew immediately to Houston, and when he arrived, found himself surrounded by reporters who wanted to know what he thought of the Bork nomination. The President had "consulted," but obviously had determined his course before talking to Biden, hoping to appear to follow the "advice" part of the Constitution by talking to Biden.

When the President decided on Bork, the White House went all out for the nominee. Baker's analysis of what had happened: "Bork was brilliant, but he turned off the Committee."

Having learned his lesson with Bork's loss, when the next vacancy occurred, the President genuinely consulted with Biden and showed him a list that included David Souter and Anthony Kennedy. Without committing himself, Biden indicated to the President that he felt Kennedy would be approved by the Senate, as he was.

When Bush became President, even a gesture toward consulting with the Senate ended.

Further Resources

BOOKS

Bork, Robert H. *The Tempting of America: The Political Seduction of the Law.* New York: Free Press, 1990.

Bronner, Ethan. *Battle for Justice: How the Bork Nomination Shook America.* New York: W.W. Norton, 1989.

Gitenstein, Mark. *Matters of Principle: An Insider's Account of America's Rejection of Robert Bork's Nomination to the Supreme Court.* New York: Simon and Schuster, 1992.

Mersky, Roy M., J. Myron Jacobstein, and Robert H. Bork. *The Supreme Court of the United States: Hearings and Reports on Successful and Unsuccessful Nominations of Supreme Court Justices by the Senate Judiciary Committee, 1916–1987: Robert H. Bork.* Buffalo, N.Y.: W.S. Hein, 1990.

Witt, Elder. *A Different Justice: Reagan and the Supreme Court.* Washington, D.C.: Congressional Quarterly, 1986.

WEBSITES

Ideology in Judicial Nominations. Available online at http://judiciary.senate.gov/oldsite/te062601cs.htm; website home page: http://judiciary.senate.gov (accessed February 11, 2003).

7

LIFESTYLES AND SOCIAL TRENDS

TIMOTHY G. BORDEN

Entries are arranged in chronological order by date of primary source. For entries with one primary source, the entry title is the same as the primary source title. Entries with more than one primary source have an overall entry title, followed by the titles of the primary sources.

Important Events in Lifestyles and Social Trends, 1980–1989

1980

- A survey finds that although smoking has dropped among men, women, and teenage boys during the last ten years, smoking among teenage girls has increased by more than 50 percent.

- Rum outsells vodka in the United States and outsells whiskey for the first time since the nineteenth century.

- Opposition to President Jimmy Carter grows as inflation continues to rise. Ronald Reagan wins the presidential and vice-presidential election on November 4 after basing his campaign on supply-side economics and a promise to reduce the size of government.

- On January 4, Bert Parks is relieved of his duties as master of ceremonies for the Miss America pageant after twenty-five years.

- On February 4, a Census Bureau study estimates that there are between 3.5 million and 4 million illegal aliens living in the United States.

- On March 1, more than a thousand people attend a national Conference on a Black Agenda for the 1980s in Richmond, Virginia, and call for the election of more African American public officials.

- From May 17 to 19, rioting occurs in African American neighborhoods in Miami after an all-white jury acquits four police officers who had been charged with beating an African American insurance executive to death. In the wake of the rioting Miami is declared a disaster area.

- On June 27, President Carter signs a law requiring males between the ages of eighteen and twenty to register for the military draft. No reinstatement of the draft is anticipated however.

- On July 22, racial strife erupts in Chattanooga, Tennessee, after two Ku Klux Klansmen are acquitted in the random shootings of four African American women.

- On November 21, an estimated 83 million Americans—the largest audience for a television series episode in history—tune in to the CBS prime-time soap opera *Dallas* to find out the answer to the question "Who Shot J.R.?"

1981

- AIDS (acquired immunodeficiency syndrome) begins to take a worldwide toll and is found to be more widely spread among homosexual males and drug addicts who share needles.

- Kellogg introduces Nutri-Grain wheat cereal, one of its many healthy breakfast foods to be marketed during the decade. Later introductions include Just Right (1987) and Common Sense Oat Bran (1988).

- The 6.2 million cars built during the year mark a twenty-year low in American auto production.

- A record 1.2 million divorces are granted during the year.

- On January 30, millions of New Yorkers attend a ticker-tape parade to honor the American hostages released by Iran.

- On February 23, the 1980 U.S. Census Bureau reports that the African American and Hispanic population grew at a faster rate than the overall U.S. population during the 1970s.

- On May 23, the Census Bureau reports that the number of Americans older than sixty-five grew by 28 percent compared to an 11 percent general population growth during the 1970s.

- On August 4, the first Mexican-American is elected mayor of a major city when Henry Cisneros becomes mayor of San Antonio.

- On August 22, the Kinsey Institute releases a major study announcing that homosexuality is a deep-rooted predisposition, perhaps inborn.

- On September 1, a study released by the Equal Employment Opportunity Commission finds that women's earnings remain about 60 percent of men's earnings in comparable jobs.

- On September 21, appointed by President Reagan, Sandra Day O'Connor is the first woman confirmed to the U.S. Supreme Court.

1982

- Reebok aerobic shoes, introduced in fashion colors, overtake Nike running shoes in sales.

- Rubik's Cube, a puzzle for which the solution proves frustrating and even obsessive for many, sells wildly in the United States and in other countries.

- Unemployment reaches its highest rate in more than forty years, and the number of Americans living below the poverty line is the highest in seventeen years.

- On January 5, a federal court strikes down an Arkansas law mandating that creation science, a theory of creation based on the Bible, be taught in all public schools. The court rules that the law violated the constitutionally-required separation of church and state.

- On March 15, the city of Kennesaw, Georgia, passes an ordinance that requires the head of every household to "maintain a firearm and ammunition."

- On June 12, a peace rally in New York City that coincides with a United Nations special session on disarmament draws between 500,000 and 750,000 participants.

- On June 15, the Supreme Court rules that the children of illegal aliens have a right to a free public school education.

- On June 30, the Equal Rights Amendment misses the deadline for ratification after it fails to get the support of three more states; thirty-five state legislatures had already voted in favor of the amendment.

- On October 5, after seven people die in the Chicago area in late September from taking Extra-Strength Tylenol capsules laced with cyanide, Johnson & Johnson recalls the product. Tylenol is reintroduced in triple-safety-sealed packages and within a year regains most of its consumer sales.

- On October 14, President Reagan announces a war on drugs. A report estimates that more than 25 million Americans smoke marijuana, spending about $24 billion on the substance.

- On November 13, in Washington, D.C., 150,000 observers witness the dedication of the Vietnam Veterans Memorial.

1983

- More than 4.1 million videocassette recorders (VCRs) are sold this year. The number of cable TV subscribers reaches 25 million, and cable viewers comprise 16 percent of the prime time audience. These events signal major changes in television viewing habits.

- First Lady Nancy Reagan begins a nationwide program to combat drug abuse and uses the slogan "Just Say No."

- U.S. soft-drink companies begin using NutraSweet artificial sweetener in diet beverages.

- On January 1, the Census Bureau reports that the U.S. population numbers well over 200 million at the start of the new year.

- On February 24, a congressional committee concludes that the World War II internment of more than one hundred thousand Japanese Americans was an injustice caused by a "long and ugly history of racism" and "failure of political leadership."

- On June 15, in three decisions, the U.S. Supreme Court limits the power of state and local governments to restrict access to legal abortions.

- On August 21, a group of Milwaukee youths break into some sixty computers around the country. Among the computers they "hack" are those of the Los Alamos National Laboratory, the nation's top nuclear science facility.

- On September 17, New York's Vanessa Williams becomes the first African American to win the title of Miss America.

- On October 17, *The New York Times* announces that the video-game craze of the early 1980s is over.

- On November 2, a federal holiday to honor slain civil rights leader Dr. Martin Luther King, Jr., is created. King's birthday will be observed on the third Monday of January. His is the first such holiday created since George Washington's birthday was made a federal holiday.

- In November, Cabbage Patch Kids are the year's must-have Christmas toys, prompting long lines and short tempers at stores around the country.

- In December, after the Federal Communications Commission (FCC) authorizes placement of low-power transmitters throughout the city, Chicago motorists talk on cellular telephones available for $3,000 plus $150-per-month service fees.

1984

- U.S. economic growth rises to a rate of 6.8 percent, the highest rate since 1951. Despite this growth, however, seventy-nine banks fail during the year, the most since 1938. The FDIC keeps watch on another 817 that are in danger of failing.

- According to a Gallup Poll, swimming, bicycling, and fishing are the most popular activities of adult Americans.

- More than 450,000 people are in prison in the United States, more than double the number in 1974.

- The board game Trivial Pursuit is introduced into U.S. stores by a Canadian entrepreneur and revitalizes the board-game industry.

- On January 17, the U.S. Commission on Civil Rights renounces the use of numerical quotas for promotion of African American workers and executives, releasing a statement saying that "such racial preferences merely constitute another form of unjustified discrimination" that "offends the constitutional principle of equal protection of the law for all citizens."

- On March 15, a jury awards a woman $390,000 when she sues a Church of Christ congregation that publicly condemned her for the sin of "fornication."

- On April 7, Los Angeles surpasses Chicago as the second most populous city in the United States. New York City remains first.

- On April 9, San Francisco public-health director Mervyn Silverman announces a controversial plan to curb sexual activity in the city's bath houses, which are popular meeting places for homosexuals.

- On April 16, a two-year study of religious television reports that more than 13 million Americans watch religious television programming on a regular basis.

- On May 1, a report by the Department of Housing and Urban Development estimates the nation's homeless population as numbering between 250,000 and 350,000. Many other national organizations claim that there are actually ten times that many homeless Americans.

- On May 10, the United Methodist Church passes legislation barring homosexuals from the ministry.

- On June 7, the House of Representatives passes legislation to cut federal highway funds to any state with an alcoholic beverage drinking age below twenty-one.

- On July 11, the Olympic committees of six Asian and African nations report that their athletes received death threats from the Ku Klux Klan in the United States. The Summer Olympic Games open in Los Angeles on July 28.

- On July 20, Geraldine Ferraro becomes the first woman on the presidential ticket of a major political party when she is named the Democrats' candidate for vice president.

- On August 17, the U.S. Court of Appeals holds that "private, consensual homosexual conduct is not constitutionally protected," thus affirming the U.S. Navy's right to dismiss homosexuals automatically.

- On September 25, Texas billionaire Ross Perot buys a seven-hundred-year-old copy of the Magna Carta—one of only seventeen copies in existence—for $1.5 million and donates it to the National Archives in Washington, D.C.

- On October 11, Brown University undergraduates vote to request that the campus health service "stockpile suicide pills for optional student use exclusively in the event of nuclear war."

- In November, more than 3 million Americans quit smoking in the American Cancer Society's Great American Smokeout.

- On November 22, about one-third of homosexual men in San Francisco respond in a survey that they continue to practice unsafe sex despite the danger of AIDS.

1985

- After noting that more than 80 percent of athletic shoes are bought for fashionable attire as opposed to strict athletic use, Robert Greenberg closes his L.A. Gear athletic apparel store and begins importing Korean-made fashion sneakers to sell under the L.A. Gear name.

- The demand for compact discs and CD players far exceeds the supply, giving credence to earlier predictions that this technology would replace records and audio tapes. People are buying books on tape, however, and enjoying literature while driving to work.

- Purchases of VCRs continue to climb, while the sale of movie tickets drops 7 percent.

- Crack—crystallized cocaine that can be smoked to produce a short but intense high—is introduced into the United States. Abuse of the drug is blamed for criminal and violent offenses, especially in urban areas, during the next years.

- A congressional investigation finds that over 500,000 persons have false degrees or other credentials in professions and fields ranging from architecture to medicine to zoology.

- On January 22, President Reagan speaks to antiabortion marchers in Washington, D.C., telling them, "I feel a great solidarity with all of you."

- On February 15, according to an Electronic Industries Association report, 98 percent of U.S. households have at least one television, 24 percent have video games, and 13 percent have videocassette recorders.

- On February 26, a panel of doctors and public-health officials concludes that hunger has reached epidemic proportions in the United States. Twenty million Americans go hungry at least two days a month, and the problem is worsening because of cuts in federal food programs.

- On April 23, Coca-Cola announces that it is replacing its ninety-nine-year-old formula with a sweeter-tasting formula. Protests induce the company into reintroducing the old formula under the name Coca-Cola Classic later in the year.

- On May 15, according to a U.S. Census Bureau report, a March 1984 survey finds that one-fourth of all U.S. families with children have only one parent present.

- On June 4, the U.S. Supreme Court affirms a federal appellate ruling against an Alabama law authorizing a one-minute period of silence in public schools "for meditation or voluntary prayer."

- On August 2, retail giant Montgomery Ward announces that it will cease its mail-order catalog business, the first in the nation, after 113 years. Long an institution on farms and in small towns, the catalog's end reflects the nation's changed demographics.

- On August 5, the Recording Industry Association of America announces that nineteen leading record companies will begin using a parental advisory label on popular music albums and cassettes that contain "blatant explicit lyric content."

- On September 9, approximately twelve thousand New York City children are kept home by their parents when the city permits an AIDS-infected seven-year-old girl to attend public-school classes. The school is following guidelines issued on August 29 by the U.S. Centers for Disease Control that "casual person-to-person contact appears to pose no risk" of AIDS infection.

- On October 2, when movie actor Rock Hudson, fifty-nine, dies of AIDS in Beverly Hills, Americans are shocked into an awareness of the disease and its growing number of victims.

- On October 28, in Oregon, U.S. authorities arrest Indian guru Bhagwan Shree Rajneesh, whose wealthy followers have given him funds that he has used to buy a fleet of Rolls-Royce automobiles.

- On November 11, according to the U.S. Centers for Disease Control, 14,739 AIDS cases have been reported in the United States and 7,418 of these patients have died.

- On December 14, Wilma Mankiller is the first woman in history to lead a major American tribe when she is sworn in as principal chief of the Cherokee Nation of Oklahoma, the largest Native American tribe in the United States after the Navajos.

1986

- European immigration is declining. About half of the legal immigrants entering the United States now arrive from Asia.

- After fifty years of popularity, the twin-stick Popsicle becomes a single-stick treat.

- Nintendo video games, featuring high-tech, sophisticated graphics, debut in the United States and reach $300 million in U.S. sales.

- The Census Bureau reports that there are 2.2 million unwed couples in the United States, nearly four times the number in 1970.

- More than sixty thousand U.S. farms are sold or foreclosed as depression continues in the rural West and Midwest.

- On January 3, Rev. Jerry Falwell announces that he is forming a political group to rally support for conservative Christian causes on many domestic and foreign issues.

- On January 23, the National Urban League reports that during 1985 the United States came closer to becoming "permanently divided between the haves and have-nots."

- On February 8, a New York woman dies after ingesting a cyanide-laced Tylenol capsule. Nine days later Johnson & Johnson ends production of nonprescription capsule medicines.

- On February 13, fourteen-year-old Ryan White, who is infected with AIDS, wins a county medical ruling that he poses no health threat to his classmates and should be allowed to attend classes at his middle school in Indiana.

- On March 9, in what is purported to be the largest rally ever staged by the National Organization of Women, abortion rights demonstrators gather in Washington, D.C.

- On May 1, the African American community of Indianola, Mississippi, calls off a five-week boycott of local white-owned businesses after the town's school district board appoints the protesters' candidate as school superintendent.

- On May 25, more than 5 million people form a human chain from New York City to Long Beach, California, in Hands Across America to call attention to poverty, hunger, and homelessness in the United States.

- On July 2, the U.S. Supreme Court upholds affirmative action and the use of numerical quotas as a remedy for past job discrimination.

- On July 3, President Reagan ceremonially relights the torch of the Statue of Liberty to mark the beginning of a four-day international centennial celebration of the newly restored statue.

- On July 8, a Johns Hopkins University study finds that teen participants in an experimental public-school sex-education program that includes free contraceptives and open discussions about sex are more likely to seek contraceptives, less likely to become pregnant, and refrain longer from sex.

- On July 9, the U.S. Attorney General's Commission on Pornography releases a report stating that violent pornography probably leads to sexual violence. The report calls for a crackdown on obscenity by federal, state, and local authorities.

- On July 10, the National Institute on Drug Abuse reports that the number of Americans killed each year in cocaine-related deaths rose from 185 in 1981 to at least 563 in 1985.

- On July 14, reports surface that white supremacists and anti-Semites gathered in Hayden Lake, Idaho, for a two-day meeting of the Aryan Nations World Congress.

- On October 7, President Reagan signs into law a measure designating the rose as the national flower of the United States.

- On November 7, President Reagan signs the Immigration Control and Reform Act, which grants amnesty to immigrants who have resided within U.S. borders since January 1, 1982. The act will expire in 1988.

- On November 14, stock broker Ivan Boesky agrees to pay a $100 million fine for insider trading and to give up his securities license for life. Boesky's troubles presage a series of ethical and criminal scandals that will rock Wall Street in the 1980s and 1990s.

1987

- U.S. sales of microwave ovens reach a record 12.6 million.

- Although sales of compact discs are nearly double those of 1986, at $1.6 billion, they are still dwarfed by cassette tape sales of $2.9 billion. However, sales of record albums decline another 15 percent to $793 million.

- U.S. spending on health care rises almost 10 percent from 1986.

- On February 2, the Children's Defense Fund, a nonprofit Washington, D.C.—based organization, releases a report showing that the U.S. infant mortality rate is one of the highest in the industrialized world.

- On February 10, Surgeon General C. Everett Koop tells a House subcommittee that condom commercials should be allowed on television to fight the AIDS epidemic.

- On March 3, many well-known actors and politicians take part in the "Grate American Sleep Out" by sleeping on heating grates in Washington, D.C., to draw attention to the plight of U.S. homelessness.

- On March 19, PTL televangelist Jim Bakker resigns after his cheating on his wife, Tammy Faye, by having a sexual encounter with church secretary Jessica Hahn is made public. Rev. Jerry Falwell takes over the PTL ministry.

- On March 31, a Bergen County, New Jersey, superior court rules that a surrogate mother contract is "constitutionally protected," awarding custody of "Baby M" to her biological father, William Stern, and terminating all parental rights for surrogate mother Mary Beth Whitehead.

- On May 4, the U.S. Supreme Court rules that Rotary Clubs must admit women.

- On June 7, the Ku Klux Klan stages its first march and rally in Greensboro, North Carolina, since 1979, when five Communist anti-Klan demonstrators were shot to death at a rally.

- On June 19, the Supreme Court rules that the creationist theory of human origins cannot be required teaching in public schools, as it promotes specific religious beliefs. The decision is a setback to fundamentalist Christians, who have long been engaged in a campaign to shape public education to their beliefs.

- In August, *Ebony* magazine reports that the number of middle-class African Americans more than doubled between 1969 and 1984, and that more than one-third of this group has some college education. The report defines "middle class" as Americans with annual incomes between $20,000 and $50,000. About 30 percent of all African American families now fit this category, compared to nearly 50 percent of white families.

- On August 28, a fire suspected as arson destroys the Arcadia, Florida, home of a couple whose three hemophiliac sons carry HIV, the virus that causes AIDS. The boys recently had returned to public school.

- On September 1, Lovastatin, a cholesterol-lowering drug, is approved by the U.S. Food and Drug Administration (FDA). High blood-cholesterol levels have been linked with arterial disease and heart attacks, and an estimated 20 million Americans have cholesterol levels that put them at risk of heart attacks. Previously the U.S. surgeon general warned that obesity also poses a serious health risk to Americans.

- On September 16, the United States joins other nations meeting at Montreal, Canada, to agree on measures to protect the environment, including a gradual ban on chlorofluorocarbons that deplete the earth's ozone layer and increase incidence of skin cancer.

- On October 11, homosexuals and their advocates demonstrate in Washington, D.C., to demand an end to discrimination and more federal funds for AIDS research. Six hundred people are arrested when they try to enter the Supreme Court to protest a sodomy decision.

- On November 7, following a disclosure that he had smoked marijuana in the past, U.S. Appeals Court Judge Douglas H. Ginsburg withdraws as President Reagan's nominee to the U.S. Supreme Court.

- In December, *Time* magazine's Man of the Year is Soviet leader Mikhail S. Gorbachev.

- On December 31, a program to resettle in the United States children fathered by Americans during the Vietnam War is restarted after a two-year suspension. The program began in 1979 and has resettled four thousand Vietnamese American children and their family members. At least ten thousand more are still in Vietnam.

1988

- Bob Barker, longtime host for the Miss USA pageant, resigns his position because one of the prizes included is a mink coat. Barker is a crusader for animal rights.

- Despite the highest number of births in twenty-five years, the nation's population is aging. The Census Bureau reports that the average age of Americans is 32.1 years, the first time it has exceeded 32.

- On February 21, speaking to a crowd of six thousand at his ministry's Family Worship Center in Baton Rouge, Louisiana, televangelist Jimmy Swaggart tearfully confesses to an unspecified sin. Swaggart loses 69 percent of his viewers and is defrocked by the Assemblies of God on April 8 after it is discovered that he has had sex with a prostitute.

- On March 7, the famous sex therapists Masters and Johnson announce at a press conference that the AIDS virus is spreading uncontrollably through the heterosexual population. A wave of panic spreads across the nation.

- In April, U.S. unemployment falls to 5.4 percent, the lowest percentage since 1974.

- On April 23, the airline industry imposes a no-smoking rule on all passenger flights of two hours or less, except for charter flights and flights to foreign destinations. Northwest Airlines announces that it will ban smoking on all its flights.

- On May 4, as the 1986 Immigration Control and Reform Act expires, more than a hundred thousand applicants jam U.S. immigration offices.

- On May 5, Eugene Antonio Marino becomes the first African American Catholic archbishop in the United States when he is installed as head of the Archdiocese of Atlanta.

- On May 23, Maryland becomes the first state to ban the manufacture and sale of so-called "Saturday night specials"—small, cheap handguns that are poorly made and easily concealed. The ban takes effect on January 1, 1990.

- On May 23, the FDA approves cervical cap contraceptives long available in Europe.

- On May 26, the U.S. government begins a nationwide mailout of approximately 114 million copies of an eight-

page brochure on AIDS that has been prepared by Surgeon General C. Everett Koop.

- On June 15, the Census Bureau reports that for the first time more than half of all working new mothers are remaining in the job market. Nearly two-thirds of new mothers with college degrees continue to work, compared to 38 percent of those with a high school education. The difference is attributed to the belief that since women in the former group have more education and more work experience before becoming mothers, they are better able to afford child care.

- On June 20, the Supreme Court upholds a New York City law that requires women be permitted to join large, private clubs that play important roles in professional and business life. Old, exclusive men's clubs across the country begin to admit women.

- On July 31, the last Playboy Club, in Lansing, Michigan, closes. The first club opened in Chicago in 1960, and by 1972 there were twenty-two Playboy Clubs across the nation. Featuring pretty young waitresses in skimpy costumes with bunny ears and tails, the clubs were very risqué at the time. However, attendance had fallen off sharply in recent years.

- On August 12, the movie *The Last Temptation of Christ,* based on the novel by Nikos Kazantzakis, which traces the life of a more human, less godlike Jesus plagued by fears and desires, opens to street protests in seven U.S. cities.

- On September 6, the Census Bureau reports that the nation's Hispanic population has grown 34 percent since 1980 and now totals 8.1 percent of the total population. More than half of Hispanic Americans live in Texas and California.

- On September 20, President Reagan names Lauro Cavazos as secretary of education and the first Hispanic Cabinet member in history.

- On December 24, a Gallup Poll report finds that 56 percent of Americans are content with "the way things are going" in the nation, despite the problems of homelessness, drugs, AIDS, and the rising cost of living.

1989

- The government reports that despite the much-publicized War on Drugs, 14.5 million Americans use illegal drugs at least once a month.

- Americans' donations to charitable causes have increased 173 percent since 1950

- On average, one of every forty-two automobiles is stolen or broken into during the year.

- The Roman Catholic Church continues to be the nation's largest religious denomination, with the Southern Baptists second, and the United Methodist Church third.

- On January 23, the U.S. Supreme Court invalidates a Richmond, Virginia, program requiring that 30 percent of the city's public works funds be set aside for minority-owned construction firms; the court calls it reverse discrimination.

- On March 8, a *Harvard Business Review* article sparks controversy by proposing that women in managerial positions must choose between a "career-primary" and a "career-and-family" (or "mommy track") career path.

- On January 31, the Educational Testing Services reports that American thirteen-year-olds rank last in math and science competency when compared with South Korean, British, Irish, Spanish, and Canadian students of the same age.

- On April 9, some 450,000 demonstrate in Washington, D.C., in support of a woman's right to have an abortion.

- In June, the FDA departs from its usual practice and announces that doctors will be allowed to prescribe the experimental anti-AIDS drug DDI while it is still being tested. The policy decision follows reports of nearly 106,000 AIDS cases in the United States, of which 61,000 have already died, and predictions of as many as 200,000 new cases by 1992.

- On June 21, the U.S. Supreme Court rules, 5-4, that burning the U.S. flag in public is a right protected by the First Amendment. President Bush asks for a constitutional amendment to prohibit flag-burning.

- On July 3, the U.S. Supreme Court upholds a Missouri abortion law when it rules, 5-4, that states can limit access to abortion.

- On August 23, racial tensions are inflamed throughout New York City when an African American teen is fatally shot after he and three African American friends respond to a used-car advertisement in a Brooklyn neighborhood and are attacked by seven white youths.

- On August 30, millionaire New York hotel owner Leona Helmsley, sixty-nine, is convicted on thirty-three counts of income tax evasion and massive tax fraud and is sentenced to four years in prison and fined $7.1 million. A former housekeeper has testified that Mrs. Helmsley told her, "Only the little people pay taxes."

- On October 17, registering 7.1 on the Richter scale, the most destructive earthquake in North America since 1906 hits San Francisco, buckling highways and the Bay Bridge, killing at least ninety people, and causing an estimated $6 billion in property damage.

- On November 17, President Bush signs a law raising the minimum wage from $3.35 an hour to $3.80 effective April 1, 1990, and to $4.25 the following year.

- On November 20, genetic tests show that ten-year-old Kimberly Michelle Mays is the biological daughter of Ernest and Regina Twigg, who maintain that the girl was switched at birth for a baby whom they raised as their own until the child died the previous year.

Jane Fonda's Workout Book
| Handbook

By: Jane Fonda

Date: 1981

Source: Fonda, Jane. *Jane Fonda's Workout Book.* New York: Simon and Schuster, 1981, 9–10, 35, 67–68.

About the Author: Jane Fonda (1937–), the daughter of actor Henry Fonda, grew up in California and New York. Gaining fame in a series of light comedies in the 1960s, Fonda eventually was acclaimed as one of the greatest actresses of her generation with Academy Award-winning roles in *Klute* (1971) and *Coming Home* (1978). She also provoked measures of admiration and criticism for her role in the anti-war movement, including a controversial trip to North Vietnam to protest America's involvement in Southeast Asia. In 1979 Fonda established the first of her Workout studios in Los Angeles; the publication of *Jane Fonda's Workout Book* followed in 1981. The book sold more than two million copies, and an accompanying record album, released in 1982, sold two million more copies. Fonda remained one of Hollywood's leading actresses until announcing her retirement upon her marriage to media mogul Ted Turner in 1991, her third marriage. Fonda separated from Turner in 2000. ■

Introduction

Like many American women, Jane Fonda absorbed the standard ideals of femininity while she was growing up—especially the desire to be thin. Embarking on a series of crash diets and using potentially dangerous diet drugs throughout her young adulthood, Fonda developed eating disorders that took years to overcome. Debuting as a stage and movie actress in the late 1950s and working as a model to make ends meet, Fonda also felt career pressures to stay thin for the camera and her costumes. Even after a string of commercial and critical successes in the 1960s and 1970s, Fonda battled a poor self-image and destructive eating habits that kept her thin, yet came close to ruining her health. Gradually, Fonda was able to overcome her bulimia and incorporate a more sensible, long-range fitness plan that included better eating habits and regular exercise. A fan of aerobics, the entrepreneurial Fonda opened up three Workout centers in California by 1979. Soon she was known as much for her call

to "go for the burn" as she was for her Academy Award-winning movies or her peace activism.

Fonda was far from alone in cashing in on the fitness craze in the 1980s. Phil Knight, the co-founder of the Nike Corporation, leaped onto the list of wealthiest Americans based on his ownership of an athletic shoe and sportswear empire. Knight and track coach Bill Bowerman had pioneered technologically advanced running shoes in the early 1970s, at the start of the jogging and fitness boom, and by the end of the decade the Nike brand was the country's most popular running shoe. In the 1980s the company branched out to sell a particular shoe for every sport and signed multi-million-dollar contracts with professional athletes to promote the brand. Its most lucrative endorsement made Air Jordans, worn by Chicago Bulls basketball star Michael Jordan, into one of the most sought-after items of clothing around the world. By the end of the 1980s, with its ubiquitous advertising campaigns featuring baseball and football star Bo Jackson under the tag line "Bo Knows," and its perennial slogan, "Just Do It," Nike reached annual revenues exceeding $1 billion.

Significance

The fitness craze seemed everywhere in the 1980s, from Olivia Newton-John's song "Physical," which spent ten weeks as the country's number-one single in 1981–1982, to the John Travolta movie *Perfect,* in which he played a reporter writing about health clubs, to the never-ending stream of television and print ads for Nike, Reebok, and Adidas. Whereas the bestseller lists in the 1970s were dominated by books about sex and relationships, the 1980s' lists were topped by exercise, diet, and fitness guides.

In light of the commercial extremes that the fitness industry spawned, some social critics viewed the fitness obsession of the 1980s as another example of yuppie indulgence by baby boomers who had lots of money to spend on expensive health club memberships, personal trainers, fitness guides, exercise gear, and specialized clothing for specific activities. The sporting goods industry, which had revenues of $17 billion in 1980, was a $45 billion industry by 1989. For those who were less active but still interested in sports, about $50 billion was spent on tickets to major-league sports and other sports-related entertainments in 1988 alone.

Ironically, just as their interest in sports and fitness soared, Americans became less physically fit than ever before in the 1980s. As television viewing increased and more people spent time sitting in front of computers, a more sedentary lifestyle took hold of many Americans. Pressed for time, more people ate their meals at fast-food restaurants such as McDonald's, Burger King, and Wendy's, which competed for customers by offering "super-sized" meals loaded with more calories, fat, and salt. By the 1990s approximately sixty percent of Americans were overweight and twenty percent were classified as "obese," which meant that their health was seriously compromised by their excess weight. Part of the trend toward being less physically fit, of course, was explained by simple demographic trends: as baby boomers aged into their forties and fifties, they inevitably had a harder time maintaining their sleek, aerobicized look. Even Jane Fonda admitted in an interview with Barbara Walters in 2002 that she no longer worked out, but relied on a sensible diet and her "good genes" to keep her physically fit.

Primary Source

Jane Fonda's Workout Book [excerpt]

SYNOPSIS: A mixture of personal anecdotes, diet guidelines, and exercise programs, *Jane Fonda's Workout Book* was the best-selling nonfiction book in 1982, when four of the top ten bestsellers were diet-and-exercise books. The success of the volume spawned a fitness empire for Fonda, who released several more albums, videos, and books in the 1980s, along with a line of exercise clothing. In these excerpts, Fonda recounts her own difficulties in establishing healthy diet and exercise habits and urges the reader to "go for the burn" by sticking to a regular fitness routine.

Like a great many women, I am a product of a culture that says thin is better, blond is beautiful and buxom is best.

From as early as I can remember, my mother, her friends, my grandmother, governesses, my sister—all the women who surrounded me—talked anxiously about the pros and cons of their physiques. Hefty thighs, small breasts, a biggish bottom—there was always some perceived imperfection to focus anxieties on. None of them seemed happy the way they were, which bewildered me because the way they were seemed fine to my young eyes.

In pursuit of the "feminine ideal"—exemplified by voluptuous film stars and skinny fashion models—women, it seemed, were even prepared to do violence to themselves. My mother, for example, who was a rather slender, beautiful woman, was terrified of getting fat. She once said that if she ever gained weight she'd have the excess flesh cut off! I remember a friend of hers talking about being injected with the urine of pregnant cows, which was reputed to make fat dissolve.

Maybe I simply wasn't privy to their more intimate conversations, but I don't remember the men

The cover of *Jane Fonda's Workout Book* by Jane Fonda. SCHAPIRO, STEVE, PHOTOGRAPHER. COVER OF *JANE FONDA'S WORKOUT BOOK*. SIMON & SCHUSTER. REPRODUCED BY PERMISSION OF THE PHOTOGRAPHER.

in my life being as concerned about how they looked. Not with the same angst at any rate. If anything, they seemed more interested in performance: making the team, doing the job, being brave. The message that came across was clear: men were judged by their accomplishments, women by their looks.

Like many young girls, I internalized this message and, in an effort to conform to the sought-after female image, I abused my health, starved my body, and ingested heaven-knows-what chemical drugs. I understood very little about how my body functioned, and what it needed to be healthy and strong. I depended on doctors to cure me, but I never relied on myself to stay well.

It wasn't until I was thirty, and pregnant for the first time, that I began to change the way I treated myself. As the baby grew inside me, I began to realize my body needed to be listened to and strengthened, not ignored and weakened. I discovered that with common sense, a bit of studying and a good deal of commitment, I could create for myself a new approach to health and beauty; an approach which would not only make me look better, but would enable me to handle the intense, multifaceted life I live with more clarity and balance, to say nothing of more energy and endurance.

I decided to write this book, not because I consider myself an expert in the pedigreed sense, but because I want to share what I've had to learn the hard way with other women. I only wish someone had shared these things with me earlier in my life. That's why I've dedicated this book to my daughter.

Seven Guidelines for a Healthy Diet

1. Substitute low-fat foods for high-fat foods
2. Cut down on meat—eat low on the food chain
3. Avoid salt and salty foods
4. Cut down on sugar
5. Emphasize whole grains
6. Beware of alcohol
7. Emphasize the Healthy Five: Raw unsalted nuts and sesame seeds, sprouted seeds such as soybeans, fresh raw wheat bran and wheat germ, yogurt and kefir, fresh fruits and vegetables

My Workout Program

The exercises that follow are basically the ones I do myself. I did not invent them, but I have worked with them, modified them and placed them in a sequence that works for me and for the people who come to my Workout Studios. They are designed to build strength, develop flexibility and increase endurance. And there is no question that this exercise program can alter the shape of your body, burn away those fatty deposits and develop muscle tone where you never knew you could have any. It will make you feel good, physically and psychologically. But you must commit yourself to regular, vigorous exercise, eat properly and get enough sleep.

The exercises are carefully structured to use each part of the body in a specific sequence. You may be tempted to go straight to the ones that attack your trouble spots. This is all right once in a great while when you are short of time, but it is really missing the point of the workout. An effective workout requires the vigorous and sustained use of your entire body for at least 20 to 40 minutes. This will not only tone muscles in a specific area, but burn up calories, improve your circulation, eliminate toxins, and strengthen your heart and lungs.

The basis of the Workout is the repetition of certain movements that use a single muscle group against the resistance of your own body weight. We work each muscle group to its maximum. The repetitions are followed by stretches to develop flexibility and to keep your muscles long. The stretches are every bit as important as the repetitions.

The Burn

From this point on, I will often mention the "burn" and exhort you to "go for the burn." This burn is a unique sensation that you get when you have used a muscle very strenuously. You feel the burn and you find that you have difficulty contracting that muscle for a moment. Newcomers to exercise often worry about it, but don't be concerned; it is simply a sign that you are exercising that particular muscle vigorously and effectively, working hard and deep.

The burn is the result of a chemical reaction in your body. During the normal metabolic process, the carbohydrate fuel in your muscle is converted to a chemical known as pyruvate. Pyruvate combines with oxygen and then the combination breaks down into carbon dioxide and water which is carried away in the blood and expelled from the body as waste gases.

If there is not enough oxygen available to combine with the pyruvate, the pyruvate turns into lactic acid, which is a toxin. The build-up of lactic acid is what causes the burning sensation and impedes muscle contraction.

There is absolutely nothing harmful or dangerous about it. It just slows you down until the oxygen supply is replenished, which is a matter of seconds. Once there is enough oxygen again, the lactic acid converts back into pyruvate.

If you are very fit, you will be able to exercise longer before you feel that burn than someone who is out of shape. When I first did the buttocks exercise described on pages 124–126, my muscles burned so much I had to stop three or four times during the exercise. Now the burn comes later and I don't have to stop. I've even come to look forward to it. It lets me know that I'm really working hard.

Further Resources
BOOKS

Andersen, Christopher P. *Citizen Jane: The Turbulent Life of Jane Fonda.* New York: Holt, 1990.

Collier, Peter. *The Fondas: A Hollywood Dynasty.* New York: Putnam, 1991.

Critser, Greg. *Fat Land: How Americans Became the Fattest People in the World.* Boston: Houghton Mifflin, 2003.

Katz, Donald R. *Just Do It: The Nike Spirit in the Corporate World.* New York: Random House, 1994.

WEBSITES

Krentzman, Jackie. "Phil Knight: The Force Behind the Nike Empire." Available online at http://www.stanfordalumni.org /news/magazine/1997/janfeb/articles/knight.html; website home page: http://www.stanfordalumni.org/news/magazine /home.html (accessed March 27, 2003).

"A Voice of Her Own: Barbara Walters Interviews Jane Fonda." ABCNews.com. Available online at http://more.abcnews.go .com/sections/2020/dailynews/2020_010202_fonda.html; website home page: http://abcnews.go.com/ (accessed March 27, 2003).

AUDIO AND VISUAL MEDIA

Jane Fonda: A New Workout. Original release, 1985. A Vision. VHS, 1997. A Vision Video.

Jane Fonda Workout Album. Columbia Records, 1982.

Perfect. Original release, 1985. Columbia/Tristar. Directed by James Bridges. VHS, 1997. Columbia/Tristar Video.

Megatrends: Ten New Directions Transforming Our Lives

Nonfiction work

By: John Naisbitt

Date: 1982

Source: Naisbitt, John. *Megatrends: Ten New Directions Transforming Our Lives.* New York: Warner Books, 1982, 249–250, 251, 252.

About the Author: John Naisbitt (1929–) was born in in Salt Lake City and graduated from the University of Utah. He worked at IBM and Eastman Kodak before becoming a business consultant in the 1970s. His company, the Naisbitt Group, gathered information from hundreds of daily newspapers to formulate predictions on emerging social trends, a practice known as content analysis. Billing himself as "the world's leading futurist" and "the global philosopher among futurists," Naisbitt built a multimedia empire in the 1980s based on his best-selling books, seminars, and frequent talk-show appearances. Although criticized by social scientists as more of a public relations survey than a rigorous study of American society, Naisbitt's methods formed the basis of much of his later work, including his 1982 bestseller, *Megatrends.* ∎

Introduction

The digital electronic computer age began with the ENIAC (electronic numerical integrator and computer), a thirty-ton device with 17,468 electronic vacuum tubes built at the University of Pennsylvania between 1943 and 1946. Commissioned by the U.S. War Department to calculate weapons trajectories, the ENIAC could perform 5,000 additions and 300 multiplications per second, reducing a task that took humans twenty hours and the then-most advanced calculators fifteen minutes down to thirty seconds. At the conclusion of World War II (1939–1945), various private companies entered the field of super-computing, but given the size and expense of the computers, their use was limited to only the largest companies and government agencies such as the Census Bureau.

Through technological advances that made the use of bulky and hot vacuum tubes unnecessary, the size and cost of computers gradually declined in the 1960s and 1970s. Seeing opportunities to make computers and programs that would perform a wider array of functions, many entrepreneurs started their own companies in anticipation of demand for personal and office computers in the 1970s. In 1975 Harvard University dropout Bill Gates founded Microsoft with his childhood friend, Paul Allen, to write software programs to serve as a platform for the new personal computer. In 1976 Steve Jobs and Steve Wozniak founded Apple Computing as a company that produced its own software operating system and its own line of personal computers.

With its line of desktop computers that boasted easy-to-use interfaces and reliable operating systems, Apple set the standard for personal computers throughout much of the 1980s. Because Microsoft licensed its software to numerous computer manufacturers, however, its operating system eventually became the prevalent one in the personal computer field. Apple's shortsightedness in retaining the rights to its operating system caused it to lose much of its market share in the 1990s, while Microsoft became so dominant that it faced charges of monopolizing the software market by the U.S. Justice Department.

Significance

As the personal computer came onto the consumer market in the late 1970s, many social observers predicted that it would transform American society. Commentators such as George Gilder and John Naisbitt foresaw the computer as the vanguard of a social and economic revolution in which America would be liberated from its industrial, insular, and hierarchical past. The future of the country in the "information age" would encourage participatory democracy, self-fulfillment, and international engagement.

The American public embraced the personal computer as avidly as any of the pundits. By 1984 the personal computer was in 8.2 percent of American homes and 18.3 percent of Americans used a computer at home, work, or school. In 1989 personal computer ownership jumped to fifteen percent, a figure that increased to 36.6

Bill Gates, co-founder and head of computer software company Microsoft, works in a computer lab at Microsoft headquarters in 1983. © DOUG WILSON/CORBIS. REPRODUCED BY PERMISSION.

percent in 1997. At work, home, or school, 47.1 percent of Americans used a computer in 1997 and 22.2 percent had access to the Internet. The popularity of the personal computer made media celebrities out of Gates, Jobs, and Wozniak and turned Gates into a billionaire, with a net worth of $1.2 billion by 1987.

For all of the talk about an information age revolution, however, the pundits' predictions proved somewhat optimistic. Although Microsoft, Apple, and some of the other software and computer companies gained a reputation for progressive employment policies, including stock options, profit sharing, and a host of company benefits, the widespread use of computers in America after the 1970s did not make the work place noticeably less hierarchical and more democratic and decentralized. The use of computers contributed to impressive gains in workforce productivity in the 1980s—output per hour from 1981–1989 increased by 1.8 percent annually in the business sector and by 3.8 percent annually in the manufacturing sector—but these gains did not translate, for the most part, into wage or benefits increases for workers. Between 1979–1987 investors more than doubled their incomes, as measured in comparison with the consumer price index, and corporate executives gained about fifty percent. During the same period, American workers lost more than five percent of their income.

Primary Source

Megatrends: Ten New Directions Transforming Our Lives [excerpt]

SYNOPSIS: In these excerpts Naisbitt offers an optimistic reading on the transformation of the American economy from an industrial base to a service-oriented one. In Naisbitt's analysis, the new economy will be more international in nature, technology-intensive, and more egalitarian through its decentralization and less hierarchical structure. Although few of Naisbitt's predictions came true, *Megatrends* ranked as the second best-selling nonfiction book of 1983 and he followed it with numerous works in a similar vein.

We are living in the *time of the parenthesis,* the time between eras. It is as though we have bracketed off the present from the past and the future, for we are neither here nor there. We have not quite left behind the either/or America of the past—centralized, industrialized, and economically self-contained. With one foot in the old world where we lived mostly in the Northeast, relied on institutional help, built hierarchies, and elected representatives, we approached problems with an eye toward the high-tech, short-term solutions.

But we have not embraced the future either. We have done the human thing: We are clinging to the known past in fear of the unknown future. This book outlines one interpretation of that future in order to make it more real, more knowable. Those who are willing to handle the ambiguity of this in-between period and to anticipate the new era will be a quantum leap ahead of those who hold on to the past. The time of the parenthesis is a time of change and questioning.

As we move from an industrial to an information society, we will use our brainpower to create instead of our physical power, and the technology of the day will extend and enhance our mental ability. As we take advantage of the opportunity for job growth and investment in all the sunrise industries, we must not lose sight of the need to balance the human element in the face of all that technology.

Yet, the most formidable challenge will be to train people to work in the information society. Jobs will become available, but who will possess the high-tech skills to fill them? Not today's graduates who cannot manage simple arithmetic or write basic English. And certainly not the unskilled, unemployed dropouts who cannot even find work in the old sunset industries.

Farmer, laborer, clerk. The next transition may well be to technician. But that is a major jump in skill level. . . .

This newly evolving world will require its own structures. We are beginning to abandon the hierarchies that worked well in the centralized, industrial era. In their place, we are substituting the network model of organization and communication, which has its roots in the natural, egalitarian, and spontaneous formation of groups among like-minded people. Networks restructure the power and communication flow within an organization from vertical to horizontal. One network form, the quality control circle, will help revitalize worker participation and productivity in American business. A network management style is already in place in several young, successful computer firms. And the computer itself will be what actually smashes the hierarchical pyramid: With the computer to keep track of people and business information, it is no longer necessary for organizations to be organized into hierarchies. No one knows this better than the new-age computer companies.

> The computer will smash the pyramid: We created the hierarchical, pyramidal, managerial system because we needed it to keep track of people and things people did; with the computer to keep track, we can restructure our institutions horizontally.

. . . Such is the time of the parenthesis, its challenges, its possibilities, and its questions.

Although the time between eras is uncertain, it is a great and yeasty time, filled with opportunity. If we can learn to make uncertainty our friend, we can achieve much more than in stable eras.

In stable eras, everything has a name and everything knows its place, and we can leverage very little.

But in the time of the parenthesis we have extraordinary leverage and influence—individually, professionally, and institutionally—if we can only get a clear sense, a clear conception, a clear vision, of the road ahead.

My God, what a fantastic time to be alive!

Further Resources

BOOKS

Butcher, Lee. *Accidental Millionaire: The Rise and Fall of Steve Jobs at Apple Computer.* New York: Paragon House, 1988.

Frank, Thomas. *One Market Under God: Extreme Capitalism, Market Populism, and the End of Economic Democracy.* New York: Doubleday, 2000.

Gates, Bill, with Nathan Myhrvold and Piner Rinearson. *The Road Ahead.* New York: Viking, 1995.

Naisbitt, John, with Nana Naisbitt and Douglas Philips. *High Tech/High Touch: Technology and Our Search for Meaning.* New York: Broadway Books, 1999.

Naisbitt, John, with Patricia Aburdene. *Re-Inventing the Corporation: Transforming Your Job and Your Company for the New Information Society.* New York: Warner Books, 1985.

Phillips, Kevin. *The Politics of Rich and Poor: Wealth and the American Electorate in the Reagan Aftermath.* New York: Random House, 1990.

Toffler, Alvin. *Powershift: Knowledge, Wealth, and Violence at the Edge of the 21st Century.* New York: Bantam Books, 1990.

WEBSITES

"Computer Use in the United States." U.S. Census Bureau. Available online at http://www.census.gov/prod/99pubs /p20-522.pdf; website home page: http://www.census.gov/ (accessed March 27, 2003).

President Ronald Reagan's Inaugural Address, January 21, 1985

Speech

By: Ronald Reagan

Date: January 21, 1985

Source: Reagan, Ronald. President Ronald Reagan's Inaugural Address, January 21, 1985. Ronald Reagan Library and Museum. Available online at http://www.reagan.utexas.edu /resource/speeches/1985/12185a.htm; website home page: http://www.reagan.utexas.edu/ (accessed March 21, 2003).

About the Author: The fortieth President of the United States, Ronald Reagan (1911–) served two terms in office, from 1981 to 1989. Appearing as an actor in fifty-three movies from the 1930s through the 1950s, Reagan entered politics with a successful bid for the California governor's office in 1966. Reelected in 1970, Reagan became one of the leading conservative politicians in the United States. His 1980 presidential campaign emphasized patriotism, reduced government regulation, and lower taxes. In the early 1990s Reagan was diagnosed with Alzheimer's disease and thereafter ceased his public appearances. ∎

Introduction

Former California governor and movie actor Ronald Reagan won the presidency in 1980 by asking Americans a simple question throughout his campaign: "Are you better off now than you were four years ago?" After the high inflation, energy shortages, rising interest rates, and plant closings of the late 1970s, many Americans believed that they were not, in fact, any better off. Voting for Reagan, who demonstrated an optimism about the country's future with the promise to make it "Morning in America" again, many people hoped to put the economic and social turmoil of the 1970s behind them.

The cornerstone of Reagan's first-term agenda was the implementation of supply-side economic policies, which came to be known as Reaganomics. Viewing entrepreneurs as the most productive and wealth-creating group in the American economy, Reagan advocated tax cuts for businesses and wealthy Americans to free up more money for investment, which would in turn create more jobs. The top tax rate for individual Americans dropped from seventy to twenty-eight percent and the corporate tax rate dropped from forty-eight to thirty-four percent. To make up for the tax cut, Reagan promised to cut government spending, in part by dismantling the regulatory agencies that, in his view, stifled business efficiency and growth. Reaganomics also carried broad social implications through its economic policies. If welfare programs were cut deeply enough, some of Reagan's supporters predicted, jobless Americans would redis-

George Gilder's *Wealth and Poverty*

George Gilder (1939–), Harvard-educated pundit, became one of the leading voices in the supply-side economics chorus of the 1980s. Gilder's opinions were often cited by President Ronald Reagan to support his own programs to reduce spending on social welfare programs; his 1981 book, *Wealth and Poverty,* became a surprise bestseller.

Appearing the same year that Ronald Reagan took office as president, it was one of the most influential social critiques of the day. Linking the persistence of poverty in America with the growth of welfare programs since the 1960s, Gilder argued that welfare destroyed individual initiative and trapped its recipients in a never-ending cycle of dependency. "There is no panacea," Gilder writes in *Wealth and Poverty,* "Overcoming poverty still inexorably depends on work."

Gilder also states: "The goal of welfare should be to help people out of these dire but temporary problems, not to treat temporary problems as if they were permanent ones, and thus make them so. This goal dictates a system nearly the opposite of the current one."

cover their personal initiative, find jobs, and become productive members of society once again.

Reagan's critics, who labeled his policies as "trickle down economics," decried the wholesale giveaway of tax breaks and benefits to those who were already wealthy. Because there was no way to force those who had received tax cuts to put the money into business creation, much of it indeed ended up fueling a stock market boom, which did little to create new jobs. Opponents of Reaganomics also observed that by the time any money trickled down to the middle and lower classes, there were few, if any, tangible benefits left for them to share. As for the proposed cuts in programs to benefit the poor, Reagan's critics viewed him as a heartless, out-of-touch leader whose policies caused unnecessary suffering among those who were already mired in poverty.

Significance

At the end of Reagan's second term in office, experts debated the effect of eight years of Reaganomics on the nation's economy and society. Boosters of Reaganomics pointed to the steady economic growth of the 1980s, which had taken off after a recession in 1981 and 1982. Although Wall Street was stunned by a dramatic market collapse in 1987, the stock market performed well for investors throughout the decade. After interest rates

President Reagan delivers his second inaugural address, January 21, 1985. © BETTMANN/CORBIS. REPRODUCED BY PERMISSION.

came down in the early 1980s, home construction and automobile purchases also rebounded from the doldrums of the 1970s.

Even its supporters admitted the "Reagan Revolution" failed to reign in government spending, in large part due to increases in military expenditures—which climbed thirty-five percent during Reagan's two terms—and the reluctance of Congress to cut spending in other areas. Instead of government becoming smaller, as Reagan had aimed to do, it instead grew larger, with the exception of regulatory agencies that his administration dismantled. The government ran up budget deficits every year during Reagan's presidency and the share of privately held federal debt soared from about twenty-two to more than thirty-eight percent under Reagan's watch.

Some critics dubbed Reagan's presidency as America's "New Gilded Age," in reference to the late nineteenth century, another period of mighty capitalists, little government regulation, and poverty and social tension that persisted despite economic progress. Given the unequal economic gains in the 1980s, it was true that the rich got richer, the poor got marginally poorer, and the middle class struggled to keep up its standard of living, mostly by working more hours and taking on consumer debt. The legacy of Reagan's emphasis on deregulation

also came to haunt the country as a series of savings-and-loan failures in the deregulated banking industry cost the American taxpayer at least $125 billion in bailouts. The deregulation of the gas and electric industries also led to volatile energy markets and culminated a decade later in the Enron corporate scandal, which forced a company once valued at $100 billion into bankruptcy.

Primary Source

President Ronald Reagan's Inaugural Address, January 21, 1985 [excerpt]

SYNOPSIS: As he began his second term as president, Ronald Reagan summarized his basic philosophy: less government—including lower taxes and fewer regulations—was better; individualism—especially in the form of an entrepreneur—was a positive force in society; and the United States—the greatest country on earth—would eventually triumph over the Soviet Union. Reagan's characteristic idealism and optimism, obvious in this excerpt, earned him the nickname "The Great Communicator."

There are no words adequate to express my thanks for the great honor that you've bestowed on me. I'll do my utmost to be deserving of your trust. . . .

When I took this oath four years ago, I did so in a time of economic stress. Voices were raised saying that we had to look to our past for the greatness and glory. But we, the present-day Americans, are not given to looking backward. In this blessed land, there is always a better tomorrow.

Four years ago, I spoke to you of a New Beginning, and we have accomplished that. But in another sense, our New Beginning is a continuation of that beginning created two centuries ago when, for the first time in history, government, the people said, was not our master, it is our servant; its only power that which we the people allow it to have.

That system has never failed us, but for a time we failed the system. We asked things of government that government was not equipped to give. We yielded authority to the National Government that properly belonged to States or to local governments or to the people themselves. We allowed taxes and inflation to rob us of our earnings and savings and watched the great industrial machine that had made us the most productive people on Earth slow down and the number of unemployed increase.

By 1980 we knew it was time to renew our faith, to strive with all our strength toward the ultimate in individual freedom, consistent with an orderly society.

We believed then and now: There are no limits to growth and human progress when men and women are free to follow their dreams. And we were right to believe that. Tax rates have been reduced, inflation cut dramatically, and more people are employed than ever before in our history.

We are creating a nation once again vibrant, robust, and alive. But there are many mountains yet to climb. We will not rest until every American enjoys the fullness of freedom, dignity, and opportunity as our birthright. It is our birthright as citizens of this great Republic.

And if we meet this challenge, these will be years when Americans have restored their confidence and tradition of progress; when our values of faith, family, work, and neighborhood were restated for a modern age; when our economy was finally freed from government's grip; when we made sincere efforts at meaningful arms reductions and by rebuilding our defenses, our economy, and developing new technologies, helped preserve peace in a troubled world; when America courageously supported the struggle for individual liberty, self-government, and free enterprise throughout the world and turned the tide of history away from totalitarian darkness and into the warm sunlight of human freedom.

My fellow citizens, our nation is poised for greatness. We must do what we know is right, and do it with all our might. Let history say of us: "These were golden years—when the American Revolution was reborn, when freedom gained new life, and America reached for her best." . . .

At the heart of our efforts is one idea vindicated by 25 straight months of economic growth: Freedom and incentives unleash the drive and entrepreneurial genius that are the core of human progress. We have begun to increase the rewards for work, savings, and investment; reduce the increase in the cost and size of government and its interference in people's lives.

We must simplify our tax system, make it more fair and bring the rates down for all who work and earn. We must think anew and move with a new boldness, so every American who seeks work can find work, so the least among us shall have an equal chance to achieve the greatest things—to be heroes who heal our sick, feed the hungry, protect peace among nations, and leave this world a better place.

The time has come for a new American emancipation—a great national drive to tear down economic barriers and liberate the spirit of enterprise in the most distressed areas of our country. My friends, together we can do this, and do it we must, so help me God. . . .

History is a ribbon, always unfurling. History is a journey. And as we continue our journey, we think of those who traveled before us. We stand again at the steps of this symbol of our democracy—well, we would have been standing at the steps if it hadn't gotten so cold. [Laughter] Now we're standing inside this symbol of our democracy, and we see and hear again the echoes of our past: a general falls to his knees in the hard snow of Valley Forge; a lonely President paces the darkened halls and ponders his struggle to preserve the Union; the men of the Alamo call out encouragement to each other; a settler pushes west and sings a song, and the song echoes out forever and fills the unknowing air.

It is the American sound. It is hopeful, big-hearted, idealistic, daring, decent, and fair. That's our heritage, that's our song. We sing it still. For all our problems, our differences, we are together as of old. We raise our voices to the God who is the Author of this most tender music. And may He continue to hold us close as we fill the world with our sound—in unity, affection, and love—one people under God, dedicated to the dream of freedom that He has placed in the human heart, called upon now to pass that dream on to a waiting and hopeful world.

God bless you, and God bless America.

Further Resources

BOOKS

Gilder, George. *Microcosm: The Quantum Revolution in Economics and Technology.* New York: Simon and Schuster, 1989.

Niskanen, William A. *Reaganomics: An Insider's Account of the Policies and the People.* New York: Oxford University Press, 1988.

Phillips, Kevin. *The Politics of Rich and Poor: Wealth and the American Electorate in the Reagan Aftermath.* New York: Random House, 1990.

Reagan, Ronald. *An American Life.* New York: Simon and Schuster, 1990.

Schaller, Michael. *Reckoning with Reagan: America and Its President in the 1980s.* New York: Oxford University Press, 1992.

Schor, Juliet B. *The Overworked American: The Unexpected Decline of Leisure.* New York: Basic Books, 1991.

Stockman, David A. *The Triumph of Politics: How the Reagan Revolution Failed.* New York: Harper and Row, 1986.

Strober, Deborah Hart, and Gerald S. Strober. *Reagan: The Man and His Presidency.* Boston: Houghton Mifflin, 1998.

WEBSITES

Niskanen, William A. "Reaganomics." Available online at http://www.econlib.org/library/Enc/Reaganomics.html; website home page: http://www.econlib.org (accessed March 21, 2003).

"Ronald Reagan Presidential Library." Available online at http://www.reagan.utexas.edu/; website home page: http://www.archives.gov/index.html (accessed March 21, 2003).

Less Than Zero
Novel

By: Bret Easton Ellis

Date: 1985

Source: Ellis, Bret Easton. *Less Than Zero.* New York: Penguin Books, 1985, 39–43.

About the Author: Bret Easton Ellis (1964–) was born in Los Angeles. He published *Less Than Zero* at age twenty-one while still a college student. His subsequent novels have not had the success of his debut effort, and his violence-drenched 1991 novel, *American Psycho,* resulted in a boycott of his publisher. Ellis and Jay McInerny were two of the best-known members of the so-called "Literary Brat Pack" of the 1980s, when a flood of young authors gained fame for their best-selling books, high media profiles, and celebrity friends. ∎

Introduction

In contrast to the idealism of the 1960s and the search for self-fulfillment in the 1970s, the 1980s were dominated by more material concerns. The individual quest for the trappings of wealth and status, as well as Reagan administration policies that resulted in an increase of wealth for the upper class, resulted in booming sales of luxury items from multimillion-dollar mansions to art works to yachts. New "upscale" restaurants, nightclubs, health clubs, and spas appeared with regularity from New York City to Los Angeles and in major urban centers in between. Gossip columnist Robin Leach capitalized on the public's fascination with wealth and status by creating a new series in 1983, *The Lifestyles of the Rich and Famous,* which was little more than an advertisement for wealthy celebrities and their hobbies.

On a more mundane level, the decade also saw the much-hyped appearance of a new social archetype, the "Yuppie," or young urban professional. Geographically, the yuppie was found not in just any urban area—like Tulsa, Buffalo, or Boise—but rather in one of the cities booming with new technology industries, like San Francisco and Seattle, or established media centers such as New York, Boston, or Atlanta. Defined by having the right clothing and accessories for any occasion, the Yup-

pie also sported a prestigious job title, enviable address, and luxury automobile, such as a BMW or Mercedes. Although Yuppies often engaged in casual sex and drug use, their politics were invariably Republican in recognition for the party's endorsement of self-interest as an inalienable right.

Although they often appeared in the media as figures of satire or derision, Yuppie characters cropped up in some of the leading literary works of the 1980s and 1990s, including Jay McInerny's *Bright Lights, Big City* and Bret Ellis's *Less Than Zero* and *American Psycho.* Both novels were the first for their author and were critical and commercial successes, although they raised speculation about how much of the works were fictionalized accounts of the writers' real lives. Accused of glamorizing drug use, sex, violence, and the trappings of status-symbol materialism in their fiction, McInerny and Ellis countered that their works merely reflected the values of contemporary society. Yuppie characters also appeared in *The Bonfire of the Vanities, Slaves of New York,* and in the pompous but sympathetic character portrayed by Michael J. Fox on the television series *Family Ties.*

Significance

The media's unbridled celebration of the wealthy and famous ebbed by the end of the decade, when the era of excess spiraled into a series of headline-grabbing scandals. In 1986 New Yorkers were shocked by the handsome, yet smug, face of yuppie Robert Chambers, who was accused of killing Jennifer Levin during a sexual tryst in Central Park. The trial, dubbed the "Preppy Murder," hinged on Chambers's claim that he had accidentally killed Levin during a session of "rough sex." After two years of legal maneuvering, Chambers was finally found guilty and sentenced to fifteen years in prison. In Los Angeles, the media were transfixed by the case of Lyle and Erik Menendez, who killed their wealthy, movie-studio executive father and mother in 1989. The two later claimed that they had been sexually abused by their father, but the jury refused to believe the claim and the two were given life sentences.

Retribution for the decade's excesses also seemed to be visited on figures that the media had previously lionized. Leona Helmsley had been praised for her renovations of some of the city's historic hotel properties and appeared in her company's ads as a regal overseer devoted to ensuring that her guests were pampered in luxurious surroundings. Put on trial for evading payment on $1.7 million in taxes in 1989, Helmsley's comment that "only the little people pay taxes" caused an uproar that turned her into "the queen of mean" before she was sent away for an eighteen-month prison term. New York City cultural affairs commissioner and former Miss America

Bess Myerson also plunged from fame to infamy after reports surfaced that she had successfully lobbied a judge to lower her then-boyfriend's alimony payments by giving the judge's daughter a job. The resulting "Bess Mess" ended in an acquittal on bribery and conspiracy charges for everyone involved in 1988.

Primary Source

Less Than Zero [excerpt]

> **SYNOPSIS:** Filled with descriptions of sex, drugs, and violence, *Less Than Zero* details the lives of a group of wealthy, college-aged friends on the Los Angeles party scene. Critics were divided on whether the book's value as a cautionary tale outweighed its nihilistic vision of lives filled with superficial pleasures but little real emotion. A movie version of the novel was released in 1987, starring Robert Downey, Jr. and Andrew McCarthy, two actors who were part of Hollywood's "Brat Pack" of young actors.

My house lies on Mulholland and as I press the gate opener, I look out over the Valley and watch the beginning of another day, my fifth day back, and then I pull into the circular driveway and park my car next to my mother's, which is parked next to a Ferrari that I don't recognize. I sit there and listen to the last lines of some song and then get out of the car and walk to the front door and find my key and open it. I walk upstairs to my bedroom and lock the door and light a cigarette and turn the television on and turn the sound off and then I walk into the closet and find the bottle of Valium that I hid beneath some cashmere sweaters. After looking at the small yellow pill with the hole in the middle of it, I decide that I really don't need it and I put it away. I take off my clothes and look at the digital clock, the same kind of digital clock that Griffin has, and notice that I only have a few hours to sleep before I have to meet my father for lunch, so I make sure the alarm is set and I lay back, staring at the television hard, because I once heard that if you stare at the television screen for a long enough time, you can fall asleep.

The alarm goes off at eleven. A song called "Artificial Insemination" is playing on the radio and I wait until it's over to open my eyes and get up. Sun is flooding the room through the venetian blinds and when I look in the mirror it gives the impression that I have this wild, cracked grin. I walk into the closet and look at my face and body in the mirror; flex my muscles a couple of times, wonder if I should get a haircut, decide I do need a tan. Turn away and open the envelope, also hid beneath the sweaters. I cut myself two lines of the coke I bought from Rip last

The so-called Queen of Mean, Leona Helmsley. Manager of New York's premier hotel and wife of a billionaire, Helmsley became a symbol of greed after a highly publicized conviction for tax evasion in 1989. © **BETTMANN/CORBIS. REPRODUCED BY PERMISSION.**

night and do them and feel better. I'm still wearing my jockey shorts as I walk downstairs. Even though it's eleven, my mother's door is closed, probably locked. I walk outside and dive into the pool and do twenty quick laps and then get out, towel myself dry as I walk into the kitchen. Take an orange from the refrigerator and peel it as I walk upstairs. I eat the orange before I get into the shower and realize that I don't have time for the weights. Then I go into my room and turn on MTV really loud and cut myself another line and then drive to meet my father for lunch.

I don't like driving down Wilshire during lunch hour. There always seem to be too many cars and old people and maids waiting for buses and I end up looking away and smoking too much and turning up the radio to full volume. Right now, nothing is moving even though the lights are green. As I wait in the car, I look at the people in the cars next to mine. Whenever I'm on Wilshire or Sunset during lunch hour I try to make eye contact with the driver of the car next to mine, stuck in traffic. When this doesn't happen, and it usually doesn't, I put my sunglasses back on and slowly move the car forward.

Young New Yorkers gather near the bar inside of Studio 54, one of New York City's top nightclubs, in 1980. © CORBIS. REPRODUCED BY PERMISSION.

As I pull onto Sunset I pass the billboard I saw this morning that read "Disappear Here" and I look away and kind of try to get it out of my mind.

My father's offices are in Century City. I wait around for him in the large, expensively furnished reception room and hang out with the secretaries, flirting with this really pretty blond one. It doesn't bother me that my father leaves me waiting there for thirty minutes while he's in some meeting and then asks me why I'm late. I don't really want to go to lunch today, would rather be at the beach or sleeping or out by the pool, but I'm pretty nice and I smile and nod a lot and pretend to listen to all his questions about college and I answer them pretty sincerely. And it doesn't embarass me a whole lot that while on the way to Ma Maison he puts the top of the 450 down and plays a Bob Seger tape, as if this was some sort of weird gesture of communication. It also doesn't really make me angry that at lunch my father talks to a lot of businessmen, people he deals with in the film industry, who stop by our table and that I'm introduced only as "my son" and the businessmen all begin to look the same and I begin to wish that I had brought the rest of the coke.

My father looks pretty healthy if you don't look at him for too long. He's completely tan and has had a hair transplant in Palm Springs, two weeks ago, and he has pretty much a full head of blondish hair. He also has had his face lifted. I'd gone to see him at Cedars-Sinai when he had it done and I remember seeing his face covered with bandages and how he would keep touching them lightly.

"Why aren't you having the usual," I ask, actually interested, after we order.

He smiles, showing off the caps. "Nutritionist won't allow it."

"Oh."

"How is your mother?" he asks calmly.

"She's fine."

"Is she really feeling fine?"

"Yes, she's really feeling fine." I'm tempted, for a moment, to tell him about the Ferrari parked in the driveway.

"Are you sure?"

"There's nothing to worry about."

"That's good." He pauses. "Is she still seeing that Dr. Crain?"

"Uh-huh."

"That's good."

There's a pause. Another businessman stops by, then leaves.

"Well, Clay, what do you want for Christmas?"

"Nothing," I say after a while.

"Do you want your subscription to *Variety* renewed?"

"It already is."

Another pause.

"Do you need money?"

"No," I tell him, knowing that he'll slip me some later on, outside Ma Maison, maybe, or on the way back to his office.

"You look thin," he says.

"Hmmm.

"And pale."

"It's the drugs," I mumble.

"I didn't quite hear that."

I look at him and say, "I've gained five pounds since I've been back home."

"Oh," he says, and pours himself a glass of white wine.

Some other business guy drops by. After he leaves, my father turns to me and asks, "Do you want to go to Palm Springs for Christmas?"

Further Resources

BOOKS

Alexander, Shana. *When She Was Bad: The Story of Bess, Hortense, Sukhreet, and Nancy.* New York: Random House, 1990.

Janowitz, Tama. *Slaves of New York.* New York: Crown, 1986.

Pierson, Ransdell. *The Queen of Mean: The Unauthorized Biography of Leona Helmsley.* New York: Bantam, 1989.

Piesman, Marissa, and Marilee Hartley. *The Yuppie Handbook: The State-of-the-Art Manual for Young Urban Professionals.* New York: Pocket Books, 1984.

Trump, Donald, with Tony Schwartz. *Trump: The Art of the Deal.* New York: Random House, 1987.

Wolfe, Tom. *Bonfire of the Vanities.* New York: Farrar, Straus Giroux, 1987.

PERIODICALS

Waters, Harry F., et al. "A Queen on Trial: Real Estate Made Leona Helmsley Royalty. Charges of Fraud Could Send Her to Jail." *Newsweek,* August 21, 1989, 46–51.

AUDIO AND VISUAL MEDIA

Bright Lights, Big City. Original release, 1988, MGM/United Artists. Directed by James Bridges. VHS, 1996. MGM/UA.

Less Than Zero. Original release, 1987, Twentieth-Century Fox. Directed by Marek Kanievska. VHS, 2000. Widescreen DVD, 2003. Twentieth-Century Fox Home Video.

Lifestyles of the Rich and Famous: Classic Collectors Edition. Directed by Jim Cross II. VHS, 1997. Multimedia Home Video.

The Closing of the American Mind

Nonfiction work

By: Allan Bloom

Date: 1987

Source: Bloom, Allan. *The Closing of the American Mind.* New York: Simon and Schuster, 1987, 73–75, 78–79.

About the Author: Allan Bloom (1930–1992) demonstrated his intellectual brilliance by earning his bachelor's degree from the University of Chicago at the age of nineteen. He stayed at the institution to earn his doctorate in philosophy in 1955 and taught at a series of prestigious universities before returning to the University of Chicago in 1979. He also co-directed the John M. Olin Center for Inquiry into the Theory and Practice of Democracy, a conservative think-tank, from 1984 until his death in 1992. With the publication of *The Closing of the American Mind* in 1987, Bloom became the leading neo-conservative thinker and social critic of his generation. ■

Introduction

When Allan Bloom's *The Closing of the American Mind* hit the top of the bestseller list in 1987, it kicked off a contentious debate among academics, policy makers, and the public at large. Few could have predicted that a book about the failure of America's higher-education system to teach its students central and lasting values would have had such an impact. Yet it became one of the most talked-about books of the decade, with its influence lasting far beyond the life of its author.

Well known in conservative political circles as the co-director of the John M. Olin Center, Bloom and his work were unlikely candidates for mass-media celebrity. A professor of philosophy and political science at the University of Chicago, Bloom argued that modern American society had been corrupted by the hedonism and self-indulgence of the 1960s and 1970s. As a result, the country no longer had a core set of beliefs to unite it, a characteristic that was especially true of young people, in Bloom's opinion. No longer did students read the classics and debate the meaning of democracy, citizenship, and nationhood. Instead, they listened to rock and roll music, had promiscuous sex, and studied what Bloom judged to be trivial subjects such as African-American, women's, and gay studies.

Although reviewers were divided on the validity of Bloom's conclusions, few disputed the author's vision and brilliance. Writing in the *New York Times,* Christopher Lehmann-Haupt noted, "By turns passionate and witty, sweetly reasoned and outraged, it commands one's attention and concentrates one's mind more effectively than any other book I can think of in the past five years." In the wake of its publication, *The Closing of the American Mind* indeed inspired a vigorous debate on the values of American society as well as a host of imitative books, notably former Secretary of Education William J. Bennett's *The Book of Virtues.*

Significance

Although Bloom insisted that he had no political agenda in writing *The Closing of the American Mind,* its harsh criticism of the liberal agenda of the 1960s and 1970s was adopted by the political right, which trumpeted its defense of "family values" against the perceived permissiveness of modern society. In the decade after Bloom's book appeared, more than one billion dollars was funneled through the leading twenty conservative think tanks, including Bloom's own Olin Foundation, the Heritage Foundation, the American Enterprise Institute, and other groups on the right. The groups worked to restrict abortion laws, prevent gay rights measures from being enacted, end affirmative-action programs, lessen governmental regulation, and privatize government programs such as Social Security. On the educational front, the political right urged prayer to be allowed back in public schools as well as using federal money to fund private, religious schools.

Each of these issues cropped up regularly on the political landscape over the next decade. Yet it was difficult to attribute many real political successes to the neo-conservative movement. Affirmative action programs remained in place; gay rights ordinances were enacted in more communities; abortion, although restricted by various Supreme Court rulings, remained legal. Public opinion polls indeed showed that the typical American was not nearly as concerned about "family values" issues as conservative lobbyists seemed to think. With the exception of abortion, which still produced deep divides in public opinion, the rest of the liberal agenda of the 1960s—from the Civil Rights movement to demands for equality for women to calls for tolerance for gays—had more or less been incorporated into the American mainstream. As for Bloom himself, the scholar continued to provoke controversy even after his 1992 death. When his friend Saul Bellow published a novel in 2000 intimately based on Bloom's life, *Ravelstein,* the public learned that Bloom was gay and had died from AIDS,

facts which his friends and colleagues had previously kept secret in deference to his public image.

Primary Source

The Closing of the American Mind [excerpt]

SYNOPSIS: Bloom's work was a wide-ranging critique of western society and the permissiveness that it generated. Among his targets were the impact of divorce, sexual promiscuity, and drug use among young people. He reserved special venom for his distaste of rock-and-roll music, which he compared unfavorably to classical music. In this excerpt, Bloom takes aim at Rolling Stones lead singer Mick Jagger, whom Bloom calls "the hero and model for countless young persons in universities, as well as elsewhere."

This is the significance of rock music. I do not suggest that it has any high intellectual sources. But it has risen to its current heights in the education of the young on the ashes of classical music, and in an atmosphere in which there is no intellectual resistance to attempts to tap the rawest passions. Modern-day rationalists, such as economists, are indifferent to it and what it represents. The irrationalists are all for it. There is no need to fear that "the blond beasts" are going to come forth from the bland souls of our adolescents. But rock music has one appeal only, a barbaric appeal, to sexual desire—not love, not *eros,* but sexual desire undeveloped and untutored. It acknowledges the first emanations of childhood's emerging sensuality and addresses them seriously, eliciting them and legitimating them, not as little sprouts that must be carefully tended in order to grow up into gorgeous flowers, but as the real thing. Rock gives children, on a silver platter, with all the public authority of the entertainment industry, everything their parents always used to tell them they had to wait for until they grew up and would understand better.

Young people know that rock has the beat of sexual intercourse. That is why Ravel's *Bolero* is the one piece of classical music that is commonly known and liked by them. In alliance with some real art and a lot of pseudo-art, an enormous industry cultivates the taste for the orgiastic state of feeling connected with sex, providing a constant flood of fresh material for voracious appetites. Never was there an art form directed so exclusively to children.

Ministering to and according with the arousing and cathartic music, the lyrics celebrate puppy love as well as polymorphous attractions, and fortify them against traditional ridicule and shame. The words implicitly and explicitly describe bodily acts that satisfy sexual desire and treat them as its only natural and routine culmination for children who do not yet have the slightest imagination of love, marriage, or family. This has a much more powerful effect than does pornography on youngsters, who have no need to watch others do grossly what they can so easily do themselves. Voyeurism is for old perverts; active sexual relations are for the young. All they need is encouragement. . . .

Picture a thirteen-year-old boy sitting in the living room of his family home doing his math assignment while wearing his Walkman headphones or watching MTV. He enjoys the liberties hard won over centuries by the alliance of philosophic genius and political heroism, consecrated by the blood of martyrs; he is provided with comfort and leisure by the most productive economy ever known to mankind; science has penetrated the secrets of nature in order to provide him with the marvelous, lifelike electronic sound and image reproduction he is enjoying. And in what does progress culminate? A pubescent child whose body throbs with orgasmic rhythms; whose feelings are made articulate in hymns to the joys of onanism or the killing of parents; whose ambition is to win fame and wealth in imitating the drag-queen who makes the music. In short, life is made into a nonstop, commercially prepackaged masturbational fantasy. . . .

This strong stimulant, which Nietzsche called Nihiline, was for a very long time, almost fifteen years, epitomized in a single figure, Mick Jagger. A shrewd, middle-class boy, he played the possessed lower-class demon and teen-aged satyr up until he was forty, with one eye on the mobs of children of both sexes whom he stimulated to a sensual frenzy and the other eye winking at the unerotic, commercially motivated adults who handled the money. In his act he was male and female, heterosexual and homosexual; unencumbered by modesty, he could enter everyone's dreams, promising to do everything with everyone; and above all, he legitimated drugs, which were the real thrill that parents and policemen conspired to deny his youthful audience. He was beyond the law, moral and political, and thumbed his nose at it. Along with all this, there were nasty little appeals to the suppressed inclinations toward sexism, racism and violence, indulgence in which is not now publicly respectable. Nevertheless, he managed not to appear to contradict the rock ideal of a universal classless society founded on love, with

British pop star Boy George, appears as a guest on *The Joan Rivers Show* in 1983. Conservatives tended to be horrified by Boy George's feminine appearance and flamboyant behavior, and attacked him as a corrupter of America's youth. © BETTMANN/CORBIS. REPRODUCED BY PERMISSION.

the distinction between brotherly and bodily blurred. He was the hero for countless young persons in universities, as well as elsewhere. I discovered that students who boasted of having no heroes secretly had a passion to be like Mick Jagger, to live his life, have his fame. They were ashamed to admit this in a university, although I am not certain that the reason has anything to do with a higher standard of taste. It is probably that they are not supposed to have heroes. Rock music itself and talking about it with infinite seriousness are perfectly acceptable. It has proved to be the ultimate leveler of intellectual snobbism. But is it not respectable to think of it as providing weak and ordinary persons with fashionable behavior, the imitation of which will make others esteem them and boost their own self-esteem. Unaware and unwillingly, however, Mick Jagger played the role in their lives that Napoleon played in the lives of ordinary young Frenchmen throughout the nineteenth century. Everyone else was so boring and unable to charm the youthful passions. Jagger caught on.

In the last couple of years, Jagger has begun to fade. Whether Michael Jackson, Prince or Boy George can take his place is uncertain. They are even weirder than he is, and one wonders what new strata of taste they have discovered. Although each differs from the others, the essential character of musical entertainment is not changing. There is only a constant search for variations on the theme. And this gutter phenomenon is apparently the fulfillment of the promise made by so much psychology and literature that our weak and exhausted Western civilization would find refreshment in the true source, the unconscious, which appeared to the late romantic imagination to be identical to Africa, the dark and unexplored continent. Now all has been explored; light has been cast everywhere; the unconscious has been made conscious, the repressed expressed. And what have we found? Not creative devils, but show business glitz. Mick Jagger tarting it up on the stage is all that we have brought back from the voyage to the underworld.

Further Resources

BOOKS

Bellow, Saul. *Ravelstein.* New York: Viking, 2000.

Cheney, Lynne V. *Telling the Truth: Why Our Culture and Our Country Have Stopped Making Sense, and What We Can Do About It.* New York: Simon & Schuster, 1995.

Hunter, James Davison. *Culture Wars: The Struggle to Define America.* New York: Basic Books, 1991.

Kelley, Robin D.G. *Yo' Mama's Disfunktional!: Fighting the Culture Wars in Urban America.* Boston: Beacon Press, 1997.

Levine, Lawrence W. *The Opening of the American Mind: Canons, Culture, and History.* Boston: Beacon Press, 1996.

Nash, Gary B., Charlotte Crabtree, and Ross E. Dunn. *History on Trial: Culture Wars and the Teaching of the Past.* New York: Knopf, 1997.

Stone, Robert L., ed. *Essays on "The Closing of the American Mind."* Chicago: Chicago Review Press, 1989.

Williams, Mary E. *Culture Wars: Opposing Viewpoints.* San Diego: Greenhaven Press, 1999.

PERIODICALS

Klein, Joe. "Whose Values?" *Newsweek,* June 8, 1992, 18–22.

Lehmann-Haupt, Christopher. "*The Closing of the American Mind*" [Book Review]. *New York Times,* March 23, 1987, 13.

WEBSITES

Johnson, Dave. "Who's Behind the Attack on Liberal Professors?" Available online at http://hnn.us/articles/1244.html; website home page, http://hnn.us/ (accessed March 25, 2003).

Racial Fault Lines

Go and Tell Pharaoh: The Autobiography of the Reverend Al Sharpton
Autobiography

By: Al Sharpton and Anthony Walton
Date: 1996
Source: Sharpton, Al, and Anthony Walton. *Go and Tell Pharaoh: The Autobiography of the Reverend Al Sharpton.* New York: Doubleday, 1996, 125, 127, 139, 141–142.
About the Author: The Reverend Al Sharpton (1954–) grew up in the Queens and Brooklyn boroughs of New York City. Ordained as a Pentecostal minister at the age of ten, Sharpton later joined the Baptist Church. Politically active during his youth, Sharpton was mentored in the 1970s by prominent civil rights leaders such as Jesse Jackson, Shirley Chisholm, and Adam Clayton Powell. He emerged as a national figure by organizing protests against the racially motivated attacks at Howard Beach in Queens in 1986. His role in the Tawana Brawley case the following year proved controversial and Sharpton was later found liable for defamation against one of the accused figures in the event. Sharpton remained in the public eye as an unsuccessful political candidate and leading civil rights activist.

Report of the Grand Jury Concerning the Tawana Brawley Investigation
Report

By: Grand Jury of the State of New York, County of Dutchess
Date: October 1988
Source: "Court TV Legal Documents: Grand Jury Report on Tawana Brawley Investigation." Court TV Online. Available online at http://www.courttv.com/legaldocs/newsmakers/tawana/part4.html; website home page: http://www.courttv.com/ (accessed March 26, 2003). ■

Introduction

A spirit of cross-racial cooperation infused the Civil Rights movement and produced social and economic gains for minorities in the 1960s and 1970s. By the 1980s, however, the racial landscape had changed. The consensus among most Americans on racial issues, which had torn down Jim Crow, no longer existed; instead, the politics of race became increasingly polarized. The new dynamic was nowhere more evident than in New York City, long considered to be a bastion of American liberalism. Although its residents elected an African-American mayor, David Dinkins, in 1989, a series of events in the 1980s showed just how fractious race relations had become in the Big Apple.

In December 1986 a gang of white youths in the Howard Beach neighborhood of Queens chased down three African Americans whose car had broken down. One of the victims, Michael Griffith, was beaten severely before he escaped from the mob by running through a fence and onto the Shore Parkway, where he was struck and killed by a passing car. When the police arrived, they seemed to treat the victims as criminals by searching them and asking them about various crimes committed in the neighborhood. When three of the defendants were convicted of manslaughter in the case, not the more serious charge of murder, activists such as the Reverend Al Sharpton accused the criminal justice system of racism and discrimination.

Sharpton repeated the charges during the investigation of the alleged abduction and rape of Tawana Brawley, a fifteen-year-old resident of upstate New York, in November 1987. Acting as the Brawley family's adviser, Sharpton refused to have the teenager cooperate in the investigation because, he claimed, no African American could expect to be treated fairly by the police and prosecutors. Even when Brawley's allegations were proved to be false—she had concocted the story to avoid getting in trouble for playing hooky from school—Sharpton continued to characterize the justice system as inherently racist and biased against African Americans.

Through the Howard Beach and Tawana Brawley incidents, Sharpton became one of the country's preeminent civil rights spokespersons. When race riots erupted in the Crown Heights neighborhood in Brooklyn in 1991 after a Hasidic Jewish man struck and killed an African American boy in a car accident, Sharpton served as a negotiator between the city leaders and African-American community groups. One person was killed and more than two-hundred police officers and civilians were injured in three days of fighting in Crown Heights.

Significance

Although African American leaders such as the Reverend Jesse Jackson urged cross-racial activism to reform American society, separatists such as Sharpton and Louis Farrakhan of the Nation of Islam symbolized the growing racial polarization of the 1980s. Farrakhan, who had ties to Libyan dictator Muammar Khadafi and routinely made threatening, anti-Semitic remarks in his speeches, was continually criticized in the mainstream press for his controversial agenda and confrontational rhetoric. Yet his popularity among many African Americans demonstrated the alienation that many felt toward the dominant political and social institutions and the economic system, all of which were perceived as being controlled by white Americans to the detriment of minority groups.

The Rev. Al Sharpton leads a demonstration in support of Tawana Brawley on March 22, 1988, in Poughkeepsie, N.Y. © BETTMANN/ CORBIS. REPRODUCED BY PERMISSION.

For many Americans, the rise of leaders such as Sharpton and Farrakhan drove them further away from the political agenda that had empowered the Civil Rights Movement. Fiery rhetoric that accused white people of being inherently racist was often perceived as political grandstanding for the personal gain of African American activists, not to support equality and fairness in American life. The Republican Party, which had pursued a "southern strategy" since the 1960s of attracting white voters by opposing affirmative action, busing, and other liberal measures, used the fears and anger of many voters over racial issues to help elect Ronald Reagan in 1980. The typical "Reagan Democrat" was a blue-collar suburbanite who had previously voted for the Democrats, but had turned to the Republican Party and its avowed agenda against liberalism, often phrased as a return to "law and order" and the defeat of "special interest groups."

In 1988 presidential candidate George Bush's (served 1989–1993) campaign resorted to a law-and-order pitch that played on racial tensions among voters by running an ad showing the African American face of Willie Horton, a convicted murderer who had committed a kidnapping and rape against a white couple while out on a prison-release program in Massachusetts, the home state of Bush's opponent, Michael Dukakis. Although he was roundly condemned for playing the race card with the Willie Horton ads, Bush pulled ahead in the polls and won the election.

Primary Source

Go and Tell Pharaoh: The Autobiography of the Reverend Al Sharpton [excerpt]

SYNOPSIS: In these excerpts, Sharpton describes his initial reaction to the Tawana Brawley case, in which a young African American woman claimed to have been abducted and assaulted by a group of white men. Arguing that the criminal justice system was hopelessly racist, Sharpton led a series of rallies to publicize the case, which turned out to have been fabricated. In 1998 Sharpton and his colleagues were ordered to pay damages for defaming Steven Pagones, a Dutchess County Assistant District Attorney, whom they had accused of taking part in the assault.

I cannot describe the horror I felt upon hearing the full details of this story. No black person is without historical memory of the outrages visited upon black women throughout slavery and into the twentieth century. I was interested in this case because I felt someone had to stand up and defend this young girl; I felt like I was defending my mother, my wife, my daughters, my sisters, all the black women I know and love, black women in general, even. Something had to be done. I had spent some time up in the area talking to people, interviewing the family. I personally talked to the EMS technicians who had brought Tawana into the hospital. According to ambulance records, she was unconscious, unresponsive, and 30 percent of the hair had been torn out of her head. Eighty percent of her body was covered with excrement, and she had burns. She could not speak. For some unstated reason, Tawana was not taken to the closest hospital, but all the way to Poughkeepsie.

I also finally met Tawana personally—I hadn't actually met her at the rally in December—and talked with her in a serious manner about what had happened. I was totally convinced that Tawana Brawley was telling the truth, that she had been raped and kidnapped as she had said. I didn't believe that she could just make these things up. She was describing law enforcement suspects who resembled actual persons, and other aspects of the case seemed to be lining up just as she said. . . .

The Tawana Brawley case quickly took on an aspect of "through the looking glass," Alice in Wonderland, nothing-makes-sense, as everything that was said was quickly and easily contradicted by the other actors in the situation. For example, Abrams stated unequivocally near the end of the investigation that Tawana had not been raped, and this is what was submitted to the grand jury. He said there was no finding of rape in the hospital examinations, but there are problems with this analysis. First of all, there are two sets of records, one that says "rape," another that does not. She was bathed before her pelvic examination, which is not supposed to be done in a rape situation, because you can destroy evidence. Bathing her was probably just a humanitarian response to a very bad circumstance; the person who so acted was not trying to participate in a cover-up or anything like that, but rather wanted to make Tawana more comfortable and remove the filth. So an act of kindness complicates the investigation and contributes to the "he said, she said" conflicts in the situation. . . .

I don't know if it is possible for us to deal with these racially charged cases in the United States. The Rodney King case would be the second biggest hoax of all time—no white person would have believed Rodney's story—if a white man named George Holliday hadn't been standing there with a video camera. And, *even with the tape and a white man swearing what he saw,* twelve white folks out in Simi Valley still thought it was a hoax. If you look at the Brawley situation through the eye of Al Sharpton, it might look different.

People say, "Can't you see how this looks fishy?" and I say yes, I can see that, I've always had to look at Tawana Brawley through their eyes, but they've never had to look at her through mine. They see another black telling lies, disturbing the peace. But what I don't understand is why there couldn't be a trial based on what had been discovered and uncovered. What everyone forgets is that the grand jury is secret, we don't know what happened unless it goes to trial. We don't know what was said by whom. And everything that happens is only the presentation of the prosecution. You don't get to hear what the defense has to say. . . .

I represent an element that is rising up in this country and saying that all the problems are far from solved. People haven't liked me saying it, but more and more are coming to agree. The problem is still the color line, the problem of race. The American Dilemma. From Du Bois to King to now, it's still the American Dilemma. And I won't let them ignore it. Jimmy Breslin wrote a story several years ago about me being the black man that haunts suburban living rooms with "Hey, it isn't over yet. Racism isn't over yet." And rather than working at solving the problems, they try to wipe me off the screen. And every time they start doing that, it only makes the screen dirtier, more opaque, more difficult to see. But they're not going to wipe me off. Whether it's Bernhard Goetz, Howard Beach, Bensonhurst, Tawana Brawley, or anything else, I'm still there.

Primary Source

Report of the Grand Jury Concerning the Tawana Brawley Investigation [excerpt]

SYNOPSIS: The Grand Jury Report issued in October 1988 found unequivocally that Tawana Brawley had lied about her abduction and rape and that no public officials had taken part in an assault or cover up. On the advice of Sharpton, Brawley had refused to appear before the Grand Jury.

The Discovery of Tawana Brawley

Tawana Brawley was found on Saturday, November 28, 1987, in the common area several feet from the rear of her former residence at 19A Carnaby Drive in the Pavillion Apartments, Town of Wappingers, New York.

She was first observed between 1:30 and 1:44 p.m. stepping into a large plastic garbage bag and pulling it up around her. She remained stationary for a couple of seconds, looked around, hopped a few feet, and then, while still inside the bag, lay on the ground near the back wall of 17 Carnaby Drive.

At approximately the same time Tawana Brawley was observed behind 17-19 Carnaby Drive, her mother, Glenda Brawley, was present in front of Apt. 19A Carnaby Drive.

Tawana Brawley's Condition

When discovered, Tawana Brawley was not suffering from exposure. If an individual had been outdoors continuously from Tuesday evening, November 24, to Saturday afternoon, November 28, when the temperature several times dropped to the freezing

Tawana Brawley, flanked by attoney Alton Maddox (left) and the Reverend Al Sharpton (right), speaks to the press on Sept. 28, 1988. Brawley and her supporters continued to vigorously insist that her accusations of kidnapping and rape were true even after a grand jury decided against her. AP/WIDE WORLD PHOTOS. REPRODUCED BY PERMISSION.

point, there is a high probability the individual would have suffered from exposure.

When discovered, Tawana Brawley was not malnourished. If an individual had been deprived of food for four days, there is a high probability that there would have been evidence of malnourishment.

When discovered, Tawana Brawley did not have a bad odor to her breath. If an individual was prevented from practicing oral hygiene for a four day period, there is a high probability that there would have been a bad odor to the breath.

When discovered, there were no burns on any part of Tawana Brawley's body. The jeans that Tawana Brawley was wearing when found had been burned in the crotch area. If an individual had been wearing the jeans in which Tawana Brawley was found when the jeans were burned, there would be burns on the body.

When discovered, Tawana Brawley had no injuries, broken bones, discolorations, contusions, or bruises, other then a slight scratch on her right breast and a quarter-sized bruise behind her left ear. The bruise was not tender or fresh, there was no collection of fluid underneath, and she did not wince or pull away when it was touched. The bruise was one to several days old and whatever caused it was unlikely to have been able to cause unconsciousness. . . .

No Evidence of Sexual Assault

There was no medical or forensic evidence that a sexual assault was committed on Tawana Brawley. If a 15-year old girl had been forcibly raped or sodomized by multiple assailants over a four day period, there is a high probability that medical or forensic evidence would have been found.

There were no bruises, lacerations, tenderness or blood in the rectal area of Tawana Brawley;

There was no trauma to the mouth or the back of the throat of Ms. Brawley;

There were no cuts, dried blood, bruising, swelling, deep redness or other injury to Ms. Brawley's vaginal and pelvic area or the surrounding skin;

There was no semen found in Ms. Brawley's mouth, or on her body;

There was no motile sperm found in a microscopic examination of vaginal slides prepared at St. Francis Hospital;

Laboratory tests on the rape kit found no blood, sperm cells, or P-30 (a prostate antigen that is a substance unique to semen) on any of the materials gathered from Ms. Brawley's fingernails, or in the specimens taken from the swabs of her mouth, rectum, or vagina;

There were no semen stains or blood on any of the clothes Ms. Brawley was wearing;

There was no urine found in Ms. Brawley's mouth;

There were no foreign pubic hairs in the pubic combings taken from Ms. Brawley;

There was no plant material found on Ms. Brawley or her clothing. If an individual was sexually assaulted in a wooded area or spent significant time in a wooded area, there is a high probability that there would have been plant materials on the individual's body and clothing. . . .

No Evidence of a Cover-up

There is no evidence that a cover-up occurred or was attempted in this case. The actions of the law enforcement agencies and officials involved were inconsistent with any attempt at a cover-up.

Significant numbers of personnel were assigned to the investigation by the Dutchess County Sheriff's Office and District Attorney's Office;

The Federal Bureau of Investigation was contacted by the Sheriff's Office while Tawana Brawley was still in St. Francis Hospital. The FBI was con-tacted based on the racial epithets on her body even before she indicated that a "white cop" was involved;

All of the key evidence in the case was sent to the FBI Laboratory in Washington, D.C.;

The State Police were brought into the investigation;

The agencies involved in the investigation assigned both blacks and women to the investigation. The agencies involved in the investigation assigned personnel with specialized expertise including expertise in civil rights cases and sexual abuse cases;

Persistent efforts were made to secure the co-operation of Tawana Brawley and her family.

Further Resources

BOOKS

Edsall, Thomas Byrne, and Mary D. Edsall. *Chain Reaction: The Impact of Race, Rights, and Taxes on American Politics.* New York: Norton, 1991.

Frady, Marshall. *Jesse: The Life and Pilgrimage of Jesse Jackson.* New York: Random House, 1996.

Freedman, Samuel G. *The Inheritance: How Three Families and America Moved from Roosevelt to Reagan and Beyond.* New York: Simon & Schuster, 1996.

Gardell, Mattias. *In the Name of Elijah Muhammad: Louis Farrakhan and the Nation of Islam.* Durham, N.C.: Duke University Press, 1996.

Rieder, Jonathan. *Canarsie: The Jews and Italians of Brooklyn against Liberalism.* Cambridge, Mass: Harvard University Press, 1985.

PERIODICALS

Duggan, Dennis. "Howard Beach: Has Anything Changed?" *Newsday,* January 12, 2003.

Ruffins, Paul. "Interracial Coalitions: 'New Moderation' Doesn't Account for the Dramatic Gains that Black Politicians Made in the Last Elections." *The Atlantic* 265, no. 6, June 1990, 28–32.

WEBSITES

"Pagones v. Maddux, Mason, and Sharpton." Available online at http://www.courttv.com/legaldocs/newsmakers/tawana/index.html; website home page: http://www.courttv.com/legaldocs/ (accessed March 26, 2003).

The Specter of AIDS

San Francisco AIDS Foundation Advertisements

Advertisements

By: San Francisco AIDS Foundation

Date: 1986–1987

Source: San Francisco AIDS Foundation. Advertisements. 1986–1987. Available online at http://www.sfaf.org/prevention /gallery/index.html; website home page: http://www.sfaf./org/ (accessed August 20, 2003.)

About the Organization: The San Francisco AIDS Foundation started out as the Kaposi Sarcoma Research and Education Foundation in 1981. A grassroots, volunteer organization to help men suffering from Kaposi's sarcoma, a formerly rare skin cancer that was a symptom of AIDS, the foundation evolved into a full support-service agency for AIDS patients as well as an outreach organization to educate the public about AIDS.

AIDS Doctors: Voices from the Epidemic

Oral history

By: Ronald Bayer and Gerald M. Oppenheimer, eds.

Date: 2000

Source: Bayer, Ronald, and Gerald M. Oppenheimer, eds. *AIDS Doctors: Voices from the Epidemic.* New York: Oxford University Press, 2000, 21–25.

About the Authors: Ronald Bayer and Gerald M. Oppenheimer both practiced medicine in the late 1970s and early 1980s, when the Acquired Immune Deficiency Syndrome (AIDS) first became recognized. Twenty years after the beginning of the epidemic, the doctors sat down to share their memories of the gradual realization that they were seeing a new and deadly virus in their patients. Given the sudden appearance and rise of the disease, the physicians sometimes felt helpless as they searched for appropriate medical treatments to combat it. Medical journals began reporting in June 1981 about rare cancers that seemed to strike gay men, although it was not until later that the cases were categorized as AIDS. Over the next three years, five thousand AIDS cases were reported; in May 1985, less than a year later, the ten thousandth AIDS case was reported. ∎

Introduction

For many gay men and lesbians, the 1970s were a time of optimism. Various forms of legal discrimination and social repression against homosexuals had ebbed during the decade and the conservative backlash, personified by Anita Bryant's "Save Our Children" campaign against gay rights, served to energize a national gay movement. Although homophobia was still prevalent in the mainstream media and culture, gay culture flourished,

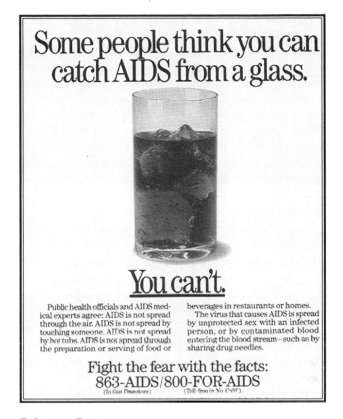

Some people think you can catch AIDS from a glass.

You can't.

Public health officials and AIDS medical experts agree: AIDS is not spread through the air. AIDS is not spread by touching someone. AIDS is not spread by hot tubs. AIDS is not spread through the preparation or serving of food or beverages in restaurants or homes.

The virus that causes AIDS is spread by unprotected sex with an infected person, or by contaminated blood entering the blood stream—such as by sharing drug needles.

Fight the fear with the facts:
863-AIDS/800-FOR-AIDS
(In San Francisco)   (Toll-free in No. Calif.)

Primary Source

San Francisco AIDS Foundation Advertisement

SYNOPSIS: As the medical establishment struggled to identify the virus that caused AIDS and its methods of transmission, rumors about the disease were widespread. To dampen unsubstantiated fears about the disease and educate the public about it, the San Francisco AIDS Foundation conducted ad campaigns throughout the 1980s. COURTESY OF THE SAN FRANCISCO AIDS FOUNDATION.

especially in New York City and San Francisco, where gay men and lesbians supported their own magazines and newspapers, social organizations, and businesses.

In early 1981, disturbing reports in gay newspapers speculated about a mysterious disease, dubbed the "gay cancer," which seemed to be striking down dozens of men who had been healthy and vital until just months before their deaths. By the summer of 1981 doctors had begun to piece together a picture of an emerging epidemic, one that indeed seemed to be afflicting gay men. Some in the medical community theorized that the disease was spread by numerous sexual contacts, while others were hesitant to speculate on its transmission, fearful of being deemed puritanical or homophobic. After cases of the disease, later named the Acquired Immune Deficiency Syndrome (AIDS), were found among intravenous drug users, it became more clear that the virus was indeed spread by the transmission of blood or semen from an infected person.

While the medical establishment worked to define the pathology of AIDS, the gay community struggled to respond to the emerging crisis. As it became clear that AIDS was spread by sexual contact involving the exchange of blood or semen, some groups urged gay men to practice "safe sex," that is, intercourse only when using condoms. In New York City and San Francisco, political battles raged over the closing of bath houses, where gay men gathered to socialize and have sex. Public health officials deemed the bathhouses breeding grounds for AIDS cases, while bathhouse patrons insisted that their choice to engage in sexual behavior should not be restricted.

Significance

Given the Reagan administration's hesitancy to address the AIDS crisis, local gay organizations took the lead in demanding medical research, providing care for AIDS patients, and conducting ad campaigns to educate the public about the disease. In New York, author Larry Kramer helped to found the Gay Men's Health Crisis (GMHC) in early 1982 to combat the perceived indifference from local health and governmental organizations to the growing AIDS crisis. Across the country the San Francisco AIDS Foundation (SFAF) worked hand-in-hand with local officials to create a network of health services for AIDS sufferers and educational resources for the gay community and the public at-large. As more became known about the nature of AIDS, the SFAF devoted much of its attention to promoting "safe sex," which counseled people to avoid the exchange of potentially dangerous bodily fluids. In contrast, the GMHC argued through the mid-1980s that gay men should merely assess the health of their potential sexual partners and limit their number of sexual partners to decrease their risk of contracting AIDS. Motivated by a fear of stigmatizing the gay community by labeling their sexual habits as dangerous, the GMHC's policy proved to be woefully inadequate in halting the spread of AIDS, which reached epidemic proportions among gay men in New York City.

By the time actor Rock Hudson died of AIDS on July 25, 1985, AIDS was a household word to most Americans. Although sixty-five percent of AIDS cases through 1985 were linked to homosexual behavior, the disease was also devastating to hemophiliacs, who typically contracted the virus through blood transfusions of tainted blood, a tragically common occurrence before screening procedures by the Red Cross were introduced in 1985. In the twenty years since the recognition of AIDS in 1981, more than 800,000 Americans have been diagnosed with the disease and almost a half million had died from it. Globally, an estimated forty million people were living with AIDS or the human immunodeficiency virus (HIV) in 2002.

Primary Source

AIDS Doctors: Voices from the Epidemic [excerpt]

SYNOPSIS: Doctors in New York and California were puzzled by a series of fatal illnesses that struck several of their formerly healthy, young, male patients in the late 1970s. Their symptoms included *Pneumocystis carinii* pneumonia, Kaposi's sarcoma, and a host of other illnesses related to a compromised immune system. In the summer of 1981 the cases, which had been informally labeled "gay cancer," were reported in medical journals, and soon afterward categorized as Acquired Immune Deficiency Syndrome, or AIDS.

Epidemic Fears

The official early history of AIDS could be told with the headlines of five articles in *Morbidity and Mortality Weekly Report* that appeared subsequent to those published in June and July 1981:

- July 9, 1982. Opportunistic Infections and Kaposi's Sarcoma Among Haitians in the United States.
- July 16, 1982. *Pneumocystis Carinii Pneumonia* Among Persons with Hemophilia A.
- December 10, 1982. Possible Transfusion Acquired Immune Deficiency Syndrome (AIDS)— California.
- January 7, 1983. Immunodeficiency Among Female Sexual Partners of Males with Acquired Immune Deficiency Syndrome (AIDS)— New York.

In that 18-month period, the contours of the epidemic as a sexually transmitted, blood-borne disease were made clear, although the extent of infection in the gay and drug-using population would not be known until the viral agent responsible for AIDS was discovered and a blood test developed.

But the landmark reports in *MMWR* tell only the public part of the story; they do not capture the extent to which those who first encountered patients with AIDS struggled with the epidemiological significance of their clinical experiences, or the extent to which their growing fears of their clinical experiences, or the extent to which their growing fears of a potentially catastrophic spread of the new disease met with resistance from colleagues. Even those who would commit themselves to AIDS work had no reason to believe initially that a grim clinical picture would produce a grave social burden.

Treating patients with Kapsoi's sarcoma in Los Angeles, Jerome Groopman thought, "This was possibly just an isolated occurrence in certain areas and

Primary Source

San Francisco AIDS Foundation Advertisement
A poster sponsored by the San Francisco AIDS Foundation to promote AIDS prevention among heterosexuals. It was displayed on the sides of buses in San Francisco during 1987. COURTESY OF THE SAN FRANCISCO AIDS FOUNDATION.

would probably be a relatively unusual disease." Never having seen an AIDS patient, Neil Schram heard about the new disease at a conference organized by the gay doctors' organization, Bay Area Physicians for Human Rights (BAPHR): "I remember thinking, That's peculiar. It can't mean anything." Fourteen years later, recalling that period, Schram noted sardonically: "I was insightful at that time." Even as late as 1984, when many had become seized with anxiety, infectious disease specialist Stephen Follansbee recalled:

> I think there was certainly the idea that this was a flash in the pan, that this was going to come and go and would die out. I can remember something around '83, maybe '84, when we thought actually that cases were dropping off. . . . So therefore this was dying out, and that this was some sort of epidemic phenomenon that is reproducible in other epidemics where the most vulnerable people get it and die and everyone else develops immunity. That little window of optimism didn't last long

. . . The reluctance to acknowledge the extent to which AIDS would take on epidemic proportions was not unique to the world of hemophilia. Those who already believed that a menacing new disease was taking hold face what, from the perspective of a few short years later, would seem like sheer blindness. Donna Mildvan, who acknowledged her own failure to recognize AIDS in an intravenous drug user because he wasn't gay, was nevertheless troubled by the resistance she witnessed.

> Everybody was resistant in states . . . or maybe believed it and couldn't deal with it. I don't know. But it was like nothing was going away; nothing was untrue of our worst fears, and they were just growing, because there would be new fears and new implications, and new populations were getting drawn into this to the point that it had gotten very very awful. . . . The reality was a lot worse than anybody would have ever dreamt.

Dan William, who had worked with Mildvan, was especially concerned about the extent to which the new disease would spread among gay men.

> The anxiety of those early years was palpable. It was very, very much greater than you can describe, because people like Donna and myself, and I think other physicians recognized the potential for the devastation that eventually would ensue. . . . I had very strong feelings about it, and many people didn't want to believe it. If you listen to Jim Curran [head of the CDC's AIDS Program] in the early days of the epidemic, he always used to end on an optimistic basis, that epidemics come, and they go, so we may be at the peak, we may not; maybe this is just a little quirk. Keep calm, and don't be too upset. It was beyond frightening. . . . Realizing early on that this is probably sexually transmitted, that it's sexually transmitted the same way as hepatitis B, that the prevalence of hepatitis B in the gay community [may be 40 percent], and the end result is death or disability, you're talking about a major disaster. . . . History is full of situations like AIDS; it's really not unique. I mean it's our own holocaust. . . . And [in] every holocaust there were warnings. There was Crystal Night in Germany.

For many gay men, a lifestyle involving the broad acceptance of multiple sexual partners and the thrill of sexual abandon was part of a precious and newly won freedom. To be told this freedom was implicated in a life-threatening disease was especially disturbing, even oppressive. To counsel restraint was tantamount to a rejection of their liberation. In looking back to the first years of the AIDS epidemic, William Owen, a founding member of the gay doctors organization, BAPHR, was especially concerned to place gay anxieties in historical perspective and to provide a justification for those who were circumspect in their warnings about sex.

> It's very easy to look through the retrospective, but the fact of the matter is this was a group of people who for many years had been repressed in terms of their sexuality. And for the first time in the mid-'70s and after Stonewall in '69, with the dawning of the gay revolution, people really felt the ability to express themselves sexually, like they couldn't do before; and in some ways it's like a kid in a candy store. They suddenly had the ability to do something that they were previously restricted from doing; so sometimes they go a little bit too far and have too many contacts. . . . *Basically the kind of diseases that we saw people coming in for were essentially treatable diseases. The gonorrhea was treatable; syphilis was treatable. Giardiasis, shigella infections, they were all treatable things.* If doctors were to have

Primary Source

San Francisco AIDS Foundation Advertisement
This ad was put out in 1986 by the San Francisco AIDS Foundation to combat stereotype that only gay men were at risk of AIDS. COURTESY OF THE SAN FRANCISCO AIDS FOUNDATION.

come out then [by warning about the dangers of an exuberant sexuality], they would have been seen as some sort of fringe element aligned with either the church or the state or the psychiatric profession, all of whom were not held in very high esteem. And so I think our voices would not have been listened to anyway.

While BAPHR did ultimately issue guidelines on sexual risk reduction in 1983, the reaction of many to those who sought to sound the tocsin was dismay. As an openly gay physician, Dan William was especially troubled.

I can remember very vividly: I was scared and anxious and afraid. Not for my own personal safety but for the health of the community. And 95 percent of people were pooh-poohing it. . . . Any kind of intrusion on sexual behavior was looked at as an intrusion upon one's gayness, and that got in the way. And in those early years . . . I got into a little bit of hot water with the community for implying that people had to consider making changes and altering behavior to lessen the probability of transmission of this illness which we did not understand at all.

. . . Even as some like Dan William struggled to convey a message of caution, others continued to embrace denial. Stosh Ostrow describes what may have been the first national conference of AIDS in 1983, a meeting sponsored by the American Association of Physicians for Human Rights and the National Gay and Lesbian Health Education Fund. It was, he recalls, a "horrible meeting."

The physicians were conservative; the others very radical. We were talking about this disease and lack of government response and blah, blah, blah, and Bernice Goodman got up and said it was a CIA plot to kill the homosexuals. . . . And it was very, very, strange, now looking back on it, that we were talking

about this disease that was killing people, and [we] knew at that point that it was sexually transmitted but didn't clearly know that we had a responsibility to behave differently. I can remember having sex with another physician there and using Phisohex as a lubricant, thinking, well, it's antibacterial, maybe it'll help. Never considered the idea of a condom.

Further Resources

BOOKS

Andriote, John-Manuel. *Victory Deferred: How AIDS Changed Gay Life in America.* Chicago: University of Chicago Press, 1999.

Garrett, Laurie. *The Coming Plague: Newly Emerging Diseases in a World Out of Balance.* New York: Farrar, Strauss and Giroux, 1994.

Kramer, Larry. *Reports from the Holocaust: The Making of an AIDS Activist.* New York: St. Martin's Press, 1989.

Patton, Cindy. *Fatal Advice: How Safe-Sex Education Went Wrong.* Durham, N.C.: Duke University Press, 1996.

Selwyn, Peter A. *Surviving the Fall: The Personal Journey of an AIDS Doctor.* New Haven, Conn.: Yale University Press, 1998.

Shilts, Randy. *And the Band Played On: Politics, People, and the AIDS Epidemic.* New York: St. Martin's Press, 1987.

WEBSITES

"GMHC: HIV and AIDS Information." Gay Men's Health Crisis. Available online at http://www.gmhc.org (accessed March 22, 2003).

"National Center for HIV, STD, and TB Prevention: Divisions of HIV/AIDS Prevention." Centers for Disease Control and Prevention. Available online at http://www.cdc.gov/hiv /dhap.htm; website home page: http://www.cdc.gov/ (accessed March 22, 2003).

San Francisco AIDS Foundation. Available online at http:// www.sfaf.org (accessed March 22, 2003).

Army Recruiting Advertisements

"Be All That You Can Be: 95 Bravo"; "Take Something Valuable to College"

Magazine advertisements

By: NW Ayer
Date: 1980s
Source: Gaslight Advertising Archives, Inc. Available online at http://www.gaslightarchives.com (accessed March 27, 2003).
About the Organization: Anticipating a shortfall in its recruiting goals, the U.S. Army hired the NW Ayer advertising

Primary Source

"Be All That You Can Be: 95 Bravo"

SYNOPSIS: From 1980 to 1987, the "Be All You Can Be" ads created by the NW Ayer agency appeared in print, radio, and television spots. Of the $162 million advertising budget of the federal government in 1983, about $89 million went to promote Army recruitment. The first series of ads promoted the military as a path to a professional career, whereas later ads portrayed life in the Army as a character-building experience that fostered team work and discipline. ARMY MATERIALS COURTESY OF U.S. GOVERNMENT. REPRODUCED BY PERMISSION.

PVT Bob Doyle, Fort Gordon, GA, is not only accumulating money for college—he's also acquiring skills in communication electronics.

TAKE SOMETHING VALUABLE TO COLLEGE.

THE ARMY COLLEGE FUND

The Veterans' Educational Assistance Program with extra Active benefits

Some people choose the Army instead of college. But today, more and more bright young people are choosing the Army and college.

One reason is the Army College Fund. If you qualify, it means you can accumulate as much as $20,100 for tuition in just three years.

The Army College Fund works like a savings plan. For every $1 you save from your Army salary (salaries start at more than $570 a month), the government adds $5 or more.

But financial aid isn't the only benefit.

You also get the benefits of Army skill training. Today's Army runs on technology. So you could find yourself working with microprocessors, electronic microscopes or troposcatter radios.

All in all, it's the kind of training and experience that could tell you what you want to gain from college.

To find out what the Army College Fund offers you, call for a free booklet, toll free, 1-800-USA-ARMY.

ARMY.
BE ALL YOU CAN BE.

Primary Source

"Take Something Valuable to College"
The "Be All That You Can Be" campaign stressed that serving in the army could help someone prepare for later civilian life, by providing skills and also helping pay for college. ARMY MATERIALS COURTESY OF U.S. GOVERNMENT. REPRODUCED BY PERMISSION.

A U.S. Navy Lieutenant inducts a new group of recruits into the military. AP/WORLD WIDE PHOTOS. REPRODUCED BY PERMISSION.

agency to launch a promotional campaign in 1980. NW Ayer was founded in 1869 and is responsible for such famous lines as DeBeers' "A diamond is forever" and AT&T's "Reach out and touch someone." For the Army, the agency developed a series of ads under the slogan "Be All You Can Be," which was heard on radio and television spots and featured heavily in its print ads. The campaign became one of the most successful in advertising history; in addition to winning dozens of awards, it accomplished its goal of helping the U.S. Army meet—and even exceed—its recruiting target in the 1980s ■

Introduction

Few politicians invoked patriotic themes more effectively than Ronald Reagan (served 1981–1989), who was elected in part on his pledge to restore pride and dignity in America's foreign relations. His presidency kicked off on a high note with the release of fifty-two American hostages from the U.S. Embassy in Tehran, Iran, on the very day of his inauguration in 1981. In October 1983 Reagan ordered an invasion of the Caribbean island of Grenada, where he claimed that Marxist rebels posed a threat; his critics accused him of using the event to detract attention from the country's foreign policy problems, which included the deadly bombing of an American

barracks in Lebanon just days earlier, killing 241 marines and other military personnel.

Reagan focused most of his foreign policy efforts on strengthening America's position against the Soviet Union and its allies in the Cold War. Although the two major superpowers avoided overt military conflicts, relations between them remained tense and filled with suspicion. Portraying the struggle between the capitalist democracies of the West and the communist, totalitarian regimes of the Eastern Bloc in moral terms, Reagan took to calling the Soviet Union the "evil empire." Arguing that the western allies could best bargain from a position of "peace through strength," Reagan endorsed a military buildup that increased budget expenditures on defense by thirty-five percent during his two terms in office. Part of the budget increase went to promote enlistments into the various military branches, which had a more difficult time filling their ranks since the draft had ended in 1973. Facing competition from the private sector, a smaller pool of post-baby boom potential recruits, and higher standards for incoming enlistees, the U.S. Army embarked on an aggressive public-relations campaign in 1980 under the slogan "Be All You Can Be."

Significance

The "Be All You Can Be" campaign, which ran throughout the 1980s, highlighted the job skills and upward career mobility that serving in the U.S. Army could offer its recruits. Its appeal to individual interests differed significantly from past recruiting efforts, which often invoked patriotic sentiments of self-sacrifice for the good of the nation. Although some critics carped that the picture of military life rendered by the "Be All You Can Be" ads was unrealistic, Army officials insisted that all of the ads were screened carefully for their authenticity. With $89 million spent on the campaign in 1983 alone, the Army reached about fourteen million people in its target audience of eighteen- to twenty-four-year-olds every month. The ads featured real Army soldiers of a variety of ethnic backgrounds, although very few women were featured. The ads were so successful that the Army consistently met or exceeded its recruitment goals during the 1980s, although economic uncertainties early in the decade also played a role in attracting recruits to its ranks.

The barrage of ads for the Army also mirrored a rise in military and patriotic themes in the popular culture of the 1980s. From the popularity of country singer Lee Greenwood's religious-themed "God Bless the U.S.A." to the glamor of Tom Cruise's fighter-pilot in *Top Gun* to the action of Sylvester Stallone's *Rambo* series, Americans asserted feelings of national pride in the music they listened to and the movies they watched. Even Bruce Springsteen's critical portrait of a Vietnam veteran in "Born in the U.S.A." was adopted by Ronald Reagan in his 1984 reelection campaign as a sign of a national reawakening of patriotism. Reagan dropped his reference to Springsteen's hit, however, after the singer protested that the president was misinterpreting his lyrics. Reagan also deemphasized his association with America's military after the Iran-Contra scandal—in which members of his staff illegally funneled money to anti-Communist forces in Nicaragua—made headlines in 1986.

Further Resources

BOOKS

Ehrenreich, Barbara. *Blood Rites: Origins and History of the Passions of War.* New York: Metropolitan Books, 1997.

Jeffords, Susan. *The Remasculinization of America: Gender and the Vietnam War.* Bloomington: Indiana University Press, 1989.

Kimmel, Michael S. *Manhood in America: A Cultural History.* New York: The Free Press, 1996.

Melanson, Richard A. *Reconstructing Consensus: American Foreign Policy Since the Vietnam War.* New York: St. Martin's Press, 1991.

Schnakenberg, Robert. "Be All That You Can Be Campaign." In *Encyclopedia of Major Marketing Campaigns.* Thomas Riggs, ed. Detroit: Gale Group, 2000, 1828–1832.

Slotkin, Richard. *Gunfighter Nation: The Myth of the Frontier in Twentieth-Century America.* New York: Atheneum, 1992.

WEBSITES

"Ronald Reagan: Evil Empire Speech." Internet Modern History Sourcebook. Available online at http://www.fordham.edu/halsall/mod/1982reagan1.html; website home page: http://www.fordham.edu/ (accessed March 25, 2003).

"President Reagan's Speech Before the National Association of Evangelicals." The Ronald Reagan Home Page. Available online at http://reagan.webteamone.com/speeches/empire.cfm; website home page: http://www.presidentreagan.info/ (accessed March 25, 2003).

"U.S. Army." Available online at http://www.goarmy.com (accessed January 1, 2003).

AUDIO AND VISUAL MEDIA

Top Gun. Paramount Video, 1986.

First Blood. Artisan/Fox Video, 1982.

Under Fire: An American Story
Memoir

By: Oliver L. North with William Novak

Date: 1991

Source: North, Oliver L., with William Novak. *Under Fire: An American Story.* New York: HarperCollins, 1991, 9–11, 14–15, 409.

About the Author: Oliver L. North (1943–), the son of a U.S. Army lieutenant colonel, graduated from the U.S. Naval Academy and served on active duty in Vietnam in 1968–1969. In the 1970s he taught guerilla warfare tactics at U.S. Marine training centers in Virginia and Okinawa. In 1981 North joined the staff of the National Security Council. After Congress prohibited funding of the Contras, an anti-Communist rebel group dedicated to the overthrow of the Nicaraguan government, North began secretly raising funds for the group. When he was authorized to sell arms to Iran in 1985 with the intent to enlist that country's efforts to secure the release of American hostages in Lebanon, North decided to overcharge the Iranians and funnel the rest of the proceeds to the Contras. When the Iran-Contra affair, with North at its center, hit the headlines in late 1986, it damaged the credibility of the Reagan administration, even though it was never clear who authorized the deal and who knew about it. ■

Introduction

The election of Ronald Reagan (served 1981–1989) in 1980 marked a resurgence in American patriotism. Not only did the president-elect invoke images of national pride and references to America's destiny as the leader of the free world, he also sharpened his rhetoric against the Soviet Union and its Communist satellites. In October 1983 Reagan directly confronted the spread of communism when he ordered the invasion of the Caribbean island of Grenada, which had been taken over by a government of avowed Marxists. One of the key military planners of the invasion was Lieutenant Colonel Oliver L. North, whom Reagan called "my favorite Marine."

Like Reagan, North believed that America had a destiny to bring democracy and capitalism to countries under repressive communist rule. North was especially disturbed at the presence of a communist government in the Central American nation of Nicaragua, which had been taken over by the Sandinistas after years of corrupt, dictatorial rule by the Somoza family, who had the backing of the United States. Although the Reagan administration supported the Contras, a group dedicated to ousting the Sandinistas, Congress banned funding to the group in 1984. To get around the ban, North started to raise money for the Contras from private groups. He also hit upon a blatantly illegal plan to funnel money to the Contras by diverting funds from a secret arms sale to Iran that the Reagan administration had authorized. North later claimed that he acted with the full knowledge of CIA director William J. Casey (who was, by then, deceased) and National Security Director John Poindexter. After reports of the Iran-Contra deal surfaced during a Congressional probe, North was dismissed from the National Security Council on November 25, 1986. As the extent of the administration's involvement became known, Iran-Contra grew into the decade's biggest scandal.

Significance

Most Americans were shocked that the Reagan administration would engage in negotiations with the regime of Iran's Ayatollah Khomeini, who had held fifty-two Americans hostage only a few years before. More shocking was the realization that the CIA had apparently created a secret espionage agency that funded military operatives abroad in defiance of Congress. The popularity of President Reagan also suffered as he maintained that he either did not know of the Iran-Contra plans or could not remember them. Although Reagan emerged from the scandal relatively intact, his administration limped to its conclusion in 1989. In 1994, Reagan announced that he was suffering from Alzheimer's disease, a major factor in his memory loss.

North, on the other hand, presented himself as a true American patriot in the Cold War tradition. Appearing before Congressional hearings in July 1987 in his Marine uniform with his wife, Betsy, at his side, North insisted that he acted on the orders of his superiors in carrying out the Iran-Contra mission. Although North made some startling admissions of wrongdoing, he maintained that he had only acted to help the Contras because of his anti-Communist beliefs. Later convicted of obstructing Congress, destroying documents, and accept-

President Reagan spoke to the nation on March 4, 1987, to admit that government agencies under his administration traded arms for hostages with Iran, and funneled profits from this to help the Contras in Nicaragua. © BETTMANN/CORBIS. REPRODUCED BY PERMISSION.

ing an illegal gratuity as a government employee, North avoided more serious charges when the Reagan administration refused to release certain classified documents to the prosecution. After North's convictions were overturned on a technicality, he ran unsuccessfully for the U.S. Senate in 1994.

In hindsight, the Iran-Contra scandal was the one of the last acts of America's Cold War with the Communist bloc. By the time the Iran-Contra affair settled down, America's long-standing fears of communist domination had indeed undergone a fundamental shift: In 1989 the Berlin Wall, separating democratic West and communist East Germany, was torn down and less than two years later the Soviet Union ceased to exist as several of its captive republics broke away.

Primary Source

Under Fire: An American Story [excerpt]

SYNOPSIS: North claimed to be surprised that the Reagan administration placed the blame for the Iran-Contra affair squarely on his shoulders. Looking back, however, even North had a difficult time proving that the president was aware of the secret

Oliver North testifies on the Iran-Contra affair before a joint committee of the U.S. Senate and House in July 1987. **AP/WIDE WORLD PHOTOS. REPRODUCED BY PERMISSION.**

arms-for-hostages deal that became public in 1986. In this excerpt, North explains the political fallout over Iran-Contra and Reagan's ability to keep the scandal from sticking to him, one of the reasons he earned the nickname "The Teflon President."

I had just been fired by the President on national television. If that was really necessary, I could live with it. But what was that the Attorney General had said? That there might be *criminality* involved?

Was he serious? I knew we were facing a political disaster, and that there would be political consequences. But never in my darkest nightmares did I imagine that anything I had done in the service of the President, my commander-in-chief, could lead to criminal charges.

I wasn't part of the President's inner circle, but one thing I knew: Ronald Reagan was in no danger of being impeached. For one thing, nobody wanted

to go through *that* again, one such crisis in a generation was enough, thank you. For another, President Reagan was loved and trusted by a vast majority of the American people.

With a few exceptions, even his critics did not want to see him impeached. Although the President's approval rating underwent a sharp decline, the word "impeachment" was rarely spoken in public— not even by congressional Democrats. Lee Hamilton, chairman of the House Intelligence Committee, used the dreaded "I" word as part of a hypothetical response to a question on ABC's "This Week with David Brinkley." And on March 5, 1987, Congressman Henry Gonzalez introduced a resolution of impeachment in the House of Representatives, which went nowhere. But these were isolated exceptions.

In the fall of 1986, President Reagan was still so popular that he and Nancy could have invited Fi-del Castro to a testimonial dinner at the White House for Ayatollah Khomeini without suffering overwhelming political damage. People would have shaken their heads, they would have wondered, but Ronald Reagan would have remained popular. If the Constitution had allowed him to seek a third term, I have no doubt that he would have run again in 1988. And, just as in 1984 against Mondale, he would have been reelected in a landslide. Iran-contra would have hurt him, certainly, but it wouldn't have been fatal.

By going public so quickly with the "diversion," the President's top advisers were essentially trading one risk for another. They could have decided to batten down the hatches and weather out the storm while we made one final effort to get the hostages out. But when our government announced, in effect, that the Iranians had been overcharged for the arms they had purchased, and that Iran had been subsidizing the Nicaraguan resistance without even knowing it—what about *those* political damages? Who knew how the government leaders in Tehran, or the hostage-takers in Beirut, might react to this humiliation from Washington? Wasn't it possible that this announcement might lead to further recriminations against the hostages or other acts of violence against the United States?

President Reagan could have handled the whole thing very differently. He could have said, "The buck stops here. I knew about the diversion. I approved it because I would have done just about anything to get our hostages out of Iran, and to avoid abandoning the contras in the midst of their life-and-death struggle. It's the President's mandate to determine our foreign policy, and as your President, I accept responsibility for everything that happened on my watch.

If the President had said that, what would Congress have done? Sure, many Democrats would have been angry, but were they any less angry when the President said he *didn't* know?

As soon as the press conference was over, everybody's favorite Watergate question began to reverberate around the nation like a battle cry: what did the President know, and when did he know it? . . .

President Reagan didn't always know what he knew. I believe he was *told* about the transfer of funds to the contras, but that doesn't mean he paid attention to it or remembered it. Early in 1987, the President made clear to his own Tower Commission that he wasn't really sure *what* he recalled about the Iran initiative, or whether he had approved a No-

vember 1985 arms shipment by the Israelis. He testified that he didn't know anything about the early TOW shipments to Iran, although by the time he wrote his memoirs he apparently remembered again.

The 1989 videotape of his testimony at the Poindexter trial showed us a terribly sad portrait of an aging and confused man who appeared to recall astonishingly little about his own administration. But even in better years, President Reagan preferred to concentrate on broad policies and values. He was never very inquisitive or curious, and he generally left the details to his subordinates. It seemed to me that he sometimes wanted to ask a question, but then didn't do so because it would have seemed to be a "stupid question" and he didn't want to appear not to know something others would think he should have known.

Admiral Poindexter has said that, hypothetically speaking, if he had discussed the "diversion" with the President, the President would have okayed it. "I was convinced," the admiral testified at the hearing, "that I understood the President's thinking on this, and that if I had taken it to him that he would have approved it."

I agree. Ronald Reagan knew of and approved a great deal of what went on with both the Iranian initiative and the private support efforts on behalf of the contras, and he received regular, detailed briefings on both topics. He met on several occasions with private donors to the resistance, and at least once, it appears, he personally solicited a foreign leader—King Fahd of Saudi Arabia—and asked him to double his contribution. Given President Reagan's policies and directives, I have no doubt that he was told about the use of residuals for the contras, and that he approved it. Enthusiastically. . . .

Later, when the whole thing blew up in his face, President Reagan claimed to accept responsibility for Iran-contra. But his professions rang hollow as he evaded real responsibility for what had happened by claiming that he just didn't know. It was a weak defense, and it reflected badly on him and his presidency.

Further Resources

BOOKS

Bradlee, Jr., Ben. *Guts and Glory: The Rise and Fall of Oliver North.* New York: Fine, 1988.

Draper, Theodore. *A Very Thin Line: The Iran-Contra Affairs.* New York: Hill and Wang, 1992.

Fried, Amy. *Muffled Echoes: Oliver North and the Politics of Public Opinion.* New York: Columbia University Press, 1997.

Liman, Arthur L., with the assistance of Peter Israel. *Lawyer: A Life of Counsel and Controversy.* New York: Public Affairs, 1998.

Tower, John, R.W. Apple, Jr., and Edmund S. Muskie. *The Tower Commission Report: The Full Text of the President's Special Review Board.* New York: Bantam, 1987.

Walsh, Lawrence E. *Firewall: The Iran-Contra Conspiracy and Cover Up.* New York: Norton, 1998.

PERIODICALS

Hackett, George, and Richard Sandza. "With Ollie North in the 'Eye of the Hurricane': A Lifetime of Service, a Cynical View of Government." *Newsweek,* July 13, 1987, 16–18.

Martz, Larry. "Ollie Takes the Hill: The 'Fall Guy' Becomes a National Folk Hero." *Newsweek,* July 20, 1987, 12–20.

AUDIO AND VISUAL MEDIA

Cover-Up: Behind the Iran-Contra Affair. Directed by Barbara Trent. MPI Home Video. Videocassette, 1988.

Deindustrializing America

Rivethead: Tales from the Assembly Line

Autobiography

By: Ben Hamper

Date: 1991

Source: Hamper, Ben. *Rivethead: Tales from the Assembly Line.* New York: Warner Books, 1991, 117–119.

About the Author: Ben Hamper (1958–), a native of Flint, Michigan, went to work on a General Motors assembly line in 1977. He was the fourth generation in his family to become an autoworker, or "shoprat," as he called it. The deadening pace of the line and uncertainty of constantly being laid off and recalled induced panic attacks in Hamper, who finally left his factory job to pursue writing full-time as a columnist for the *Michigan Voice* and other publications. After appearing in Michael Moore's documentary of deindustrialization and its impact on Flint, *Roger and Me,* Hamper published *Rivethead* in 1991.

End of the Line: Autoworkers and the American Dream

Oral history

By: Richard Feldman and Michael Betzold, eds.

Date: 1990

Source: Feldman, Richard, and Michael Betzold, eds. *End of the Line: Autoworkers and the American Dream.* Urbana: University of Illinois Press, 1990, 111–114, 191, 195, 196–197.

About the Authors: The oral histories collected in *End of the Line* were solicited from workers at the Ford Motor Company's Michigan Truck Plant, located just outside of Detroit.

Workers at a General Motors plant in California watch as the last car rolls off of the assembly line before the plant closes due to high costs and low sales. **AP/WIDE WORLD PHOTOS. REPRODUCED BY PERMISSION.**

Most of the plant's workers had suffered layoffs during the recessions of the 1970s and early 1980s. By the mid-1980s truck sales had picked up enough that most of the workers had been called back to work, yet the fears of economic insecurity remained paramount in their minds. ∎

Introduction

In the 1980s the long-term effects of the energy crisis of the mid-1970s became fully apparent in the American economy. Many of the country's industries—from steel making to ship building to apparel and shoe manufacturing—went into sharp decline. In some cases the plant closures were directly related to the higher energy prices that by then were being felt in the global marketplace. Other companies had not invested in new product lines and technologies and floundered when consumer tastes and demands began to change quickly. High interest rates, put into place to dampen the rising inflation of the late 1970s, also made borrowing money to reinvest in aging factories more expensive. Some corporate officials also blamed higher wages in the American work force as driving manufacturing plants to low-wage locations in developing nations, especially Mexico.

No industry seemed harder hit by the economic crunch in the years around 1980 than the American automobile industry. The "Big Three" auto makers—General Motors, Ford, and Chrysler—had served as the gauge of the country's industrial might and economic progress for most of the twentieth century. Steady profits on larger cars stifled their interest in building smaller, more fuel-efficient cars, a policy that proved disastrous as gasoline prices climbed and consumers bought Japanese economy cars in droves. Although industry and labor union officials tried to get consumers to "Buy American," the Big Three's problems continued to mount. When the Chrysler Corporation faced bankruptcy in January 1980, the Carter administration took the unprecedented step of ordering a $1.2 billion loan guarantee to keep the company open.

Not everyone was disturbed by the plant shutdowns in the industrial Northeast and Midwest. Supporters of President Ronald Reagan's (served 1981–1989) laissez-faire economic policies argued that the global marketplace should determine the course of America's economic changes, regardless of the social costs to American workers. It was up to individual workers to retrain for jobs in the information age instead of calling for the government to subsidize outdated and inefficient industries.

Significance

Although some criticized Reagan's policies toward American workers as uncaring, his administration nonetheless moved aggressively to remove labor unions from the workplace. In a highly symbolic move, Reagan ousted all of the federal air traffic controllers who refused to end their strike in 1981. With the National Labor Relations Board staffed with administrators who were hostile to organized labor, the rate of union membership dropped drastically throughout Reagan's two terms, from twenty-five to sixteen percent of the work force. The trend was reinforced by the ongoing shift to a service-oriented economy, and many observers predicted that America was entering a "post-industrial" age.

By the mid-1980s lower interest rates, foreign investment, and falling energy prices had restored some of the vitality to American industry. Although the word "downsizing" entered the American vocabulary to describe the smaller number of workers who were employed, plant closures made the headlines less often. Despite the economic expansion that took off after the recession of 1981–1982, workers who returned to their former jobs retained a sense of uncertainty in the rapidly changing economy. Autoworker Sheryl Jackson, who worked at a Ford plant in Michigan, described her feelings after being called back to work after a six-year lay-off: "Now that my foot's back in the door," she said, "I'm going to try to save some money, so when they kick me out again, I'll have something to fall back on."

Jackson's outlook was shared by millions of other Americans, from blue-collar workers to white-collar professionals, who also experienced the layoffs generated by leveraged buyouts financed by junk-bond financiers. By the end of the decade the symbol of America's economic uncertainty was no longer the closed auto plant or steel mill, but rather Wall Street barons such as Henry Kravis, who bought up companies only to dismantle them in search of quick profits, and Michael Milken and Ivan Boesky, who became multimillionaires through illegal financial transactions. Milken and Boesky were both sent to jail on securities fraud and insider-trading charges, but emerged from jail with much of their fortunes intact.

Primary Source

Rivethead: Tales from the Assembly Line [excerpt]

SYNOPSIS: Like many industrial workers in the 1980s, Ben Hamper constantly worried about his job security. After enduring one particularly long layoff, Hamper was glad to hear that General Motors had secured a defense contract that put him back to work.

Another layoff swallowed me up, this time, the grandpappy of 'em all. I was out of work for nearly a year, far too long a span when you stopped to consider Reagan was now in power. Ron wasn't nearly as charitable as our old pal Jimmy Carter. He had his own designs on what he wanted to do with the budget and they surely didn't include funnelling any of it into the frayed pocket lining of Joe Lunchpail. No more safety nets for the urchins of the fickle industry.

On the verge of poverty, Dave Steel and I were really beginning to sweat it. We began calling up co-workers who were still clinging to their jobs in the plant. We started hittin' them up for every two-bit rumor they could hustle down. Bob-A-Lou informed me that there was some heavy chatter making the rounds regarding a new product being introduced at out plant. No one was sure what this mystery vehicle would be, but the grapevine was practically smoldering. Dave was receiving the same scuttlebutt from his sources.

We'd both been fortunate up until then. Each time we'd been shelved, GM reeled us back in just

Americans at work in a Mitsubishi auto plant in Normal, Ill., in November 1988. The establishment of Japanese car factories in the United States highlighted the decline of traditional American manufacturers during the 1980s. AP/WIDE WORLD PHOTOS. REPRODUCED BY PERMISSION.

before our benefits were set to dissolve, so our lay-offs seemed more like paid vacations. But this was before Reaganomics, before the merry-go-round rusted to a standstill. We weren't carefree spuds anymore. We were thirty . . . something and we had budgets that had entwined themselves around those hefty blue-checkered pay stubs.

All we could do was wait. Wait, wait, wait and pray that the simmering rumors were true. Once again, Richard Dawson's eyes began boring tiny holes little holes in my skull. I'd jump into my Camaro and drive around aimlessly. It wasn't fair. Eleven months of lame luck for a five foot six and a half meat loaf with red eyes and a soul in need of one colossal enema. Seventh Heaven closed for repairs, please proceed to 7-Eleven for as much over-priced beer as you can lug to your car and drive seven miles outta town, plow 'em all down and vomit

out the T-top as the crows all scream your name. I was experiencing shoprat withdrawal. From thoroughbred to sawhorse. I became the third-base coach for my brother's Little League baseball team. I volunteered to take retards to the zoo. I conned my way into my own radio show on the city's Public Broadcasting station, playing Black Flag and Annette Funicello records for a small cult of adolescent skinheads.

And then . . . finally . . . it was HIM! The date: July 26, 1983. The time: 10:00 A.M. EST. The place: General Motors Executive Headquarters, Top Dog Suite, Detroit Michigan.

In one fluid motion, GM Chairman Roger Smith reared back in his leather chair, cocked his arm high above his head, and hurled out the half-eaten remainder of a lemon-filled jelly doughnut out his four-teenth-story window.

A decision had been reached. A nervous smile crept through and replaced the morning-long grimace. Roger Smith—Chairman of the Bored, honcho of a thousand wretched levers—tapped the intercom button for his secretary.

"Miss Henderson, it is time to place the call."

"Oh, Mr. Smith, surely you don't mean—"

"Precisely, Miss Henderson. Tell him we mean it. Tell him to show up promptly and leave his blasphemous notepads behind. Tell him damn the torpedos and damn the Toyotas and damn Iacocca if he gets in our way. Tell him . . . goddamit . . . just tell him we NEED him!"

RINNNNNNNG! RINNNNNNNNG!

. . . he loves me not. He loves me, he loves me not. He loves me . . . well, hell yes that squat little gerbil loves me. After all, who else would rumble outta bed between dreary daymares of life and death and Eve Plumb in turquoise hotpants if not I, the Rivethead, thoroughbred of all thoroughbreds, the quickest triggerman this side of the River Rouge.

"Hello."

"Mr. Hamper?" It was that same sultry monotone, I got goosebumps the size of hubcaps.

"Yes?" I responded breathlessly."

"You are to report back to work at the GM Truck & Bus plant tomorrow morning at 6:00 A.M. for re-hiring."

"I love you."

CLICK!!!!

Apparently my callback to GM was necessitated when the Corporation landed this enormous contract with Uncle Sam to build a shitload of army trucks. This was the mystery product that Bob-A-Lou had been hinting about. Besides Smith, I now had another man to thank for this well turn of events—Caspar (The Friendly) Weinberger. It was this man's dogged lust for a few billion dollars worth of military vehicles that reopened the doors and pumped new life into my sagging shoprat career.

Primary Source

End of the Line: Autoworkers and the American Dream [excerpt]

SYNOPSIS: To Sheryl Jackson, her job as a union-ized employee at Ford's Michigan Truck Plant pro-

vides better wages and benefits that allowed her to afford a middle-class lifestyle. She describes the changes caused by a six-year layoff, including the struggle to make ends meet by cleaning houses while she searched for another job. Jerry Conrad, who started working at Ford in 1966, takes pride in the trucks he builds, which he calls "world-class." Yet he remains frustrated by the callous attitudes of management and the favoritism that he sees in union affairs. He is particularly irritated by American consumers who buy foreign-made cars: "If I saw someone with a broken-down foreign car on the road and it was raining snowballs, I wouldn't stop to help them."

Sheryl Jackson

Born June 29, 1952, in Detroit

Hired July 21, 1977

Assembler on the Engine Line

I grew up in the projects in Detroit, and my mom was on welfare. I remember when I was in junior high, they took us on a tour of an auto plant, and I decided that's where I wanted to work. Before that I had always wanted to be a singer or a seamstress.

After I got married and got a job at Wayne Assembly, I joined the middle class. My husband and I were both working at Ford, and we had financial security. His mother was wealthy. We owned a fish market and a record shop. We were going to move out to the suburbs, get a big trailer home, and travel the world. But all those plans weren't worth the price for me. I finally left my husband because I got tired of him being mean to me. He had served in Vietnam and had seen his buddy get killed, and he would fly off the handle for no reason. Once he even pointed a gun at me. I finally decided I didn't have to live with that. I didn't have to be punished for Vietnam.

Even after the divorce I maintained a comfortable life-style. I stayed in the middle class until they kicked me out the door in February 1980. I was really hurt the way they laid me off. "Here's your pink slip. Just get out; we don't need you anymore." That's how it was. They weren't nice about it.

In a way I was glad to get laid off because I wanted to be with my three kids. I had been working afternoons and didn't get to see them much. Plus I hated working in that place. I had paid my car off, and I wasn't worried because I knew I had ADC [Aid to Dependent Children] to fall back on. And I collected my unemployment for a year. But when that ran out, I had to get by on ADC and food stamps, and that was peanuts, about $500 a month. Out of that I had to pay my house note and the gas and lights.

Things were tight. I couldn't get my kids what they wanted for Christmas. I didn't go to church much because I couldn't afford nice clothes and I didn't have a car. But I read the Bible a lot, and that helped. It said, "Don't worry about what you are going to wear for tomorrow, what you are going to eat. I'll feed you and I'll clothe you." The only way to survive in this world is to be strong. You just have to keep going. Things may be tight now, but don't give up. There is always a brighter day.

I was laid off for six years. I never thought I'd get called back. I looked for other jobs. I took the post office test twice. I took a test for corrections officers twice, but they never called me. After three years with no job I met a lady who has a cleaning business. I started working with her. We would clean houses for rich white folks out in the suburbs for $25 a day. But the work wasn't steady.

I was one of about twenty-nine people who got called back in April 1986 to the truck plant. The first day back we had an orientation. We met all the supervisors, the superintendents, the plant managers. We had coffee and doughnuts, and they told us about the plant, and they had videos and pamphlets about all the chemicals they use. They let us ask questions. Then they took us on the line and showed us the work and we met the foremen. I couldn't believe how nice the people were. They smiled at you and said hi. It's like one big happy family at the truck plant. Everybody talks to everybody.

Now that I'm working, I feel like a human being again. I'm in the work force. I'm in the big leagues. I can take care of my own. I can walk around with my head up high.

If you're on ADC, people don't respect you. They figure all you want to do is sit around and wait for the check. Maybe some women do that, but not me. When I was collecting ADC, I didn't feel like they were giving me anything that I didn't deserve. I felt I was getting back what I had put in from the years I was working and the money they took out of my paycheck for taxes. Now I'm back to work, and I can help somebody else. They take my taxes out and give the money to somebody who can use it.

I get angry about people working overtime. The plant has been on ten hours for a long time. That is a lot of work for one person. Why not split it up and let somebody else get some of that money?

There are a lot of people out there who want work. They don't like sitting around in their houses. They have family and kids, too. Eight hours in enough. Share some of that work. Let everybody have some of the goodies.

I have a friend who was working at an auto plant in the suburbs. She got laid off and never got called back. She is doing housecleaning now.

I'm not greedy to work overtime. Just as long as I have a job, I'm happy. Working all that overtime, what kind of life is that? You don't have time to do anything. You are tired when you come home.

Jerry Conrad

Born September 8, 1939, in Webster Springs, West Virginia

Hired October 27, 1966

Relief man on the Trim Line

The union has changed. When I hired in, the union was really anticompany. That plant chairman who the company sued for stealing the alternators was great. He hated authority. He would put out bulletins that said, "Watch that big fat-ass guard up there; he is watching you." If an assembler was pushing a broom, he'd break the broom because it wasn't in his job classification. I respected that plant chairman for having some balls against the company.

But the union has mellowed on that stuff now. They go along with that EI bullshit. EI is just a bunch of psychology. It benefits the company more than it does the hourly guy. Some guys participate in it just to get an hour off the line. That's tempting, but I don't get involved. Just leave me over on the side, and I'll do my thing and goodbye. I'm a relief man, so I don't work the first hour, I take two hours for lunch and break, and I'm done an hour before quitting time, so I can't bitch. They don't say anything, so I just do my job and don't say anything to them. . . .

The truck plant is making gobs of money now because we're putting out a world-class unit and they are not paying a second shift. They're overloaded with jobs. The best thing for quality would be so slow down the line so people could do their jobs better.

Meanwhile, the politicians are letting these Japanese imports in. They're getting their kickbacks and we're getting shit. It's a damn rip-off. The politicians are getting richer, and we are busing our butts trying to make a buck. I'm a registered Democrat, I always vote Democrat, but I have no sympathies with the son of a guns. I know they are getting kickbacks for these imports.

The foreign companies are smart. They're bringing their auto plants over here, but they are still selling a foreign-made product. I don't blame the people who work there; a guy has to work.

If I saw someone with a broken-down foreign car on the road and it was raining snowballs, I wouldn't stop to help them. Not here in the Detroit area, no way in hell. I was at a picnic at my wife's uncle's house the other day. He was driving a damn Toyota. He is making American bucks and buys a foreign product, and I resent that.

I remember it used to be you wouldn't even buy another American company's car. Some guy was telling me he had to park across the street because he had a Chrysler car and worked in a Ford plant. If he parked in the lot, he'd find his tires flat and his windows busted out. Now I got a friend on Line One and he went out last week and bought a General Motors truck for $18,000, and I said, "I hope it blows up on you." I couldn't believe that. The guy is biting the hand that feeds him. He could have gotten the same pickup here a lot cheaper. But he didn't like the Ford product.

I remember back in 1980 when this TV newsman was reporting on the big recession live from the parking lot of the Michigan Truck Plant. He was talking about how foreign orders are killing Detroit and how the truck plant went down to one shift, and all the time he's on TV he's backed up against this repairman's Toyota pickup. Boy, did we give that repairman hell. About a week later he traded in the Toyota and got a Ford pickup.

Further Resources
BOOKS
Dudley, Kathryn Marie. *The End of the Line: Lost Jobs, New Lives in Postindustrial America.* Chicago: University of Chicago Press, 1994.

Freeman, Joshua, Norman Lichtenstein, and Stephen Brier. *Who Built America?: Working People and the Nation's Economy, Politics, Culture, and Society.* New York: Pantheon Book, 1992.

Geoghegan, Thomas. *Which Side Are You On?: Trying to Be for Labor When It's Flat on Its Back.* New York: Farrar, Straus, Giroux, 1991.

Ingrassia, Paul, and Joseph B. White. *Comeback: The Fall and Rise of the American Automobile Industry.* New York: Simon & Schuster, 1994.

Keller, Maryann. *Rude Awakening: The Rise, Fall, and Struggle for Recovery of General Motors.* New York: Morrow, 1989.

Sugrue, Thomas. *The Origins of the Urban Crisis: Race and Inequality in Postwar Detroit.* Princeton, N.J.: Princeton University Press, 1996.

Terkel, Studs. *Working: People Talk About What They Do All Day and How They Feel About What They Do.* New York: Pantheon Books, 1974.

PERIODICALS
"Rivethead on the Road." *Detroit Free Press Magazine,* June 7, 1992, 6–20.

Cry of the Invisible: Writings from the Homeless and Survivors of Psychiatric Hospitals
Nonfiction work

By: Michael A. Susko, ed.
Date: 1991
Source: Susko, Michael A., ed. *Cry of the Invisible: Writings from the Homeless and Survivors of Psychiatric Hospitals.* Baltimore. The Conservancy Press, 1991, 214–215, 230–231, 233, 235.
About the Author: Michael A. Susko, a Baltimore-based counselor who had worked for more than a decade with the homeless, collected the narratives in *Cry of the Invisible.* By focusing attention on the lives of the "invisible" people of the street, Susko also hoped to help the individuals find validation and healing. Rob, who describes his first day of being homeless, had graduated from medical school before schizophrenia left him unable to hold a job and alienated from his family. Like Rob, Jan was also diagnosed with mental disorders that resulted in several hospitalizations, which she resented. As her narrative shows, the institutional response to homelessness was often ineffective, and even counterproductive. ∎

Introduction

There has always been at least a small number of people who lived without permanent shelter throughout American history. Known in different eras as "hoboes," "vagrants," or "street people," it was not until the 1970s that the term "homeless" came into wide usage to refer to people who spent their days and nights in public places or in shelters that did not require payment. Given the difficulties of tracking the homeless population, estimates of their numbers ranged from half a million to three million in the 1980s; even with the imprecise measurements, experts agreed that the incidence of homelessness rose sharply around 1980. As in the past, most of the homeless were single men who performed odd jobs or panhandled during the day but did not make enough money to pay for a place to spend the night. A growing number of single women, sometimes dismissed as "bag ladies," and families, typically single mothers and their children, also began appearing on the streets.

As homelessness developed into a chronic and growing problem in the 1980s, experts struggled to explain why more people were out on the streets during an era of apparent prosperity. Many Americans had memories of hoboes traveling the country during the Great Depression, but the presence of so many homeless in some of the country's wealthiest cities was a jarring contrast. Part of the problem stemmed from changes in the real estate market and housing codes in most cities, which reduced the number of cheap, single-occupancy hotel rooms available for a couple of dollars per night in the 1970s. The shortage of affordable, if temporary, housing also had an impact on people who were released from mental institutions with the belief that "deinstitutionalizing" them would help them readjust to mainstream society. Anywhere from ten to thirty percent of the homeless in the 1980s suffered from some form of mental illness, which made it even more difficult for them to find housing.

Significance

Although the reasons for the increase in homelessness were complex, the government came in for the greatest share of the blame. Between 1980 and 1987 the percentage of federal spending devoted to human resources fell from twenty-eight to twenty-two percent, while defense expenditures increased from twenty-three to twenty-eight percent. Some human resources programs, such as the Aid to Families with Dependent Children and low-income housing subsidies, were particularly hard hit. When Ronald Reagan (served 1981–1989) took office in 1981, the budget for the Department of Housing and Urban Development was $36 billion; six years later, it had been slashed to $14 billion. President Reagan did little to quell the criticism of his administration when he claimed that some of the homeless were sleeping on the streets "by choice" and that there was nothing to be done to help them.

With the federal government slow to act on the homelessness problem, local governments and nonprofit organizations dealt with the crisis as best they could. The most publicized anti-homelessness effort was the Hands Across America celebration in 1986, which raised $16 million in pledges for antipoverty programs as citizens attempted to link hands across the continent. Religious groups also continued to operate missions and outreach centers, where homeless men could get a meal, bed, and dose of spiritual instruction. Unable to keep up with the demand and the changing nature of the homeless population, which included more women and children, the

missions were joined by municipal shelters, battered women's shelters, and other temporary housing solutions in most American cities. The public outcry over homelessness indeed translated into some effective efforts to provide adequate shelter in many communities; the ongoing lack of affordable housing and job opportunities for the poor, however, meant that thousands of Americans routinely spent the night outdoors, in abandoned buildings, or on public property throughout the 1980s.

Primary Source

Cry of the Invisible: Writings from the Homeless and Survivors of Psychiatric Hospitals [excerpt]

SYNOPSIS: Both Rob and Jan suffered from mental illness as adults and alternated between hospitalizations in psychiatric wards and time on the streets. Critical of the mental health care system's reliance on therapeutic drugs for patients, Jan describes the difficulty of reestablishing her independence after being institutionalized. Rob was also frustrated by his experience with social workers; as he writes elsewhere in his essay, "Never take anyone else's vision of the truth as your own. . . . At the very last moment when I was about to get off the streets I never had more people telling me what I should do. And if I had taken their advice I would still be on the streets today."

Rob's Story

Part Two

With only pennies in my pocket, I spent my first day walking around the city. Food consisted of a package of leftover bread. By nightfall it began to get chilly and as I only had a sweater on, I thought of going to the mission. But I had too much pride and put it out of my mind. I couldn't see myself sharing living quarters with bums and derelicts. . . . It grew colder and colder. I began to shake. I decided I would walk past the Salvation Army just to see what the building looked like. When I got there the door was closed for the night. "Good," I thought, "I didn't want to spend the night there anyway."

Three hours later after the temperature plummeted and I continued to shake, I returned to the mission and knocked on the door. Now I was principally concerned with getting out of the cold. I learned that the mission was closed but there was a sleeping area for drunks along the side—an alley way along a chain-link fence. Unlike the drunks, I didn't have any whiskey in my belly to warm me. "Some protection from the cold" I thought, "a chain link fence with holes in it." I walked on.

A homeless man rests on a bench in Lafayette Square, Washington, D.C., on November 11, 1987. The White House, home to the president of the United States, is behind him. © BETTMANN/CORBIS. REPRODUCED BY PERMISSION.

My legs were stiff and my feet numb. I got some respite from the cold at 5 A.M. when a gas-station attendant let me use the rest room. At 8:45 A.M. I was in the crowd waiting outside the main branch of the city library waiting for the doors to open. Not having slept, my head began to nod as I sat pretending to read a newspaper. Before long, a guard warned me that if I fell asleep I would be asked to leave. For the next three hours my head bobbed up and down like a human bob-o-link.

That evening, I showed up at the mission at 4:15 P.M. when the doors opened. I was not about to be locked out in the cold again.

Thanksgiving came and went, and the weather was getting colder. I had had enough exploring. I called up the parents of a friend from the religious cult and asked if I could stay with them for a few days. I walked through their house with my head bent down, wrapped in thoughts. I was afraid that if I loosened up, my friend's parents would ask me to leave. During meals I kept my eyes glued on the plate and made forced conversation when it seemed appropriate. I braced myself for the inevitable request to leave.

In the meantime my friend's parents had called my family to tell them where I was. They saw no reason why a grown man with so many accomplishments should be locked away in a state mental hospital. On the other hand they didn't want to interfere. So on day five my parents came to pick me up and informed me I was to be taken to a state hospital.

Homeless

by Jan

. . . It's hard to recall what happens when you're out on the streets. At the time, I could only think of the day and my two priorities: where am I going to sleep? Where am I going to eat? I did things always with one eye open. The way I kept track of things was by keeping a calendar. And now, although I'm not a homeless person, I still think as though I'm homeless, i.e. will I sleep OK tonight?

My becoming homeless goes back to being labeled so-called mentally ill in 1987. I wasn't getting along with my family. I was only working part time. I didn't have enough money in my bank account. Two or three months earlier, I had been in a car accident and hadn't received proper treatment. I never really considered how I was going to support myself and added to that was the fact that I wasn't feeling well due to the accident. I was overwhelmed by the responsibility in front of me: I hadn't really been taught living skills. It wasn't that I was out of touch with reality. I was just not prepared to take care of myself, not only as a normal person, but as a person who wasn't in good health. So I checked in at a shelter. It gave me this incredible sense of being overwhelmed.

Someone at the shelter told me to try the Mental Health Center. So I walked in there and tried to explain that I had been in this car accident, and that I was trying to get a job. They said to me, "You look tired, you look depressed."

They gave me Imipramine, an anti-depressant and never told me about the side effects—one being that you get a dry mouth and you need to keep drinking. I just assumed that a psychiatrist was like a normal doctor and would tell me if something could go wrong. After about a week of taking the drug, I was dehydrated. Within a week and a half I was severely dehydrated. Within two week I lost twelve pounds; I wasn't feeding myself properly.

In two weeks I was supposed to check back with the psychiatrist. He said that my eyes were dilated, my skin yellow and that I was severely dehydrated. I was admitted to the medical side of the hospital and was treated. A counselor there said I looked near to death.

While I was lying there, completely exhausted, somebody from the psychiatric unit came and asked me some questions. They asked where I was from. I had lived in twelve to fifteen states. I said, "Well, I guess I'm from Washington D.C. or Maryland or Connecticut. . . ." I was not coming up with a concrete answer which those tests are designed to look for. When they asked for my name, I said, well, you can call me this, this, or this—because I've been called different names, especially depending where I lived. They ended up telling my family I was a very confused person. In reality I was just exhausted. . . .

Within a month after I left, they finally diagnosed me. Although I still had dreams of things I wanted to do, I couldn't hold down a job. Three times I tried—I couldn't sit still. But I could go to school. One summer I took a psychology class and got an A in it.

I had grown dependent on the system to the point of abusing it, only because I was being abused myself and didn't realize it. I didn't realize I was a victim of the mental health system. Even if someone offered me the kind of benefits that you can get in a hospital—I didn't have to pay for it, medicaid did—free food, a country club atmosphere, no responsibilities, I wouldn't go. I did choose to go when I was on drugs because no one, none of my so-called normal friends could tolerate me being around. First of all, I could not sit still—I would just pace back and forth. I would do little annoying things like tap the table. The only people that could stand to be around me were people with the same problems. So we would all go to the same place where we just didn't have to deal with things.

These hospitals were more or less luxury places, with a swimming pool, art therapy, music therapy, dance therapy, psychodrama—and all my friends were in there. It is really difficult to leave the system. I absolutely admire anyone who does. The told me countless times that *I* had a *mental illness,* that *they* were the *mental health system.* They encourage you to depend on them: "they" being the doctors, the drugs, the hospital. They want you to depend on them and when you start showing any sense of independence—which is what they say they are trying to help you obtain—they backtrack. They say, "Well, you're getting a job but if you need us, we will write up a contract for your safety." There's an incredible amount of mixed messages. . . .

I chose to leave the system in 1988. I chose to go off drugs after watching what it had done to myself and to a friend. My friend was on his way to becoming homeless before he committed suicide. He had come from a family background that could have helped him find a place to live, but didn't help him out, which was similar to my situation. The death of my friend really shook me up. I had to ask myself if I wanted to end up like him.

I had never been to a funeral before and I became obsessed with the fact that he was gone. I was obsessed with grieving. I went overboard. I did anything I could to understand why he had died. I began to see similarities between his situation and mine.

I told my social worker that the best thing I could do for myself was to go to the funeral. She said, "Absolutely not. You won't be able to handle it." It was at that point that I realized that somebody was trying to deny me the right to feel something, which was supposedly what therapy was all about. I though, "Wait a minute—hold everything."

I went to the funeral. At that point a lot of things happened, things that these therapists were supposed to be working for. When I came back and said, "I feel better about this, I want to leave the system." They tried to keep me. In fact, they suggested I go into the hospital because I was "obviously" out of control. I wasn't screaming. I wasn't threatening to hurt myself or others. I would just go there and sob and grieve.

My friend's death was an awakening point for me of the reality of the mental health system. Somebody close to me was dead due to falling through the cracks. He went for help constantly and the system failed him. Did *he* commit suicide? Or did the system? I felt I was heading this way, if I didn't get out.

Further Resources

BOOKS

Baum, Alice S., and Donald W. Burnes. *A Nation in Denial: The Truth About Homelessness.* Boulder, Colo.: Westview, 1993.

Blau, Joel. *The Visible Poor: Homelessness in the United States.* New York: Oxford University Press, 1992.

Harrington, Michael. *The New American Poverty.* New York: Holt, Rinehart and Winston, 1984.

Nunez, Ralph da Costa. *The New Poverty: Homeless Families in America.* New York: Insight Books, 1996.

O'Flaherty, Brendan. *Making Room: The Economics of Homelessness.* Cambridge, Mass.: Harvard University Press, 1996.

Phillips, Kevin. *The Politics of Rich and Poor: Wealth and the American Electorate in the Reagan Aftermath.* New York: Random House, 1990.

PERIODICALS

Cowley, Geoffrey, with Elizabeth Ann Leonard and Mary Hager. "Tuberculosis: A Deadly Return." *Newsweek,* March 16, 1992, 52–57.

Morganthau, Tom, et al. "Children of the Underclass." *Newsweek,* September 11, 1989, 16–23.

WEBSITES

National Alliance to End Homelessness. Available online at http://www.naeh.org/ (accessed March 23, 2003).

"Profile of Homelessness." U.S. Department of Health and Human Services. Available online at http://aspe.hhs.gov /progsys/homeless/profile.htm; website home page: http:// www.hhs.gov/ (accessed March 23, 2003).

AUDIO AND VISUAL MATERIALS

Samaritan: The Mitch Snyder Story. Original release (made for TV), 1986. Directed by Richard T. Heffron. VHS, 1991. Fries Home Video.

Televangelism

Son of a Preacher Man: My Search for Grace in the Shadows
Memoir

By: Jay Bakker, with Linden Gross.

Date: 2001

Source: Bakker, Jay, with Linden Gross. *Son of a Preacher Man: My Search for Grace in the Shadows.* New York: HarperCollins, 2001, 6–8.

Tammy: Telling It My Way
Memoir

By: Tammy Faye Messner

Date: 1996

Source: Messner, Tammy Faye. *Tammy: Telling It My Way.* New York: Villard, 1996, 128–129, 145, 147.

I Was Wrong
Memoir

By: Jim Bakker, with Ken Abraham

Date: 1996

Source: Bakker, Jim, with Ken Abraham. *I Was Wrong.* Nashville: Nelson, 1996, 514–515, 517–518.

About the Authors: Jim Bakker (1940–) and Tammy Faye LaValley (1942–) met as students at the North Central College run by the Assemblies of God in Minneapolis, Minnesota. The two dropped out to get married and in 1961 traveled around the country as Jim Bakker preached in various evangelical churches. In 1965 the couple began broadcasting a religious-themed puppet show for children on Pat Robertson's CBN Network in Virginia. A year later Jim Bakker began hosting *The 700 Club,* a variety-talk show aimed at an evangelical audience, in 1966. After leaving Robertson to work in California, the Bakkers relocated to Charlotte and created *The PTL ("Praise the Lord") Club* in 1974. The show was the basis for an evangelical broadcasting and entertainment empire that flourished until 1987, when details emerged of a cover-up of an extramarital affair in which Bakker had been involved seven years earlier. Jim Bakker later served five years in prison for criminal fraud and rival minister Jerry Falwell took over the PTL empire. The Bakkers divorced in 1993 and each subsequently remarried. Both of the Bakkers's children, Tammy Sue (1970–) and Jay (1976–), became ministers, with Jay serving as pastor of Revolution, a ministry devoted to young people. ∎

Introduction

The use of the mass media for religious programming dated back to the live services and gospel hours that were broadcast on radio stations in the 1920s. With the arrival of television in the 1940s and its increasing popularity in the 1950s, figures such as Bishop Fulton J. Sheen, the Reverend Billy Graham, and the Reverend Oral Roberts used the new medium to reach a nationwide audience. In the 1960s a more sophisticated set of religious broadcasters, dubbed "televangelists," offered programs that differed little in style from secular fare—including children's shows, talk shows, and variety shows—with the exception of their religious and spiritual content. Among the most popular of the new media stars were Jim and Tammy Faye Bakker, a young married couple who presented a puppet show to teach children moral and spiritual values. The show, broadcast on Pat Robertson's fledgling Christian Broadcasting Network (CBN) in 1965, led to Jim Bakker's creation of *The 700 Club,* named for an appeal for 700 people to pledge $10 per month to support CBN. The program adopted a talk-show format, albeit with frequent requests for additional donations.

Robertson edged Bakker out of CBN in 1973 to take over *The 700 Club,* which served as the cornerstone for his own lucrative mass-media empire. Bakker went on to found *The PTL Club* in Charlotte, North Carolina in 1974. According to Bakker, the show's initials stood for "Praise the Lord" or "People That Love." Both Bakker and his wife were enthusiastic and telegenic personalities and the PTL soon matched Robertson's success with CBN. As the money from their televised fundraising appeals rolled in, the Bakkers branched out with Heritage USA, a Christian vacation center, amusement park, and campground. Robertson and the Bakkers were joined by other Pentecostal or evangelical ministers in the 1970s and 1980s who preached a message of God's desire for their followers to be prosperous, including Oral Roberts, Jimmy Swaggart, and Jerry Falwell.

Significance

In addition to their gospel of wealth, most of the televangelists preached a conservative political agenda to demand an end to abortion, gay rights, and the ban on prayer in public schools. Although President Jimmy Carter's identity as a "born-again" Christian heartened many evangelicals, his administration's agenda was not conservative enough to secure support from the religious right. In response, Jerry Falwell founded the Moral Majority in 1979 as a political lobbying group on the extreme right wing of the political spectrum. The Moral Majority took credit for helping to elect Ronald Reagan to the presidency in 1980 and indeed, Reagan did secure the support of most religious, conservative voters. In 1988 Pat Robertson decided to follow Falwell's political lead by announcing his own bid for the presidency. Like the Moral Majority's lobbying, Robertson's campaign raised fears among many Americans about the separation of church and state. In the end his bid was more about making headlines than any political impact.

Robertson's presidential bid was also marred by a series of explosive scandals that discredited the televangelists in the late 1980s. In the spring of 1987 reports surfaced of a cover-up of Jim Bakker's brief affair with church secretary Jessica Hahn, which had taken place several years earlier. Within a year the Bakkers had been ousted from PTL and replaced by Jerry Falwell. A criminal investigation eventually led to Jim Bakker's conviction on fraud charges for selling time-share condominiums at Heritage USA that did not actually exist. Following on the heels of the PTL crisis, Oral Roberts demanded $8 million in pledges from his television viewers and threatened that God would "call him home" if he didn't receive the money. His fundraising pitch failed, but Roberts didn't die; he did, however, become a national laughingstock for his desperate bid for money. Further diminishing the reputation of the televangelists, Jimmy Swaggart was caught in a tryst with a prostitute in February 1988; he regained the trust of some of his followers with a tearful confession in which he admitted, "I have sinned," but another publicized liaison with a prostitute in October 1991 seemed to belie his earlier quest for redemption.

Primary Source

Son of a Preacher Man: My Search for Grace in the Shadows [excerpt]

> **SYNOPSIS:** As the son of the PTL's founders, Jay Bakker had perhaps the best perspective of anyone on its mission and the way it operated. In this excerpt he explains how his parents were part of a "gospel of prosperity" movement that dated back to the 1950s in American religion.

My parents met in North Central Bible College in Minnesota, where they were both studying for the ministry. They married soon after, on April 1, 1961, left school, and became itinerant evangelists. Mom played the accordion and sang, and Dad preached. During Sunday school, they would perform a puppet show for children; Mom provided the voices and action for Suzy Moppett and Allie the Alligator, while Dad stood in front and talked to the puppets.

In 1966, that show landed them on Pat Robertson's new TV network. The audience loved them, and what was supposed to be a one-time appearance became a regular feature. The puppet show's success also led to Dad's hosting a Christian TV show called the *700 Club,* which he had modeled after Johnny Carson's *Tonight Show.* The talk show proved an instant hit, and the station's viewership and donations soared. Since the new television ministry didn't sell advertising, its existence was completely dependent on donations. And with this new format, TV religion began to sweep across the nation and eventually the world.

After eight years, Mom and Dad moved away from Pat Robertson. After helping found TBN (Trinity Broadcasting Network), they launched PTL. Their show was so popular in Charlotte, North Carolina, where they'd moved, that Dad decided to buy time on some fifty stations—one station at a time—across the country to see how it would do nationally. The overwhelming success that washed over them seemed heaven-sent.

Indeed, throughout their careers God had provided for them whenever they were in need. This was no different. PTL grew 7,000 percent in its first year and a half. The rise was so swift that there was no way to accurately chart the TV ministry's growth projections.

The money that followed this growth allowed my parents to build Heritage Village, a miniature reproduction of Colonial Williamsburg, complete with red brick buildings, a steepled church, and landscaped grounds. By 1978, Dad had his own satellite network (one of only four in the world), with over twelve hundred cable systems carrying his show into 13 million households across the country. (At its peak, nine thousand cable systems and two hundred broadcast stations would be connected to that network.) It seemed obvious—God wanted them to thrive.

My parents didn't invent the gospel of prosperity. Oral Roberts and others started preaching that God wanted His people to live well in the 1950s. The message took root and became almost a tradition, especially in the charismatic movement. "God wants you to prosper" became almost as common a message as "God wants you to do good," "God loves you," and "Rock 'n' roll is the devil's music." With his satellite network, Dad was simply spreading the word to more people than ever before. And because they liked what they heard, his ministry reaped the financial benefits. Meanwhile on Wall Street, of course, prosperity was taking off in another direction. It was the perfect religion for the time.

Primary Source

Tammy: Telling It My Way [excerpt]

SYNOPSIS: During the PTL's "Glory Years" in the 1980s, Tammy Faye Bakker became one of the leading women in the evangelical movement. Known for

her elaborate wardrobe and makeup, Bakker enjoyed the limelight and the lavish lifestyle that PTL's revenues provided. Although she insisted in her memoir that the mistakes she and her husband made in managing PTL were unintentional, Bakker acknowledged, "I take full responsibility for any part I played in the eventual downfall and destruction of our beautiful Heritage USA and the PTL ministry that occupied it."

"So where did the money go?" Over and over I'm asked that question. To those of you who have already condemned me, I'm afraid no answer will suffice. I can't account for every single dime that went in and out of PTL, nor would I ever attempt to. All I can recount is what we achieved, what we delivered, and where we fell short. I hope you will judge me on my own words, not on any preconceptions.

From 1983 through 1986 PTL underwent its greatest period of expansion, often referred to as "The Glory Years." During Christmas, tens of thousands of visitors would make their pilgrimage to Heritage USA, and they would never be disappointed. Ringing the grounds was a dazzling spectacle of lights, a breathtaking extravaganza of more than a million colored bulbs. It took almost a year to plan and execute this display, the grandest celebration of the year. Long lines of cars trying to enter the grounds would stretch for more than twelve miles.

Every Fourth of July, Jim would organize an immense pageant to commemorate our country's day of independence. A colorful parade of marching bands and patriotic floats was the central highlight of the festivities. In 1985 more than sixty thousand people streamed into Heritage USA for that single occasion. With over six million visitors in 1986, the theme park was the third-biggest tourist destination, second only to Disneyland and Disney World.

During this three-year period the number of employees swelled from just under seven hundred to over two thousand. Contributions quadrupled, rising from $40 million to $160 million annually.

Jim Bakker was a human locomotive barreling down the rails at breakneck speed; there was no way to keep up with him. He wasn't slowing down for anybody. Because of this Jim frequently appeared impulsive; sometimes bordering on obsessive. The urgency of his vision seemed to transcend all rhyme and reason. Once he got a plan into his mind, there was no talking him out of it, or slowing him down. Many people thought he should slow down, even Roe Messner. "What's your rush, Jim?" Roe used to ask him. I too begged Jim to please slow down, but it was no use.

Jim had to have everything finished yesterday. He wanted to give the partners everything they deserved as quickly as possible. As a result, construction costs often doubled and occasionally tripled. There seemed to be no end in sight. As the erection of more buildings got under way, we had to hire more people.

Add in the hotels and restaurants, entertainment such as water parks, and colossal productions such as the Passion Play and other extravaganzas, and you can just imagine the number of men and women needed to bring it off. And all these people needed to make a living, they needed to be paid. Therefore salaries siphoned a huge chunk of our income. But the more salaries we paid out, the more airtime we had to buy to keep contributions coming in. It became a vicious circle. . . .

Our "Extravagant" Lifestyle

People have this romantic image of how a preacher should live, but that's all it is—a romantic image. It has nothing to do with reality. I have often wondered where this came from. People say Jesus was born in a manger, that he had no place to lay his head. They give me scripture after scripture about how Christians are supposed to not care about possessions or money.

But for every scripture they quote I can find just as many or more that say the opposite. That God wants us to prosper. That God wants us to have life and have it more abundantly. That if we give to Him, He will give back to us pressed down, shaken together, and running over. To me that does not speak of living meagerly. And it certainly does not say "except for ministers."

I think this theory got started in the Catholic church when their priests were commanded to take the vow of poverty. And I must say, I admire them for that. I think it is noble to be able to live on the barest subsistence, without earthly possessions. It takes special people with a special calling to be able to do that. And I believe that God is pleased with such sacrifice. But I don't think the fact that you have money and possessions has any bearing on how much you love God.

Primary Source

I Was Wrong [excerpt]

SYNOPSIS: It was Jim Bakker's charismatic and persuasive presence on television screens that turned the PTL ministry into a religious and entertainment

empire. Convicted in 1989 of criminal fraud, Bakker initially received a forty-five-year sentence. He ended up spending five years in prison and returned to religious work after his release. In this excerpt Bakker attempts to answer one of the lingering questions of the PTL scandal: Where did the money go?

I attempted to explain to the parole commission in simple terms how our original Lifetime Partnership program expanded with the full knowledge of those people involved. I told them we began in January 1984 to build a Partner lodging center at Heritage USA, our church-sponsored retreat center. This new project became the Heritage Grand Hotel. To help defray construction costs, we offered a "Lifetime Partnership" to anyone who donated $1,000 to the ministry of PTL. As a way of saying thank you for their gift, Lifetime Partners received four days and three nights free lodging at the Hotel every year for life. I had said on television and in mailings sent out to our mailing list that only twenty-five thousand of these Partnerships were available. Once they were gone, we would close the offer.

We didn't. We kept on receiving more Lifetime Partners and simply changed our original lodging offer by adding to the program other already built properties such as the ninety-six room Heritage Inn and the massive Fort Heritage camping facilities to accommodate them. This brought the Partner total to 69,142. All the while, we were dramatically expanding every fact of Heritage USA and the ministries that flowed out of there. The crowds kept coming, both in person and by means of television, and soon I announced the second expansion of the Lifetime Partnership program. We began building the twenty-one story, five hundred-room Heritage Grand Towers, which was nearing completion at the time I foolishly resigned from the PTL in March 1987 on the advice of Jerry Falwell, Richard Dortch, and others.

The reason I was accused of fraud, I explained to the parole commission, was because by 1987, we had more than 150,000 Lifetime Partners. The government's case against us said that there was no way we could accommodate all those people and that we did not intend to do so, but were merely pocketing the money for ourselves. It was like being stopped in the middle of building a house and being told, "You never really planned to build it, anyhow!" Regardless, we were not prepared for the landslide of response we received from people who wanted to become Lifetime Partners and the thousands more who were coming to Heritage USA every

Televangelist Jim Bakker stands in front of a water park, part of his ministry's Heritage U.S.A. development, in 1986. **AP/WIDE WORLD PHOTOS. REPRODUCED BY PERMISSION.**

week to enjoy the eighty-six religious services and Christian fellowship. . . .

Shirley Fulbright and Jim Toms sent some books and brochures from which I cut pictures with my prison-purchased, mustache scissors and pasted them onto separate pages, laying the spread out in such a way to tell the story so even a child could see the many projects and buildings on which the money was spent. Again and again, I pasted in the question, "Where did the money go?" and then tried to show a photo of some aspect of Heritage USA, with the amount is cost to build and maintain it. For instance, using the auditor's figures only from the years 1984 to 1987, the years during which we had implemented the Lifetime Partnership programs, I listed and illustrated with photos:

$171 million to build and equip Heritage USA between 1984 and 1987 (many structural parts of Heritage USA had already been built before that time period).

$35 million for general operating expenses.

$13 million to build Heritage Island (the famous water slide and giant swimming area).

$22 million for food, retail shops, and lodging costs besides the Grand Hotel and the Grand Towers. This included food and housing for the many guests on our programs, as well as the cost of food available throughout the grounds.

$1 million for the Passion Play presented in the amphitheater nightly during the summer months.

$17 million to pay interest on loans, accounting fees, and legal fees.

$91 million to pay for television time to stations that aired our program and broadcasting on our own satellite broadcasting system.

$101 million for wages and salaries. In 1987, we employed approximately 2,400 people and had a $25-million payroll.

$17 million for Bibles and books

$15 million for printing and postage.

Jim and Tammy Faye Bakker at a May 1987 press conference.
© BETTMANN/CORBIS. REPRODUCED BY PERMISSION.

$21 million for real estate development. This was the area in which we were building houses and condominiums for the people who wanted to live at Heritage USA all year long.

$1 million per year to put on our annual Christmas City display.

$15 million for maintenance and utilities. This included water towers, wells, sewage treatment plants, phone systems, electric power, roads, landscaping, maintenance, and warehousing. These things are often take for granted by the average visitor to a public place, but the costs are gigantic.

Further Resources

BOOKS

Abelman, Robert, and Stewart M. Hoover, eds. *Religious Television: Controversies and Conclusions.* Norwood, New Jersey: Ablex, 1990.

Alexander, Bobby C. *Televangelism Reconsidered: Ritual in the Search for Human Community.* Atlanta: Scholars Press, 1994.

Frankl, Razelle. *Televangelism: The Marketing of Popular Religion.* Carbondale: Southern Illinois University Press, 1987.

Hadden, Jeffrey K. and Anson Shupe. *Televangelism: Power and Politics on God's Frontier.* New York: Holt, 1988.

Schultze, Quentin J. *Televangelism and American Culture: The Business of Popular Religion.* Grand Rapids, Mich.: Baker Book House, 1991.

AUDIO AND VISUAL MEDIA

ABC News Nightline: Jim and Tammy Faye Bakker. Original release (TV), May 27, 1987. ABC News Production. Directed by Katerina Monemvassitis. VHS, 1990. MPI Home Video.

The Eyes of Tammy Faye. Original release, 2000. Universal. Directed by Randy Barbato and Fenton Bailey. DVD/VHS, 2001. Universal Studios.

8

THE MEDIA

MILLIE JACKSON

Entries are arranged in chronological order by date of primary source. For entries with one primary source, the entry title is the same as the primary source title. Entries with more than one primary source have an overall entry title, followed by the titles of the primary sources.

Important Events in the Media, 1980–1989

1980

- On June 1, Atlanta entrepreneur Ted Turner debuts the twenty-four-hour news channel, Cable News Network (CNN).

- On July 2, in *Richmond Newspapers v. Virginia,* the Supreme Court rules that the press and the public have a right to attend criminal trials.

- From September 15 to September 19, NBC's miniseries *Shogun,* starring Richard Chamberlain and Toshiro Mifune, captivates audiences.

- On October 14, President Carter signs a law forbidding the unannounced search of newsrooms except in special circumstances.

- On November 21, the nighttime television soap opera *Dallas* captures the largest audience in history for an episode of a TV series. The episode answers the question from the spring season concerning an attempted assassination of the lead character J.R. Ewing: "Who Shot J.R.?" Some 83 million viewers find out.

1981

- Warner Communications, owners of the Superman character, sue the students of Richard J. Daley College in Chicago for trademark infringement when they name their student newspaper *The Daley Planet.*

- On January 12, ABC debuts the prime-time soap opera *Dynasty.*

- On January 15, *Hill Street Blues,* a police drama produced by Steven Bochco, debuts on NBC.

- On March 6, CBS news anchorman Walter Cronkite relinquishes his duties after thirty years in broadcasting. He is replaced at the anchor desk by veteran newsman Dan Rather.

- On August 8, the Washington *Evening Star* ceases publication after 128 years. In 1978, it had been purchased by Time, Inc., which spent $85 million in an unsuccessful effort to make the paper profitable.

- On October 8, *Cagney and Lacey,* a police drama featuring two female leads, debuts on ABC.

1982

- Technological improvements in facsimile communications make the fax machine a popular business tool.

- Music Television (MTV), a cable channel playing music videos twenty-four hours a day, debuts.

- On January 8, following an eight-year antitrust suit, American Telephone and Telegraph (AT&T) agrees to divest itself of its twenty-two Baby Bell telephone systems.

- On January 29, the *Philadelphia Bulletin* ceases publication.

- On August 16, the *Saturday Review,* a monthly featuring art and literary criticism, ceases publication after fifty-eight years, after losing $3 million in 1980 and 1981.

- On September 15, Gannett's national daily, *USA Today,* begins publication. It differs from most other newspapers in that it features heavy use of color and short articles that touch on only the highlights of the story.

- On September 29, NBC debuts the television sitcom *Cheers,* set in a Boston bar.

- On November 23, the FCC ends its limit on the number and length of TV commercials, currently at 8.5 minutes per hour. Stations are now free to broadcast as many commercials as they wish.

1983

- The Federal Communications Commission (FCC) authorizes the testing of a cellular telephone system in Chicago.

- On March 2, the farewell episode of the popular sitcom *M*A*S*H* attracts an audience of 125 million, making it the highest-rated nonsports show to date.

- On August 8, a federal jury awards five hundred thousand dollars to female newscaster Christine Craft, who claimed that the owners of KMBC in Kansas City considered her "too old, unattractive, and not deferential enough to men."

- On November 20, ABC airs *The Day After,* a controversial movie simulating the effects of a nuclear war on a Kansas town.

- On November 20, in the largest magazine acquisition in history, CBS pays more than $362 million for twelve publications—including *Popular Mechanics, Car & Driver,* and *Stereo Review*—owned by the Ziff-Davis Publishing Company. The next day, Australian publisher Rupert Murdoch buys twelve trade journals from Ziff-Davis for $350 million.

- On December 18, the *New York Review of Books* is purchased by cable TV executive Rea Hederman for about $5 million.

1984

- On January 17, in a decision condemned by the film industry, the Supreme Court rules that home videotape recording of movies does not infringe upon copyright law.

- On March 4, a television hall of fame is established. Among its first inductees are comedians Lucille Ball and Milton Berle, playwright Paddy Chayefsky (posthumously), producer Norman Lear, and industry magnates William S. Paley and David Sarnoff.

- On May 9, the Johnson Publishing Company, publisher of *Ebony* and *Jet* magazines, replaces Motown Records as the nation's largest black-owned business.

- On June 9, at Disneyland, Donald Duck's fiftieth birthday is celebrated.

- On September 16, the postmodern police drama *Miami Vice,* starring Don Johnson, debuts on NBC.

- On September 20, NBC debuts the television sitcom *The Cosby Show,* starring comedian Bill Cosby.

1985

- On January 24, New York courts acquit *Time* magazine of libel in a suit filed by Israeli politician Ariel Sharon.

- On February 17, former commander of American forces in Vietnam, Gen. William Westmoreland, drops a $120 million libel suit against CBS.

- On March 4, the avant-garde publisher Grove Press is bought by Britain's Weidenfeld Limited, for $2 million.

- On March 8, *The New Yorker* magazine is bought by Newhouse Publications for $142 million.

- On March 18, Capital Cities Communications buys the American Broadcasting Corporation (ABC) for $3.5 billion.

- On July 13, Live Aid, an all-star concert telethon held simultaneously in Philadelphia and London to benefit African famine victims, becomes the most-watched television program in history when it is televised in more than one hundred countries, attracts approximately 1.5 billion viewers, and raises more than $40 million in pledges.

- On July 19, the U.S. Court of Appeals rules that the FCC's "must carry" provisions, which require cable systems to carry local broadcast stations, are a violation of the First Amendment.

- On September 22, Farm Aid, an all-star concert telethon inspired by Live Aid, is held in Champaign, Illinois, to raise funds for American farmers. Dubbed as a "Concert for America," the concert is televised nationwide on cable television, attracts approximately 20 million viewers, and raises approximately $10 million.

- On December 5, a jury awards Brown & Williamson Tobacco Company $5 million in damages from CBS for an on-the-air statement that B&W was trying to lure children to smoke, and for calling company's spokespersons liars.

- In December, General Electric buys the Radio Corporation of America (RCA) and the National Broadcasting Company (NBC) for $6.3 billion.

1986

- The national trend away from evening newspapers continues. Twenty-six evening papers shift to morning publication during the year.

- On January 14, the FCC rules against local laws that forbid the use of backyard satellite dishes.

- On April 27, a video pirate interrupts the broadcast of an HBO movie and replaces it with a message protesting the high cost of cable service. Broadcasters and the FCC are dismayed that TV signals can be so easily overridden by an outside party.

- On May 19, the Gannett newspaper group acquires the *Louisville Times* and *Courier-Journal,* which have been family owned for nearly seventy-five years, for $305 million.

- On May 28, the Times Mirror Company of Los Angeles buys *The Baltimore Sun* and *Evening Sun* for $450 million.

- On June 1, televised coverage of Senate proceedings begins on an experimental basis. The House of Representatives has broadcast its proceedings since 1979.

- On September 10, CBS president and chairman Thomas Wyman resigns. He is replaced as president by Laurence Tisch, the company's largest stockholder. Company founder William Paley becomes acting chairman.

- On September 15, the television drama *L.A. Law* debuts on NBC.

- On September 28, German publisher Bertelsmann AG buys American publisher Doubleday & Co. for $475 million.

- On September 29, American journalist Nicholas Daniloff, arrested by the Soviet Union for spying, is released in a spy exchange.

1987

- Australian media baron Rupert Murdoch buys Harper & Row for $300 million.

- Experts estimate that 43.2 million homes, or more than 49 percent of households, have cable television, an increase of 2 million from the previous year.

- Harcourt Brace Jovanovich successfully repels a $1.7 billion takeover bid by British publishing entrepreneur Robert Maxwell.

- The baby-boomer melodrama *Thirty Something* debuts on ABC.

- On January 16, San Francisco TV station KRON airs a commercial for condoms as a protection against AIDS. It is the first condom commercial to appear in a major TV market. In February, Surgeon General C. Everett Koop calls for such commercials to be allowed on all television.

- On March 13, on appeal, a $2 million libel judgment against the *Washington Post* is overturned.

- On August 4, the FCC scraps its thirty-eight-year-old Fairness Doctrine, which required broadcasters to air all sides of a controversial issue. The agency says that the number of radio and TV stations serving the nation makes the requirement unnecessary. The decision arouses a storm of protest among citizen groups and in Congress.

- On September 14, the A.C. Nielsen Company introduces a new means of measuring television viewing audiences. A new system of push-button "people meters" replaces its old-fashioned television diary system.

1988

- On January 25, in a live interview, Vice President George Bush and CBS news anchor Dan Rather begin shouting at each other over Bush's involvement in the Iran-Contra affair.

- On February 24, the Supreme Court strongly endorses the media's right to criticize public figures by ruling that *Hustler* magazine's satires of evangelist Jerry Falwell are constitutionally protected speech.

- On April 13, by purchasing American publisher Diamandis Communications, Inc., French book and magazine publisher Hachette S.A. becomes the largest magazine publisher in world, printing over seventy-five publications in ten countries.

- On May 17, Pepsico Inc. becomes the first American company to buy advertising time on Soviet television.

- On August 7, in the largest takeover in publishing yet, Australian media mogul Rupert Murdoch buys Walter Annenberg's Triangle Publications (*TV Guide, Daily Racing Form,* and *Seventeen*) for $3 billion.

1989

- News Corporation Limited buys William Collins and Sons of Great Britain, forming HarperCollins.

- The New York Times Company sells all of its cable television properties for $420 million. CBS buys television station WCIX in Miami, Florida, for $59 million.

- Book publishing continues to show an upward trend, with paperback sales growing at an annual rate of 6.5 percent since 1982 and adult hardback sales increasing 12.4 percent per year.

- Magazine publishing continues to decline as advertising revenues fall. This is due in part to the competition of five hundred to six hundred new titles each year, although eighty percent of these new publications will fail.

- On April 18, it is announced that the ABC, NBC, and CBS TV networks have lost viewers for the sixth year in a row. Only two-thirds of viewers watch network TV during prime time. The remaining third are watching cable channels.

- On July 24, Warner Communications and Time, Inc. merge to create Time Warner, Inc. the world's largest media and entertainment company. The new company will have annual revenues of $10 billion.

- On September 27, Japanese company Sony purchases Columbia Pictures Entertainment for $3.4 billion. It is the largest Japanese acquisition of an American company to date.

"Toxic Shock"

Newspaper article

By: Nan Robertson

Date: September 19, 1982

Source: Robertson, Nan. "Toxic Shock." *The New York Times,* September 19, 1982, 30.

About the Author: Nan Robertson (1926–) worked for *The New York Times* for more than thirty years in Washington, Paris, and New York. She was a reporter and a feature writer. Before that, Robertson was employed by the *New York Herald Tribune European Edition* and the *Milwaukee Journal.* Robertson taught at the University of Maryland after retiring. ∎

Introduction

Toxic shock syndrome (TSS) is a rare disease mainly seen in menstruating women who use high-absorbency tampons. It is caused by a bacterial strain of staph. The disease came to the public's attention in the 1980s when women began contracting it. Some victims died. Robertson cites a June 1980 study by the Centers for Disease Control that escalated awareness across the nation. The disease comes on quickly, with a high fever, rash, diarrhea, faintness, and aches. It was frequently misdiagnosed by doctors who were not used to seeing the symptoms or who did not connect the symptoms with TSS.

TSS became the focus of the medical community and Congress. Congress conducted hearings on the disease, and the United States Food and Drug Administration enacted regulations for labeling tampons with warnings. Companies who manufactured and marketed tampons found themselves in court, being sued for deaths and for illness caused by their products.

Nan Robertson felt she had to write an article on toxic shock after contracting, and surviving, TSS. She said, "I wrote it because I wanted to save lives. Doctors were misdiagnosing toxic shock over and over again as scarlet fever, a very serious case of influenza or as food poisoning." Her story was not just a personal account of her illness; it was a well researched, factually accurate article meant to draw attention to a potentially deadly disease. The piece won the Pulitzer Prize in April 1983. Robertson was only the third woman at *The New York Times* to be honored with journalism's highest award.

Significance

Nan Robertson's editor first approached her about writing the story of her experience while she was still hospitalized. She was less than enthusiastic when he contacted her, but after she had recovered she did write the article, which was used as a cover story for *The New York Times.*

Robertson brought attention not only to the disease, but also to the fact that it can strike anyone and is not always related to tampon use. The bacteria, *Staphylococcus aureus,* releases toxins into the bloodstream, causing the symptoms. Robertson's story highlights the facts surrounding the disease and the misconceptions about it. She says that the disease is most often linked to menstruating women who use super-absorbent tampons. She also describes the flurry of press reports and warnings in advertisements, especially by Proctor & Gamble, one of the manufacturers of a brand linked to the disease.

This is Nan Robertson's personal story, but it is also the story of how a dangerous disease can go undetected. Robertson mixes her personal experience and anecdotes with the factual information garnered from interviews with doctors and other health professionals. The resulting narrative is effective and moving. Robertson's vivid language provides images for the reader. For example, she describes the horror and rage that she experienced when she was told she would have to have her fingers amputated. Later in the story, Robertson recounts the agony of waiting for the surgery and the relief she felt when it was over.

Robertson recalls the letter she received from the chairman of the Pulitzer Prize jury for feature writing. The chairman called "Toxic Shock" "a stunning achievement, one that students of our craft will be reading for several years to come . . . as fine and heroic a piece of newspapering as I expect to see."

Primary Source

"Toxic Shock" [excerpt]

> **SYNOPSIS:** The opening paragraphs of "Toxic Shock" provide a picture contrasting the lively woman out dancing with the woman who was near death following Thanksgiving dinner with her family. The photograph accompanying the article shows Robertson working at her typewriter, with amputated fingers which resulted from the gangrene that set in from the disease.

That was how it began: almost discreetly. I felt drained; my legs were slightly numb. The manager, apologizing all the way, drove us back to my sister's

Gangrene caused by the bacterium *Staphylococcus aureus* led to the partial amputation of eight of Nan Robertson's fingers. Here, she uses leather nooses to give her stiffened fingers more flexibility. © 1983. PHOTO BY SARA KRULWICH. REPRODUCED BY PERMISSION.

house in the hotel van. I was put to bed in the downstairs den.

I awoke, trancelike, in the middle of the night to find myself crawling and crashing up the stairs to the bathroom. The vomiting and diarrhea were cataclysmic. My only thought was to get to the bathtub to clean myself. I sat transfixed in my filthy nightgown in the empty tub, too weak to turn on the water. Warren and my sister, Jane, awakened by the noise of my passage, carried me back downstairs, with exclamations of horror and disgust at the mess I had created. Warren, an engineer who is strong on detail, remembers it as five minutes before 3 A.M.

As I lay in the darkened den, I could hear their voices, wrangling. Jane said it must be the 24-hour flu: "Let's wait until morning and see how she is." Warren said: "No, I can't find a pulse. It's serious. I'm calling an ambulance. Nan, do you want to go to the hospital now?'" "Yes," I said. His choice, of course, was Rockford Memorial—the status Protes-

tant hospital in Rockford where my family's doctors practiced.

The ambulance came within a few minutes, in the wake of a sheriff's car and a fire truck. People in uniform spoke to me gently, gave me oxygen. Lying in the ambulance, I could feel it surging forward, then beginning to turn right, toward Rockford Memorial, 15 minutes across town. I heard an emergency medical technician, 18-year-old Anita Powell, cry out: "Left! Left! Go to St. Anthony! She has no pulse! Rockford Memorial is 15 minutes away—she'll be D.O.A. [dead on arrival] if we go there! St. Anthony is three minutes from here—she'll have a chance."

"Do what she says," my sister told the driver. We turned left to St. Anthony Hospital, and my life may have been saved for the second time that night, following Warren's decision to call the ambulance.

In the early hours of Friday, Nov. 27, the baffled young medical staff on holiday emergency-room duty telephoned several physicians. One of them was Dr. Thomas E. Root, an infectious-diseases consultant for the Rockford community. He arrived at 7:30 A.M.

Dr. Root was informed about the vomiting, the diarrhea, the plummeting blood pressure. By then, a faint rash was also beginning to stipple my body. I did not develop the last of the disease's five classic acute symptoms—a fever of more than 102 degrees—until later. But Dr. Root is a brilliant diagnostician. And, incredibly, he and his colleagues had treated two similar cases within the previous year. "I think she has toxic shock syndrome," Dr. Root said to his colleagues. "Let's get going."

Further Resources

BOOKS

Riley, Tom. *The Price of a Life: One Woman's Death from Toxic Shock.* Bethesda, Md.: Adler & Adler, 1986.

United States Senate. Committee on Labor and Human Resources, Subcommittee on Health and Scientific Research. *Toxic Shock Syndrome, 1980 . . . June, 6, 1980.* Washington: U.S. Government Printing Office, 1980.

PERIODICALS

"FDA Will Propose Formal Plan to Rate Tampon Absorbency." *The Wall Street Journal,* July 2, 1984, 1.

MacDonald, K.L., et. al. "Toxic Shock Syndrome: A Newly Recognized Complication of Influenza and Influenzalike Illness." *JAMA* 257, no. 8, February 27, 1987, 1053–1058.

WEBSITES

Tampons and Asbestos, Dioxin, & Toxic Shock Syndrome. Available online at http://www.fda.gov/cdrh/consumer/tamponsabs.html; website home page: http://www.fda.gov (accessed June 11, 2003).

Toxic Shock Syndrome Information Service. Available online at http://www.toxicshock.com (accessed June 11, 2003).

"*M*A*S*H*: RIP"

Magazine article

Date: March 1983
Source: "*M*A*S*H*: RIP." *Life,* March 1983, 40–45. ∎

Introduction

Television comedy series had always portrayed war in a farcical or goofy way, until the series *M*A*S*H*. Previous shows like *McHale's Navy, F Troop,* and *Gomer Pyle, U.S.M.C.* contained loveable and irreverent characters. *M*A*S*H* presented the comic, the satiric, and the devastating sides of war. Robert Altman directed a movie version of *M*A*S*H* in 1970 based on Richard Hornberger's book. Larry Gelbart and Gene Reynolds were the first producers and the creators of the television series. Burt Metcalfe took over as producer in the fifth season. The series, which ran for 11 years, was inspired by the movie. Aired on CBS, it was one of the most popular comedies on television between 1972 and 1983. The show was set in Korea at a MASH (Mobile Army Surgical Hospital) unit. Although a comedy, the show integrated dramatic plotlines as well.

The show's mainstays were Alan Alda as Hawkeye Pierce, Loretta Swit as Major Margaret Houlihan, Gary Burghoff as "Radar" O'Reilly, and Jamie Farr as Corporal Maxwell Klinger. Other characters came and went, the most significant being Trapper John, played by Wayne Rogers, and Dr. B.J. Honicutt, his replacement, portrayed by Mike Farrell. The 4077 MASH was under the command of Col. Henry Blake (McLean Stevenson) until he was discharged and his plane was shot down on the way home. Col. Sherman Potter, a career military man, took his place, complete with horse, and was played by Harry Morgan. Gary Burghoff was the only cast member who had also been in the movie version.

M*A*S*H, like other successful sitcoms, produced a few spinoffs, but none survived. The final episode, "Good-bye, Farewell, and Amen," bid a fond farewell to a cast of characters that America had come to know in the groundbreaking series.

Significance

Meatball surgery mixed with comedic wit to create a show that topped the Nielsen ratings the majority of its 11 seasons and earned numerous awards. This wasn't always the story of *M*A*S*H*, however. During the first few seasons, it was almost cancelled. The show was moved to Saturday night between *All in the Family* and *The Mary Tyler Moore Show.* This is where it found its loyal audience. The show remained in the top ten for nine seasons.

The cast of *M*A*S*H* developed into a fine example of ensemble acting. The Swamp (the tent where Hawkeye Pierce, Trapper John, and Capt. Frank Burns lived) and the operating room were the two main scenes for the show. Trapper and Burns were replaced by Dr. B.J. Honicutt (Mike Farrell) and Dr. Charles Emerson Winchester, played by David Ogden Stiers, but the Swamp continued to be a place of practical jokes and gin drinking.

Rick Mitz is quoted as saying, "This was a comedy that showed war. Not like a John Wayne epic, but one of small-scale, more human dimensions." The humanity of the characters, as well as the respect for the audience's intelligence, was a hallmark of the show's writing team. Incidents portrayed in the show often came from real life through interviews with doctors who had actually served in Korea. The creative team for *M*A*S*H* was not limited to a group of writers, however. The cast had input about how the characters would be portrayed, and changes were made when a script seemed out of character. Alan Alda directed many episodes in addition to playing Hawkeye Pierce.

M*A*S*H began as a dark comedy attacking war in general and Vietnam in particular, despite the Korean conflict as the setting. The comedy softened as the seasons progressed. Satiric humor remained part of the survival skills for the doctors of the 4077th. Compassionate scenes revealed the humanity of each character in the series, which lasted four times as long as the Korean conflict itself.

Primary Source

"*M*A*S*H*: RIP"

SYNOPSIS: The final episode of *M*A*S*H* drew a larger audience than any single television episode had in the past. With more than 60 percent of the audience, Hawkeye Pierce and the other doctors, nurses, and staff of the 4077 bid their final farewell. The show lives on in reruns on late-night television and on cable stations.

"I am relieved to learn that peace is at hand finally . . ." wired Henry Kissinger as the 4077th Mobile Army Surgical Hospital unit ended its distinguished service in Korea. Ronald Reagan, Jimmy Carter and Gerald Ford (three of the 32 million regular viewers) sent congratulations too. After 99 Emmy nominations and 15 Emmy awards, *M*A*S*H* was filming its last episode (air date February 28). Commercial time on the final show cost $450,000 for 30 seconds—the most expensive spots in TV history.

Scenes from four of the two-hundred-fifty-one total episodes of M*A*S*H. The television show was on the air for eleven seasons and lasted four times as long as the Korean conflict. AP/WIDE WORLD PHOTOS. REPRODUCED BY PERMISSION.

This past season *M*A*S*H* ranked third in the Nielsen ratings, and the decision to stop the cameras came not from CBS, but from the creative staff. "We ran the risk of squeezing it dry," explains Alan Alda, 47. The star (Hawkeye Pierce) of all 250 episodes, Alda was author and director of the final two-and-a-half-hour show, whose audience is expected to exceed 65 million. Back in 1972, its first season, *M*A*S*H* was as ailing as some of its make-believe patients. Critics called it a dimwitted offspring of Robert Altman's darkly comic 1970 hit movie. Some viewers saw it as a protest against Vietnam and turned off their sets. In its second season *M*A*S*H* writers became more adept at combining comedy with ironic contempt for war. The performers grew into an ensemble where off-camera discussions about their on-camera lives were used as dialogue. Says Alda, "We dug a little deeper so the characters were like real people. We wanted something more than just high jinks at the front."

Says executive producer Burt Metcalfe, "America loves these characters. They also sense that they love one another." Next season three *M*A*S*H* regulars—Harry Morgan (Colonel Potter), Jamie Farr (Sergeant Klinger) and William Christopher (Father Mulcahy) may be reunited in a spin-off set in a VA hospital. Alda, Mike Farrell (Captain B.J. Hunnicutt), Loretta Swit (Major Margaret "Hot Lips" Houlihan) and David Ogden Stiers (Major Winchester) are considering new projects. Abandoning M*A*S*H hurt a lot. "Suicide is Painless" is the title of the show's haunting theme song—but it wasn't true for the *M*A*S*H* "family." Another family member, Arlene Alda, Alan's wife of 25 years, photographed the final days for *LIFE*.

A Few Last Laughs and a Week Full of Tears

"We hugged each other a lot this week," says Swit, 45. "We had difficulty remembering lines. Everybody had his turn at falling apart. We joked about what we were going to do when school let out. I was the only one who couldn't handle that. Maybe you could call it creative interruptus."

"Do you know how many actors were dying to work on this show?" Farr's character of Klinger, who dressed as a woman in hopes of getting a psycho discharge from the Army, was created by writer Larry Gelbart as a one-time joke. By the third year, Farr was a regular cast member and Klinger was allowed to become less wacky. In the eighth season he was promoted to company clerk. "I'm glad *M*A*S*H* is over," Farr cracks. "I'm sick of all those dress jokes. I'm glad Gelbart wrote *Tootsie* and gave my wardrobe to Dustin Hoffman." But Farr admits he's interested in the idea of a spin-off. "It takes some of the depression away."

"This is the last time I'll have these boots on," says Alda. "When I started the show I didn't need glasses to read my dog tags. . . . I don't expect anything to live up to this experience. When you've spent 12 to 13 hours a day for so many years, you're leaving something that's un-leavable."

"When I first [started] I was 21," says Nakahara, 33, who played a nurse. "I've spent most of my adult life here. These people taught me so much about myself. They helped me grow up."

"There has never been a congregation of actors put together that could come within a mile of this bunch," says Harry Morgan, an actor who has made "a hundred-plus" movies (he was in *High Noon* and *The Oxbow Incident* and seven other TV series including *Dragnet*). "Someone asked me whether *M*A*S*H* has made me a better actor. I don't know about that, but I can say it has made me a better human being." Says Stiers, who once taught drama at Harvard, "All of us are going to be dealing with potent postpartum feelings. It'll probably hit me three weeks later." William Christopher, whose first role was as a groundhog in the third grade, recalls that "from the beginning it's been a happy set. Something very special has happened because of our long, long life. We're welded together."

His War Days Over, Alda Counts His Battle Stars

"*M*A*S*H* was about people who were sent to a war, people under stress, standing around in other people's blood, hating being there . . . we had a seriousness of purpose, but we enjoyed the craziness. We had both—a series with a purpose, but we did it with a light touch. We always tried to get together at the end of the week, have pizza, schmooze." Alda, who became the first ever to win Emmys as writer,

actor and director for his work on the show, was asked how much he would miss *M*A*S*H*. His reply: "How much would you miss your arm?"

Further Resources

BOOKS

Reiss, David S. *M*A*S*H: The Exclusive Inside Story of TV's Most Popular Show.* Indianapolis: Bobbs-Merrill, 1980.

PERIODICALS

Ehrmann, Paul. "Will "M*A*S*H" Go On Forever?" *Horizon* 24, May 1981, 36–43.

Gelbart, Larry. "This . . . is CBS." *Electronic Media* 21, no. 35, September 2, 2002, 11.

Gehring, Wes. "M*A*S*H Turns 30." *USA Today* 131, September 2002, 66–69.

Worland, Rick. "The Other Living-Room War: Prime Time Combat Series, 1962–1975." *Journal of Film and Video* 50, no. 3, Fall 1998, 3–23.

WEBSITES

M*A*S*H. Available online at http://www.mash4077.co.uk /index.php (accessed June 11, 2003).

The Museum of Broadcast Communications. Available online at http://www.museum.tv/archives/etv/index.html (accessed June 11, 2003).

"Hussein's Decision"

Newspaper article

By: Karen Elliott House

Date: April 14, 1983

Source: House, Karen Elliott. "Hussein's Decision." *The Wall Street Journal,* April 14, 1983, 1, 16; April 15, 1983, 1, 19.

About the Author: Karen Elliott House (1947–) earned her bachelor's degree in journalism from the University of Texas, Austin. Her first reporting job was at *The Dallas Morning News.* She joined *The Wall Street Journal* in 1974, where she became recognized for her work writing about foreign affairs. House became president of the international group of Dow Jones & Company in 1995. ■

Introduction

King Hussein of Jordan (1935–1999) became the monarch of Jordan following his grandfather's assassination in 1953. The Middle East region has been a volatile area for decades, and King Hussein dealt with several conflicts and crises during his reign. He carried the burden of history with him as he attempted to negotiate peace.

A number of wars throughout the last half of the twentieth century escalated tensions in the region. During the Six Day War in June 1967, Israel attacked Egypt, Iraq, Jordan, and Syria. After capturing the Syrian Golan

Heights, Jordanian West Bank, and the Egyptian Sinai Peninsula and Gaza Strip, the Isralis began forming settlements. "Black September," the war in 1970, forced the Palestinian refugees out of Jordan. Wars between other countries in the region also affected Jordan and King Hussein's peacekeeping efforts. Along with wars, there were negotiations and ongoing talks between leaders, including leaders from the United States. The 1979 Camp David Accords, written to normalize relations between Egypt and Israel and facilitated by President Jimmy Carter, were not viewed as a solution in much of the Arab world. King Hussein and many other leaders denounced the treaty, and talks broke down. In 1982, President Ronald Reagan appealed to leaders in the Middle East once again and tried to revisit the Camp David process. Reagan's plan included a "Jordanian option." He sought King Hussein as a representative of the Palestinians and had consulted with him prior to the announcement. The Arab Summit was scheduled to meet shortly after Reagan's initial announcement. The Palestinians did not want to be represented by Hussein, however; they wanted representation from the Palestine Liberation Organization (PLO). Hussein and Arafat, leader of the PLO, met to discuss options. This is the point where Karen House Elliott's interview ends. Tensions continued in the region, complicated by politics, history, and personal feelings about one's country and people. No easy solutions have been found regarding occupation of the territory. The Reagan administration continued to be involved, but cautiously. Subsequent administrations have also attempted to aid the peace process in the Middle East.

Significance

Karen Elliott House was awarded the Pulitzer Prize in 1984 for her series of interviews with King Hussein of Jordan. Editors from *The Wall Street Journal* noted that her coverage not only chronicled the unfolding story of the Reagan peace plan in "vivid detail," but also "analyzed and accurately foreshadowed the course of events." The series of articles, which appeared April 14 and 15, 1983, were based on House's interviews with King Hussein of Jordan over a period of several months. The articles "deal with a whole range of issues—Arab divisiveness, American naiveté, Soviet meddling, and the intricacies of high-stakes diplomacy played out in half a dozen world capitals," according to the letter nominating House for the Pulitzer Prize. House captures King Hussein's character and "his private hopes, fears, and frustrations" as a ruler and as a human being.

House chronicles the Middle East peace talks and King Hussein's ongoing conversations with President Reagan from 1982 through the spring of 1983. She details Hussein's frustrations and the "tangled tale" of talks between the two leaders and Henry Kissinger. She re-

counts a relationship between the men that was almost paternal. Through personal quotes and feelings, House describes Hussein's reactions to Reagan's promises to convince Congress to give Jordan F-16s and his disappointment and disbelief when he learns that Henry Kissinger met with Arafat.

In an obituary printed in the online edition of the *Washington Post* Thomas W. Lippman wrote, "Everyone in the Middle East—and in Washington, London and Moscow—was furious at Hussein at one time or another, but he proved as skillfully evasive as a hummingbird, always darting to safety just as the pressures of the day seemed about to overwhelm him." At the time of his death in 1999, King Hussein had ruled Jordan for 46 years. The most important element of House's interviews was her depiction of Hussein's integrity and his passion for peace which kept him "darting to safety" and made him a respected leader. House continued to write about the Middle East and King Hussein for *The Wall Street Journal*.

Primary Source

"Hussein's Decision" [excerpt]

> **SYNOPSIS:** The excerpt from the first article in the series depicts the struggle for peace in the Middle East region and King Hussein of Jordan's desire for peace. House reveals the anguish of a ruler who has struggled to find a solution. Her access to the king over a four-month period allows House to show the reader both his private and public sides.

King Had U.S. Pledges On Peace Talks but Met A Maze of Arab Foes

Amman, Jordan—The peace effort, in King Hussein's mind, was at an end. He had been refused a Palestinian negotiating mandate, and now he was sending an urgent private message to President Reagan telling where things stood on the Reagan plan for West Bank talks with Israel: "I am unable to identify a single ray of hope I haven't pursued. . . ."

It was a bitter outcome to an effort that had once seemed full of promise. Four months earlier, another Hussein-Reagan contact had filled the king with confidence that he could enter Mideast negotiations with Arab approval. Mr. Reagan—in the strongest indication he has yet given of his political plans—promised. King Hussein at the White House in December: "We'll be partners for the next six years."

Mr. Reagan also made a more concrete pledge at the December meeting. In a private letter marked SECRET, he promised that if the Jordanian monarch merely offered to enter peace talks with Israel, the U.S. would try to halt the building of Israeli settlements in the West Bank and Gaza—a promise that the State Department publicly acknowledge last Friday.

If the U.S. failed, Jordan would have no further obligation, Mr. Reagan added, declaring: "You will not be pressed to join negotiations on transition arrangements until there is a freeze on new Israeli settlement activity."

The months between that December meeting and last Sunday, when King Hussein finally announced with exasperation that he would take no part in any West Bank talks, were a time of personal trial for him and of political portent for the Middle East. The chronicle of his struggle to decide whether he should—or could—join the peace talks is one of great-power politics, of Arab intrigue and of a monarch caught in the middle. It is a tangled tale in which even former Middle East negotiator Henry Kissinger reappears.

The story of those months is based on a score of confidential conversations with King Hussein, as well as on access to letters and documents and on interviews with other actors in the drama. The king, a lonely and very private man, shared not only intimate details of his talks with world leaders but also his personal hopes, fears and frustrations. The tension of those roller-coaster months had the king at various times brimming with confidence, exploding in anger or, as at one point, collapsing with a heart problem that sent him for a secret hospital stay.

As King Hussein weighed the peace plan President Reagan offered last September, among the many things influencing his thinking may have been the close, almost paternal relationship between the 72-year-old U.S. president and the 47-year-old monarch. King Hussein says Mr. Reagan is the first president he can fully relate to and rely upon since Dwight Eisenhower, who was a genuine father figure to him.

Dark Chapters

The king's family history is tragic. His father was schizophrenic, and he was largely reared by his grandfather, King Abdullah. While just a teen-ager, he saw his grandfather stabbed to death as the two were visiting Jerusalem. He has himself survived at least 11 assassination attempts.

Mr. Reagan's occasional bluff, fatherly advice seems to reinforce the king's regard for him. For instance, when Palestine Liberation Organization Chairman Yasser Arafat arrived in Amman for his fi-

King Hussein of Jordan. Karen Elliott House was awarded the Pulitzer Prize in 1984 for her series of interviews with King Hussein. © CORBIS. REPRODUCED BY PERMISSION

nal critical talks with the king, Mr. Reagan woke King Hussein with an early-morning phone call to say, "Don't let the bastards get you down."

Those Arafat-Hussein talks proved to be the end of the king's search for a way to take part in negotiations with Israel. The nine hours of talks at first appeared fruitful, producing a tentative agreement that, among other things, would have led to a negotiating team of Jordanians and of non-PLO Palestinians (of whom the PLO approved). It was this agreement that was blocked last week by more-radical PLO officials, in a possibly mortal blow to the Reagan peace plan.

The Reagan plan calls for Jordanian-Israeli negotiations aimed at creating a Palestinian self-government on the West Bank and Gaza in "association" with Jordan. After the U.S. offered the proposal last Sept. 1, the king publicly hailed it as "courageous and positive." But the Arab League had in 1974 named the PLO as the Palestinians' sole representative. So even though the West Bank had been part of Jordan before 1967, King Hussein feels he can't negotiate over it without Arab and PLO authorization.

And strong opposition from outside the region soon surfaced. We may pick up the story in early December, with King Hussein leading an Arab delegation to Moscow. Inside the Kremlin, Yuri Andropov, the new Soviet leader, takes him aside and, as the king recalls it, delivers this warning: "I shall oppose the Reagan plan, and we will use all our resources to oppose it. With due respect, all the weight will be on your shoulders, and they aren't broad enough to bear it."

The king flies on to Peking, where he meets with less hostility but little optimism. "I don't envy you your decision," he is told by Chinese leader Deng Xiaoping. "On the one hand, you have the Russians with all their aims on your region. And on the other, you have an American president worrying about votes."

The next stop for King Hussein is the White House, where those votes apparently come up again. Mr. Reagan reportedly says he knows he is going to lose the Jewish vote in 1984 by pressing a peace plan Israel opposes but he confidently predicts he can win reelection without that bloc. (Asked for response, a White House spokesman said the administration generally doesn't comment on private exchanges with world leaders.)

In his secret letter pledging to pressure Israel to halt West Bank settlement, Mr. Reagan also promises that once peace talks have started, the U.S. will put forward an "American draft" of ideas for a possible agreement. He also promises to push the notions that any transitional arrangement for the occupied lands should be effective as soon as negotiated, and that talks would then have to begin immediately on deciding the final status of the territories.

The president further offers to reward King Hussein for joining the peace talks by pressing Congress to let Jordan buy a squadron of F-16s, America's most sophisticated fighter planes. This is the plane Mr. Reagan more recently said he would withhold from Israel to pressure it to withdraw from Lebanon. (A White House spokesman wouldn't confirm the president's offer, but he noted that the administration has said on "a number of occasions" that it is willing to help meet Jordan's security needs.)

Finally, Mr. Reagan gives the king a second letter, one that he can show to doubting Arabs. In it, the president records his "personal commitment" to the talks and to United Nations Resolution 242, which calls on Israel to yield occupied lands in exchange for peace.

With the letters and pledges, King Hussein leaves Washington for home, confident his secret arrangements with the U.S. president will win him Arab approval to negotiate. His confidence holds through exploratory talks with Mr. Arafat about a joint Jordanian-Palestinian negotiating team. But in February, it meets a severe setback: A radical-dominated Palestinian National Congress in Algiers rejects the Reagan peace plan.

This is unexpected bad news to the king. But worse is soon to come.

The king learns that Mr. Arafat, while discussing a negotiating team with him, has secretly arranged for Saudi Arabia to try to wrest a better deal from President Reagan than the king had won. On March 3, Prince Bandar bin Sultan, a nephew of Saudi King Fahd and his special emissary, flies to Amman to tell of his own talks with Mr. Reagan.

As always, King Hussein must take the Saudis seriously. Jordan is a poor country, and its economic stability is heavily dependent on Saudi aid. He gets a further reminder during this visit: a notice that his oil bill is long overdue.

One thing the Saudis have asked Mr. Reagan is whether his envisioned "association" between the West Bank and Jordan means a "confederation"; a confederation would imply a link between two countries and thus might be a back-door U.S. endorsement of a Palestinian state. As the king listens to Prince Bandar, he realizes that Mr. Reagan's answers to the Saudis don't square with those he had himself received. For Mr. Reagan has told the Saudis in writing that "confederation is one of the possible outcomes."

The president had told King Hussein no such thing. The effect of the discrepancy is to undermine the king's credibility with Mr. Arafat and to lead the PLO to believe that more-generous concessions can be wrung from the U.S. than those the king had obtained. The U.S. later tries to correct this impression, but the damage has been done.

After his talks with Prince Bandar, the king sits in his palace living room and fumes. "There are too many cooks," he complains.

But above all he is worried about U.S. credibility. "My fear is that the U.S. position is eroding," he says. "The American answers to the Saudis aren't as firm as those President Reagan gave me in December."

It is clear to the king that he must have a face-to-face meeting with Mr. Arafat, who has assiduously avoided coming to Amman ever since the Palestinian congress's rejection of the Reagan peace plan. The conference of nonaligned nations is about to begin in New Delhi, and the king hopes to corner Mr. Arafat there. But in New Delhi he is to learn of still more intrigue, the kind of infighting that again and again stymies Arab efforts to reach consensus.

March 5, the day he must head to India, offers the king a brief chance to get away from the problems preoccupying him. On a cold and drizzly day, the king, a pilot, enters the cockpit of a Boeing 707 and straps himself in. He pushes the throttle and the plane speeds over the wet runway and into the clouds, emerging after a few bumpy minutes into bright sunshine. His mood lifts, too. When one of his copilots fails to see a Kuwaiti jet ahead visible to the king, he grabs a brush and playfully dusts off the copilot's eyeglasses.

Such gaity is rare for the king these days. "Flying is the only time I forget the Reagan peace plan," he says. His wife, Queen Noor, says he sometimes wakes up with nightmares about the negotiations.

The New Delhi conference begins well. King Hussein meets with Egyptian President Hosni Mubarak, the first time he has seen an Egyptian president in the nearly six years since the late Anwar Sadat went to Jerusalem. Mr. Mubarak, representing the one Arab country at peace with Israel, urges the king to step forward. But he cautions him against expecting too much of either PLO or American leadership. "I doubt the Americans can deliver," the king recalls Mr. Mubarak saying.

Further Resources

BOOKS

The Middle East. 9th ed. Washington, D.C.: CQ Press, 2000.

Queen Noor. *Leap of Faith: Memoirs of an Unexpected Life.* New York: Miramax, 2003.

Snow, Peter John. *Hussein: A Biography.* Washington, D.C.: R.B. Luce, 1972.

PERIODICALS

Greenberger, Robert S. "Hussein and Reagan Seek Formula for Viable Mideast Peace Process." *The Wall Street Journal,* October 1, 1985, 1.

"Journal's Karen House, Vermont Royster Win Pulitzers for Foreign News, Comment." *The Wall Street Journal,* April 17, 1984, 1.

WEBSITES

Israel/Arab Relations and the Middle East Peace Process. Available online at http://www.columbia.edu/cu/lweb/indiv/mideast/cuvlm/Isr-Arab.html; website home page: http://www.columbia.edu (accessed June 11, 2003).

King Hussein: A Man of Peace. Available online at http://www.pbs.org/newshour/bb/middle_east/jan-june99/hussein_index.html; website home page: http://www.pbs.org (accessed June 11, 2003).

Lippman, Thomas. "Hussein: A Lifetime Balancing Act." Available online at http://www.washingtonpost.com/wp-srv/inatl/longterm/hussein/hussein.htm; website home page: http://www.washingtonpost.com (accessed May 22, 2003).

"NBC Comedy 'Cheers' Has Turned Into a Success"

Newspaper article

By: Peter Kerr

Date: November 29, 1983

Source: Kerr, Peter. "NBC Comedy 'Cheers' Has Turned Into a Success." *The New York Times,* November 29, 1983, C19.

About the Author: Peter Kerr spent fourteen years as a reporter and bureau chief at *The New York Times*. His major stories were on substance abuse and the cocaine trade. Kerr has worked in communications since he left the *Times*. He was named the chief communications officer for the Markle Foundation in 2001. ∎

Introduction

The set for *Cheers* was based on a bar on Boston's Beacon Hill named the Bull & Finch Pub. Like many other comedies that went on to become long-running successful series, *Cheers* was almost cancelled during its first season. The show went on to become part of the Thursday night lineup of NBC "Must See TV." The plot revolved around the bar and the loveable group of bar flies who hung out there. Sam Malone, played by Ted Danson, was the bar's owner and a former major league baseball player. Coach, the bartender played by Nicholas Colasanto, was the funny guy who didn't realize how funny he was. He died in 1985 and was replaced by Woody, the goofy bartender who was played by Woody Harrelson. The women of *Cheers* included Diane (Shelley Long), Sam's on-again off-again love interest and a graduate student; Carla (Rhea Perlman), the curmudgeonly bar maid; and later, Rebecca (Kirstie Alley), who played the new owner. The trivia-spouting mailman Cliff (John Ratzenberger); Norm (George Wendt), the accountant who never seems to hold a job; and psychiatrists Dr. Frasier Crane (Kelsey Grammer) and Dr. Lilith Sternin (Bebe Neuwirth) rounded out the regulars on the bar stools.

Cheers was the place "where everyone knows your name" and the place where everyone called out Norm's

Although the television show *Cheers* was nearly canceled after its first season, the series went on to gain top ten ratings for eight of its eleven seasons.
THE KOBAL COLLECTION/PARAMOUNT TV. REPRODUCED BY PERMISSION.

name as he walked through the door. The Boston setting distinguished the show from other comedies mainly set in California. Characters traded witty remarks and satiric jibes. The jokes fit the characters, as Diane threw in literary references and Norm concentrated on food and his wife. The series became a hit for NBC in a season when other shows did not do as well. The crowd at *Cheers* was one happy dysfunctional "family" full of politically incorrect actions and comments.

Significance

Cheers united a group of writers, producers, and network executives who already had proven success in television comedy. Glen and Les Charles were fresh from the hit series *Taxi* when they began writing for *Cheers*. The two men started as part of the MTM team of writers who produced quality television shows throughout the 1970s to the 1990s. James Burrows, the producer, was also an MTM alum. Grant Tinker, who had created MTM with Mary Tyler Moore, became a network executive at NBC in 1981, the year before the series launched. He

brought the idea of quality television to the network and promoted it with shows like *Cheers*.

The sparks between the characters were only part of the success for *Cheers*. The fact that the show remained true to its mission—entertainment—was the key to success. This series did not attempt high-handed moral lessons through comedy. The characters and the writers produced adult scripts that were truly funny. Flashbacks to previous episodes tied the seasons together, particularly regarding Diane and Sam's relationship. While the show usually remained in the bar, the characters would venture out to Frasier's home for a party, to Carla's house where her huge clan of children abused the other characters as much as Carla did, or on the road when the boys would take a trip for one reason or another. The show ended while it was still popular. Ted Danson wanted to move on to other projects, and the production costs had risen dramatically when the bar closed in 1993.

Cheers gained top ten ratings for eight of its eleven seasons. In 1990–1991 it was rated number one. Twenty-three more Emmy awards were added to the show's five Emmys from the first season. The show also produced the successful spinoff *Frasier,* starring Kelsey Grammer.

Primary Source

"NBC Comedy 'Cheers' Turns Into a Success"

SYNOPSIS: The tensions between characters often provided the plots for *Cheers.* Sam, the woman-chasing bartender, was the foil for Diane, the snobbish graduate student. The relationship between the two turned from disdain to romance as the seasons progressed, but always with a humorous twist.

The scene is a Boston bar, where the regulars hoot, back-slap and dissolve into giggles when somebody makes a joke about sex. Diane Chambers (Shelley Long), a former graduate student working as a waitress, once again is offended. She begins to lecture the customers in her most professorial tone.

DIANE: Ah yes, unlimited sex. The adult male version of owning a candy store. But once you've consumed as much sex as you want for as long as you want, what do you do then?

(The crowd is silent.)

NORM (a regular): I'd help the poor.

So goes the dialogue in "Cheers," a half-hour NBC television comedy that is one of the network's few success stories this season. After months of dismally low ratings last year, the show has managed this season to gather a respectable audience. And it has done so, critics say, with good acting and witty writing, the type of quality programming that Grant Tinker, the president of NBC, has said he wants on the network.

Won Five Emmy Awards

The show was a particular point of pride for NBC executives this fall when it won five Emmy Awards, including the categories for outstanding comedy, for writing and for direction. Miss Long received the award for outstanding actress in a comedy series for her portrayal of Diane.

"'Cheers' is a very important comedy for us," said Brandon Tartikoff, the president of the NBC entertainment division. "It is classy, sophisticated and for adults. We never for a second doubted that we would renew it for this year."

The show revolves around the inhabitants of the bar, including the owner, a retired baseball pitcher, and Diane, the snobbish but vulnerable former graduate student.

So far this season, "Cheers" has scored a modest success in the ratings. But to NBC executives, who have seen program after program go down to defeat in recent years, "Cheers" is a major victory. (The shelves of the NBC gift shop in Rockefeller Center are stocked with "Cheers" T-shirts these days.)

Has Competed Well

The program surpassed ABC's entry in the 9:30 P.M. time period, the now-canceled comedy, "It's Not Easy," and has competed well with one of the most popular shows on prime-time television, CBS's "Simon and Simon." In the first seven weeks of the season it has averaged a 17.6 rating and a 27 share of the audience, according to the A. C. Nielsen Company.

By comparison, eight of NBC's nine new prime-time shows have averaged at or below an 11 rating and an 18 share and most have finished third in their time periods. "Simon and Simon" received a 24.3 rating and a 37 share. A rating point represents one percent of all the households with televisions in the United States, or 838,000 homes. A share is the percent of all televisions turned on at a specific time.

Another point of pride for NBC is that the dialogue on the show at times reaches a sophistication that is rare on network television. Jokes have included references to Shakespeare, John Donne and Spinoza. Among other affections, Diane has the unfortunate habit of dropping phrases in French.

"John Cheever is pretty small pommes de terre," she offers as other bar inhabitants wince.

Developed by Three Men

The show was created and developed by three men who have had considerable experience with award-winning television programs, such as "M*A*S*H" and "Taxi"—two brothers, Glen and Les Charles, and James Burrows, who directs the program.

"We wanted to create a show around a Katharine Hepburn-Spencer Tracy-type relationship," Mr. Burrows said in a recent telephone interview, referring to the characters of the bar owner, Sam Malone, and Diane. "She is uptown, he is downtown."

Throughout the program's development, Glen Charles said, the creators attempted to draw ideas for the set, the characters and the dialogue from reality. Glen Charles traveled to Boston to find a bar that could be used as a model for the set. They settled on an establishment named The Bull & Finch. In the program, it took the name "Cheers."

Rhea Perlman, the actress in "Cheers" who plays a tiny, sharp-tongued waitress named Carla Tortelli, was sent to The Bull & Finch to watch the bar in operation. Ted Danson, who plays Sam Malone, the handsome, ex-alcoholic bar owner, spent two weeks attending a bartending school in Burbank, Calif., preparing for his part. The character of Norm, a bloated, unemployed accountant on a regimen of one beer every half hour, is based on a real character Les Charles said he encountered when he worked as a bartender in college.

The three creators of the show also visited bars around Los Angeles, picking up bits of conversation that would later be used in the show. "Cheers" dialogue that was taken from real bars, included a discussion of which is "the sweatiest movie ever made," and what is the best flavor of canned soup.

Further Resources

BOOKS

Brooks, Tim. *The Complete Directory to Prime-Time Network TV Shows.* New York: Ballantine, 1992.

Gwinn, Alison, ed. *The 100 Greatest TV Shows of All Time.* New York: Entertainment Weekly Books, 1998.

Thompson, Robert J. *Television's Second Golden Age: From Hill Street Blues to ER.* New York: Continuum, 1996.

PERIODICALS

Christensen, Mark, and Cameron Stauth. "Everybody Knows Their Names: The Improbable Rise to Fame of 'Cheers' and Its Offbeat Cast of Characters." *American Film.* 10, November 1984, 48–52.

Higgins, George. "Prime Time Discovers Boston." *The Wall Street Journal,* June 11, 1984, 1.

Stauth, Cameron. "Cheers, the Hit That Almost Missed." *Esquire* 101, February 1984, 85–88.

WEBSITES

Cheers. Available online at http://www.cheersboston.com (accessed June 11, 2003).

"Bill Cosby: The Doctor Is In"

Magazine article

By: Todd Gold

Date: April 1985

Source: Gold, Todd. "Bill Cosby: The Doctor Is In." *Saturday Evening Post* 257, April 1985, 42–44.

About the Author: Todd Gold (1958–) writes about television and television stars. He has coauthored numerous celebrity autobiographies, including those of actress Drew Barrymore and Brian Wilson of the Beach Boys. Gold also edited *Comic Relief,* which brings together routines by comedians such as Billy Crystal, Robin Williams, Whoopi Goldberg, Dennis Miller, and Gary Shandling. The contributions of these and other comics have helped raise millions of dollars for the homeless since the founding of Comic Relief in 1986. ■

Introduction

The Cosby Show broke ground in American television by portraying a normal, upper-middle-class black family dealing with the joys and problems that all families encounter. Prior to its appearance on NBC in 1984, the everyday life of a black family was not part of the usual comedy lineup. A few shows, such as *The Jeffersons* and *Good Times,* featured black families, but the humor was not focused around daily life. Rather, it tended to be self-deprecating and counted on the joke for a laugh. Bill Cosby saw a need to change that view.

Bill Cosby was a known commodity as a comedian by the time *The Cosby Show* appeared. In *I Spy,* a TV comedy from the 1960s, he broke the color barrier as the first black to have a lead role on a television sitcom. He went on to star in several other sitcoms. Cosby's brand of comedy is deadpan. He makes daily life or childhood memories hilarious. Fat Albert, Old Weird Harold, and their cast of friends were already well known to a wide audience from comedy routines when they turned up on Saturday morning cartoons. His *Bill Cosby Show* extended his audience and his vision for funny shows portraying characters who were multidimensional. The family consisted of Clair, the mother and an attorney, played by Phylicia Rashad, as well as four daughters and a son. As the children grew up, cast members were added as friends and as spouses.

Bill Cosby's personal experiences as a parent, his own youth, and his interest and training in education all contributed to the shaping of *The Cosby Show.* The show featured his values depicting a family that cared about one another. Bill Cosby stressed the importance of shared experiences between human beings, not just black families.

Significance

The Cosby Show relied on life to teach life's lessons. The parents in the show held professional jobs (a doctor and a lawyer), and the five children experienced the trials and tribulations of childhood without getting into serious trouble. Shows dealt with the trauma of the first day of school, finding and keeping friends, and going off to college. The extended family was also an important part of the *Cosby Show* experience. Grandparents, in particular, played an important role as teachers of family history and as moral guides. Friends of the family also contributed to the cohesiveness of life in the Huxtable home. *The Cosby Show* provided subtle cues to the life of the family through the art that hung on the walls and the music and entertainment which was favored.

Bill Cosby's theories about education and parenting were integral to the show. Many viewers may not have realized that the same funny man they had just spent a half hour laughing at was the William H. Cosby, Jr., Ed.D. in the credits who had written a dissertation on television and learning. Cosby also made sure that other experts were part of the planning and writing process for the series.

The show received praise and criticism. The loving relationships of the family members, the humor, the revival of the comedy series, and the weekly presence of a nuclear black family were all praised. Critics thought that the show did not address social issues or racism, however. The show was also criticized because Cliff was not given enough to do in the community and because Clair's work was invisible. Some thought plots depicted the problems of raising children, while others though they only dealt with trivial matters.

The Cosby Show was part of NBC's Thursday night lincup from 1984 to 1992. The show was at the top of the Nielson ratings throughout the eight-year run. The series ended in April 1992 when Los Angeles was being torn apart by riots after the Rodney King incident. Like most successful comedies, the show continues in reruns.

Primary Source

"Bill Cosby: The Doctor Is In" [excerpt]

SYNOPSIS: Bill Cosby draws on his own family life for his comedy *The Cosby Show*. Like the Huxtables, Camille and Bill Cosby have five children who they were raising during the time *The Cosby Show* aired. His research and interest in education and the images that children see on television also contribute to the show and its contents.

A party-time mood buoys the racially mixed audience watching "The Bill Cosby Show" being taped inside the NBC studios in Brooklyn, New York—despite a tedious string of takes and retakes. The reason for the spectators' mirth? The star's penchant for improvisation has turned the rest of the cast into cackling groupies. Finally Bill Cosby, greeted by applause and hoots, steps into the darkened portion of the set to admonish the onlookers. A spotlight illuminates him. "Stop laughing," he says. "I'm doing it all wrong and you're just encouraging me." The crowd breaks up once more and Cosby returns to the scene and plays it the same as before—only this time the actors hold themselves together and go with the Cos. It's the best take yet.

The following afternoon finds Cosby hunched under a gray baseball cap in the back booth of a dimly lit Greenwich Village coffee shop, his fingers drumming an irregular beat on the tabletop in time with the cool jazz filtering through the cafe's stereo system. A large man, Cosby's is a presence to reckon with. Even the most self-absorbed New Yorker stops to stare at Cosby's face, a face that shelves an encyclopedia of comic expressions. A waiter carrying a tray above his head turns the corner and, noticing Cosby, does a double take that causes him to spill the dishes. "That's not funny," says Cosby, the master of the deadpan. "Now do it again and make it funny." It's the waiter's turn to laugh now.

Bill Cosby, at 47 years old, is not the avuncular, joke-a-minute sort you might expect him to be, based on his numerous comedy albums and those ingratiating commercials for Jell-O pudding. He is, instead, a sagacious, serious fellow, a man of many interests and strong opinions, who speaks slowly and chooses his words carefully. His observations come forth in a folksy manner, much like the stories of Mark Twain, full of truths of human behavior that teach as well as tickle—emphasized, of course, by Cosby's patented mug.

At the moment, Cosby is ensconced in the role of concerned parent as he discusses the domestic problems that inspired his return to television, troubles that began several years ago when he and his wife, Camille, purchased a "dish" antenna that brought 25 different TV channels into their Massachusetts home—much to the immediate delight of their five children. "But we created a new problem," Cosby explains. "It was no longer that they were watching too much television. Instead, we had to monitor the content of the shows."

What passed for entertainment on the airwaves was of special interest to William Henry Cosby, Ed. D., whose 242-page dissertation examined television as an aid to learning. He found little educational value in the gaggle of shows his new antenna plucked from orbiting satellites. "My kids, if unmonitored, could watch four different movies with cars smashing, people getting drunk and sex without permission as entertainment," Cosby says. Dr. Cosby thus prescribed no more television: "We told the children that later on in life, when we are very old and cannot take care of ourselves, they could beat us up for not letting them watch."

Prior to the appearance of *The Cosby Show* on NBC in 1984, the everyday life of a black family was not part of the usual comedy lineup. **THE KOBAL COLLECTION. REPRODUCED BY PERMISSION.**

Cosby didn't put himself in a position like the patriot Patrick Henry and holler at the network brass: "Give me better programming or give me death." Cosby, instead, chose to lead by example and decided to return to television, after an eight-year absence, with a series of his own, much like a parent who joins the PTA and hopes he can make a difference. "It was cheaper to do a series than to throw out my family's TV sets, " he says. But CBS and ABC turned him down. "I walked in at a bad time," he says, "because everybody in the gray suits and paisley ties said that, according to marketing reports, sitcoms were over.

"So here I come, with all these marketing negatives: a black family that is not going to be of the street-level humor,; a wife who's a professional person; five children; and a show that deals with the human behavior of the people in the series more than making up situations so the breasts can come out and the pants can come down."

The third time was the charm. NBC finally gave Cosby the go-ahead, and what he developed is an absolutely fetching sitcom. "The Cosby Show," ranked consistently among the ten most popular pro-

grams and watched each week by an estimated 38.3 million people, is this season's prime-time sensation, a dignified jewel among half-hour duds. No one is more pleased than the man listed on the show's credits as creator, producer, writer and star. "I'm pleasantly surprised at the show's success," Cosby says with a grin. "I was just hoping it could stay on, because I have so much to give."

An insightfully funny portrait of an upper-middle-class family and their five children, "The Cosby Show" is crammed with the sort of amusing fancies and foibles of contemporary family life that spark a smile of instant recognition among viewers. "The show is really a love story to people," Cosby says. "It's about what I studied for at the university; it's about my gratitude that I finally woke up as a youngster and went to college; and it's about my love for telling and writing stories. Most of all, though, it's entertainment for the entire family."

The show breaks new ground in television because it transcends questions of race and concentrates on the people themselves. Cosby himself emphasizes that the show has nothing to do with black people on television. "My point is," he says, "that they are black and you can see it. We don't have to tell anybody. What we are telling everyone is that we are human beings, and we have all the same wants and needs that everyone else has."

The message is strong and forceful, like the man himself. But then this is Cosby's show, totally. It's his idea. He contributed to the casting of the actors who make up his TV family. He selected paintings by Varnette Honeywood, a black artist whose work is in Cosby's own home, to hang on the walls of the set. And he frequently contributes ideas to the show's writers; he draws on his experience as husband and parent to make certain the show resembles situations encountered by real families. "He never will let something just go by," says Caryn Sneider, one of the show's producers. "He works very hard to make each moment special."

More revealing of the man, however, is that "The Cosby Show" is about as close a look at his personal life as the extremely private Cosby has ever allowed. He even acknowledges that the series is almost a mirror image of his own family—his wife of 20 years, whom he met on a blind date when she was a psych major at the University of Maryland; his daughters Erika, 19, Erinn, 18, Ensa, 11, Evin, 8, and his son Ennis, 5. Cosby finds this only natural. "This is what I know best," he says. "Family and kids. But you have to understand that the show would not be this successful if my life wasn't so much like the lives of so many human beings.

"Look, we're all dealing with the same problems. Parents, regardless of what color they are, or how much money they have, perceive themselves as people who work hard and have wisdom to hand down, and they see their children as people who repel hard work and wisdom. Understand that I have wealth and fame, and I have found it's impossible to buy a kid who's going to do homework. And it's nearly as hard to find a kid who's going to return a car with a full tank of gas."

Such Cosbyisms have their origin in the North Philadelphia ghetto where Cosby grew up. His father, a career Navy man, separated from his wife during Cosby's youth. Cosby himself was a restless child. "I played my whole youth," he says, "and every day I'm sorry for it." Though his mother stressed the importance of education, Cosby dropped out of the tenth grade, an admitted mistake. "I had hit the bottom—I was out of school, I could get a job and go party—and it really wasn't any fun." The big turnaround came after Cosby enlisted in the Navy and found himself awakened at four in the morning by a snarling chief petty officer clanging a stick in a metal trash can. "I knew then and there that there were alternatives to this life," he says. The one Cosby chose was a high-school-equivalency degree via a service correspondence course and then three years at Temple University on an athletic scholarship.

Perfoming before an audience wasn't always in Cosby's plans. Many years ago he fell in love with jazz music and seriously considered becoming a drummer. Cosby still composes music, like the opening theme to his show, and counts among his close friends the musical legends Dizzy Gillespie and Miles Davis. He also thought about playing professional football after the New York Giants offered him a tryout. And then for a long time he wanted to teach junior high school. But, eventually, the young, street-wise Cosby yielded to his aching funny bone and moved to New York to launch a show-biz career. "I think that no matter what career I would have chosen—medicine, law or teaching—I would have inevitable gone into performing," he says.

The decision was, obviously, the correct one.Thanks to more record sales than any other comedian's (and eight Grammys), and numerous movie roles, two previous TV series and his ubiquitous presence as a commercial pitchman, Cosby is a millionaire many times over. He resides in princely fashion with his family in a 19th-century farmhouse on more than 200 acres near Amherst, Massachusetts. (The house was completely renovated by Camille and filled with the antique furniture and American art that are their passions.) "The Cosby Show" is produced in Brooklyn so Cosby can remain close to his family. He lives in a midtown-Manhattan brownstone during the week and returns weekends to the ongoing love story he shares with his wife. "To see her face, to hug her, to see her laugh and smile, it's the only way I know I want to feel," he says. As for parenting their large brood, Cosby says both he and Camille are "committed to not giving up."

The seed that led Bill Cosby into another weekly TV series began germinating long ago. In the late '60s, Cosby resumed his education at the University of Massachusetts at Amherst. After seven years of course work and practice teaching at prisons and on "Sesame Street" and "The Electric Company," plus a fat dissertation, he stepped forward in his hooded gown and accepted a sheep-skin as "Doctor of Education." "I did it because I had something to say about Orwell, 1984, and the fact that I felt we could use the television set to help educate people," says Cosby.

This new show seems to be just what the doctor ordered. Through humor, the only medicine he's allowed to dispense, Cosby hopes he might be able to teach people an important lesson, that things like "segregation, sexism and racism are ways that we only set ourselves back," in Cosby's words.

And Cosby is already hearing positive response to his hilarious half hour of humanity. People have written him that the show is a time the entire family gathers around the TV set to watch; others have written that they've changed their day off in order to catch the show. This is exactly the type of response Cosby is seeking: "I want to put a show on the air that people feel good about, one that they can be proud of and identify with, and, most important, a show where children can laugh at the behavior of parents and parents can laugh at the behavior of children."

The funny thing is, Cosby is doing just that. So let's all be thankful that the doctor has decided to make a house call.

Further Resources
BOOKS

Fuller, Linda K. *The Cosby Show: Audiences, Impact, and Implications.* Westport, Conn.: Greenwood Press, 1992.

Jhally, Sut, and Justin Lewis. *Enlightened Racism: The Cosby Show, Audiences, and the Myth of the American Dream.* Boulder, Colo.: Westview, 1992.

PERIODICALS

Frazer, June, and Timothy Frazer. *"Father Knows Best* and *The Cosby Show*: Nostalgia and the Sitcom Tradition." *Journal of Popular Culture* 27, no. 3, Winter 1993, 163–172.

Merritt, Bishetta D. "Bill Cosby: TV Auteur?" *Journal of Popular Culture* 24, no. 4, Spring 1991, 89–102.

WEBSITES

Nick at Nite: The Cosby Show. Available online at http://www .tvland.com/nickatnite/cosby_show/; website home page: http://www.tvland.com (accessed June 12, 2003).

Bill Cosby. Available online at http://www.delafont.com/co-medians/Bill-Cosby.htm; website home page: http://www .delafont.com (accessed June 12, 2003).

"Thousands Watch a Rain of Debris"

Newspaper article

By: William J. Broad

Date: January 29, 1986

Source: Broad, William J. "Thousands Watch a Rain of Debris." *The New York Times,* January 29, 1986, Section A.

About the Author: William J. Broad has been a science reporter for *The New York Times* since 1983. He is a two-time Pulitzer Prize winner for his work at the *Times.* Broad is also the author of several books on outer space. ∎

Introduction

Between 1958 and 1973, NASA launched a number of space flights under the Apollo program. As the next step, NASA envisioned a "skylab" where people could work and live for extended periods of time. This phase was instituted in 1973 and 1974. The space shuttle program was the next step. Budget cuts at NASA and shifting national priorities changed the vision for the program. Instead of a shuttle that would carry people and supplies back and forth to the skylab, NASA searched for alternatives. International agreements were signed, and it appeared that the space program would continue in cooperation with the Russians. The political climate did not allow for the agreement to go forward in the late 1970s, however. The first space shuttle flight of the *Columbia* took place in 1981, and the program received a boost in 1984 as President Reagan reaffirmed a commitment to space travel and exploration. The program and the international agreements continued in the 1980s. The *Challenger* mission was to be the space shuttle's 25th flight and the 10th for this spacecraft. *Columbia* had launched on January 12 and landed on January 18, a successful mission following several delays. *Challenger* had also been delayed but was set to lift off on January 28,

1986. After 74 seconds into the flight, the shuttle exploded in front of thousands on the ground at Cape Canaveral and millions more who were watching on television. Part of the *Challenger's* mission was to renew interest in space travel, which had been waning since the end of the Apollo program. Instead, onlookers witnessed the deaths of the seven crew members.

The eerie photographs of the *Challenger* explosion spread across the front pages of newspapers throughout the world and were replayed on television newscasts. Following the explosion of *Challenger,* no space shuttles were launched until September 1988.

Significance

The space shuttle *Challenger* carried a crew of experienced scientists and engineers. Some had already flown on previous space shuttle missions, while others boarded the craft for the first time. Christa McAuliffe, a teacher, had grown up watching space flight. As women began to enter the space program, she looked to her students for the future of the space program. The opportunity to become the first civilian on the space shuttle provided McAuliffe with the prospect of living part of a dream. Instead of writing a journal of her experiences, she perished with the other astronauts. Although people tend to associate the mission with McAuliffe, the other crew members were seasoned astronauts. Dick Scobee was the mission's commander. Scobee, an Air Force pilot since 1965, had flown on previous missions. Michael J. Smith, a Naval Academy graduate and naval captain, had been selected for astronaut training in 1980. Ronald E. McNair had already flown on the shuttle. McNair was a physicist and the second African American to travel into space. A scholarship program was established in his name for students at universities across the country. Ellison Onizuka fulfilled a childhood dream when he became an astronaut. He looked forward to seeing Halley's Comet on this flight. Judith Resnik, an engineer, worked on projects supporting the Orbiter development. She flew her first mission in 1984. Gregory Jarvis was the payload specialist on the mission. He had worked as an engineer in conjunction with space programs for several years.

Following tragic accidents, the space program steps back and reevaluates its missions and the equipment. The report issued on the investigation into the space shuttle explosion indicated that the "O"-ring failed. This is a "synthetic rubber ring designed to ensure that the separate sections of the booster rocket held together." Problems had already been noted concerning the design of the part; however, the reports were not coordinated, according to the investigation. Chapter six of *The Presidential Commission on the Space Shuttle Challenger Accident Report* notes a number of problems with the "O"-ring

The crew of the space shuttle *Challenger* included experienced scientists and engineers as well as a New Hampshire schoolteacher selected to be the first civilian in space. AP/WIDE WORLD PHOTOS. REPRODUCED BY PERMISSION.

which both Morton Thiokol, Inc., the contractor, and NASA were aware. Commissioner Feyman called it "a kind of Russian roulette" because they knew the part may fail, though it had not done so up to this point. The accident and investigation caused greater scrutiny of the space program.

The shuttle program was reinstated in September 1988 and continued without a serious accident until February 1, 2003, when the *Columbia* exploded upon reentry during its 113th flight. Again, all the crew members were killed.

Primary Source

"Thousands Watch a Rain of Debris"

SYNOPSIS: The expedition of the space shuttle *Challenger* was to be historic for carrying the first ordinary citizen, Christa McAuliffe, into space. Instead, it became historic for the tragic accident that ended her life and the lives of the rest of the crew. As thousands watched at Cape Canaveral and millions on television, the shuttle exploded shortly after takeoff.

Cape Canaveral, Fla., Jan. 28—The space shuttle Challenger exploded in a ball of fire shortly after it left the launching pad today, and all seven astronauts on board were lost. The worst accident in the history of the American space program, it was witnessed by thousands of spectators who watched in wonder, then horror, as the ship blew apart high in the air.

Flaming debris rained down on the Atlantic Ocean for an hour after the explosion, which occurred just after 11:39 A.M. It kept rescue teams from reaching the area where the craft would have fallen into sea, about 18 miles offshore.

It seemed impossible that anyone could have lived through the terrific explosion 10 miles in the sky, and officials said this afternoon that there was no evidence to indicate that the five men and two women aboard had survived.

No Ideas Yet as to Cause

There were no clues to the cause of the accident. The space agency offered no immediate explanations, and said it was suspending all shuttle flights indefinitely while it conducted an inquiry. Officials discounted speculation that cold weather at Cape Canaveral or an accident several days ago that slightly damaged insulation on the external fuel tank might have been a factor.

Americans who had grown used to the idea of men and women soaring into space reacted with shock to the disaster, the first time United States astronauts had died in flight. President Reagan canceled the State of the Union Message that had been scheduled for tonight, expressing sympathy for the families of the crew but vowing that the nation's exploration of space would continue.

Killed in the explosion were the mission commander, Francis R. (Dick) Scobee; the pilot, Comdr. Michael J. Smith of the Navy; Dr. Judith A. Resnik; Dr. Ronald E. McNair; Lieut. Col. Ellison S. Onizuka of the Air Force; Gregory B. Jarvis, and Christa McAuliffe.

Mrs. McAuliffe, a high-school teacher from Concord, N.H., was to have been the first ordinary citizen in space.

After a Minute, Fire and Smoke

The Challenger lifted off flawlessly this morning, after three days of delays, for what was to have been the 25th mission of the reusable shuttle fleet that was intended to make space travel commonplace. The ship rose for about a minute on a column of smoke and fire from its five engines.

Suddenly, without warning, it erupted in a ball of flame.

The shuttle was about 10 miles above the earth, in the critical seconds when the two solid-fuel rocket boosters are firing as well as the shuttle's main engines. There was some discrepancy about the exact time of the blast: The National Aeronautics and Space Administration said they lost radio contact with the craft 74 seconds into the flight, plus or minus five seconds.

Two large white streamers raced away from the blast, followed by a rain of debris that etched while contrails in the cloudless sky and then slowly headed toward the cold waters of the nearby Atlantic.

The eerie beauty of the orange fireball and billowing white trails against the blue confused many onlookers, many of whom did not at first seem aware that the aerial display was a sign that something had gone terribly wrong.

There were few sobs, moans, or shouts among the thousands of tourists, reporters and space agency officials gathered on an unusually cold Florida day to celebrate the liftoff, just a stunned silence as they began to realize that the Challenger had vanished.

Among the people watching were Mrs. McAuliffe's two children, her husband and her parents and hundreds of students, teachers and friends from Concord.

"Things started flying around and spinning around and I heard some oh's and ah's, and at that moment, I knew something was wrong," said Brian Ballard, the editor of *The Crimson Review* at Concord High School.

"I felt sick to my stomach. I still feel sick to my stomach."

Ships Searching the Area

At an outdoor news conference held here this afternoon, Jesse W. Moore, the head of the shuttle program at NASA, said:

"I regret to report that, based on very preliminary searches of the ocean where the Challenger impacted this morning, these searches have not revealed any evidence that the crew of the Challenger survived." Behind him, in the distance, the American flag waved at half-staff.

Coast Guard ships were in the area of impact tonight and planned to stay all night, with airplanes set to comb the area at first light for debris that could provide clues to the catastrophe. Some material from the shattered craft was reported to be washing ashore on Florida beaches tonight, mostly the small heat-shielding tiles that protect the shuttle as it passes through the earth's atmosphere.

Films of the explosion showed a parachute drifting toward the sea, apparently one that would have lowered one of the huge reusable booster rockets after its fuel was spent.

Pending an investigation, Mr. Moore said at the news conference this afternoon, hardware, photographs, computer tapes, ground support equipment and notes taken by members of the launching team would be impounded.

The three days of delays and a tight annual launching schedule did not force a premature launching, Mr. Moore said in answer to a reporter's question.

The space shuttle *Challenger* explodes 74 seconds after lift off. Part of the *Challenger's* mission was to renew public interest in space travel. AP/WIDE WORLD PHOTOS. REPRODUCED BY PERMISSION.

'Flight Safety a Top Priority'

"There was no pressure to get this particular launch up," he said. "We have always maintained that flight safety was a top priority in the program."

Several hours after the accident, Mr. Moore announced the appointment of an interim review team, assigned to preserve and identify flight data from the mission, pending the appointment of a formal investigating committee.

The members of the interim panel are Richard G. Smith, the director of the Kennedy Space Center; Arnold Aldridge, the manager of the National Space Transportation System, Johnson Space Center; William Lucas, director of the Marshall Space Flight Center; Walt Williams, a NASA consultant, and James C. Harrington, the director of Spacelab, who will serve as executive secretary.

A NASA spokesman said a formal panel could be appointed as soon as Wednesday by Dr. William R. Graham, the director of the space agency.

All American manned space launchings were stopped for more than a year and a half after the worst previous American space accident, in January 1967, when three astronauts were killed in a fire in an Apollo capsule on the launching pad.

"Hope We Go Today"

This year's schedule was to have been the most ambitious in the history of the shuttle program, with 15 flights planned. For the Challeneger, the workhorse of the nation's shuttle fleet, this was to have been the 10th mission.

Today's launching had been delayed three times in three days by bad weather. The Challenger was to have launched two satellites and Mrs. McAullife was to have broadcast two lessons from space to millions of students around the country.

All day long, well after the explosion, the large mission clocks scattered about the Kennedy Space Center continued to run, ticking off the minutes and seconds of a flight that had long ago ended.

Long before liftoff this morning, skies over the Kennedy Space Center were clear and cold, reporters and tourists shivering in leather gloves, knit hats and down coats as temperatures hovered in the low 20s.

Icicles formed as ground equipment sprayed water on the launching pad, a precaution against fire.

At 9:07 A.M., after the astronauts were seated in the shuttle, wearing gloves because the interior was so cold, ground controllers broke into a round of applause as the shuttle's door, whose handle caused problems yesterday, which was closed.

"Good morning, Christa, hope we go today," said ground control as the New Hampshire schoolteacher settled into the space plane.

"Good morning," she replied, "I hope so, too." Those were her last known words.

The liftoff, originally scheduled for 9:28 A.M., was delayed two hours by problems on the ground caused first by a failed fire-protection device and then by ice on the shuttle's ground support structure.

The launching was the first from pad 39–B, which had recently undergone a $150 million overhaul. It had last been used for a manned launching in the 1970's.

Just before liftoff, Challenger's external fuel tank held 500,000 gallons of liquid hydrogen and oxygen, which are kept separate because they are highly volatile when mixed. The fuel is used in the shuttle's three main engines.

At 11:38 A.M. the shuttle rose gracefully off the launching pad, heading into the sky. The shuttle's main engines, after being cut back slightly just after liftoff, a normal procedure, were pushed ahead to full power as the shuttle approached maximum dynamic pressure when it broke through the sound barrier.

"Challenger, go with throttle up," said James D. Wetherbee of mission control in Houston at about 11:39 A.M.

"Roger," replied the commander, Mr. Scobee, "go with throttle up."

Those were the last words to be heard on the ground from the winged spaceplane and her crew of seven.

As the explosion occurred, Stephen A. Nesbitt of Mission Control in Houston, apparently looking at his notes and not the explosion on his television monitor, noted that the shuttle's velocity was "2,900 feet per second, altitude 9 nautical miles, down-range distance 7 nautical miles." That is a speed of about 1,977 miles an hour, a height of about 10 statute miles and a distance down range of about 8 miles.

The first official word of the disaster came from Mr. Nesbitt of Mission Control, who reported "a major malfunction." He added that communications with the ship had failed 1 minute 14 seconds into the flight.

"We have no downlink," he said, referring to communications from the Challenger. "We have a report from the flight dynamics officer that the vehicle has exploded."

His voice cracked. "The flight director confirms that," he continued. "We're checking with the recovery forces to see what can be done at this point."

Tapes Showed Small Fire

In the sky above the Kennedy Space Center, the shuttle's two solid-fuel rocket boosters sailed into the distance.

The explosion, later viewed in slow-motion televised replays taken by cameras equipped with telescopic lenses, showed what appeared to be the start of a small fire at the base of the huge external fuel tank, followed by the quick separation of the solid rockets. A huge fireball then engulfed the shuttle as the external tank exploded.

At the news conference, Mr. Moore would not speculate on the cause of the disaster.

The estimated point of impact for debris was 18 to 20 miles off the Florida coast, according to space agency officials.

"The search and rescue teams were delayed getting into the area because of debris continuing to fall from very high altitudes, for almost an hour after ascent," said Mr. Nesbitt of Mission Control in Houston.

Speaking at 1 P.M. in Florida, Lieut. Col. Robert W. Nicholson Jr., a spokesman for the rescue operation, which is run by the Defense Department, said range safety radars near the Kennedy Space Center detected debris falling for nearly an hour after the explosion. "Anything that went into the area would have been endangered," he said in an interview.

In addition, the explosion of the huge fuel supply would have created a cloud of toxic vapors. NASA officials said tonight that the hazardous gases presented no danger to land, but the Coast Guard was advising boats and ships to avoid the area.

'Not a Good Ditcher'

In an interview last year, Tommy Holloway, the chief of the flight director office at the Johnson Space Center in Houston, talked about the possibility of a shuttle crash at sea.

"This airplane is not a good ditcher," he said. "It will float O.K. if it doesn't break apart, and we have hatches we can blow off the top. But the orbiter lands fast, at 190 knots. You come in and stop in 100 yards or so. You decelerate like gangbusters, and anything in the payload bay comes forward. We don't expect a very good day if it comes to that."

On board Challenger was the world's largest privately owned communication satellite, the $100 million Tracking and Data Relay Satellite, which with its rocket boosters weighed 37,636 pounds.

This morning, water froze on the shuttle service structure, used for fire-fighting equipment and for emergency showers that technicians would use if they were exposed to fuel. The takeoff was delayed because space agency officials feared that during the first critical seconds of launching, icicles might fly off the service structure and damage the delicate heat-resistant tiles on the shuttle, which are crucial for the vehicle's re-entry through the earth's atmosphere.

Further Resources

BOOKS

Cooper, Henry S.F. *Before Lift-off: The Making of a Space Shuttle Crew.* Baltimore: Johns Hopkins University Press, 1987.

Heppenheimer, T.A. *The Space Shuttle Decision: NASA's Search for a Reusable Space Vehicle.* Washington: NASA, NASA History Office, Office of Policy and Plans, 1999.

Neal, Arthur G. *National Trauma and Collective Memory Major Events in the American Century.* Armonk, N.Y.: M.E. Sharpe, 1998.

PERIODICALS

Elliot, Norbert, Eric Katz, and Robert Lynch. "The Challenger Tragedy: A Case Study in Organizational Communication and Professional Ethics." *Business & Professional Ethics Journal* 12, Summer 1993, 91–108.

McGinley, Laurie, and Arlen J. Large. "The Challenger Disaster: In the Beginning, Few Understood What They Saw." *The Wall Street Journal,* January 29, 1986, 1.

WEBSITES

51-L Challenger Accident. Available online at http://www.fas.org/spp/51L.html; website home page: http://www.fas.org (accessed June 12, 2003).

The Challenger Disaster: 10 Years Later. Available online at http://www.life.com/Life/space/challenger.htmll; website home page: http://www.life.com (accessed June 12, 2003).

Report of the Presidential Commission on the Space Shuttle Challenger Accident. Available online at http://science.ksc.nasa.gov/shuttle/missions/51-l/docs/rogers-commission/table-of-contents.html; website home page: http://science.ksc.nasa.gov (accessed June 12, 2003).

"Street Questions"
Magazine article

Date: April 21, 1986
Source: "Street Questions." *The New Yorker* 62, April 21, 1986, 40–41. ∎

Introduction

Talk shows have been part of the television and radio landscape for decades. Jack Parr, Arthur Godfrey, Paul Harvey, and others popularized different formats of talk shows. Parr and Godfrey are products of the 1950s and 1960s, when talk shows were part standup comedian and part interview. Harvey's commentaries on life, politics, and news in general are part of a shorter format that is not interactive. Harvey's show has attracted listeners since 1951.

AM radio slumped in popularity in the 1970s and 1980s. FM radio took over as the place to find music, current news, and interesting programming. The talk show format seemed like it might be dead. But Larry King changed that with his overnight radio program featuring audience participation. The same was true for late-night television. It was "traditionally a throwaway time filled with direct-response ads for kitchen utensils and trade schools." This changed with King's talk show, *Larry King Live,* and with *Late Show With David Letterman.*

AM radio and late-night television became a place to attract listeners and viewers who were "well educated, affluent audiences favored by advertisers." The personalities of the hosts made the difference, as did the format of the shows. Audience participation, interesting guests, and humor that seemed off the cuff were part of the formula that made late night the place to be.

The talk-show circuit became crowded as the 1980s progressed. Shock radio, controversial and contentious talk-show hosts, and political commentary became the norm on many stations. Rush Limbaugh, the conservative talk show host, and Howard Stern, the shock jock, represent opposite spectrums of hosts who took over the airwaves.

Significance

Larry King's voice spread across the media in the 1980s. He hosted an all-night radio show, as well as a

Larry King on the set of his CNN television talk show, *Larry King Live*. Larry King helped to reinvigorate AM radio and late-night television with his call-in talk shows. THE KOBAL COLLECTION/CNN. REPRODUCED BY PERMISSION.

nightly talk show on CNN, and wrote for *USA Today*. He did each one with his own distinct style, looking for what he calls "street questions." King does not want to be the regular interviewer; he wants to ask the questions people are curious about and to probe for unusual information. King became the leader in the talk-show industry by being interactive with his audience. He asks questions of them and then listens.

Larry King Live became part of the CNN nightly lineup in 1985. The show is the only international call-in talk show. King features "celebrity interviews, contemporary issue debates, and politics—all with the input of the audience." This formula is also part of the overnight radio show. Larry King's "credence is in the value of unfiltered talk and in the viewers, listeners, and callers who are partners in his career."

Larry King has received credit for renewing interest in AM radio. In 1981, King received a letter from veteran radio commentator Paul Harvey, thanking him for bringing press attention back to radio. King's programs started a generation of radio talk shows. He remains a popular figure and host both on television and for the millions who stay up all night to listen to him on the radio.

Primary Source

"Street Questions"

SYNOPSIS: Guests are scheduled day by day on King's shows. On the call-in segments, King never knows what to expect or who to expect on the other end. He says these are the elements of the radio and television programs that keep him sharp and asking good questions.

For each of the eight years that Larry King has had his current radio show, five nights a week (it's now heard on two hundred and eighty-two Mutual stations, including WOR in New York, where it runs from 11:06 P.M. until 5 A.M.), he has devoted one program to the question "Why are you up?" The last time, when listeners phoned in from all over the country, sixty-four per cent said they were King-aholics, and regularly stayed up with Larry at least four nights a week; twenty-six per cent said they were working or coming off work; twelve per cent said they were doing homework; and eight per cent identified themselves as insomniacs. We missed that program, but late one recent evening we visited the studio, near Washington, D.C., where Larry broadcasts, to talk with him and then see how he goes about his business. He is a medium-sized man of fifty-two, with graying hair and a focussed look, and he wore a red Dior sweater over a button-down shirt open at the collar. After greeting us with a quick pump of our hand, he sat down and fiddled with his watch.

Some notes on technique: Larry delivers comments that are packaged like aphorisms. (Example: "Every day is weird.") He likes numbers, he told us ("Forget about the three million people who listen to me. Over two per cent of the people in this country can't sleep at night"), and free association ("Dean Rusk doesn't sleep, Jerry Lewis doesn't sleep, Jackie Gleason doesn't sleep") and putting things straight ("If I have an author on and I read his book ahead of time, I feel terrible. I lose my curiosity. I forget to ask a question about the book"). He tries to offer a different kind of show ("Talk-show heaven is hysteria, and I don't like to jump on that"), and he tries not to use "I" when he's interviewing someone, so he gets it out of his system when he's not. "My idea is 'Go for the moment,'" he said to us. "When I started out, twenty-eight years ago, at a little AM station in Miami called WAHR, there used to be a sign up in the studio. It said, 'If in doubt, leave it out.' I always break that rule. I do a TV show five nights a week on the Cable News Network, and I write a weekly column for *USA Today*. I was commentator last fall on the NBC pregame football show with Bob Costas, and I used to do a column for a sports magazine. I'm a real sports nut. Until recently, I did a radio show for the Voice of America, the first Sunday of each month—it was fascinating, because I took calls from all over the world. Once, I got a call from China. Hunan, China."

Larry uses a code of his own, as in "I'm still the streets of New York" (he grew up in Brooklyn), and puts headlines of his own on questions, as in "True or False: Truman wanted Eisenhower to run as a Democrat." (True.) That question he delivered to Harold Stassen, who arrived not long after we did, to talk with Larry and dozens of callers about his proposal for a new United Nations charter. ("I'm curious about everything," Larry told us.) Stassen is a stocky, not very talkative man with a famous toupee, who became governor of Minnesota at thirty-one, in 1938, and has since held a variety of positions (one of the drafters of the original United Nations charter, adviser to President Eisenhower, president of the University of Pennsylvania) while earning a reputation as a perennially unsuccessful candidate for President of the United States. (He's run eight times.) Stassen slipped off his tie, pulled up a chair, and faced Larry across a table. While they waited for the second hand on a studio clock to tick down the last minute before showtime, Larry flicked some ashes off the shoulder of his sweater and talked with his guest about Hawaii.

Larry being introduced on the air by a taped voice: "And now America's most talked-about interviewer and the host of our program, Larry King." Larry responding live to the tape: "Thank you, Paul." Larry in an aside to Stassen during a break at 12:40: "Living Through History: You know, Adlai Stevenson had the most twinkling blue eyes I have ever seen. I'm talking Paul Newman, Frank Sinatra, the whole bit." Larry on the air at 1:08, with fourteen phone lines blinking in front of him, taking his first call of the night: "Laurel, Maryland. Good morning." Larry drinking a cup of coffee during another break, at 2:04: "The question is, When do you take your last cup? If this is it, I go home and sleep fine until midmorning. If not, I'm in big trouble." A caller from Milwaukee, Wisconsin, whose voice sounds far away, with a hypothetical for Stassen: "Imagine that you and Larry and I are sitting around in 1945 . . ." Larry on another break, after Stassen has left, and before the start of the show's "Open Phone America" segment, when people call in to talk about whatever is on their minds: "I interviewed Casey Stengel once.

I asked him one question, and he went on for twenty-eight and a half minutes."

When Larry is thinking, he pats his hair, his mouth turns down, and he slumps in his chair. He pushes his studio mike away, smokes through a cigarette, and then dumps his ashtray. His eyes droop, and his voice, which is naturally dusky, drops to a hush—especially if he seems to like what he has come up with. He picks at the carpet on the table, and stares at a glossy photo of himself (red Dior sweater, focussed look) that hangs on the studio wall, surrounded by shots of Bette Midler, Alexander Haig, and Jesse Jackson, and of Sid Caesar doing his show.

Toward dawn, he told us, "I ask a human kind of question. Like, if I had President Reagan on here the first thing I'd ask him about would be movies. That was his career. Does he read *Variety*? If I were President, I'd read *Broadcasting*.' Mr. President, do you follow the film grosses every week? What do you think of De Niro? Pacino? Are there any actors around who are what you were: Ronald Reagans, Gig Youngs, Tony Randalls—third-star best friends?' So then you could go from talking about movies to questions about using acting skills as President, without ever being discourteous. 'Could we take a Gregory Peck, in your opinion, Mr. President, school him, train him, and make him an effective leader?' Those are street questions he's never going to get at a press conference."

Further Resources

BOOKS
Munson, Wayne. *All Talk: The Talkshow in Media Culture.* Philadelphia: Temple University Press, 1993.

Murray, Michael D., ed. *The Encyclopedia of Television News.* Phoenix: Oryx Press, 1999.

PERIODICALS
"King of Radio: Ten Years and Counting." *Broadcasting,* January 25, 1988, 66–67.

Rosellini, Lynn. "The Audience That Loves Late Shows." *U.S. News & World Report,* June 23, 1988, 77–78.

WEBSITES
Larry King Live. Available online at http://www.cnn.com/CNN/Programs/larry.king.live; website home page: http://www.cnn.com (accessed June 12, 2003).

"Jeff MacNelly: One Cartoon Not Enough"

Magazine article

By: Tricia Drevets

Date: August 30, 1986

Source: Drevets, Tricia. "Jeff MacNelly: One Cartoon Not Enough." *Editor & Publisher,* August 30, 1986, 38–39. ∎

Introduction

Daily comic strips and editorial cartoons differ in nature and topic. The daily cartoon follows a cast of characters through a story line that generally continues. Characters tend to be stable, and relationships between characters are established through the plot lines of the strip. Editorial/political cartoons comment on current news and social or controversial issues. Several national editorial cartoonists are syndicated in papers across the country, and their cartoons provide commentary on national as well as international topics. Daily comic strips tend to focus on lighter topics.

It is the rare cartoonist who carries off both forms of cartoon art. Jeff MacNelly (1947–2000), however, created both editorial/political cartoons and the comic strip *Shoe.* The daily strip is planned and drawn ahead of its appearance in the newspaper. While current news and issues appear in some daily strips, like Gary Trudeau's *Doonesbury,* most are topical. The older cartoons, such as *Peanuts, Beetle Bailey,* and *Hi & Lois,* follow the group of characters through humorous events, sometimes making a point in a subtle way. Younger strips, like *Cathy, Garfield,* and *For Better or for Worse,* depend on humor of one or more main characters for the content. Garfield, the grumpy cat, tortures his owner Jon and other characters. Cathy's trials as a single woman make people laugh every day. *For Better or for Worse* follows the daily life of a family.

Jeff MacNelly followed the tried and true advice that helps make cartoons a success: use what you know. The characters of *Shoe* and the subject of the comic strip were based on newspapers and newspaper people whom MacNelly had worked with over the years. He also said that many of the characters were versions of himself. MacNelly used birds rather than humans in the comic strip, but the caricatures of daily life in the world of journalism have captured the hearts of readers and of his fellow cartoonists.

Significance

Jeff MacNelly's success came through finding the humor in everyday life. His focus for the strip *Shoe* was the newsroom, a world he knew. In his editorial cartoons,

the reader needed some knowledge of the event or whom he was satirizing. Successfully pulling off *Shoe* plus editorial cartoons would have been more than enough, but MacNelly drew more. He regularly illustrated Dave Barry's humorous column and books as well.

Syndication was a key aspect for MacNelly's widespread popularity. Appearing on both the editorial pages and in the comic section gave him a venue for voicing his opinions. Editorial cartoonists are under pressure to provide timely, humorous frames. Like others in his field, MacNelly was passionate about his art. James D. Squires wrote that "one slip of Mr. MacNelly's pen is likely to cause me more grief in a day than all the words written by all Tribune reporters in a year." Though he could be a "nasty sort" in his editorials, the Tribune Media Services supported his work and his opinions. Editorial cartoonists as a group can influence public opinion or bring a subject to the attention of the public quicker than a long-winded written editorial.

MacNelly's daily strip was also syndicated by the Tribune Media Services. In *Shoe,* the comic strip that he began drawing in 1977, he captures the humor of the newsroom through the exploits of the Treetop Tattler. The cast of characters, which includes Shoe, the editor, Perfesser Cosmo Fishhawk, and Skyler, represent the underachievers and overachievers we all find in day-to-day work. The goof-ups of the paper's staff provide laughter about the world of work in general as well as the newspaper world specifically. Taking a break from the editorial pages, MacNelly also earned the respect of his peers and earned awards for the comic strip, in addition to those he had won for editorial cartooning. The greatest tribute to Jeff MacNelly may be the commitment of Chris Cassatt, Gary Brookins, and Susie MacNelly to carry on with the strip after he died in June 2000.

Primary Source

"Jeff MacNelly: One Cartoon Not Enough"

SYNOPSIS: This profile of Jeff MacNelly focuses on his ability to draw both the political-oriented editorial cartoon and the daily comic strip. The deadlines and demands of keeping up with production of both types of comic art generally limit the artist to one or the other, but MacNelly found topics for both until his death in 2000.

There's a little bit of Jeff MacNelly in all the characters in his "Shoe" comic strip.

The editor bird Shoe is roughly patterned after Jim Shumaker, the editor at the Chapel Hill, North Carolina, weekly newspaper where MacNelly had his first cartooning position. "Jim Shumaker used to

Jeff MacNelly draws a character from his cartoon *Shoe* for a young girl. AP/WIDE WORLD PHOTOS. REPRODUCED BY PERMISSION.

wear sneakers to work and smoke cigars just like Shoe," said MacNelly. "He had a wonderful sense of what a newspaper should be. He was the one who convinced me I could make it in this business.

"The other characters in 'Shoe' are more or less composites of people I know, and they're all part of me. The professor is me; Skyler is me."

MacNelly, whose comic strip and editorial cartoons are syndicated by Tribune Media Services, gets ideas for "Shoe" from "hanging around the newspaper, listening to what's going on."

When he started "Shoe" in 1977, the newspaper MacNelly was "hanging around" was the *Richmond* (Va.) *News-Leader,* where he served as editorial cartoonist for 11 years.

At the time he created "Shoe," MacNelly was drawing five editorial cartoons a week for the News-Leader. "I was always curious about doing a comic strip," he recalled. "As a kid, I was a big 'Pogo' fan, but I didn't know if I could ever do a strip."

When MacNelly finally decided to give his ideas for a comic a try, he rented a small room in Richmond, furnished it with only a table, chair, and radio—and later an air conditioner—and forced himself to commit his strip to paper.

"It was really hard going to that room," MacNelly said with a grimace. "But I knew I wouldn't get anything done at the office or at home."

The comic's characters were humans at first, but MacNelly said he found them too dull and soon changed them to birds.

"I knew it was going to be about newspapers because that's what I know," he continued. "A cartoonist should do what he knows. If you're going to live with these people you create, you'd better be pretty familiar with them."

After about five to six months of after-hours work in his hideaway, MacNelly had finished creating "Shoe."

Today, readers of about 950 newspapers are familiar with the colorful birds on the staff of the *Treetop Tattler Tribune.* And the comic's fans includes journalists. "I really get a kick out of it when I see 'Shoes' on computer terminals in newsrooms," MacNelly said. "It shows I'm communicating with the audience."

He noted: "The great thing about a strip is you can be silly and fun. You can write a week's worth of strips complaining about anything—even pencil sharpeners."

MacNelly "complains" about more serious matters in his editorial cartoons. The three-time Pulitzer Prize winner (and two-time recipient of the National Cartoonists Society's Reuben Award for "Outstanding Cartoonist of the Year") draws three editorial cartoons a week for the *Chicago Tribune.* And his work is syndicated to about 400 newspapers.

While putting the finishing touches on a cartoon commemorating Chicago's Vietnam Veterans Day Parade, MacNelly discussed his decision to put his editorial cartooning on hold for awhile in 1981.

"I thought I had a pretty good career in political cartooning, and I was ready to do something else," recalled the 38-year-old MacNelly, who won his first Pulitzer when he was only 24. "I think everyone hits that point sometime in a career when you feel you've seen everything. I was doing my cartoons sort of automatically, and that's not good. I was disenchanted with politics, too.

"Here I'd been yelling about all this conservative stuff for years, and Ronald Reagan gets in office. I didn't have any complaints. A cartoonist needs something to complain about. Plus I'd always had this idea that it would be the life to start a second strip and live in the Bahamas or something."

But MacNelly found, when he began doing only "Shoe" out of his Richmond home, that his inspiration for the comic had been cut off. "I discovered I really couldn't do 'Shoe' without the daily contact with people," MacNelly said.

When his friend James Squires, editor of the Tribune, asked MacNelly to come to Chicago, he agreed. MacNelly had been away from political cartooning for only about nine months when he joined the Tribune's editorial staff in March 1982.

MacNelly said he tries to keep about four to five weeks ahead of the dailies in preparing "Shoe," which will be featured in another collection this fall. *One Shoe Fits All* will be the eighth "Shoe" book published by Henry Holt and Company.

Although he is happy with his current workload, MacNelly said he has ideas for a second comic in the back of his mind. "It would be a goofball kind of thing with both animals and human characters," he stated. "But I don't know when and if I'll get around to doing it." With one strip already and his editorial cartooning, MacNelly said he would probably need to work with an assistant on a second comic, and he's hesitant about that.

"I've used assistants occasionally in the past," he noted. "My editors can't tell the difference, but I can tell. Plus it takes me longer with an assistant because I have to sketch everything out first in pencil."

MacNelly, whose wife was expecting a baby this month, is also formulating ideas for a humorous book for "pregnant fathers."

"It would be a parody on books for pregnant women," he said. "My wife's pregnant, but I've put on about 20 pounds, my feet hurt, and I can't sleep. It's crazy."

The father of two sons, ages 12 and 14, from a previous marriage, MacNelly realizes that a new baby is going to change his life. "I work a lot at home now," he said. "I'll probably be doing more work here at the office."

That shouldn't be too much of a problem since MacNelly lives only a short distance from Tribune Tower. "I walk to work," he said. "That's part of what's great about Chicago. It's so liveable." However, the New York-born cartoonist admits to thinking of Virginia as home.

"I'm in a period of solidification right now," he stated. "I like the strip and I'm having fun with it. . . . I'm always changing the ink, the brushes.

"When I look back at some of my work, I'm pretty critical of myself. Sometimes I think the work holds up well, but, for the most part, I'm pretty embarrassed by it. I think that's a good thing, though. When I lose that feeling, I'll be in trouble."

Further Resources

BOOKS
Colldeweih, Jack, and Kalman Goldstein, eds. *Graphic Opinions: Editorial Cartoonists and Their Art.* Bowling Green, Ohio: Bowling Green State University Popular Press, 1998.

Somers, Paul, P., Jr. *Editorial Cartooning and Caricature: A Reference Guide.* Westport, Conn.: Greenwood Press, 1998.

PERIODICALS
Astor, David. "MacNell on 'Telly' Led to Cartooning?" *Editor & Publisher* 128, no. 38, September 23, 1995, 40.

Squires, James D. "Quick Draw Artists: Cartoon Kings and Mere Pretenders." *Wall Street Journal,* April 16, 1984, 1.

WEBSITES
MacNelly Chicago Tribune. Available online at http://www .macnelly.com/editorial.html (accessed June 12, 2003).

Tributes to Jeff MacNelly. Available online at http://cagle.slate .msn.com/news/macnelly/ (accessed June 12, 2003).

AUDIO AND VISUAL MEDIA
MacNelly, Jeff. "Reflection on My Career." Shaw Video Services, VHS, 1995.

"AIDS in the Heartland"

Newspaper article

By: Jacqui Banaszynski

Date: June 21, 1987

Source: Banaszynski, Jacqui. "AIDS in the Heartland." *St. Paul Pioneer Press*, June 21, 1987. Reprinted in *Pulitzer Prize Feature Stories*, David Garlook, ed. Ames, Iowa: Iowa State University Press, 1998, 276–277.

About the Author: Jacqui Banaszynski is the associate managing editor for special projects and staff development at the *Seattle Times.* She has worked as a news reporter for thirty years. Banaszynski also teaches journalism at the University of Missouri School of Journalism and Poynter Institute in St. Petersburg, Florida. ∎

Introduction

The AIDS epidemic first struck the United States in 1981. Initially viewed as a disease of gay men, it spread to a wider community, touching men, women, and children from all walks of life. Fear surrounded the disease, and myths abounded about how the HIV virus that causes AIDS was contracted. Educational efforts from public health organizations, schools, and media outlets attempted to correct the misconceptions through facts. HIV/AIDS is spread through needle exchange, sexual contact, or blood transfusions from infected persons. Some health care workers may be at risk because of contact with needles containing HIV-infected blood.

Although awareness was heightened, many still thought the disease was limited to big cities or urban areas. As of December 1999, statistics from the Centers for Disease Control showed that more than 410,000 Americans had died from AIDS. These people were in every state in the union, from cities both large and small.

Stigma and fears still surround the illness. This is a part of the story that Banaszynski relays in her series "AIDS in the Heartland," which chronicles the story of Dick Hanson, a 37-year-old farmer from Glenwood, Minnesota, and his partner, Bert Henningson, as Hanson was dying of AIDS. Goldie Kadushin's study of gay men in the Midwest with HIV/AIDS shows that the men "are more likely to seek and receive social support from friends and partners than from the family of origin." There are many reasons for this, but the absense of contact with one's family because of sexual orientation is one factor. The reactions of Hanson's family are the focal part of the second article in the series. There were family members who did not like the attention of a newspaper series.

Banaszynski relays the story of Hanson and Henningson in a humane manner. She "noted one of her greatest challenges [was] recognizing she was becoming emotionally involved in the story." In the end, she was able to write passionately and forcefully about an issue that challenges society and individuals.

Significance

The story of Dick Hanson came to Banaszynski through the photographs of Jean Pieri. The two journalists had worked together on stories before and collaborated on this one as well.

Hanson's story was important because of his political affiliations. He was the first openly gay member of the Democratic National Committee. Although this was one of the facts that first drew her, the human story of pain, prejudice, fear, and death kept Banaszynski working on the story. The three parts appeared in the Sunday section of the St. Paul, Minnesota *Pioneer Press.* The series brought a "big city" disease home to the rural communities of the Midwest. Through her narrative of the two men's lives, Banaszynski tells the story not only of a devastating disease but also of life in the community and with families and friends. She tells how the men "use their story to personalize the AIDS epidemic and to debunk some of the stereotypes and myths about AIDS and its victims." The fight was now to make people aware of AIDS and educate them about the realities of the disease.

Dick Hanson lost his battle with AIDS in July 1987. Bert Henningson also contracted the disease and died in 1988. Jacqui Banaszynski won the 1988 Pulitzer Prize for her groundbreaking portrait of two men whose lives were changed by a deadly disease and of the people they touched through their honesty about it.

Primary Source

"AIDS in the Heartland" [excerpt]

> **SYNOPSIS:** The optimism of Dick Hanson comes across through Baraszynski's sensitive portrayal. She relates the positive spirit through Hanson's words and through his actions as a political activist and as a farmer. Hanson's own words about his life and his illness are perhaps the strongest part of the story.

Hanson sat with his partner, Bert Henningson, in the small room at Minneapolis' Red Door Clinic on April 8, 1986, waiting for the results of Hanson's AIDS screening test.

He wouldn't think about how tired he had been lately. He had spent his life hefting hay bales with ease, but now was having trouble hauling potato sacks at the Glenwood factory where he worked part time. He had lost 10 pounds, had chronic diarrhea and slept all afternoon. The dishes stayed dirty in the sink, the dinner uncooked, until Henningson got home from teaching at the University of Minnesota-Morris.

It must be the stress. His parents had been forced off the farm and now he and his brothers faced foreclosure. Two favorite uncles were ill. He and Henningson were bickering a lot, about the housework and farm chores and Hanson's dark mood.

He had put off having the AIDS test for months, and Henningson hadn't pushed too hard. Neither was eager to know.

Now, as the nurse entered the room with his test results, Hanson convinced himself the news would be good. It had been four years since he had indulged in casual weekend sex at the gay bathhouse in Minneapolis, since he and Henningson committed to each other. Sex outside their relationship had been limited and "safe," with no exchange of semen or blood. He had taken care of himself, eating homegrown food and working outdoors, and his farmer's body always had responded with energy and strength. Until now.

"I put my positive thinking mind on and thought I'd be negative," Hanson said. "Until I saw that red circle."

The reality hit him like a physical punch. As he slumped forward in shock, Henningson—typically pragmatic—asked the nurse to prepare another needle. He, too, must be tested.

Then Henningson gathered Hanson in his arms and said, "I will never leave you, Dick."

Hanson is one of 210 Minnesotans and 36,000 Americans who have been diagnosed with AIDS since the disease was identified in 1981. More than half of those patients already have died, and doctors say it is only a matter of time for the rest. The statistics show that 80 to 90 percent of AIDS sufferers die within two years of diagnosis; the average time of survival is 14 months after the first bout of pneumocystis—a form of pneumonia that brought Hanson to the brink of death last August and again in December.

Further Resources

BOOKS

Bellenir, Karen, ed. *AIDS Sourcebook,* 2nd ed. Detroit: Omnigraphics, Inc., 1995.

Roleff, Tamara L., ed. *AIDS: Opposing Viewpoints.* San Diego, Calif.: Greenhaven Press, 1998.

PERIODICALS

Kadushin, Goldie. "Barriers to Social Support and Support Received From Their Families of Origin Among Gay Men

With HIV/AIDS." *Health & Social Work* 24, no. 3, August 1999, 198–209.

WEBSITES

AIDS.org. Available online at http://www.aids.org/index.html (accessed June 12, 2003).

CDC, National Center for HIV, STD, and TB Prevention. Divisions of HIV/AIDS Prevention. HIV/AIDS Fact Sheets. Available online at http://www.cdc.gov/hiv/pubs/facts.htm; website home page: http://www.cdc.gov (accessed June 12, 2003).

Johns Hopkins AIDS Service. Available online at http://www.hopkins-aids.edu/ (accessed May 27, 2003).

The Making of McPaper: The Inside Story of USA Today

Nonfiction work

By: Peter Prichard

Date: 1987

Source: Prichard, Peter. *The Making of McPaper: The Inside Story of USA Today.* Kansas City: Andrews, McMeel & Parker, 1987, 1–3.

About the Author: Peter Prichard (1944–) is the president of the Freedom Foundation in Arlington, Virginia. The Freedom Foundation is the home of the Newseum. He worked as editor in chief for *USA Today* between 1988 and 1994. Prichard has worked in journalism for his entire career in such areas as sportswriting, police and court reporting, assistant city editing, and feature editing. ∎

Introduction

In the 1980s, newspaper readership was on the decline as cable television increased in popularity. News shows and news channels competed directly with the daily newspapers that had been the source of information for most Americans. Along with the television competition, local dailies were being bought by companies, which resulted in a loss of local control and feel. Gannett, Knight Ridder, and the Tribune Company own most of the newspapers in the United States.

Newspapers began trying to appeal to a broader audience of readers by including feature articles that would be interesting. *The New York Times* and *The Wall Street Journal* catered to a certain class of readers, not to a broad majority. Neither paper could be distributed throughout the country the day it was published. So that the paper could be delivered the same day instead of arriving in the mail several days late, *The New York Times* formed affiliations with regional and large city newspapers since the early 1980s.

However, there were no true national newspapers prior to *USA Today.* Its launch signaled a new era in newspaper publishing. The paper did not make a profit for several years, but it continued to challenge the larger, more established papers, which thought of themselves as the national press. *USA Today* pushed newspapers like *The New York Times* to examine content and format. Critics predicted that the paper would not last more than a few months. It has not only survived, but has grown to become the most widely circulated daily newspaper in the United States.

Significance

USA Today was a bold experiment headed by a man who wanted it to succeed at any cost. Allen H. Neuharth, then the chairman and president of Gannett, envisioned a general daily newspaper delivered across the United States. He dubbed the paper the Nation's Newspaper in its inaugural issue, September 15, 1982. Critics, especially journalists, had harsh words for *USA Today,* claiming that it watered down the news and did not constitute serious journalism. Neuharth and his staff, however, found their niche and became a successful daily newspaper across the country within a decade of its founding. While many daily newspapers were folding or combining, *USA Today* drew readership by catering to the general reader interested in current news that was short, timely, and interesting.

The editors and reporters who launched the newspaper worked endless hours to produce *USA Today.* The stress and long hours caused some turnover in the staff. As the paper stabilized, new reporters joined the publication

The newspaper broke several rules, content being the biggest one. The use of color photographs, mastheads, and other nontraditional formats gave the paper a different look. The boldest commitment the paper made was to become the business traveler's newspaper. While *The Wall Street Journal* remained the serious newspaper for business, *USA Today* carved out a place in hotels and on airlines across the nation. *USA Today* appears in front of the doors of all classes of hotels and is given to customers free of charge. By 2002, *USA Today* claimed 2.2 million readers per day. This is a major milestone in a market that no longer supports a newspaper in every city in the United States.

Primary Source

The Making of McPaper: The Inside Story of USA Today [excerpt]

> **SYNOPSIS:** Pressure to succeed was a key factor for *USA Today.* Staffers worked 18-hour days to publish the newspaper and keep the product true to its orig-

Allen H. Neuharth, then chairman and president of the Gannett newspaper chain, envisioned *USA Today* as a general daily newspaper delivered across the United States. © BETTMANN/CORBIS. REPRODUCED BY PERMISSION.

inal vision—to be a different kind of paper. The paper turned a profit and met goals more quickly than expected.

Launch

Allen H. Neuharth sat alone in the back seat of a limousine as it slipped across a bridge into Washington, moving against the sluggish flow of commuters heading home at the end of another muggy, late summer day in the nation's capital.

For Neuharth, that Wednesday—September 15, 1982—was a momentous day. He was chairman and president of the Gannett Company, which already published eighty-eight daily newspapers. That morning, his company had launched *USA Today,* the country's first national, general-interest daily newspaper. Its first edition had sold out. Readers in the Washington-Baltimore area, its initial market, had snapped up all 155,000 copies.

The night before, Neuharth had been up until 4 A.M. He rewrote headlines in the newsroom until midnight, checked the first copies that came off the press at 1:30 A.M., did some television interviews,

The use of color photographs, mastheads, and other non–traditional formats gave *USA Today* a different look. Other newspapers adopted the same look based in part on *USA Today*'s original design. **AP/WIDE WORLD PHOTOS. REPRODUCED BY PERMISSION.**

ate linguine with clams at 3 A.M., and went to bed in his suite at the Capital Hilton Hotel. At 6 A.M. he was up, jogging in Lafayette Park and checking the *USA Today* newsracks around the White House.

Now, at dusk, he was on the way to the Washington Mall to promote the birth of what was, in many ways, his newspaper. The launch gala was an extraordinary event: Neuharth, the head of the nation's largest newspaper chain, a man who was the closest thing the country had to a press lord, had managed to persuade the president of the United States, the Speaker of the House of Representatives, and the Senate majority leader to stand together on the same dais in a tent at the foot of Capitol Hill to celebrate the arrival of Vol. 1, No. 1, of *USA Today.*

Neuharth later told his son Dan—then a *USA Today* reporter—that this day seemed too good to be true. Here he was, "a little guy from South Dakota," and the three most important leaders of the most powerful nation on earth were standing under his tent, promoting the birth of his newspaper. In his speech, the Speaker of the House, Thomas P. "Tip" O'Neill, remarked that these three leaders were not together often. That was true, and they certainly had never gathered before to promote the introduction of a commercial product.

Although Ronald Reagan, Howard Baker, and O'Neill had come to praise *USA Today,* plenty of others wanted to bury it. In the American newspaper establishment, Neuharth had more than his share of critics. They sneered at this new newspaper, his pet project. They were also put off by his vaulting ambition, his drive to acquire so many newspapers, his desire to leave his mark on journalism. Many of them distrusted Gannett, disliked Neuharth, and despised *USA Today.*

Neuharth's flair for showmanship was well known in the newspaper business, and that, too, offended his critics. The launch of this newspaper was his ultimate promotion. The centerpiece was a huge tent, 140 feet long and 60 feet wide, with "USA TODAY" banners draped all over it.

The tent's flaps had been left up, despite early objections from the Secret Service. They had to be up; Neuharth wanted to make sure everyone could see the Capitol and the Washington Monument. This christening had to come off just as he had choreographed it, with liberal doses of drama and patriotism. "The Nation's Newspaper" would debut in the nation's capital, flanked by the nation's two greatest monuments, surrounded by the nation's highest leaders, all of it wrapped up in red, white, and blue.

The eight hundred guests invited to *USA Today*'s "Salute to Congress" included senators and representatives, cabinet members, and the board of directors of the American Newspaper Publishers Association. That board included some of the most powerful publishers in the country, and many of them thought the new newspaper would surely fail. After the reception, the publishers and their spouses were coming to dinner at *USA Today*'s new headquarters in a thirty-story silver skyscraper in Rosslyn, a section of Arlington, Virginia, across the Potomac River from the Mall. Construction crews had been working day and night to finish the seventeenth floor executive dining room, catching naps when they could in sleeping bags on the floor. The work had been completed that very day, and the view of the Mall and the monuments from its windows was gorgeous. "From here we can look down on Washington," Neuharth liked to joke.

But on the afternoon of *USA Today*'s first day, much of official Washington was busy checking out this lavish bash on the Mall. No expense had been spared; the food alone cost $45,000. Like the newspaper, the buffet had an "Across the USA" theme. Just as there was news from every state, there was food from every state. The guests ate king crab from Alaska, walleyed pike from Minnesota, crab cakes from Maryland, oysters from New York and barbecued beef from Texas—washed down with wine from California. Then President Reagan stepped to the microphone, and for a moment the crowd was still.

The president's toast was short and simple. *USA Today,* he said, is "a testimony to the kind of dreams free men and women can dream and turn into reality here in America."

Neuharth thought the president had struck just the right note. For him, this new newspaper's first day was the beginning of a dream come true, a fairy tale he hoped would have a happy ending.

Further Resources

BOOKS

Mayer, Martin. *Making News.* Boston: Harvard Business School Press, 1993.

Nord, David. *Communities of Journalism: A History of American Newspapers and Their Readers.* Urbana: University of Illinois Press, 2001.

Squires, James D. *Read All About It!: The Corporate Takeover of America's Newspapers.* New York: Times Books, 1993.

PERIODICALS

Gordon, Richard. "USA Today Steps Up Market Rollout Plans." *Advertising Age* 53, no. 44, October 18, 1982, 3–4.

Stein, Nicholas. "Deadline U.S.A." *Fortune,* July 8, 2002, 78–80.

WEBSITES

Gannett: The Information Company. Available online at http://www.gannett.com/ (accessed June 12, 2003).

USA Today. Available online at http://www.usatoday.com/ (accessed June 12, 2003).

"Dialogue on Film: Steven Bochco"

Interview

By: Steven Bochco

Date: July–August 1988

Source: Bochco, Steven. "Dialogue on Film: Steven Bochco." *American Film,* July–August 1988, 14, 16–18.

About the Author: Steven Bochco (1943–) was born in Manhattan, New York and trained as a classical musician. He attended Carnegie Tech in Pittsburgh, Pennsylvania, where he received a degree in theater. Bochco has used his combined talents to create, write, and produce television shows which break the rules of genre television. ∎

Introduction

In the 1970s, cop shows were about detectives in trenchcoats or comedic cops chasing cars. However, the king of the television genre at this time was the sitcom, not the drama. Shows like *The Mary Tyler Moore Show, Taxi, Barney Miller,* and *M*A*S*H* were the hits on the three main network channels. In the 1980s, quick-paced dramas based on the more realistic side of life filled the schedule. Quality drama became the norm with shows like Bochco's *Hill Street Blues* and *L.A. Law.* Other dramas, such as *St. Elsewhere,* a show centered on a hospital, also became known for the quality of script and acting. These television shows began replacing the vapid series of the 1970s. Aaron Spelling's *Charlie's Angels,* for example, had been popular but lacked the kind of substance seen in the next decade of television police shows.

The MTM studio was a training ground for writers who would go on to create award-winning, groundbreaking television. Steven Bochco was part of this group. It was there that he began his work on *Hill Street Blues,* a show that, like many hits, began slowly. As was the case with all television in the 1980s and thereafter, the networks were feeling the pressure of new offerings on cable and needed different approaches for series. Bochco was able to carve out his place in television because he had new ideas. His shows not only drew audiences, but also became commercial successes for the networks.

Significance

Steven Bochco breaks the rules and not only comes up with television programs that are hits, but also are quality television. In the 1970s, Bochco became part of the creative group of writers at MTM, where James Burrows, Les and Glen Charles, and other award-winning writers also learned and honed their craft. Bochco went in a different direction, however. In 1980, he and co–creator Michael Kozoll conceived and filmed a pilot for *Hill Street Blues,* a police drama that would shake up the way the genre was viewed. *Hill Street Blues* first convinced many serious artists that television had finally come of age. Bochco was tired of the usual format of television cop shows, so he reinvented it. *Hill Street Blues* opened with roll call and assignments in a precinct. This opening scene also provided clues for the plot line of the episode. There were few pretty cops here; instead, these were the street cops who now fill television shows. Bochco created stories that were more interesting and realistic than the ones viewers were used to seeing. He continued this trend after being fired from MTM and *Hill Street Blues.* Creating *L.A. Law* provided an opportunity to redefine television about lawyers. Set in upscale offices, *L.A. Law* was about a powerful and successful group of lawyers who interacted in the office and courtroom as well as outside world.

Stephen Bochco's creative talents continue to be the source for redefining television and for creating new formats from old standbys. He challenges boundaries of acceptable content and language on television. Unique camerawork marks his shows. The single camera panning the station in *Hill Street Blues* and the jerkier motion of the camerawork in *L.A. Law* changed the way directors and producers thought about filming television. His innovative work reshaped the way television drama was conceived and created in the final decades of the twentieth century. Bochco is certain to continue being influential in the years to come.

Primary Source

"Dialogue on Film: Steven Bochco"

SYNOPSIS: Steven Bochco talks about his career, the frustrations of writing for television, and the show that he created and produced. The interview takes place in the Elton H. Rule Lecture Series held under the auspices of the American Film Institute's Center for Advanced Film and Television Studies.

In his twenty-two years in television, Steven Bochco has been awarded eight Emmys, two Humanitas Awards, two Peabodys, three Image Awards (from the NAACP), four Golden Globes, six People's Choices, two Writers Guild awards, and an Edgar Allen Poe. This for a man who has described his work life as "something like that of an insurance salesman. I go to an office every day, I do my job, and I go home. And I like that." But Bochco's image of himself as a clock-punching bureaucrat is contradicted by the television industry, which has usually viewed him—with both admiration and trepidation—as a Young Turk.

The son of a concert violinist, Bochco was raised in Manhattan; after graduating from the city's High School of Music and Art he received a bachelor's degree in theater from Carnegie Tech in Pittsburgh. In 1966 he moved to Hollywood and for the next twelve years honed his writing skills at Universal Studios on such shows as "The Name of the Game," "Columbo," and "McMillan and Wife." His work on movies of the week (including *Double Indemnity* in 1973, *The Invisible Man* in 1975, and *Vampire* in 1979), as well as his writing-producing credits on "Griff" and "Delvecchio," earned him a reputation as a crime-show specialist. But it was after he moved to MTM in 1978 that his career took off in earnest. "Hill Street Blues," a 1980–81 midseason replacement, sealed Bochco's reputation as a creative force. The show won a record twenty-six Emmys over its span, and spawned a number of look-alikes, including Bochco's own—unsuccessful—"Bay City Blues." In 1985, operational and financial differences forced Bochco to leave MTM. Moving to Twentieth Century-Fox, he co-created, with Terry Louise Fisher, two hot new shows: "L.A. Law" and "Hooperman," which have already garnered sixteen awards. And last fall he signed a ten-series deal with ABC.

"Television is my medium of choice," Bochco has said. "I love the idea of communicating ideas to, and entertaining, a mass audience. And I love the idea of doing it with, hopefully, some grace and style and wit and complexity."

Question: How did you get such an early start in the business?

Steven Bochco: In my last year of college, I was in the enviable position of having a job to go to at Universal—I'd had a summer-job stint there earlier. I wish I could tell you that I've had to struggle in my career, but I haven't. I've had just three jobs in twenty-two years: Universal, MTM, and the last three at Twentieth Century-Fox.

Universal in those days—and I think to a great extent today, as well—was sort of like a sausage factory. In the best sense of the word, in that they used every single part of the pig to make a product. Nothing got thrown out. What I did when I first started there—and it was tremendous hands-on training—was take unsold pilots and episodes of "Chrysler Theatre" and write an additional hour's material for them. It would be filmed, spliced in, and the whole thing released as an overseas movie package for television. Really, it was very smart business. So they started me off doing these things, and they said, "Well, now you're going to join the Writers Guild." I said, "All right, I'll join the Writers Guild."

Probably the single most fortunate thing that ever happened to me was going to work on "Columbo" for Dick Levinson and Bill Link. You know, the episode of "Columbo" that Steven [Spielberg] directed was the first one I ever wrote. And the two of us were really the baby boys at Universal. Dick and Bill were the old guys—I think they were thirty-five at the time, and I was twenty-six and Steven was twenty-two. Because of "Columbo's" success, I gained a degree of professional recognition in the business that I hadn't had before.

Question: How did you cross the line from writing into producing, and why?

Bochco: Self-defense. The fundamental production chores, be they important casting decisions or real control over the direction of a show—its conceptual underpinnings, so to speak—were in the hands of the suits. Occasionally, those suits had bodies in them. It didn't much matter.

Anyway, I had written a screenplay in a very short time—a week and a half—for the first film that Douglas Trumbull ever directed, Silent Running. And they just went, whoosh! "Give me that!" I mean, that was it. I did some rewrites on the fly. And then they said, "Great going, kid." And, "Feel free to come down to the aircraft carrier any time." I watched them make this thing, and I hated it. I was so disturbed, as I guess most writers are, at seeing the terrible disparity between what was in my head and what they

Steven Bochco, creator of the television shows *Hill Street Blues* and *L.A. Law*. AP/WIDE WORLD PHOTOS. REPRODUCED BY PERMISSION.

were putting on the screen, that I thought: I've got to be able to do something about this. And I never had an impulse to be a director, ever, so I thought: Well, at least if I produced the thing, I'd have some significant input. I started producing the next year. I was a god-awful producer.

Question: How did the radical rethinking of television's formats on "Hill Street Blues" happen?

Bochco: Well, I wish I could take credit for it, but that show came out of a process that I think typifies television at its best: It was a genuine ensemble invention. I just wound up having the mouth. And we—Michael Kozoll and I—did not approach it from the point of view of wanting to do something that had never been done before, but from the point of view of not wanting to do a whole bunch of things that we'd been doing for the last six or seven years in television.

Neither of us really felt that we had anything more to add to the police-show genre. It was NBC that made it click when they said that Fred Silverman was interested in having a television series like Fort Apache: The Bronx. Of course, they didn't flat out say, "Steal," but you never have to actually utter the "s" word in television—everybody knows

A still from Steven Bochco's *Hill Street Blues*. Bochco's unique camera work and other innovative contributions reshaped the way television drama was conceived and created in the final decades of the twentieth century. **NBC-TV/THE KOBAL COLLECTION. REPRODUCED BY PERMISSION.**

that's what you're doing. But we really stole the style of "Hill Street Blues" from something called *The Police Tapes,* which was shot in the South Bronx—Fort Apache, in fact—in black and white. The crew just followed a bunch of cops around—domestic violence, crime, street-gang murders, whatever—and put together a remarkable couple of hours of stuff that was very stark and all hand-held. It was one of the most arresting things I'd ever seen in my life. We said, "This is the feeling we want. We want to create something that gives the illusion of random event."

Anyway, the deal with NBC—we thought about it for a few days and finally agreed to do the show under one condition: that they absolutely leave us alone. And they agreed. Which was pretty surprising, but necessity being the mother . . . They needed a pilot desperately; there was very little time. This form sort of evolved without us really knowing what we were doing. I mean, we just knew we had a lot of characters—initially we had, I think, eight regulars. And as we began to develop these characters, we knew that we couldn't tell conventional stories and

also meet the needs of eight fully fleshed-out characters. So we began to think of it more in terms of a tapestry.

Of course, what happened is we shot the pilot and by the end of the pilot, the eight characters had become twelve. And then over the course of some years, the twelve officially became seventeen, but it really was more like thirty, because we had a whole group of satellite characters who evolved around this little universe.

Over the years of working on cop shows, you really do develop a treasure chest of oddball characters. I've actually gotten to know a lot of cops—in this town, you know, a lot of them want to be writers. I did a cop show once called "Delvecchio," with Judd Hirsch and Charlie Haid. It was a more standard, linear kind of show—a good one, I thought—and I met about four cops who wrote. These guys would come in in their suits and spin you some yarn that was just god-awful, usually a variation of some other cop show they'd seen on television. And I'd say, "Wait a second, wait a second. I don't want that; I want something else. But I don't know what."

Suddenly the tie and the jacket would come off and the gun's hanging out. You give them a drink. Or two or three. And they would start to tell you the most remarkable, bizarre stories. I'd ask, "Well, why don't you write that?" And they'd say, "Because we don't think anyone would ever believe that." But in a show like "Hill Street," those things were actually the building blocks of what we were doing.

So the show kept getting denser and denser, with more and more information packed into the frame. Sometimes we'd think we had put something on film that was in fact falling off the edge, there was so much going on. But when we looked back at early episodes of "Hill Street" in the third year, it was like staring into an empty room.

Question: When you're mapping out a year's worth of episodes, do you construct a twenty-two-hour dramatic unit and decide where you're going to cut it up into twenty-two episodes?

Bochco: No, no. I'm embarrassed to tell you how ragged the process really is. I wish we were that organized. I wish one could sit down and conceive of a coherent twenty-two-hour anything. That would be great. But I sure can't. And, in particular, when you have a show that has ten, eleven, twelve regular characters, it becomes impossible. What we tried to do is sit down at the beginning of the year and arc a few things. For instance, I knew in the third season of "Hill Street" that by show nineteen I wanted to marry Davenport and Furillo. And the reason I knew it had to be in show nineteen is that the networks always hold the last three shows for May sweeps, which means that there is like a six-week period where you are down in reruns or something. So in a sense you have a nineteen-show season and then a mini, three-show season, and that kind of shaped certain things in the relationship that led to the marriage. But that's about as specific as it gets.

Question: What do you look for when you're selecting a director for a particular project?

Bochco: I do have some input in the selection, but by and large it's a function that I give away, because I don't trust my instincts that much. In twenty-plus years of working in this business and writing continually, I don't really see what I write. I hear it. I don't have a director's eye. And because of my perceived lack of that sensibility, I've always tried to associate myself with director-producers. Somehow I figure that between the writer-producers and director-producers we'll cover all of our bases. But in television, you're always going to have damage of one kind or another. You don't have enough time,

people are overworked, you're understaffed, relatively speaking, you're doing so much on the run. Things fall through the cracks.

Question: So how do you protect yourself?

Bochco: Well, you do it sometimes by reshooting things. You do it sometimes by some wizardry in the cutting room. And sometimes, after all of that, you wind up with something that's ordinary, that you know was better on the page.

Question: You make it sound frustrating—is that what "Hill Street" was like?

Bochco: The truth is that even though the rewards of doing "Hill Street" were enormous, creatively and professionally, it wasn't a fun show to make. We were at war every single day. We were doing something we had no business trying to do, making forty-eight-minute movies in seven, eight days. And, of course, MTM hated us, because they thought we were spending them into oblivion. Though I maintain to this day that it was one of the most responsibly produced shows in the history of television—given what we were able to put on the screen for the amount of money we spent. But it was a runaway train. At all times.

With "L.A. Law," I very specifically set out to design a show that was at least physically producible. I had several ideas that I took over to Twentieth Century-Fox, a law show being one of them. I chose that one because I felt that, of the two or three that I was seriously considering, it was the one that I could guarantee would be responsibly produced—in economic terms. Which I was highly sensitive to at the time because I got my brains beat out when I was fired by MTM. And so among the several things that I wanted to prove under the "F—k you" category was that I could, in fact, produce a successful show, very responsibly, for the price.

Question: With "Hill Street" and "L.A. Law," you have really pushed the line as far as what you can do on network television.

Bochco: We're going to go further.

Question: You don't think that you've already gone further than any other shows?

Bochco: Yeah, but not enough. I want more.

Question: A lot of the dialogue is stuff that you would never have heard five years ago.

Bochco: That's true. It's actually beginning to sound like how grown-ups really talk. If you give me about five more years [laughs], I think we'll get the rest of the way. I'll tell you what I'd love to be able to do on television: I'd love to have characters speak the way you and I do. And use language that you and I use. You know, your vast array of four-letter words that are common usage in virtually every venue of life, whether you're checking your groceries or in your college classroom. And I'd like us to be able to be sexier, legitimately sexier. I think that you're going to see all kinds of things in the next half-dozen years on television that you can't even imagine today.

Question: There's already an awful lot of sex in "L.A. Law." How come?

Bochco: I think it's part and parcel of the show—adults tend to jump into bed occasionally. Of course, I'm not sure we'd be doing that if the show was at eight o'clock. Then again, if you have young kids, it's your responsibility as a parent to monitor what they see. There's a button there. Turn it on; turn it off. That's a big thing of mine. But I am actually against any kind of broadcast standards. If you eliminated them tomorrow, there would be some excesses—the same bad taste that you see in movie theaters and in literature and magazines and newspapers—but the pressures of the marketplace would ultimately determine what is acceptable fare for a substantial number of viewers.

Question: Do you take audience demographics into consideration when deciding what story to tell, and how?

Bochco: Quite frankly, I've always tried to avoid figuring out an audience, and I've never tried to structure a story to accommodate an audience. I don't think you can. You never know who's out there—except that at ten o'clock at night, you know you're not going to get a bunch of nine-year-olds. Beyond that, I just don't think in those terms. I mean, if I'm doing a law show, there are countless fascinating themes and stories. I'm interested in finding something that is really complicated: If we're telling a story in which the most interesting aspect is whether a lawyer wins or loses or whether a client is guilty or innocent, then we have failed. "Perry Mason" does that.

We're always trying to find ways in which you can illuminate the gray that exists in the law. Trying to do things that aren't so much hinged on outcome as they are on consequence, in personal terms. Being a lawyer is, I think, really schizophrenic. You know, you have one kind of ethical mind-set for your work life, which you conveniently turn off for your nonwork life. It's very fracturing for a lot of attorneys. It's why I think it's a very, very unhappy profession.

At least, judging from the mail I've been getting. [*Laughs*]

Question: Are you interested in doing more thirty-minute shows like "Hooperman"?

Bochco: Yeah, I'd like to. As a matter of fact, we did an episode in the "Hooperman" run that is sort of a spin-off for another half-hour show which, if I had my way, I would bracket with "Hooperman" in an hour. Do you know the actor David Rappaport, the dwarf? We've spun him off in "Nick Derringer, P.I."—it's about a sleazy, womanizing private detective in San Francisco. Typified by lines like "Have you ever had a man stand behind you and kiss the back of your knees?" And aside from the fact that I think it could be a fun half hour, I would love to see it programmed side by side with "Hooperman," because I think we could then sort of fuzz up the line between those two shows and bleed through. You could start a story in a "Hooperman" and legitimately finish it in a "Derringer." There are some interesting things that could actually expand the limitations of a half hour, without literally going over length.

Question: Is a network-programming position something that would interest you then?

Bochco: Yeah, I've always fantasized about doing that. Maybe even running a network. What more powerful thing could you do in the business? But it's just not the time in my life to do that. I'm looking to work less hard, not harder than I already do.

Further Resources

BOOKS
Gitlin, Todd. *Inside Prime Time.* New York: Pantheon, 1983.

Thompson, Robert J. *Television's Second Golden Age From Hill Street Blues to ER.* New York: Continuum, 1996.

PERIODICALS
Christensen, Mark. "Bochco's Law." *Rolling Stone* 524, April 21, 1988, 75–78.

Higgins, George V. "Television: The View from the Hill." *Wall Street Journal,* September 30, 1985, 1.

WEBSITES
Hill Street Blues. Available online at http://www.tvtome.com /tvtome/servlet/ShowMainServlet/showid-269/ (accessed June 12, 2003).

Steven Bochco. Available online at http://www.museum.tv /archives/etv/B/htmlB/bochcosteve/bochcosteve.htm (accessed June 12, 2003).

"The Importance of Being Oprah"

Magazine article

By: Barbara Grizzuti Harrison

Date: June 11, 1989

Source: Harrison, Barbara Grizzuti. "The Importance of Being Oprah." *The New York Times Magazine,* June 11, 1989, 28–30, 46, 48.

About the Author: Barbara Grizzuti Harrison (1934–2002) was an essayist and author. She wrote a highly acclaimed book about the Jehovah's Witnesses titled *Visions of Glory,* a travel history titled *Italian Days,* and a book called *An Accidental Autobiography.* ■

Introduction

Talk shows were a staple of daytime television by the 1980s. There is not a single format for this television genre. One of the unifying aspects is that the hosts and shows explore topics which are controversial in the public eye. Live audiences are also a part of the format.

Shows are classified as subject-based format, service format, or magazine format. In the 1980s, Dr. Ruth hosted the *Ask Dr. Ruth* show on the subject of sex advice. *Donahue* and *The Oprah Winfrey Show* fall into the service format—providing information for the audience meant to be helpful to their lives. The magazine format includes shows such as *Today, Good Morning America,* and *Sunday Morning.* Each of these shows filled a niche for the viewing public. The popularity of Winfrey's show resulted from the relevant topics she selected for her audience.

Winfrey moved from Nashville, where she attended college and began her career, to Baltimore and then to Chicago, where she remains. Oprah Winfrey appeared on local television in Chicago on a program called *A.M. Chicago,* which was transformed into *The Oprah Winfrey Show* by September 1984. Winfrey's show began syndication in 1986 and now appears throughout the country.

Significance

Oprah Winfrey rose through the journalistic ranks from a news reporter in Nashville, Tennessee to a successful talk-show host in Chicago. Oprah's personality and her compassion for her guests and her audience challenged every other talk-show host on the air for first place. Winfrey not only created a program which drew audiences, but also created her own production company, Harpo Studios, Inc.

Winfrey's show, *A.M. Chicago,* was expanded from half an hour to an hour-long format, which is now *The Oprah Winfrey Show.* Richard Zoglin wrote that although Winfrey was not as tough as other talk-show hosts, "she makes up in plainspoken curiosity, robust humor and, above all, empathy." Her early shows were not always the most stringent journalistically; however, she went on with the show and improved her skills. "America got a talk-show host who laughed and cried right along with her guests, shared her troubles and tragedies, made people feel comfortable talking to millions of viewers about the most intimate stuff." However, Oprah does not mince words if she disagrees with a guest or a reviewer.

Harrison addresses the subject of Oprah's image. Oprah has risen from her Southern background to celebrity status. By the time this article was published in 1989, Winfrey had already battled her weight on national television, won daytime Emmy Awards for her show, and earned millions of dollars. The recognition brought her wealth and material goods, but according to all reports, she remains down to earth.

Oprah's loyal staff is also a significant part of her success. She remains in control of the production. Oprah also draws strength from a circle of friends who include Maya Angelou and Quincy Jones.

Oprah Winfrey has gone on to start the Oxygen Network, a television station aimed at women, as well as O! Magazine. She also became the first African American female to make the *Forbes* list of billionaires in 2003.

Primary Source

"The Importance of Being Oprah" [excerpt]

> **SYNOPSIS:** In the 1980s, Oprah Winfrey was still forming her identity and carving out her place as a talk-show host and as a media icon. Her role in the film version of Alice Walker's *The Color Purple* and her production of Gloria Naylor's *The Women of Brewster Place* broadened her influence and visibility.

Looking at pictures of herself as a young girl—"A *nappy*-haired little colored girl"—Oprah Winfrey sees herself on a porch swing, "scared to death of my grandfather. I feared him. Always a dark presence. I remember him always throwing things at me or trying to shoo me away with his cane. I lived in absolute terror.

"I slept with my grandmother, and my job was to empty the slop jar every morning. And one night my grandfather came into our room, and he was looming over the bed and my grandmother was saying to him, 'You got to get back into bed now, come on, get back in the bed.' I thought maybe

Oprah Winfrey in 1986, the same year *The Oprah Winfrey Show* went into syndication. AP/WIDE WORLD PHOTOS. REPRODUCED BY PERMISSION.

he was going to kill both of us. I was 4. Scared. And she couldn't get him to get back in his room. And there was an old blind man who lived down the road, and I remember my grandmother going out on the porch screaming. 'Henry! Henry!' And when I saw his light going on I knew that we were going to be saved.

"But for years I had nightmares that he would come in the dark and strangle me."

The girl who emptied out the slop jar is the woman who now wears Valentino, Ungaro, Krizia clothes; powerful, glamorous, rich. She doesn't know what got her from there to here. How does one make a self? Why? Oprah Winfrey's rushed headlong to get the answers, sometimes in advance of framing the questions.

Her audiences are co-creators of the self and the persona she crafts. Her studio is a laboratory. She says hosting a talk show is as easy as breathing.

Here she is, an icon, speaking:

"I just do what I do—it's amazing. . . . But so does Madonna. . . . Everybody's greatness is rela-

tive to what the Universe put them here to do. I always knew that I was born for greatness. . . .

"If it's not possible for everybody to be the best that they can be, then it has to mean that I'm special, and if I'm special then it means the Universe just goes and picks people, which you know it doesn't do. . . . I've been blessed—but I create the blessings. . . . Most people don't seek discernment; it doesn't matter to them what the Universe intended for them to do. I hear the voice, I get the feeling. If someone without discernment thinks she hears a voice and winds up being a hooker on Hollywood and Vine, it is meaningful for the person doing it, right *now*. She is where the Universe wants her to be. . . .

"According to the laws of the Universe, I am not likely to get mugged, because I am helping people be all that they can be. I am all that I can be. . . . I am not God—I hope I don't give that impression—I'm not God. I keep telling Shirley MacLaine, 'You can't go around telling people you are God.' It's a very difficult concept to accept."

■ ■ ■

Her amber eyes fill with tears. We are talking about the fact of human misery, and about her phenomenal success; and she has adopted a metaphysical theory that encompasses both—several metaphysical theories, actually, partaking of Eastern religion and Western religion and of what is called New Age. She says she has achieved peace and the serenity of total understanding. (She is 35.) Knotty contradictions in the fabric of her belief have not, up to now, impeded the progress of what she calls a "triumphal" life. If her comfortable truths do not entirely cohere—if on occasion they collide—they are, nevertheless, perfect for the age of the soundbite. They make up in pith for what they lack in profundity.

She is as likely to rest her beliefs on Ayn Rand as on Baba Ram Dass. She brings the baggage of her contradictions to her television talk show, which she calls her "ministry." An avowed feminist, she does not challenge or contradict when a guest psychologist repeatedly attributes lack of self-esteem (a favorite daytime talk-show subject) to a negative "tape" . . ."the internalized mother" (talk shows are full of language like this). Her contradictions work for her: they act to establish kinship with an avid audience, whose perplexities they reflect; they insure that she will be regarded as spontaneous, undogmatic.

Her great gift for making herself likable is married to a message smooth as silk: *Nothing is random.* Whether Oprah Winfrey is in her fatalistic mode ("if you were abused as a child, you will abuse someone else as an adult") or espousing free will ("I was a welfare daughter, just like you . . . how did you let yourselves become welfare mothers? Why did you choose this? I didn't"), she chases away the fear that things may sometimes happen by malicious accident, or by the evil offices of others. In Winfrey's scheme of things, the mugger and the mugged were fated to meet—*and* they chose this fate . . . the starving man from India chose the path that led to his death. The fact of human suffering she manages to erase by divesting it of its apparent aimlessness. This is what commercially successful television programs do, no matter what the format: in an hour or less, they *resolve.*

"I want it to be for a reason, Oprah. . . ." a recovering alcoholic (with four alcoholic children) says, deploring the anarchy of fate. By the time the hour is over, the audience, if not the woman, will be convinced both that it had to be and that it *has* been for a reason. Oprah Winfrey—sassy, sisterly, confiding—has said so.

■ ■ ■

She brings her audiences into her life. No one who watches Oprah Winfrey—and an estimated 16 million people do—does not know about her weight loss—by her reckoning, 67 pounds on a 400-calories-a-day liquid diet (Optifast), not her meanest achievement—or about her hairdresser, her seamstress, her history of childhood abuse, her golden retriever, her boyfriend, Stedman Graham. There appears to be no membrane between the private person and the public persona.

The woman herself embodies a message, and a sanguine one. It says: You can be born poor and black and female and make it to the top.

In a racist society, the majority needs, and seeks, from time to time, proof that they are loved by the minority whom they have so long been accustomed to oppress, to fear exaggeratedly, or to treat with real or assumed disdain. They need that love, and they need to love in return, in order to believe that they are good. Oprah Winfrey—a one-person demilitarized zone—has served that purpose.

Last year, Oprah Winfrey made $25 million. Her production company, Harpo Productions Inc., gained ownership and control of her top-rated television talk show; she secured the unprecedented guarantee that ABC would carry "The Oprah Winfrey Show" on its owned and operated stations for five additional years. She also bought, reputedly for $10 million (including partial renovation costs), an 88,000-square-foot studio in Chicago, which, when renovated. will provide facilities for producing motion pictures and television movies, as well as her talk show. It will, says Harpo's chief operating officer, Jeffrey Jacobs, be "*the* studio in between the coasts, the final piece in the puzzle" that will enable Winfrey to do "whatever it is she wants to do, economically, and under her own control." It is also in the path of Chicago real-estate development.

Winfrey, whose television production of Gloria Naylor's "The Women of Brewster Place" won its time-period ratings on two successive nights, owns the screen rights to Toni Morrison's "Beloved" and to "Kaffir Boy," the autobiography of the South African writer Mark Mathabane. She has bought a 162-acre farm in Indiana. She is part-owner of three network-affiliated stations. She has an interest in The Eccentric, a Chicago restaurant which she often works three nights a week, going from table to table, shaking every hand. She says she entered into partnership because she "wanted a place to dance."

■ ■ ■

. . . When she walks from room to room in her large apartment which receives cool light from Lake Michigan, she talks to herself, little purring, self-approving speeches—as if to reproach the silence, as if silence were a form of inactivity, a vacuum that called out to be filled. . . .

■ ■ ■

She brings a practiced wit, an evangelist's anecdotal flair and a revivalist fervor to the dozens of speeches she gives every year. When she spoke to 6,000 women who attended an AWED (American Woman's Economic Development Corporation) conference in New York in February, the audience—nearly half of whom were black, atypical for an AWED gathering—loved her from the moment she bounded onto the stage in form-hugging black and peach. Her speech didn't bear close scrutiny, as it advanced at least two opposing ideas, which may, in fact, be part of her appeal—her audiences are seldom called upon to follow a difficult path either of reasoning or of action; they seem to be able to draw from her words an affirmation of that which they already believe to be true.

"There is," she said, "a false notion that you can do and be anything you want to be . . . a very false notion we are fed in this country . . . there's a condition that comes with being and doing all you can: you first have to know who you are before you can do that. . . . The life I lead is good, it is good . . . people ask me what temperature I would like to have my tea. . . . What the Universe is trying to get you to do is . . . to look inside and see what you feel . . . all things are possible."

They loved her. Perhaps they saw that in spite of perceived anomalies—(once) fat in a world of thin, female in an industry dominated by males, black in a racist society—she is, her flamboyance notwithstanding, deeply conventional in her thinking: a born-again capitalist, she believes goodness is always rewarded, and that the reward takes the form of money, "if you expect it to take the form of money."

When Winfrey found demands on her time and on her new money overwhelming, the author Maya Angelou told her: "Baby, all you *have* to do is stay black and die. . . . The work is the thing, and what matters at the end of the day is, were you sweet, were you kind, did you get the work done."

Winfrey calls upon Angelou, Bill Cosby, Quincy Jones and Sidney Poitier for counsel; they are available to discuss anything from investments to the criticism she has received from time to time from the black community. "You are their hope," Poitier says.

She calls Quincy Jones "the first person I have unconditionally loved in my whole life. He walks in the light. He is the light. If something were to happen to Quincy Jones, I would weep for the rest of my life."

Celebrities need one another—they ratify one another's myths. They are one another's truest fans.

Having refused to hire an agent, a manager and an attorney—"I don't get why anyone would want to pay 40 percent of their earnings in commissions or retainers"—she lavishly praises Harpo's Jeffrey Jacobs, who fills all those roles: "If something were to happen to him, I don't know what I would do, I don't know."

She has "weeded out" the people who "get on my nerves and just take up my time."

■ ■ ■

Her living room is white on white—white pickled oak walls and floors and white rugs with silver threads and fat white sofas and skinny white chairs; crystal obelisks and vases, brushed chrome, white marble and white onyx and vaguely deco wall sconces, steel and Lalique; a heroic Elizabeth Catlett

sculpture (a gift from Cosby) and two architectural plants, unwatered, droopy. The light that enters the room is silvery . . .

■ ■ ■

Winfrey embodies the entrepreneurial spirit; she is an Horatio Alger for our times. Salve to whites' burdened consciences? She shoves the idea aside. Role model for black women? For all women, she says, her aim being to "empower women."

An active fund-raiser, not necessarily for glamorous causes, she is philanthropic and fabulously generous.

She set up a "Little Sisters" program in Chicago's Cabrini-Green housing projects, to which she devotes time. She annually endows 10 scholarships to Tennessee State University, her alma mater. The story that she made her longtime and best friend Gayle King, a newscaster in Hartford, a millionaire with a Christmas check of $1,250,000 is part of the Oprah legend.

Two Christmases ago, she took three producers and her publicist to New York. At the hotel, she sent them a note saying: "Bergdorf's or Bloomingdale's— you have 10 minutes to decide."

Reliving the enacted fantasy with a breathy mix of chumminess and adulation that is characteristic of the staff of Harpo Inc. and peculiar to devotees of a guru, Christine Tardio, then one of her producers, says: "We go to Bergdorf's and she hands us each an envelope and in the envelope is a slip of paper and it says you have one hour to spend X amount of money. So we are frantically running around shopping and then she walks around and pays for everything.

"The next morning a little piece of paper is slipped under the door and it says, you have five minutes to decide where you want to buy boots and shoes—Walter Steiger or Maud Frizon. And then while she is paying for the boots at Frizon, she hands us another slip of paper and it says you have like two minutes to decide, leather or lingerie. So we all pick leather; so again we're like throwing clothes around the store, and half an hour later we get into the limo and she blindfolds us with terrycloth sweat bands.

"We're drinking champagne, driving around New York. We get to our destination and we're helped out of the car, through a revolving door, into an elevator and through another door and she says, 'O.K., on the count of three take off your blindfolds,' and we're in the middle of a furrier's. And she hands us another note that says, 'You can have anything in the store you want, except sable.' So three of us got minks and one of us got fox. And she was a little kid through the whole thing. Oh! She's wonderful!"

The producer Mary Kay Clinton says: "I would take a bullet for her."

Further Resources

BOOKS
Brands, H.W. *Masters of Enterprise: Giants of American Business From John Jacob Astor to J.P. Morgan to Bill Gates and Oprah Winfrey.* New York: Free Press, 1999.

Brunsdon, Charlotte, Julie D'Acci, and Lynn Spigel, eds. *Feminist Television Criticism: A Reader.* Oxford: Clarendon Press, 1997.

King, Norman. *Everybody Loves Oprah!: Her Remarkable Life Story.* New York: W. Morrow, 1987.

PERIODICALS
Gillespie, Marcia Ann. "Winfrey Takes All." *Ms.,* November 1988, 50–55.

Zoglin, Richard. "Lady with a Calling." *Time* 132, no. 6, August 8, 1988, 62–64.

WEBSITES
Oprah.com. Available online at http://www.oprah.com/ (accessed June 12, 2003).

9

MEDICINE AND HEALTH

JACQUELINE LESHKEVICH

Entries are arranged in chronological order by date of primary source. For entries with one primary source, the entry title is the same as the primary source title. Entries with more than one primary source have an overall entry title, followed by the titles of the primary sources.

Important Events in Medicine and Health, 1980–1989

1980

- On January 3, the Food and Drug Administration (FDA) allows the National Cancer Institute to do the first clinical study of the effects of the controversial and allegedly ineffective drug, Laetrile, on humans.

- On January 8, Virginia authorities approve the opening of the first "test-tube baby" clinic in the United States.

- On January 10, University of California Medical Center at San Francisco researchers devise a fetal test to predict the skin disease epidermolytic hyperkeratosis in an unborn child.

- On January 14, the U.S. Surgeon General reports the first signs of an epidemic of smoking-related diseases among women.

- On January 15, a federal judge rules the Hyde Amendment, restricting federal financing of abortions under Medicaid, unconstitutional.

- On January 16, genetically-engineered bacteria produce human interferon, a disease-fighting protein effective against some viral diseases and cancers.

- On January 25, studies report an increased risk of miscarriage or premature births in daughters of women who took the steroid DES (diethylstilbestrol) when they were pregnant.

- On January 31, the drug sulfinpyrazone is reported to reduce the incidence of sudden death among heart attack victims in the first seven months after a coronary attack.

- On February 2, a new drug, buprenorphine, is reported to treat heroin addiction.

- On February 4, the U.S. Departments of Agriculture and Health, Education, and Welfare issue guidelines to reduce fat, sugar, cholesterol, salt, and alcohol in the diet.

- On February 7, the FDA upholds a federal ban on the sale of cyclamates, sugar substitutes banned since 1969 as carcinogens.

- On February 14, research at the Baylor College of Medicine in Houston, Texas, reports that jogging reduces the risk of heart attacks.

- On February 15, a widespread outbreak of influenza B and associated deaths is reported.

- On February 28, a Rutgers Medical School study links SIDS (Sudden Infant Death Syndrome), or "crib death," to hereditary respiratory defects.

- On March 6, National Cancer Institute, U.S. Public Health, and American Health Foundation studies dispute earlier studies linking the artificial sweetener saccharin to cancers of the bladder and urinary tract.

- On March 20, the U.S. Cancer Society recommends the elimination of such cancer tests as chest X rays and a reduction in the frequency of others such as the annual Pap smear for women to "at least once every three years."

- On March 24, Duke University researchers report the active ingredient in marijuana, THC (tetrahydrocannabinol), may reduce nausea and vomiting in chemotherapy patients.

- On March 26, the *New England Journal of Medicine* reports that cigarette smoke deteriorates air tubes and sacs in the lungs of nonsmokers.

- On April 17, Donald A. Henderson, Johns Hopkins University physician and head of the World Health Organization campaign against smallpox, announces its eradication.

- On April 24, the U.S. Drug Enforcement Administration limits production of the active ingredient in Darvon, a mild painkiller that turned out to be addictive and may have caused hundreds of accidental deaths and suicides.

- On June 6, a U.S. Senate health subcommittee learns of a baffling, recently discovered disease called toxic shock syndrome that strikes young women and can cause death within days.

- On June 9, the FDA approves a new rabies vaccine requiring only five shots in the arm instead of twenty-three injections in the abdomen.

- On June 30, the U.S. Supreme Court affirms the Hyde Amendment, ruling neither the federal government nor states must fund abortions for poor women.

- On July 11, the FDA requires manufacturers of Valium, Librium, and other widely used tranquilizers to warn physicians not to overprescribe these drugs for "everyday" stress.

- On July 13, the National Center for Health Statistics finds birth control pills to be the most effective contraception.

- On July 22, the American Medical Association adopts a revised code of medical ethics allowing doctors to advertise their fees and services and to refer patients to chiropractors.

- On August 19, the FDA and U.S. Department of Agriculture reject a ban on the preservative sodium nitrate from food, reporting a 1978 study claiming that nitrate caused cancer in animals is inconclusive.

- On September 4, the FDA advises pregnant women to stop or reduce consumption of coffee, tea, cola drinks, and other caffeine-containing products because of the danger of birth defects.

- On September 7, the U.S. National Oceanic and Atmospheric Administration reports 1,265 deaths, mostly among the elderly or poor who did not live in air-conditioned homes, from the 1980 summer heat wave.

- On September 22, the FDA recalls Rely tampons because federal studies link their use to increased risks of toxic shock syndrome.

1981

- Scientists find that spirochetes, a type of virus, named Borrelia burgdorferi, cause Lyme disease.

- Surgeons at the University of Denver insert a valve into the skull of an unborn baby to drain off excess fluid from the brain and prevent hydrocephalus.

- On January 8, studies confirm the health benefits of reducing cholesterol and saturated fats in the diet.

- On January 13, a three-month study links toxic shock to the use of high-absorbency tampons and confirms earlier findings that teenagers have the highest risk of developing the syndrome.

- On February 26, an influenza outbreak ebbs after sweeping thirty-one states.

- In March, the *New England Journal of Medicine* reports that acyclovir, an experimental drug, suppresses the herpes simplex virus.

- On March 2, the New York State Legislature approves a tissue-typing procedure for use as court evidence in paternity cases.

- On March 11, Harvard University scientists link coffee consumption and pancreatic cancer, the fourth most fatal cancer.

- On March 26, a National Cancer Institute study links chewing tobacco and snuff to cancer of the mouth.

- On April 30, a five hundred thousand dollar National Cancer Institute study finds Laetrile ineffective against cancer, even though advocates of the controversial drug derived from apricot pits continue to defend it as the last hope for terminal patients.

- On May 21, the Centers for Disease Control and Prevention announce that in 1980 and 1981 influenza killed sixty thousand to seventy thousand, the most since the 1968–1969 epidemic of Hong Kong flu, and recommend that the strength of flu vaccines be doubled in the future.

- In June, physicians in California and New York detect a new disease that will come to be known as AIDS among gay men and intravenous drug users.

- On June 18, molecular biologists create a vaccine against foot-and-mouth disease through gene splicing.

- On July 9, the President's Commission for the Study of Ethical Problems in Medicine and Biomedicine and Behavioral Research recommends legislation to standardize the definition of death in every state.

- On July 15, the FDA approves aspartame, a combination of two amino acids, as an artificial sweetener.

- On July 17, the U.S. Surgeon General advises pregnant women to abstain from alcohol.

- On July 20, the *New England Journal of Medicine* reports that women who use birth control pills increase their risk of heart attacks even after stopping their use.

- On August 4, doctors and scientists from twenty-five nations warn of antibiotic overuse and abuse, resulting in the development of antibiotic-resistant bacteria.

- On August 14, a *Journal of the American Medical Association* study says heart pacemakers are being implanted more often than necessary.

- In October, the *New England Journal of Medicine* reports the first successful operation to destroy a defective fetus in a pair of fraternal twins.

- On October 7, a study reveals that American life expectancy dropped in 1980 for the first time since 1968 because of an increase in deaths from flu and pneumonia.

- On October 29, National Heart, Lung, and Blood Institute scientists announce that the drug propranolol could reduce the risk of second heart attacks by 26 percent.

- On November 16, the FDA approves the first vaccine against the hepatitis B virus.

1982

- Evidence grows that children living near traffic routes suffer from lead poisoning from auto emissions.

- The first commercial product of genetic engineering appears when human insulin produced by bacteria is marketed.

- Combined heart lung and kidney-pancreas transplants are carried out successfully.

- On January 21, a *New England Journal of Medicine* study contradicts earlier studies suggesting coffee drinking during pregnancy contributes to premature births and birth defects.

- On January 22, the Centers for Disease Control and Prevention reports a penicillin-resistant strain of gonorrhea.

- On January 24, statistics show the cost of medical care increased 12.5 percent in 1981, the highest increase since the government began reporting medical costs in 1935.

- On February 18, a *New England Journal of Medicine* study indicates that the ability of women to conceive after age thirty declines more sharply than previously thought.

- On February 25, the American College of Obstetricians and Gynecologists challenges the previously held view that once a woman has a caesarean delivery, all her subsequent deliveries must also be surgical.

- On March 30, the FDA approves the drug acyclovir to treat genital herpes.

- On April 21, a federal jury finds the Proctor & Gamble Company, the makers of Rely tampons, liable for the toxic-shock-syndrome death of a twenty-five-year-old woman and awards three hundred thousand dollars in damages.

- On June 4, parents and doctors are warned against using aspirin to treat children suffering from flu, chicken pox, and other viral infections because of its association with Reye's syndrome, a rare but often fatal children's disease.

- On June 23, a weeklong slowdown by surgeons in southern Florida ends when the governor signs a compromise bill on malpractice insurance rates.

- On July 1, the U.S. Supreme Court rules that the nursing school at the Mississippi University for Women cannot refuse to admit a male student.

- On July 9, a report in *Science* challenges 1970s studies suggesting that alcoholics can be trained to drink in moderation.

- On July 15, the *Journal of the American Medical Association* publishes a study suggesting many apparently "senile" nursing home patients actually suffer from treatable conditions.

- On July 17, doctors admit their inability to identify the cause of a new disease known as acquired severe immuno-deficiency disease (ASID), which almost exclusively afflicts gay males and heavy drug users when it was first detected in June 1981.

- On August 12, the U.S. Census Bureau reports the aging of the U.S. population: the median age as of July 1981 was 30.3 years.

- On September 29, the first of seven people dies in Chicago after taking Extra-Strength Tylenol capsules tainted with cyanide.

- On October 1, the FDA warns consumers not to take Extra-Strength Tylenol.

- On October 5, following the discovery of Extra-Strength Tylenol laced with strychnine in California, the manufacturer announces a nationwide recall of all Tylenol capsules.

- On October 7, a *New England Journal of Medicine* study warns women against using aspirin during pregnancy because of the danger of fetal bleeding.

- On October 15, a tourist in Florida reports throat burns after using mouthwash tainted with hydrochloric acid.

- On October 29, the FDA reports more than 270 cases of possible product contamination, with thirty-six cases verified as "true tampering."

- On November 4, the FDA and the Department of Health and Human Services approve new packaging regulations to protect consumers from product tampering.

- On November 13, the General Accounting Office makes public a report that abuse of prescription drugs results in many more deaths and drug emergencies than the use of illegal drugs.

- On November 20, the U.S Supreme Court hears arguments on a variety of laws to make it more difficult for women to obtain legal abortions in several states.

- On December 2, physicians at the University of Utah Medical Center in Salt Lake City implant a permanent artificial heart, the Jarvik-7, in a sixty-one-year-old retired dentist.

- On December 9, the Centers for Disease Control and Prevention in Atlanta announces that the disease now known as Acquired Immunodeficiency Syndrome (AIDS) is spreading to infants and children.

- On December 15, *New England Journal of Medicine* warns that a diet high in meat and low in fiber may increase the risk of breast cancer in women.

- On December 24, a California jury awards $10.5 million in damages to a woman who suffered from toxic shock syndrome after using tampons made by Johnson & Johnson.

1983

- The first liposuction surgery to reduce subcutaneous body fat is performed in the United States.

- On January 6, the Department of Health and Human Services announces that death rates have declined for Americans, except those aged fifteen to twenty-four, for whom violent deaths have increased.

- On January 21, the Bureau of Labor Statistics reports that health-care costs outpace inflation.

- On January 25, the Food Resource and Action Center links an eight-state increase in infant mortality to poverty brought on by the economic recession.

- On February 18, a federal district judge in Washington, D.C. blocks the implementation of a Health and Human Services Department rule requiring federally funded birth control clinics to notify parents after providing prescription contraceptives to persons under eighteen.

- On February 19, the FDA approves aspartame as an artificial sweetener in soft drinks.

- On March 3, after hemophiliacs contract AIDS, the Public Health Service urges that several groups, including gay men, intravenous drug users, and Haitians, not donate blood because of the possibility of AIDS transmission through transfusions.

- On March 4, the pharmaceutical company Johnson & Johnson withdraws the painkiller Zomax from the market following reports of five deaths from allergic reactions to the drug.

- On March 21, a presidential panel recommends that patients have the choice to discontinue life-support treatment.

- On March 22, the Reagan administration implements the so-called "Baby Doe" rules to prevent federally funded hospitals from denying food or medical care to handicapped infants.

- On March 25, a *Journal of the American Medical Association* article concludes that birth control pills do not increase a woman's risk of breast cancer and may lower the risk of uterine and ovarian cancer.

- In April, scientists identify genes that predispose people to Duchenne muscular dystrophy and Huntington's disease.

- On April 6, the FDA approves a contraceptive sponge that does not require a doctor's prescription.

- On April 27, the *New England Journal of Medicine* reports that physicians misdiagnosed nearly a quarter of patients who died in hospitals.

- On May 1, the FDA approves the immunosuppressant drug cyclosporine for use during organ transplants to prevent the body from rejecting its new organ.

- On May 4, the *New England Journal of Medicine* reports that interferon, an infection-fighting protein, appears helpful against a rare form of cancer, Kaposi's sarcoma, that often afflicts AIDS victims.

- On May 19, the *New England Journal of Medicine* reports the possibility of AIDS transmission in heterosexual intercourse.

- On May 24, the U.S. Public Health Service calls AIDS the nation's "number one priority."

- On June 6, a Minnesota jury awards $1.5 million to a woman who suffered an infection from a Dalkon Shield intrauterine contraceptive device (IUD).

- On July 21, a *New England Journal of Medicine* study says supposedly low-nicotine cigarettes deliver about as much nicotine to smokers as regular brands.

- On July 25, Accutane, an acne drug, is linked to birth defects.

- On August 2, the American Cancer Society urges women over forty to have regular mammograms to detect breast cancer.

- On August 31, the Reagan administration imposes standard hospital rates in an attempt to curb increases in Medicare spending.

- On September 21, the Tennessee Supreme Court orders chemotherapy for a twelve-year-old girl whose fundamentalist parents resisted treatment for her rare form of bone cancer.

- On October 26, a ten-year national study suggests about 15 percent of patients who had heart bypass surgery could have postponed or avoided the operation.

- On December 19, the Robert Wood Johnson Foundation reports one American in eight has "serious trouble" getting medical care, and one in nine has no regular source of care.

- On December 22, the Equitable Life Insurance Society of the United States reports hospital costs rose at about double the rate of inflation.

1984

- A National Institutes of Health study links smoking to low birth weights.

- The San Francisco public-health director announces steps to curb sexual activity in the city's gay bathhouses to reduce the spread of AIDS.

- On January 4, the Centers for Disease Control and Prevention reports that AIDS can spread through heterosexual intercourse.

- On January 10, the University of Utah approves guidelines for artificial-heart patients permitting the operation at earlier rather than later stages of heart disease.

- On January 11, the Centers for Disease Control and Prevention reports that infected blood can transmit AIDS to recipients of transfusions.

- On January 12, the National Heart, Lung, and Blood Institute reports that reducing cholesterol consumption lowers the risk of heart disease.

- On February 8, a National Institutes of Health panel advises physicians to limit ultrasound use on their pregnant patients.

- From February 13 to February 14, a six-year-old Texas girl becomes the first dual heart and liver transplant recipient.

- On February 16, the American Heart Association, American Lung Association, and American Cancer Society denounce cigarette ads.

- On February 23, the American Medical Association asks doctors to freeze their fees for one year to curb inflation.

- On April 1, the American Cancer Society reports a 7 percent drop in cigarette smoking, the largest in a single year.

- On April 9, the FDA recalls a vitamin E solution linked to the death of premature infants.

- On April 21, the Centers for Disease Control and Prevention confirms reports that French researchers have identified a virus thought to cause AIDS.

- On May 7, Vietnam veterans win a $180 million settlement for injuries from the herbicide Agent Orange.

- On May 10, the FDA approves the new drugs glipizide and glyburide to treat diabetes.

- On May 18, the FDA approves over-the-counter sale of ibuprofen, a drug that reduces pain.

- On May 31, the *New England Journal of Medicine* reports the success of a chicken pox vaccine in trials.

- On June 7, the *New England Journal of Medicine* reports health maintenance organizations (HMOs) could cut health-care costs 25 percent over the traditional fee-for-service system.

- On June 13, Wyeth Laboratories announces an end to production of pertussis (whooping cough) vaccine because rare complications of the vaccine expose Wyeth to lawsuits.

- On June 16, record numbers of foreign-trained physicians fail medical tests necessary for internship or residency in the United States.

- On September 10, the House of Representatives passes a measure to require stronger warnings on cigarette packages and ads.

- On September 12, the American Psychiatric Association reports that the policy of discharging mentally ill patients from institutions into local communities has failed with the result that many are homeless.

- On September 24, low-cost generic versions of many widely used prescription drugs will be available to consumers with the signing of legislation.

- On October 20, the Centers for Disease Control and Prevention reports that lung cancer will soon become the leading cause of cancer deaths among women.

- On October 26, doctors in Loma Linda, California, replace the defective heart of a newborn baby girl known as "Baby Fae" with a baboon heart, the first heterograft (cross-species organ transplant) of a heart.

- On November 5, federal health officials announce that exposure to the AIDS virus is much wider than previously thought.

- On November 15, the infant who received the baboon heart transplant dies of complications from rejection of the organ.

- On November 25, Humana Heart Institute doctors perform the second permanent artificial-heart operation, provoking controversy that the technology is a misapplication of medical research funds better spent on preventive health.

- On November 28, San Francisco gay bathhouses reopen with strict regulations on sexual activity.

- On December 11, a medical laboratory worker suffering from AIDS is determined to have contracted the disease after accidentally pricking himself with a needle while drawing blood from an infected patient.

- On December 13, the Centers for Disease Control and Prevention reports the incidence of hepatitis B, a viral disease that can cause cancer, is on the rise and urges the vaccination of high-risk groups.

1985

- Surgeons use lasers to clean out clogged arteries.

- On January 3, a study links the AIDS virus, currently called HTLV-3, to brain damage in AIDS victims.

- On January 10, the Department of Health and Human Services announces that a new test to detect the AIDS virus will soon be available to reduce the incidence of AIDS transmission through donated blood, although the test cannot predict whether an infected person will develop AIDS.

- On January 16, the Mayo Clinic reports vitamin C ineffective against cancer.

- On January 17, the American Medical Association reports that malpractice suits have become a crisis.

- On January 23, aspirin manufacturers plan to issue warnings to consumers of a possible link between aspirin use and Reye's syndrome, a rare and often fatal disease in children when aspirin is used to treat viral infections.

- On January 24, a study questions the value and cost of routine chest X rays in symptomless patients.

- On January 29, the FDA approves the first oral drug, acyclovir, for the treatment of genital herpes.

- On February 8, the American Cancer Society predicts more women will die of lung cancer than breast cancer.

- On February 10, the National Center for Health Statistics reports one of every three American women of reproductive age is infertile.

- On February 11, U.S. life expectancy rises to 78.2 for women and 70.9 for men.

- On February 13, the National Institutes of Health calls obesity a killer in the United States.

- On February 15, the U.S. Census Bureau reports that 15 percent of Americans lack health insurance.

- On February 17, a third permanent artificial heart, the Jarvik-7, is implanted at Humana Hospital in Louisville, Kentucky.

- On February 19, the FDA approves an intravenous form of the drug indomethacin for use in premature infants instead of heart surgery to repair a congenital defect.

- On February 21, the Office of Technology Assessment criticizes the Reagan administration for spending too little on AIDS research.

- On February 26, a panel of doctors and public-health officials charges that hunger is "epidemic" in the United States because of cuts in federal food programs.

- On March 2, the Department of Health and Human Services approves the first test to screen donated blood for the AIDS virus.

- On March 12, the Alan Guttmacher Institute calls the U.S. teen pregnancy rate the highest among industrial nations.

- On March 14, the *New England Journal of Medicine* reports that removal of a malignant breast lump and radiation is as effective as removal of the entire breast in treating early breast cancer.

- On March 21, an outbreak of salmonella, a bacterial infection, traced to contaminated milk from a Chicago dairy, strikes six Midwestern states, killing at least six.

- On April 2, the A. H. Robbins Company sets up a $615 million fund to settle legal claims from women who suffered infections from the company's Dalkon Shield IUD birth control device.

- On April 11, the *New England Journal of Medicine* reports that IUD birth-control devices double the risk of infertility.

- On May 23, the *New England Journal of Medicine* reports that running and other vigorous exercise may make young women temporarily infertile.

- In June, the Renfrew Center, the first residential facility devoted exclusively to the treatment of the eating disorders anorexia nervosa and bulimia, opens in Philadelphia.

- On June 28, a National Institutes of Health panel gives cautious endorsement to electroconvulsive therapy as a treatment of last resort in severe depression.

- In July, the American Red Cross and the American Heart Association endorse the Heimlich maneuver for choking victims.

- On July 10, the *New England Journal of Medicine* reports that the AIDS virus destroys T4 helper cells, a set of blood cells that detects invading microbes.

- In August, the *Journal of the American Medical Association* links female infertility with cigarette smoking.

- On August 13, Johns Hopkins University reports progress in treating normally fatal liver cancer with radiolabeled antibodies.

- On August 29, the Centers for Disease Control and Prevention recommends that AIDS victims be able to attend school because casual person-to-person contact poses no risk of contagion.

- On September 9, parents keep children home after a New York City school permits a seven-year-old AIDS victim to attend.

- On September 26, Harvard Medical School scientists announce the discovery of an organ-growth protein.

- On October 3, the Centers for Disease Control and Prevention reports twenty-five times the risk of fetal malformation in women who used the acne drug accutane during the first trimester of pregnancy.

- On October 16, Baby Fae's death is revealed to have been caused by the wrong blood type in the transplanted baboon heart.
- On November 7, the American Medical Association reports no link between saccharin, an artificial sweetener, and bladder cancer in humans.
- On November 11, a Johns Hopkins study links coffee drinking to heart disease.
- On November 14, the Center for Science in the Public Interest indicts fast-food chains for deep frying with beef fat rather than with oils lower in saturated fats.
- On December 4, cancer therapists announce a new treatment that activates the body's immune system to combat untreatable cancers.
- On December 10, health officials announce that taking one aspirin a day can reduce subsequent heart attacks.

1986

- Scientists discover the first gene that inhibits growth. It inhibits the cancer retinoblastoma.
- A Harvard University study links exercise to a lower risk of breast cancer in women.
- Massachusetts Institute of Technology scientists announce the production of the first artificial blood vessels from cells grown in the lab.
- On January 9, the *New England Journal of Medicine* reports the drug interferon alpha 2 shows promise in preventing the spread of cold viruses.
- On January 17, a cyanide-filled Tylenol capsule kills a Yonkers, New York, woman; Johnson & Johnson, the manufacturer, ends production of all its nonprescription capsule medicine.
- On January 22, a *Wall Street Journal* poll finds 18 percent of unmarried adults have changed their sexual behavior for fear of contracting AIDS.
- On January 23, the *New England Journal of Medicine* reports that heredity determines adult body-fat levels.
- On February 6, the *New England Journal of Medicine* rules out contracting AIDS through casual contact.
- On March 6, the *New England Journal of Medicine* reports that moderate exercise in adulthood may increase longevity.
- On March 10, the FDA reports preliminary success with a new clot-dissolving drug, TPA, or tissue plasminogen activator, a genetically engineered protein.
- On March 13, public-health officials warn that the population at high risk of AIDS has a rising incidence of tuberculosis.
- On March 20, the *New England Journal of Medicine* finds that replacing saturated fats with olive oil in the diet reduces cholesterol.
- On March 25, a study links pancreatic cancer and smoking.
- On April 6, the Massachusetts General Hospital finds that infected women can transmit AIDS to men.
- In May, an international commission names the AIDS virus the human immunodeficiency virus (HIV).

- On May 20, a Senate Special Committee on Aging condemns conditions in the nation's nursing homes.
- On May 21, National Institutes of Health experts report patients suffering from pain are likely to be treated with too little or too much pain medication.
- On June 5, the FDA approves the use of alpha-interferon, a synthetic human hormone, against a rare blood cancer.
- On June 6, a Los Angeles woman gives birth to the first baby in the United States to be born from a frozen embryo.
- On June 11, the U.S. Army limits smoking to designated areas.
- On June 15, the American Medical Association urges medical schools to limit the supply of new doctors.
- On June 23, the U.S. Justice Department says federal civil rights laws do not forbid the firing of employees with AIDS.
- On June 30, the federal government announces $100 million in contracts to accelerate research for an AIDS cure.
- On July 8, the FDA bans some sulfite preservatives in fresh vegetables and fruits after linking them to deaths, primarily among asthma sufferers.
- On July 10, the National Institute on Drug Abuse reports an increase in deaths among cocaine users.
- On July 23, the FDA approves the first genetically engineered vaccine to protect against the hepatitis B virus, a cause of liver disease.
- On July 29, the Department of Health and Human Services reports 1985 health-care costs reached $425 billion.
- On August 28, scientists refute a 1981 study linking coffee drinking with pancreatic cancer.
- On September 4, the *New England Journal of Medicine* doubts that fetal heartbeat monitoring and caesarean sections improve outcomes for most babies.
- On September 19, the federal government announces that an experimental drug, azidothymidine (AZT), prolonged the lives of some AIDS victims.
- On October 7, California surgeons, in a pioneering operation, remove a twenty-three-week-old fetus from his mother's uterus, perform surgery to correct a blocked urinary tract, then return the fetus to the womb.
- On October 24, the Federal Trade Commission requires makers of smokeless tobacco to include health warnings in their ads and on packages of tobacco.
- On October 29, the National Academy of Sciences criticizes the federal effort against AIDS as inadequate.
- On November 4, the National Academy of Sciences condemns secondhand smoke for imperiling the health of children and adults.
- On November 28, the *Journal of the American Medical Association* reports that 80 percent of middle-aged American men risk death from heart disease because of high cholesterol.
- On December 5, the General Services Administration announces requirements to provide federal workers with a "reasonably smoke-free environment."

- On December 9, the National Academy of Sciences issues a report saying teens should not be forced to seek parental consent for abortion and should have easy access to contraceptives.

1987

- A bone-marrow transplant registry is created in Saint Paul, Minnesota, to match donors with patients.

- On January 13, the U.S. Supreme Court upholds a California law requiring employers to give women disability leave for pregnancy and childbirth and to guarantee they can return to their jobs.

- On January 16, San Francisco television station KRON becomes the first major-market station in the United States to lift a ban on advertising condoms on television.

- On February 2, the Children's Defense Fund reports that U.S. infant mortality is among the highest in the industrialized world.

- On March 2, the Centers for Disease Control and Prevention reports that the chance of developing AIDS rises in the seven years after HIV infection.

- On March 16, the FDA recommends approval of minoxidil (brand name Rogaine) to treat baldness.

- On March 20, the FDA approves AZT for treating AIDS symptoms.

- On April 8, the National Institutes of Health recommends that screening for sickle cell disease be routine for all infants.

- On April 17, the *Journal of the American Medical Association* reports the percentage of women who had contracted AIDS from sex with infected men more than doubled between 1982 and 1986, with the greatest increase for non-white women.

- On May 31, President Ronald Reagan closes the United States to immigrants and aliens with AIDS.

- From June 1 to June 5, the Third International Conference on AIDS meets in Washington, D.C.

- On June 1, Washington, D.C., police wear rubber gloves to protect themselves against AIDS infection while policing protestors of Vice President George Herbert Walker Bush's address to the Third International Conference on AIDS.

- On June 19, the *Journal of the American Medical Association* reports the first "clear evidence" that a cut in dietary cholesterol can benefit those with symptoms of coronary artery disease.

- On July 20, Louisiana becomes the first state to make HIV testing and disclosure of results mandatory for marriage-license applicants.

- On July 30, President Ronald Reagan bars federal funding for family-planning programs that offer abortion counseling.

- On August 18, U.S. health officials announce plans for the first human trials in the United States of an experimental AIDS vaccine.

- On September 1, the FDA approves lovastatin, described as the most effective drug for lowering cholesterol in the blood.

- On September 11, the Centers for Disease Control and Prevention reports smoking in the United States at an all-time low of 26.5 percent of adults.

- On September 21, Illinois becomes the second state to require AIDS testing for marriage licenses.

- On October 11, the AIDS quilt is unfurled for the first time on the Mall in Washington, D.C. Participants hoped to shame Congress into increasing its funding of research for a cure.

- On November 2, the *Wall Street Journal* reports that the Pap smear, a procedure to detect cervical cancer, fails in about one in four cases.

- On November 12, the American Medical Association states that U.S. physicians have a moral obligation to treat AIDS victims.

- On November 13, the FDA approves TPA, or tissue plasminogen activator (brand name Activase), a genetically engineered blood-clot dissolver, as an emergency heart attack medication.

1988

- Surgeons implant the world's first plutonium-powered pacemaker.

- On January 2, the Centers for Disease Control and Prevention links an increase in tuberculosis cases to the AIDS epidemic.

- On January 21, the *New England Journal of Medicine* asserts that up to half of the heart pacemakers may be unnecessary.

- On January 22, a study credits Retin-A, an acne drug, with reversing some of the effects of sun-induced wrinkles.

- On January 26, a study indicates an aspirin taken every other day could halve the rate of heart attacks in men.

- On January 27, NutraSweet produces a low-calorie, cholesterol-free fat substitute called Simplesse, made of milk or egg proteins.

- On January 31, New York City health authorities distribute free needles to drug addicts to fight the spread of AIDS.

- On February 2, the National Cancer Institute reports that cancer cases continue to rise 1 percent a year.

- On February 23, a Reagan panel urges a $2 billion increase in spending to expand drug treatment programs and improve health care to fight the spread of AIDS.

- On March 10, the *Journal of the American Medical Association* questions whether mammograms are worth the expense in women younger than fifty with no risk factors for breast cancer.

- On March 17, a study indicates women who smoke increase their risk of strokes.

- On April 21, a Massachusetts universal health-care bill guarantees health insurance to all residents.

- On April 23, smoking is banned on domestic airline flights lasting less than two hours.

- On May 5, a government study reports that chorionic villi sampling is nearly as safe as amniocentesis as a prenatal test for birth defects.

- On May 12, the National Institutes of Health halts funding for artificial-heart research, citing failure in all five patients who had received an artificial heart.

- On May 21, the U.S. Cancer Institute urges women who have undergone surgery for breast cancer to follow up with drug or hormone therapy.

- On May 23, the FDA approves prescription marketing to women of the cervical cap, a contraceptive device.

- On May 26, the FDA orders curbs against the anti-acne prescription drug Accutane to prevent its use by pregnant women because of its potential for serious birth defects.

- On June 1, the National Academy of Sciences criticizes the absence of federal leadership and funding in the fight against AIDS.

- On June 13, a federal jury in Newark, New Jersey, convicts a tobacco company for the death of a cigarette smoker, the first conviction in more than three hundred liability lawsuits.

- On June 21, the National Institute of Dental Research reports that nearly half of all U.S. schoolchildren have no tooth decay.

- On July 5, the FDA warns against indiscriminate use of the anti-acne drug Retin-A to erase wrinkles.

- On July 28, a study reports that 31 percent of all conceptions end in miscarriage, usually in the early months of pregnancy.

- On August 17, the FDA approves minoxidil (Rogaine) as a prescription treatment for baldness.

- On August 31, a Florida manufacturer pleads guilty to U.S. federal charges that it sold cardiac pacemakers that could malfunction.

- On September 28, the Harvard School of Public Health recommends restructuring Medicare payments, with family doctors receiving more money and specialists less.

- On October 1, the Rand Corporation reports that proper care might have prevented up to 27 percent of hospital patient deaths because of heart attack, stroke, or pneumonia.

- On October 19, the FDA adopts a new policy on drug approval to speed access to new drugs for patients suffering from life-threatening illnesses such as AIDS or cancer.

- On November 1, a new Medicare reimbursement policy aims to reduce hospital stays for Medicare patients.

- On November 11, a panel of physicians and medical school faculty recommends that medical schools train students to develop social psychology skills.

- On November 14, the Department of Transportation announces the first federal anti-drug effort in the private sector—random testing of nearly four million transportation workers.

- On November 21, the FDA approves alpha interferon to treat Kaposi's sarcoma, a skin cancer often found in AIDS victims.

- On November 25, Harvard Medical School warns against overmedication with psychoactive, or mood-altering drugs, to nursing-home patients.

- On December 1, the Department of Health and Human Services finds flaws in nursing home drug dispensing and food service.

- On December 12, a government report warns of a nursing shortage and recommends better recruitment, training, and pay for nurses.

- On December 22, the FDA reports that evidence is insufficient to justify a ban on silicone breast implants.

- On December 30, the Department of Health and Human Services announces the establishment of a nationwide computer registry of malpractice suits and disciplinary actions against doctors and dentists.

1989

- National Institutes of Health scientists inject genetically engineered nonhuman cells into a human patient for the first time.

- On January 5, the *Journal of the American Medical Association* establishes that cigarette smokers are likely to be poor, ill educated, and minorities.

- On January 11, the U.S. Surgeon General reports that smoking has caused more deaths than was previously believed—390,000 deaths in 1985, or about one-sixth of all deaths in the country.

- On February 1, the Environmental Protection Agency announces a ban on daminozide (brand name Alar), a suspected cancer-causing chemical sprayed on apples, to take effect in eighteen months.

- On February 6, the FDA announces that it will widen the availability of an experimental aerosol drug, pentamidine, to treat Pneumocystis carinii pneumonia, a once rare disease that afflicts AIDS patients.

- On March 2, the National Academy of Sciences urges Americans to eat more fruit and less fat.

- On March 5, the American Academy of Pediatrics reverses its position and states that the circumcision of male infants protects against kidney and urinary tract infections.

- On March 8, the Department of Health and Human Services says it will support programs to supply hypodermic needles to drug addicts in hopes of slowing the spread of AIDS.

- On March 9, the *New England Journal of Medicine* reports that prompt treatment of heart attack victims with blood-clot-dissolving drugs is as effective as balloon angioplasty, an expensive and widespread procedure.

- On March 16, scientists estimate that HIV incubates in the body 9.8 years on average.

- On March 17, the FDA quarantines all fruit from Chile after USDA agents discover traces of cyanide in Chilean grapes.

- On March 30, an eight-year study concludes that a lumpectomy, followed by radiation therapy, is as effective against breast cancer as a mastectomy.

- On April 27, the FDA approves an implantable contraceptive for women called Norplant.

- On April 28, the Department of Health and Human Services shows that physicians who have a financial interest in clinical laboratories order 45 percent more tests and lab services than physicians without such investments.

- On May 1, the first U.S. patient to have human fetal cells implanted into his brain as a Parkinson's disease treatment shows slow but steady improvement.

- On May 22, the American College Health Association finds that 0.2 percent of U.S. college students have HIV, a higher rate than expected.

- On June 1, the FDA approves a genetically engineered drug, epoetin, (brand name Epogen), to treat anemia in kidney patients.

- On June 9, *Science* publishes a study showing that the extent of AIDS among whites and in the Midwest is underestimated.

- On June 15, the FDA approves the aerosol pentamidine to treat Pneumocystis carinii pneumonia, the leading cause of death in AIDS victims.

- On June 28, a national survey shows as many as 25 million Americans, or 16 percent of the U.S. population over age fifteen, might be infected with the sexually transmitted herpes simplex II virus.

- On June 30, researchers pinpoint a set of genes that may predispose people to multiple sclerosis, a debilitating nerve disease.

- On July 7, the *Journal of the American Medical Association* says more than one-third of all American adults need to lower their blood cholesterol.

- On July 10, the National Institute of Allergy and Infectious Diseases announces that AZT will be given to pregnant women infected with AIDS to determine whether it can protect newborns from infection.

- On July 20, the *New England Journal of Medicine* confirms that an aspirin tablet every other day reduces the risk of heart attack in men older than fifty.

- On July 28, the Centers for Disease Control and Prevention reports a 44 percent increase in deaths from lung cancer in women from 1979 to 1986, compared to an increase of only 7 percent among men.

- On August 4, a new drug, deprenyl, appears to slow the progression of Parkinson's disease, a degenerative brain disorder.

- On August 9, the *Journal of Pediatrics* says in vitro babies are as healthy and mentally alert as those conceived normally.

- On August 15, the Gay Men's Health Crisis of New York City reverses its policy and endorses widespread voluntary testing for AIDS.

- On August 16, the *New England Journal of Medicine* says nursing mothers who drink alcohol appear to transfer enough of it to their infants to impair their muscle coordination.

- On August 18, the *Journal of the American Medical Association* estimates that only about 20 percent of the 10 million Americans afflicted with depression get treatment.

- On August 24, American and Canadian scientists announce the isolation and cloning of the gene causing cystic fibrosis.

- In September, the *New England Journal of Medicine* finds that HIV can lie dormant for up to three years before detection by a blood test.

- On September 6, the Harvard School of Public Health finds no evidence of increased cancer risk among women who started taking birth control pills in their mid twenties.

- On September 13, the University of Minnesota releases a new version of the Minnesota Multiphasic Personality Inventory, the most widely used psychological test, first published in 1942.

- On November 22, simple blood tests are introduced that can detect 60–70 percent of fetuses with Down's syndrome, a cause of mental retardation.

- On November 27, the first U.S. liver transplant using a living donor is performed with a mother who gave part of her liver to her twenty-one-month-old daughter.

- On December 2, a bipartisan report recommends that Congress lift its ban on funding research into in vitro fertilization, which antiabortion groups oppose.

- On December 8, scientists at Tulane University's Delta Regional Primate Research Center develop a vaccine that protects monkeys against a simian version of AIDS.

"First Recombinant DNA Product Approved by the Food and Drug Administration"

Press release

By: Genentech

Date: October 29, 1982

Source: Genentech. "First Recombinant DNA Product Approved by the Food and Drug Administration." Press release. Available online at http://www.gene.com/gene/nes/press-releases/printnews.jsp?detail=4193; website homepage: http://www.gene.com/gene/index.jsp (accessed February 1, 2003).

About the Organization: Genentech is a large biotechnology company, meaning that it develops new or improved biological products. It was officially incorporated on April 7, 1976, by Herbert W. Boyer and Robert A Swanson. Boyer graduated from St. Vincent's College in 1958 and went on to the University of Pittsburgh for a Ph.D in microbiology. He was a professor at the University of California, San Francisco from 1966 to 1991. Swanson was a venture capitalist from the firm Kleiner and Perkins. He received a bachelor's degree and a master's degree from the Massachusetts Institute of Technology in 1970. He succumbed to brain cancer in 1999 at the age of fifty-two. ■

Introduction

The first products of recombinant DNA technology were made possible by the discovery of the structure of DNA. No one could even comprehend the term "gene splicing," as recombinant DNA is sometimes called, until the structure of DNA was deduced in 1953. The enormous variability of all life on earth is conveyed by the linear sequence of four nucleotides: adenine (A), cytosine (C), thymine (T), and guanine (G). The revelation of this simple algorithm excited and spurred many more discoveries and technological innovations. Eventually the basic methodological foundation for recombinant DNA technology was developed. Enzymatic tools (proteins), viral vectors, and bacterial factories comprise its basic elements. Proteins such as restriction enzymes, ligases, and polymerases are the tools used to recognize, cut, join, and make DNA. Viruses that infect bacteria, called bacterio-

phages, are the vectors that transport DNA from one organism into another organism. Innocuous forms of *E. coli* are the bacterial factories that accept new DNA and churn out large quantities of the new DNA's protein product—which is what DNA does, make proteins.

Insulin and other hormones were the natural choice for the first recombinant DNA products to produce at Genentech. Insulin, produced by the pancreas, is critical for metabolizing carbohydrates, fats, and proteins. Diabetes mellitus is a group of diseases characterized by high blood sugar levels from an inability to produce or use insulin. Type I diabetics and large number of type II diabetics depend on multiple daily injections of insulin.

The founders of Genentech decided to focus their efforts on insulin for several reasons. First, the protein structure of insulin was already established. Second, there was a large demand for insulin. At the time, diabetics were using pig or cow insulin that was extracted from pancreas glands derived from slaughterhouses. Third, they calculated that they could produce recombinant insulin cheaper than cow or pig insulin. At the time, it took about eight thousand pounds of pancreas glands at $1.50 to $1.75 a pound to make one pound of insulin. Drug maker Eli Lilly had sales of about $400 million worth of insulin a year. The economics were favorable for Genentech to move forward in the production of recombinant insulin.

Significance

Recombinant DNA human insulin has become the most widely used form of insulin today. It is considered purer and generally causes fewer side effects than its cow or pig counterpart. Without recombinant human insulin, there almost certainly would have been a shortage of insulin in the United States. In the 1980s, it was predicted that cow and pig insulin would not meet the demand by the 1990s, for the incidence of diabetes mellitus was rising and is expected to keep rising in the twenty-first century.

Genentech production of human insulin demonstrated the feasibility of using recombinant DNA technology in the pharmaceutical industry. Genentech's human insulin was the first recombinant DNA product ever approved by the U.S. Food and Drug Administration (FDA). Since then, nearly a hundred recombinant DNA pharmaceutical products have been approved by the FDA, and hundreds more are in clinical trials. Biotechnology has become an industry unto itself. Companies make millions of dollars selling "kits" that contain the tools (restriction enzymes, ligases, polymerases, vectors, and bacteria) necessary to perform recombinant DNA methods.

The ethical considerations of recombinant DNA technology remain. In the mid-1970s biotech industry

"First Successful Laboratory Production of Human Insulin Announced" [Press Release from Genentech on September 6, 1978]

Insulin is a protein hormone produced in the pancreas and used in the metabolism of sugar and other carbohydrates. The synthesis of human insulin was done using a process similar to the fermentation process used to make antibiotics. The achievement may be the most significant advance in the treatment of diabetes since the development of animal insulin for human use in the 1920's. The insulin synthesis is the first laboratory production DNA technology.

Recombinant DNA is the technique of combining the genes of different organisms to form a hybrid molecule. DNA (deoxyribonucleic acid), the substances genes are composed of, contains the chemical record in which genetic information is encoded.

Scientists at Genentech and City of Hope inserted synthetic genes carrying the genetic code for human insulin, along with the necessary control mechanism, into an E. coli bacterial strain which is a laboratory derivative of a common bacteria found in the human intestine. Once inside the bacteria, the genes were "switched-on" by the bacteria to translate the code into either "A" or "B" protein chains found in insulin. The separate chains were then joined to construct complete insulin molecules.

The development of genetically engineered human insulin was funded by Genentech. However, the work was a cooperative effort between Genentech and City of Hope. The synthesis of human insulin gene was accomplished by four scientists at City of Hope Medical Center led by Roberto Crea, Ph.D., and Keichi Itakura, Ph.D. Scientists at Genentech, led by David Goeddel, Ph.D. and Dennis Kleid, Ph.D., joined the genes that were made in sections and inserted them, along with the control mechanism into the E. Coli bacterium. Arthur Riggs, Ph.D. at the City of Hope and Dr. Goeddel of Genentech were responsible for developing the final assays, purification and joining techniques.

Approximately 1.5 million diabetics take injections of insulin. At present, this insulin is extracted from the pancreas glands of swine and cattle slaughtered for food. It takes about 8,000 pounds of animal pancreas glands to produce one pound of insulin. The new process will produce ample quantities to meet the growing demand, and more importantly, produce a chemically identical human insulin.

One of the advantages of producing insulin using the recombinant DNA method is to reduce the dependency on animal glands. Also, by using insulin that chemically is identical to human insulin, scientists hope that certain allergic reactions by some diabetes to insulin derived from animals can be eliminated.

"The development of human insulin demonstrates the viability of using recombinant DNA technology to produce products with practical application," said Robert Swanson, president of Genentech.

"While extensive testing and refinement of the process is needed, we want to see human insulin and other genetically engineered products benefitting the people who need them in the shortest possible time," said Swanson.

Genentech, a privately financed corporation, and City of Hope have established a joint cooperative program to conduct basic research to develop commercial application of molecular genetic technology. Less than one year ago, Genentech announced its first product, the hormone somatostatin which was developed in a cooperative program with City of Hope Medical Center and the University of California San Francisco Medical Center.

SOURCE: Genentech. "First Successful Laboratory Production of Human Insulin Announced." Press release. Available online at http://www.gene.com/gene/nes/press-releases/printnews.jsp?detail=4160; website homepage: http://www.gene.com/gene/index.jsp (accessed February 1, 2003).

scientists and government officials tried to answer the many ethical questions surrounding recombinant DNA technology. Many groups today still oppose it. However, recombinant DNA products have proven safe, reliable, and effective for the millions of Americans who depend on them.

Primary Source

"First Recombinant DNA Product Approved by the FDA"

SYNOPSIS: This is the Genentech press release announcing the FDA approval of human insulin.

South San Francisco, CA, October 29, 1982—Robert A. Swanson, president of Genentech, Inc. said today that approval by the Food and Drug Administration of human insulin produced by recombinant DNA technology, "is a tribute to the collaboration of two great scientific teams—those at Eli Lilly and Genentech."

Humulin, the tradename of the new insulin, is being manufactured and marketed by Lilly under a license from Genentech. It is the first human health care product from recombinant DNA technology to reach the market.

Genentech president Robert Swanson (right) and scientist David Goeddel stand next to the fermentation vats used to produce the first recombinant DNA products (human insulin and growth hormone) ever, San Francisco, California, January 30, 1980. © ROGER RESSMEYER/CORBIS. REPRODUCED BY PERMISSION.

U.S. government approval followed by only one month the recent approval by British regulatory authorities for introduction of the human insulin in the United Kingdom.

Swanson pointed out that approval by the Food and Drug Administration came only four years after scientists at Genentech and City of Hope National Medical Center, working together on the Genentech-funded project, successfully produced human insulin using recombinant DNA technology. "The FDA has quickly expanded the range of its expertise in the area of genetic engineering in order to be responsive to the rapid development of new products made possible by this new technology."

Further Resources

BOOKS

Hall, S.S. *Invisible Frontiers: The Race to Synthesize a Human Gene*. New York: Atlantic Monthly Press, 1987.

Olson, Steve. *Biotechnology: An Industry Comes of Age*. Washington D.C.: National Academy Press, 1986.

Watson, James D., et al. *Recombinant DNA: A Short Course*. New York: Scientific American Books, 1983.

PERIODICALS

Hood, L. "Biotechnology and Medicine of the Future." *Journal of the American Medical Association* 259, 1988, 1837–1844.

Johnson, Irving S. "Human Insulin from Recombinant DNA Technology." *Science* 219, February 11, 1983, 632–637.

Sindelar, Robert D. "The Pharmacy of the Future."*Drug Topics* 137, no. 9, May 3, 1993, 66–79.

WEBSITES

Online Archive of California, Regional Oral History Office, University of California, Berkeley. "Herbert W. Boyer." 1994. Available online at http://ark.cdlib.org/ark:/13030 /kt5d5nb0zs/; website homepage: http://www.oac.cdlib.org/ (accessed March 2, 2003).

Online Archive of California. Regional Oral History Office, University of California, Berkeley. "Robert A Swanson." 1996 and 1997. Available online at http://ark.cdlib.org/ark: /13030/kt9c6006s1; website homepage: http://www.oac.cdlib .org/ (accessed March 2, 2003).

"The Purification and Manufacture of Human Interferons"

Magazine article

By: Sidney Pestka

Date: August 1983

Source: Pestka, Sidney. "The Purification and Manufacture of Human Interferons." *Scientific American,* August 1983, 36–44.

About the Author: Sidney Pestka (1936–) earned a bachelor's degree from Princeton University in 1957 and a doctorate in medicine from the University of Pennsylvania. He spent sixteen years working at the Roche Institute of Hoffman-La Roche in Nutley, New Jersey. Pestka is professor and chairman of the Department of Molecular Genetics, Microbiology, and Immunology at Robert Wood Johnson Medical School at the University of Medicine and Dentistry of New Jersey in Piscataway, N.J. He received the National Medal of Technology Award from President George W. Bush on June 12, 2002. ■

Introduction

Interferons are a part of the animal kingdom's arsenal of disease-fighting weapons. They were discovered in 1957 by two London researchers, Alick Isaacs and Jean Lindenmann. They isolated a protein that was released by animal cells infected with a virus. The protein seemed to make neighboring cells resistant to the viral attack. They called the protein "interferon" because it interfered with the virus.

The promise of interferon was recognized right away. Here was a protein that could interfere with, and

stop, viral infection. Antibiotics were already being used to treat bacterial infections, and the hope that interferon could be used as an effective antiviral medication to treat such diseases as Ebola, dengue, and yellow fever was very high.

By the late 1970s, some twenty years after interferon's discovery, its promise was still untapped. Interferon had not yet been purified, and there were even doubts about its existence. Interferon proved troublesome for several reasons. First, rather than just one interferon protein, there was a large family of many different interferons. Second, animal cells excrete only miniscule amounts of interferon, so enormous volumes of blood were needed to extract just a small amount of the protein. Third, no one understood how interferons worked. There was a great deal of research done on interferons during the 1960s and 1970s, but the problems and difficulties slowed any major progress.

As the 1970s turned into the 1980s several researchers overcame the challenges posed by interferon. Sidney Pestka and his team of researchers at Roche Institute of Molecular Biology were one of several groups that helped to unlock the potential of interferons. Pestka's lab was one of the first to purify human alpha interferon (there are three main types of interferon: alpha, beta, and gamma). In the article excerpted here, Pestka describes how his lab used recombinant DNA technology and high-performance liquid chromatography (HPLC) to produce and purify large amounts of human interferons. In 1986, the U.S. Federal Drug Administration (FDA) approved Pestka's synthesized interferon for use as an antiviral medication.

Significance

Historically, viral infections have been very hard to treat. Before the advent of antibiotics during the twentieth century, bacterial infections were a scourge of mankind. Viruses, however, do not respond to antibiotics. Until interferons were purified and produced on a large scale, there were few antiviral medications. Today, alpha interferon (also called interferon A) combined with another antiviral medication is the most effective treatment against hepatitis B and C. Many patients are actually virus free after undergoing the treatment.

Interferons work by interacting with cells under viral attack. They stimulate the cells to produce compounds that protect nearby cells and prevent viruses from replicating. Normally, people suffering from viral diseases produce small amounts of interferons in response to a virus. However, extra interferon administered in high doses attacks the virus with a concentrated and overwhelming force.

Interferons have proven effective against certain kinds of cancers, especially some forms of leukemia, and

Executives at Cetus Labs stand in front of the lab's interferon production facility, Emeryville, California, October 4, 1982. Interferons help fight viral infections, which do not respond to antibiotics. Before their isolation and production in the 1980s, there was little with which to fight such infections.
© ROGER RESSMEYER/CORBIS. REPRODUCED BY PERMISSION.

is used to treat metastatic malignant melanoma, kidney and bladder cell carcinoma, and AIDS-related Kaposi's sarcoma. Interferons are also used to treat multiple sclerosis. As more is learned about how interferons work, they are being used to treat more and more diseases.

Primary Source

"The Purification and Manufacture of Human Interferons" [excerpt]

SYNOPSIS: In the following excerpts, Sidney Pestka describes some of the work performed in his lab that enabled the large-scale manufacture of human interferons.

Both the sporadic cancer studies and those attempting to assess interferon's efficacy against viral diseases suffered from the serious shortage and high cost of interferon and even more from the fact that the major "interferon" available was really a mixture of various proteins of which less than 1 percent by weight was interferon itself. Aside from antiviral activity no observed effect of the mixture could dependably be attributed to interferon. Purification of the protein was therefore a matter of high priority.

In 1977 we took on the task of purifying human alpha interferon in my laboratory at the Roche Institute of Molecular Biology. The first requirement was a large supply of crude leukocyte interferon. Our method of preparing it was essentially the one developed several years before by Karl Cantell of the Finnish Red Cross Blood Center. Human leukocytes (white blood cells) are incubated with an inducing virus, either Sendai virus or Newcastle-disease virus. Where Cantell had used human or bovine blood serum as a component of the culture medium, we substituted the milk protein casein; as a single protein it proved to be easier to remove in the initial concentration steps than the multiple proteins of serum were. We found the yield could be improved by substituting leukocytes from patients with chronic myelogenous leukemia for normal leukocytes, and we were able to obtain large supplies of leukemic cells (which are removed in therapy of the disease) from the M.D. Anderson Hospital and Tumor Institute in Houston. After incubation overnight the cells and viruses are removed by centrifugation. What remains is a crude interferon preparation: it contains some induced interferon along with any other proteins

Test tube containing interferon, which was approved by the FDA for clinical use in 1986. Interferon is a protein that helps fight infection. © ZEVA OELBAUM/CORBIS. REPRODUCED BY PERMISSION.

whose secretion may have been induced by the virus and also all the normal cell secretions. The objective is to remove all the proteins other than interferon in a series of purification steps. At each step one must assay the concentrate for interferon activity in terms of standard units of "specific activity." The usual assay, measuring the extent to which a sample inhibits the destruction of cells by a virus, took three days. Philip C. Familletti and Sara Rubinstein found a way to cut the time to less than 16 hours and thereby speeded up the purification process considerably.

Knowing how much difficulty had attended efforts to purify interferon by conventional techniques, we decided to try what is called high-performance liquid chromatography. Chromatography methods in general involve adsorbing a crude mixture to some solid support and eluting different fractions with a solvent. In high-performance liquid chromatography the starting mixture is adsorbed to very fine bead-like particles packed in a column and the solvent is pumped through the column. Sidney Udenfriend, Stanley Stein and Peter Bohlen of Roche had managed to separate peptides (short chains of amino acids) by means of reverse-phase liquid chromatography, in which the solid phase (the beads) is coated with an organic material that is hydrophobic, or water-repellent; the mobile phase (the solvent) is more polar, or water-attracting. Stein, Menachem Rubinstein and I undertook to apply the method to purify the alpha interferon. Ethyl alcohol, the accepted solvent, did not work; the protein remained adsorbed to the beads. We decided to try a somewhat less polar solvent, n-propanol, even though proteins are not very soluble in it and the interferon might precipitate as it was being eluted. As it turned out, a gradient of n-propanol worked. As we pumped increasing concentrations of the solvent through the column, different protein fractions (having different affinities for the solid support) were eluted successively and collected in tubes. Each fraction was assayed for interferon activity. Fractions that were relatively rich in interferon were applied to another column for further purification. By altering the reverse-phase process with normal-phase chromatography (in which the beads are coated with hydrophilic groups and the solvent is less polar) Rubinstein purified human alpha interferon, in just a few steps, about 80,000-fold. The specific activity of the purified interferon was from 200 to 400 million units per milligram. Subjected to gel electrophoresis, which separated the proteins on the basis of molecular size, the interferon yielded a single band at a molecular weight of 17,500, and the protein in that single band was active. In other words, human alpha interferon had been purified to homogeneity.

There remained the problem of obtaining enough pure interferon for intensive study of its mode of action and for clinical trials. We might have accumulated enough by large-scale induction of leukocytes and purification of the crude material, but a better method was at hand. In the mid-1970's recombinant-DNA techniques had been developed whereby the DNA containing the gene for a particular protein can be inserted into the bacterium Escherichia coli and be cloned, or replicated in many copies, and expressed: translated into protein. We realized that by such methods we could obtain a large supply of particular interferon genes for study and also get the bacteria to manufacture a particular interferon—eventually perhaps on an industrial scale.

An antibody is a protein of the immune system that recognizes and binds to a foreign protein, or antigen. Since 1975 it has been possible to prepare large amounts of monoclonal antibodies: antibodies directed against a specific antigen. The availability of our purified interferon had enabled Theophil Staehelin of F. Hoffmann-La Roche & Co., Ltd., to prepare monoclonal antibodies directed against specific interferon molecules. Monoclonal antibodies that were specific for alpha interferon were linked to beads packed into chromatography columns. To purify bacterial interferon Staehelin, Hsiang-fu Kung and Donna S. Hobbs poured onto the column an extract of E. coli cells that had synthesized recombinant interferon A. The interferon, and only the interferon, bound to the antibodies; the other components, including any bacterial toxins, went right through the column. Then an acid solution was passed through the column to elute virtually pure interferon.

The availability of large amounts of very pure interferon opened the way to clinical trials, which I shall describe below. It also meant we could crystallize interferon, the first step toward analysis of the protein's three-dimensional structure by X-ray crystallography. David L. Miller and Kung have prepared crystals of human recombinant Interferon A.

Early clinical trials of interferon were hampered, as I have suggested, by the short supply and high cost of interferon synthesized by human cells and by the impurity of the preparations, which clouded assessment of interferon's own effect and also limited dosages (since large amounts of the crude material could not be administered to patients). The purification of recombinant human alpha interferon in quantity removed all these impediments. After appropriate tests for safety in animals, the bacterial product prepared by Hoffmann-La Roche, Inc., was approved for trials in human beings. In January of 1981 Jordan U. Gutterman of the M. D. Anderson Hospital initiated a clinical trial designed to establish the safety, toxicity and side effects of various blood levels of recombinant interferon A in cancer patients.

Interferon A is only the first bacterial interferon to be tested. Other alpha interferons are becoming available for trials; beta interferon and gamma interferon will follow. Some classes, species and combinations of interferon may be more effective than others against particular diseases and under particular conditions. Moreover, the physician will not be limited to the set of natural interferons. One can break up interferon genes and splice the pieces to make new genes that are translated into hybrid interferons. We and other workers have already experimented with such hybrid molecules. It may

become possible, as more is learned about the mechanisms of these proteins' various activities, to tailor interferon molecules to optimize particular effects.

Further Resources

BOOKS
Block, Timothy M. *Innovations in Antiviral Development and the Detection of Virus Infections.* New York: Plenum Press, 1992.

Domingo, Esteban, Robert G. Webster, and John J. Holland. *Origin and Evolution of Viruses.* San Diego, Calif.: Academic Press, 1999.

PERIODICALS
Miller, Roger. "One Patient's Experience with Interferon." *FDA Consumer,* April 1987, 11.

Mostow, Steven R., Richard J. Whitley, and Lisa A. Piermattie. "Today's Antiviral Armamentarium." *Patient Care* 22, no. 13, August 15, 1988, 162–173.

Weinstock, Cheryl Platzman. "Medicines from the Body." *FDA Consumer,* April 1987, 6–11.

Wroblewski, John J. "The Microuniverse of Antivirals." *Drug Topics,* January 3, 1983, 44–49.

WEBSITES
Fitzgerald-Docarsly, Patricia. "The History of Interferon: An Interview with Sid Pestka." Available online at http://bioinformatics.weizmann.ac.il/isicr/newsletter/Volume%204/isicr4.2.html; website home page: http://bioinformatics.weizmann.ac.il/isicr/ (accessed March 2, 2003).

Hale, Kathryn L. "Interferon: The Evolution of a Biological Therapy." *Oncolog.* Available online at http://www3.mdanderson.org/~oncolog/14_Interferon.html; website home page http://www.mdanderson.org/ (accessed March 2, 2003).

"The Stormy Legacy of Baby Doe"
Magazine article

By: *Time*
Date: September 1983
Source: Wallis, Claudia. "The Stormy Legacy of Baby Doe." *Time,* September 26, 1983, 58.
About the Author: Claudia Wallis (1954–) graduated from Yale University with a bachelor's degree in philosophy in 1976. She began her career at *Time* as a writer in 1979. She was the magazine's medical writer from 1982 through 1987 when she became the third woman in the magazine's history to be named a senior editor. She was also the founding editor of *Time for Kids* magazine and was managing editor of that publication and a contributing editor for *Time* in the early twenty-first century. ∎

Introduction

On April 9, 1982, a baby was born in a Bloomington, Indiana, hospital. The baby, known to the world as Baby Doe because his parents did not name him, was destined over his tragically short life to become the center of controversy. For after Baby Doe was born with Down syndrome (trisomy 21) and esophageal atresia, his parents declined surgical intervention and allowed their child to starve to death. According to stories in the press, the parents were told by their doctor that their baby was severely retarded, "a blob," and that his chances of surviving the surgery to correct the esophageal atresia were 50 percent.

Down syndrome is a genetic condition caused by having extra genetic material. Humans normally have twenty-three pairs of chromosomes, each pair consisting of one chromosome from the mother and one from the father. People with trisomy 21 have three number 21 chromosomes. The extra chromosome contains extra genes that produce extra doses of proteins that cause the features and characteristics typical of Down syndrome: folds over the eyes, flattened noses, decreased muscle tone, and varying degrees of mental retardation. Children with Down syndrome are at increased risk for certain health problems, such as congenital heart defects, increased susceptibility to infection, respiratory problems, obstructed digestive tracts, and childhood leukemia. However, most of these health problems are treatable. People born with Down syndrome typically live to about fifty-five years of age.

Esophageal atresia is a congenital disorder that typically occurs along with Down syndrome and other birth defects. In infants with esophageal atresia, the esophagus forms into two separate tubes. One tube connects to the throat, the other to the stomach, but they do not connect to each other. When an infant feeds, the upper pouch fills up and liquid overflows into the lungs. In addition, the baby cannot swallow his nose and throat mucous and inhales the secretions into his lungs, causing pneumonia. Before the performance of the first successful repair in 1939, this condition was fatal. In the 1980s, however, neonatal surgery could repair the malady.

Baby Doe's parents received advice from three doctors: the obstetrician who delivered Baby Doe, a pediatrician, and their family practitioner. The obstetrician advised the parents not to treat, while the other two doctors advised the parents to treat and save Baby Doe's life. The obstetrician's orders said to feed Baby Doe, not to administer intravenous fluids, and to keep Baby Doe comfortable with sedatives. Feeding an infant with esophageal astresia is highly likely to lead to choking and death. Baby Doe was transferred to a private room with a private nurse because the nurses at the hospital refused to carry out the obstetrician's orders. Four days later, Baby Doe began spitting up blood, and he was weak and near death. Once the story became publicized, several couples came forward who were interested in adopting Baby Doe, and there were several attempts to save his life in the courts, but they failed.

Significance

The Baby Doe case created an outcry from many people across the nation, especially the pro-life movement and President Reagan's administration. As a direct result of the Baby Doe case, the Department of Health and Human Services issued several sets of rules and regulations, all of which were challenged in court. The federal action reflected the viewpoint of some people that Baby Doe had been a victim of abuse and neglect (by not performing life-saving surgery) and also of discrimination against persons with disabilities (Down syndrome). They argued that if Baby Doe had just been born with one malady, he would more than likely have survived.

Important federal legislation occurred as a result of the Baby Doe case. The "Baby Doe amendment" was added to child abuse law in 1984. Under the legislation, it is *child abuse and neglect* to withhold "medically indicated" treatment unless an infant is chronically and irreversibly comatose, when treatment would be futile and merely prolong dying, or treatment is both virtually futile and inhumane. Many in the medical profession, though, are not satisfied with the law. They believe that the pain and suffering for many severely handicapped infants and premature infants is so great that it is not in the best interest of the child to keep it alive.

The Baby Doe case holds several moral and ethical dilemmas regarding whether or not the government should intervene between doctors and parents when deciding what is best for a child, whether or not some damaged children are worth saving and who should decide, and if pain and suffering are ever so great that death is better than life. There are are still no simple solutions to these dilemmas, and there likely will never be.

Primary Source

"The Stormy Legacy of Baby Doe"

> **SYNOPSIS:** This article describes the flurry of reactions from the Reagan administration and the medical community in response to the death of Baby Doe.

Should the Government try to save severely afflicted infants?

On April 9, 1982, an infant who became known to the world only as Baby Doe was born in Bloom-

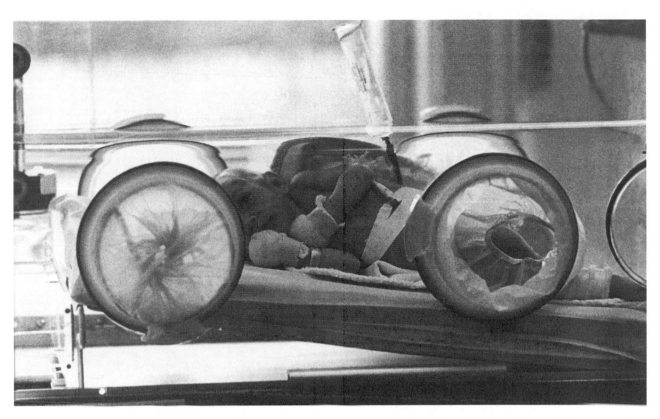

An infant lies in a neonatal unit at a hospital in Philadelphia, Pennsylvania, 1981. Advances in science allowed infants with severe inflictions to survive, with serious handicaps, which sparked heated debates as to what role the government should play and how far it should go. © ED ECKSTEIN/CORBIS. REPRODUCED BY PERMISSION.

ington, Ind. He had an incomplete esophagus and Down's syndrome, which causes moderate to severe mental retardation. Thanks to advances in neonatal medicine, surgeons could ensure Baby Doe's survival by attaching his esophagus to his stomach, but nothing could be done to prevent retardation. His parents were confronted with an agonizing dilemma: to assent to an operation that would save the life of a child who could be hopelessly retarded, or to allow him to die of starvation. Against the wishes of their pediatrician and hospital, they chose the latter. The parents' right to this choice was twice challenged in the courts by the hospital and twice upheld. On April 15, Baby Doe died.

His legacy is today one of the most fiercely debated controversies in medicine. At issue: how to protect the rights of severely handicapped infants, and what role the Federal Government should play. Locked in the battle are three factions—doctors, handicapped citizens' groups and right-to-life organizations. Last week, as the Reagan Administration reviewed its stand, it came under concerted attack by the medical profession in the form of two blistering editorials in the prestigious *New England Journal of Medicine.*

The Baby Doe debate was ignited by the President. Outraged by the case, Reagan ordered the Department of Health and Human Services to ensure that handicapped infants would receive proper medical care even if their parents or physicians were willing to let them die. In May 1982, the department informed the nation's 5,800 hospitals that they could lose federal funding if they withheld treatment or nourishment from handicapped infants. This edict was followed by a tougher regulation requiring hospitals to post large signs in public places bearing the inscription "Discriminatory failure to feed or care for handicapped infants in this facility is prohibited by federal law." The posters provided the number of a 24-hour, toll-free hotline for anonymous informers who wanted to report violations to federal investigators.

Doctors and medical organizations were outraged by this unprecedented intrusion of the Federal Government into matters that traditionally have been settled privately between physicians and parents. The new rule implied that doctors and parents could not be trusted to act in the best interest of a handicapped child. No less infuriating to physicians was the rule's assumption that all congenital defects could be handled in the same manner, that any child's life, no matter how tenuous, painful and ill-fated, should be sustained for as long as is technically possible.

The American Academy of Pediatrics, the American Hospital Association and a number of other professional organizations took the HHS to court over the Baby Doe rule and won. District Court Judge Gerhard Gesell last April found the regulation to be "arbitrary" and "ill-considered." Three months later HHS issued revised regulations, which conceded that there was no need to impose "futile therapies" on terminally ill infants.

The Government argues that the informer system developed by the hotline has been effective. As of last week, there had been 33 accusations that hospitalized infants were not receiving proper care. In eleven cases, the Government dispatched teams composed of doctors and civil rights investigators. The squads found nothing to criticize on eight visits, but were able to help save the lives of three handicapped infants whose doctors seemed to be unaware of new techniques for treating birth defects.

The pediatricians and allied medical groups argue that the best way to help such afflicted babies is by better educating doctors about medical advances, not by sending in federal watchdogs. Hospitals charge that some of the investigative teams disrupted neonatal clinics. Such disturbances led the A.A.P. to protest that "the Government's 'remedy' is potentially harmful to the very infants it seeks to protect."

As an alternative to direct federal interference under the Baby Doe rule, the pediatricians, the A.H.A. and five other medical groups propose that all hospitals be required to create "infant bioethical review committees" to protect the rights of handicapped newborns. These committees, composed of medical experts, laymen, clergy and lawyers, would be consulted in any decision to forgo treatment. The groups would also try to resolve any conflict between parents and doctors over how to proceed. Should parents refuse to approve treatment that would clearly benefit their child, the committee could ask state agencies and courts to appoint a guardian.

Such an approach is unacceptable to groups representing the handicapped and right-to-life organizations. "The problem is how to ensure the rights of the handicapped to treatment, when the parents, doctors and the hospital agree not to provide it," says Gary Curran of the American Life Lobby. Another worry is that a bioethics committee could not act quickly enough. Warns Paul Marchand, of the Association for Retarded Citizens: "If these infants are not treated within days, hours, they will die."

The Department of Health and Human Services has reservations about the proposal to create ethical review committees. "The problem is there wouldn't be any enforcement," says John Svahn, who was recently promoted from HHS Under Secretary to Assistant to the President for Policy Development. The department hopes to come to a final judgment in the next few weeks. If the hotline and what some doctors deride as investigative "goon squads" are not eliminated, the medical organizations have threatened to take the Reagan Administration to court again.

Further Resources

BOOKS

Caplan, Arthur L., Robert H. Blank, and Janna C. Merrick. *Compelled Compassion: Government Intervention in the Treatment of Critically Ill Newborns.* Totowa, N.J.: Humana Press, 1992.

Pence, Gregory E. *Classic Cases in Medical Ethics: Accounts of the Cases That Have Shaped Medical Ethics, with Philosophical, Legal, and Historical Backgrounds.* New York: McGraw-Hill, 1990.

Walter, James J. and Thomas A. Shannon. *Quality of Life: The New Medical Dilemma.* New York: Paulist Press, 1990.

PERIODICALS

Clark, Robert T. "Baby Jose—Narrative Fiction." *Medical Student Journal of the American Medical Association* 284, September 6, 2000, 1144–1145.

Clouser, K.D. "The Sanctity of Life: An Analysis of a Concept." *Annals of Internal Medicine* 78, 1973, 119–25.

Kopelman, Loretta M. "Do the "Baby Doe" Rules Ignore Suffering?" *Second Opinion* 18, no. 4, April 1993, 100–114.

Evans, Daryl. "The Psychological Impact of Disability and Illness on Medical Treatment Decision Making." *Issues in Law and Medicine* 5, no. 3, Winter 1989, 277–299.

WEBSITES

Anderson, Mark. "Preemies: Baby Doe Law Creates Miracles—at a Cost." American. Pediatric Services. Available online at http://www.pediatricservices.com/prof/prof-01.htm; website home page: http://www.pediatricservices.com (accessed March 8, 2003).

"Baby Doe, Baby Jane Doe, Baby Doe Regulations, and the 1983 Amendment to the Child Abuse Law. Our Essence." Available online at http://www.ascensionhealth.org/our_essence/ethics/affiliates/cases/case3.asp; website home page: http://www.ascensionhealth.org (accessed March 8, 2003).

"Ted Slavin's Blood and the Development of HBV Vaccine"

Letter

By: Baruch Blumberg

Date: January 17, 1985

Source: Blumberg, Baruch, et al. "Ted Slavin's Blood and the Development of the HBV Vaccine." *New England Journal of Medicine* 312, January 17, 1985, 189.

About the Author: Baruch Blumberg (1925–) was born in Brooklyn, New York. He earned a bachelor's degree in physics from Union College in Schenectady, New York, in 1946. Afterwards, he studied medicine at Columbia University, where he received his M.D. in 1951. After doing research abroad, Blumberg joined the National Institutes of Health in 1957 and Fox Chase Cancer Center in 1964. Blumberg is also a professor of Medicine and Anthropology at the University of Pennsylvania. He was awarded the 1976 Nobel Prize in medicine for his 1967 discovery of the hepatitis B virus. ∎

Introduction

The scientific foundations for vaccination were laid in eighteenth-century efforts to combat the smallpox virus, one of the world's greatest killers. Edward Jenner, who coined the term *vaccination* (derived from the Latin word for cow), used the cowpox virus, a closely related virus that induced a milder reaction, for his inoculations; Famed Puritan minister Cotton Mather performed the same technique in America. Those inoculated with the cowpox virus developed a lifelong immunity to smallpox.

Vaccines work by triggering our infection fighting memory, or immune response. In a successful immune response, proteins called antibodies seek out and destroy an invading pathogen. The immune response is very precise. Antibodies are made specifically for each invading pathogen. The first time the body is exposed to a certain pathogen, it has to "learn" how to make the antibody for it. The second time the body is exposed, however, it "remembers" the pathogen. The body quickly synthesizes vast numbers of the correct antibodies and mounts a strong immune defense. This is called immunity. The goal of vaccination is to trigger a long-term immunity through a mild first-time exposure.

Viral hepatitis is one of the most common infectious diseases. The hepatitis B virus infects liver cells and can cause causing lifelong infection, cirrhosis (scarring of liver cells), liver cancer, liver failure, and death. Baruch Blumberg discovered the virus in 1967. Later, he and Irving Millman developed a method to test for it and a vaccine to protect against it. Before Blumberg's research, the hepatitis B virus afflicted millions of people. Though still a major disease, it affects far fewer people today. Blum-

Preparations are being made to screen a patient for Hepatitis B, Massachusetts, February 1984. Through the donations of his own blood, Ted Slavin was able to help scientists prepare the first successful vaccine for hepatitis B, which was approved by the FDA in the 1980s. © TED SPIEGEL/CORBIS. REPRODUCED BY PERMISSION.

berg won a Nobel Prize for his discovery of the hepatitis B virus.

In the 1970s, Ted Slavin contacted Baruch Blumberg and others at the National Institutes of Health and offered his blood for research purposes. Slavin had persistent hepatitis B, and his blood contained an unusually large hepatitis B titer (level of virus). Blumberg and Millman used Slavin's blood to extract particles from the virus's protective protein coat, then used these "surface proteins" in an experiment to trigger an effective immune response. This approach was critical to the development of a hepatitis B vaccine, since it is extremely difficult to culture and grow the virus. In the early 1980s, the FDA approved Blumberg's vaccine, the first one against hepatitis B.

Significance

Slavin's blood contained so much hepatitis B virus that it was extremely valuable. While Slavin gave his

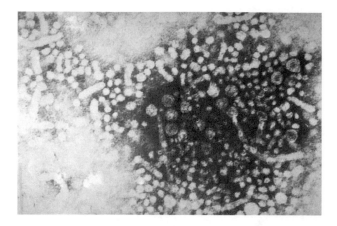

An electron micrograph shows hepatitis B viruses. Hepatitis B causes an inflammation of the liver. © LESTER V. BERGMAN/CORBIS. REPRODUCED BY PERMISSION.

blood to such noncommercial researchers as Blumberg and Millman, he also sold it to commercial entities for as much as $6,000 per pint. He even formed a company, Essential Biological, to market his blood in addition to the blood or tissue of other people with rare and valuable characteristics. Slavin died from hepatitis B complications on November 15, 1984.

The blood of chronic hepatitis B sufferers is no longer needed to produce the hepatitis B vaccine. A recombinant hepatitis B vaccine was produced shortly after Blumberg's vaccine was approved. Using recombinant DNA technology, the surface proteins of the virus are produced in yeast. Human trials showed that a three-dose regimen stimulated an immune response as effective as the vaccine prepared from the blood of infected individuals. Later, the FDA approved the recombinant vaccine.

The smallpox virus is again impacting history. During the 1980s, the smallpox virus, which provided the impetus for the discovery of vaccines, was eradicated. No human being harbors the virus. As far as is known, there are only two places in the world where the smallpox virus exists: the United States and Russia. However, in response to possible biological terrorist attacks, the United States began vaccinating health care workers and first responders against smallpox in 2003.

Primary Source

"Ted Slavin's Blood and the Development of the HBV Vaccine"

> SYNOPSIS: In this letter to the editor, Baruch Blumberg and his colleagues at the Fox Chase Cancer Center eulogized Ted Slavin and praised him for providing his valuable blood at no cost to researchers.

To the Editor:

Ted Slavin died on the 15th of November, 1984, from the ravages of hemophilia, kidney disease, and congestive heart failure. His death was a blow to all of us in the Division of Clinical Research of the Fox Chase Cancer Center.

Mr. Slavin contracted hepatitis B in the mid-1950s, and probably as a consequence of subsequent repeated exposure to hepatitis B virus in numerous transfusions (blood donors were not screened for the virus at that time), he had very high titers of antibodies against hepatitis B. In 1970 the Hemophilia Society began to test patients for hepatitis B viral markers, and the high titers of antibodies in his blood were revealed. Slavin realized the value of his blood both to commercial organizations that at the time were using human serum in manufacturing diagnostic kits for hepatitis B virus, and to laboratories attempting to advance knowledge about blood-borne human viruses. Ironically, Slavin's blood, which previously had been an enormous burden to him, then became an asset. He began to market his blood, on occasion for up to $10.00 a milliliter, and later organized a company, Essential Biologicals (a particularly appropriate name), to collect blood from persons with rare or unique blood factors. Through his energy and wit, he converted a disastrous health condition into a successful business.

In addition to its commercial use, Slavin provided his serum, at no cost, for research purposes. From the National Institutes of Health he obtained a printout of workers in the hepatitis field and selected our laboratory as a recipient of his blood. We used it in research on the radioimmunoassay test, tissue fluorescence techniques, the development of the vaccine against hepatitis B virus, and the prevention of primary cancer of the liver.

What Kind of Vaccine Is It?

There are three different kinds of vaccines, "live virus," "killed virus," or "subunit vaccines." Live virus vaccines are usually the most effective, but they also have the potential to cause serious side effects. While the virus is deactivated, it is still "alive" and can infect cells. Killed viruses are safer, but the immune response is not as strong, so booster shots are usually required. Subunit vaccines are composed of fragments of the virus, usually one of the proteins isolated from the virus's protective coating.

We will long remember Ted Slavin as a gallant man who loved life and who contributed greatly to our research efforts.

Baruch S. Blumberg, Irving Millman, W. Thomas London, and other members of the Division of Clinical Research Fox Chase Cancer Center Philadelphia, PA 19111

Further Resources

BOOKS

Blumberg, Baruch S. *Hepatitis B: The Hunt for a Killer Virus.* Princeton, N.J.: Princeton University Press, 2002.

Mack, Arien. *In Time of Plague: The History and Social Consequences of Lethal Epidemic Disease.* New York: New York University Press, 1991.

Millman, Irving, Toby K. Eisenstein, and Baruch S. Blumberg. *Hepatitis B: The Virus, the Disease, and the Vaccine.* New York: Plenum Press, 1984.

PERIODICALS

Kochler, Christopher S. W. "'Science,' 'Society,' and Immunity." *Modern Drug Discoverer* 4, no. 10, October 2001, 59–60. Available online at http://pubs.acs.org/subscribe/journals/mdd/v04/i10/html/10timeline.html; website home page: http://pubs.acs.org/journals/mdd/index.html (accessed March 5, 2003).

National Vaccine Advisory Committee. "Lessons Learned From a Review of the Development of Selected Vaccines." *Pediatrics* 104, no. 4, October 1999, 942–950.

WEBSITES

National Academy of Sciences. "The Hepatitis B Vaccine. Beyond Discovery." Available online at http://www.beyonddiscovery.org/content/view.page.asp?I=273; website home page http://www.beyonddiscovery.org (accessed March 3, 2003).

National Cancer Institute. "Understanding the Immune System." Available online at http://press2.nci.nih.gov/science behind/immune/immune00.htm; website home page: http://press2.nci.nih.gov/sciencebehind/index.htm (accessed March 3, 2003).

"The Age of AIDS: A Great Time for Defensive Living"

Editorial

By: George Lundberg, M.D.

Date: June 1985

Source: Lundberg, George. "The Age of AIDS: A Great Time for Defensive Living." *Journal of the American Medical Association* 253, no. 23, June 21, 1985, 3440–3441.

About the Author: George Lundberg (1933–) was born in Florida and grew up in southern Alabama. He earned a bachelor's degree from the University of Alabama in 1952 and re-

ceived his M.D. from the Medical College of Alabama in 1957, specializing in pathology. From 1982 to 1999, he was the editor of the *Journal of the American Medical Association.* In 2002, he became editor-in-chief emeritus of Medscape, an Internet site for health and medical information. ■

Introduction

The AIDS virus spread rapidly during the 1980s. When the virus causing AIDS first emerged in the early 1980s, it was seen predominately in gay men. By 1985, four major risk groups had emerged: gays, intravenous (IV) drug users, recipients of blood transfusions, and recent Haitian immigrants. Even though people in these groups represented the majority of AIDS cases, there was growing concern that the disease was spreading into the heterosexual population. A series of papers published in 1985 documented the sexual transmission of AIDS between straight men and women. It was apparent that anyone, young or old, male or female, rich or poor, black or white, gay or straight, was at risk for contracting the disease.

Fearing an epidemic of untold proportions if the virus took hold in the heterosexual population, Dr. George Lundberg, a pathologist and the editor of the *Journal of the American Medical Association (JAMA),* in 1985 called on leaders in government, medicine, the clergy, and society in general to educate the public about ways to avoid AIDS. He, *JAMA,* and other members of the medical community appealed for widespread AIDS testing using the enzyme-linked immunosorbent assay (ELISA) just recently developed. In addition, a change in lifestyle was suggested. As Lundberg said, "Individuals have the power to protect themselves more than science currently can."

Significance

The AIDS epidemic transcended medicine and health. The impact of the disease was felt in every area of society and changed people's ideas about sex. A demarcation line occurred in the 1980s separating the time before AIDS from the time after. If, as Dr. George Lundberg notes in his editorial, before AIDS was a time where sex was trivialized and easy, after AIDS was a time where casual sex was feared. As the disease spread, so did the fear. According to Lundberg and others, if fear of contracting the disease changed people's lifestyles, particularly as it related to sex, then it was for the good.

Several aspects of AIDS were particularly insidious and sobering. A person could have the virus for years and transmit it to others without being or looking sick, and without knowing they had the virus. In addition, in 1985 a diagnosis of AIDS was virtually a death sentence. Most of those who developed a full-blown version of the disease died, as there was no known treatment.

At the beginning of 1985, the federal government was silent on the AIDS epidemic despite its alarming spread. However, by the end of the year it was made a national priority. In early 1986, the Committee on a National Strategy for AIDS was created. Its report, *Confronting AIDS: Directions for Public Health, Health Care, and Research,* was the first major report on AIDS in the world.

Primary Source

"The Age of AIDS: A Great Time for Defensive Living"

SYNOPSIS: Dr. George Lundberg summarizes the facts known about AIDS in June 1985. In order to prevent the transmission of AIDS, he calls for widespread AIDS testing and a change in lifestyle. Note that in the United States at the time, the virus that causes AIDS was called HTLV-III.

It was the age of overindulgence. It was the age of tolerance for anything in anybody. It was the age of fear of imposing one's own social values on someone else. It was the age of the trivialization of sex. It was the age of anticelibacy. It was the age when early teenage sex was commonplace. It was the age when homosexuality came out of the closet and became almost acceptable to those who once found it intolerable. It was the age of easy, irresponsible oversex, abortion on demand, chlamydia, and genital herpes. And it was the age of AIDS.

Not since syphilis among the Spanish, plague among the French, tuberculosis among the Eskimos, and smallpox among the American Indians has there been the threat of such a scourge. Yet, the acquired immunodeficiency syndrome (AIDS) is different from any disease previously seen clinically and epidemiologically. After the torrents of words that have been written and spoken about AIDS, pre-AIDS, and all the rest, is there anything else to say? Yes, a great deal. Thus, this is another *JAMA* theme issue on AIDS with medical news stories, *MMWR,* original contributions, a brief report, a case report, a special communication, questions & answers, letters, and two editorials, all dealing with myriad aspects of this gargantuan problem.

The medical community has responded brilliantly to this new challenge with a rapid outpouring of correct new scientific information. The salient points are:

1. AIDS is caused by an infectious agent, which has been given three names but seems to be a single retrovirus.

2. Many (but not all) who are exposed to the virus become infected, but only some (perhaps 5% to 10% per year) who become infected ultimately demonstrate symptoms.

3. It is possible that cofactors may lower resistance to and promote infectivity of the virus.

4. The virus may be transmitted from an infected person many years before the onset of clinical manifestations.

5. Latency of many years may occur between transmission, infection, and clinically manifest disease.

6. Antibody testing of serum samples is a valuable method to determine who has been exposed to the virus but it does not make the diagnosis of AIDS.

7. A very high percentage of those who develop the full-blown disease die.

8. There is no known treatment for the immune deficiency, and the treatments for complications are variable and inconsistent.

The Dilemma of Serological Testing

In the application of any screening test, the basic principle is first to use a very sensitive test calibrated appropriately so as to have the smallest possible number of false-negative results. Because specificity is sacrificed by such an approach, it is necessary to confirm all positive results by a technically separate and highly specific test that is calibrated appropriately so as to have the smallest possible number of false-positives. Only a specimen positive by both procedures is considered actually positive. Applying this principle in AIDS blood testing makes sense.

The current enzyme-linked immunosorbent assay (ELISA) is excellent for detecting antibody to the third member of the human T-cell leukemia (lymphotropic) retrovirus family (HTLV-III), but it is not perfect. There will be a few false-positive and false-negative results. The problem comes with the variable sensitivity and specificity of ELISA and the extraordinary difference in disease prevalence between middle-aged married women in Kansas (for example) and young single men in San Francisco. The very low general prevalence of clinical AIDS (perhaps four per 100,000) means that with a test with a sensitivity of 95% and a specificity of 99.7%, there will be 99 false-positive results for every one true-positive result. Given the vast range of disease prevalence, it might make sense to use different calibrations for the same tests in populations with greatly differing disease prevalence. In theory, this would allow one to set the number of false-positive results at some reasonable level (such as perhaps 10% rather than 99%) to decrease the number of persons who will experience mental anguish from the false-positive result. But at this time there is no reasonable "gold standard" for the disease against which to evaluate a positive antibody test, short of actual clinical AIDS by the criteria of the Centers for Disease Control. Also, the "incubation period" after being exposed to the virus until the onset of clinical illness may be several years. So it is very difficult to know how to interpret positive serological results.

The Virus Must Be Contained

Except for the blood-donor testing programs, there seem to have been few real efforts by government, medicine, law, the clergy, or society leaders to curtail the transmission of this virus. What small efforts have been present seem, for the most part, to be trivial and ineffective. A notable exception is the response to public health officials of responsible leaders in the homosexual community in educating its members about avoiding transmission of AIDS.

In our technological age we have come to expect and to rely on pharmacologic, surgical, and immunologic methods for the prevention or treatment of disease. But, in fact, much of the greatest current progress is instead being made by changes in life-style. Exercise, diet, limitations on the use of tobacco and alcohol, automobile seatbelts, and the like are having a major influence on the incidence of many diseases.

Widespread application of HTLV-III serological testing will decrease the transmission of AIDS by transfusion, but at a very high price. It may cost as much as $2,000,000 for every case of AIDS prevented by the current blood-donor testing program. But less than 2% of AIDS cases so far have been induced by transfusion. In sharp contrast, more than 70% of AIDS cases seem to have been transmitted sexually. Thus, until a technological method of prevention and treatment can be developed, it will be necessary to contain this virus by changing the life-style of many people—by no means all of them homosexual men. People who are infectious must stop copulating indiscriminately. The chances of this change occurring, however, given our free society and sexual drives seems almost nil. One might re-

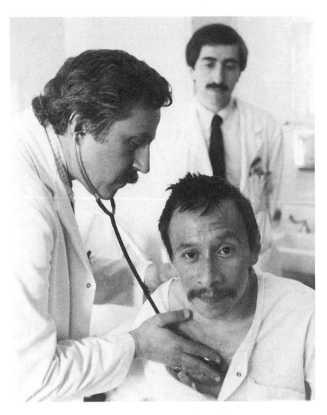

A physician checks the heart of an AIDS patient with a stethoscope at a hospital in Bronx, New York, July 21, 1986. In 1985 it was discovered that AIDS was spreading to the heterosexual population and becoming a threat to any person, regardless of race, age, sex, class, or lifestyle.
© WALLY MCNAMEE/CORBIS. REPRODUCED BY PERMISSION.

call that the natural means of world population control have always been war, famine, and disease and that the fundamental facts of human existence rarely change greatly.

Given the small likelihood of the success of this proposal, it may behoove those people who do not wish to get AIDS to adjust their life-style so as to practice living defensively—particularly in the sexual arena. Individuals have the power to protect themselves more than science currently can. As far as we know, prevention is fairly simple:

1. We should not inject blood or blood products that are infected by the AIDS virus into another person.

2. We should not share injection needles with someone who is infected.

3. Persons who are carrying the AIDS virus should not become pregnant.

4. We should not engage in sexual activity (oral, anal, or vaginal) with someone who has the AIDS virus.

5. We should consider instituting serological testing for HTLV-III before the issuing of marriage licenses.

This is a great time to practice sexual monogamy.

GEORGE D. LUNDBERG, MD

Further Resources

BOOKS

Hall, Lynn, and Tom Modl. *AIDS.* St. Paul, Minn.: Greenhaven, 1988.

Marr, Lisa. *Sexually Transmitted Diseases: A Physician Tells You What You Need to Know.* Baltimore, Md.: Johns Hopkins University Press, 1998.

National Academy of Sciences. *Confronting AIDS: Directions for Public Health, Health Care, and Research.* Washington D.C.: National Academy Press, 1986.

Shilts, Randy. *And the Band Played On: Politics, People, and the AIDS Epidemic.* New York: St. Martin's Press, 1987.

PERIODICALS

Church, Cathleen A., Phyllis T. Piotrow, and John A. Harris. "How Is the Virus Spread?" *Population Reports* 17, no. 3, September 1989, 5–8.

Marx, Jean L. "Spread of AIDS Sparks New Health Concern."*Science,* January 7, 1983, 42–44.

Raymond, Chris Anne. "Pilot Project: Preventing Further AIDS Spread Among Women, General Heterosexual Population." *Journal of the American Medical Association* 259, no. 22, June 10, 1988, 3224–3226.

WEBSITES

Divisions of HIV/AIDS Prevention. U.S. Centers for Disease Control (CDC). Available online at http://www.cdc.gov/hiv /dhap.htm; website home page: http://www.cdc.gov (accessed March 1, 2003).

U.S. CDC National Prevention Information Network. Available online at http://www.cdcnpin.org/ (accessed March 1, 2003).

"Baboon-to-Human Cardiac Xenotransplantation in a Neonate"

Journal article

By: Leonard L. Bailey

Date: December 20, 1985

Source: Bailey, Leonard L., Sandra L. Nehlsen-Cannarella, Waldo Conception, and Weldon B. Jolley. "Baboon-to-Human Cardiac Xenotransplantation in a Neonate." *Journal of the American Medical Association* 254, no. 23, December 20, 1985, 3321–3329.

About the Author: Dr. Leonard Bailey (1942–), who received an MD from Loma Linda in 1969, is a chief surgeon at the Loma Linda Children's Hospital and a member of the infant heart transplant team. The Loma Linda International Heart Institute is a world leader in infant heart transplantation. ∎

Introduction

For some time before the subject of this study, Baby Fae, received her baboon heart, Loma Linda University Medical Center was experimenting with infant heart xenotransplantation between rhesus monkeys and baboons. *Xenotransplantation* refers to the transfer of an organ (or just tissues and cells) from an individual of one species to an individual of another species. Genetically, nonhuman primates such as baboons are very close to humans. Just before Baby Fae was born, Loma Linda researchers had been given approval to begin trials transplanting hearts from infant live baboons into human infants to attempt to save the lives of babies with hypoplastic left heart syndrome (HLHS), a birth defect in which the left ventricle is completely absent or severely malformed.

In October 1984 a baby was born in a Barstow, California, hospital. The blue-eyed brown-haired baby girl was named Stephanie Fae. Premature by about two and a half weeks, Baby Fae was born with HLHS. Since the hospital in Barstow did not have the necessary heart specialists, Baby Fae was transferred to Loma Linda University Medical Center, where Dr. Leonard Bailey transferred a baboon heart into little Baby Fae to save her life.

The biggest challenge in organ transplantation was, and still is, the rejection of the organ and its subsequent destruction by the recipient. Rejection is based on the body's recognition of any foreign tissue as being "bad" and attacking it with either lymphocytes or antibodies. Our bodies identify something as being foreign using protein-based molecules found on the surface of all our cells. "Blood type" refers to molecules found on the surface of red blood cells, while "tissue type" refers to molecules found on the surface of all cells. Any organ, tissue, or cell transferred to another person will be recognized as foreign by the recipient's body if blood and tissue types are not precisely matched.

Baby Fae's transplant was not only cross-species, it was cross-blood-type. Her blood type was O, which is rare in baboons. So Dr. Bailey used a heart from an AB baboon selected because of other typing matches and a minimal reaction between the baboon's blood and the baby's blood. He administered cyclosporine to prevent her from rejecting the baboon's heart. Cyclosporine is a powerful immunosuppressant drug. It acts by suppressing the immune response of the recipient, preventing rejection and destruction of the newly transplanted organ. Cyclosporine, however, is itself a highly toxic drug with many side effects.

Baby Fae lived with her baboon heart for twenty days. According to her doctors, problems did not arise until the fourteenth day after surgery, when tests revealed that she was beginning to reject the baboon heart. Over the next five days, doctors increased her dosages of cyclosporine and other antirejection drugs, supplemented her weakening heart with digitalis, and helped her to breathe with a respirator. Despite their efforts, Baby Fae died twenty days after the transplant.

Significance

Baby Fae's life, though brief, accomplished a great deal. She helped doctors understand infant organ transplantation, and she underscored the need for human infant organ donation. The situation is particularly dire for infants. Obtaining a matching donor heart for a newborn infant is nearly impossible. However, the first successful human-to-human newborn heart transplantation procedure was accomplished at Loma Linda University Medical Center one year after Baby Fae's transplant. The recipient is alive and well today.

Baby Fae's life was also marked by controversy. Her transplant was reported around the world. Demonstrators picketed outside the hospital for different moral, ethical, and religious reasons. Some people were averse to the crossing of a "sacred line" between humans and animals. Some physicians questioned why Dr. Bailey did not even look for a matching human donor, while others wondered about the circumstances in which Baby Fae's parents consented to the procedure.

Some people objected to the use of baboons as "organ factories." At the time of Baby Fae's transplant, however, some animal tissues were already used as heart valve replacements or as temporary skin dressings. Today, some scientists even propose making animals that are genetically modified so that their organs will not trigger an immune response if transferred to humans. Many people morally oppose this practice, however.

Baby Fae's life was donated to science in the hopes that she might live. There are trade-offs in any medical experiment, especially one so dramatic as Baby Fae went through. The doctor must constantly struggle with two objectives, treating the patient and gathering data. The experiment could have saved Baby Fae's life. But she became part of something much larger: saving the lives of those who come after her.

Primary Source

"Baboon-to-Human Cardiac Xenotransplantation in a Neonate" [excerpt]

> **SYNOPSIS:** In these excepts, Dr. Bailey and his medical team report the details of the first case of heart xenotransplantation in an infant.

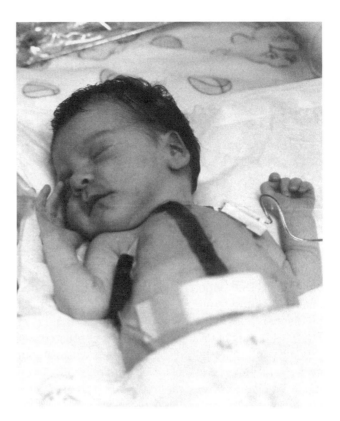

Baby Fae sleeps after being the world's first infant to receive a baboon heart transplant, Loma Linda, California, October 30, 1984. © BETTMANN/CORBIS. REPRODUCED BY PERMISSION.

Hypoplastic left heart syndrome (HLHS) is a spectrum of uniformly lethal congenital cardiovascular malformation. The syndrome is diagnosed in nearly 7.5% of patients with symptomatic heart disease presenting in the first year of life. Most victims perish in the first month of life regardless of therapy. Only one case report describes extended patient survival (3.5 years) without treatment. Experimental palliative operations are being attempted for these unfortunate infants.

These newborns are typically free of additional malformations and deserve consideration for other potentially therapeutic options. One such option is cardiac replacement by orthotopic allotransplantation or xenotransplantation. Cardiac allotransplantation during neonatal life is desirable but, as yet, impractical. Cardiac xenotransplantation has been investigated in neonatal animals in the Loma Linda University School of Medicine Surgical Research Laboratory since 1978. Clinical trials of baboon-to-human cardiac xenotransplantation in neonates with HLHS are predicated on (1) favorable results in animal models; (2) experience using cyclosporine (Sandimmune) in neonatal and young infant animal cardiac transplant hosts; (3) data suggesting variable homology between baboons and humans; and (4) relative immaturity of the newborn immune response. This is a report of the first baboon-to-human orthotopic cardiac transplant performed as investigational therapy for HLHS in a neonate.

Report of a Case

A 2,600-g female neonate was born following 36 weeks of uncomplicated gestation. The newborn's depressed Apgar score, persistent mild cyanosis, and tachypnea prompted early referral to Loma Linda University Medical Center (LLUMC) for investigation of suspected congenital heart disease.

A diagnosis of HLHS was confirmed by echocardiography. The patient's grave prognosis was discussed with the family, who requested that the infant be discharged. On the patient's sixth day of life (Oct 19, 1984), her LLUMC neonatologist contacted her parents and informed them of the possibility of surgery, including cross-species transplantation. The family decided to readmit the infant to LLUMC for life-support intervention and discussion of surgical options. Palliative surgery was rejected by the family. They chose to pursue plans for xenotransplantation and asked that pretransplant evaluation and testing commence. (The protocol and consent process was subsequently reviewed by the National Institutes of Health, Office of Protection From Research Risk.)

The patient, meanwhile, required mechanical ventilation, inotropic support, and continuous infusion of prostaglandin E-1. Central arterial and venous catheters were inserted and used for hemodynamic monitoring and vascular access. Hemodynamic and metabolic stability were achieved and maintained, although serial chest roentgenography showed progressive pulmonary edema. The patient's weight gradually stabilized at 2,200 g. Parental consent for transplantation pended results of initial immunologic and clinical screening. . . .

Cardiac Xenograft Donors

Baboons were young females, weighing 3.6 to 5.4 kg, obtained from the Southwestern Foundation for Biomedical Research, San Antonio, Tex. They were free of microfilaria, hepatitis antigen, cytomegalovirus, and skin, blood, and fecal parasites. Blood culture, complete blood cell count, sedimentation rate, HLA assays, liver profile, tuberculin test, chest roentgenogram, echocardiogram, and electro-

cardiogram had also been used to screen each animal.

Pretransplant Clinical Course

The consent form for cardiac xenotransplantation was signed by both parents on Oct 24 and again on Oct 25. . . .

Comment

Well-motivated attempts by Hardy et al and by Barnard et al to salvage adult victims of terminal heart disease were born of desperation and were unsuccessful. Favorable laboratory research now forms a basis for clinical cardiac xenotransplantation trials in neonates with HLHS.

This first newborn patient to receive an orthotopically implanted baboon heart died of progressive graft necrosis, complicated by acute renal and pulmonary insufficiency. Initial success of this transplantation endeavor was made possible, in part, because lymphocytotoxic antidonor antibodies were absent preoperatively. Hyperacute rejection did not occur. Anti-A and anti-B isoagglutinins to human erythrocytes and low-titered heteroagglutinins to baboon erythrocytes were present in the patient's circulation before transplantation but disappeared afterward. Operative exsanguination and postoperative blood sampling may have played a role in this phenomenon. Anti-A and anti-B isoagglutinins were notably absent terminally. Traces of heteroagglutinins were still detectable in terminal serum samples. Did she selectively fail to produce hemagglutinins postoperatively, or, more likely, were they immediately and continuously absorbed by the baboon graft? Both Reemtsma and Starzl et al report mismatched graft absorption of ABO isoagglutinins. Best and worst results in both these series of renal xenotransplantations correlated with the degree of ABO matching. Species-specific heterohemagglutinins were directed mainly toward donor erythrocytes transferred passively with the graft. . . .

The role played by species-specific lymphocytotoxic antibody produced after xenotransplantation is unclear. Such antibodies were present in at least three of Reemtsma's patients given chimpanzee kidneys, including the patient whose graft survived nine months.

The infant's cellular response to the cardiac xenograft was weak and played virtually no role in graft compromise. In this respect, the infant's reaction resembled that of recipients of chimpanzee kidneys described in Reemtsma's series and is in marked contrast to findings in baboon kidneys implanted into human recipients by Starzl's group. The precise position of baboon-human xenotransplants in the spectrum of concordance (described by Calne) is unclear. Chimpanzees seem to share greater homology with humans, but are virtually unavailable as organ donors. Baboons are generally less concordant with man than are chimpanzees, but it may be feasible to narrow the "disparity gap" by a careful selection process based upon suitable immunologic screening assays. *Experience with this infant recipient resembled that expected of a concordantly xenografted, if not an allografted, patient whose transplant was across ABO blood groups.*

Some degree of homology between baboon and human lymphocyte antigens must exist. Results of MLC and HLA testing between this patient and her donor panel lend credence to this concept. Although the patient failed to make vigorous responses in MLC (possibly because of the reduced tritiated thymidine pulse incubation time), it seemed appropriate to choose as the organ donor the baboon that least stimulated the baby and that responded least to the baby in reverse assay.

Attempted HLA typing of baboon lymphocytes produced interesting results. The fact that human HLA typing reagents react with baboon lymphocytes is probably due to the surprising amount of homology found between disparate members of the animal kingdom. This fact, however, does not explain why some of the typing reagents consistently reacted with baboon cells and others did not.

Cytochemical and other noninvasive testing results, including those of echocardiography and electrocardiography, were indicative of myocardial injury but nonspecific for rejection. Appearance of a pre-MM fraction of creatine kinase isoenzymes (specific to the xenograft) seemed to be a sensitive measure of graft injury. . . .

Graft changes observed in this case appear to have resulted from anoxia producing necrosis of deeper fibers and mitochondria swelling of surviving fibers. Fatty infiltration was a secondary phenomenon, since it was not prominent in necrotic myocytes. These changes are consistent with hemagglutinin-mediated injury. Very similar histologic changes, however, have been reported following myocardial injury of numerous etiologies, including anthracycline and ethanol toxicity.

Some postmortem changes identified in this clinical case have subsequently been reproduced by us in a xenograft laboratory model (pig-to-newborn goat

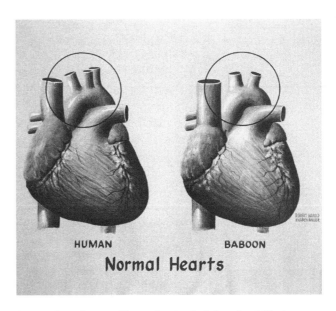

A comparison of a normal human heart and a baboon heart. The two are similar enough to allow for successful transplants between species. © BETTMANN/CORBIS. REPRODUCED BY PERMISSION.

orthotopic cardiac transplant) known to be erythrocyte incompatible (unpublished data). These laboratory hosts (surviving up to 30 days) received cyclosporine and azathioprine immunosuppression. Changes in grafts from these animals include (1) patchy myocyte necrosis; (2) vascular endothelial cell, myocardial cell, and mitochondrial edema; and (3) minimal lymphocyte and other leukocytic infiltration. These histologic findings appear to be antibody and/or complement mediated despite immunosuppression. Postmortem changes, notably missing in these pig-to-goat xenografts in comparison with the baboon-to-human graft, include (1) erythrocyte abnormalities, (2) marked interstitial hemorrhage, and (3) lipid infiltration.

In summary, it has been demonstrated that cardiac replacement by orthotopic xenotransplantation is technically feasible in the small neonate with HLHS. A gratifying early recovery and survival to 20 days were documented. Minimal cell-mediated graft rejection was observed. Factors contributing to xenograft injury may include (1) ABO hemagglutinins, (2) species-specific cytotoxic antibody, (3) lipid-induced cyclosporine myocardiotoxicity, and (4) lipid and/or antibody-induced erythrocyte aberrations (also responsible for renal and respiratory failure.)

A reasonable yet speculative explanation for graft and patient loss follows. Crossing the ABO barrier (even in a neonatal recipient) placed the graft and host in a highly vulnerable situation. Crossing this barrier does not necessarily preclude graft survival, but is generally avoided in human allotransplantation. Although human ABO antigens are expressed poorly on baboon erythrocytes, they are expressed on other baboon tissues, including salivary glands, mucous membranes, and gastrointestinal mucous and on vascular endothelium. The infant (type O) was destined to develop a significant titer of A and B hemagglutinins, particularly with the stimulus of a probable ABO mismatched graft. These ABO antibodies and/or antibaboon antibodies were gradually absorbed by the graft, producing injury to the largest endothelial bed, namely, the microcirculatory vessels. This phenomenon resulted in widespread microvascular luminal narrowing. Circulatory sludging, thrombosis, cellular hypoxia, and myocyte injury and/or necrosis followed. Edematous and porous microvascular endothelium permitted interstitial hemorrhage and lipid accumulation. Lipophylic cyclosporine may have achieved high concentrations within graft myocytes and interstitial spaces, exacerbating graft injury by direct myocyte toxicity. Erythrocytes, trapped in regions of lipid accumulations, developed secondary morphological changes.

More difficult to understand are the erythrocyte changes that appear to have produced glomerular obstruction and renal failure during the patient's last four postoperative days. In the absence of pulmonary edema, respiratory insufficiency during the patient's final 48 hours may have been on a similar basis, viz, scattered microvascular obstruction and resultant hypoxemia. Histologic sections of kidney and lung support this concept. What would produce this apparent erythrocyte "adhesiveness"? The infant was receiving small daily infusions of screened, washed, and irradiated erythrocytes. Did donor erythrocyte processing contribute to microcirculatory sludging? Did infusion of 20% lipid emulsion with cyclosporine during her posttransplant course adversely affect erythrocyte and/or microcirculatory physiology? One plausible explanation for erythrocyte pathophysiology in this case would be development of an autoimmunized state directed against the H antigen on human type O erythrocytes as an immunologic over-response to the antigenic load by the ABO-incompatible graft. Such a phenomenon has been observed (W. W. Socha, MD, J. Moor-Jankowski, MD, oral communication, June 1985).

Data derived from this first clinical trial suggest that cardiac xenotransplantation for the management of neonatal HLHS is a reasonable investiga-

tive option. Protocol changes, including a simultaneous search for an allograft donor during the preoperative workup, avoidance of an ABO mismatch, more restrained use of lipid emulsion, and, possibly, inclusion of antiplatelet agents (aspirin and dipyridamole) in small dosage, should result in extended graft and patient survival.

Further Resources

BOOKS

Fishman, Jay, David H. Sachs, and Rashid Shaikh. *Xenotransplantation: Scientific Frontiers and Public Policy.* New York: New York Academy of Sciences, 1998.

Munson, Ronald. *Raising the Dead: Organ Transplants, Ethics, and Society.* New York: Oxford University Press, 2002.

PERIODICALS

Ashwal, S., A.L Caplan, W.A. Cheatham, Evans, R.W., and J.L. Peabody. "Social and Ethical Controversies in Pediatric Heart Transplantation." *Journal of Heart and Lung Transplantation* 5, September/October 1991, 860–876.

Bailey, L.L., S. Gundry, and A. Razzouk. "Bless the Babies, 115 Late Survivors of Heart Transplantation During the First Year of Life." *Journal of Thoracic and Cardiovascular Surgery* 105, May 1993, 805–815.

O'Neil, Paul. "The Heart That Failed." *Discover,* January 1985, 14–20.

WEBSITES

Loma Linda University Medical Center International Heart Institute. Heart Transplantation. Available online at http://www.llu.edu/ihi/iheart.htm; website home page: http://www.llu.edu (accessed March 10, 2003).

United Network for Organ Sharing. Available online at http://www.unos.org/ (accessed March 10, 2003).

"The Health Consequences of Involuntary Smoking"

Journal article

By: U.S. Centers for Disease Control (CDC)

Date: December 19, 1986

Source: Centers for Disease Control and Prevention. "Perspectives in Disease Prevention and Health Promotion 1986 Surgeon General's Report: The Health Consequences of Involuntary Smoking." *Morbidity and Mortality Weekly Report* 35, no. 50, December 19, 1986, 769–770.

About the Organization: The U.S. Centers for Disease Control (CDC), an agency of the Department of Health and Human Services, is the lead federal agency protecting the health of Americans. Headquartered in Atlanta, the CDC focuses on disease control and prevention, health education, and health promotion. Part of the CDC mission is to collect and disseminate health data. The *Morbidity and Mortality Weekly Report*

(MMWR) is one vehicle used to do this. The MMWR includes reports about infectious and chronic diseases, environmental hazards, natural or human-generated disasters, occupational diseases and injuries, and other injuries, gleaned from reports by state health departments across the nation. ■

Introduction

Tobacco smoking began in the Americas. Historians believe the tobacco plant, *Nicotiana tobacum,* grew all over the Americas in the early history of civilization. The Mayas of Mexico were among the first people to begin rolling and smoking tobacco leaves. As civilization and society spread in America, so too did tobacco. Tobacco was so prominent in the southern United States that in many respects it provided the basis for the region's history. By the 1950s, cigarette ads were one of the hallmarks of radio and television advertising. Cigarettes were also a part of the persona of popular actors such as Humphrey Bogart and James Dean.

However, the 1950s also saw the beginning of public evidence that smoking was bad for health. In 1950, American and British researchers published papers presenting evidence that smoking causes lung cancer. In 1957 an extensive study commissioned by the American Cancer Society showed that heavy smoking significantly shortens life span. Then, in 1964, a landmark report was issued. The first U.S. Surgeon General's Report on smoking came out and argued that smoking is a major health risk for cancer, cardiovascular disease, and emphysema. Following this, the U.S. Congress passed a law in 1965 requiring labels on cigarette packages: "Warning: Cigarette Smoking may be Hazardous to your Health." In 1970, Congress acted again, banning cigarette advertising on television and radio and requiring stronger health warnings on cigarettes.

In the 1980s, Surgeon General C. Everett Koop waged an all-out war on smoking. Cigarette smoking was (and still is) associated with more deaths than drugs, alcohol, auto accidents, and AIDS combined. Each year in the 1980s, the surgeon general's office published a report on the health consequences of smoking. Koop was responsible for many of these. In 1980, it was about women and smoking; in 1981, about cancer and smoking; in 1982, secondhand smoke, or passive smoking, also called exposure to environmental tobacco smoke (ETS). The 1986 report *The Health Consequences of Involuntary Smoking* was the nineteenth surgeon general's report on smoking since the landmark 1964 report.

Significance

In 1981, one of the first reports on the effects of passive smoking was published. "The Hirayama Study" was conducted by Japanese scientist Takeshi Hirayama, chief of epidemiology of the Research Institute at Tokyo's Na-

A mother smokes while playing with her child. In 1986 the Surgeon General released a report on the health consequences associated with secondhand smoke. © JENNIE WOODCOCK; REFLECTIONS PHOTOLIBRARY/CORBIS. REPRODUCED BY PERMISSION.

tional Cancer Center. It contained fourteen years of research on ninety-two thousand nonsmoking wives of smoking husbands compared with a similar-sized group of nonsmoking wives whose husbands were also nonsmokers. The results were striking. The women whose husbands were smokers had a 40 to 90 percent increase in the incidence of lung cancer. There was a direct correlation between the number of cigarettes the husband smoked per day and the increased risk of lung cancer for the wife. A woman whose husband smoked up to fourteen cigarettes a day showed a 40 percent elevated risk; those whose husbands smoked fifteen to nineteen cigarettes a day had a 60 percent higher risk; and those whose husbands smoked a pack or more a day had a 90 percent heightened risk.

In 1982, a year after the Hirayama report, Surgeon General Koop published a report that said there was a possibility that secondhand smoke *may cause* lung cancer. His 1986 report, however, was definitive: Involuntary smoking *causes* lung cancer in healthy nonsmokers. The report pointed out the risk to children whose parents smoked. Children's respiratory systems are still developing, and the effect of environmental tobacco smoke on their immature lungs is especially worrisome. In general, the children of smokers have a slower start in life.

Reports on the adverse health effects of passive smoke provided a basis for a steady stream of public smoking bans. In 1987, Beverly Hills, California, banned smoking in restaurants. Pennsylvania's 1988 Clean Indoor Air Act required restaurants with 75 or more seats to provide a nonsmoking section. In 1989, Congress passed legislation banning smoking on all domestic U.S. air flights. In 1995, California banned smoking in all restaurants.

Primary Source

"The Health Consequences of Involuntary Smoking"

SYNOPSIS: The U.S. Centers for Disease Control's *Morbidity and Mortality Weekly Report* highlights the surgeon general's 1986 findings on the effects of passive smoking on healthy nonsmokers and children.

Inhalation of tobacco smoke during active cigarette smoking remains the largest single preventable cause of death and disability in the United States. The health consequences of cigarette smoking and of the use of other tobacco products have been extensively documented in the 18 previous Surgeon General's reports issued by the Public Health Service. More than 300,000 premature deaths that are directly attributable to tobacco use—particularly cigarette smoking—occur each year in the United States. The magnitude of the disease risk for active smokers, secondary to their high dose exposure to tobacco smoke, suggests that the lower doses of smoke received by involuntary smokers also puts them at risk. The 1986 Surgeon General's Report explores the health consequences incurred by involuntary smokers. It was developed by the Office on Smoking and Health, Center for Health Promotion and Education, Centers for Disease Control (CDC) as part of the U. S. Department of Health and Human Services' responsibility under Public Law 91-222 to report new and current information on smoking and health to the U. S. Congress. Data in the 1986 report present evidence that the chemical composition of sidestream smoke (smoke emitted into the environment by a smoker between puffs) is qualitatively similar to the mainstream smoke inhaled by the smoker and that both mainstream and sidestream smoke act as carcinogens in bioassay systems (1). Data on the environmental levels of the components of tobacco smoke and on nicotine absorption in nonsmokers suggest that nonsmokers are exposed to levels of environmental tobacco smoke (ETS) that would be expected to generate a lung cancer risk. In addition, epidemiological studies of populations exposed to ETS have documented an increased risk for lung cancer in those nonsmokers with increased exposure. Of the 13 epidemiological studies that were available for review in the scientific literature, 11 reported a positive relationship and six of these observed statistically significant results. It is rare to have such detailed exposure data or human epidemiologic studies on disease occurrence when attempting to evaluate the

risk of low-dose exposure to an agent with established toxicity at higher levels of exposure. The relative abundance of data reviewed in the report, their cohesiveness, and their biologic plausibility allow a judgment that involuntary smoking can cause lung cancer in nonsmokers.

The 1986 Surgeon General's Report comes to three major conclusions:

1. Involuntary smoking is a cause of disease, including lung cancer, in healthy nonsmokers.

2. Compared with children of nonsmoking parents, children whose parents smoke have an increased frequency of respiratory symptoms and infections. They also have slightly smaller rates of increase in lung function as the lung matures.

3. Simple separation of smokers and nonsmokers within the same air space may reduce, but does not eliminate, ETS exposure.

The report also reviews policies restricting smoking in public places and the workplace and states that, in the 1970s, an increasing number of public and private sector institutions began adopting policies to protect individuals from ETS exposure by restricting the circumstances in which smoking is permitted. Local governments have been enacting smoking ordinances at an increasing rate since 1980. Restrictions on smoking at the workplace have resulted from both governmental action and private initiative, and an increase in workplace smoking policies has been a trend of the 1980s. Laws restricting smoking in public places have been implemented with few problems and at little cost to state and local governments. Public opinion polls document strong and growing support for restricting or banning smoking in a wide range of public places.

The Surgeon General, in his preface to the report, states, "Cigarette smoking is an addictive behavior, and the individual smoker must decide whether or not to continue that behavior; however, it is evident from the data presented in this volume that the choice to smoke cannot interfere with the nonsmokers' right to breathe air free of tobacco smoke." Reported by Office on Smoking and Health, Center for Health Promotion and Education, CDC.

Editorial Note

A review recently published by the National Academy of Sciences states that approximately 20% of the estimated 12,200 lung cancer deaths occurring annually in nonsmokers are attributable to environmental tobacco smoke (2). This estimate falls close to the mid-point of the range published by Repace and Lowery, who state that between 500 and 5,000 lung cancer deaths may occur annually as a result of nonsmokers' exposure to tobacco smoke (3). By comparison, figures published in the Journal of the Air Pollution Control Association estimate that between 1,300 and 1,700 total cases of cancer resulting from other air pollutants in the general environment occur each year in the United States (4). Thus, while the number of lung cancer deaths that may be related to ETS exposure is small compared with those caused by active smoking, the actual number of lung cancer deaths caused annually by involuntary smoking is large. In addition, ETS causes more cases of cancer annually than many other agents in the general environment that are regulated because of their potential to cause disease.

Further Resources

BOOKS

Glantz, Stanton A. *The Cigarette Papers*. Berkeley, Calif.: University of California Press, 1996.

Kluger, Richard. *Ashes to Ashes: America's Hundred-Year Cigarette War, the Public Health, and the Unabashed Triumph of Philip Morris*. New York: Knopf, 1996.

Smoking and Health: Report of the Advisory Committee to the Surgeon General of the Public Health Service. Washington D.C.: U.S. Department of Health, Education and Welfare, Public Health Service, 1964.

PERIODICALS

Hirayama, Takeshi. "Non-smoking Wives of Heavy Smokers Have a Higher Risk of Lung Cancer: A Study from Japan." *British Medical Journal* 282, January 17, 1981, 183–185.

Ong, Elisa, and Stanton A. Glatz. "Hirayama's Work Has Stood the Test of Time."*Bulletin of the World Health Organization* 78, no. 7, 2000, 938–939.

WEBSITES

Tobacco.org. "Tobacco Timeline." Available online at http://www.tobacco.org/resources/history/Tobacco_History.html; website home page http://www.tobacco.org (accessed March 8, 2003).

U.S. Centers for Disease Control. "Tobacco Information and Prevention Source." Available online at http://www.cdc.gov/tobacco/; website home page http://www.cdc.gov (accessed March 8, 2003).

The Bill Schroeder Story

Memoirs

By: Bill Schroeder Family and Martha Barnette
Date: 1987

Source: The Schroeder Family with Martha Barnette. *The Bill Schroeder Story*. New York: William Morrow and Company, 1987, 13–15, 245–249.

About the Authors: Bill Schroeder's children—Monica Bohnert, Melvin Schroeder, Stan Schroeder, Terry Schroeder, Cheryl Schroeder, and Rod Schroeder—and his wife, Margaret wrote *The Bill Schroeder Story* with the assistance of writer Martha Barnette. For many years, the family traveled both in the United States and abroad, following Bill in his Air Force career. All of the Schroeder children, along with their mother, were by Bill Schroeder's side throughout the artificial heart transplant ordeal.

Martha Barnette (1957–) received her bachelor's degree from Vassar College in 1981. Barnette worked as a reporter for the *Louisville Times* from 1981 to 1985. She covered Bill Schroeder's artificial heart transplant for the *Washington Post*. She has been writing for national magazines since 1991 and, as of 2003, continued to work as a freelance writer ■

Introduction

In the 1980s, many medical professionals looked to artificial heart transplantations and xenotransplantations (transplanting an organ from another species, such as baboons) to overcome a chronic shortage of donated human hearts. Artificial hearts, it was reasoned, would always be available, since they could be manufactured. Implantation of artificial hearts also eliminated or lessened the need for strong, and toxic, immune-suppressing drugs like cyclosporine, since theoretically they should not trigger an immune response.

One of the best known artificial hearts, the Jarvik-7, was invented by Robert K. Jarvik, an American doctor. The Jarvik-7 was made of plastic, aluminum, and Dacron polyester. It consisted of two pumps representing the human heart's two ventricles. The Jarvik-7 was unable to obtain energy from the blood, so it needed an external power source to provide the pumping action. Two tubes connected to an air compressor pumped air in and out of the artificial heart. The tubes entered through the patient's abdomen. Implantation of the Jarvik-7 required the patient to be connected to the pumping machines (a smaller portable pump and a larger stationary one) for the rest of their lives.

Bill Schroeder was one of six patients in the 1980s to receive the Jarvik-7 artificial heart. Each of the six faced enormous physical and emotional challenges, and all eventually suffered serious complications and died. Schroeder was diabetic and had smoked cigarettes for thirty years before quitting in 1982. His heart was starved for oxygen due to severely clogged coronary arteries. Starting in 1982, he had several heart attacks, each one slowly deteriorating more and more of his heart tissue. Medication and coronary bypass surgery in 1983 failed to stabilize his heart, and his cardiac doctor began to look for options. At first, he considered a human heart transplant, but eligibility guidelines for donated organs would

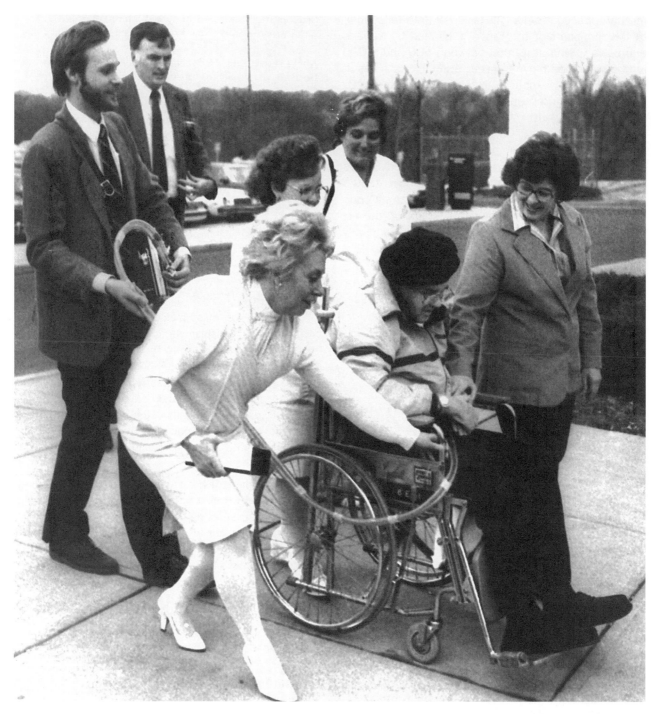

William Schroeder is accompanied into a hospital with his wife and hospital employees, Louisville, Kentucky, February 22, 1985. The man on the left holds the external compressor for his artificial heart. **AP/WIDE WORLD PHOTOS. REPRODUCED BY PERMISSION.**

likely rule out the fifty-two-year-old diabetic. Another heart attack in October 1984 compelled the cardiologist to contact Dr. William DeVries, a controversial and world-famous heart surgeon who two years before had implanted the first artificial heart in Seattle dentist Barney Clark. A month later, on November 25, 1984, Dr. DeVries inserted the Jarvik-7 into Bill Schroeder's chest.

Schroeder and his family were euphoric after he received his artificial heart. Two days later, when Dr. DeVries removed the respirator, Bill asked for a beer. The media would record virtually every moment of Bill's experience. Nearly three weeks later, however, Bill began to suffer complications: strokes, seizures, depression, fever, and flulike illnesses. He received frequent blood transfusions and a variety of drugs, including several experimental medications. Another series of strokes and ensuing lung complications finally ended his ordeal. In the end, Bill had died, but eerily the Jarvik-7 still pumped until Dr. DeVries and the Schroeder family turned it off in a symbolic gesture. The entire 620-day ordeal, the longest any one had ever survived with an artificial heart, had emotionally changed Bill Schroeder's family in ways they could not anticipate.

Significance

The Jarvik heart was implanted into six patients in the 1980s. DeVries, who implanted five of them, hoped they would provide a permanent alternative to transplanting a human heart. However, severe complications from the procedure and the death of all artificial heart recipients raised many doubts about the viability of permanent artificial hearts. Since then, artificial hearts have mainly been used as a stop-gap measure to keep severely ill patients alive while they await a donated human heart.

From the 1980s until 2001, no one had performed a complete artificial heart transplant. To many, the loss of quality of life was too high a price to pay and the procedure was largely abandoned. But because of an ongoing shortage of human heart donors, many doctors still hope that artificial hearts will provide a cure for irreparable and devastating heart damage. A new artificial heart was developed and implanted into a patient in 2001. The AbioCor heart is a self-contained titanium and plastic pump made by a Massachusetts company. Since the AbioCor is self-contained, the risk of infection is greatly reduced. However, Robert Tools, the first person to receive the AbioCor, died of internal bleeding and organ failure after living with the device for 151 days.

The heart performs a rather simple mechanical function, but the living heart has proven to be tough to replace. The heart extracts fuel and nutrients from the blood and uses them to rebuild itself continuously. No one has yet devised a self-sustaining pump that can go for seventy years or more without any maintenance.

Primary Source

The Bill Schroeder Story [excerpt]

SYNOPSIS: These excerpts provide a glimpse of the emotions the family of Bill Schroeder experienced. The initial glee and hope when Bill was told he would be given an artificial heart turned into the harsh reality of severe physical complications, conflict from being in a medical experiment, and an emotionally depleted family. Finally, the family accepted that Bill was going to die and were grateful for the extra time they had with Bill.

His strength was seeping away with every hour. Margaret sat on the side of the bed, stroking his arm, just wishing she could give him a little bit of her own life. Her husband wasn't saying anything, but she knew that even now, especially now, Bill Schroeder hated to be kept waiting. He'd been in this hospital almost two weeks, had let them run all kinds of tests—and the doctors still hadn't said for sure that he could get that artificial heart.

The doctors back home had said that without a new heart, Bill would die in less than a month. His diabetes and age ruled out the possibility of a human heart transplant. He was down to the last resort. If the doctors here really were going to choose him for the artificial heart, it would have to be soon. If not . . .

The door opened, and Dr. William DeVries walked in, trailed by several members of his medical team. The tall, sandy-haired surgeon was smiling as they formed a half-circle around Bill's bed.

"Well, Bill," DeVries said, "we've decided to go for it. You're now officially a candidate for the artificial heart."

"Fine with me," Bill said quickly. "When do we do it?"

First, DeVries explained, they'd have to read over and discuss a seven-page consent form, to make sure that Bill understood everything. DeVries would read it to him now and Bill would sign it. They'd go over the whole thing again, twenty-four hours later, then Bill would sign it again to show that he knew what he was doing. Margaret reached for Bill's hand. The lanky surgeon sat down beside them and began reading aloud.

" . . . I recognize that the ventricles—the larger two of the heart's four pumping chambers—from my own natural heart will be removed . . ."

Margaret couldn't believe it. It was like a dream. *They really are going to give him the artificial heart.*

" . . . risks include: (a) emboli or blood clots which may lead to stroke, kidney loss, liver, bowel or lung dysfunction, or damage to other organs or body functions . . ."

She squeezed Bill's hand. *We made it. We really made it! Bill's going to get himself that artificial heart.*

" . . . During his life with the Total Artificial Heart, Dr. Clark experienced kidney and lung problems, a pneumothorax, which is air in the lung cavity, valve breakage, seizures, bleeding complications, and depression. He remained hospitalized during the entire hundred-and-twelve-day period . . ."

Bill didn't say a word. He just watched DeVries and nodded every once in a while. After hanging on this long, he certainly wasn't going to quit now.

" . . . No representations or guarantees have been made to me either that the procedure will be successful, or the length of time or the level at which the Total Artificial Heart will function . . ."

At least now we have a chance. I'm going to bring him home with me and we can be a family again.

" . . . I understand that the materials which are made public, as described in this paragraph, will protect my modesty and be within generally accepted bounds of good taste . . ."

Oh, come on, Dr. DeVries. You know we trust you. You just get Bill better.

" . . . I acknowledge by my signature to this special consent form that I have read and understand the foregoing, including the risks involved . . ."

Margaret thought he would never finish reading. *Of course* she wanted the doctors to save her husband. Bill was only fifty-two, with everything to live for—their grandbaby due in the spring, their third son's wedding four months away, just the chance to come back home and live out whatever time he had left with his family. DeVries could read that thing backwards and sideways if he wanted to, as long as he gave Bill that artificial heart.

"Do you have any more questions?" DeVries asked. "Anything at all?"

"No," Bill answered. "I understand everything." He reached for the pen.

It was like an answer to prayer, the thought of Bill getting well again. He had really shown those doctors that he was their man: a positive attitude, a strong will to survive, cherished goals to live for, and a close family to support him until he got back on his feet.

Margaret couldn't wait to tell the kids.

■ ■ ■

Although Bill showed little improvement, the Schroeders took some comfort at least in the knowledge that new strides were being made in heart implantation, thanks in part to Bill's struggle. By the spring of 1986, there had been about two dozen implants of temporary artificial hearts, including not only the Jarvik heart, but others developed at Penn

State, in Phoenix, Arizona, and in Berlin, West Germany. A twenty-five-year-old Arizona man who had received a human heart transplant in September after being kept alive for several days with a Jarvik heart—and who had suffered a mild transient stroke while on the device—was back at work as a supermarket manager. The Swedish man who had received a Jarvik heart, Leif Stenberg, had been well enough to hold a press conference in July. He'd spent his days in a Stockholm apartment, and returned to the hospital each night. But he suffered a severe stroke in September, gradually lost consciousness, slipped into a coma, and died in late November. Murray Haydon remained in the hospital, since he had respiratory problems and infections.

In early April the family's regular meetings with DeVries began to take on a different tone. The doctor explained that a biopsy of Bill's liver over the past several weeks showed that the infection was getting worse, and nothing could be done to reverse it. He warned them that Bill's condition could only deteriorate.

The doctor showed the family some charts of the enzyme levels in Bill's liver, a measure of how the organ was functioning. Normally, patients whose levels were in the hundreds would be very, very ill. Bill's were slowly climbing above three thousand. Few people ever survived for long with such high enzyme levels, but again, Bill's artificial heart didn't suffer the damage which would be expected in patients with a normal heart. The focus of the Schroeders' discussions with DeVries now shifted from getting Bill well to assuring the family members that the medical world was gaining unprecedented scientific knowledge from him, that he had confounded all the doctors' predictions, and that he was still making history every day. What DeVries was saying was that they had to start preparing for Bill's death. It was most likely that the liver infection would spread, and he would lapse into a coma and never come out of it. As time went on, the kidneys might fail, in which case the family would face the question of whether to put him on dialysis. Or his lungs might collapse, and they'd have to decide whether to put him on a respirator. Ultimately, if he were to lapse into a coma for a long time, they would have to decide whether to turn off the artificial heart and let him die.

It was difficult to imagine ever turning off the heart that Bill had wanted so badly, or ending the battle he had fought so hard. But the family unanimously agreed on one thing at this point: no more artificial measures.

At this point, the Schroeders also began to reflect on their own roles in the experiment. They recognized that they had entered the artificial heart program with very little understanding of what a medical experiment entailed. They knew that from the beginning they should have asked more questions. They definitely should have asked Bill what he wanted done in certain eventualities, such as being unable to talk or make decisions on his own or refuse certain tests. They should have discussed frankly how much each member of the family would be able to help out during and after Bill's hospitalization.

If they'd had to do it over, they would have insisted that from the beginning that Bill have a small, consistent team of nurses to follow him throughout the experiment. They would have made sure that a lawyer went over the consent form to advise them of their legal rights and responsibilities. They would have quizzed their family doctors on every aspect of the complications listed in it. The consent form had clearly stated that having an artificial heart meant the risk of stroke, but it couldn't list every implication—that, in turn, stroke might mean grueling, exhausting physical therapy, or, ultimately, a suctioning of his mouth and nose every few minutes. The family would also have tape-recorded more of their meetings with the medical team —something that might have made the doctors feel threatened, but that seemed the only way to be sure that everyone understood what was happening. It was too easy to get caught up in things and never really hear what the doctors had said.

They would have insisted that Bill and the family have regularly scheduled, inviolable private time together. And that, in turn, he be informed it was impossible for the family to be with him all the time—that they should probably spend one day a week away from him, from day one and consistently throughout.

The family also began to understand the trade-offs involved in any medical experiment, whether clinical trials of a new painkilling drug or a new surgical device. Had they been asked to advise potential candidates for an artificial heart or any other experiment, they would have said:

You have to gamble on the possibility that the experiment might help you, but you also have to recognize that you will be part of a much larger project that may not save your life—that might even kill you—but could save the lives of thousands in the future. You have to accept the fact that, in a way,

Dr. William DeVries holds an artificial heart, December 2, 1982. The heart he holds is much like the Jarvik-7 that William Schroeder received. © BETTMANN/CORBIS. REPRODUCED BY PERMISSION.

you will be donating your body to science while you are still alive. And you have to understand that your doctor will constantly struggle to walk a fine line between treating you and gathering data. You must understand and expect that mistakes will be made.

The Schroeders had thought all along that it was the artificial heart which was being tested. Now they realized that the experiment extended beyond the heart, the patient, the apartment—to the family itself. So many situations had come up that had never been faced before, and everyone, medical team and family alike, had had to make things up as they went along. And all of them had changed.

The whole family found themselves more serious than before, less certain that anything in life could ever come easily. The kids found that, in drawing closer to each other, they had lost touch with many of their friends. Their lives had become so unpredictable that they couldn't be counted on to join their old pals for outings or parties, and much of their leisure time was taken up by regular trips to Louisville anyway. They found it hard to start a project at home, even something as simple as painting a fence or planning a gathering, because they never knew if it would be interrupted. Many friends hesitated to bother them, uncertain whether to ask how their parents were doing. Sometimes the ordeal was the only thing the Schroeders wanted to talk about; sometimes they wished they didn't have to talk about it at all. They often felt set apart from everyone else, as if they had moved away for a long time and no longer fit into their old circles.

The Schroeders also were struck by how much DeVries himself had changed. At the time of Bill's operation, the surgeon had looked like a skinny young man barely out of college. Within a year much of his sandy hair had turned silver, and his boyish freckled face was deeply lined.

On some level Bill himself seemed to understand that he was still accomplishing something just by being alive, helping provide information that the doctors had never dreamed of obtaining. His medical chart now occupied more than eight feet of shelf space. When DeVries came to visit and tell him how much they were learning, Bill would listen and nod.

In fact, he often seemed more alert than ever during this period. He'd play possum sometimes, but if someone exclaimed at something seen out the window, he'd snap awake and look, too. If the doctors turned their backs to discuss his medical condition, Margaret could see Bill was craning his neck to look around them and listen. The doctors told her that it was possible that he was more alert and perceptive now because the damage from the strokes was continuing to resolve itself. Every once in a while though, it took him a minute to recognize people.

There was a lot of time to think during those long days at Bill's bedside. Sometimes Margaret would get up to check the Utah console or look at the computer readouts, or just gaze in amazement at the machine that had become a part of her husband, that went wherever he went, and had never ceased its mechanical, life-giving rhythm. She would think back to her roots in the hilly farm country outside Jasper, remembering how her grandmother used to come into the cabin with her apron full of sassafras roots for tea to thin her blood in the summertime, or hang leeks and herbs from the ceiling to dry for medicines. If Margaret could observe so much change in her own lifetime, she wondered, what was going to happen by the time the grandkids were grown?

Sometimes when DeVries talked to Margaret now, she wouldn't say a word to him. She was sure the doctor must think she was being angry or moody. That wasn't the case at all—it was that he'd gestured with his hands, and she couldn't take her eyes off them. *Those hands took out Bill's heart and put in an artificial one and made him live again. Those hands gave me back my husband.* Whatever their conflicts during the past, whatever the hardships and disappointments, and whatever was down the road, this fact remained: Those giant-sized hands had given Bill and the family some more time, moments that no one could ever take away. Just as nothing could change her gratitude toward Dr. DeVries, she also knew that she could never find the words to thank him enough. And sometimes she just couldn't say anything at all to him.

Further Resources

BOOKS
DeBakey, Michael, and Antonio Gotto. *The Living Heart.* New York: D. McKay, 1977.

Fox, Renee C., and Judith P. Swazey. *Spare Parts: Organ Replacement in American Society.* New York: Oxford University Press, 1992.

Hogness, John R., and Malin VanAntwerp. *The Artificial Heart: Prototypes, Policies, and Patients.* Washington, D.C.: National Academy Press, 1991.

PERIODICALS
Breo, Dennis L. "Surgeon (William DeVries) Foresees Artificial Heart as 'Shelf Item.'" *American Medical News* 29, September 12, 1986, 1–6.

Kunzig, Robert. "The Beat Goes On." *Discover* 21, no. 1, January 2000, 33.

Lawrie, Gerald M. "Permanent Implantation of the Jarvik-7 Total Artificial Heart: A Clinical Perspective." *Journal of the American Medical Association* 259, no. 6, February 12, 1988, 892–894.

McCarthy, Patrick M., and William A. Smith. "Mechanical Circulatory Support—a Long and Winding Road." *Science,* February 8, 2002, 998–1000.

Toufexis, Anastasia. "Stilling the Artificial Beat: After 620 Days, Jarvik-7 Recipient William Schroeder Succumbs." *Time,* August 18, 1986, 58.

WEBSITES
Franklin Institute. "Building a Better Heart." Available online at http://sln.fi.edu/biosci/healthy/fake.html; website home page: http://sln.fi.edu (accessed March 9, 2003).

Alzheimer's: A Caregiver's Guide and Sourcebook
Guidebook

By: Howard Gruetzner

Date: 1988

Source: Gruetzner, Howard. *Alzheimer's: A Caregiver's Guide and Sourcebook.* New York: Wiley, 1988, 60–66.
About the author: Howard Gruetzner, M.Ed. is Director of the Heart of Texas Region Mental Health Mental Retardation Center Elder Services. He is also the founder of the Alzheimer's Family Support Group in the region. He conducts seminars on dementia and other geriatric mental health problems. ∎

Introduction

Alois Alzheimer was the first to link the mental impairment of older persons with a distinctive and abnormal brain physiology. He described the brain of what would come to be called an Alzheimer's patient in 1906. A fifty-one-year-old woman at the Munich psychiatric hospital had died after four years of progressive confusion, memory loss, and intellectual decline. Alzheimer autopsied her brain and found some unusual plaques and tangles in and around the brain cells (neurons). His mentor at the University of Munich later named this condition Alzheimer's disease.

Alzheimer's disease gained prominence in the 1980s. For most of the twentieth century, Alzheimer's was considered relatively rare. Older persons with confusion and mental decline were said to be "senile." However, in the 1980s it was realized that the majority of older persons suffering from senility in fact had Alzheimer's disease. The nation's health care system was not set up to care for Alzheimer's patients, putting most of the burden on the families, who were overwhelmed by the emotional, financial, and physical burden. The National Institutes of Health called Alzheimer's one of the biggest public health dilemmas ever encountered.

Alzheimer's disease is difficult to diagnose. The only way to verify its presence is by a meticulous examination of the brain cells. The presence of plaques and tangles, just as Alois Alzheimer observed almost one hundred years ago, is still required for a definitive diagnosis of the disease. Unfortunately, the only way this can be done is during an autopsy once the patient has died. The difficulty in diagnosing Alzheimer's is part of the reason the disease was overlooked for so many years.

During the 1980s significant insights were gained into the formation of the plaque associated with Alzheimer's. The plaque is formed from a protein called beta-amyloid (A-beta). Alzheimer's patients have too much A-beta in their brains. The A-beta accumulates and clumps together to form the plaque. As more and more plaque accumulates, it begins to block connections and eventually kills the brain cells, which do not regenerate. Most of the dead and diseased neurons are located in the parts of the brain that control thought, memory, and language. This is evidenced by the confusion, language problems, and memory loss of Alzheimer's sufferers.

Significance

Since the 1980s, conditions have improved for Alzheimer's patients and their families. There is much research activity focusing on the disease's cause, risk factors, and treatment. There are Alzheimer's support groups, and medical centers specializing in the care of Alzheimer's patients. Additionally, the nation's health care system recognizes and provides for the treatment of Alzheimer's sufferers. As a result, the families of Alzheimer's patients typically have several places to turn for help.

Diagnosing Alzheimer's disease is still challenging. Since the only way to confirm a diagnosis of Alzheimer's is through an autopsy, doctors diagnose "probable Alzheimer's" by performing several tests to rule out other causes of the symptoms. Doctors use memory, problem solving, and language tests in addition to medical tests on blood, urine, and spinal fluid. Recently, positron emission topography (PET) scans have been used to glean information about the presence of the plaques and tangles associated with Alzheimer's disease.

An early diagnosis of Alzheimer's disease is important for the quality of life for Alzheimer's patients and their families. The disease progresses slowly, starting with mild memory problems and ending with severe brain damage. It is estimated that on average, Alzheimer's patients live from eight to ten years after they are diagnosed. No treatment exists that can stop Alzheimer's or reverse it, but there are some drugs that alleviate symptoms. By helping to control sleeplessness, anxiety, wandering, and depression, these drugs can make life easier for the patient and the caregiver. However, most of these treatments have an effect only in the early to middle phases of the disease.

Scientists are studying a controversial approach, which uses stem cells to treat Alzheimer's. Stem cells, unlike most cells in the body, have the potential to turn into any kind of cell. Heart cells, liver cells, and skin cells, all start from stem cells. So, too, do brain cells. Thus, stem cells provide a way to replace the brain cells killed by Alzheimer's. However, the best stem cells are found in human embryos. Only two kinds of human embryos are available for research, those made in assisted reproductive techniques and those created by cloning. The president, the U.S. Congress, the U.S. National Institutes of Health, and researchers around the world are debating the moral and ethical implications of using embryonic stem cells to treat diseases such as Alzheimer's.

Primary Source

Alzheimer's: A Caregiver's Guide and Sourcebook [excerpt]

SYNOPSIS: Many books and guides published in the late 1980s were written to help family members cope with the stress of caring for an Alzheimer's patient. These excerpts summarize some of the common myths associated with aging, senility, and Alzheimer's.

Six Common Myths about Alzheimer's

Myth 1: Alzheimer's Symptoms Are a Normal Sign of Old Age

Alzheimer's should not be confused with the aging process.

Some of the early symptoms of Alzheimer's, such as forgetfulness, do correspond to our common notions of aging; but Alzheimer's is a disease and should not be confused with the aging process. This becomes clear as the disease progresses, and the victim's deterioration becomes more dramatic.

Old-age forgetfulness is benign.

In terms of memory loss, for example, it is true that a degree of increased forgetfulness commonly accompanies aging. Older persons may find it more difficult to recall the details of past events. However, the memory loss caused by Alzheimer's is far more severe and progressive in nature. Eventually the disease destroys not just the memory of details but all memory of the event itself. The person in time will forget not only the events of the past but what she did that morning, who her spouse is, where she lives, even her own name. These are not the normal consequences of aging.

Myth 2: Senility Is the Usual Cause of Problems in Old Age

Senility obscures real illnesses and problems of aging.

Senility is a blanket term that has long been used to cover a wide-ranging variety of symptoms. In this sense it is a damaging notion and a term to be avoided. An assumed diagnosis of senility obscures the real problem at hand and increases the difficulty of getting correct treatment for the older person's condition or impairment. The older person may suffer along assuming her condition is irreversible, when treatment may in fact be readily available. In addition, the myth of senility reinforces the negative and mistaken belief that all persons must become helpless and useless with age.

Common hearing and visual problems produce misleading views of older persons.

If an older person has difficulty relating to others or conducting her affairs, many problems other than senility or Alzheimer's disease may be the source. For example, the person may suffer from impaired hearing or vision. Her failure to clearly follow a conversation or respond to something in the environment may make it seem that her thought processes are impaired, when actually she has simply not seen or heard what happened. Additionally, the impaired person may begin to avoid situations where her problem is most apparent or troublesome. A person who is hard of hearing may avoid crowds, while a person with poor sight may become confused in social situations because everyone's face looks the same. Often older persons are unwilling to admit these impairments, which can add to confusion about the source of their problems.

Medical problems produce emotional and behavioral changes labeled as senility.

Medical conditions also may be at the root of the older person's problems. Congestive heart failure may cause weakness, fatigue, mental confusion, forgetfulness, and other symptoms mistaken for senility. Hyperthyroidism may cause apathy, depression, lethargy, impaired memory, and slow responses in the elderly. Hypothyroidism has similar symptoms in the elderly, with weakness and fatigue a little more prominent. Both of these illnesses have a slow, progressive onset similar to that of Alzheimer's disease. Persons suffering from these problems should receive a full medical evaluation, and family members should not just assume that the problem is old age.

Other conditions that may be confused with Alzheimer's include B-12 deficiencies, pernicious anemia, electrolyte imbalances, normal pressure hydrocephalus, hypoglycemia, and a range of infections. Infections of the urinary system, for example, may cause confusion, apathy, and inattentiveness before other symptoms are apparent. It is therefore essential that experienced medical personnel rule out all other possible causes for the older person's problems before arriving at a diagnosis of Alzheimer's.

Medications create Alzheimer's-type symptoms.

Often medication prescribed for a medical condition can cause side effects similar to Alzheimer's symptoms, such as confusion, forgetfulness, tremors, and slower responses. This can be a particular problem when the older person is taking several medications at one time to treat different conditions. If problems are apparent, they should be brought

An elderly woman with Alzheimer's sits with a social worker at the opening of a community healthy center's Alzheimer's program, June 1984. Increased research and knowledge of Alzheimer's have greatly increased support for patients. **AP/WIDE WORLD PHOTOS. REPRODUCED BY PERMISSION.**

promptly to the attention of the doctor or doctors involved. When a number of doctors and pharmacies are involved with different medications, there is a greater chance that medication-related problems will develop. It is therefore extremely important to provide all professionals involved with an up-to-date regimen of medications.

Depression is often mistaken for senility.

Psychological problems such as depression often are passed off as senility as well. It is common for older persons to experience some depression as they face the loss of health, friends, spouse, home, as well as their own death. Such major life changes late in life may lead to mental conditions requiring a psychiatrist's care, such as severe depression, anxiety, or paranoia. The person may not seem "crazy," but fear and insecurity in the face of real losses or perceived threats may be interfering with her ability to effectively cope with life.

Depression accentuates other difficulties.

Depression can in turn lead to complaints about memory problems. The person may see even minor memory lapses as evidence that she is becoming senile. In fact, however, she may simply be suffering from lapses in attention and concentration caused by the depression. One difference between the symptoms of depression and those of Alzheimer's is that, while the depressed person may not recognize her depression, she will rarely deny the resulting problems. Alzheimer's victims, on the other hand, tend to deny all evidence of the disease.

A belief in senility stops people from seeking help.

The myth of senility and the lack of dignity associated with it often prevent older persons from seeking treatment for conditions that are in fact reversible. Family members should encourage older persons to seek medical treatment for the problems they encounter and should not let them assume that senility is a necessary consequence of old age.

Myth 3: Nothing Can Be Done for the Alzheimer's Victim

Proper care is important in the management of the illness.

It is true that at present we have no cure for Alzheimer's disease. The disease is progressive and leads ultimately to death. However, there is much that can be done to make the victim's last months or years more meaningful, pleasant, and comfortable.

Medical care

Alzheimer's patients benefit from both proper medical care and informed behavior management. Thus the family should involve health professionals in their victim's care as early as possible, and they should continue to seek professional opinions throughout the disease.

Psychiatric care

Psychiatrists and other mental health professionals can successfully treat the depression or other psychological symptoms that frequently develop. Doctors and nutritionists can provide help with meal preparation, special diets, and nutritional supplements as the person's appetite and eating abilities deteriorate. Careful attention to the use of medications will prevent unnecessary and prolonged side effects.

Other medical problems coexist.

Treatment of coexisting medical problems is also very important. It should not be assumed that all of the person's physical and mental symptoms are caused by the disease. Persons with Alzheimer's are especially vulnerable to the common viruses, colds, and infections that affect us all, including pneumonia, and these conditions should receive prompt medical attention.

Myth 4: Alzheimer's Is Strictly a Mental Illness

Psychiatric symptoms

Many of the changes initially observed in the Alzheimer's patient seem to be personality disorders or other psychological problems. Furthermore, because Alzheimer's disease primarily affects the brain, it is in a sense a "mental" illness. However, Alzheimer's disease is a degenerative medical condition and not a psychiatric disorder.

Psychiatric symptoms are a significant part of the illness. As the brain gradually loses its capacity to perform normal functions we take for granted, the individual becomes increasingly insecure and unable to relate to her daily world. In time her personality is completely altered, and she truly becomes a "different person" than the loved one we have always known.

Insurance views the illness as psychiatric

Because society's recognition of the medical nature of the disease is fairly recent, however, Alzheimer's may be regarded at times as a psychiatric condition. Persons financially dependent on insurance or Medicaid programs, for example, may find that they do not meet the "medical" requirements that make them eligible for long-term care. It is to be hoped that these requirements and attitudes will change as the understanding of Alzheimer's becomes more widespread.

Diagnostic findings of good health are misleading.

The impression that Alzheimer's is a mental illness may be supported when a diagnosis of general "good health" is coupled with a diagnosis of Alzheimer's disease. What medical professionals mean by such a diagnosis, however, is that no other medical problems have been found, or other conditions are so successfully controlled that the individual is in otherwise satisfactory health.

Myth 5: Only the Family Should Care for the Alzheimer's Victim

Family care is supportive and necessary.

In most cases, it is certainly best if the affected person can stay at home with her spouse or family as long as possible. The love and regular interaction a family can provide usually helps the person retain her abilities longer and helps ease her difficult adjustment to the disease.

Other resources make a big difference.

However, not all spouses or children have the resources to care properly for their loved one. Even those who do have the resources eventually may have to call upon outside care when the disease reaches its later stages and caregiving becomes an utterly exhausting experience.

Caregivers should be careful about overinvolvement.

Overinvolvement, or the feeling that the caregiver must do everything herself, is a common reaction to the disease. Often it represents a stage in the family member's adjustment to the disease (see Chapter 7). The caregiver imagines that she can hold back the disease by doing everything herself, and her grief leads her to become extremely protective of the victim. She may also feel reluctant to seek outside help because of shame and the stigmas associated with mental conditions.

Primary caregivers must accept help.

However, the family, and in particular the primary caregiver, must learn to accept help. The burden of caring for an Alzheimer's patient can otherwise cause serious problems for the caregiver and alienate her from friends and family who want to share the caregiving role. The caregiver should not hesitate to call upon community resources as well, such as those discussed in detail in Chapter 10. Without these resources, the burden of care can become overwhelming.

Further Resources

BOOKS

Cohen, Donna, and Carl Eisdorfer. *The Loss of Self: A Family Resource for the Care of Alzheimer's Disease and Related Disorders.* New York: Norton, 1986.

Cutler, Neal R., and John J. Sramek. *Understanding Alzheimer's Disease.* Jackson, Miss.: University Press of Mississippi, 1996.

Shenk, David. *The Forgetting: Alzheimer's, Portrait of an Epidemic.* New York: Doubleday, 2001.

PERIODICALS

McGuire, Rick. "Alzheimer's: New Breakthroughs." *Total Health* 12, no. 6, December 1990, 28–30.

Starr, Cynthia. "Alzheimer's: The Stranger Amongst Us." *Drug Topics* 134, no. 17, September 3, 1990, 34–41.

WEBSITES

Alzheimer's Disease Education and Referral. "Alzheimer's Disease: Unraveling the Mystery." Available online at http://www.alzheimers.org/unraveling/06.htm; website home page http://www.alzheimers.org (accessed March 5, 2003).

Who Named It.com. "Alois Alzheimer." Available online at http://www.whonamedit.com/doctor.cfm/177.html; website home page: http://www.whonamedit.com(accessed March 5, 2003).

"The Cystic Fibrosis Gene Is Found"

Magazine article

By: Jean L. Marx

Date: September 1, 1989

Source: Marx, Jean, L. "The Cystic Fibrosis Gene Is Found." *Science.* September 1, 1989, 923–925.

About the Author: Jean L. Marx Marx received a bachelor's degree in chemistry from the College of Mt. St. Joseph-on the Ohio in 1961; a master's degree in biochemistry from Purdue in 1964; and a Ph.D. in biochemistry from Purdue in 1967. She was a 1970 winner of a National Science Foundation Summer Research Grant as well as other awards. She was named a Purdue University Old Master in 1983. Marx is a senior correspondent for *Science* magazine. ∎

Introduction

Three papers were published in the September 1, 1989, issue of *Science*. The three papers described the three major research milestones that guided codiscoverers Lap-Chee Tsui and Francis Collins to the cystic fibrosis (CF) gene. In the paper "Identification of the Cystic Fibrosis Gene: Genetic Analysis," Lap-Chee Tsui describes how he and his team got very close to the cystic fibrosis gene using genome mapping. A genome map is like any map; it reflects the relative locations of different landmarks to each other. Since genes are organized and arranged on chromosomes in a linear manner, a genome map is like a long "yellow brick road" of adenine (A), cytosine (C), thymine (T), and guanine (G). Researchers identify signposts as they traverse down the road. The signposts consist of special patterns of A, C, T, and G and are referred to as "DNA markers." Researchers map a gene's location on the genome map by bracketing it in between different DNA markers. The closer the DNA markers are to each other, the closer researchers are to the location of the gene they are seeking.

In "Identification of the Cystic Fibrosis Gene: Chromosome Walking and Jumping," Collins and Tsui zeroed in on the CF gene using a method developed by Collins that allowed them to traverse the genome road map at an accelerated speed. Collins' technique speeded up the process by allowing researchers to do two things. First they could jump over impediments and obstacles called "unclonable regions," which normally halted the entire mapping process. Second, from each jumping point, they could move in both directions (forward and backward) along the map. Collins's technique of "chromosome jumping" made it possible to locate the CF gene.

Once the researchers had found the cystic fibrosis gene using Collins' technique, they were anxious because it did not seem as though the gene was expressed. Expression is the act of turning the gene sequence into a protein. Messenger RNA (mRNA) is an intermediary between the genomic DNA (gene) and the protein. If researchers can find mRNA for a gene, they know the gene is expressed. The third paper, "Identification of the Cystic Fibrosis Gene: Cloning and Characterization of Complimentary DNA," describes how they found that the CF gene was in fact expressed. They found the CF mRNA by using a cDNA (DNA complementary to mRNA) library created by John Riordan.

Significance

Considerable hope was centered on the discovery of the CF gene. Its identification led to the development of tests to identify gene *carriers,* people who have no symptoms but carry one copy of the gene. It takes two copies of the defective gene to cause cystic fibrosis. Many medical professionals and parents are grateful to be able to test for the CF gene. Additionally, people with cystic fibrosis and their families were hopeful that identification of the defective gene would provide enough information to design effective treatments to counter the disease. Gene therapy was an especially tantalizing idea. Introducing the normal counterpart of the cystic fibrosis gene into the lung cells of CF patients has the promise of alleviating many of their symptoms. As of 2003, though, scientists have been unable to target the gene to the lung cells where it is needed.

Cloned genes are invaluable for diagnostic purposes and potentially for gene therapy, but the protein product of a gene that confers disease can prove even more valuable in leading to a treatment. The CF protein, cystic fibrosis transmembrane conductance regulator (CFTR), is found in the membrane of lung cells. It transverses the entire cell membrane and acts as a gatekeeper to regulate the number of chloride ions allowed into and out of the cell. The isolation of the CFTR protein confirmed what CF researchers had suspected, that the lung cells of CF patients are unable to secrete chloride ions into the mucous present in their lungs.

Primary Source

"The Cystic Fibrosis Gene Is Found"

> **SYNOPSIS:** The September 1, 1989, issue of *Science* was dedicated to the discovery of the cystic fibrosis gene. It contained the three technical reports detailing the discovery of the gene, an editorial by the magazine's editor, and this "News and Comment" article providing a detailed description of the research leading up to the discovery.

Researchers have identified the major gene defect that causes cystic fibrosis. The discovery should lead to better diagnosis and perhaps improved therapies for the now fatal disease

The race to find the cystic fibrosis gene is over. In three papers to be published in the 8 September issue of *Science,* researchers from Toronto and Ann Arbor report that they have cloned the gene and pinpointed the gene defect that causes most cystic fibrosis cases. "The data are virtually irrefutable that they have the right gene," says Louis Kunkel of Children's Hospital Medical Center in Boston, a cloning expert who led the successful search for the gene causing Duchenne muscular dystrophy.

Cystic fibrosis researchers have looked long and hard for their gene—and with good reason. The disease is the most common genetic disorder of Caucasians. In the United States, it strikes one child in every 2000. An estimated 30,000 people have the disease today, and their prospects are grim. Most will die before their thirtieth birthday. Perhaps not surprisingly then, news of the gene discovery began to leak out before the scheduled publication of the papers describing the research, and this in turn prompted the editors of *Science* to drop their normal embargo policy (also see box on p. 924).

The discovery means that scientists can improve cystic fibrosis diagnosis, including prenatal diagnosis, and also devise better screening tests for people who carry a defective copy of the gene and run the risk of having children with disease. It also raises hopes for better cystic fibrosis treatments, perhaps new drugs or even gene therapy to replace the defective gene itself.

None of this could have even been considered until scientists could get a handle on the basic protein defect that causes cystic fibrosis. "Now we can really study what the basic defect is and we may be able to treat the defect directly, not just the symptoms," says Lap-Chee Tsui, the leader of one of the groups that cloned the gene. No one can now predict, however, how long it might take to do this or even if it will prove to be possible.

The search for the cystic fibrosis gene has been highly competitive, if not out-and-out contentious at times (*Science,* 8 April 1988, p. 141, and 15 April 1988, p. 282). But in the end, a collaborative effort by the groups of Tsui and John Riordan at Toronto's Hospital for Sick Children, together with Francis Collins at the Howard Hughes Medical Institute at the University of Michigan, bagged the gene.

The researchers appear to have a clear victory. "We have a lot of papers in press, but we don't have the gene," says chief competitor Robert Williamson of Saint Mary's Hospital Medical School in London, who has also been rumored to be close to cloning the cystic fibrosis gene. "If we couldn't get it, we're very pleased that Francis and Lap-Chee were the ones to do it."

The collaboration between Tsui and Collins began in the fall of 1987, when the two researchers, who had previously been working independently, got together in San Diego at the annual meeting of the American Society for Human Genetics. "It was clear by then that this was a very hard problem that was not going to be solved without a great deal of labor," Collins says.

The cystic fibrosis gene was such a tough nut to crack because, in the absence of information

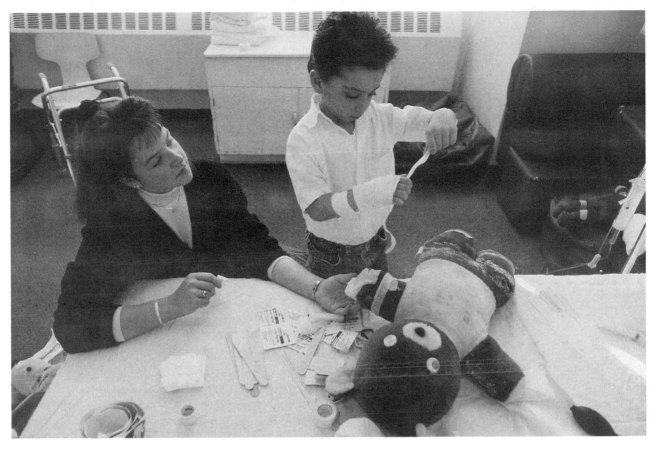

A young boy with cystic fibrosis plays in a hospital's pediatrics playroom, Boston, November 1989. The discovery of the cystic fibrosis gene led to better diagnosis and therapies for sufferers. © DAVID H. WELLS/CORBIS. REPRODUCED BY PERMISSION.

about the protein it encodes, researchers did not know what they were looking for among the estimated 100,000 genes in the human genome. Researchers have managed to clone a few other genes without knowing what their products were—the Duchenne muscular dystrophy gene is one of them—but some of the defects responsible for the malfunction of these genes were large rearrangements that made them relatively easy to spot once their approximate locations in the genome were known. The cystic fibrosis gene did not carry any such convenient tag, unfortunately.

In 1985, however, 2 years before Tsui and his colleagues joined forces with Collins and his team, the Toronto group had provided a big boost to efforts to find the gene when they mapped it to chromosome 7. Williamson and Ray White of the Howard Hughes Medical Institute at the University of Utah in Salt Lake City further narrowed its location by identifying two "markers," the *met* oncogene and a DNA sequence designated J3.11 that flanked the gene. . . .

Once flanking markers have been identified, they can serve as starting points for zeroing in on a target gene. But *met* and J3.11 are almost 1600 kilobases apart—too great a distance to be traversed in a reasonable time by standard chromosome "walking" techniques. (A researcher walks a chromosome by identifying overlapping cloned fragments of DNA until the final destination is reached.)

Tsui consequently decided to use a brute force approach known as saturation mapping to find new marker sequences that were closer to the cystic fibrosis gene than either *met* or J3.11. To do this, the Toronto workers had to look for identifiable DNA sequences that are inherited along with the cystic fibrosis gene in the members of families with cystic fibrosis. The frequency with which a particular marker is transmitted along with the target gene gives an estimate of how close together they are. "Lo and behold, after screening 250 markers," Tsui says, "we found two that happened to be between *met* and J3.11." The genetic studies indicated that both were closer to the cystic fibrosis gene than either *met* or J3.11.

Dr. Lap-Chee Tsui stands in his laboratory. Tsui was the leader of one of the teams that discovered the cystic fibrosis gene in 1989.
REPRODUCED BY PERMISSION OF LAP-CHEE TSUI.

It was at that point that Tsui joined forces with Collins, who had developed a technique called chromosome jumping that can skip over lengthy segments of DNA. Not only is jumping faster than walking, but it also has the advantage of being able to move over unclonable DNA sequences. The human genome is studded with such sequences and they can stop a walk in its tracks.

It would have been ideal if the two new markers identified by Tsui had flanked the cystic fibrosis gene. But they didn't. They were located close together between *met* and another gene that the Williamson group had originally identified in the spring of 1987.

At the time, the London workers thought that they had the cystic fibrosis gene itself and said as much in an article published in *Nature:* By the fall of that year, however, their hopes were cruelly dashed when additional work showed that it was not. But the gene, which became known as the IRP (for *int*-related protein) gene because the protein it encodes resembles the product of the *int* oncogene, did prove to be the closest marker yet for the cystic fibrosis gene.

Despite some initial disappointment at the location of the new markers, Tsui, Collins, and their colleagues decided to plunge ahead. They began walking and jumping at one marker, moving at first in both directions. "You have to move in both directions until you cross a landmark that tells you which way you are going," Collins explains. The IRP gene was one of the first landmarks crossed, and the researchers knew that they were heading in the right direction.

The researchers had to jump and walk across 280 kilobases of DNA before encountering the beginning of the cystic fibrosis gene. Along the way they searched for potential genes by comparing the DNA sequences they were traversing with DNAs from other organisms. If structurally related sequences could be found in other organisms, that would mean that the sequence had been conserved during evolution, a good indication that it has an essential function. They found three conserved DNA sequences but were quickly able to eliminate two of them as candidates for the cystic fibrosis gene.

The third proved to be the key to the prize—but not without some initial anxiety. Genetic studies in cystic fibrosis families indicated that the potential gene segment was in the right location, but when the researchers looked for signs that it might be actively expressed, they could not find any after an extensive search. "That was quite disappointing," Tsui says. It looked as if the DNA sequence was not part of any active gene.

And this is the point where Tsui's Toronto colleague Riordan made an essential contribution. The Riordan group had made "libraries" of DNAs copied from the messenger RNAs present in sweat gland cells, which is one of the cell types in which the cystic fibrosis gene is supposed to be expressed. Each DNA copy corresponds to an active gene, and one of those from the sweat gland library proved to contain a segment matching the conserved sequence that Tsui, Collins, and their colleagues had found.

The extent of the match-up was quite small. The two DNAs shared only 113 base pairs of sequence, a circumstance that may explain why the researchers originally had so much trouble showing that the conserved sequence was part of an active gene. Further analysis showed, however, that those 113 base pairs were likely to come from the starting end of the cystic fibrosis gene. This provided the probe they needed to clone the whole gene. But even that did not come easily. "To finish the cloning we spent night and day with lots of people," Tsui remarks. "We could only get bits and pieces and then had to fit everything together."

The gene proved to be quite large, extending across nearly 250 kilobases of genomic DNA. Like other genes of higher organisms, it consists of a mosaic of protein-coding exons—24 in this case—separated by nonprotein-coding introns.

Sequence analysis revealed that the protein encoded by the gene contains 1480 amino acids and that it has all the earmarks of a membrane protein, possibly of an ion channel. The protein sequence resembles those of several other proteins known to be involved in transporting substances across membranes. And that, says Robert Beall of the Cystic Fibrosis Foundation, "is very compatible with our current hypothesis of what causes cystic fibrosis."

The patients' main problem is the abnormally thick mucus that they produce, especially in the lungs. As a result, they fall prey to repeated infections that destroy the lung tissue, eventually leading to the patients' deaths. Although researchers had not been able to identify the protein defect causing the excessively thick mucus, recent evidence has indicated that the fault may lie in the inability of the lung cells to secrete chloride ions, and therefore water, into the mucus.

The structure of the cystic fibrosis protein now suggests that it may be a membrane channel for chloride ions. Moreover, Tsui, Riordan, Collins, and their colleagues have found that the gene encoding the protein is altered in cystic fibrosis patients, a change that might well cause the protein to malfunction.

Approximately 70% of the gene mutations are caused by the loss of a single specific trinucleotide codon. As a result, the corresponding protein is lacking just one amino acid, the phenylalanine at position 508. The researchers never see this change in the gene on normal chromosomes. This observation provides the proof that they have the correct gene, Tsui says. They are now looking for the remaining 30% of the mutations that alter this gene.

The site of the phenylalanine deletion may provide some clues as to how the protein malfunctions in cystic fibrosis patients. It affects what may be an important region regulating the protein's activity. The region contains an apparent binding site for adenosine triphosphate (ATP), a compound that provides energy for many cell functions. A nearby region also contains several target sequences for phosphate addition by the protein kinases A and C, both important protein regulators.

The loss of the phenylalanine may therefore interfere with chloride ion transport by preventing ATP binding to the cystic fibrosis protein and depriving it of the energy it needs or by rendering it unresponsive to activation by the protein kinases.

Currently, clinicians can only treat cystic fibrosis patients by attempting to control their infections and other symptoms. But now that the cystic fibrosis gene and protein are in hand it may at last be possible to design more rational therapies aimed at the specific defect itself. One possibility is to develop drugs that can act through the protein to restore normal chloride transport. "This will require a long period of research and development," Tsui says, "but we have at least reached a starting point."

Ultimately, it may even be possible to use gene therapy to correct the defect. Introducing the normal gene into lung cells should be sufficient to help patients, Beall suggests. They have other symptoms, but these can be controlled. It is the lung defect that kills. Until a way can be found to deliver a functioning cystic fibrosis gene into lung cells, gene therapy will remain something of a long shot, however.

Improved detection of carriers of defective cystic fibrosis genes is a much more immediate prospect. A person has to inherit two bad genes to get the disease. A carrier has only one defective copy and does not have any symptoms by which he or she might be identified. But if two carriers have a baby, their child has a 25% chance of being affected.

Before the cystic fibrosis gene was discovered, carriers could only be detected in families already known to carry the defective gene because some of their members had the disease. Genetic counselors were forced to look for markers known to be inherited with the cystic fibrosis gene, rather than the gene itself, and this procedure requires a knowledge of family genetics.

But the new work should make it possible to identify defective cystic fibrosis genes in anyone. This will require, Tsui points out, that the remaining 30% of the mutations in the cystic fibrosis gene be identified. But the researchers are hard at work on this project, and it may be completed in a year or two.

The long march to the cystic fibrosis gene was obviously arduous. But the successful procedures worked out by Tsui, Collins, and their colleagues for isolating the gene should also be applicable to the identification of the genes causing other genetic diseases. "It was a long task," Kunkel says, "but it shows that it can be done. It can be done again."

Further Resources

BOOKS

Annas, George J., and Sherman Elias. *Gene Mapping: Using Law and Ethics as Guides.* New York: Oxford University Press, 1992.

Cystic Fibrosis and DNA Tests: Implications of Carrier Screening. Washington D.C.: Congress of the U.S., Office of Technology Assessment, 1992.

Tsui, Lap-Chee. *The Identification of the CF (Cystic Fibrosis) Gene: Recent Progress and New Research Strategies.* New York: Plenum, 1991.

PERIODICALS

Cowley, Geoffrey. "Closing in on Cystic Fibrosis: Researchers Are Learning to Replace a Faulty Gene." *Newsweek,* May 3, 1993, 56.

Hasegawa, Hajime, et al. "A Multifunctional Aqueous Channel Formed by CFTR." *Science,* November 27, 1992, 1477–1480.

Roberts, Leslie. "To Test or Not to Test (for Cystic Fibrosis Gene)." *Science,* January 5, 1990, 17–20.

WEBSITES

Cystic Fibrosis Foundation. Available online at http://www.cff.org/ (accessed March 9, 2003).

Gene Gateway–Exploring Genes and Genetic Disorders. "The Cystic Fibrosis Gene." Available online at http://www.ornl.gov/TechResources/Human_Genome/posters/chromosome/cftr.html; website home page: http://www.ornl.gov (accessed March 9, 2003).

"The Cholesterol Myth"
Magazine article

By: Thomas J. Moore

Date: September 1989

Source: Moore, Thomas J. "The Cholesterol Myth." *The Atlantic,* September 1989, 37–62.

About the Author: Thomas J. Moore received a bachelor's degree from Cornell. He is the author of several books including *Heart Failure* and *Prescription for Disaster.* He is a lecturer and consultant on the safety of prescription drugs, a senior scientist for drug safety and policy at the Institute for Safe Medication Practices (ISMP), and a fellow at the Center for Health Services Research and Policy. ∎

Introduction

Heart disease is a major killer of Americans. In 1921, coronary heart disease became the leading cause of death in the United States, and it remains a top killer today. Heart disease includes a host of ailments of the cardiovascular system, which is made up of the heart and blood vessels: coronary artery disease (narrowing of arteries), ischemic heart disease (lack of oxygen in the heart), stroke (brain attack), high blood pressure (hypertension), and rheumatic heart disease. Tens of millions of Americans have heart disease of one form or another.

The most common form of heart disease is coronary heart disease, which results from a gradual buildup of plaque or a thickening of the inside walls of the artery. As a result, the heart has to work harder and the flow of oxygenated blood, and thus the supply of oxygen to vital organs and the arms and legs are significantly reduced. A heart attack may occur if the oxygenated blood supply to the heart is reduced. A stroke may occur if the oxygenated blood supply to the brain is cut off. Gangrene may occur if the oxygenated blood supply is reduced to the arms and legs. Generally coronary heart disease is a result of lifestyle and genetic factors. High blood cholesterol levels, obesity, stress, smoking, and high-fat diets are all lifestyle factors implicated in coronary heart disease.

Cholesterol, a lipid (a waxy substance) steroid found in all eukaryotic (plant and animal) cells, is essential for life. It comprises a major component of eukaryotic cell membranes and is a precursor to vitamin D and steroid hormones such as progesterone, testosterone, and estrogen. Cells obtain cholesterol from two sources: the liver and to a lesser extent the intestines, which synthesize it from scratch; and from the foods we eat. Egg yolks, fatty meats, and shellfish contain high amounts of cholesterol.

Cholesterol metabolism is highly regulated. It is transported in the blood serum (the liquid portion) to the body's cells packaged with other fats in vesicles made of lipoproteins (composed of fats and proteins). There are several types of vesicles, which vary by their weight or density. Low-density lipoprotein (LDL) vesicles are important in cholesterol metabolism. If there are too many LDL vesicles floating around in the blood serum, they start to aggregate, or clump together, and form plaque in the arteries. Atherosclertotic (pertaining to the arteries) plaque leads to heart disease by clogging arteries and making the heart work harder.

A lack of LDL receptors on the surface of cells leads to heart disease. Cholesterol floating around in LDL in the blood serum is essentially useless for cells. LDL receptors are docking stations on the outside of cells that function to bring cholesterol into the cell, where it can be used. A landmark study published by Brown and Goldstein in the 1980s reported that a defective gene can lead to varying degrees of LDL receptor deficiencies. People who inherit the defective gene from both parents have absolutely no LDL receptors. Their arteries become full of atherosclerotic plaque, and they usually die from coronary heart disease in childhood.

Significance

A nationwide program was launched in the 1980s to educate medical professionals and the public about the association of cholesterol and coronary heart disease. In October 1987, the National Heart, Lung, and Blood Institute (NHLBI) issued guidelines telling doctors how to evaluate and treat people with high blood cholesterol. The guidelines were a part of the National Cholesterol Education Program (NCEP) the goal of which was to reduce coronary heart disease.

The basis of the link between cholesterol and heart disease was established in a famous study known as the Framingham study. Framingham researchers meticulously followed and collected health, dietary, and lifestyle habits for an entire Massachusetts town starting in 1948. Many important health findings came out of the Framingham study, including a connection between cigarette smoking and heart disease, high-blood pressure and stroke, and cholesterol and coronary heart disease.

Since the 1980s many drugs have been developed to lower the levels of cholesterol in the blood. An enzyme called 3-hydroxy-3-methylglutaryl-coenzyme A reductase (HMG CoA reductase) is important in cholesterol formation. Statins are cholesterol drugs that inhibit this enzyme. The NHLBI recommends cholesterol-lowering drugs when necessary, along with lifestyle changes to lower blood cholesterol levels. A blood cholesterol level of 240 milligrams per deciliter (mg/dL) is considered high. People with high blood cholesterol levels are two times more likely to have a heart attack than people with normal levels (less than 200 mg/dL).

Primary Source

"The Cholesterol Myth" [excerpt]

> **SYNOPSIS:** These excerpts are from an article drawn from Thomas J. Moore's book, *Heart Failure*. Here he provides an interesting story about the origins of the discovery of cholesterol's link to coronary heart disease.

One morning in early October of 1987 the U.S. health authorities announced that 25 percent of the adult population had a dangerous condition requiring medical treatment. Since there were no symptoms, it would be necessary to screen the entire population to identify those in danger. More than half of those screened would be dispatched to their physicians for medical tests and evaluation. Then for one out of four adults treatment would begin. The first step would be a strict diet under medical supervision. If within three months the dieting had not achieved specified results that could be verified by laboratory tests, a more severe diet would be imposed. The final step for many patients would be powerful drugs to be taken for the rest of their lives.

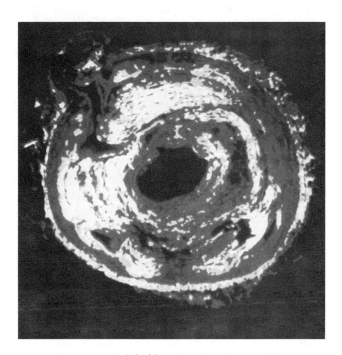

A view of an artery occluded with cholesterol. In October 1987, the National Heart, Lung, and Blood Institute (NHLBI) issued guidelines telling doctors how to evaluate and treat people with high blood cholesterol in efforts to reduce the occurrence of coronary heart disease. © **HOWARD SOCHUREK/CORBIS. REPRODUCED BY PERMISSION.**

Considering that this was expected to be one of the most important medical interventions in the nation's history, the formal announcement was deceptively low-key. It was to be called the National Cholesterol Education Program. And while cholesterol was surely a household word, the official sponsor was less familiar: the National Heart, Lung, and Blood Institute, a major division of the federal government's National Institutes of Health. Although the heart institute's main job is to coordinate and finance medical research, this departure into medical intervention was not unprecedented. At first glance the program's objective sounded positively innocuous: "To reduce the prevalence of elevated blood cholesterol in the United States and thereby contribute to reducing coronary heart disease morbidity and mortality." But the National Cholesterol Education Program was a medical landmark in several ways. It was the culmination of an extraordinary and sustained medical-research effort targeting the nation's biggest killer—coronary heart disease. One experiment had taken forty years and was still in progress. Another involved examining 361,622 middle-aged men. A famous experiment by two Nobel Prize winners had penetrated the innermost recesses of the human cell to identify a single gene with a dramatic effect on cholesterol levels.

Researchers had studied the arteries of rabbits, given highfat diets to monkeys, and fed egg yolks to college students. It would be hard to find another medical issue that had been explored with such vigor, by so many researchers, and at such great expense. Just two important experiments took twelve years, cost more than $300 million, and consumed 60 percent of the heart institute's clinical-research budget.

There were serious risks to consider. Not since the introduction of oral contraceptives would so many people be exposed to powerful new prescription drugs over decades. Among the most elusive hazards of any drug are damaging or even deadly side effects that are recognized only after the drug has been administered to thousands of people for years. Nor is dietary therapy quite as simple as it sounds. So complex are the interactions among food compounds, and so varied are the behavior and the chemistry of individuals, that dietary intervention has proved to be one of the most complicated of all medical treatments, subject to unexpected difficulties and disappointing results.

Finally, the National Cholesterol Education Program represented a major change in strategy in the prevention of coronary heart disease. Previous efforts, led mainly by the American Heart Association, had relied on advice and persuasion. Now the federal government was calling on the authority of physicians to prescribe a medically supervised regimen of treatment. This was not just friendly advice from the family doctor to cut down on cholesterol. It was, in the words of the treatment guidelines, a program of "behavior modification" backed by laboratory tests to ensure adherence and measure results. People still might abandon drugs that made them sick—and some cholesterol-lowering drugs were famous for doing so—or refuse to eat foods they didn't like. But now they would be violating explicit doctor's orders. . . .

The story of cholesterol began in 1951, when the Pentagon dispatched a team of pathologists to the combat zone of the Korean War on a grisly mission to learn from the bodies of the dead. The principal assignment of the team, led by Major William E Enos and Lieutenant Colonel Robert H. Holmes, was to examine wound ballistics, and in three years the team performed autopsies on 2,000 dead soldiers. As a group, battle casualties differ greatly ftom the subjects a pathologist normally examines, who were mostly old and very sick when they died. The soldiers on whom Enos and Holmes performed

autopsies had been vigorous young men. So when the pathologists began to notice signs of coronary heart disease, it was surprising, because practically nobody under thirty-five dies of coronary heart disease, and these war dead were, on the average, twenty-two. So the pathologists launched a systematic study of the hearts of soldiers killed in battle. In 300 consecutive cases they dissected the single most vulnerable component of the heart—the network of tiny coronary arteries that nourish the heart muscle with blood. These small arteries are considerably more sophisticated than hollow tubes. Their inside surface is a thin layer of very smooth, almost slick cells. The surface needs to be smooth because when the platelets and proteins in the blood encounter a break or irregularity, they lay down a deposit of fibrous material. Such a fibrous deposit on the skin is the familiar scab, and would be undesirable in an artery unless there were a leak or other damage that needed repair. The next major layer in the artery consists of smooth muscle, which can expand and contract, like other muscles in the body. One of the mechanisms by which the heart muscle can increase its blood supply is by dilating the coronary arteries, thus increasing the flow. Enos and Holmes expected to find mostly slick interior surfaces surrounded by healthy smooth muscle. Instead they found stringy, streaky yellow deposits of fat and fiber in 35 percent of the casualties. These particular deposits had posed no immediate threat. But they meant that degeneration of the arteries was well under way more than twenty years before these men would have been likely to experience heart attacks. In another 42 percent of the casualties the coronary arteries were in even worse shape. In this group the fatty streaks had already grown into full-fledged lesions, structures that somewhat resemble warts. Such lesions are usually capped by hard, fibrous plaque. Inside is a mass of debris that can include cholesterol compounds, dead tissue, and calcium. Some lesions are soft, like pimples; others are rock hard. Once these lesions are established they slowly increase in size. Fortunately for human life expectancy, they can block about 75 percent of the diameter of an artery without seriously inhibiting the blood flow. Also, some areas of the heart muscle are nourished by more than one branch of the arterial network; if one artery becomes blocked, the tissue can get blood through another. One out of ten soldiers already had lesions severe enough to reduce or block entirely the flow of blood in at least one artery.

Thus 77 percent of the Korean War casualties examined showed gross evidence of coronary heart disease. This was a shock to the medical community, for it meant that the process underlying coronary heart disease began much earlier than anyone had thought. Here were fully developed lesions, some entirely obstructing arteries, in twenty-two-year-olds. Furthermore, practically all the casualties showed at least some signs of coronary heart disease.

Arterial lesions would remain at the center of medical interest in coronary heart disease for decades to come. Cholesterol-lowering diets would aim to slow their growth; bypass surgery would attempt to route blood around them; in angioplasty a tiny balloon would squeeze the lesions open. In 1953, however, researchers faced a more immediate problem. Without examining the coronary arteries directly, how were doctors going to tell who was in danger? The answer to that question was just then beginning to take shape eighteen miles west of Boston, in an industrial town called Framingham.

A Town Under Examination

If doctors could pinpoint what was different about people with coronary heart disease, maybe they could learn to save them. Tracing the development of such a universal peril would require the careful surveillance of thousands of people for years on end. One might as well examine the population of an entire town—and that is exactly the task that a team of Boston University Medical School physicians undertook, in Framingham, Massachusetts. It was among the first large-scale projects of the heart institute, which paid for and directed the study. The researchers, led by Thomas R. Dawber, hoped to recruit most of the adult residents of Framingham and study them for the rest of their lives. The project, which continues today, began in 1948.

The researchers set up shop in the mostly blue-collar community of 28,000, primarily ethnic Irish and Italians, and recruited two out of every three healthy men and women from age thirty to sixty-two. Every two years the participants would undergo physical examinations, fill out detailed questionnaires about their living habits and diet, and be tested with exercise treadmills and electrocardiographs.

Probably in no other city in the United States have the population's health, weight, diet, exercise, and living habits been measured so meticulously for so many years. A substantial fraction of everything that medical science knows today about the epidemiology of coronary heart disease has been learned from the residents of Framingham. But the public-health policies that have unfolded in the forty years since the study began have been heavily influenced by the strengths—and weaknesses—of the particular kind of knowledge that emerges from a study like this one. . . .

The Framingham experimenters built a detailed portrait of coronary heart disease from a sample of 5,127 adults, of whom 404 died of coronary heart disease over twenty-four years. When epidemiological studies are complete, the tidy mathematical charts and tables tend to conceal the crude and approximate character of the entire exercise. The Framingham study was no exception. Just deciding which residents had coronary heart disease involved significant amounts of medical guesswork. The typical participant failed to appear for about one out of five physical examinations. It has been hard to keep some laboratory tests uniform over so many years.

Further Resources

BOOKS
Moore, Thomas J. *Heart Failure.* New York: Random House, 1989.

Pollock, M.L., and D.H. Schmidt. *Heart Disease and Rehabilitation.* New York: Wiley, 1986.

Roth, Eli, and Sandra L. Streicher-Lankin. *Good Cholesterol, Bad Cholesterol.* Rocklin, Calif.: Prima Publishing and Communcations, 1988.

PERIODICALS
Brown, M.S., and J.L. Goldstein. "How LDL Receptors Influence Cholesterol and Atherosclerosis." *Scientific American* 251, no. 5, 1984, 58–66.

Castelli,W.P., et al. "Incidence of Coronary Heart Disease and Lipoprotein Cholesterol Levels. The Framingham Study." *Journal of the American Medical Association* 256, 1986, 2835–2838.

Ross, R. "The Pathogenesis of Atherosclerosis—an Update. *New England Journal of Medicine* 314, 1986, 488–500.

WEBSITES
American Heart Association. "Cholesterol." Available online at http://www.americanheart.org/presenter.jhtml?identifier=1516; website home page: http://www.americanheart.org (accessed March 8, 2003).

National Heart, Lung, and Blood Institute. "Framingham Heart Study." Available online at http://www.nhlbi.nih.gov/about/framingham/index.html; website home page: http://www.nhlbi.nih.gov (accessed March 8, 2003).

"The Underground Test of Compound Q"

Magazine article

By: Dennis Wyss

Date: October 9, 1989

Source: Wyss, Dennis. "The Underground Test of Compound Q: Desperate Activists Try to Speed Up the Discovery of a Cure for AIDS." *Time,* October 9, 1989, 18–20.

About the Organization: Project Inform was created in San Francisco in 1985 when the AIDS epidemic was reaching its peak and reliable information about the disease and its treatment was difficult to obtain. It is a national, nonprofit, community-based HIV/AIDS treatment information and advocacy organization. Project Inform serves many interest groups, including those infected with HIV, their caregivers, and their health-care and service providers. Project Inform operates a national, toll-free treatment hotline and publishes the *PI Perspective* (a Project Inform newsletter) online. ∎

Introduction

In 1989, eight years after the first cases of AIDS were recognized, AIDS patients had few treatment options, and there was still no cure. The immune system of people with full-blown AIDS is virtually nonexistent, making them easy prey for rare and exotic opportunistic infections caused by microbes (bacteria, viruses, or fungi) that are harmless to someone with a healthy immune system. The first opportunistic diseases to strike were typically those that targeted the skin and mucous membranes. As a result, those with AIDS suffered with unsightly and painful ulcers of the skin, mouth, or genital area. The purple skin lesions of Kaposi's sarcoma were an easily recognizable symbol of the AIDS disease. Oral hairy leukoplakia, which causes fuzzy white patches on the tongue, often occurred. Next were life-threatening diseases that affected major organs, like the lungs, liver, and brain. *Pneumocystis carinii* pneumonia (PCP) was the primary cause of death for three out of five AIDS patients. Toxoplasmosis affected the brain, causing seizures and coma. *Cryptococcus,* a fungus typically found in pigeons, caused meningitis (brain and spinal cord inflammation). Cryptosporidiosis caused chronic diarrhea, sometimes leading to death from dehydration. The list of diseases that affected early AIDS sufferers went on and on, and few drugs were available to treat these uncommon diseases.

By the end of the 1980s, though, a large amount of basic science had been performed on HIV, the virus causing AIDS. The virus was identified and grown in mass quantities in the lab, a blood test was developed that was used to protect the blood supply from contamination, the virus was characterized, its RNA was sequenced, and its proteins were identified. However, patients were still suf-

fering from the horrific symptoms of the disease. Many of the initial drugs used against AIDS were highly toxic and caused significant side effects. However, doctors were beginning to find dosages that worked safely and still made some dent in the disease. Zidovudine (AZT), the only drug in 1989 approved by the Federal Drug Administration to treat AIDS, was at first thought too toxic to use. But by using lower doses and taking "time outs" from treatment, AZT was tolerated and was prolonging the life of some AIDS patients.

Significance

Underground AIDS treatments like compound Q illustrated the controversy over the speed of the U.S. Federal Drug Administration's (FDA) drug approval process. Federal regulators had to consider the need to get drugs out on the market as quickly as possible in order to save lives. However, they also had to make sure the drugs were safe. On March 8, 1990, the FDA approved a retreatment study of compound Q. It was implemented by Project Inform and conducted by doctors in San Francisco, Los Angeles, Miami, and New York.

The end of the 1980s would signal somewhat of a turning point in AIDS treatment. In the 1980s, doctors felt completely helpless against AIDS, but that would change in the 1990s. Doctors were able to alleviate suffering, and new and better treatments were prolonging the life of AIDS patients. AZT was at least partly able to slow the HIV virus. Protease inhibitors and drugs that inhibited reverse transcriptase were showing great promise. Proteases are proteins that act by chopping up other proteins. Since a protease is necessary for HIV to infect cells, blocking the protease disabled HIV. Reverse transcriptase is necessary for HIV to convert its RNA into DNA. By inhibiting reverse transcriptase, HIV is also disabled. Thanks to new and promising drugs, AIDS in the 1990s was no longer a death sentence.

Primary Source

"The Underground Test of Compound Q"

SYNOPSIS: This *Time* magazine article conveys the desperate situation AIDS patients faced in the 1980s. While new AIDS drugs were beginning to be developed, many AIDS activists were impatient with the processes of the U.S. Food and Drug Administration, and many AIDS sufferers desperately sought hope from any new drug in development.

Bob Barnett sits on an examination table in San Francisco while an intravenous needle drips an experimental AIDS drug into his veins. The drug, called Compound Q, is a purified protein extracted from a cucumber-like Chinese plant and one of the latest promising glimmers in the search for a cure for AIDS. Across town, researchers at San Francisco General Hospital Medical Center are conducting cautious, federally approved Phase 1 toxicity trials with minute dosages of GLQ223, as Compound Q is officially known. But for Barnett, a 37-year-old former radio sales manager, as for thousands of others afflicted with AIDS, precious time is running out. Barnett wants to know if Compound Q works in larger therapeutic doses. He wants to know now. "My options are death and doing this," he says. Barnett is one of 51 AIDS patients who, along with six doctors, took part in underground trials of Compound Q this past spring and summer. The clandestine study was organized by Project Inform, a San Francisco-based group of activists who believe the Food and Drug Administration's system for testing potentially life-saving new drugs is unconscionably slow. On Sept. 19, Project Inform director Martin Delaney revealed the preliminary results of the underground trials to an intent crowd of some 500 predominantly gay men in San Francisco. Although many of the trial's volunteers, including Barnett, showed a marked decrease in activity of the human immunodeficiency virus (HIV) that causes AIDS, Delaney said, Compound Q could not be considered a cure. But the desperation of the epidemic guarantees that underground drug trials will continue; AIDS activists say at least two dozen such experiments are under way across the U.S.

Hope flashed through the nation's AIDS community last April, when researchers from the University of California at San Francisco announced that, in test tubes at least, Compound Q could kill HIV-infected cells while leaving healthy cells unaffected. The substance quickly found its way into the U.S. and to desperate AIDS patients, who administered the drug on their own. "Word was out," says Dr. Alan Levin, medical director of the Project Inform trials in San Francisco. "People started getting it and injecting themselves in their kitchens."

To Delaney, such haphazard self-medication posed its own threats. "We said, 'Instead of just passing it out to see what happens, let's channel it into controlled clinical use,'" Delaney recalls. He contacted James Corti, a Los Angeles-based activist and importer of AIDS drugs who shipped 400 doses of Compound Q out of China.

Delaney then asked a group of doctors to design a protocol, or test model, based on an FDA trial for a similar drug called Ricin Toxin. Delaney says several FDA and National Institutes of Health officials in Washington were told of Project Inform's proposed

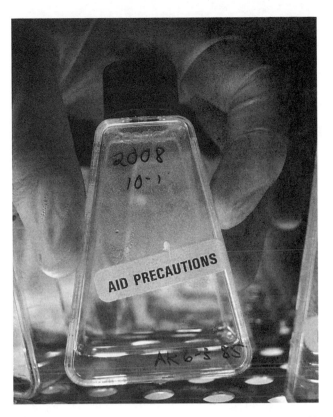

A laboratory bottle marked for AIDS researchers, June 11, 1985. In April 1989, researchers announced that they had discovered a compound that would kill HIV-infected cells while leaving healthy cells alone—at least in a test-tube environment. © NATHAN BENN/CORBIS. REPRODUCED BY PERMISSION.

trial, which was planned for patients in San Francisco, Los Angeles and New York City. "At no time did anyone tell us to stop," he says. An FDA spokesman in Washington claims officials did not hear about the clandestine trials until well after they began. Without revealing the purpose, Project Inform asked Genelabs, Inc., a California biotechnology firm that manufactures the drug in the U.S., to test samples of Compound Q that Corti brought back from China. They wanted to make sure it was identical to the Compound Q used in the FDA-approved study. An attorney drew up guidelines that would keep the trials within federal law. Each patient made a videotaped statement, in the presence of an attorney and a witness, that he was entering the trial of his own free will. "What we wanted was a trial that was faster than the FDA, yet as safe," says Dr. Larry Waites of San Francisco.

The trial's volunteers were all men who had failed to respond to conventional AIDS therapy, including AZT, so far the only FDA-approved drug for treating the AIDS virus. To obtain accurate readings on Compound Q's effectiveness, volunteers were asked to stop using any other approved or unapproved drugs.

The secret trials began on May 24 in San Francisco. For three weeks, patients received infusions of Compound Q, some as high as 17 times the dosage given patients in the San Francisco General Hospital toxicity trials. For the first 48 hours, the carefully monitored volunteers suffered side effects of sore muscles, nausea, fever and fatigue. The side effects eventually went away, and many patients, including Bob Barnett, began to feel more energetic.

The clandestine study became public in late June after a San Francisco volunteer suffocated on his vomit after coming out of a coma ten days following his first dose of Compound Q. The FDA launched an investigation into the underground trials, which Project Inform suspended. Two other volunteers have since died, one in San Francisco and one in New York. Levin says the death of one of the San Francisco men was indirectly related to Compound Q, while the cause of the New York man's death has yet to be determined. Some researchers raise serious doubts about the methodology of guerrilla drug tests. Project Inform is strongly criticized for bypassing an initial phase to establish Compound Q's safety before proceeding to larger, therapeutic dosages and for not having the trials reviewed by an external monitoring group. Says Jere Goyan, dean of the University of California at San Francisco School of Pharmacy and a former FDA commissioner: "If you get people taking these drugs willy-nilly around the country, you'll lose valuable information, and it will be at the expense of future patients."

To Delaney, such reasoning is flawed because it suggests that some victims who might be helped by experimental drugs may die while the traditional methods of testing drugs work their slow and cumbersome way. Pressure from AIDS activists has resulted in the FDA's allowing wider use of such experimental AIDS drugs as r-erythropoietin, which is used to treat AIDS-related anemia, before studies have been completed. Compound Q faces much more rigorous testing despite the hint of promise. "It's not a one-shot cure," Delaney warned the packed community meeting. But Bob Barnett, a true believer in his right to receive another dose of Compound Q, leaped to his feet with the rest of the crowd to give Delaney a standing ovation.

Further Resources

BOOKS

Arno, Peter S., and Karyn Feiden. *Against the Odds: The Story of AIDS Drug Development, Politics, and Profits.* New York: HarperCollins, 1992.

Joseph, Stephan D. *Dragon Within the Gates: The Once and Future AIDS Epidemic.* New York: Carroll & Graf, 1992.

PERIODICALS

Alexander, Charles P. "Medical Progress—Live! On CNN! An Experimental AIDS Treatment Tests the Judgment of Journalists." *Time,* June 25, 1990, 50.

Berger, Timothy G., Marian L. Obuch, and Ronald H. Goldschmidt. "Dermatologic Manifestations of HIV Infection." *American Family Physician* 41, no. 6, June 1990, 1729–1733.

Fettner, Ann Giudici. "Scientists Juggle '1,000 Drugs.'" *Medical World News* 30, no. 18, September 25, 1989, 66–68.

Palca, Joseph. "A Storm over Steroid Therapy." *Science,* November 30, 1990, 1196–1199.

WEBSITES

Berger, Daniel S. "Diary of an HIV Doctor: Life During the Early Years of the Epidemic." November/December 2000. Available online at http://www.thebody.com/tpan/novdec_00/diary.html; website home page:http://www.thebody.com/index.shtml (accessed March 1, 2003).

Project Inform. "The Body: An AIDS and HIV Information Resource." Available online at http://www.thebody.com/pinf/pinfpage.html; website home page: http://www.thebody.com/index.shtml (accessed March 1, 2003).

Koop: The Memoirs of America's Family Doctor
Memoir

By: C. Everett Koop

Date: 1991

Source: Koop, C. Everett. *Koop: The Memoirs of America's Family Doctor* New York: Random House, 1991, 3–8.

About the Author: Charles Everett Koop (1916–) was born in Brooklyn, New York. He received his bachelor of science degree from Dartmouth College in 1937 and his M.D from Cornell University Medical School in 1941. Koop served on the faculty of the University of Pennsylvania for over thirty years and served as the nation's surgeon general during the Reagan administration. ∎

Introduction

The office of surgeon general has a long history. The first national department concerned with the health of Americans was the U.S. Marine Hospital Service established by Congress in 1798. This department became the U.S. Public Health Organization under the control of a "Supervising Surgeon" appointed by the president of the United States. In the early 1950s, the Department of Health, Education and Welfare was created and the surgeon general position became nearly obsolete. Except for one report published in 1964 (concerning putting warning labels on cigarette packs) by Surgeon General Luther Terry, most people did not even realize that the nation had a surgeon general. The position was left vacant during the Nixon (served 1969–1974) administration, and President Jimmy Carter (served 1977–1981) combined the duties of surgeon general with those of the assistant secretary of health and human services.

Ronald Reagan (served 1981–1989), elected president in 1980, revived the position of surgeon general. By all accounts, he wanted to fill it with someone who would promote his beliefs—especially his stance against abortion. C. Everett Koop was passionate about abortion. He communicated his antiabortion philosophy in books, speeches, and lectures, whenever and wherever he could. Reagan felt Koop was a perfect fit for surgeon general. Koop, for his part, was nearing mandatory retirement age at the University of Pennsylvania Children's Hospital, where he was chief surgeon. The chance to affect the health of the entire country was an opportunity the altruistic, hardworking, and energetic Koop could not turn down.

Koop distinguished himself and the position of surgeon general in the 1980s. His chief goal was to make Americans healthier, and he did. His tenure is most notable for three issues: smoking, abortion, and AIDS. Koop's fair-minded and thoughtful handling of these issues earned him the respect and admiration of those on all sides of the issue. In spite of intense pressure from the Reagan administration, and even at times putting aside his own passionate beliefs, his reports and advice were based on what he felt was best for the nation.

Significance

C. Everett Koop redefined the position of surgeon general in the 1980s. Before Koop, the surgeon general's office was largely symbolic. Koop, however, was diligent, determined, and fervent. His Surgeon General Reports were highly regarded. In them, he tried to answer the questions of the American public and dispense advice as America's doctor. He is most proud of his antismoking campaign, in which he opened the eyes of the nation about the health hazards of cigarette smoking. During Koop's tenure, the percentage of the smoking population declined, the numbers of cigarette packs purchased dropped, and hundreds of antismoking laws were put on the books.

Koop's years as surgeon general included the emergence of HIV and AIDS. Much to the dismay of the Reagan administration, his 1986 report on AIDS faced the issue head-on. He advocated sex education, safe sex, and the use of condoms to prevent the spread of AIDS. Conservative members of Reagan's team even asked him to take the word *condom* out of the report, but Koop refused. In addition, he called for the compassionate treatment of AIDS victims. He urged doctors not to refuse to

Surgeon General C. Everett Koop speaks on his new campaign against drunk driving, Washington, D.C., May 1989. Koop redefined the position of surgeon general, which had previously been largely symbolic. © BETTMANN/CORBIS. REPRODUCED BY PERMISSION.

treat AIDS patients, reminding them of the Hippocratic oath. The surgeon general's AIDS pamphlet was one of the largest government mailings of all time (excluding tax forms). The report and pamphlet had a valuable effect on public thinking and helped to prevent the spread of AIDS.

The abortion issue exemplifies Koop's integrity and respect for the office of the surgeon general. Abortion is a highly contentious issue. In 1987, President Reagan asked Koop to write a report detailing the adverse health effects of abortion on women. But Koop's commitment to good science compelled him to write a straightforward letter to President Reagan saying, "I believe that the issue of abortion is so emotionally charged that it is possible that many who might read this letter would not understand it because I have not arrived at conclusions they can accept. But I have concluded in my review of this issue that, at this time, the available scientific evidence about the psychological sequelae [following from or caused by] of abortion simply cannot support either the preconceived beliefs of those pro-life or of those pro-choice." Koop was the health conscience of the country during the tumultuous 1980s, and he wouldn't have had it any other way.

Primary Source

Koop: The Memoirs of America's Family Doctor
[excerpt]

SYNOPSIS: C. Everett Koop reflects on his appointment as President Ronald Reagan's surgeon general and his first day on the job.

On an ordinary day in August 1980, a call slipped through the screening system in my office at the Children's Hospital of Philadelphia.

"Don't you think it's time the Surgeon General was a surgeon?"

"Who is this?"

"It doesn't matter—don't you think it's time the Surgeon General was a surgeon?"

I didn't have a ready answer. In fact, like most Americans, I didn't think about the Surgeon General very much, if at all. But my caller urged me to consider the opportunity to serve a new Republican administration. The presidential election was still fifteen weeks away, and I was anything but a politician, but instinctively I decided to keep my options open. I said I might be available. I took the caller's name and number and tucked it under the corner of my desk blotter. He was Carl Anderson, administrative aide to North Carolina Senator Jesse Helms.

The next day the Heritage Foundation called.

"You've turned up in our memory bank as a conservative Republican, one who is pro-life with a credible experience in academia. How would you like to be Surgeon General?"

I repeated to the second caller—whose name I no longer remember—that yes, I might be available. A new name and number joined its predecessor under the corner of the blotter.

A few days later came the third call.

"Dr. Koop, this is John Condon. We met at Billy Graham's when you briefed him on some biomedical issues. I am now a headhunter for Reagan–Bush. How would you like to be the Surgeon General?"

"What makes you so sure they'll be elected?"

"Don't worry about that!"

"This is the third call I've had on this subject. Do you guys work together? Do you know what each other is doing? . . . You can say I might be available."

That name and number found its place with the others.

Stretching back in my desk chair, I wondered about the timing of the calls. I was entering the last year of my academic career. I would turn sixty-five the next calendar year, and it was customary at the University of Pennsylvania School of Medicine to retire in June of the year when the magic number sixty-five rolled around.

A member of the medical school faculty since 1942, I had climbed the academic ladder to hold two professorships. In addition, as a pediatric surgeon, my clinical interests and credentials had put me in the role of surgeon-in-chief of the Children's Hospital of Philadelphia—the first in the country—since 1948. My retirement had already been planned for April: a farewell party in combination with a scientific program to which some of my colleagues in pediatric surgery from around the world had been invited. Then I would be old Mr. Chips at the Children's Hospital, with my successor already in my office.

Over the next few weeks, the three telephone calls about the Surgeon General position crossed my mind only infrequently. My wife, Betty—I alone usually call her Liz—mentioned it occasionally, but the prospect never seemed very real to me.

After work on election day in November 1980, Betty and I drove down to Deerfield, New Jersey, about an hour away from our suburban Philadelphia home, to watch the election returns with our son Norman and his wife, Anne. As I say, I was not a political animal, my only involvement in politics being limited to membership on the Committee of 70, a political watchdog committee striving to keep voting honest on election day in Philadelphia—no small chore. I wanted to see a Republican victory in 1980 because I—like most of the electorate, as it turned out—was fretting about the apparent inability of our country to achieve its potential during the Carter administration. As we watched the Reagan landslide, I felt an optimism unlike anything I had previously felt on an election evening.

As we drove home, Betty, with her customary good sense, gave me a bit of advice that changed my life: As usual, she was filling her role as my most valued counselor. Over the years, her advice had repeatedly—and wisely—steered our course.

"You do know you're going to be miserable in the job you've chosen for yourself next year after you retire. Have you really thought what it would be like, after being chief for thirty-some years, to be floating around the hospital—operating, teaching, and so on, but with someone else at the helm? You will still be regarded by many as the boss, and they'll bring you all their dissatisfactions that come with a new regime—but you'll be powerless to do anything about it. You'll be miserable. Why don't you call those people about being Surgeon General?"

Driving along in the Pennsylvania darkness, I knew she was right. I didn't have a shred of enthusiasm as I looked at my future. So Wednesday morning, first thing, I found tucked under the leather border of my desk blotter the wrinkled scraps of paper with the three names and phone numbers.

Rather miraculously, I found the first two immediately at the other end of the line. John Condon called me back. I remember being surprised that his wife knew who I was. I said the same thing to each: "When we last spoke, I said in reference to the appointment of Surgeon General that I 'might be available.' I would like to change that now to 'enthusiastically seeking.'" . . .

Once I had decided I wanted the position of Surgeon General, I found myself whipsawed between optimism and pessimism. After my name was announced as one of several possible candidates for Surgeon General, I began to receive newspaper editorials and copies of letters sent to congressmen urging my appointment. I didn't know if and when I would ever hear anything official from the Reagan people. Each day brought more reports, rumors, and suggestions that I was "in," only to be followed by similar signs and clues that could only mean I was "out."

When Richard Schweiker was appointed Secretary of Health and Human Services, the first of three with whom I would work, I saw that as a good sign. I had met Schweiker before and saw this as a good appointment. On Valentine's Day Schweiker told me that President Reagan had appointed me as deputy assistant secretary of health, with the promise that I would be nominated as Surgeon General and that shortly thereafter there would be a reorganization of HHS. No one ever said explicitly that the price of my job was to be the zealous pursuit of the pro-life agenda. I don't think even Schweiker fully understood this.

I was excited. And I was not at all concerned about one little technical problem. I was too old. Schweiker called me one night to say he had just learned that existing legislation mandated that the Surgeon General could be no more than sixty-four years and twenty-nine days old. I had been alive for about one hundred days longer than that. But, he assured me, the Senate, which by statute had to offer its "advice and consent" to the president regarding the appointment, could see that Congress changed the law. After all, the nation had just elected seventy-year-old Ronald Reagan as our oldest president. Certainly no one could imagine that a sixty-four-year-old would be barred from serving as Surgeon General. . . .

My first day on the job, March 9, 1981, I felt worse than when I was a little boy on the first day at a new school. I had received a letter to report to a room on the seventh floor of the Department of Health and Human Services' Humphrey Building, two blocks down the Mall from the Capitol. The little office was starkly empty except for a desk and a chair. Following instructions, I sat there and waited for someone to show up. And waited. I busied myself by cleaning the telephone. Through my window I could see the dome of the Capitol, the American flag crowning it flapping in the breeze. It was a stirring sight, and as I gazed out the window, I felt a sense of mission and purpose that I had not felt since that day early in 1946 when I had first walked into the Children's Hospital to begin my career in pediatric surgery. Now I stood on the brink of a new career. How could it possibly top the sense of accomplishment and joy that pediatric surgery had brought?

My sense of expectancy and enthusiasm diminished as the hours crept by. In the early afternoon, Charlie Miller, retiring deputy assistant secretary of health, took me to meet Ed Brandt, my new boss, who had recently been designated assistant secretary of health. A laconic Oklahoman apparently preoccupied by his own confirmation concerns, Ed simply told me I would have to be sworn in. He gave me no further explanations or instructions. Tom McFee, deputy assistant secretary of health (personnel) did the honors. I went back to my cheerless office with its uncluttered desk, looked again at the Capitol dome and the American flag, and wondered if my new role would ever make sense. My sense of isolation began to grow.

If ever I believed in the sovereignty of God, it was during those first lonely minutes in that vacant Washington office. I felt a great sense of God and country, of mission and opportunity. In spite of my misgivings that first day, I believed the only clouds on the horizon were small. There was that technical problem about my age, but I trusted the people who said it was nothing to worry about. Although I had seen a few articles in the press noting the dissatisfaction expressed by some pro-abortion groups about my appointment, it had not yet dawned on me what vicious opposition I would face from both them and other groups as I awaited confirmation.

I faced a long uphill climb against formidable foes. I would need to prove myself each day, each time I met someone. It was going to be just like my first days as a surgeon at the Children's Hospital of Philadelphia, when I had to prove myself to people who said I was not needed, who told me I was unwanted. It was going to be lonely and tough, just like my first days at PS 124 back in Brooklyn.

Further Resources

BOOKS

Bianchi, Anne. *C. Everett Koop: The Health of the Nation.* Brookfield, Conn.: Millbrook Press, 1992.

Cooper, Terry L. *Exemplary Public Administrators: Character and Leadership in Government.* San Francisco: Jossey-Bass, 1992.

Easterbrook, Gregg. *Surgeon Koop.* Knoxville, Tenn.: Whittle Direct Books, 1991.

PERIODICALS

Bowman, James S., and Brent Wall. "Koop as an Exemplar of Moral and Democratic Decision Making: An Axial Approach to Ethical Theory." *Administration and Society* 29, no. 3, July 1997, 251–276.

Koop, C. Everett. "A to Z. Medical Advice from C. Everett Koop, Surgeon General of the United States." *U.S. News & World Report,* May 30, 1988, 64.

Pollner, Fran. "Dr. Koop Assesses His Record." *Medical World News* 30, no. 13, July 10, 1989, 15–17.

Wallace, Carol. "C. Everett Koop." *People Weekly,* April 21, 1986, 91–95.

WEBSITES

National Library of Medicine. *Reports of the Surgeon General.* Available online at http://sgreports.nlm.nih.gov/NN/ListBy Date.html; website home page: http://profiles.nlm.nih.gov /(accessed March 7, 2003).

Office of the Surgeon General. Available online at http:// www.surgeongeneral.gov/sgoffice.htm (accessed March 7, 2003).

Prozac Diary

Diary

By: Lauren Slater
Date: 1998
Source: Slater, Lauren. *Prozac Diary.* New York: Random House, 1998. 3–6, 9–10, 15–16, 24–25.
About the Author: Lauren Slater (1962–) was born in Boston, Massachusetts. She has a master's degree in psychol-

ogy from Harvard and a doctorate from Boston University. She is the director of AfterCare Services, a mental health clinic, teaches creative nonfiction writing at Goucher College, and has written several nonfiction books. ■

Introduction

A sequence of electrochemical events form the basis of the human mind. Neurons (brain and nerve cells) are different from other cells in our body in that they directly communicate with each other. The flow of information between neurons is sequential, proceeding in an electrical-to-chemical-to-electrical order. Information originates and flows from what is called a presynaptic neuron in the form of an electrical signal. As the electrical signal exits the neuron it is converted into a chemical. This chemical crosses the gap between the presynaptic neuron (the sending neuron) and the postsynaptic neuron (the receiving neuron). The gap between the two neurons is called the synapse—hence the terms *pre* synaptic and *post* synaptic. Finally, the chemical enters the postsynaptic neuron, where it is converted back into an electrical signal. Our thoughts occur by these signals traveling from neuron to neuron.

The chemical messengers that cross the synaptic gap play a major role in neuron communication and in determining much of who we are and what we feel, think and do. These chemical messengers are called neurotransmitters. An imbalance of neurotransmitters, either too much or too little, is related to the symptoms of various mental diseases. There are several different neurotransmitters that modulate activity in the brain. One group of neurotransmitters, called "monoamines," includes acetylcholine, norepinephrine, dopamine, and serotonin. The first pharmaceuticals prescribed for depression included monoamine oxidase inhibitors (MAOIs). These antidepressants work by stopping the action of a certain enzyme (called monamine oxidase) that degrades the monoamine neurotransmitters. So, MAOIs work by getting rid of the "hit man" (monoamine oxidase) that normally gets rid of the monoamine. The overall effect is that there is an increase in the levels of monoamines in the synaptic space.

Fluoxetine hydrochloride (Prozac is the trade name), introduced in 1987, represented the first of a new type of antidepressant called a selective serotonin reuptake inhibitor (SSRI). Serotonin is an important monoamine neurotransmitter derived from the amino acid tryptophan. Fluoxetine achieves its therapeutic effect by interfering *solely* with the reabsorption of serotonin within the synaptic space between neurons. Thus, it increases the levels of serotonin. Fluoxetine often relieves cases of depression that have failed to yield to other antidepressants, and it also produces fewer and less serious side effects. Fluoxetine became one of the most widely used antidepressants by the end of the twentieth century.

Significance

Fluoxetine was the first selective serotonin reuptake inhibitor (SSRI) to hit the commercial market in the 1980s. It led to several other SSRIs, which are now the most widely used antidepressants in the United States: citalopram (Celexa), fluvoxamine (Luvox), paroxetine (Paxil), and sertraline (Zoloft). The primary uses for the SSRIs include unipolar and bipolar major depression, obsessive-compulsive disorder (OCD), and anxiety disorders.

Some research has suggested that Prozac does more than eliminate the symptoms of mental illness and actually improves one's personality. In her book *Prozac Diary,* Slater supports this view: "Prior to Prozac, when asked to describe my early history, I would tell a story of depression with roots so far-reaching even my earliest memories came up gray. . . . But, having been on Prozac for ten years now, I notice my memory of my early life changing a bit. I still vividly recall the whiteness, the fear, the cold, the cuts. But the lifting of illness, incomplete though it is, has brought other, more colorful glints as well. In altering my present sense of who I am, Prozac has demanded a revisioning of my history, and this revisioning is, perhaps, the most stunning side effect of all."

Primary Source

Prozac Diary [excerpt]

SYNOPSIS: In these excerpts, Lauren Slater describes her first encounter with Prozac and the "miraculous" changes it worked in her.

To get there, you turn left off the highway and drive down the road bordered on one side by pasture. And then, a radio song or so later, you turn right into the hospital's gated entrance, easing your car up the slope that leads to the turreted place where he waits. Safety screens cover all the windows. The stairs are steep, and exit signs cast carmine shadows on the concrete floors. Four flights you must travel, and then down several serpentine corridors, before you finally come to his office.

I had never been here before. I had never heard the word *Prozac* before. It was 1988, the drug just released. I was to be one of the first to take Prozac, and, even though I didn't know this then, one of the first to stay on it for the next ten years, experienc-

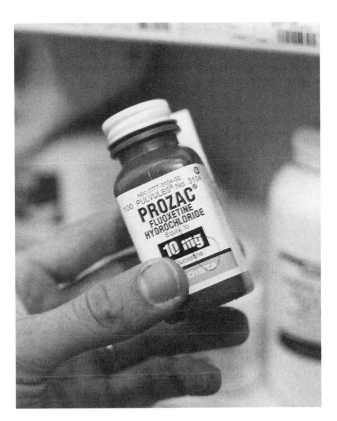

A pharmacist displays a bottle of Prozac. Prozac was the first of a new generation of antidepressant drugs called selective serotonin uptake inhibitors (SSRIs). It entered the market in 1988. © DAVID BUTOW/ CORBIS SABA. REPRODUCED BY PERMISSION.

ing what longterm existence on this new medication is actually like.

The Prozac Doctor is a busy man. He sees thirty, forty, sometimes fifty patients a day. He is handsome in ways you don't expect your medicine man to be. He has shining black hair and beautiful loafers made of leather so fresh you can practically see the hide still ripple with life. He wears one simple gold band on a finger as tapered as a pianist's, topped with a chip of nacreous nail sanded to perfect smoothness. He is host as well as doctor, and that first time, as well as every time thereafter, he invites me in, standing behind his desk and ushering me forward with stately sweeps of his hand, bowing ever so slightly in a room where you half expect caterers carrying platters of shrimp to emerge from the shadows.

"Sit, Ms. Slater," he said to me the morning we met. He gestured to a deep seat, and I sat. There was a silence between us then, a kind of weighted silence, a grand silence, like the sort you hear before a symphony begins.

And that day was the beginning, the bare beginnings of a story very little like the popular Prozac myths—a wonder drug here, a drug that triggers violence there. No. For me the story of Prozac lies not between these poles but entirely outside of them, in a place my doctor was not taught to get to—the difficulty and compromise of cure, the grief and light of illness passing, the fear as the walls of the hospital wash away and you have before you this—this strange planet, pressing in.

But that first day, there was just Prozac pressing in. I looked around me at the office. On the doctor's desk I saw a Lucite clock with the word PROZAC embossed across the top. I saw a marble mount holding four pens with PROZAC etched down their flanks. The pads of paper resting on his bookshelf were the precise size and shape of hors d'oeuvre napkins, and all had PROZAC in fancy script across their borders, like the name of some new country club.

"What is this stuff?" I asked. I heard my voice repeat itself in my ears, as so many sounds seemed to do lately, the screech of brakes, birdsong nipping at my brain.

The doctor leaned back in his seat. "Prozac," he said, "is the chemical compound fluoxetine hydrochloride." He told me it had a three-ring chemical structure similar to that of other medications I'd tried in the past but that its action on the body's serotonin system made it a finer drug. He told me about the brain chemical serotonin and its role in OCD—obsessive-compulsive disorder—the most recent of my many ills, for me the nattering need to touch, count, check, and tap, over and over again. He told me about synapses and clefts, and despite the time he took with me that day, I felt him coming at me across a gulf. . . .

"We will start," he said to me, "with twenty milligrams a day, a single capsule, although OCD, unlike depression, usually requires a higher dose." He showed me how, if the dose made me nauseous, I could split the pill and try half, and when I asked him what, exactly, was inside, he told me the story of the drug's design. He told me about Eli Lilly's campus in Indiana, where Prozac was first made, how a man raised rats and then ground their brains into something called a synaptosome, which became this medicine. He told me how Prozac marked a revolution in psychopharmacology because of its selectivity on the serotonin system; it was a drug with the precision of a Scud missile, launched miles away

from its target only to land, with a proud flare, right on the enemy's roof.

I pictured the proud flare. I pictured the grounds of Eli Lilly, green and winding. Inside, the labs were clean. White-coated technicians were plucking the gray matter from rats, extracting the liquid transmitters, some kind of healing wet.

I hoped then.

I hoped to be helped. . . .

Evaluation and Treatment Plan

Patient Name: Lauren J. Slater

Patient Age: 26

Evaluating Physician: Dr. Morris Koskava

Date of Evaluation: May 22, 1988

1. Presenting Problem and History:

Patient currently presents with symptoms that meet the criteria for Obsessive-Compulsive Disorder. However this diagnosis can be seen as secondary as opposed to primary. Patient reports OCD, with its attendant compulsions to count, check, and wash, emerged rather suddenly and unexpectedly w/in last few months. However, patient does have a long history of psychopathology prior to the manifestation of her present complaint. Has in the past attempted suicide, and engaged in self-mutilating behaviors, including anorexia, that resulted in psychiatric hospitalizations: dates, 1977, 1979, 1983, 1984, 1985, Record indicates patient has carried a diagnosis of Borderline Personality Disorder since 19 years of age, and a diagnosis of major depression, severe and recurrent, beginning in her early— . . .

To describe the subtle but potent shift caused by Prozac is to tussle with failing words, sensations that seep beyond language. But that doesn't make it any less miraculous. Doctors assure the public that psychotropic drugs don't get a patient high; rather, supposedly, they return the patient to a normal state of functioning. But what happens if such a patient, say, myself, for instance, has rarely if ever experienced a normal state of functioning? What happens if such a patient has spent much of her life in mental hospitals, both pursuing and pursued by one illness after another? What happens if "regular life" to such a person has always meant cutting one's arms, or gagging? If this is the case, then the "normal state" that Prozac ushers in is an experience in the surreal, Dali's dripping clock, a disorientation so deep and sweet you spin. Thus Prozac, make no mistake about it, blissed me out and freaked me out and later on, when the full force of health hit me, sometimes stunned me with grief.

Further Resources

BOOKS

Breggin, Peter R. *Talking Back to Prozac: What Doctors Aren't Telling You about Today's Most Controversial Drug.* New York: St. Martin's Press, 1994.

Fieve, Ronald R. *Prozac: Questions and Answers for Patients, Family and Physicians.* New York: Avon, 1994.

Kramer, Peter D. *Listening to Prozac.* New York: Penguin, 1993.

LeDoux, Joseph. *Synaptic Self.* New York: Viking Penguin, 2002.

PERIODICALS

"The Chemistry of Despair." *The Economist (US),* June 16, 1990, 95–97.

Wernicke, J. "The Side Effect Profile and Safety of Fluoxetine."*Journal of Clinical Psychiatry* 46, 1985, 59–67.

WEBSITES

National Institute of Mental Health. "Depression." Available online at http://www.nimh.nih.gov/publicat/depressionmenu.cfm; website home page http://www.nimh.nih.gov (accessed March 9, 2003).

Virtual Hospital. "Selective Serotonin Reuptake Inhibitors." Available online at http://www.vh.org/adult/provider/psychiatry/CPS/13.html; website home page: http://www.vh.org (accessed March 9, 2003).

10

RELIGION

DENNIS A. CASTILLO

Entries are arranged in chronological order by date of primary source. For entries with one primary source, the entry title is the same as the primary source title. Entries with more than one primary source have an overall entry title, followed by the titles of the primary sources.

Important Events in Religion, 1980–1989

1980

- On January 24, delegates from ten Protestant denominations seeking church unity approve a proposal for a common ministry for a projected united church. The new church would be known as the Church of Christ Uniting.

- In April, the Church of Jesus Christ of Latter-Day Saints (Mormons) celebrates 150 years of institutional existence.

- On April 29, more than two hundred thousand evangelical Christians gather in Washington, D.C., for a "Washington for Jesus" rally and march.

- On May 4, Pope John Paul II issues a directive banning all Roman Catholic priests and nuns from serving in public office.

- On August 4, Roman Catholic nun and 1979 Nobel Prize winner Mother Teresa visits the United States on a four-day mission.

- On October 11, Rev. Jerry Falwell says that he believes that God hears the prayers of Jews, reversing his earlier position.

- On November 4, Ronald Reagan is elected president after being greatly supported by the New Christian Right.

1981

- Richard A. Viguerie's book *The New Right: We're Ready to Lead,* revised after the national elections, is published.

- The Dalai Lama conducts a six-week tour of the United States.

- On March 26, the Moral Majority launches an advertising campaign to counter criticism that it is anti-Semitic, opposed to women's rights, and that its concerns are really political and not moral.

- On April 17, the National Council of Churches and several major Protestant denomination leaders stage a Good Friday protest in Washington, D.C., against the United States' giving military aid to El Salvador.

- On May 13, Pope John Paul II is shot in the abdomen by a Turkish terrorist, Mehmet Ali Agca, while being driven into Saint Peter's Square in Vatican City.

- On July 28, antiwar activists Father Daniel Berrigan and his brother, former priest Philip Berrigan, are sentenced to three to ten years in prison for participating in an antinuclear protest and damaging warheads in Pennsylvania.

1982

- On March 4, the Coalition for Better Television calls for a nationwide boycott of the National Broadcasting Company (NBC) and its parent company, RCA Corporation, claiming too much violence, sex, and anti-Christian messages are on the airwaves.

- On March 23, President Ronald Reagan is given a humanitarian award by the National Conference of Christians and Jews.

- On May 6, President Reagan endorses a constitutional amendment authorizing voluntary group prayer in public schools.

- On May 7, Baptist evangelist Billy Graham leads more than six hundred religious leaders in a weeklong antinuclear conference held in the Soviet Union.

- On June 3, the Equal Rights Amendment (ERA), having been under fire from the "Religious Right" and the Catholic Church since its inception, is defeated after falling three states short of ratification.

- On July 16, the Rev. Sun Myung Moon, leader of the Unification Church (the "Moonies"), is sentenced to eighteen months in prison and fined twenty-five thousand dollars for tax fraud and conspiracy to obstruct justice.

- On August 29, a Gallup poll shows American public opinion almost evenly divided between belief in biblical accounts of creation and belief in the theory of evolution.

- On November 3, a federal appeals court in Pawtucket, Rhode Island, rules that the city has violated the constitutional prohibition on the establishment of religion by displaying a Christian nativity scene.

- On November 22, a federal district judge rules unconstitutional a Louisiana law requiring the teaching of "scientific creationism" in the state's public schools.

1983

- The White House declares 1983 as the Year of the Bible.

- On February 23, the Synagogue Council of America issues a statement urging President Reagan and Soviet leader Yuri V. Andropov to seek a "total cessation of the production and deployment of nuclear weapons."

- On May 3, the National Conference of Catholic Bishops publishes "The Challenge of Peace: God's Promise and Our Response."

- The California State Board of Equalization strips away the tax-exempt status of the Rev. Robert H. Schuller's $18 million Crystal Cathedral.

- On June 8, a diverse group of U.S. religious leaders calls for Congress to limit genetic research and ban genetic engineering.

- On June 10, the Presbyterian Church U.S.A. is formed by the merger of the Northern and Southern branches of the denomination.

- On October 14, the National Council of Churches publishes a translation of the Bible that attempts to avoid referring to God and humanity exclusively in the masculine.

- On November 3, the Rev. Jesse Jackson declares his candidacy for the 1984 Democratic presidential nomination.
- On November 8, the People's Temple is officially dissolved as a legal and corporate entity nearly five years after the tragic suicides of hundreds in Jonestown.
- On November 20, conservative organizations condemn the antinuclear television film *The Day After,* calling it leftist, disarmament propaganda.

1984

- The Assemblies of God church creates a satellite television network to broadcast across the nation.
- Membership in religious congregations in the United States rises almost 1 percent in 1984, according to the National Council of Churches.
- On January 10, the United States and the Vatican establish full diplomatic relations after an eleven-year hiatus.
- On February 26, the Rev. Jesse Jackson apologizes for referring to Jews as "Hymies" and New York City as "Hymietown."
- On April 5, the Reorganized Church of Jesus Christ of Latter-Day Saints votes to accept a revelatory document authorizing the ordination of women.
- In May, the United Methodist Church celebrates the two hundredth anniversary of American Methodism.
- On June 24, John Cardinal O'Connor of New York declares that no Catholic "in good conscience" can vote for a pro-choice candidate for elected office.
- On June 28, the Rev. Jesse Jackson disavows minister Louis Farrakhan and his Nation of Islam for their anti-Semitic remarks.
- On November 11, the National Conference of Catholic Bishops releases the first draft of its pastoral letter on the state of the United States' economy

1985

- On January 24, the heads of the three major Lutheran Churches protest the indictments of the Sanctuary Movement supporters.
- On February 14, the U.S. Rabbinical Assembly of Conservative Judaism announces its acceptance of women rabbis.
- On April 24, the Procter & Gamble Company announces that it is phasing out its distinctive emblem carried on its products because of intense criticism from Christian groups who believe the emblem is a symbol for Satan.
- On May 5, President Reagan infuriates American Jews with his visit to a West German cemetery at Bitburg.
- On August 19, the Rev. Jerry Falwell, after visiting South Africa, declares his support for the Pretoria regime and vows to oppose U.S. economic sanctions on that nation.
- On October 2, Rabbi Meir Kahane is stripped of his U.S. citizenship after assuming a seat in the Israeli parliament in 1984.
- On October 28, U.S. authorities arrest Indian guru Bhagwan Shree Rajneesh in Oregon after he had made his rich followers give him money to buy a fleet of Rolls Royces.

1986

- *The Christian Science Monitor* expands its monthly television news broadcast to a weekly program.
- The American Baptist Churches in the U.S.A. announces a new $30 million national church-building campaign titled "Alive in Mission."
- On January 3, Rev. Jerry Falwell founds his Liberty Federation.
- On January 16, the British government announces that it has barred minister Louis Farrakhan from entering Great Britain, saying his presence there "would not be conducive to the public good."
- On June 23, the Unitarian-Universalist Church marks the twenty-fifth anniversary of the two churches' merger.
- On August 18, Father Charles E. Curran is barred by the Vatican from teaching theology because of his dissenting views on sexual matters.
- On October 1, the Christian Broadcasting Network (CBN) celebrates its twenty-fifth anniversary.

1987

- Robert Peel's *Spiritual Healing in a Scientific Age* is published and reaffirms the Christian Scientist belief in faith healing.
- In March, evangelical preacher Oral Roberts begins his month-long campaign to raise $4.5 million or he claims "God could call Oral Roberts home."
- On March 19, Praise the Lord (PTL) founder Jim Bakker resigns after revelations that he committed adultery and stole funds from his ministry.
- On June 30, the United Church of Christ adopts a declaration on Judaism acknowledging the continuing religious validity of the Jewish faith.
- In July, the North American Congress on the Holy Spirit, in the largest Pentecostal gathering of the year, adopts the goal of converting half the world's population to Jesus Christ by the year 2000.
- On August 16, the Harmonic Convergence, a two-day gathering of New Agers, begins.
- On September 7, a *Time* magazine poll reveals that 53 percent of Catholics in the United States believe priests should be allowed to marry.
- On September 10, Pope John Paul II begins his ten-day tour of the United States, titled "Unity in the Work of Service."
- On December 7, *Time* magazine devotes its cover story, "New Age Harmonies," to the growing New Age movement in the nation.
- On December 10, U.S. Catholic bishops release a position paper on AIDS that allows for the teaching of condom usage.

1988

- The National Missionary Baptist Convention is founded.
- On January 1, the Evangelical Lutheran Church in America is formed.

- On April 6, the Rev. Marion "Pat" Robertson declares that he will no longer campaign actively for the Republican presidential nomination.

- On April 8, the Rev. Jimmy Swaggart is defrocked by the Assemblies of God for refusing to accept discipline by church leadership.

- On May 3, the United Methodist Church revises its hymnal and book of worship to reflect the Church's position on non-gender-specific language.

- On May 15, the Rev. Pat Robertson files papers to create a new PAC, Americans for the Republic, that will train and fund conservative Christian political candidates.

- On August 12, the film *The Last Temptation of Christ* opens to much criticism and protest by Christian and Jewish groups.

1989

- On January 22, President George Bush signs a proclamation establishing a National Day of Prayer and Thanksgiving.

- On February 11, the Rev. Barbara Clementine Harris becomes the first woman consecrated as a bishop in the Episcopal Church.

- The Vatican officially condemns racism as sinful and identifies the United States and South Africa as nations with major racial problems.

- On February 25, more than four thousand American Muslims pray and burn effigies of writer Salman Rushdie in front of the New York offices of Viking Penguin, the American publisher of *The Satanic Verses*.

- On June 2, the Episcopal Synod of America is formed after dissenting conservative Episcopalians splinter from the main branch because of their opposition to the ordination of female priests and bishops.

- On June 10, the Moral Majority is officially dissolved.

- On July 2, Father George A. Stallings, Jr., establishes an African American Catholic congregation.

- On October 24, former PTL leader Jim Bakker is sentenced to forty-five years in prison and fined five hundred thousand dollars for fraud and conspiracy convictions.

Religion in America, 1981

Survey

By: The Gallup Organization

Date: 1981

Source: *Religion in America, 1981*. Princeton, N.J.: The Gallup Organization & The Princeton Religion Research Center, 1981.

About the Organization: George Gallup (1901–1984) was born in Jefferson, Iowa, and he died in Switzerland at eighty-two. Trained as a journalist, he earned his Ph.D. from the University of Iowa in 1928. His dissertation, "A New Technique for Objective Methods for Measuring Reader Interest in Newspapers," laid the foundation for his future career as a professional pollster and public opinion statistician. In 1935, he founded the American Institute of Public Opinion. ■

Introduction

Between 1860 and 1960, the United States could be described as a predominately Protestant country, with the odd twist that its largest single denomination was Roman Catholic. The religious map was a patchwork of groups dominating specific areas of the country—Catholics in the urban areas and Northeast, Baptists in the South, and Methodists in the Midwest. Until the 1960s, this semi-establishment of Protestantism (composed of Baptists, Congregationalists, Episcopalians, Methodists, and Presbyterians) dominated the religious scene. The only significant non-Christian group were the Jews.

In the decade of the 1950s, there were increases in religious membership and finances, as well as church construction. The role of these traditional churches looked very stable at the time. During the 1960s and early 1970s, however, this peaceful landscape was challenged on multiple fronts. The Civil Rights movement, the "Sexual Revolution," the Vietnam War (1964–1975), and Women's Liberation shook the pastoral world of most Americans. New specifically religious developments also appeared and appealed to many of the young. These included new "alternative" spiritualities—most of Eastern origin, including yoga, transcendental meditation, Buddhism, and Hinduism.

Traditional American religious institutions were grouped together with the government, military, and big business as part of "the Establishment." The protest movement led many young people out of organized religion, and, during the 1960s and early-1970s, many observers predicted that religious practice would become extinct. During the 1980s, this was proven untrue. While religious groups have not recovered to their pre-1960 level, they are still an important part of American society.

Significance

The document below is an excerpt of a joint publication by the Gallup Organization and the Princeton Religion Research Center, *Religion in America in 1981*. It documents two phenomenon: first, the decline in church and synagogue membership in the United States since the middle of the twentieth century; and second, despite this decline, it shows how prominent religious practice remained in the 1980s, in particular within certain groups.

The peak year for church and synagogue membership was 1947, with the poll showing a membership rate of seventy-six percent, as compared to sixty-nine percent in 1980. The poll did note, however, that evangelical and more conservative groups were growing. This would be a phenomenon more closely examined in the selection on fundamentalism.

As far as the characteristics of American religion in 1980, the poll revealed many interesting items of information. First, there were significant geographic differences in church and synagogue membership. The South led this category with a rate of seventy-five percent, followed closely by the Midwest at seventy-three percent. The East came in at sixty-nine percent, and the West had a fifty-three percent rate.

Despite struggles over the ordination of women, seventy-three percent of women belonged to a religious community. Those least likely to belong to a church or synagogue were those living in the West (fifty-three percent), the divorced (fifty-seven percent), young adults (fifty-nine percent), and those with no more than a high school education (seventy percent). It is interesting to note that while critics of religion will say that it is a superstitious practice preying on the weak-minded, those with a college education were more likely to be members of a church or synagogue.

Primary Source

Religion in America, 1981

SYNOPSIS: While not as prominent as in other periods of American history, religious groups in the United States still could count a significant majority of the population as members. This influence was further reinforced through the large number of

Worshippers attend a church service, Detroit, Michigan, c. 1982. According to Gallup Polls in 1980, 93 percent of Americans indicated a religious preference; nearly all said they preferred Judaism or one of the Christian religions. © DAVID TURNLEY/CORBIS. REPRODUCED BY PERMISSION.

primary and secondary schools, colleges and universities, hospitals, and charitable activities that the various denominations operated.

In 1980, a total of 93% of adults indicated a religious preference, with 61% saying their preference was Protestant, 28% Catholic, 2% Jewish, one percent Eastern Orthodox, and one percent other religious preferences. A total of 7% in the 1980 surveys said they have no religious preference.

An examination of trends in religious preference over the last three decades shows the proportion of Catholics in the U.S. adult population to have increased by nearly one-half since 1947.

In 1947, one adult in five (20 percent) stated his or her religious preference as Catholic. In 1979, the figure was 29 percent. The 1980 figure is 28%, statistically the same.

Various factors contributing to the dramatic growth in the proportion of Catholics in the U.S. populace could include a relatively higher birth rate and the influx of Hispanics.

Over the same period of time, the proportion of Protestants in the adult population has declined from 69 percent in 1947 to 59 percent in 1979. The 1980 figure is virtually the same, 61%. A decline in the proportion of those giving their religious preference as Jewish has also been recorded—from five percent in 1947 to two percent in 1972 and in subsequent surveys.

The appeal of religious faiths *other* than the four major communities (Protestantism, Catholicism, Judaism, and Orthodoxy) appears to have been greatest in the early and mid-seventies. This group includes Buddhists, Hindus, Moslems and numerous other faiths.

Particular attention should be given to the "none" category. While the overwhelming majority of American adults continue to state a religious preference, the proportion who say they have "no preference" quadrupled between 1967 when the proportion was two percent and 1979 when the comparable figure was eight percent. The 1980 figure is 7%.

The 33-year downtrend in church and synagogue membership appears to have levelled out in 1980, with 69% of the 10,982 adults surveyed saying they are members.

In 1979 and 1978 the membership figure was 68%.

Church and synagogue membership had been on a steady overall downtrend since 1947 when the Gallup Poll showed 76% to be members. Here is the trend:

Church or Synagogue Membership

1937	73%
1938	73
1939	72
1940	72
1942	75
1944	75
1947	76
1952	73
1965	73
1975	71
1976	71
1977	70
1978	68
1979	68
1980	69

It is important to note that while overall church membership for all faiths has been on the decline, certain denominations (primarily those in the evangelical group) have reported membership gains in recent years.

Furthermore, it is important to bear in mind that the percentages represent *self-classifications:* the proportion of people who *say* they are members of a church. They thus may include some who are not actually on the rolls of a local church. Furthermore, it should be noted that adherents of certain faiths—such as Roman Catholics and the Eastern Orthodox—are considered to be members at birth.

73% of Women are Members

Most likely to say they are members of a church are women (73 percent), non-whites (71 percent), adults 50 years of age and older (76 percent), persons living in the Midwest (73 percent) and South (75 percent), and married persons (72 percent).

Little difference is found on the basis of formal education, with 70 percent of persons with a college background saying they are members compared to 68 percent among those with only a high school background and 70 percent among those with only a grade school background.

As perhaps would be expected, demographic patterns for church membership closely parallel patterns for church attendance. As determined by the 1980 Gallup Audit of Church Attendance, the most regular attenders, for example, are found among women, non-whites, older adults, persons living in the Midwest and South, and Catholics.

Following is the question asked to measure church membership on the basis of self-classification:

> Do you happen to be a member of a church or synagogue, or not?

The following table shows church membership by key groups, based on an average of the results of surveys taken in 7 selected weeks during 1980:

Church Membership
(Self-classification)

Major faiths:

Catholics	80%
Protestants	72
Jews	51

5 Major Protestant Churches:

Baptists	75
Methodists	72
Lutherans	76
Presbyterians	75
Episcopalians	70

By Demographics:

East	69
Midwest	73
South	75
West	53
18–29 years	59
30–49 years	68
50 and over	76
College background	70
High school	68

Further Resources

BOOKS

Greeley, Andrew M. *Religious Change in America.* Cambridge, Mass.: Harvard University Press, 1996.

Lawrence, Bruce B. *New Faiths, Old Fears: Muslims and other Asian Immigrants in American Religious Life.* New York: Columbia University Press, 2002.

Robbins, Thomas. *In Gods We Trust: New Patterns of Religious Pluralism in America.* New Brunswick, N.J.: Transaction Publishers, 1990.

The Fundamentalist Phenomenon: The Resurgence of Conservative Christianity

Nonfiction work

By: Jerry Falwell

Date: 1981

Source: Falwell, Jerry. *The Fundamentalist Phenomenon: The Resurgence of Conservative Christianity.* Garden City, N.Y.: Doubleday, 1981.

About the Author: Jerry Falwell (1933–), a prominent fundamental religious leader of the 1980s, was born in Lynchburg, Virginia. Ordained in 1956, Rev. Falwell founded a Baptist congregation in his hometown that grew to 22,000, and he established the Moral Majority, a political organization that sought to promote conservative religious values. ∎

Introduction

The Moral Majority was a political organization founded in 1979 by the Rev. Jerry Falwell, a Baptist minister from Lynchburg, Virginia. Falwell was a successful minister, founding the Thomas Road Baptist Church in Lynchburg, with an original congregation of thirty-five families. Eventually the congregation grew to a membership of 22,000. Among its various activities were a day school, rehabilitation center for alcoholics, summer camp for children, transportation services, missionary and poverty programs in Latin America and Asia. Falwell started a radio program, "The Old-Time Gospel Hour," that transformed into a national television show in 1971. Educational institutions also were formed to promote Falwell's conservative religious views. These were the Thomas Road Bible Institute in 1972, and the Lynchburg Baptist Theological Seminary in 1973.

Throughout the 1970s Falwell addressed a variety of political issues. He supported school prayer, capitalism and free enterprise, balanced budgets, a strong military, and support for Israel. Falwell also opposed the Equal Rights Amendment, pornography, homosexuality, and sought to have *Roe v. Wade* (the U.S. Supreme Court decision that legalized abortion in America) overturned. Falwell's entry into the political arena took a dramatic step, in 1979, when he founded the Moral Majority, a conservative Christian lobbying organization. Falwell's timing was very good, as the nation was becoming more conservative politically. The Moral Majority was credited with being a major contributing factor to the election of President Ronald Reagan (served 1981–1989) in 1980, and they basked in that political success. The Moral Majority became a major force in Republican politics, supporting Reagan's re-election, the election of President George H. W. Bush (served 1989–1993) in 1988, as well as the nomination of conservative Supreme Court justices.

Significance

Religious groups have played a prominent role in social and political movements in American history. Examples include the Abolitionism, Temperance, and Civil Rights movements. The major figure in the Civil Rights movement, the Rev. Dr. Martin Luther King Jr., was a Baptist minister with a doctorate in theology, and who was also president of the Southern Christian Leadership Conference.

In the early twentieth century, the liberal Federal Council of Churches had been active in political and economic issues. Conservative Christians criticized these actions, saying that it was inappropriate for churches to be involved in political issues. The liberals countered that political issues had religious and moral consequences. With the rise of the Moral Majority, conservatives have shown that they overcame their earlier reluctance and began to get directly involved in the political process to advance their agenda.

The success of the Moral Majority in the 1980s brought about the rise of the Christian Right in American politics. Like other conservative movements of the time, it too was a reaction against the liberal developments associated with the 1960s—civil rights conflicts, Vietnam protests, the alternative youth culture, the women's liberation movement, and the sexual revolution. Government itself also seemed to threaten American values, with excessive regulation that seemed anti-capitalistic, and with Supreme Court decisions that banned prayer and Bible readings in public schools (*Engel v. Vitale* in 1962) and that legalized abortion (*Roe v. Wade* in 1973).

Led by charismatic, energetic figures like Jerry Falwell, Pat Robertson, and Phyllis Schlafly, activists sought to defend traditional Christian values, such as the authority of the Bible in all areas of life, the necessity of faith in Jesus Christ, and the relevance of biblical values in sexual relations and marital arrangements. In the excerpt listed below, Falwell describes his agenda for the 1980s. This agenda is politically conservative and promotes traditional family values. The irony of the Moral Majority was that its first political victory, the election of Ronald Reagan in 1980, saw President Jimmy Carter (served 1977–1981), a happily married evangelical Christian with liberal views, defeated by a man who had been divorced and who attended church services irregularly.

Primary Source

The Fundamentalist Phenomenon: The Resurgence of Conservative Christianity [excerpt]

SYNOPSIS: American politics was shocked by the sudden reemergence of fundamentalism, a movement thought to be discredited nationally after the Scopes Trial in the 1920s. In the form of the Moral Majority, religious conservatives had found a vehicle to advance their conservative agenda politically. The Moral Majority was disbanded in 1989, but religious conservatives continue to be prominent in the Republican Party and American political life.

Imperative of Morality

As a pastor, I kept waiting for someone to come to the forefront of the American religious scene to lead the way out of the wilderness. Like thousands of other preachers, I kept waiting, but no real leader appeared. Finally I realized that we had to act ourselves. Something had to be done now. The government was encroaching upon the sovereignty of both the Church and the family. The Supreme Court had legalized abortion on demand. The Equal Rights Amendment, with its vague language, threatened to do further damage to the traditional family, as did the rising sentiment toward so-called homosexual rights. Most Americans were shocked, but kept hoping someone would do something about all this moral chaos.

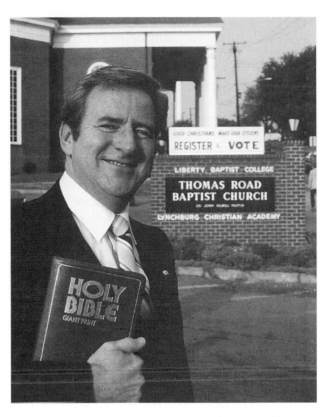

Jerry Falwell poses outside Thomas Road Baptist Church, Lynchburg, Virginia, August 31, 1980. In 1979 Falwell organized the Moral Majority. A conservative political action group, Moral Majority helped elect Ronald Reagan in the 1980 election. © **WALLY MCNAMEE/CORBIS. REPRODUCED BY PERMISSION.**

Organizing the Moral Majority

Facing the desperate need in the impending crisis of the hour, several concerned pastors began to urge me to put together a political organization that could provide a vehicle to address these crucial issues. Men like James Kennedy (Fort Lauderdale, Florida), Charles Stanley (Atlanta, Georgia), Tim La Haye (San Diego, California), and Greg Dixon (Indianapolis, Indiana) began to share with me a common concern. They urged that we formulate a nonpartisan political organization to promote morality in public life and to combat legislation that favored the legalization of immorality. Together we formulated the Moral Majority, Inc. Today Moral Majority, Inc., is made up of millions of Americans, including 72,000 ministers, priests, and rabbis, who are deeply concerned about the moral decline of our nation, the traditional family, and the moral values on which our nation was built. We are Catholics, Jews, Protestants, Mormons, Fundamentalists—blacks and whites—farmers, housewives, businessmen, and businesswomen. We are Americans from all walks of life united by one central concern: to serve as a special-interest group providing a voice for a return to moral sanity in these United States of America. Moral Majority is a political organization and is not based on theological considerations. We are Americans who share similar moral convictions. We are opposed to abortion, pornography, the drug epidemic, the breakdown of the traditional family, the establishment of homosexuality as an accepted alternate life-style, and other moral cancers that are causing our society to rot from within. Moral Majority strongly supports a pluralistic America. While we believe that this nation was founded upon the Judeo-Christian ethic by men and women who were strongly influenced by biblical moral principles, we are committed to the separation of Church and State.

Here is how Moral Majority stands on today's vital issues:

1. *We believe in the separation of Church and State.* Moral Majority, Inc., is a political organization providing a platform for religious and nonreligious Americans who share moral values to address their concerns in these areas. Members of Moral Majority, Inc., have no common theological premise. We are Americans who are proud to be conservative in our approach to moral, social, and political concerns.

2. *We are pro-life.* We believe that life begins at fertilization. We strongly oppose the massive "biological holocaust" that is resulting in the abortion of one and a half million babies each year in America. We believe that unborn babies have the right to life as much as babies that have been born. We are providing a voice and a defense for the human and civil rights of millions of unborn babies.

3. *We are pro-traditional family.* We believe that the only acceptable family form begins with a legal marriage of a man and woman. We feel that homosexual marriages and common-law marriages should not be accepted as traditional families. We oppose legislation that favors these kinds of "diverse family form," thereby penalizing the traditional family. We do not oppose civil rights for homosexuals. We do oppose "special rights" for homosexuals who have chosen a perverted life-style rather than a traditional life-style.

4. *We oppose the illegal drug traffic in America.* The youth in America are presently in the midst of a drug epidemic. Through education, legislation, and other means we want to do our part to save our young people from death

on the installment plan through illegal drug addiction.

5. *We oppose pornography.* While we do not advocate censorship, we do believe that education and legislation can help stem the tide of pornography and obscenity that is poisoning the American spirit today. Economic boycotts are a proper way in America's free-enterprise system to help persuade the media to move back to a sensible and reasonable moral stand. We most certainly believe in the First Amendment for everyone. We are not willing to sit back, however, while many television programs create cesspools of obscenity and vulgarity in our nation's living rooms.

6. *We support the state of Israel and Jewish people everywhere.* It is impossible to separate the state of Israel from the Jewish family internationally. Many Moral Majority members, because of their theological convictions, are committed to the Jewish people. Others stand upon the human and civil rights of all persons as a premise for support of the state of Israel. Support of Israel is one of the essential commitments of Moral Majority. No anti-Semitic influence is allowed in Moral Majority, Inc.

7. *We believe that a strong national defense is the best deterrent to war.* We believe that liberty is the basic moral issue of all moral issues. The only way America can remain free is to remain strong. Therefore we support the efforts of our present administration to regain our position of military preparedness—with a sincere hope that we will never need to use any of our weapons against any people anywhere.

8. *We support equal rights for women.* We agree with President Reagan's commitment to help every governor and every state legislature to move quickly to ensure that during the 1980s every American woman will earn as much money and enjoy the same opportunities for advancement as her male counterpart in the same vocation.

9. *We believe ERA is the wrong vehicle to obtain equal rights for women.* We feel that the ambiguous and simplistic language of the Amendment could lead to court interpretations that might put women in combat, sanction homosexual marriages, and financially penalize widows and deserted wives.

10. *We encourage our Moral Majority state organizations to be autonomous and indigenous.* Moral Majority state organizations may, from time to time, hold positions that are not held by the Moral Majority, Inc., national organization.

Facing the Opposition

We have been labeled by our critics as arrogant, irresponsible, and simplistic. They accuse us of violating the separation of Church and state. However, the National Council of Churches (NCC) has been heavily involved in politics for years, and virtually no one has complained. Since many moral problems, such as abortion, require solutions that are both legal and political, it is necessary for religious leaders to speak on these matters in order to be heard.

Further Resources

BOOKS

Bromley, David G. *New Christian Politics.* Macon, Ga.: Mercer, 1984.

Fackre, Gabriel J. *The Religious Right and Christian Faith.* Grand Rapids, Mich.: Eerdmans, 1982.

Goodman, William R. *Jerry Falwell: An Unauthorized Profile.* Lynchburg, Va.: Paris & Associates, 1981.

Willoughby, William. *Does America Need the Moral Majority?* Plainfield, N.J.: Haven Books, 1981.

The Challenge of Peace: God's Promise and Our Response

Letter

By: National Conference of Catholic Bishops

Date: May 3, 1983

Source: National Conference of Catholic Bishops. *The Challenge of Peace: God's Promise and Our Response: A Pastoral Letter on War and Peace, May 3, 1983.* Washington, D.C.: United States Catholic Conference, 1983, v–viii.

About the Organization: The National Conference of Catholic Bishops, is a national organization representing the approximately 300 bishops in the United States. This organization originated in 1917, and is currently known as the United States Conference of Catholic Bishops. ∎

Introduction

Christianity has two approaches to the issues of war and peace. The more radical of these is a commitment to total pacifism. This can be traced to the early Church where, despite being persecuted for the first three centuries of its existence, there is no recorded incident of Christian retaliation or rebellion against Roman oppression. It was later reemphasized by St. Francis of Assisi in the thirteenth century, and this approach continues to be advocated by the various "peace" churches, such as the Amish, Hutterites, Mennonites, and Quakers—as well as elements within the Catholic Church.

Another approach, dating back to St. Augustine in the fifth century, is the Just War Theory. This holds that while war should be avoided, under certain circumstances, going to war may be permitted as the lesser of two evils. The Just War Theory specifies seven criteria that must all be met before it is morally permissible to go to war. These are:

1. Just cause.

2. Only a competent authority can declare war.

3. Right intention, that is war can only be fought for the just cause, no other war aims.

4. War must be the last resort.

5. The cost of the war must be proportionate to the worth of the value of the just cause.

6. Probability of success.

7. Goal is to restore peace, a peace preferable to the peace that existed before the war.

Even if, however, all the criteria have been met and the conflict is deemed a just war, there are two additional moral conditions to be observed in conducting the war: proportionality and discrimination. While at the beginning of the conflict the estimated cost of the war was proportionate to the good to be attained, if the costs become disproportionate, then the conflict must be ended. Furthermore, in fighting the war, combatants must discriminate between civilian and military targets. Civilians are never to be harmed.

Significance

In 1983, the National Conference of Catholic Bishops (NCCB) approved the pastoral letter *The Challenge of Peace: God's Promise & Our Response.* It was not the first time the Catholic bishops had addressed the problem of war. The NCCB had issued ten statements addressing war and peace issues in the two decades prior to *The Challenge of Peace.* These included statements on Vietnam (1966 and 1971) and the conflict in the Middle East (1967, 1973, and 1978). In 1983, however, the Catholic bishops openly questioned the morality of the nuclear policy of the United States—particularly the policy of Mutually Assured Destruction in the event of an atomic exchange with the Soviet Union.

Protesters in a parade against the use of nuclear weapons, New York, June 12, 1982. As the arms race with the Soviet Union grew, many protested nuclear weapons, including the Catholic bishops who declared their use immoral. AP/WIDE WORLD PHOTOS. REPRODUCED BY PERMISSION.

The document, approved on May 3, 1983, is divided into four major sections: Peace in the Modern World; War and Peace in the Modern World; The Promotion of Peace; and the Pastoral Challenge. The bishops questioned whether any nuclear war could ever be a just war, as it would clearly violate the criteria of proportionality and discrimination. Further, the document challenged the concept of the military policy of Mutually Assured Destruction—stressing that under no circumstances could nuclear weapons be used for the purpose of destroying population centers. Retaliatory action that would indiscriminately and disproportionately take many innocent lives was also condemned. To promote peace, the document called for a halt to developing new nuclear weapons, and reductions in the arsenals of both superpowers.

In the decade of the 1980s, the American bishops followed up *The Challenge of Peace* with other pastoral letters and statements. These included expressing concerns on arms control (1984), rejection of the MX missile system (1985), and opposition to military aid for the

Contras (1986). *The Challenge of Peace* has since become an important part of the social teachings curriculum in Catholic parishes and schools.

Primary Source

The Challenge of Peace: God's Promise & Our Response [excerpt]

> **SYNOPSIS:** During the Cold War, American Catholics were considered by the United States government to be strong supporters in the struggle against Communism. Thus, it was very noteworthy when this community's spiritual leaders, representing approximately one out of every five Americans, questioned the morality of American nuclear policy, in 1983, with the pastoral letter, *The Challenge of Peace.*

II. Moral Principles and Policy Choices

As bishops in the United States, assessing the concrete circumstances of our society, we have made a number of observations and recommendations in the process of applying moral principles to specific policy choices.

A. On the Use of Nuclear Weapons

1. *Counter Population Use:* Under no circumstances may nuclear weapons or other instruments of mass slaughter be used for the purpose of destroying population centers or other predominantly civilian targets. Retaliatory action which would indiscriminately and disproportionately take many wholly innocent lives, lives of people who are in no way responsible for reckless actions of their government, must also be condemned.

2. *The Initiation of Nuclear War:* We do not perceive any situation in which the deliberate initiation of nuclear war, on however restricted a scale, can be morally justified. Non-nuclear attacks by another state must be resisted by other than nuclear means. Therefore, a serious moral obligation exists to develop non-nuclear defensive strategies as rapidly as possible. In this letter we urge NATO to move rapidly toward the adoption of a "no first use" policy, but we recognize this will take time to implement and will require the development of an adequate alternative defense posture.

3. *Limited Nuclear War:* Our examination of the various arguments on this question makes us highly skeptical about the real meaning of "limited." One of the criteria of the just-war teaching is that there must be a reasonable

hope of success in bringing about justice and peace. We must ask whether such a reasonable hope can exist once nuclear weapons have been exchanged. The burden of proof remains on those who assert that meaningful limitation is possible. In our view the first imperative is to prevent any use of nuclear weapons and we hope that leaders will resist the notion that nuclear conflict can be limited, contained or won in any traditional sense.

B. On Deterrence

In concert with the evaluation provided by Pope John Paul II, we have arrived at a strictly conditional moral acceptance of deterrence. In this letter we have outlined criteria and recommendations which indicate the meaning of conditional acceptance of deterrence policy. We cannot consider such a policy adequate as a long-term basis for peace.

C. On Promoting Peace

1. We support immediate, bilateral verifiable agreements to halt the testing, production and deployment of new nuclear weapons systems. This recommendation is not to be identified with any specific political initiative.

2. We support efforts to achieve deep cuts in the arsenals of both superpowers; efforts should concentrate first on systems which threaten the retaliatory forces of either major power.

3. We support early and successful conclusion of negotiations of a comprehensive test ban treaty.

4. We urge new efforts to prevent the spread of nuclear weapons in the world, and to control the conventional arms race, particularly the conventional arms trade.

5. We support, in an increasingly interdependent world, political and economic policies designed to protect human dignity and to promote the human rights of every person, especially the least among us. In this regard, we call for the establishment of some form of global authority adequate to the needs of the international common good.

This letter includes many judgments from the perspective of ethics, politics and strategy needed to speak concretely and correctly to the "moment of supreme crisis" identified by Vatican II. We stress again that readers should be aware, as we have been, of the distinction between our statement of moral principles and of official Church teaching and our application of these to concrete issues. We urge that special care be taken not to use passages out of context; neither should brief portions of this document be cited to support positions it does not intend to convey or which are not truly in accord with the spirit of its teaching.

In concluding this summary we respond to two key questions often asked about this pastoral letter:

Why do we address these matters fraught with such complexity, controversy and passion? We speak as pastors, not politicians. We are teachers, not technicians. We cannot avoid our responsibility to lift up the moral dimensions of the choices before our world and nation. The nuclear age is an era of moral as well as physical danger. We are the first generation since Genesis with the power to threaten the created order. We cannot remain silent in the face of such danger. Why do we address these issues? We are simply trying to live up to the call of Jesus to be peacemakers in our own time and situation.

What are we saying? Fundamentally, we are saying that the decisions about nuclear weapons are among the most pressing moral questions of our age. While these decisions have obvious military and political aspects, they involve fundamental moral choices. In simple terms, we are saying that good ends (defending one's country, protecting freedom, etc.) cannot justify immoral means (the use of weapons which kill indiscriminately and threaten whole societies). We fear that our world and nation are headed in the wrong direction. More weapons with greater destructive potential are produced every day. More and more nations are seeking to become nuclear powers. In our quest for more and more security we fear we are actually becoming less and less secure.

In the words of our Holy Father, we need a "moral about-face." The whole world must summon the moral courage and technical means to say no to nuclear conflict; no to weapons of mass destruction; no to an arms race which robs the poor and the vulnerable; and no to the moral danger of a nuclear age which places before humankind indefensible choices of constant terror or surrender. Peacemaking is not an optional commitment. It is a requirement of our faith. We are called to be peacemakers, not by some movement of the moment, but by our Lord Jesus. The content and context of our peacemaking is set not by some political agenda or ideological program, but by the teaching of his Church.

Ultimately, this letter is intended as an expression of Christian faith, affirming the confidence we have that the risen Lord remains with us precisely in moments of crisis. It is our belief in his presence and power among us which sustain us in confronting the awesome challenge of the nuclear age. We speak from faith to provide hope for all who recognize the challenge and are working to confront it with the resources of faith and reason.

To approach the nuclear issue in faith is to recognize our absolute need for prayer: we urge and invite all to unceasing prayer for peace with justice for all people. In a spirit of prayerful hope we present this message of peace.

Further Resources

BOOKS

Anscombe, G.E.M. *Nuclear Weapons and Christian Conscience.* London: Merlin Press, 1961.

Bainton, Roland. *Therefore Choose Life: Essays on the Nuclear Crisis.* London: Fellowship of Reconciliation, 1961.

Clancy, William. *The Moral Dilemma of Nuclear Weapons.* New York: Church Peace Union, 1961.

O'Brien, William Vincent. *Nuclear War, Deterrence, and Morality.* Westminster, Md.: Newman Press, 1967.

"Jewish-Christian Relations: A Jewish Perspective"

Journal article

By: David Berger

Date: 1983

Source: Berger, David. "Jewish-Christian Relations: A Jewish Perspective." *Journal of Ecumenical Studies* 20, Winter, 1983. Reprinted in Cohen, Naomi W., ed. *Essential Papers on Jewish-Christian Relations in the United States.* New York: New York University Press, 1990, 328–330.

About the Author: David Berger (1943–) was born in Brooklyn, New York. Ordained a rabbi in 1967, he received his doctorate in 1970 from Columbia, and he is a faculty member of the Department of History at Brooklyn College of the City University of New York. Trained as a medievalist, Dr. Berger's area of scholarly activity has been in the area of Jewish-Christian relations. ∎

Introduction

In 1850, there were 50,000 Jews in the United States, including 16,000 in New York City. At the beginning of the twentieth century, there were approximately one million Jews in the United States. This was the third largest Jewish population in the world, following Russia and Austria-Hungary. Approximately half of the American Jewish population lived in New York City, making it the world's most populous Jewish city, more than twice the population of Warsaw, the next largest Jewish city.

This tremendous growth was due primarily to immigration, and it continued in the early decades of the twentieth century. Between 1900 and 1924, another 1.75 million Jews came to the United States, the majority of these from Eastern Europe. Before 1900, American Jews made up less than one percent of the total population. By 1930, Jews constituted 3.5 percent of America's population.

Just as with Catholic immigration, this great increase in the Jewish population elicited nativist reactions, and there was an increase in anti-Semitism. The American Jewish community responded to this rise in bigotry by forming the Anti-Defamation League in 1913. Its purpose was to identify the causes of religious and racial prejudice, followed by education to try and change these mindsets.

There were many obstacles to overcome. Prejudice was not limited to the uneducated, as educational institutions and government entities also discriminated against Jews. During the 1920s, quotas were set to limit the enrollment of Jews in major universities. Furthermore, housing covenants excluded Jews from many neighborhoods.

One response was to turn within the community and avoid interaction with non-Jews. The Reformed and Conservative movements, however, believed that Jews needed to integrate into American culture, while at the same time preserving the Jewish community. A big part of this required fostering dialogue with non-Jews, particularly Christians. As a result, Jews have been at the forefront on interreligious dialogue.

Significance

The excerpt below is an example of the continuing dialogue on Jewish-Christian relations in the 1980s, appearing in the Winter 1983 issue of the *Journal of Ecumenical Studies.* Professor David Berger, a Jewish scholar and ordained rabbi, begins by assessing the great strides that have occurred in the twenty years prior to his writing.

Dr. Berger recognized the revolutionary changes in the official positions of many Christian denominations toward Jews. In the 1930s Father Charles Coughlin pilloried Jews in anti-Semitic radio broadcasts; during the Second Vatican Council, the Catholic Church issued its famous document, *Nostra Aetate* in 1965. That document acknowledged past discrimination, declared that Jews of today should not be held accountable for the crucifixion of Jesus, and that there exists a special relationship between Christians and Jews. Many Protestant churches have made similar declarations as well, either singly, in denominational statements, or collectively—through the National Council of Churches in Christ or the World Council of Churches.

These statements have resulted in the establishment of committees and other structures to continue the discussion. In continuing this dialogue, Dr. Berger recommended five areas that needed to be addressed; the problem of dialogue, mission and covenant, Anti-Semitism, the State of Israel, and moral questions affecting public policy.

Dr. Berger writes with a spirit of hope, but also with a degree of caution. Despite tremendous gains, anti-Semitism still remains in the United States. Anti-Jewish acts, including vandalism of Jewish property, continued. Polls taken by the Anti-Defamation League reveal that prejudices regarding Jews in the business world and fears of a worldwide Jewish conspiracy continue.

Primary Source

"Jewish-Christian Relations: A Jewish Perspective" [excerpt]

> **SYNOPSIS:** Like Catholics and Lutherans, Jewish immigrants suffered from nativist bigotry. In addition to this obstacle, Jews bore the additional burden of many centuries of anti-Semitism. There had been improvement in this area by the 1980s, but much more remained to be done. As can be seen in this document, much still needed to be done in establishing the basis for constructive dialogue.

Our generation has seen some fundamental, even revolutionary changes in the official position of many Christian churches toward Jews and Judaism. Antisemitism has been denounced, contemporary Jewish responsibility for the crucifixion denied, missionizing reexamined, textbooks revised, and dialogue encouraged. These changes, though welcomed by most Jews, have left many lingering problems unresolved, and, especially in the case of dialogue, they have raised new, complex questions about the propriety and character of interfaith relations.

The most famous Christian statement on the Jews in recent years is, of course, the widely heralded and much debated document issued by Vatican II in 1965 (Nostra Aetate 4), which spoke of a special bond between Christians and Jews. Since then, a series of Catholic statements both in Rome and in various national churches has attempted to grapple with the ambiguities and omissions in Nostra Aetate 4, and in January 1975, official guidelines were issued for the implementation of the council's declaration and the encouragement of continuing contacts between Catholics and Jews.

Protestant churches have also moved toward a reassessment of their attitudes concerning Jews and Judaism in a number of statements by the World Council of Churches, international conferences of individual denominations, and national organizations. Although the decentralized character of Protestantism makes generalization difficult, most of the major trends in the Catholic declarations appear among Protestants as well, and here, too, the call for interfaith dialogue is a prominent and recurring feature.

To further such contacts, both Christians and Jews have set up institutional mechanisms whose primary function is interfaith relations. The Pontifical Commission for Religious Relations with the Jews and the Consultation on the Church and the Jewish People of the World Council of Churches are major examples of Christian bodies which function on a worldwide scale. In the United States, the Catholic Secretariat for Christian-Jewish Relations, the Committee on Christian-Jewish Relations of the National Council of Churches, and a substantial number of national officials of individual Protestant churches deal primarily with Jewish issues. Jews reciprocate with significant programs for interreligious affairs at the American Jewish Committee, Anti-Defamation League, American Jewish Congress, Synagogue Council of America, Union of American Hebrew Congregations, and elsewhere, while the National Conference of Christians and Jews continues to expand its longstanding efforts. Though the scope and intensity of such activities vary greatly from country to country, some increase in interfaith contacts is noticeable in virtually every Western nation with a significant Jewish population. . . .

The Problem of Dialogue

At first glance, the case for dialogue is self-evident, straightforward, and deceptively simple. Communication is preferable to isolation; friendship and trust can be established only by people who talk to one another. Nevertheless, although dialogue is often initiated by the Jewish side, the history of Jewish-Christian relations has bequeathed to many Jews a legacy of mistrust and suspicion which makes them perceive the Christian advocacy of such discussions as a subtle and more sophisticated expression of the missionary impulse. We shall have to examine the question of mission later on, but to the extent that this perception could be defended, the argument for dialogue—at least in the eyes of many Jews—would be severely undermined.

The conviction that the motivation for dialogue is a sincere desire for mutual understanding is indispensable for the legitimation of such conversations, but it does not define their content. The most interesting questions, in fact, arise only in the context of a favorable decision about the fundamental enterprise. What should be discussed? Are some subjects too sensitive, or does the exclusion of such topics contradict the essential objective of interfaith dialogue? Should discussants direct their efforts toward the solution of clearcut problems in Jewish-Christian relations, or should they address essential matters of faith as well? If a separation between such issues is desirable, is it in fact possible?

In a thoughtful and perceptive article, Henry Siegman argued that Jews and Christians bring different agendas to what is essentially an asymmetrical discussion. Since Jews can understand their faith without reference to Christianity, there is no internal Jewish need to engage in theological discussion with Christians; Christianity, on the other hand, confronts Judaism the moment it "searches into the mystery of the Church." The Jewish agenda is historical rather than theological and focuses on such issues as Antisemitism, the Holocaust, and the State of Israel. Although each side may recognize some value in the other's agenda, the basic impulses leading to dialogue are profoundly different.

Further Resources

BOOKS

Croner, Helga B. *More Stepping Stones to Jewish-Christian Relations.* New York: Paulist Press, 1985.

Neusner, Jacob. *Judaism and Christianity: The New Relationship.* New York: Garland Publications, 1993.

Rousseau, Richard W. *Christianity and Judaism: The Deepening Dialogue* Scranton, Pa.: Ridge Row Press, 1983.

In Memory of Her: A Feminist Theological Reconstruction of Christian Origins

Nonfiction work

By: Elisabeth Schüssler Fiorenza

Date: 1983

Source: Schüssler Fiorenza, Elisabeth. *In Memory of Her: A Feminist Theological Reconstruction of Christian Origins.* New York: Crossroad, 1983.

About the Author: Elizabeth Schüssler Fiorenza (1938–) was born in Romania. After moving with her family to then West Germany, she decided to become a professional theologian in the Roman Catholic Church. She moved to the United States in 1970, and she joined the Theology Department of the University of Notre Dame. ■

Introduction

Women have played a prominent role in American religion. Some took leading roles in social reform, such as Frances Willard and the Temperance Movement. Others gained fame as evangelists and founders of churches, such as Mary Baker Eddy and Aimee Semple McPherson.

Still, for most of American history, women were subjected to the same limitations in religion as they were in the rest of society. With the exception of those who founded religious communities, women were denied positions of leadership in denominations. They were not allowed to be ordained and were expected to assume subservient, domestic roles.

In explaining this state of affairs, the male clergy would often point to the Bible, in particular some of the letters of St. Paul (the Timothy and Titus letters to be exact), where woman are called upon to be submissive. There were strong female figures in the Bible—such as Judith who saved the people of Israel by beheading the Assyrian general Holofernes—but for the most part these episodes are few and far between. As these biblical images are crucial to defining the role of women in Judaism and Christianity, feminist scholars have focused much of their research on these texts.

A prominent feminist in the 1980s Christian tradition was Elisabeth Schüssler Fiorenza. She received a Masters in Divinity degree from the University of Wurtzburg in 1962, a licentiate in theology from the same institution, and received her doctorate in theology from the University of Munster in 1970. She immigrated that year to the United States to take a teaching position at the University of Notre Dame. In 1984, Schüssler Fiorenza became the Krister Stendahl Professor of Divinity at Harvard University. She was also the founder and co-editor of *The Journal of Feminist Studies in Religion*.

Significance

Schüssler Fiorenza's contribution to feminist thought began early with the publication of her thesis, *The Forgotten Partner: Foundations, Facts, and Possibilities for the Participation of Women in the Church* in 1964. By 2001, she had published sixteen books in both English and German in the areas of feminist and scriptural studies, as well as serving as the editor for ten other volumes.

Schüssler Fiorenza's most famous book was *In Memory of Her: A Feminist Theological Reconstruction of Christian Origins,* an excerpt of which is featured below. Published in 1983 by Crossroad, this book describes Christianity as being originally an egalitarian movement, including women as well as men. This is not readily apparent in the sources of Early Christianity, including the New Testament writings.

These writings are not only silent for the most part about the activities of women in Christianity, at times belittling their roles. This is not reflective of Jesus or the Christian message, but rather of the patriarchal culture within which these texts were composed, as well as the later generations that interpreted them. By acknowledging this influence, Schüssler Fiorenza argues, it is possible to reconceive and reconstruct these texts. This work, she believes, reveals a Jesus and early Christian community that was egalitarian and inclusive of women.

In the selection from *In Memory of Her* below, Schüssler Fiorenza calls for a reclamation of the Christian heritage of women. This heritage was present from the very beginning, but has been hidden by patriarchal oppression. The first step in this liberation, she believes, is for women to reclaim their history, to revive the original spiritual communities shared by women (the ekklēsia of women), and restore the coequal discipleship of women in Christianity.

Primary Source

In Memory of Her: A Feminist Theological Reconstruction of Christian Origins [excerpt]

SYNOPSIS: Feminists have often targeted religious groups as examples of patriarchal institutions that have oppressed women throughout history and continue to do so today. Christian feminists acknowledge the problem of patriarchy, but argue that Christianity was originally a movement where women enjoyed equality. Their argument is that churches must be purged of patriarchal control and be restored to original Christianity.

A feminist Christian spirituality, therefore, calls us to gather together the *ekklēsia of women* who, in the angry power of the Spirit, are sent forth to feed, heal, and liberate our own people who are women. It unmasks and sets us free from the structural sin and alienation of sexism and propels us to become children and spokeswomen of God. It rejects the idolatrous worship of maleness and articulates the divine image in female human existence and language. It sets us free from the internalization of false altruism and self-sacrifice that is concerned with the welfare and work of men first to the detriment of our own and other women's welfare and calling. It enables us to live "for one another" and to experience the presence of God in the *ekklēsia* as the gathering of women. Those of us who have heard this calling respond by committing ourselves to the liberation struggle of women and all peoples, by being accountable to women and their future, and by nurturing solidarity within the *ekklēsia* of women. Commitment, accountability, and solidarity in community are the hallmarks of our calling and struggle.

Two major objections are usually raised at this point. The first is that the church of women does not share in the fullness of church. This is correct, but neither do exclusive male hierarchical assemblies. Women's religious communities have always existed within the Catholic tradition. They were generated as soon as the local church structures became patriarchal and hierarchical and therefore had to relegate women to subordinate roles or to eliminate them from church office altogether. The male hierarchical church in turn has always sought to control these communities by colonizing them through male theology, liturgy, law, and spirituality, but was never quite able to do so. By abolishing these religious communities of women the Protestant Reformation has strengthened patriarchal church structures and intensified male clerical control of Roman Catholic women's communities in modern times. In the past centuries, however, women founders and leaders of their people have arisen again and again who sought to gather communities of women free from clerical and monastic control. A Christian feminist spirituality claims these communities of women and their history as our heritage and history and seeks to transform them into the *ekklēsia* of women by claiming our own spiritual powers and gifts, by deciding our own welfare, by standing accountable for our decisions, in short, by rejecting the patriarchal structures of laywomen and nun-women, of laywomen and clergywomen, which deeply divide us along patriarchal lines.

The second objection made is the charge of "reverse sexism" and the appeal to "mutuality with men" whenever we gather together as the *ekklēsia* of women in Her name. However, such an objection does not face sufficiently the issues of patriarchal oppression and power. It looks too quickly for easy grace, having paid lip service to the structural sin of sexism. Do we call it "reverse imperialism" if the poor of South and Central America gather together as a people? Or do we call it "reverse colonialism" whenever Africans or Asians gather together as a people? We do not do so because we know too well that the coming together of those exploited does not spell the oppression of the rich or that the oppressed are gaining power over white men and Western nations, but that it means the political bonding of oppressed people in their struggle for economic and cultural survival. Why then do men feel threatened by the bonding of women in our struggle for liberation? Why then can churchmen not understand and accept that Christian women gather together for the sake of our spiritual survival as Christians and women persons? It is not over and against men that we gather together but in order to become *ekklēsia* before God, deciding matters affecting our own spiritual welfare and struggle. Because the spiritual colonialization of women by men has entailed our internalization of the male as divine, men have to relinquish their spiritual and religious control over women as well as over the church as the people of God, if mutuality should become a real possibility.

Women in turn have to reclaim their spiritual powers and to exorcise their possession by male idolatry before mutuality is possible. True, "the dream of a common language" belongs to God's alternative world of cohumanity in the power of the Spirit. Yet it can only become reality among the people of God, when male idolatry and its demonic structures are rejected in the confession of the structural and personal sin of sexism and when the fullness of *ekklēsia* becomes a possibility in a genuine conversion of individual persons and ecclesiastical structures. Not women, but churchmen exclude women from "breaking the bread and sharing the cup" in eucharistic table community.

Further Resources

BOOKS

Carmody, Denise. *Biblical Woman: Contemporary Reflections on Scriptural Texts.* New York: Crossroad, 1988.

Carr, Anne. *Transforming Grace: Christian Tradition and Women's Experience.* New York: Continuum, 1996.

Coll, Regina. *Christianity and Feminism in Conversation.* Mystic, Conn.: Twenty-Third Publications, 1994.

Ruether, Rosemary Radford. *Sexism and God-Talk: Toward a Feminist Theology.* Boston: Beacon Press, 1983.

"On Racial Justice"
Statement

By: National Council of the Churches of Christ in the U.S.A.

Date: 1984

Source: National Council of the Churches of Christ in the U.S.A. "On Racial Justice." Racial Justice Working Group of the Division of Church and Society, 1984. Reprinted in Jerslid, Paul T., and Dale A. Johnson, eds. *Moral Issues and Christian Response.* New York: Harcourt Brace, 1993, 78–80.

About the Organization: The National Council of the Churches of Christ was founded in 1950. It can trace its roots back even further to the Federal Council of Churches, founded in 1908, the first permanent, inter-denominational organization in the United States. From its beginning, this alliance of thirty-five churches has supported a variety of progressive causes, including the rights of labor, civil rights, and the struggle against poverty and racism. It is part of the World Council of Churches. ∎

Introduction

The issue of racial justice has a long history in American religion, beginning with the abolition of slavery, and again in the promotion of civil rights. In the area of abolition, the Quakers took the lead. In 1775, a group of Philadelphia Quakers organized the first anti-slavery society. In 1776, the Quakers forbid members to hold slaves and expelled those who did.

Whether it was moral for a Christian to own slaves became a major moral issue in American Protestantism in the nineteenth century. The Baptists divided into northern and southern branches over this issue in 1845, followed by the Methodists in the same year, and the Presbyterians in 1861.

The Abolitionist movement drew much of its strength from the revivalist fervor of these churches that reduced a complex social problem to a simple dichotomy of right and wrong. The notion of gradual, compensated emancipation was replaced with an insistence on immediate freedom and punishment for the slave-holding evildoers. This was achieved by means of the bloody Civil War (1861–1865), but after obtaining the goal of abolishing slavery, the churches turned their attention to other issues, ignoring the problem of enforcing the civil rights of the newly freed slaves. It would take almost 100 years before the churches took up the cause for liberty again, this time in the Civil Rights movement.

There were, of course, other important efforts as well. The NAACP did significant work in the courts, challenging unjust laws. The Congress on Racial Equality would also succeed in promoting voting registration. Still, it would not be until the churches became involved that the Civil Rights movement would gain momentum.

Ku Klux Klansmen hold white unity signs during a rally, Connecticut, September 1980. In 1984 the National Council of the Churches of Christ in the U.S.A. adopted a policy statement asserting that "the church is called to identify racism . . . and is summoned to eliminate it." © OWEN FRANKEN/CORBIS. REPRODUCED BY PERMISSION.

Once again, the revivalist spirit of these church communities energized the Civil Rights movement, just as it had the Abolitionist movement.

Significance

The Southern Christian Leadership Conference (founded 1957), under its president, Rev. Dr. Martin Luther King Jr., succeeded in bringing about the Civil Rights Act of 1964. Much was also done in the area of promoting black involvement in the political process, as well as trying to overcome centuries of discrimination through affirmative action programs in education and hiring.

By the 1980s, however, the goal of an egalitarian society had not been achieved. Furthermore, there was concern that, as the country was becoming more conservative politically, it was turning its back on civil rights—and that the hard won gains of the 1960s and 70s would be lost. Rather than allowing another lapse to take place, as was the case after Abolitionism, liberal Christians resolved to address the issue directly.

It is in this spirit that the document below was written. "On Racial Justice" was approved by the NCCC in 1984. The document condemns racism as a form of idol-

atry, as a sin against God, in whose image all humanity has been created. The document defined racism as more than simply prejudice. It was prejudice combined with power, and the consequence, whether intentional, was the repression of those deemed inferior.

The document points out that this problem of racism has been present since the early colonial years. It continues in American society and can be found particularly in the area of economics, called "the heart of racism in the United States." The NCCC called for aggressive economic policies that would ensure equal opportunity for employment and freedom from job discrimination. While locating most of racism in the area of economics, the document does confess that racial injustice also continues in the churches as well, and the NCCC committed itself to addressing the problem.

Primary Source

"On Racial Justice" [excerpt]

> **SYNOPSIS:** During the 1980s, many civil rights leaders believed that the country was regressing in the area of racism. The National Council of Churches in Christ, a liberal association of Christian churches, composed of both African American and European

American congregations, continued the struggle against this social sin.

God's Creation

All humanity is created in the image of God. Christians are called to oneness in Christ which unites all particularities and reaffirms the Biblical image of God as a universal affirmation of faith.

Racism is an expression of idolatry, replacing faith in the God who made all people and who raised Jesus from the dead with the belief in the superiority of one race over another or in the universality of a particular form of culture. When this idolatry is expressed by those who possess economic and political power, it leads to a cruel and extensive repression of selected peoples and a negation of their identity and value as given by God.

The Church's Mission

The church is called to identify racism as sin against God and is summoned to eliminate it. As Christians hear and respond to the Gospel, they confess that all people are called into the fellowship of Christ, and through the Holy Spirit create such a fellowship. The grace of God is needed in this task because sin exerts its power over all people (Romans 3:23). Racism can be vanquished, finally, by nothing less than God's redemptive action to liberate both victims and victimizers from this evil.

The struggle against racial injustice continues to be waged by the Lord Jesus, confessed by Christians together as the Christ. In Christ, God challenges racism and promises its defeat. That challenge is part of the meaning of the Cross and is a part of the resurrection promise.

Through the Holy Spirit, God calls and gathers the church in obedience to the gospel of Jesus Christ. Although no one, not even those called by the name of Jesus Christ, can claim to be free from racism or its effects, those who have been baptized into the death and resurrection of Christ are called to walk in newness of life (Romans 6:4). In each generation the faithful of the church are to struggle against racial injustice. . . .

Definitions

Prejudice is a personal attitude towards other people based on a categorical judgment about their physical characteristics, such as race or ethnic origin.

Racism is racial prejudice plus power. Racism is the intentional or unintentional use of power to isolate, separate, and exploit others. This use of power is based on a belief in superior racial origin, identity, or supposed racial characteristics. Racism confers certain privileges on and defends the dominant group, which in turn sustains and perpetuates racism. Both consciously and unconsciously, racism is enforced and maintained by the legal, cultural, religious, educational, economic, political, and military institutions of societies.

Racism is more than just a personal attitude—it is the institutionalized form of that attitude.

Institutional Racism is one of the ways organizations and structures serve to preserve injustice. Intended or not, the mechanisms and function of these entities create a pattern of racial injustice.

Racism is one of several sub-systems of domination in the modern world. It interacts with these other sub-systems to produce broad patterns of oppression and exploitation that plague the world. Among these sub-systems are class and sexual oppression. Women who are victimized by racism face a compound burden. They not only have to deal with oppression due to their racial origin or identity, but they are also confronted with economic and political exploitation and oppression based on their sex and/or class.

Racism in U.S. History

The United States has prided itself on its grounding in religious values, especially its founding claim that "all [people] are created equal." Yet historically it has uncritically placed a priority on being white, male, and English-speaking.

Historically, people of European ancestry have controlled the overwhelming majority of the financial resources, institutions, and levers of power. Racism in the United States can therefore be defined as white racism: racism as promulgated and sustained by the white majority. White racism is not peculiar to the U.S. it permeates much of the world. The complete dominance and institutionalization of white racism in the United States make "reverse racism" nearly impossible because the victims of racism lack power.

The colonists who invaded North America came with some preconceived notions of economic exploitation and white superiority. They institutionalized racism by the creation of dual economic, educational, social and political systems that made clear distinctions between Europeans and Africans, Asians, Hispanics, and Indigenous People. To the colonist, life was significant only if it was of European ancestry. Africans were enslaved, maimed, and killed. Asians and Hispanics were paid low wages, imprisoned, and slaughtered. Indigenous People were removed from their land and massacred.

From the early colonial years through the westward expansion, the general pattern of racial exploitation and oppression continued. This westward expansion did not end at the Pacific Ocean; it continued on with Western imperialism extending to the Hawaiian Islands, the Philippines, Samoa, Puerto Rico, the Caribbean, and Latin America. Even now racial exploitation is still clearly visible in U.S. international policies and practices towards Africa, the Caribbean, Latin America, Asia, the Pacific Islands, and the Middle East.

Racism In the Church

During the early colonial years and through the westward expansion, in the U.S. the general pattern of most Christian traditions was either to condone, participate in and develop a religious rationale for racism, or to keep silent. Yet, at points in U.S. history, some national and local churches were exceptions to this pattern and championed the call for equality, human rights, and the dignity of all people.

Within many of the denominations, there have been prophetic streams which have advanced the cause of justice in the face of slavery, racial segregation, religious intolerance, racial violence, and human suffering. At other times, the church has been silent in the face of appalling injustice. For example, some congregations joined the "underground railroad" to rescue Africans from slavery while other congregations profited from slavery. During World War II, when Japanese-Americans were imprisoned in concentration camps, only a few Christian communions publicly protested. Some individual Christians, however, assisted in the resettlement of Japanese-Americans after the war.

At the national level, Christian denominations have recently failed to give adequate support to immigrants who are victims of racism, especially those who have migrated to the U.S. to escape political and economic oppression. A sign of hope has been that some churches have offered sanctuary to victims of persecution from Central America.

However, despite the significant involvement of some Christian denominations in attempting to combat racism, racial injustice still continues in both the church and society. Christians must no longer assume that racial justice is a matter of overcoming individual attitudes and personal bigotry, nor that well-intentioned and non-racist attitudes can, in and of themselves, effectively eliminate racism. Christians must acknowledge that, despite their good intentions, religious and societal structures, institutions and systems can and do perpetuate racism. They must confess that by its style of organization and management, the white institutional church excludes those who are victims of racism. . . .

Racism in Society

Christians share with people of good will a deep concern for the dignity of humankind and a profound respect for the inalienable rights with which we have been endowed by our Creator, including life, liberty, and the pursuit of happiness.

A responsible society is one in which freedom and social responsibility are practiced by all. Those who administer justice and public order and who hold political authority or economic power are accountable for its exercise to God and to the people whose welfare is affected by that authority or power. The responsibility of the church is to call attention to the injustices of society and to empower the victims of injustice in their struggle against the systems and individuals that oppress them.

Since racism knows no boundaries and penetrates religious and secular communities throughout the world, we are compelled to monitor its evolution and destructiveness in its entirety and create strong and effective strategies for combatting it. . . .

Racism in the United States

As we see the connection between global racism and racism in the United States, we affirm that our public and private treatment of all of God's people should exemplify not only our commitment to racial justice, but also our vision of an inclusive and caring society. Our strategies should include resignation from racist professional, civic, service and social clubs, monitoring negative media stereotypes, and identifying racist legislation at all levels of government. Our public pronouncements and witness should also include promotion and financial assistance for racial justice education, compensatory programs, fair and non-discriminatory housing, and land rights. The following issues have been selected on the basis of their direct relationship to racial justice. But commitment in these areas should not exclude the many other areas of human life affected by racism.

Further Resources

BOOKS

Beals, Ivan. *Our Racist Legacy: Will the Church Resolve the Conflict.* Notre Dame, Ind.: Cross Cultural Publications, 1997.

Davies, Susan E. *Ending Racism in the Church.* Cleveland, Ohio: United Church Press, 1998.

McKenzie, Steven. *All God's Children: A Biblical Critique of Racism.* Louisville, Ky.: Westminster John Knox Press, 1997

The Pope's Secrets
Pamphlet

By: Tony and Susan Alamo Christian Foundation

Date: 1984

Source: Alamo, Tony. *The Pope's Secrets.* Alma, Ark.: End Time Books, 1984. Available online at http://www.alamoministries.com/Anti-Christ/popes_secrets.htm; website home page: http://www.alamoministries.com/ (accessed July 29, 2003).

About the Organization: The Tony and Susan Alamo Christian Foundation was founded in 1969. Susan Alamo claimed to have been supernaturally healed of tuberculosis as a child and to have been told by God that she would be preaching the Gospel in the last days before the Second Coming of Christ. Tony Alamo, born Bernie Lazar Hoffman, was a popular entertainer who converted to Christianity in the 1960s and began a new career as an evangelist with his wife. ∎

Introduction

Anti-Catholicism in the United States, also known as nativism, has roots going back to the Anglican Reformation. The memories of violent acts by Catholics during that period, such as Queen Mary Tudor's (1516–1558) execution of over 300 Protestants and English traitor Guy Fawkes' (1570–1606) attempt to blow up Parliament in the Gunpowder Plot, contributed to the notion that Catholics were a threat to liberty. When English Protestants settled in the New World, they brought this concern with them. It was prominent in the colonial period, and continued on after independence. Outbreaks occurred in the 1830s, 1850s, 1880s, and 1920s. Fears of the large waves of Irish, German, Italian, and Polish immigration continued to feed much of this bigotry. This fear of a Catholic takeover resulted in discrimination against these immigrants, and it would directly influence the American presidential elections in 1928 and 1960.

The right of Catholics to have a full participation in American life became a big issue in 1928, when Catholic Alfred Smith ran for president of the United States. Methodist Bishop J.M. Cannon (1864–1944) urged Protestants to "vote as you pray," and in the South the traditional Democratic vote was reduced. The Ku Klux Klan also lobbied heavily against Smith; in some states Smith's train would pass by rows of burning crosses.

The religion issue did help Smith gain two states with large Catholic populations that had gone Republican in 1924 (Massachusetts and Rhode Island), but it cost him six traditionally Democratic southern states. The loss of the southern states resulted in his gaining only 87 electoral votes, the worst showing in the electoral college for the Democrats since President Grant's (served 1869–1877) victory in 1872.

The last serious outbreak of nativism occurred in the election of 1960, with opposition to John F. Kennedy (served 1961–1963), a Catholic, running for president of the United States. It is notable that the support of liberal Protestants was necessary help offset the religious opposition to Kennedy.

Significance

Anti-Catholicism declined a great deal after the election of Kennedy in 1960. When it became obvious that the first Catholic president was not going tear up the Constitution or appoint Jesuits to Cabinet posts, many of the fears of Catholics were laid to rest. Enough of it remained, however, to keep the conspiracy theory of papal plans to overthrow the United States alive and well.

An example is listed below. This material appeared in a pamphlet that was widely distributed in the 1980s in both English and Spanish. Produced by the Tony and Susan Alamo Christian Foundation, it sought to warn the people of the United States of the great threat posed by the Roman Catholic Church. In typical conspiracy theory fashion, practically all problems in the nation can be traced to this diabolical papal plot. This sinister plot, it was claimed, had already taken control of the United Nations, IRS (called "Rome's collection agency"), FBI, Customs, the Department of Labor, and labor unions.

Next to the pope, the next most threatening group is the Jesuit Order, the pope's special agents. Through the use of Jesuit assassins, it is claimed, the pope has already executed Presidents Lincoln (served 1861–1865) and Kennedy for attempting to thwart his plans. Castro, Jim Jones, and Timothy Leary are all labeled as Jesuit-trained.

In the attempt to expose this evil, the pamphlet tries to affix blame on the Vatican for every calamity in world history, even if some of these are inconsistent. The Vatican is accused of working with both Communism, and Nazism, as well as being pro-homosexuality and pro-ecumenism. The Vatican is also claimed to have started both world wars as part of its campaign for global domination.

Primary Source

The Pope's Secrets [excerpt]

SYNOPSIS: One of the oldest conspiracy theories in the United States is the threat of Roman Catholicism to democracy and the American way of life. These fears became heightened when Catholics tried to run for high office. Even though the election of John F. Kennedy in 1960 disproved many of these fears, this conspiracy theory is still alive in the United States.

The Vatican is posing as Snow White, but the Bible says that she is a prostitute, "the great whore," a cult. She uses government agency branches in every country, including the United States, as her vicious little dwarfs. The more power and control she gets in government, the more she will fade away into the background in her "Snow White" disguise so that government will be used and blamed for all her evil deeds.

REASON: To enforce laws that harass, malign, destroy and censor everyone, and every idea that is not Roman Catholic, so she can sit as the satanic queen (the big whore).

Because of her age-old desire to control the world government and church, the serpent like Vatican has infested the world and the U.S. government with so many of her zealous, highly-trained and dedicated Jesuit devotees, that she now controls the United Nations (which she created); the White House; Congress; every state, federal, civic, and social government agency including the U.S. Department of Labor, the IRS, the FBI, Supreme Court, judicial systems, the armed forces; state, federal and other police; also the international banking and federal reserve systems (called the Illuminati and Agentur); labor unions, the Mafia and most of the heavy-weight news media.

This cult (the Vatican) is very close to replacing our U.S. Constitution with her one-world satanic canon laws of death to the "heretic" (anyone that is not Roman Catholic). General Lafayette, President George Washington's most respected aide and general, prophetically stated: "If the liberties of the American people are ever destroyed, they will fall by the hand of the Roman Catholic institution's clergy."

Today we see the climax of detailed plans given in excerpts from a speech given nearly fifty years ago in Australia by Roman Catholic Archbishop Gilroy:

The Roman Catholic motto is ourselves alone for fellow Roman Catholics. We must defeat all heretics (non-Roman Catholics) at the ballot box. The holy father states that negative tactics are fatal. The demands of the holy father (the pope) are that the public services should be 100% Roman Catholic soon. Care must be taken that no suspicion may be raised when Roman Catholics are secretly given more government jobs than Protestants, Jews and other heretics.

Multi-millions of people have been slaughtered by the Vatican, thus saith the Lord (Rev. 18:24). History bears record to this fact. During the Roman Catholic Inquisition in Europe, 68 million people were tortured, maimed, and murdered by this huge sect. The St. Bartholomew's Day Massacre accounted for the butchering of as many as 100,000 Protestants. President Abraham Lincoln blamed the papacy with the Civil War in these words:

This war would never have been possible without the sinister and secretive influence of the Jesuits. We owe it to popery that we now see our land reddened with the blood of her noblest sons.

Lincoln added,

I am for liberty of conscience in its noblest, broadest and highest sense. But I cannot give liberty of conscience to the pope and to his followers, the papists, so long as they tell me, through all their councils, theologians, and canon laws that their conscience orders them to burn my wife, strangle my children, and cut my throat when they find their opportunity.

Because of Abraham Lincoln's many exposés of the Vatican, he was put to death, just as he foretold. Yes, assassinated by the Jesuits under Rome's instructions. The Vatican hasn't changed since Mr. Lincoln's time.

J.F.K.'s Fatal Mistake

When John F. Kennedy was asked by the Vatican, "Are you going to go along with the Roman canon law or the U.S. Constitution?" Mr. Kennedy answered them by saying, "The U. S. Constitution." This was President Kennedy's fatal mistake. His assassination was ordered by Rome, then planned and carried out by Jesuits, just as President Lincoln's was. Anyone who knew too much about Mr. Kennedy's assassination was taken care of too.

When America cried out for an investigation, Chief Justice Earl Warren (a member of the Vatican's secretive Knights of Columbus) was recruited to do the investigation. He did a lot of double-talking and shuffling—as he was supposed to—and then, after a sufficient period of time, closed the investigation.

Pope John Paul II, left, walks with President Ronald Reagan, Miami, Florida, September 10, 1987. In a 1984 tract "The Pope's Secrets," Tony Alamo writes that the Pope and the Vatican control the U.S. government, the United Nations, the IRS, the FBI, the Mafia, and other oranizations. AP/WIDE WORLD PHOTOS. REPRODUCED BY PERMISSION.

Like the pope says, "Negative actions are fatal." Remember that President Kennedy was a great admirer and a student of Abraham Lincoln and knew what Mr. Lincoln knew.

World War II with its casualties of over 30 million deaths (6 million Jews—the Holocaust) was conjured up and sponsored by the Vatican—Hitler, Mussolini and Franco were all members of this sect (the Roman Catholic institution)—to win the world, not for Christ, but for the Vatican, the Antichrist.

The turmoil in Central and South America, the tyranny under Jesuit trained Castro Cuba and throughout the Caribbean, and the terrorism in Lebanon and Ireland today are the Vatican's handiwork. Now can you see why God calls the Roman Catholic institution the mother of every abomination on earth? (Rev. 17:5)

The Vatican knew that after World War II many people were wise that the war was a Vatican inquisition, so they had to use one of their famous diversionary tactics and open the John Birch Society to get everybody thinking and talking about commu-

nism (which the Vatican also sponsors) instead of the true culprit (the Vatican). This was a great success for them.

The Vatican also sponsors every major terrorist group in the world. The reason for this is to keep people's thoughts on unexplainable, insane tragedies that their terrorist groups are committing while the Vatican is busy undermining all the governments of the world so they can have world dominion (papal power). When terrorist news hits, it is so shocking that it minimizes the news of the Vatican taking away the U.S. Constitution and of people being deprived of their religious freedoms (being jailed, schools and churches being closed). This is the real thing that the Vatican is after though, world control of our religion and our government. The more insane, bizarre, unreasonable and unexplainable the terrorism is, the better. The Vatican's heavy weight news media also keeps you busy thinking about it all. Now that they are exposed with their modus operandi, they will soon (with their media and the President of the United States, who just joined them) be the driving force of a campaign to stop all this terrorism (that they have created themselves) to make everyone believe that they are good and godly, and that they could have never sponsored anything like this.

Jim Jones, a Roman Catholic Jesuit deacon posing as a Christian, was sacrificed (not with poisoned Kool-aid) murdered, along with his flock by the Vatican to make the world look narrowly and suspiciously upon innocent Christian retreats.

> These six things doth the Lord hate: yea, seven are an abomination unto him: A proud look, a lying tongue, and hands that shed innocent blood, An heart that deviseth wicked imaginations, feet that be swift in running to mischief, A false witness that speaketh lies, and he that soweth discord among brethren.
>
> *(Pro. 6:16-19).*

(All these things that God hates the devilish Vatican is.)

Did you ever notice that with the Vatican-controlled U.S. Customs and Immigrations we cannot get out of this country without going through the third degree (searches, radar, etc.). But in the 1960's when Jesuit Vatican-trained Timothy Leary led our nation's youth into drug addiction, Immigration and Customs seemed unable (then, as they do now) to detect tens of thousands of pounds of narcotics and drugs entering into our once fair nation via the Mafia, which launders all of its illicit, ill-gotten gain (all its black market money) through the Vatican. Maybe this is why President Abraham Lincoln said: "I see a very dark cloud on America's horizon, and that dark cloud is coming from Rome."

Look at what the Bible says about the Antichrist that caused all this corruption and shed all this blood:

> And I saw the woman (the Vatican) drunken with the blood of the saints, and with the blood of the martyrs of Jesus: and when I saw her, I wondered with great admiration.
>
> *(Rev. 17:6)*

> How much she hath glorified herself, and lived deliciously, so much torment and sorrow give her: for she saith in her heart, I sit a queen, and am no widow, and shall see no sorrow.
>
> *(Rev. 18:7)*

> These (governments) have one mind, and shall give their power and strength unto the beast (that is one-world government, state and federal, civic and social government agencies included, powered by Satan, giving that power to the Antichrist by carrying out her orders).
>
> *(Rev. 17:13)*

These are some of the very last signs in the Bible's book of Revelation before Jesus comes back to earth again, and time shall be no more. God destroyed the world by water, Sodom and Gomorrah by fire and brimstone. On both occasions God sent messengers preaching the forthcoming doom. Today, God, in His infinite mercy, warns all Roman Catholics: "Come out of her, my people, that ye be not partakers of her sins, and that ye receive not of her plagues" (Rev. 18:4). And now, when the Word quickens unto you, is the time for this—now is the acceptable time of the Lord (11 Cor. 6:2).

Many Vatican state and federal government agencies such as the IRS, OSHA, and the U.S. Department of Labor along with labor unions have destroyed wonderfully the economic backbone of our country by harassing and forcing hundreds of businesses and industries into bankruptcy and out of business. This leaves millions of Americans out of work and hungry, while Vatican enterprises are not harassed at all but do flourish, because they run the government agencies. Look at what God says about the Antichrist when he will be thrown into hell:

> They that see thee shall narrowly look upon thee, and consider thee, saying, Is this the man (the Antichrist) that made the earth to tremble, that did shake kingdoms; That made the world as a wilderness, and destroyed the cities thereof.
>
> *(Isa. 14:16,17)*

Feds OK Vatican Slave Labor Camps

Just one of the Vatican's many multi-billion dollar enterprises is their liquor and wine slave labor camps which have no labor problems whatsoever because they unlawfully use free labor (thousands of Roman Catholic monks). These federal government agencies will not allow anyone else to enjoy the same privileges of volunteering our labor to God, our Father, and our Saviour, the Lord Jesus Christ, because we are all "heretics" (non-Roman Catholics). Yes, their enterprises do prosper, with no harm or harassment, using free labor in their Christian Brothers, La Salle, and Benedictine liquor and wine distilleries (slave labor camps) and in many others, all the way from Napa Valley, California, to New York State.

The Vatican's IRS and U.S. Department of Labor cross now the constitutional dividing line of separation between church and state and in every way are attempting to destroy all fundamental Christian churches and schools—one way is by taking away their tax-exempt status. This anti-American, anti-U.S. Constitution organization (the IRS), however, has given tax exempt status to all communist organizations in America, under Internal Revenue Code 501c3. They have never made any attempt to take this status away from them. Rome's collection agency (the IRS) has also made sure that the Roman Catholic institution is the only religious organization in the U.S. that doesn't have to pay property tax or even tax on their multi-billion dollar businesses. This is done under Sec. 892 of the Internal Revenue Code. The Vatican is the only religion that receives multi-millions of dollars of federal aid each year for their parochial schools. This comes out of your tax dollars. Like Archbishop Gilroy says: "Ourselves alone for fellow Roman Catholics" and "we must defeat all heretics."

The Vatican has used the Communist Party to help destroy the Russian Orthodox churches. And she used the Nazi Party in her attempt to do away with the Jews and their synagogues. (Because the Vatican says that all others than themselves are "heretics"—non-Roman Catholics.)

IRS—Roman Cult's Collection Agency

The Roman Catholic Jesuits started the international banking system called the Illuminati and the Agentur (and blamed the Jews for this). Rome's motto is "He that holds the money bags runs the nations." The Vatican started all the wars (inquisitions) to rid the world of heretics (non-Roman Catholics) and then made loans from her banks to nations so they would have enough money to fight them. We foolishly permitted this cult's collection agency into our country (the IRS—which answers only to Rome).

Further Resources

BOOKS

Greeley, Andrew M. *An Ugly Little Secret: Anti-Catholicism in North America.* Kansas City, Mo.: Sheed Andews and McMeel, 1977.

Lockwood, Robert P. *Anti-Catholicism in American Culture.* Huntington, Ind.: Our Sunday Visitor, 2000.

Perea, Juan F. *Immigrants Out! The New Nativism and the Anti-Immigrant Impulse in the United States.* New York: New York University Press, 1997.

Respect Life
Booklet

By: Committee for Pro-Life Activities

Date: 1985

Source: United States Conference of Catholic Bishops. *Respect Life.* Washington, D.C.: Committee for Pro-Life Activities, National Conference of Catholic Bishops, 1984.

About the Author: Joseph Cardinal Bernardin (1928–1996), chairman of the Pro-Life Committee of the National Conference of Catholic Bishops, was born in Columbia, South Carolina. He was ordained a Catholic priest in 1952 and served in the Diocese of Charleston. Bernardin was ordained a bishop in 1966. He became Archbishop of Cincinnati in 1972, and Archbishop of Chicago in 1982, being named a cardinal in 1983. Cardinal Bernardin died of pancreatic cancer on November 14, 1996. ∎

Introduction

During the decade of the 1980s, the Catholic Church in the United States began to promote a new approach to ethical issues, the Consistent Ethic of Life. Popularly known among Catholic progressives as "the Seamless Garment," it was an attempt to cease dealing with ethical issues separately, in a random fashion, and, instead, weave all Catholic moral and social positions into a single ethic of life.

While already noted for its pro-life position, Catholicism was attempting through this new approach to broaden the definition of "pro-life" beyond simply opposing abortion. Attempting to be pro-life in a consistent and comprehensive fashion, it opposed the inconsistency of being anti-life on one issue and pro-life on another. Regarding abortion, Catholic leaders continued to hold the view that every conceived life is sacred, and that the right to birth of this life should be defended. But, they

reasoned, is not that life just as sacred after birth? Should not every one of these precious lives have a right to adequate food, shelter, clothing and educational opportunities? Furthermore, would not it be inconsistent to argue that the life of an unborn child is sacred but, if that person should later commit murder, then he or she should be executed? To be truly pro-life, the bishops argued, meant not only to be anti-abortion. It also meant to be anti-capital punishment, anti-war, and anti-poverty.

This approach greatly expanded the scope of the bishops' understanding of the pro-life movement. It was no longer to be limited to the nine months of gestation. Rather, the issue of life, both its existence and its quality, should be advocated from conception to natural death. Abortion was no longer to be the whole of the pro-life effort, but merely the first major life issue that is necessary for the exercise of all the others.

Significance

The principle spokesperson for the Consistent Ethic of Life or Seamless Garment approach to the pro-life movement was Joseph Cardinal Bernardin, Archbishop of Chicago. Bernardin wanted to link all Catholic moral teachings together in a consistent manner. He stated: "Life, before and after death, from the moment of conception until natural death is like a seamless garment . . . If we become insensitive to the beginning of life and condone abortion, or if we become careless about the end of life and justify euthanasia, we have no reason to believe that there will be much respect for life in between." He believed that weakness on any one life issue undermined the rest—a just and moral society cannot successfully promote life in one area if it is anti-life in another.

In 1983, Bernardin became chairman of the Pro-Life Committee of the National Conference of Catholic Bishops. The influence of the Consistent Ethic of Life on Catholic moral teaching can be seen in the Respect Life Program, an annual publication of the national bishop's conference intended as a resource for parishes. An excerpt from this document is listed below. It shows this new approach, which broadens the concept of what it means to be pro-life, extending beyond protecting the unborn to protecting human life at every stage of existence. Consequently, the following issues now fall under this expanded definition what it means to be pro-life:

1. Abortion
2. Poverty
3. Education
4. Suicide
5. Euthanasia
6. Discrimination against the physically and mentally challenged

Anti-abortion activists carry signs urging people to "Stop abortion. America. . . Return to God," as they demonstrate in front of the U.S. Supreme Court in Washington, DC. © **BETTMANN/CORBIS. REPRODUCED BY PERMISSION.**

7. Racism

8. Religious Persecution

9. Capital Punishment

10. War

Critics of the Seamless Garment as a pro-life approach stated that abortion should stand as an issue of its own, that to link this issue with other issues would weaken the fight against abortion. In particular, opponents objected to linking abortion with capital punishment—as abortion is viewed as intrinsically evil, and the Catholic Church historically has recognized the right of the state to employ capital punishment. Proponents countered that the use of the death penalty by the state to punish criminals further decreases the respect for life in society, with negative consequences for everyone, including the unborn.

Primary Source

Respect Life [excerpt]

SYNOPSIS: The Catholic Church in the United States has long been an opponent of abortion. In the 1980s, under the leadership of Cardinal Joseph Bernardin of Chicago, the Catholic Church in America broadened its pro-life efforts to include a variety of other issues, including poverty, racism, capital punishment, euthanasia, and war.

Morality requires a consistent commitment to the good of human life in oneself and others. No one, however, can put this commitment into practice with equal diligence in regard to all the "life" issues of our time. Prudence requires particular individuals and groups to concentrate on particular issues and concerns—on correcting the intolerable circumstances of legalized abortion, for example, or working for worldwide disarmament and an end to war. Such concentration of effort is not merely a matter of practical necessity; it is virtuous in its own right, inasmuch as it heightens the chances of success.

But absolute consistency, not selectivity, is required of us all in negative terms: We may never in any context choose and act *against* the good of life.

Consistency is also required of us at the level of moral principle, where we are obliged to recognize

Cardinal Joseph Bernardin, Washington, D.C., November 16, 1987. Cardinal Bernardin, chairman of the National Conference of Catholic Bishops' Committee for Pro-Life Activities, wrote that life should be respected in all stages "from the moment of conception until death." © BETTMANN/CORBIS. REPRODUCED BY PERMISSION.

the sanctity of life at every stage and to endorse appropriate efforts directed to its protection and promotion. The logic of a consistent ethic of life applauds all realistic measures on behalf of life—from a constitutional amendment to protect the unborn to positive initiatives to achieve arms control; it endorses even those measures to which, in practice, one can lend only limited active support because one's energies are taken up in the defense of life in some other cause or context. . . .

The message of the Respect Life Program is that human life must be protected at every stage of its existence and in every circumstance of human living. It is critical to put an end to whatever directly threatens life, such as war, abortion and euthanasia. Moreover, respect for life also requires efforts to overcome obstacles to the proper enjoyment of life—hunger, poverty, disease, inequity and ignorance. This year

we focus on the value of children and the importance of family life, human experimentation and society's efforts to deal with the escalating incidence of suicide as some promote the idea of "rational" suicide. We review, too, the unsatisfied needs of nations struggling to provide food for their people. We focus on the story of abortion in the United States from 1973 to the present, and on the continuing need to become a caring community that is supportive of pregnant women and their children.

The Respect Life Program addresses a diversity of issues that, seen together, dramatize a commitment to a consistent ethic of life—an ethic linking the Church's teaching on issues concerning human life from conception until natural death.

Further Resources

BOOKS

Bernardin, Joseph Louis. *A Moral Vision for America.* Washington, D.C.: Georgetown University Press, 1998.

Fuechtmann, Thomas G. *Consistent Ethic of Life.* Kansas City, Mo.: Sheed & Ward, 1988.

McMunn, Richard. *Religion in Politics.* Milwaukee, Wisc.: Catholic League for Religious and Civil Rights, 1985.

"Abortion and the Sexual Agenda"
Journal article

By: Sidney Callahan

Date: April 25, 1986

Source: Callahan, Sidney. "Abortion and the Sexual Agenda." *Commonweal* 112, April 25, 1986. Reprinted in *Moral Issues and Christian Response,* 5th ed. Paul T. Jersild, and Dale A. Johnson, eds. Fort Worth, Tex.: Harcourt Brace Jovanovich, 1993, 346, 348, 349.

About the Author: Sidney Cornelia Callahan (1933–) was born in Washington, D.C. An educator in the field of psychology, she received her master's degree from Sarah Lawrence College in 1971, a doctorate from CUNY in 1980, and numerous honorary doctorates. She has taught in the field of psychology at Mercy College in New York and Fairfield University in Connecticut. ∎

Introduction

The Supreme Court legalized abortion in 1973 in *Roe v. Wade.* Religious conservatives saw this decision to legalize abortion on demand as an affront to the Judeo-Christian moral tradition, and as an approval of the most immoral aspect of the sexual revolution of the 1960s. The main religious opponents of abortion have been evangelical and fundamentalist Protestants, the Church of Jesus Christ of Latter-day Saints, and, most notably, the Roman Catholic Church. It has also included members of other faith communities who do not agree with their denominations' pro-choice stance.

In general, the position of the pro-life movement has been that all life is sacred from the moment of conception, and that the rights of the mother need to be balanced with the right of the unborn child to life. In a conflict between the two, the right of the child to life had priority, although there would be disagreement within the group over abortions to save the life of the mother or in cases of rape or incest.

The controversy over abortion has been the most divisive social issue in American religion since Abolition. Both sides use emotional labels, "pro-life" and "pro-choice," as banners for their respective clauses. Certainly, no one would want to be labeled as "anti-life." Likewise, in a society which favors freedom from any restrictions upon individual liberty, respondents to surveys are likely to agree that people should have the right to do things that they themselves would never do or encourage.

Various actions were proposed—including demonstrations at abortion clinics, marches on Washington on the anniversary of *Roe v. Wade,* appointment of conservatives to the Supreme Court and reverse the decision, and, finally, bypassing the Supreme Court and amending the Constitution. A major anti-abortion strategy that emerged in the 1980s was to limit the role of the federal government and apply abortion restrictions at the state level.

Significance

New developments in 1980s included the development of the Seamless Garment theory and emergence of Christian feminists. In the former case, this has been an initiative by the Catholic Church to be more consistent in advocating on a variety of ethical issues—to be pro-life on issues such as capital punishment and poverty, as well as abortion. While this has by no means resolved the controversy, it has taken some of the animosity of the debate, as pro-choice individuals acknowledge that this is a reasonable position that can be the basis of dialogue and be intellectually respected as consistent. It has caused controversy, however, among those who feel it has watered down the anti-abortion effort.

Regarding the Christian feminist position, an example is listed below. It is an excerpt from an article written by Sidney Callahan, which appeared in *Commonweal,* a Catholic magazine, on April 25, 1986. She begins by listing the four major feminist arguments for the morality of abortion: (1) the moral right to control one's own body; (2) the right to autonomy and personal responsibility; (3) the contingent value of the life of the fetus; and

(4) the right of women to social equality. Callahan responds to each in turn from a feminist position.

Callahan argued that while our legal tradition does guarantee the right to control our bodies, it also requires us not to harm other bodies—however immature or lacking full development they may be, such as in the case of the handicapped and newborns. On the second point, Callahan regarded this as an overemphasis on autonomy that undermined the moral responsibility that comes from living in an interdependent human community. Third, Callahan rejected the argument that the value of the fetus was contingent on the judgment of others. While dependent on others for its support and defense, fetal life has intrinsic value. Finally, Callahan argued that " . . . feminine and fetal liberation are ultimately one and the same cause." The pro-choice position, she claimed, freed society in general, and men in particular, from any responsibility for assisting women with their pregnancies. Whether they chose to abort or keep the fetus, having a baby was a woman's choice and, thereby, responsibility.

Primary Source

"Abortion and the Sexual Agenda" [excerpt]

SYNOPSIS: The pro-life movement includes a variety of religious groups and points of view. Some oppose abortion on any condition, while others would allow it to save the life of the mother. While usually associated with conservative views, some pro-life advocates tied the issue to other, more progressive causes, such as the abolition of the death penalty. Others opposed abortion on feminist grounds.

The Moral Right to Control One's Own Body

Pro-choice feminism argues that a woman choosing an abortion is exercising a basic right of bodily integrity granted in our common law tradition. If she does not choose to be physically involved in the demands of a pregnancy and birth, she should not be compelled to be so against her will. Just because it is *her* body which is involved, a woman should have the right to terminate any pregnancy, which at this point in medical history is tantamount to terminating fetal life. No one can be forced to donate an organ or submit to other invasive physical procedures for however good a cause. Thus no woman should be subjected to "compulsory pregnancy." And it should be noted that in pregnancy much more than a passive biological process is at stake.

From one perspective, the fetus is, as Petchesky says, a "biological parasite" taking resources from the woman's body. During pregnancy, a woman's whole life and energies will be actively involved in the nine-month process. Gestation and childbirth

Anti-abortion protestors rally in Tallahassee, Florida, October 9, 1989. After the court granted minors the same rights as adults in choosing abortions, pro-lifers argued that the rights of the unborn should be respected as well. © BETTMANN/CORBIS. REPRODUCED BY PERMISSION.

involve physical and psychological risks. After childbirth a woman will either be a mother who must undertake a twenty-year responsibility for child-rearing, or face giving up her child for adoption or institutionalization. Since hers is the body, hers the risk, hers the burden, it is only just that she alone should be free to decide on pregnancy or abortion.

This moral claim to abortion, according to the pro-choice feminists, is especially valid in an individualistic society in which women cannot count on medical care or social support in pregnancy, childbirth, or childrearing. A moral abortion decision is never made in a social vacuum, but in the real life society which exists here and now. . . .

From the Moral Right to Control One's Own Body to a More Inclusive Ideal of Justice

The moral right to control one's own body does apply to cases of organ transplants, mastectomies,

contraception, and sterilization; but it is not a conceptualization adequate for abortion. The abortion dilemma is caused by the fact that 266 days following a conception in one body, another body will emerge. One's own body no longer exists as a single unit but is engendering another organism's life. This dynamic passage from conception to birth is genetically ordered and universally found in the human species. Pregnancy is not like the growth of cancer or infestation by a biological parasite; it is the way every human being enters the world. Strained philosophical analogies fail to apply: having a baby is not like rescuing a drowning person, being hooked up to a famous violinist's artificial life-support system, donating organs for transplant—or anything else.

As embryology and fetology advance, it becomes clear that human development is a continuum. Just as astronomers are studying the first three minutes in the genesis of the universe, so the first moments, days, and weeks at the beginning of human life are the subject of increasing scientific attention. While neonatology pushes the definition of viability ever earlier, ultrasound and fetology expand the concept of the patient in utero. Within such a continuous growth process, it is hard to defend logically and demarcation point after conception as the point at which an immature form of human life is so different from the day before or the day after, that it can be morally or legally discounted as a non-person. Even the moment of birth can hardly differentiate a nine-month fetus from a newborn. It is not surprising that those who countenance late abortions are logically led to endorse selective infanticide.

The same legal tradition which in our society guarantees the right to control one's own body firmly recognizes the wrongfulness of harming other bodies, however immature, dependent, different looking, or powerless. The handicapped, the retarded, and newborns are legally protected from deliberate harm. Pro-life feminists reject the suppositions that would except the unborn from this protection.

After all, debates similar to those about the fetus were once conducted about feminine personhood. Just as women, or blacks, were considered too different, too underdeveloped, too "biological," to have souls or to possess legal rights, so the fetus is now seen as "merely" biological life, subsidiary to a person. A woman was once viewed as incorporated into the "one flesh" of her husband's person; she too was a form of bodily property. In all patriarchal unjust systems, lesser orders of human life are granted rights only when wanted, chosen, or invested with value by the powerful.

Fortunately, in the course of civilization there has been a gradual realization that justice demands the powerless and dependent be protected against the uses of power wielded unilaterally. No human can be treated as a means to an end without consent. The fetus is an immature, dependent form of human life which only needs time and protection to develop. Surely, immaturity and dependence are not crimes. . . .

It also seems a travesty of just procedures that a pregnant woman now, in effect, acts as sole judge of her own case, under the most stressful conditions. Yes, one can acknowledge that the pregnant woman will be subject to the potential burdens arising from a pregnancy, but it has never been thought right to have an interested party, especially the more powerful party, decide his or her own case when there may be a conflict of interest. If one considers the matter as a case of a powerful versus a powerless, silenced claimant, the pro-choice feminist argument can rightly be inverted: since hers is the body, hers the risk, and hers the greater burden, then how in fairness can a woman be the sole judge of the fetal right to life?

Further Resources

BOOKS

Burtchaell, James Tunstead. *Rachel Weeping and Other Essays on Abortion.* Kansas City, Mo.: Andrews and McNeel, 1982.

Fairweather, Eugene Rathbone. *The Right to Birth: Some Christian Views on Abortion.* Toronto: Anglican Book Centre, 1976.

Noebel, David A. *The Slaughter of the Innocent* Tulsa, Okla.: American Christian College Press, 1977.

Economic Justice for All

Letter

By: Archbishop Rembert Weakland

Date: November 18, 1986

Source: National Conference of Catholic Bishops. *Economic Justice for All: Pastoral Letter on Catholic Social Teaching and the U.S. Economy.* Washington, D.C.: United States Catholic Conference, 1986, ix–xii.

About the Author: Archbishop Rembert Weakland (1927–) of Milwaukee chaired the committee of the National Conference of Catholic Bishops that wrote the pastoral letter, *Economic Justice for All.* Weakland was born in Patton, Pennsylvania. He entered the Benedictine Order in 1945, was ordained a priest in 1951, and was appointed Archbishop of Milwaukee in 1977. ∎

Introduction

In 1980, the American Catholic bishops approved a letter critiquing Marxism. While content with the statement, some expressed the view that it would make more sense for the bishops of the most affluent society in the world to make a statement on capitalism.

Toward this end, a committee was established, chaired by Rembert Weakland, O.S.B., the Archbishop of Milwaukee. Extensive consultation took place, including wide circulation of draft copies and providing opportunities for the laity (non-ordained members) to express their opinions. In order to avoid the impression that the views expressed in these drafts favored one political party over the other, the release of one draft was delayed until after the 1984 presidential election.

This statement on economic justice is part of a long tradition of Catholic social teaching. Throughout the Middle Ages, the Church emphasized the need for all in society to work for the common good. The Industrial Revolution changed the European economy drastically, and modern Catholic social teaching dates from 1893, when Pope Leo XIII issued his encyclical, *Rerum Novarum* (On the Condition of Labor). In this letter, Leo argued strongly for the right of labor to organize and the payment of living wages.

The American response to *Rerum Novarum* was *Social Reconstruction: A General Review of the Problems and Survey of Remedies,* approved by the Catholic bishops on February 12, 1919. In this document, the bishops supported a whole range of political and economic issues. These included a minimum wage law, workman's compensation, the right of labor to organize unions, social security, housing assistance, child labor laws, job placements, and vocational training.

Much of this agenda was achieved in the New Deal and, in the post-war period, Catholic leaders focused on other issues. By the 1980s, however, with changes in the American and global economy, the bishops came back to the issue of economics.

Significance

On November 18, 1986, the National Council of Catholic Bishops voted to approve *Economic Justice for All: Pastoral Letter on Catholic Social Teaching and the U.S. Economy.* A critique of the U.S. economic system, the letter stated that all economic decisions must ultimately be judged by how they affect people—whether they hinder or promote human dignity.

The document begins with a review of general Christian economic principles, then goes into a detailed review of specific issues and makes specific policy recommendations. It was felt that the document would be more effective if it addressed specific issues, rather than address only generalities. The problem was that the letter became dated within a few years. The six principal themes of economic justice specified in the letter, included in the excerpt below, continue to be used by Catholic social justice activists and applied to current situations.

The letter received much criticism from conservative Catholics, who believed that capitalism was a morally superior economic system. It was known at the time that Pope John Paul II was composing a new encyclical letter on economic matters, and conservatives were sure it would justify their views regarding capitalism. In the 1988 encyclical, *Sollicitudo Rei Socialis* (The Social Concern of the Church), Pope John Paul II critiqued both Marxism and Capitalism, stating: "It is in the light of the dignity of the human person . . . that all economic and political systems are to be judged . . . a system is inhuman and immoral when people become cogs in the wheel of state determination or profit-determined goals submerge the individual."

The American bishops followed *Economic Justice for All* with additional political and economic statements on welfare reform (1987), international debt (1987), the Fair Housing Amendments Act (1987), and testimony to the Democratic and Republican platform committees (1988).

Primary Source

Economic Justice for All [excerpt]

> **SYNOPSIS:** A major source of conflict in America between conservatives and liberals in the Catholic Church was the 1986 pastoral letter, *Economic Justice for All.* Some conservatives believed it to be an unfair condemnation of capitalism, while some liberals were encouraged by it and Pope John Paul II's 1988 encyclical on capitalism and Marxism.

Principal Themes of the Pastoral Letter

12. The pastoral letter is not a blueprint for the American economy. It does not embrace any particular theory of how the economy works, nor does it attempt to resolve the disputes between different schools of economic thought. Instead, our letter turns to Scripture and to the social teachings of the Church. There, we discover what our economic life must serve, what standards it must meet. Let us examine some of these basic moral principles.

13. *Every economic decision and institution must be judged in light of whether it protects or undermines the dignity of the human person.* The pastoral letter begins with the human person. We believe the person is sacred—the clearest reflection of God among us. Human dignity comes from God, not from nationality, race, sex, economic status, or any human accomplishment. We judge any economic system by what it does *for* and *to* people and by how it permits all to *participate* in it. The economy should serve people, not the other way around.

14. *Human dignity can be realized and protected only in community.* In our teaching, the human person is not only sacred but also social. How we organize our society—in economics and politics, in law and policy—directly affects human dignity and the capacity of individuals to grow in community. The obligation to "love our neighbor" has an individual dimension, but it also requires a broader social commitment to the common good. We have many partial ways to measure and debate the health of our economy: Gross National Product, per capita income, stock market prices, and so forth. The Christian vision of economic life looks beyond them all and asks, Does economic life enhance or threaten our life together as a community?

15. *All people have a right to participate in the economic life of society.* Basic justice demands that people be assured a minimum level of participation in the economy. It is wrong for a person or group to be excluded unfairly or to be unable to participate or contribute to the economy. For example, people who are both able and willing, but cannot get a job are deprived of the participation that is so vital to human development. For, it is through employment that most individuals and families meet their material needs, exercise their talents, and have an opportunity to contribute to the larger community. Such participation has a special significance in our tradition because we believe that it is a means by which we join in carrying forward God's creative activity.

16. *All members of society have a special obligation to the poor and vulnerable.* From the Scriptures and church teaching, we learn that the justice of a society is tested by the treatment of the poor. The justice that was the sign of God's covenant with Israel was measured by how the poor and unprotected—the widow, the orphan, and the stranger—were treated. The kingdom that Jesus proclaimed in his word and ministry excludes no one. Throughout Israel's history and in early Christianity, the poor are agents of God's transforming power. "The Spirit of the Lord is upon me, therefore he has anointed me. He has sent me to bring glad tidings to the poor" (Lk 4:18). This was Jesus' first public utterance. Jesus takes the side of those most in need. In the Last Judgment, so dramatically described in St. Matthew's Gospel, we are told that we will be judged according to how we respond to the hungry, the

An assistant for Detroit's Good Samaritan hands out bread to the hungry, Detroit, Michigan, April 17, 1981. In a pastoral letter on the U.S. economy, the National Conference of Catholic Bishops wrote that "it is a social and moral scandal that one of every seven Americans is poor." © BETTMANN/ CORBIS. REPRODUCED BY PERMISSION.

thirsty, the naked, the stranger. As followers of Christ, we are challenged to make a fundamental "option for the poor"—to speak for the voiceless, to defend the defenseless, to assess life styles, policies, and social institutions in terms of their impact on the poor. This "option for the poor" does not mean pitting one group against another, but rather, strengthening the whole community by assisting those who are most vulnerable. As Christians, we are called to respond to the needs of *all* our brothers and sisters, but those with the greatest needs require the greatest response.

17. *Human rights are the minimum conditions for life in community.* In Catholic teaching, human rights include not only civil and political rights but also economic rights. As Pope John XXIII declared, "all people have a right to life, food, clothing, shelter, rest, medical care, education, and employment." This means that when people are without a chance to earn a living, and must go hungry and homeless, they are being denied basic rights. Society must ensure that these rights are protected. In this way, we

will ensure that the minimum conditions of economic justice are met for all our sisters and brothers.

18. *Society as a whole, acting through public and private institutions, has the moral responsibility to enhance human dignity and protect human rights.* In addition to the clear responsibility of private institutions, government has an essential responsibility in this area. This does not mean that government has the primary or exclusive role, but it does have a positive moral responsibility in safeguarding human rights and ensuring that the minimum conditions of human dignity are met for all. In a democracy, government is a means by which we can act together to protect what is important to us and to promote our common values.

19. These six moral principles are not the only ones presented in the pastoral letter, but they give an overview of the moral vision that we are trying to share. This vision of economic life cannot exist in a vacuum; it must be translated into concrete measures. Our pastoral letter spells out some specific applications of Catholic moral principles. We call for

a new national commitment to full employment. We say it is a social and moral scandal that one of every seven Americans is poor, and we call for concerted efforts to eradicate poverty. The fulfillment of the basic needs of the poor is of the highest priority. We urge that all economic policies be evaluated in light of their impact on the life and stability of the family. We support measures to halt the loss of family farms and to resist the growing concentration in the ownership of agricultural resources. We specify ways in which the United States can do far more to relieve the plight of poor nations and assist in their development. We also reaffirm church teaching on the rights of workers, collective bargaining, private property, subsidiarity, and equal opportunity.

20. We believe that the recommendations in our letter are reasonable and balanced. In analyzing the economy, we reject ideological extremes and start from the fact that ours is a "mixed" economy, the product of a long history of reform and adjustment. We know that some of our specific recommendations are controversial. As bishops, we do not claim to make these prudential judgments with the same kind of authority that marks our declarations of principle. But, we feel obliged to teach by example how Christians can undertake concrete analysis and make specific judgments on economic issues. The Church's teachings cannot be left at the level of appealing generalities.

21. In the pastoral letter, we suggest that the time has come for a "New American Experiment"— to implement economic rights, to broaden the sharing of economic power, and to make economic decisions more accountable to the common good. This experiment can create new structures of economic partnership and participation within firms at the regional level, for the whole nation, and across borders.

Further Resources

BOOKS

Lindsell, Harold. *Free Enterprise: A Judeo-Christian Defense.* Wheaton, Ill.: Tyndale House, 1982.

Ryan, John Augustine. *Economic Justice: Selections from Distributive Justice and a Living Wage.* Louisville, Ky.: Westminster John Knox Press, 1996.

Wuthnow, Robert. *God and Mammon in America.* New York: Free Press, 1994.

"Womanist Theology: Black Women's Voices"

Magazine article

By: Delores S. Williams

Date: March 2, 1987

Source: Williams, Delores S. "Womanist Theology: Black Women's Voices." *Christianity and Crisis* 47, no. 3, March 2, 1987. Reprinted in *Black Theology: A Documentary History. Vol. 2, 1980–1992.* Maryknoll, N.Y.: Orbis Books, 1993, 265, 266, 267, 271.

About the Author: Delores S. Williams is the Paul Tillich Professor of Theology and Culture at Union Theological Seminary in New York. She received her Ph.D. from Union in 1991. Dr. Williams' areas of teaching and research interests focus on the emergence of womanist theology, in addition to religion and culture. ∎

Introduction

Historically, African American women have suffered a two-fold oppression; first as people of color, and second as women. This was not only encountered in society at large, but in the churches as well. This situation did not prevent many pioneering African American women from embarking after slavery's end upon careers as preachers and missionaries. These women found inspiration in such texts as Joel 2:28-29, "After this I shall pour my spirit on all mankind: / your sons and your *daughters* will prophesy. . . . I shall pour out my spirit in those days even on slaves and *slave-girls* (emphasis added)."

They traveled all over the country. Denied the opportunity to preach on pulpits, they preached in tents, meeting halls, and private homes. Many more remained home, serving as lay leaders on various committees and boards of their churches. In fact, the contribution of women has been substantial in the historically black denominations such as the Church of God in Christ, African Methodist Episcopal, African Methodist Episcopal Zion and Progressive Baptist churches, where women make up approximately two-thirds of the membership. These large numbers in the pews do not have a parallel in the pulpit, with African American women only making up about five percent of leadership positions, such as pastor, in these denominations.

While the black churches themselves have been at the forefront of the Civil Rights movement, as a whole they have been less active in the area of women's rights. One African American woman found this to be true even in the more generally radical environment of the Black Theology movement, stating: "Black males have gradually increased their power and participation in the male-dominated society, while Black females have continued to endure the stereotypes and oppressions of an earlier period." (*A Religious History of America*, 346). Despite these limitations, black women theologians and religious leaders have made significant contributions.

Significance

A major theme in Black Theology is that of liberation, rooted in the powerful scriptural account of Israel's liberation in the Book of Exodus. Black women's theology, represented by such writers as bell hooks, goes even further by emphasizing the freedom of all peoples, moving beyond racial discrimination to address oppression in the areas of gender, race, class, sexuality, and ecology as well. Womanist theology draws on sources that range from traditional church doctrines, African American fiction and poetry, nineteenth century black women leaders, poor and working class black women in holiness churches, and African American women under slavery.

In the excerpt below, Dr. Delores Williams draws on the writings of novelist Alice Walker to express her view what it means to be a womanist and to do womanist theology. A womanist, she writes, is a black feminist. Williams sees much of womanist thought as rooted in the tradition of black mothers passing on wisdom to their daughters. This wisdom, so necessary for survival in communities dominated by whites and men, has been preserved in slave narratives, folk tales, and contemporary literature.

This struggle for liberation by African American women has resulted in significant gains, particularly in the churches. Barbara Harris became the first Anglican bishop in 1989. In 2000, the 2.5 million-member African Methodist Episcopal Church elected its first female bishop, Vashti McKenzie. Currently 3,000 of the AME's 10,000 ministers are women. The future looks even brighter. According to the Association of Theological Schools, a third of all graduate-level seminary students are now women. In 2002, there were 2,030 African American women working towards seeking a master's of divinity degree, compared to 133 in 1977.

Primary Source

"Womanist Theology: Black Women's Voices"
[excerpt]

> **SYNOPSIS:** African Americans have long suffered discrimination in the United States. Women likewise have suffered from patriarchy, making the situation of African American women doubly problematic. This has also provided a context that has made the theological contributions of black women unique. While part of Black Theology as a whole, it also has a distinctive voice.

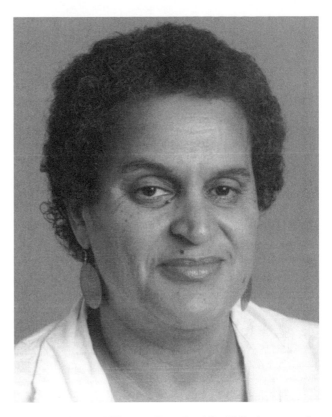

Delores S. Williams. Williams applies author Alice Walker's concept of "womanism" to theology in an essay on black women's voices in modern religion. **PHOTO COURTESY OF DELORES S. WILLIAMS. REPRODUCED BY PERMISSION.**

> Daughter: Mama, why are we brown, pink, and yellow, and our cousins are white, beige, and black?
>
> Mother: Well, you know the colored race is just like a flower garden, with every color flower represented.
>
> Daughter: Mama, I'm walking to Canada and I'm taking you and a bunch of slaves with me.
>
> Mother: It wouldn't be the first time.

In these two conversational exchanges, Pulitzer Prize-winning novelist Alice Walker begins to show us what she means by the concept "womanist." The concept is presented in Walker's *In Search of Our Mothers' Gardens* (Harcourt Brace Jovanovich, 1983) and many women in church and society have appropriated it as a way of affirming themselves as *black* while simultaneously owning their connection with feminism; and with the African-American community, male and female. The concept of womanist allows women to claim their roots in black history, religion, and culture.

What then is a womanist? Her origins are in the black folk expression "You acting womanish," meaning, according to Walker, "wanting to know more and in greater depth than is good for one . . . outrageous, audacious, courageous and willful behavior." A womanist is also "responsible, in charge, serious." She can walk to Canada and take others with her. She loves, she is committed, she is a universalist by temperament.

Her universality includes loving men and women, sexually or non-sexually. She loves music, dance, the spirit, food and roundness, struggle, and she loves herself. "Regardless."

Walker insists that a womanist is also "committed to survival and wholeness of entire people, male and female." She is no separatist, "except for health." A womanist is a black feminist or feminist of color. Or as Walker says, "Womanist is to feminist as purple to lavender." . . . in male-female roles, and more respect for female intelligence and ingenuity than is found in bourgeois culture.

The black folk are poor. Less individualistic than those who are better off, they have, for generations, practiced various forms of economic sharing. For example, immediately after Emancipation mutual aid societies pooled the resources of black folk to help pay for funerals and other daily expenses. *The Book of Negro Folklore* describes the practice of rent parties which flourished during the Depression. The black folk stressed togetherness and a closer connection with nature. They respect knowledge gained through lived experience monitored by elders who differ profoundly in social class and world view from the teachers and education encountered in American academic institutions. Walker's choice of context suggests that womanist theology can establish its lines of continuity in the black community with nonbourgeois traditions less sexist than the black power and black nationalist traditions.

In this folk context, some of the black female-centered cultural codes in Walker's definition (e.g., "Mama, I'm walking to Canada and I'm taking you and a bunch of slaves with me") point to folk heroines like Harriet Tubman, whose liberation activity earned her the name "Moses" of her people. This allusion to Tubman directs womanist memory to a liberation tradition in black history in which women took the lead, acting as catalysts for the community's revolutionary action and for social change. Retrieving this often hidden or diminished female tradition of catalytic action is an important task for womanist theologians and ethicists. Their research may well reveal that female models of authority have been absolutely essential for every struggle in the black community and for building and maintaining the community's institutions. . . .

Who Do You Say God Is?

Regardless of one's hopes about intentionality and womanist theological method, questions must be raised about the God-content of the theology. Walker's mention of the black womanist's love of the spirit is a true reflection of the great respect Afro-American women have always shown for the presence and work of the spirit. In the black church, women (and men) often judge the effectiveness of the worship service not on the scholarly content of the sermon nor on the ritual nor on orderly process. Rather, worship has been effective if "the spirit was high," i.e., if the spirit was actively and obviously present in a balanced blend of prayer, of cadenced word (the sermon), and of syncopated music ministering to the pain of the people.

The importance of this emphasis upon the spirit is that it allows Christian womanist theologians, in their use of the Bible, to identify and reflect upon those biblical stories in which poor oppressed women had a special encounter with divine emissaries of God, like the spirit. In the Hebrew Testament, Hagar's story is most illustrative and relevant to Afro-American women's experience of bondage, of African heritage, of encounter with God/emissary in the midst of fierce survival struggles. Kate Cannon among a number of black female preachers and ethicists urges black Christian women to regard themselves as Hagar's sisters.

In relation to the Christian or New Testament, the Christian womanist theologian can refocus the salvation story so that it emphasizes the beginning of revelation with the spirit mounting Mary, a woman of the poor (" . . . the Holy Spirit shall come upon thee, and the power of the Highest shall overshadow thee . . ." Luke 1:35). Such an interpretation of revelation has roots in nineteenth century black abolitionist and feminist Sojourner Truth. Posing an important question and response, she refuted a white preacher's claim that women could not have rights equal to men's because Christ was not a woman. Truth asked, "Whar did your Christ come from? . . . From God and a woman! Man had nothin' to do wid Him!" This suggests that womanist theology could eventually speak of God in a well-developed theology of the spirit. The sources for this theology are many. Harriet Tubman often "went into the spirit" before her liberation missions and claimed her strength for liberation activity came from this way of meeting God. Womanist theology has grounds for shaping a theology of the spirit informed by black women's political action.

Further Resources

BOOKS

Bassard, Katherine Clay. *Spiritual Interrogations: Culture, Gender, and Community in Early African American Women's Writing.* Princeton, N.J.: Princeton University Press, 1999.

Gayles, Gloria. *My Soul Is a Witness: African-American Women's Spirituality.* Boston: Beacon Press, 1995.

Frederick, Marla Faye. *Between Sundays: Black Women and Everyday Struggles of Faith.* Berkeley: University of California Press, 2003.

"The New Lutheran Church: The Gift of Augustana"

Magazine article

By: Richard F. Koenig

Date: June 17, 1987

Source: Koenig, Richard. "The New Lutheran Church: The Gift of Augustana." *The Christian Century* 104, no. 19, June 17–24, 1987, 555, 556, 557, 558. ∎

Introduction

Some of the earliest settlers in the Americas were Scandinavian, Dutch and German Lutherans. By the 1620s, there were settlements of Lutherans along the Hudson River, in what are now New York and New Jersey. As the number of congregations grew, scattered groups would form a "synod" or church body, and as the nation expanded, so did the number of Lutheran church bodies.

By the late-nineteenth century, the twenty or so Lutheran church bodies that would eventually merge to become the American Lutheran Church and the Lutheran Church in America had been established. Massive immigration from traditionally Lutheran countries had started, and between 1840 and 1875 alone fifty-eight Lutheran synods were formed in the United States. The result of this immigration from so many different countries was the creation of a myriad of Lutheran churches. A town may have had three Lutheran churches, one each for the Swedes, Danes, and Norwegians.

Nineteenth-century Lutherans still looked to their homelands to supply pastors and worship materials. As second and third generation Americans spoke English more than German, Norwegian or Danish, a need arose to provide formal theological training, hymnals, catechisms and other materials. As these communities gradually assimilated into American society, maintaining the ethnic divisions within Lutheranism became less important.

The twentieth century witnessed a great deal of consolidation. In 1960, the American Lutheran Church (German), the United Evangelical Lutheran Church (Danish) and the Evangelical Lutheran Church (Norwegian) merged to form the American Lutheran Church (ALC). The Lutheran Free Church (Norwegian), which had dropped out of merger negotiations, came into the ALC in 1963. In 1962 the ULCA (German, Slovak and Icelandic) joined with the Augustana Evangelical Lutheran Church (Swedish), Finnish Evangelical Lutheran Church and American Evangelical Lutheran Church (Danish) to form the Lutheran Church in America (LCA).

Significance

By the middle of the twentieth century, the Lutheran World Federation became increasingly active in ecumenical initiatives. Discussions were held with Roman Catholics and churches of the Reformed tradition, including Presbyterians. This ecumenical spirit also was exhibited by American Lutherans among themselves, as they took the process of Lutheran consolidation even further.

In the late 1970s, the American Lutheran Church (ALC), the Lutheran Church in America (LCA), and the Association of Evangelical Lutheran Churches (AELC) began talks toward merger. The latter group had emerged from the German Lutheran Church–Missouri Synod, which unfortunately did not participate. A Committee on Lutheran Unity was formed in 1979.

Eight years later, the new denomination, the Evangelical Lutheran Church in America (ELCA), was finally born at its constituting convention in Columbus, Ohio from April 30 to May 3, 1987. The three separate churches had "closing conventions" the day before, voting themselves out of existence, and coming together in the new communion. The Columbus convention elected the ELCA's first bishop, Herbert Chilstrom, as well as the various other officers required to staff the many activities of this larger denomination of 5.3 million members.

The selection below is from an article in the *Christian Century* magazine written shortly after the Columbus convention. It describes the various streams of Lutheran traditions that had merged into the larger body, as well as the many personalities involved—particularly that of the new denomination's first bishop, Herbert W. Chilstrom. While merger with the Missouri Synod would have made the new denomination complete, the story of unification among Lutherans is an inspiring one. Religion is all too often depicted as a divisive force, with isolated acts of violence and bigotry making the headlines,

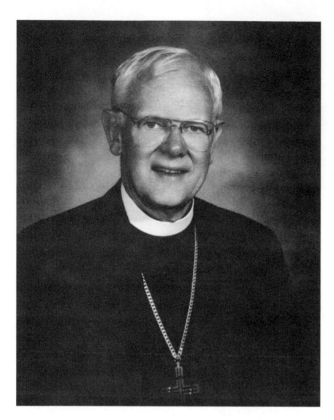

Herbert W. Chilstrom. Rev. Chilstrom was elected presiding bishop of the Evangelical Lutheran Church in America at its inception in 1987 and served in that position until October 1995. COURTESY OF EVANGELICAL LUTHERAN CHURCH IN AMERICA (ELCA). REPRODUCED BY PERMISSION.

while the ongoing work of preaching the Gospel, feeding the hungry, educating children, and operating hospitals goes largely unnoticed. Examples such as the formation of the ELCA show how past divisions can be overcome.

Primary Source

"The New Lutheran Church: The Gift of Augustana" [excerpt]

SYNOPSIS: The Lutherans came to the United States from many different countries where their churches were the official state churches. The Lutheran Church of Denmark, Norway, Sweden, and a whole host of others established offshoots in the United States. Throughout the twentieth century, an ecumenical spirit led these various national churches to come together as one church, united by faith, and no longer divided by ethnicity. The establishing of the Evangelical Lutheran Church in America in 1987 was a major step in this process.

The power of symbols and symbolic actions to make real to people what would otherwise remain remote or abstract was abundantly evident in the constituting convention of the new Evangelical Lutheran Church in America held in Columbus, Ohio, April 30–May 1. Whereas the actual vote creating the new church evoked not so much as a ripple of emotion on the part of the 1,045 delegates, both the delegates and the thousands of visitors were profoundly moved by the rites included in the worship services. The meeting began with bishops James R. Crumley, Jr., of the Lutheran Church in America, David W. Preus of the American Lutheran Church, and Will L. Herzfeld of the small Association of Evangelical Lutheran Churches each pouring water from separate containers into a great baptismal font set in the midst of the congregation. On Saturday evening the bishops filled a common chalice from three flagons before the thousands gathered for the closing Eucharist in Batelle Hall of the Ohio Center. At Columbus, Lutherans engaged in actions that not only made them one, but made them feel as one. . . .

Lutherans came to America (before and after the American Revolution) speaking more than a dozen different languages, not counting dialects. Liturgical traditions and church orders were equally many and various. But the churches to which the immigrants belonged all professed formal adherence to the Augsburg Confession and the other Lutheran confessions. In addition, and of utmost significance, both earlier and later immigrants were deeply influenced by the powerful surges of Pietism that swept the churches of Europe and Scandinavia in the 18th and early 19th centuries. Lutherans in America were confessional Pietists.

According to the late Sydney Ahlstrom of Yale, himself a member of the Augustana Church, the twin challenge for Lutherans upon reaching America was, first, the separation of church and state, and second, denominational pluralism, the predominant stream of which was Reformed, but in some places "drastically re-formed and given a more radical turn by the exigencies of America's westward expansion . . . which led inexorably to a root-and-branch abandonment of the ancient catholic tradition."

For many Lutherans the problems posed by the American situation proved to be too much. Millions joined other churches or simply chose not to affiliate with any group. For those who strove to remain Lutheran, the American milieu acted as a stimulus for a fresh discovery of confessional identity. But even with that discovery their problems were not over. In the founding of church organizations, Lutherans were required to pass through the fiery waters of doctrinal controversy before reaching some stability. In this respect Augustana's experience was benignly different. As Ahlstrom says:

> The most salient fact in Augustana's history is the relatively smooth and untroubled course of its history. The Danish, Norwegians, Finnish, and German Lutheran groups which were organized more or less at the same time have histories that are filled with controversy, schism, mergers, and reunions. But the history of Augustana is clouded by only one period of dissensus and one relatively minor withdrawal.

In the matrix of such a history, graced by fruitful contact with a thousand years of Christian tradition in the Church of Sweden and enlivened by gifted leaders, Augustana developed the "distinctive character," the "ethos," which historians have noted and which later would mature into "evangelical catholicity." That ethos kept together in a special, calm way what other groups tended to find difficult: the combination of a firm Lutheran confessionalism and a warm pietism. In addition the Augustana ethos embraced a centralization in church polity without sacrificing congregational autonomy, a growing churchliness in matters of worship and liturgy, a settled doctrine of the ordained ministry, missionary zeal, an active social concern and an emphasis on higher education and culture. All of these elements were present in other Lutheran groups, but in Augustana they seem to have come together as a tradition to liberate the synod for a career in fostering Lutheran unity and wider ecumenical contacts. . . .

Lutherans, especially midwestern Lutherans, love to dwell on the trek that brought their ancestors to the new land and the dedication they exhibited in forming the church bodies that nourished them. The stories are tales of hardship overcome by faith, and the telling of them reveals admiration and gratitude on the part of the children. It was risky business. Lutherans have now set out on another kind of trek.

Further Resources

BOOKS

Flesner, Dorris A. *American Lutherans Help Shape World Council: The Role of the Lutheran Churches of America in the Formation of the World Council of Churches.* St. Louis, Mo: Lutheran Historical Conference, 1981.

Martin, Janet Letnes. *Growing Up Lutheran.* Hastings, Minn.: Caragana Press, 1997.

Reuss, Carl F. *Profiles of Lutherans in the U.S.A.* Minneapolis, Minn.: Augsburg Publishing House, 1982.

"The Future Is Now for Southern Baptists"

Magazine article

By: Bill J. Leonard

Date: July 16, 1988

Source: Leonard, Bill J. "The Future Is Now for Southern Baptists." *The Christian Century* 105, no. 21, July 6–13, 1988, 628–630.

About the Author: Bill J. Leonard (1946–) was born in Decatur, Texas. A religion educator and minister, he attended Southwestern Baptist Seminary and was ordained a Baptist minister in 1971, and received his Ph.D. from Boston University in 1975. He has served as a pastor in Southboro, Massachusetts, and taught at Southern Baptist Theological Seminary in Louisville, Kentucky. ■

Introduction

Fundamentalism originated in the early-twentieth century as a reaction against liberal developments in theology, particularly in applying modern methods to the study of the Bible. Fundamentalists believed that liberal theology had surrendered too much of the core beliefs of Christianity to modernism, and that the essentials of the faith had to be preserved. Much of the focus of fundamentalism was on preserving the Bible as the sole, inerrant, and unchanging source of authority for Protestant Christianity.

On the national scene, the major episode in this earlier period was the famous Scopes Monkey Trial in 1925, where a high school teacher in Tennessee was found guilty of teaching evolution. As far as the general public was concerned, fundamentalism disappeared after the circus trial in Dayton, Tennessee, concluded. In reality, it never went away; the struggle within many Protestant denominations between Modernists and Fundamentalists continued. Liberal theologians continued to try and demonstrate an affinity between religion and progress. To do this, religion in general, and the Bible in particular, need to be subjected to the same critical standards as any other field of study. Such an analysis and questioning of traditional beliefs and texts was regarded as impious by religious conservatives.

The general public rediscovered fundamentalism in the 1980 presidential election. The Moral Majority, a political organization advancing a conservative religious agenda, was credited with being a major contributing factor to the election of President Ronald Reagan (served 1981–1989) that year. While the American news media was surprised by its reemergence, in many denominations the decades since the Scopes Trial had seen long struggles between religious liberals and conservatives. Much of this struggle was internal, dealing with denominational organizations and seminaries.

Significance

Just as in its earlier phase, modern fundamentalism continues to stress biblical inerrancy. A major development, however, is the origin of the Christian Right, a political movement to advance the religious conservative agenda—advocating school prayer and traditional family values, while opposing abortion and homosexuality.

In his 1988 article for *Christian Century,* Bill J. Leonard gave an inside look at the struggles taking place within the largest Protestant denomination in the United States, the Southern Baptist Convention. The Southern Baptists had always been a conservative denomination, and their struggle over Modernism did not last long. The issue, however, was whether moderates could feel at home in the denomination, or would the fundamentalist faction in the church gain complete control.

Dr. Leonard, a Baptist who taught church history at Southern Baptist Theological Seminary in Louisville, Kentucky, observed the annual meeting of the Southern Baptist Convention held in San Antonio from June 14–16, 1988. Leonard commented that moderates had failed to have any of their candidates elected convention president, and saw the election of Jerry Vines as decisive, stating: "For all practical purposes, Vines' election means that the denomination, at least in its national organization, is now controlled by a fundamentalist faction." One concern was that the Southern Baptist Convention will shift its resources out of certain social action efforts, and support, instead, conservative projects and political agendas.

Primary Source

"The Future Is Now for Southern Baptists"

> **SYNOPSIS:** In the early religious history of the United States, denominations were distinguished from one another on issues such as church government, or the degree to which the religious community should adapt to American culture. Increasingly, religious communities are dividing along liberal and conservative lines, with moderates experiencing great difficulty in maintaining unity. In many ways, conservative Baptists have more in common with conservative Methodists, than with liberal or moderate Baptists.

The future collided with the present at the Southern Baptist Convention held in San Antonio June 14–16. The election of Jerry Vines, co-pastor of the 18,000-member First Baptist Church of Jacksonville, Florida, as convention president effectively ended years of speculation as to what a fundamentalist takeover of the denomination might mean "sometime in the future." For all practical purposes,

Vines's election means that the denomination, at least in its national organization, is now controlled by a fundamentalist faction. It is a sobering reality for convention moderates and fundamentalists alike.

Moderates are now forced to recognize that time has run out in their attempt to thwart the fundamentalists' ten-year plan to dominate convention boards and agencies. Since 1979, moderates have failed to elect any of their candidates to the SBC presidency, a post with a one-year term. Rather, a succession of fundamentalist-oriented presidents—Adrian Rogers, Bailey Smith, Jimmy Draper and Charles Stanley—has continued to appoint to convention leadership biblical inerrantists. They aim to direct the denomination to follow theological, political and social agendas that are even more conservative than those promoted by the convention in the past. The election of Vines, who has pledged to continue their trend, means that fundamentalist control of all convention agencies is now a fait accompli. Even if moderates should regain the presidency in the foreseeable future, it would take years—perhaps another decade—to displace fundamentalist majorities on boards and agencies and re-establish a moderate agenda. Indeed, the fundamentalists' control is so thorough that other than the election of the president, moderates have no real influence on the business carried out at the annual meeting. This circumstance has led the Southern Baptist Alliance, a moderate group formed over two years ago as an alternative to fundamentalism, to declare that "the SBC is now a fundamentalist-dominated convention."

Moderates' attempt to elect Richard Jackson, pastor of the 18,000-member North Phoenix Baptist Church, Phoenix, Arizona, failed by a relatively small margin (692 out of 31,291 votes cast). Now they are divided over what to do next. Some talk of trying to elect a moderate at next year's convention in Las Vegas. Others call for churches to withhold donations to convention funds. Some note that if moderates cannot succeed in electing Jackson, a staunch theological conservative, they probably cannot elect anyone. Still others speculate that fundamentalists now have such power over the convention that it may be impossible to retake control and keep the convention intact. For the present, prospects for moderates' regaining momentum are bleak.

Fundamentalists, on the other hand, have little time to savor their victory. The future caught up with them also in San Antonio. Though they now control the denomination, it is badly fragmented, perched on the edge of serious decline. The day after Vines's election, Joel Gregory, a popular convention preacher and conservative Texas pastor, warned messengers that "we are at a flash-point. Southern Baptists cannot survive many more months of personal animosity in our midst." Even fundamentalist messengers acknowledged that the Southern Baptist rift has extended into local congregations. They overwhelmingly passed a resolution stating that "there is an ever-increasing number of our local Southern Baptist churches experiencing conflict and inner-church power struggles." The resolution also noted that "love involves trust, and our choice not to trust one another has diminished our witness and our mission at home and around the world." It was a surprisingly candid confession.

Many messengers apparently believe that conflicts in local churches would be resolved if laypeople would submit to their pastors' authority. This attitude was reflected in Resolution Five, "On the Priesthood of the Believer," which declared that "none of the five major writing systematic theologians in Southern Baptist history have given more than passing reference to the doctrine of the Priesthood of the Believer in their systematic theologies," and that "the high-profile emphasis on the doctrine of the Priesthood of the Believer in Southern Baptist life is a recent historical development."

The resolution repudiated the idea that the doctrine can be used to justify "that a Christian may believe whatever he [sic] so chooses and still be considered a loyal Southern Baptist." It suggested that the doctrine of the priesthood of the believer "in no way contradicts the biblical understanding of the role, responsibility, and authority of the pastor" and affirmed "the truth that elders, or pastors, are called of God to lead the local church (Acts 20:28)." That resolution infuriated many moderates who saw it as an example of the fundamentalists' reinterpretation of historic Baptist principles and their obsession with ministerial authority. It confirmed their feelings that they have been disenfranchised by the convention. Resolution Five, perhaps more than the presidential election, solidified divisions and heightened debates. One group of about 200 protested its passage by marching to the Alamo, where they wrote "heresy" across copies of the resolution, ripped them up, then prayed and sang hymns.

Predictions of how the controversy might harm the denomination seem to have come true this year. Membership, programs and funding have declined. Baptisms, the lifeblood of the denomination's self-understanding, decreased from 363,124 in 1986 to 338,495 in 1987. Membership in Southern Baptist churches in 1987 increased by the smallest percentage since 1936. Leaders of the Foreign Mission Board announced that they will need to take $5.1 million from current cash reserves to meet a shortfall in the annual Christmas foreign-missions offering. They also reported that their 1988 budget would be cut by 12 per cent because of declining revenues.

Enrollment in master of divinity programs at the six denominational seminaries is shrinking. Finances are tight; for several years seminaries have been receiving fewer Cooperative Program dollars. Money from the Cooperative Program for collective budget funding is stretched to the limit. The Woman's Missionary Union, a missions-education organization, reported that the average Southern Baptist church now contributes about 8 per cent of its budget to the Cooperative Program, and that percentage is decreasing annually.

Financial problems are plaguing the state associations as well. The Baptist Convention of North Carolina expects a $750,000 budget deficit for this fiscal year. In addition, Cooperative Program giving from North Carolina churches has declined by about 3.5 per cent. An informal survey of churches in the state discovered three basic reasons for this development. First, many conservative churches are by passing the Cooperative Program and sending funds directly to the Home Mission Board, now directed by Larry Lewis, a well-known advocate of biblical inerrancy. Second, many moderate churches are sending some of their offerings to the Southern Baptist Alliance. Third, some North Carolina congregations are simply not taking in enough funds to meet their own church budgets, and are therefore sending less money to the Cooperative Program.

Now the fundamentalists must confront the denomination's decline and fragmentation. From the beginning of their takeover activities, fundamentalists have promised to save the denomination from the declines evident among United Methodists, Presbyterians and other mainline denominations. They have blamed such declines almost entirely on the rise of theological liberalism.

But they may discover that extremism on the right can also foster such decline. Many Southern Baptists who criticize mainline churches for their involvement in liberal political causes now want the SBC to expand its support for certain right-wing political agendas. Fundamentalist leaders will probably respond by reorganizing the denomination's political and social-action efforts, which are now expressed through the Christian Life Commission and the Baptist Joint Committee on Public Affairs. The new director of the Christian Life Commission, to be chosen this year, will have to meet fundamentalist approval. The SBC's relationship with the Washington-based Baptist Joint Committee has already been modified considerably and may soon be severed entirely. Many fundamentalist leaders are active, to varying degrees, in New Right organizations such as Eagle Forum, Roundtable, the Council for Public Policy and Christian Reconstructionism. Can fundamentalists continue to carry the convention toward the political right at a time when public sentiment seems to be moving toward the center of the political spectrum? Will right-wing politics contribute to the further decline of the denomination?

However, the fundamentalists seem to believe that most Southern Baptists now support their cause or will ultimately acquiesce to their views on Scripture, doctrine, polity and pastoral authority. Perhaps they are right. The convention may have done such an excellent job of inculcating Baptist identity into its people that many will accept whatever convention leaders demand as long as they can continue to call themselves Southern Baptists. This loyalty may help explain why the SBC has endured so long without a major schism and why it has until now avoided the inevitable membership and funding declines that sooner or later confront every major religious group. From a demographic perspective, the convention would probably have experienced these declines regardless of the current controversy. Indeed, many fundamentalist leaders anticipated the declines and capitalized on them in their phenomenal rise to power. Rather than resolving denominational difficulties, however, fundamentalists may help hasten the impact of these difficulties on the churches.

Faced with seemingly unending controversy, fragmentation and decline, many Southern Baptists seem content to take refuge in traditional piety. Indeed, some prefer to practice the piety of denial—burying their considerable problems in rhetoric, denouncing one faction or both factions while calling for a nebulous spiritual renewal that will somehow transcend the hard questions, deep hurts and institutional struggles rampant in the agencies and churches. They seem to believe they can hurt each other and then gloss over injuries with pious slogans of a bygone era. Some of the same people who at the convention applauded Dallas pastor W. A. Criswell's denunciation of liberal "skunks" also ap-

plauded Joel Gregory's call for peace and reconciliation and apparently saw no contradiction in their actions.

For the past ten years, many Southern Baptists ignored the controversy and hoped that it would have only a limited effect on convention programs, funding and ministries. Many now hope that something will happen to save the SBC from itself. Such notions seem increasingly impossible. Both time and controversy have inexorably caught up with America's largest Protestant denomination. For Southern Baptists, the future is now.

Further Resources

BOOKS

Green, Clifford. *Prayers in the Precincts: The Christian Right in the 1998 Elections.* Washington, D.C.: Georgetown University Press, 2000.

Marty, Martin E. *Fundamentalism and Evangelicalism.* New York: K.G. Saur, 1993.

Sekulow, Jay. *From Intimidation to Victory: Regaining the Christian Right to Speak.* Lake Mary, Fla.: Creation House, 1990.

Neighbors: Muslims in North America

Nonfiction work

By: Muhammed Halabi and Elias D. Mallon

Date: 1989

Source: Halabi, Muhammed. Interview by Elias D. Mallon. In Mallon, Elias D. *Neighbors: Muslims in North America.* New York: Friendship Press, 1989, 80–81, 82–83.

About the Authors: Muhammad Halabi was a Ph.D. candidate in American Drama at New York University at the time of the interview. He is a native of Syria, and he taught English and American drama at the University of Damascus before coming to the United States.

Elias D. Mallon was associate director of the Graymoor Ecumenical Institute in New York, where he coordinated interfaith relations. An ordained member of the Society of the Atonement, Fr. Mallon chaired the Roman Catholic-Muslim Dialogue in the Archdiocese of New York. He has a Ph.D. in Near Eastern Languages from the Catholic University of America. ∎

Introduction

Thousands of Muslims began to arrive in the United States in the 1880s. These first Islamic immigrants were Arabs from what was then Greater Syria. These Syrian, Jordanian, and Lebanese migrants were unskilled laborers seeking greater economic opportunities. Many returned, but those that stayed endured prejudice, but they were able to establish fledgling Islamic communities. By 1920, Arab immigrants worshiped in a rented hall in Cedar Rapids, Iowa, and they built a mosque of their own in 1935. Lebanese-Syrian communities did the same in Ross, North Dakota, and later in Detroit, Pittsburgh, and Michigan City, Indiana. The first wave of Muslim immigration ended in 1924, when the Johnson-Reed Immigration Act allowed only a trickle of Arabs to enter the nation.

In addition to Arab immigrants, conversion has also added to the Muslim population in the United States. While there have been a few Euro-American converts, the vast majority have been African Americans. A black nationalist Islamic community, the Moorish Science Temple, began in Newark, New Jersey, in 1913. In 1930, Wallace D. Ford, who changed his name to Wali Farad, founded the Nation of Islam in 1930. After Farad's unexplained disappearance in 1934, Elijah Muhammed (1897–1975) took over, and he attracted disenchanted and poor African Americans from the urban North.

Muslim immigration began to pick up again with Palestinian refugees arriving after the creation of Israel in 1948. More important for the history of American Islam, the McCarran-Walter Act of 1952 relaxed the quota system established in 1924, thereby allowing greater Muslim immigration. Further revision of the immigration law in 1965 resulted in even greater numbers of Muslims entering the United States. In addition to economic opportunity, Muslim migrants have also come to escape oppressive regimes in Egypt, Iraq, and Syria. Furthermore, South Asian Muslims from Pakistan have also arrived, bringing even greater diversity to the American Muslim population.

Significance

Until recently, the United States has been a predominately Protestant country, with its largest single denomination being Roman Catholic. For much of American history, Jews were the major exception to this Christian monopoly. The Muslims represent a major contribution to American diversity. By the 1980s there were approximately 3,000,000 Muslims in North America.

While diversity can be very enriching, for others this was unsettling. For many Americans, Muslims were violent people inspired to commit acts of terrorism by their religion. In order to help dispel such prejudices, Fr. Elias Mallon published *Neighbors: Muslims in North America*, a portion of which is excerpted below.

In this work, Fr. Mallon interviewed numerous Muslims from a variety of backgrounds. They had come to the United States from many nations, including Ghana, Egypt,

China, and Yugoslavia. They are students, professionals, and laborers. In these interviews, Muslims talked about their families, their work, and their spiritual journeys. Some were first-generation immigrants, and others had been studying or working in the United States for a number of years. Like all other immigrant groups, these Muslims came to the United States for economic and political reasons. Still, like the Pilgrims, Irish, Germans, Jews, and other immigrants, they also wanted to raise their children in their own faith, to establish houses of worship in their communities, and try to find a way of fitting into American society without abandoning their culture.

This religious community has continued to grow in the United States. By the 1990s, Muslims had established more than six hundred mosques and centers across the United States. Like the United States in general, it is a diverse community of Arabs, Asians, and African Americans. It is hoped that the tragedy of September 11, 2001 will not foster a new round of anti-Muslim Nativism.

Primary Source

Neighbors: Muslims in North America [excerpt]

SYNOPSIS: Until the middle of the twentieth century, one could address religious diversity in the United States by speaking of Protestants, Catholics, and Jews. Other religions have made the United States increasingly diverse in the area of religion, and chief among these are Muslims. In addition to contending with preserving their faith and religious identity, American Muslims also must deal with the stereotype that they practice a religion that preaches violence.

EM: Getting back to what you were talking about before. How have you been perceived as a Muslim or how is Islam perceived by non-Muslims that you know professionally or socially?

MH: As I said, from my first name you can pick up what religion I belong to. But there is a real dilemma for somebody who believes in his religion but tries not to stress it as far as society's concerned. For example, I have applied for different jobs, and I've been denied four or five. Just last week. One of them was open and nobody had applied for this job and the lady was trying to persuade me, "Muhammad, this is the job for you. You have that kind of résumé. . . ." I set up the time for an interview. The guy seemed to be unhappy or uncomfortable with me. I expected to be denied. I called him back and he said they got somebody else.

EM: Have you any indication why that might be?

MH: Every time I gave my name I felt like they paused. Before I gave my name I was talking to them

A teacher reads as students listen at a weekend school of the American Muslim Society, Dearborn, Michigan. In an interview with Elias Mallon, Muhammad Halabi recounts the prejudice and stereotyping he faced as a muslim in North America in the late 1980s. **PAUL S. CONKIN. REPRODUCED BY PERMISSION.**

very comfortably. But when they asked for my name, my address, my phone number, I felt that pause as they spelled the name. This kind of pause gives me the impression that they're uncomfortable.

EM: So it's when you give your name. Among the students at NYU obviously a good number of your fellow students would know that you're a Muslim. What kind of a reaction do you get there?

MH: They do associate Islam with terrorism nowadays. It's known from the media that in the civil war in Lebanon different sects of Muslims are fighting each other. So they ask for some explanation—what's going on? How do you explain to me the militias? And the *hizbullah?* (*Hizbullah*, Arabic for "Party of God," is a pro-Iranian faction in the Lebanese civil war.) Whatever. As far as Ramadan is concerned, they ask me how can I tolerate the fasting from dawn to sunset. Why am I doing this? Do I go to prayer? Just general questions. But I do have the impression that they're really open-minded.

EM: They would be open minded and curious?

MH: Oh, curious, of course. If somebody's practicing, they are curious about what's going on. Can you explain this or that?

EM: What about people in general, besides those you have dealt with recently for jobs. In other words, what are some of the North American stereotypes that you have to deal with?

MH: Terrorism.

EM: Terrorism. That has come up in many of the interviews.

MH: Right, right, I was expecting that. The "Muslim"—this term still seems vague to North Americans. They do know something about it. But they don't know the facts. . . .

EM: In terms of your experiences both here in the United States and at home in Syria, what would you say that Islam has to deal with as we move towards the twenty-first century and the fifteenth century of the Hijra? (The Muslim era, reckoned from the date of the emigration (hijra) *of Muhammad from Mecca to Medina in 622 C.E.)*

MH: As we've seen lately in the Middle East, there is a kind of Muslim fundamentalist movement or underground organization, the Muslim brotherhood. It seems to me ironic that there where Islam was born it's oppressed. But here it's open. When it is open, there is misconception. Where it's oppressed, they do know the facts. Those people who live in North America don't know the facts and very few read books about Islam. In the Middle East the Muslim communities do practice Islam in a sense fully, but they are under great stress from their governments. They cannot do whatever they want to in terms of religion because there is no belief in the separation of state and religion. What really strikes me is that many Muslims in North America practice prayer differently from the way we practice back home. They follow different rules.

EM: What do you wish North Americans understood about Islam and your non-Muslim friends and colleagues understood about your religion from knowing you?

MH: I would like them to know that they should not associate Islam with Arabs. Islam is a religion. We do not discriminate between one culture and another, one color and another. Very few white Americans convert to Islam. The majority of converts are black. Black people have always been looking for a community to get them together to strengthen their ties. They thought that Islam, since it does not discriminate in skin color, would be a kind of asylum to them. I really think many of them feel happy when they come to prayer shoulder to shoulder with all different kinds of people. I've felt that kind of joy in them. Especially when after the prayer they go and shake hands and say, "May God accept your prayer." This is the typical expression that we use after prayer. So you feel then that they want to get closer to you but they don't know how.

Further Resources

BOOKS

Athar, Shahid. *Reflections of an American Muslim.* Chicago: Kazi Publications, 1994.

Haddad, Yvonne Yazbeck. *The Muslims of America.* New York: Oxford University Press, 1991.

Wolfe, Michael. *Taking Back Islam: American Muslims Reclaim Their Faith.* Emmaus, Pa.: Rodale, 2002.

"Human Beings: In God's Image"

Magazine article

By: John M. Swomley

Date: 1990

Source: Swomley, John M. "Human Beings: In God's Image." *Christian Social Action.* 1990. Reprinted in *Moral Is-* sues and Christian Response, 5th ed. Paul T. Jersild, and Dale A. Johnson, eds. Fort Worth, Tex.: Harcourt Brace Jovanovich, 1993, 340–342.

About the Author: John M. Swomley Jr. (1915–) was born in Harrisburg, Pennsylvania. He received a master's degree from Boston University in 1939 and a Ph.D. from the University of Colorado in 1958. Swormley was ordained a Methodist minister in 1956, and he became professor of social ethics at St. Paul School of Theology in Kansas City, Missouri in 1960. He has been active in civil rights and peace activities. ■

Introduction

The Supreme Court legalized abortion in 1973 in *Roe v. Wade.* Most religious groups in the United States agreed that abortion was an undesirable practice, but became deeply divided as to what actions to take about it. The more liberal religious communities considered abortion to be the lesser evil of the social costs stemming from unwanted pregnancies. They also believed that a woman's right to choose and to have control over reproduction was an important part of their advocacy for women's rights. The moderate Christian position has been that the presumption should first be to preserve and protect life, with abortion being an option of last resort. There is also the need to address the circumstances that lead individuals to consider abortion. While accepting the right to choose an abortion, addressing these circumstances is also important.

Liberal Protestant denominations have had longstanding pro-choice positions. The United Church of Christ has maintained a consistently strong pro-choice stance since 1970. The Unitarian Universalist Association affirmed a woman's right to choose in 1963, ten years before the Supreme Court decision. This position was reaffirmed in 1993—the most recent General Assembly—with a resolution adopted urging members to support federal legislation that would guarantee the basic right to abortion, provide federal funds for abortion to low-income women and military personnel, and protect doctors and clinics providing abortion services from violence and harassment. Judaism, likewise, is divided on the issue, with liberal Jewish groups supporting the right to choice as part of a women's rights platform. Both the Union of American Hebrew Congregations, representing Reform congregations, and the United Synagogue of Conservative Judaism have opposed attempts to overturn *Roe v Wade.* Even the Orthodox have maintained a long standing tradition that abortion was permissible in order to save the life of the mother.

Significance

In the document listed below, Dr. John Swomley, Professor Emeritus of Social Ethics from St. Paul School of Theology and an ordained Methodist minister, gives the pro-choice Christian position. He begins with a review of the biblical literature on the questions of the value of the fetus compared with that of the woman, as well as the origin of life. Swomley then reviews biological data on the development of the brain and the frequency of successful pregnancies, and makes the assertion that " . . . a fetus, as well as a fertilized egg, is a potential rather than an actual human being." Since a woman is a living being, Swomley states, her life has priority over that of the fetus, who is a potential being. The excerpt concludes with a reference to women's rights. He asserts that women, who for centuries have been at the mercy of male control, must make these decisions that concern their lives so profoundly. In the following decades, more denominations made explicit statements supporting abortion rights. The Evangelical Lutheran Church in America issued a social statement on abortion, adopted by the 1991 Churchwide Assembly. While insisting that there needs to be a presumption to preserve and protect life, as well as the need to address the circumstances that create the need for an abortion, the church did recognize that there could be sound reasons for electing abortion. At the 1992 General Conference of The United Methodist Church, the principles of *Roe v. Wade* were reaffirmed. In 1993, the General Assembly of the Presbyterian Church (USA) strongly reaffirmed support for legal abortion and comprehensive family planning. In 1994, the General Convention of the Episcopal Church adopted a resolution opposing any legislation that would limit a woman from access to an abortion.

Primary Source

"Human Beings: In God's Image" [excerpt]

SYNOPSIS: Religious liberals, whether Protestant, Catholic, or Jewish, have shared the concerns of feminists that women in the United States have been repressed by a patriarchal culture. This has led to their advocacy of various women's issues, including abortion rights. This has often set them at odds with anti-abortion activists within their religious communities.

The tragedy of an unwanted pregnancy that threatens a woman's life or health existed in the ancient world, as it does today. At the time the Bible was written, abortion was widely practiced in spite of heavy penalties. The Assyrian code prohibited abortion with this statement: "Any woman who causes to fall what her womb holds shall be tried, convicted and impaled upon a stake and shall not be buried." In Assyria the fetus was given more value than the woman.

Although the Hebrews were influenced by many of the laws of their Assyrian, Sumerian and Baby-

lonian neighbors, all of which forbade abortion, the Hebrew scriptures had no laws forbidding abortion. This was chiefly because of the higher value placed upon women. There are, however, some references to the termination of pregnancy. In Exodus 21:22–25 a pregnant woman has a miscarriage as a result of a fight between two men. The penalty for the loss of the fetus was a fine; if the woman was killed, the penalty was "life for life." It is obvious from this passage that the men who terminated the woman's pregnancy are not regarded as murderers unless they killed the woman. The woman, undeniably, had greater moral and religious worth than the fetus.

There is also reference in the Mosaic law to "abortion on request" (Numbers 5:11–31) if a husband suspects his wife is pregnant by another man. The "husband shall bring his wife to the priest" who shall mix a drink that was intended to make her confess or be threatened with a miscarriage if she had been unfaithful to her husband.

No Biblical Condemnation

Aside from these passages, the Bible does not deal with the subject of abortion. Although both Testaments generally criticized the practices of their neighbors, such as idol worship and prostitution, as well as various immoral acts in their own land, there is no condemnation or prohibition of abortion anywhere in the Bible in spite of the fact that techniques for inducing abortion had been developed and widely used by the time of the New Testament.

A key question in the abortion controversy is, "When does human life begin?" The Bible's clear answer is that human life begins at birth with breathing. In Genesis 2, God "breathed into his nostrils the breath of life and man became a living being" (in some translations, "a living soul"). The Hebrew word for a human being or living person is *nephesh,* the word for breathing. "Nephesh" occurs hundreds of times in the Bible as the identifying factor in human life. This is consistent with modern medical science, as a group of 167 distinguished scientists and physicians told the Supreme Court in 1989 that "the most important determinant of viability is lung development," and "viability has not advanced to a point significantly earlier than 24 weeks of gestation" because critical organs, "particularly the lungs and kidneys, do not mature before that time."

In the Christian scriptures, the Incarnation, or "the Word made Flesh" was celebrated at Jesus' birth, not at a speculative time of conception. The biblical tradition is followed today by counting age

Pro-choice supporters demonstrate at a rally sponsored by NOW, Hollywood, Florida, September 17, 1989. Pro-choice supporters argue along with scientists that a human life has begun not at conception, but when the brain and lungs are fully functional—a distinction John Swomley argues the bible also supports. **AP/WIDE WORLD PHOTOS. REPRODUCED BY PERMISSION.**

from the date of birth rather than from conception, a date people do not know or seek to estimate. The state issues no conception certificates, only birth certificates.

The Vatican assumption that human life begins at conception is derived from Greek philosophy, rather than the Bible, and implies that a human being is created at a specific moment instead of by a process that takes about nine months. To focus on the biological realities of genes and chromosomes present at conception or to think of personhood solely in materialist or biological terms neglects the spiritual nature and characteristics of humans, which the Bible describes as created "in the image of God" (Genesis 1:26–27). This does not refer to biological similarities but to the abilities to love and to reason, self awareness, transcendence, and freedom to choose, rather than to live by instinct.

The brain is crucial to such human abilities. The 167 scientists mentioned above said, "It is not until sometime after twenty-eight weeks of gestation that the fetal brain has the capacity to carry on the same range of neurological activity as the brain in a full-term newborn."

"Conflict of Life with Life"

Fifty-one percent of all abortions in the United States occurs before the eighth week of pregnancy; more than 91 percent by the twelfth week, in the first trimester; and more than 99 percent by twenty weeks, which is about four weeks before the time of viability when 10 to 15 percent of fetuses can be saved by intensive care. This means that in the "tragic conflict of life with life that may justify abortion" (from the United Methodist Social Principles) there is no brain or neo-cortex, and hence no pain in cases of early abortion.

Every termination of potential human life is a normal problem to be justified only because of the "damage [that] may result from an unacceptable pregnancy" (United Methodist statement). Contrary to the statement, abortion is rarely used as a method of birth control, and, according to the Guttmacher Institute, is so seldom used as a means of gender selection, except for a few Mideastern couples, that no data are available.

Abortion is viewed by most women as an extreme measure to be considered only when there is no other reasonable alternative. Those who claim abortion is a method of birth control refer to the fact that some birth control devices function immediately after conception to prevent implantation. The argument that conception is more crucial to the birth process than implantation is irrelevant, as both are necessary steps before the formation of individual biological life can begin.

Up to 50 percent of fertilized eggs do not implant. Of those that do, between 20 percent and 50 percent miscarry. Of all implantations, only about 10 percent are successful pregnancies. If there is objection to the prevention of implantation as a method of abortion, on the assumption that this is the taking of life, then nature or God is the greatest killer, because there are more spontaneous preventions of implantation than those performed medically. In other words, God does not will that every conception should eventuate either in implantation or in birth. This is consistent with our previous assertion that a fetus, as well as a fertilized egg, is a potential rather than an actual human being.

Further Resources

BOOKS

Gregory, Hamilton. *The Religious Case for Abortion: Protestant, Catholic, and Jewish Perspectives.* Asheville, N.C.: Madison & Polk, 1983.

Maguire, Daniel C. *Sacred Choices: The Right to Contraception and Abortion in Ten World Religions.* Minneapolis.: Fortress Press, 2001.

Wenz, Peter S. *Abortion Rights as Religious Freedom.* Philadelphia: Temple Univeristy Press, 1992.

11

SCIENCE AND TECHNOLOGY

CHRISTOPHER CUMO

Entries are arranged in chronological order by date of primary source. For entries with one primary source, the entry title is the same as the primary source title. Entries with more than one primary source have an overall entry title, followed by the titles of the primary sources.

Important Events in Science and Technology, 1980–1989

1980

- On January 16, the Boston office of Biogen, a Swiss bio-engineering firm, announces it has produced a disease-fighting protein, interferon.

- On February 2, *Science News* reports that 170 Adirondack lakes have lost their fish due to acid rain.

- On February 26, the nuclear containment building at Crystal River, Florida, spills thousands of gallons of radioactive water.

- On March 20, *New Scientist* publishes the discovery of a binary star system—two stars that rotate around each other every six hours.

- On April 2, William J. Schopf at the University of California at Los Angeles discovers evidence that life on earth is 3.5 billion years old—a finding that corroborates earlier estimates.

- On May 18, in Washington State, Mount St. Helens erupts, spewing forth 51 million cubic yards of volcanic ash, dirt, and rocks, leveling nearby forests and killing sixty-one people.

- On June 6, physicists Luis Alvarez and Walter Alvarez (father and son) propose that the collision of an asteroid with the earth caused the extinction of the dinosaurs 65 million years ago.

- On June 16, in *Diamond v. Chakrabarty* the Supreme Court grants biotechnology firms and scientists the right to patent genetically-engineered organisms.

- On November 12, the spacecraft *Voyager 1* reaches Saturn, making new discoveries about Saturn's moons and rings.

1981

- On March 3, in *Diamond v. Diehr,* the Supreme Court rules that a technological process that relies on a computer program can be patented.

- On April 12, NASA launches a reusable spacecraft, the space shuttle *Columbia,* from Cape Canaveral, Florida.

- In May, entomologists at the U.S. Department of Agriculture confirm the presence of Mediterranean fruit flies in California, leading to fears of infestation and devastation of the state's crops. The Department authorizes quarantine and insecticide use against the flies.

- On August 12, International Business Machines (IBM) introduces its first personal computer, with an operating system by Microsoft.

- On August 25, the spacecraft *Voyager 2* comes within sixty-three thousand miles of Saturn.

1982

- On January 5, a federal judge in Arkansas, citing the separation of church and state, strikes down a law mandating the teaching of creationism in the public schools.

- On January 28, the Federal aviation administration announces efforts to update the nation's twenty-year-old air traffic control system.

- On January 29, the Nuclear Regulatory Commission (NRC) fines Boston Edison Company five hundred thousand dollars for violations at its Pilgrim Station Unit 1 in Plymouth, Massachusetts.

- In February, a Gallup poll reports the American public is evenly divided between supporters of the theory of evolution and those who believe the Biblical account of creation.

- In March engineers complete, in the Mojave Desert, the largest solar energy generating plant to date, capable of producing ten thousand kilowatts of electricity.

- On March 1, two unmanned Soviet probes land on Venus, surviving long enough to transmit data on the soil and atmosphere.

- In April, Boeing introduces the commercial airliner 767, which it claims is 35 percent more fuel efficient than older jets.

- On August 30, British anthropologist Richard Leakey, son of Louis S. B. and Mary Leakey, and a team of anthropologists report the discovery in Kenya of a "humanlike" jawbone 8 million years old.

- On December 10, two Soviet cosmonauts set a new record for time in space, 211 days.

- On December 23, the Centers for Disease Control and Prevention (CDC) calls for the evacuation of Times Beach, Missouri, after soil samples reveal toxic levels of dioxin contamination.

- On December 30, Harvard scientists receive federal permission to begin genetic engineering experiments with the lethal diphtheria bacterium.

1983

- On January 26, scientists announce the discovery of one of the four basic forces in nature. The W, for weak force, assumed to be the force responsible for the radioactive splitting of atoms, joins gravity, electromagnetism, and the strong force (which holds atomic nuclei together) as the physical constants of nature.

- On March 8, Apple Computer introduces a new machine, called Lisa, that features a hand-held electronic pointer, or "mouse."

- On March 30, at the San Diego Zoo the first California condor is born outside its natural environment.

- On May 11, the newly discovered IRAS-Araki-Alcock comet comes within 2.9 million miles of Earth, the closest a comet has come since 1770.

- On August 9, scientists at the Jet Propulsion Laboratory announce the discovery of evidence that there are solar systems other than Earth's. Satellites had detected objects orbiting the star Vega.

- On September 14, IBM announces the development of a computer chip capable of storing 512,000 bits of information.

1984

- On January 13, for the first time in history, the Nuclear Regulatory Commission refuses an operating license for a nearly completed nuclear plant.

- On January 24, Apple Computer unveils its long-awaited personal computer, the Macintosh.

- On February 7, two shuttle astronauts, Bruce McCandless and Robert Stewart, become the first humans to fly freely in space. Rather than being tethered to their spacecraft, they maneuver in jet backpacks.

- On March 26, in the first major eruption since 1950, Hawaii's Mauna Loa volcano erupts.

- On May 16, U.S. District Judge John J. Sirica orders a delay in outdoor experiments with genetically engineered organisms.

- On July 3, American physicists Steven Weinberg and Brian Greene announce they have found evidence of the "top" quark—one of the building blocks of subatomic theory.

- On August 22, British anthropologist Richard Leakey and American anthropologist Alan Walker announce the discovery of 18-million-year-old bones of the common ancestor of humans and the African apes.

- On September 24, the Carnegie Museum of Natural History in Pittsburgh announces a rich find of dinosaur fossils in central Wyoming.

- On December 11, University of Arizona at Tucson astronomers announce their discovery of the first planet outside our solar system.

- On December 20, Bell Laboratories introduces a one-megabyte random access memory (RAM) chip, capable of storing four times as much information as any previous computer chip.

1985

- IBM physicists develop the scanning microscope, making it possible to resolve the atoms in a solid.

- On February 17, British scientists report the existence of a giant "hole" in the ozone layer over Antarctica.

- On March 4, the EPA bans most leaded gasolines in the United States because they spew lead pollutants into the air.

- On March 13, Congress agrees to clean up Bikini Atoll, a ring of tiny islands in the Pacific where U.S. physicists conducted nuclear tests after World War II.

- On April 12, Senator Jake Garn of Utah becomes the first non-astronaut to fly aboard a space shuttle.

- On September 1, explorer Robert D. Ballard, leading a joint French-U.S. team, discovers the wreck of the *Titanic* in the Atlantic Ocean five hundred miles south of Newfoundland.

- On September 24, the Congressional Office of Technology Assessment declares the Reagan administration's Strategic Defense Initiative (SDI) beyond the capability of U.S. technology and engineering.

- On October 11, University of Chicago scientists announce evidence that continent-sized wildfires raged across the globe 65 million years ago, when dinosaurs went extinct.

- On October 13, the Fermi National Accelerator Laboratory in Illinois activates a new cyclotron that is the world's most powerful atom accelerator and smasher.

- In November, British anthropologist Richard Leakey and American anthropologist Alan Walker made what biochemist and historian of paleoanthroplogy Roger Lewin called "the paleontological discovery of the century": a 1.6 million-year-old skeleton in Kenya missing only an arm bone and some bones in the hands and feet. The press dubbed the discovery the Turkana Boy because Leakey and Walker had found it near Lake Turkana, Kenya, and because the remains were of a nine-year-old boy, Leakey and Walker estimated.

- On November 14, the EPA approves the release into the environment of the first genetically engineered microorganisms, bacteria designed to prevent frost damage in strawberries.

1986

- On January 24, the space probe *Voyager 2* passes within fifty-one thousand miles of Uranus.

- On January 28, the space shuttle *Challenger* explodes following liftoff in Cape Canaveral, Florida. All crew members die, including Christa McAuliffe, a New Hampshire schoolteacher who was to be the first "citizen-observer" in space.

- On March 6, Congress again appoints James C. Fletcher, NASA administrator from 1971 to 1977, head of the space program.

- On March 14, the European Space Agency's *Giotto* spacecraft passes within 335 miles of the core of Halley's Comet.

- In April, Swiss, German, and American physicists make news as they explore zero electrical resistance—"superconductivity"—in ceramic materials frozen below −283°F.

- On April 26, the Chernobyl power plant near Kiev, Ukraine, releases fallout across much of Europe and renders thousands of acres of land near the accident site uninhabitable and unarable for thousands of years.

- On June 3, President Reagan names William R. Graham his chief science adviser.

- On June 9, a presidential commission investigating the *Challenger* disaster blames NASA for inadequate attention to the crew's safety.

- On July 31, American and Japanese trade representatives sign a five-year accord resolving a dispute over computer chips.

- On December 2, a University of Minnesota study claims the genetic makeup of a child is a stronger influence on personality than child rearing.
- On December 23, Pilots Richard Rutan and Jeana Yeager complete the first nonstop flight around the globe on a single load of fuel in the experimental airplane *Voyager.*

1987

- On January 1, American molecular biologists Rebecca L. Cann, Mark Stoneking, and Allan C. Walker announce that evidence from mitochondrial DNA traces the ancestry of all modern humans to a single woman who lived in Africa between one hundred thousand and two hundred thousand years ago. The press dubbed her Mitochondrial Eve.
- On January 15, the British journal *Nature* announces that scientific fraud is far more common than scientists had assumed.
- On January 30, President Ronald Reagan approves the construction of a $6 billion atomic particle accelerator.
- From February 16 to March 27 physicists announce progress in their search for materials capable of superconductivity at higher temperatures.
- On March 9, scientists testifying before Congress announce that the ozone layer has thinned in the last ten years.
- On April 2, IBM unveils the next generation of its personal computer.
- On April 3, President Ronald Reagan approves a scaled-down version of the proposed space station.
- On April 16, the U.S. Patent Office announces it will grant patents for genetically engineered animals, although it will not patent genetic engineering of humans.
- On April 19, biologists capture the last California condor left in the wild forty miles southwest of Bakersfield in hopes of preventing the species' extinction.
- On April 24, molecular biologists at Advanced Genetic Sciences, Inc., release the first of a genetically engineered organism, Frostban, a frost-retardant bacteria, into a strawberry patch in northern California to protect strawberries from frost.
- On June 17, Canadian geologists announce the discovery of a vast meteor impact crater on the North Atlantic Ocean floor.
- On June 19, the Supreme Court invalidates the teaching of creationism in public schools, striking down a Louisiana law.
- On July 26, physicists announce the discovery of black holes in nearby galaxies.
- On September 16, a world environmental summit in Montreal passes measures to reduce the presence of ozone-depleting chlorofluorocarbons.
- On November 4, Genentech, Inc., a bioengineering firm, wins a broad patent covering basic techniques of bioengineering.

1988

- On January 28, the Public Service Corporation of New Hampshire, a power company responsible for building the controversial Seabrook, New Hampshire nuclear plant, files for bankruptcy.
- On March 14, the U.S. Senate ratifies an international agreement to phase out the use of ozone depleting chlorofluorocarbons.
- On April 12, scientists at Harvard University patent a genetically engineered mouse susceptible to cancer and thus of use in medical experiments.
- On April 15, the Reagan administration bans research with fetal tissues.
- On May 13, the journal *Nature* announces that scientists have succeeded in deciphering a second genetic code responsible for the synthesis of proteins inside cells, a problem geneticists had been working on for over twenty years.
- On September 29, NASA launches the space shuttle *Discovery,* the first since the 1986 *Challenger* explosion.

1989

- On March 23, Stanley Pons of the University of Utah and Martin Fleischmann of the University of Southampton, England, announce they have achieved nuclear fusion at room temperature.
- On March 24, in the worst oil spill in American history, the oil tanker *Exxon Valdez* runs aground in Alaska, spilling 240,000 barrels of oil into Prince William Sound.
- On April 12, President George Herbert Walker Bush chooses Rear Admiral Richard Truly to replace James C. Fletcher as head of NASA.
- On May 23, IBM, AT&T, and the Massachusetts Institute of Technology form the Consortium for Superconducting Electronics to advance research into room-temperature superconductors.
- On June 21, seven leading computer firms form U.S. Memories, Inc., a consortium to produce dynamic random access memory (DRAM) chips for computers.
- On August 24, the *Voyager 2* spacecraft passes within 3,000 miles of the planet Neptune.
- On August 27, McDonnell-Douglas Space Systems Co. launches the first privately owned rocket carrying a satellite.
- On October 17, San Francisco suffers its worst earthquake since 1906, measuring 7.1 on the Richter scale, killing ninety people, and causing $6 billion in property damage.
- On November 19, scientists at the California Institute of Technology announce they have discovered the oldest and most distant object yet known, a quasar at the edge of the observable universe.

Mount St. Helens Erupting, May 18, 1980

Photograph

By: Austin Post

Date: May 18, 1980

Source: Post, Austin. Mount St. Helens Erupting, May 18, 1980. Cascades Volcano Observatory, U.S. Geological Survey. Available online at http://vulcan.wr.usgs.gov/Volcanoes/MSH /Images/may18_images.html; website home page: http:// vulcan.wr.usgs.gov/home.html (accessed May 22, 2003). ∎

Introduction

Conventional wisdom identifies the Sun as the source of heat in our solar system. This belief has much truth, but it is incomplete. Earth has its own heat source. Eighteen hundred miles beneath Earth's surface is the core, which contains radioactive elements. As these elements disintegrate into lighter elements, they convert part of their mass into energy in accord with Albert Einstein's equation: energy equals mass times the speed of light squared. Because the speed of light squared is ninety million billion meters per second squared, even a small amount of matter multiplied by ninety million billion meters per second squared will equal a huge number. That small amount of mass yields tremendous energy. This energy heats Earth's core to between 4,000 and 8,000 degrees Fahrenheit, only a little below the 10,000 degrees Fahrenheit of the Sun's surface.

The heat from Earth's core melts rock and generates tremendous pressure on Earth's mantle and crust, rock that surrounds Earth in layers. Earth cannot withstand this pressure and must release it through hot springs, geysers, and volcanoes. The most savage eruptions have claimed a place in history. One of the most famous occurred in 79 C.E., when Mount Vesuvius in Italy erupted with such fury that its lava (melted rock), ash, and debris buried Herculaneum and Pompeii, two towns along the Mediterranean coast. The eruption buried Herculaneum within hours, killing many of its residents, while the residents of Pompeii, being further from Vesuvius than Herculaneum, were able to flee during the first few hours. Those who stayed suffocated from toxic gases or were consumed by lava. Today, the towns display casts of victims, a grisly reminder of volcanoes' fury.

Significance

Unlike Mount Vesuvius, Mount St. Helens in southwestern Washington State is not near large population centers. The nearest city, Portland, Oregon, lies seventy miles from it. On March 27, 1980, Mount St. Helens began emitting smoke and ash. Authorities alerted as many as 250,000 people of the potential for an eruption and many fled their homes. Unlike Vesuvius, which gave Romans little warning before its eruption, Mount St. Helens did not erupt until May 18, 1980, nearly two months after it first emitted smoke.

When it came, the eruption was ferocious. Mount St. Helens spewed millions of tons of lava and debris sixty-five thousand feet into the atmosphere. Wind carried debris east and northeast. The blast blew off more than one thousand feet of the volcano's cap, scarring it with a crater over two miles long and a mile wide. The eruption may have equaled the detonation of five hundred uranium bombs of the kind that leveled Hiroshima, Japan, in 1945.

In human terms, Mount St. Helens was less lethal than Mount Vesuvius. Mount St. Helens' eruption killed sixty-one people, although thousands of elk and coyotes may have perished, along with deer, bobcats, bears, mountain lions, and many other animals. The eruption blanketed half of the state of Washington with ash.

The volcano erupted again on May 25, 1980, and April 11, 1981, though both eruptions lacked the fury of the initial blast. In May and June 1985, minor earthquakes shook the volcano, but no eruption followed. Geologists fear, however, that Mount St. Helens may erupt again in the twenty-first century. Italian geologists likewise fear that Vesuvius may also erupt, two millennia after it buried Herculaneum and Pompeii.

Further Resources

BOOKS

Bilderback, David E. *Mount St. Helens, 1980*. Berkeley: University of California Press, 1987.

Flaherty, David C. *Mount St. Helens: The Aftermath*. Washington, D.C.: U.S. Department of the Interior, 1983.

Lipman, Peter W., ed. *The 1980 Eruptions of Mount St. Helens*. Washington, D.C.: U.S. Government Printing Office, 1981.

Rosenfeld, Charles, and Robert Cooke. *Earth Fire: The Eruption of Mount St. Helens*. Cambridge: MIT Press, 1982.

Tilling, Robert I., Lyn Topinka, and Donald A. Swanson. *Eruptions of Mount St. Helens*. Washington, D.C.: U.S. Government Printing Office, 1990.

PERIODICALS

Decker, Robert, and Barbara Decker . "The Eruption of Mount St. Helens." *Scientific American,* March 1981, 68–80.

Primary Source

Mount St. Helens Erupting, May 18, 1980

SYNOPSIS: This photo captures Mount St. Helens in the initial moments of its May 18, 1980, eruption. Lava and debris rocketed from the volcano, drifting east and northeast with the wind. USGS/CASCADES VOLCANO OBSERVATORY; PHOTO BY AUSTIN POST, MAY 18, 1980.

A member of the U.S. Army searches a pickup truck for victims ten days after the eruption of Mount St. Helens, Washington, May 28, 1980.
© BETTMANN/CORBIS. REPRODUCED BY PERMISSION.

"Mount St. Helens Is Calm." *Science News,* June 29, 1985, 6.

"Volcano, Dormant for 123 Years, Begins Erupting in Washington State." *The New York Times,* March 28, 1980, A2.

WEBSITES

"Eruptions of Mount St. Helens: Past, Present, and Future." U.S. Geological Survey. Available online at http://pubs.usgs.gov/publications/msh; website home page: http://www.usgs.gov/ (accessed May 22, 2003).

"Mount St. Helens." University of North Dakota. Available online at http://volcano.und.nodak.edu/vwdocs/msh/msh.html; website home page: http://.und.nodak.edu (accessed October 13, 2002).

"Mount St. Helens—From the 1980 Eruption to 2000." U.S. Geological Survey. Available online at http://geopubs.wr.usgs.gov/fact-sheet/fs036-00; website home page: http://www.usgs.gov/ (accessed May 22, 2003).

Mount St. Helens National Volcanic Monument. Available online at http://www.fs.fed.us/gpnf/mshnvm (accessed May 22, 2003).

VIDEOCASSETTES

Mount St. Helens: Keeper of the Fire. Finley-Holiday Film Corporation, 1980, VHS.

"Extraterrestrial Cause for the Cretaceous-Tertiary Extinction"

Journal article

By: Luis W. Alvarez, Walter Alvarez, Frank Asaro, and Helen V. Michel

Date: June 6, 1980

Source: Alvarez, Luis W., Walter Alvarez, Frank Asaro, and Helen V. Michel. "Extraterrestrial Cause for the Cretaceous-Tertiary Extinction." *Science* 208, no. 4448, June 6, 1980, 1095–1097, 1100–1101, 1105–1107.

About the Authors: Luis W. Alvarez (1911–1988) received a doctorate in physics from the University of Chicago in 1936. In 1946, he invented a proton accelerator. His work with subatomic particles won him the 1968 Nobel Prize in physics.

Walter Alvarez (1940–), son of Luis W. Alvarez, received a doctorate in geology in 1967 from Princeton University. In 1983, he was a Guggenheim Fellow and in 1991 he was elected to the National Academy of Sciences. He is a professor of earth and planetary science at the University of California, Berkeley.

Frank Asaro received his doctorate in chemistry from the University of California, Berkeley, in 1953 and is emeritus senior scientist at the Ernest Orlando Lawrence Berkeley National Laboratory in Berkeley, California. He is an authority on analyzing artifacts with X rays.

Helen V. Michel received a doctorate in chemistry from Boston University in 1962 and is a research scientist at the Ernest Orlando Lawrence Berkeley National Laboratory in Berkeley, California. She is a member of the American Association for the Advancement of Science, the American Chemical Society, and the National Academy of Sciences. ∎

Introduction

Though we know many things about dinosaurs, they still remain mysterious. At the end of the Permian era 245 million years ago, more than 90 percent of terrestrial and aquatic animals became extinct. In the wake of this greatest of all extinctions arose dinosaurs, who dominated Earth as no animal has with the exception of humans. For nearly two hundred million years, dinosaurs reigned supreme, only to become extinct as suddenly as they had arisen at the end of the Cretaceous era sixty-five million years ago.

Their abrupt demise after such longevity demands explanation. One hypothesis is that global temperatures rose at the end of the Cretaceous. The temperature of cold-blooded dinosaurs rose with that of Earth. As dinosaur temperatures rose, so did that of male testes, thereby heating sperm. Since sperm can only endure a narrow temperature range, the increase in body temperature killed them. As a result, male dinosaurs were sterilized and could not breed, which led to the eventual extinction of all dinosaurs. Though this sounds plausible, there is no evidence that temperatures rose at the end of the Cretaceous. Nor is it clear that all dinosaurs were cold-blooded.

A second hypothesis notes that flowering plants evolved toward the end of the Cretaceous. Many contain alkaloids that may have been toxic to dinosaurs. Dinosaur herbivores that ate these flowering plants may have died, which led to the eventual death of the carnivores. One cannot know, however, whether dinosaur herbivores ate flowering plants or that such plants were toxic to them.

Even if these hypotheses were plausible, they apply only to dinosaurs and do not explain why sixty-five million years ago nearly all marine plankton died, as did 15 percent of marine invertebrate families. A hypothesis that explains the extinction of dinosaurs must be comprehensive enough to explain these other extinctions as well.

Significance

Luis W. Alvarez, Walter Alvarez, Frank Asaro, and Helen V. Michel announced such an explanation in 1980. They proposed that sixty-five million years ago a large asteroid smashed into Earth, throwing up huge clouds of dust and debris that blocked sunlight from reaching Earth, perhaps for months. The lack of sunlight stopped photosynthesis, which, in turn, killed plants and plankton. Dinosaur herbivores and marine invertebrates, which

depended on plants and plankton for food, died soon thereafter. Carnivorous dinosaurs likewise died as the number of herbivores plummeted. This hypothesis explains the extinction of dinosaurs and marine invertebrates, as well as the death of most plankton.

Though this explanation may seem fanciful, Alvarez, Alvarez, Asaro, and Michel found evidence for it in the geological record. Worldwide, sixty-five-million-year-old rock contains large amounts of iridium, an element that is rare in Earth's crust but abundant in asteroids and other extraterrestrial debris. The presence of iridium in rocks sixty-five million years old must mean that an asteroid hit Earth, spewing iridium into the atmosphere. The iridium would have fallen back to Earth, covering it with a blanket of debris. Sediment would have covered the iridium, preserving it in the geological record.

This explanation comes with a warning. A nuclear war between two or more countries might also throw up huge clouds of debris, particularly if it ignited widespread fires. This debris might once more block sunlight from Earth, killing crops and causing global temperatures to fall. Humans would die of famine, disease, and perhaps hypothermia and many species, including our own, might teeter on the brink of extinction.

Primary Source

"Extraterrestrial Cause for the Cretaceous-Tertiary Extinction" [excerpt]

SYNOPSIS: In the following excerpt, Alvarez, Alvarez, Asaro, and Michel propose that an asteroid smashed into Earth sixty-five million years ago, throwing up clouds of debris that blocked sunlight. The lack of sunlight stopped photosynthesis, killing plants and plankton. Dinosaur herbivores and marine invertebrates, which depended on the plants and plankton for food, died, as did the dinosaur carnivores when the number of herbivores decreased.

In the 570-million-year period for which abundant fossil remains are available, there have been five great biological crises, during which many groups of organisms died out. The most recent of the great extinctions is used to define the boundary between the Cretaceous and Tertiary periods, about 65 million years ago. At this time, the marine reptiles, the flying reptiles, and both orders of dinosaurs died out, and extinctions occurred at various taxonomic levels among the marine invertebrates. Dramatic extinctions occurred among the microscopic floating animals and plants; both the calcareous planktonic foraminifera and the calcareous nannoplankton were nearly exterminated, with only a few species surviving the crisis. . . .

Scientists Walter Alvarez, Luis Alvarez, Helen Michel, and Frank Asaro, Berkely, California, February 19, 1985. Luis Alvarez led this team of researchers who theorized that an asteroid's colliding with the earth was responsible for the extinction of the dinosaurs. © ROGER RESSMEYER/CORBIS. REPRODUCED BY PERMISSION.

Identification of Extraterrestrial Platinum Metals in Deep-Sea Sediments

This study began with the realization that the platinum group elements (platinum, iridium, osmium, and rhodium) are much less abundant in the earth's crust and upper mantle than they are in chondritic meteorites and average solar system material. Depletion of the platinum group elements in the earth's crust and upper mantle is probably the result of concentration of these elements in the earth's core.

Pettersson and Rotschi and Goldschmidt suggested that the low concentrations of platinum group elements in sedimentary rocks might come largely from meteoritic dust formed by ablation when meteorites passed through the atmosphere. Barker and Anders showed that there was a correlation between sedimentation rate and iridium concentration, confirming the earlier suggestions. Subsequently, the method was used by Ganapathy, Brownlee, and Hodge to demonstrate an extra-terrestrial origin for silicate spherules in deep-sea sediments. Sarna-Wojcicki *et al.* suggested that meteoritic dust accumulation in soil layers might enhance the abundance of iridium sufficiently to permit its use as a dating tool. Recently, Crocket and Kuo reported iridium abundances in deep-sea sediments and summarized other previous work.

Considerations of this type prompted us to measure the iridium concentration in the 1-centimeter-thick clay layer that marks the C-T boundary in some sections in the Umbrian Apennines, in the hope of determining the length of time represented by that layer. . . .

Italian Stratigraphic Sections

Many aspects of earth history are best recorded in pelagic sedimentary rocks, which gradually accumulate in the relatively quiet waters of the deep sea as individual grains settle to the bottom. In the Umbrian Apennines of northern peninsular Italy there are exposures of pelagic sedimentary rocks representing the time from Early Jurassic to Oligocene, around 185 to 30 million years ago. The C-T boundary occurs within a portion of the sequence formed by pink limestone containing a variable amount of clay. This limestone, the *Scaglia rossa,* has a matrix of coccoliths and coccolith fragments (calcite platelets, on the order of 1 micrometer in size, secreted by algae living in the surface waters) and a rich assemblage of foraminiferal tests (calcite shells, generally in the size range 0.1 to 2.0 millimeters, produced by single-celled animals that float in the surface waters).

In some Umbrian sections there is a hiatus in the sedimentary record across the C-T boundary, sometimes with signs of soft-sediment slumping. Where the sequence is apparently complete, foraminifera typical of the Upper Cretaceous (notably the genus *Globotruncana*) disappear abruptly and are replaced by the basal Tertiary foraminifer *Globigerina eugubina*. This change is easy to recognize because *G. eugubina,* unlike the globotruncanids, is too small to see with the naked eye or the hand lens. . . . The coccoliths also show an abrupt change, with disappearance of Cretaceous forms, at exactly the same level as the foraminiferal change, although this was not recognized until more recently.

In well-exposed, complete sections there is a bed of clay about 1 cm thick between the highest Cretaceous and the lowest Tertiary limestone beds. This bed is free of primary $CaCO_3$, so there is no record of the biological changes during the time interval represented by the clay. The boundary is further marked by a zone in the uppermost Cretaceous in which the normally pink limestone is white in color. This zone is 0.3 to 1.0 meter thick, varying from section to section. Its lower boundary is a gradational color change; its upper boundary is abrupt and coincides with the faunal and floral extinctions. In one section (Contessa) we can see that the lower 5 mm of the boundary clay is gray and the upper 5 mm is red, thus placing the upper boundary of the zone in the middle of the clay layer.

The best known of the Umbrian sections is in the Bottaccione Gorge near Gubbio. Here some of the first work on the identification of foraminifera in thin section was carried out; the oldest known Tertiary foraminifer, *G. eugubina,* was recognized, named, and used to define the basal Tertiary biozone; the geomagnetic reversal stratigraphy of the Upper Cretaceous and Paleocene was established, correlated to the marine magnetic anomaly sequence, and dated with foraminifera; and the extinction of most of the nannoplankton was shown to be synchronous with the disappearance of the genus *Globotruncana*. . . .

Twenty-eight elements were selected for study because of their favorable nuclear properties. . . .

Twenty-seven of the 28 elements show very similar patterns of abundance variation, but iridium shows a grossly different behavior; it increases by a factor of about 30 in coincidence with the C-T boundary, whereas none of the other elements as much as doubles with respect to an "average behavior." . . .

A Sudden Influx of Extraterrestrial Material

To test whether the anomalous iridium at the C-T boundary is of extraterrestrial origin, we considered the increases in 27 of the 28 elements measured by NAA that would be expected if the iridium in excess of the background level came from a source with the average composition of the earth's crust. . . .

We conclude that the pattern of elemental abundances is compatible with an extraterrestrial source for the anomalous iridium and incompatible with a crustal source. . . .

Size of the Impacting Object

If we are correct in our hypothesis that the C-T extinctions were due to the impact of an earth-crossing asteroid, . . .

We conclude that the data are consistent with an impacting asteroid with a diameter of about 10 ± 4 km.

Biological Effects

A temporary absence of sunlight would effectively shut off photosynthesis and thus attack food chains at their origins. In a general way the effects to be expected from such an event are what one sees in the paleontological record of the extinction.

The food chain in the open ocean is based on microscopic floating plants, such as the coccolith-producing algae, which show a nearly complete extinction. The animals at successively higher levels in this food chain were also very strongly affected, with nearly total extinction of the foraminifera and complete disappearance of the belemnites, ammonites, and marine reptiles.

A second food chain is based on land plants. Among these plants, existing individuals would die, or at least stop producing new growth, during an interval of darkness, but after light returned they would regenerate from seeds, spores, and existing root systems. However, the large herbivorous and carnivorous animals that were directly or indirectly dependent on this vegetation would become extinct. Russell states that "no terrestrial vertebrate heavier than about 25 kg is known to have survived the extinctions." Many smaller terrestrial vertebrates did survive, including the ancestral mammals, and they may have been able to do this by feeding on insects and decaying vegetation. . . .

Implications

Among the many implications of the asteroid impact hypothesis, if it is correct, two stand out prominently. First, if the C-T extinctions were caused by an impact event, the same could be true of the earlier major extinctions as well. There have been five such extinctions since the end of the Precambrian, 570 million years ago, which matches well the probable interval of about 100 million years between collisions with 10-km-diameter objects. Discussions of these extinction events generally list the organisms affected according to taxonomic groupings; it would be more useful to have this information given in terms of interpreted ecological or food-chain groupings. It will also be important to carry out iridium analyses in complete stratigraphic sections across these other boundaries. However, E. Shoemaker (private communication) predicts that if some of the extinctions were caused by the collision of a "fresh" comet (mostly ice), the Ir anomaly would not be seen even though the extinction mechanism was via the same dust cloud of crustal material, so the absence of a higher Ir concentration at, for example, the Permian-Triassic boundary would not invalidate our hypothesis. According to Shoemaker, cometary collisions in this size range could be twice as frequent as asteroidal collisions.

Second, we would like to find the crater produced by the impacting object. Only three craters 100 km or more in diameter are known. Two of these (Sudbury and Vredefort) are of Precambrian age. For the other, Popigay Crater in Siberia, a stratigraphic age of Late Cretaceous to Quaternary and a potassium-argon date of 28.8 million years (no further details given) have been reported. Thus, Popigay Crater is probably too young, and at 100-km-diameter probably also too small, to be the C-T impact site. There is about a 2/3 probability that the object fell in the ocean. Since the probable diameter of the object, 10 km, is twice the typical oceanic depth, a crater would be produced on the ocean bottom and pul-

Asteroid Impact, by Don Davis. The heat from a catastrophic asteroid impact would result in a huge fireball scorching much of the vicinity, while the dust and debris created would blanket the sky, obscuring the sun, cooling the earth, and impairing plants' photosynthesis. **ILLUSTRATION BY DON DAVIS. NASA. REPRODUCED BY PERMISSION.**

verized rock could be ejected. However, in this event we are unlikely to find the crater, since bathymetric information is not sufficiently detailed and since a substantial portion of the pre-Tertiary ocean has been subducted.

Further Resources

BOOKS

Eldredge, Niles. *Life Pulse: Episodes From the Story of the Fossil Record.* New York: Facts on File, 1987.

Gould, Stephen Jay. *The Flamingo's Smile: Reflections in Natural History.* New York: Norton, 1985.

PERIODICALS

Alvarez, Luis W. "Experimental Evidence That an Asteroid Impact Led to the Extinction of Many Species 65 Million Years Ago." *Proceedings of the National Academy of Sciences,* 1982, 627–642.

Alvarez, Walter, and Richard A. Muller. "Evidence From Crater Ages for Periodic Impacts on the Earth." *Nature,* 1984, 718–720, 801–805.

Whitmore, Daniel P., and Albert A. Jackson. "Are Periodic Mass Extinctions Driven by a Distant Solar Companion?" *Nature,* 1984, 713–715.

WEBSITES

"A Blast from the Past." Department of Paleobiology, National Museum of Natural History, Smithsonian Institution. Available online at http://www.nmnh.si.edu/paleo/blast; website home page: http://www.nmnh.si.edu/paleo/ (accessed May 22, 2003).

"Dinosaur Extinction." Morrison Natural History Museum's Guide to the Dinosaurs of Colorado. Available online at http://town.morrison.co.us/dinosaur/extinction/; website home page: http://town.morrison.co.us/dinosaur/ (accessed May 22, 2003).

Dinosaur Extinction—Compelling New Theory. Available on-line at http://www.dinosaur-extinction.com (accessed May 22, 2003).

Dinosaur Extinction Page. Available online at http://web.ukonline.co.uk/a.buckley/dino.htm; website home page: http://web.ukonline.co.uk (accessed May 22, 2003).

Diamond v. Chakrabarty

Supreme Court decision

By: Warren Burger

Date: June 16, 1980

Source: *Diamond v. Chakrabarty.* 447 U.S. 303 (1980). Available online at http://laws.findlaw.com/us/447/303.html; website home page: http://www.findlaw.com (accessed May 22, 2003).

About the Author: Warren Burger (1907–1995) received a doctorate in law from St. Paul College of Law in 1931. In 1953, President Dwight Eisenhower (served 1953–1961) appointed him to the U.S. Court of Appeals, and, in 1969, President Richard Nixon (served 1969–1974) nominated him chief justice of the U.S. Supreme Court. Burger retired from the Court in 1986. ∎

Introduction

Thomas Jefferson (served 1801–1809) and Benjamin Franklin, America's leading scientists and statesmen of the eighteenth century, valued applied science more than basic science. A scientist who discovers useful knowledge is doing applied science, whereas one who discovers knowledge for its own sake without regard to utility is doing basic science. The breeding of a new variety of wheat is an example of applied science, whereas the knowledge that the universe is some fifteen billion years old is basic science because such knowledge has no utility.

Jefferson and Franklin wanted the U.S. Congress to promote applied science. Accordingly, Article 1 of the U.S. Constitution grants Congress the authority to "promote the Progress of Science and useful Arts, by securing for limited Times to Authors and Inventors the exclusive Right to their respective Writings and Discoveries." Jefferson supplemented the Constitution with the Patent Act of 1793, which he wrote to grant Congress authority to issue patents for "any new and useful art, medicine, manufacture, or composition of matter, or any new or useful improvement."

In 1930, Congress passed the Plant Patent Act, extending its authority to grant scientists patents for breeding new varieties of plants with the intent of encouraging the breeding of new crop varieties. This act gave Congress the authority to patent life, at least to the extent that it could patent new plant varieties. Congress affirmed its authority to patent new crop varieties by passing the Plant Variety Protection Act in 1970.

Significance

Neither the Constitution nor the Plant Patent Act nor the Plant Variety Protection Act made clear whether congressional authority to grant patents extended to genetically engineered organisms. In 1980, Ananda Chakrabarty, a microbiologist at General Electric Company, sought to patent a bacterium in which he had inserted genes that enabled it to break down petroleum. Companies might use this bacterium to clean up oil spills. The bacterium's utility was clear, but could Congress grant Chakrabarty a patent for it?

In a 5-4 decision, the U.S. Supreme Court on June 16, 1980, ruled for Chakrabarty. Chief Justice Warren Burger, writing for the majority, cited Article 1 of the Constitution and the Plant Patent Act of 1930 as granting Congress broad authority in issuing patents. He cited the bacterium's "potential for significant utility" in accordance with the Constitution's expectation that Congress would extend patents for useful inventions.

The decision confirmed the new science of biotechnology as a commercial enterprise. After the Chakrabarty decision, scientists and investors began establishing biotechnology firms. These Wall Street newcomers tempted investors with the promise of genetically engineered crops, chemicals, and medicines. The U.S. biotech firm Genentech was one of the first to court investors after the Chakrabarty decision. On October 14, 1980, it offered one million shares of stock at $35 a share. The stock leapt to $89 a share in the first twenty minutes of trading. By day's end, Genentech had raised $36 million and held a value of $532 million. Ironically, Genentech had not patented a single organism, plant, medicine, or chemical. It was enough that it promised such inventions as forthcoming. The success of Genentech and other biotech firms proved that science and technology had by 1980 come to dominate the U.S. economy. The industrial era had ended, while computer manufacturers and biotech firms heralded a new economy of microchips and genes.

Primary Source

Diamond v. Chakrabarty [excerpt]

SYNOPSIS: Chief Justice Burger, writing for the majority, affirms that Congress has authority to grant scientists patents for genetically engineered organisms. Burger cites Article 1 of the Constitution and the Plant Patent Act of 1930 as precedent for granting Congress broad authority in granting patents.

Mr. Chief Justice Burger delivered the opinion of the Court.

We granted certiorari to determine whether a live, human-made micro-organism is patentable subject matter under 35 U.S.C. 101.

In 1972, respondent Chakrabarty, a microbiologist, filed a patent application, assigned to the General Electric Co. The application asserted 36 claims related to Chakrabarty's invention of "a bacterium from the genus Pseudomonas containing therein at least two stable energy-generating plasmids, each of said plasmids providing a separate hydrocarbon degradative pathway." This human-made, genetically engineered bacterium is capable of breaking down multiple components of crude oil. Because of this property, which is possessed by no naturally occurring bacteria, Chakrabarty's invention is believed to have significant value for the treatment of oil spills.

Chakrabarty's patent claims were of three types: first, process claims for the method of producing the bacteria; second, claims for an inoculum comprised of a carrier material floating on water, such as straw, and the new bacteria; and third, claims to the bacteria themselves. The patent examiner allowed the claims falling into the first two categories, but rejected claims for the bacteria. His decision rested on two grounds: (1) that micro-organisms are "products of nature," and (2) that as living things they are not patentable subject matter under 35 U.S.C. 101.

Chakrabarty appealed the rejection of these claims to the Patent Office Board of Appeals, and the Board affirmed the examiner on the second ground. Relying on the legislative history of the 1930 Plant Patent Act, in which Congress extended patent protection to certain asexually reproduced plants, the Board concluded that 101 was not intended to cover living things such as these laboratory created micro-organisms.

The Court of Customs and Patent Appeals, by a divided vote, reversed on the authority of its prior decision in In re Bergy, 563 F.2d 1031, 1038 (1977), which held that "the fact that microorganisms . . . are alive . . . [is] without legal significance" for purposes of the patent law. Subsequently, we granted the Acting Commissioner of Patents and Trademarks' petition for certiorari in Bergy, vacated the judgment, and remanded the case "for further consideration in light of *Parker v. Flook,* 437 U.S. 584 (1978)." 438 U.S. 902 (1978). The Court of Customs and Patent Appeals then vacated its judgment in Chakrabarty and consolidated the case with Bergy for reconsideration. After re-examining both cases in the light of our holding in Flook, that court,

with one dissent, reaffirmed its earlier judgments. 596 F.2d 952 (1979).

The Commissioner of Patents and Trademarks again sought certiorari, and we granted the writ as to both Bergy and Chakrabarty. 444 U.S. 924 (1979). Since then, Bergy has been dismissed as moot, 444 U.S. 1028 (1980), leaving only Chakrabarty for decision.

The Constitution grants Congress broad power to legislate to "promote the Progress of Science and useful Arts, by securing for limited Times to Authors and Inventors the exclusive Right to their respective Writings and Discoveries." Art. I, 8, cl. 8. The patent laws promote this progress by offering inventors exclusive rights for a limited period as an incentive for their inventiveness and research efforts. *Kewanee Oil Co. v. Bicron Corp.,* 416 U.S. 470, 480–481 (1974); *Universal Oil Co. v. Globe Co.,* 322 U.S. 471, 484 (1944). The authority of Congress is exercised in the hope that "[t]he productive effort thereby fostered will have a positive effect on society through the introduction of new products and processes of manufacture into the economy, and the emanations by way of increased employment and better lives for our citizens." Kewanee, supra, at 480.

The question before us in this case is a narrow one of statutory interpretation requiring us to construe 35 U.S.C. 101. which provides:

> Whoever invents or discovers any new and useful process, machine, manufacture, or composition of matter, or any new and useful improvement thereof, may obtain a patent therefor, subject to the conditions and requirements of this title.

Specifically, we must determine whether respondent's micro-organism constitutes a "manufacture" or "composition of matter" within the meaning of the statute.

In cases of statutory construction we begin, of course, with the language of the statute. *Southeastern Community College v. Davis,* 442 U.S. 397, 405 (1979). And "unless otherwise defined, words will be interpreted as taking their ordinary, contemporary, common meaning." *Perrin v. United States,* 444 U.S. 37, 42 (1979). We have also cautioned that courts "should not read into the patent laws limitations and conditions which the legislature has not expressed." *United States v. Dubilier Condenser Corp.,* 289 U.S. 178, 199 (1933).

Guided by these canons of construction, this Court has read the term "manufacture" in 101 in ac-

Dr. Ananda Chakrabarty in front of the Supreme Court, Washington, D.C., August 1983. He displays his patent and Supreme Court decision validating the issuance of a patent on life forms. In front of him are vials of his materials. © TED SPIEGEL/CORBIS. REPRODUCED BY PERMISSION.

cordance with its dictionary definition to mean "the production of articles for use from raw or prepared materials by giving to these materials new forms, qualities, properties, or combinations, whether by hand-labor or by machinery." *American Fruit Growers, Inc. v. Brogdex Co.,* 283 U.S. 1, 11 (1931). Similarly, "composition of matter" has been construed consistent with its common usage to include "all compositions of two or more substances and . . . all composite articles, whether they be the results of chemical union, or of mechanical mixture, or whether they be gases, fluids, powders or solids." *Shell Development Co. v. Watson,* 149 F. Supp. 279, 280 (DC 1957) (citing 1 A. Deller, Walker on Patents 14, p. 55 (1st ed. 1937)). In choosing such expansive terms as "manufacture" and "composition of matter," modified by the comprehensive "any," Congress plainly contemplated that the patent laws would be given wide scope.

The relevant legislative history also supports a broad construction. The Patent Act of 1793, authored by Thomas Jefferson, defined statutory subject matter as "any new and useful art, machine, manufacture, or composition of matter, or any new or useful improvement [thereof]." Act of Feb. 21, 1793, 1, 1 Stat. 319. The Act embodied Jefferson's philosophy that "ingenuity should receive a liberal encouragement." 5 Writings of Thomas Jefferson 75–76 (Washington ed. 1871). See *Graham v. John Deere Co.,* 383 U.S. 1, 7–10 (1966). Subsequent patent statutes in 1836, 1870 and 1874 employed this same broad language. In 1952, when the patent laws were recodified, Congress replaced the word "art" with "process," but otherwise left Jefferson's language intact. The Committee Reports accompanying the 1952 Act inform us that Congress intended statutory subject matter to "include anything under the sun that is made by man." S. Rep. No. 1979, 82d Cong., 2d Sess., 5 (1952); H. R. Rep. No. 1923, 82d Cong., 2d Sess., 6 (1952).

This is not to suggest that 101 has no limits or that it embraces every discovery. The laws of nature, physical phenomena, and abstract ideas have been held not patentable. See *Parker v. Flook,* 437 U.S. 584 (1978); *Gottschalk v. Benson,* 409 U.S. 63, 67 (1972); *Funk Brothers Seed Co. v. Kalo Inoculant Co.,* 333 U.S. 127, 130 (1948); *O'Reilly v. Morse,* 15 How. 62, 112–121 (1854); *Le Roy v. Tatham,* 14 How. 156, 175 (1853). Thus, a new mineral discovered in the earth or a new plant found in the wild is not patentable subject matter. Likewise, Einstein could not patent his celebrated law that $E=mc^2$; nor could Newton have patented the law of gravity. Such discoveries are "manifestations of . . . nature, free to all men and reserved exclusively to none." Funk, supra, at 130.

Judged in this light, respondent's micro-organism plainly qualifies as patentable subject matter. His claim is not to a hitherto unknown natural phenomenon, but to a nonnaturally occurring manufacture or composition of matter—a product of human ingenuity "having a distinctive name, character [and] use." *Hartranft v. Wiegmann,* 121 U.S. 609, 615 (1887). The point is underscored dramatically by comparison of the invention here with that in Funk. There, the patentee had discovered that there existed in nature certain species of root-nodule bacteria which did not exert a mutually inhibitive effect on each other. He used that discovery to produce a mixed culture capable of inoculating the seeds of leguminous plants. Concluding that the patentee had discovered "only some of the handiwork of nature," the Court ruled the product nonpatentable.

Each of the species of root-nodule bacteria contained in the package infects the same group of leguminous plants which it always infected. No species acquires a different use. The combination of species produces no new bacteria, no change in the six species of bacteria, and no enlargement of the range of their utility. Each species has the same effect it always had. The bacteria perform in their natural way. Their use in combination does not improve in any way their natural functioning. They serve the ends nature originally provided and act quite independently of any effort of the patentee. 333 U.S., at 131.

Here, by contrast, the patentee has produced a new bacterium with markedly different characteristics from any found in nature and one having the potential for significant utility. His discovery is not nature's handiwork, but his own; accordingly it is patentable subject matter under 101.

Further Resources

BOOKS

Malinowski, Michael J. *Biotechnology: Law, Business and Regulation.* Gaithersburg, Md.: Aspen Law and Business, 1999.

Rifkin, Jeremy. *The Biotech Century.* New York: Putnam, 1998.

Smith, George P. *The New Biology: Law, Ethics and Biotechnology.* New York: Plenum, 1989.

PERIODICALS

Hettinger, Ned. "Patenting Life: Biotechnology, Intellectual Property, and Environmental Ethics." *Boston College Environmental Affairs Law Review,* Winter 1995, 267–306.

Johnson, B. Julie. "Patenting Life." *Ms.,* November–December 1992, 82–84.

Kevles, Daniel J. "Patenting Life: A Historical Overview of Law, Interests, and Ethics." Legal Theory Workshop, Yale Law School, December 20, 2001. Available online at http://www.yale.edu/law/ltw/papers/ltw-kevles.pdf (accessed May 22, 2003).

Kluger, Jeffrey. "Who Owns Our Genes?" *Time,* January 11, 1999, 51.

Marshall, Eliot. "Legal Fight Over Patents on Life." *Science,* June 25, 1999, 2067–2109.

"Patenting Life." *New Scientist,* July 26, 1997, 7.

Thorpe, Nick. "Patenting Life." *World Press Review,* November 1997, 41.

WEBSITES

"New Developments in Biotechnology: Patenting Life-Special Report." The OTA Legacy, Woodrow Wilson School of Public and International Affairs, Princeton University. Available online at http://www.wws.princeton.edu/~ota/disk1/1989/8924_n.html; website home page: http://www.wws.princeton.edu/~ota (accessed May 22, 2003).

"Patenting, Genes and Living Organisms." Society, Religion and Technology Project. Available online at http://dspace.dial.pipex.com/srtscot/scsunpat.shtml; website home page: http://dspace.dial.pipex.com/srtscot/srtpage3.shtml (accessed May 22, 2003).

"The Fossil Footprints of Laetoli"

Magazine article

By: Richard L. Hay and Mary D. Leakey

Date: February 1982

Source: Hay, Richard L., and Mary D. Leakey. "The Fossil Footprints of Laetoli." *Scientific American* 246, no. 2, February 1982, 50, 55–57.

About the Authors: Richard L. Hay (1926–) received a doctorate in geology from Princeton University in 1952. Between 1948 and 1949, he was a geologist with the U.S. Geological Survey in Washington, D.C. He then taught at Louisiana State University and in 1957 he joined the faculty at the University of California, Berkeley. In 1983, he became the Ralph E. Griu Professor of Geology at the University of Illinois, Urbana.

Mary D. Leakey (1913–1996) was born in London. In the 1930s, she began searching for fossils of early humans in East Africa. In 1959, she discovered a nearly complete skull of an *Australopithecine.* The find won her and her husband, Louis S.B. Leakey, worldwide fame. In 1977, she discovered 3.5-million-year-old *Australopithecine* footprints, which were evidence that our human ancestors walked upright early in their evolution. ∎

Introduction

Charles Darwin supposed that humans shared a common ancestor with the African apes: the two species of chimpanzee and the gorilla. Both species of chimpanzee and the gorilla are knuckle walkers with brains only one-third the size of the modern human brain, leading paleoanthropologists to suspect that our human ancestors had been small-brained knuckle walkers early in their evolution. How and when did our human ancestors walk upright and evolve a large brain? Debate swirled around the issue of whether we had walked upright first and only later evolved a big brain, had evolved a big brain first and only later stood upright, or had done both in concert.

Darwin believed human ancestors walked upright first. Bipedalism freed the hands to build and use tools and weapons, activities that favored the evolution of a big brain. Evidence for this view surfaced when Charles Dawson in 1912 unearthed in Piltdown, England (hence the Piltdown man), a skull that had housed a brain as large as that of modern humans but that also had an apish jaw. But in 1953, three British scientists proved that Piltdown man was a fraud: it was a modern skull and with an orangutan jaw, both stained to appear ancient and the teeth filed to disguise their identity.

Piltdown man's collapse rejuvenated the bipedalism-first argument, a position Raymond Dart had taken in 1924 when he discovered a toddler's skull (the Taung baby) in the Taung quarry of South Africa that would

Parallel tracks of hominid footprints preserved in the 3.5-million-year-old cemented volcanic ash at Laetoli in Tanzania, published in *Scientific American,* February 1982. The left trail was made by the smallest of three upright walkers; the other was made by a large individual whose prints were partially obliterated by another smaller individual who stepped in them. © **J. READER/PHOTO RESEARCHERS, INC. REPRODUCED BY PERMISSION.**

have housed a brain the size of a chimpanzee's. What was different, though, was that the hole through which the spine passed was centered beneath the skull as it is in modern humans, whereas it is toward the rear of the skull in apes and monkeys. Dart concluded that the Taung baby had walked as upright as modern humans.

The belief that bipedalism preceded the evolution of a big brain gathered strength in 1974 when Donald C. Johanson discovered a 40 percent complete skeleton of a female (Lucy) more than three million years old. She had walked upright but, like the Taung baby, had a brain little larger than a chimpanzee's.

Significance

By the 1980s, the crucial issue was how long ago human ancestors had walked upright. In 1967, Vincent M. Sarich and Allan C. Wilson had put the date for the divergence between humans and African apes at five million years ago. How soon after the five-million-year divergence had our ancestors walked upright?

In answering this question, Mary D. Leakey discovered human-like footprints in soil 3.5 million years old. Richard L. Hay and Leakey wrote that the tracks had formed when three Australopithecines (a genus of hominid, one of whose species is thought to be ancestral to humans) walked across fresh volcanic ash. Rain fell after their departure, hardening the tracks, and debris filled them in until Leakey discovered them. The footprints resemble those of modern humans in revealing an arch. This fine-tuning of the foot's anatomy led Hay and Leakey to infer that human ancestors had walked upright earlier than 3.5 million years ago.

During the 1990s, Tim White and Richard Potts discovered pelvic fragments nearly 4.5 million years old. These suggested that human ancestors walked upright some 4.5 million years ago. That is, in half a million years or less our ancestors had evolved from knuckle walkers to bipeds. Darwin had supposed evolution took millions of years, yet here was an anatomical transformation that took at most five hundred thousand years. Evolution does not occur in the gradual accumulation of small changes as Darwin thought but in rapid bursts. In our case, the rapid evolution of bipedalism set the stage for the evolution of the modern human brain.

Primary Source

"The Fossil Footprints of Laetoli" [excerpt]

> **SYNOPSIS:** In the following excerpt, Richard L. Hay and Mary D. Leakey describe her discovery of 3.5-million-year-old footprints of three Australopithecines. The tracks lead Hay and Leakey to infer that Australopithecines walked upright earlier than 3.5 million years ago because the prints reveal a foot with

an arch, the kind of anatomical fine-tuning that suggests that our ancestors walked upright soon after they split from the line leading to the African apes five million years ago.

Near Lake Eyasi in Tanzania is a series of layers of volcanic ash notable for having yielded the remains of early hominids that are among the oldest known: they date back between 3.5 and 3.8 million years. The layers of ash hold an even more unusual example of preservation: fossil footprints. Several tens of thousands of animal tracks have now been discovered in these ash deposits. The survival of these normally ephemeral traces, ranging from early hominid footprints to the trail of a passing insect, gives a vivid glimpse of life on the African savanna well before the Pleistocene epoch. . . .

The Footprint Tuff was deposited over a short span, perhaps in a few weeks beginning near the end of the savanna dry season and extending into the early part of the rainy season. The excellent preservation of footprints and rainprints alike shows that the tuff layers must have been buried by fresh ash falls soon after the prints were made. Further evidence that the burial process was quick is provided by the continuity of layers, some only a few millimeters thick, over an area 70 square kilometers in extent.

There is other evidence of the short span of the event. The absence of grass blades at the base of the tuff suggests that the first volcanic eruptions came in the dry season. The rainprints in the lower unit were most probably made by brief showers as the dry season neared its end. In contrast, the redeposition of ash falls in the upper unit by runoff water points to a period of heavier rains, presumably the early part of the rainy season. Moreover, the widespread erosion at the base of the upper unit and between layers No. 2 and No. 3 of the upper unit is clearly attributable to heavy rainfall. Finally, the scarcity of rainprints on the surface of the upper-unit layers can be laid to the fact that rain-saturated sediments do not preserve such prints.

Since the Footprint Tuff is well cemented and more resistant to erosion than the underlying and overlying deposits, it has survived exposure to erosion over wide areas. Where the tuff is weathered it splits readily along the bedding planes between layers, revealing any footprints on the surface of the layer exposed. The footprints have now been examined in 16 localities at Laetoli; the exposures have been labeled sites A through P. . . .

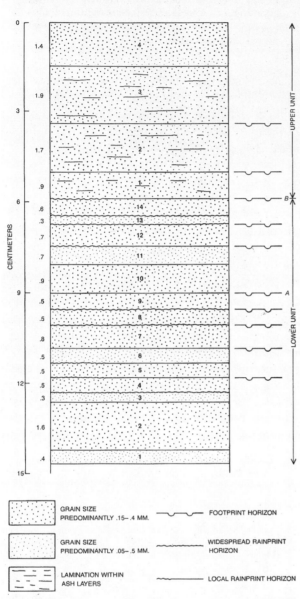

GRAIN SIZE
PREDOMINANTLY .15– .4 MM.

FOOTPRINT HORIZON

GRAIN SIZE
PREDOMINANTLY .05– .5 MM.

WIDESPREAD RAINPRINT
HORIZON

LAMINATION WITHIN
ASH LAYERS

LOCAL RAINPRINT HORIZON

FOOTPRINT TUFF is seen in section at a point where it is almost 15 centimeters thick. Of the 14 subdivisions of the lower unit eight are imprinted with tracks; the tracks are most abundant on horizons *A* and *B*. Two of the upper-unit subdivisions also bear tracks. The hominid tracks appear on horizon *B*. Numerals indicate the average thickness of the layers at Site *A*.

55

Cross-section of the 3.5-million-year-old volcanic strata from the laetoli site in which are found hominid footprints, published in *Scientific American*, February 1982. **ILLUSTRATION BY ANDREW M. TOMKO III.**

The five footprints found in 1977 that were probably made by hominids are at Site *A*. The two parallel tracks of hominid prints, first uncovered in 1978, are at Site *G*. The tracks are 25 centimeters apart and have been exposed over a distance of 25 meters. The best-defined of the footprints are from one centimeter to three centimeters deep and have clear margins. They show the rounded heel, uplifted arch and forward-pointing big toe typical of the human foot. One of the tracks was made by a single small individual. The other is a composite: the original prints were made by a comparatively large individual, and a second set of prints was superposed on the first set by a smaller individual who stepped in the original prints.

The hominid tracks are clear proof that 3.5 million years ago these East African precursors of early man walked fully upright with a bipedal human gait. This was at a time when both in stature and in brain size the hominids of Africa were still small by later human standards. Assuming that, as is true of modern human populations, the length of the Laetoli hominids' feet was about 15 percent of their height, then the smallest of the three who left their tracks at Site *G* was 1.2 meters tall (about three feet 10 inches). The next-largest would have been 1.4 meters tall (four feet seven inches). The length of the footprints made by the third and largest individual cannot be measured because they are overprinted and partly obliterated by the tracks of the next-largest.

An upright posture this early in the course of human evolution is of great importance. It freed the hands both for carrying and for toolmaking and tool use. In spite of diligent searching, no stone tools have been found in the Laetolil Beds. Hence it seems likely that the hominids who left their tracks in the Footprint Tuff had not arrived at the stage of making stone tools. The fact remains that their upright posture gave them full-time use of the first of all primate tools: unencumbered hands. . . .

To summarize, a most unusual set of conditions gave rise to the Footprint Tuff. Approximately 3.5 million years ago the Laetoli area supported an abundant and diverse animal population. The showers of volcanic ash that fell in the area were not heavy enough to drive the animals away. The excellent definition of a multitude of footprints, tracks and trails made in the fresh ash was a result of the admixture of carbonatite, an uncommon igneous material, with the more typical particles of volcanic ash; the imprinted ash layers were then buried at frequent intervals by fresh falls. Finally a heavy ash fall deeply buried the Footprint Tuff, protecting it from erosion, and the imprinted layers were cemented and became hard rock. When recent weathering split the layers of tuff along their bedding planes, it opened a unique window on the world of early hominids and the animals with which they lived.

Further Resources

BOOKS

Bowler, Peter J. *Theories of Human Evolution.* Baltimore, Md.: Johns Hopkins University Press, 1986.

Inman, Verne T., Henry J. Ralston, and Frank Todd. *Human Walking.* New York: Williams and Wilkins, 1981.

Leakey, Richard E., and Roger Lewin. *Origins: What New Discoveries Reveal About the Emergence of Our Species and Its Possible Future.* New York: Dutton, 1977.

Lewin, Roger. *In the Age of Mankind: A Smithsonian Book of Human Evolution.* Washington, D.C.: Smithsonian, 1988.

———. *Principles of Human Evolution: A Core Textbook.* Malden, Mass.: Blackwell Science, 1998.

PERIODICALS

Junger, William L. "Relative Joint Size and Hominid Locomotor Adaptations with Implications for the Evolution of Hominid Bipedalism." *Journal of Human Evolution,* 1988, 247.

Lovejoy, C. Owen. "Evolution of Human Walking." *Scientific American,* November 1988, 118–125.

Tague, Robert G., and C. Owen Lovejoy. "The Obstetric Pelvis of AL 288-1 (Lucy)." *Journal of Human Evolution,* May 1986, 237–255.

Weaver, Kenneth F., Richard E. Leakey, and Alan Walker. "The Search for Early Man." *National Geographic,* November 1985, 560–629.

WEBSITES

"Human Evolution: The Fossil Evidence in 3D." Department of Anthropology, University of California, Santa Barbara. Available online at http://www.anth.ucsb.cdu/projects/human; website home page: http://www.anth.ucsb.edu/index .html (accessed May 22, 2003).

"Human Evolution: Lucy in the Earth." A Science Odyssey, You Try It, Public Broadcasting Service. Available online at http://www.pbs.org/wgbh/aso/tryit/evolution/lucy.html; website home page: http://www.pbs.org/wgbh/aso/tryit/ (accessed May 22, 2003).

The Human Origins Program: In Search of What Makes Us Human. Available online at http://www.mnh.si.edu/anthro/humanorigins (accessed May 22, 2003).

"Carbon Dioxide and World Climate"

Magazine article

By: Roger Revelle

Date: August 1982

Source: Revelle, Roger. "Carbon Dioxide and World Climate." *Scientific American* 247, no. 2, August 1982, 35, 39–40.

About the Author: Roger Revelle (1909–1991) became an oceanographer at Scripps Institute of Oceanography in California in 1936. In 1960, he helped found the University of California, San Diego, and four years later he founded the Center for Population Studies at Harvard University. In 1990, President George Bush (served 1989–1992) honored him with the National Medal of Science. ∎

Introduction

During the 1960s, scientists warned that technology and industry might be harming the environment. In *Silent Spring* (1962), aquatic biologist Rachel Carson alerted Americans to this danger, charging that dichlorodiphenyl trichloroethane (DDT) and other chemicals were polluting soil, water, and air. But the effects of cars and factories spewing gases into the atmosphere was unclear.

In 1962, geophysicist Arthur Beiser warned that factories and cars had during the last 100 years poured 360 billion tons of carbon dioxide into the atmosphere. He also believed that the clearing of land for farming had released an equal amount of carbon dioxide. Carbon dioxide acts as an insulator. Sunlight that is not captured by plants, soil, or water reflects off Earth to return to the atmosphere. This light would ordinarily travel into space, but atmospheric carbon dioxide reflects light back to Earth where it heats the planet. The more carbon dioxide in the atmosphere, the more heat it will trap on Earth. Beiser estimated that atmospheric carbon dioxide had increased 13 percent during the past century and warned that such an amount might have raised Earth's temperature by 1 degree Fahrenheit. He predicted that additional carbon dioxide might increase Earth's temperature 3.6 degrees Fahrenheit by 2000 and 12.5 degrees by 3000. Such an increase would melt polar ice, raising sea levels and thus flooding coastlines around the globe.

Yet in 1967, meteorologists Robert A. McCormick and John H. Ludwig at the National Center for Air Pollution Control in Cincinnati, Ohio, warned that aerosol pollutants in the atmosphere blocked sunlight from reaching Earth, lowering global temperatures. They calculated that atmospheric aerosols reduced the sunlight that reached Earth by 5 percent and pointed to a cooling trend that had begun in the 1940s.

Significance

Two different arguments had produced different claims. In one, an increase in atmospheric carbon dioxide was increasing global temperatures, whereas the other concluded that an increase in atmospheric aerosols was lowering global temperatures. Only one argument could be right, but which one?

In 1982, Roger Revelle agreed with Beiser, estimating that atmospheric carbon dioxide had increased 15 percent in the past century. Yet, he noted that even this increase had not raised global temperatures. An increase in temperatures, however, might melt polar ice, raising sea levels "five to six meters." He warned that such an

Scientist Roger Revelle, 1982. Revelle asserted that the consequences of the "greenhouse effect" may not all be bad. SAN DIEGO HISTORICAL SOCIETY PHOTOGRAPH COLLECTION. REPRODUCED BY PERMISSION.

increase would submerge the Netherlands, Bangladesh, half of Florida, and much of the world's coastline.

However, an increase in atmospheric carbon dioxide might also benefit humans. Plants grow more rapidly as atmospheric carbon dioxide increases. Moreover, carbon dioxide stimulates plants to close some of their stomata (leaf pores), reducing water loss through these pores. Crops should therefore yield more food as carbon dioxide levels increase and should yield well even during arid periods because they will conserve water.

Scientists had labeled a rise in temperature due to increases in atmospheric carbon dioxide the Greenhouse Effect. But not all scientists believe that the Greenhouse Effect is responsible for raising global temperatures or even that temperatures have risen. Temperatures have fluctuated over time for reasons that have nothing to do with carbon dioxide levels. During the dinosaurs' reign, temperatures were higher than they are today, converting much of Earth into tropical and subtropical climates. Palm trees grew in Alaska one hundred million years ago. At the other extreme, the ice ages of the last one million years have periodically spread ice sheets across the land. These fluctuations hamper scientists' ability to predict the effects of an increase in atmospheric carbon dioxide.

Primary Source

"Carbon Dioxide and World Climate" [excerpt]

SYNOPSIS: In this excerpt, Revelle asserts that an increase in atmospheric carbon dioxide might raise sea levels, flooding coastlines around the world. On the other hand, it might increase crop yields, even during arid periods. The results of the Greenhouse Effect may be mixed rather than unequivocally positive or negative.

The "carbon dioxide question," which has become the subject of extensive concern in recent years, is actually three questions. The first is how much carbon dioxide will be added to the atmosphere in future years, and at what rate, from the burning of fossil fuels and the clearing of forests. These human activities have already increased atmospheric carbon dioxide by about 15 percent in the past century. The second question is whether the increase in carbon dioxide will cause an important global rise in average temperature and other changes in the climate of various regions. Mathematical models of the world's climate indicate that the answer is probably yes, but an unambiguous climatic signal has not yet been detected. The third question is whether possible climatic changes and other effects of the growing concentration of carbon dioxide in the atmosphere would have major consequences for human societies. Here too the answer is probably yes, with the qualification that the consequences would be complex: some regions and some human activities would benefit, whereas others would be harmed.

Carbon dioxide alters the heat balance of the earth by acting as a one-way screen. It is transparent to radiation at visible wavelengths, where most of the energy of sunlight is concentrated, so that the sun is able to warm the oceans and the land. On the other hand, molecules of carbon dioxide in the atmosphere absorb and reradiate some of the longer-wavelength, infrared radiation that otherwise would be transmitted back into space from the surface of the earth. This is the "greenhouse effect." If there were no carbon dioxide at all in the atmosphere, heat would escape from the earth much more easily. The surface temperature required for a balance between incoming and outgoing radiation would be lower and the oceans might be a solid mass of ice.

Over geologic time vast quantities of carbon dioxide have been emitted by volcanoes. Almost all of it has been chemically transformed into calcium carbonate and magnesium carbonate or into organic matter and has been buried in marine sediments.

The amount of carbon in sedimentary carbonates is estimated to be about 50 million gigatons (a gigaton is a billion tons) and the amount in sedimentary organic matter is estimated to be about 20 million gigatons. The total of some 70 million gigatons is almost 2,000 times larger than all the carbon in the atmosphere, the oceans and the biosphere, namely about 42,000 gigatons. The atmospheric component is itself a small fraction of this latter amount: roughly 700 gigatons. The fact that most of the carbon in the earth's surface layers has passed through the atmosphere and has been buried in sediments accounts for the moderate strength of the greenhouse effect in the earth's atmosphere. On Venus, which has no oceans, the atmosphere consists mainly of carbon dioxide, so that the greenhouse effect is much severer and the surface temperature is 400 degrees Celsius; on Mars, where the atmosphere is very thin, the effect is weaker and the surface temperature is −50 degrees C. . . .

All these uncertainties suggest that the mathematical modeling of changes in climate should be evaluated and controlled by studies of past climates, and particularly of past warm periods. A study of this kind has recently been done by Hermann Flohn of the University of Bonn. From his findings he has estimated the changes in average temperature and precipitation that are likely in several latitude belts if the concentration of atmospheric carbon dioxide rises into the range from 560 to 680 parts per million (about twice the level of a century ago) and other infrared absorbing gases also become more abundant. . . .

Flohn's analysis of the historical record suggests there could be appreciable decreases in precipitation and increases in temperature (and hence in evaporation) in bands of latitude centered on 40 degrees North and 10 degrees South. Precipitation would be greater, on the other hand, between 10 and 20 degrees North and in the regions north of 50 degrees North and south of 30 degrees South. These changes could have profound effects on the distribution of the world's water resources. For example, in the Colorado River system of the U.S. the major drainage basin is at about 40 degrees North. Not only would rainfall diminish in this area but also the higher temperature would augment evaporation. At present about 85 percent of the precipitation evaporates and only 15 percent is carried by the river. With a rise of several degrees C. in air temperature and a 10 to 15 percent decline in precipitation the average flow of the Colorado could diminish by 50 percent or more. Even today's flow,

backed up by large volumes of water stored in reservoirs, is barely enough to meet the demands of irrigated agriculture.

Major changes in surface and underground water supplies would be likely in other parts of the world. In northern Africa the average flow of the Niger, Chari, Senegal, Volta and Blue Nile rivers could increase substantially because their basins would receive from 10 to 20 percent more precipitation while temperatures at the surface would rise only slightly. In many other rivers the flow could greatly decrease: the Hwang Ho in China, the Amu Darya and Syr Darya in one of the prime agricultural areas of the U.S.S.R., the Tigris-Euphrates system in Turkey, Syria and Iraq, the Zambezi in Zimbabwe and Zambia and the São Francisco in Brazil. Somewhat smaller runoff and underground storage could be expected in the Congo River in Africa, the Rhone and the Po in western Europe, the Danube in eastern Europe, the Yangtze in China and the Rio Grande in the U.S. Many of these rivers form the basis of extensive and highly productive irrigated-agriculture systems, and the projected slackening of their flow could have grave consequences. At the same time large increases in the flow of the Mekong and the Brahmaputra rivers could lead to frequent destructive floods over wide areas of Thailand, Laos, Cambodia, Vietnam, India and Bangladesh.

The large-scale effects of increased atmospheric carbon dioxide on rain-fed agriculture would be complex and are more difficult to estimate than the effects on irrigated agriculture. Carbon dioxide is an essential plant nutrient; it is one of the raw materials from which organic matter is formed in photosynthesis. As Sylvan H. Wittwer of Michigan State University and Norman J. Rosenberg of the University of Nebraska at Lincoln have emphasized, experiments both in the greenhouse and in the field show that a higher concentration of carbon dioxide promotes photosynthesis and gives rise to faster growth. Other things being equal, a higher atmospheric content of carbon dioxide should lead to increased production of such crops as rice, wheat, alfalfa and soybeans.

Of perhaps equal importance is the fact that many plants tend to partly close their stomata, or leaf pores, in an environment high in carbon dioxide, with a resulting reduction in the transpiration of water. Hence with marginal rainfall maize, sugarcane and sorghum, as well as the crops already named, are likely to be less affected by water stress as the atmospheric content of carbon dioxide increases. At high latitudes the higher temperatures

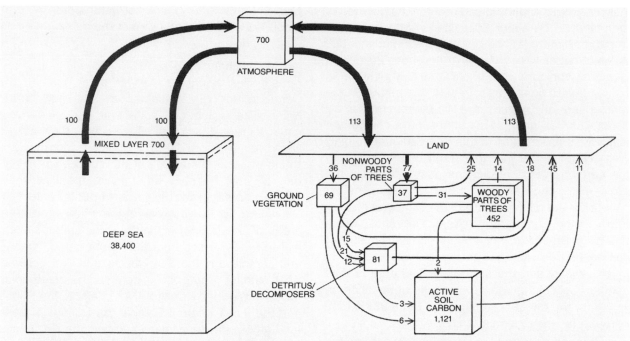

CARBON CYCLE is shown in terms of the amount of carbon stored in various reservoirs and the annual flows between reservoirs. The flows are indicated by the arrows. The numbers are in gigatons, or billions of tons. In the cubes representing stored carbon the numbers show the present carbon content of the reservoir. The numbers associated with the arrows give the equilibrium flow of carbon in gigatons per year, which would take place without any human inter- **vention. Human activities such as the burning of fossil fuels and the clearing of forests are increasing the amount of carbon (as carbon dioxide) in the atmosphere. The increase could lead to a global warming because molecules of carbon dioxide in the atmosphere absorb and reradiate some of the infrared radiation from the earth's surface. The estimates of stored carbon and carbon flows from the land biosphere were made by Jerry Olson of the Oak Ridge National Laboratory.**

38

Earth's carbon cycle, quantifying the storage and movement of carbon between the land, sea, and atmosphere, published in *Scientific American,* August 1982.

induced by carbon dioxide may lengthen the growing season, making it possible to expand rain-fed agricultural areas.

A possible consequence of climatic warming that has been widely discussed is the disintegration of the West Antarctic ice sheet, which many glaciologists think is unstable because much of it is below sea level. The volume of ice above sea level is about two million cubic kilometers. If it were all carried into the ocean, the sea would rise by five to six meters, inundating many coastal cities and much farmland in the Netherlands, Bangladesh, the coastal lowlands of the southern U.S. and populated river deltas throughout the world. Half of the state of Florida would be covered by seawater.

Further Resources

BOOKS

Abrahamson, Dean E., ed. *The Challenge of Global Warming.* Washington, D.C.: Island Press, 1989.

Cline, William R. *The Economics of Global Warming.* Washington, D.C.: Institute for International Economics, 1992.

Grubb, Michael. *Energy Policies and the Greenhouse Effect.* Brookfield, Vt.: Dartmouth, 1990.

Oppenheimer, Michael, and Robert H. Boyle. *Dead Heat: The Race Against the Greenhouse Effect.* New York: Basic, 1990.

Rosenzweig, Cynthia, and Daniel Hillel. *Climate Change and the Global Harvest: Potential Impacts of the Greenhouse Effect on Agriculture.* New York: Oxford University Press, 1998.

PERIODICALS

"Greenhouse Effects: Global Warming Is Well Underway." *Time,* December 13, 1999, 54.

WEBSITES

"Global Warming—Climate." U.S. Environmental Protection Agency. Available online at http://yosemite.epa.gov/oar /globalwarming.nsf/content/Climate.html; website home page: http://www.epa.gov/ (accessed May 23, 2003).

"The Greenhouse Effect." Environmental Database for Use in Schools, University of Southampton. Available online at http://www.soton.ac.uk/~engenvir/environment/air/green house.effect.html; website home page: http://www.soton.ac .uk/~engenvir/ (accessed May 23, 2003).

"The Greenhouse Effect." Global Warming: Kids Site, U.S. Environmental Protection Agency. Available online at http://

www.epa.gov/globalwarming/kids/greenhouse.html; website home page: http://www.epa.gov/globalwarming/kids/ (accessed May 23, 2003).

"Greenhouse Effect and Enhanced Greenhouse Effect." Welcome to Zuotao Li's Home Page, School of Computational Sciences, George Mason University. Available online at http://www.science.gmu.edu/~zli/ghe.html; website home page: http://www.science.gmu.edu/~zli/ (accessed May 23, 2003).

"On Stars, Their Evolution and Their Stability"

Lecture

By: Subramanyan Chandrasekhar

Date: December 8, 1983

Source: Chandrasekhar, Subramanyan. "On Stars, Their Evolution and Their Stability." Nobel lecture, December 8, 1983. Published in Nobelstiftelsen, and Gösta Ekspong, ed. *Physics 1981–1990*. Vol. 6. *Nobel Lectures*. Singapore: World Scientific, 1993, 162–163. Available online at http://www.nobel.se/physics/laureates/1983/chandrasekhar-lecture.html; website home page: http://www.nobel.se (accessed May 23, 2003).

About the Author: Subramanyan Chandrasekhar (1910–1995) was born in Lahore, India, and received a doctorate in physics from Cambridge University in 1933. In 1937, he joined the faculty at the University of Chicago. His work on stellar evolution won him the 1983 Nobel Prize in physics. ■

Introduction

Life is not alone in evolving. The universe and every object in it has evolved. The American physicist and astronomer Hans A. Bethe won the 1967 Nobel Prize in physics for elaborating on many of the details of stellar evolution. Stars are born from the gravitational attraction of gases, much of them hydrogen gas, and debris. The inward tug on the gases and debris generates friction, which heats them as they coalesce. As temperatures rise, hydrogen atoms at the core of the nascent star begin to fuse into helium, releasing tremendous energy. This nuclear reaction signals a star's birth. It will continue burning hydrogen until it has consumed roughly 40 percent of the element, when it will begin fusing helium atoms together to make the heavier elements in the universe.

As a star fuses heavier elements, it releases more energy and grows hotter. At 1.4 billion degrees Fahrenheit, it will begin to fuse neon atoms into magnesium atoms. At 2.7 billion degrees, it fuses magnesium into aluminum, silicon, sulfur, and phosphorus atoms. At 4 billion degrees, it fuses these elements into still heavier elements: titanium, chromium, manganese, iron, cobalt, nickel, copper, and zinc.

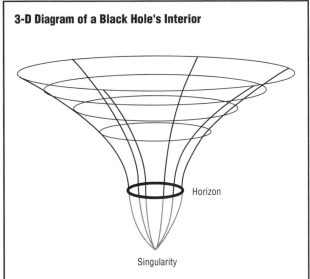

3-D Diagram of a Black Hole's Interior

Horizon

Singularity

SOURCE: Illustration from "Black Hole Structure." Cosmic Journeys. Available online at http://perry.sonoma.edu/journeys/black_holes/pages/schwarzchild.html; website home page: http://perry.sonoma.edu/journeys/ (accessed April 10, 2003).

These temperatures swell a star into a red giant, a stage in which it, being larger and hotter, burns its elements more rapidly. As it begins to exhaust its fuel, the red giant will no longer be able to stave off gravity, which will begin to collapse a star in on itself.

Significance

A small star will collapse into a dense ball of matter that gradually cools until it emits no more heat. The collapse of a large star opens another possibility. The gravity of a large star will be massive. According to Albert Einstein's theory of general relativity, gravity is the curvature of space. That is, any massive object curves the space surrounding it as a bowling ball curves a mattress on which it rests. Moreover, Einstein fused the concepts of space and time, describing them together as space-time; though we perceive them separately, each is simply one aspect of a single unity.

In a massive star that collapses in on itself, the curvature of space will be so great that it curves space into an infinite loop. If space and time are equivalent, the curvature of an infinite loop means time without end. We can write these statements despite an inability to conceive of space infinitely curved, translating into eternal time. Yet, the condition of eternal time means that a massive star will continue collapsing in on itself without end; it will never reach a point at which it stops collapsing. Astronomers call such an eternally collapsing star a black hole.

A black hole strains our understanding. One might conclude, for example, that if black holes collapse in infinite time, then time exists in an eternal now. If one could imagine oneself in a black hole (an impossibility), no time would pass for that person. Therefore, such a person would not be able to send a wave of light or any other signal, as Subramanyan Chandrasekhar noted, to someone outside a black hole. This is a way of saying that the gravitational attraction of a black hole permits nothing to escape it. Anything that approaches a black hole too closely is pulled in by its enormous force of gravity, never to exit. Even light itself cannot escape, making black holes utterly dark, hence their name.

As strange as black holes are, British physicist Stephen Hawking thinks they are even stranger. Contrary to Einstein and Chandrasekhar, he believes that black holes emit heat and given enough time will dissipate in a heat death. That is, black holes will lose all of their heat and cease to exist. If so, then time is not eternal after all for black holes. If this is the fate of black holes, then it must also be the fate of the universe. It will cease to exist after losing all its mass as heat. Just as it had a beginning far in the past, the universe will end far in the future.

Primary Source

"On Stars, Their Evolution and Their Stability"
[excerpt]

> **SYNOPSIS:** In the following excerpt, Chandrasekhar postulates that stars that are massive enough collapse into black holes, whose properties Einstein's mathematics describe with precision. A black hole separates itself from the rest of the universe in the sense that no light or other information can travel from within a black hole to any part of the universe.

The Mathematical Theory of Black Holes

So far, I have considered only the restrictions on the last stages of stellar evolution that follow from the existence of an upper limit to the mass of completely degenerate configurations and from the instabilities of relativistic origin. From these and related considerations, the conclusion is inescapable that black holes will form as one of the natural end products of stellar evolution of massive stars; and further that they must exist in large numbers in the present astronomical universe. In this last section I want to consider very briefly what the general theory of relativity has to say about them. But first, I must define precisely what a black hole is.

A black hole partitions the three-dimensional space into two regions: an inner region which is bounded by a smooth two-dimensional surface called the *event horizon;* and an outer region, external to the event horizon, which is asymptotically

Subramanyan Chandrasekhar, October 19, 1983. Dr. Chandrasekhar's work on stellar evolution won him the 1983 Nobel Prize in physics. © **BETTMANN/CORBIS. REPRODUCED BY PERMISSION.**

flat; and it is required (as a part of the definition) that no point in the inner region can communicate with any point of the outer region. This incommunicability is guaranteed by the impossibility of any light signal, originating in the inner region, crossing the event horizon. The requirement of asymptotic flatness of the outer region is equivalent to the requirement that the black hole is isolated in space and that far from the event horizon the space-time approaches the customary space-time of terrestrial physics.

In the general theory of relativity, we must seek solutions of Einstein's vacuum equations compatible with the two requirements I have stated. It is a startling fact that compatible with these very simple and necessary requirements, the general theory of relativity allows for stationary (i.e., time-independent) black-holes exactly a single, unique, two-parameter family of solutions. This is the Kerr family, in which the two parameters are the mass of the black hole and the angular momentum of the black hole. What is even more remarkable, the metric describing these solutions is simple and can be explicitly written down.

I do not know if the full import of what I have said is clear. Let me explain.

Black holes are macroscopic objects with masses varying from a few solar masses to millions of solar masses. To the extent they may be considered as stationary and isolated, to that extent, they are all, every single one of them, described *exactly* by the Kerr solution. This is the only instance we have of an exact description of a macroscopic object. Macroscopic objects, as we see them all around us, are governed by a variety of forces, derived from a variety of approximations to a variety of physical theories. In contrast, the only elements in the construction of black holes are our basic concepts of space and time. They are, thus, almost by definition, the most perfect macroscopic objects there are in the universe. And since the general theory of relativity provides a single unique two-parameter family of solutions for their descriptions, they are the simplest objects as well.

Turning to the physical properties of the black holes, we can study them best by examining their reaction to external perturbations such as the incidence of waves of different sorts. Such studies reveal an analytic richness of the Kerr space-time which one could hardly have expected. This is not the occasion to elaborate on these technical matters. Let it suffice to say that contrary to every prior expectation, all the standard equations of mathematical physics can be solved exactly in the Kerr space-time. And the solutions predict a variety and range of physical phenomena which black holes must exhibit in their interaction with the world outside.

The mathematical theory of black holes is a subject of immense complexity; but its study has convinced me of the basic truth of the ancient mottoes,

The simple is the seal of the true

and

Beauty is the splendour of truth.

Further Resources

BOOKS

Chandrasekhar, Subramanyan. *The Mathematical Theory of Black Holes.* New York: Oxford University Press, 1983.

Hawking, Stephen W. *Hawking on the Big Bang and Black Holes.* New York: Bantam, 1993.

Nicolson, Iain. *Gravity, Black Holes and the Universe.* New York: Wiley, 1981.

Thorne, Kip S. *Black Holes and Time Warps: Einstein's Outrageous Legacy.* New York: Norton, 1994.

PERIODICALS

Irion, Robert. "Rings of Light Could Reveal Black Holes." *Science Now,* September 29, 2002, 4–7.

Svitil, Kathy A. "Black Holes Flip Out." *Discover,* November 2002, 11.

Thomas, Vanessa. "When Black Holes Collide." *Astronomy,* November 2002, 20.

WEBSITES

"Black Holes." Cambridge Relativity Public Home Page, Department of Applied Mathematics and Theoretical Physics, University of Cambridge. Available online at http://www.damtp.cam.ac.uk/user/gr/public/bh_home.html; website home page: http://www.damtp.cam.ac.uk/user/gr/public/ (accessed May 23, 2003).

"Black Holes." Imagine the Universe, High Energy Astrophysics Science Archive Research Center, National Aeronautics and Space Administration. Available online at http://imagine.gsfc.nasa.gov/docs/science/know_l2/black_holes.html; website home page: http://imagine.gsfc.nasa.gov/ (accessed May 23, 2003).

"Black Holes and Beyond." Cyberia, National Center for Supercomputing Applications. Available online at http://archive.ncsa.uiuc.edu/Cyberia/NumRel/BlackHoles.html; website home page: http://archive.ncsa.uiuc.edu/Cyberia/ (accessed May 23, 2003).

"Virtual Trips to Black Holes and Neutron Stars." Robert Nemiroff, Astronomy Picture of the Day, National Aeronautics and Space Agency. Available online at http://antwrp.gsfc.nasa.gov/htmltest/rjn_bht.html; website home page: http://antwrp.gsfc.nasa.gov/apod/astropix.html (accessed May 23, 2003).

"The Climatic Effects of Nuclear War"

Magazine article

By: Richard P. Turco, Owen B. Toon, Thomas P. Ackerman, James B. Pollack, and Carl Sagan

Date: August 1984

Source: Turco, Richard P., Owen B. Toon, Thomas P. Ackerman, James B. Pollack, and Carl Sagan. "The Climatic Effects of Nuclear War." *Scientific American* 251, no. 2, August 1984, 33, 37–38, 41, 43.

About the Authors: Richard P. Turco (1943–) earned a doctorate in physics from the University of Illinois, Urbana, in 1971. Between 1971 and 1988, he was a research scientist and program manager at R&D Associates in Los Angeles. In 1988, he joined the department of atmospheric sciences at the University of California, Los Angeles, which he chaired from 1993 to 1996. He is also the codirector of the Southern California Particle Center and Supersite in Los Angeles.

Owen B. Toon (1947–) received a doctorate in physics from Cornell University in 1975 and is a professor of oceanic sciences at the University of Colorado. His research focuses on the effects of human activity on atmospheric conditions. He also studies the climate of other planets.

Thomas P. Ackerman received a doctorate in atmospheric science in 1976 from the University of Washington. Since 1988, he has been a professor of meteorology and an associate director of the Earth System Science Center at Pennsylvania State University.

James B. Pollack (1938–1994) was a senior space research scientist at the National Aeronautics and Space Administration (NASA) Ames Research Center in California. He helped design several space probes, such as *Mariner, Viking, Voyager,* and *Galileo.* He discovered that Venus's clouds contain sulfuric acid and studied Saturn's rings and the evolution of Jupiter and Saturn.

Carl Sagan (1934–1996) received a doctorate in astronomy from the University of Chicago in 1960. He taught at the University of California, Berkeley, and Harvard University and between 1962 and 1968 was an astrophysicist at the Smithsonian Astrophysical Observatory. In 1968, he became the director of Cornell University's Laboratory of Planetary Studies. ■

Introduction

World War II (1939–1945) unleashed the fury of the atom. As early as 1939, physicists understood that the fission (splitting) of uranium atoms yielded energy in accord with Albert Einstein's equation: energy equals mass times the speed of light squared. Because the speed of light squared equals ninety million billion meters per second squared, this number multiplied by even a small mass would yield enormous energy. In 1939, Einstein alerted President Franklin Roosevelt (served 1933–1945) that German scientists were trying to build an atomic bomb and urged him to establish a project to beat the Germans to it. The American effort, known as the Manhattan Project, resulted in the dropping of two atomic bombs on Japan, thus ending World War II and ushering in a new era: the atomic age, in which physicists around the globe raced to amass nuclear bombs and missiles more powerful than the bombs dropped on Japan.

Until the 1980s, policy makers and scientists supposed that a nuclear war between two nations would kill hundreds of thousands of people, perhaps millions, in the combatant nations and would devastate their agriculture, transportation network, and central government. Combatant nations would therefore suffer acutely, but the rest of the world would escape damage.

In 1980, American scientists Luis W. Alvarez, Walter Alvarez, Frank Asaro, and Helen V. Michel forced their colleagues to reexamine their beliefs. They argued that an asteroid had smashed into Earth sixty-five million years ago, extinguishing the dinosaurs, 15 percent of marine invertebrate families, and innumerable plankton by throwing up huge clouds of dust and debris on impact. This dust and debris had blocked sunlight from Earth, stopping photosynthesis, perhaps for months. Herbivores starved as did the carnivores who feed on them. The asteroid impact had thus caused a mass extinction that exterminated even the dinosaurs.

Significance

As a result of Alvarez, Alvarez, Asaro, and Michel's work, scientists came to understand that a nuclear war might cause the same damage as an asteroid had done sixty-five million years ago. Richard P. Turco, Owen B. Toon, Thomas P. Ackerman, James B. Pollack, and Carl Sagan called this catastrophe "nuclear winter." As the asteroid had done, nuclear explosions would throw up clouds of dust and debris. Moreover, the fires that nuclear explosions would cause would add to the airborne debris. The result would again be clouds that would block sunlight from Earth. Crops would fail and global temperatures would plummet. In addition, nuclear explosions might blow holes in the ozone layer, allowing ultraviolet radiation to sicken animals and humans once the clouds had abated. Humans and other animals would die from starvation, hypothermia, and radiation exposure. In such a weakened state, humans would be vulnerable to epidemics. A nuclear war might do more than devastate combatant nations; it might extinguish humans and other life all over the globe.

Turco and his colleagues raised the possibility that no nation could win a nuclear war, for such a war would imperil life everywhere on Earth. Science, a source of so much good, had given humans the power to exterminate themselves and other life. The threat of extinction led Pope John Paul II to convene in 1982 an international panel of scientists that included Sagan and Harvard University biologist Stephen Jay Gould. The panel declared that "nuclear war could thus carry in its wake a destruction of life unparalleled at any time during the tenure of humans on Earth, and might therefore imperil the future of humanity." Religion and science, so often at odds over the issue of evolution, had joined to condemn nuclear war as a threat to all life.

Primary Source

"The Climatic Effects of Nuclear War" [excerpt]

SYNOPSIS: In this excerpt, Turco and his colleagues warn that a nuclear war, like the asteroid that struck Earth sixty-five million years ago, might throw up clouds of dust and debris, blocking sunlight from Earth. Crops would fail and temperatures would plummet. Humans and other animals would suffer from starvation, hypothermia, and radiation exposure. Nuclear war might do more than devastate combatant nations; it might exterminate humans and other life everywhere on Earth.

Since the beginning of the nuclear arms race four decades ago it has been generally assumed that the most devastating consequence of a major nuclear war between the U.S. and the U.S.S.R.

Firestorm develops in the aftermath of a one-megaton nuclear explosion over the heart of New York City in the hypothetical sequence of events depicted, published in *Scientific American,* August 1984. The skyline of the city, viewed here from the west, is drawn to scale; the detonation point is assumed to be at a height of 6,500 feet directly over the Empire State Building. The initial flash of thermal radiation from the fireball would spontaneously ignite fires in combustible materials (1). Many of these fires would be snuffed out by the passage of the spherical blast wave (black arcs) and the accompanying high winds, but these affects could also start secondary fires (2). Some the primary and secondary fires could merge (3) and turn into a single massive fire covering the city (4). If the firestorm reached a high enough intensity and meteorological conditions were favorable, a full-scale firestorm could ensue (5). Eventually the fire would burn itself out, leaving a smoldering residue (6). The smoke and dust thrown up by these explosions could effectively block sunlight and drastically reduce the surface temperature. If such firestorms were common in a nuclear war, the authors contend the resulting nuclear winter would be much more severe than the one predicted by the existing computer models. **ILLUSTRATION BY IAN WORPOLE.**

would be a gigantic number of human casualties in the principal target zones of the Northern Hemisphere. Although in the wake of such a war the social and economic structure of the combatant nations would presumably collapse, it has been argued that most of the noncombatant nations—and hence the majority of the human population—would not be endangered, either directly or indirectly. Over the years questions have been raised about the possible global extent of various indirect, long-term effects of nuclear war, such as delayed radioactive fallout, depletion of the protective ozone layer in the upper atmosphere and adverse changes in the climate. Until recently, however, the few authoritative studies available on these added threats have tended to play down their significance, in some cases emphasizing the uncertainty inherent in any attempt to predict the combined effects of multiple nuclear explosions.

This comparatively optimistic view of the potential global impact of nuclear war may now have to be revised. Recent findings by our group, confirmed by workers in Europe, the U.S. and the U.S.S.R., suggest that the long-term climatic effects of a major nuclear war are likely to be much severer and farther-reaching than had been supposed. In the aftermath of such a war vast areas of the earth could be subjected to prolonged darkness, abnormally low temperatures, violent windstorms, toxic smog and persistent radioactive fallout—in short, the combination of conditions that has come to be known as "nuclear winter." The physical effects of nuclear war would be compounded by the widespread breakdown of transportation systems, power grids, agricultural production, food processing, medical care, sanitation, civil services and central government. Even in regions far from the conflict the survivors would be imperiled by starvation, hypothermia, radiation sickness, weakening of the human immune system, epidemics and other dire consequences. Under some circumstances, a number of biologists and ecologists contend, the extinction of many species of organisms—including the human species—is a real possibility. . . .

In brief, our initial results showed that "the potential global atmospheric and climatic consequences of nuclear war . . . are serious. Significant hemispherical attenuation of the solar radiation flux and subfreezing land temperatures may be caused by fine dust raised in high-yield nuclear surface bursts and by smoke from city and forest fires ignited by airbursts of all yields." Moreover, we found that long-term exposure to nuclear radiation from the radioactive fallout of a nuclear war in the Northern Hemisphere could be an order of magnitude greater than previous studies had indicated; the radioactivity, like the other nuclear-winter effects, could even extend deep into the Southern Hemisphere. "When combined with the prompt destruction from nuclear blast, fires and fallout and the later enhancement of solar ultraviolet radiation due to ozone depletion," we concluded, "long-term exposure to cold, dark and radioactivity could pose a serious threat to human survivors and to other species." Subsequent studies, based on more powerful models of the general circulation of the earth's atmosphere, have tended to confirm both the validity of our investigative approach and the main thrust of our findings. . . .

Nuclear explosions over forests and grasslands could also ignite large fires, but this situation is more difficult to evaluate. Among the factors that affect fires in wilderness areas are the humidity, the moisture content of the fuel, the amount of the fuel and the velocity of the wind. Roughly a third of the land area in the North Temperate Zone is covered by forest, and an equal area is covered by brush and grassland. Violent wildfires have been known to spread over tens of thousands of square kilometers from a few ignition points; in the absence of a nuclear war such fires occur about once every decade. Although most wildfires generated by nuclear explosions would probably be confined to the immediate area exposed to the intense thermal flash, it is possible that much larger ones would be started by multiple explosions over scattered military targets such as missile silos.

The total amount of smoke likely to be generated by a nuclear war depends on, among other things, the total yield of the nuclear weapons exploded over each type of target, the efficiency of the explosions in igniting fires, the average area ignited per megaton of yield, the average amount of combustible material in the irradiated region, the fraction of the combustible material consumed by the fires, the ratio of the amount of smoke produced to the amount of fuel burned and the fraction of the smoke that is eventually entrained into the global atmospheric circulation after local rainfall has removed its share. By assigning the most likely values to these parameters for a nuclear war involving less than 40 percent of the strategic arsenals of the two superpowers we were able to calculate that the total smoke emission from a full-scale nuclear exchange could easily exceed 100 million metric tons. In many respects this is a conservative estimate. Crutzen and his co-workers Ian Galbally of the Commonwealth Scientific and Industrial Research Organization (CSIRO) in Australia and Christoph Brühl of the Max Planck Institute at Mainz have recently estimated that the total smoke emission from a full-scale nuclear war would be closer to 300 million tons.

One hundred million tons of smoke, if it were distributed as a uniform cloud over the entire globe, could reduce the intensity of sunlight reaching the ground by as much as 95 percent. The initial clouds would not cover the entire globe, however, and so large areas of the Northern Hemisphere, particularly in the target zones, would be even darker; at noon the light level in these areas could be as low as that of a moonlit night. Daytime darkness in this range, if it persisted for weeks or months, would trigger a climatic catastrophe. Indeed, significant disturbances might be caused by much smaller amounts of smoke.

Wildfires normally inject smoke into the lower atmosphere to an altitude of five or six kilometers. In contrast, large urban fires have been known to inject smoke into the upper troposphere, probably as high as 12 kilometers. The unprecedented scale of the fires likely to be ignited by large nuclear explosions and the complex convective activity generated by multiple explosions might cause some of the smoke to rise even higher. Studies of the dynamics of very large fires suggest that individual smoke plumes might reach as high as 20 kilometers, well into the stratosphere. . . .

We find that for many scenarios a substantial reduction in sunlight may persist for weeks or months after the war. In the first week or two the clouds would also be patchy; hence our calculations probably underestimate the average light intensity at these early stages. Nevertheless, within the target zones it would be too dark to see, even at noon.

The large amount of smoke generated by a nuclear exchange could lead to dramatic decreases in continental temperatures for a substantial period. In many of the scenarios represented in the illustrations accompanying this article land temperatures remain below freezing for months. Average temperature decreases of only a few degrees Celsius in spring or early summer could destroy crops throughout the North Temperate Zone. Temperature drops of some 40 degrees C. (to an absolute temperature of about −25 degrees C.) are predicted for the baseline case, and still severer cooling effects are possible with the current nuclear arsenals and with those projected for the near future. . . .

Of course, the actual consequences of a nuclear war can never be precisely foreseen. Synergistic interactions among individual physical stresses might compound the problem of survival for many organisms. The long-term destruction of the environment and the disruption of the global ecosystem might in the end prove even more devastating for the human species than the awesome short-term destructive effects of nuclear explosions and their radio-active fallout. The strategic policies of both superpowers and their respective military alliances should be reassessed in this new light.

Further Resources

BOOKS

Ehrlich, Paul R., and Carl Sagan. *The Cold and the Dark: The World After Nuclear War.* New York: Norton, 1984.

Gould, Stephen Jay. *The Flamingo's Smile: Reflections in Natural History.* New York: Norton, 1985.

Greene, Owen, Ian Percival, and Irene Ridge. *Nuclear Winter: The Evidence and the Risks.* New York: Blackwell, 1985.

McCuen, Gary E. *Nuclear Winter.* Hudson, Wisc.: McCuen, 1987.

Sagan, Carl, and Richard P. Turco. *A Path Where No Man Thought: Nuclear Winter and the End of the Arms Race.* New York: Random House, 1990.

PERIODICALS

Bowden, Mark. "Despite Warming in Cold War, Nuclear Winter Still a Possibility." *The Philadelphia Inquirer,* May 17, 2002, B4.

Sagan, Carl. "Nuclear War and Climatic Catastrophe: Some Policy Implications." *Foreign Affairs,* Winter 1983–1984, 257–292.

WEBSITES

"Nuclear Winter." James Schombert, Department of Physics, University of Oregon. Available online at http://zebu.uoregon.edu/~js/glossary/nuclear_winter.html; website home page: http://zebu.uoregon.edu/~js/ (accessed May 23, 2003).

"Nuclear Winter: Science and Politics." Brian Martin, Science, Technology and Society, University of Wollongong. Available online at http://www.uow.edu.au/arts/sts/bmartin/pubs/88spp.html; website home page: http://www.uow.edu.au/arts/sts/bmartin/ (accessed May 23, 2003).

"Nuclear Winter and Other Scenarios." Jon Roland, Starflight Corporation. Available online at http://www.pynthan.org/vri/nwaos.htm; website home page: http://www.pynthan.org/ (accessed May 23, 2003).

"Nuclear Winter Revisited." Alan Phillips, Canadian Centres for Teaching Peace. Available online at http://www.peace.ca/nuclearwinterrevisited.htm; website home page: http://www.peace.ca/ (accessed May 23, 2003).

"What Is Nuclear Winter?" Available online at http://nyny.essortment.com/whatisnuclear_rioc.htm (accessed May 23, 2003).

"The Return of Halley's Comet"

Journal article

By: Larry Gedney and John Olson

Date: March 4, 1985

Source: Gedney, Larry, and John Olson. "The Return of Halley's Comet." *Alaska Science Forum,* March 4, 1985. Available online at http://www.gi.alaska.edu/ScienceForum/ASF7/705.html (accessed May 23, 2003).

About the Authors: Larry Gedney (1938–) earned a master's in seismology from the University of Nevada in 1964. That same year he became a geophysicist at the U.S. Earthquake Mechanism Laboratory in Chicago, and in 1977 he became a seismologist at the Geophysical Institute at the University of Alaska.

John Olson (1943–) received a doctorate in physics from Michigan State University in 1971. That same year he became a physicist at the Geophysical Institute at the University of Alaska. ∎

Scientists at the Space Research Institute, Moscow, March 1986. They evaluate data on Halley's Comet transmitted by the VEGA II spacecraft. The comet last passed the earth in 1910, though it was much closer and easier to observe that time around. © BETTMANN/CORBIS. REPRODUCED BY PERMISSION.

Introduction

In addition to the Sun, the planets, and their moons, the Solar System has an estimated one hundred billion comets, which consist of frozen gases and debris. Like the planets, comets travel around the Sun in elliptical orbits. Their orbits take some comets ten trillion miles from the Sun, while others burn up when they pass too near the Sun. In space, comets have no tail but as they near the Sun, solar energy vaporizes their outer layer, driving it away to form a bright tail that adds to their spectacular appearance.

Comets sometimes pass near Earth. Astronomers first noticed Biela's comet in 1772, which reappeared every six and a half years. But in 1869 it disintegrated into a shower of meteorites as it passed through Earth's atmosphere. Others have hit Earth. In 1908, one struck Siberia, toppling trees in a thirty-mile radius and knocking over people and breaking windows one hundred miles away from the impact. Even the Trans-Siberian Railway, four hundred miles distant, shuddered. In 1960, a Soviet scientist estimated that the comet weighed approximately one million tons.

The most celebrated comet is Halley's comet, which is named after British astronomer Edmund Halley, the first astronomer to identify it as a comet. Its brilliance led Chinese and Japanese astronomers to record its appearance beginning in 240 B.C.E. The comet swings as far as 3.2 billion miles from the Sun and comes as near as 50 million miles to it, thus making it visible to observers on Earth every seventy-six years.

Significance

Larry Gedney and John Olson warned in March 1985 that the 1986 return of Halley's comet would not be as spectacular as its 1910 visit. In 1910, its close approach to the Sun fired a brilliant tail, but Gedney and Olson predicted that in 1986 the comet would pass thirteen million miles further from the Sun than it had in 1910. Moreover, they predicted that the comet would be most brilliant when on the opposite side of the Sun, which would block the view of observers on Earth. In addition, much of the comet's path would cross the southern rather than northern hemisphere, obscuring the view of observers in the United States. Lastly, Gedney and Olson predicted that Halley's comet would be "about as bright as a faint star."

Despite these dour predictions, humans all over the globe awaited Halley's comet with anticipation. Its return was a highlight of the 1980s and made the grandeur of the heavens apparent to people who otherwise had little interest in science and technology in general and in astronomy in particular. Halley's comet reminded people that the movement of celestial bodies was predictable, a regularity that has impressed humans since antiquity. Those of us fortunate enough to be alive in 2061 will greet Halley's comet on its next return. Perhaps, it will be more spectacular that year than it was in 1986.

Primary Source

"The Return of Halley's Comet"

SYNOPSIS: In the following article, Gedney and Olson predict that the 1986 return of Halley's comet will be less spectacular than its 1910 appearance. It will not approach the Sun as close as it had in 1910 and the Sun will obscure it during its nearest approach. Moreover, the comet will be more visible in the southern than the northern hemisphere.

The Orbit of Halley's Comet

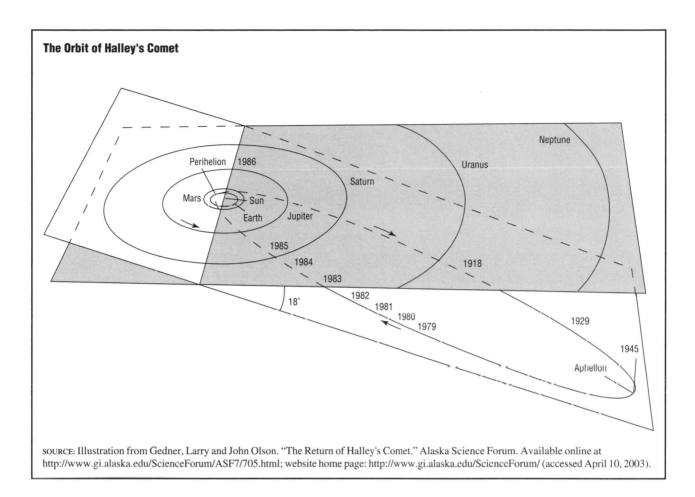

SOURCE: Illustration from Gedner, Larry and John Olson. "The Return of Halley's Comet." Alaska Science Forum. Available online at http://www.gi.alaska.edu/ScienceForum/ASF7/705.html; website home page: http://www.gi.alaska.edu/ScienceForum/ (accessed April 10, 2003).

By now, just about everybody has heard that during the latter part of this year, Halley's Comet will be making its first appearance in earth's skies since the famous visitation of 1910. How many of us have wondered since we were children if we'd be alive to see its return? But don't reserve any seats just yet—Alaska is not going to be on the 50 yard line. Sadly, this time around, it's likely that it will require a good pair of binoculars and a knowledge of just where to look in order to be able to see it at all. To understand this, it is helpful to recount what can be expected from the comet, based on observations made during its return at 76-year intervals, throughout history.

In order to visualize more easily the comet's path in the sky, we'll speak of distances in terms of the Astronomical Unit (AU). This is the mean orbital distance of the earth from the sun, about 93 million miles.

Halley's comet moves in a highly elliptical orbit, ranging from a distance of over 35 AU from the sun at aphelion (greatest distance from the sun) to just over one-half AU at perihelion (closest approach to

the sun). It follows that it was last at perihelion during the 1910 appearance, and invisible from earth at aphelion in 1948. Perihelion during this orbit will occur on February 9, 1986. It is then that the comet will be at its most brilliant and will produce the longest "tail." Unfortunately, it is also then that it will be on the opposite side of the sun from the earth, and it will be invisible to viewers during the time of its greatest display.

Yet another factor will prevent the comet from being easily visible from the northern latitudes: the comet's orbital plane is tipped so that most of the path is below the ecliptic—south of the plane in which the sun and most of the planets' orbits lie. That, combined with the tilt of the earth on its axis, means that the comet will be below the horizon in the northern hemisphere most of the time. Only for a relatively short period from late November 1985 into January 1986 will circumstances combine so that the comet is near enough to the sun, near enough to the earth, and traveling high enough above the ecliptic so that it will be visible from most of Alaska. Even then it will not be spectacular, but it

Halley's Comet, March 7, 1986. Though it only comes within sight of the earth every 76 years, due to its orbit some visits are more spectacular than others. © BETTMANN/CORBIS. REPRODUCED BY PERMISSION.

should be dimly visible (about as bright as a faint star) low on the southern horizon.

The comet will be above the ecliptic at perihelion, and soon after emerging from behind the sun in mid-February, it will again cross to below the ecliptic plane between the orbits of earth and Venus and be visible only to more southerly observers. As luck would have it, during the time that it can be viewed from earth, this is probably when it will be at its brightest. Comets typically exhibit more of a tail after, rather than before, their closest encounter with the sun, and the closest approach to the earth will occur after perihelion.

Unfortunately, although scientists stand to learn a great deal from their measurements and observations, there can be no escaping the conclusion that this year's visit by Halley's Comet will not be nearly as spectacular as the one in 1910. During that event, the approach to earth was much closer (0.14 AU, compared with a closest approach of 0.42 AU on April 11, 1986), and the comet was visible at perihelion. It was a worldwide sensation. Cartoonists had a field day playing on the fears of kings,

Kaisers, and the common man. New products and brand names sprang up overnight, and sideshow hucksters sold "comet pills" by the handful and gas masks to ward off the perils that would ensue when the earth passed through the tail of the comet (which actually may have occurred).

It was all good fun, but not likely to be repeated this time around. For the optimist, though, there's always 2061 to look forward to.

Further Resources

BOOKS

Bergamini, David. *The Universe.* New York: Time-Life, 1962.

Calder, Nigel. *The Comet Is Coming!: The Feverish Legacy of Mr. Halley.* New York: Viking, 1980.

Flaste, Richard. *The New York Times Guide to the Return of Halley's Comet.* New York: Times, 1985.

Harper, Brian. *The Official Halley's Comet Book: 1986.* London: Hodder and Stoughton, 1985.

Littmann, Mark, and Donald K. Yeomans. *Comet Halley: Once in a Lifetime.* Washington, D.C.: American Chemical Society, 1985.

Reddy, Francis. *Halley's Comet!* Milwaukee, Wisc.: AstroMedia, 1985.

PERIODICALS

Kellerstrom, Nicholas. "The Path of Halley's Comet and Newton's Late Apprehension of the Law of Gravity." *Annals of Science,* October 1999, 331–357.

Kerr, Richard A. "Halley's Origins Mysterious No More?" *Science,* November 10, 2000, 1071.

WEBSITES

"Comet Halley." Bill Arnett, The Nine Planets, University of Arizona. Available online at http://seds.lpl.arizona.edu /nineplanets/nineplanets/halley.html; website home page: http://seds.lpl.arizona.edu/nineplanets/ (accessed May 23, 2003).

"Comet Halley." Online Journey Through the Astronomy, Department of Physics and Astronomy, University of Tennessee. Available online at http://csep10.phys.utk.edu /astr161/lect/comets/halley.html; website home page: http:// csep10.phys.utk.edu/ (accessed May 23, 2003).

"Halley's Comet." Calvin J. Hamilton, Views of the Solar System. Available online at http://www.solarviews.com/eng /halley.htm; website home page: http://www.solarviews .com/eng/homepage.htm (accessed May 23, 2003).

"Halley's Comet Returns in Bits and Pieces." Science@NASA. Available online at http://science.nasa.gov/newhome/head lines/ast20oct98_1.htm; website home page: http://science .nasa.gov/ (accessed May 23, 2003).

"MWO Museum Exhibit: Halley's Comet." Astronomical Museum, Mt. Wilson Observatory. Available online at http:// www.mtwilson.edu/Tour/Museum/Exhibit_H/m_halley .html; website home page: http://www.mtwilson.edu/Tour /Museum/ (accessed May 23, 2003).

"Homo Erectus Unearthed"

Magazine article

By: Richard Leakey and Alan Walker

Date: November 1985

Source: Leakey, Richard, and Alan Walker. "Homo Erectus Unearthed." *National Geographic* 168, no. 5, November 1985, 625, 627, 629.

About the Authors: Richard Leakey (1944–) was born in Nairobi, Kenya. The son of anthropologists, he refused at first to follow them into the profession, but his discovery in 1963 of an australopithecine jaw sparked his interest in paleoanthropology. Numerous finds of early humans followed this initial discovery. The most famous, with Alan Walker, is the nearly complete skeleton of a nine-year-old male *Homo erectus.* Leakey's books on human evolution have won him a wide audience.

Alan Walker (1938–) earned a doctorate in anthropology from London University in 1967. The next year he joined Richard Leakey in the search for early humans in East Africa. He is the Distinguished Professor of Anthropology and Biology at Pennsylvania State University. ■

Introduction

In *On the Origin of Species* (1859), Charles Darwin restricted himself to a single sentence on human evolution, "Light will be thrown on the origin of man and his history." His caution did not prevent Thomas Huxley and Ernest Haeckel from writing books about human evolution in the 1860s, though they had little fossil evidence to draw on for support. The lone fossil was a partial skeleton quarry workers had unearthed in the Neander Valley, Germany (hence the name Neanderthal man), in 1856. Others had found Neanderthal remains in 1829 in Belgium and in 1848 in Gibraltar, but only in the twentieth century did paleoanthropologists recognize them as such. In 1886, an amateur fossil hunter found a fourth Neanderthal. Then in 1897, Eugene Dubois found a partial cranium and femur of a more ancient early human, *Homo erectus,* in Indonesia.

The discovery fueled the conviction of most anthropologists that Asia was humanity's birthplace. Yet, in 1924, Raymond Dart discovered a toddler's skull in South Africa. It resembled that of a chimpanzee, but the hole through which the spine passed was centered beneath the skull as it is in modern humans, not located toward the back of the skull as it is in apes. This showed that the toddler had likely walked on two legs, an inference Dart used to support his claim that our human ancestors arose in Africa, not Asia. Indeed, the fossil, which Dart christened *Australopithecus africanus,* at more than two million years was the oldest hominid fossil discovered at that time.

Dart's discovery brought Robert Broom and Louis S.B. Leakey and Mary D. Leakey to Africa. Their finds proved Dart and Darwin correct: Africa was humanity's birthplace. Yet, all pre-Neanderthal finds had been fragmentary, including Donald C. Johanson's 1974 discovery of a 40 percent complete australopithecine female (Lucy). A complete skeleton would yield anatomical details that no amount of guesswork could surmise.

Significance

In 1985, Richard Leakey and Alan Walker found a 1.6-million-year-old skeleton in Kenya missing only an arm bone and some bones in the hands and feet. They named it *Homo erectus,* as it was a member of the species Dubois had found in 1897.

The skeleton was of a 12-year-old boy. Despite his youth, he already stood over five feet and would have surpassed six feet as an adult. Moreover, his bones were thicker than those of modern humans and the insertions for tendons were larger, evidence that the boy was both taller and more muscular than modern humans. Neanderthals likewise had been more muscular than modern humans. This evidence disproved the widespread belief that human evolution had built each species larger, culminating in modern humans.

The fact that modern humans are smaller and weaker than *Homo erectus* and weaker than *Homo sapiens neanderthalensis* led Stephen Jay Gould to believe that no compelling reason exists why Neanderthals became extinct and we survived. One might retort that we survived because of superior intelligence. Yet, Neanderthals had a brain slightly larger than ours and may not have trailed us in intellect. Their burial of the dead, a practice unknown in any other species except modern humans, indicates that they engaged in ritual that is strikingly human.

With the traditional arguments for human superiority in doubt, perhaps we alone survived because of luck. Gould surmised that no cosmic force preordained our survival. No logic programmed the cosmos for us. *Homo erectus* or *Homo sapiens neanderthalensis* could as easily be here instead of us. We were lucky. They were not.

Primary Source

"Homo Erectus Unearthed" [excerpt]

SYNOPSIS: In the following excerpt, Leakey and Walker recount the elation of discovering a nearly complete *Homo erectus* skeleton. They note that the 12-year-old boy would have surpassed six feet as an adult, taller than most modern humans. Moreover, he had been more muscular than modern humans. This evidence disproves the myth that greater size and strength helped modern humans survive.

The story opens 1.6 million years ago, that we know. But did the boy actually perish in the mud and

Richard Leakey and Kamoya Kimeu search under a thorn tree near Lake Turkana, Kenya, 1984. Here they discovered shattered facial bones belonging to a 1.6-million-year-old skeleton of *Homo Erectus,* an early human. **AP/WIDE WORLD PHOTOS. REPRODUCED BY PERMISSION.**

water weeds fringing the prehistoric shore of Kenya's Lake Turkana? Or did he die elsewhere, his body swept down to the shallows in a flash flood?

However he came there, the 12-year-old's body rocked lifelessly for some time in the lake's western backwaters. Later only catfish may have noticed his scattered white bones, trampled into the mud by hippos and elephants visiting the marsh. In time even fish grew indifferent to the fragmented skeleton, until without witness it disappeared beneath layers of lake sediment and river-borne ash from distant volcanoes.

Recently this boy's bones—his skull, his teeth, and most of the rest of his skeleton—came to light in one of the most remarkable finds in human evolutionary studies. This skeleton, the best preserved of an early human ever found, gives us definitive evidence of the size and anatomy of *Homo erectus,* a species intermediate between the first upright-walking hominids and modern man. Moreover, it may help explain whether early humans evolved from ape-

like ancestors gradually or through abrupt changes in brain size and body shape.

The circumstances of this discovery were extraordinary. Since 1968 the slopes and gullies bordering Lake Turkana have yielded the fossil remains of more than 200 early humans. Until last year all had been found east of the lake by teams from the National Museums of Kenya in Nairobi. In 1971, for example, near Koobi Fora, deputy team leader Kamoya Kimeu recovered *Homo erectus* skull and bone fragments 1.5 million years old. Among these was the partial skeleton of an adult female. In life she had been large, but her disease-distorted bones allowed no firm conclusions about the average size of her kind. . . .

That day some expedition members washed clothes or wrote letters. Kamoya's irrepressible energy compelled him to take a walk. Crossing the sand river, he paused occasionally to pry among black lava pebbles strewn across a hillock. Kamoya's diligence is impressive, but it is unlikely that he would have scouted the unprepossessing mound if not for his day of enforced leisure. Nor would he have spotted, in sight of the camp kitchen, a piece of skull. Recognizably human, it was from the frontal section of a cranium, but no bigger than a matchbook.

A skull fragment so small tells you very little. Over the years we had stumbled on countless such fossils that, after tedious excavation, led no further. But as always, Kamoya kept his find to show us.

A few days later great clouds of dust drifted over the hill as we sieved its pebbly soil with mosquito screens. By dusk elated voices spread the word: "*Tume pata kichwa!*—We've found the skull!"

Even by lantern light we could see that we now had additional scraps of a *Homo erectus* skull—and that they would fit back together. A few more days of sieving and a blackened skull began to take shape, pains-takingly glued like broken crockery. Yet large sections were still missing, including the face, likely lost forever through erosion, the usual fate of fossil skulls here. We'd give this specimen one more day of investigation.

Impatience never pays. During what we thought would be our last excavation, delicate digging with a dental pick at the foot of a thorn tree suddenly rewarded us. Stones and soil loosened and fell away, revealing the missing facial bones. Though shattered like the rest of the skull, beside them lay both halves of a tooth-studded upper jaw.

Analysis of the teeth and of pelvic, arm, and leg bones recovered later showed that this fossil skull was that of a boy, no more than 12 years old at death.

During the next three weeks we had the exquisite pleasure of unearthing almost an entire *Homo erectus* skeleton, the first recovered of such antiquity— 1.6 million years old—and the earliest set of one individual's bones found in situ. Limb, rib, and collarbones appeared, along with vertebrae and the lower jaw, one of the very few ever to be matched to its skull. To find a more complete skeleton, we must jump forward in time to 100,000 years ago, when Neandertal man began to bury his dead.

This spectacular find dramatically confirms the antiquity of the human form. In its parts and proportion only the skull of the Lake Turkana boy would look odd to someone untrained in anatomy. The rest of his skeleton, essentially human, differs only subtly from that of a modern boy.

And too, because it is a youth's skeleton and so complete, it offers us a unique glimpse of growth

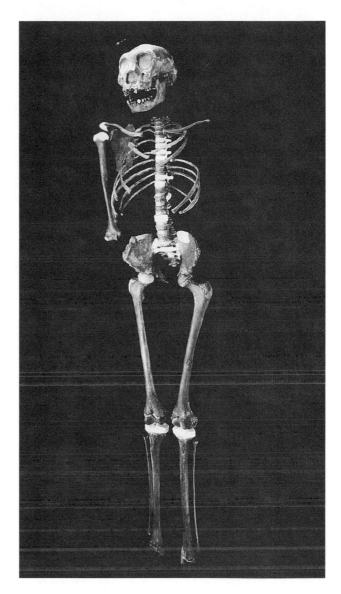

Cast reproduction of the fossilized boy found in Kenya, 1985. The boy, designated KNM-WT 15000, died of unknown causes; his bones were scattered and trampled in a swamp before sediment covered them. Under him was volcanic tuff dating from 1.65 million years ago, the period when *Homo Erectus* enters the fossil record. © 1985 DAVID L. BRILL. REPRODUCED BY PERMISSION.

and development in early humans. At five feet four inches tall, the boy from Turkana was surprisingly large compared with modern boys his age; he could well have grown to six feet. Suitably clothed and with a cap to obscure his low forehead and beetle brow, he would probably go unnoticed in a crowd today.

This find combines with previous discoveries of *Homo erectus* to contradict a long-held idea that humans have grown larger over the millennia. Our ancestors on the African savanna may have been much taller than we ever imagined. Indeed, we may have reached our present general size more than a million and a half years ago, with some populations in poorer environments becoming smaller fairly recently.

Only luck, the presence of a supply of underground water, and the scanty shade of a few parched thorn trees first drew us to the Nariokotome River and the skeleton of the boy from Lake Turkana. During the 1985 excavation, we began to uncover the last of the missing bones, adding another page to his biography—and to mankind's.

Further Resources

BOOKS

Bowler, Peter J. *Theories of Human Evolution.* Baltimore, Md.: Johns Hopkins University Press, 1986.

Lewin, Roger. *In the Age of Mankind: A Smithsonian Book of Human Evolution.* Washington, D.C.: Smithsonian, 1988.

———. *Principles of Human Evolution: A Core Textbook.* Malden, Mass.: Blackwell Science, 1998.

Walker, Alan, and Richard Leakey, eds. *The Nariokotome Homo Erectus Skeleton.* Cambridge, Mass.: Harvard University Press, 1993.

PERIODICALS

Brown, Frank H. "Early Homo Erectus Skeleton from West Lake Turkana, Kenya." *Nature,* 1985, 788–792.

Rightmire, George P. "Homo Erectus: Ancestor or Evolutionary Sidebranch?" *Evolutionary Anthropology,* 1992, 43–49.

Swisher, Carl C. "Age of the Earliest Known Hominids in Java, Indonesia." *Science,* 1994, 1118–1121.

Weaver, Kenneth F., Richard Leakey, and Alan Walker. "The Search for Early Man." *National Geographic,* November 1985, 560–629.

Wood, Bernard. "Origin and Evolution of the Genus Homo." *Nature,* 1992, 783–790.

Wood, Bernard, and Alan Turner. "Out of Africa and into Asia." *Nature,* 1995, 239–240.

WEBSITES

"Human Evolution: The Fossil Evidence in 3D." Department of Anthropology, University of California, Santa Barbara. Available online at http://www.anth.ucsb.edu/projects/human; website home page: http://www.anth.ucsb.edu/index.html (accessed May 22, 2003).

"The Human Origins Program: In Search of What Makes Us Human." Available online at http://www.mnh.si.edu/anthro/humanorigins (accessed May 22, 2003).

"Mitochondrial DNA and Human Evolution"

Journal article

By: Rebecca L. Cann, Mark Stoneking, and Allan C. Wilson

Date: January 1, 1987

Source: Cann, Rebecca L., Mark Stoneking, and Allan C Wilson. "Mitochondrial DNA and Human Evolution." *Nature* 325, January 1, 1987, 31–36.

About the Authors: Rebecca L. Cann received a doctorate in genetics from the University of California, Berkeley, in 1982. She is a professor of genetics and molecular biology at the University of Hawaii. Her research focuses on quantifying the genetic diversity of Polynesians and of endangered Hawaiian birds.

Mark Stoneking (1956–) received a doctorate in genetics from the University of California, Berkeley, in 1986. After serving as a staff scientist at the Human Genome Center in Berkeley and teaching at Pennsylvania State University, since 1999 he has been a professor at the Max Planck Institute for Evolutionary Anthropology in Leipzig, Germany.

Allan C. Wilson (1934–1991) was a professor of biochemistry at the University of California, Berkeley, for thirty-five years. He held a MacArthur "Genius" Award, was a visiting professor at Harvard University, St. Louis University, and Massachusetts Institute of Technology, and was nominated for a Nobel Prize. ∎

Introduction

Charles Darwin believed that all life had evolved from primitive ancestors. The fossil record, then too meager to help, led him in 1871 to concentrate on modern humans. He noted that they resembled two species of chimpanzee and the gorilla more than any other animal. He proposed that because these apes lived only in Africa, they must have arisen there. Since humans shared many similarities with the apes, they, too, must have arisen in Africa. Furthermore, he believed that evolution was a slow process, leading him to suspect that humans had separated from the apes millions of years ago.

Other scientists agreed that humans must have arisen millions of years ago, though many favored Asia rather than Africa as humanity's birthplace. In 1897, Eugene Dubois discovered in Indonesia a partial cranium and femur of the oldest human unearthed to that date, strengthening the case for an Asian origin for humanity. In 1924, Raymond Dart discovered a toddler's skull in South Africa of what he believed to be our most ancient ancestor. Only Mary D. Leakey's discovery in 1959 of a nearly complete skull in East Africa tilted the evidence toward Africa.

By then, a new technique had emerged to settle the question of human origins. In 1953, James Watson and Francis Crick discovered the chemistry of heredity: deoxyribonucleic acid (DNA). DNA has a double helix structure, similar to a spiral staircase, each rung of which comprises two of the four nucleotide bases: adenine, thymine, guanine, and cytosine. By splitting a double helix down the middle, a molecular biologist can read the sequence of nucleotide bases that form the half-strand of DNA. The more nucleotide bases two species share in a sequence, the closer they are related.

In 1967, Vincent Sarich and Allan C. Wilson compared blood proteins as a measure of genetic relatedness between humans and chimpanzees and found that they share a common ancestor who lived five million years ago. This work implied that humans had arisen in Africa and that they could not be millions of years old, for modern humans represented only a fraction of the five million years since the African apes and humans had diverged from a common ancestor.

Significance

Rebecca L. Cann, Mark Stoneking, and Wilson clinched the argument in 1987. They understood that every cell in the human body contains DNA in the nucleus and in the mitochondria, the sites that metabolize energy for a cell. Humans inherit mitochondrial DNA (mtDNA), unlike DNA in the nucleus, only from their mother. Furthermore, this mtDNA passes through the maternal line unchanged except for mutations (chemical changes to DNA) that it accrues.

Cann, Stoneking, and Wilson quantified the differences in nucleotide sequence in mtDNA from 147 people. Because they knew how fast mtDNA accumulated mutations, they were able to calculate back to the time when all humans shared the same mtDNA. Moreover, they found the greatest mtDNA diversity among Africans. The African population must be the oldest to have accumulated the most mutations; that is, humanity had originated in Africa as Darwin had supposed. Most astonishing of all, Cann, Stoneking, and Wilson traced human mtDNA back to a single woman who lived in Africa about two hundred thousand years ago.

This work electrified the media, which christened her "mitochondrial Eve" in reference to the biblical Eve. The comparison may mislead readers. Whereas Genesis, if interpreted literally, relates that Eve was the only woman at the beginning of human history, mitochondrial Eve could not have been the only African woman alive two hundred thousand years ago, but rather the only woman whose mtDNA survived to the present. Luck had favored her, because she was the only woman whose descendents had at least one daughter in every generation to pass on mtDNA to the present. Cann, Stoneking, and Wilson demonstrated that Darwin had been right to seek human origins in Africa but wrong to suppose modern humans

had arisen millions of years ago. At most, we are two hundred thousand years old as a species, making us the newcomer on Earth.

Primary Source

"Mitochondrial DNA and Human Evolution" [excerpt]

SYNOPSIS: In this excerpt, Cann, Stoneking, and Wilson quantify the differences in nucleotide sequence in mtDNA from 147 people. Because they know how fast mtDNA accumulates mutations, they are able to calculate back to the time when all humans shared the same mtDNA. Moreover, they find the greatest mtDNA diversity among Africans, meaning, humanity originated in Africa two hundred thousand years ago.

Molecular biology is now a major source of quantitative and objective information about the evolutionary history of the human species. It has provided new insights into our genetic divergence from apes and into the way in which humans are related to one another genetically. Our picture of genetic evolution within the human species is clouded, however, because it is based mainly on comparisons of genes in the nucleus. Mutations accumulate slowly in nuclear genes. In addition, nuclear genes are inherited from both parents and mix in every generation. This mixing obscures the history of individuals and allows recombination to occur. Recombination makes it hard to trace the history of particular segments of DNA unless tightly linked sites within them are considered.

Our world-wide survey of mitochondrial DNA (mtDNA) adds to knowledge of the history of the human gene pool in three ways. First, mtDNA gives a magnified view of the diversity present in the human gene pool, because mutations accumulate in this DNA several times faster than in the nucleus. Second, because mtDNA is inherited maternally and does not recombine, it is a tool for relating individuals to one another. Third, there are about 10 mtDNA molecules within a typical human and they are usually identical to one another . . .

Restriction maps

MtDNA was highly purified from 145 placentas and two cell lines, HeLa and GM 3043, derived from a Black American and an aboriginal South African (!Kung), respectively. Most placentas were obtained from US hospitals, the remainder coming from Australia and New Guinea. In the sample, there were

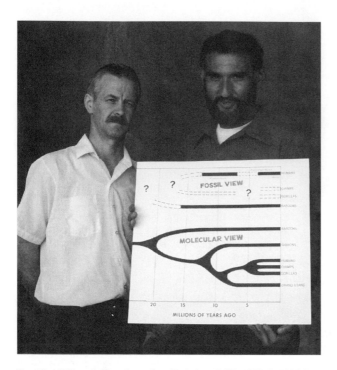

Dr. Allan Wilson (left) and associate, Berkeley, Calif., 1979. In 1987 Dr. Wilson participated in a DNA study with colleagues Dr. Rebecca L. Cann and Dr. Mark Stoneking, leading to their theory that all humans living today are descended from one woman who lived in Africa about 200,000 years ago. © ROGER RESSMEYER/CORBIS. REPRODUCED BY PERMISSION.

representatives of 5 geographic regions: 20 Africans (representing the sub-Saharan region), 34 Asians (originating from China, Vietnam, Laos, the Philippines, Indonesia and Tonga), 46 Caucasians (originating from Europe, North Africa, and the Middle East), 21 aboriginal Australians, and 26 aboriginal New Guineans. Only two of the 20 Africans in our sample, those bearing mtDNA types 1 and 81 . . . were born in sub-Saharan Africa. The other 18 people in this sample are Black Americans, who bear many non-African nuclear genes probably contributed mainly by Caucasian males. . . .

Evolutionary tree

A tree relating the 133 types of human mtDNA and the reference sequence . . . was built by the parsimony method. To interpret this tree, we make two assumptions, both of which have extensive empirical support: (1) a strictly maternal mode of mtDNA transmission (so that any variant appearing in a group of lineages must be due to a mutation occurring in the ancestral lineage and not recombination between maternal and paternal genomes) and (2) each individual is homogeneous for its multiple mtDNA genomes. We can therefore view the tree as

a genealogy linking maternal lineages in modern human populations to a common ancestral female (bearing mtDNA type a).

Many trees of minimal or near-minimal length can be made from the data; all trees that we have examined share the following features with the tree [relating the 133 types of human mtDNA and the reference sequence]: (1) two primary branches, one composed entirely of Africans, the other including all 5 of the populations studied; and (2) each population stems from multiple lineages connected to the tree at widely dispersed positions. Since submission of this manuscript, Horai *et al.* built a tree for our samples of African and Caucasian populations and their sample of a Japanese population by another method; their tree shares these two features.

Among the trees investigated was one consisting of five primary branches with each branch leading exclusively to one of the five populations. This tree, which we call the population-specific tree, requires 51 more point mutations than does the tree of minimum length. . . . The minimum-length tree requires fewer changes at 22 of the 93 phylogenetically-informative restriction sites than does the population-specific tree, while the latter tree required fewer changes at four sites; both trees require the same number of changes at the remaining 67 sites. The minimum-length tree is thus favoured by a score of 22 to 4. The hypothesis that the two trees are equally compatible with the data is statistically rejected, since 22:4 is significantly different from the expected 13:13. The minimum-length tree is thus significantly more parsimonious than the population-specific tree.

African origin

We infer from the tree of minimum length . . . that Africa is a likely source of the human mitochondrial gene pool. This inference comes from the observation that one of the two primary branches leads exclusively to African mtDNAs . . . while the second primary branch also leads to African mtDNAs. . . . By postulating that the common ancestral mtDNA (type a) was African, we minimize the number of intercontinental migrations needed to account for the geographic distribution of mtDNA types. It follows that b is a likely common ancestor of all non-African and many African mtDNAs. . . .

Tentative time scale

A time scale can be affixed to the tree . . . by assuming that mtDNA sequence divergence accumulates at a constant rate in humans. One way of estimating this rate is to consider the extent of differentiation within clusters specific to New Guinea . . . , Australia and the New World. People colonised these regions relatively recently: a minimum of 30,000 years ago for New Guinea, 40,000 years ago for Australia, and 12,000 years ago for the New World. These times enable us to calculate that the mean rate of mtDNA divergence within humans lies between two and four percent per million years: a detailed account of this calculation appears elsewhere. This rate is similar to previous estimates from animals as disparate as apes, monkeys, horses, rhinoceroses, mice, rats, birds and fishes. We therefore consider the above estimate of 2%–4% to be reasonable for humans, although additional comparative work is needed to obtain a more exact calibration.

. . . [T]he common ancestral mtDNA (type a) links mtDNA types that have diverged by an average of nearly 0.57%. Assuming a rate of 2%–4% per million years, this implies that the common ancestor of all surviving mtDNA types existed 140,000–290,000 years ago. Similarly, ancestral types b–j may have existed 62,000–225,000 years ago. . . .

When did the migrations from Africa take place? The oldest of the clusters of mtDNA types to contain no African members stems from ancestor c and included types. . . . The apparent age of this cluster . . . is 90,000–180,000 years. Its founders may have left Africa at about that time. However, it is equally possible that the exodus occurred as recently as 23,000–105,000 thousand years ago. . . . The mtDNA results cannot tell us exactly when these migrations took place. . . .

Relation to fossil record

Our tentative interpretation of the tree . . . and the associated time scale . . . fits with one view of the fossil record: that the transformation of archaic to anatomically modern forms of *Homo sapiens* occurred first in Africa, about 100,000–140,000 years ago, and that all present-day humans are descendants of that African population. Archaeologists have observed that blades were in common use in Africa 80–90 thousand years ago, long before they replaced flake tools in Asia or Europe. But the agreement between our molecular view and the evidence from palaeoanthropology and archaeology should be treated cautiously for two reasons. First, there is much uncertainty about the ages of these remains. Second, our placement of the common ancestor of

all human mtDNA diversity in Africa 140,000–280,000 years ago need not imply that the transformation to anatomically modern *Homo sapiens* occurred in Africa at this time. The mtDNA data tell us nothing of the contributions to this transformation by the genetic and cultural traits of males and females whose mtDNA became extinct.

An alternative view of human evolution rests on evidence that *Homo* has been present in Asia as well as in Africa for at least one million years and holds that the transformation of archaic to anatomically modern humans occurred in parallel in different parts of the Old World. This hypothesis leads us to expect genetic differences of great antiquity within widely separated parts of the modern pool of mtDNAs. It is hard to reconcile the mtDNA results with this hypothesis. The greatest divergences within clusters specific to non-African parts of the World correspond to times of only 90,000–180,000 years. This might imply that the early Asian *Homo* (such as Java man and Peking man) contributed no surviving mtDNA lineages to the gene pool of our species. Consistent with this implication are features, found recently in the skeletons of the ancient Asian forms, that make it unlikely that Asian *erectus* was ancestral to *Homo sapiens.* Perhaps the non-African *erectus* population was replaced by *sapiens* migrants from Africa; incomplete fossils indicating the possible presence of early modern humans in western Asia at Zuttiyeh (75,000–150,000 years ago) and Qafzeh (50,000–70,000 years ago) might reflect these first migrations.

If there was hybridization between the resident archaic forms in Asia and anatomically modern forms emerging from Africa, we should expect to find extremely divergent types of mtDNA in present-day Asians, more divergent than any mtDNA found in Africa. There is no evidence for these types of mtDNA among the Asians studied. Although such archaic types of mtDNA could have been lost from the hybridizing population, the probability of mtDNA lineages becoming extinct in an expanding population is low. Thus we propose that *Homo erectus* in Asia was replaced without much mixing with the invading *Homo sapiens* from Africa.

Conclusions and prospects

Studies of mtDNA suggest a view of how, where and when modern humans arose that fits with one interpretation of evidence from ancient human bones and tools. More extensive molecular comparisons are needed to improve our rooting of the mtDNA tree and the calibration of the rate of mtDNA divergence within the human species. This may provide a more reliable time scale for the spread of human populations and better estmates of the number of maternal lineages involved in founding the non-African populations.

It is also important to obtain more quantitative estimates of the overall extent of nuclear DNA diversity in both human and African ape populations. By comparing the nuclear and mitochondrial DNA diversities, it may be possible to find out whether a transient or prolonged bottleneck in population size accompanied the origin of our species. Then a fuller interaction between palaeoanthropology, archaeology and molecular biology will allow a deeper analysis of how our species arose.

Further Resources

BOOKS

Lewin, Roger. *Bones of Contention.* New York: Simon and Schuster, 1987.

———. *Principles of Human Evolution: A Core Textbook.* Malden, Mass.: Blackwell Science, 1998.

PERIODICALS

Moore, William S. "Inferring Phylogenies From mtDNA Variation: Mitochondrial-Gene Trees versus Nuclear-Gene Trees." *Evolution,* 1995, 718–726.

Pritchard, J.K, and M.W. Feldman. "Genetic Data and the African Origin of Humans." *Science,* 1996, 1548–1549.

Rogers, Jeffrey. "The Phylogenetic Relationships Among Homo, Pan, and Gorilla." *Journal of Human Evolution,* 1993, 201–215.

Ruvolo, Maryellen. "Molecular Evolutionary Processes and Conflicting Gene Trees: The Hominoid Case." *American Journal of Physical Anthropology,* 1994, 89–114.

Stoneking, Mark. "In Defense of 'Eve.'" *American Anthropology,* 1994, 131–141.

———. "DNA and Recent Human Evolution." *Evolutionary Anthropology,* 1993, 60–73.

Templeton, Alan R. "'Eve': Hypothesis Compatibility versus Hypothesis Testing." *American Anthropology,* 1994, 141–155.

———. "The 'Eve' Hypothesis: A Genetic Critique and Reanalysis." *American Anthropology,* 1993, 51–72.

Wilson, Allan C., and Rebecca L. Cann. "The Recent African Genesis of Humans." *Scientific American,* April 1992, 68–73.

WEBSITES

"An Example: Mitochondrial Eve." Kent Holsinger, University of Connecticut. Available online at http://darwin.eeb.uconn.edu/eeb348/lecture-notes/coalescent/node3.html; website home page: http://darwin.eeb.uconn.edu/ (accessed May 25, 2003).

"Mitochondrial 'Eve.'" John Brookfield. Available online at http://www.fitzroydearborn.com/Samples/Genesmp2.pdf (accessed May 25, 2003).

"Mitochondrial Eve." Jonathan Marks, Department of Sociology and Anthropology, University of North Carolina, Charlotte. Available online at http://www.uncc.edu/jmarks/2141/mtEve.pdf; website home page: http://www.uncc.edu/jmarks/ (accessed May 25, 2003).

"The Verdict on Creationism"

Magazine article

By: Stephen Jay Gould

Date: July 19, 1987

Source: Gould, Stephen Jay. "The Verdict on Creationism." *New York Times Magazine,* July 19, 1987, 32, 34.

About the Author: Stephen Jay Gould (1941–2002) received a doctorate from Columbia University in 1967. That same year, he joined the faculty at Harvard University, rising to be a professor of biology, geology, and history of science. His books and articles found an audience among both scholars and the wider public. ■

Introduction

Clerics in Europe and the United States, taking their cue from Genesis, believed God had created humans in his image. Beginning in the eighteenth century, scientists advanced the claim, with caution at first, that all life, including humans, had evolved from primitive ancestors. There was no moment when God created humans.

Clerics savaged Jean Baptiste Lamarck and Robert Chambers when they proposed evolution in earnest during the first half of the nineteenth century. Charles Darwin sat on the theory of evolution by natural selection for twenty years out of fear of religious controversy, publishing it only in 1859 after Alfred Russell Wallace arrived at the same theory a year earlier. Anglican bishop Samuel Wilberforce attacked Darwin at the 1860 meeting of the British Association for the Advancement of Science, but by century's end European clerics had either made their peace with Darwinism or ignored it.

Only in the United States did fundamentalists (those who believe in a literal reading of the Bible) oppose evolution into the twentieth century. They first tried to ban the teaching of evolution in public schools, a movement that peaked in the 1920s. By executive order, Texas governor Miriam Ferguson outlawed the use of textbooks in public schools that referred to evolution, and in 1925 the Tennessee legislature banned the teaching of evolution in public schools. When biology teacher John Scopes defied the law, attorney Clarence Darrow and journalist Henry L. Mencken used the trial to discredit fundamentalists as intolerant and ignorant of science.

The embarrassment of the trial led fundamentalists to a second tactic. If they could not ban the teaching of evolution in public schools, they could try to sneak creationism into the classroom by proclaiming it science. Henry Morris founded the Institute for Creation Research, and in the 1960s and 1970s tried to refashion the Genesis account of creation into a science. If creationism were really a science, then students should learn both the theory of evolution and the theory of creation, asserted Morris. Under the guise of equal time for both theories, Morris and his supporters won victories in California in 1972 and in Arkansas and Louisiana in the early 1980s.

Significance

These victories alarmed scientists, almost all of whom opposed creationism. Stephen Jay Gould led a group of prominent scientists and philosophers of science in challenging these laws. Gould and others testified at a dramatic trial in Arkansas. In response, the court struck down the law, and in June 1987 the U.S. Supreme Court struck down the Louisiana law.

The next month, Gould celebrated the Court's decision in an article in the *New York Times Magazine*. He branded creation science a ruse. It was religion not science, and public schools are in the business of teaching science rather than religion. The U.S. Supreme Court's ruling, Gould believed, freed public school teachers from the tyranny of having to teach religion as though it were science. The ruling freed them to teach science.

Yet, creationists have not conceded defeat. They now assert that the chemistry of even the simplest bacterium is too complex to have evolved. An intelligence (God) had to have designed life. Supporters and detractors call this rationale Intelligent Design. In 2002, supporters tried to convince the Ohio Board of Education to add Intelligent Design to state education standards, a move that would prompt public schools to add it to their curriculum. The board refused, but it also did not endorse the teaching of evolution in Ohio public schools. More than a century after Darwin's death, evolution remains controversial.

Primary Source

"The Verdict on Creationism" [excerpt]

SYNOPSIS: In this excerpt, Gould brands creation science a ruse. According to Gould, it is religion not science, and public schools are in the business of teaching science rather than religion. Gould feels the U.S. Supreme Court's ruling against the teaching of creationism in Louisiana's public schools frees teachers to teach science, rather than religion under the guise of science.

Americans, like people of all cultures, I suppose, have been deluged throughout history with our

American paleontologist Stephen Jay Gould, New York, January 1982. In an article in *The New York Times Magazine,* Gould celebrated the Supreme Court's decision in *Edwards v. Agyillard* (1987) that declared unconstitutional the Louisiana Act specifying equal classroom time for creation science and evolution. © BETTMANN/CORBIS. REPRODUCED BY PERMISSION.

share of Philistines and Yahoos. We tend, as Mencken did, to treat the fundamentalist anti-evolution movement as a primary example of Know-Nothingism, an aberrant phenomenon meriting only our ridicule. But it would be a bad mistake to banish these important chapters of American history to the sidelines of humor.

One such prominent chapter ended before the United States Supreme Court last month. By a decisive 7-2 vote, the Court struck down the last bill in a long lineage, the Louisiana act specifying "equal time" in the classroom for "creation science" if evolution were taught. . . .

The argument that the literal story of Genesis can qualify as science collapses on three major grounds: the creationists' need to invoke miracles in order to compress the events of the earth's history into the biblical span of a few thousand years; their unwillingness to abandon claims clearly disproven, including the assertion that all fossils are products of Noah's flood, and their reliance upon distortion, misquote, half-quote, and citation out of context to characterize the ideas of their opponents.

Against these negative assessments, we must counterpose the overwhelming judgment provided by consistent observations and inferences by the thousands. The earth is billions of years old and its living creatures are linked by ties of evolutionary descent. Scientists stand accused of promoting dogma by so stating, but do we brand people illiberal when they proclaim that the earth is neither flat nor at the center of the universe? Science *has* taught us some things with confidence! Evolution on an ancient earth is as well established as our planet's shape and position. Our continuing struggle to understand how evolution happens (the "theory of evolution") does not cast our documentation of its occurrence—the "fact of evolution"—into doubt.

But creation science is also a sham because the professed reason for imposing it upon teachers—to preserve the academic freedom of students to learn alternative viewpoints—is demonstrably false. Creationists are right in identifying academic freedom as the key issue, but they have the argument perversely backward.

It was their law that abridged the most precious meaning of academic freedom, the freedom of teachers to follow the dictates of their consciences, their training and their professional commitments. Creationists claim that their law broadened the freedom of teachers by permitting the introduction of controversial material. But no statute exists in any state to bar instruction in "creation science." It could be taught before, and it can be taught now.

"Creation science" has not entered the curriculum for a reason so simple and so basic that we often forget to mention it: because it is false, and because good teachers understand exactly why it is false. What could be more destructive of that most fragile yet most precious commodity in our entire intellectual heritage—good teaching—than a bill forcing honorable teachers to sully their sacred trust by granting equal treatment to a doctrine not only known to be false, but calculated to undermine any general understanding of science as an enterprise?

This victory belongs to the teachers. Not to us few who thrive unharassed in elite universities, but to those thousands who labor without adequate recompense or recognition in the nation's public schools, and who uphold, often at personal peril and for no reward beyond its righteousness the ideal that truth—to which we so feebly aspire in all our mortality—shall make us free.

Further Resources

BOOKS

Hanson, Robert W., ed. *Science and Creation: Geological, Theological, and Educational Perspectives.* New York: Macmillan, 1986.

Kitcher, Philip. *Abusing Science: The Case Against Creationism.* Cambridge: MIT Press, 1982.

Larson, Edward J. *Trial and Error: The American Controversy Over Creation and Evolution.* New York: Oxford University Press, 1985.

Whitcomb, John C., and Henry M. Morris. *The Genesis Flood: The Biblical Record and Its Scientific Implications.* Philadelphia: Presbyterian and Reformed Publishing, 1961.

Zetterberg, J. Peter, ed. *Evolution versus Creationism: The Public Education Controversy.* Phoenix, Ariz.: Oryx, 1977.

PERIODICALS

Callaghan, Catherine A. "Evolution and Creationist Arguments." *American Biology Teacher,* 1980, 422–427.

Cavanaugh, Michael A. "Scientific Creationism and Rationality." *Nature,* 1985, 185–189.

Gatewood, Willard B. "From Scopes to Creation Science: The Decline and Revival of the Evolution Controversy." *South Atlantic Quarterly,* 1984, 363–383.

Nelkin, Dorothy. "The Science-Textbook Controversies." *Scientific American,* April 1976, 33–39.

Numbers, Ronald L. "Creationism in Twentieth-century America." *Science,* 1986, 538–544.

Scott, Eugenie C., and Henry P. Cole. "The Elusive Scientific Basis of Creation Science." *Quarterly Review of Biology,* 1985, 21–30.

WEBSITES

Institute for Creation Research. Available online at http://www.icr.org (accessed May 25, 2003).

"The Next Computer Revolution"

Magazine article

By: Abraham Peled

Date: October 1987

Source: Peled, Abraham. "The Next Computer Revolution." *Scientific American* 257, no. 4, October 1987, 57, 59, 64.

About the Author: Abraham Peled (1945–) earned a master's and doctorate in electrical engineering from Princeton University. From 1974 to 1993, he was the research division vice president of Systems and Software at IBM. From 1993 to 1995, he was the senior vice president of business development for Elron Electronic Industries. Since 1995, he has been the director, president, and chief executive officer of NDS, a digital television manufacturer in Middlesex, England. ■

Introduction

The ways information is organized and transmitted are a central aspect of technology. The Sumerians (an ancient people in what is today Iraq) ushered in the first advance by codifying language into a written text five thousand years ago. The invention of an alphabet enabled humans to encode language in a discrete set of letters, and the rise of the Roman Empire after 200 B.C.E. brought the Roman alphabet to the Mediterranean basin, an alphabet that is the foundation of written language throughout the Western world. In the fifteenth century, Johannes Gutenberg invented the printing press, apparently independent from and later than the Chinese ninth-century invention of moveable type.

The nineteenth century's telegraph and telephone gave humans the technology to transfer information instantaneously. In the twentieth century, radio and television augmented the technology of instantaneous information transfer. The computer revolution of the present generation may be the most far-reaching information technology. The personal computer (PC) that gives users access to electronic mail (email) and Internet chat rooms approximates the telephone in allowing users to interact with the medium of communication. The chat room participant is not bound to passively receive information as is the case with radio and television, but can communicate ideas to others in an exchange of information.

Intel scientist Theodore Hoff sparked the PC revolution in 1971 by inventing the microchip, and in 1974 the American company MITS marketed the first PC, the Altair, which used Intel chips. Three years later, American entrepreneurs Steven Jobs and Stephen Wozniak founded Apple Computer Inc. and introduced the Apple II, a PC they mass-produced at low cost as Henry Ford had mass-produced the Model T earlier in the century. In 1977, U.S. companies Radio Shack and Commodore Business Machines introduced their own PCs.

Significance

Abraham Peled wrote in 1987 that the PC would become as ubiquitous as the telephone within fifteen years. He cited the relentless miniaturization of the PC along with increasing speed and memory at low cost as factors that would make PCs attractive to Americans. Peled estimated that computer prices had fallen 20 to 30 percent a year for thirty years and predicted that the number of components on a chip would soon increase fortyfold and the speed of PCs would increase twelve times. Moreover, one could access software by mouse and icons, making it possible for novices to use PCs; no longer did one need to program a PC. Taken together, Peled believed that these developments would create an information revolution.

Peled was right, though he did not foresee how sweeping this revolution would be. In 1969, the U.S. Defense Department created an electronic network, the forerunner of the Internet, for the exchange of email. As academics came to use it, the National Science Foundation financed its growth, and in 1989 Tim Berners-Lee at CERN, a scientific organization in Geneva, Switzerland, launched the World Wide Web (WWW), an information retrieval system. By the mid-1990s, millions of users worldwide were linked to the Internet through their PCs.

We have only an inkling of how the PC as a gateway to the Internet is changing our world. The Internet's international reach, its strenuous defense of free speech, and its eclectic mix of information make it and the PC technologies rooted in the democratic exchange of ideas. Indeed, anyone with a PC or access to a library with PCs can travel the information superhighway. The PC has the potential to connect anyone to information, a quantum leap beyond the ancient and medieval worlds, when the elite restricted literacy and thus information to themselves.

Primary Source

"The Next Computer Revolution" [excerpt]

SYNOPSIS: In the following excerpt, Peled cites, in 1987, the miniaturization of the PC, the increasing memory and speed, and the low cost as factors that will make PCs as widespread as telephones within fifteen years. Just as factories had powered the industrial revolution, PCs are powering an information revolution.

And now computing appears to be entering a new passage. In this phase, by means of developments in hardware and software, computing will grow more powerful, sophisticated and flexible by an order of magnitude in the next decade. At the same time the technology will become an intellectual utility, widely available, ultimately as ubiquitous as the telephone. Visual and other natural interfaces will make the machines easier to use, and a flexible high capacity network will be capable of linking any combination of individuals who need computing, whether they are physicians trying to reach a difficult diagnosis, investment bankers structuring a deal, aeronautical engineers creating a new airframe, astrophysicists modeling the evolution of the universe or students studying for an examination.

Although the emergence of such an intellectual utility represents a profound change in society's relation to the computer, it is the direct result of well-established trends that have been carrying the industry forward since the end of World War II. The most important of these forces is the miniaturization of electronic components. Miniaturization has been primarily responsible for a sustained reduction in the cost of computing at a rate of from 20 to 30 percent per year over a period of three decades. As the size of a transistor, gate or other element etched on a chip declines, the speed of operation increases proportionately and the density of the elements per area of chip rises geometrically.

The process of miniaturization can be expected to continue at its current pace for at least the next 10 or 15 years, pushed forward by difficult yet feasible engineering refinement of current technologies. X-ray lithography using synchrotron radiation, new materials and better device structures will probably improve the density of components on a chip by a factor of 20 to 40. Such processors will probably be from six to 12 times faster than existing ones.

These improvements will be compounded by the steady increase of parallelism in computing systems. Virtually all computers perform calculations in sequence one step at a time. Parallel processing is much more powerful, as it enables a computer to operate many times faster by carrying out all or many of the steps in a problem or task simultaneously.

If miniaturization sets the pace for technological progress, the rate at which software can be developed and deployed will ultimately determine the speed with which computing systems penetrate and transform the industrial, service and scientific enterprises. The reason is that software transforms a computer from a tool that can solve a particular problem in principle to one that can solve it in practice. There is no single or even predominant software technology, progress will come from better structure, more powerful languages and more efficient programming environments.

In the context of software the term "structure" refers to the efficiency or even elegance with which the subroutines that make up a complete program are put together to enable the machine to carry out its task. The language allows the user to tell the machine how to implement the program or some part of it to carry out a task. The power of a computer language is gauged by the degree of detail that needs to be specified. The most powerful languages enable the user simply to state the mathematical or logical formulation of the problem, in the expectation that the computer can fill in the details.

The programming environment, the array of physical and logical means by which a programmer transmits instructions, has evolved from toggle switches to the keyboard and the mouse, from flow charts and coding sheets to interactive text and graphic representations. Advances in technology promise still more natural means of communication. A major part of the software effort is clearly directed at removing the mechanical difficulties impeding the use of a computer so that the only difficulty left will be the conceptual one of solving the problem at hand. . . .

The progress in computing systems will continue—perhaps exponentially and certainly unabated—for at least the next 10 or 15 years. The widespread availability of computers to a growing community of users will amplify creativity and fuel the continued progress.

Currently computing can amplify only simple, relatively routine mental capacities, but steady progress is being made toward an ability to enhance the more analytical and inferential skills. Just as machines capable of extending and amplifying human physical abilities created the Industrial Revolution, so computing—through its ability to extend man's mental abilities—is the engine propelling the current and as yet inadequately named revolution. The journey has only begun.

Further Resources

BOOKS

Berners-Lee, Tim. *Weaving the Web.* San Francisco: HarperSanFrancisco, 1999.

Freiberger, Paul, and Michael Swaine. *Fire in the Valley: The Making of the Personal Computer.* Berkeley, Calif.: Osborne/McGraw-Hill, 1984.

Gates, Bill. *The Road Ahead.* New York: Penguin, 1995.

Yourdon, Edward. *Nations at Risk: The Impact of the Computer Revolution.* New York: Yourdon, 1986.

PERIODICALS

Kay, Alan C. "Microelectronics and the Personal Computer." *Scientific American,* September 1977, 230–244.

Smarte, Gene, and Andrew Reinhardt. "1975–1990: Fifteen Years of Bits, Bytes, and Other Great Moments." *Byte,* September 1990, 369–400.

Thompson, Tom. "The Macintosh at Ten." *Byte,* February 1994, 47–54.

WEBSITES

"Chronology of Personal Computers." Ken Polsson. Available online at http://www.islandnet.com/~kpolsson/comphist; website home page: http://www.islandnet.com/~kpolsson/ (accessed May 25, 2003).

"PC-History." Available online at http://www.pc-history.org (accessed May 25, 2003).

"Personal Computer History." Dan Knight, Low End PC. Available online at http://lowendpc.com/history/; website home page: http://lowendpc.com/ (accessed May 25, 2003).

Personal Computer Milestones, Blinkenlights Archaeological Institute. Available online at http://www.blinkenlights.com/ (accessed May 25, 2003).

"Personal Computers: History and Development." Jones Media and Information Technology Encyclopedia. Available online at http://www.digitalcentury.com/encyclo/update/pc_hd .html; website home page: http://www.jonesencyclo.com/ (accessed May 25, 2003).

"Evolution of Human Walking"

Magazine article

By: C. Owen Lovejoy

Date: November 1988

Source: Lovejoy, C. Owen. "Evolution of Human Walking." *Scientific American* 259, no. 5, November 1988, 118, 122–123, 125.

About the Author: C. Owen Lovejoy received a doctorate in physical anthropology from the University of Massachusetts and is a professor of anthropology at Kent State University, an adjunct professor of anatomy at Northeastern Ohio Universities College of Medicine, a consultant for the Cuyahoga County Coroner's Office in Cleveland, Ohio, and a member of the Department of Orthopaedic Surgery at Case Western Reserve University. He is an authority on australopithecine anatomy and locomotion. ■

Introduction

In *The Descent of Man* (1871), Charles Darwin proposed that humans were most closely related to the African apes, the two species of chimpanzee and the gorilla. Because chimpanzees and gorillas are knuckle walkers, Darwin reasoned that the common ancestor of both the African apes and humans must have also been a knuckle walker. This rationale raised the issue of when our human ancestors began to walk upright.

Darwin suspected that our human ancestors must have walked upright early in their evolution, for only bipedalism would have freed the hands to make and manipulate tools and weapons. Such activities must have favored those of our ancestors with larger brains and greater intellect. Yet, for Darwin the evolution of bipedalism and later of a large brain took millions of years, because he believed that evolution is a gradual process that moves by innumerable small changes.

In 1967, Vincent Sarich and Allan C. Wilson compared the differences in blood proteins of humans and

Anthropologist C. Owen Lovejoy sits at a table with a spectrum of early hominid bones. PHOTO BY BOB CHRISTY, KENT STATE UNIVERSITY. REPRODUCED BY PERMISSION.

chimpanzees as a way of measuring genetic differences between them. They knew that genes accumulate mutations (chemical changes to deoxyribonucleic acid [DNA]) at a fixed rate and that blood proteins must reflect these mutations by changing at a fixed rate. By calculating back to the time when no differences existed, Sarich and Wilson arrived at the common ancestor of humans and the African apes. The common ancestor had lived only five million years ago. The evolution of bipedalism, therefore, occurred within the last five million years, but when?

In 1974, Donald C. Johanson discovered a 40 percent complete skeleton of a female (Lucy) that was a little over three million years old. Her pelvis, leg bones, and vertebrae proved that human ancestors walked upright during her lifetime. In 1977, Mary D. Leakey discovered 3.5-million-year-old footprints in East Africa. The footprints resembled ours to the detail of having an arch. This fine-tuning of the foot's anatomy implied that human ancestors must have walked upright soon after their five-million-year-old divergence from the line leading to the African apes.

Significance

C. Owen Lovejoy went further than Johanson or Leakey by placing bipedalism at five million years ago.

Yet, the fossil record is sparse earlier than four million years ago and nonexistent at five million years. In making the case for early bipedalism, Lovejoy relied on Lucy, the most complete skeleton at three million years or earlier. Lovejoy had taken the principal role in reconstructing her skeleton. This work led him to conclude that the muscle attachments to her pelvis and legs would have made her a more efficient biped than modern humans. This conclusion implied that bipedalism had arisen early in our human ancestors to have reached a state of such efficiency more than three million years ago.

Bipedalism could only have evolved so early, Lovejoy believed, if it conveyed an advantage to human ancestors. Bipedalism was so successful because it favored the development of the nuclear family, asserted Lovejoy. It would have freed the hands of women to care for infants and children, while fathers used their hands to gather food and to hunt. They would return to camp laden with food for their women and children. Bipedalism thus gave our human ancestors a reproductive advantage because more young would survive to maturity given such care. The newly mature would in turn have more children of their own, on which they would lavish the same care. Thus, these genetic improvements were slowly passed on to future generations.

The power of Lovejoy's explanation lay in its linking together important human traits early in our evolution: bipedalism, the monogamous pairing of male and female adults, and with this pairing the origin of the nuclear family. Our ancestors were thus human in their behavior early in their evolution. All that remained was for our ancestors to develop technology, religion, and other attributes of culture. (Culture is everything nongenetic that humans pass from generation to generation.) According to Lovejoy, from the beginning our ancestors stood on the brink of being human.

Primary Source

"Evolution of Human Walking" [excerpt]

> **SYNOPSIS:** In this excerpt, Lovejoy bundles together important traits early in human evolution: bipedalism, the monogamous pairing of male and female adults, and with this pairing the origin of the nuclear family.

I have proposed that bipedality accompanied a set of behavioral adaptations that became the key evolutionary innovation of humanity's earliest ancestors. These adaptations included, in effect, the nuclear family: lasting monogamy together with care of the offspring by both parents. The male's contribution took the form of providing high-energy food, which expanded the mother's ability to nurture and protect each infant and also enabled her to give birth more often. Bipedality figured in this new reproductive scheme because by freeing the hands it made it possible for the male to carry food gathered far from his mate. These developments must have come long before the current hominid fossil record begins.

Upright walking should therefore have been perfected by the time of an australopithecine female whose fossil has become a test case for early walking. In 1974 the continuing search for human ancestors in the Afar Triangle of Ethiopia, led by Donald C. Johanson of the Institute of Human Origins in Berkeley, Calif., was splendidly rewarded by the recovery of the "Lucy" skeleton, known formally as A.L. 288–1. Although the skeleton is not quite complete, it preserves far more detail than any comparable fossil. In particular, it includes many of the lower-limb bones, one of the innominate bones that, in a mirror-image pair, make up the primate pelvis, and an intact sacrum (the fused vertebrae at the back of the pelvis). Upright walking is so dependent on this structure that an analysis of Lucy's pelvis can reveal how well she and her contemporaries walked. . . .

In one respect Lucy seems to have been even better designed for bipedality than we are. Her ilia flare outward more sharply than those of a modern pelvis and her femoral necks are longer. Her abductor muscles thus enjoyed a greater mechanical advantage than these muscles do in modern females. Some of the abductors' advantage merely compensated for the slightly wider separation of her hip joints (which gave her trunk a longer lever arm). Yet accurate measurements of both the abductor and the trunk lever arms—possible because the Lucy pelvis is so complete—show that her abductor advantage is still greater than our own. Her abductors had to exert less force to stabilize the pelvis, which also reduced the pressure on the hip-joint surfaces.

Why should a three-million-year-old hominid have had this mechanical advantage over her descendants? The answer lies in the accelerated growth of the human brain during the past three million years. Lucy's pelvis was almost singularly designed for bipedality. The flaring ilia and long femoral necks increased her abductors' lever arm, but they yielded a pelvis that in top view was markedly elliptical, resulting in a birth canal that was wide but short from front to back. The constriction was tolerable because Lucy predated the dramatic expansion of the brain; her infant's cranium would have been no larger than a baby chimpanzee's. The process of birth in Lucy

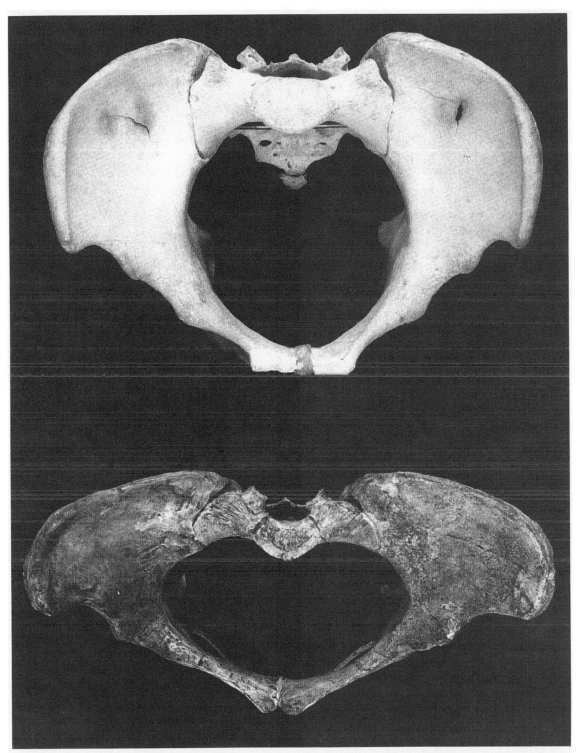

PELVISES of a modern human female (*top*) and Lucy (*bottom*) are separated by three million years of evolution but bear the same hallmarks of upright walking. The major change visible in this view—the more ovoid form of the human pelvis—ac- companied an expansion of the birth canal, needed because of the increase in brain size since Lucy. The author and Barbara Brown restored the Lucy pelvis from the fragmented fossil; Larry Rubens of Kent State University made the photograph.

SCIENTIFIC AMERICAN *November 1988* 119

Pelvis of modern human female (top) compared to that of 3-million-year-old Lucy (bottom), published in *Scientific American,* November 1988. **LARRY RUBENS, KENT STATE UNIVERSITY. REPRODUCED BY PERMISSION.**

and her contemporaries would have been slightly more complex than in an ape, but much easier than the modern human birth process. . . .

As human ancestors evolved a larger brain, the pelvic opening had to become rounder. The pelvis had to expand from front to back, but at the same time it contracted slightly from side to side. In the process the flare of the ilia was reduced, leaving us with a somewhat shorter abductor lever arm than Lucy's. (These changes are less pronounced in the modern male pelvis, where the abductors retain some of their former mechanical advantage.) Meanwhile the head of the modern femur has become enlarged to withstand increased pressure from the harder-working abductors. The difficulty of accommodating in the same pelvis an effective bipedal hip joint and an adequate passage for a large infant brain remains acute, however, and the human birth process is one of the most difficult in the animal kingdom.

The close resemblance of Lucy's pelvis to that of a modern human and its dramatic contrast to the pelvis of a chimpanzee make it clear that she walked fully upright. But was her bipedal progression truly habitual? Had she forsaken all other kinds of locomotion? The muscular rearrangements that enabled her to walk upright would not have allowed efficient quadrupedal movement on the ground. Perhaps, however, she often took to the trees and climbed, as most primates do, using all four limbs.

Basic evolutionary principles provide one kind of verdict on the possibility. A species cannot develop detailed anatomical modifications for a particular behavior, such as bipedality, unless it consistently employs that behavior. For natural selection to have so thoroughly modified for bipedality the skeleton Lucy inherited, her ancestors must already have spent most of their time on the ground, walking upright. . . .

I have concentrated on the pelvic anatomy of Lucy because the hallmarks of bipedality are so vivid there. A review of the rest of her skeleton and of other *Australopithecus* skeletons would reveal equally dramatic modifications that favor bipedality and rule out other modes of locomotion. The knee, for example, is adapted for withstanding greater stress during complete extension than the knee of other primates, and its design brings the femur and the tibia together at a slight angle, so that the foot can easily be planted directly under the body's center of mass when body weight is supported on one leg. The ankle is also modified for supporting the entire body weight, and a shock-absorbing arch helps the foot to cope with the added load. The great toe is no longer opposable, as it is in quadrupedal apes, but runs parallel to the other digits. The foot is now a propulsive lever for upright walking rather than a grasping device for arboreal travel. The arms have also become less suited to climbing: both the limb as a whole and the fingers have grown shorter than they are in the apes.

Lucy's ancestors must have left the trees and risen from four limbs onto two well before her time, probably at the very beginning of human evolution. I have suggested an explanation of why bipedality, with its many disadvantages, appeared long before our ancestors could have put their freed hands to use in carrying tools or weapons: it was part of a novel reproductive strategy that included provisioning by the male, a strategy that enabled the first hominids to flourish and diversify. The explanation will continue to be debated, but the evidence is conclusive that this curious form of locomotion was among the first anatomical characteristics to mark the ascent to cognitive life.

Further Resources

BOOKS

Bowler, Peter J. *Theories of Human Evolution.* Baltimore, Md.: Johns Hopkins University Press, 1986.

Inman, Verne T., Henry J. Ralston, and Frank Todd. *Human Walking.* New York: Williams and Wilkins, 1981.

Johanson, Donald C., and Edey Maitland. *Lucy: The Beginning of Humankind.*

Lewin, Roger. *In the Age of Mankind: A Smithsonian Book of Human Evolution.* Washington, D.C.: Smithsonian, 1988.

———. *Principles of Human Evolution: A Core Textbook.* Malden, Mass.: Blackwell Science, 1998.

PERIODICALS

Junger, William L. "Relative Joint Size and Hominid Locomotor Adaptations With Implications for the Evolution of Hominid Bipedalism." *Journal of Human Evolution,* 1988, 247.

Lovejoy, C. Owen. "The Origin of Man." *Science,* January 23, 1981, 341–350.

Tague, Robert G., and C. Owen Lovejoy. "The Obstetric Pelvis of AL 288-1 (Lucy)." *Journal of Human Evolution,* May 1986, 237–255.

Weaver, Kenneth F., Richard Leakey, and Alan Walker. "The Search for Early Man." *National Geographic,* November 1985, 560–629.

WEBSITES

"Finding Lucy." Evolution, Public Broadcasting Service. Available online at http://www.pbs.org/wgbh/evolution/library/07/1/l_071_01.html; website home page: http://www.pbs.org/wgbh/evolution/index.html (accessed May 22, 2003).

"Human Evolution: Lucy in the Earth." A Science Odyssey, You Try It, Public Broadcasting Service. Available online at http://www.pbs.org/wgbh/aso/tryit/evolution/lucy.html; website home page: http://www.pbs.org/wgbh/aso/tryit/ (accessed May 22, 2003).

"Physical Mapping of Human DNA: An Overview of the DOE Program"

Journal article

By: Anthony V. Carrano

Date: Summer 1989

Source: Carrano, Anthony V. "Physical Mapping of Human DNA: An Overview of the DOE Program." *Human Genome Quarterly* 1, no. 2, Summer 1989. Available online at http://genome.gsc.riken.go.jp/hgmis/publicat/hgn/v1n2/01phymap.htm (accessed February 26, 2003).

About the Author: Anthony V. Carrano (1942–) received a doctorate in biophysics from the University of California, Berkeley, in 1972. Since 1987, he has been a geneticist at Lawrence Livermore National Laboratory and since 1990 the director of the Human Genome Center. He is also an adjunct professor at the University of California Davis School of Medicine. ∎

Introduction

In 1866, Gregor Mendel announced that particles (genes) code for traits in pea plants and that pea plants passed these traits unaltered from generation to generation. This implied that genes code for traits in other plants and animals including humans. Scientists ignored his work until three scientists rediscovered his paper on pea hybridization in 1900. This discovery launched the science of genetics.

Early in the twentieth century, scientists understood that genes code for traits through a chemical pathway, implying that genes are made of molecules. This realization led chemists to seek the chemistry of genes. In 1953, James Watson and Francis Crick identified deoxyribonucleic acid (DNA) as the molecule of heredity. DNA is a spiral ladder with each rung formed by the bonding of two of the four nucleotide bases: adenine, guanine, cytosine, and thymine. Adenine always bonds with thymine and guanine with cytosine. If half a strand of DNA contains cytosine, cytosine, guanine, thymine, and guanine, the other half must contain guanine, guanine, cytosine, adenine, and cytosine.

In the early 1970s, Hamilton Smith and others discovered that a class of enzymes acted as a knife in cutting out a series of nucleotide bases from a strand of DNA. Moreover, each enzyme cut out only a specific sequence of nucleotide bases. Enzyme A, for example, might cut out only the sequence adenine, adenine, cytosine, and guanine, whereas enzyme B might cut out only the sequence thymine and guanine. Every time enzyme A cut out a strand of DNA, a scientist would know he or she had the sequence adenine, adenine, cytosine, and guanine. In this way, scientists could use this class of enzymes to decode DNA strands of great length.

Genes and thus DNA are in a line on chromosomes, the linear units in the nucleus of every cells. Each gene and its chromosome are analogous to a roll of breath mints, with each mint analogous to a gene and a roll to a chromosome. Every species (all plants or animals that can interbreed to produce fertile offspring) has a fixed number of chromosomes. Scientists who decode the sequence of nucleotide bases on each chromosome will have a DNA map of that species.

Significance

Every human has twenty-three pairs of chromosomes, having inherited half from the mother and the other half from the father. The twenty-three chromosomes from each parent pair to form the full complement of forty-six chromosomes in every human. Scientists number these chromosomes 1 through 23, with each number corresponding to 1 or the other of the pair of chromosomes that occupy that number. Chromosome 1 means either chromosome 1A or 1B, either of which can occupy the position of chromosome 1.

In 1989, Anthony V. Carrano announced that scientists throughout the United States would work with the U.S. Department of Energy's (DOE) Office of Health and Environmental Research to map the human genome (all the genes in the forty-six chromosomes of humans). That is, scientists would work to map the sequence of nucleotide bases in all twenty-three pairs of human chromosomes. Already, Carrano stated, Columbia University molecular biologists Cassandra Smith and Charles Canter were mapping chromosome 21. They were also mapping a portion of chromosome 4 in hopes of identifying the genes that cause Huntington's disease.

This example suggests that the promise of the Human Genome Project (the mapping of the sequence of all nucleotide bases in all twenty-three pairs of chromosomes) lies in the identification of genes that cause diseases in humans. Beyond this, however, scientists must learn how to disable (turn off) genes that cause diseases if they are to use the mapping of the human genome to its fullest. The ability to disable genes that cause diseases would revolutionize medicine, moving it beyond the treatment of diseases to the prevention of them. Such a revolution would increase both longevity and quality of life.

Primary Source

"Physical Mapping of Human DNA: An Overview of the DOE Program" [excerpt]

SYNOPSIS: In the following excerpt, Carrano announces that scientists throughout the United States will work with the DOE's Office of Health and Environmental Research to map the human genome.

Introduction

Just as a map of the earth's surface details geographical landmarks and distances, a map of DNA provides similar information about the human genome. For the DNA map, however, the landmarks are not cities, but genes or restriction enzyme recognition sites, and the distances between landmarks are not in miles, but in numbers of base pairs (bp). DNA maps can have either a genetic or a physical basis and offer various degrees of resolution. Generally, a strategy for physical mapping is chosen that is consistent with the interests of the scientists and with the laboratory's general programmatic effort.

There are two primary types of physical maps: a *macrorestriction map* and an *ordered-clone map.* The highest resolution physical map is, of course, the DNA sequence itself—the ultimate goal of the human genome effort. Given the present state of sequencing technologies, it is neither economically feasible nor technologically appropriate to begin a large-scale project now to sequence the entire genome of man. Rather, the construction of physical maps, as a first priority, will facilitate future sequencing efforts. Knowledge of the physical map and its correlation to the genetic map will guide the scientific community in assigning priorities to regions of the genome to be sequenced. A physical map of DNA clones can provide the raw material for sequencing.

Macrorestriction Maps

A macrorestriction map is a linearly ordered set of large fragments of DNA representing a chromosome region or, potentially, an entire human chromosome. The fragments are derived by cutting very high molecular weight DNA with restriction enzymes whose recognition sites are of low occurrence in the genome. Since the dinucleotide sequence CpG is estimated to be underrepresented in the human genome by about fivefold, restriction enzymes that contain such dinucleotides as part of their recognition site will cut the DNA infrequently. Typical of the restriction enzymes in this category are *Not* I (GCG-GCCGC) and *Mlu* I (ACGCGT), which theoretically cut,

on the average, every million or 300,000 bp, respectively.

To obtain such large fragments of DNA, shearing must be minimized during the DNA isolation process. First, the cells are embedded in agar blocks, and then the DNA fragments are electrophoresed out of the agar blocks and separated using an alternating-field electrophoresis system. Depending on the conditions of electrophoresis, fragments ranging in size from about 50 kilobases (Kbp) to 10 megabases (Mbp) can be seen either by staining the gel with ethidium bromide or by performing Southern blots and identifying specific fragments by hybridization to radiolabeled probes.

Even with the rare-cutting restriction enzymes, the human genome contains too many fragments to separate on a single gel lane. Thus for most mapping studies, hybrid cells containing a single human chromosome are used, and the human chromosome-specific fragments are identified by Southern hybridization using total human repetitive DNA, human Alu-sequence probes, or human unique sequence probes.

A macrorestriction map, developed by using rare-cutting enzymes, provides information at a level of organization between the intact chromosome and cloned fragments of DNA. It serves as a global map of fragments spanning large regions of DNA. More detailed maps will then be related to the global macrorestriction map.

Obtaining relative order of the restriction fragments is also possible. For example, techniques have been developed to construct probes that contain rare-cutting restriction sites and their flanking DNA. These are called *linking probes* because they uniquely identify adjacent restriction fragments. If DNA is digested with *Not* I and hybridized to a *Not* I linking probe, the two adjacent fragments will be identified on the gel. A collection of such linking probes would then allow one to order the *Not* I restriction fragments for the chromosome or region of interest.

Another interesting application exploiting the rare-cutting restriction sites is to identify DNA polymorphisms. Since these sites are rich in CpG, which are also targets for methylation, the methylation sensitivity of many of the rare-cutters prevents them from cleaving the methylated site. In comparing two sources of DNA, differences in restriction fragment patterns might, therefore, identify patterns of DNA methylation. Finally, it has been shown that *Not* I sites will often cluster in islands that are located adjacent to gene sequences. This information can be used to signal gene locations in a segment of DNA.

The Human Genome Program in the Department of Energy (DOE) Office of Health and Environmental Research supports a number of projects that develop or make use of macrorestriction maps of DNA. To highlight the various strategies and techniques, a few of these research activities are delineated here.

At Columbia University, Cassandra Smith and Charles Cantor have been constructing maps of the entire human chromosome 21 and the Huntington's region on the short arm of chromosome 4. Using somatic cell hybrids containing human chromosome 21 and several rare-cutting restriction enzymes, as well as human repetitive, unique sequence, and linking probes, Smith and Cantor estimate that about 40 Mbp of the chromosome can be recognized by the rare-cutter fragments on a gel. The researchers are in the process of determining the order of the fragments.

Thomas Caskey and his colleagues at the Baylor College of Medicine have established a macrorestriction map spanning a 7-Mbp region on the human X chromosome containing the G6PD gene cluster.

A group under the direction of Michael McClelland at the University of Chicago is exploiting the methylation sensitivity of some of the rare-cutting enzymes. By using methylation-sensitive restriction enzymes together with modification methyltransferases, McClelland's group is able to control partial digest reactions. Moreover, by first methylating adenine with a methyltransferase and then using methylation-dependent rare-cutters, very large DNA fragments (3-5 Mbp) are produced in some genomes. In conjunction with Carol Westbrook, also at Chicago, the researchers plan to apply these techniques to create a macrorestriction map for a region of chromosome 5.

While the rare-cutter restriction map is extremely useful, it does not provide cloned DNA for further analysis. Complementary methods which make use of cloned DNA are necessary.

Ordered Clone Maps

An ordered clone map is a collection of cloned DNA fragments arranged in the same linear position that they would have along the native chromosome. The clones are generally derived from primary arrayed libraries, and each clone is maintained either in the well of a microtiter tray or in an individual tube.

A researcher conducts DNA electrophoresis analysis to compare DNA fragments. This is one technique used to map the structures of genes. © **VISUALS UNLIMITED. REPRODUCED BY PERMISSION.**

The DNA may be cloned in any one of the vector systems [e.g., yeast artificial chromosomes (YACs), cosmids, phage, or even plasmids]. The larger the cloned insert, the lower the map resolution; but, fewer clones must be analyzed to construct the map. Three of the DOE-supported efforts to create clone maps rely primarily on cosmids which contain about 40 Kbp of insert. However, large, human DNA inserts of more than 100 Kbp are being cloned by YAC cloning vectors now being developed at Los Alamos National Laboratory (LANL), Lawrence Berkeley Laboratory (LBL), and Lawrence Livermore National Laboratory (LLNL), in collaboration with university-based investigators.

Clones from multiple libraries, and possibly from multiple vector systems, are believed to be necessary to complete a map of the entire chromosome. At least two factors contribute to this assumption:

1. The inability to clone certain DNA sequences in some vector systems results in nonrepresentative libraries.

2. The nonuniform growth of individual clones leads to sample bias during clone selection. . . .

In this overview, some of the physical mapping strategies currently being supported by the DOE Human Genome Program have been summarized. The laboratory techniques used to implement these strategies are state of the art and continually being improved. There is no *one optimal strategy* for physical mapping. In fact, new methods probably will be developed that replace or refine all of the present approaches. As those who are involved in physical mapping quickly realize, none of these techniques alone will produce a complete map. The final map likely will be derived from a combination of the strategies discussed above, as well as others yet to come.

The Genetic Map: A Tool to Locate Relative Position of Genes

The genetic map is an important and complementary tool in human genome research. It can be used to locate the relative positions of genes, to assist in the study of the heritability of genetic diseases, and, ultimately, to validate the physical map. A genetic map of DNA provides information on the relative location of genes or gene markers (e.g., restriction fragment length polymorphisms, RFLPs). The distances on the genetic map are measured in centimorgans (cM), a measure of the recombination frequency between loci. The greater the distance between two loci, the greater the probability a meiotic recombination event will occur. While the genetic map does provide relative order for the loci on a chromosome, the frequency of recombination is not an accurate measure of physical distance. It is now well documented that some regions of DNA recombine much more frequently than others; therefore, the recombination frequency will either over- or underestimate the true distance in base pairs. The resolution of the genetic map is dependent upon the

number of meiotic recombination events observed between loci as detected by RFLPs in two- or three-generation families with a large number of sibs.

Further Resources

BOOKS

Bodmer, Walter F., and Robin McKie. *The Book of Man: The Human Genome Project and the Quest to Discover Our Genetic Heritage.* New York: Scribner, 1995.

Copper, Necia G. *The Human Genome Project: Deciphering the Blueprint of Heredity.* Mill Valley, Calif.: University Science Books, 1994.

David, Joel. *Mapping the Code: The Human Genome Project and the Choices of Modern Science.* New York: Wiley, 1990.

Lee, Thomas F. *The Human Genome Project: Cracking the Genetic Code of Life.* New York: Plenum, 1991.

Shostak, Stanley. *Evolution of Sameness and Difference: Perspectives on the Human Genome Project.* Amsterdam: Harwood Academic, 1999.

Yudell, Michael, and Robert DeSalle, eds. *The Genomics Revolution: Unveiling the Unity of Life.* Washington, D.C.: Joseph Henry, 2002.

PERIODICALS

Kluger, Jeffrey. "Who Owns Our Genes?" *Time,* January 11, 1999, 51.

Wade, Nicholas. "Human Genome Sequence Has Errors, Scientists Say." *The New York Times,* June 11, 2002, F4.

WEBSITES

"Human Genome Project Information." DOEGenomes.org, Oak Ridge National Laboratory. Available online at http://www.ornl.gov/hgmis (accessed May 25, 2003).

"Human Genome Research." Office of Biological and Environmental Research, Office of Science, U.S. Department of Energy. Available online at http://www.er.doe.gov/production/ober/hug_top.html; website home page: http://www.er.doe.gov/ (accessed May 25, 2003).

National Human Genome Research Institute. Available online at http://www.genome.gov/ (accessed May 25, 2003).

12

SPORTS

JACQUELINE LESHKEVICH

Entries are arranged in chronological order by date of primary source. For entries with one primary source, the entry title is the same as the primary source title. Entries with more than one primary source have an overall entry title, followed by the titles of the primary sources.

Important Events in Sports, 1980–1989

1980

- On January 1, Alabama defeats Arkansas, 24-9, in the Sugar Bowl and is later voted the national champion of college football for 1979.

- On January 7, the Philadelphia Flyers' National Hockey League (NHL) record-setting streak of thirty-five games without a loss comes to an end when they are beaten by the Minnesota North Stars, 7-1.

- On January 20, the Pittsburgh Steelers win their fourth Super Bowl in six years with a 31-19 victory over the Los Angeles Rams; also, the United States announces that it will not participate in the 1980 Summer Olympics in Moscow in protest of the Soviet Union's invasion of Afghanistan.

- On February 12, the XXIII Winter Olympic Games open in Lake Placid, New York. Bobsledders Willie Davenport and Jeff Gadley become the first African American athletes to represent the United States in the Winter Olympics.

- On February 22, the United States Olympic ice hockey team upsets the Soviet Union, 4-3. Two days later the U.S. team wins the gold medal by defeating Finland, 4-2.

- On February 23, American speed skater Eric Heiden wins the gold medal in the 10,000-meter event in a world-record-setting time of 14 minutes, 28.13 seconds. It is his fifth gold medal in five events.

- On March 24, Louisville defeats UCLA, 59-54, to win their first men's NCAA basketball championship.

- On March 26, Nancy Lieberman of Old Dominion University wins her second straight Margaret Wade Trophy as the player of the year in women's college basketball.

- On April 6, hockey legend Gordie Howe, age fifty-two, plays the final regular season game of his thirty-two-year career.

- On April 12, Milwaukee Brewers' Cecil Cooper and Don Money both hit grand slams in the second inning against the Boston Red Sox.

- On April 16, Arthur Ashe, the first black man to win major professional tennis tournaments, announces his retirement.

- On April 21, Rosie Ruiz apparently wins the eighty-fourth Boston Marathon, but is later disqualified when it is discovered that she cheated by cutting the course.

- On May 16, the Los Angeles Lakers win the National Basketball Association (NBA) championship by defeating the Philadelphia 76ers in six games.

- On June 6, nineteen-year-old Wayne Gretzky of the Edmonton Oilers wins the Hart Memorial Trophy (the league's MVP award) and the Lady Byng Memorial Trophy, thus becoming the youngest player ever to win two major NHL awards in the same season.

- On June 7, Temperence Hill, a 53-1 longshot, wins the Belmont Stakes.

- On June 12, Jack Nicklaus sets a record for the lowest seventy-two-hole score in any U.S. Open championship, with a total of 272. It is his fourth Open win since 1962.

- On June 20, Roberto Duran defeats Sugar Ray Leonard in fifteen rounds to win the World Boxing Council (WBC) welterweight championship.

- On July 5, Bjorn Borg defeats John McEnroe in the Wimbledon finals in five sets.

- On July 19, the XXII Summer Olympic games in Moscow begin, the first Olympics ever staged in a Communist nation. The United States and sixty-four other countries boycott the games to protest the Soviet invasion of Afghanistan.

- On July 30, Houston Astros pitcher J.R. Richard suffers a stroke during practice.

- On August 3, Al Kaline and Duke Snider are among those inducted into the Baseball Hall of Fame.

- On August 10, Jack Nicklaus wins the nineteenth major tournament of his career by winning the Professional Golf Association (PGA) championship in Rochester, New York.

- On August 11, Reggie Jackson of the New York Yankees hits his four hundreth home run.

- On August 19, the *Los Angeles Times* reports that between 40 and 75 percent of the players in the NBA use cocaine.

- On September 7, John McEnroe beats Bjorn Borg to win his second straight U.S. Open singles championship.

- On September 25, the U.S. yacht *Freedom* completes the twenty-fourth consecutive defense of the America's Cup.

- On October 2, WBC heavyweight champion Larry Holmes defeats Muhammad Ali in ten rounds in Ali's penultimate fight.

- On October 4, Alabama football coach Paul "Bear" Bryant wins his 300th game.

- On October 5, George Brett finishes the season with a .390 batting average, the highest major-league mark in thirty-nine years.

- On October 15, Manny Mota of the Los Angeles Dodgers collects his major-league record 150th career pinch hit.

- On October 21, the Philadelphia Phillies defeat the Kansas City Royals in six games to win the World Series.

- On November 3, in Los Angeles, British and European bantamweight champion Johnny Owen dies as the result of injuries suffered in a September 19 title bout with WBC champion Lupe Pintor.

- On November 25, Sugar Ray Leonard avenges his loss to Roberto Duran to regain the WBC welterweight championship when Duran turns his back on Leonard in the eighth round and says, "No más."

- On November 29, the three-point field goal line is used in college basketball for the first time on an experimental basis by the Southern Conference.

- On December 20, as an experiment NBC broadcasts an NFL game between the Miami Dolphins and the New York Jets without a play-by-play announcer and color commentator.

1981

- On January 1, Georgia defeats Notre Dame, 17-10, in the Sugar Bowl and is later voted the college football national champion for 1980.

- On January 13, the NCAA votes to sponsor Division I women's championships in twelve sports after the 1981–1982 season.

- On January 25, the Oakland Raiders defeat the Philadelphia Eagles, 27-10, in Super Bowl XV.

- On March 29, Phil Mahre is the first American to win the men's overall World Cup skiing championship.

- On March 30, led by sophomore guard Isiah Thomas, Indiana beats North Carolina, 63-50, to win the men's NCAA basketball championship.

- On April 5, Edmonton Oiler Wayne Gretzky, age twenty, becomes the youngest player to win an NHL points title, with 55 goals and 109 assists for a league-record 164 points.

- On April 9, Frank Robinson of the San Francisco Giants becomes the first African American manager in the National League.

- On April 24, jockey Bill Shoemaker wins his eight thousandth race.

- On April 29, Steve Carlton of the Philadelphia Phillies becomes the first left-handed pitcher to strike out three thousand batters.

- On May 14, the Boston Celtics defeat the Houston Rockets in six games to win their fourteenth NBA championship.

- On May 15, Len Barker of the Cleveland Indians pitches a perfect game.

- On May 27, Julius "Dr. J" Erving of the Philadelphia 76ers wins the NBA's Most Valuable Player (MVP) award, the first noncenter to do so in sixteen years.

- On June 23, the longest game in the history of organized baseball ends when the Triple-A Pawtucket Red Sox beat the Rochester Red Wings, 3-2, in 33 innings.

- On July 3, Chris Evert Lloyd wins her third women's singles lawn tennis championship at Wimbledon by defeating Hana Mandlikova.

- On July 4, John McEnroe upsets Bjorn Borg to win his first men's singles tennis championship at Wimbledon.

- On July 31, a midseason strike by Major League Baseball players comes to an end. The forty-nine-day strike, which saw 713 games canceled, is the longest in the history of professional sports.

- On August 2, the Baseball Hall of Fame inducts Bob Gibson, Johnny Mize, and Rube Foster.

- On August 10, Pete Rose collects his 3,631st hit, breaking Stan Musial's all-time National League mark.

- On September 12, Tracy Austin wins her second U.S. Open women's singles title by defeating Martina Navratilova.

- On September 13, John McEnroe beats Bjorn Borg to win his third consecutive U.S. Open men's singles title.

- On September 16, Sugar Ray Leonard defeats Thomas Hearns in the fourteenth round of their bout to unify the welterweight championship of the world. It is the single richest sports event in history to that point, grossing approximately $35 million.

- On September 20, Gary Gaetti, Kent Hrbek, and Tim Laudner of the Minnesota Twins all hit home runs in their first major-league game.

- On September 26, Nolan Ryan of the Houston Astros pitches his major-league record fifth no-hitter; also, the Chicago Sting beat the New York Cosmos, 1-0, in a shootout to win the Soccer Bowl, the championship of the North American Soccer League (NASL).

- On October 25, Alberto Salazar sets a record for the fastest time in the New York City Marathon: 2 hours, 8 minutes, 13 seconds; Allison Roe of New Zealand sets a record for the best women's time: 2 hours, 25 minutes, 28 seconds.

- On October 28, the Los Angeles Dodgers defeat the New York Yankees to win the World Series in six games after trailing two games to none.

- On November 28, Alabama coach Bear Bryant becomes the all-time winningest coach in major-college football with his 315th victory.

- On December 2, less than a month after winning the National League Cy Young award, Fernando Valenzuela of the Los Angeles Dodgers wins the National League Rookie of the Year award. Valenzuela is the first player to win both awards in the same season.

- On December 22, John Henry, a six-year-old gelding, is named Horse of the Year at the annual Eclipse Awards.

1982

- On January 1, Clemson beats Nebraska, 22-15, in the Orange Bowl and is later voted the national champion of college football for 1981.

- On January 11, WBC heavyweight champion Larry Holmes knocks out Gerry Cooney in the thirteenth round of their title bout; each man earns $7 million for his efforts.

- On January 10, Joe Montana of the San Francisco 49ers completes a 6-yard touchdown pass to Dwight Clark with 51 seconds left to beat the Dallas Cowboys in the National Football Conference (NFC) championship game, 28-27.

- On January 24, the San Francisco 49ers win Super Bowl XVI by beating the Cincinnati Bengals, 26-21.

- On February 27, Earl Anthony becomes the first bowler to win $1 million in his career.

- On March 13, Scott Hamilton and Elaine Zayak win gold medals at the world figure skating championships in Copenhagen, Denmark.

- On March 18, the first NCAA women's swimming and diving championship is held in Gainesville, Florida.

- On March 28, Louisiana Tech defeats Cheyney State of Pennsylvania, 76-62, to win the first women's Division I NCAA basketball championship.

- On March 29, freshman guard Michael Jordan hits a game-winning jump shot with 32 seconds left to lead North Carolina over Georgetown, 63-62, winning the men's NCAA basketball championship.

- On April 4, Edmonton Oiler center Wayne Gretzky sets three NHL single-season records: in goals (92), assists (120), and total points (212).

- On April 18, George Gervin of the San Antonio Spurs wins his fourth NBA scoring title by averaging 32.3 points per game.

- On May 6, Gaylord Perry of the Seattle Mariners wins his three hundredth career game.

- On May 7, a federal district court decides in favor of the Oakland Raiders in that team's civil antitrust suit against the NFL, clearing the way for the team to move to Los Angeles.

- On May 12, the twelve-team United States Football League (USFL) is founded.

- On May 16, the New York Islanders sweep the Vancouver Canucks, four games to none, to become the first U.S.-based NHL team to win three consecutive Stanley Cups.

- On May 30, Gordon Johncock wins the Indianapolis 500 by the narrowest margin in the race's history, 0.16 of a second ahead of Rick Mears; also, Cal Ripken, Jr., of the Baltimore Orioles begins his record-setting consecutive-games-played streak.

- On June 8, Wayne Gretzky of the Edmonton Oilers becomes the first player to win an NHL MVP award by a unanimous vote.

- On July 3, Martina Navratilova wins her third women's singles championship at Wimbledon by defeating Chris Evert Lloyd. The following day Jimmy Connors wins his second men's Wimbledon singles title by defeating John McEnroe.

- On August 1, Hank Aaron and Frank Robinson are among those inducted into the Baseball Hall of Fame.

- On August 4, Joel Youngblood gets hits for two different teams in two different cities on same day when he is traded from the New York Mets to the Montreal Expos.

- On August 8, Ray Floyd wins the sixty-fourth PGA championship at the Southern Hills Country Club in Tulsa, Oklahoma.

- On September 12, Jimmy Connors wins his fourth U.S. Open men's singles championship. The previous day Chris Evert Lloyd won her sixth U.S. Open women's singles title.

- On September 19, the New York Cosmos win their fourth NASL title in five years by edging the Seattle Sounders, 1-0, to win the Soccer Bowl.

- On September 21, NFL players strike for the first time in the league's sixty-three-year history.

- On September 25, Eddie Robinson, head football coach at Grambling, wins his 300th game as Grambling beats Florida A & M, 42-21.

- On October 20, the St. Louis Cardinals win the World Series four games to three over the Milwaukee Brewers.

- On October 26, Steve Carlton of the Philadelphia Phillies wins a record fourth Cy Young award.

- On November 13, Duk Koo Kim suffers fatal brain damage in a fight with Ray "Boom Boom" Mancini for the World Boxing Association (WBA) lightweight championship.

- On November 17, the NFL players' strike comes to an end after fifty-seven days. The strike led to the cancellation of 112 of 224 scheduled games and lost players, owners, television networks, cities, and businesses an estimated $450 million.

- On November 20, On the last play of the game, trailing Stanford, 20-19, the California football team receives a kickoff. Thinking the game is over, Stanford's marching band takes the field. California runs the ball back, through the band and utilizing five laterals, to score a game winning touchdown.

- On November 28, the United States wins its twenty-eighth Davis Cup by beating France, 4-1.

- On December 24, Chaminade defeats number-one-ranked Virginia, 77-72, in one of the biggest upsets in men's college basketball history.

1983

- On January 1, Penn State defeats Georgia, 27-23, in the Sugar Bowl and is later awarded its first national championship in college football.

- On January 3, Dallas Cowboy running back Tony Dorsett runs for a 99-yard touchdown against the Minnesota Vikings.

- On January 11, at the annual NCAA convention Proposition 48 is passed by a 4-1 margin. Applying only to Division I schools, the proposal mandates minimum scores on entrance tests and graduation from high school with a 2.0 GPA in a core curriculum for all student athletes.

- On January 13, the International Olympic Committee (IOC) presents Jim Thorpe's children with two Olympic gold medals, reversing the decision to strip Thorpe of his 1912 decathlon and pentathlon victories.

- On January 30, the Washington Redskins defeat the Miami Dolphins, 27-17, in Super Bowl XVII. The game draws a record 111.5 million national television viewers.

- On February 23, Heisman Trophy running back Herschel Walker signs a contract with the New Jersey Generals of the USFL.

- On April 2, seven-foot four-inch Ralph Sampson of Virginia wins his third consecutive Adolph Rupp Trophy as the men's college basketball player of the year.

- On April 4, North Carolina State upsets Houston, 54-52, on a last-second shot to win the men's NCAA basketball championship. The game draws a record fifty million television viewers.

- On April 18, Joan Benoit sets a world record for women in the Boston Marathon, winning the race in 2 hours, 22 minutes, 42 seconds.

- On April 27, Nolan Ryan of the Houston Astros breaks Walter Johnson's career strikeout record with strikeout number 3,508.

- On May 17, the New York Islanders defeat the Edmonton Oilers in four games to win their fourth Stanley Cup in a row, only the second NHL team to do so.

- On May 27, Tom Sneva wins the sixty-seventh Indianapolis 500. His average speed of 162.117 MPH is the second fastest in the race's history.

- On May 31, the Philadelphia 76ers win the NBA championship by sweeping the Los Angeles Lakers.

- On July 2, Martina Navratilova wins her fourth women's singles championship at Wimbledon. The following day John McEnroe wins his second men's Wimbledon singles title.

- On July 6, the American League breaks its eleven game losing streak in the All-Star Game by beating the National League, 13-3, at Comiskey Park.

- On July 17, golfer Tom Watson wins his fifth British Open; also, the Michigan Panthers beat the Philadelphia Stars, 24-22, to win the first USFL championship.

- On July 24, George Brett of the Kansas City Royals hits his famous "pine tar" home run against the New York Yankees to give the Royals a 5-4 lead in the 9th. The homer was disallowed at the time because the pine tar extended too far on the barrel of the bat, but the umpire's decision was reversed on appeal.

- On July 29, Steve Garvey's National League record 1,207 consecutive-games-played streak ends when he breaks his thumb.

- On July 31, Brooks Robinson, Juan Marichal, George Kell, and Walter Alston are inducted into the Baseball Hall of Fame.

- On August 19, Billy Cannon, college football's Player of the Year in 1959, is sentenced to five years in prison and fined ten thousand dollars for masterminding a multimillion-dollar counterfeiting scheme.

- On September 11, Jimmy Connors wins his fifth U.S. Open men's singles championship. The previous day Martina Navratilova won her first U.S. Open women's singles title.

- On September 16, Philadelphia Phillies pitcher Steve Carlton wins his three hundredth game.

- On September 26, *Australia II* beats the U.S. yacht *Liberty* to win the America's Cup, the first American loss in the competition in the 132-year history of the event.

- On October 16, the Baltimore Orioles defeat the Philadelphia Phillies to win the World Series four games to one.

- On November 8, Dale Murphy of the Atlanta Braves wins his second consecutive National League MVP award.

- On November 10, middleweight champion "Marvelous" Marvin Hagler scores a unanimous fifteen-round victory over Roberto Duran.

- On November 16, Cal Ripken, Jr., becomes the first player in major-league history to win Rookie of the Year in his first season and Most Valuable Player in his second season.

- On November 21, Darryl Strawberry of the New York Mets is named National League Rookie of the Year.

- On December 3, Ray Meyer, men's basketball coach at De-Paul for more than forty years, wins his seven hundredth game.

1984

- On January 2, Miami defeats Nebraska, 31-30, in the Orange Bowl and is later voted its first national championship in college football.

- On January 22, the Los Angeles Raiders win Super Bowl XVIII by beating the Washington Redskins, 38-9.

- On January 27, Edmonton Oiler Wayne Gretzky's NHL record-setting fifty-one game scoring streak comes to an end against the Los Angeles Kings.

- On February 8, the XIV Winter Olympic Games open in Sarajevo, Yugoslavia.

- On February 16, Bill Johnson becomes the first American to win a gold medal in the Olympic downhill skiing event.

- On February 19, the XIV Winter Olympic Games end. The Soviet Union wins the most medals, twenty-five, while the United States finishes tied for fifth, with eight medals.

- On March 29, the Baltimore Colts of the NFL leave Baltimore for Indianapolis. The team had been in Baltimore since 1953.

- On April 1, Southern California (USC) defeats Tennessee, 72-61, to win its second consecutive women's Division I NCAA basketball championship.

- On April 2, Georgetown beats Houston, 84-75, to win the men's college basketball championship. John Thompson becomes the first African American coach to win an NCAA Division I basketball title.

- On April 5, Kareem Abdul-Jabbar of the Los Angeles Lakers becomes the NBA's all-time scorer by breaking Wilt Chamberlain's record of 31,419 points. Abdul-Jabbar finishes his career in 1989 with 38,387 points.

- On April 13, twenty-one years to the day after his first major-league hit, Pete Rose of the Cincinnati Reds doubles against the Philadelphia Phillies to become the first National League player to accumulate four thousand hits.

- On May 7, the Soviet Union announces that it will not attend the 1984 Summer Olympic games in Los Angeles.

- On May 15, Magic Johnson of the Los Angeles Lakers sets an NBA playoff-game record by passing for twenty-four assists.

- On May 19, the Edmonton Oilers, led by Wayne Gretzky, win their first Stanley Cup with a 5-2 victory over the New York Islanders, taking the NHL championship series four games to one.

- On June 12, the Boston Celtics defeat the Los Angeles Lakers in seven games to win the NBA championship.

- On June 18, Fuzzy Zoeller wins the eighty-fourth U.S. Open in a 18-hole playoff against Greg Norman.

- On June 19, after the Houston Rockets select Hakeem Olajuwan and the Portland Trail Blazers choose Sam Bowie, the Chicago Bulls take Michael Jordan with the third pick in the NBA college draft.

- On June 27, the United States Supreme Court rules, 7-2, that the NCAA had violated federal antitrust law by preventing individual schools from negotiating the rights to football telecasts

- On June 29, Pete Rose of the Cincinnati Reds sets a major-league record by playing in his 3,309th baseball game.

- On July 28, the XXIII Summer Olympics open in Los Angeles.

- On August 3, Mary Lou Retton wins the Olympic gold medal in the all-around women's gymnastic competition by earning perfect scores in the floor exercise and the vault.

- On August 4, Carl Lewis wins the gold medal in the 100-meter dash, his first of four in the Summer Olympics.

- On August 8, Greg Louganis wins the springboard and platform Olympic diving competitions, setting world records in both events.

- On August 10, Mary Decker and Zola Budd collide during the 3,000-meter run at the Olympics. Maricica Puica of Romania wins the race.

- On August 20, Nancy Lopez wins the richest prize on the Ladies' Professional Golf Association (LPGA) tour, sixty-five thousand dollars, with a victory in the World Championship of Women's Golf.

- On August 23, controversial television sportscaster Howard Cosell quits ABC's *Monday Night Football* after fourteen years of telecasts.

- On September 17, Reggie Jackson of the California Angels hits the five hundredth home run of his career.

- On September 30, California Angel Mike Witt pitches a perfect game against the Texas Rangers; also, New York Yankee Don Mattingly goes 4 for 5 to finish the season with .343 batting average, and thus becomes only the seventh major-league player since 1900 to win a batting crown in his first full season.

- On October 1, Peter Ueberroth succeeds Bowie Kuhn as baseball commissioner.

- On October 7, Walter Payton of the Chicago Bears rushes for 154 yards against the New Orleans Saints to bring his career rushing total to 12,400 yards, breaking the previous mark of 12,312 held by Jim Brown. Payton finished his career in 1987 with 16,726 yards.

- On October 11, Mario Lemieux makes his NHL debut with the Pittsburgh Penguins.

- On October 14, the Detroit Tigers, who started the season with a 35-5 record, beat the San Diego Padres four games to one to win the World Series.

- On October 17, the USFL files a $1.3 billion antitrust suit against the NFL.

- On October 27, running back Ruben Mays rushes for 357 yards for Washington State against Oregon, setting an NCAA record for most rushing yards in a game; also, Mississippi Valley State wide receiver Jerry Rice sets a Division I-AA record with five touchdown catches in one game.

- On November 6, relief pitcher Willie Hernandez of the Detroit Tigers wins the American League MVP award to go with his American League Cy Young award.

- On November 19, twenty-year-old New York Mets pitcher Dwight Gooden becomes the youngest player to win the National League Rookie of the Year award.

- On November 23, with six seconds left in the game, Boston College quarterback Doug Flutie scrambles and then completes a 64-yard touchdown pass to lead Boston College over Miami, 47-45. A week later Flutie wins the Heisman Trophy.

- On December 9, Eric Dickerson of the Los Angeles Rams rushes for 215 yards against the Houston Oilers to break O.J. Simpson's single-season mark of 2,003 yards. Dickerson finishes the season with 2,105 yards.

- On December 16, Washington Redskins wide receiver Art Monk catches eleven passes against the St. Louis Cardinals to set an NFL record for receptions in a season with 106.

- On December 17, Dan Marino of the Miami Dolphins throws his forty-eighth touchdown of the year, setting an NFL single-season record.

1985

- On January 3, Brigham Young University, the nation's only undefeated and untied football team, narrowly becomes the 1984 college football champion.

- On January 14, Martina Navratilova wins her hundredth career singles title.

- On January 19, Mary Decker sets a world indoor record in the 2,000 meters with a time of 5:34.52.

- On January 20, the San Francisco 49ers win Super Bowl XIX by beating the Miami Dolphins, 38-16. Las Vegas bookmakers report that a record $40 million is bet on the game.

- On January 22, O.J. Simpson, Joe Namath, Roger Staubach, Pete Rozelle, and Frank Gatski are elected into the Pro Football Hall of Fame.

- On January 27, Chris Evert Lloyd beats Martina Navratilova for the first time in more than two years.

- On February 6, Diann Roffe becomes the first American woman to win a gold medal at the World Alpine Skiing Championships.

- On February 18, Olympic diver Greg Louganis wins the 1984 Sullivan Award as the amateur athlete of the year.

- On March 3, Bill Shoemaker becomes the first jockey to win $100 million in purses.

- On March 6, heavyweight Mike Tyson knocks out Hector Mercedes in the first round to win his first professional fight.

- On March 28, the North American Soccer League announces that it will not operate an outdoor league in 1985.

- On April 1, Villanova University upsets Georgetown, 66-64, to win the NCAA men's basketball championship.

- On April 4, a New Orleans grand jury indicts eight people, including three members of the Tulane men's basketball team, on charges connected to point shaving during the 1984–1985 season.

- On April 14, Steve Garvey of the San Diego Padres plays in his 193rd straight game without committing an error, a major-league record for first basemen.

- On April 15, Marvin Hagler knocks out Thomas Hearns in the third round of their fight for the undisputed middleweight world championship.

- On April 26, Utaz Jazz center Mark Eaton blocks ten shots versus the Houston Rockets to set an NBA playoff-game record.

- On May 16, Michael Jordan of the Chicago Bulls is named the NBA Rookie of the Year.

- On May 30, the Edmonton Oilers win their second consecutive Stanley Cup by beating the Philadelphia Flyers in five games.

- On June 9, the Los Angeles Lakers beat the Boston Celtics, four games to two, to win their third NBA championship of the decade.

- On June 11, Von Hayes of the Philadelphia Phillies leads off a game against the New York Mets with a home run. Later that same inning he hits a grand slam, becoming the first player ever to hit two home runs in the first inning.

- On July 11, Nolan Ryan, thirty-eight, of the Houston Astros strikes out his four thousandth batter.

- On July 14, the Baltimore Stars beat the Oakland Invaders, 28-24, to win their second straight USFL championship. It is the USFL's final game.

- On August 4, Tom Seaver of the Chicago White Sox wins his three hundredth game; also, Rod Carew of the California Angels raps his three thousandth hit.

- On August 7, a major-league players' strike is settled after just one day when a new five-year basic agreement is reached.

- On August 23, Martina Navratilova and Pam Shriver beat Vitas Gerulaitis and sixty-seven-year-old Bobby Riggs to win three hundred thousand dollars in a battle-of-the-sexes doubles tennis exhibition.

- On August 25, twenty-year-old Dwight Gooden of the New York Mets becomes the youngest major-league pitcher to win twenty games in a season.

- On September 11, Pete Rose, the forty-four-year-old player-manager of the Cincinnati Reds, cracks his 4,192nd career hit, breaking Ty Cobb's fifty-seven-year-old record for career hits. Rose retires as a player in 1986 with 4,256 hits.

- On September 21, light-heavyweight champion Michael Spinks upsets previously undefeated heavyweight world champion Larry Holmes by winning a unanimous fifteen-round decision.

- On October 5, Eddie Robinson of Grambling becomes the winningest coach in college football history with his 324th win.

- On October 6, New York Yankees pitcher Phil Niekro, forty-six, wins the three hundredth game of his twenty-two-year career.

- On October 8, former college basketball all-American and 1984 Olympic team captain Lynette Woodward is the first woman to make the Harlem Globetrotters' roster.

- On October 13, Dallas Cowboy Tony Dorsett becomes only the sixth player in NFL history to rush for more than 10,000 yards.

- On October 26, Patrick Ewing of the New York Knicks makes his NBA debut.

- On October 27, after being down three games to one, the Kansas City Royals beat the St. Louis Cardinals in seven games to win the World Series.

- On November 9, running back Joe Dudek of Plymouth State, a Division III college in New Hampshire, sets three NCAA records against Curry College: he rushes for his seventy-sixth touchdown, the seventy-ninth touchdown of his career, and scores the 474th point of his career.

- On November 13, Dwight Gooden of the New York Mets becomes the youngest winner of the National League's Cy Young award after leading the league in wins (24), earned run average (1.53), and strikeouts (268).

- On December 7, Auburn University running back Bo Jackson wins the Heisman Trophy.

- On December 22, Roger Craig of the San Francisco 49ers becomes the first player in NFL history to gain 1,000 yards rushing and receiving in a season.

1986

- On January 1, Oklahoma defeats Penn State, 25-10, in the Orange Bowl and is named the national champion of college football for the 1985 season.

- On January 4, Navy basketball center David Robinson sets an NCAA record with fourteen blocked shots in a game against North Carolina-Wilmington.

- On January 13, NCAA adopts Proposition 48, which had been passed in early 1983.

- On January 25, Mike Tyson knocks out his seventeenth straight opponent to break Rocky Marciano's heavyweight record.

- On January 26, the Chicago Bears rout the New England Patriots, 46-10, in Super Bowl XX.

- On January 28, Denis Potvin of the New York Islanders scores his 271st goal to break Bobby Orr's goal-scoring record for defensemen.

- On February 8, five-foot seven-inch Spud Webb of the Atlanta Hawks wins the NBA's slam dunk competition.

- On February 24, marathoner Joan Benoit Samuelson wins the Sullivan Award as the nation's top amateur athlete.

- On February 25, Alvin Robertson of the San Antonio Spurs achieves a "quadruple double"—20 points, 11 rebounds, 10 assists, and 10 steals; also, Micheal Ray Richardson of the New Jersey Nets is banned from the NBA for cocaine use. It is his third such violation.

- On March 13, Susan Butcher wins the 1,158-mile Iditarod dogsled race.

- On March 15, the University of Iowa wins its ninth consecutive NCAA wrestling championship.

- On March 21, Debi Thomas becomes the first African American to win a women's world figure skating championship.

- On March 30, Texas thrashes USC, 97-81, to win the NCAA women's basketball championship. Texas finishes the season 34-0.

- On March 31, Louisville beats Duke, 72-69, to win the NCAA men's basketball championship.

- On April 2, the NCAA approves the use of the 19-foot 9-inch three-point field goal in college basketball for the 1986–1987 season.

- On April 8, with the first swing of his first major-league at-bat, Will Clark of the San Francisco Giants hits a home run off Houston Astro pitcher Nolan Ryan.

- On April 13, Jack Nicklaus becomes the oldest player to win the Masters, his record-setting sixth victory at Augusta.

- On April 20, Michael Jordan of the Chicago Bulls scores an NBA playoff-record sixty-three points in a losing cause against the Boston Celtics.

- On April 29, the Boston Red Sox's Roger Clemens strikes out twenty Seattle Mariners, including eight in a row.

- On May 3, riding Ferdinand, fifty-four-year-old Bill Shoemaker becomes the oldest jockey to ever win the Kentucky Derby.

- On May 15, Patrick Ewing is honored as the NBA's Rookie of the Year.

- On May 28, Larry Bird wins his third consecutive NBA MVP award.

- On May 31, Bobby Rahal sets a record for the fastest Indianapolis 500, averaging almost 171 MPH.

- On June 1, Pat Bradley wins the LPGA championship and becomes the first woman to win all four of the top women's tournaments: the du Maurier Classic, the U.S. Open, the Dinah Shore, and the LPGA.

- On June 8, the Boston Celtics win their sixteenth NBA championship in six games over the Houston Rockets.

- On June 10, former college star Nancy Lieberman becomes the first woman to play in a men's professional basketball league, the U.S. Basketball League.

- On June 18, forty-one-year-old pitcher Don Sutton wins his three hundredth career game.

- On June 19, Maryland basketball player Len Bias dies from a drug overdose. Two days before, Bias was selected in the NBA college draft by the Boston Celtics.

- On July 6, the Atlanta Braves' Bob Horner hits four home runs in a game, which the Braves lose.

- On July 27, Greg LeMond wins pro cycling's Tour de France, an American first.

- On July 29, the USFL is awarded one dollar in their federal antitrust civil suit against the NFL.

- On August 26, with less than two months to live, former Washington Redskins tight end Jerry Smith discloses that he is suffering from AIDS (acquired immunodeficiency syndrome). Smith is the first prominent athlete known to have AIDS.

- On September 23, Jim Deshaies of the Houston Astros sets a major-league record by striking out the first eight batters of a game.

- On September 25, Mike Scott of the Houston Astros pitches a no-hitter to clinch the National League Western Division title.

- On October 12, in game five of the American League Championship Series (ALCS) Donnie Moore of the California Angels gives up a two-out, two-run home run to Dave Henderson of the Boston Red Sox in the ninth inning, propelling the Red Sox to a 7-6 victory in eleven innings. Three years later the game is said to be a contributory cause in Moore's suicide.

- On October 25, in game six of the World Series Bill Buckner's fielding error on a slow roller in the tenth inning enables the New York Mets to defeat the Boston Red Sox, 6-5. Two nights later the Mets win game seven and the World Series.

- On November 18, Roger Clemens of the Boston Red Sox wins the American League MVP; he already had won the American League Cy Young award after going 24-4 with a 2.24 earned-run average and 238 strikeouts.

- On November 22, Mike Tyson knocks out WBC champion Trevor Berbick in the second round to become, at twenty, the youngest heavyweight champion in history.

- On December 13, Augustana wins its fourth straight Amos Alonzo Stagg Bowl to claim the NCAA Division III national championship.

- On December 25, linebacker Brian Bosworth of Oklahoma is prohibited from playing in the upcoming Orange Bowl because he tests positive for steroids.

- On December 27, Doug Jarvis of the Hartford Whalers plays in his record-breaking 915th consecutive NHL game.

1987

- On January 2, Penn State defeats Miami, 14-10, in the Fiesta Bowl and is later voted the 1986 national college football champion.

- On January 25, the New York Giants beat the Denver Broncos, 39-20, in Super Bowl XXI.

- On February 4, *Stars & Stripes,* captained by Dennis Conner, wins the America's Cup trophy for yachting, avenging Conner's 1983 loss.

- On February 8, with her 35th career victory Nancy Lopez qualifes for the LPGA Hall of Fame.

- On February 25, the NCAA announces sanctions for the scandal-ridden Southern Methodist University (SMU) football program, including the cancellation of its 1987 season.

- On March 7, Mike Tyson wins the WBA title by beating James "Bonecrusher" Smith in twelve rounds.

- On March 9, George Foreman, former heavyweight world champion, ends his ten-year retirement by knocking out Steve Zouski.

- On March 21, Iowa State snaps Iowa's NCAA wrestling championship streak at nine.

- On March 30, Bobby Knight wins his third NCAA men's national college basketball championship when Indiana beats Syracuse, 74-73, on a shot by Keith Smart with five seconds left in the game.

- On April 6, Sugar Ray Leonard defeats Marvin Hagler on points to win the WBC middle-weight championship. It is Leonard's first fight in three years; also, Los Angeles Dodgers' vice president Al Campanis reveals racist attitudes during an interview on *Nightline.*

- On April 9, Wayne Gretzky of the Edmonton Oilers breaks the all-time NHL playoff scoring mark of 176 points set by Jean Beliveau.

- On April 12, golfer Larry Mize wins the Masters in a sudden death playoff when he holes an improbable pitch from 140 feet.

- On May 18, Magic Johnson of the Los Angeles Lakers becomes the first guard in twenty-three years to win the NBA's MVP award.

- On May 24, Al Unser, Sr., wins his fourth Indy 500.

- On June 4, Edwin Moses loses in the 400-meter hurdles. It is his first loss in almost ten years and ends his record-setting victory streak at 122.

- On June 14, the Los Angeles Lakers win the NBA championship by beating the Boston Celtics in six games.

- On June 27, the longest winning streak in baseball history comes to an end as the Salt Lake Trappers, a rookie-league team, loses for the first time in 30 games.

- On July 18, New York Yankee first baseman Don Mattingly ties a major-league record by hitting a home run in eight straight games.

- On August 1, Mike Tyson defeats Tony Tucker in twelve rounds to become the undisputed world heavyweight champion by unifying the IBF, WBA, and WBC titles.

- On August 9, golfer Larry Nelson wins the PGA Championship in sudden death.

- On August 26, Paul Molitor of the Milwaukee Brewers sees his 39-game hitting streak come to an end, the longest streak in the American League since Joe DiMaggio's 56-game streak in 1941.

- On September 19, freshman running back Emmitt Smith, in his first start, rushes for a school-record 224 yards as Florida upsets Alabama, 23-14.

- On September 21, an arbitrator rules that Major-League Baseball owners are guilty of collusion after they fail to sign free agents following the 1985 season.

- On September 29, Don Mattingly hits his sixth grand slam of the season to set a major-league record.

- On October 19, Billy Martin is hired by George Steinbrenner to manage the New York Yankees for the fifth time. He is fired June 23, 1988.

- On October 25, the Minnesota Twins beat the Saint Louis Cardinals four games to three to win the World Series.

- On November 1, Kansas City Royals outfielder Bo Jackson makes his NFL debut with the Los Angeles Raiders. Jackson says professional football will be a "hobby."

- On November 6, Jack Ramsay sets an NBA record for most games coached with 1,559.

- On December 4, Kareem Abdul-Jabbar of the Los Angeles Lakers is held to only seven points by the Milwaukee Bucks, breaking his streak of 787 games in which he scored at least ten points a game.

- On December 6, San Francisco 49er quarterback Joe Montana completes an NFL record 22 straight passes against the Green Bay Packers.

- On December 8, Philadelphia Flyer goaltender Ron Hextall is the first goalie in NHL history to shoot and score a goal.

1988

- On January 1, unbeaten Miami defeats previously unbeaten Oklahoma, 20-14, on their way to winning the 1987 college football national championship.

- On January 9, Brian Boitano wins his fourth straight U.S. men's figure-skating championship.

- On January 17, in the American Football Conference (AFC) championship game, Cleveland Browns running back Ernest Byner fumbles at the goal line as the Browns lose, 38-33, to the Denver Broncos.

- On January 31, the Washington Redskins score 35 points in the second quarter on their way to winning Super Bowl XXII over the Denver Broncos, 42-10.

- On February 13, the Calgary Winter Olympic Games open.

- On February 22, Bonnie Blair wins the 500-meter speed-skating gold medal at the Winter Games.

- On February 28, the Winter Olympic Games close with the Soviet team winning the most medals (29). The United States finishes a disappointing ninth with 6 medals.

- On March 15, the NFL approves the St. Louis Cardinals' proposed move to Arizona.

- On March 24, the NFL announces that referee John Grier will lead an umpiring crew in the upcoming season. He is the first African American official to head a crew.

- On April 4, George Bell of the Toronto Blue Jays becomes the first player to hit three home runs on opening day.

- On April 28, the Baltimore Orioles lose their record-setting 21st game in a row.

- On May 2, National League president A. Bartlett Giamatti suspends Cincinnati Reds manager Pete Rose for thirty days and fines him ten thousand dollars—the toughest penalty ever imposed for an on-field infraction—for twice shoving umpire Dave Pallone during an argument.

- On May 17, John Stockton of the Utah Jazz passes for 24 assists in a playoff game to tie Magic Johnson's NBA record.

- On May 26, the Edmonton Oilers win the Stanley Cup, their fourth in five years.

- On May 29, Rick Mears wins the Indy 500 for the third time.

- On May 30, more than twenty thousand people witness Syracuse defeat Cornell in the Carrier Dome to win the NCAA lacrosse championship.

- On June 21, by defeating the Detroit Pistons, 108-105, the Los Angeles Lakers become the first team since 1969 to win back-to-back NBA championships.

- On June 27, heavyweight champion Mike Tyson knocks out former champ Michael Spinks in the first round.

- On July 2, Steffi Graf defeats Martina Navratilova to win the women's singles championship at Wimbledon, ending Navratilova's record streak of 6 straight Wimbledon titles.

- On July 9, baseball manager Sparky Anderson wins his 800th game with the Detroit Tigers to become the first manager to win 800 games in both the American National Leagues. He had won 863 with the Cincinnati Reds (1970–1978).

- On July 16, Florence Griffith Joyner sets a world record time of 10.49 in the 100-meter dash at the U.S. Olympic trials.

- On July 17, first baseman Willie Stargell of the Pittsburgh Pirates is inducted into the Baseball Hall of Fame.

- On August 8, the first night game at Wrigley Field in Chicago is played.

- On August 9, the Edmonton Oilers trade superstar Wayne Gretzky to the Los Angeles Kings in a multiplayer, multi-million-dollar deal.

- On September 16, Cincinnati Reds' pitcher Tom Browning throws a perfect game.

- On September 17, the Summer Olympic Games open in Seoul, South Korea.

- On September 18, Arnold Palmer wins his first golf tournament in three years, the Crestar Classic for Seniors in Richmond, Virginia.

- On September 23, José Canseco of the Oakland Athletics becomes the first major leaguer to steal forty bases and hit forty home runs in the same season.

- On September 24, Canadian runner Ben Johnson wins the 100-meter dash at the Olympics and sets a world record with a time of 9.79. Two days later Johnson is stripped of his gold medal when he tests positive for steroids.

- On September 25, swimmer Matt Biondi wins his fifth gold medal (and seventh medal overall) at the Olympics by helping the U.S. team win the 400-meter medley relay.

- On September 27, on his final dive Greg Louganis wins the 10-meter platform event, becoming the first man to win two diving gold medals in two Olympics in a row.

- On September 29, sisters-in-law Jackie Joyner-Kersee and Florence Griffith Joyner both win gold medals and set world records in their respective events: Joyner-Kersee in the heptathlon and Griffith Joyner in the 200-meter dash.

- On October 8, the Columbia College football team snaps its 44-game losing streak by beating Princeton 16-13.

- On October 9, in Bayston, Texas, Eddie Hill sets a record for the fastest time in drag racing, completing the quarter-mile race in 4.936 seconds.

- On October 20, the Los Angeles Dodgers win the World Series by upsetting the Oakland Athletics, four games to one.

- On October 24, Mike Bossy, whose 573 goals is sixth on the NHL all-time list, retires.

- On November 11, Dallas beats John Brown, 76-68, to snap college basketball's longest losing streak at 86 games.

- On November 20, the North Carolina women's soccer team wins its seventh NCAA national championship in eight years.

- On December 3, Oklahoma State running back Barry Sanders wins the Heisman Trophy.

- On December 19, Oklahoma's football program is penalized for "numerous and major" violations of NCAA rules.

1989

- On January 1, undefeated Notre Dame defeats West Virginia, 34-21, in the Fiesta Bowl and is later voted the national champion for the 1988 college football season.

- On January 11, the NCAA passes controversial Proposition 42, which disallows athletic scholarships to those students who fail to meet minimum academic standards set by Proposition 48.

- On January 14, Georgetown basketball coach John Thompson walks off the court before a game against Boston College to protest the passage of Proposition 42.

- On January 20, Mario Lemieux of the Pittsburgh Penguins becomes only the second player in NHL history (Wayne Gretzky is the other) to score 50 goals in less than 50 games. Lemieux scores goal number fifty in the forty-fourth game of the season.

- On January 22, the San Francisco 49ers win Super Bowl XXIII by coming from behind to beat the Cincinnati Bengals, 20-16.

- On January 25, Chicago Bulls guard Michael Jordan scores his ten thousandth NBA point in his 303rd game. Only Wilt Chamberlain scored as many points in fewer games.

- On January 31, the Loyola Marymount and U.S. International men's basketball teams combine to score a record 310 points in a game, which Loyola Marymount wins, 181-130.

- On February 3, former St. Louis Cardinal outfielder Bill White is named president of the National League. White is the first African American man to head a major U.S. professional sports league.

- On February 13, Oklahoma quarterback Charles Thompson is arrested for selling cocaine.

- On February 25, the Dallas Cowboys of the NFL are sold to Jerry Jones. Coach Tom Landry is replaced by former University of Miami coach Jimmy Johnson.

- On March 17, Julie Croteau of St. Mary's becomes the first woman to play in a men's college baseball game.

- On March 22, Pete Rozelle, commissioner of the NFL for twenty-nine years, announces his resignation.

- On April 3, Rumeal Robinson sinks two free throws with three seconds left in overtime to help Michigan defeat Seton Hall, 80-79, in the NCAA's men's basketball championship final.

- On April 7, the International Basketball Federation (FIBA) votes to allow professional basketball players to participate in the Olympics beginning in 1992.

- On April 23, Kareem Abdul-Jabbar plays his final NBA regular season game; also, the NFL holds its annual college draft: the first five picks are quarterback Troy Aikman (Dallas), offensive lineman Tony Mandarich (Green Bay), running back Barry Sanders (Detroit), linebacker Derrick Thomas (Kansas City), and defensive back Deion Sanders (Atlanta).

- On April 28, high-school pitcher Jon Peters wins his record fifty-first consecutive game. His streak is snapped at fifty-three a month later.

- On May 4, Soviet hockey player Alexander Mogilny defects to Sweden and thereafter immigrates to the United States to play for the Buffalo Sabres of the NHL.

- On May 21, Nancy Lopez wins the LPGA Championship.

- On May 26, Hobart College wins its tenth consecutive NCAA division III lacrosse championship.

- On June 12, Sugar Ray Leonard and Thomas Hearns fight to a draw in their twelve-round WBC super-middleweight title fight.

- On June 13, the Detroit Pistons complete a sweep of the Los Angeles Lakers in the NBA finals to win their first world championship.

- On June 18, golfer Curtis Strange wins his second consecutive U.S. Open Championship.

- On June 19, pitcher Dwight Gooden of the New York Mets, twenty-four, wins his hundredth career game.

- On July 23, Greg LeMond wins cycling's Tour de France for the second time; also, the Baseball Hall of Fame inductees include Johnny Bench and Carl Yastrzemski.

- On August 22, Nolan Ryan, forty-two, of the Texas Rangers collects the five thousandth strikeout of his career.

- On August 24, Cincinnati Reds manager Pete Rose agrees to a lifetime suspension from baseball for gambling.

- On August 24, Victoria Brucker becomes the first girl from the United States to play in the Little League World Series.

- On August 26, a team from Trumbull, Connecticut, wins the Little League World Series.

- On September 1, baseball commissioner A. Bartlett Giamatti dies of a heart attack.

- On September 2, SMU plays its first football game since the NCAA "death penalty" was imposed in 1987.

- On September 5, Chris Evert Lloyd plays her last match at the U.S. Open, losing to Zina Garrison.

- On September 13, Fay Vincent is named baseball commissioner.

- On September 16, in college football action number one Notre Dame defeats number two Michigan 24-19. Raghib "Rocket" Ismail returns two kickoffs of 88 and 92 yards for touchdowns.

- On October 3, Art Shell is hired as the Los Angeles Raiders coach, making him the first African American NFL coach since Fritz Pollard was a player-coach for the Hammond (Indiana) Pros (1923–1925).

- On October 15, Wayne Gretzky of the Los Angeles Kings scores a goal against the Edmonton Oilers to become the NHL's all-time leading scorer with 1,850 points.

- On October 17, an earthquake in the San Francisco Bay area prior to game three of the World Series forces a ten-day delay in the Series, which the Oakland Athletics eventually win by sweeping the San Francisco Giants.

- On October 26, Paul Tagliabue is named commissioner of the NFL.

- On November 9, the Milwaukee Bucks defeat the Seattle Supersonics, 155-154, after five overtime periods. The game takes four hours and seventeen minutes to complete, the third-longest game in NBA history.

- On November 19, the U.S. soccer team wins a berth in the final round of the World Cup.

- On December 7, Sugar Ray Leonard wins a unanimous twelve-round decision against Roberto Duran to retain his WBC super-middleweight championship.

- On December 23, wide receiver Steve Largent of the Seattle Seahawks plays his final game. He retires as the NFL's all-time leader in touchdown receptions (100), total catches (819), and receiving yardage (13,089).

"United States 4—Soviet Union 3 . . . And the Fireworks Explode"

Newspaper article

By: Gerald Eskenazi and Dave Anderson

Date: February 23, 1980

Source: Eskenazi, Gerald, and Dave Anderson. "United States 4—Soviet Union 3 . . . And the Fireworks Explode." *The New York Times,* February 23, 1980. Reprinted as chapter 11 in *Miracle on Ice.* New York: Bantam, 1980.

About the Authors: Gerald Eskanazi (1936–) was born in Brooklyn, New York. Eskanazi joined *The New York Times* in 1959, and he was a sports reporter for the paper until his retirement in 2000. He has written over eight thousand stories that appeared in *The New York Times,* as well as thirteen books and hundreds of articles.

Dave Anderson (1929–) was born in Troy, New York. After graduating from Holy Cross, Anderson wrote for several newspapers prior to joining *The New York Times* in 1966 as a reporter. He became a columnist in 1971, and as of 2003 he continues to write the "Sports of the Times" column. Anderson won a Pulitzer Prize in 1981 for distinguished sports commentary, and he was inducted into the National Sports Writers and Sportscasters Hall of Fame in 1990. Anderson has written twenty-one books and more than 350 magazine articles. ∎

Introduction

Prior to 1980, only the 1960 Unites States Olympic ice hockey team had won a gold medal. After 1960, the U.S. Olympic hockey program weakened due to expansion by the National Hockey League (NHL), when the best American players signed professional contracts rather than participate in amateur competitions, including the Olympics.

The 1980 U.S. Olympic ice hockey team was seeded seventh in a field of twelve teams. It was composed largely of current and former college hockey players, and the expectations for the team were modest. Only three days before the start of the Olympic competition, the Soviet Union's Olympic team humiliated the Americans in an exhibition game, 10-3.

By contrast, the Soviet Union had built an impressive hockey program. While technically amateurs, the Soviets fielded arguably the best hockey team in the world at any level, amateur or professional—featuring legendary defenseman Vyacheslav Fetisov and goalie Vadislav Tretiak among its many stars. With skilled players at every position, the Russians dominated in all aspects of the game, emphasizing speed and precision passing. In 1979, the Soviets soundly defeated a collection of NHL all-stars in a series of exhibition games. Called "The Big Red Machine," the Soviet Union had won four consecutive Olympic gold medals, and they were prohibitive favorites to win a fifth in Lake Placid, New York, the site of the 1980 Winter Olympics.

Olympic ice hockey divides the field into two division of six, and each team plays the other five teams in its division. The top two teams from each division advance to the semifinals, where the teams are reseeded. The U.S. team tied its first game in the closing seconds, and then won four consecutive divisional games. The United States, the Soviet Union, Sweden, and Finland advanced to the medal round.

As the lowest seed in the medal round, the Americans played the Soviet Union in the semifinals, with the winner to go on to the gold medal game. The Soviets were considered invincible, and few gave the United States team a chance to win the game. However, the unexpected success of the hockey team—just to make it to the medal round without a loss—created considerable national attention. Fans, chanting "U.S.A." and waving American flags, packed the arena, and even casual hockey fans watched the game on television.

The Soviets dominated the play in the first period, but U.S. goalie Jim Craig was outstanding, holding the Russians to two goals. The Americans managed to tie the game, 2-2, on a disputed goal scored less than one second before the end of the period. The Soviets held a 3-2 lead into the third period; however, the Americans tied the game, and then went ahead on a goal by their captain, Mike Eruzione, with ten minutes left in the game. The Soviets created several excellent scoring chances, but Craig stopped them all. Over the roar of the crowd—as the clock ticked toward zero, with America's victory certain—ABC announcer, Al Michaels, shouted, "Do you believe in miracles? Yes!" The unheralded American team had stunned the Soviet Union, in one of the great upsets in sports history, to advance to the gold medal game against Finland.

Significance

The monumental upset became the central story of the Olympic games. The resulting fervor spread throughout America, and the gold medal game remains the most watched hockey game in American history. After falling behind 2-1, the Americans scored three unanswered goals to capture the gold medal. The flag-waiving crowd cheered and chanted "U.S.A." throughout the game. Amidst the bedlam within the stadium after the game ended, Jim Craig searched the stands to make eye contact with his father. For the gold medal ceremony, Craig wrapped himself in a large American flag. These images of Craig immediately after the game remain vivid to those who watched the "Miracle on Ice" end in golden glory for the 1980 U.S. ice hockey team.

Adding to the drama of the incredible upset of the Soviet Union was the charged political climate existing at the time. At the height of the Cold War, the United States and the Soviet Union were locked in an escalating nuclear arms race, and they were competing for political influence across the globe. The upset was significant to the American psyche. The Soviet Union invaded Afghanistan in 1979, and the threat of a boycott of the 1980 Summer Olympics in Moscow loomed. Also, the American economy was mired in a period of little growth, rising inflation, and high interest rates. On top of that, forty-four Americans were being held hostage in Iran. The victory over the Soviet Union lifted the spirits of the entire nation, and it is viewed as one of the greatest moments in the history of American sports. ESPN, the American sports cable network, declared the victory over the Soviet Union the greatest game in twentieth century athletics.

The victory over the Soviet Union is so memorable because it was so unexpected. Although several U.S. players went on to the NHL, this was a team that was overmatched by the talent and experience of the Soviets. The overachieving American team, for at least one sixty-minute stretch, was the best team in the world.

Primary Source

"United States 4—Soviet Union 3 . . . And the Fireworks Explode"

> **SYNOPSIS:** In the first part of this article, *New York Times* reporter Gerald Eskenazi provides a detailed description of the semifinal game, as the U.S. hockey team upsets the Soviet Union to advance to the gold medal game. In the second part, Pulitzer Prize-winning columnist Dave Anderson describes the bedlam after the shocking upset.

"United States 4—Soviet Union 3"

In one of the most startling and dramatic upsets in Olympic history, the underdog United States hockey team, composed in great part of collegians, defeated the defending champion Soviet squad by 4-3.

The victory brought a congratulatory phone call to the dressing room from President Carter and set off fireworks over the tiny Adirondack village. The tri-

The U.S. players celebrate their victory in the final moments of the semifinals against the Soviet Union, Lake Placid, New York, February 22, 1980. It was one of the greatest upsets in sports history. **AP/WIDE WORLD PHOTOS. REPRODUCED BY PERMISSION.**

umph also put the Americans in a commanding position to take the gold medal in the XIII Olympic Winter Games.

If the United States defeated Finland, which tied Sweden, 3-3, the Americans would win the gold medal regardless of the outcome of the game between Sweden and the Soviet Union later that day. If the United States tied Finland, the Americans were assured of at least a bronze medal.

The American goal that broke a 3-3 tie against the Russians was scored midway through the final period by a player who typified the makeup of the United States team.

His name is Mike Eruzione, he is from Winthrop, Mass., he is the American team's captain and he was plucked from obscurity. His opponents included world-renowned stars, some of them performing in the Olympics for the third time.

The Soviet team had captured five of the last six Olympics. The only club to defeat them since 1956 was the United States team of 1960, which won the gold medal at Squaw Valley, Calif.

The United States's winning goal gets by Soviet goaltender Vladimir Myshkin in the Olympic Games, Lake Placid, New York, February 22, 1980. The United States beat the heavily favored Soviets, 4-3, to earn a spot in the gold medal game. AP/WIDE WORLD PHOTOS. REPRODUCED BY PERMISSION.

Few victories in American Olympic play have provoked reaction comparable to that provoked by the decision in the red-seated, smallish Olympic Field House at the end of the United States–Soviet Union game. At the final buzzer, after the fans had chanted the seconds away, fathers and mothers and friends of the United States players dashed onto the ice, hugging everyone they could find in red, white and blue uniforms. Truly, they had witnessed a miracle on ice.

Meanwhile, in the stands, most of the 10,000 fans—including about 1,500 standees, who paid $24.40 apiece for a ticket—shouted "U.S.A." over and over, and hundreds outside waved American flags. Later, the orchestrator of the team, Coach Herb Brooks took out a yellow piece of paper, displayed the almost illegible scrawl on it, and said, "I really said this to the guys. I'm not lying to you."

Before the game, Brooks had taken out that card in the locker room and read his remarks.

"You were born to be a player," he read. "You were meant to be here." They proved him right.

From the opening minutes fans and players fed off one another in the festive atmosphere at the arena. The tempo and emotion of the game was established early, when a longtime Soviet star, Valery Kharlamov, wearing the traditional lipstick-red uniform, was sandwiched between two Americans.

Suddenly, he was lifted between them and, looking like a squirt of ketchup, sailed into the air and then flopped to the ice. Beyond the constant pressure of intimidating body checks, though, were the intricate passing patterns of the Americans, who have derived many of their techniques from the Russians.

The Soviet system is based on attack. The Russians more than doubled the shots on goal of the Americans, 39-16, but almost every one that the Russians took was stopped, often dramatically, by Jim Craig.

As a result of the victory, the hockey players would be among the prouder contingents of the 150 American Olympians to be honored at the White House at a two-hour session with the President.

The Americans struggled until the final period, however, never leading until Eruzione's goal. They trailed by 3-2 going into the last 20-minute period. No hockey game is played nonstop for 60 minutes, but this one came close. The Russians have been famed for their conditioning techniques. They also were considered the finest hockey team in the world.

The Soviet Union broke through first, with its new young star, Valery Krutov, getting his stick in the way of Aleksei Kasatonov's whistling slap shot. The puck changed direction and sailed beyond Craig's reach in the first period.

Midway through the period, the only American who has been an Olympian, Buzz Schneider, drilled a shot over the left shoulder of Vladislav Tretyak, the Soviet goalie.

The goal was Schneider's fifth of the series, giving him the team lead. That is a surprising performance for a player who once failed the tryout with the lowly Pittsburgh Penguins in the National League, and since has bounced around American leagues of less stature.

But there were other highlights of that first period. The Russians had one when Sergei Makarov punched the puck past Craig while fans screamed in vain for Referee Karl-Gustav Kaisla of Finland to notice an American who was being held.

Only a few seconds remained when Ken Morrow slammed an 80-foot desperation shot toward the goal. The puck caromed out to Mark Johnson, who struck it home with no seconds showing on the clock.

A goal cannot be scored with no time remaining. Actually, when the puck had sailed in there was a second left. It took another second for the goal judge to press the button signaling the score and stopping the clock.

The Soviet skaters left the ice, contending time was over, but after Kaisla spoke to other officials, the goal was allowed. The arena rocked with applause with the verification of the 2-2 tie.

Back came the disappointed Russians from their dressing room, adjusting their shiny red helmets. They had a new player on the ice, too—Vladimir Myshkin had replaced Tretyak in goal for the final faceoff of the period. Later, the assistant Soviet coach, Vladimir Jursinov, explained the removal of Tretyak, saying through an interpreter, "He is not playing well and my feeling is he is nervous."

Myshkin kept the Americans at bay for the second period, although they tested him with only two shots. The Russians took a 3-2 lead when one of their veterans, Aleksandr Maltsev, scored with a man advantage.

But in the last period Johnson swatted home a shot that Dave Silk had gotten off while being hauled down, and the puck eluded Myshkin to tie the score. About a minute and a half later, with exactly half of the period over, Eruzione picked up a loose puck in the Soviet zone, skated to a point between the face-off circles and fired a screened, 30-foot shot through the pads of Myshkin for the winning score.

The goal set off cheering that lasted through the remainder of the game, as the youngest team of all the American squads, average age 22, put itself in a position to win only the second gold medal ever for an American hockey team.

" . . . And the Fireworks Explode"

Outside the Olympic Field House, fireworks exploded above Main Street in the tiny Adirondack Mountain village of Lake Placid. Four searchlights lit up the dark sky. On the snow-muddied sidewalks, thousands of people stood around, still transfixed by the United States's 4-3 upset of the Soviet Union in the XIII Winter Olympics hockey tournament. To most hockey people, the Soviet national team was the world's best team, better than any National Hockey League team.

But the best team lost.

A platoon of Americans, mostly from colleges in cold-weather states like Minnesota and Massachusetts, ambushed the renowned Soviet national team gathered from the Central Red Army and the Moscow Wings and the Moscow Dynamo, virtually the same Soviet players who had embarrassed the N.H.L. all-stars in the Challenge Cup at Madison Square Garden a year ago.

Throughout the second game against the Russians, the chant of "U.S.A., U.S.A." appeared to inspire the American team as it had throughout the Olympic tournament. And all through the small arena that has only 8,500 seats, dozens of American flags, large and small, had been waved.

When the game finally ended, the spectators who had paid up to $67.40 for a seat at center ice—if not $150 to a scalper—stood and shouted as American players jumped and hugged each other while the Soviets grouped silently at the other end of the ice, staring in shock at the scene around them.

Now, outside the arena, the "U.S.A., U.S.A." chant could be heard every so often—from down

Main Street past the speed-skating oval, from the lot where the buslines were, from a third-floor window in Lake Placid High School that serves as the Olympic press center.

Near the players' entrance, goalie Jim Craig was surrounded by people who unknowingly were shoving him toward one of the arena's huge plate-glass windows. In the game he had stopped 36 shots, including nine in the third period as the Americans rallied for two goals. But now he appeared to be unnerved by the plate-glass window and the fireworks bursting above.

"Hey, don't push me into the window," he was saying now. "Don't push me into the window."

But then he talked about the Soviets' desperate rushes for the tying goal they never obtained.

"They panicked at the end," he said. "I couldn't believe it. They were just throwing the puck in and hoping for a break. Hey, what was the final score? Was it 4-3? Does anybody know the final score?"

Yes, it was 4-3, he was told.

"That was my kind of game," he said. "I had to concentrate all the way. My ear was hurting from the flu I've had the last few days. I took a penicillin shot but I wouldn't let myself believe I could get sick. I'll get sick next week."

Just as he was asked a question, a dazzle of fireworks burst high in the sky, startling him.

"Would you please repeat that question?" he said.

"Would you please repeat that question?"

Against the Soviets, he had resembled a goaltender carved in ice. But now he appeared frightened by the fireworks bursting above him.

"Would you please repeat that question?" he said again.

"How did you feel in there at the end?" he was asked.

"If we lost," he finally replied, "I was determined they would have to beat me with a good goal—all I was trying to do was keep us in the game. We were just lucky we got the breaks."

Not far away Mark Johnson, who scored the Americans' second and third goals, was wearing his red-white-and-blue jacket.

"I can't believe it. I can't believe we beat them. But we did. And now we're only 60 minutes away from the gold medal, baby, only 60 minutes away."

The United States still had to face Finland, a game that was to be followed by the Soviet Union–Sweden showdown in the afternoon.

"We only had two shots on net in the second period," Mark Johnson continued. "But we were only losing by 3-2 and that's when we knew we had a chance to win. When we lost to the Russians, 10-3, two weeks ago at Madison Square Garden, we were down 7-1 after two periods. But being behind by only one goal this time we knew we were younger, we knew we could outskate them, we knew we were going to break our butts to beat 'em. And we did." Mike Eruzione, the American captain, scored the winning goal.

"On a line change too," the 25-year-old left-winger said from under the brim of his Olympic cowboy hat. "My buddy Buzz Schneider came off early, so I was out there with John Harrington and Mark Pavelich when Harrington gave me the puck inside the blue line. I shot, the defenseman screened the goaltender, and it went in. Very simple."

"Did the Afghanistan situation affect you?" somebody asked.

"That doesn't concern us now," he said. "All we're concerned about now is winning this tournament. Hey, we had champagne in our locker room but nobody touched it. We put it away until after Sunday's game. This is a dream that nobody can say they're a part of except us." And except all those people chanting, "U.S.A., U.S.A."

Further Resources

BOOKS

Baker, Eugene, H., and Donna Baker. *XIII Olympic Winter Games, Lake Placid, 1980.* Chicago: Rand McNally, 1979.

Greenspan, Bud. *Frozen in Time: The Greatest Moments at the Winter Olympics.* Los Angeles: General Publishing Group, 1997.

Powers, John, and Arthur C. Kaminsky. *One Goal: A Chronicle of the 1980 U.S. Olympic Hockey Team.* New York: Harper & Row, 1984.

PERIODICALS

Klobuchar, Jim. "U.S.–Russia Puck Drama Plays On: It's Not 1980 and the Cold War Is Gone, but This Remains a Great Hockey Rivalry." *Christian Science Monitor,* February 19, 2002, 12.

Koppett, Leonard. "Olympic Boycott Makes Sense." *The Sporting News* 189, January 26, 1980, 17.

Swift, E.M. "The Original Miracle on Ice: U.S. Olympic Hockey Team in 1960." *Sports Illustrated* 91, no. 21, November 29, 1999, 102–105.

WEBSITES

Levine, Russell. "20 Years Ago Today: U.S. Shocks Soviets." NHL.com. Available online at http://www.nhl.com/olympics

2002/1980_miracle.html; website home page:http://www
.nhl.com (accessed July 17, 2003).

Reflecting on a Miracle. ESPN.com. Available online at http://
espn.go.com/gen/miracle; website home page: http://espn.go
.com (accessed July 17, 2003).

AUDIO AND VISUAL MEDIA

Miracle on Ice. Directed by Steven Hilliard Stern. Trylon
Video, 1990, VHS.

"Convention Acts on Key Athletic Issues"

Journal article

By: National Collegiate Athletic Association

Date: January 19, 1983

Source: "Convention Acts on Key Issues." *The NCAA News*
20, no. 3, January 19, 1983, 1, 12.

About the Organization: The National Collegiate Athletic
Association (NCAA), founded in 1905, is a voluntary association of approximately twelve hundred American colleges,
universities, and athletic conferences designed to foster the
sound administration of intercollegiate athletics. The NCAA
establishes recruiting guidelines and academic standards for
eligibility of its member institutions, as well as investigating
violations and enforcing penalties for violations of its regulations. Approximately twenty percent of the member institutions participate in Division I-A, institutions with substantial
athletic programs, including the University of Michigan,
Notre Dame, and Duke. ∎

Introduction

In the 1980s, many criticized universities and colleges maintaining high-profile athletic programs for failing to provide student-athletes a quality education. A
1985 Pulitzer Prize–winning series in the *Macon Telegraph and News* highlighted the situation. The series
compared the graduation rates for athletes at the University of Georgia and Georgia Tech University to the general student body over a ten-year period. At the University of Georgia, only 4 percent of African American
basketball players and 17 percent of African American football players graduated from 1975 to 1985; graduation of
white basketball and football players was 63 percent and
50 percent respectively, while the non-athlete graduation
rate was 61 percent. In response to this criticism, the
NCAA examined various alternatives to ensure that member institutions would provide student-athletes quality educational opportunities.

After careful study and heated debate, in 1983 the
NCAA adopted Proposal 48 to establish mandatory academic eligibility requirements for entering freshman var-
sity athletes at Division I schools. To be eligible to
participate in athletics, freshman were required to have a
minimum SAT score of 700 or an ACT score of 15 *and*
a minimum GPA of 2.0 in eleven identified high school
core subjects. Athletes meeting only one of the criteria
were deemed "partial qualifiers" and allowed to receive
athletic scholarships. The student-athlete would have
three years of eligibility remaining if satisfactory
progress toward a degree was made freshman year.

Significance

The passage of Proposition 48 prompted law suits
and protests. Courts upheld the regulation, and it became
effective in 1986. In 1989, the NCAA passed an amendment precluding partial qualifiers from receiving athletic
scholarships as freshmen. After protests and the threat of
a boycott by the Black Coaches Association, the NCAA
rescinded the amendment in 1990. In 1992, the NCAA
again amended the freshman academic eligibility requirements by passing Proposition 16.

More stringent than Proposition 48, Proposition 16's
provisions increased the high school core subject requirement to encompass thirteen subjects beginning in
1995. In 1996, two significant additions became effective under Proposition 16: the core requirements for high
school English and math were raised; and a sliding scale
combining GPA and SAT/ACT test scores was implemented. The most controversial provision of Proposition
16 was the adoption of a minimum standardized test score
(SAT score of 820—the same as the previous standard
as the test's scoring was modified—or an ACT score of
17) as a perquisite for eligibility, irrespective of high
school GPA. Students with 2.0 GPA need to score a 900
on the SAT or 21 on the ACT to be eligible, while students with over a 2.5 need only meet the minimum scores
required.

While implementing Proposition 48 has achieved
many of the goals established by the NCAA member
institutions, it undoubtedly has impacted minority students—especially African Americans—disproportionately and negatively. The NCAA's experience since 1986
demonstrates the tension between raising eligibility requirements for athletes and allowing access to a finite
number of athletic scholarships.

Propositions 48 and 16 have significantly impacted
the academic performance of student-athletes and those
seeking scholarships at Division I-A schools. NCAA
studies demonstrate an increased number of core academic courses by prospective student-athletes, an increase
in academic performance by prospective scholarship recipients in both GPA and standardized test scores, and a
significant increase in percentage of students from all ethnic groups in attaining the initial eligibility requirement.
Since Proposition 48 became effective, student-athletes

Coach Bobby Knight speaks to a group of players attending the Bobby Knight Basketball School, Bloomington, Indiana, June 16, 1983. In a move to make schools more responsible for educating athletes, the NCAA passed Proposal 48, which required student-athletes to achieve a minimum standard of academic success. AP/WIDE WORLD PHOTOS. REPRODUCED BY PERMISSION.

are graduating in greater numbers, graduating at a higher rate than non-athletes, realizing improved first year GPAs, and remaining eligible at higher rates.

Despite the positive results by student-athletes in general, Propositions 48 and 16 have been justly criticized for their negative impact on minority students, especially in the first year that each was in effect. The same NCAA study that documented the positive results of Proposition 48 showed that the enrollment of African Americans declined dramatically immediately following the implementation of the proposals. As of 1998, the number of African American student-athletes was still below pre-Proposition 48 levels.

Fair Test, a national civil rights group, has been the leading critic of Propositions 48 and 16. Fair Test's substantive criticism of the NCAA eligibility requirements includes charges that the test requirements are discriminatory. NCAA research shows that the requirements disqualify African American student-athletes at ten times the rate of white student-athletes. Also, Fair Test argues that these standards are unnecessary as minority student-athletes have always graduated at rates higher than their non-athlete counterparts. And Fair Test argues that the standardized tests are inherently biased against minori-

ties, and further that there exists no rational basis for establishing cutoff scores.

While the criticisms of Propositions 48 and 16 remain valid, there was no easy solution to the original problem. Minority students were affected disproportionately, especially in the first years that the standards were in place. However, the actions of the NCAA members have been consistent with their missions as academic institutions. By establishing higher standards, the NCAA has provided prospective athletes a strong incentive to select more difficult high school curriculums and better prepare for the standardized tests—both to the benefit of the student-athletes. The true impact of the eligibility requirements remains to be determined, and they are subject to revision if better alternatives become available.

Primary Source

"Convention Acts on Key Athletic Issues" [excerpt]

SYNOPSIS: This article from the NCAA newsletter published after the 1983 convention describes several proposals, including Proposal 48, debated by NCAA delegates to improve the quality of education of student-athletes.

More than 1,400 delegates, including a record number of chief executive officers, took significant steps at the 77th annual Convention January 10–12 to correct a number of problems facing intercollegiate athletics today.

The most significant action was the passage of Proposal No. 48, which produced more than two hours of debate and will implement tougher academic standards for incoming high school student-athletes.

"This Convention represented one of the most, if not the most, determined and forceful effort to deal with the serious problems of intercollegiate athletics that I have ever observed," Executive Director Walter Byers said at a press conference after the final business session.

"The Convention was very successful in concentrating on what we believe the leadership of higher education has concluded are rather grave problems that need treatment. I don't recall any Convention in which colleges and universities have taken such a substantial, if not gigantic step, forward."

The passage of No. 48 establishes, for the first time, a specific core curriculum for which a student must record a minimum 2.000 grade-point average in high school. It also requires an incoming student-athlete to register a minimum 700 combined score on the SAT verbal and math sections or a 15 composite score on the ACT for initial eligibility at a Division I institution.

Included in the core curriculum of at least 11 academic courses are three courses in English, two in mathematics, two in social science and two in natural or physical science, including at least one laboratory class, if offered by the high school. This amendment becomes effective August 1, 1986.

Delegates also approved Proposal No. 49-B, which will allow student-athletes who have an overall 2.000 grade-point in high school but who do not meet the above requirements, to receive financial aid; however, any such student-athlete will lose one season of eligibility.

A total of 23 speakers debated Proposal No. 48 on the Convention floor, including 15 CEOs, six faculty athletic representatives, one commissioner and one football coach.

The proposal was sponsored by the NCAA Council and the American Council on Education. Although the subject produced rather heated debate at times, the proposal passed without a count.

"This legislation is necessary to uphold the integrity of the NCAA and the institutions," said L. Donald Shields, president, Southern Methodist University. "These are reasonable standards for freshman eligibility, and our stewardship and integrity as leaders of higher education are at stake."

Five CEOs spoke in opposition to No. 48, including Luna I. Mishoe, president, Delaware State College. "The SAT is a restraint that penalizes low-income students and does not indicate whether a student can perform college work. Test scores have nothing to do with ability."

Further Resources

BOOKS

Funk, Gary. *Major Violation: The Unbalanced Priorities in Athletics and Academics.* Champaign, Ill.: Leisure Press, 1991.

Lapchick, Richard. *Five Minutes to Midnight: Race and Sport in the 1990s.* New York: Madison Books, 1991.

Smith, Ronald A. *Sports and Freedom: The Rise of Big-Time College Athletics.* New York: Oxford University Press, 1988.

Thelin, John, R., and Lawrence L. Wiseman. *The Old College Try: Balancing Academics and Athletics in Higher Education.* Washington, D.C.: School of Education and Human Development, George Washington University, 1989.

PERIODICALS

Bennett, Bruce. "Scholars or Slaves: The Story of Athletic Scholarships." *Journal of Popular Culture* 20, Winter 1986, 167–178.

"Division I Academic Reform." *NCAA News,* September 16, 2002. Available online at http://www.ncaa.org/news/2002/20020916/active/3919n04.html; website home page: http://www.ncaa.org (accessed June 23, 2003).

Hawes, Kay. "Opportunity or Exploitation: Concerns Over Standards and Higher-Education Access Sparked Debates in the '90s." *NCAA News,* December 20, 1999. Available online at http://www.ncaa.org/news/1999/19991220/active/3626n28.html; website home page: http://www.ncaa.org (accessed June 23, 2003).

Kirshenbaum, Jerry. "The NCAA's Options." *Sports Illustrated* 58, February 21, 1983, 11.

"NCAA Division I Initial Eligibility Standards." NCAA Report. July 22, 1998. Reprinted as Attachment A, Supplement No. 4-c to Report of Division I Board of Directors. October 1998. Available online at http://www.ncaa.org/databases/reports/1/199810bd/199810_di_bd_agenda_s04c_a.html; website home page: http://www.ncaa.org (accessed June 23, 2003).

Sanoff, Alvin, P. "It's Cleanup Time for College Sports." *News & World Report* 99, July 1, 1985, 62–65.

WEBSITES

"Ethics and College Sports." The Sports Ethics Institute. Available at http://www.sportsethicsinstitute.org/college_sports.htm; website home page: http://www.sportsethicsinstitute.org (accessed July 17, 2003).

"What's Wrong with the NCAA's Test Score Requirements?" *FairTest*. Available online at http://www.fairtest.org/facts /prop48.htm; website home page: http://www.fairtest.org (accessed June 23, 2003).

Martina
Autobiography

By: Martina Navratilova, with George Vecsey

Date: 1985

Source: Navratilova, Martina, with George Vecsey. *Martina.* New York: Alfred A. Knopf, 1985, 261–269.

About the Author: Martina Navratilova (1956–) was born in Prague, Czechoslovakia. Navratilova began playing tennis at an early age, and she competed in tournaments across the world. She defected to the United States after the 1975 U.S. Open Championship, becoming a citizen in 1981. Over the course of her career, Navratilova won eighteen singles and thirty-seven doubles titles in Grand Slam events. She also established a career record 167 singles and 165 doubles titles. Navratilova was inducted into the International Tennis Hall of Fame in 2000. After retiring from tennis she became a writer and an advocate for gay and lesbian causes. ∎

Introduction

Martina Navratilova burst onto the women's tennis scene, dominated by Americans Billie Jean King and Chris Evert, with her defection to the United States in 1975. She was only eighteen, and Navratilova's decision required her to break ties with her family in Czechoslovakia, a communist country. She struggled with her newfound freedom and her weight for several years—tennis commentator, Bud Collins, referred to her as the "Great Wide Hope." Uniquely talented, Navratilova achieved success on the tour despite her lack of the top conditioning and mental toughness that would later allow her to dominate the sport. She became the top-ranked player in the world in 1978 and 1979; but her play slipped, and she lost the number one spot in 1980.

After becoming a U.S. citizen in 1981, Navratilova dedicated herself to reaching her full potential, hiring basketball superstar Nancy Lieberman as her conditioning coach, and Renee Richards as her hitting coach. Navratilova became the first star on the women's tour to incorporate weightlifting into an exercise program, and she significantly improved her strength, power, and quickness. Already gifted, her training regimen and growing confidence and mental toughness allowed her to dominate the tour. As described below, she won the only Grand Slam event title that eluded her, the U.S. Open, in 1983 over Evert, solidifying her as the women's number-one-ranked player, a rank she held continuously for five years, from 1982 to 1986.

Significance

The 1983 U.S. Open was significant for Navratilova as it answered the one question that remained about her game: could she win at Flushing Meadows? Despite her many accomplishments, she had not performed well over the years at the U.S. Open. In the 1981 finals, the favored Navratilova lost to Tracy Austin in a third-set tiebreaker—double faulting on match point. In 1982, Navratilova suffered from a viral infection, losing to her doubles partner, Pam Shriver, in the quarterfinals.

Navratilova did not lose a set—and only nineteen games in seven matches—in the entire 1983 tournament, with only her finals match lasting more than one hour. The 1983 title was also significant because she convincingly beat Evert, her long-time nemesis, 6-1, 6-3. Their rivalry was one of sport's greatest, and many fans and experts refused to credit Navratilova until she defeated Evert at the U.S. Open. After losing twenty-one of their first twenty-five matches, Navratilova won thirty-nine of the final fifty-five matches between the great rivals.

Navratilova's 1983 U.S. Open title resulted in large part from her conditioning program. Nancy Lieberman, her conditioning coach, created a disciplined, structured regimen that allowed Navratilova to thrive physically and mentally. Lifting weights and achieving excellent cardiovascular fitness provided Navratilova a tremendous advantage on her competition. Previously, tennis coaches had focused largely on mechanics and match strategy. Navratilova became the first female tennis player to train like other world-class athletes, with an intensity and focus that translated into dominance on the court.

Navratilova evoked a wide range of reactions from American tennis fans over the years. Fans viewed her as distant and temperamental early in her career, pulling for Chris Evert when they played. She also became the first prominent athlete to acknowledge being a bisexual, costing her many endorsements. As she matured and became more comfortable with the fans, they grew to appreciate her. By the end of her career, she became among the most beloved figures in sports.

Primary Source

Martina [excerpt]

> **SYNOPSIS:** In this excerpt, Navratilova recounts her excellent play during the 1983 U.S. Open. Finally "getting the monkey off her back," Navratilova describes her victory over Chris Evert in the finals to win the one Grand Slam event title that had eluded her.

Off My Back

I felt so wonderful throughout the 1983 Open that I almost had to ask myself what was wrong. I felt as if I had willed away all the problems of the past. The weather was hot, but there weren't the swirling winds of earlier Opens. The airplanes had been routed onto another flight pattern for the entire tournament—just a matter of prevailing winds, but I felt it was an omen. There was no blood disorder to make my knees tremble. And it seemed just about everybody at the brawling, sprawling Open was my personal friend, smiling benignly at me and asking what they could do to help.

Maybe they saw something in me. I went around with a smile on my face, enjoying things. During the press conferences, when reporters brought up the past, I just smiled. Everything was in slow motion. Now I could look around and smell the roses.

After I beat Emilse Rapponi in an early round, one of the reporters asked me if I considered the Open to be a jinx. I said: "No, I don't feel jinxed at all. I like the city too much to feel jinxed here."

Somebody else asked me about pressure and I said: "I've never won this tournament before, so I'm really the underdog."

Asked if it was stimulating to have easy matches, I said: "This is the U.S. Open, so everything is stimulating, including the practices. First- and second-round matches are fun here as opposed to other tournaments. I always find myself more nervous before my first match in a big tournament because I want to get it under way. It's a good nervous, though. I'm excited—excited nervous, not 'Oh, my God,' nervous."

We did everything to avoid the tensions of the past. I had rented a house in Little Neck, a few miles east of Flushing Meadow, to insure my privacy. The whole two weeks went by like a dream. Quick matches, friendly faces, peace and quiet at home. We even discouraged friends from dropping in so I could relax between matches.

The only people at the house were me, Nancy, and Pam Derderian. For the entire two weeks, we kept this joke going about the magic number, like in baseball, where you only need a certain number of games to win the pennant. Every day they'd say: "Well, Tini, the magic number is four now," or whatever.

Nancy wanted me to be in a good mood during the Open, so she told me not to watch the evening highlights of the Open. I guess she was worried I'd hear something controversial that would interrupt my

Martina Navratilova leaps into the air after winning her first U.S. Open championship, New York, September 10, 1983. After amassing many victories in three of the four major tennis tournaments, Navratilova won the U.S. Open for the first time in 1983. © BETTMANN/CORBIS. REPRODUCED BY PERMISSION.

peace of mind. She would say: "All right, Tini, the highlights are coming on now. Leave the room." And I would leave the room while she took mental notes on who said what.

The only thing that went wrong during those two weeks was when some kids stole the sponsor's $40,000 Porsche 944 from right in front of the house. It was discovered a few blocks away the next day, with the kids driving it. They weren't too smart, driving a car like that near the house.

I cruised to the finals, beating six opponents without losing a set. Against Sylvia Hanika in the quarters, I played some of the most overwhelming tennis I've ever played, winning the first eleven points on smashes and aces. In the semifinals, Pam and I got to stage a rematch of the previous year's Toxoplasmosis Cup. Early in the match, Pam pulled even with me at 2-all and I could hear people saying, "Here goes Martina again," but I just smiled to myself and said out loud: "Wrong."

Pretty soon I was so far ahead that one loudmouth down near the court started to pick on my partner for not making it closer. I confess, I felt like making the schoolyard salute at him, but I concentrated on beating Pam, 6-2, 6-1. Afterward Pam went into the press conference and with her usual arched eyebrows told the reporters: "If she comes in here and says she has anything, I'll kill her."

When somebody asked Pam if she thought I could get any better, she said: "God, I hope not."

Pam said the match with Chris would be "a big test" for me, adding: "When you're twenty-six years old and have won as many tournaments as Martina has and you've never won here, that's not easy for anybody."

Someone asked Pam if I could be beaten, and she said yes. But she added: "I wouldn't bet my house on somebody else besides Martina."

Later that day, Chris was asked the same question. She replied: "I'd bet my three houses on it," but then she added: "I wouldn't bet my life on it."

Chris also said: "I have confidence I can beat her, I don't know how many other people can. It's up to me and the other players. There's no reason she should get worse. Even if she gets stale or drained, with her physical ability there are only three or four people who can beat her."

This was to be the thirty-ninth time Chris and I would meet in a final, and we were even at 19-all. She was still ahead of me, 30-24, in overall matches since our first meeting in 1973, but I had won nineteen of the most recent twenty-nine, including three Wimbledon finals.

Remembering all the hokum between me and Chris the year before, I tried to avoid comparisons this time. But Arthur Ashe said of me: "She's still not as good as Billie Jean or Margaret Court. Her record is not yet as good as Chrissie's." Going into the final, I had merely won all but one of my last sixty-six matches and 155 of my last 159. I thought I was having the best streak of tennis any woman had ever had. But I know how people don't like to hear women talk assertively about themselves, so I held back my responses.

Saturday, September 10, 1983, was a day I'll remember all my life: good weather, good vibrations.

I got to the courts early and was working out with Mike when I spotted my friend Jane Leavy of the Washington *Post,* leaning over the fence. Jane had been writing throughout the tournament that the only fitting script for the Open was for me to meet Chris in the final, since Chris had won the tournament six times. I had kept insisting it didn't matter to me, but when Jane arrived on Saturday morning, I called over: "You got your wish." Then I paused and gave her the punch line: "So did I." I knew it was too late for Jane to turn my comment into a headline that Chris could see.

After the workout I changed and was sitting around with Mike in the lounge outside the locker room. It's pretty quiet the last two days because most of the players have already been eliminated and have moved on, somewhere cheaper than New York. The locker room is pretty generic, with no sense that you are at a Grand Slam event, the only personal effect being your name taped on your locker. But even in these sterile surroundings, I couldn't help thinking about the past champions of the U.S. Open: Maureen Connolly, Margaret Court, Billie Jean, Chris, Tracy. It seemed a little ludicrous that I had gotten to be twenty-six without putting my name on that list, but I was the only one who could do anything about that.

"I've waited two years and I'd better do it now," I said out loud.

I'll admit it, my knees started knocking as I told myself: The time is now. I had worked so hard to get here and I knew time was running out.

"God, I want to win so bad, I'll die if I don't," I said.

And Mike, who had never come close to a U.S. Open or any other major final, had all the poise in the world. In his raspy Texas voice, he said: "Relax, you've already won it in your mind. You just have to prove it to everybody else." That logic carried me through the quiet grounds and into the hot, sunny madness of the stadium, where 20,819 fans were waiting to see if I could finally win this big one.

From the start, everything went just as Mike had told me. I was charging Chris, forcing her to go for winners. Once in a while she would hit a super passing shot into the corner and the crowd would roar, thinking that Chris was finding her game. But I knew there was only a tiny patch on each side available to her, and if she could find it, more power to her.

When I won the first set, 6-1, in twenty-five minutes, with a forehand cross-court volley, I banged my racquet down hard on the surface, twice. One down, one to go.

I broke Chris in the first game of the second set with a hard forehand down the line, and then we both held serve to make it 2-1. I looked in the air and saw an airplane overhead and I remembered the plane at Wimbledon advertising the postal codes. I wondered what message was coming this time, and then I saw the little puffs of smoke coming out, spelling "Good Luck Chrissie—Lipton Tea." I'm no fool. I know Lipton uses Chris for endorsements, so I didn't bother keeping my eyes on the sky to see if they would add, "And Martina."

Chrissie didn't need luck from the sky. She had her lob and some great returns and my own dumb double fault to break me and make it 2-2. Then she won four straight points on her serve to go ahead, 3-2. But I held serve and then broke back with my own love game to take a 4-3 lead.

I understood why the crowd was pulling for Chris—they thought I was the favorite. They always want the favorite to sweat it out, no matter who it is. I started getting pumped up, hearing them root for Chris, and knew I had to hit better shots than what I had been hitting.

The big point came with me serving at 4-3 in the second set, when she pulled back to deuce by hitting a winner at the net. I knew if she broke me and made it 4-all, it would be a close one. But I went to advantage, and on game point I chased down a great get by Chris and managed to come around it on my forehand. Then I hit a winner down the line that handcuffed her. God, she was playing well. She had almost played herself right back into the match, but now I was only one game away.

Never believe it when athletes say they don't know what's happening in the stands. I always know what's going on, and so do most of the others. I could hear the applause from some fans who noticed the digital clock in the corner had inched its way from fifty-nine minutes to one hour. It was the first time in this tournament anybody had extended me that far.

Hearing the fans applaud a one-hour match was a moral victory for Chris, but it was also a compliment for me. People were shouting "We love you, Chris" while she was serving, but at the end some of the fans got excited for me because they knew I hadn't won it before. I heard their support, I felt I deserved it, and it was fun. How could you not hear people screaming "Go, Martina"?

I went ahead, 30-love, by flicking a winner at the net and then chasing down a lob and hitting a shot into the corner—two of the best back-to-back shots in my life. I was feeling so good, so confident. Then Chris served back to deuce, but I went to advantage with a long backhand lob.

On the fourth match point of the day, Chris hit a simple backhand past me, much like a million others she has hit by me in our lifetimes. I was standing near the net and I watched the ball float toward the baseline and I waited for it to come down, and it did—outside the line. I had won the U.S. Open. I had won my national championship.

I jumped into the air, but I quickly remembered the champion on the other side of the net, and how gracious she had always been to me. I had to show her the same respect. I rushed to the net, and Chris Evert Lloyd—my grandmother's favorite player—was there waiting. She put her arm around me and patted my head with her racquet. Then, arm in arm, we walked off the court.

The 6-1, 6-3 victory was my longest match of the tournament: sixty-three minutes. I had lost only nineteen games while winning eighty-four, and had averaged only fifty-two minutes per victory.

After I thanked the umpire, I rushed off to the corner of the stands where the dreaded Team Navratilova was lurking—Mike and Barbara Estep, Nancy, Pam, Lynn Conkwright, and a few other friends.

Some people had wondered how Nancy and I would greet each other after a victory. Would we hug, the way some friends do after a big victory? Nancy had had a dream a few weeks earlier about the two of us celebrating by giving high-fives, like basketball players, and that's just what we did.

I was shaking my fist and jumping up and down, shouting: "Off my back! Off my back!" because I had finally gotten rid of that monkey, that reputation for choking in the Open. I gave high-fives to the whole corner before I headed back to my bench.

Sitting there for a moment, drying off and fixing my hair, I was wondering whether my skirt was on right. After having my skirt almost fall off at Wimbledon, I didn't need it to happen again, not with all the photographers around.

Another crazy thought I had: I saw the champions' box in the corner of the stands and thought to myself: Now I get to sit there anytime I want to.

I knew I'd be interviewed live by CBS, with the sound piped into the stadium. So many thoughts go through your head at a moment like that. At some of the smaller tournaments, I have been known to sing a few bars of "Turn Out the Lights, the Party's Over," when I know I've got it won. Since this was the Big Apple, I got this crazy thought that when the CBS people came over to me I was going to start off by singing the opening line of *New York, New York:* "Start spreading the news, I'm leaving today . . ." But I didn't want to expose the national audience to my singing voice.

When they did come over with the camera, I had tears in my eyes and I thought to myself, All they have to do is play the national anthem and I'll break down for sure. I was so proud to have finally won my country's championship.

I made sure to praise Chris for being a great player, and to thank Mike Estep and Nancy Lieberman for all they had done for me, and, thank God, I remembered to praise Renee Richards, too. It's so hard to say the right thing at a time like that, but supposing I had forgotten her, just because of our disagreement? I wasn't happy about the way our working relationship ended, but she had helped me a lot, and she was still my friend, and later she sent me a telegram that said: WELL DONE. Well done both ways.

After the television interview, I was ushered into the press room, and one of the first people I saw was Frank Deford of *Sports Illustrated.* I had been teasing him for a long time because his magazine had never put me on the cover, and he knew I was pretty touchy about it because I had won Wimbledon four times and felt I had been snubbed. This seemed like the right time to ask him in something more than a whisper: "Do I make the cover now?"

Frank, who's a great writer and a lovely guy, mumbled something about hearing I might have to share it with Ivan Lendl if he won the men's division the next day. I would have bet one of my Porsches on the cover headline: "Czech and Double Czech." But Ivan lost to Connors, so I had it all to myself: "Martina Navratilova: U.S. Open Champion at Last."

When the questions started, one of the reporters noted that my $120,000 prize and $500,000 Playtex bonus gave me $6,089,756 for the year to date, the most ever in one year by any tennis player, male or female.

I said: "I know New York is an expensive city to live in. Maybe this can go toward a down payment somewhere."

Then I told the reporters about my real reward for winning the Open: "Wimbledon was worth three days' bingeing. This is worth a week."

Asked how long I could dominate women's tennis, I said: "Maybe you can compare me to *M*A*S*H.*"

Somebody raised the question about whether it was unfair to win so many tournaments by this big a margin. That raised my temperature a few degrees and I said: "They can do everything I do: all the line drills, the quarter-miles on the track, the full-court basketball games. . . . If they want to, they can do it. I know I'm blessed with talent and genes, but so are a lot of people. I've put in the work. I'm a size eight; the only thing big about me are my feet. How is it unfair?"

The tone of the interview, after I had thought I had gotten the monkey off my back, told me I might never totally get rid of it. If I lost, I was a choker. If I won big, I was unfair to women's tennis. How could I arrange to win by a narrow margin?

We celebrated my "unfair" victory at an Italian restaurant in Little Neck, with about thirty of my friends seated around one long table. They toasted me with champagne and I broke training with some garlic butter and a few other forbidden foods. I hoped Nancy was looking the other way.

When we got back to the house, all the tensions of the tournament seemed far behind. I felt total satisfaction. We had a little more champagne, but only a taste because I had a doubles match the next day, and then we sat back and watched television. This time Nancy let me watch the highlights.

Further Resources

BOOKS

Blue, Adrianne. *Martina: The Lives and Times of Martina Navratilova.* Secaucus, N.J.: Carol Publishing Group, 1995.

King, Billie Jean, and Cynthia Starr. *We Have Come a Long Way: The Story of Women's Tennis.* New York: McGraw-Hill, 1988.

Zwerman, Gilda. *Martina Navratilova.* Lives of Notable Gay Men and Lesbians, ed. Martin B. Duberman. New York: Chelsea House, 1995.

PERIODICALS

Bodo, Peter. "One More Wimbledon for Martina." *Tennis* 31, April 1996, 22–23.

"She Put Herself Into High Gear and Headed North." *Sports Illustrated,* September 19, 1983, 29–31.

Starr, Mark. "Martina Redux." *Newsweek* 129, June 2, 1997, 60–61.

WEBSITES

"Martina Navratilova." Women's Sports Foundation. Available online at https://www.womenssportsfoundation.org/cgi-bin/iowa/athletes/record.html?record=585; website home page: https://www.womenssportsfoundation.org (accessed July 17, 2003).

United States Football League v. National Football League

Court case

Date: October 2, 1986

Source: *United States Football League v. National Football League.* 84 Civ. 7484 (PKL), United States District Court, 644 F.Supp. 1040 (S.D.N.Y. 1986). ∎

Introduction

The United States Football League (USFL) was formulated in the mind of Louisiana entrepreneur David Dixon. He envisioned a professional football league that played in the spring. Football was so popular that Dixon believed people wanted more of it, and that they would watch pro football in the spring in addition to the fall.

The USFL's season started in May, and the championship game would be held in July. It would compete with other sports, but not with the already well-established National Football League (NFL). The hockey and basketball seasons would be drawing to an end and, as Dixon reasoned, basketball was at a low point as the 1980s began and hockey was only popular in the Midwest and northeast parts of the country. Baseball could be a significant distraction, but it was very early in the season.

The USFL began on May 11, 1982, at a press conference. The first players named to the twelve-team, three-division league were mostly players recently released from the NFL. However, a few notable college players began their careers with the USFL, including Reggie White, Jim Kelly, Anthony Carter, and Steve Young. Herschel Walker was the league's biggest star.

In its inaugural season, 1983, the USFL had an immediate impact. The league had television contracts with ABC and ESPN, and a marquee player in Hershel Walker, whom league directors hoped would draw large numbers of fans. The average game attendance for the league's first week was just under forty thousand, and television ratings were higher than expected, as curiousity drew many fans to the new league. By midseason, both television ratings and attendance dropped off significantly. Still, it was an encouraging first year for the new league, and team owners were optimistic heading into their second season.

However, the owners created many financial difficulties for themselves. To achieve legitimacy, USFL team owners signed multimillion-dollar contracts with many prominent college stars. Steve Young, Mike Rozier, Reggie White, Doug Flutie, and Jim Kelly all signed

USFL Commissioner Chet Simmons speaks at a meeting, Washington, D.C., August 31, 1982. Originally created as a spring professional football league, the USFL moved to the fall, resulting in its losing players and television network contracts to the NFL. The USFL then sued its rival league before disbanning. © BETTMANN/CORBIS. REPRODUCED BY PERMISSION.

big contracts with teams that lost money. More financial woes followed for the spring league when team owners announced that, beginning in 1986, the USFL would play its games in the fall—competing head-to-head with the NFL. Team owners, most prominently Donald Trump, were thinking about bigger television revenues in the fall, and hoping for a USFL-NFL merger, similar to the merger between the NFL and the AFL in 1970.

Switching seasons to compete with the NFL threw the young league into turmoil. The USFL, after starting with twelve teams, fielded only eight in 1985. Many prominent USFL players signed contracts with NFL teams in the summer of 1985, and television contracts for the next season, to be played in the fall, were not yet signed. The USFL team owners blamed the NFL. Finally, late in 1985, the owners decided the only way to save the league was to file an antitrust lawsuit against the NFL.

The trial began in the summer of 1986. Among those testifying were Howard Cosell, Donald Trump, and Pete Rozelle. After forty-eight days, the trial ended. After five days of deliberation, the jury found that the NFL did indeed constitute a monopoly, and that it had used predatory practices. However, instead of the 567 million dollars in damages the USFL sought, the jury awarded the league one dollar.

Significance

Without a big jury award, USFL team owners decided to suspend the 1986 season and examine their options. USFL players scrambled to the NFL and Canadian Football League. League stars Herschel Walker (Dallas Cowboys) and Jim Kelly (Buffalo Bills) signed with NFL teams. The USFL would never resume play.

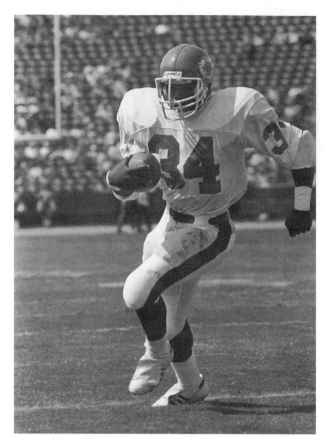

The New Jersey Generals' Herschel Walker scores a touchdown, Los Angeles, March 6, 1983. The Generals were one of the many teams operating in the newly formed United States Football League. © BETTMANN/CORBIS. REPRODUCED BY PERMISSION.

The move of the USFL season from the spring to the fall is considered one of the worst self-inflicted wounds in sports history. Most of the initial USFL franchises were in cities with NFL teams and big-time college teams nearby. The Pittsburgh and Chicago teams disbanded, while the Michigan team was folded into the Oakland franchise rather than competing for fans in the fall.

After the trial, the jury made a statement. Although the NFL did harm the USFL with its monopolistic and predatory actions, the jury felt that the major reasons for the USFL's problems were its own actions. The jury cited the multimillion-dollar player contracts and the league's switch from spring to fall, leading to the abandonment of major television markets. The jury concluded that the USFL failed due to its own mismanagement.

The USFL did not survive, but it did impact the NFL. The USFL made many bold moves to challenge the venerable NFL. The upstart league signed big name players including Hershal Walker and two other Heisman Trophy winners, paying its stars huge salaries, forcing the NFL to start doing the same. Thus it contributed to the increase of salaries in professional football.

The failure of the USFL also demonstrated the power and success of the NFL in the 1980s. Unlike the earlier challenge of the AFL, the NFL was much more firmly established and prepared to fight the USFL successfully. By the 1980s, successful expansion and strong television ratings had helped the NFL establish a superior level of football that the USFL could not match.

Primary Source

United States Football League v. National Football League [excerpt]

SYNOPSIS: The jury in the *United States Football League v. National Football League* case issued its findings that, although the NFL constituted a monopoly, it was not responsible for the USFL's problems.

LEISURE, District Judge:

In this action, the United States Football League and certain of its member clubs (hereinafter collectively referred to as the "USFL") have brought suit against the National Football League, its commissioner and certain of its member clubs (hereinafter collectively referred to as the "NFL") for the NFL's alleged violations of Sections 1 and 2 of the Sherman Anti-Trust Act, 15 U.S.C. §§ 1 and 2, and of the common law. After ten weeks of trial, the jury unanimously rendered a series of general verdicts and answered numerous special interrogatories by entering their responses on a jury verdict sheet, Court Exhibit 16, which had been prepared by the Court after consultation with the parties and due consideration of their respective objections.

With regard to the USFL's claim of actual monopolization, the jury found the NFL liable, concluding that defendants had willfully acquired or maintained monopoly power in a relevant market consisting of major league professional football in the United States. *See* Court Exhibit 16 at 3 (Question No. 4). The jury also found that the NFL's unlawful monopolization of a relevant market had caused injury to plaintiffs' business or property. *Id.* (Question No. 5). Despite these findings, the jury chose to award plaintiffs only nominal damages, concluding that the USFL had suffered only $1.00 in damages as a result of the NFL's unlawful conduct. *See id.* at 11 (Question No. 17).

Plaintiffs were less successful on the remainder of their antitrust claims. The jury found that none of the defendants had violated Section 2 of the Sherman Act by attempting to monopolize a relevant market, *id.* at 5 (Question No. 7), or by conspiring to monopolize. *See id.* at 8–9 (Questions Nos. 12–14). In addition, the jury found that even though one or more of the defendants had participated in a contract, combination or conspiracy to exclude competition within major league professional football, *id.* at 12 (Question No. 20), that combination did not constitute an unreasonable restraint of trade in violation of Section 1 of the Sherman Act. *See id.* (Question No. 21). The jury also found that the NFL's contracts with all three television networks for the right to broadcast the league's regular season and championship games through the 1986–87 season were not an unreasonable restraint of trade violative of Section 1. *See id.* at 14 (Question No. 24). Finally, the jury rejected plaintiffs' "essential facilities" claim, specifically finding that defendants did not have the ability to deny actual or potential competitors access to a national broadcast television contract. *Id.* at 17 (Question No. 33).

Further Resources

BOOKS

Bryne, Jim. *The $1 League: The Rise and Fall of the USFL.* New York: Prentice Hall, 1986.

Patton, Phil. *Razzle Dazzle: The Curious Marriage of Television and Professional Football.* Garden City, N.Y.: Dial Press, 1984.

Quirk, James, P. *Pay Dirt: The Business of Professional Team Sports.* Princeton, N.J.: Princeton University Press, 1992.

PERIODICALS

Higgins, John M. "TBS, NBC Huddle on New Ball Game: Losers in NFL Bidding Talk About Forming Own League." *Broadcasting & Cable* 128, February 2, 1998, 9.

Lieber, Jill. "So Long, USFL—Now What?" *Sports Illustrated* 65, August 18, 1986, 30–32.

Staudohar, Paul D. "The Scope of Pro Football's Antitrust Exemption." *Labor Law Journal* 50, no. 1, March 1999, 34–42.

WEBSITES

Michigan Panthers. Available online at http://members.tripod.com/scimini/Default.htm (accessed July 18, 2003).

"USFL." OurSports Central. Available online at http://www.oursportscentral.com/usfl/index.htm; website home page: http://www.oursportscentral.com (accessed July 18, 2003).

"They Were Just One Pitch Away"

Magazine article

By: Leigh Montville
Date: October 26, 1986

Source: Montville, Leigh. "They Were Just One Pitch Away." *Boston Globe,* October 26, 1986.

About the Author: Leigh Montville was a sports columnists for the *Boston Globe* for twenty-one years. He later became a senior writer for *Sports Illustrated,* as well as a contributing commentator on *CNN/SI,* a twenty-four hour television sports news network. Montville wrote two books, *At the Altar of Speed: The Fast Life and Tragic Death of Dale Earnhart* and *Manute: Center of Two Worlds,* and coauthored another one with Connecticut basketball coach Jim Calhoun. ■

Introduction

The 1986 Boston Red Sox had a remarkable season. Predicted to finish fifth in the tough American League East, the Red Sox won the division title, finishing 95-66, improving from eighty-one wins in 1985. Roger Clemens emerged as the top pitcher in baseball, winning his first fourteen decisions, finishing 24-4 for the season, striking out a major league record twenty batters in a nine-inning game, and winning both the American League MVP and Cy Young Awards. Third baseman Wade Boggs won the batting title, hitting .357, as well as leading the league in walks (105) and on-base percentage (.450). Other Red Sox hitters had excellent seasons: Jim Rice (.320, 20 HR, 110 RBI), Bill Buckner (18 HR, 102 RBI), Dwight Evans (26 HR, 97 RBI), and Don Baylor (31 HR, 94 RBI). And Manager John McNamara won the AL Manager of the Year.

In the American League playoffs, the Red Sox faced the AL West champion California Angels, led by future Hall of Famers Reggie Jackson and Don Sutton. After four games, the Red Sox trailed three games to one in the best-of-seven series. The Red Sox were within one out of losing the AL Championship Series when reserve outfielder David Henderson, who earlier in the game had turned a long fly ball into a California home run, hit a two-out, two-run homer in the ninth inning to give the Red Sox the lead. After California rallied to tie the score, Henderson hit a sacrifice fly to win the game for Boston in the eleventh inning. Boston completed the remarkable comeback by winning games six and seven to advance to the World Series.

Boston's opponent in the World Series was the New York Mets, baseball's best team during the season with a 108-53 record. The Mets featured hitters Keith Hernandez and Daryl Strawberry, and the best pitching rotation in the major leagues. Adding to the drama of the series was talk of "The Curse of the Bambino." Despite fielding perennially strong teams, the Red Sox had not won a World Series since trading Babe Ruth to the Yankees in 1920 for cash and a loan enabling the building of Fenway Park. Since the Ruth trade, the Red Sox had appeared in three previous World Series, suffering heartbreaking losses in the seventh game of each of these series.

Bill Buckner shrinks off the field after committing an error in game six of the World Series, New York, October 25, 1986. Buckner's error came with Boston needing one out to win the game and helped the Mets's comeback victory. AP/WIDE WORLD PHOTOS. REPRODUCED BY PERMISSION.

The Red Sox appeared to be a team of destiny after winning the first two World Series games at New York's Shea Stadium. However, they lost games three and four at Fenway Park, before rallying to win game five. Ahead three games to two, Boston prepared to celebrate its first championship since 1918, sixty-eight long years of frustration.

Game six of the 1986 World Series at Shea Stadium was a classic, one that will live forever in baseball lore. Boston jumped out to leads of 2-0 and 3-2, but the Mets rallied to tie the game in the eighth inning. In the top of the tenth inning, Boston scored two runs. The first two Mets made outs, and the Red Sox were one out away from the championship. After two singles, the Mets's Ray Knight, on an 0-2 count, singled in one run and advanced the tying run to third. Manager McNamara brought in Red Sox closer Bob Stanley to preserve the win. The count went to 2-2, and Mookie Wilson fouled off two pitches. Then Stanley threw a wild pitch, allowing the tying run to score and moving the winning run to second base. Wilson then hit a weak groundball to first baseman Bill Buckner—a routine play that should have gotten the Red Sox out of the inning. Amazingly, the ball went between Buckner's legs, allowing Ray Knight to score from second for a Mets victory. One strike away from the World Series title, the Boston players had to put the devastating loss behind them and think about game seven.

The Red Sox jumped to a 3-0 lead in game seven, but the Mets tied the game in the fifth inning. The Mets went ahead for good with three runs in the seventh, as reliever Calvin Schiraldi—after giving up eight earned runs all season—surrendered his fifth, sixth, and seventh earned runs of the 1986 World Series. Boston scored two in the eighth inning to make it 6-5; but the Mets then added two insurance runs in the bottom of the inning, and they held on to win game seven, 8-5.

Significance

"The Curse of the Bambino" and the agony of long-suffering Red Sox fans continued. Despite all of the previous heartbreaking World Series game seven losses, game six remains the most bitter defeat in Boston Red Sox history. To allow the tying run to score on a wild pitch and the winning run to score on a routine ground-ball was devastating, even by Red Sox standards—particularly as the first two Mets hitters in the ninth inning made outs. The notoriety of "The Curse of the Bambino" has grown since the crushing 1986 defeat. It became the title of an incredibly popular musical in Boston—in which the baseball gods console suffering Red Sox fans—and the topic of a popular website, http://bambinoscurse.com. All of the Red Sox's historic heartbreaks are chronicled at http://www.soxsuck.com. The subtitle of the site is: "A Chronological History of Amazing Boston Red Sox Losses, Remarkable Collapses and Other Record Breaking Feats." The 1986 Red Sox appeared to be a team of destiny after its dramatic comeback against the Angels in the AL Championship Series, but it turned out not to be.

Sports fans routinely use the phrase "pulled a Buckner" to describe a collapse or failure at a critical juncture. While Bill Buckner's error in the tenth inning of game six is generally considered the key play that allowed the Mets to win, there were plenty of others worthy of the label "goat." The Red Sox's closer Bob Stanley allowed the tying run on a wild pitch with two outs; the Red Sox stranded fourteen batters in game six; and McNamara failed to replace Buckner for defensive purposes, as was his habit throughout the season. McNamara later admitted that he did not replace Buckner so that he could be on the field when the Red Sox won the championship. Also, the Red Sox still had a chance to win game seven, but lost a three-run lead, as its pitching failed the team.

Primary Source

"They Were Just One Pitch Away"

SYNOPSIS: This article illustrates the wild swing in emotions for the Boston Red Sox, from "almost euphoria" to "bitter disappointment," produced during game six of the 1986 World Series.

One pitch away from a world championship. One pitch from an end to 68 years of frustration. One pitch.

Not close enough.

In a heartbreak that ranks with all of the heartbreaks ever recorded in the long book of Boston Red Sox heartbreak history, the Olde Towne Team let that world championship bounce away in the red dirt of Shea Stadium last night. One wild pitch. One error by first baseman Bill Buckner. One pitch away. The New York Mets scored three runs in the bottom of the 10th and final inning after allowing the Red Sox two in the top of the inning to post a wild, 6-5 win in the sixth game of this World Series and force a seventh game tonight at 8:35 (NBC-TV).

Never have the Red Sox come this close and failed. Never in the Bucky Dent game or the Enos Slaughter game or the Jim Burton game or all the recorded games of frustration had the finish been this close to a championship. Never. Not since 1918. Never.

"We didn't get that final out," manager John McNamara said. "That's all I can say. We needed that one more out, and we didn't get it.

"Yes, it's disappointing, but at least we have another chance tomorrow. That's something they (the Mets) didn't have."

How much of a heartbreak was this? A simple recitation of the roller-coaster events of the 10th is enough to show how bad this one was. In the top of the 10th, Dave Henderson, apparently God's favorite baseball player of this October, homered to

left. The Red Sox added another run, and they had a 5-3 lead and an apparent win.

What more could they want? Relief ace Calvin Schiraldi was on the mound. There was dancing in the dugout. There was a party in half the houses in New England—tell the truth—crepe paper being strung everywhere, the civic reception and parade virtually ready to go.

Schiraldi took care of leadoff hitter Wally Backman with a fly ball to left. One out. Schiraldi took care of slugger Keith Hernandez with a fly to center. Two outs. Two outs? Two outs!!!!!

The moon suddenly fell out of the sky and landed on the Red Sox' heads. Ker-plunk! Kaboom! Ouch and double ouch!

How to describe the unraveling? Gary Carter singled to left. So what? Pinch hitter Kevin Mitchell singled to center. Carter moving to second. Big deal. Third baseman Ray Knight, husband of pro golfer Nancy Lopez, swinging with two strikes, singled to center to score Carter and move Mitchell to third. Uh-oh. The lead now was 5-4 and the tying run was on third.

Schiraldi was taken from the game and replaced by Bob Stanley. Wouldn't this be the story of stories? Wouldn't that be the perfect final picture, Stanley hugging catcher Rich Gedman as the 68 years of frustration ended? Here was the man who has endured the longest run of wrath from the Fenway Park fans. Couldn't he celebrate the loudest?

The batter was Mookie Wilson, the Mets' left fielder, a man who will swing at most pitches thrown anywhere near the plate, a swinger's swinger.

Stanley pitched. Mookie swung. Foul ball. Stanley pitched. Ball one. Stanley pitched. Ball two. Stanley pitched three straight times. Mookie fouled all three pitches backwards. The count was stuck at 2-2.

On the next pitch, Stanley ran the ball inside. Mookie jumped backward. Gedman reached for the ball, but not far enough. Wild pitch. Kevin Mitchell ran home as if he were yelling ollie-ollie-in-free and setting the Mets and the entire city of New York free in a giant game of hide and seek. Tie game, 5-5.

Knight now was on second with the winning run. Stanley still was on the mound. Mookie still was at the plate. The count now was 3-2. Stanley pitched again. Mookie fouled the ball backward again. Stanley pitched again. Mookie fouled again.

On the next pitch, Mookie hit a weak ground ball toward first. Half the crowd of 55,078 began to

The New York Mets celebrate their World Series victory after defeating Boston in the seventh and final game, New York, October 27, 1986. The victory completed the embarrassment for the Red Sox, who were one out from the championship in game six. **AP/WIDE WORLD PHOTOS. REPRODUCED BY PERMISSION.**

record the easy, unassisted out in the scorebook. The other half breathed nervously, relaxing for the inevitable 11th inning.

Red Sox first baseman Bill Buckner bent low to pick up the ball. Bill Buckner, the man of a million aches and hurts, didn't bend low enough. The ball skipped directly through Buckner's legs and down the first base line. Knight, running all the way with two outs, virtually cartwheeled to the plate, landing so hard to officially score the run that he thought he hurt himself.

Pandemonium landed as if it were a giddy disease. The Mets gave curtain call after curtain call, handshake after handshake, while the Red Sox walked off the field with the dumbstruck look of accident vicims. The worst. The absolute worst.

"Thinking about the team's history . . . ," manager McNamara was asked in the interview room.

"I don't know anything about history," he said with a toneless voice, "and don't tell me anything about that choke crap."

Due to the lateness of the game, added to early deadlines at most metropolitan newspapers, story after story was ripped up in a hurry. How many leads had been written about this game that had the Red Sox winning, 5-3, and ending all that frustration? How many actually made the newspapers? How many happy stories, traded for sad? How fast? How unbelievably fast?

"This is the worst yet," a man in the press box said. "This is the game that truly will be remembered forever."

"Not yet," he was told. "It all will depend on what happens in the final game. If the Red Sox win that game, the story will be a sidelight. But if they don't . . ."

Never easy with this team. Never easy.

Further Resources

BOOKS

Frommer, Harvey. *Baseball's Greatest Rivalry: The New York Yankees and Boston Red Sox.* New York: Atheneum, 1982.

Shaughnessy, Dan. *The Curse of the Bambino.* New York: Dutton, 1990.

PERIODICALS

Creamer, Robert C. "When New York and Boston Played 74 Years Ago." *Sports Illustrated* 65, October 27, 1986, 27.

Fimrite, Ron. "Good to the Very Last Out." *Sports Illustrated,* November 3, 1986.

Gammons, Peter. "The Hub Hails Its Hobbling Hero." *Sports Illustrated* 65, November 10, 1986, 26–30.

Gergen, Joe. "Red Sox Couldn't Erase Ghosts of Series Past." *The Sporting News* 202, November 10, 1986, 7.

WEBSITES

Cossette, Edward. "The Curse of the Bambino." Available online at http://bambinoscurse.com (accessed June 26, 2003).

"The Curse of the Bambino." CNN/Sports Illustrated. Available online at http://sportsillustrated.cnn.com/baseball/mlb/news/2000/03/22/the_curse_timeline; website home page: http://sportsillustrated.cnn.com (accessed July 16, 2003).

"1986 Boston Red Sox." BaseballLibrary.com. Available online at http://www.baseballlibrary.com/baseballlibrary/teams/1986redsox.stm; website home page: http://www.baseballlibrary.com (accessed June 26, 2003).

"1986 World Series." Baseball-Reference.com. Available online at http://www.baseball-reference.com/postseason/1986_WS.shtml; website home page: http://www.baseball-reference.com (accessed June 16, 2003).

Soxsuck.com: A Chronological History of Amazing Boston Red Sox Losses, Remarkable Collapses and Other Record Breaking Feats. Available online at http://www.soxsuck.com (accessed June 26, 2003).

AUDIO AND VISUAL MEDIA

MLB: 1986 World Series Game 6 Boston Red Sox vs. New York Mets. Hackensack, N.J.: Major League Baseball Home Video, 1992, VHS.

"'Everything I Did Worked'"

Magazine article

By: William Nack

Date: April 20, 1987

Source: Nack, William. "'Everything I Did Worked.'" *Sports Illustrated* 66, April 20, 1987, 50–52.

About the Author: William Nack was born in Chicago, Illinios, and he graduated from the University of Illinois before serving in the U.S. Army in the Vietnam War (1964–1975). Prior to joining *Sports Illustrated* in 1979, Nack served as a reporter and columnist for *Newsday.* Nack has won six Eclipse Awards from the Thoroughbred Racing Association for excellence in magazine writing. He has also published two books, *Secretariat: The Making of Champion* and *My Turf: Horses, Boxers, Blood Money, and the Sporting Life.* ∎

Introduction

Sugar Ray Leonard began boxing at fourteen. He won three National Gold Glove titles, two AAU championships, and the 1975 Pan-Am Games gold medal. He capped his brilliant amateur career by winning the welterweight gold medal at the 1976 Olympics in Montreal.

Early in Leonard's professional career, four boxers emerged—nicknamed "The Fantastic Four"—who would dominate the boxing world during the 1980s: Leonard, Marvin Hagler, Roberto Duran, and Tommy "Hit Man" Hearns. They would all fight each other during the decade, staging some of the greatest matches in boxing history. After taking the WBC welterweight title from Wilfred Benitez in 1979, Leonard fought Duran twice in 1980. Duran won their first fight by a unanimous decision; but Leonard controlled the second fight, forcing Duran to quit in the middle of the eighth round, after uttering *"no mas"* (Spanish for "no more").

Leonard then fought Hearns in an epic 1981 bout. Leonard started quickly, but Hearns rallied in the middle rounds. In the fourteenth round, Leonard—behind on all three cards—landed twenty-five consecutive punches, knocking Hearns down. Although Hearns got to his feet, the fight was stopped and Leonard was awarded a technical knockout. His victory over Hearns proved costly, as Leonard sustained a serious injury to his retina during the fight, forcing him to retire and undergo extensive surgery after his following bout.

Marvin Hagler was the undisputed middleweight champion from 1980 to 1987. He successfully defended his title twelve times over that period. Hagler defeated Duran in 1983; and, in 1985, he knocked out Tommy Hearns in the fourth round—a bout where the fighters stood toe-to-toe and punched for the entire match, widely considered the most intense and entertaining fight in boxing history. Hagler, a fearsome puncher who could fight right-handed or left-handed, appeared invincible.

During this time, Sugar Ray Leonard stayed in shape and served as a commentator for several fights. Then, despite having fought only one bout in the past five years, Leonard signed to meet Hagler in a twelve-round middleweight fight in Las Vegas on April 6, 1987. Leonard trained as never before, adding eleven pounds of muscle to fight Hagler as a middleweight. Hagler was a prohibitive favorite, and many were fearful that Leonard's comeback would end his career in disgrace and defeat, as well as risk further damage to his eye. Hagler trained hard for three months, and both fighters came to the fight in excellent condition.

Sugar Ray Leonard (right) taunts Marvin Hagler during their title bout, Las Vegas, Nevada, April 6, 1987. At points during the fight, defending champion Hagler, the overwhelming favorite, had trouble even landing a punch. © BETTMANN/CORBIS. REPRODUCED BY PERMISSION.

Just as he had with Duran and Hearns, Leonard started strongly and seemed to confuse Hagler. Leonard moved constantly, frustrating Hagler and making him miss and then tying him up. After the fight, Hagler described Leonard's style by saying, "He fought like a girl. He ran from me." Leonard fought a brilliant tactical fight, throwing enough scoring punches to steal several rounds. As the fight wore on, Hagler began to take control. However, Leonard summoned the strength to begin the final round with a three-punch combination that brought the crowd to its feet. The fight ended in a split decision victory for Leonard. Hagler was not gracious in defeat, claiming that the judges gave the fight to Leonard unfairly. Leonard again retired, refusing to give Hagler a rematch. Hagler also retired, as he would only agree to fight Leonard.

Significance

Leonard came out of retirement again in 1988 to beat Donny Lelonde and pick up two additional championship titles. Over the course of his career, Leonard held titles in five divisions; welterweight, junior middleweight, middleweight, super middleweight, and light heavyweight. In 1989, Leonard again fought Hearns; the fight ended in a draw (although the crowd and experts felt that

Hearns had won decisively). Leonard then won a decision over Duran, once again retiring after the bout. Leonard's third retirement ended when he lost to reigning welterweight champion, Terry Norris, in 1991. Amazingly, Leonard came out of retirement a fourth time to fight Hector "Macho" Camacho in 1997. Camacho completely dominated the fight, and it was stopped in the fifth round. Leonard finished his illustrious career 36-3-1.

Leonard's victory over Hagler ensured that he would be considered the top fighter of the 1980s. While the 1970s featured great heavyweight champions—including Ali, Frazier, Foreman, Norton and Holmes—the best fighters in the 1980s were in the welterweight and middleweight divisions. Leonard beat all three of his main rivals, and avenged his only loss of the decade with a convincing victory over Duran. Leonard's ring mastery enabled him to beat his stronger opponents, scoring points and moving throughout the bouts. But Leonard did not just rely on dancing and outpointing his opponents; Leonard knocked out Hearns when trailing late in the bout. His opponents typically underestimated Leonard's strength and punching ability because he was so effective in scoring while minimizing his opponents' opportunities for landing clean blows. Unlike most decades, the best fighters of the 1980s met in the ring to fight each other; Leonard emerged as the best boxer of the 1980s.

The fight also marred Hagler's reputation both in the short and long term. Seen as virtually unbeatable, Hagler could not solve Leonard, who kept changing his angles and avoiding Hagler. Hagler could not put Leonard away, and experts generally agree that Leonard won the fight by a narrow margin, although Hagler believed that he was robbed of his title. Hagler was viewed negatively by the public when complaining about the judging after the fight and for his blunt criticism of Leonard. The Leonard fight was the last of Hagler's career, and he left the sport embittered and frustrated.

The fight was also important because it showed how attention to small details can make the difference in a championship fight. Leonard may well have won the fight with Hagler during the negotiations for the bout. As he was willing to give Hagler a larger share of the purse and agreed to fight in Las Vegas, Leonard ensured that the fight would only last twelve rounds—not fifteen as customary for championship bouts. Leonard was also able to negotiate a relatively big ring for the fight. Both of these factors played a key role in Leonard's upset. Leonard devised a perfect fight plan for Hagler and carried it out beautifully.

Primary Source

"'Everything I Did Worked'" [excerpt]

SYNOPSIS: On April 10, four days after he defeated Marvin Hagler, Sugar Ray Leonard talks to *Sports Illustrated* about the amazing fight.

Sugar Ray Leonard couldn't help exulting over his upset of Marvelous Marvin Hagler

I went against history, and now they'll have to rewrite the books. They talked about logic, that the fight was not supposed to be. Someone said before the fight, "Two things will not happen this year: Oliver North will not be back in the White House, and Sugar Ray Leonard will not beat Marvin Hagler."

I think they better check the White House.

Sugar Ray Leonard

They were ensconced at a back table in Jameson's Restaurant in the Washington suburb of Bethesda, Md., early on Friday afternoon. The two men were swapping tales from that twilight zone that falls somewhere between nightmare and dream. Just four days earlier, Sugar Ray Leonard had beaten Marvelous Marvin Hagler to pull off the most extraordinary comeback in recent sports history. Mike Trainer, Leonard's attorney, financial adviser and close friend since the fighter turned pro 10 years ago, recalled

Some of Boxing's Weight Divisions

HEAVYWEIGHT: 190 pounds and over
CRUISERWEIGHT: Up to 190 pounds
LIGHT HEAVYWEIGHT: Up to 175 pounds
SUPER MIDDLEWEIGHT: Up to 168 pounds
MIDDLEWEIGHT: Up to 160 pounds
JUNIOR MIDDLEWEIGHT: Up to 154 pounds
WELTERWEIGHT: Up to 147 pounds
JUNIOR WELTERWEIGHT: Up to 140 pounds

how he had awakened in his Maryland home on Wednesday morning, a couple of days after the fight, thinking he was still at Caesars Palace.

"I thought, Was the fight postponed, or what?" Trainer recounted to Leonard at Jameson's. "Did this fight really happen yet?" Trainer then recalled that he had looked over and had seen his wife, Jill, who had traveled to Las Vegas with him, asleep. "I thought, Am I still at Caesars?" Trainer said. After he had sat in bed, befuddled for a moment, Trainer spotted the family cat, Gigi, and the sight of that familiar animal jogged him back to Maryland and the real world. "I said, 'It's over,'" Trainer recalled. "'We're home.'"

Leonard looked at Trainer with a wondering expression. "Is that right?" he said. Leonard shook his head. That same Wednesday morning Leonard had been walking through his father-in-law's suburban Washington home when he had suddenly lapsed into his own trancelike world. "I didn't feel nothing," Leonard said, "and I didn't hear nothing." He had been sore after the fight—his sides, his neck, his biceps, even the back of his head—but when he had felt himself that morning, the aches were nonexistent.

Like Trainer, momentarily disoriented, Leonard had begun to wonder whether the fight had really happened. He had gone to a mirror to check his face. It was unmarked. Seeing his old friend Joe Broddie, who was an overnight guest in the house, Leonard asked him earnestly, "Is the fight over?"

"Yeah, it's over, Ray," Broddie said. "It's all over." The next night, Broddie says he found the fighter at 10 o'clock in the driveway of Leonard's Potomac, Md., home. He was shadowboxing his dog, a chow chow named Caesar.

Sugar Ray Leonard holds the middleweight championship belt aloft after winning it from Marvin Hagler, Las Vegas, Nevada, April 6, 1987. The victory capped Leonard's comback after retiring five years earlier. AP/WIDE WORLD PHOTOS. REPRODUCED BY PERMISSION.

"Ray, you O.K.?" Broddie asked.

Leonard was just fine, parachuting slowly down from the heights he had attained, but still so restlessly hyper that on Friday he rolled out of bed at 6 a.m. and told his wife, Juanita, that he was going running. "Lay your butt down!" she said to him.

What Leonard had passed through was so physically and emotionally draining that it left him groping to fathom what he had done. What he had done, of course, was emerge out of a virtual five-year retirement and lift the title from Hagler, a man who had held it for nearly seven years, since Sept. 27, 1980, and through 12 defenses, a man regarded as one of the finest middleweight champions of all time.

"It was like a revelation," Leonard said on Friday afternoon. "I wish I could really describe it. My head is so clogged up now. Sometimes, during the day, I'm so tired I just lie down. I say, 'What the hell's wrong? I'm O.K. now.' We'll sit here and have a few beers, and I'll try to reminisce and think about it and create the vivid scenario to see it. But it's not clear enough, not clear enough to say, 'That's it!' I know what I accomplished, but I don't feel anything

yet. I'm mentally exhausted. I busted my chops in training. People don't know what I went through."

Although he says he felt numb last week, Leonard was animated in Trainer's law office on Friday as he watched a tape of the bout on a small black-and-white screen. Looking at the third round, as Hagler chased him and swung and missed, Leonard cried out, "Look at that! He can't catch me."

To be sure, his speed and his ability to move frustrated Hagler. "I was so fast, man!" said the 30-year-old former welterweight and junior middleweight champion of the world. "He couldn't hit me for nothing! When he finally did hit me, it was like, 'This is it?' He was more of a pusher than a puncher. I couldn't believe he was that slow, that vulnerable, that susceptible to punches. It was my speed that upset him, my movement that threw him off. People said I lost the zip, but my hands are just as fast as they were when I was 20 years old!"

Looking at the fifth round, Leonard watched his opponent dogging him and throwing one punch at a time. "Look!" Leonard said. "He never threw combinations. He always threw, like, one punch and that was all."

"The only time he threw more than one punch was when you were on the ropes," said Trainer.

"Yeah, but never short combinations," said Leonard.

Here Hagler landed a solid uppercut that would win him the fifth round on all three judges' cards. "That was a good shot," Leonard admitted. "He stunned me. But he didn't know I was hurt. Watch this!" As the bell rang, ending the round, Hagler pushed Leonard away. "He was so mad!" said Leonard with a laugh.

Leonard went flat-footed in the sixth. "I'm a little tired here," he said. "Five years ago he couldn't have touched me!" That was when the two men had been expected to have their first joust, the one that never came off because Leonard suffered a detached retina in his left eye and retired.

As he viewed the seventh round, Leonard mused about what Thomas Hearns must have thought about the fight. Instead of boxing Hagler, as Leonard had done, Hearns had gone toe-to-toe with the champ two years ago, and he was knocked out in the third round. "You realize how Hearns must feel looking at this?" Leonard asked. "He must be sick. I was in a totally different world in this fight." Watching Hagler chase and miss once again, Leonard said, "Marvin's like an amateur."

"One of the greatest middleweights who ever lived," said Trainer.

"But I'm matching him, Mike!" said Leonard. "I told you what I would do—taunt him, frustrate him, cross his wires, make him mad. Didn't I? And I'm doing it! I was like radar out there. I could see all his punches coming."

No, said Leonard, he was not hurt in the wild ninth round, when it appeared that Hagler had Sugar Ray in trouble in his own corner. "I was just tired," he said. The camera zoomed in on Hagler measuring Leonard for each punch. Then the perspective suddenly widened as Leonard flurried his way out of trouble. Just seconds later, at mid-ring, Leonard caught Hagler with another flurry. "Oh, I love it!" said Leonard with a laugh.

What he loved most of all about watching the fight was listening to his trainer, Angelo Dundee, exhort him between rounds. Before the seventh, Dundee yelled, "Round number 7! Yeah, baby, Rooooouuund 7!" Leonard howled as he heard that again. "Look at Angie! He's like a kid. I'm telling you, Angelo was great!" Before the last round Dundee screamed, "Three minutes, champ!"

"Boy, Angelo pumped me up there," said Leonard.

Moments after the fight ended, Leonard leaped on a ring rope. "I was on cloud nine," he said. "I gazed out at the audience and saw currency being exchanged [bets being paid off]. I knew I had it. I just knew."

What he had known, and what others at ringside had sensed, was that he had indeed achieved this most improbable of upsets. As Leonard watched ring announcer Chuck Hull declare it was a split decision and then begin to read off the third judge's card, he leaned forward in the office chair in Trainer's office. "Listen to this!" he said. "This is the greatest feeling in the world, to hear this."

Hull's voice then intoned, "The winner and new. . . ."

"Yeah!" Leonard said. "Jeez, God, I mean. . . ." Trainer, clapping, burst out laughing.

When asked what he said to Hagler in the ring when he was seen tapping the former champion on the shoulder, Leonard said, "I was saying, 'Hey, we're still friends, right? Still friends?'" To which, according to Leonard, Hagler replied, "It's not fair." Leonard pressed: "No, we're still friends, right?"

Because of the commotion and noise around the ring, the new champion was not sure what Hagler then said. "I think he said, 'Yeah, good fight, good fight,'" Leonard said. He emphatically denied that he said to Hagler, as Hagler later insisted he had, "You beat me." Said Leonard, "I told Marvin, 'You're still the champ.'"

The tape then showed Hagler telling HBO commentator Larry Merchant, "That flurry stuff didn't mean nothing." Leonard leaned forward once more. This time he addressed Hagler's unhappy visage on the screen, "It meant points. Points!"

So what began almost a year ago, when Leonard issued his challenge to Hagler on a Washington, D.C., television broadcast, ended late last week with Leonard talking to a TV set outside that same city, trying to explain to a man who could not hear him what he had done to that man. It had been a long year for Leonard, the most difficult and agonizing in his professional life. He had worked his head and body into the kind of shape required for him to do what no fighter had ever done.

Further Resources

BOOKS

Hauser, Thomas. *The Black Lights: Inside the World of Professional Boxing.* New York: Simon & Schuster, 1986.

Oates, Joyce Carol. *On Boxing.* New York: Simon & Schuster, 1987.

Toperoff, Sam. *Sugar Ray Leonard and Other Noble Warriors.* New York: McGraw-Hill, 1987.

PERIODICALS

McDonough, John. "Dream Fight. S.R. Leonard vs. M. Hagler." *Sport* 78, December 1987, 56–63.

Nack, William. "Comeback for the Ages." *Sports Illustrated,* April 13, 1987, 18–26.

Unger, Norman O. "Sugar Ray Leonard: Why I Am Fighting Again." *Ebony* 42, April 1987, 92–94.

WEBSITES

"Ali Helped Make Sugar." *ABC Sports Online.* ESPN.com. Available online at http://espn.go.com/abcsports/wwos/leonard/ali.html; website home page: http://www.espn.go.com (accessed July 16, 2003).

"A Conversation With Marvin Hagler." Secondsout.com. Available online at http://secondsout.com/usa/news_52052; website home page: http://secondsout.com (accessed June 26, 2003).

The Official Website of Marvelous Marvin Hagler. Available onlie at http://marvelousmarvin.com (accessed June 26, 2003).

"Sugar Ray's 'Marvellous' Comeback." BBC Sport. Available online at http://news.bbc.co.uk/sport1/hi/boxing/1593089.stm; website home page: http://news.bbc.co.uk (accessed July 16, 2003).

AUDIO AND VISUAL MEDIA

Hagler vs. Leonard. Chico, Calif.: Tamarelle's International Films, 1987, VHS.

Comeback: My Race for the America's Cup

Memoir

By: Dennis Conner, with Bruce Stannard

Date: 1987

Source: Conner, Dennis, with Bruce Stannard. *Comeback: My Race for the America's Cup.* New York: St Martin's Press, 1987, 15–22.

About the Author: Dennis Conner (1943–) was born in San Diego, California. Conner has been sailing for most of his life, joining the San Diego Yacht Club at eleven. In addition to winning the America's Cup four times, he has won many sailing competitions—including the prestigious Etchell's World Championships, Congressional Cups, and a bronze medal in the 1976 Olympic Games. As of 2003, Conner was still actively involved in many aspects of current America's Cup campaigns. He also has authored several sailing and motivational books, and started a business. ∎

Introduction

In June, a few months before the final races of the 1983 America's Cup challenge, the *Australia II* arrived in Newport, Rhode Island. In a shroud of secrecy, the yacht was measured and inspected by the International Yacht Racing Union Measures Committee. Those who saw her were immediately amazed at her unusual looking keel. The keel is a protruding section under the boat that provides stability and prevents sideways drift. The *Australia II* sported a revolutionary "winged keel." Instead of just protruding straight down, the *Australia II*'s keel protruded straight down with its two wings sticking out on either side, resembling an upside down T or Y.

Word of *Australia II*'s winged keel spread to Dennis Conner who, along with other team members, was busy preparing the yacht *Liberty* for the America's Cup competition. The New York Yacht Club (NYYC) had not yet chosen the American defender of the Cup, and the *Liberty* was one of three teams competing for the honor. Conner and members of his team tried to convince the NYYC and the International Yacht Racing Union Measures Committee that the winged keel design was illegal, breaking the rule that a yacht "shall draw no more than nine feet."

The New York Yacht Club's attitude toward defending the America's Cup had become lackadaisical. The Manhattan-based NYYC held the deed to the "100 Guinea Cup," as it was originally known, since it was first presented to the team of the yacht *America* in 1851. The America's Cup stayed in New York through twenty-four foreign challenges over 132 years of competition. At first the NYYC did not take Conner's claims seriously. But, they started actively pursing the matter as the *Aus-*

tralia II won competition after competition, and it became apparent that it would be the foreign challenger for the Cup (only one foreign team races against the defender).

In September 1983, the *Australia II* challenged the *Liberty*, (chosen by the NYYC as the defender) for the America's Cup. Conner and the NYYC were disappointed, but the *Australia II*'s winged keel design was permitted by the International Yacht Racing Union. After four races at the Newport, Rhode Island, seaport—home to America's Cup races since 1930—Dennis Conner, his crew, and the *Liberty* were leading 3-1 in the best-of-seven match. However, the *Australia II* won the final three races to wrench the "100 Guinea Cup" away from the Americans. For the first time ever, the America's Cup left New York and the U.S.A.—it headed down under.

Significance

The America's Cup is sailing's Holy Grail. It is the oldest trophy in sport, first awarded on August 22, 1851. For most of the twentieth century, the Cup has sat within the confines of the New York Yacht Club. However, after 132 years the Cup left New York when the U.S. team, led by Dennis Conner, lost the cup to the Australians. The reaction in the United States was one of shock and sadness. However, the Aussies were jubilant. Taking the America's Cup away from the mighty United States had a significant impact on the psyche of Australia. The Australian Prime Minister wept openly on television and declared a national holiday for the nation.

Although no prize money is associated with the America's Cup, when the competition is held racing syndicates from around the world pay tens of millions of dollars organizing campaigns to demonstrate their technological superiority at sea. The economic impact for the city hosting the America's Cup race is worth billions of dollars.

From the beginning, the event has been associated with technological prowess of the competing countries. The first race at Cowes, Isle of Wight, on August 22, 1851, was held in conjunction with Prince Albert's Great London Exhibition of 1851, paying tribute to the technological achievements of the time. The tradition of technological superiority remains a basis for the America's Cup. The 1983 America's Cup race had a huge impact on the technology of future races. Adding "wings" to the keel greatly enhances maneuverability and speed. After the *Australia II*'s defeat of the *Liberty*, keels with wings became the norm on 12-meter yachts.

After losing the Cup, several significant events occurred within America. In a controversial move, Conner ended his association with the NYYC. For the first time, the NYYC would not automatically be the U.S. sponsor

American yacht *Liberty* (left) falls behind to *Australia II* in the America's Cup, Newport, Rhode Island, September 14, 1983. *Australia II* won the race—the first time in its history that it was won by a non-American. © BETTMANN/CORBIS. REPRODUCED BY PERMISSION.

of the America's Cup team. Also, for the first time the American team would not be the Cup defender. Conner sought supporters to fund his quest to win back the Cup, making this his sole goal for the following three years. Conner raised necessary funding and created the technologically perfect "super yacht."

In addition to technological savvy, winning the America's Cup also requires superior seamanship. Though he lost in 1983, Dennis Conner and America would rebound. He showed his superior sailing skills in 1987 when he staged a remarkable comeback to claim the Cup, this time under the auspices of the San Diego Yacht Club. The 1987 victory introduced many Americans outside the sailing world to the competition and instilled renewed pride and patriotism in America. The Cup was back where it belonged.

Primary Source

Comeback: My Race for the America's Cup
[excerpt]

> **SYNOPSIS:** In this excerpt from his 1987 book, Dennis Conner talks about the 1983 America's Cup race in which his team lost to the *Australia II* (The "White Shark"). It was the first time ever that the United States lost the America's Cup.

The White Shark

. . . The fourth race was perhaps the finest race we had ever sailed up to that point. Bertrand tried to get us in a circle game during the prerace maneuvers, but with about three and a half minutes to go before the gun, I just peeled *Liberty* off and sailed way off to the left. I had a feeling Bertrand thought we'd gone too far and he let his guard down. We'd never been too impressed with his starting ability—he was always hunched over the wheel looking so white and nervous and sick—and I had an idea we could stick one to him today.

When I turned to make the dash for the line, I was pretty confident I was spot on. I was on port tack and *Australia II* was on starboard tack, which under sailing's rules of the road meant Bertrand had right of way. I had to stay clear *if* we were on a collision course. We both headed for the line, going right at each other. Fifty tons of aluminum and lead were bearing down on each other and something had to give. Bertrand was trying to make me take his stern, but I thought I sensed some daylight in front of his bow.

I asked Tom Whidden, "Can we cross their bow?" He said, "Probably not," but I took a hard

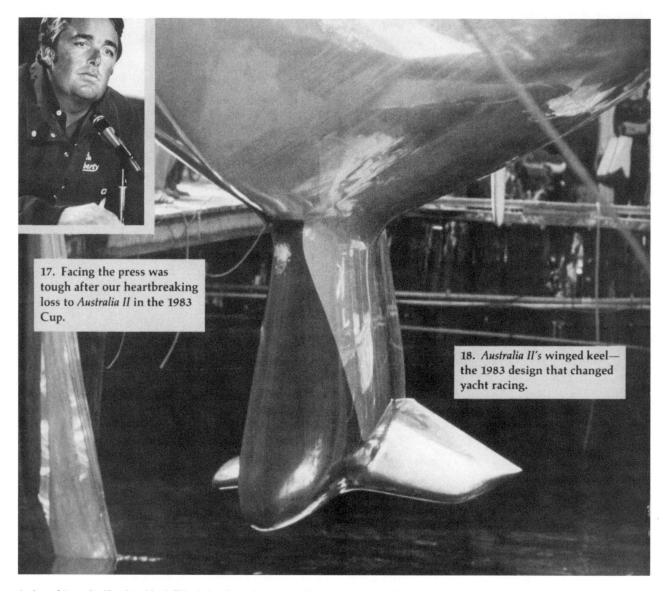

17. **Facing the press was tough after our heartbreaking loss to *Australia II* in the 1983 Cup.**

18. *Australia II's* **winged keel— the 1983 design that changed yacht racing.**

A view of *Australia II*'s winged keel. This design changed the sport of yacht racing. (Inset) Dennis Conner at a press conference after losing the 1983 America's Cup and surrendering the trophy to a foreigner. **PHOTOS FROM *COMEBACK: MY RACE FOR THE AMERICA'S CUP* BY DENNIS CONNER WITH BRUCE STANNARD. ST. MARTIN'S PRESS, 1987. © DANIEL FORSTER AND ADAM J. STOLTMAN/DUOMO. REPRODUCED BY PERMISSION OF DUOMO PHOTOGRAPHY INC.**

look and said, "Hell, we can make it." I flicked up on the wheel and took him by maybe ten or fifteen feet. We were over the starting line first by six seconds, but by port-tacking him I think he got pretty demoralized. You're just not supposed to let something like that happen if you're an America's Cup helmsman with the starboard tack advantage. It was a real faux pas. He completely miscalculated time and distance. I had to laugh at that. There are five moves in match-racing that you should never let happen, and that was one of them. It was the ultimate insult, and I believe it hurt the Australians psychologically because they were never really in the race

after that. Bertrand said after we won the race by forty-three seconds, "I'll never endure a humiliation like that again."

Some people have described that race as the "most perfect America's Cup race ever sailed." I'm not sure I go along with that, but I will admit it was memorable. What made it so satisfying wasn't just that we made the right moves at the right time, but that we were able to neutralize a faster boat.

Now we only had to win one race before the Aussies could win three. We felt good to have gotten there by sheer sailing ability, because without question the White Shark was the faster boat. All we needed now was to keep sailing hard and a little racing luck.

Racing luck. I'm not a very superstitious person. I don't go in for rabbit's feet or garlic cloves or lucky pennies or any of that. To me, luck is work, preparation, ability, attitude, confidence, skill. When something breaks or the wind shifts, I don't see it as a result of the stars being aligned in a certain pattern or because our bowman walked under a ladder. But if there is such a thing as racing luck, ours ran out about an hour before the fifth race in 1983.

For me, the most dramatic, traumatic, and suspenseful part of the '83 series was before the start of that race. I joke with John Marshall about what happened, but back then he felt dismal about it. While tuning up we were on a starboard tack, and John was pumping out the hydraulic pistons in the jumper struts that control the top third of the mast. What he didn't realize was that he had left both valves open so all the fluid drained out and the pistons froze. There was some pressure in the windward piston, so it wasn't too badly damaged, but the leeward rod went out 20 percent farther than it had ever been before. When we tacked, it broke off and the jumper strut bent over like the skin of a peeled banana. This occurred just one hour before the start.

That was just the beginning of a comedy of errors. Our first big mistake was that we didn't have a spare part on the water. I immediately radioed to Ed du Moulin, our syndicate chairman, who in turn requested help from the Coast Guard. They denied the request. That left us with only a couple of options, one of which was to hacksaw the piston off and then reattach it.

To accomplish this, we sent Scotty Vogel and Tom Rich up the mast. It was blowing twenty knots true and those two guys performed a Herculean job in adverse conditions. In the meantime, our chase boat raced to our dock, picked up a spare, and got it to us just a few minutes before the ten-minute gun. However, our problems were far from over. The new piston was about two inches too long. It was absolute agony waiting for the gun, with the minutes ticking away, and realizing that we were in deep trouble.

Scotty and Tom came down after fifty minutes aloft, tired and beat to hell. They immediately went back into action to hoist the jib we had chosen especially for the wind condition. No sooner was it up than it ripped. Down it came to be replaced by another. All this was happening about eight minutes before the start, while we were supposed to be concentrating on prestart maneuvers.

The White Shark smelled blood again and came at us. But Bertrand was still having problems with the start, and despite being wounded, we came back at him aggressively. We were to leeward of the starting line and I got the better position and just forced him over the line by about one second. *Australia II* had to reround and by the time she got squared away, we had a thirty-seven-second lead on him.

You had to like our situation at that moment. We were ahead on the board 3-1, we were ahead on the course by more than a half-minute, the wind conditions suited us perfectly, and right then, we had *Liberty* moving well.

But about four minutes into the race, the jumper strut broke again. Without proper tension, the mast sagged and we were just unable to point up into the wind. With blood on the water, the white shark started charging and soon she was just a few boatlengths behind us. We were both on port tack and then Bertrand tacked to clear his air. As he took off to the left side of the course, I kept driving on our same heading.

In his book, Bertrand criticizes us for not covering. What he does not mention is that in our crippled state we couldn't have possibly engaged in a tacking duel. There was no way we could have won the race on boat speed in close proximity. Actually, he gave us the only chance we had by splitting away. The only way for us to win was to be a mile apart and have the windshifts come in our direction. Unfortunately, it just didn't happen that way.

Australia II won by 1:47. I still feel we should have won that race. It was the kind of breeze in which the boat didn't heel over too much but she could still use her waterline. She had enough sail area so that she could go full speed, but not so much that she would heel over and have to reduce power. She was a longer boat than *Australia II* so she had a little more potential when she was able to use her full power. That's one of the reasons we were faster reaching.

Race Five was a lesson we took into the 1986/87 Cup. We now have an even more comprehensive list of spare parts on our tender *Betsy* (named of course after Betsy Ross, maker of the first American flag). One of the reasons *Betsy* is such a satisfactory tender is that she is big enough to stow all sorts of gear on board. We had booms, spinnaker poles, winches, mainsheets, halyards, guys, blocks, pump handles, and yes—pistons for the jumper struts.

The sixth race was a real ballbreaker. It started off with Bertrand misjudging his start yet again. He was too close with too much time so he had to jibe, circle, and cross behind us. We were over seven seconds in front of him.

The story of that race was that *Australia II* caught a spectacular windshift on the first leg and just kept powering out ahead of us. Bertrand had taken the boat to the left and we got the first lift, but then God must have come back from His day off and decided to help the Aussies. We had a good breeze, about 16 knots true, but then *Australia II* got her own private blast several knots more than we had and almost 20 degrees closer to the mark. I remember watching that damn boat go faster and faster and get farther and farther away. Who *are* those guys? They're the ones who got to the first mark two minutes, twenty-nine seconds before we did. Yes, 2:29. Kiss that one good-bye. In the end, they won by 3:25, the largest margin ever recorded by a challenging yacht.

So we went into the seventh race, the first time in history the America's Cup had gone the distance. At the press conference after the sixth race, Bertrand said something about how not even Hollywood scriptwriters could have cooked up a better scenario. Where he saw this as some big drama, I saw it as just another boat race.

A lot of people who don't know me imagine that the final race was the cause of all sorts of anxiety and that the result must have been heartbreaking. It's difficult to convince them that none of the eleven people on board felt that the end of the world was near. The fact is that we just shook hands and told each other we'd raced well.

What I remember most about that last race was that the Aussies called a lay-day, which enabled us to change the mode of our boat. Lee Davis, our meteorologist, gave us a firm prediction for light wind the next day, so we decided to take *Liberty* to Cove Haven Marina (the same place the Aussies' wing keel was first discovered) and make her as light as possible. *Australia II,* because of her shorter size, came out of the box a good deal lighter than we so she had always been a good light-air boat.

If the casual fan only understood what nerve it took for us to take the risk we did, there might be a greater appreciation of just how gutsy we were.

Making the boat lighter would make her fast in 10 knots or less wind, but hopelessly slow in fresh air. We took out 1,000 pounds of ballast and we stripped the boat clean, trying to get every bit of weight we could off her. Normally we sailed with six jibs, six spinnakers, and several staysails. When we hit the starting line for Race Seven, we had just two jibs and two spinnakers. We had also taken off the spare winch drum, the spare afterguys, the spare halyards—every bit of weight that wasn't absolutely essential. The guys even left their sweaters and boots on the dock. They wore nothing but shorts and T-shirts.

But then on the way out to the course, the wind was blowing 15 true. We had been counting on 10 or less. We began to think Lee had made a colossal mistake, but just before the start the breeze died down as he had predicted. In the seventh race, *Liberty* was faster than she had ever been in such light air.

There were no pep talks, no "come on guys, let's go get 'em" talk. There never has been on any of my boats. Anyone who sails with me is at the top of his sailing career. He is the best, otherwise he wouldn't be there. And at that level there's no need for hype. The most that is ever said is, "Let's have a good one."

The early difference between the two boats in that final race was not so much that we sailed spectacularly well but that the Australians really screwed up by not covering us. We were almost to the starboard lay line, and they let us get back to the inside of the course. That was better for us because the wind went to the left, making the first reach so lopsided, and ultimately that's what won them the race. It meant that we couldn't make any gains to add to our 31-second lead. We got 15 seconds on the first reach and then gave it all back when change in the direction of the wind turned the second reach into a run downwind. The rest of the race was fairly uneventful except that on the second windward leg we got quite a long way ahead, and right at the end we got in a little lighter wind up by the spectator fleet and got a little out of phase with the wind. It was my fault, not Tom's, that they closed up on us. The same left-hand shift that let us pass them on the first beat allowed them to pass and saved their ass. We knew that the Australians had been gaining an average of a minute on every spinnaker run and since we were only 49 seconds ahead at the last windward mark we knew we were in deep ca-ca. We were not at all confident that we were going to win.

We started the run by heading out to the right, but then we found there was more pressure on port than starboard so we jibed to port to get to the inside of the course. People who say we didn't cover just don't know what they're talking about. The truth is that we did exactly the right thing to cover. We got to the inside of the course so that we could have clear air on the jibe and when we got to the inside we jibed back to starboard. The Aussies came down on us with a real bone in their teeth. I could see them out of the corner of my eye gaining bearing, gaining bearing, gaining bearing. Tommy was calling out the number of diminishing boat-lengths that once was our lead, but no one was getting excited. That's when I said, "Anyone got any ideas?"

I don't think I had any emotions one way or another. I certainly didn't say to myself, oh boy, here goes the Cup. As far as we were concerned it was still a boat race that we were going to win. When we converged on opposite jibes they were very close to being able to pass before us so we jibed onto a course parallel to theirs and they still just sailed up right through us. The fact that the lead had changed didn't make a scrap of difference. After we both rounded the leeward mark and bore upwind toward the finish line we said right, we'll tack them down and we did. There were 47 tacks on that last leg and a lot of times I went head to wind and got Bertrand all screwed up. At the end I took him over into the spectator fleet. I thought I might get lucky and someone might run him down! In Bertrand's book he claims there was a fist fight on board *Liberty*. If you will pardon the expression that's just plain bullshit. It's an absolute fabrication. It never happened and what's worse when the author called to check the story, he was told it definitely did not happen. It wasn't true, they knew it wasn't true, but they included it anyway. That's the way history gets distorted.

Going across the line 41 seconds astern was no big deal either. When it happened the guys shook hands and said, "Nice going. Good race. We gave it our best shot." There were no tears shed by anyone except Kyle Smith, the biggest, toughest, meanest guy on the boat. Of course there was a lot of emotion later, especially when I went aboard *Australia II*'s tender, *Black Swan*. That's when I said hi to Sir James Hardy, one of the world's great yachtsmen, who sailed for Australia in several America's Cups. I said, "Jim, I can't sail any better than that." He replied, "You sailed a great race, Dennis. You were beaten by a faster boat." I tried to put a brave face on, but the truth is I was ready to go home.

Further Resources

BOOKS

Bertrand, John, and Patrick Robinson. *Born to Win: A Lifelong Struggle to Capture the America's Cup.* New York: Hearst Marine Books, 1985.

Conner, Dennis, and Michael Levitt. *The America's Cup: The History of Sailing's Greatest Competition in the Twentieth Century* New York: St. Martin's Press, 1998.

Riggs, Doug. *Keelhauled: Unsportsmanlike Conduct and the America's Cup.* Newport, R.I.: Seven Seas Press, 1986.

Whipple, A.B.C. *The Racing Yachts.* Alexandria, Va.: Time-Life Books, 1980.

PERIODICALS

"Cliffhanger." *The New Yorker* 59, November 7, 1983, 113–126.

"An Impish Aussie Designer and His Magic Keel Haul America's Cup Down Under After 132 Years of U.S. Ownership, Work of B. Lexcen." *People Weekly,* 20, December 26, 1983, 44.

"Quest for the America's Cup." *Technology Review* 86, October 1983, 66–69.

WEBSITES

"About the America's Cup." AmericaOne. Available online at http://www.americaone.org/cup/aboutac.html; website home page: http://www.americaone.org (accessed July 17, 2003).

Levitt, Michael. "150th Anniversary of the America's Cup." The New York Yacht Club. Available online at http://www.nyyc.org/popup.cfm?content=viewthenews&thenewsid=139; website home page: http://www.nyyc.org (accessed May 29, 2003)

Official America's Cup website. Available online at http://americascup.yahoo.com (accessed July 17, 2003).

AUDIO AND VISUAL MEDIA

Conner, Dennis. "The America's Cup: Past, Present and Future." Speech given at the Harvard Law School Forum, October 21, 1987. Available online at http://www.law.harvard.edu/studorgs/forum/audio.html; website home page: http://www.law.harvard.edu (accessed May 29, 2003).

Pete Rose is Banned from Baseball

"The Rose Probe"

Magazine article

By: Craig Neff

Date: March 21, 1989

Source: Neff, Craig. "The Rose Probe." *Sports Illustrated,* March 21, 1989, 13.

"Statement of Commissioner A. Bartlett Giamatti, August 24, 1989"

Press statement

By: A. Bartlett Giamatti

Date: August 24, 1989

Source: Giamatti, A. Bartlett. "Statement of Commissioner A. Bartlett Giamatti, August 24, 1989." Reprinted in The Baseball Archive. Available online at http://www.baseball1 .com/bb-data/rose/abg_statement.html; website homepage: http://www.baseball1.com (accessed June 16, 2003).

About the Author: Angelo Bartlett (Bart) Giamatti (1938–1989) was born in South Hadley, Massachusetts. At sixteen, Giamatti attended the Phillips Academy in Andover, Massachusetts. He entered Yale University in 1956, and eventually became a professor of Renaissance Literature there. In 1978, he became Yale's youngest president. In 1986, he was appointed president of baseball's National League. He became Commissioner of Baseball on April 1, 1989, serving for five months until his untimely death from a heart attack on September 1, 1989. ∎

Introduction

Pete Rose was one of the greatest baseball players in history. He set records for most career hits (4,256), games played, and at bats. He played in six World Series (winning three), batted over .300 fifteen times, won three batting titles, established a National League record forty-four-game hitting streak (tied for second-longest in major league history), and was selected as the National League's MVP in 1973.

In addition to his statistical accomplishments, Rose played baseball with reckless abandon. Nicknamed "Charlie Hustle," Rose sprinted to first base after walks, dove headfirst into bases, and crashed violently into Ray Fosse in the 1970 All-Star game, seriously injuring Fosse's shoulder. His determination, work ethic, and competitive drive made him the leader of the Cincinnati Red's "Big Red Machine" of the 1970s. Unlike most baseball superstars, Rose lacked exceptional natural talent. By virtue of his hard work he accomplished tremendous feats, including playing as a regular at five different positions over the course of his twenty-four year career (second base, third base, left field, right field, and first base).

After sixteen seasons with the Reds, Rose went to the Philadelphia Phillies as a free agent. He spent five years with the Phillies, and then played for the Montreal Expos for a part of the 1984 season, before returning to the Reds in August as player-manager. He retired from playing in the 1986 season, but he continued as the Reds' manager.

In March 1989, the commissioner of major league baseball, Peter Ueberroth, announced that the league was investigating allegations that Pete Rose bet on baseball games, including games involving the Cincinnati Reds while he managed them. The baseball world was shocked by the allegations. After a preliminary investigation in which Ueberroth and incoming commissioner Bart Giamatti questioned Rose, major league baseball hired attorney John Dowd as a special counsel to investigate the charges against Rose. Dowd produced a 235-page report concluding that Rose bet on Reds' games in 1985, 1986, and 1987, together with the testimony and documentary evidence supporting the conclusion. This evidence included the testimony of thirty witnesses—including individuals who bet on baseball games for Rose; betting slips in Pete Rose's handwriting; corresponding records in Rose's possession and various bookmakers, telephone records, and bank records.

After receiving the report, Giamatti scheduled a hearing for Rose to answer the special counsel's report and present evidence in his defense. Rose filed a lawsuit rather than appear before the commissioner. After his injunction request was denied, Rose approached the commissioner's office to settle the matter. Rose agreed to acknowledge that there was credible evidence to believe that he bet on baseball and to accept a lifetime ban from the sport—although Rose was allowed to apply for reinstatement after one year. The agreement stated that Rose's consent was not an admission that he bet on baseball. On August 24, 1989, Giamatti issued a statement explaining his lifetime ban of Rose. Eight days later, Giamatti died unexpectedly of a heart attack.

Significance

In 1990, Rose was convicted of federal tax evasion for failing to declare substantial winnings on a "pick-six" bet on horse races worth over $200,000. Rose served five months in federal jail.

Rose has admitted gambling on various sports, but continues to deny that he bet on baseball. He applied for reinstatement in 1997, but commissioner Bud Selig stated that no response was necessary as Rose had presented no new evidence with his petition. Rose has been permitted to participate in various major league events where fans have selected him for an honor, including a ceremony for the All-Century Team. Rose and Selig met in November 2002, and representatives have exchanged proposals for what steps Rose would need to take to be reinstated.

Americans were shocked at the allegations that Pete Rose bet on baseball. Rose was a fan favorite because he played the game with such intensity. He was one of the most recognized and popular players of his generation, and the news brought disbelief to so many who had rooted for Rose over the years. After the release of the Dowd Report and the commissioner's deciding on a lifetime ban—together with Rose's 1990 conviction for tax evasion—most came to believe that Rose bet on games involving the Reds. This scandal was especially damaging because Pete Rose had long been an ambassador for the game, and fans could question why Rose bet on the Reds only on certain days and whether the integrity of all Reds' games during that period was undermined.

The Rose scandal also has caused a rift within baseball circles as to whether Rose should be reinstated and made eligible for the Hall of Fame. Many feel that Rose has suffered long enough, and that he should be given another chance. Others, including Hall of Fame pitcher Bob Feller are outspoken in believing that since Rose bet on games involving his own team, he should remain banned for life. Even if readmitted, a number of Hall of Fame players believe that Rose should not be eligible for induction into Baseball's Hall of Fame because of the disgrace that Rose brought to the sport. While Rose's accomplishments as a player merit induction in the Hall of Fame, his case has raised issues as to whether he should be so honored. In 1991, the Hall of Fame members and trustees adopted a specific regulation precluding the nomination of any individual banned by baseball for induction.

Rose likely would be required to admit betting on baseball, and on games involving the Reds in particular, as a condition of his reinstatement. Rose steadfastly has denied betting on baseball, despite overwhelming evidence to the contrary. Fans generally want Rose reinstated, but not without his admitting and expressing remorse for betting on baseball and for lying about it since 1989. That Rose and the commissioner's office have not yet reached an agreement for Rose to be reinstated raises an interesting possibility: that Rose will not admit that he bet on baseball and the Reds in the 1980s, since that would require him to admit that he has lied continuously about the matter since 1986, thus allowing him to keep the popularity he now enjoys,.

Primary Source

"The Rose Probe"

> In this article from *Sports Illustrated*, Craig Neff discusses the accusations mounting against Pete Rose for his involvement in betting on professional baseball games and what the likely consequences will be.

Baseball commissioner Peter Ueberroth announced on Monday that his office "has for several months been conducting a full inquiry into serious allegations" about Cincinnati Reds manager Pete Rose. Ueberroth, who on Feb. 20 summoned Rose from spring training in Florida to New York City for an unspecified purpose, did not divulge the nature of the inquiry, but SI has been told that the commissioner has information that Rose may have bet on baseball games. Under major league rules, if

Major League Baseball commissioner A. Bartlett Giamatti speaks at a press conference, New York, August 24, 1989. Giamatti announced his decision to ban Pete Rose from baseball for gambling. AP/WIDE WORLD PHOTOS. REPRODUCED BY PERMISSION.

Rose bet on games in which his team was not involved, he would be suspended for one year. If he bet on games in which his team was involved, he would be banned for life.

One man linked to possible baseball betting with Rose is Ron Peters, the owner of Jonathan's Cafe in Franklin, Ohio, 40 miles north of Cincinnati. Alan Statman, an attorney for Peters, describes Peters as Rose's "principal bookmaker" and approached SI last week in hopes of selling Peter's story. Statman told SI's Jill Lieber and Martin F. Dardis that he and his client had been asked by Kevin Hallinan, baseball's security chief, "if we had information on Pete Rose betting on baseball. We said we can supply that information." Statman said Hallinan "told me that if we could deliver what we say we could, in general, that means Pete Rose could be banned from baseball." Statman said Peters would not tell his story to baseball authorities without first selling it to a publication. SI declined to buy Peters's story.

Another man said by sources to have been involved with Rose in baseball betting is Paul Janszen, a body-builder friend of Rose's. Janszen pleaded

Cincinnati Reds manager Pete Rose holds a press conference in the dugout prior to a game during spring training, Plant City, Florida, March 23, 1989. At the time Rose was under investigation for alleged gambling. © BETTMANN/CORBIS. REPRODUCED BY PERMISSION.

guilty in January to a charge of evading taxes on income from the sale of steroids and is serving a six-month sentence in a Cincinnati halfway house. Janszen recently discussed with SI the possible sale of a story about Rose. Although SI did not buy the story, a source with knowledge of Janszen's dealings with federal investigators said that while in the dugout at Riverfront Stadium, Rose exchanged signals somehow relating to baseball betting with Janszen, who was in the stands. And a fellow weightlifter told SI he heard Janszen using a phone at Gold's gym in suburban Cincinnati to place baseball bets he understood had come from Rose.

"Janszen used to come into the gym, pull out a newspaper and go over all the baseball games," the weightlifter said. "He'd mark them with a pen, then he'd go into the office and phone in bets for Pete Rose. He never said he was doing it for Pete. But that's what the talk was around the gym."

Rose makes no secret of his passion for betting at the racetrack, but he told SI he has never wagered with bookies on any sport: "I'd be willing to bet you, if I was a betting man, that I have never bet on baseball," he said. A former handyman and friend of Rose's, Chuck Beyersdoerfer, says Rose did place bets through a bookie on football and basketball games and that the Reds skipper kept three TV sets going at once in his living room to monitor the action. And Michael Fry, a former co-owner of Gold's now serving an eight-year federal prison sentence for cocaine trafficking and income-tax evasion, told SI's Bruce Selcraig that he heard a crony of Rose's,

Tommy Gioiosa, regularly place bets to bookies on college and pro basketball and football games. Fry said he understood those bets to be for Rose. According to Fry, Rose, who promoted Gold's in various ways, including a newspaper ad identifying the establishment as Pete Rose's Gold's Gym, said he never bet baseball. But Fry said Rose often talked about which baseball teams would be good to bet on. Gioiosa identifies himself as a professional gambler but says he never placed bets for Rose.

Rose denied knowing Peters and said, "I don't know if I've ever been to Jonathan's or any other café." However, three people told SI they have seen Rose in Jonathan's; two of them said they saw him in Peters's company. Asked why Rose would make a trek to an eatery in Franklin, Peters cracked. "He liked my beer."

If Rose is found to have bet on baseball, it could jeopardize his otherwise certain election to the Hall of Fame when he becomes eligible in 1992. Reds owner Marge Schott, asked if Rose had bet on the national pastime, spoke for all of baseball when she said, "I hope not. I hope not. God, I hope not."

Primary Source

"Statement of Commissioner A. Bartlett Giamatti, August 24, 1989"

SYNOPSIS: In this press statement, commissioner Giamatti banishes all time hit leader and Cincinnati Reds Manager Pete Rose from baseball for life because Rose did not provide any evidence to defend himself from accusations that he bet on games in which he managed.

The banishment for life of Pete Rose from baseball is the sad end of a sorry episode. One of the game's greatest players has engaged in a variety of acts which have stained the game, and he must now live with the consequences of those acts. By choosing not to come to a hearing before me, and by choosing not to proffer any testimony or evidence contrary to the evidence and information contained in the report of the Special Counsel to the Commissioner, Mr. Rose has accepted baseball's ultimate sanction, lifetime ineligibility.

This sorry episode began last February when baseball received firm allegations that Mr. Rose bet on baseball games and on the Reds' games. Such grave charges could not and must never be ignored. Accordingly, I engaged and Mr. Ueberroth appointed John Dowd as Special Counsel to investigate these and other allegations that might arise and to pursue the truth wherever it took him. I believed then and believe now that such a process, whereby an experienced professional inquires on behalf of the Commissioner as the Commissioner's agent, is fair and appropriate. To pretend that serious charges of any kind can be responsibly examined by a Commissioner alone fails to recognize the necessity to bring professionalism and fairness to any examination and the complexity a private entity encounters when, without judicial or legal powers, it pursues allegations in the complex, real world.

Baseball had never before undertaken such a process because there had not been such grave allegations since the time of Landis. If one is responsible for protecting the integrity of the game of baseball—that is, the game's authenticity, honesty and coherence—then the process one uses to protect the integrity of baseball must itself embody that integrity. I sought by means of a Special Counsel of proven professionalism and integrity, who was obliged to keep the subject of the investigation and his representatives informed about key information, to create a mechanism whereby the integrity we sought to protect was itself never violated. Similarly, in writing to Mr. Rose on May 11, I designed, as is my responsibility, a set of procedures for a hearing that would have afforded him every opportunity to present statements or testimony of witnesses or any other evidence he saw fit to answer the information and evidence presented in the Report of the Special Counsel and its accompanying materials.

That Mr. Rose and his counsel chose to pursue a course in the courts rather than appear at hearings scheduled for May 25 and then June 26, and then choose to come forward with a stated desire to settle this matter is now well known to all. My purpose in recounting the process and the procedures animating that process is to make two points that the American public deserves to know:

> First, that the integrity of the game cannot be defended except by a process that itself embodies integrity and fairness;

> Second, should any other occasion arise where charges are made or acts are said to be committed that are contrary to the interests of the game or that undermine the integrity of baseball, I fully intend to use such a process and procedure to get to the truth and, if need be to root out offending behavior. I intend to use, in short, every lawful and

ethical means to defend and protect the game.

I say this so that there may be no doubt about where I stand or why I stand there. I believe baseball is a beautiful and exciting game, loved by millions—I among them—and I believe baseball is an important, enduring American institution. It must assert and aspire to the highest principles—of integrity, of professionalism of performance, of fair play within its rules. It will come as no surprise that like any institution composed of human beings, this institution will not always fulfill its highest aspirations. I know of no earthly institution that does. But this one, because it is so much a part of our history as a people and because it has such a purchase on our national soul, has an obligation to the people for whom it is played—to its fans and well-wishers—to strive for excellence in all things and to promote the highest ideals.

I will be told that I am an idealist. I hope so. I will continue to locate ideals I hold for myself and for my country in the national game as well as in other of our national institutions. And while there will be debate and dissent about this or that or another occurrence on or off the field, and while the game's nobler parts will always be enmeshed in the human frailties of those who, whatever their role, have stewardship of this game, let there be no doubt or dissent about our goals for baseball or our dedication to it. Nor about our vigilance and vigor—and patience—in protecting the game from blemish or stain or disgrace.

The matter of Mr. Rose is now closed. It will be debated and discussed. Let no one think that it did not hurt baseball. That hurt will pass, however, as the great glory of the game asserts itself and a resilient institution goes forward. Let it also be clear that no individual is superior to the game.

Further Resources

BOOKS

Reston, James Jr. *Collision at Home Plate: The Lives of Pete Rose and Bart Giamatti.* New York: Edward Burlingame Books, 1991.

Rose, Pete, and Roger Kahn. *Pete Rose: My Story.* New York: Macmillan, 1989.

Sokolove, Mike. *Hustle: The Myth, Life, and Lies of Pete Rose.* New York: Simon and Schuster, 1990.

Valerio, Anthony. *Bart: A Life of A. Bartlett Giamatti By Him and About Him.* New York: Harcourt, Brace, Jovanovich, 1991.

PERIODICALS

Leland, John. "Baseball: Pete Rose Hustles for the Hall." *Newsweek* 134, no. 24, 1999, 72–75.

Lieber, Jill, and Steve Wulf. "Sad Ending for a Hero." *Sports Illustrated* 73, no. 5, July 30, 1990, 22–25.

WEBSITES

"Answers to Frequently Asked Questions About Pete Rose." Baseball Archives. Available online at http://www.baseball1 .com/bb-data/rose; website home page: http://www .baseball1.com (accessed June 16, 2003).

"Bart Giamatti." BaseballLibrary.com. Available online at http://www.baseballlibrary.com/baseballlibrary/ballplayers /G/Giamatti_Bart.stm; website home page: http://www .baseballlibrary.com (accessed July 22, 2003).

Carter, Bob. "Hustle Made Rose Respected, Infamous." ESPN.com. Available online at http://espn.go.com /sportscentury/features/00016443.html; website home page: http://espn.go.com (accessed June 27, 2003).

Dowd, John. "The Dowd Report." The Baseball Archive. Available online at http://www.baseball1.com/bb-data/rose/dowd /dowd_cover.html; website home page: http://www .baseball1.com (accessed June 27, 2003).

"A Red-Letter Day"

Magazine article

By: Crosbie Cotton

Date: April 10, 1989

Source: Cotton, Crosbie. "A Red-Letter Day." *Sports Illustrated* 70, April 10, 1989, 38–39.

About the Author: Cotton Crosbie is the president of Cotton Crosbie Communications. Prior to forming that company, Crosbie served as the editor in chief for the *Calgary Herald*. Crosbie also serves as a board member and media consultant for the Association for Mountain Peaks Protection in Banff, Alberta, and he serves as the director of the National Parks Ski Area Association. ■

Introduction

During the Cold War, the government of the Soviet Union placed great emphasis on its sports programs, especially ice hockey. By the start of the 1970s, three million Russian boys were involved in the intensive hockey program. This national emphasis on the sport resulted in Russian dominance of amateur hockey from the mid-1950s until the 1990s. Once the program became established and it was able to compete with North American professional players, the Soviet Hockey Federation (SHF) arranged an eight-game tournament, "The Summit Series," with the best Canadians from the National Hockey League (NHL) in 1972—four games in Canada and then four in Russia. While many across the world expected the Canadians to win all eight games handily, they were shocked when the Russians won the first game, 7-3, led by the stellar play of goalie Vladislav Tretiak.

While the Canadians won the series, 4-3-1, the Russians proved that they could compete at the highest levels of hockey. The SHF then won several exhibition series with the NHL over the next decade, establishing Russian hockey as the best in the world.

Despite its willingness to compete with the NHL, Russia refused to release its players to play in North America. The Russians continued to enjoy success in international and Olympic hockey competitions throughout the 1980s, despite losing in a large upset to the Americans in the 1980 Olympics. At the close of the decade, major political changes happened within Russia and Eastern Europe. President Mikhail Gorbachev brought some democratic reforms to the Soviet Union, and major hockey stars, especially Igor Larionov and Viacheslav Fetisov, publicly complained about being "caged and drilled for Soviet hockey praise nearly eleven months a year." Fetisov was dismissed from the Red Army team, but his teammates refused to play unless he was reinstated for the 1989 world championships. Fetisov rejoined the team, leading them to victories in every game and being named the outstanding defenseman for the competition.

In the late 1970s, NHL teams started drafting most of the top Russian players in the event that they might receive permission to leave the Soviet Union to play professional hockey. Due to the poor Russian economy, the SHF agreed in 1989 to grant some players permission to play in the NHL, a decision left to Viktor Tikhonov, head of SHF. Tikhonov at first allowed Sergei Priakin—a solid player, but not a star—to play for Calgary in early 1989. On May 25, 1989, Tass, the Soviet news agency, announced that stars Igor Larionov, Viacheslov Fetisov, and Sergei Makarov were free to play anywhere in the world. The Russian revolution was on. At the end of the 2002–2003 season, there were sixty-five Russian players in the NHL—about ten percent of the NHL rosters. Europeans comprised nearly twenty-five percent of NHL players.

Significance

The full impact of Russian players on the NHL was not felt for a couple of years after the Russians began playing in the NHL. Other than defector Alexander Mogilny of the Buffalo Sabres, the first Russian players were generally over thirty. They struggled in the face of hostile treatment by North American players and referees—one commentator called Fetisov "The Jackie Robinson of hockey"—as well as difficulties in adjusting to the NHL style of play, the NHL's smaller rink sizes, and a different culture and language. However, the fortitude that allowed the Russian stars to endure the Soviet system eventually won over their teammates and the fans. Fetisov and Larionov were reunited with fellow countrymen Viacheslav Koslov, Sergei Fedorov, and Vladimir

Konstantinov under Scotty Bowman with the Detroit Red Wings. Bowman played them together as a unit—dubbed the "Russian Five"—a key element in the Wings 1996–1997 Stanley Cup championship. Captain Steve Yzerman, after receiving the Stanley Cup, handed it first to Larionov and Fetisov to carry to honor them and their role in fighting the Soviet Hockey Federation. That summer Larionov, Fetisov, and Koslov brought the Stanley Cup to Russia, and they drank champagne from it with the Russian prime minister in Moscow.

Also significant was the continuation of a trend of mixing the finesse, precision passing, and discipline of the traditional Russian style with the rough-and-tumble physical play of the NHL. After the 1972 exhibition games against the Soviets, the NHL realized that it needed to infuse certain elements of Russian and European play to improve the quality of the league. The infusion of talented Russians—particularly Mogilny, Federov, and Pavel Bure—elevated the level of play throughout the NHL, as their playmaking, skating, and vision have became the standards of excellence. Federov became the first Russian to earn awards in the NHL when he was named the league's Most Valuable Player and Top Defensive Forward in 1993–1994. Also, the Russian leagues, after playing the North Americans, have became much more physical.

The Russian revolution of the NHL has impacted Russian hockey significantly. Russia no longer dominates international competitions, and most of its top players elect to play in the NHL or European leagues.

Primary Source

"A Red-Letter Day"

SYNOPSIS: This *Sports Illustrated* article from April 1989 provides a glimpse of the game in which the first Soviet player to play in the NHL, Sergei Priakin, debuted. It describes some of the game's action, Priakin's thoughts, and the reaction of other Calgary Flames and Winnipeg Jets players.

The Soviet Union's Sergei Priakin Made His NHL Debut With the Flames

Fifteen seconds after Sergei Priakin stepped onto the ice and made hockey history in Calgary last Friday night, Winnipeg Jet center Dale Hawerchuk had the newest Flame player exactly where he wanted him deep in the Calgary zone, head down and ready for the slaughter. Welcome to the NHL, you job stealer. Hawerchuk launched himself at full bore and slammed Priakin to the Saddledome ice with a clean but oh-so-vicious bodycheck.

Twenty seconds later Priakin was at the other end of the ice, perfectly setting up rugged linemate

Vyacheslav Fetisov turns and looks up-ice during the Olympic Winter Games, Calgary, Alberta, February 1988. Captain of the Soviet National Team and Central Red Army team, Fetisov helped break down the barriers that prevented Soviet players from competing in the NHL. © WALLY MCNAMEE/CORBIS. REPRODUCED BY PERMISSION.

Tim Hunter, who was alone 50 feet in front of the Winnipeg net. Although Hunter flubbed the pass, the point had been made: Priakin, the first Soviet allowed by his country to play in the NHL, can handle the pain.

"It was a case where I was in a good place to hit him, and that's our game," Hawerchuk said. "I know it is a touchy thing to say, but I don't think it's a good idea to have the Soviets play over here.

"He's taking a job from North Americans. If this leads to league expansion, then I'm for it. If not, I don't like it."

Priakin, 25, the former captain of the Soviet Wings of the U.S.S.R.'s Elite League, shrugged off the Hawerchuk remarks, much as he did that first hit. "I thought the game would be more physical than it was," he said. "I expected the game would be somewhat faster, but perhaps that can be explained because Winnipeg won't be in the playoffs."

Take that one, Hawerchuk. How about another?

"This is like a great holiday for me," said Priakin. "The rink is packed with people [a sellout crowd of 20,002 watched his debut]. It is great to play under conditions like that." Priakin is used to performing before fewer than 2,000 spectators in Moscow.

Sergei Priakin of the Calgary Flames prepares to pass the puck during a game. Priakin was the first player from the Soviet Union to play in the National Hockey League. **PAUL BERESWILL/HOCKEY HALL OF FAME. REPRODUCED BY PERMISSION.**

As for the accusation that he's putting North American hockey players on the breadlines, Priakin said, "I don't want to talk politics. I am here to play hockey. I think it is hockey that will benefit from having Soviets in the NHL."

For the record, Priakin played 14 minutes and four seconds on Friday; he had no goals, no assists and no penalties, and had one shot on goal in the Flames' 4-1 win. On Sunday against the Oilers, he had one penalty in a 4-2 Calgary victory. The Flames do not plan to use him extensively in the playoffs.

Priakin, who plays right wing, is no superstar back home in Moscow, where he plans to marry a Russian-language teacher named Larissa in June (she will be allowed to join him in Calgary next fall). In 43 international appearances with the Wings, dating back to the 1983 world championships, he has scored four goals and 11 assists.

But don't let the numbers fool you.

"I'll guarantee you he'll get 20 goals in this league easy, maybe a lot more," said Edmonton Oiler coach and general manager Glen Sather, who watched the performance of the 6'3', 210-pound Priakin from the press box. "Everybody would love to have a few Soviets. They come from a strong, disciplined background. They're rugged."

But why Calgary, and why Priakin? Why not star defenseman Vyacheslav Fetisov, for whom the New Jersey Devils have offered Fort Knox?

"I just can't answer those questions, because I don't know," said Flame president Cliff Fletcher, who negotiated the deal—a hard-currency, no-trade, no-cut, fully guaranteed contract for the balance of this season, plus two more seasons. Although details have not been released, insiders indicate getting Priakin will cost Calgary more than $500,000 total. He will get only a percentage of the money; the largest portion will go to the U.S.S.R. Ice Hockey Federation.

"Priakin is on a budget," says Roman Dacyshyn, executive vice-president of Intercan Sports, the Canadian company that represents the Soviets. "The Flames pay the money to [Intercan] three times a year, and we divide it up. He gets pocket money. He

Interview: Vyacheslav Fetisov

When did you first decide that you wanted to play hockey in North America? Is that something that you grew up with as a boy?

No, never. I grow up with only one dream in my mind: to play for national team and [win] Olympic gold medals for my country, and play for World Championship.

So when did your ambition change? When did you decide and why?

My ambitions never change. It was, they gave me offer before [1988] Olympic Games in Calgary. They said, You probably a Soviet player who wants to play in National Hockey League? And I said okay, fine. And then, Olympic Games in '88, [I] came to Calgary and talk to the high officials in the Pro Sport Committee in Soviet Union. And they promised they let me go. . . .

So you were the beginning . . .

But was one year [afterward] and they [did not] let me go right away. I was supposed to stay [in North America] after Olympic Game, but it was long year for me . . . I was fighting for my rights, human rights and all this stuff, and the system didn't like those situations. For [the Army and Communists] it was easy to present separation as a conflict between [Central Red Army Coach Victor] Tikhonov and Sasha [Fetisov] . . .

And there was more of a conflict between Fetisov and the system, as opposed to Fetisov and an individual.

Oh yeah . . . It was biggest war I would say in my life . . . Almost nobody want to support me in this situation because you know it's—it's understandable. It's never happened before and I was in a double trap.

It's almost like a defection.

It's not defection. I had so many possibilities to defect but I was, I got too big of name to just run away from this situation. And like Gary Kasparov the World Champion chess[master], he told me you can open different possibility for Soviet people, not only athletes. You got big name, you got good support and you can do it. But you have to be strong mentally. It's not a situation many people can do. And I said, I got a few possibilities to defect . . . and they said I got too big a name to just run away. And I think in those time if I going to do this, I going to have my friends too. I think if I going to defect, they going to close the gate and I think I got kind

of mission to fight through all this situation to get the gate open. . . .

Get the gate open.

To get the gate open in the right way. And I mean it took too much energy from me, and mostly it was mental kind of disaster. And I remember when the situation was over and, and I get here . . . [I faced] another challenge to play in National Hockey League. But I was empty, empty physically and, and empty mentally. I was tired and I never think they let me go but they give me passport and airline ticket. . . . They were thinking at the last moment to let me go or not. . . . I was the first Soviet citizen who got multiple entrance from the American embassy. And there are many people from different professions call me and send the letters to say thank you because they got the opportunities in their life, and they got chance to go somewhere, do something different.

What do you think about what happened subsequently and the extent to which the National Hockey League has almost become dependent on Russians?

It's different hockey right now than was twenty years ago. I played so many games against NHL team those years then. I would say it's better hockey right now . . .

What do you think it did to the morale of young Russians when a bunch of Russian hockey players from Detroit took the Stanley Cup over there last year? What was the reaction?

The reaction was unbelievable. I was a little bit nervous when I ask [NHL Commissioner] Gary Bettman first time to let us bring the Cup and there was millions of questions, how they gonna be, how is security, how this? Like don't worry about it, it's going to be first class, and they send security people. . . . [Russian] people know about Stanley Cup, people know about NHL and I think it's great. . . . I never forget when it was opening night in soccer stadium, 90,000 people, president of Russia and Prime Minister and all big shots there. And it's in between periods and three of us was, you know, walking with the Cup around, you know, on soccer field and nobody was left in the seats. And next morning we went to the [Russian] White House and drink champagne from the cup with Prime Minister. . . . And I think it's no more question Russian tough enough to play for Stanley Cup. . . .

SOURCE: "Interview: Vyacheslav Fetisov." Originally aired on *Frontline*, October 12, 1999. Reprinted in PBS Online. Available online at http://www.pbs.org/wgbh/pages/frontline/shows/hockey/interviews/fetisov.html; website home page: http://www.pbs.org (accessed June 27, 2003).

gets a clothing allowance. Obviously, he needs more money for clothing now than he will later. We have to protect him. He can't go into a store and buy four suits just because the clerk says he needs them."

Fletcher says that solid drafting and a little luck landed Priakin. "We took an educated guess last

year that the first player to come out of the Soviet Union would not be a star," he says. "We looked at the middle level and decided Priakin was a likely player to release if they released anyone."

As the 1988 NHL draft ground to a halt last June, the Flames announced Priakin's name. The son of a Moscow chauffeur, he was the 252nd and last player taken in the draft.

Sather has a theory about what happened: "I'm told he's a cut above the rest in terms of presentation. He dresses well, he acts well, he has a good image. I think he was released because he'll make a good ambassador."

Flames public relations director Rick Skaggs has another theory: "What the Soviets have to fall back on are their superstars. If Priakin does well, they can say, 'Now you want our superstars, get out your checkbooks.'"

When he arrived in Calgary from Hamilton, Ont.—where he was on tour with the Soviet National Team—Priakin's first stop was at a clothing store. Dacyshyn says, "I get a call from my son Greg, who's going to travel with Sergei for a couple of weeks, and he's saying, 'Dad, he's trying on a Hugo Boss suit and it's $850.' I tell him to look at suits a little more conservative. They settled on one a couple hundred dollars cheaper. Heck, the kid's got to look good."

Upon arrival in Calgary, Priakin did some more spending as soon as he learned where the players like to shop. "He has great taste, but expensive tastes," says Greg.

Such is the cost of *glasnost* in the NHL.

Further Resources

BOOKS

Edelman, Robert. *Serious Fun: A History of Spectator Sports in the USSR.* New York: Oxford University Press, 1993.

Martin, Lawrence. *The Red Machine: The Soviet Quest to Dominate Canada's Game.* Toronto: Doubleday Canada, 1990.

Peppard, Victor, and James Riordan. *Playing Politics: Soviet Sports Diplomacy to 1992.* London: JAI Press, 1993.

Sanful, John. *Russian Revolution: Exodus to the NHL.* London: Profile Publishing, 2002.

PERIODICALS

Farber, Michael. "Boris Good Enough? You Bet He Was! Players From the Former Soviet Union, Who Ten Seasons Ago Arrived in the NHL to Loathing and Mistrust, Have Made the League Bigger, Better and Brassier." *Sports Illustrated* 92, no. 9, February 28, 2000, 62–69.

Harvey, Randy. "They're Here." *Sport* 80, December 1989, 68–72.

Howse, John. "Soviet Invasion. National Hockey League." *Maclean's* 102, October 9, 1989, 46–47.

WEBSITES

A to Z Hockey. Available online at http://www.azhockey.com (accessed June 16, 2002).

Dolezar, Jon A. "Sweeping Changes: Russian Hockey Looked Different After '72 Summit Series." CNN/Sports Illustrated, September 27, 2002. Available online at http://sportsillustrated.cnn.com/hockey/news/2002/09/27/soviet_legacy; website home page: http://sportsillustrated.cnn.com (accessed July 23, 2003).

Samoilov, Georg. "History." Sergei Makarov and Soviet Hockey Fanpage. Available online at http://www.russianrocket.de/History/hauptteil_history.html; website home page: http://www.russianhockey.de (accessed July 23, 2003).

"Sergei Priakin." Legends of Hockey. Available online at http://www.legendsofhockey.net:8080/LegendsOfHockey/jsp/SearchPlayer.jsp?player=14040; website home page: http://www.legendsofhockey.net (accessed June 16, 2003).

"Soviet Sports Wars." *The Red Files.* PBS. Available online at http://www.pbs.org/redfiles/sports; website home page: http://www.pbs.org (accessed July 23, 2003).

"Viacheslav Fetisov." Legends of Hockey. Available online at http://www.legendsofhockey.net:8080/LegendsOfHockey/jsp/LegendsMember.jsp?mem=P200101#photo; website home page: http://www.legendsofhockey.net (accessed July 23, 2003).

Never Too Young to Die: The Death of Len Bias

Nonfiction work

By: Lewis Cole

Date: 1989

Source: Cole, Lewis. *Never Too Young to Die: The Death of Len Bias.* New York: Pantheon Books, 1989.

About the Author: Lewis Cole is an author and freelance writer. In addition to his book about the death of Len Bias, Cole has published *Dream Team,* a review of the New York Knick's 1969–1970 championship team, and coauthored *This Side of Glory* with David Hilliard, an autobiography of a leader of the Black Panther Party. ■

Introduction

Len Bias (1963–1986) was a hero in his hometown. He was a young African American who came from the street and worked to be successful. People in the African American communities in the Washington D.C. area identified with him; he was religious and a hard worker—a "good boy." No one thought he would have anything to do with drugs. On the basketball court, Bias combined power, finesse, and stunning acrobatics. He was an All-American player for the local University of Maryland Terrapins, the pride of the Washington D.C. community.

Bias was primed to be a superstar in the NBA. Maryland was a top basketball school in the Atlantic Coast Conference, and Bias was in the national spotlight. When chosen second in the first round of the NBA draft by the Boston Celtics on June 15, 1986, Bias was ecstatic.

Tragically, he never became a famous Boston Celtic. Instead, he is famous for his death shortly after the draft. Bias collapsed unconscious in his dorm room while celebrating his selection by the Celtics with a group of friends. He never regained consciousness. The cause of death: cocaine intoxication.

Bias's tragic death shocked the nation—especially the Washington D.C. area. Questions abounded. Len Bias's image was one of a religious young man who did not smoke or drink. Had he really been using cocaine? Why? Was it his first time? How long had he been doing it? Who did he get it from? Who else knew that he used cocaine? Who was to blame? It seemed Len Bias had been seriously involved with cocaine. Why would talented Len Bias, future Boston Celtic, such a "nice young man," succumb to the lures of drugs? Many people, institutions, and organizations attempted to answer these questions.

After his death, a massive investigation ensued. There were accusations that evidence was removed from Bias's dorm room to hide any connection with cocaine. Bias's friend, Brian Tribble, who was with him the night he died, was indicted for obstruction of justice, although later acquitted of the charges. Lefty Driesell, head coach of Maryland basketball team, was also accused of obstructing justice. However, he was never charged.

Significance

Len Bias's death in June 1986 from "cocaine intoxication" cast a shadow over Maryland for many years. Internal reviews found that the athletic department's social, academic, and drug policies were lax, and several top Maryland officials resigned. Terrapin basketball coach Lefty Driesell resigned under pressure, as did athletic director Dick Dull.

Based on a medical examiner's speculation, it was widely reported that Bias had been using crack cocaine. However, it was the powdered form of the drug—not "rocks" of cocaine mixed with sodium bicarbonate—that killed Bias. Still, the early association of Bias's death with crack cocaine influenced federal lawmakers working on anti-drug laws. They ended up enacting stronger penalties for crack than for powdered cocaine in the Anti-Drug Abuse Act in late 1986. Subsequently, groups have charged that the stiffer crack penalties unfairly target African Americans, as they are more likely to use crack.

Many people, including Bias's mother, hoped that Bias's death sent a message to young people of the dan-

Len Bias sports a Boston Celtics cap after being drafted second overall, New York, June 17, 1986. Just a couple days later, Bias died of a cocaine overdose during a party to celebrate his success. **AP/WIDE WORLD PHOTOS. REPRODUCED BY PERMISSION.**

gers of drug use. Many lawmakers were motivated to pass the Anti-Drug Abuse Act because of Len Bias. In 1987, the U.S. Department of Health and Human Services reported that drug use among high school students fell by twenty percent in 1987. This was an indication that perhaps Bias's death caused a greater awareness among young people of the dangers of drug abuse.

Primary Source

Never Too Young to Die: The Death of Len Bias
[excerpt]

> **SYNOPSIS:** This excerpt from *Never Too Young to Die: The Death of Len Bias* describes the day the young basketball star died from a cocaine overdose, during a party to celebrate his being drafted second overall in the NBA rookie draft.

The youth and his father arrived home a little before ten that night. Later the father testified he had never seen his son so happy. In the last two days the twenty-two-year-old had fulfilled the dream of a lifetime. He had become a professional basketball player. And not simply a player, but a star. At the National Bas-

Friends carry the casket of University of Maryland basketball star Len Bias from the college chapel, Washington, D.C., June 23, 1986. Bias's death was a national story and helped raise awareness of the dangers of cocaine. AP/WIDE WORLD PHOTOS. REPRODUCED BY PERMISSION.

ketball Association's annual draft, he had been chosen second by the most prestigious team in the league. The Boston Celtics, the commissioner had announced, pick . . . Leonard Bias! Confident, elegant—style meant a lot to him—Leonard had stood up and the fans in New York's Felt Forum had erupted, yelling his name, their crescendo of chants and cheers announcing one thing: the future belonged to him.

For the next half hour he answered the reporters' predictable questions. "He's a pretty cool guy," his father, who was to accompany him through the thirty-six-hour whirlwind, told one reporter. "It's hard to know what he's thinking." Not that afternoon. Leonard was effusive and poetic. Yes, he was going to buy a Mercedes with his new contract. Yes, he was eager to join a squad that featured other stars. Yes, he was looking forward to winning a championship with his new team. Yes, this was a dream come true—a dream to play in the NBA, a dream to play for the Celtics, a dream within a dream.

Then his professional responsibilities—already!—called. A flight to his new home was waiting: the

Celtics wanted him to appear on the local six o'clock news.

Leonard, his father James, and a vice-president from the sports representation firm Leonard had hired to handle all legal and financial matters—he wasn't only a player, but a property, something of value—flew to Boston. There the royal treatment continued: a press conference; luxury hotel accommodations; lavish praise from Red Auerbach, the legendary Celtics president, who said no rookie in the team's storied history—not even Bob Cousy, not even Bill Russell—had ever excited keener anticipation or quicker acceptance from the fans. "He's the guy we wanted," Auerbach told the press. "He's a great kid."

The next morning Leonard began to reap the material rewards of his success. A limousine drove him and James Bias—Big James, Leonard sometimes called him—to the Reebok offices. While his agent worked out the final terms of the endorsement deal, company executives gave Leonard and Mr. Bias a tour of the plant. When they were finished the agent announced they had come to terms: one million dollars for five years, a mutually beneficial pact that in one stroke, the agent claimed, assured Leonard of lifelong financial security. Celebrating the agreement, the executives took Leonard and Mr. Bias to a promotional party. There he met some members of the Celtics and was introduced by the president of Reebok as the firm's newest "family member," before leaving with his father for the last shuttle home.

Now, finally, the plane was landing; in moments he would be safe, out from under the lights, free from questions, home.

In the airport parking lot, Leonard and Mr. Bias got into Leonard's new cobalt-blue Nissan X-Z. As soon as he had signed with his agent, Leonard had secured a fifteen-thousand-dollar loan. In school he had never seemed to have enough money and would work any job, even helping his friend Brian Tribble clean government offices, to get some cash. The car was the first thing he had acquired with his borrowed riches, arranging a lease and saying a happy goodbye to the broken-down Cutlass he had endured during his four years in college. Cars meant a lot to him; they were one of your personal signatures in the world, a measure of achievement.

They cruised past Northeast Washington and the galaxy of suburbs surrounding the capital city: Anacostia, Seat Pleasant, Landover Hills. The whole area was one world, a de facto black city that included the slums of H Street, the mansions of Kenilworth Gardens, the suburban tracts of Maryland. Here he was already a legend: Len Bias, the player who came from the street and made good, the born-again Christian who sported a thick gold chain around his neck, the boy-next-door who was a millionaire, the brother off the block who could bring the crowd to their feet with basket-rattling dunks.

The family home was in Landover. The house was a comfortably sized brown suburban ranch set on a street of tidy lawns, generous backyards, two-car garages. Though only minutes from both modern malls and desolate housing projects, the street had a fifties' feel about it, a place where teenage boys would spend their Saturday afternoons washing their fathers' sedans. That afternoon his mother had spoken about her son's fortune in the naive tone of an Andy Hardy mom. "I'm thrilled that Len was picked by the Number One team in the country," she said. "We'll celebrate as soon as he and his dad get back. I think that everything has worked out perfectly for Len in his basketball career. He played three years in high school and carried his team. He played four

years in college and carried the team his last two years, and now he's going on to a team where he'll have a year or so to prepare himself to start."

When the two men reached the house, she hadn't yet returned from her church meeting. Later she said she had felt low all day, not "hurt or pain, but just a lowness I couldn't describe." Leonard waited a while, unloading free sneakers he had brought back for his family. Then, worried about other gifts left unattended in his open car, he told his father he would come back tomorrow, and took off.

It was less than ten miles from his house to the University of Maryland's College Park campus. He roomed in Washington Hall with Jeff Baxter, another hometown star. The two of them shared a three-bedroom suite with three other players from the basketball team. The sprawling university was the players' turf, where they were pampered and protected by their coach, the nationally famous Lefty Driesell. Leonard had arrived here four years earlier as a local star of still questionable ability and had emerged as an All-American, the team's adored, envied leader, arguably the most popular, best-known man on campus. A shot of him slamming the ball over his head backward into the basket adorned the cover of that season's yearbook, while the next two pages were filled with stats and awards and color shots of him at *Playboy*'s All-American Team Weekend. For his teammates and buddies Leonard was more than simply a friend. He was a natural resource. His stardom rewarded everyone he was close to: for his coaches, new respect; for a teammate, perhaps an entrance through the back door into the NBA; for his friends, the thrill of leading the life of a celebrity.

Some of his teammates were there when he arrived; they joked and congratulated him. He dumped his bags—the Celtics and Reebok had loaded him down with freebies—and called one of his many girl-friends.

The young woman came to visit for a short time. When she left, he told the other guys he was going out. Shortly past twelve he showed up at the home of his friend Brian Tribble, an ex-student who shared an apartment in the university area. Around one o'clock he was stopped on campus by a college cop who congratulated him on his success. After that he went into a College Park liquor store and bought a six-pack of Private Stock beer and a bottle of cognac, then autographed a picture for the star-struck store manager.

No one knows where he went after that—or if they do, they have not yet said. But when he reap-

"Maryland Basketball Star Len Bias is Dead at 22" [excerpt]

University of Maryland all-America basketball player Len Bias collapsed in his dormitory suite early yesterday morning and two hours later was pronounced dead of cardiac arrest at Leland Memorial Hospital in Riverdale.

Evidence of cocaine was found in a urine sample taken at the hospital as an emergency medical team labored from 6:50 to 8:50 a.m. to revive him, police sources said. Maj. James Ross, head of criminal investigations for Prince George's County police, said even if cocaine had been detected, it would not be possible to tell if that had contributed to Bias' death without further tests.

Medical experts said sudden cardiac arrest in a 22-year-old in apparent top physical shape could have been caused by cocaine, by a heart ailment that even frequent examinations might have missed, or by a combination of the two.

Sources said Bias passed a physical—including a urinalysis to test for drugs—administered May 27 by the Boston Celtics, who Tuesday made him the No. 2 over-all pick in the National Basketball Association draft. Bias showed no sign of a heart ailment in yearly team physicals, including a special study to look for hidden heart disease, and no evidence of drug use in urine tests last season, according to University of Maryland physicians.

From interviews with Bias' family, teammates and friends, a picture of his last hours emerges: He flew in from Boston with his father, went to the family home in Landover about 11 p.m., arrived at College Park around midnight, ate crabs in his dormitory suite with teammates and a member of the football team until about 2 a.m., drove off alone and was seen at an off-campus gathering, and returned to his dorm about 3 a.m. He collapsed some time after 6 a.m., while talking with teammate Terry Long.

Bias was unconscious and was not breathing when county ambulance attendants arrived at his dormitory suite at 6:36 a.m.—four minutes after they were called and six minutes before a mobile intensive care unit arrived—and he never regained consciousness nor breathed on his own, said Dr. Edward Wilson, chief emergency room physician at Leland Memorial.

SOURCE: Harriston, Keith, and Sally Jenkins. "Maryland Basketball Star Len Bias is Dead at 22: Evidence of Cocaine Reported Found." *Washington Post,* June 20, 1986, C1.

---

peared at the dorm two hours later with Tribble, he wanted to have some fun. They roused two teammates, an easygoing center named Terry Long and a tall, thin sophomore forward named David Gregg. It was between two and three in the morning, the end of Leonard's long day. In the room were the six-pack, the cognac, and approximately an ounce of 88 percent pure cocaine. The boys shut the door and began to party.

Further Resources

BOOKS

Carroll, Jim. *The Basketball Diaries.* New York: Bantam, 1978.

Smith, Fraser C. *Lenny, Lefty, and the Chancellor: The Len Bias Tragedy and the Search for Reform in Big Time College Basketball.* Baltimore, Md.: Bancroft Press, 1992.

Wetzel, Dan, and Don Yaeger. *Sole Influence: Basketball, Corporate Greed, and the Corruption of America's Youth.* New York: Warner Books, 2000.

PERIODICALS

McCallum, Jack. "Back From the Depths." *Sports Illustrated* 82, February 20, 1995, 20–24.

———. "'The Cruelest Thing Ever.' Death of NBA Draftee L. Bias." *Sports Illustrated* 64, June 30, 1986, 20–22.

Neff, Craig, and Bruce Selcraig. "One Shock Wave After Another. Death of L. Bias and Resignation of Maryland Basketball Coach L. Driesell." *Sports Illustrated* 65, November 10, 1986, 76–80.

WEBSITES

"The Len Bias Tragedy." *The Washington Post.* Available online at http://www.washingtonpost.com/wp-srv/sports/longterm/memories/bias/launch/biasfrnt.htm; website home page: http://washingtonpost.com (accessed May 29, 2003).

"Remembering Len Bias, 15 Years Later." *South Coast Today,* June 19, 2001. Available online at http://www.s-t.com/daily/06-01/06-19-01/c01sp091.htm; website home page: http://www.southcoasttoday.com (accessed July 18, 2003).

AUDIO AND VISUAL MEDIA

I'll Never Forget You. Directed by Tom Emmi. Evanston, Ill.: Perennial Education, 1987, VHS.

Gretzky: An Autobiography

Autobiography

By: Wayne Gretzky, with Rick Reilly

Date: 1990

Source: Gretzky, Wayne, with Rick Reilly. *Gretzky: An Autobiography.* New York: HarperCollins, 1990.

About the Author: Wayne Gretzky (1961–) was born in Brantford, Ontario, and quickly was recognized as a hockey prodigy. He could skate at age two, and he was famous in Canada by six. Nicknamed "The Great One," he played for the Edmonton Oilers, Los Angeles Kings, St. Louis Blues, and New York Rangers in the NHL. During his career Gretzky set more records than any other hockey player ever, including most career goals, assists, and points. He retired from hockey in 1999, and he was immediately inducted into the Hockey Hall of Fame. In 2000, Gretzky became a minority owner in the NHL's Phoenix Coyotes. ■

Introduction

In one of the biggest deals in sports history, Wayne Gretzky was traded from the Edmonton Oilers to the Los Angeles Kings on August 10, 1988. The trade sent a twenty-seven-year-old Gretzky, along with forward Mike Krushelnyski and defenseman Marty McSorley, to the Kings for centerman Jimmy Carson and forward Martin Gelinas. In addition, the Kings gave Edmonton their first round picks for 1988, 1989, 1991, and 1993, and eighteen million dollars in the trade.

At the time of the trade, Gretzky was the preeminent player in the game and still in his prime. Gretzky's nickname, "The Great One," is truly fitting. He drew fans wherever he went. People who never went to hockey games would go just to see Gretzky play. In his ten seasons with Edmonton, Gretzky garnered endless trophies. He won the Hart Trophy (league MVP) eight times, the Art Ross Trophy (league's leading scorer) seven times, and the Conn Smythe Trophy (outstanding player in the playoffs) twice.

Gretzky's last season in an Edmonton uniform was memorable. In the 1987–1988 season, Gretzky was second in league scoring behind Mario Lemieux of the Pittsburgh Penguins. He scored forty goals and had 109 assists, despite missing sixteen games with eye and knee injuries. When the Oilers swept the Boston Bruins to win the Stanley Cup in 1988, Gretzky was awarded his second Conn Smythe Trophy as the most valuable player in the playoffs.

Gretzky made an immediate impact in Los Angeles. The year before the Kings acquired Gretzky, they were eighteenth in the league with a 0.375 winning percentage. In his first year in L.A., Gretzky catapulted the Kings to a 0.525 winning percentage, and he was named the NHL's most valuable player. In 1993, the Kings made it to their first Stanley Cup finals because of Gretzky. However, not even Gretzky could stop the Montreal Canadiens from winning their NHL-leading twenty-third Stanley Cup.

Significance

It is said that hockey is a religion in Canada. It is part of the fabric of Canadians. The game was made for Canada, and Canada was made for the game. Hockey Night in Canada is the country's most watched television

An emotional Wayne Gretzky announces his trade from the Edmonton Oilers to the Los Angeles Kings, August 9, 1988. The Gretzky trade was perhaps one of the biggest and most monumental trades in all of sports history. AP/WIDE WORLD PHOTOS. REPRODUCED BY PERMISSION.

show. There is no Canadian Tinsel town, no New York. Canadian celebrities are, for the most part, hockey players. During the 1980s, Wayne Gretzky was the preeminent Canadian celebrity.

The trade that sent Wayne Gretzky from the Edmonton Oilers to the Los Angeles Kings made front pages throughout Canada. Canadians were shocked and hurt by the trading of their national hero to a United States team. Some fans blamed Wayne Gretzky's new wife, California actress Janet Jones, for the trade. However, newly married Wayne and Janet had been house hunting in Edmonton earlier in the year and they had wished to stay.

The effects of the Gretzky trade to Los Angeles, a major media market, were felt immediately. Suddenly tickets to Kings games were hard to get, team merchandise soared in popularity, and ice rinks sprang up all over California to accommodate the huge increase in youth hockey participants.

Gretzky was a major catalyst behind the increasing popularity of U.S. hockey in the 1980s. For over fifty years, the NHL had only its "original six" teams; Montreal, Toronto, Detroit, Chicago, Boston, and New York. The league's first expansion in 1967 included one Western team: Los Angeles. The "Miracle on Ice" U.S. Olympic ice hockey victory in 1980, and Gretzky's trade to L.A. in 1988 led to increased United States visibility for hockey. In the 1990s, teams based in Florida, Atlanta, Texas, and Arizona entered the NHL. Not only did Gretzky raise the interest level in hockey in the L.A. market, he helped the game gain a wider audience across the United States. In 1994, the NHL awarded Gretzky the Lester Patrick Trophy for his "outstanding service to hockey in the United States."

Primary Source

Gretzky: An Autobiography [excerpt]

SYNOPSIS: In this excerpt from Wayne Gretzky's 1990 autobiography, he talks about the events leading up to his being traded to the Los Angeles Kings—among the biggest trades ever made in sports history.

The Day I Made "Transactions"

Not two hours after we'd won the Cup, we were having a celebration dinner. The season was over, the title was ours and I was feeling elated and exhausted at the same time. My wife was there and my dad and a few friends. But somewhere between the appetizer and the salad they all dropped a bomb on me.

I was in the middle of telling my dad that Janet and I were going to see if we could buy Pat Bowlen's old house in Edmonton. Bowlen owns the Denver Broncos and he was selling and we just wanted to see . . . And that's when I saw a real weird look on my dad's face.

"What's wrong?" I said.

"Uh, Wayne," he said, "I'd forget about the house if I were you."

This didn't sound good.

"Why?"

"They're trying to deal you."

"What?"

"They're trying to trade you. I swear. I know for a fact. You don't believe me, you call Nelson Skalbania. He's already called me a couple times. I've been wanting to tell you so bad. But I didn't want to upset you during the playoffs."

I couldn't believe it, but I could tell from my dad's expression that it was true. The team wanted to trade me? The team that just two hours before I'd helped to win its fourth Stanley Cup in the last five years? The team that was still young enough to win

another three or four in a row? The team I assumed I'd retire with? Amazing how fast you can lose your appetite.

How could this happen? Janet and I were looking at homes in Edmonton. She'd already had her car shipped up. She'd made friends. We were about to start Lamaze classes. It was the beginning of a whole new life for us. And now they were going to deal me?

My world was rocked. Even more amazing than that was that all these people—my dad, Janet, Mike Barnett, Angie Bumbacco—they'd all kept this from me for three months. You don't know what an achievement that is for my dad. We talked two or three times a week through that stretch. I'm surprised he didn't explode.

Now they couldn't stop telling me all the details. Apparently Pocklington had been talking about dealing me for two years. He even approached Jerry Buss about it when Buss owned the L.A. Kings. The possible teams now had boiled down to the Kings, Detroit, the Rangers and Vancouver. Skalbania, back from the dead, was in on the Vancouver deal. He and the billionaire Jimmy Pattison would buy fifty-one percent of the Vancouver Canucks, then give me twenty-five percent. Skalbania was going to pay Pocklington $15 million for me and Peter was going to give me $2 million of it if I approved the deal. I was going to be the only person in sports history to own himself.

No wonder Skalbania had been calling me for months. And the other part of the deal was, I'd only have to play three years if I wanted and then I could become coach and general manager. One hitch: since a player can't technically be an owner, they were going to give my share to my dad until I retired. That worked out to about $10 million to my dad.

But I didn't want any part of that deal. I didn't want to leave Edmonton. I didn't want to be a coach. I knew Skalbania. He'd have me standing in Vancouver shopping malls wearing funny hats and selling tickets. Most important, I didn't want to leave the team. Put yourself in my position. Would you want to leave all of your closest friends in the world, just like that?

I knew what was behind all this. Peter's other businesses were rumored to be in serious trouble—oil, meat packing, land development, trust company, car dealership—and he needed cash. He'd sold his expensive art collection. He'd even put the Oilers up as collateral against a loan. My contract was an asset he held. In 1987, I had signed a personal services contract with him. When Peter's businesses started going south, he decided he'd take the Oilers public, the way the Boston Celtics are public. He thought it would be a great way to raise cash. After all, he'd bought the team for about $7 million and people said it was worth near $100 million now. But to go public, he needed to get me out of the personal service contract and make me the property of the team. I had him. I was on top.

I didn't nail him so much for money as for privileges. The biggest one I wrote in was that I could leave after five years and be an *unrestricted* free agent. There's supposed to be no such thing as an unrestricted free agent in the NHL—the team that gets the player is supposed to cough up big-time draft picks—but this was no-strings-attached scot-free free agency. In 1992, I'd be able to go to any team I wanted. I'd be a free man. I could sign a contract for my fair market value.

Naturally, Peter wanted me to waive the right to free agency, because that would reduce my value in a trade. Then he wanted me to sign an extension. I said I'd think about it. What I really wanted was to sign one last very big, six- or seven-year contract and end my career with Edmonton. But Peter never made us any offer. He knew what he needed and it wasn't more Stanley Cups. He didn't need to sell more tickets. His arena was already sold out. He needed cash.

While I was waiting to hear from him, I was on my honeymoon in L.A. One day the phone rang and it was Bruce McNall, the Kings owner, saying, "Wayne, I've been given permission to talk to you."

Just like that. No call from Peter Pocklington or anyone in the organization. That was a slap in the face. I'd been loyal as hell to the Oilers, busted my butt, been part of one of the greatest dynasties in hockey history, and here I was getting thrown around from team to team like a piece of meat.

"So," said Bruce. "Do you wanna have lunch tomorrow?"

Bruce and I were acquainted. We'd had dinner a couple times in L.A. with mutual friends. I liked him. And if I was going to be traded, I liked the idea of going to L.A., where Janet could resume her career.

Bruce told me he was prepared to pay $20 million to $25 million plus three first-round draft picks and two players. In return, he'd get me and two or three other Oilers.

"Fine," I said, "As long as one of them is Marty McSorley."

I knew Slats wasn't going to give up Jari or Anderson or Mess or Kevin. And I knew the Kings needed some grit and some defense. Edmonton always had great role players for that: Pat Hughes and Kevin McClelland, Marty, Dave Hunter, Krusher, guys who would come off the bench, bust their butts, never complain and win.

Of course, I wasn't about to tell Marty or Krush. I wanted to, but if I did, the story would start leaking, the town would be all over Pocklington and he'd back out of the deal. I told my dad and my wife and that's it.

Meanwhile, I was starting to have some doubts. This was a huge step for me and a huge risk, too. I really felt that the Oilers had at least two or three Cups left in them. That's not easy to kiss away. And what if I fell flat on my face in Los Angeles? The Kings were a team that had been running brutal for twenty years. They were eighteenth in the league that year. What if I went down there and couldn't help them a bit?

I stared at a lot of 3:00 A.M. ceilings wondering what was ahead for me. I was only twenty-seven. Janet said she was behind whatever decision I made, but she said one thing I'll never forget. "Don't underestimate your own ability."

I called Cof.

"Gretz," he said, "you'll miss the players and the friendships and the fans, but you won't even look back. It's just nice to go somewhere with a challenge."

I knew I wasn't appreciated anymore by Puck. At the awards dinner where I was to receive my eighth Hart Trophy, neither Peter nor Glen congratulated me. Nothing. Not even a handshake.

And if *that* didn't seal it for me, then what happened next did. I was in L.A., meeting with Bruce in his office, when his secretary yelled, "Mr. Pocklington for you."

Bruce always takes his calls on his speaker phone and we both knew what was going to happen next. He looked at me and I looked at him. He took the call and that's when I heard all the trash Peter was heaping on me, how I had a huge ego and how selfish I was. He even said my dad was a big pain in his side. I don't know where that came from. My dad never called Peter in all my years in Edmonton.

Now I was sure I wanted to leave. Besides, the more I got to know Bruce the more I liked him. But

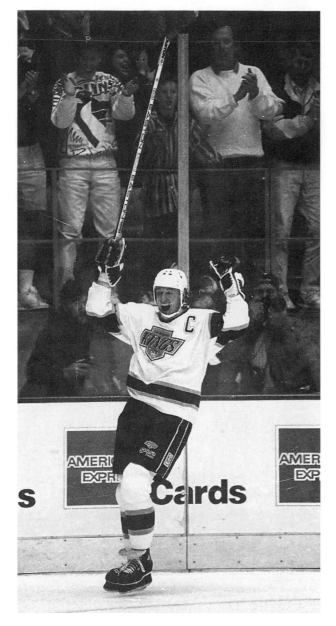

Los Angeles King Wayne Gretzky celebrates his 802nd goal, in Inglewood, California, March 23, 1994. The goal broke Gordie Howe's record for career goals. **AP/WIDE WORLD PHOTOS. REPRODUCED BY PERMISSION.**

there was a complication. Sather was refusing to give up Marty. Pretty soon, it looked like things were falling totally apart. Peter was hedging and Glen wasn't giving up anybody. Finally I called Bruce.

"Bruce, tell Peter they gotta give up Marty or there's no deal. I'm not leaving Edmonton without Marty." I knew Slats wouldn't budge, but Peter could budge him for us.

The next morning, Bruce called Peter and said he had to have Marty and Krusher and the three draft picks had to be staggered, not consecutive. Take it or leave it.

Peter took it. Bruce gave him Carson, Martin Gelinas—the Kings' new first-round draft pick—the money and the picks. The funny thing is, all Peter got was $15 million instead of the $20 million Bruce was willing to go. And why should he have received the full price? The whole time, throughout the dealings, he kept telling Bruce what a selfish player I was.

Of course, Peter saved himself some money, too. He refused to pay me the $2 million he'd promised for okaying the deal, no matter what the deal was. "I'm not paying him, you pay him," Peter told Bruce. "I'm tired of paying him." Afterwards, everybody asked me, "How could you pass up the $2 million? You should have fought for it." But I just said, "Listen, I went home with $2 million worth of happiness."

So this was it. Bruce said to me, "Wayne, you phone Peter back now and ask to be traded and he'll do the deal tomorrow. If you don't, he might not make the trade."

So I swallowed hard and dialed up Peter that night from Bruce's office. It was about 5:00. I was sweating. I said, "Peter, I've thought a lot about it. You and I have got our differences right now. I feel that in the ten years I was there, I worked very hard. I feel that I was as loyal as any employee could be for you. But I think it's best for both of us—I'm asking you to trade me. Please trade me to L.A."

I wasn't choked up about it. I was past that. That's what Peter wanted, what he'd set as a condition of the trade—me to ask him—and I was willing to play the game. He said that the feelings were mutual and he was sorry to see me go.

Then Bruce said one more thing to me before it became a done deal.

"You know," he said, "you once told me you'd always dreamed as a kid of playing in Detroit. If you want to play in Detroit, I'll back out of the deal right now and you can go to Detroit."

Right then, I knew more than ever that I was making the right move. I told him L.A. was where I wanted to be and that was that. The next morning, Bruce faxed his signed contract to Edmonton and Peter signed it and . . . Bruce's fax broke.

The two of us almost had coronaries. What if Peter suddenly got cold feet? I was ready to get on a plane and deliver it myself.

Twenty minutes later, it was fixed and the contracts came through. I was now a King. All of a sudden, I realized I had a whole new life ahead of me.

Janet and I were shocked and excited, but we couldn't tell anybody for two weeks. The Oilers season-ticket drive didn't close until then and Peter had insisted the trade be kept secret during that time.

Bruce, his wife, Janet and I went to Chasen's that night and tried to pin the corners of our mouths down to keep from grinning. We couldn't believe it had happened. We tried to act nonchalant, but every now and then someone would walk by whom Bruce knew and he'd say, "What would you think if I got Wayne here to L.A.? Wouldn't that be something?"

"Get him out of Edmonton? Good luck."

And we'd toast our good luck.

The deal started to leak before the two weeks were up. I was staying at Alan Thicke's house while he was in Europe. Janet and I had been out to dinner. We got back about 12:30 and Bruce called at 1:00.

"We're leaving tomorrow morning at 7:00 for Edmonton," he said.

"Bruce, I don't know if I'm ready for this," I said.

And I wasn't, but we had to go. The next twelve hours looked scary.

When our private plane landed in Canada, the lady from Customs came aboard. I guess she'd heard the rumors because she looked at us and said, "Are you guys *sure* you want to do this?"

I looked Bruce right in the face and I said, "Bruce, are you sure we want to do this?"

We were sure. Mike Barnett picked us up at a private airport in Edmonton and this time the drive that I'd done hundreds of times—from the airport into the city—was one I'll never forget.

The first thing we did was go to my apartment. I wanted to tell Kevin and I wanted to tell Mess and a few other guys. Mess must have called me eight or nine times during the negotiations, but I knew I couldn't call him back. I knew if I called him, he'd go crazy and maybe talk Peter out of the deal. Mess is just that persuasive.

I made those calls while four Edmonton city policemen that Mike had arranged for stood in my apartment for my own protection. As if it wasn't wild enough, when we got to Molson House before the press conference, in walked this public relations pest hired by Peter. He said he was there to "coach me" on what to say at the press conference.

"I've written a speech for you," he said. "You might want to read it over."

Bruce and Mike were both flabbergasted, but I knew what Peter was trying to accomplish. Obviously, he was worried. In the "speech," I was supposed to tell everybody that it was all my idea, that Peter had nothing to do with it. "And then right about in here," this flack said, "would be a good time to drop in the fact that Janet's going to have your baby."

That was the last straw. I blew up. "Hey, just get out of my face!"

That's about when Peter and Glen decided they wanted to have one last private talk with me. I looked at Bruce. He looked worried. I'm sure he thought they'd try to talk me out of the whole thing.

Peter and I sat down, eye-to-eye. But it wasn't a fistfight or anything. In fact, we thanked each other for the good years. I asked him if he would take care of Joey Moss, make sure that Joey always had a job and he said he would. We shook hands and I left.

Looking back on it, the biggest mistake Peter made was not letting me just play out my four years into free agency. I refused to sign a contract that didn't have a no-trade clause in it and Peter refused to give me one that had one in it, so we were stuck. He should have let me play out the four years. As Mike Barnett put it, I would then have been a 31-year-old veteran with fourteen years on one team. I probably would have been firmly fixed in Edmonton. So Peter could've then said, "There's the door. *You* tell Edmonton you're leaving." But it never happened.

Then Glen and I sat down by ourselves. As soon as he closed the door he said, "Wayne, if you don't want to do this deal, we can call the whole thing off right now."

Despite our differences, I really don't think Glen ever wanted to trade me, but his hands were tied. He worked for Peter and Peter had to take care of the bottom line. Simple as that. Peter and I couldn't agree and he knew the deal was going through, so he fought for everything he could get. He's a hockey man, first, last and always. Although I wonder how he had the face to tell the press afterwards that he didn't know a thing about the deal. "That trade broke my heart," he kept saying.

I did say one thing to him, though.

"I was disappointed you didn't call me through all of this. That doesn't sound very much like a coach who wants to keep a player."

"I did call," he said. "Last night."

We stood to go. "Glen," I said, "you've taught me a lot about hockey and a lot about life. I don't know if there's another man besides my father I respect as much." And I meant it. As bad as it had become between us at the end, he still had done so much for me. He believed in a small skinny center who was never where he was supposed to be, always flitting here and there, looking like he was lost. He played me a lot, even at eighteen. He understood me. If I had a big night going, he would just kind of look at me and I'd look back and he'd leave me in. He changed hockey. He was the first guy to use his four best offensive guys to kill penalties. I played a lot of minutes that way and we won a ton of hockey games that way. Is there another coach who would've gotten as much out of me? We both cried a little bit. He's a very emotional man. I am, too.

Through the glass of the office, I could see Bruce about to turn blue. So as I came out I turned my head and gave him a little wink. You could have heard him sigh in Manitoba.

The press conference was covered by everybody. Programming on the Canadian networks was interrupted to show the press conference live. My wife sat at home in L.A. and watched it by satellite. The first thing people saw was Pocklington laying it on thick. He said it was with "mixed emotions" and "a heavy heart" that he granted my request to leave the Oilers. "What do you do when an outstanding, loyal employee approaches you and asks for an opportunity to move along? You know you don't want to lose him, but at the same time, you don't want to stop him from pursuing his dreams."

Then it was my turn and I just tried to keep it simple and take the heat like I said I would. But then came the question.

"What will you remember about Edmonton?"

That question cut right to my heart. It hit me like a jolt that I was leaving my best friends and the best team in the world. Mark and Kevin and Jari and Joey and everybody. I'd joined this team, really, as a child, at seventeen—I'd literally grown up with these guys—and the roots that I was cutting off were deep. I started thinking of real basic things like scoring and congratulating each other and kidding around. Everything with us was a celebration. We were constantly celebrating something: scoring, winning, championships, records. And now, at least for me, it was about to end. I just started to cry. And every time I started to try to talk again, I couldn't. For a

guy who was getting what he wanted, it sure didn't feel very good.

The date was August 9, 1988, exactly twenty-five days after my wedding.

It was also the same day workers came to my dad's house to start digging up the old backyard where I first learned to play hockey. They were putting in a present I'd given my parents. A swimming pool.

Further Resources

BOOKS

Christopher, Matt. *On the Ice With—Wayne Gretzky.* Boston: Little, Brown, 1997.

Macgregor, Roy, and Steve Dryden. *Total Gretzky: The Magic, the Legend, the Numbers.* Tundra Books, 1999.

Messier, Mark. *Wayne Gretzky: The Making of the Great One.* Beckett, 1998.

PERIODICALS

Lupica, Mike. "Hockey's Only Hope." *Esquire* 111, February, 1989, 55–57.

Underwood, Nora. "The Great One Becomes a King." *Maclean's* 101, August 22, 1988, 38–39.

WEBSITES

"Greatness Personified." NHL.com. Available online at http://www.nhl.com/hockeyu/history/gretzky; website home page: http://www.nhl.com (accessed June 16, 2003).

The Wayne Gretzky Home Page. Available online at http://www.upperdeck.com/athletes/waynegretzky (accessed June 16, 2003).

"Every Time They Met"

Box scores

Date: December 14, 1992

Source: "Every Time They Met." *Sports Illustrated* 77, December 14, 1992. ∎

Introduction

Earvin "Magic" Johnson (1959–) was born in Lansing, Michigan. A high school basketball star in Michigan, he has been "Magic" Johnson since age fifteen when a local sports writer decided Johnson needed a nickname. Johnson went on to play basketball for the Michigan State Spartans and the Los Angeles Lakers. In 1991, Johnson learned he had the HIV virus. As of 2003 he had not developed AIDS. He remained healthy, and he has been a spokesperson and an inspiration for those stigmatized with the disease.

Magic Johnson (left) and Larry Bird reach for a loose ball in game four of the NBA Finals, Boston Garden, June 10, 1987. Helped by the rivalry of two of the greatest players in NBA history, interest in basketball skyrocketed—the NBA's revenue tripled in the 1980s. AP/WIDE WORLD PHOTOS. REPRODUCED BY PERMISSION.

Larry Bird (1956–) was born in West Baden, Indiana. Bird moved often as a youngster, as his mom and dad struggled financially. At nineteen, his parents divorced. Tragically, soon after this his dad took his own life. Bird did not become interested in basketball until he was thirteen. How-

ever, it did not take long for him to become a star. In his illustrious career, he played for Indiana State University and the Boston Celtics. He later coached the Indiana Pacers.

After meeting in the 1979 NCAA championship game, both Larry Bird and Magic Johnson headed to the

National Basketball Association (NBA). The Boston Celtics had picked Bird in the first round of the 1978 draft, but he elected to play his senior season with Indiana State before joining the Celtics. The Lakers selected Johnson with the first pick of the 1979 draft.

Johnson and Bird entered the NBA when the league's popularity was in decline. With talent stretched thin by expansion, the NBA's television ratings, attendance, and revenues were down significantly. The league lacked a dominant franchise, with five different teams winning the NBA title in the five years before Johnson and Bird entered the league. The league was doing so poorly that the 1979–1980 NBA finals were shown on tape delay throughout the country, not live on national television. After the 1979–1980 season, the NBA signed a lucrative television contract with CBS, and the network featured Johnson and Bird in its promotion of the league.

The Lakers and the Celtics dominated the NBA during the 1980s. The storied franchises won eight of the nine NBA titles from 1980 to 1988. While the Lakers won in 1979–1980 and 1981–1982 and Boston won in 1980–1981, the two teams did not play each other in the finals until 1983–1984, the fifth NBA season for Johnson and Bird. The two teams met in three finals over the next four years.

Beyond Bird and Johnson, both the Lakers and the Celtics had tremendous talent and depth. Nine individuals selected to the NBA's 50 Greatest Players in NBA History (selected in 1996) played in the Lakers-Celtics championship series clashes in 1983–1984, 1984–1985, and 1986–1987. Besides Johnson and Bird, these series featured the NBA's all-time leading scorer, Kareem Abdul-Jabbar, in addition to James Worthy and Bob McAdoo for the Lakers; and Kevin McHale, Larry Parish, Nate Archibald, and Bill Walton for the Celtics. The 1985–1986 Celtics and the 1986–1987 Lakers were selected in 1996 as two of the top ten individual teams in the history of the NBA.

The Celtics and Lakers met three times in the NBA finals. The Lakers won in 1984–1985 (Johnson averaged 18.3 points, 14 assists, and 6.8 rebounds per game) and 1986–1987 (Johnson, named series MVP, averaged 26.2 points, 13 assists, and 8 rebounds per game), and the Celtics won in 1983–1984 (Bird, named series MVP, averaged 27 points and 14 rebounds per game). Game seven of the 1984–1985 NBA finals drew the largest television ratings in the history of the NBA up to that point.

Significance

Johnson and Bird, together with the rivalry of the Lakers and Celtics, revived the NBA's popularity and ushered in a golden era for the league. Johnson and Bird provided fresh faces for a league that was struggling to maintain its national audience. During the 1980s, either the Lakers or the Celtics played on national television nearly every week—attracting fans throughout the country. Johnson played with an infectious enthusiasm and passion that quickly made him the most popular player in the league. The Lakers played a very entertaining fast break style of basketball, nicknamed "Showtime," and Magic led the way with uncanny no-look and alley-oop passes. By contrast, Bird's style was far less flashy than Johnson's—but his uncanny shooting ability, feel for the game, and competitive spirit attracted the attention of basketball fans. Johnson and Bird were the NBA's brightest stars during the 1980s, eventually relinquishing the spotlight to Isiah Thomas of the Detroit Pistons and Michael Jordan of the Chicago Bulls as the 1990s began.

The Johnson-Bird rivalry also was significant because the two stars elevated the play of their teammates. In addition to their individual brilliance, both Johnson and Bird had tremendous instincts for the game and were sound fundamentally, making everyone around them better. It is rare that two stars, recognized as two of the greatest to ever play, and their teams, recognized as two of the best in NBA history, all peak at the same time. The series also marked a distinct contrast in styles, with the Lakers favoring a wide-open, fast-break attack, and the Celtics concentrating on tough defense and a patient half-court offense. Many basketball experts consider their NBA championship series as the greatest basketball ever played, and Johnson and Bird performed brilliantly in all three series.

The Johnson-Bird rivalry brought out the best in both players. Building on their highly publicized NCAA championship matchup, the stars continued their rivalry in the NBA. Older and more advanced in his basketball skills, Bird immediately impacted the league. While Johnson was an instant superstar, he continued to develop his game—especially his outside shooting—over his first several years in the league. Johnson publicly stated that Bird's excellence compelled him to practice harder and improve. By the time the two stars met in the 1983–1984 NBA finals, both were at the top of their games. The NBA finals provided an appropriate stage for the Johnson-Bird rivalry. Both players, tremendous when the game was on the line, responded to the challenge and provided some of basketball's most electrifying moments when competing against each other.

(continued on page 681)

Every Time They Met

Here, for posterity, are the box scores of each of the 38 games in which Bird and Magic took the floor against each other.

March 26, 1979
Michigan State 75 Indiana State 64

MICHIGAN STATE: Brkovich 1–2 3–7 5, Kelser 7–13 5–6 19, Charles 3–3 1–2 7, Donnelly 5–5 5–6 15, Johnson 8–15 8–10 24, Vincent 2–5 1–2 5. TOTALS: 26–43 23–33 75.
INDIANA STATE: Miley 0–0 0–1 0, Gilbert 2–3 0–4 4, Bird 7–21 5–8 19, Nicks 7–14 3–6 17, Reed 4–9 0–0 8, Heaton 4–14 2–2 10, Staley 2–2 0 1 4, Nemcek 1–1 0–0 2. TOTALS: 27–64 10–22 64.

Michigan State	37	38	75
Indiana State	28	36	64

Rebounds: Johnson 7, Bird 13.
Assists: Johnson 5, Bird 2.

Dec. 28, 1979
Boston 105 at Los Angeles 123

BOSTON: Bird 7–15 2–3 16, Maxwell 6–12 7–9 19, Cowens 2–11 0–0 4, Archibald 4–13 6–7 14, Ford 7–12 2–4 18, Carr 8–14 0–0 16, Robey 3–9 0–2 6, Henderson 4–7 0–0 8, Chaney 1–2 0–0 2, Judkins 0–3 2–2 2. TOTALS: 42–98 19–27 105.
LOS ANGELES: Chones 6–8 4–6 16, Wildes 11–21 0–0 22, Abdul-Jabbar 4–9 7–8 15, Johnson 7–14 9–10 23, Nixon 7–13 3–4 17, Cooper 4–7 0–0 8, Haywood 6–11 4 6 16, Ford 3–3 0–0 6, Mack 0–1 0–0 0. TOTALS: 48–87 27–34 123

Boston	25	27	25	28	105
L.A.	30	31	28	34	123

Rebounds: Johnson 8, Bird 4.
Assists: Johnson 6, Bird 3.
Three-point goals: Johnson 0–0, Bird 0–0.

Jan. 13, 1980
Los Angeles 100 at Boston 98

LOS ANGELES: Haywood 4–13 2–2 10, Wilkes 10–18 1–1 21, Abdul-Jabbar 14–29 5–7 33, Nixon 2–9 7–8 11, Johnson 0–2 1–2 1, Chones 7–10 1–1 15, Cooper 4–6 1–1 9. TOTALS: 41–87 18–22 100.
BOSTON: Maxwell 5–9 3–4 13, Bird 7–10 0–0 14, Cowens 11–21 0–0 22, Archibald 4–10 5–10 13, Ford 5–16 0–0 11, Chaney 1–3 0–0 2, Carr: 3–5 2–5 8, Henderson 3–7 2–2 8, Rodney 3–8 1–2 7. TOTALS: 42–90 13–23 98.

L.A.	21	30	26	23	100
Boston	34	28	12	24	98

Rebounds: Johnson 3, Bird 1.
Assists: Johnson 2, Bird 1.
Three-point goals: Johnson 0–0, Bird 0–1.

Feb. 14, 1982
Boston 108 at Los Angeles 103

BOSTON: Bird 4–11 4–5 12, Maxwell 10–16 7–8 27, Parish 10–17 2–4 22, Archibald 5–13 6–8 17, Ford 1–4 0–0 2, McHale 2–4 2–2 6, Henderson 3–9 1–2 7, Robey 3–4 0–3 6, Carr 4–6 1–2 9. TOTALS: 42–84 23–34 108.
LOS ANGELES: Johnson 6–11 7–9 19, Wilkes 11–21 3–4 25, Abdul-Jabbar 7–16 7–10 21, Cooper 4–13 1–1 9, Nixon 3–11 0–6 6, Jordan 7–9 0–0 14, McAdoo 3–11 3–4 9. TOTALS: 41–93 21–28 103.

Boston	24	28	22	34	108
L.A.	25	32	22	24	103

Rebounds: Johnson 10, Bird 9.
Assists, Johnson 8, Bird 9.
Three-point goals: Johnson 0–0, Bird 0–0.

Jan. 30, 1983
Los Angeles 95 at Boston 110

LOS ANGELES: Rambis 1–5 4–5 6, Wilkes 9–19 2–3 20, Abdul-Jabbar 12–22 3–3 27, Nixon 3–7 0–0 6, Johnson 5–10 4–4 14, Cooper 2–6 2–3 6, Worthy 3–8 1–2 7, McAdoo 4–11 1–2 9. TOTALS: 39–88 17–22 95.
BOSTON: McHale 8–19 0–0 16, Bird 9–22 3–3 21, Parish 11–18 2–4 24, Buckner 2–6 0–0 4, Ainge 6–13 0–0 12, Archibald 3–8 1–2 7, Maxwell 6–8 4–5 16, Henderson 2–7 0–0 4, Carr 3–5 0–0 6. TOTALS: 50–106 10–14 110.

L.A.	26	24	27	18	95
Boston	24	36	32	18	110

Rebounds: Johnson 9, Bird 13.
Assists: Johnson 10, Bird 8.
Three-point goals: Johnson 0–0, Bird 0–0.

Feb. 23, 1983
Boston 113 at Los Angeles 104

BOSTON: Bird 13–23 4–6 32, Maxwell 10–16 10–13 30, Parish 7–13 2–4 16, Ainge 1–9 0–0 2, Archibald 5–13 2–4 12, McHale 3–7 0–0 6, Henderson 4–4 0–0 8, Buckner 1–6 0–0 2, Carr 1–2 1–2 3, Wedman 0–0 2–2 2. TOTALS: 45–93 21–31 113.
LOS ANGELES: Rambis 1–3 1–1 3, Wilkes 8–19 1–2 17, Abdul-Jabbar 7–18 0–0 14, Johnson 9–21 2–3 20, Nixon 7–14 2–2 16, Worthy 8–12 4–7 20, Cooper 4–10 1–1 9, Jones 2–3 1–2 5. TOTALS: 46–100 12–18 104.

Boston	28	30	32	23	113
L.A.	27	31	29	17	104

Rebounds: Johnson 13, Bird 17.
Assists: Johnson 10, Bird 9.
Three-point goals: Johnson 0–1 Bird 2–3.

Feb. 8, 1984
Los Angeles 111 at Boston 109

LOS ANGELES: Worthy 7–10 3 3 17, Wilkes 11–18 3–4 25, Abdul-Jabbar 12–19 3–3 27, Scott 3–6 0–0 6, Johnson 9–13 2–2 20, Cooper 1–2 0–0 2, Rambis 4–4 2–2 2, McAdoo 6–10 0–0 12. TOTALS: 49–91 13–14 111.
BOSTON: Maxwell 2–8 4–4 8, Bird 12–19 5–5 29, Parish 8–18 1–1 17, Johnson 5–16 1–2 11, Henderson 7–12 1–1 15, Ainge 3–13 0–0 6, McHale 9–15 3–3 21, Carr 1–2 0–0 2. TOTALS: 47–103 15–16 109.

L.A.	30	31	27	23	111
Boston	29	30	26	24	109

Rebounds: Johnson 8, Bird 11.
Assists: Johnson 10, Bird 7.
Three-point goals: Johnson 0–0, Bird 0–0.

Feb. 24, 1984
Boston 108 at Los Angeles 116

BOSTON: Bird 6–12 2–2 14, Maxwell 7–14 3–3 17, Parish 8–19 1–1 17, Henderson 5–10 3–3 13, Johnson 4–18 3–3 11, Ainge 0 2, 0–0 0, Buckner 1–2 0–1 2, McHale 11–19 4–4 26, Wedman 4–8 0–0 8. TOTALS: 46–104 16–17 108.
LOS ANGELES: Cooper 7 16 5–6 20, Rambis 1–2 3–4 5, Abdul-Jabbar 11–18 9–10 31, Johnson 4–11 1–2 9, Scott 7–18 0–0 14, Worthy 11–15 5–5 27, McGee 4–10 2–2 10, Garrett 0–2 0–0, Nater 0–1 0–0 0. TOTALS: 45–93 25–29 116.

Boston	26	24	37	21	108
L.A.	23	30	31	32	116

Rebounds: Johnson 8, Bird 11.
Assists: Johnson 18, Bird 5.
Three-point goals: Johnson 0–0, Bird 0–0.

May 27, 1984
Los Angeles 115 at Boston 109

LOS ANGELES: Rambis 3–3 1–1 7, Worthy 8–16 4–4 20, Abdul-Jabbar 12–17 8–9 32, Cooper 4–11 2–2 11, Johnson 7–11 4–4 18, Scott 5–7 4–4 14, McAdoo 2–12 3–4 7, Nater 1–2 1–2 3, Wilkes 1–4 1–2 3. TOTALS: 43–83 28–32 115.

[CONTINUED]

Primary Source

"Every Time They Met" (1 OF 5)

SYNOPSIS: In 1992, after the first NBA season without Bird and Magic, *Sports Illustrated* published the box scores of every game in which the two players faced off against each other.

Every Time They Met [CONTINUED]

Here, for posterity, are the box scores of each of the 38 games in which Bird and Magic took the floor against each other.

BOSTON: Maxwell 3–8 0–0 6, Bird 7–17 9–11 24, Parish 6–13 1–4 13, Johnson 7–20 9–11 23, Henderson 5–12 2–2 12, McHale 10–16 5–6 25, Buckner 0–3 0–0 0, Ainge 0–0 0–0 0, Kite 0–0 0–0 0, Wedman 3–5 0–0 6. TOTALS: 41–94 26–24 109.

L.A.	34	31	27	23	115
Boston	22	30	36	21	109

Rebounds: Johnson 6, Bird 14.
Assists: Johnson 10, Bird 5.
Three-point goals: Johnson 0–1, Bird 1–1.

May 31, 1984
Los Angeles 121 at Boston 124

LOS ANGELES: Rambis 0–1 0–0 0, Worthy 11–12 7–9 29, Abdul-Jabbar 9–22 2–4 20, Cooper 4–13 1–2 9, Johnson 10–14 7–7 27, McAdoo 6–9 4–6 16, Scott 2–3 1–3 5, Nater 1–2 0–0 2, Wilkes 5–8 3–4 13. TOTALS: 48–84 25–35 121.
BOSTON: Maxwell 3–7 10–10 16, Bird 8–22 11–15 27, Parish 9–14 0–4 18, Johnson 4–10 2–2 10, Henderson 7–14 2–3 16, Buckner 0–1 2–4 2, McHale 3–8 7–10 13, Ainge 6–10 0–0 12, Wedman 5–12 0–0 10. TOTALS: 45–98 34–48 124.

L.A.	26	33	28	26	8	121
Boston	36	25	29	23	11	124

Rebounds: Johnson 10, Bird 13.
Assists: Johnson 9, Bird 3.
Three-point goals: Johnson 0–0, Bird 0–0.

June 3, 1984
Boston 104 at Los Angeles 137

BOSTON: Bird 9–16 12–15 30, Maxwell 3–6 3–4 9, Parish 3–9 3–4 9, Henderson 4–9 2–4 10, Johnson 2–8 0–1 4, McHale 5–13 2–3 12, Wedman 7–18 0–0 16, Buckner 3–5 0–0 6, Ainge 1–5 0–0 2, Carr 1–5 0–0 2, Kite 0–2 0–0 0, Clark 2–5 0–0 4. TOTALS: 40–101 22–31 104.
LOS ANGELES: Rambis 7–7 3–5 17, Worthy 6–11 1–3 13, Abdul-Jabbar 9–19 6–9 24, Cooper 6–13 5–5 17, Johnson 4–6 6–10 14, McAdoo 8–16 5–7 21, Wilkes 2–6 2–2 6, Scott 1–2 0–0 2, Nater 3–6 0–0 6, McGee 6–15 3–3 15, Kupchak 0–0 0–0 0, Spriggs 1–2 0–0 2. TOTALS: 53–103 31–44 137.

Boston	26	20	33	25	104
L.A.	29	28	47	33	137

Rebounds: Johnson 11, Bird 7.
Assists: Johnson 21, Bird 2.
Three-point goals: Johnson 0–0, Bird 0–0.

June 6, 1984
Boston 129 at Los Angeles 125

BOSTON: Bird 9–24 10–10 29, Maxwell 3–6 5–7 11, Parish 11–23 3–3 25, Henderson 5–10 3–5 13, Johnson 9–23 4–4 22, Wedman 2–2 0–0 5, McHale 3–13 3–4 9, Buckner 0–0 0–0 0, Ainge 4–7 1–2 9, Carr 2–3 2–2 6. TOTALS: 48–111 31–37 129.
LOS ANGELES: Rambis 4–5 1–4 9, Worthy 14–17 2–3 30, Abdul-Jabbar 12–25 8–11 32, Cooper 4–8 2–4 10, Johnson 8–12 4–7 20, McAdoo 5–10 3–4 13, Nater 1–4 5–6 7, Wilkes 1–1 0–0 2, Scott 1–3 0–0 2. TOTALS: 50–85 25–39 125.

Boston	32	26	30	25	16	129
L.A.	33	35	22	23	12	125

Rebounds: Johnson 11, Bird 21.
Assists: Johnson 17, Bird 2.
Three-point goals: Johnson 0–0, Bird 1–3.

June 8, 1984
Los Angeles 103 at Boston 121

LOS ANGELES: Rambis 1–2 0–0 2, Worthy 10–17 2–5 22, Abdul-Jabbar 7–25

5–6 19, Cooper 3–5 0–0 8, Johnson 3–9 4–6 10, Wilkes 1–3 0–0 2, McAdoo 7–12 4–8 18, McGee 3–8 2–4 8, Nater 1–3 4–4 6, Scott 2–6 0–0 4, Spriggs 1–1 0–0 2, Kupchak 0–0 2–2 2. TOTALS: 39–91 23–35 103.
BOSTON: Maxwell 2–4 9–9 13, Bird 15–20 2–4 34, Parish 5–12 3–4 13, Johnson 10–20 2–3 22, Henderson 2–9 0–0 4, McHale 5–8 9–10 19, Ainge 2–4 0–2 5, Buckner 2–7 0–0 4, Carr 1–1 3–4 5, Kite 1–2 0–0 2, Clark 0–0 0–0 0. TOTALS: 45–87 28–36 121.

L.A.	26	27	24	26	103
Boston	26	29	33	33	121

Rebounds: Johnson 5, Bird 17.
Assists: Johnson 13, Bird 2.
Three-point goals: Johnson 0–0, Bird 2–2.

June 10, 1984
Boston 108 at Los Angeles 119

BOSTON: Bird 8–11 12–13 28, Maxwell 3–7 6–8 12, Parish 6–13 4–6 16, Henderson 10–17 2–2 22, Johnson 8–20 3–4 20, McHale 3–9 0–0 6, Ainge 1–6 2–2 4, Buckner 0–1 0–0 0, Kite 0–0 0–0 0. TOTALS: 39–84 29–35 108.
LOS ANGELES: Rambis 4–9 0–0 8, Worthy 9–18 2–2 20, Abdul-Jabbar 14–26 2–6 30, Cooper 9–15 5–5 23, Johnson 10–18 1–2 21, McAdoo 0–2 0–0 0, McGee 0–1 0–0 0, Nater 1–2 2–2 4, Wilkes 1–4 0–0 2, Scott 5–10 0–0 11. TOTALS: 53–105 12–17 119.

Boston	33	32	22	21	108
L.A.	29	30	24	36	119

Rebounds: Johnson 6, Bird 14.
Assists: Johnson 10, Bird 8.
Three-point goals: Johnson 0–0 Bird 0–0.

June 12, 1984
Los Angeles 102 at Boston 111

LOS ANGELES: Rambis 3–8 1–1 7, Worthy 9–14 3–6 21, Abdul-Jabbar 12–22 5–8 29, Cooper 6–12 2–4 16, Johnson 5–14 6–7 16, Wilkes 2–3 0–0 4, Scott 2–7 0–0 4, Nater 0–0 0–0 0, Kupchak 2–4 1–2 5. TOTALS: 41–84 18–28 102.
BOSTON: Maxwell 5–10 14–17 24, Bird 6–18 8–8 20, Parish 4–16 6–9 14, Johnson 5–13 12–12 22, Henderson 4–8 1–2 9, Carr 0–2 0–0 0, Ainge 5–12 0–0 10, Buckner 1–1 0–0 2, McHale 4–6 2–3 10, Clark 0–0 0–0 0. TOTALS: 34–86 43–51 111.

L.A.	30	22	26	24	102
Boston	30	28	33	20	111

Rebounds: Johnson 5, Bird 12.
Assists: Johnson 15, Bird 3.
Three-point goals: Johnson 0–0, Bird 0–0.

Jan. 16, 1985
Los Angeles 102 at Boston 104

LOS ANGELES: Spriggs 1–4 2–2 4, Worthy 5–11 0–0 10, Abdul-Jabbar 12–19 9–11 33, Scott 8–15 0–1 16, Johnson 4–11 0–0 8, Cooper 3–12 0–0 7, McAdoo 2–4 2–2 6, McGee 3–6 0–2 6, Rambis 3–3 0–0 6, Wildes 3–4 0–0 6. TOTALS: 44–89 13–18 102.
BOSTON: Maxwell 3–4 2–3 8, Bird 9–16 1–1 19, Parish 8–15 3–3 19, Johnson 10–22 0–0 20, Ainge 8–13 0–0 16, McHale 4–13 2–5 10, Wedman 2–5 0–0 4, Clark 4–8 0–0 8. TOTALS: 48–96 8–12 104.

L.A.	33	23	28	18	102
Boston	31	27	29	17	104

Rebounds: Johnson 7, Bird 11.
Assists: Johnson 13, Bird 7.
Three-point goals: Johnson 0–1, Bird 0–0.

Feb. 17, 1985
Boston 111 at Los Angeles 117

[CONTINUED]

Primary Source

"Every Time They Met" (2 OF 5)

Continuation of box scores for the Bird and Magic games.

Every Time They Met [CONTINUED]

Here, for posterity, are the box scores of each of the 38 games in which Bird and Magic took the floor against each other.

BOSTON: Bird 14–22 4–5 33, Maxwell 4–9 4–4 12, Parish 1–3 1–2 3, Ainge 5–11 0–0 10, Johnson 8–20 4–4 20, McHale 6–8 3–4 15, Clark 1–2 0–0 2, Wedman5–8 0–0 10, Carr 2–5 0–0 6, Kite 0–0 0–0 0. TOTALS 46–88 16–19 111.
LOS ANGELES: Rambis 2–5 0–0 4, Worthy 8–18 8–10 24, Abdul-Jabbar 7–14 6–10 20, Johnson 10–16 17–19 37, Scott 8–12 0–0 16, Cooper 3–7 0–0 6, McAdoo 4–8 2–2 10, McGee 0–2 0–0 0. TOTALS 42–82 33–41 117.

Boston	29	33	20	29	111
L.A.	34	25	27	31	117

Rebounds: Johnson 3, Bird 15.
Assists: Johnson 13, Bird 3.
Three-point goals: Johnson 0–0, Bird 1–3.

May 27, 1985
Los Angeles 114 at Boston 148

LOS ANGELES: Rambis 4–6 0–0 8, Worthy 8–19 4–6 20, Abdul-Jabbar 6–11 0–0 12, Scott 5–14 0–0 10, Johnson 8–14 3–4 19, Cooper 1–5 2–2 4, McAdoo 6–13 0–0 12, Spriggs 4–7 0–2 8, Kupchak 3–3 1–2 7, McGee 4–7 4–5 14, Lester 0–1 0–0 0. TOTALS: 49–100 14–21 114.
BOSTON: McHale 10–16 6 9 26, Bird 8–14 2–2 19, Parish 6–11 6–7 18, Johnson 6–14 1–1 13, Ainge 9–15 0–0 19, Wedman 11–11 0–2 26, Buckner 3–5 0–0 6, Williams 3 5 0–0 6, Kite 3–5 1–2 7, Maxwell 1–1 1–2 3, Carr 1–3 0–0 3. Clark 1–2 0–0 2. TOTALS: 62–102 17–25 148.

L.A.	24	25	30	35	114
Boston	38	41	29	40	148

Rebounds: Johnson 1, Bird 6.
Assists: Johnson 12, Bird 9.
Three-point goals: Johnson 0–0, Bird 1–2.

May 30, 1985
Los Angeles 109 at Boston 102

LOS ANGELES: Rambis 1–6 1–2 3, Worthy 6–14 4–6 16, Abdul-Jabbar 15–26 0–0 30, Scott 5–17 1–2 11, Johnson 6–9 2–4 14, McAdoo 1–7 4–5 6, Cooper 8–9 5–6 22, Kupchak 2–4 1–2 5, Spriggs 0–0 2–2 2. TOTALS: 44–92 20–29 109.
BOSTON: McHale 6–13 3–8 15, Bird 9–21 11–11 30, Parish 6–8 6–7 18, Johnson 6–18 3–4 15, Ainge 7–13 1–2 15, Wedman 2–5 0–4 4, Kite 0–0 0–0 0, Buckner 0–0 0–0 0, Maxwell 0–1 3–4 3. TOTALS: 37–82 27–36 102.

L.A.	31	33	23	22	109
Boston	26	20	29	27	102

Rebounds: Johnson 4, Bird 12.
Assists: Johnson 13, Bird 3.
Three-point goals: Johnson 0–0, Bird 1–3.

June 2, 1985
Boston 111 at Los Angeles 136

BOSTON: Bird 8–21 4–5 20, McHale 10–13 11–12 31, Parish 6–14 5–7 17, Ainge 2–8 3–4 7, Johnson 3–14 2–2 8, Maxwell 1–2 2–2 4, Wedman 4–6 1–2 10, Buckner 2–3 0–0 4, Williams 2–5 0–0 4, Kite 0–3 0–0 4, Carr 2–4 0–0 4, Clark 0–0 2–2 2. TOTALS: 40–93 30–36 111.
LOS ANGELES: Rambis 3–7 0–1 6, Worthy 12–22 5–6 29, Abdul-Jabbar 10–13 6–8 26, Johnson 6–13 4–4 17, Scott 5–12 1–2 12, McAdoo 9–16 1–2 19, Cooper 2–4 3–3 8, Kupchak 2–3 3–4 7, Spriggs 2–3 0–0 4, McGee 1–2 2–2 5, Lester 0–1 2–2 2, Nevitt 0–0 1–2 1. TOTALS: 52–96 28–36 136.

Boston	29	30	26	26	111
L.A.	25	40	35	36	136

Rebounds: Johnson 9, Bird 7.
Assists: Johnson 16, Bird 3.
Three-point goals: Johnson 1–2, Bird 0–0.

[CONTINUED]

June 5, 1985
Boston 107 at Los Angeles 105

BOSTON: Bird 8–16 10–12 26, McHale 11–19 6–8 28, Parish 4–10 2–2 10, Ainge 4–10 0–0 8, Johnson 11–20 5–6 27, Wedman 0–4 1–2 1, Maxwell 1–2 1–2 3, Williams 1–1 0–0 2, Carr 0–1 0–0 0, Buckner 1–3 0–0 2, Kite 0–0 0–0 0. TOTALS: 41–86 25–32 107.
LOS ANGELES: Rambis 5–8 2–4 12, Worthy 7–14 2–2 16, Abdul-Jabbar 7–12 7–9 21, Johnson 5–12 10–11 20, Scott 7–17 1–1 16, Kupchak 1–3 0–0 2, McAdoo 5–12 0–0 10, Cooper 3–5 2–2 8, Spriggs 0–0 0–0 0. TOTALS: 40–83 24–29 105.

Boston	28	31	23	25	107
L.A.	32	26	26	21	105

Rebounds: Johnson 11, Bird 11.
Assists: Johnson 12, Bird 5.
Three-point goals: Johnson 0–0, Bird 0–0.

June 7, 1985
Boston 111 at Los Angeles 120

BOSTON: Bird 8–17 3–5 20, McHale 10–18 4–5 24, Parish 11–22 4–6 26, Ainge 4–8 2–2 11, Johnson 10–21 2–2 22, Maxwell 0–0 0–0 0, Wedman 3–7 1 1 8. TOTALS: 46–93 16–21 111.
LOS ANGELES: Rambis 2–6 3–4 7, Worthy 13–17 7–11 33, Abdul-Jabbar 16–28 4–5 36, Johnson 11–20 4–4 26, Scott 2–3 0–0 4, Cooper 4–7 2–3 10, Kupchak 2–2 0–0 4, McAdoo 0–5 0–0 0, McGee 0 0 0–0 0. TOTALS: 50–88 20–27 120.

Boston	31	20	30	30	111
L.A.	35	29	31	25	120

Rebounds: Johnson 6, Bird 7.
Assists: Johnson 17, Bird 7.
Three-point goals: Johnson 0–0, Bird 1–2.

June 9, 1985
Los Angeles 111 at Boston 100

LOS ANGELES: Rambis 4–5 1–2 9, Worthy 11–15 6–9 28, Abdul-Jabbar 13–21 3–4 29, Scott 6–13 2–4 14, Johnson 5–15 4–4 14, Cooper 2–4 5–5 9, Kupchak 1–5 4–6 6, McAdoo 1–5 0–0 2, McGee 0–1 0–2 0. TOTALS: 43–84 25–36 111.
BOSTON: McHale 11–18 10–13 32, Bird 12–29 4–5 28, Parish 5–14 4–6 14, Johnson 3–15 5–6 11, Ainge 3–16 0–0 7, Wedman 2–3 2–2 7, Kite 1–1 0–0 2. TOTALS: 37–96 25–32 100.

L.A.	28	27	27	20	111
Boston	26	29	18	27	100

Rebounds: Johnson 10, Bird 10.
Assists: Johnson 14, Bird 3.
Three-point goals: Johnson 0–0, Bird 0–2.

Jan. 22, 1986
Los Angeles 95 at Boston 110

LOS ANGELES: Lucas 4–11 1–3 9, Worthy 5–15 0–1 12, Abdul-Jabbar 6–20 5–6 17, Scott 7–13 1–1 16, Johnson 6–10 3–3 15, Cooper 2–5 0 0 4, Kupchak 2–9 2–3 6, Green 2–6 0–0 4, McGee 2–5 2–2 6, Spriggs 2–4 0–1 4, Lester 1–3 0–0 2. TOTALS: 39–101 16–22 95.
BOSTON: McHale 3–14 6–8 12, Bird 8–16 4–4 21, Parish 7–14 2–3 16, Johnson 9–19 4–4 22, Ainge 5–9 0–0 11, Walton 5–6 1–2 11, Sichting 3–4 1–1 7, Wedman 2–6 0–0 4, Carlisle 1–3 0–0 2, Vincent 2–3 0–0 4, Kite 0–2 0–0 0, Thirdkill 0–2 0–0 0. TOTALS: 45–98 18–22 110.

L.A.	25	24	26	20	95
Boston	31	26	31	22	110

Rebounds: Johnson 5, Bird 12.
Assists: Johnson 6, Bird 7.
Three-point goals: Johnson 0–0, Bird 1–1.

[CONTINUED]

Primary Source

"Every Time They Met" (3 OF 5)

Continuation of box scores for the Bird and Magic games.

Every Time They Met [CONTINUED]

Here, for posterity, are the box scores of each of the 38 games in which Bird and Magic took the floor against each other.

Feb. 16, 1986
Boston 105 at Los Angeles 99

BOSTON: Bird 7–17 8212 22, Wedman 5–9 0–0 11, Parish 5–8 1–1 11, Ainge 2–7 0–0 4, Johnson 11–23 1–2 23, Walton 5–10 0–1 10, Thirdkill 1–3 1–1 3, Sichting 4–9 222 11, Carlisle 5–7 0–0 10, Kite 0–0 0–0 0. TOTALS: 45–93 13–19 105.

LOS ANGELES: Rambis 0–2 4–4 4, Worthy 14–26 7–9 35, Abdul-Jabbar 7–17 9–11 23, Johnson 0–4 6–6 6, McGee 1–2 1–1 4, Cooper 6–13 0–0 15, Scott 5–11 0–0 10, Kupchak 0–1 0–0 0, Lucas 1–1 0–0 2, Green 0–1 0–0 0. TOTALS: 34–78 27–32 99.

| Boston | 30 | 28 | 28 | 19 | 105 |
| L.A. | 29 | 26 | 25 | 19 | 99 |

Rebounds: Johnson 6, Bird 18.
Assists: Johnson 12, Bird 7.
Three-point goals: Johnson 0–0, Bird 0–1.

Dec. 12, 1986
Los Angeles 117 at Boston 110

LOS ANGELES: Worthy 12–24 1–2 25, Green 2–3 3–4 7, Abdul-Jabbar 11–16 4–4 26, Scott 4–6 0–0 9, Johnson 13–25 5–7 31, Rambis 2–5 0–1 4, Cooper 5–13 0–0 11, Smrek 1–1 0–0 2, Thompson 1–6 0–0 2. TOTALS: 51–99 13–18 117.

BOSTON: McHale 10–17 2–2 22, Bird 11–13 3–3 26, Parish 9–19 5–6 23, Johnson 10–19 1–2 21, Ainge 6–13, 0–0 12, Roberts 2–2 2–2 6, Sichting 0–1 0–0 0, Daye 0–0 0–0 0, Thirdkill 0–0 0–0 0, Carlisle 0–0 0–0 0. TOTALS: 48–84 13–15 110.

| L.A. | 35 | 24 | 29 | 29 | 117 |
| Boston | 39 | 26 | 29 | 16 | 110 |

Rebounds: Johnson 7, Bird 3.
Assists: Johnson 8, Bird 6.
Three-point goals: Johnson 0–0, Bird 1–1.

Feb. 15, 1987
Boston 103 at Los Angeles 106

BOSTON: Bird 7–12 5–7 20, McHale 9–17 5–6 23, Parish 9–13 2–2 20, Ainge 3–11 2–4 10, Johnson 8–18 6–8 22, Kite 0–0 0–0 0, Daye 0–1 0–0 0, Sichting 3–4 0–0 6, Vincent 1–3 0–2 2, Roberts 0–0 0–0 0, Henry 0–0 0–0 0. TOTALS: 40–79 20–27 103.

LOS ANGELES: Green 2–3 1–2 5, Worthy 12–16 2–2 26, Abdul-Jabbar 4–11 2–2 10, Johnson 12–20 14–15 39, Scott 4–17 1–1 9, Cooper 1–7 4–4 7, Rambis 0–1 0–0 0, Thompson 5–7 0–0 10. TOTALS: 40–82 24–26 106.

| Boston | 32 | 26 | 23 | 22 | 103 |
| L.A. | 28 | 22 | 27 | 29 | 106 |

Rebounds: Johnson 7, Bird 5.
Assists: Johnson 10, Bird 7.
Three-point goals: Johnson 1–1, Bird 1–2.

June 2, 1987
Boston 113 at Los Angeles 126

BOSTON: Bird 14–25, 4–4 32, McHale 6–11 3–4 15, Parish 7–14 2–4 16, Ainge 4–6 0–0 11, Johnson 3–7 1–2 7, Walton 1–1 0–0 2, Vincent 2–5 3–4 7, Daye 2–4 3–3 7, Sichting 1–2 0–0 2, Roberts 1–2 2–2–3 4, Henry 3–4 2–2 8, Kite 1–1 0–0 2. TOTALS: 45–82 20–26 113.

LOS ANGELES: Green 4–7 2–3 10, Worthy 16–23 1–4 33, Abdul-Jabbar 5–12 4–4 14, Johnson 13–25 3–3 29, Scott 9–15 2–2 20, Cooper 4–9 1–1 10, Rambis 0–1 0–0 0, Thompson 1–1 2–2 4, Matthews 2–2 0–0 4, Branch 1–2 0–0 2, Smrek 0–2 0–0 0. TOTALS: 55–99 15–19 126.

| Boston | 26 | 28 | 31 | 28 | 113 |
| L.A. | 35 | 34 | 32 | 25 | 126 |

[CONTINUED]

Rebounds: Johnson 8, Bird 7.
Assists: Johnson 13, Bird 6.
Three-point goals: Johnson 0–0, Bird 0–0.

June 4, 1987
Boston 122 at Los Angeles 141

BOSTON: Bird 9–17 4–5 23, McHale 9–12 2–2 20, Parish 6–16 5–8 17, Ainge 3–4 0–0 6, Johnson 9–18 2–2 20, Sichting 1–3 0–0 2, Daye 3–4 0–0 6, Vincent 4–6 2–4 10, Walton 0–0 0–0 0, Roberts 6–8 4–6 16, Kite 0–1 0–0 0, Henry 1–4 0–2 2. TOTALS: 51–93 19–29 122.

LOS ANGELES: Green 5–8 2–2 12, Worthy 10–15 3–5 23, Abdul-Jabbar 10–14 3–6 23, Johnson 10–17 2–2 22, Scott 9–11 6–7 24, Cooper 7–10 1–1 21, Rambis 2–3 4–4 8, Thompson 2–6 0–1 4, Matthews 0–3 0–0 0, Branch 0–3 2–4 2, Smrek 1–1 0–0 2. TOTALS: 56–91 23–32 141.

| Boston | 34 | 22 | 36 | 30 | 122 |
| L.A. | 38 | 37 | 32 | 34 | 141 |

Rebounds: Johnson 5, Bird 10.
Assists: Johnson 20, Bird 4.
Three-point goals: Johnson 0–0, Bird 1–1.

June 7, 1987
Los Angeles 103 at Boston 109

LOS ANGELES: Worthy 6–18 1–4 13, Green 1–3 0–0 2, Abdul-Jabbar 9–16 9–13 27, Scott 2–9 0–0 4, Johnson 12–18 8–8 32, Thompson 4–7 2–2 10, Cooper 6–10 0–0 15, Rambis 0–0 0–0 0. TOTALS: 40–81 20–27 103.

BOSTON: McHale 8–15 5–5 21, Bird 10–24 10–11 30, Parish 6–7 4–7 16, Johnson 11–22 3–4 26, Ainge 5–11 2–2 12, Kite 0–0 0–0 0, Sichting 0–1 0–0 0, Daye 1–2 0–2 2, Roberts 1–1 0–0 2, Walton 0–0 0–0 0. TOTALS: 42–86 24–29 109.

| L.A. | 29 | 27 | 22 | 25 | 103 |
| Boston | 22 | 38 | 26 | 23 | 109 |

Rebounds: Johnson 11, Bird 12.
Assists: Johnson 9, Bird 4.
Three-point goals: Johnson 0–0, Bird 0–1.

June 9, 1987
Los Angeles 107 at Boston 106

LOS ANGELES: Worthy 9–18 3–3 21, Green 3–4 1–2 7, Abdul-Jabbar 5–17 6–10 16, Scott 3–10 2–2 8, Johnson 12–20 5–6 29, Thompson 6–9 4–7 16, Cooper 3–6 2–2 10, Rambis 0–1 0–0 0. TOTALS: 41–85 23–32 107.

BOSTON: McHale 10–14 5–8 25, Bird 7–19 5–5 21, Parish 9–14 0–0 18, Johnson 6–15 3–3 15, Ainge 11–21 0–0 23, Kite 0–0 0–0 0, Sichting 1–2 0–0 2, Daye 1–1 0–0 2. TOTALS: 45–86 13–16 106.

| L.A. | 22 | 25 | 31 | 29 | 107 |
| Boston | 29 | 26 | 30 | 21 | 106 |

Rebounds: Johnson 8, Bird 10.
Assists: Johnson 5, Bird 7.
Three-point goals: Johnson 0–0, Bird 2–3.

June 11, 1987
Los Angeles 108 at Boston 123

LOS ANGELES: Worthy 6–19 0–0 12, Green 5–10 0–1 10. Abdul-Jabbar 8–21 2–2 18, Scott 3–10 0–0 7, Johnson 12–21 4–4 29, Thompson 4–6 10–11 18, Cooper 4–5 0–0 10, Rambis 1–2 0–0 2, Matthews 0–1 1–2 1, Smrek 0–0 0–0 0, Branch 0–0 1–2 1. TOTALS: 43–95 18–22 108.

BOSTON: McHale 8–15 6–8 22, Bird 7–18 8–9 22, Parish 10–12 1–2 21, Johnson 11–22 3–4 25, Ainge 7–11 2–2 21, Kite 0–3 1–2 1, Sichting 1–3 0–0 2, Daye 1–2 2–2 4, Roberts 0–0 0–0 0, Walton 1–1 0–2 2, Vincent 0–1 2–2 2, Henry 0–1 0–0 0. TOTALS: 46–89 25–31 123.

| L.A. | 25 | 23 | 29 | 31 | 108 |
| Boston | 25 | 38 | 33 | 27 | 123 |

[CONTINUED]

Primary Source

"Every Time They Met" (4 OF 5)

Continuation of box scores for the Bird and Magic games.

Every Time They Met [CONTINUED]

Here, for posterity, are the box scores of each of the 38 games in which Bird and Magic took the floor against each other.

Rebounds: Johnson 8, Bird 12.
Assists: Johnson 12, Bird 7.
Three-point goals: Johnson 1–1, Bird 1–2.

June 14, 1987
Boston 93 at Los Angeles 106

BOSTON: Bird 6–16 4–4 16, McHale 7–15 6–6 20, Parish 4–8 4–6 12, Ainge 1–9 0–0 2, Johnson 11–22 11–11 33, Walton 1–3 0–0 2, Kite 1–1 0–0 2, Sichting 0–4 0–0 0, Daye 2–3 2–2 6, Roberts 0–0 0–2 0, Vincent 0–0 0–0 0, Henry 0–0 0–0 0. TOTALS: 33–81 27–31 93.
LOS ANGELES: Green 2–8 2–2 6, Worthy 10–16 2–3 22, Abdul-Jabbar 13–18 6–10 32, Johnson 7–21 2–2 16, Scott 4–7 0–0 8, Thompson 6–12 3–4 15, Cooper 3–10 0–0 6, Rambis 0–0 1–2 1, Branch 0–1 0–0 0, Smrek 0–0 0–0 0, Matthews 0–0 0–0 0. TOTALS: 45–93 16–23 106.

| Boston | 32 | 24 | 12 | 25 | 93 |
| L.A. | 25 | 26 | 30 | 25 | 106 |

Rebounds: Johnson 8, Bird 9.
Assists: Johnson 19, Bird 5.
Three-point goals: Johnson 0–1, Bird 0–1.

Dec. 11, 1987
Los Angeles 115 at Boston 114

LOS ANGELES: Worthy 4–9 0 0 8, Green 4–7 5–6 13, Abdul-Jabbar 10–14 3–4 23, Scotts 8–15 4–5 21, Johnson 6–11 5–6 18, Cooper 8–12 2–2 21, Thompson 3–9 3–4 9, Rambis 0–0 2–2 2. TOTALS: 43–77 24–29 115.
BOSTON: McHale 4–12 2–2 10, Bird 14–26 6–8 35, Parish 6–9 3–3 15, Johnson 8–19 3–4 19, Ainge 6–10 2–4 15, Roberts 1–3 1–2 3, Sichting 8–10 0–0 17, Acres 0–0 0–0 0, Daye 0–2 0–0 0. TOTALS: 47–91 17–23 114.

| L.A. | 32 | 26 | 25 | 32 | 115 |
| Boston | 30 | 30 | 29 | 25 | 114 |

Rebounds: Johnson 8, Bird 9.
Assists: Johnson 17, Bird 8.
Three-point goals: Johnson 1–1, Bird 1–1.

Feb. 14, 1988
Boston 106 at Los Angeles 115

BOSTON: Bird 8–22 9–11 25, McHale 11–14 2–2 24, Parish 0–4 0–0 0, Ainge 6–11 2–2 16, Johnson 10–20 1–1 21, Gilmore 0–0 1–2 1, Minniefield 0–4 0–0 0, Lohaus 3–5 2–2 9, Acres 0–1 0–0 0, Roberts 3–3 0–0 6, Daye 1–2 0–0 2, Lewis 1–2 0–0 2. TOTALS: 43–88 17–20 106.
LOS ANGELES: Green 0–3 2–2 2, Worthy 5–10 0–0 10, Abdul-Jabbar 8–19 1–1 17, Johnson 9–19 4–7 22, Scott 15–19 6–8 38, Thompson 5–8 2–5 12, Cooper 1–8 9–9 12, Smrek 1–1 0–0 2. TOTALS: 44–87 24–32 115.

| Boston | 24 | 20 | 36 | 26 | 106 |
| L.A. | 31 | 33 | 12 | 39 | 115 |

Rebounds: Johnson 5, Bird 17.
Assists: Johnson 14, Bird 4.
Three-point goals: Johnson 0–1, Bird 0–0.

Dec. 15, 1989
Los Angeles 119 at Boston 110

LOS ANGELES: Cooper 4–9 2–2 12, Worthy 13–19 2–2 28, Green 8–12 9–12 25, Scott 9–15 2–2 21, Johnson 4–12 8–8 16, McNamara 0–1 0–0 0, Drew 0–1 2–2 2, Divac 4–9 2–3 10, Woolridge 2–3 1–1 5. TOTALS: 44–81 28–32 119.
BOSTON: Bird 9–27 2–2 21, Pinckney 1–2 0–0 2, Parish 10–16 3–5 23, Johnson 11–15 2–2 24, Paxson 3–5 0–0 6, McHale 9–11 3–3 21, Upshaw 1–5 0–0 3, Lewis 3–7 0–0 6, Kleine 2–3 0–1 4, Gamble 0–0 0–0 0, M. Smith 0–0 0–0 0. TOTALS: 49–91 10–13 110.

| L.A. | 28 | 32 | 25 | 34 | 119 |
| Boston | 30 | 25 | 27 | 28 | 110 |

Rebounds: Johnson 6, Bird 12.
Assists: Johnson 21, Bird 2.
Three-point goals: Johnson 0–1, Bird 1–2.

Feb. 18, 1990
Boston 110 at Los Angeles 116

BOSTON: Bird 9–17 2–2 20, Pinckney 1–2 0–0 2, Parish 9–12 2–4 20, Johnson 5–10 0–0 10, Lewis 10–13 4–4 24, McHale 8–14 5–6 21, Kleine 1–1 0–0 2, Gamble 1–2 0–0 3, Paxson 3–5 0–0 6, M. Smith 1–2 0–0 2, C. Smith 0–0 0–0 0. TOTALS: 48–78 13–16 110.
LOS ANGELES: Green 3–5 0–0 6, Worthy 12–26 1–2 25, Thompson 2–7 2–2 6, Johnson 10–21 7–7 30, Scott 8–16 5–7 24, Divac 4–8 5–7 13, Cooper 0–1 2–2 2, Woolridge 4–7 0–0 8, Drew 1–2 0 0 2. TOTALS: 44–93 22–27 116.

| Boston | 30 | 28 | 36 | 16 | 110 |
| L.A. | 29 | 23 | 40 | 24 | 116 |

Rebounds: Johnson 4, Bird 7.
Assists: Johnson 13, Bird 7.
Three-point goals: Johnson 3–6, Bird 0–0.

Feb. 15, 1991
Boston 98 at Los Angeles 85

BOSTON: Bird 4–16 2–2 11, Gamble 6–13 2–2 14, Parish 13–16 3–3 29, Lewis 12–23 2–2 26, Shaw 5–10 0–0 10, Pinckney 2–3 0–0 4, Kleine 0–0 0–0 0, Brown 1–3 0–0 2, M. Smith 1–1 0–0 2. TOTALS: 44–85 9–9 98.
LOS ANGELES: Green 3–5 2–2 8, Worthy 10–19 3–6 23, Divac 4–10 2–3 10, Johnson 7–13 6–8 21, Scott 2–9 0–0 4, Thompson 0–2 0–0, Perkins 3–10 1–2 7, Teagle 6–13 0 0 12, Smith 0–2 0–0 0, Campbell 0–0 0–0 0. TOTALS: 35–83 14–21 85.

| Boston | 35 | 23 | 23 | 17 | 98 |
| L.A. | 27 | 20 | 25 | 13 | 85 |

Rebounds: Johnson 9, Bird 11.
Assists: Johnson 16, Bird 11.
Three-point goals: Johnson 1–4, Bird 1–3.

SOURCE: "Every Time They Met." *Sports Illustrated*, December 14, 1992.

Primary Source

"Every Time They Met" (5 OF 5)

Continuation of box scores for the Bird and Magic games.

The debate among basketball fans raged during the 1980s as to who was the better player—Magic or Bird—with compelling arguments on both sides. At 6' 9," Johnson revolutionized the point guard position and became the greatest guard ever in transition and on the fast break. Bird became arguably the greatest pure shooter in league history, and he is widely recognized as the greatest clutch shooter ever to play the game. Johnson and Bird staged one of the great rivalries in the history of sports, and they will forever be honored as two of the greatest players and competitors in NBA history. Their careers will always be linked in the minds of basketball fans.

Over the years, they also became close friends as well as competitors. Bird introduced Johnson when Johnson was inducted into basketball's Hall of Fame. Fittingly, Johnson and Bird finally played together on the 1992 U.S. Olympic gold medal team—The Dream Team—along with Michael Jordan, when professionals were first allowed to play in Olympic competition. At the time, Johnson had retired after being diagnosed as HIV-positive, and Bird was suffering from severe back problems that eventually ended his career. However, the two great stars played exceptionally well in leading the United States to a gold medal. It was an appropriate ending to one of the great rivalries in all of sports.

Further Resources

BOOKS

Bird, Larry, with Bob Ryan. *Drive: The Story of My Life.* New York: Doubleday, 1989.

Bird, Larry, with Jackie MacMullan. *Bird Watching: On Playing and Coaching the Game I Love.* New York: Warner Books, 1999.

Johnson, Earvin, with William Novak. *My Life: Earvin "Magic" Johnson.* New York: Random House, 1992.

PERIODICALS

Halbertsam, David. "The Stuff Dreams Are Made Of." *Sports Illustrated,* June 29, 1987, 38–43.

MacMullan, Jackie. "A Jewel of a Duel: 1979 NCAA Championship Game Between Michigan State Led by M. Johnson vs. Indiana State Led by L. Bird." *Sports Illustrated* 91, no. 21, November 29, 1999, 133–134.

Ryan, Bob. "Tuesday, June 9, 1987." *Sports Illustrated,* December 14, 1992.

WEBSITES

Biography of Earvin "Magic" Johnson. "NBA History." NBA.com. Available online at http://www.nba.com/history /players/johnsonm_bio.html; website home page: http:// www.nba.com (accessed June 16, 2003).

Biography of Larry Bird. "NBA History." NBA.com. Available online at http://www.nba.com/history/players/bird_bio .html; website home page: http://www.nba.com (accessed June 16, 2003).

For the Love of the Game
Autobiography

By: Michael Jordan

Date: 1998

Source: Jordan, Michael. *For the Love of the Game.* Mark Vancil, ed. New York: Crown Publishing, 1998.

About the Author: Michael Jordan (1963–) was in Brooklyn, New York. He grew up in Wilmington, North Carolina, attended North Carolina University, and was drafted by the

NBA's Chicago Bulls in 1984. Jordan was named the Most Valuable Player in the NBA five times, selected ten times to the All-NBA First Team, and led the Chicago Bulls to six NBA championships. In 2000, ESPN named Jordan the greatest athlete of the twentieth century. ■

Introduction

Michael Jordan is widely regarded as the greatest basketball player ever. In the 1980s and 1990s, Jordan dominated the NBA as no player had since Wilt Chamberlain. Jordan possessed phenomenal natural talent, strength, quickness, and mental toughness. Able to shoot and drive to the basket, on offense he was a prolific scorer, averaging over thirty-one points per game for his career—best in league history. He led the NBA in scoring for seven consecutive seasons, from 1986–1987 to 1992–1993. On defense, he was named the 1987–1988 NBA Defensive Player of the Year and chosen a record nine-times for the NBA's All-Defensive First Team selection. He led the Chicago Bulls to six NBA championships, and he was selected as the Most Valuable Player in each of those finals.

Magic Johnson of the L.A. Lakers and Larry Bird of the Boston Celtics ignited a resurgence of interest in the NBA during the early 1980s. The league was riding a new wave of popularity when Jordan joined the Bulls for the 1984–1985 season. Jordan quickly adapted to the NBA, but it took several years for the Bulls to contend for the NBA championship. Early in his professional career, Jordan proved capable of taking over games and scoring nearly at will when necessary. Eventually, Chicago surrounded Jordan with other talented players— including Scottie Pippin—and the Bulls won six championships in seven years. Jordan's play remained at an incredibly high level throughout that span. Many feel that only Jordan's ill-fated retirement from basketball for two years in an attempt to play professional baseball kept the Bulls from winning additional championships.

At the beginning the 1990s, after the retirement of Bird and Johnson, Jordan emerged as the face of the NBA. His popularity translated into high ratings for the league, and Jordan became one of the most influential and recognizable people in the world. He also captured the attention of Madison Avenue, successfully endorsing products for Pepsi, McDonalds, his "Air Jordan" shoes for Nike, and starring in the movie *Space Jam.* He amassed a staggering personal net worth in the process.

Significance

On May 20, 1986, Jordan scored sixty-three points against the Boston Celtics. Jordan's account of the game and his reaction to Larry Bird's praise of him are excerpted here. This game was significant in that it provided a glimpse of how dominant Jordan would eventually become. Jordan broke his foot three games into the 1985–1986 season, and his return enabled the team to grab the final playoff position, pitting them against the top seed Boston Celtics. Despite a strong Celtic defense, Jordan was able to score with little trouble, averaging over forty points a game in the series. Larry Bird, one of the greatest players in NBA history, marveled publicly at Jordan's ability. Jordan had no weakness. His talent stood out in a league of talented players.

Also significant in the excerpted material is Jordan's growing realization of how good he could become. Although he had been the College Player of the Year in 1983 and 1984, he played on an excellent North Carolina team and had not been featured as he would be in the NBA. He had grown up watching Bird and Magic and other NBA legends, and Jordan had to convince himself that he could play at the highest levels. Praise such as the accolades Bird gave appeared to help convince Jordan that he belonged in that top group of players in the NBA.

Michael Jordan is fortunate to have come of age in the 1980s. He received excellent coaching: at North Carolina from legend Dean Smith, as well as Doug Collins and Phil Jackson with the Chicago Bulls. More importantly, he developed in a time when there was more focus on fundamentals. Many top high school players with Jordan's physical skills have since begun focusing on dunking and shooting three-pointers as this is often what makes the highlights on all-sports cable channels. Jordan learned all aspects of the game and was able to continue to develop as a professional because he had mastered the finer points of the game. Also, he did not face the expectations and pressure that many high-profile draft picks now feel to become "the next Michael Jordan." Additionally, the league has added salary cap provisions that would have made it impossible for the Bulls' core nucleus to have remained together for so long.

Primary Source

For the Love of the Game [excerpt]

SYNOPSIS: Michael Jordan talks about Larry Bird's comments after Jordan's record-breaking sixty-three-point playoff game.

I think he's God disguised as Michael Jordan. He is the most awesome player in the NBA. Today in Boston Garden, on national TV, in the playoffs, he put on one of the greatest shows of all time. I couldn't believe someone could do that against the Boston Celtics.

Larry Bird, April 21, 1986

I remember reading what Larry said about that game. I really couldn't believe he would say some-

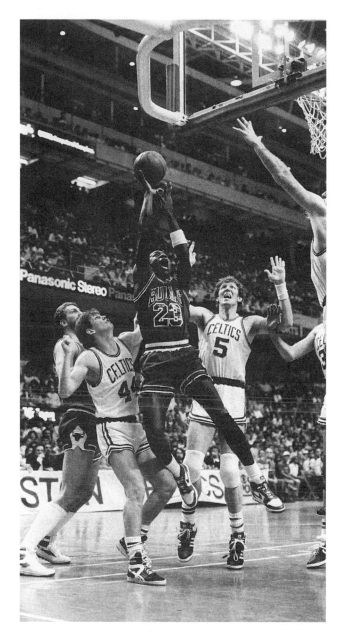

Michael Jordan (23) drives past Danny Ainge and Bill Walton of the Celtics during a playoff game at Boston Garden, May 20, 1986. Jordan set an NBA record with sixty-three points in the game; however, the Celtics won in double overtime. © BETTMANN/CORBIS. REPRODUCED BY PERMISSION.

thing like that. Here was a guy who had been in the league seven years and was in a class I was trying to enter. To that point I don't think I had ever played a game as good as that one, but I knew I still had a long way to go.

Larry Bird's comments gave me credibility. Up to that point I was still perceived as a hotshot rookie, not a real player. When Bird acknowledged my performance, I became a player. I still wasn't up to his level, but I was now a player who was marked as a star, a potential Hall of Famer depending upon how I took those comments. At the time, I really didn't understand what his statements meant to me. In other words, his praise wasn't going to change how I would try to establish myself as a player. I didn't see myself in the same way Larry did. If I did, I probably wouldn't have accomplished as much as I did later. I took those words as a compliment and nothing more. He confirmed I was on the right path, but nothing he or anyone else might have said would have altered that path. Off the court, Larry Bird intimidated me because of who he was, what he had accomplished, and the fact that he was Larry Legend. I felt the same way about all the stars at that time: Magic Johnson, Julius Erving, all of them. I wasn't scared of them on the court because I believed I had the skills to compete with anybody. But their presence off the court intimidated me. Now that I look back I realize how much I had to learn to attain their level. I'm glad I didn't know then how much I had yet to learn. If I hadn't evolved at my own pace, I wouldn't have been able to paint the tiny details that defined my career. I remember every little step, every little crease. Now when I look back I see one big beautiful picture. Some of these young kids just have that big blob of paint without any detail. Their careers are just a mass of color without any definition because they haven't taken the time to work on the details or they don't appreciate or understand the process.

Further Resources

BOOKS

Beahm, George W. *Michael Jordan: Shooting Star.* Kansas City, Mo.: Andrews and McMeel, 1994.

Greene, Bob. *Rebound: The Odyssey of Michael Jordan.* New York: Viking, 1995.

Greene, Bob. *Hang Time: Days and Dreams with Michael Jordan.* New York: Doubleday, 1992.

Halbestam, David. *Playing for Keeps: Michael Jordan and the World He Made.* New York: Random House, 1999.

Smith, Sam. *The Jordan Rules.* New York: Simon and Schuster, 1992.

PERIODICALS

Leershen, Charles. "Rampaging Rookies." *Newsweek* 104, November 26, 1984, 121–122.

"Sportsman of the Year: The Everywhere Man." *Sports Illustrated* 75, no. 27, December 21, 1991, 64–101.

WEBSITES

"Chicago Bulls History." Bulls.com. Available online at http://www.nba.com/bulls/history/Chicago_Bulls_History-24393-42.html; website home page: http://www.nba.com/bulls (accessed July 18, 2003).

Maiorana, Sal. "Today We Expect Him to Do It, but Back in 1986 Michael Jordan's 63-Point Playoff Outburst Against

the Celtics Was Actually Considered to Be a Monumental Feat." CBS Sportsline Historian. Available online at http://cbs.sportsline.com/u/page/historian/jordan63.htm; website home page: http://www.cbs.sportsline.com (accessed May 29, 2003).

AUDIO AND VISUAL MEDIA

Michael Jordan: His Airness. New York: Polygram Video, 1999, VHS.

Never Die Easy
Autobiography

By: Walter Payton, with Don Yeager

Date: 2000

Source: Payton, Walter, and Don Yaeger. *Never Die Easy.* New York: Villard, 2000.

About the Author: Walter Payton (1954–1999) was born in Columbia, Mississippi. Walter graduated with a degree in special education from Jackson State College in Mississippi, where he was a star running back. He was drafted fourth overall by the Chicago Bears in the 1975 NFL draft, and he went on to become, as former Bear coach Mike Ditka commented at Walter's memorial service, "the greatest Bear of all." Payton was named All-Pro seven times, holds the record for most rushing yards in a single game (275), and was elected to Pro Football's Hall of Fame in 1993. ∎

Introduction

Walter Payton, called "Sweetness" by fans, broke Jim Brown's professional football career rushing record at Chicago's Soldier Field on October 7, 1984, against the New Orleans Saints. Jim Brown had set the previous record—12,312 yards—twenty years before during nine seasons with the Cleveland Browns. It was Payton's tenth year with the Chicago Bears.

If anyone were going to break his record, Jim Brown had wanted it to be Payton. Brown made it clear that he did not want Franco Harris to break it. Brown had been critical of Harris for running out of bounds too often; Brown also felt that the thirty-four-year-old Harris, in his twelfth season, was past his prime.

Both Harris's and Payton's career rushing totals were close at the start of the 1984 season. Harris actually began the year with 325 more rushing yards than Payton. But by the conclusion of the fourth week Payton had erased the gap. Ironically, the game that pushed Payton ahead of Harris featured Payton's Bears against Harris's Seattle Seahawks. Payton, helped in the record chase by a tough Bears defense that only allowed Harris twenty-three yards that game, gained 116 himself. Payton was then only sixty-six yards from Jim Brown's record.

Bears running back Walter Payton (34) carries the ball against the New Orleans Saints at Soldier Field, Chicago, October 7, 1984. During the game, Payton broke Jim Brown's NFL record for career rushing yards. © BETTMANN/CORBIS. REPRODUCED BY PERMISSION.

Payton broke the record in his next game. The record-breaking play was a typical Walter Payton run. Early in the second half, Payton, from the I-formation, took a pitch around the left end, following his blockers, Matt Suhey and Mark Bortz, for six yards—making him the NFL's new career rushing leader. The fans, the officials, the players, and the coaches immediately recognized the achievement. Saints players were the first to congratulate him, while an official tossed him the ball. Cameramen and journalists streamed onto the field. Payton ran over, shook hands with Saints coach Bum Phillips, and then ran to the Bear sideline to gave the ball to running backs coach Johnny Roland. After a brief ceremony, Payton shooed photographers off the field so that he and the other Bear players could huddle for the next play.

Payton finished the game with thirty-two carries and 154 yards rushing. It marked the fifty-ninth time in his career that Payton had rushed for over one hundred yards in a game, breaking another Jim Brown record.

Significance

When Walter Payton broke Jim Brown's record, the entire country took note. Jim Brown was proud that Payton broke his record. Payton's style was similar to Brown's—straightforward, hard driving, and workmanlike. Brown called to congratulate Payton, as did President Ronald Reagan (served 1981–1989), who called from Air Force One.

Payton is considered one of the finest football players of all time. Two seasons before retiring from football following the 1987 season, Payton led the 1985 Bears to a Super Bowl championship. In Payton's 190 games for the Bears, he carried 3,838 times for 16,726 yards, scoring 110 of his 125 touchdowns rushing.

Payton was a beloved figure in America. Grief poured forth from across the country when he died from a rare liver disease. He meant more than his records to football players and fans. Though a highly private man, he had the ability to deeply touch all those who came in contact with him.

In 2002, Dallas Cowboy star Emmet Smith broke Payton's career rushing record. However, nothing could diminish the impact of Walter Payton's career; he was a great man and a great football player, inducted into the Pro Football Hall of Fame in 1993. "Sweetness" will always be considered one of the greatest football players in the history of the National Football League.

Box Score for the October 7, 1984 Chicago Bears–New Orleans Saints Football Game

Bears 20, Saints 7

New Orleans	0	7	0	0— 7
BEARS	6	7	0	7—20

Chi–FG Thomas 48, 5:17, 3–0
Chi–FG Thomas 46, 14:32, 6–0
NO–Wilson 15 pass from Todd [Andersen kick], 12:15, 6–7
Chi–Payton 1 run [Thomas kick], 14:57, 13–7
Chi–McKinnon 16 pass from McMahon [Thomas kick], 5:15, 20–7
A–53,752

Team	N Orl	BEARS
First downs	14	20
Rushes-yards	31–176	49–246
Passing yards	145	097
Return yards	05	62
Passes	07–26–0	10–14–0
Sacks by	4–31	1–13
Punts	7–46	7–40
Fumbles-lost	1–1	0–0
Penalties-yards	10–68	5–35
Time of possession	24:50	35:10

Individual statistics

RUSHING—New Orleans, Rogers 16–99, Gajan 7–51, Wilson 6–19, Todd 2–7. BEARS, Payton 32–154, Suhey 11–44, McMahon 4–25, McKinnon 1–21, Gentry 1–2.
PASSING—New Orleans, Todd 7–26–0, 158 yards. BEARS, McMahon 10–14–0, 128 yards.
RECEIVING—New Orleans, Young 2–93, Wilson 2–27, Brenner 1–19, Tice 1–17, Gajan 1–2. BEARS, Suhey 3–45, Gault 2–33, Payton 2–11, Moorehead 1–18, McKinnon 1–16, Saldi 1–5.
MISSED FIELD GOALS—None.

SOURCE: "Bears 20, Saints 7." *Chicago Tribune*, October 8, 1984.

Primary Source

Never Die Easy [excerpt]

SYNOPSIS: In this excerpt, running back Walter Payton discusses breaking Jim Brown's NFL career rushing record, and what it meant to him to break it. Yet he concludes by stating that, in his mind, Brown's record has not even been broken.

At the time I could barely comprehend what it meant. I couldn't conceive of what it meant to break that record. I tried to keep things low-key and not get too off the ground with it, but breaking Jim's record was just something else. It was always the ultimate individual goal because it represented not just great individual performances, but the culmination of years of consistency and sustained excellence.

I've always thought that consistency is the most difficult thing to attain in life. Anyone can be good for a day, or a year. But can you consistently be great? That is so much more difficult. It requires a person to continue to work hard even after they have achieved success. It requires sacrifice, even after

sacrifice is no longer required. It requires a hunger in a person that is about more than just making it. It is about staying there.

Whether it is an athlete, or an actor, or a musician, or a businessman, I think people will tell you that staying on top of your profession for a long period is the most difficult thing. A lot of actors have won one Academy Award, but how many have won a number of them, consistently throughout their career? You can start one successful business, but how about being successful in a number of ventures?

That was what motivated me about the record. I've always needed something to motivate me. Because I worked out so often on my own, I needed something to drive me. I didn't want coaches telling me to get in shape, and that never happened. I was always in shape. But I needed something to push me over the edge to get in the best possible shape. That had to come from within. The record gave me something to focus on during some of those years when our team wasn't very good. It kept me at the top.

I was always fearful that I wasn't in the best shape I could be. I always wondered if I had slipped a little bit. That motivated me. At Jackson State I used to say that my goal was to be able to play all-out on every play for a ninety-minute game. I figured if I could play all-out on every play of a game that long, then I was ready for an NFL game. I'd probably only play thirty minutes a game in the NFL, so I figured I would have enough to go that extra mile to make it.

Entering the season I wanted to break Jim's record first. I wanted to pass Franco Harris even though at the start of the season that seemed unrealistic. He had a 325-yard lead on me and I thought he might break the record by the end of September. While I did want to break the record first, it wasn't because I disliked Franco Harris or didn't respect the man. That is completely untrue. The man had four Super Bowl rings and this is a team game first and foremost. I also liked Franco, I had some business dealings with him, and off the field he and I were friends, our families really liked each other.

A lot of people tried to make a big deal of the fact that two of us—Franco Harris and myself—were going after Jim Brown's record at the same time. People tried to compare the two of us, compare our styles. It was as if the good news of two men going after a record wasn't enough.

I was asked at least a hundred times how I felt about Franco's running style, that he was known for running out-of-bounds, while my style was more physical. How was I supposed to answer that question? I said what I thought, which was that whatever style works for each runner is the style they should use, and Franco's style works for him. I got knocked for not being honest. I couldn't have been more honest. I consider Franco a friend. We've worked out together, played basketball together. He is a super person and one of the best running backs of all time. There was no way I was going to get drawn into any controversy about him versus me.

In my opinion, Franco was the best in clutch situations—third-and-two, third-and-three, goal line. He had a great offensive line and used them and they won a lot of games. How can you question his success? Numbers don't show greatness anyway. It's how you feel and the desire you bring to the field.

I said after the game that the motivating drive for me has been for the athletes who have tried but yet still failed to reach that certain achievement. And also the athletes who didn't get an opportunity to, like the Overstreets and the Delaneys and the Brian Piccolos. This simplifies what the game is made of. What I did out there that day was a reflection of those guys because they made the sacrifices as well. It was a tribute to me to bestow this honor on them.

As I got close, I have to admit that it was a lot more pressure than I let on. I tried to pretend it was no big deal and I didn't want to talk about it. But it was. I sure was glad to get it over with, I was glad I didn't have to do that every week. The funny thing is, if people didn't remind me about the specific play, I wouldn't even remember it. I really don't think about that play often. It was all a blur. It was a career thing anyway, so one run didn't do it.

And you know what? In the end, it is just like anything else. When Barry Sanders, Emmitt Smith, Jerry Rice, all those guys, when they come up to break somebody's record or they come up to push my stats, the media is gonna make so much out of it. They're gonna realize, Oh man, what's happening? It's gonna make them nervous, it's gonna make them anticipate, it may even change what they do or how.

I didn't let it bother me. I tried to maintain my own personal level of whatever it was, my own space, my own drum, and keep it away. The thing with records is if you play long enough you're gonna break some records. It is almost a matter of time. I used to joke that I probably gained an extra hundred yards over my career by inching the ball ahead every time I was tackled. When a referee would catch me and

move it back to where it belonged I would always say, "Hey, how do you expect me to catch Jim Brown if you do that to me?" Instead of worrying about numbers, what you try to do is you try to do better than what everybody expected. Everybody's pointing at Jim Brown's record and saying, You gotta shoot for that. I wanted to go past that and I did. It really doesn't stand out. I think that is why I talked about the sixteen thousand yards. That immediately became the next unreachable goal. It's one of those things, to chase dreams, to chase goals. Once it happens it tends to lose some of the glimmer.

I don't want, in any way, to minimize the records. Especially this one, because it is special. But football is a team game. The more you win as a team, the better your team gets, and as your team gets better it becomes easier to achieve things individually. But if you're just out there setting records as an individual, it actually gets harder to keep things happening at a high level. Eventually, other guys you play with start to ask why they're not getting the same opportunities you are. Some of them might stop playing as hard. Then you get killed. That's why I'd rather play for a winning team than play for a team where I would set a bunch of records.

So that's why I want to say this. I'm not saying breaking the record or my statistics weren't important to me, but I don't believe I ever broke Jim Brown's record. I don't think anybody has broken it. I think it is still standing. I don't think the record books need to be rewritten, because if you can't do it in nine years and eight games, then you can't break his record. I didn't do it in the amount of time that Jim Brown did. I had more games and I played longer. So I didn't break it.

Further Resources

BOOKS

Barber, Phil, and John Fawaz. *NFL's Greatest: Pro Football's Best Players, Teams, and Games.* New York: DK, 2000.

Johnson, Tom, and David Fantle. *Sweetness: The Courage and Heart of Walter Payton.* Chicago: Triumph Books, 1999.

Payton, Walter, and Jerry B. Jenkins. *Sweetness.* Chicago: Contemporary, 1978.

PERIODICALS

Attner, Paul. "Lessons in Greatness: Walter Payton." *The Sporting News* 223, November 15, 1999, 8–10.

Telander, Rick. "Up and Over, to the Record and Beyond." *Sports Illustrated* 60, October 15, 1984, 44–48.

WEBSITES

Huber, Jim. "Walter Payton: A Tribute to Sweetness." CNN/Sports Illustrated. Available online at http://sportsillustrated.cnn.com/football/nfl/news/1999/11/01

/payton_tribute; website home page: http://sportsillustrated .cnn.com (accessed May 29, 2003).

"Walter Payton." Pro Football Hall of Fame. Available online at http://www.profootballhof.com/players/enshrinees /wpayton.cfm; website home page: http://www .profootballhof.com (accessed May 29, 2003).

"Walter Payton: 'Sweetness'." ChicagoBears.com. Available online at http://www.chicagobears.com/history/index .cfm?cont_id=70225; website home page: http://www .chicagobears.com (accessed May 29, 2003).

You Cannot Be Serious
Autobiography

By: John McEnroe, with James Kaplan

Date: 2002

Source: McEnroe, John, with James Kaplan. *You Cannot Be Serious.* New York: G. P. Putnam's Sons, 2002, 120–124.

About the Author: John McEnroe (1959–) was born at Wiesbaden Air Force Base in Germany, but his parents returned to New York City shortly after. As a freshman at Stanford, McEnroe won the NCAA singles championship in tennis before turning professional at nineteen. In McEnroe's sixteen-year professional career he won 154 tournaments, seventy-seven in both singles and doubles, the most of any player in tennis history. McEnroe held the top ranking in doubles for record 257 consecutive weeks. He also led the United States to five Davis Cup titles. As of 2003, McEnroe still plays on the Master's tennis circuit and serves as a tennis commentator. ■

Introduction

At the start of the 1980s, tennis was quite popular in the United States and abroad. Tennis exposure had expanded greatly around the world due to television, and players' earnings reflected this. Total prize money for Wimbledon had increased by a factor of ten from 1976 to 1980.

In 1980, Bjorn Borg was one of tennis's top stars, having won four consecutive Wimbledon titles. Possessing a powerful serve and groundstrokes, Borg was the top seed. He easily advanced to the 1980 finals to meet John McEnroe—a young, brash New Yorker competing in his fourth Wimbledon. After an impressive debut in 1977, McEnroe's 1978 and 1979 Wimbledon appearances were disappointments. McEnroe then defeated his rival, Jimmy Connors, to advance to the 1980 finals.

The 1980 Wimbledon final was a classic, featuring the world's two best players playing brilliantly. The tension and excitement during the match were palpable. The legendary fourth set started with Borg leading two sets to McEnroe's one. Six times Borg was denied match point, as McEnroe rallied with skillful shot-making. In the tiebreaker, McEnroe eventually prevailed to win the fourth set, 18-16—the second-longest tiebreaker (lasting twenty-two minutes) in Wimbledon history. However, Borg won the final set 8-6. Three hours and fifty-three minutes after the match began, Borg sent a backhand winner past McEnroe to win his fifth consecutive Wimbledon championship. Arguably the most famous photograph of Borg showed him kneeling at Centre Court after the match, hands in the air triumphant, exhausted, ecstatic, and relieved.

Significance

The Sporting News ranked the 1980 Wimbledon finals as the fifth-greatest sporting event of the twentieth century. It is widely considered the greatest tennis match in history. Featuring two of the greatest tennis players ever, the match was a study in contrasting styles. Borg had a strong serve and preferred to stay on the baseline. McEnroe excelled at volleying and took the net whenever possible. With both Borg and McEnroe playing at the top of their games, the match featured spectacular shots and drama at Wimbledon, the sport's most prestigious venue.

The 1980 Wimbledon Mens Singles Championship represented the end of an era. For Borg, the tournament marked his fifth consecutive Wimbledon title—but proved to be his last. Borg lost to McEnroe in a rematch in the 1981 Wimbledon finals, and he retired at twenty-five. For McEnroe, the loss was a pivotal moment. Although exhausted and drained, McEnroe realized that he could beat Borg even at Wimbledon. Later in 1980, McEnroe beat Borg in the U.S. Open, a championship Borg never won.

In addition to winning his first singles title at Wimbledon in 1981, McEnroe's verbal outbursts during the tournament caused much controversy. McEnroe's bad behavior was televised around the world, and his post-match confrontation with the game umpire led to the London tabloids to nickname him "Superbrat." That moniker is still applied to him.

Primary Source

You Cannot Be Serious [excerpt]

SYNOPSIS: In this except, McEnroe talks about participating in his first Wimbledon final against Bjorn Borg in 1980, considered one of the greatest tennis matches ever played. Borg won the four-hour match in five sets.

After people talk about my temper, the main thing everybody always wants to discuss is my first

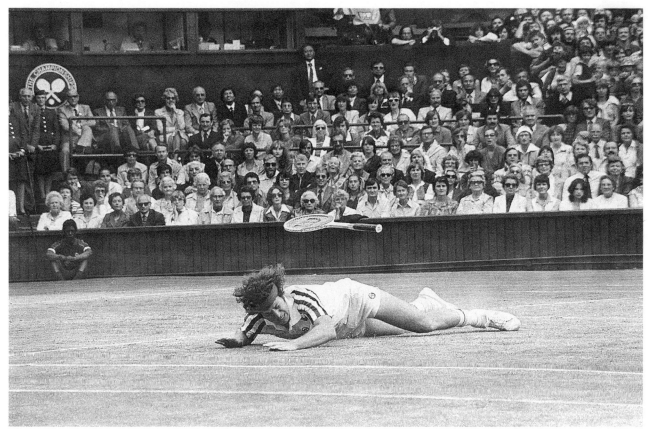

John McEnroe falls to the ground during his finals match with Bjorn Borg at Wimbledon, 1980. McEnroe eventually lost the marathon match—which featured a fourth-set tiebreaker that went thirty-four points—in the fifth set. © BETTMANN/CORBIS. REPRODUCED BY PERMISSION.

Wimbledon final against Borg in 1980, the one with the fourth-set tiebreaker that went thirty-four points. It's funny: People usually think I won that match, even though I lost it in the fifth. That's OK with me. In fact, in a way it's OK that I *didn't* win that one.

Unfortunately, I almost always feel like a loser after I'm beaten in a tennis match. It's a sad fact about tennis—and probably other sports as well—that when you lose your confidence in your game, you lose a bit of confidence in yourself as a person. It's hard to overcome that feeling. You always have to fight the thought, "I'm a loser; I'm not the same person I was," when, in fact, you may very well be a better person in certain ways.

Of course, there have been a fair number of times in my career when I not only lost a match that I probably shouldn't have, but also acted like a complete jerk.

However, when you lose the final at Wimbledon 8-6 in the fifth set to Bjorn Borg, that's different. I never acted like a jerk when I played Borg: I re-spected him too much; I respected the *occasion*. Whether I won or lost was always less important than that I got to be a part of history.

It was the first time I'd ever played Bjorn on grass, and I thought my game matched up perfectly against his on that surface. For one thing, I had beaten him in that final at Dallas in May, on a fast indoor carpet not totally dissimilar to grass. He had a habit of standing way back to receive; I knew I could get to net quickly on most of my serves and take command of the angles. Also, while Borg's first serve was stronger than most people realize, he was never known as a volleyer, and his second serve could be a bit dicey.

From the beginning, everything went according to plan. Early on, in fact, I was amazed at how easily I was winning. To tell the truth, I think I actually let up a little bit—which was my first mistake. I'd won the first set 6-1, and I was up 5-4 in the second, very close to taking a two-sets-to-love lead, at which point I could have just kicked his behind—which is what I expected I was going to do. But my plan went off the rails.

Some of it was just bad luck. First, I had had to play Connors the day before—which, because it was the first time I'd played him at Wimbledon since our '77 semifinal, was obviously an emotional match. To make matters worse, though, since I had spent the past year pushing Jimmy out of his number-two spot in the rankings, there was bad blood between us, and now it was showing itself in the form of some serious testiness.

At that point, my relationship with Connors was the exact opposite of my relationship with Borg—there was little respect for the man or the occasion of playing him. Like two club fighters, we trash-talked each other on the changeovers: Jimmy called me a baby, and I told him what he could kiss. It was exciting, in a perverse way, but it also turned out to be a very draining four-set win.

As if that weren't enough, because of a rain delay earlier, I had had to play the doubles semifinal right after my match with Connors!

Borg, however, had played his singles semi on Friday, so he got to spend his Saturday resting.

Borg never played doubles. Connors stopped playing them very early in his career, and Lendl rarely played them—but I loved playing doubles, for two reasons: First, I liked being part of a team. Second, it kept me sharp for singles, and I preferred it to practicing. Most of the time at Wimbledon, the scheduling worked to my advantage—I could play singles one day, doubles the next. But looking back, I do wonder whether pulling out of the doubles semifinal that year at Wimbledon would have given me the extra energy to win that fifth set against Borg. Still, I know now—and knew then—that I could never have done that to Peter, my friend and partner. It just wasn't my style.

That final was when I saw for the first time how Bjorn's incredible athletic ability and physical fitness could cost me.

At 5-4 in that second set, I got a little tight—maybe at the thought of the match coming too easily—and he got his serve going, which let him come back and win the set 7-5. At that point, something in me deflated. I felt I should have been up two sets to love, and the fact that I wasn't opened the gates to mental and physical fatigue, and I lost the third set, 3-6.

Then he broke my serve once in the fourth set, and suddenly I was serving at 3-5. It felt like a nightmare—it had all happened so quickly. Here I'd honestly thought I was going to win 6-1, 6-4, 6-3; now, all of a sudden, I was almost out of the match.

Which was when something magical happened. I held my serve; saved a couple of match points, then on Borg's serve, I got my fight back. By the time we got to the tiebreaker, I was back to feeling I could win the match.

Greatness is a judgment that's bestowed long after the fact, but I can tell you that while I was in that tiebreaker, I knew something special was going on. In those days, there was still a standing-room section at Wimbledon finals (great seats if you're willing to stand in line for three days), and the crowd was very excited: very vociferous, and then dramatically hushed at other moments. Somehow—maybe because I'd saved those match points earlier—I could sense that even the people who didn't want me to win the match wanted me to win the tiebreaker.

They just didn't want this match to *end*.

And the match *itself* didn't seem to want to end. The tiebreaker kept going back and forth, back and forth, both of us hitting a lot of winners, neither of us able to put it away. I had been feeling tired, but now the crowd pumped me up so much that I forgot about it.

I don't know why it stands out in my mind after so many years, but I hit one running forehand—a winner down the line, as it turned out—and ended up practically in the crowd when I stopped, and Centre Court at Wimbledon is pretty wide. I could feel the excitement coming off those people in waves—to the extent that I actually had to make an effort not to get too excited myself. The further we got into that tiebreaker, though, the less I could hold it in.

And then when I finally won it, 18-16, I knew I'd won the match. *Knew* it.

I thought Bjorn would be utterly deflated after losing that tiebreaker—but whatever he had inside him was beyond anything I could imagine. He was not only undiscouraged, but physically, he was still going strong.

I wondered how this could even be possible. I had forgotten my fatigue during the tiebreaker, but now I was beginning to remember it. Borg served the first game of the fifth set, and I hit a couple of good returns to go up 30-love—and then he started coming up with big first serves. As fatigued as I was, I wasn't making him work hard enough on his serve.

I lost that first game, then held, and then we went into a pattern in which he was holding serve at love or 15 every time. I kept saying to myself, *Oh, my God, I've got to break him now.*

It never happened. When I saw how completely unperturbed he seemed about that fourth-set loss, and how he just kept getting stronger in the fifth—something in me wilted. He seemed totally fresh, and I was drained.

I was amazed. He had won four Wimbledons in a row! I kept thinking, *Come on, isn't enough enough?* As the last set wore on, it became a war of attrition, which was exactly what I hadn't wanted to happen: I just didn't have enough gas left in the tank. Finally, I was barely hanging on: I couldn't even win points on his serve.

And then we were shaking hands at the net. I knew I could beat Borg. But Wimbledon still belonged to him.

Further Resources

BOOKS

Borg, Bjorn, and Eugene L. Scott. *My Life and Game.* New York: Simon and Schuster, 1980.

Evans, Richard. *McEnroe, a Rage for Perfection: A Biography.* New York: Simon and Schuster, 1982.

Garner, Joe. *And the Crowd Goes Wild: Relive the Most Celebrated Sporting Events Ever Broadcast.* Naperville, Ill.: Sourcebooks, 1999.

PERIODICALS

Bonk, Thomas. "Down the Stretch." *Sport* 83, October, 1992, 76–79.

Stern, Richard. "Tennis Anyone?" *Commentary* 95, April, 1993, 48–51.

WEBSITES

Maiorana, Sal. "Bjorn Borg's Fifth Straight Wimbledon Championship in 1980, a Five-Set Victory Over John McEnroe, Set a New Standard of Tennis Excellence." CBS Sportsline Historian. CBS.Sportsline.com. Available online at http://www.cbs.sportsline.com/u/page/historian/borg.htm; website home page: http://www.sportsline.com (accessed July 17, 2003).

The Official Website of Wimbledon. Available online at http://www.wimbledon.org (accessed May 29, 2003).

AUDIO AND VISUAL MEDIA

Wimbledon 1980 Final: Borg vs. McEnroe. London: BBC Productions, 2000, VHS.

GENERAL RESOURCES

General

Carnegy, Vicky. *Fashions of a Decade. The 1980s.*New York: Facts on File, 1990.

Congressional Quarterly. *America in the 1980s.* Washington, D.C.: Congressional Quarterly, 1980.

Demac, Donna A. *Keeping America Uninformed: Government Secrecy in the 1980s.* New York: Pilgrim, 1984.

Duden, Jane, and Gail B. Stewart. *1980s.* New York: Crestwood Press, 1991.

Duignan, Peter, and Alvin Rabushka. *The United States in the 1980s.* Stanford, Calif.: Hoover Institution, 1980.

Ferguson, Marilyn. *The Aquarian Conspiracy: Personal and Social Transformation in the 1980s.* New York: J.P. Tarcher, 1980.

Godfrey, Tony. *The New Image: Painting in the 1980s.* New York: Abbeville Press, 1986.

Holt, Sid. *The Rolling Stone Interviews: The 1980s.* New York: St. Martin's Press, 1989.

Kahn, Herman. *Thinking About the Unthinkable in the 1980s.* New York: Simon and Schuster, 1984.

Marsh, David. *Glory Days: Bruce Springsteen in the 1980s.* New York: Pantheon, 1987.

Marx, Robert. *Famous American Plays of the 1980s.* New York: Dell, 1988.

McKenzie, Richard B. *What Went Right in the 1980s.* San Francisco: Pacific Research Institute for Public Policy, 1994.

Mills, Nicolaus. *Culture in the Age of Money: The Legacy of the 1980s in America.* Chicago: I.R. Dee, 1990.

Schaller, Michael. *Reckoning with Reagan: America and its President in the 1980s.* New York: Oxford University Press, 1992.

Torr, James D. *The 1980s.* San Diego: Greenhaven, 2000.

Vonnegut, Kurt. *Fates Worse than Death: An Autobiographical Collage of the 1980s.* New York: Putnam, 1991.

The Arts

Andersen, Christopher. *Madonna: Unauthorized.* New York: Simon & Schuster, 1991.

Beardsley, John and Livingston, Jane. *Hispanic Art in the United States.* New York: Abbeville Press, 1987.

Boyle, Donald. *Blacks in American Films and Television: An Encyclopedia.* New York: Garland, 1988.

Brode, Douglas. *The Films of Robert De Niro.* Secaucus, N.J.: Carol Publishing Group, 1993.

———. *The Films of the Eighties.* New York: Citadel Press, 1990.

Bronson, Fred. *The Billboard Book of Number One Hits.* New York: Billboard Publications, 1992.

Campbell, Edward D. C. *The Celluloid South: Hollywood and the Southern Myth.* Knoxville: University of Tennessee Press, 1981.

Carroll, Dennis. *David Mamet.* New York: St. Martin's Press, 1987.

Celant, Germano, ed. *Keith Haring.* Munich: Prestel, 1992.

Christgau, Robert. *Grown Up All Wrong: 75 Great Rock and Pop Artists from Vaudeville to Techno.* Cambridge: Harvard University Press, 1998.

Craven, Wayne. *American Art: History and Culture.* New York: Harry N. Abrams, Inc., 1994.

Cross, Charles R. and the editors of *Backstreets Magazine*. *Backstreets: Springsteen, The Man and His Music*. New York: Harmony Books, 1989.

Davis, Francis. *In the Moment: Jazz in the 1980s*. New York: Oxford University Press, 1986.

Dean, Anne. *David Mamet: Language as Dramatic Act*. Rutherford, N.J.: Fairleigh Dickinson University Press, 1990.

Eliot, Mark with Mike Appel. *Down Thunder Road: The Making of Bruce Springsteen*. New York: Simon & Schuster, 1992.

Fineburg, Jonathan. *Art Since 1940: Strategies of Being*. New York: Abrams, 1995.

Frank, Peter and Michael McKenzie. *New, Used & Improved: Art for the '80s*. New York: Abbeville Press, 1987.

Friedman, Benjamin. *Day Of Reckoning: The Consequences of American Economic Policy Under Reagan and After*. New York: Random House, 1988.

Giddins, Gary. *Rhythm-a-ning: Jazz Tradition and Innovation in the '80s*. New York: Oxford University Press, 1986.

————. *Riding on a Blue Note: Jazz and American Pop*. New York: Oxford University Press, 1981.

Godfrey, Tony. *The New Image: Painting in the 1980s*. Oxford: Phaidon, 1986.

Goodman, Fred. *The Mansion on the Hill: Dylan, Young, Giffen, Springsteen and the Head-on Collision of Rock and Commerce*. New York: Random House, 1997.

Greiner, Donald J. *Women Without Men: Female Bonding and the American Novel of the 1980s*. Columbia: University of South Carolina Press, 1993.

Grenier, Richard. *Capturing the Culture: Film, Art, and Politics*. Washington, D.C.: Ethics & Public Policy Center, 1991.

Grossberg, Lawrence. *We Gotta Get Out of This Place: Popular Conservatism and Postmodern Culture*. New York: Routledge, 1992.

Haskell, Molly. *From Reverence to Rape: The Treatment of Women in the Movies*. Chicago: University of Chicago Press, 1987.

Honeyford, Paul. *The Thrill of Michael Jackson*. New York: Quill, 1984.

Hughes, Robert. *American Visions: The Epic History of Art in America*. New York: Alfred A. Knopf, 1997.

Jackson, Michael. *Moonwalk*. New York: Doubleday, 1988.

Kane, Leslie. *David Mamet: A Casebook*. New York & London: Garland, 1992.

Kingsbury, Paul and Alan Axelrod, eds. *Country: The Music and the Musicians*. New York: Abbeville Press, 1988.

Kruger, Barbara. *Love for Sale, with Text by Kate Linker*. New York: Abrams, 1990.

————. *Remote Control: Power, Culture, and the World of Appearance*. Cambridge, Mass.: MIT Press, 1993.

Kuhn, Annette. *Women's Pictures: Feminism and Cinema*. London & Boston: Routledge & Kegan Paul, 1982.

Kurtz, Bruce K., ed. *Keith Haring, Andy Warhol, and Walt Disney*. Munich: Prestel / Phoenix: Phoenix Art Museum, 1992.

Livingstone, Marco. *Pop Art: A Continuing History*. New York: Abrams, 1990.

Lourdeaux, Lee. *Italian and Irish Filmmakers in America*. Philadelphia: Temple University Press, 1990.

Lucie-Smith, Edward. *Race, Sex, and Gender in Contemporary Art*. New York: Abrams, 1989.

Marsh, Dave. *Glory Days: Bruce Springsteen in the 1980s*. New York: Pantheon, 1987.

Maychick, Diana. *Meryl Streep: The Reluctant Superstar*. New York: St. Martin's Press, 1984.

Medved, Michael. *Hollywood vs. America: Popular Culture and the War on Traditional Values*. New York: HarperCollins, 1992.

Miller, Mark Crispin, ed. *Seeing Through Movies*. New York: Pantheon, 1990.

Mott, Donald R. and Saunders, Cheryl McAllster. *Steven Spielberg*. Boston: Twayne, 1986.

Nelson, George. *Buppies, B-boys, Baps & Bohos: Notes on Post-Soul Black Culture*. New York: HarperCollins, 1992.

Nite, Norm N. *Rock On Almanac: The First Four Decades of Rock 'n' Roll*. New York: Harper & Row, 1989.

O'Brien, Tom. *The Screening of America: Movies and Values from "Rocky" to "Rain Man"*. New York: Continuum, 1990.

Papadakis, Andreas, Clare Farrow, and Nicola Hodges, eds. *New Art: An International Survey*. New York: Rizzoli, 1991.

Raven, Arlene. *Crossing Over: Feminism and Art of Social Concern*. Ann Arbor, Mich.: UMI Research Press, 1988.

Rozelle, Robert V., Alvia Wardlaw, and Maureen A. McKenna, eds. *Black Art: The African Impulse in African-American Art*. New York: Abrams, 1989.

Scorsese, Martin. *Scorsese on Scorsese*. London & Boston: Faber & Faber, 1990.

Sexton, Adam. *Desperately Seeking Madonna: In Search of the Meaning of the World's Most Famous Woman*. New York: Delta, 1993.

Szatmary, David P. *Rockin' in Time: A Social History of Rock and Roll*. Englewood Cliffs, N.J.: Prentice-Hall, 1987.

Thomson, David. *A Biographical Dictionary of Film*, 3rd ed., rev. New York: Knopf, 1994.

Varnedoe, Kirk, and Adam Gopnik. *High and Low: Modern Art and Popular Culture*. New York: Abrams, 1990.

Vineberg, Steve. *No Surprises, Please: Movies in the Reagan Decade*. New York: Schirmer, 1993.

Walker, John, ed. *Halliwell's Film Guide*, 10th ed., rev. New York: HarperCollins, 1994.

————. *Halliwell's Filmgoer's and Video Viewer's Companion*, 11th ed., rev. New York: HarperCollins, 1995.

Whitburn, Joel. *The Billboard Book of Top 40 Hits*. New York: Billboard Publications, 1991.

————. *Billboard Hot 100 Charts: The Eighties*. Menomonee Falls, Wis.: Record Research, 1991.

Wiley, Mason and Damien Bona. *Inside Oscar: The Unofficial History of the Academy Awards*. New York: Ballantine, 1992.

Websites

"1980." The 1900s. Available online at http//www.archer2000
.tripod.com/1980.html (accessed August 26, 2003).

The Artchive. Available online at http://www.artchive.com
/artchive (accessed August 26, 2003).

The Greatest Films. Available online at http://www.filmsite.org
(accessed August 26, 2003).

Internet Broadway Database. Available online at http://www
.ibdb.com (accessed August 26, 2003).

"Timeline: Significant Events in the History of Rock Music."
Available online at http://pages.prodigy.net/cousinsteve/rock
/feat4.htm (accessed August 26, 2003).

Business and the Economy

Alesina, Alberto, and Geoffrey Carliner, eds. *Politics and Economics in the Eighties.* Chicago: University of Chicago Press, 1991.

Block, Fred, Richard A. Cloward, Barbara Ehrenreich, and Frances F. Piven. *The Mean Season: The Attack on the Welfare State.* New York: Pantheon Books, 1987.

Bluestone, Barry, and Bennett Harrison. *The Deindustrialization of America: Plant Closings, Community Abandonment, and the Dismantling of Basic Industry* New York: Basic Books, 1982.

Bruck, Connie. *The Predators Ball: The Junk Bond Raiders and the Man Who Staked Them.* New York: American Lawyer/Simon & Schuster, 1988.

Carroll, Paul. *Big Blues: The Unmaking of IBM.* New York: Crown, 1993.

Cohen, Stephen S., and John Zysman. *Manufacturing Matters: The Myth of the Post-Industrial Economy.* New York: Basic Books, 1987.

Dertouzos, Michael L., Richard K. Lester, and Robert M. Solow. *Made in America: Regaining the Productive Edge.* New York: Harper & Row Perennial Library, 1989.

Dobson, James M. *A History of American Enterprise.* Englewood Cliffs, N.J.: Prentice Hall, 1988.

Farman, Irvin. *Tandy's Money Machine: How Charles Tandy Built Radio Shack Into the World's Largest Electronics Chain.* Chicago: Mobium Press, 1992.

Feldstein, Martin, ed. *American Economic Policy in the 1980s.* Chicago: University of Chicago Press, 1994.

Friedman, Benjamin M. *Day of Reckoning: The Consequences of American Economic Policy Under Reagan and After.* New York: Random House, 1988.

Gambardella, Alfonso. *Science and Innovation: The U.S. Pharmaceutical Industry in the 1980s.* Cambridge: Cambridge University Press, 1995.

Garson, Barbara. *The Electronic Sweatshop: How Computers Are Transforming the Office of the Future into the Factory of the Past.* New York: Penguin Books, 1989.

Gilpin, Toni. *On Strike for Respect: The Clerical and Technical Workers' Strike at Yale University, 1984–1985.* Urbana, Illinois: University of Illinois Press, 1995.

Green, Hardy. *On Strike at Hormel: The Struggle for a Democratic Labor Movement.* Philadelphia: Temple University Press, 1990.

Harl, Neil E. *The Farm Debt Crisis of the 1980s.* Ames: Iowa State University Press, 1990.

Harrison, Bennett, and Barry Bluestone. *The Great U-Turn: Corporate Restructuring and the Polarizing of America.* New York: Basic Books, 1990.

Holland, Max. *When the Machine Stopped: A Cautionary Tale from Industrial America.* Boston: Harvard Business School Press, 1989.

Hooks, Linda M. *Bank Failures and Deregulation in the 1980s.* New York: Garland, 1994.

Kennedy, Paul M. *The Rise and Fall of the Great Powers: Economic Change and Military Conflict from 1500 to 2000.* New York: Random House, 1987.

Long, Robert Emmit, ed. *The Farm Crisis.* New York: Wilson, 1987.

Lowy, Martin. *High Rollers: Inside the Savings and Loan Debacle.* New York: Praeger, 1991.

Pilzer, Paul Zane, and Robert Deitz. *Other People's Money: How Bad Luck, Worse Judgment, and Flagrant Corruption Made a Shambles of a $900 Billion Industry.* New York: Simon & Schuster, 1989.

Prestowitz, Clyde V. *Trading Places: How We Allowed Japan to Take the Lead.* New York: Basic Books, 1988.

Reich, Robert. *The Work of Nations: Preparing Ourselves for 21st Century Capitalism.* New York: Knopf, 1991.

Robinson, Michael A. *Overdrawn: The Bailout of American Savings: The Inside Story of the $2 Billion S & L Debacle.* New York: Dutton/Penguin, 1990.

Schlosstein, Steven. *The End of the American Century.* New York: Congdon & Weed, 1989.

Slater, Robert. *Portraits in Silicon.* Cambridge: MIT Press, 1987.

Tiffany, Paul A. *The Decline of American Steel: How Management, Labor, and Government Went Wrong.* New York: Oxford University Press, 1988.

Phillips, Kevin. *The Politics of Rich and Poor: Wealth and the American Electorate in the Reagan Aftermath.* New York: Random House, 1990.

Vance, Sandra Stringer, and Roy V. Scott. *Wal-Mart: A History of Sam Walton's Retail Phenomena.* New York: Twayne, 1994.

Yergin, Daniel. *The Prize: The Epic Quest for Oil, Money, and Power.* New York: Simon & Schuster, 1991.

Zieger, Robert. *American Workers, American Unions, 1920–1985.* Baltimore: Johns Hopkins University Press, 1986.

Websites

"Exports and Imports of Goods and Services, 1980–2010." Available online at http://www.infoplease.com/cgi-bin/id
/A0855074.html.

"FRB Minneapolis Research Archives—The U.S. Economy in 1980." Available online at http://www.minneapolisfed.org
/research/qr/qr412.html.

"Lessons of PATCO." Available online at http://www.socialist worker.org/2001/374/374_10_PATCO.shtml.

"Lessons from the Strike of 1981." Available online at http://www.roadsidephotos.com/baseball/bb01-4.htm.

"Power Plant: Honda's Ohio Factory Sparked a Revolution in U.S. Auto Industry." Available online at http://www.wsjclassroomedition.com/archive/03jan/AUTO.htm.

"Reganomics." Available online at http://www.wikipedia.org/wiki/Reaganomics.

"Supply Side Economics." Available online at http://www.pages.stern.nyu.edu/nroubini/SUPPLY.HTM.

"The Tax Reform Act of 1986." Available online at http://cwx.prenhall.com/bookbind/pubbooks/dye4/medialib/docs/tax1986.htm.

"TWU Local 553 vs. Eastern Airlines/Frank Lorenzo: 1989." Available online at http://www.corporatecampaign.org/twaeast.htm.

"U.S. Labor History, 1980–1989." Available online at http://members.tripod.com/Norrit1/afl-cio/1980.htm.

Education

Adler, Mortimer. *The Paideia Proposal: An Educational Manifesto.* New York: Macmillan, 1982.

Benbow, Charles P, and John C. Stanley, eds. *Academic Precocity.* Baltimore: Johns Hopkins University Press, 1984.

Berube, Maurice R. *American School Reform: Progressive, Equality, and Excellence Movements, 1883–1993.* Westport, Conn: Praeger, 1994.

Bettelheim, Bruno, and Karen Zelan. *On Learning to Read: The Child's Fascination With Meaning.* New York: Knopf, 1982.

Bloom, Allan. *The Closing of the American Mind: How Higher Education Has Failed Democracy and Impoverished the Souls of Today's Students.* New York: Simon & Schuster, 1987.

Brademas, John. *The Politics of Education: Conflict and Consensus on Capitol Hill.* Norman: University of Oklahoma Press, 1987.

Brandt, Godfrey. *The Realization of Anti-Racist Teaching.* Philadelphia: Falmer Press, 1986.

Clements, John. *Changed Lives: The Effects of the Perry Preschool Project on Youths Through Age Nineteen.* Ypsilanti, Mich.: High Scope Press, 1984.

A Common Destiny: Blacks and American Society. Washington, D.C.: National Research Council, 1989.

Cusick, Philip. *The Egalitarian Ideal and the American High School.* New York: Longman, 1983.

Delfattore, Joan. *What Johnny Shouldn't Read: Censorship In America.* New Haven, Conn.: Yale University Press, 1992.

Eaton, Judith S. *The Unfinished Agenda: Higher Education and the 1980s.* New York: Macmillan, 1991.

Escobedo, Thersa, ed. *Early Childhood Bilingual Education: A Hispanic Perspective.* New York: Teachers College Press, 1982.

Flesch, Rudolf. *Why Johnny Still Can't Read.* New York: Harper & Row, 1981.

Franzosa, Douglas, and Karen Mazza, comps. *Integrating Women's Studies into the Curriculum: An Annotated Bibliography.* Westport, Conn.: Greenwood Press, 1984.

Gardner, Howard. *Frames of Mind: The Theory of Multiple Intelligences.* New York: Basic Books, 1983.

Gilligan, Carol. *In a Different Voice: Psychological Theory and Women's Development.* Cambridge: Harvard University Press, 1982.

Goodman, Kenneth. *Language and Literacy.* Boston: Routlege & Kegan Paul, 1982.

Graham, Hugh Davis. *The Uncertain Triumph: Federal Education Policy in the Kennedy and Johnson Years.* Chapel Hill: University of North Carolina Press, 1984.

Heath, Shirley Brice. *Ways With Words.* Cambridge: Cambridge University Press, 1983.

Hirsch, Eric D. *Cultural Literacy: What Every American Needs to Know.* New York: Vintage Books, 1988.

Klein, Karen, and Deborah Strother, eds. *Planning for Microcomputers in the Curriculum.* Bloomington, Ind.: Phi Delta Kappa, 1984.

Kohl, Herbert. *Basic Skills: A Plan for Your Child, A Program for All Children.* Boston: Little, Brown, 1982.

Kozol, Jonathan. *Savage Inequalities: Children in America's Schools.* New York: Crown, 1991.

Levine, Arthur, ed. *Higher Learning in America 1980–2000.* Baltimore, Md.: Johns Hopkins University Press, 1993.

Macrorie, Ken. *Twenty Teachers.* New York: Oxford University Press, 1984.

Murphy, Joseph, ed. *The Educational Reform Movement of the 1980s: Perspectives and Cases.* Berkeley, Calif.: McCutcheon, 1990.

Oakes, Jeannie. *Keeping Track: How Schools Structure Inequality.* New Haven, Conn.: Yale University Press, 1985.

Owen, David. *None of the Above: Behind the Myth of Scholastic Aptitude.* Boston: Houghton Mifflin, 1985.

Powell, Arthur G., Eleanor Farrar, and David Cohen. *The Shopping Mall High School: Winners and Losers in the Educational Marketplace.* Boston: Houghton Mifflin, 1985.

Pride, Richard A. *The Political Use of Racial Narratives: School Desegregation in Mobile, Alabama, 1954–1997.* Urbana: University of Illinois Press, 2002.

Ravitch, Dianne. *The Schools We Deserve: Reflections on the Educational Crises of Our Time.* New York: Basic Books, 1985.

Seller, Maxine Schwartz, ed. *Women Educators in the United States, 1820–1993: A Bio-Bibliographical Sourcebook.* Westport, Conn.: Greenwood Press, 1994.

Sharp, Stanley. *The REAL Reason Johnny Still Can't Read.* Smithtown, N.Y.: Exposition Press, 1983.

Shor, Ira. *Culture Wars: School and Society in the Conservative Restoration.* Boston: Routledge & Kegan Paul, 1986.

Silver, Larry. *The Misunderstood Child: A Guide for Parents of Learning Disabled Children.* New York: McGraw-Hill, 1984.

Sykes, Charles J. *The Hollow Men: Politics and Corruption in Higher Education.* Washington, D.C.: Regnery Gateway, 1990.

———. *ProfScam: Professors and the Demise of Higher Education.* Washington, D.C.: Regnery Gateway, 1988.

Timpane, Michael, and Laurie Millar McNeill. *Business Impact on Education and Child Development Reform.* New York: Committee for Economic Development, 1991.

Turkle, Sherry. *The Second Self: Computers and the Human Spirit.* New York: Simon & Schuster, 1984.

Websites

"Act 590 of 1981." Available online at http://www.antievolution.org/projects/mclean/new_site/legal/act_590.htm.

"The Drug-Free Schools and Communities Act." Available online at http://www.cu.edu/policies/Personnel/drugfree.html.

"Edwards v. Aguillard, 482 U.S. 578 (1987) (USSC+)." Available online at http://www2.law.cornell.edu/cgi-bin/foliocgi.exc/historic/query=[Group 482.

"Hazelwood School District v. Kuhlmeier." Available online at http://www.ux1.eu.edu/~cfjat/classes/4101/casebook/Hazelwood.html.

"History of Indian Education in the United States." Available online at http://www.aiefprograms.org/history_facts/history.html#1920.

"McLean v. Arkansas Board of Education." Available online at http://www.talkorigins.org/faqs/mclean-v-arkansas.htm.

"New Jersey v. T.L.O." Available online at http://www.fausett.com/Seminars/Education/TLO.html.

"U.S. Supreme Court: Bender v. Williamsport Area School District, 475 U.S. 534 (1986)." Available online at http://caselaw.lp.findlaw.com/scripts/getcase.pl?court=us&vol=475&invol=534.

"U.S. Supreme Court: Karcher v. May, 484 U.S. 72 (1987)." Available online at http://caselaw.lp.findlaw.com/scripts/getcase.pl?court=us&vol=484&invol=72.

"U.S. Supreme Court: Valley Forge College v. Americans United, 454 U.S. 464 (1982)." Available online at http://caselaw.lp.findlaw.com/scripts/getcase.pl?court=us&vol=454&invol=464.

Fashion and Design

Barna, Joel Warren. *The See-Through Years: Creation and Destruction in Texas Architecture and Real Estate 1981–1991.* Houston: Rice University Press, 1992.

Capella, Juli and Quim Larrea. *Designed by Architects in the 1980s.* New York: Rizzoli, 1988.

Carnegy, Vicky. *Fashions of a Decade: The 1980s.* New York: Facts On File, 1990.

Chenoune, Farid. *A History of Men's Fashion.* Paris: Flammarion, 1993.

Cowan, Thomas. *Living Details: More than 500 Ways to Make a House a Home.* New York: Whitney Library of Design, 1986.

The Encyclopedia of Fashion. New York: Abrams, 1986.

Garreau, Joel. *Edge City.* New York: Doubleday, 1991.

Gold, Annalee. *90 Years of Fashion.* New York: Fairchild Fashion Group, 1991.

Goldberg, Paul. *On the Rise: Architecture and Design in a Postmodern Age.* New York: Penguin, 1983.

Hunt Jr., William Dudley. *Encyclopedia of American Architecture.* New York: McGraw-Hill, 1990.

Kemp, Jim. *American Vernacular: Regional Influences in Architecture and Interior Design.* New York: Viking, 1987.

Kostof, Spiro. *History of Architecture: Settings and Rituals.* Oxford: Oxford University Press, 1995.

Kultermann, Udo. *Architecture in the 20th Century.* New York: Reinhold, 1993.

LeBlanc, Sydney. *20th Century American Architecture.* New York: Watson-Guptill, 1993.

Maddex, Diane, ed. *Master Builders: A Guide to Famous American Architects.* Washington, D.C.: Preservation Press, 1985.

Martin, Richard and Harold Koda. *Jocks and Nerds: Men's Style in the Twentieth Century.* New York: Rizzoli, 1989.

Milbank, Caroline Rennolds. *Couture: The Great Designers.* New York: Stewart, Tabori & Chang, 1985.

———. *New York Fashion: The Evolution of American Fashion.* New York: Abrams, 1989.

Moor, Jonathan. *Perry Ellis: A Biography.* New York: St. Martin's Press, 1988.

Morgan, Ann Lee and Colin Naylor, eds. *Contemporary Architecture.* Chicago: St. James Press, 1987.

Mulvagh, Jane. *"Vogue" History of 20th Century Fashion.* New York: Viking, 1988.

Payne, Blanche. *The History of Costume.* New York: HarperCollins, 1992.

Peacock, John. *20th Century Fashion: The Complete Sourcebook.* New York: Thames & Hudson, 1993.

Phillips, Lisa. *The American Century: Art and Culture 1950–2000.* New York: W.W. Norton & Co., 1999.

Reid, Aileen. *I. M. Pei.* New York: Crescent Books, 1995.

Russell, Beverly. *Architecture and Design 1970–1990: New Ideas in America.* New York: Abrams, 1989.

Schurnberger, Lynn. *Let There Be Clothes.* New York: Workman, 1991.

Smith, Ray. *Interior Design in 20th Century America: A History.* New York: Harper & Row, 1987.

Stegemeyer, Anne. *Who's Who in Fashion.* New York: Fairchild, 1988.

Wilson, Elizabeth. *Adorned in Dreams: Fashion and Modernity.* Berkeley: University of California Press, 1987.

Wolfe, Tom. *From Bauhaus to Our House.* New York: Farrar, Straus & Giroux, 1981.

Yarwood, Doreen. *Fashion in the Western World: 1500–1990.* New York: Drama Book Publishers, 1992.

Websites

"1980's Lifestyle and Fashion." Fashion-Era. Available online at http://www.fashion-era.com/1980s_lifestyle_and_fashion .htm

"The Costume Gallery." Women Fashions: 1980s–1990s. Available online at http://costumegallery.com/1980.htm (accessed August 26, 2003).

Government and Politics

Auletta, Ken. *The Underclass.* New York: Random House, 1982.

Barker, Lucius J., and Ronald W. Walters, eds. *Jesse Jackson's 1984 Presidential Campaign: Challenge and Change in American Politics.* Urbana: University of Illinois Press, 1989.

Bell, Terrel. *The Thirteenth Man: A Reagan Cabinet Memoir.* New York: Free Press, 1988.

Beschloss, Michael R., and Strobe Talbott. *At the Highest Levels: The Inside Story of the End of the Cold War.* Boston: Little, Brown, 1993.

Blumenthal, Sidney. *Our Long National Daydream: A Political Pageant of the Reagan Era.* New York: Harper & Row, 1988.

———. *Pledging Allegiance: The Last Campaign of the Cold War.* New York: HarperCollins, 1990.

Broder, David, and Bob Woodward. *The Man Who Would Be President: Dan Quayle.* New York: Simon and Schuster, 1992.

Bush, George H., and Brent Scowcroft. *A World Transformed.* New York: Knopf, 1998.

Cannon, Lou. *Reagan.* New York: Putnam, 1982.

Cockburn, Leslie. *Out of Control: The Story of the Reagan Administration's Secret War in Nicaragua, the Illegal Arms Pipeline, and the Contra Drug Connection.* New York: Atlantic Monthly Press, 1987.

Colton, Elizabeth O. *The Jackson Phenomenon: The Man, the Power, the Message.* Doubleday, 1989.

Dallek, Robert. *Ronald Reagan: The Politics of Symbolism.* Cambridge: Harvard University Press, 1984.

Deaver, Michael, and Mickey Hershkovits. *Behind the Scenes.* New York: Morrow, 1987.

Draper, Theodore. *A Very Thin Line: The Iran Contra Affair.* New York: Hill & Wang, 1991.

Edel, Wilbur. *The Reagan Presidency: An Actor's Finest Performance.* New York: Hippocrene Books, 1992.

Faw, Bob. *Thunder in America: The Improbable Presidential Campaign of Jesse Jackson.* Austin: Texas Monthly Press, 1986.

Freedman, Samuel G. *The Inheritance: How Three Families and America Moved from Roosevelt to Reagan.* New York: Simon and Schuster, 1996.

Galbraith, John Kenneth. *A Journey Through Economic Time: A Firsthand View.* Boston: Houghton Mifflin, 1994.

———. *Reaganomics: Meaning, Means, and Ends.* New York: Free Press, 1983.

Germond, Jack W., and Jules Witcover. *Wake Us When It's Over: Presidential Politics of 1984.* New York: Macmillan, 1985.

Gerston, Larry, Cynthia Fraleigh, and Robert Schwab. *The Deregulated Society.* Pacific Grove, Calif.: Brooks/Cole, 1988.

Gutman, Roy. *Banana Diplomacy: The Making of American Policy in Nicaragua, 1981–1987.* New York: Simon & Schuster, 1988.

Haig, Alexander M. *Caveat: Reaganism, Realism, and Foreign Policy.* New York: Macmillan, 1984.

Hodgson, Godfrey. *The World Turned Right Side Up: A History of the Conservative Ascendancy in America.* Boston: Houghton Mifflin, 1996.

Hoeveler, J. David, Jr. *Watch on the Right: Conservative Intellectuals in the Reagan Administration.* Madison: University of Wisconsin Press, 1990.

House, Ernest R. *Jesse Jackson & the Politics of Charisma: The Rise and Fall of the Push/Excel Program.* Boulder, Colo.: Westview Press, 1988.

Jackson, Jesse, and others. *Straight From the Heart.* Philadelphia: Fortress Press, 1987.

Johnson, Haynes. *Sleepwalking Through History: America in the Reagan Years.* New York: Norton, 1991.

Jordan, Hamilton. *Crisis: The Last Year of the Carter Presidency.* New York: Putnam, 1982.

Katz, Michael B. *The Undeserving Poor: From the War on Poverty to the War on Welfare.* New York: Pantheon, 1982.

Kimball, Penn. *Keep Hope Alive!: Super Tuesday and Jesse Jackson's 1988 Campaign for the Presidency.* Washington, D.C.: Joint Center for Political and Economic Studies Press, 1992.

Kirkpatrick, Jeane J. *The Reagan Phenomenon, and Other Speeches on Foreign Policy.* Washington, D.C.: American Enterprise Institute, 1983.

LaFeber, Walter. *Inevitable Revolutions: The United States in Central America..* New York: Norton, 1983.

Leebaert, Derek. *The Fifty-Year Wound: the True Price of America's Cold War Victory.* Boston: Little, Brown and Company, 2002.

Mayer, Jane, and Doyle McManus. *Landslide: The Unmaking of the President, 1984–1988.* Boston: Houghton Mifflin, 1988.

Morris, Edmund. *Dutch: A Memoir of Ronald Reagan.* New York: Random, 1999.

Noll, Mark A. *Religion and American Politics: From the Colonial Period to the 1980s.* New York: Oxford University Press, 1990.

O'Neill, Thomas P. *All Politics Is Local, and Other Rules of the Game.* New York: Times Books, 1994.

———. *Man of the House: The Life and Memoirs of Speaker Tip O'Neill.* New York: Random House, 1987.

Parmet, Herbert S. *George Bush: The Life of a Lone Star Yankee.* New York: Scribner, 1997.

Pemberton, William. *Exit with Honor: The Life and Presidency of Ronald Reagan.* Armonk, N.Y.: M.E. Sharpe, 1997.

Phillips, Kevin P. *The Politics of Rich and Poor: Wealth and the American Electorate in the Reagan Aftermath.* New York: Random House, 1990.

———. *Post-Conservative America: People, Politics and Ideology in a Time of Crisis.* New York: Random House, 1982.

Pomper, Gerald M., and others. *The Election of 1980: Reports and Interpretations.* Chatham, N.J.: Chatham House, 1981.

———. *The Election of 1984: Reports and Interpretations.* Chatham, N.J.: Chatham House, 1985.

———. *The Election of 1988: Reports and Interpretations.* Chatham, N.J.: Chatham House, 1989.

Quayle, Dan. *Standing Firm: A Vice-Presidential Memoir.* New York: HarperCollins, 1994.

Ranney, Austin, ed. *The American Elections of 1984.* Durham, N.C.: Duke University Press, 1985.

Reagan, Nancy, and William Novak. *My Turn: The Memoirs of Nancy Reagan.* New York: Random House, 1989.

Reagan, Ronald. *An American Life: The Autobiography.* New York: Simon & Schuster, 1990.

Regan, Donald T. *For the Record: From Wall Street to Washington.* San Diego, New York: Harcourt Brace Jovanovich, 1988.

Reich, Robert. *The Next American Frontier.* New York: Times Books, 1983.

Runkel, David R. *Campaigning for President: The Managers Look at '88.* Dover, Mass.: Auburn House, 1989.

Schweizer, Peter. *Reagan's War: The Epic Story of His Forty-Year Struggle and Final Triumph Over Communism.* New York: Doubleday, 2002.

Shultz, George P. *Turmoil and Triumph: My Years as Secretary of State.* New York: Scribners, 1993.

Sick, Gary. *All Fall Down: America's Tragic Encounter With Iran.* New York: Random House, 1985.

———. *October Surprise: America's Hostages in Iran and the Election of Ronald Reagan.* New York: Times Books/Random House, 1991.

Slansky, Paul. *The Clothes Have No Emperor: A Chronicle of the American '80s.* New York: Simon & Schuster, 1989.

Smith, Geoffrey. *Reagan and Thatcher.* New York: Norton, 1991.

Speakes, Larry, and Robert Pack. *Speaking Out: The Reagan Presidency from Inside the White House.* New York: Scribners, 1988.

Stockman, David A. *The Triumph of Politics: Why the Reagan Revolution Failed.* New York: Harper & Row, 1986.

Talbott, Strobe. *Deadly Gambits: The Reagan Administration and the Stalemate in Nuclear Arms Control.* New York: Knopf, 1988.

———. *The Master of the Game: Paul Nitze and the Nuclear Peace.* New York: Knopf, 1988.

Virga, Vincent. *The Eighties: Images of America.* New York: Burlingame, 1992.

Weinberger, Caspar W. *Fighting For Peace: Seven Critical Years in the Pentagon.* New York: Warner, 1990.

Wills, Garry. *Reagan's America: Innocents at Home.* Garden City, N.Y.: Doubleday, 1987.

Woodward, Bob. *Veil: The Secret Wars of the CIA, 1981–1987.* New York: Simon & Schuster, 1987.

Law and Justice

Abraham, Henry J. *Justices, Presidents, and Senators: A History of the U.S. Supreme Court Appointments from Washington to Clinton.* Rowman & Littlefield, 1999.

Belsky, Martin H. *The Rehnquist Court: A Retrospective.* Oxford University Press, 2002.

Douglas, John. *Mindhunter: Inside the FBI's Elite Serial Crime Unit.* New York: Pocket Books, 1996.

Hall, Kermit L., ed. *The Oxford Companion to the Supreme Court.* New York: Oxford University Press, 1992.

Harrison, Maureen, and Steve Gilbert, eds. *Landmark Decisions of the United States Supreme Court II.* Beverly Hills: Excellent Books, 1992.

Kelly, Alfred H., Winfred A. Harbison, and Herman Belz. *The American Constitution: Its Origins and Development.* 7th ed. Vol. 2. New York: Norton, 1991.

Mikula, Mark F., and L. Mpho Mabunda, eds. *Great American Court Cases.* Detroit: Gale Group, 2000.

Palmer, Kris E., ed. *Constitutional Amendments: 1789 to the Present.* Detroit: Gale Group, 2000.

Sifakis, Carl. *The Encyclopedia of American Crime.* New York: Facts On File, 2002.

Woodward, Bob. *Veil: The Secret Wars of the CIA, 1981–1987.* New York: Simon & Schuster, 1987.

West's Encyclopedia of American Law. 2d ed. 12 vols. St. Paul, Minn.: West Publishing Co.

Websites

"U.S. Supreme Court Opinions." Available online at http://www.findlaw.com/casecode/supreme.html; website home page: http://www.findlaw.com (accessed March 16, 2003).

"The Presidents of the United States." Available online at http://www.whitehouse.gov/history/presidents/; website home page: http://www.whitehouse.gov (accessed April 20, 2003).

"The Oyez Project of Northwestern University, a U.S. Supreme Court Multimedia Database." Available online at http://www.oyez.com (accessed April 20, 2003).

"The John Hinckley Trial." Available online http://www.law.umkc.edu/faculty/projects/ftrials/hinckley/hinckleytrial.html; website home page: http://www.law.umkc.edu/faculty/projects/ftrials/ftrials.htm (accessed April 20, 2003).

"The McMartin Preschool Abuse Trials." Available online-http://www.law.umkc.edu/faculty/projects/ftrials/mcmartin/mcmartin.html; website home page: http://www.law.umkc.edu/faculty/projects/ftrials/ftrials.htm (accessed April 20, 2003).

Lifestyles and Social Trends

Allen, David F., and James F. Jekel. *Crack: The Broken Promise.* New York: St. Martin's Press, 1991.

Allen, Henry. *Going Too Far Enough: American Culture at Century's End*. Washington: Smithsonian Institution Press, 1994.

Ambry, Margaret K. *Consumer Power: How Americans Spend Their Money*. Ithaca, N.Y.: New Strategists Publications, 1991.

Barone, Michael. *Our Country: The Shaping of America from Roosevelt to Reagan*. New York: Free Press, 1990.

Berman, Morris. *The Twilight of American Culture*. New York: Norton, 2000.

Borstelmann, Thomas. *The Cold War and the Color Line: American Race Relations in the Global Arena*. Cambridge: Harvard University Press, 2001.

Brooks, David. *Bobos in Paradise: The New Upper Class and How They Got There*. New York: Simon & Schuster, 2000.

Carabillo, Toni, Judith Meuli, and June Bundy Csida. *Feminist Chronicles: 1953–1993*. Los Angeles: Women's Graphics, 1993.

Christensen, F. M. *Pornography: The Other Side*. New York: Praeger, 1990.

Clausen, Christopher. *Faded Mosaic: The Emergence of Post-Cultural America*. Chicago: Ivan R. Dee, 2000.

Cooke, Alistair. *America Observed: From the 1940s to the 1980s*. New York: Knopf, 1988.

Coontz, Stephanie. *The Way We Really Are: Coming To Terms With America's Changing Families*. New York: Basic Books, 1997.

———. *The Way We Never Were: American Families and the Nostalgia Trap*. New York: Basic Books, 1992.

Ehrenreich, Barbara. *The Worst Years Of Our Lives: Irreverent Notes From A Decade of Greed*. New York: Pantheon, 1990.

Fairclough, Adam. *Better Day Coming: Blacks and Equality, 1890–2000*. New York: Viking, 2001.

Faludi, Susan. *Backlash: The Undeclared War against American Women*. New York: Crown, 1991.

Fantasia, Rick, and Maurice Isserman. *Homelessness: A Sourcebook*. New York: Facts On File, 1994.

Gaslin, Glenn, and Rick Porter. *The Complete, Cross-Referenced Guide to the Baby Buster Generation's Collective Unconscious*. New York: Boulevard Books, 1998.

Giamatti, A. Bartlett. *Take Time for Paradise: Americans and Their Games*. New York: Summit Books, 1989.

Gillon, Steven M., and Diane B. Kunz. *America During the Cold War*. Fort Worth: Harcourt Brace Jovanovich, 1993.

Gitter, Michael, and Sylvie Anapol. *Do You Remember?: The Book That Takes You Back*. San Francisco: Chronicle Books, 1996.

Gregory, Ross. *Cold War America, 1946 to 1990*. New York: Facts on File, 2003.

Gross, Michael. *My Generation: Fifty Years of Sex, Drugs, Rock, Revolution, Glamour, Greed, Valor, Faith, and Silicon Chips*. New York: Cliff Street Books, 2000.

Hampton, Henry, and Steven Fayer. *Voices of Freedom: An Oral History of the Civil Rights Movement From the 1950s Through the 1980s*. New York: Bantam Books, 1990.

Harris, Jonathan. *Drugged America*. New York: Four Winds Press, 1991.

Hoff-Wilson, Joan. *Rights of Passage: The Past and Future of the ERA*. Bloomington: Indiana University Press, 1986.

Katz, Milton S. *Ban the Bomb: A History of SANE, the Committee for a Sane Nuclear Policy, 1957–1985*. New York: Greenwood Press, 1986.

Klassen, Albert D., and others. *Sex and Morality in the U.S.* Middletown, Conn.: Wesleyan University Press, 1989.

Kowinski, William Severini. *The Malling of America: An Inside Look at the Great Consumer Paradise*. New York: Morrow, 1985.

Kuznick, Peter J., and James Gilbert, eds. *Rethinking Cold War Culture*. Washington: Smithsonian Institution Press, 2001.

Landry, Bart. *The New Black Middle Class*. Berkeley: University of California Press, 1987.

Loeb, Paul Rogat. *Hope in Hard Times: America's Peace Movement and the Reagan Era*. Lexington, Mass.: Lexington Books, 1987.

Maltby, Richard. *Passing Parade: A History of Popular Culture in the Twentieth Century*. New York: Oxford University Press, 1989.

Mansbridge, Jane J. *Why We Lost the ERA*. Chicago: University of Chicago Press, 1986.

Marty, Myron A. *Daily Life in the United States, 1960–1990: Decades of Discord*. Westport, Conn.: Greenwood Press, 1997.

McKenzie, Nancy F., ed. *The AIDS Reader: Social, Political, and Ethical Issues*. New York: Meridian, 1991.

Moore, Joan, and Harry Pachon. *Hispanics in the United States*. Englewood Cliffs, N.J.: Prentice-Hall, 1985.

Panati, Charles. *Panati's Parade of Fads, Follies, and Manias: The Origins of Our Most Cherished Obsessions*. New York: HarperPerennial, 1991.

Phillips, Kevin. *The Politics Of Rich and Poor: Wealth and the American Electorate in the Reagan Aftermath*. New York: Random House, 1990.

Queenan, Joe. *Balsamic Dreams: A Short But Self-Important History of the Baby Boomer Generation*. New York: Henry Holt and Co., 2001.

Rosenberg, Rosalind. *Divided Lives: American Women in the Twentieth Century*. New York: Hill & Wang, 1992.

Sale, Kirkpatrick. *The Green Revolution: The American Environmental Movement, 1962–1992*. New York: Hill & Wang, 1993.

Steele, Shelby. *The Content of Our Character: A New Vision of Race in America*. New York: St. Martin's Press, 1990.

Torr, James D., ed. *The 1980s*. San Diego, Calif.: Greenhaven Press, 2000.

Wachtel, Paul L. *The Poverty Of Affluence: A Psychological Portrait of the American Way of Life*. New York: Free Press, 1988.

Weiss, Michael J. *The Clustered World: How We Live, What We Buy, and What It All Means About Who We Are*. Boston: Little, Brown, 2000.

———. *Latitudes & Attitudes: From Abilene, Texas, to Zanesville, Ohio: An Atlas of American Tastes, Trends, Politics, and Passions.* Boston: Little, Brown, 1994.

Weitzman, Lenore J. *The Divorce Revolution.* New York: Free Press, 1985.

Websites

"1989 Earthquake History." Available online at http://www.sfmuseum.org/1906/89.html (accessed April 28, 2003).

"American Cultural History, 1980–1989." Available online at http://kclibrary.nhmccd.edu/decade80.html (accessed April 28, 2003).

"The Christian Right." Available online at http://www.nhc.rtp.nc.us:8080/tserve/twenty/tkeyinfo/chr_rght.htm (accessed April 28, 2003).

"The Chronology of the Equal Rights Amendment, 1923–1996." Available online at http://www.now.org/issues/economic/cea/history.html (accessed April 28, 2003).

"The Eighties Nostalgia Site." Available online at http://www.inthe80s.com/index.shtml (accessed April 28, 2003).

"1980s General Images" Available online at http://www.authentichistory.com/images/1980s/general_1980s/1980s_images_01.html; website homepage: http://www.authentichistory.com/ (accessed April 28, 2003).

The Media

Altschuler, Glenn C., and David I. Grossvogel. *Changing Channels: America in TV Guide.* Urbana: University of Illinois Press, 1992.

Auletta, Ken. *Three Blind Mice: How the TV Networks Lost Their Way.* New York: Random House, 1991.

Aylesworth, Thomas G. *Great Moments of Television.* New York: Exeter Books, 1987.

Bagdikian, Ben H. *Media Monopoly.* Boston: Beacon, 1990.

Barnouw, Eric. *Tube of Plenty: The Evolution of American Television.* 2d ed. New York: Oxford University Press, 1990.

Blair, Gwenda. *Almost Golden: Jessica Savitch and the Selling of the American News.* New York: Simon & Schuster, 1988.

Block, Alex Ben. *Outfoxed: Marvin Davis, Barry Diller, Rupert Murdoch, Joan Rivers, and the Inside Story of America's Fourth Television Network.* New York: St. Martin's Press, 1990.

Brinkley, David. *Everyone Is Entitled To My Opinion.* New York: Ballantine Books, 1997.

Broder, David S. *Behind the Front Page.* New York: Simon & Schuster, 1987.

Casserly, Jack. *Scripps: The Divided Dynasty.* New York: Donald I. Fine, 1993.

Collins, Jim, ed. *High-Pop: Making Culture into Popular Entertainment.* Malden, Mass.: Blackwell Publishers, 2002.

Cook, Philip S., Douglas Gomery, and Lawrence W. Lichty, eds. *The Future of News: Television-Newspapers-Wire Services-Newsmagazines.* Baltimore: Johns Hopkins University Press, 1992.

Dates, Jannette L., and William Barlow, eds. *Split Image: African Americans in the Mass Media.* Washington, D.C.: Howard University Press, 1990.

Denisoff, R. Serge. *Inside MTV.* New Brunswick, N.J.: Transaction Books, 1988.

Diamond, Edwin, and Stephen Bates. *The Spot: The Rise of Political Advertising on Television.* Cambridge: MIT Press, 1988.

Douglas, Susan J. *Listening In: Radio and the American Imagination: From Amos 'n' Andy and Edward R. Murrow to Wolfman Jack and Howard Stern.* New York: Times Books, 1999.

Draper, Robert. *Rolling Stone Magazine: The Uncensored History.* New York: Doubleday, 1990.

Emery, Michael, and Edwin Emery. *The Press and America: An Interpretive History of the Mass Media.* 7th ed. Englewood Cliffs, N.J.: Prentice Hall, 1992.

Goldberg, Robert, and Gerald Jay Goldberg. *Citizen Turner.* New York: Harcourt Brace, 1995.

Goodwin, Andrew. *Dancing in the Distraction Factory: Music Television and Popular Culture.* Minneapolis: University of Minnesota Press, 1992.

Hertsgaard, Mark. *On Bended Knee: The Press and the Reagan Presidency.* New York: Farrar, Straus & Giroux, 1989.

Hosley, David H., and Gayle K. Yamada. *Hard News: Women In Broadcast Journalism.* Westport, Conn.: Greenwood Press, 1987.

Kellner, Douglas. *Media Culture: Cultural studies, identity and politics between the modern and the postmodern.* London: Routledge, 1995.

Kiernan, Thomas. *Citizen Murdoch.* New York: Dodd, Mead, 1986.

Kinsella, James. *Covering the Plague: AIDS and the American Media.* New Brunswick, N.J.: Rutgers University Press, 1989.

Kluger, Richard. *The Paper: The Life and Death of the New York Herald Tribune.* New York: Knopf, 1986.

MacDonald, J. Fred. *Black and White TV: Afro-Americans in Television Since 1948.* Chicago: Nelson-Hall, 1983.

———. *One Nation Under Television: The Rise and Decline of Network TV.* New York: Pantheon Books, 1990.

Maier, Thomas. *Newhouse: All the Glitter, Power, and Glory of America's Richest Media Empire and the Secretive Man Behind It.* New York: St. Martin's Press, 1994.

Mair, George. *Oprah Winfrey: The Real Story.* New York: Birch Lane Press, 1994.

Marc, David, and Robert J. Thompson. *Prime Time, Prime Movers.* Boston: Little, Brown, 1992.

Marrill, Alvin H. *Movies Made For Television: The Telefeature and the Miniseries, 1964–1986.* New York: New York Zoetrope, 1987.

Montgomery, Kathryn C. *Target Prime Time: Advocacy Groups and the Struggle Over Entertainment Television.* New York: Oxford University Press, 1989.

Powers, Ron. *The Beast, the Eunuch, and the Glass-eyed Child: Television In the '80s.* San Diego: Harcourt Brace Jovanovich, 1990.

Rowan, Carl. *Breaking Barriers: A Memoir*. Boston: Little, Brown, 1991.

Schudson, Michael. *The Power of News*. Cambridge: Harvard University Press, 1995.

Shawcross, William. *Murdoch*. New York: Simon & Schuster, 1992.

Smith, Anthony. *Goodbye Gutenberg: The Newspaper Revolution of the 1980s*. New York: Oxford University Press, 1980.

Smith, Ronald L. *Cosby*. New York: St. Martin's Press, 1986.

Squires, James D. *Read All About It: The Corporate Take-over of America's Newspapers*. New York: Times Books, 1993.

Stark, Steven D. *Glued to the Set: The 60 Television Shows and Events That Made Us Who We Are Today*. New York: Free Press, 1997.

Underwood, Doug. *When MBAs Rule the Newsroom: How the Marketers and Managers Are Reshaping Today's Media*. New York: Columbia University Press, 1993.

Veciana-Suarez, Ana. *Hispanic Media, USA*. Washington, D.C.: Media Institute, 1987.

Whittemore, Hank. *CNN: The Inside Story*. Boston: Little, Brown, 1990.

Winship, Michael. *Television*. New York: Random House, 1988.

Websites

"1980s News." Available online at http://www.authentichistory.com/audio/1980s/1980s_news_01.html; website homepage: http://www.authentichistory.com/(accessed April 28, 2003).

"The 1980s and 1990s on CNN" (CNN Video Almanac). Available online at http://www.cnn.com/resources/video.almanac/ (accessed April 28, 2003).

"Invasion of the Corporate Bodysnatchers." Available online at http://lcweb.loc.gov/rr/print/swann/herblock/invasion.html; website homepage: http://www.loc.gov/rr/print/swann/herblock/ (accessed April 28, 2003).

Medicine and Health

Altman, Drew. *AIDS in the Mind of America*. Garden City, N.Y.: Anchor, 1986.

Altman, Drew, Richard Greene, and Harvey M. Sapolsky. *Health Planning and Regulation: The Decision-Making Process*. Washington, D.C.: AUPHA, 1981.

Andrews, L. B. *New Conceptions: A Consumer's Guide to the Newest Infertility Treatments*. New York: St. Martin's Press, 1984.

Baby Fae: Ethical Issues Surrounding Cross-Species Organ Transplantation. Washington, D.C: Georgetown University, 1985.

Bachrach, L., ed. *New Directions for Mental Health Services: Deinstitutionalization*. San Francisco: Jossey-Bass, 1983.

Baldessarini, Ross J. *Chemotherapy in Psychiatry: Principles and Practice*. Rev. ed. Cambridge: Harvard University Press, 1985.

Baltimore, David, and S. Wolf, eds. *Confronting AIDS: Directions for Public Health, Health Care and Research*. Washington, D.C., National Academy Press, 1986.

Baskin, Yvonne. *The Gene Doctors*. New York: Morrow, 1984.

Bender, Arnold E. *A Dictionary of Food and Nutrition*. NewYork: Oxford University Press, 1995.

Bennett, William, and Joel Gurin. *The Dieter's Dilemma*. New York: Basic Books, 1982.

Bergdoll, Merlin S., and P. Joan Chesney. *Toxic Shock Syndrome*. Boca Raton, Florida: CRC Press, 1991.

Berk, R. A., ed. *The Social Impact of AIDS in the USA*. Cambridge, Mass.: Abt, 1988.

Berman, Henry, and Louisa Rose. *Choosing the Right Health Plan*. Mount Vernon, N.Y.: Consumer Reports Books, 1990.

Black, D. *The Plague Years: A Chronicle of AIDS, the Epidemic of Our Times*. New York: Simon & Schuster, 1986.

Bolognesi, D., ed. *Human Retroviruses, Cancer and AIDS: Approaches to Prevention and Therapy*. New York: Liss, 1988.

Boskind-White, Marlene, and William White. *Bulimarexia: The Binge/Purge Cycle*. New York: Norton, 1987.

Brandt, A. M. *No Magic Bullet: A Social History of Venereal Disease in the United States since 1800. With a New Chapter on AIDS*. 2d ed. New York: Oxford University Press, 1987.

Breo, Dennis L., and Noel Keane. *The Surrogate Mother*. New York: Everest House, 1981.

Brumberg, Joan Jacobs. *Fasting Girls: The Emergence of Anorexia Nervosa as a Modern Disease*. Cambridge: Harvard University Press, 1988.

Cantwell, A., Jr. *AIDS, the Mystery and Solution*. Los Angeles: Aries Rising Press, 1986.

Chung, Edward K. *One Heart, One Life*. Englewood Cliffs, N.J.: Prentice-Hall, 1982.

Cole, H. M., and G. D. Lundberg. *AIDS: From the Beginning*. Chicago: American Medical Association, 1986.

Connor, S., and S. Kingman. *The Search for the Virus: The Scientific Discovery of AIDS and the Quest for a Cure*. Harmondsworth, U.K.: Penguin, 1988.

Corea, Gene. *The Mother Machine: Reproductive Technologies from Artificial Insemination to Artificial Wombs*. New York: Harper & Row, 1985.

Crandall, Keith A. ed. *The Evolution of HIV*. Baltimore: Johns Hopkins University Press, 1999.

Crosignani, P. G. *In Vitro Fertilization and Embryo Transfer*. London: Academic Press, 1983.

Dalton, H. L., and S. Burris. *AIDS and the Law*. New Haven: Yale University Press, 1987.

Davidson, S., and R. Hudson. *Rock Hudson, His Story*. New York: Morrow, 1986.

Edwards, R. G., and P. C. Steptoe. *A Matter of Life*. New York: Morrow, 1980.

Elkington, John. *The Gene Factory: The Science and Business of Biotechnology*. New York: Carroll & Graf, 1987.

Enthoven, Alain C. *Health Plan: The Only Practical Solution to Soaring Health Costs*. Reading, Mass.: Addison-Wesley, 1980.

Farthing, C. F., and others. *A Colour Atlas of AIDS.* Chicago: Yearbook Medical Publications, 1986.

Fein, Rashi. *Medical Care, Medical Costs: The Search for a Health Insurance Policy.* Cambridge: Harvard University Press, 1986.

Fettner, A. G., and W. A. Check. *The Truth about AIDS: Evolution of an Epidemic.* New York: Holt, Rinehart & Winston, 1984.

Fisher, Seymour, and Roger Greenberg. *The Scientific Credibility of Freud's Theories and Therapy.* New York: Basic Books, 1985.

Fleming, A. F., ed. *The Global Impact of AIDS.* New York: Liss, 1988.

Fox, Renee C. *Spare Parts: Organ Replacement in American Society.* New York: Oxford University Press, 1992.

Gallo, Robert C., and F. Wong-Staal, eds. *Retrovirus Biology: An Emerging Role in Human Diseases.* New York: Dekker, 1988.

Galton, Lawrence. *Med Tech: The Layperson's Guide to Today's Medical Miracles.* New York: Harper & Row, 1985.

Garfield, Paul E., and David M. Garner. *Anorexia Nervosa: A Multidimensional Perspective.* New York: Brunner/Mazel, 1982.

Gerety, Robert J. *Hepatitis B.* Orlando, Florida: Academic Press, 1985.

Goldsmith, Jeff Charles. *Can Hospitals Survive? The New Competitive Health Care Market.* Homewood, Ill.: Dow Jones-Irwin, 1981.

Gottlieb, M. S., and others, eds. *Current Topics in AIDS.* New York: Wiley, 1987.

Greenfield, Ellen. *House Dangerous: Indoor Pollution in Your Home and Office—and What You Can Do About It.* New York: Vintage, 1987.

Gross, Cynthia S. *The New Biotechnology: Putting Microbes to Work.* New York: Lerner, 1987.

Haug, M., and Lavin, B. *Consumerism in Medicine.* Beverly Hills, Calif.: Sage, 1983.

Health & Medical Horizons 1986. New York: Macmillan Educational Co., 1986.

Hollis, Judi. *Fat Is a Family Affair.* Center City, Minn.: Hazelden Educational Materials, 1985.

Holmes, H. B., B. B. Hoskins, and M. Gross, eds. *The Custom-Made Child.* Clifton, N.J.: Humana Press, 1981.

Ide, A. F. *AIDS Hysteria.* Dallas: Monument Press, 1986.

Institute of Medicine, National Academy of Sciences. *Confronting AIDS: Directions for Public Health, Health Care, and Research.* Washington, D.C.: National Academy Press, 1986.

Kübler-Ross, Elisabeth. *AIDS, the Ultimate Challenge.* New York: Macmillan, 1987.

Landau, Elaine. *Surrogate Mothers.* New York: Franklin Watts, 1988.

———. *Why Are They Starving Themselves: Understanding Anorexia Nervosa and Bulimia.* New York: Julian Messner, 1983.

Lappe, Mark. *Broken Code: The Exploitation of DNA.* San Francisco: Sierra Book Clubs, 1984.

Lasker, Judith, and Susan Borg. *In Search of Parenthood: Coping with Infertility and High Tech Conception.* Boston: Beacon, 1988.

Leinwald, Gerald. *Transplants.* New York: Franklin Watts, 1985.

Lipp, Martin R. *The Bitter Pill.* New York: Harper & Row, 1980.

Marion, John Francis. *The Fine Old House: Smith Kline Corporation's First 150 Years.* Philadelphia: Smith Kline, 1980.

Masson, Jeffrey M. *The Assault on Truth: Freud's Suppression of the Seduction Theory.* New York: Farrar, Straus & Giroux, 1984.

Masters, W. A., E. Johnson, and R. C. Kolodny. *Crisis: Heterosexual Behavior in the Age of AIDS.* New York: Grove Press, 1988.

Milunsky, Aubrey, ed. *Genetic Disorders and the Fetus.* New York: Plenum Press, 1986.

Mitroff, Ian I., and Ralph H. Kilmann. *Corporate Tragedies: Product Tampering, Sabotage, and Other Catastrophes.* New York: Praeger, 1984.

National Research Council, National Academy of Sciences. *Indoor Pollutants.* Washington, D.C.: National Academy Press, 1981.

Nayak, Ranganath, and John M. Ketteringham. *Breakthroughs!* New York: Rawson, 1986.

Nelkin, Dorothy, and Laurence Tancredi. *Dangerous Diagnostics: The Social Power of Biological Information.* New York: Basic Books, 1989.

Nichols, Eve K. *Mobilizing against AIDS: The Unfinished Story of a Virus.* Cambridge: Harvard University Press, 1986.

———, ed. *Human Gene Therapy.* Cambridge: Harvard University Press, 1988.

Nungesser, L. G. *Epidemic of Courage: Facing AIDS in America.* New York: St. Martin's Press, 1986.

Panem, S. *The AIDS Bureaucracy: U.S. Government Response to AIDS in the First Five Years.* Cambridge: Harvard University Press, 1988.

Parascandola, John, ed. *The History of Antibiotics: A Symposium.* Madison, Wis.: American Institute of the History of Pharmacy, 1980.

Peabody, B. *The Screaming Room: A Mother's Journal of Her Son's Struggle with AIDS.* San Diego, Calif.: Oak Tree, 1986.

Pope, Harrison G., Jr., and James I. Hudson. *New Hope for Binge Eaters: Advances in the Understanding and Treatment of Bulimia.* New York: Harper & Row, 1984.

President's Commission for the Study of Ethical Problems in Biomedical Research. *Splicing Life: A Report on the Social and Ethical Issues of Genetic Engineering.* Washington, D.C.: U.S. Government Printing Office, 1982.

Preston, Richard. *The Hot Zone.* New York: Random House, 1994.

Professional Guide to Diseases. 6th ed. Springhouse, Penn: Springhouse, 1998.

Riley, Tom. *The Price of a Life: One Woman's Death From Toxic Shock.* Bethesda, Md.: Adler & Adler, 1986.

Rothman, B. K. *The Tentative Pregnancy: Prenatal Diagnosis and the Future of Motherhood.* New York: Viking, 1986.

Rousseau, David, W. J. Rea, and Jean Enwright. *Your Home, Your Health, and Well-Being.* Berkeley, Calif.: Ten Speed Press, 1988.

Shaw, Margery W., ed. *After Barney Clark.* Austin: University of Texas Press, 1984.

Shilts, Randy. *And the Band Played On: Politics, People, and the AIDS Epidemic.* New York: St Martin's Press, 1987.

Shorter, Edward. *Bedside Manners: The Troubled History of Doctors and Patients.* New York: Simon & Schuster, 1985.

———. *The Health Century.* New York: Doubleday, 1987.

———. *History of Women's Bodies.* New York: Basic Books, 1982.

Singer, P., and D. Wells. *Making Babies: The New Science and Ethics of Conception.* New York: Scribner, 1985.

Sneader, Walter. *Drug Discovery: The Evolution of Modern Medicine.* New York: Wiley, 1985.

Spallone, Patricia. *Beyond Conception: The New Politics of Reproduction.* Granby, Mass.: Bergin & Garvey Publishers, 1989.

Starkweather, David B. *Hospital Mergers in the Making.* Ann Arbor, Mich.: Health Administration Press, 1981.

Starr, Paul. *The Social Transformation of American Medicine: The rise of a sovereign profession and the making of a vast industry.* New York: Basic Books, 1982.

Steten, DeWitt, Jr. *NIH: An Account of Research in Its Laboratories and Clinics.* Orlando, Fla.: Academic Press, 1984.

Thomas, Lewis. *The Lasker Awards: Four Decades of Scientific Medical Progress.* New York: Albert & Mary Lasker Foundation, 1985.

Turiel, Isaac. *Indoor Air Quality and Human Health.* Stanford, Calif.: Stanford University Press, 1985.

U.S. Department of Health and Human Services. *The Health Consequences of Smoking: Report of the Surgeon General.* Washington, D.C.: GPO, 1982.

Valenstein, Elliot. *Great and Desperate Cures: The Rise and Decline of Psychosurgery and Other Radical Treatments for Mental Illness.* New York: Basic Books, 1986.

Westheimer, Ruth. *All in a Lifetime.* New York: Warner Books, 1983.

———. *Dr. Ruth's Guide to Good Sex.* New York: Warner, 1983.

———. *First Love: A Young People's Guide to Sexual Information.* New York: Warner, 1983.

Wheale, P. R., and Ruth McNulty. *Genetic Engineering: Catastrophe or Utopia?* New York: St. Martin's Press, 1987.

Whitehead, Mary Beth, and Loretta Schwartz-Nobel. *A Mother's Story: The Truth About the Baby M Case.* New York: St. Martin's Press, 1989.

Wood, C., and A. Westmore. *Test-Tube Conception.* Englewood Cliffs, N.J.: Prentice-Hall, 1984.

Wormser, G. P., R. E. Stahl, and E. J. Bottone, eds. *AIDS: Acquired Immunodeficiency Syndrome and Other Manifestations of HIV Infection.* Park Ridge, N.J.: Noyes, 1987.

Zimmerman, Burke K. *Biofuture: Confronting the Genetic Era.* New York: Plenum Press, 1984.

Zimmerman, Burke K., and Raymond A. Zilinkas, eds. *Reflection on the Recombinant DNA Controversy.* New York: Macmillan, 1984.

Websites

"American SIDS Institute." Available online at http://www.sids.org.

"Ebola Reston Outbreaks." Available online at http://www.stanford.edu/group/virus/filo/ebor.html.

"HEPATITIS B VACCINE." Available online at http://www.cdc.gov/nip/publications/VIS/vis-hep-b.pdf.

"The History of Medicine: 1966–Present." Available online at http://www.medhelpnet.com/medhist10.html.

Hull, Richard T. "The Baby Fae Case: Treatment, Experiment, or Animal Abuse?" Available online at http://www.richard-t-hull.com/publications/baby_fae_case.pdf.

"Jarvik-7: Total Artificial Heart." Available online at http://www.tmc.edu/thi/j7tah.html.

"Medicine and Madison Avenue—Timeline." Available online at http://scriptorium.lib.duke.edu/mma/timeline.html.

"MEDLINEplus Medical Encyclopedia: Toxic Shock Syndrome." Available online at http://www.nlm.nih.gov/medlineplus/ency/article/000653.htm.

"Surgeon General's Reports on Smoking and Health, 1964–2001." Available online at http://govpubs.lib.umn.edu/guides/surgeongeneral.phtml.

"Timeline: A Brief History of AIDS/HIV." Available online at http://www.aegis.com/topics/timeline/default.asp.

"United States Cancer Mortality from 1900 to 1992." Available online at http://www.healthsentinel.com/Vaccines/DiseaseAndRelatedData_files/she.

"WHO Declares Smallpox Eradication in 1980." Available online at http://www.vaccinationnews.com/Scandals/feb_8_02/WHOEradicationNotice.htm.

Religion

Ammerman, Nancy Tatom. *Bible Believers: Fundamentalism in the Modern World.* New Brunswick, N.J.: Rutgers University Press, 1987.

Armstrong, Karen. *The Gospel According to Women: Christianity's Creation of the Sex Wars in the West.* Garden City, N.Y.: Anchor/Doubleday, 1987.

Bainbridge, William Sims. *The Future of Religion: Secularization, Revival and Cult Formation.* Berkeley: University of California Press, 1985.

Balmer, Randall. *Mine Eyes Have Seen the Glory: A Journey into the Evangelical Subculture of America.* New York: Oxford University Press, 1989.

Bellah, Robert N., and others. *Habits of the Heart: Individualism and Commitment in American Life.* Berkeley: University of California Press, 1985.

Brown, Richard C. *The Presbyterians: Two Hundred Years in Danville, 1784–1984*. Danville, Ky.: Presbyterian Church, 1983.

Callahan, Kennon L. *Twelve Keys to an Effective Church*. San Francisco: Harper & Row, 1983.

Castelli, Joseph, and Jim Gremillion. *The Emerging Parish: The Notre Dame Study of Catholic Life Since Vatican II*. San Francisco: Harper & Row, 1987.

Cohen, Steven M. *American Assimilation or Jewish Revival*. Bloomington: Indiana University Press, 1988.

Cooney, John. *The American Pope*. New York: Times Books, 1984.

Cox, Harvey. *Religion in the Secular City*. New York: Simon & Schuster, 1984.

Danzger, Herbert M. *Returning to Tradition: The Contemporary Revival of Orthodox Judaism*. New Haven: Yale University Press, 1989.

Deedy, John. *American Catholicism: And Now Where?* New York: Plenum Press, 1987.

Draper, James T., and Forrest E. Watson. *If the Foundations Be Destroyed*. Nashville: Oliver Nelson, 1984.

Edel, Wilber. *Defenders of the Faith: Religion and Politics from the Pilgrim Fathers to Ronald Reagan*. New York: Praeger, 1987.

Falwell, Jerry. *The Fundamentalist Phenomenon: The Resurgence of Conservative Christianity*. Garden City, N.Y.: Doubleday, 1981.

Ferguson, Marilyn. *The Aquarian Conspiracy: Personal and Social Transformation in the 1980s*. Los Angeles: J. P. Tarcher, 1980.

Fishwick, Marshall, and Ray B. Browne, eds. *The God Pumpers: Religion in the Electronic Age*. Bowling Green, Ohio: Bowling Green University Popular Press, 1987.

Fore, William F. *Television and Religion: The Shaping of Faith, Values, and Culture*. Minneapolis: Augsburg Publishing House, 1987.

Fowler, J. W. *Stages of Faith*. New York: Harper & Row, 1981.

Greeley, Andrew. *Religious Change in America*. Cambridge: Harvard University Press, 1989.

Groothuis, Douglas R. *Unmasking the New Age*. Downers Grove, Ill.: InterVarsity Press, 1986.

Guerrero, Andres Gonzales. *A Chicano Theology*. Maryknoll, N.Y.: Orbis Books, 1987.

Hadden, Jeffrey K., and Anson Shupe. *Televangelism: Power and Politics on God's Frontier*. New York: Holt, 1988.

Hennesey, James. *American Catholics: A History of the Roman Catholic Community in the United States*. Oxford: Oxford University Press, 1981.

Horsefield, Peter G. *Religious Television: The American Experience*. New York: Longman, 1984.

Hunter, James Davidson. *American Evangelicalism: Conservative Religion and the Quandary of Modernity*. New Brunswick, N.J.: Rutgers University Press, 1983.

Hutchenson, William R. *Between the Times: The Travail of the Protestant Establishment in America, 1900–1960*. Cambridge: Cambridge University Press, 1989.

Jorstad, Erling. *Being Religious in America*. Minneapolis: Augsburg Publishing House, 1986.

Kaiser, Robert B. *The Politics of Sex and Religion*. Kansas City: Leaven Press, 1985.

Lader, Lawrence. *Politics, Power and the Church: The Catholic Crisis and Its Challenge to American Pluralism*. New York: Macmillan, 1987.

Lippy, Charles H., ed. *Twentieth-Century Shapers of American Popular Religion*. New York: Greenwood Press, 1989.

Lovin, Robin W., ed. *Religion and American Public Life*. New York: Paulist Press, 1986.

Lucas, Isidro. *The Browning of America: The Hispanic Revolution in the American Church*. Chicago: Fides/Claretian, 1981.

MacLaine, Shirley. *Dancing In the Light*. Toronto: Bantam, 1985.

Martire, Gregory, and Ruth Clark. *Anti-Semitism in the United States*. New York: Praeger, 1982.

Marty, Martin E. *Modern American Religion*. Chicago: University of Chicago Press, 1986.

Mayer, Egon. *Love and Tradition: Marriage Between Jews and Christians*. New York: Schocken, 1985.

Meyer, Michael A. *Response to Modernity: A History of the Reform Movement in Judaism*. New York: Oxford University Press, 1988.

Mukenge, Ida Rousseau. *The Black Church in Urban America*. Lanham, Md.: University Press of America, 1983.

Noll, Mark A., and others. *The Search for Christian America*. Westchester, Ill.: Crossway Books, 1983.

Quebedeaux, Richard. *By What Authority: The Rise of Personality Cults in American Christianity*. San Francisco: Harper & Row, 1982.

Randi, James. *The Faith-Healers*. Buffalo: Prometheus Books, 1987.

Reich, James A. *Religion in American Public Life*. Washington, D.C.: Brookings Institution, 1985.

Robertson, Pat. *America's Dates with Destiny*. Nashville: Thomas Nelson, 1986.

Roof, Wade Clark, and William McKinney. *American Mainline Religion: Its Changing Shape and Future*. New Brunswick, N.J.: Rutgers University Press, 1987.

Sklare, Marshall, ed. *Understanding American Jewry*. New Brunswick, N.J.: Transaction Books, 1982.

Smith, Timothy L. *Revivalism and Social Reform in the Mid-Nineteenth Century America*. Baltimore, Md.: Johns Hopkins University Press, 1980.

Viguerie, Richard A. *The New Right: We're Ready to Lead*. Falls Church, Va.: Viguerie, 1981.

Wald, Kenneth D. *Religion and Politics in the United States*. New York: St. Martin's Press, 1987.

Weigel, George. *Catholicism and the Renewal of American Democracy*. New York: Paulist Press, 1989.

Welch, Sharon D. *Communities of Resistance and Solidarity: A Feminist Theology of Liberation.* Maryknoll, N.Y.: Orbis Books, 1985.

Wilson, Bryan R., ed. *The Social Impact of New Religious Movements.* New York: Rose of Sharon Press, 1981.

Woocher, Jonathan. *Sacred Survival: The Civic Religion of American Jews.* Bloomington: Indiana University Press, 1986.

Wood, James E., Jr., ed. *Religion and the State.* Waco: Baylor University Press, 1985.

Wuthnow, Robert. *The Restructuring of American Religion: Society and Faith Since World War II.* Princeton: Princeton University Press, 1988.

Science and Technology

Asimov, Isaac. *Frontiers: New Discoveries about Man and His Planet, Outer Space, and the Universe.* New York: Dutton, 1989.

———. *The Universe: From Flat Earth to Black Holes—And Beyond.* New York: Walker, 1980.

Aveni, Anthony. *Empires of Time: Calendars, Clocks, and Cultures.* New York: Basic Books, 1989.

Barrow, John D., and Frank J. Tipler. *The Anthropic Cosmological Principle.* Oxford: Oxford University Press, 1988.

Boslough, John. *Stephen Hawking's Universe.* New York: Morrow, 1985.

Carrigan, Richard A., Jr., and W. Peter Trowers, eds. *Particle Physics in the Cosmos.* New York: Freeman, 1989.

Cohen, Nathan. *Gravity's Lens.* New York: Wiley, 1988.

Davies, Paul. *Superforce.* New York: Simon & Schuster, 1984.

Dyson, Freeman. *Infinite in All Directions.* New York: Harper & Row, 1985.

Feynman, Richard P. *QED: The Strange Theory of Light and Matter.* Princeton, N.J.: Princeton University Press, 1983.

———. *Surely You're Joking Mr. Feynman!.* New York: Norton, 1985.

Fraser, Julius T. *Time: The Familiar Stranger.* Boston: University of Massachusetts Press, 1987.

Gould, Stephen Jay. *The Flamingo's Smile.* New York: Norton, 1985.

———. *Wonderful Life: The Burgess Shale and the Nature of History.* New York: Norton, 1989.

Hawking, Stephen. *A Brief History of Time: From the Big Bang to Blackholes.* New York: Bantam, 1988.

Heisenberg, Werner. *Encounters with Einstein.* Princeton: Princeton University Press, 1989.

Lewin, Roger. *In the Age of Mankind: A Smithsonian Book of Human Evolution.* Washington, D.C.: Smithsonian Books, 1988.

———. *Principles of Evolution: A Core Text.* Malden, Mass: Blackwell Science, 1998.

Macaulay David, and Neil Ardley. *The Way Things Work.* London: Kindersley, 1988.

Pagels, Heinz. *The Cosmic Code.* New York: Simon & Schuster, 1982.

Rifkin, Jeremy. *The Biotech Century: Harnessing the Gene and Remaking the World.* New York: Putnam, 1998.

Sagan, Carl. *Cosmos.* New York: Random House, 1980.

Taubes, Gary. *Nobel Dreams.* New York: Random House, 1986.

Weinberg, Steven. *The First Three Minutes.* New York: Bantam, 1984.

Websites

Carrano, Anthony V. "Physical Mapping of Human DNA: An Overview of the DOE Program." Available online at http://genome.gsc.riken.go.jp/hgmis/publicat/hgn/v1n2/01phymap.htm

"The Challenger Accident." Available online at http://www.fas.org/spp/51L.html.

Chandrasekhar, Subramanyan. "On Stars, Their Evolution and Their Stability." Available online at http://www.nobel.se/physics/laureates/1983/chandrasekhar-lecture.pdf. *New York: Putnam, 1998.*

"The Greenhouse Effect." Available online at http://www.epa.gov/globalwarming/kids/greenhouse.html.

Kevles, Daniel J. "Patenting Life: A Historical Overview of Law, Interests, and Ethics." Available online at http://www.yale.edu/law/ltw/papers/ltw-kevles.pdf.

"KNM-WT 15000 (Turkana Boy)." Available online at http://www.talkorigins.org/faqs/homs/15000.html.

Martin, Brian. "Nuclear Winter: Science & Politics." Available online at http://www.uow.edu.au/arts/sts/bmartin/pubs/88spp.html.

"Mitochondrial Eve." Available online at http://www.uncc.edu/jmarks/2141/mtEve.pdf.

"Mount St. Helens National Volcanic Monument." Available online at http://www.fs.fed.us/gpnf/mshnvm.

"National Museum of Natural History—Dinosaur Extinction." Available online at http://www.nmnh.si.edu/paleo/blast.

Sports

Abdul-Jabbar, Kareem, and Mignon McCarthy. *Kareem.* New York: Random House, 1990.

Aeseng, Nathan. *Carl Lewis: Legend Chaser.* Minneapolis: Lerner, 1985.

———. *Steve Carlton, Baseball's Silent Strongman.* Minneapolis: Lerner, 1984.

Ashe, Arthur, Jr., and Arnold Rampersad. *Days of Grace.* New York: Knopf, 1993.

———. *A Hard Road to Glory: A History of the African-American Athlete Since 1946.* New York: Warner, 1988.

Bird, Larry, and Bob Ryan. *Drive: The Story of My Life.* New York: Doubleday, 1989.

Boswell, Thomas. *Strokes of Genius.* New York: Doubleday, 1987.

Bosworth, Brian, and Rick Reilly. *The Boz: Confessions of an Anti-Hero.* New York: Doubleday, 1988.

Bradshaw, Terry, and David Fisher. *It's Only a Game.* New York: Pocket, 2001.

Burchard, Marshall. *Sports Hero, Jimmy Connors.* New York: Putnam, 1976.

Cohen, Neil. *Jackie Joyner-Kersee.* Boston: Little, Brown, 1992.

Evert, Chris, and Neil Amdur. *Crissy, My Own Story.* New York: Simon and Schuster, 1984.

Feinstein, John. *Hard Court: Real Life on the Professional Tennis Tours.* New York: Villard, 1991.

———. *A Season Inside: One Year in College Basketball.* New York: Villard, 1988.

———. *A Season on the Brink: A Year with Bob Knight and the Indiana Hoosiers.* New York: MacMillan, 1986.

Garvey, Steve, and Skip Rozin. *Garvey.* New York: Doubleday, 1989.

Gloeckner, Carolyn, and Howard Schroeder. *Marvelous Marvin Hagler.* Mankato, Minn.: Crestwood House, 1985.

Golenbock, Peter. *American Zoom: Stock Car Racing—From the Dirt Tracks to Daytona.* New York: Macmillan, 1993.

Greene, Bob. *Rebound: The Odyssey of Michael Jordan.* New York: Viking, 1995.

Gretzky, Wayne, and Rick Reilly. *Gretzky: An Autobiography.* New York: HarperCollins, 1990.

Halberstam, David. *Playing for Keeps: Michael Jordan and the World He Made.* New York: Random, 1999.

Herskowitz, Mickey. *The Legend of Bear Bryant.* New York: McGraw, 1987.

Illingworth, Montieth. *Mike Tyson: Money, Myth, and Betrayal.* New York: Carol Publishing Group, 1991.

Johnson, Earvin, Jr., and Roy S. Johnson. *Magic's Touch.* Reading, Mass.: Addison-Wesley, 1989.

Knapp, Ron. *Sports Great Isiah Thomas.* Hillside, N.J.: Enslow, 1992.

Lazenby, Roland. *The Lakers: A Basketball Journey.* New York: St. Martin's Press, 1993.

Lopez, Nancy, and Peter Schwed. *The Education of a Woman Golfer.* New York: Simon and Schuster, 1979.

Macht, Norman. *Jim Abbott: Major League Pitcher.* New York: Chelsea House, 1994.

McEnroe, John, and James Kaplan. *You Can't Be Serious.* New York: Putnam, 2002.

Navratilova, Martina, and George Vecsey. *Martina.* New York: Knopf, 1985.

Pemberton, Cynthia. *More Than a Game: One Woman's Fight for Gender Equity in Sport.* Boston: Northeastern University Press, 2002.

Powers, John, and Arthur C. Kaminsky. *One Goal: A Chronicle of the 1980 Olympic Hockey Team.* New York: Harper and Row, 1985.

Raber, Thomas. *Joe Montana, Comeback Quarterback.* Minneapolis: Lerner, 1989.

Reston, James, Jr. *Collision at Home Plate: The Lives of Pete Rose and Bart Giamatti.* New York: HarperCollins, 1991.

Retton, Mary Lou, and others. *Mary Lou: Creating an Olympic Champion.* New York: McGraw-Hill, 1986.

Ripkin, Cal, and Mike Bryan. *The Only Way I Know.* New York: Viking, 1997.

Robinson, Eddie, and Richard Edward Lapchick. *Never Before, Never Again: The Stirring Autobiography of Eddie Robinson, the Winningest Coach in the History of College Football.* New York: St. Martin, 1999.

Rose, Pete, and Roger Kahn. *Pete Rose: My Story.* New York: MacMillan, 1989.

Schembechler, Bo, and Mitch Albom. *Bo.* New York: Warner, 1989.

Shaikin, Bill. *Sport and Politics: The Olympics and the Los Angeles Games.* New York: Praeger, 1988.

Shoemaker, Bill, and Barney Nagler. *Shoemaker.* New York: Doubleday, 1988.

Toperoff, Sam. *Sugar Ray Leonard and Other Noble Warriors.* New York: McGraw-Hill, 1987.

PRIMARY SOURCE TYPE INDEX

Primary source authors appear in parentheses. Page numbers in italics indicate images, and those followed by the letter t indicate tables.

Primary source authors appear in parentheses. Page numbers in italics indicate images, and those followed by the letter *t* indicate tables.

Primary source authors appear in parentheses. Page numbers in italics indicate images, and those followed by the letter *t* indicate tables.

Primary source authors appear in parentheses. Page numbers in italics indicate images, and those followed by the letter *t* indicate tables.

GENERAL INDEX

Page numbers in bold indicate primary sources; page numbers in italic indicate images; page numbers in bold italic indicate primary source images; page numbers followed by the letter t indicate tables. Primary sources are indexed under the entry name with the author's name in parentheses. Primary sources are also indexed by title. All primary sources can be identified by bold page locators.

A

AbioCor (artificial heart), 487

Abolitionist movement, 532

Abortion
court cases, 293–297
position of C. Everett Koop, 507
position of Catholic Church, 540–541
position of Christian feminists, 542–545
position of Moral Majority, 524
position of Robert Bork, 350
position of Sandra Day O'Connor, 238–241
protests, *295, 541, 544*
religious liberal position, 559–562

"Abortion and the Sexual Agenda," 542–545
journal article (Callahan), **543–545**

Academic freedom, 332, 604

Academics
Bloom, Allan, 150–154, 373–376
Callahan, Sidney, 542–545
Freeman, Sue Joan Mendelson, 200
Heath, Shirley Brice, 130–133
Schüssler Fiorenza, Elisabeth, 530–532
Thurow, Lester, 85–88
Williams, Delores S., 548–551, *549*

Accidents. *See* Disasters and accidents

Ackerman, Thomas P.
magazine article, **588–591**

Acquired Immune Deficiency Syndrome. *See* AIDS

Activism
African Americans, 377
Guerrilla Girls, 57–61
judges, 237–238, 348–349
South Africa and *Graceland* (album), 47

Activists
Farrakhan, Louis, 377
Goodman, Mark, 158–161
King, Martin Luther, Jr., 533
Parker, Mike, 104–109
Sharpton, Al, *377,* 377–379, *379*

Actors
Alda, Alan, 414–415
Alice, Mary, *43*
Cosby, Bill, 422–426
Douglas, Michael, *99*
Farr, Jamie, 415
Fonda, Jane, 361–364
Jones, James Earl, *43*
Keaton, Diane, *21*
Lange, Jessica, *21*
Madonna, 32
Olmos, Edward James, *167*
Shields, Brooke, *176*
Spacek, Sissy, *21*

Admissions, college, 143

Adult education, 132, 144–146

Advertising
Air Jordans, 186–187, *187*
Army recruiting, *385, 386*
Calvin Klein jeans, *176,* 176–177
Calvin Klein suits, *201*
cash for Panamanian weapons, *279–280,* 281
Empire Bay tracksuit, *195*
Guerrilla Girls, *59*
San Francisco AIDS Foundation, *381, 383, 384*
sports figures in, 361
Willie Horton political ads, 378

Advice and Consent, 347–352
memoir (Simon), **349–352**

Affirmative action programs, 289–293, 326–330, 338–342

Africa
origin of man, 599, 600
"We Are the World" aid, 30

African Americans
affirmative action programs, 289, 338
churches, 548–549
college athletes, 141–143, 631–632
cultural identity, 550
discrimination at Bob Jones University, 138–141
language education, 130–131
Muslims, 557, 559

Page numbers in bold indicate primary sources; page numbers in italic indicate images;
page numbers in bold italic indicate primary source images; page numbers followed by the letter *t* indicate tables.

Page numbers in bold indicate primary sources; page numbers in italic indicate images; page numbers in bold italic indicate primary source images; page numbers followed by the letter *t* indicate tables.

Page numbers in bold indicate primary sources; page numbers in italic indicate images; page numbers in bold italic indicate primary source images; page numbers followed by the letter *t* indicate tables.

Page numbers in bold indicate primary sources; page numbers in italic indicate images;
page numbers in bold italic indicate primary source images; page numbers followed by the letter *t* indicate tables.

Page numbers in bold indicate primary sources; page numbers in italic indicate images;
page numbers in bold italic indicate primary source images; page numbers followed by the letter *t* indicate tables.

Page numbers in bold indicate primary sources; page numbers in italic indicate images;
page numbers in bold italic indicate primary source images; page numbers followed by the letter *t* indicate tables.

Page numbers in bold indicate primary sources; page numbers in italic indicate images;
page numbers in bold italic indicate primary source images; page numbers followed by the letter *t* indicate tables.

Page numbers in bold indicate primary sources; page numbers in italic indicate images;
page numbers in bold italic indicate primary source images; page numbers followed by the letter *t* indicate tables.

Page numbers in bold indicate primary sources; page numbers in italic indicate images; page numbers in bold italic indicate primary source images; page numbers followed by the letter *t* indicate tables.

Page numbers in bold indicate primary sources; page numbers in italic indicate images;
page numbers in bold italic indicate primary source images; page numbers followed by the letter *t* indicate tables.

Page numbers in bold indicate primary sources; page numbers in italic indicate images;
page numbers in bold italic indicate primary source images; page numbers followed by the letter *t* indicate tables.

Page numbers in bold indicate primary sources; page numbers in italic indicate images; page numbers in bold italic indicate primary source images; page numbers followed by the letter *t* indicate tables.

Page numbers in bold indicate primary sources; page numbers in italic indicate images;
page numbers in bold italic indicate primary source images; page numbers followed by the letter *t* indicate tables.

Page numbers in bold indicate primary sources; page numbers in italic indicate images;
page numbers in bold italic indicate primary source images; page numbers followed by the letter *t* indicate tables.

Page numbers in bold indicate primary sources; page numbers in italic indicate images; page numbers in bold italic indicate primary source images; page numbers followed by the letter *t* indicate tables.

Page numbers in bold indicate primary sources; page numbers in italic indicate images;
page numbers in bold italic indicate primary source images; page numbers followed by the letter *t* indicate tables.

Page numbers in bold indicate primary sources; page numbers in italic indicate images; page numbers in bold italic indicate primary source images; page numbers followed by the letter *t* indicate tables.

Page numbers in bold indicate primary sources; page numbers in italic indicate images;
page numbers in bold italic indicate primary source images; page numbers followed by the letter *t* indicate tables.

Page numbers in bold indicate primary sources; page numbers in italic indicate images;
page numbers in bold italic indicate primary source images; page numbers followed by the letter *t* indicate tables.

Page numbers in bold indicate primary sources; page numbers in italic indicate images;
page numbers in bold italic indicate primary source images; page numbers followed by the letter *t* indicate tables.

Page numbers in bold indicate primary sources; page numbers in italic indicate images;
page numbers in bold italic indicate primary source images; page numbers followed by the letter *t* indicate tables.

Page numbers in bold indicate primary sources; page numbers in italic indicate images; page numbers in bold italic indicate primary source images; page numbers followed by the letter *t* indicate tables.

Page numbers in bold indicate primary sources; page numbers in italic indicate images;
page numbers in bold italic indicate primary source images; page numbers followed by the letter *t* indicate tables.

Page numbers in bold indicate primary sources; page numbers in italic indicate images;
page numbers in bold italic indicate primary source images; page numbers followed by the letter *t* indicate tables.

Page numbers in bold indicate primary sources; page numbers in italic indicate images; page numbers in bold italic indicate primary source images; page numbers followed by the letter *t* indicate tables.